About the Author

The author was born in Glasgow in 1946 and emigrated to Australia in 1960, at which time he started to collect information on prominent Scots. By 2005, he had details of over 15,000 Scots whose influence went far beyond Scotland. This book is a result of some of that research.

Dedication

This book is dedicated to my wife, Vicki, my daughter, Alana, and my grandson, Nicholas, as well as to all those people named in this book who have contributed to the advance of knowledge and to the improvement of human life.

Andrew Gordon Paterson

BRILLIANT!

SCOTTISH INVENTORS, INNOVATORS, SCIENTISTS AND ENGINEERS WHO CHANGED THE WORLD

AUSTIN MACAULEY PUBLISHERS™

LONDON • CAMBRIDGE • NEW YORK • SHARJAH

A CIP catalogue record for this title is available from the British Library.

ISBN 978-1-78629-437-1 (Paperback)
ISBN 978-1-78629-436-4 (Hardback)
ISBN 978-1-78629-435-7 (E-Book)

www.austinmacauley.com

First Published (2017)
Austin Macauley Publishers Ltd.™
25 Canada Square
Canary Wharf
London
E14 5LQ

INTRODUCTION

In the first decade of the 21st century the People's Republic of China underwent the fastest industrialisation of any nation in history, a period that has been called the second industrial revolution.[1] It was, however, in the United Kingdom, more than two centuries earlier, that the first industrial revolution occurred – an event that ultimately and irrevocably changed the way of life for almost every human being now on this planet. Many of the initial key elements that brought about this event were innovations that led to the mass production of textiles and were invented in England – the spinning jenny, the water frame, the spinning mule, and the power loom. Other factors sustaining the progress of the original industrial revolution included, but were not limited to: improved iron and steel production, improved transportation, a rising population, better and more widespread education (particularly in Scotland), and the advent of scientific investigation; but the most iconic symbol of the industrial revolution is undoubtedly the steam engine. And, like all good stories, the invention of the particular steam engine that was the genesis of the first industrial revolution has its own foundation myth. The story goes that a local instrument-maker was given a model Newcomen steam engine to repair for Glasgow University. He realised that this engine was highly inefficient and sought to improve it, but he was a busy man trying to make a living in tough times, so he had little time to think about it until one Sunday in May 1765 (the actual date, like all good legends, is suitably imprecise), he was strolling through Glasgow Green letting his thoughts wander. Suddenly, in a flash of inspiration, he realised the solution was to create a separate condensing chamber which, after a number of years and a failed business partnership, he succeeded in producing.

The inspirational moment may be factual or myth, but it spawned the most famous name of the industrial revolution – James Watt. His fellow Scots had been actively involved with innovation before this time, particularly in medicine, agriculture and warfare, but following the advent of Watt's efficient steam engine, Scots, like no other race of people (in proportion to population), produced a profusion of inventors, innovators, engineers and scientists, placing Scotland and Scots at the heart of innovation, the end result of which was an entirely different world from the one that humans had experienced prior to the 19th century.

Scotland was so much to the fore in engineering that it produced the first three presidents of the Institution of Civil Engineers (ICE), the first such national professional body in the world. Their combined presidencies covered the period 1820 to 1848. Another 22 presidents of ICE have been born in Scotland with at least five others who had one or both parents born in Scotland. It was also a Scot, James Laurie, who was a co-founder and the first President of the American Society of Civil Engineers (ASCE). James Pugh Kirkwood, born in Edinburgh was also a president of ASCE, as was Glasgow-born Alexander Dow; and John Thomson of Fochabers in Morayshire was Treasurer. The first British university professorship in engineering was founded at Glasgow University in 1840 with Lewis Dunbar Brodie Gordon in the chair, and the first professor of engineering in the English-speaking world was James Renwick, born in 1792 in Liverpool, England. He served as Columbia University's all-round applied scientist and engineer-in-all-but-title for 33 years[2] (officially he was Professor of Natural and Experimental Philosophy at Columbia College). His mother was Jane Jeffrey who was born in Ruthwell, Dumfries-shire on 29 May 1774.

The total number of civil engineering projects published in Britain in the 130 years from 1700 to 1830 (excluding reports printed in Parliamentary Papers) comprised 219 printed reports and 114 engraved plans, of which 90 reports (41%) and 40 plans (35%) were by just four civil engineers: Thomas Telford, John Rennie, Robert Mylne and Robert Stevenson – all born in Scotland.[3]

Engineering and Scotland became so inextricably linked that, when the iconic 1960s television series *Star Trek* was created, it was almost inevitable that the Starship engineer would be a Scot, and a new phrase entered the world's lexicon - "Beam me up, Scotty".

Scots came late to the world of invention – even whisky was first recorded in Ireland – but by the 18th and 19th centuries, Scottish innovators had more than made up lost ground and were well represented in technological achievement; and they have continued innovating into the present day.

In deciding who to include in this book I first had to determine what actually made someone Scottish, or sufficiently Scottish to qualify for inclusion. Even being born in Scotland is not necessarily enough to make a person inherently Scottish. For example, Sir Nigel Gresley, designer of the *Flying Scotsman* locomotive, was born in Scotland to English parents whose ancestors had resided in England for centuries. He was born in Edinburgh during a visit by his mother to see her gynaecologist and returned to Derbyshire shortly afterwards. He grew up and spent his life working in England and he saw himself as English. His Scottishness is tenuous to say the least, despite his Scottish birth. Similarly, many famous English men and women have been born outside of England, including Alan Brooke (WWII field marshal), Henry Cavendish (scientist), Julie Christie (actress), Richard Dawkins (biologist), John Fisher (admiral), C.S. Forester (novelist), Guy Gibson (pilot and V.C. war hero of dambuster fame), Sir George Gray (explorer, governor and politician), Rudyard Kipling (novelist), Vivien Leigh (actress), William Somerset Maugham (novelist), Spike Milligan (comedian), Florence Nightingale (founder of modern nursing), Sir Thomas Stamford Raffles (founder of Singapore), Sir Cliff Richard (singer), and Arthur Wellesley (first Duke of Wellington, hero of Waterloo and British prime minister). Although not born in England each of these people were (and are) considered by many as quintessentially English. Thus, each individual has a personal view of his or her sense of belonging and nationality that is not necessarily predicated by their country of birth. Sir Compton Mackenzie was born in England but saw himself as Scottish, whereas the similarly English-born historian, Thomas Babington Macaulay, was an archetypal Englishman despite having a famous Highland father.

The descendants of immigrants often have an attachment to the "home country" of their ancestors. In the United States, many of its citizens describe themselves as Polish-American, Italian-American, Irish-American, Lebanese-American, Chinese-American, and so on, even though many of them have had *only* American-born ancestors for many generations. In 2014, many Russian-speaking people in Crimea successfully broke away from Ukraine and integrated with Russia on the basis of their ancestry. Likewise, many people of British ancestry belonged to the third or fourth generation of their family born in places such as India, Jamaica, Kenya and Ceylon (Sri Lanka), but they always considered themselves to be British. So, clearly, ancestry matters for many people in determining their emotional ties to a distant "homeland", which they may never have seen let alone lived in.

Additional complications in identifying how to assign nationality arise because some people are claimed as nationals of a particular country simply because they have resided in that country for a period of time. Thus, we find that Ian Wilmut (Dolly, the cloned sheep), Robert Lister (a pioneer of antiseptic surgery), Stan Laurel (comic actor who teamed up with Oliver Hardy), Graham Teasdale (co-inventor of the Glasgow coma scale), and Hubert Booth (inventor of the vacuum cleaner) are often claimed as Scots, though all of them were born and raised in England and had English ancestry.

Furthermore, nationality is not set in concrete – it can be changed. Many immigrants choose citizenship of their country of adoption, as I did – I was born in Scotland of Scottish ancestry and became an Australian citizen. This option is, however, not open to people settling in Scotland, England, Wales or Northern Ireland from outside the United Kingdom. Immigrants to Britain cannot take out Scottish, English, Welsh or Northern Irish citizenship; only British. So, the people named in the previous paragraph could not, in any event, have become Scots in any legal sense.

As it is not always possible to determine someone's personal view of their cultural heritage, the only approach I felt was acceptable was one that could be measured objectively, so I have determined that anyone born in Scotland (including, for consistency, Sir Nigel Gresley), or who has a Scottish-born parent or grandparent, qualifies for entry in this book. Having an ancestor born in Scotland any further back than a grandparent makes the Scottish connection too tenuous for Scotland to have much influence on their achievements, even though the Scottish connection is still valid. (As always, there is an exception to the rule – I have included Canadian-born Chalmers Jack Mackenzie as *all* eight of his great grandparents were born in Scotland).

The 867 inventors, scientists, innovators and engineers included in this book span a period of more than half a millennium and range over many fields of endeavour – aeronautics, agriculture, air-conditioning, archaeology, architecture, astronomy, banking, biology, chemistry, communications, computing, construction, economics, electrics, electronics, engineering, entertainment, finance, forensic science, gas technology, genetics, geology, insurance, iron and steel technology, management, manufacturing, mathematics, medicine, meteorology, mining, music, oceanography, oil technology, photography, physics, physiology, plastics, printing, publishing, refrigeration, sanitation, seismology, shipping, sport, steam engine technology, surveying, tool-making, transportation, warfare – and many more.

The entries are laid out in chronological order by year of birth, and alphabetically by surname within any given year. Where the year of birth is not known, I have deducted 25 years from the period of their most important achievement, thus David Donald, fl. 1727, appears in 1702. While this is inaccurate, it does place them closer to their true date of birth. The entries concentrate on each individual's achievements and contain no information (or very little) on their personal lives or their personal struggles to bring their ideas to fruition.

There are many direct quotations in the book, such as the reference to Robert Davidson who invented, "in the early 1840s a lathe, a saw, and a small printing machine, all electrically operated, and a model electric locomotive that would carry two people on a railway." To minimise "visual clutter", I have used quotation marks sparingly, but all citations have the source reference included. I have also changed the spelling of some words in direct quotations to conform to British English. One effect of so many direct citations is that the book speaks with many voices, including that of the author, which may affect continuity of style, but the achievements of the subjects included speak for themselves – and what a story they tell!

A.G. Paterson

CHAPTER 1

1453-1749

Scotland, located on the outer north-western reaches of the European Atlantic littoral, was for much of its history considered a primitive backwater compared to the more sophisticated, better educated, and the much more technologically adept peoples of the Mediterranean. Even by the primitive standards of medieval Western Europe and England, the Scots lagged behind on almost every measurable criterion of civilised endeavour. Only in one area did Scotland hold its own against its European neighbours – warfare. The Scots defended their freedom against a much more powerful southern neighbour, and they constrained the fearsome Vikings of Scandinavia to settlements on Scotland's periphery, unlike in what is now modern England, Ireland, France and Russia where the Norsemen took some of the best land available. To the south, the Saxons and Angles had to do homage to a Danish invader – King Cnut – and, some three decades after his death, England was again in thrall to the descendants of other Norsemen who had first seized Normandy then conquered southern Britain. Scotland's resources were often consumed in keeping invaders at bay, and its most productive land was close to the border and easily ravaged by invading armies from the south, with the result that it was economically poor and fared badly in technological innovation. It should come then as no surprise that the first entry in this book was involved in warfare and, appropriately – given the low profile of Scots in the eastern Mediterranean – there was confusion about where he originated.

Not until the 16th century would Scotland produce someone of European renown in the world of invention, but even in the century that followed John Napier's logarithms, Scottish inventors, scientists and engineers were rare. From the 15th to the 17th centuries, Europe was swept by the Renaissance and the Reformation, bringing new ways of thinking and seriously challenging the old ways. In Scotland, this was manifested in a religious fervour which gave impetus to the education of the "small people" rather than just the more privileged classes. In the same period, a Scottish king united the British Isles under one monarch and later, in 1707, the Scottish Parliament voted to join in union with the English Parliament to form the United Kingdom (the Scottish Parliament had voted for union with England a century earlier on 11 August 1607 but Westminster refused to pass it in the form desired by King James). The number of Scottish technologists and innovators born after this period began to climb dramatically and, by 1800, Scotland had already produced a remarkable array of innovative men who would make their mark in many fields, particularly science, medicine and technology. Some of these people, and their contributions to invention, science, engineering, and innovation, are recorded in this chapter and those following.

Johannes Grant birth unknown-died 1453 was an engineer employed by the Byzantine Empire at the fall of Constantinople in 1453. Contemporary Greek accounts referred to him as being

German, although more recent scholarship has suggested he was more likely a Scot, named John Grant. His use of counter-tunneling prevented the Turks from weakening or invading Constantinople, the world's greatest city, from under the walls. Under torture, a captured Turkish officer of the miners trying to tunnel into the city revealed to the Byzantines where all the Turkish mines were placed. Grant managed to locate each of the mine shafts and either undermine them or destroy the attackers inside with explosives, flooding, or the incendiary Greek fire. None of the fourteen mines succeeded and the Turks abandoned their mining activities.[1]

Historian Sir Steve Runciman has in recent times identified Grant as a Scot who played a pivotal role in Medieval Greek folklore. Previously, it was thought he was actually German, but Runciman says "Grant, usually described as a German but … may well have been a Scottish adventurer who had found his way through Germany to the Levant."[2]

George Bruce c1550-1625 designed an apparatus to drain his coalmine in Culross, including "innovative mechanical drainage, ventilation, and haulage techniques – notably an 'Egyptian wheel' [chain and bucket system] – to solve the problems of exploiting deep and under-sea coalmines."[1]

Bruce extended a coal mine under the tidal Forth River by building an artificial island in the river, thereby allowing the entrance shaft to stay well above the high-water mark. On the island, he then had a shaft dug that was, at least, 12 metres deep, but may have been more than twice this depth. This shaft was connected to one on the mainland and a third shaft was used to drain water from the mine with water power that was generated by a dam. The three shafts also provided much greater ventilation in the mine than was usual at the time.[2] Bruce's mine was the first successful undersea mine known – it was the "earliest example of undersea mining [being] commenced about 1588 at Culross, Perthshire, Scotland"[3] with the mine shaft extending quarter of a mile (0.4 km) from the shore. In 1617, James VI (James I of England) did a tour of the mine and went down into the Culross colliery. When he ascended the shaft at the Moat Pit he panicked at finding he was on an island, fearing treachery and possible assassination (his father had been murdered and he himself had been kidnapped in his youth). Sir George quickly explained the situation to him and the king calmed down when he saw a tethered boat intended to return them to the mainland. The mine operated from around 1588 until it was inundated by a storm in 1625.[4]

John Napier 1550-1617 invented a form of abacus, using rods made from materials such as wood, metal or ivory (hence "Napier's Bones") that were placed in a rimmed board with the numbers 1-9 aligned vertically in squares on the left edge. Each rod had nine squares with the top square containing an integer in the range 0-9. The other eight squares were diagonally divided and corresponded to a multiple of the top integer, with the first number of the multiple placed in the top diagonal and the second part of the multiple in the lower diagonal. For example, if the top square held the number 7, the first diagonally divided square would have 1/4 (7x2=14), the second diagonally divided square would have 2/1 (7x3=21), the third 2/8 (7x4=28) and so on to the last diagonally divided square for the number 7, which would be 6/3 (7x9=63).

With these rods multiplication could be performed by simple addition, and division by simple subtraction – even square roots could be calculated with an extra three-column rod attached. In the days before the calculator, this was an important aid in the advance of complex mathematical calculations, particularly in astronomy. Napier first publicly described his invention in *Rabdologiæ* (1617). He also made a card version that let the user multiply numbers up to 200 digits in length – an amazing innovation in its day. He built a calculator called the Promptuary which "could be said to be the world's first calculating machine. Napier invented it for larger calculations"[1] because using his "bones" required some degree of skill to make good use of them. "The High Speed Promptuary for Multiplication", as Napier called it, avoided that problem but [unlike his "bones"] performed only multiplication.[2]

Napier's rods could also be used as a slide rule, as noted by the Oughtred Society in their *Slide Rule History*, since "logarithms are the foundation on which the slide rule is built, its history rightly begins with him [Napier]. His early concept of simplifying mathematical calculations through logarithms makes possible the slide rule as we know it today."[3]

"Logarithms proved to be a vitally important advance in mathematics, and not just as a theory for academics – the concept led directly to the invention of the slide rule by Englishman William Oughtred around 1622, and paved the way for mechanical and [much later] electronic calculation and computation."[4]

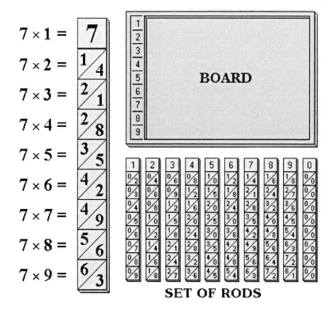

Image 1 – Napier's Bones

Napier first brought his invention of logarithms to public attention in *Mirifici Logarithmorum Canonis Descriptio* (1614). Jost Bürgi of Switzerland may have conceived logarithms as early as 1588, but he didn't publish until 1620 when Napier's logarithms had been in well-established use by European scientists. Bürgi's method was geometric whereas Napier used an algebraic method for his logarithms. Napier thought of logarithms as a ratio between two distances in a geometric form and it wasn't until later that they were thought of as exponents. English mathematician Henry Biggs and Napier adapted logarithms to their modern practice by using 10 as a base, giving them exponential functionality.

Napier was also interested in improving agricultural output and quality. He experimented so successfully with the use of common salts to help kill weeds and to fertilise soil that the government granted a monopoly to his family for this practice, and he published his findings in *The new order of gooding and manuring all sorts of field land with common salt*.[5]

He invented "several war machines for defence against Spain, including two types of 'burning mirror' intended to be used for setting fire to ships at a distance, a rapid-fire artillery gun that would kill men and horses, and an armoured chariot that was effectively a primitive form of tank which permitted occupants to fire in any direction through holes while being safely inside the armed vehicle. In 1597, he was granted a patent for the invention of a hydraulic screw controlled by a revolving axle, used as a pump to control the water level in coalmines."[6]

Napier's rules of circular parts used spherical triangles, that is, the shape enclosed when three points on the surface of a sphere are joined. "Text-books and treatises are considerably at variance as to the importance and status of these rules. They are continually referred to as mere mnemonics requiring independent proof in each case; and not infrequently their role in this capacity is discouraged, analogies with corresponding formulae in the plane being offered as preferable substitutes. These much-abused individuals [i.e. Napier's rules of circular parts] are entitled to more generous consideration and should be invested with the dignity of a theorem."[7]

Despite his inventive success, Napier's main concern was religion. He was fanatically Protestant and published what he considered his most important work – *Plaine Discovery of the Whole Revelation of St. John* – the first book by a Scot to interpret the Scriptures. It acquired a reputation in parts of the Continent, including Catholic countries.

Napier is sometimes, incorrectly, credited with inventing the decimal point to separate fractions from integers, but he did play a major role in making it popular. The decimal point as a separator may have originated as early as the 9th century in Persia [Iran] – although it was not then a point or comma but a bar above the fraction. The decimal dot was first recorded by a German Jesuit priest, Christopher Clavius, in *Tabula Sinuum* (1593) well before Napier first used it around 1616.

Napier's *Logarithmorum Canonis Descriptio* has been described as "one of the most influential books ever published. It introduced the world to logarithms that were the principle behind most of the methods of computation prior to the invention of the electronic computer. They are also fundamental in the theory behind many mathematical systems."[8]

His tables of logs enabled Johannes Kepler to analyse Tycho Brahe's observations and deduce the orbits of the planets. Napier's rods were, in essence, the first practical calculating machines, being described thus: "One of the greatest seventeenth-century advances in computation was the invention of logarithms by John Napier. His *Description of the wonderful table of logarithms* is unique in the history [of] science as being the result of original speculation by one individual unaided by either the work of precursors or contemporaries."[9]

Robert Scott after 1568-died 1631 developed a leather-covered cannon, also known as the leather gun, in competition with that of Austrian Melchior von Wurmbrand-Stuppach, and Philip Eberhard of Switzerland. It was widely copied in all corners of Europe[1] and became the most celebrated of the new types of light artillery introduced in the first three decades of the 17th century. Originally invented by Eberhard, it was copied by Wurmbrand who took it to Sweden where it was first tested on 15 July 1625.[2]

The "leather was in fact the least important element of this innovative new gun's construction, the strength of the design being a central tube of copper wound with wire – a similar idea to the wire windings used in the nineteenth century."[3] These cannon were revolutionary in that they were light enough to be carried by two men, they fired the same size shot as conventional cannon with half the powder, and they could fire up to a hundred times without having to be left to cool down.

Scott used different proportions to Wurmbrand in the construction of his cannon. He also told the Swedish king Gustavus Adolphus that he had contrived a way of reloading his cannon ten times before a soldier could reload his musket once. Some Danish noblemen witnessed a demonstration of the leather cannon in Stockholm at which the Swedish king was said to have been suitably impressed. However, Scott wished payment of 20,000 Swedish riksdaler for his invention, a sum which Gustavus Adolphus refused to pay. Scott transferred to serve the Danish King and was made Master-General of Artillery on 6 September 1628, apparently the first time this position ever existed in Denmark.

"Gustavus Adolphus is sometimes given credit for these guns, but with little proof; yet there is little doubt that he used them extensively in the Thirty Years War where they produced the desired effect of shock."[4] The effectiveness of the leather cannon has, however, been doubted,[5] but there is ample evidence of its being regarded as an excellent weapon during the Wars of the Three Kingdoms [England, Scotland and Ireland] between 1638 and 1651. It first saw service with the Scottish Covenanters in the version developed by General Alexander Hamilton, known as "Dear Sandy's stoup". Later, leather cannons could be found in the English parliamentarian and Cromwellian service in the Scott model, as developed and refined by his nephew James Wemyss.[6]

David Ramsay c1575-1660 took out the first patent for something resembling a water jet propulsion system in 1631 – English Patent No. 50. This was at a time when the use of steam power to lift water out of mines and to operate fountains was of great interest, so Ramsay would probably have used steam power for his invention. Ramsay was clockmaker to King James VI of Scotland and I of England and he appears to have been of an inventive mind as witnessed by his patents "for the manufacture and use of numerous inventions and engines: to plough without horses in 1619; to make an engine invented by John Jack and David Ramsay, Page of the Bedchamber, to raise water, for draining land and mines; an engine to turn spits; and others dealing with the manufacture of saltpetre and a scarlet dye."[1] In 1630, Ramsay took out another patent of nine claims, the second of which reads, "To raise water from lowe pittes by fire;" and this is considered the earliest notice of an engine for raising water by fire (i.e. steam) in England.[2] This is 68 years before Thomas Savery's steam engine, which is credited with being the first ever commercially used steam engine, its only use being to pump out water from coal mines.

Some of his other patents included: propelling ships and boats, making tapestry without a loom, refining copper, bleaching wax, separating gold and silver from the base metals, dyeing fabrics, heating boilers, kilns for drying and burning bricks and tiles, and smelting and refining iron by means of coal.[3]

Robert Murray [Moray] 1609-1673 was the prime mover in founding The Royal Society of London, the world's oldest scientific academy in continuous existence, and which has played a part in some of the most fundamental, significant, and life-changing discoveries in scientific history.[1] Following the restoration of Charles II after the rule of Oliver Cromwell and, later, his son Richard, Murray began to take a prominent part in the deliberations of a club instituted in London for the discussion of natural science, or, as it was then called, the "new philosophy". When it was proposed to obtain a charter for the society, he undertook to interest the king in the matter, the result being that on 15 July 1662 the club was incorporated by charter under the designation of The Royal Society. Murray was its first president.[2]

While there were other important people involved in the foundation of The Royal Society, including Robert Boyle, Sir Christopher Wren and Robert Hooke, it was Murray who made it happen. He was "a mover and shaker who actively served the King during his exile. [And] he was the only person able to deliver a Royal Charter to this ramshackle bunch of philosopers."[3] "*The Journal Book* of the Society shows that Moray was the driving force behind building an organisation which was structured well enough to be able to request a Royal Charter. Sir Henry Lyons says of this period: 'Moray was extremely active throughout the year 1661 and this was recognised by his colleagues who elected him to the presidency of the new Society oftener than any other of its members. He undoubtedly had much to do with the preliminary drafting of the First Charter.'"[4]

John Winthrop, Governor of Connecticut, and son of a founder of Massachusetts, came "to London looking for a Royal Charter for his colony. Moray, who had met Winthrop at Oxford in 1643, invited him into the Society and once more took on his old role of negotiator, helping Winthrop to get the charter he sought."[5] This territory was much larger than the present state of Massachusetts and covered much of what is New England.

On 1 March 1665, Sir Robert had put a motion to the Council which said that: "The Philosophical Transactions, to be composed by Mr Oldenburg, be printed the first Monday of every month, if he have sufficient matter for it, and that the tract be licensed and that the President be now desired to license the first papers thereof." This was the first regular publication of scientific knowledge! "The importance of this new venture to the development of science was enormous. Modern science, we have seen, develops by a process of observation, prediction and finally control. The idea of a journal, recording and spreading the detail of observations and allowing the sharing of predictions, was an enormous step forward for the development of science". The idea originated with Murray, being "conceived from his experience of sharing ideas [while in exile with the future King Charles II] with a correspondence circle".[6]

Alexander Bruce c1629-1680 was co-patentee, with Christiaan Huygens, of the short pendulum clock which could measure longitude at sea better than previous methods (although not well enough to be of any real use on voyages of great distance).

Huygens invented the pendulum in 1656, but five years later Bruce used an inverted F-crutch design to improve its accuracy. Huygens' final patent drawings around 1664 clearly depict Bruce's double-fork crutch in the form of an inverted F. In 1662, Dutch watchmaker Severijn Oosterwijck made two copies of Bruce's "first Longitude pendulum clock fitted with a double-fork F-crutch, shown to Huygens in London in 1661, both tested by Robert Holmes.

Oosterwijck then constructed Huygens' Longitude design and, by August 1664, he also had incorporated Huygens' ingenious but flawed weight-remontoir, for which Huygens would obtain a Dutch patent."[1] Thus, the very first marine pendulum was developed by both Huygens and Bruce in the last two months of 1662. Over the course of the next three years, Bruce and The Royal Society supervised sea trials of the clocks. "Huygens had already toyed with various ways of suspending the clock from a pivot so as to render it independent of the ship's motion, but Bruce's idea of a steel ball encased in a brass cylinder proved most effective in tests at The Hague. Two of the clocks went with Bruce to London early in 1663 and, after minor setbacks prompting the intervention of The Royal Society, accompanied Captain Robert Holmes on voyages first to Lisbon and then to Guinea and out into the Atlantic. The first voyage yielded a log with encouraging data, including clocked longitudes that agreed well with accepted values in well-known waters."[2]

When Holmes returned to London in 1665 he presented his report to an expectant Royal Society. The clocks had performed spectacularly well. Indeed, he declared, they had actually saved the expedition from disaster. On the return journey, Holmes had been obliged to sail several hundred nautical miles westwards in order to pick up a favourable wind. Having done so, the *Jersey* and the three ships accompanying her sailed several hundred more miles north-eastwards, at which point the four captains found that water was running worryingly low on board. Holmes' three fellow-captains produced three competing sets of calculations of their current positions based on traditional reckoning, but all agreed they were dangerously far from any potential source of water. Not so, declared Holmes. According to his calculations – based on the pendulum clocks – they were a mere 90 miles (144 km) west of the island of Fuego, one of the Cape Verde islands. He persuaded the party to set their course due east whereupon, the very next day, around noon, they indeed made landfall on Fuego, exactly as predicted.[3]

Despite parsimony in his public credit of co-inventors, there is no doubt, from first concept right up to his patent, Huygens always had committed himself to Bruce's new F-crutch.[4]

Bruce finally received the "credit due to him, which Christiaan Huygens had been loath to give publicly; both in his 1664 Patent applications for his weight-remontoir with Bruce's crutch, and in his great 1673 Opus, *Horologium Oscillatorium*. ... these sea-clocks, [should be] properly attributed to their acknowledged *inventor*, the 2nd Earl Kincardine Alexander Bruce between 1660/1 and 1665."[5]

"Bruce did produce enough evidence to show that a suitable clock could be used to measure longitude with a useful degree of accuracy."[6] Not long afterwards the Dutch and English were at war, competing for overseas trade and empire – competition unwittingly fostered by the navigational advances Bruce and Huygens had made possible.[7] It would not be until 1761 that Englishman John Harrison created the first effective marine chronometer at the instigation of the Royal Navy, who offered the phenomenal sum of up to £20,000 for one that worked accurately in all weather conditions. Simultaneously, Frenchman Pierre Le Roy had been working on an even more accurate marine chronometer which used his detent escapement invention (1748), with his marine chronometer being completed in 1766.

James Gregory 1638-1675 proposed, in 1663, that the distance between the Earth and sun could be found using the parallax of Venus when it crossed the surface of the sun as seen from Earth –

the so-called Transit of Venus. This distance is now referred to as the Astronomical Unit whose current value is some 8.794 arc-seconds. Gregory (he preferred Gregorie) also was the first to provide the first proof of the fundamental theorem of calculus, also in 1663. He provided a formula that allows a definite integral of a function to be expressed by its sum and differences, or its sum by its integral and difference. Gregory demonstrated his advanced knowledge on series expansions; they also show that he discovered the binomial theorem independently of Newton (although it was also known to ancient Greek, Indian and Persian mathematicians). In February 1671, he communicated to John Collins, without proof, several trigonometric series. The printing of Gregory's manuscripts in 1939 made it clear that he obtained these series by the method now known as the Taylor Expansion of a function.[1]

In 1667, he published *Vera Circuli et Hyperbolae Quadratura* where he introduced the terms *convergent* and *divergent* for series, when he demonstrated how the areas of the circle and hyperbola could be obtained in the form of infinite convergent series.

Today, Gregory is best remembered for the reflecting telescope. Refractor telescopes had been around since the Dutch first built them around 1608. The next improvement was the reflecting telescope, employing a combination of curved and flat mirrors to reflect light to form an image. One was designed in 1616 by Italian Niccolo Zucchi, but he encountered problems and gave up on developing it. In 1663, Gregory published *Optica Promota*, describing the compact reflecting telescope which was to dominate astronomical observation for more than 150 years. It was built by English polymath Robert Hooke and was the first practical reflecting telescope. The Gregorian reflecting telescope used a concave secondary mirror which gave an upright image suitable for use on land as well as in astronomy. Isaac Newton designed his own reflecting telescope around 1670 and this is sometimes, incorrectly, called the first practical reflecting telescope. Newton's design was superior, but that doesn't negate Gregory's achievement.

Gregory's method of determining the value of the Astronomical Unit using parallax, also described in *Optica Promota*, was the basis for the major scientific endeavour of the 18th century – to observe the Transit of Venus during its paired crossings of the sun in 1761 and 1769, the latter date being part of the reason for the voyage of Lieutenant James Cook to Tahiti and thence to look for the "missing" Southern Land (Australia).

Gregory was given a professorship in mathematics at St Andrews but its provincialism at that time stifled his ability to do further effective research. "Denied by geography much knowledge of the parallel mathematical work in Britain and abroad, James Gregorie nevertheless discovered for himself the general interpolation and binomial theorems, derived a number of trigonometric series, notably for the natural and logarithmic tangent and secant, and found a series solution to a problem posed by Kepler, employing 20 years before Newton a Taylor development of a function in terms of its nth order derivatives. In applied science, in dynamics in particular, he bridged Galileo's *Discorsi* and Newton's *Principia*, proposing solutions to dozens of astronomical problems, ranging from planetary ellipses to designing the 'catadioptric' telescope of mirrors and lenses. Much of the correspondence from his short career is lost to us, and he was reluctant to publish. But all evidence suggests that James Gregorie was a weightier figure than tradition has allowed. Newton, in particular, almost certainly owes him more than anyone has yet recognised."[2]

Hugh MacKay c1640-1692 is claimed as the inventor of the ring bayonet which soon came into general use, the idea being suggested to him by the failure of the plug-bayonet to stop the rush of the Jacobite Highlanders at Killiecrankie in 1689. Prior to this battle, soldiers had used plug bayonets, invented in France and named for the city of Bayonne, but there were obvious drawbacks to this form of bayonet as the rifle could not be loaded or fired when the bayonet was in place. "The person who first invented the ring bayonet is uncertain. Hugh Mackay … wrote that his men had no time to place or remove their plug bayonets when the Highland clansmen charged them firing their pistols and brandishing their swords. He had rings put on the bayonets so his men could fire while their bayonets were in place."[1]

There are also strong claims that the socket (ring) bayonet was invented in 1688 by French engineer Sebastien Le Prestre de Vauban. Certainly, the British army was slower than the French to adopt the ring bayonet as indicated in *Military Antiquities* – It is not known "when the present mode of fixing bayonets took place, nor by whom it was invented; the improvement is said to have originated in France, which seems to be corroborated by the following anecdote communicated to me by Lieut. Col. Christopher Maxwell of the 30th regiment of foot, who had it from his grandfather, formerly Lieutenant Colonel of the 25th regiment of foot. In one of the campaigns of King William III in Flanders, in an engagement, the name of which my informant has forgot, there were three French regiments, whose bayonets were made to fix after the present fashion, a contrivance then unknown in the British army; one of them advanced against the 25th regiment with fixed bayonets; Lieutenant Colonel Maxwell who commanded it, ordered his men to screw their bayonets into their muzzles to receive them; but to his great surprise, when they came within a proper distance, the French threw in a heavy fire, which for a moment staggered his people, who by no means expected such a greeting, not conceiving how it was possible to fire with fixed bayonets; they nevertheless recovered themselves, charged and drove the enemy out of the line."[2]

William Paterson 1658-1719 was the chief projector of the plan to establish the Bank of England and the concept of The National Debt. Paterson was among the first to submit a proposal that, although rejected in its early form, established the use of public debt borrowed from a bank.[1] People in England sensed that the country was on the brink of a tremendous expansion of trade, but one vital element was lacking: what was needed was a bank or "fund of money" – more liquidity, in modern parlance – to drive the trade of the country. They looked with some envy across to the continent at the example of the Dutch who were then pre-eminent in Europe.

Central to the success of the Dutch was the Amsterdam Wisselbank, which had been founded in 1609. It provided the motive power for the Dutch economy by lending to the City of Amsterdam, to the State in the form of the Province of Holland, and to trade in the shape of the Dutch East India Company, as well as being responsible for coinage and, of course, exchange. Much later, in 1683, it was empowered to lend to private customers. Payments over a certain amount had to pass through it and it therefore was convenient for the important finance houses to hold accounts with it. Thus, not only was it in a position to oversee the Dutch financial scene, it was also able to act as a stabilising influence on it.

Dutch-born King William III of Great Britain had brought to his adopted country an understandable desire to help his native country in its war against the French and this proved to be the catalyst necessary for the idea of a national bank to be accepted, albeit grudgingly by some.[2]

Paterson first came to public notice in 1691, when he joined a group of London merchants who proposed that England should set up a bank of credit on the Dutch model. The proposal was initially rejected by a Parliamentary Committee in January 1692. In 1694, Parliament approved a plan drawn up by Paterson, the merchant Michael Godfrey, and the Treasury commissioner Charles Montagu, for a fund to support long-term public borrowing, a bank to administer it, and the mortgaging of future revenue for payment of interest to investors.[3]

The founding of the Bank of England revolutionised public finance and put an end to defaults. "From now on there would be no more regular defaulting (the 'Stop of the Exchequer' of 1672 when, with the crown deep in debt, Charles II had suspended payment of his bills, was still fresh in the memories of London investors). There would be no more debasement of the coinage, particularly after the adoption of the gold standard in 1717. There would be parliamentary scrutiny of royal finances. And there would be a sustained effort to consolidate the various debts that the Stuart dynasty had incurred over the years".[4] From then on, the British Government would never fail to repay its creditors. In the following centuries, other countries in Europe and, later, around the world adopted similar financial institutions to manage their government debt.

Despite an earlier proposal, it was Paterson's scheme that eventually found favour. He had first put forward a proposal in 1691, but this had been rejected for several reasons, including: "Others said this project came from Holland and therefore would not hear of it, since we had too many Dutch things already". Under his scheme, in return for a loan of £1 million, the bills issued by his company should be made legal tender. This idea proved to be more than a century ahead of its time, and consequently unacceptable to the Parliamentary Committee. After several more rejections, Paterson put forward a plan for a 'Bank of England' and a 'Fund for Perpetual Interest' although this time bills were not mentioned. Supported by two powerful personalities – Charles Montagu, Chancellor of the Exchequer, who looked after the Parliamentary lobbying, and Michael Godfrey a leading merchant who ensured the idea's acceptance in the City – it was all but inevitable, given the Government's pressing need for funds, that the scheme should be approved by Parliament. So, Paterson's plan was accepted and the necessary act passed. The public were invited to invest in the new project and it was these subscriptions totalling £1.2 million that were to form the initial capital stock of the Bank of England and were to be on-lent to Government in return for a Royal Charter.[5]

To start with, the Bank was the Government's banker: managing the Government's accounts; managing (at some expense to itself) the recoinage of 1696; providing and arranging loans to the Government. It was also a commercial bank, dealing in bills – the then equivalent of overdraft finance, furnishing finance for trade. It took deposits and issued notes, and with the development of the issue function, it began to realise the dreams of some of the original projectors, of a Bank that would "double the Effect of out our coined Money". One particularly significant development around this time lay in the perception of credit or 'imaginary money' as it was then called. It represented a fundamental and distinctive principle in the new thinking that was so prevalent during this age of ideas and experiments. Projectors had begun to recognise the existence of an untapped source of assets, albeit non-metallic, such as stocks of merchandise, tax receipts, revenues on land and commercial obligations, against which 'credit' or 'imaginary money' could be raised. Credit could be, they argued, the seed corn of wealth. But what was the money? To the man in the street, money simply meant coins, but the new thinking was overturning that Shibboleth: it was suggesting that money could take other forms which would have no intrinsic value and yet still possess qualities to enable it to be used to make payments thereby fuelling and lubricating the economy. It was inevitable, therefore, that when theory became practice and the funded National Debt was born, that crucial element, paper money, almost simultaneously completed the equation.

An early exponent of free trade decades before Adam Smith rewrote modern economics with *The Wealth of Nations*, Paterson would pen: "Trade will increase trade, and money will beget money, and the trading world shall need no more want work for their hands, but will rather want hands for their work." Before his departure from the board of the Bank of England, Paterson successfully lobbied the Scottish Parliament for the passage of the Act for a Company Trading to Africa and the Indies. The act led to the erecting of the Bank of Scotland in 1696. Paterson is also remembered for the disaster of the Darien Scheme with Scotland losing over half its national wealth alongside the lives of over 2,000 colonists who died attempting to set up a trading post in what is now Panama. The failed experiment was caused in no small measure by England's withdrawal of investment and assurances of safety on the colony, alongside similar promises and withdrawal by the Dutch (the English and Dutch East India companies had united in procuring orders from the king forbidding any one to render the colonists any assistance).[6]

It was an economic disaster too. The company had lost over £232,884, made up of the life savings of many of the Scottish people. Scotland was now completely incapable of going it alone. Just seven years after the failure at Darien, it was forced to concede to the Act of Union, joining Scotland with England as the junior partner in the United Kingdom of Great Britain. As part of the deal, England paid off Scotland's debts with the "Equivalent", a sum of £398,000, most of which went to cover the Company of Scotland's losses. The institution established to administer this money eventually became the Royal Bank of Scotland.[7]

Hans Sloane 1660-1753 invented milk chocolate as a drink and he was one of the earliest to use statistics in respect of medicine. He was also the "Great Collector" who became one of the founding fathers of the British Museum. Sloane was a foundation Governor to Captain Coram's Foundling Hospital, opened in Bloomsbury, London, in 1741. Seven years later, in 1748, at the age of 88 he wrote to the Vice President of the hospital a letter on the nursing of infants that reveals his exceptional common sense and intelligence. "Upon examining the books of the Hospital, I found as follows, by which it plainly appears, that what I said was agreeable to matter of fact:

March 25th, 1741: admitted 30 children; to wett nurses, 2: dyed, 0: to dry nurses, 28; dyed, 15.
April 17th, 1741: admitted 30 children; to wett nurses, 7; dyed, 1: to dry nurses, 22; dyed, 11.
May 8th, 1741: admitted 30 children; to wett nurses, 17; dyed, 4: to dry nurses, 13; dyed 8.
Total children admitted = 90.
Total to wett nurses, 26; dyed 5.
Total to dry nurses, 63; dyed, 34. Taken out, 1."

From these figures, it can be seen that the mortality for infants who were dry-nursed was nearly three times greater than that for those who were wet-nursed (54% v 19%), a highly significant difference. Although retrospective and non-randomised (i.e. a clinical trial in which the participants are not assigned by chance to different treatment groups) this observation must be one of the earliest, if not the earliest, to use audit and statistics to guide medical practice.[1] Note: Englishman John Gaunt is considered the founder of medical statistics with his 1662 publication *Natural and Political Observations*, and he was followed by William Petty and Matthew Hale before Sloane's publication.

In 1687, Sloane became a fellow of the College of Physicians and went that year to Jamaica as a physician in the suite of the Duke of Albemarle. The duke died soon after landing and Sloane's visit lasted only fifteen months. During that time, he noted about 800 new species of plants, the island being virgin ground to the botanist. Of these, he published an elaborate catalogue in Latin in 1696; and at a later date (1707-1725) he made the experiences of his visit the subject of two folio volumes. He became secretary to The Royal Society in 1693 and edited the *Philosophical Transactions* from then until 1714.[2] While he was in Jamaica, Sloane had observed that "Chocolate is here used by all Peoples, at all times". However, the natives in the West Indies drank chocolate mixed with honey and pepper, a concoction quite unpalatable as far as Europeans were concerned; Hans himself recorded that he "found it in great quantities nauseous" whilst also noting that it "colours the Excrements of those feeding on it a dirty colour". Sloane saw babies being fed on a mixture of cocoa beans and their mother's breast milk.[3]

Sloane was unhappy with the taste of the cocoa drink favoured by the Jamaicans and on his return to England his great innovation was to find a way of making chocolate palatable for European tastes, which was simply to mix it with hot milk. He began the commercial production of "Sir Hans Sloane's Milk Chocolate" which was marketed as a medicine noted "For its Lightness on the Stomach and its great Use in all Consumptive Cases". Chocolate soon joined coffee as one of the fashionable drinks of the age and made Sloane yet another fortune. In 1849, Cadbury Brothers released bars of "Sir Hans Sloane's Milk Chocolate" as their first drinking milk chocolate. This was soon followed by milk chocolate bars for eating, the predecessors of today's Cadbury's *Dairy Milk*.[4]

His purchase, in 1712, of the manor of Chelsea in London provided the grounds for the Chelsea Physic Garden as well as perpetuating his memory in the name of a "place," a street, and a square. His great stroke as a collector was to acquire (by bequest, conditional on paying of certain debts), in 1701, the cabinet of William Courten, who had made collecting the business of his life.[5] In 1716, Sloane was created a baronet, the first medical practitioner to receive a hereditary title and, in 1719, he became president of the College of Physicians, holding the office sixteen years. In 1727, he succeeded Sir Isaac Newton as president of The Royal Society and he retired from it at the age of eighty.

When Sloane died in 1753 he left over 50,000 books and 250,000 natural history specimens to science which became the core of the British Museum. He bequeathed his books, manuscripts, prints, drawings, pictures, medals, coins, seals, cameos and other curiosities to the nation, on condition that Parliament should pay to his executors £20,000, payable to his daughters – a large sum for the time but an amount far less than the collection's actual worth. Funds from a lottery were used to make the purchase during the year of his death and the British Museum of Bloomsbury was created. It was to be the founding core of the British Museum and, later, The Natural History Museum.[6]

Sloane was appointed as Physician Extraordinary to Queen Anne (1712-1714) and to King George I (1716), President of the Royal College of Physicians (1719-1735) when he succeeded Sir Isaac Newton, and Physician in Ordinary (i.e. in regular service) to King George II (1727). He dedicated the first volume of his *Natural History* to Queen Anne and the second to King George I. At a critical juncture, Sloane preserved the life of Anne for two days more than she was expected to live and may thus have preserved the Hanoverian succession. This observation was based on the dismissal of Robert Harley, Lord Treasurer, on 27 July 1714, a few days before Anne's death on 1 August. Harley was a Jacobite sympathiser and it was believed that he would try to orchestrate the return of the Old Pretender, James Stuart (whom Jacobites referred to as James VII and III).[7]

William Ged 1690-1749 developed stereotyping, an important innovation in the era before computers. Today, television, radio, telephone, email, fax, web documents, text messaging and the word processor are major forms of communication, but before the advent of electricity and electronics, the most common methods of communicating over distances or to the multitude were by mail and printed documents. Printing has a long history traceable to ancient China, but it was the German goldsmith Johannes Gutenberg who, in 1447, brought printing to Europe, from where it spread to the rest of the world. Minor improvements were made over time, but the next three and a half centuries were really a period of stasis in the printing industry. A forerunner of modern stereotype did originate in Germany early in the 15th century but never caught on. Dutchmen Johannes Muller and J. Van der Mey re-introduced it in the 1690s with little success. Their process required separate composition of the types for each form made as Muller soldered his plates together. This process is different from "true" stereotyping, as developed by William Ged.

Ged was an Edinburgh goldsmith at a time when metal type castings were often transported from London, and Ged realised that substantial savings could be made if the current process could be made more efficient. Starting around 1725, Ged sought to reduce overheads and within two years he had produced an effective means of making copies of print runs for re-publication with papier-mâché moulds of the original work. This allowed the metal to be re-used for another job while retaining the capacity to quickly re-publish stereotyped works. A few years later Frenchman Gabriel Valleyre developed a similar solution by using clay for his moulds, but these were more prone to damage. Ged's process involved setting up his page with movable type, before he "locked his form and then the page was laid upon gypsum or plaster of Paris, or some other semi-liquid substance, just as it was drying; when it was dried completely he removed the form from the gypsum cast, and using this cast as a matrix, he formed solid plates of lead. From these he printed on the ordinary letter-press. The letters on the edges of the plates stood up rather higher than those in the centre."[1]

Ged went into partnership with a London stationer, William Fenner, but they met with opposition from other printers and Ged suffered financial hardship. In 1736, he made a complete stereotype copy of *Sallus* (the *Nome de plume* of Roman historian Gaius Sallustius Crispus). Following his support for the Jacobite rebellion – he served with James Drummond, the Duke of Perth's regiment – Ged was imprisoned and later left Britain for Jamaica to join his brother, but died the following year.

Image 2 – Stereotype

For some obscure reason, William Ged is frequently claimed as the inventor of the Lost Wax Process used by jewellers to reproduce delicate designs. This method involves carving or modelling a design in wax, making a "positive" mould of the design which is then placed in a heated oven until the wax melts and drains away to leave a "negative" design. Hot metal is then injected into this mould and, when cooled, the mould is broken open and the design is cleaned and polished. It is unclear why Ged is hailed as the inventor for the Lost Wax Process, which has been known since 3,000BC.

James Stirling 1692-1770 completed Isaac Newton's classification of cubic curves in his work *Lineaetertii ordinis Neutonianae* (1717). While in London, Stirling published his most important work, *Methodus Differentialis*, in 1730. This book is a treatise on infinite series, summation, interpolation and quadrature. The asymptotic formula for n! for which Stirling is best known appears as Example 2 to Proposition 28 of the *Methodus Differentialis*. One of the main aims of the book was to consider methods of speeding up the convergence of series.[1]

The *Methodus Differentialis* is one of the early classics of numerical analysis. It contains not only the results for which Stirling is chiefly remembered today (the Stirling numbers, Stirling's interpolation formula, Stirling's formula for 1n n!) but also a wealth of material on transformations of series and limiting processes.[2]

William Smellie 1697-1763 was "the real pioneer in the use of obstetric forceps"[1] and was one of the most important obstetricians of all times and all countries. He was the first to teach obstetrics and midwifery on a scientific basis.[2] He arranged for students to pay a fee of six shillings into a fund out of which he gave charity to necessitous patients. By having his medical students attend the delivery of poor women, who were delivered free of charge, a trend was established that led to the use of medically trained men in childbirth, for many centuries a practice that had been enjoyed solely by midwives, often sorely untrained.

Smellie (pronounced Smiley) ignored folklore and refused to believe anything which he could not prove by personal observation, much of which was very painstaking. It had been taught that the foetus lay as a breech until term, and then when it got hungry it turned round around and crawled out. "Smellie dismissed all of that and described accurately the mechanisms of labour using his illustrations, so that we cannot improve on his teaching to this very day". He taught conservatism in the third stage of pregnancy and recommended light traction on the umbilical cord. He laid down rules for the use of forceps which are almost identical to those being taught today.[3]

Although forceps were invented by Frenchman Peter Chamberlen (or one of his sons), it was kept a secret for three generations. The real pioneer in the use of obstetric forceps was William Smellie, whose great achievement was their proper use. His forceps were either wood or steel padded with leather, and they were short. He advocated their use only after the head had entered the pelvis.[4] Smellie was one of the first to accurately describe how the forceps should be used, because people had a habit of shoving the forceps way up inside to get them around the hips of the foetus, and this caused enormous destruction to the uterus and to the woman. Smellie invented forceps with both pelvic and cephalic curves, as well as inventing mannequins for instruction.[5]

Smellie controlled the use of forceps by a scientific study of pelvic measurements, introducing the diagonal conjugate measurement, measured by the fingers from the arch of the pubis to the sacrum. He realised that most of those who had suffered rickets in their infancy have a pelvis that is commonly narrow and distorted, and consequently subject to tedious and difficult labours.[6] Smellie invented the English lock-forceps which allowed the blades to be inserted separately into the vagina and then brought together.[7]

He treated asphyxia in newborns by inserting catheters inside the upper respiratory tract. He was the first to realise that the foetal head rotated during labour and was first to describe how to rotate with forceps a head that is in the occipito-posterior position (i.e. where the back part of the head is turned towards either the right or left rear quarter of the mother's pelvis). Being the first to apply forceps to the aftercoming head in breech deliveries, he invented long forceps with both a pelvic and cephalic curve especially for the purpose.[8]

He was the first to correctly describe the bony pelvis and the different shapes and forms it could take. He designed a perforator to work like a scissors, with the operator being required to use both hands to open the blades and cut the tissue. The end of the short, pointed blades had a shoulder, which prevented the device from being introduced to too great a depth.

In Smellie's day, obstructed labour was often completed by performing an internal version through the vagina, to turn the head in to the upper part of the uterus and bring the breech down. The baby was then extracted by pulling on a leg or by using breech hooks. This method caused great infant mortality, so in 1737 Smellie tried a pair of French forceps (Dusée's) that had been recommended to him by a Scottish obstetrician, Alexander Butter. Smellie not only designed several better forceps which enabled him to avoid the internal version, he also wrote textbooks and produced a very important atlas, which contains, among other things, illustrations and descriptions of how to apply forceps and deliver the baby.[9]

His 1754 publication *A set of anatomical tables, with explanations, and an abridgment, of the practice of midwifery* is probably the most important anatomical atlas ever produced.

Smellie is especially known for his discovery and description of "the mechanism of labour", or how the infant's head adapts to changes in the pelvic canal during birth.[10] For the first time in the history of midwifery, there was a clear and coherent description of the movements of the head in relation to the pelvis during birth.[11]

Perhaps his greatest contributions to childbirth were the rejections of superstition and the mystery of delivery, the introduction of anatomically designed instruments as standard items in obstetrical practice, and the acceptance of the physician as the trained accoucheur.[12] No other individual did so much to augment and clarify our basic knowledge and understanding of the process of childbirth, at the same time clearing away the superstition, magic and myths which had stifled progress for more than a millennium. Smellie has been described as "the greatest figure in the history of British obstetrics."[13]

Professor Miles Phillips of Sheffield wrote: "It is my belief that no other man ever advanced in his own lifetime knowledge of the theory and practice of midwifery to an extent in any way comparable with that achieved by Smellie."[14]

Robert Wallace 1697-1771 invented modern life insurance in 1744 by creating the Scottish Ministers' Widows' Fund with fellow Scot **Alexander Webster 1708-1784**[1] "The Scottish Ministers' Widows' Fund was the first such fund, and its foundation was truly a milestone in financial history. It established a model not just for Scottish clergymen, but for everyone who aspired to provide against premature death. ... Within the next twenty years similar funds sprung up on the same model all over the English-speaking world. ... By 1815 the principle of insurance was so widespread that it was adopted even for those men who lost their lives fighting against Napoleon."[2]

Wallace and Webster were Church of Scotland ministers from Edinburgh, who were acutely aware of the harsh conditions that people in their parish lived under. They were particularly concerned about the vulnerability of widows and children of ministers, who received half the year's stipend in the year of death, but not much else. Together, with fellow Scot and mathematician, Colin Maclaurin, they created the first true life insurance fund. Scottish Widows, as the fund became known, is still a major force.[3] Together, Wallace, Webster and Maclaurin, worked out actuarial tables showing the risk of death each year of a Protestant (Presbyterian) minister. The three men proposed that the Protestant ministers pool a small contribution to form an insurance fund. The fund would be invested with a percentage yield large enough to support eventual widows and their children. This, the first life insurance fund, was born in 1776 (a propitious year with the US Declaration of Independence and publication of Adam Smith's *The Wealth of Nations*). The Scottish Widows Insurance Fund grew to be the largest life insurance company in Britain and became a model for life insurance companies in England and eventually the rest of the world.[4]

In 1753, Webster was the author of *A dissertation on the numbers of mankind in ancient and modern times*, one of the early works on population. In his 1761 *Various Prospects of Mankind, Nature, and Providence*, a metaphysical, economical, and theologically dogmatic treatise, Wallace anticipated Thomas Malthus in respect of his population theories. Webster, a minister whose favourite subject was mathematics, planned the first census of Scotland in 1755 and the papers for this are in the Advocates Library.[5]

Wallace's 1761 publication of *Various Prospects of Mankind, Nature and Providence* set out his belief that the human population was steadily increasing and would at some point exceed the ability to sustain it from existing resources. Thomas Malthus' seminal and famous work on population growth was first published 37 years later in 1798 as *An Essay of the Principle of*

Population and was an attempt to intervene in a debate on the question of the future improvement of society, which had its historical beginning in Webster's 1761 publication.[6]

Colin Maclaurin 1698-1746 is considered by many to be the best British mathematician of the generation after Newton. Maclaurin published the first logical and systematic exposition of the method of fluxions (the rate of change of a function, especially the instantaneous velocity of a moving body), and the correct theory for distinguishing between maximum and minimum values of a function. In solving problems, whether they dealt with mathematics, gravitational theory of the earth, taxation, actuarial theories, map-making or theology, he employed a combination of sophisticated mathematical modelling and empirical data.[1]

Maclaurin published the first systematic formulation of Isaac Newton's methods in *A Treatise of Fluxions* (1742). In this work, he developed a method for expanding functions about the origin in terms of series now known as Maclaurin Series.[2]

His chief works are his: *Geometria Organica* (1720); *De Linearum Geometricarum Proprietatibus* (1720); *Treatise on Fluxions* (1742); *Algebra* (1748); and *Account of Newton's Discoveries* (1748).

The first section of the first part of the *Geometria Organica* is on conics; the second on nodal cubics; the third on other cubics and on quartics; and the fourth section is on general properties of curves. Newton had shown that, if two angles bounded by straight lines turn round their respective summits so that the point of intersection of two of these lines moves along a straight line, the other point of intersection will describe a conic; and, if the first point moves along a conic, the second will describe a quartic. Maclaurin gave an analytical discussion of the general theorem, and showed how by this method various curves could be practically traced. This work contains an elaborate discussion on curves and their pedals, a branch of geometry which he had created in two papers published in the *Philosophical Transactions* for 1718 and 1719.

The *Geometria Organica* has been subjected to a most careful and exhaustive analysis by statistician Maurice Charles Kenneth Tweedie, and the main result of his investigations has been to prove that Maclaurin's treatise has been strangely neglected and that in this work he has anticipated many of the discoveries of a much later date. It is quite impossible in a short note to summarise the contents of the treatise, but it may be pointed out that many of the well-known properties of Circular Cubics are due to Maclaurin, that the whole theory of Pedals, and more particularly of the Pedals of the Conic Section, is given in the *Geometria Organica*, and that he discovered "a whole host of new curves never before discussed and which have since been named and investigated with but scant acknowledgment of their true inventor." After noting that Maclaurin's use of the Cartesian geometry is, as compared with modern developments, somewhat cumbersome, Tweedie emphasises the "consummate skill" with which Maclaurin applies the methods of the ancient geometry. Of the two parts into which the treatise is divided, the first treats the cases in which the loci along which the vertices of constant angles are made to move are straight lines. In the second part, the curves so found in the first part are added to the loci to obtain curves of higher order. It contains, in particular, the theory of pedals and the epicycloidal generation of curves by rolling one curve on a congruent curve. The last section contains some general theorems in curves forming the foundation of the theory of Higher Plane

Curves. It also contains what is erroneously termed Cramer's Paradox; in fact, Cramer quotes Maclaurin as his authority.[3]

Maclaurin also determined the attraction of a homogeneous ellipsoid at an internal point, and gave some theorems on its attraction at an external point; in attacking these questions he introduced the conception of level surfaces, that is, surfaces at every point of which the resultant attraction is perpendicular to the surface. No further advance in the theory of attractions was made until Joseph-Louis Lagrange in 1773 introduced the idea of the potential. Maclaurin also showed that a spheroid was a possible form of equilibrium of a mass of homogeneous liquid rotating about an axis passing through its centre of mass. Finally, he discussed the tides; this part had been previously published (in 1740) and had received a prize from the French Academy.

The *Treatise of fluxions* is a major work of 763 pages, much praised by those who read it but usually described as having little influence. Maclaurin's influence on the continental Europeans, however, has been underrated as revealed by mathematics historian, Judith Victor Grabiner, who gave five areas of influence of Maclaurin's treatise: his treatment of the fundamental theorem of the calculus; his work on maxima and minima; the attraction of ellipsoids; elliptic integrals; and the Euler-Maclaurin summation formula.[4]

It was said that during the 18th century Maclaurin and Matthew Stewart, who succeeded him in the mathematical chair at Edinburgh, were the only prominent mathematicians in Great Britain. Writing towards the end of the century, Joseph Jérôme Lefrançois de Lalande, in his *Life of Condorect*, maintained that in 1764 there was not a single first-rate analyst in the whole of England. When a Highland army marched upon Edinburgh in the uprising of 1745, Maclaurin wholeheartedly organised the defence of the city. With tireless energy, he planned and supervised the hastily erected fortifications, and, indeed, drove himself to a state of exhaustion from which he never recovered. The city fell to the Jacobites and Maclaurin was forced to flee to England.[5]

Michael Menzies c1699-1766 designed one of the earliest threshing machines, if not the earliest, in 1732, and it reportedly did the work of six labourers. It had a series of flails drawn by a water wheel but, although it operated at 1,320 strokes a minute, it was not commercially successful because it left a lot of seed on the ground. "Trials made with these machines [i.e. those made by Menzies] were so far satisfactory, that a great deal of work was done in a given time, but, owing to the velocity required to work perfectly, they soon broke, and the invention fell into disgrace."[1]

Though not a practical success, Menzies' invention seems to have been the first for the mechanical threshing of grain. His idea of imitating non-mechanised action also influenced his invention of a coal cutter, for which he took out a patent in 1761 and which copied miners' tools for obtaining coal. He proposed to carry heavy chains down the pit so that they could be used to give motion to iron picks, saws or other chains with cutting implements. The chains could be set into motion by a steam-engine, by watermills or windmills, or by horses' gins. Although it is quite obvious that this apparatus could not work, Menzies was the first to have thought of mechanising coal production in the style that was in use in the late 20th century. Menzies had successfully used the power of a steam-engine on the River Wear eight years beforehand, when he obtained a patent for raising coal. According to his device, a descending bucket filled with water raised a basket of coals, while a steam-engine pumped the water back to the surface; the balance-tub system, in various forms, quickly spread to other coalfields. Menzies' patent from

1750 for improved methods of carrying the coals from the coalface to the pit-shaft had also been of considerable influence: this device employed self-acting inclined planes, whereon the descending loaded wagons hauled up the empty ones.[2]

Archibald Cleland c1700-1771 described, in 1729, a nasal illumination device that consisted of biconvex lenses placed in front of a wax candle in order to magnify and redirect the light. Though little more is known of the circumstances surrounding Cleland's innovation, including whether he was in fact the first to use lenses in this manner, we do know for certain that his work represents an important turning point in the history of endoscopy, certainly a big step up from the early days of using drinking glasses filled with water! Though this milestone is rarely mentioned in other histories of endoscopy, it is a significant first that brought the field closer than ever to modern-day techniques.[1]

While surgeon to the 3rd Dragoon Guards, Cleland found time to develop several novel instruments which he demonstrated before members of The Royal Society. These included a catheter facilitating suprapubic lithotomy, a candle-powered illuminator for inspecting ear drums, instruments for eye surgery, and a vacuum tube for correcting the retracted tympanic membranes of soldiers whose drums had been blown inwards by the force of nearby explosions. Cleland was also the first British practitioner to describe how to catheterise the Eustachian tube.[2] Note: British surgeon Sir William Wilde attempts to claim the use of the catheter as a British discovery. He makes Edmé-Gilles Guyot a mere suggester of the operation of catheterisation, but the evidence seems to favour Guyot, a French postmaster.

Cleland's ear inspections were performed thus: "The passage should be lubricated by throwing a little warm water into it by a syringe fixed to a silver tube which is introduced through the nose into the oval opening of the duct at the posterior part of the nares … the pipes of the syringe are made small, of silver, to admit of bending them, as occasion offers, and for the most part, resemble small catheters. They are mounted with a sheep's ureter, the other end of which is fixed to an ivory pipe which is fitted to the syringe, whereby warm water may be injected, or they will admit to blow into the Eustachian tube and so force air into the barrel of the ear and dilate the tube sufficiently for the discharge of excrementitious matter."[3]

Cleland also used probes of the same size as the catheter to explore the tube. He does not allude to Edmé-Gilles Guyot's suggestions to the French Academy, but this is not proof that he did not know of them. However, as Wilde states, Cleland was the first one to introduce the catheter through the nose, "the only proper way of performing the operation"; and he says that Guyot never practiced the operation which he recommended, and that it was on this ground rejected by the French Academy, as they "wanted the recommendation of facts to support and enforce it."[4]

David Donald (dates unknown) "invented a flax-beating machine driven by water-power" in 1727. The British Linen Company appraised it and in the "Extracts from the Minutes and Annual Reports of the Trustees" commented "1727. David Donald invented a machine for beating and bruising flax. Tried and approved of."[1]

Donald's machine used a roller mechanism for scutching the flax. Prior to this, the most advanced method of treating flax had been the Dutch brake method of crushing flax with a hand-held beater which required a large labour force and was arduous work.[2]

George Moir c1704-1792 made a device that was useful for threshing oats, but was less successful for other grains. His thresher was made in 1764 and had four horizontal scutches enclosed in a cylinder into which sheaves were hand-fed through the open top with the grain being separated by riddles and fanners. Although it wasn't particularly successful, it pointed the way to using rotary motion and provided a launching point for the next step by Andrew Meikle, who developed the first really effective threshing machine in 1786.[1]

Michael Stirling 1708-1796 made a thresher that processed wheat, barley and some other grain, although it couldn't process oats, Scotland's most commonly grown cereal. He originally built it in miniature, resembling a water mill "in which two iron springs, made to rise and fall alternately, represented the motion of two flails, by which a few stalks of corn put under them might be speedily thrashed".[1] By 1758, he had built one that had a drum rotating within a cylinder, although it wasn't sufficiently efficient to be commercially successful.

William Cullen 1710-1790 took the first step towards the discovery and development of refrigeration, which finally came to fruition from the work of British, French and American enterprise, with several Scots making their mark in this field. "The first known demonstration of refrigeration was carried out in 1748 at the University of Glasgow by the Scottish physician William Cullen. This technique worked by allowing ethyl ether to boil in a partial vacuum."[1] Cullen published the results in *An Essay on the Cold Produced by Evaporating Fluids and Some Other Means of Producing Cold*. This was the first publication and first known instance of artificial refrigeration as distinct from using snow or ice for freezing.

Cullen was a co-founder of the Glasgow Medical School in 1744, the Royal Medical Society of Edinburgh (1734) – one of the oldest medical societies in Europe – and The Royal Society of Edinburgh (1783). Cullen was probably the most famous lecturer in any university in his day and was a teacher *par excellence*, introducing voluntary practical work and helping make Edinburgh the leading medical training centre in the world. In 1777, he published *First Lines of the Practice of Physic*, which became the main reference book on classifying and treating disease, and postulated that disease arose from disturbances in the nervous system. He opposed laxatives and purgatives, preferring tonics such as quinine, camphor or wine to stimulate or tranquilise the nervous system. The book became Europe's principal text on the classification and treatment of disease.[2] In the English-speaking world, he was the single most influential medical lecturer, although his theories have little relevance today (as are those of Aristotle, who had a profound influence on medicine for two millennium), but his observations on artificial freezing were the true foundations of modern refrigeration.

James Short 1710–1768 was the first to calculate the solar parallax and he invented the first parabolic and elliptic, distortionless mirror for reflecting telescopes. He was closely involved with the Transit of Venus observations made throughout the world on 6 June 1761 and his instruments travelled on the ship *Endeavour* with First Lieutenant James Cook to observe a second Transit of Venus on 3 June 1769.[1]

The extraordinary attention devoted to these transits, especially in 1761 and 1769, was due to their usefulness in determining the length of the Astronomical Unit, that is, the mean distance from Earth to the Sun, in terms of terrestrial distance units such as miles. Indeed, one estimate of the Astronomical Unit, computed from observations of the 1769 transit and published in 1771, differs from modern radar-based values by a mere eight-tenths of a percent.[2]

James Short sifted many reports received from observers of the Transit of Venus in 1761, and from them he calculated an authoritative solar parallax.[3] Short derived a solar parallax of 8.25", which calculation he published in the *Philosophical Transactions* (1764). The way in which Short handled the times of contact collected from many different stations highlights a striking limitation (from our standpoint) of 18th century means of handling multiple observations of the same phenomenon; statistical knowledge had not advanced to the point where anyone knew how to deal with many observations. All they could do was to combine them, as Short did, two at a time and then average the results. Eventually, when statistical analysis had matured, Simon Newcomb (1891) was able to carry out an exhaustive study of the two 18th century transits, and he arrived at a solar parallax of 8.79" with a mean error of ±0.051".[4]

Short was Britain's pre-eminent telescope manufacturer at the time long-standing rivals, France and Britain, were the two main nations involved in the observation of the Transit of Venus. He was Britain's principal coordinator for the project, although he died almost a year before Cook's observations on 3 June 1769.

Short invented the first parabolic and elliptic, distortionless mirror ideal for reflecting telescopes and he accomplished this in a very practical manner: since parallel rays nearer the centre of a spherical mirror overshoot the marginal rays coming from the edge of the mirror, he realised the rays of light could be brought to the same point of focus by deepening the centre. This telescope was known as the *Short telescope* and is based on the principles of James Gregory. Short built over 1,360 telescopes, all of which had speculum mirrors (speculum metal is a mixture of around two-thirds copper and one-third tin making a white brittle alloy that can be polished to make highly reflective surface mirrors). It wasn't until the 1850s that silver replaced speculum (silver has a longer lifespan, but still loses reflectivity quickly over time due to oxidation. By 1930, telescope mirrors were being coated with aluminium, which is further overcoated with a clear coating).[5] Short was reckoned to be the leading maker of reflecting telescopes in this era and was the first to produce parabolic mirrors in quantity.[6] He made three telescopes in 1734, 1750 and 1752 that were the largest three in the world, the last being made for the Spanish king, Ferdinand VI, costing the royal sum of £1,200.[7]

George (Andrew) Gordon 1712-1751 invented the electrostatic reaction motor and the electric chime (bell), and he developed what was probably the first compact portable generator. He took the Latinised name of Andreas when he became a Benedictine monk. He was a professor of natural philosophy (physics) at Erfurt University in Germany and became the first person to observe that water evaporated faster when electrified. He ignited a bowl of alcohol by turning a stream of electrified water upon it, thus presenting the seeming paradox of fire produced by a stream of water.[1] In 1663, German-born Otto von Guericke devised a primitive friction machine using a sulphur ball. Isaac Newton then suggested using a glass globe instead of the sulphur, following which, in 1671, Gordon substituted a glass cylinder and made an efficient frictional machine. He mounted his cylinder on an axle, which he turned back and forth against its rubbing pad by means of a bow, similar to the method used to drive a watchmaker's lathe. This enabled the cylinder to turn at 680 revolutions a minute.[2] His second model was driven by a large pulley wheel that turned the cylinder against a leather cushion. Gordon's machines were probably the first compact portable generators.[3]

One of Gordon's other inventions was a light metallic star supported on a sharp pivot with the pointed ends bent at right angles to the rays of the star and commonly called the "electrical whirl", which was an electrostatic reaction motor – the earliest of its kind. Another invention of his was an electric chime – the first electric bell.

While these inventions are described in many textbooks of the pioneering days of electricity, the name of Gordon is rarely mentioned, though both inventions are fully described by him in his *Versuch einer Erklarung der Electricital* (Erfurt 1745). Benjamin Franklin, who is usually credited with the electric chime, simply adopted the "German chimes" in 1752 to serve as an electrical annunciator in connection with his experimental lightning rod. The "Franklin chimes" (or, more correctly, "Gordon chimes") "constituted the first device that converted electrical energy into mechanical energy in the form of continuous mechanical motion, in this case, the moving of a bell clapper back and forth between two oppositely charged bells."[4]

Gordon's other experiments showed, in 1745, that small animals could be killed by electricity travelling through wires about 250 metres long when he killed a chaffinch in Saxony, the first record of an animal being killed by human-generated electricity.

Alexander Wilson 1714-1786 was the first person, with his friend Thomas Melville, to use kites for meteorological purposes. In 1749, he flew a series of kites – each between one and two metres in length – in train to measure upper air temperatures to determine if the air above the ground was colder or warmer than the air on the ground. They required a controllable flying machine for their experiments, and since it was 30 years before the first balloon flight, and 150 years before the aeroplane, a kite flew to the rescue. Wilson and Melville put kites on a career path that would last for more than two centuries.

Each kite had a thermometer that was wrapped up in strips of cloth to prevent the delicate instruments from breaking when they hit the ground. Each bundle had a slow burning fuse and a white ribbon attached. As the fuse burned through the string that bound the bundle to the kite, it would fall to the ground. The white ribbons would surf the wind on a downward descent, making it easier to see where they landed so that they could be found quicker for more accurate readings. This was the first recorded attempt at obtaining scientific data using kites as well as the first recorded use of kites in a train.[1] Flying in train is the technique of flying two or more kites from a common line and Wilson's experiment is the first recorded account of the train technique being used.[2]

The experiments of Wilson and Melville were successful and they published their research. However, their work was overlooked for over seventy years until Wilson's memoirs were published in England in 1825 and reprinted two years later in America.[3]

He observed what is now termed the Wilson Effect in relation to sunspots: the penumbra and umbra vary in the manner expected by perspective effects if the umbrae of the spots are in fact slight depressions in the surface of the photosphere. The magnitude of the depression is difficult to determine but may be as large as 1,000 km. "To explain the effect, Wilson suggested that sunspots represent saucer-shaped depressions in the sun's surface formed by the removal of the bright luminous material which, he believed, covered the darker interior. While this explanation may appear rather naïve today, it nevertheless represented the first attempt to infer the physical properties of a sunspot from the centre-limb observations."[4]

Hugh Orr 1715-1798 designed machinery for making ropes and for carding and spinning textiles. He had been a gunsmith in Scotland but adapted his skills when he arrived in America. He became a flax seed (linseed) exporter and seemingly, in 1753, the first person to invent a feasible machine for flax dressing – the process of removing fibres from the straw and cleaning it sufficiently to be spun. Flax was an important crop in early America as it was used for the manufacture of linen (damasks, lace and sheeting), linseed oil, dye, paper (especially banknotes), soap, medicines, twine, rope and fishing nets.[1]

"In many respects, the most extraordinary of the Scotch inventors whose ingenuity has helped to swell the business of the Patent Office was Hugh Orr, a Renfrewshire man. ... In 1753 Mr Orr invented a machine for dressing flax, and in the cultivation of that plan he took a deep interest, and succeeded, in the long run, in making it a profitable agricultural industry around his home town. [His] flax-raising experiments deserve the highest commendation. In company with two Scotch mechanics, Robert and Alexander Barr, he constructed some carding, roping, and spinning machines, and he had become so thorough a Yankee as to ask for an appropriation from the Legislature to complete them, and got it. The machines were the first of their kind ever seen in America, so that Orr may be called the introducer into the United States of the spinning jenny."[2]

James Lind 1716-1794 was a pioneer in improved shipboard hygiene and the treatment of scurvy. Scurvy "was responsible for more deaths at sea than storms, shipwreck, combat and all the other diseases combined. Historians have conservatively estimated that over two million sailors perished from scurvy during the Age of Sail" (1500-1850 AD).[1] English admiral Lord George Anson circumnavigated the world in 1740-1744, setting out with seven ships and 1,955 men. His objective was to harass the Spanish-held west coast of Latin America. When he returned to England, he had one ship and 145 men. The biggest single cause of death of Anson's sailors was scurvy, either causing death or so impairing the sailors that their ships were lost. Anson was a good sailor who enforced cleanliness and ensured supplies of fresh water, as well as providing medication in the form of (Joshua) Ward's Pill and Drop, made from balsam, wine and antimony, the favoured treatment for all kinds of ailments. The medical profession of the time was utterly perplexed as to why there was such a high mortality. During the Seven Years' War (1756-1763) Britain had 184,899 sailors in service of whom 133,708 died from disease (largely from scurvy) and only 1,512 died in combat.[2] these numbers illustrate the enormous toll scurvy took on the navies of Europe, killing orders of magnitude more men than battle.

Ironically, the cure for scurvy had been known for some time. Scurvy grass (*Cochlearia* species) –a herb related to cabbages – had been used with some effect since the 16th century and probably earlier. English sailor Richard Hawkins had used oranges and lemons during a 1593 Pacific voyage. The Dutch had established orange groves near Cape Town specifically to counter scurvy on their long voyages to the Spice Islands (Indonesia). Another Englishman, James Lancaster, issued three spoonfuls of lemon juice daily to his crew on a voyage to India in 1601. But by the time of Anson, this knowledge had been forgotten, ignored or disputed, not just in Britain but elsewhere, until James Lind investigated the malady of scurvy.

Lind, from Edinburgh, is considered the founder of naval hygiene in the British Royal Navy. He served as a naval surgeon in the Mediterranean, West Indies, English Channel, and off the coast of West Africa. In May-June 1747, Lind conducted what is often claimed as "the first controlled trial in medical history and determine[d] that citrus juice is 'a virtual specific' for scurvy"[3] ("spccific" in this sense means any drug used to treat a particular disease). The trial was small – only 12 participants – and it didn't include the "double blind" methodology of today. "Recent reassessments have mentioned the fact that Lind's experiment constituted not a controlled study in the very strict sense, since the patients were not chosen at random and since there was no group without treatment."[4] "But the Treatise of this 'man of observation', as his disciple [Thomas] Trotter called him, proved to be a most influential guide for future work in naval medicine: in its three editions [1753, reprinted 1754, 1757, 1772] Lind taught and stressed the use of the experimental trial in clinical conditions; this message in itself 'was just as important as his famous cure for scurvy'"[5] His "trial" also had numerous other shortcomings but, nevertheless, it was an important first step in the use of clinical trials, now widespread and *de rigueur* in any etiological investigation.

The experiment was conducted on HMS *Salisbury* in the English Channel, and the scorbutic sailors were divided into six pairs with each pair having an extra item added to their normal diet, which consisted of salted meat and bread – or biscuit – known as hard tack. Biscuit (bis coctus = twice baked) had been given to sailors since, at least, the days of ancient Greece and the bread dough could be baked as often as four times, and sometimes the cooked biscuits were ground up and baked again. The flour was usually full of weevils and the recommended way of eating the weevilly hardtack was to sharply tap the biscuits on the table and the weevils would crawl out. Because sailors' teeth were in a poor state, the biscuits were generally broken with a knife or in the crook of the elbow. In port, sailors would receive fresh bread, known as *soft Tommy*, with fresh fruit and vegetables, so scurvy wasn't normally a problem on short voyages. It was, however, catastrophic during long voyages or long blockades of ports during war. Scurvy resulted in horrendous loss of life and even those who survived were too weak to be of use in servicing their ship, which could leave the whole crew in peril during a storm or action against enemy ships.

Added to the sailors' basic diet of gruel with sugar for breakfast, broth with mutton or pudding for dinner; barley and raisins, rice, and currants for supper, the dozen men in Lind's experiment were, for each pair, given a quart of hard cider; drops of elixir vitriol (aromatic sulphuric acid); two spoonfuls of vinegar three times a day; half a pint of sea water; a paste of garlic, mustard seed, balsam of Peru, dried radish root, and gum myrrh; and two oranges and one lemon.[6] The pair on citrus fruit (which ran out after six days so they were switched to elixir vitriol) fared best, followed by the patients given cider. The others did not improve at all.

Lind's *Treatise of the Scurvy* was published in 1753 although he missed the chance to directly target lemons as a cure for scurvy. He considered the current sailors' fare as adequate provided they had lots of exercise and fresh air (two things already in abundance for most sailors). Lind believed that scurvy was a digestive disorder causing "blocked perspiration" which builds up toxins in the body. His recommended treatment did include "fruit and greenstuff" to help the digestion and removal of waste products, but it also included fighting melancholia (partly with the issue of naval uniforms); cleanliness of body; warm and dry bedding; and exercise in dry, pure air (he even suggested building an exercise machine to simulate the action of a horse to counteract scurvy on board ship).[7]

Lind stressed in his *Treatise* that his work was to be founded "on attested facts and observations, without suffering the illusions of theory to influence and pervert the judgement." Such were "the surest and most necessary guides".[8]

Lind had to compete with a multitude of other remedies and he lacked sufficient social standing or patronage in an era when it was critical to advancement (his erstwhile patron, Anson, died in 1762). As such he was in no position to seriously challenge the many people who had alternative remedies or who disputed his method of combating scurvy – these opponents included the great medical reformer of army hospitals, John Pringle, and the far more famous James Cook, explorer extraordinaire. Cook felt that malt wort was the main dietary factor in preventing scurvy, although he issued other additives to crew, including lemons, and it was this that enabled him to sail to Australia and back without loss from scurvy. The Admiralty, along with the Board of Directors at Haslar Hospital (built to treat sailors of the Royal Navy), needed to be absolutely convinced of the merits of lemon juice before they would make the necessary changes, and Lind had not provided the proof. In fact, Lind undertook experiments at Haslar which seemed to support Cook and Pringle's belief that malt wort was anti-scorbutic, although this observation may have arisen because "many of his scurvy patients probably suffered from a mixed deficiency of both vitamins B and C, and wort was rich in vitamin B complex."[9]

More telling, though, is that Lind didn't actually consider fresh citrus fruit to be a cure for scurvy. This is apparent during his 25 years at Haslar, where he probably had the greatest concentration of scurvy victims on the planet. At no time did Lind routinely prescribe fresh citrus fruit or juice and he lost many patients to scurvy. His publications were not well structured and he appeared to support fresh fruit and vegetables in some parts and downplay them elsewhere. His 1753 *Treatise on Scurvy* referred to other authors who recommended that scurvy could be cured by change of diet, including Dutchman Johannes Bachstrom, who categorically stated that scurvy "is solely owing to a total abstinence from fresh vegetable food, and greens; which alone is the primary cause of the disease". But Lind denies "that health and life cannot be preserved long, without the use of green herbage, vegetables, and fruits; and that a long abstinence from these is alone the cause of the disease". His premise is that there are people who remain scurvy-free yet "eat few or no vegetables".[10]

This is consistent with his earlier analysis of the various useful anti-scorbutic properties of different foodstuffs. Lemon juice, when it was used, was conceived by Lind rather as a powerful medicine, than as a basic food, or occasional dietary supplement. Moreover, in neat doses, lemon juice had, he says, a tendency to make weak patients vomit. But undoubtedly Lind did regard it as a potent anti-scorbutic, for he proudly relates his successful diagnosis and cure, using lemons, of two local female patients to whom he had been called as a private consultant.

Lind produced two other publications: *An Essay on the Most Effectual Means of Preserving the health of Seamen in the Royal Navy* in 1757 just before starting at Haslar and *An Essay on Diseases Incidental to Europeans in Hot Climates* in 1768. The former publication "gives a very full account of measures of naval hygiene for ships at sea, directions for disinfection and for the destruction of vermin, for filtering water through casks of sand, or by charcoal, for the wearing of special clothes by surgeons who attend the sick, and the strict ventilation and cleanliness of the sick-berth. Before his day none of these things received attention."[11] The latter publication was based on Lind's observations of sailors who had been in the Americas, Asia, Africa, and the Pacific Islands and, to avoid fevers at home and abroad, "he advised people to live on high ground away from stagnant water" – sound advice to avoid mosquito-transmitted diseases, although Lind would not have known that mosquitoes were disease carriers.[12] In this publication Lind was prescient in "pointing out that geography and weather in some parts of the world determine the presence or absence of certain diseases."[13]

Lind's versatility is evident in his three great classics on scurvy, hygiene, and tropical medicine, in each of which he was a pioneer and an original investigator. Lind, indeed, has claims to be the founder of vitamin therapy, social medicine, and tropical climatology.[14] In 1816, Britain suffered a major typhus epidemic but the "Royal Navy remained free of typhus by adopting the recommendations of James Lind, that sailors should be stripped, scrubbed, shaved and issued with clean clothes."[15] "Lind associated tropical fever with stinging insects, flies and mosquitoes and in his book on tropical medicine he mentions their absence as one of the four most important factors in the selection of a healthy human habitation. In preparing a site for a dwelling place, he recommends what are unwittingly anti-mosquito measures, i.e. choosing high dry ground, cutting back the scrub around human habitations, and efficient drainage. Similarly, he associated typhus, also called gaol fever, with vermin in the infested clothes of the press-gang's victims, and his recommendations for the prevention of typhus could be a paraphrase of the delousing instructions to be found in any modern manual of military hygiene before the discovery of D.D.T. Lind of course had no idea of lice or mosquitoes as the direct agents of fever, but his unique powers of observation had taught him, consciously or unconsciously, the almost invariable association between the prevalence of these insects and the occurrence of typhus and tropical fevers."[16]

In 1758, Lind also found a satisfactory process for distilling water on board ship to provide fresh drinking water. Techniques to do this had been known for many centuries, but the distilled water had a foul, burnt taste that made it unpopular with sailors. Remedies to make it more palatable included the addition of ground bone, powdered chalk and even soap. Lind discovered that the burnt taste of distilled water disappeared if the water was exposed to air and that there was no need to use additives. "After a study of this problem, and the development of an ingenious and practical still made from a large kettle used as a distillation pot, a tea kettle for a still head, and a cast and a musket barrel for a condenser, Lind had this to say: "In the year 1761, I was so fortunate as to discover, that the steam arising from boiling sea water was perfectly fresh, and that sea water, simply distilled, without the addition of any ingredient, afforded a water as pure and wholesome as that obtained from the best springs." The term, 'I was so fortunate,' indicates the tone of modesty which prevails in Lind's writing. Not only did Lind develop this procedure, but he described and recommended the use of a still head and condenser which fitted as a cover over the large copper vessels used in cooking on shipboard. This afforded a most efficient use of the available fuel, a fact which must have been particularly satisfying to this thrifty Scot. Although Lind had definitely established priority in this discovery, the British Parliament in 1771 awarded a gift of £5,000 to another naval surgeon, Charles Irving, for the development of a method of distilling fresh water from sea water. The most interesting aspect of this, and a good insight into the character and generosity of Lind, is indicated by the fact that he served on the official board which appraised the merits of Irving's work.[17]

Lind died in 1794, the same year as HMS *Suffolk*, carrying plentiful supplies of lemons, arrived in Madras without a single case of scurvy having appeared during the 23-week voyage. Lind's recommendations, with the dubious exception of cold baths, are sometimes claimed to have played a major part in the dominance of the Royal Navy throughout the world for, unlike other nations, the British were able to greatly reduce sickness and mortality, giving them the upper hand in combat and blockade. The British navy's later success in blockading Napoleonic France owed in part to its ability to control scurvy.[18] Earlier, during the Seven Years War "Anson, in his anxiety to limit the incursion of scurvy into the Western Squadron, which was charged with blockading Brest and other French ports, took Lind's advice and sent out provisioning ships carrying fresh fruit and live animals. This measure proved a great success, and remained Admiralty policy thereafter."[19] Ironically, "the merchant crews of the supply ships were themselves decimated by scurvy while carrying to the King's ships antiscorbutics which they were not allowed to touch themselves. Here the unfortunate scurvy-stricken merchant sailors acted as a control to the protected Royal Naval ratings."[20]

In summing up achievements in improved naval medicine which may be credited to Lind, Louis Harry Roddis cites these points:

1. The classic experiment proving the importance of citrus fruits or their juices in prevention of, and in treatment for, scurvy. Application of these principles late in the 18th century and early in the 19th century led to virtual elimination of scurvy in men of the Royal Navy.

2. Recommendation that new recruits be brought first to receiving ships for quarantine, and that they be bathed and issued clean clothing. This did more to eliminate shipboard typhus fever than any other measure.

3. The suggestion that special ships be run between England and naval blockading squadrons to supply fighting ships with fresh provisions, fruits, and green vegetables. Adoption of this suggestion for maintaining ships' crews in fighting trim is believed to have been a definite deciding factor in favour of the British in their war with Napoleon.

4. Demonstration of a practical method of obtaining fresh water from sea water by simple distillation, adapting utensils normally found on shipboard.

5. Recommendations for physical examination of naval recruits with maintenance of records thereof.

6. Suggestion of issuance of naval uniforms to seamen, a measure favourably affecting both health and morale of these men.

7. Insistence of physical exercise and on cold baths as "toughening-up" processes.

8. Use of cinchona bark for prevention of malaria.

9. Recommendations that, in the tropics, ships be anchored well off shore and that crew not be given work details or liberty ashore at night. This did much to reduce the incidence of malaria.[21]

Without the Royal Navy, there would have been no British Empire, and without Lind the British navy would have had to find another advantageous edge to give them the upper hand against French, Spanish and Dutch warships. While this does have an element of truth, it is only indirectly linked to Lind, for his publications on scurvy were published in German, French and Dutch, so Europeans would have been familiar with his recommendations in combating the great malady of seamen – scurvy.

Patrick Mackellar 1718-1778 was a military engineer with experience in the Mediterranean and in North America under Major-General Edward Braddock. He was briefly in captivity when the French captured Fort Oswego in 1756. He subsequently ended up as the engineer responsible for taking Louisbourg under the direction of James Wolfe. "Although James Wolfe was impatient with the slow progress of the siege, it appears that not a little of the credit for the capitulation of Louisbourg on 27 July was due to Mackellar's professional skill."[1] Mackellar became a trusted adviser to Wolfe during the siege of Quebec and, having been held in that city during his imprisonment, he was able to provide Wolfe with plans of the city, although not altogether accurate as he had restricted movement within the city. "He sited the British batteries and conducted all preliminary siege operations, despite a serious wound suffered during the attack on the Beauport shore on 31 July, and he devised and tested methods of landing infantry from floating stages. By 12 July these batteries began a bombardment of the upper and lower towns that was to last throughout the many weeks of stalemate while Wolfe struggled to find the key to the conquest of a city the French were convinced was impregnable."[2]

Mackellar also advised Wolfe against a frontal attack upon the city and accompanied the general on his final reconnaissance. Immediately after the victory on the Plains of Abraham on 13 September, Mackellar engaged in preparations to besiege Quebec, but its capitulation five days later made these efforts redundant.

"It is curious that Mackellar, despite a most respectable and distinguished career, was never the recipient of honours. His promotions, however, prove that he was one of the most esteemed military engineers of his generation, and certainly he deserves recognition for his contribution to the British successes in Canada during the final campaigns of the Seven Years' War."[3]

Mackellar was the engineer in charge of siege operations on the attack against Fort Royal in Martinique (1762) and, in the same year, during the Battle of Havana he played an important role in the capture of the Morro fortress by building consecutive lines of breastworks to protect the British batteries that were eventually able to fire up to 600 shells a day. "On 17 July Mackellar began a trench so that the batteries could be moved closer to the fortress; despite continued Spanish counter-attacks the British finished mining the walls and stormed the fortress on 30 July."[4] Mackellar had the distinction of a major role in what Syrett has referred to as 'the most difficult siege undertaken by the British army between the great sieges of Marlborough's campaigns and those of the Peninsular War.'"[5] In 1764, Mackellar was in Minorca and successfully recommended moving the town of St Philips, which was too close to the fortress. It was relocated and is now known as Es Castell. It was in Minorca that he died, although his burial place is unknown.

John Campbell 1719-1790 invented the sextant when he greatly improved on the octant invented in 1731 by two Englishmen working independently – John Hadley and Thomas Godfrey. The octant could measure latitude but not longitude. This shortcoming was overcome by Campbell's invention of the sextant in 1757, as it could measure both longitude and latitude. The Industrial Revolution would have been greatly hindered if there hadn't been an improvement in transportation, both by land and sea. Ships and barges could carry goods by sea, rivers and canals more readily than packhorses and wagons could carry freight by land, but canals were rare and travel by sea was slow and hazardous. One difficulty with ocean travel was the inability of a ship's crew to accurately determine their precise location, and, in the early 18th century, the British Royal Navy was locked in an escalating contest with France for control of the seas. Superiority depended upon technological improvements, one of which was to accurately determine the actual location of a ship at any given time. The sextant became the most important instrument of navigators, and many explorers used it too, including Lewis and Clark on their expedition across continental America. The sextant is included in *100 Greatest Science Inventions of All Time* (Kendall F. Haven, Libraries Unlimited, Westport, CT, 2006, p 69) citing the reason: "In 1676, the English government declared that navigation was the greatest scientific problem of the age. European countries were poised to expand into global trade and conquest. But they couldn't do it if their ships had no way to accurately know their position when out of sight of land." This need was dramatically demonstrated on 22 October 1707 when Rear Admiral Cloudesley Shovell died with some 1,400 (some reports say almost 1,800) sailors off the Scilly Islands when four ships of the line, and a treasure trove, were lost on rocks because they couldn't determine their location in a storm. The admiral's body was washed up at Porthellick Cove on St Marie's Island where his body was stripped of its clothes and his emerald ring stolen (some sources say he was murdered for his ring but this is unlikely).

Campbell had conducted the first sea trials of Hadley's octant and he realised that by enlarging the arc to a sixth of a circle – hence *sextant* – it would give much greater accuracy in determining the altitude of objects such as stars. It also permitted better measurement of lunar distances – the distance between certain known stars and the moon – and it was this feature which allowed longitude to be measured. According to William Wales, Campbell was the first person to use a Hadley quadrant for actually measuring, "for his own amusement", the angular distance between the moon and fixed stars.[1]

Campbell had been flag captain of the *Royal George* under Admiral Hawke at the decisive battle of Quiberon Bay in 1759. He became a vice-admiral and Governor of Newfoundland, as well as Commander-in-Chief in the period 1782-1786, permitting religious freedom for all Newfoundlanders, including Catholics – a rather radical step at the time. In conjunction with Englishman John Harrison's chronometer, the sextant greatly improved navigation and gave British ships an increased degree of safety.

Andrew Meikle 1719-1811 and his brother **George Meikle 1712-1811** made some innovative changes to farm equipment. George almost certainly knew of another early design, initiated by

Michael Stirling, farmer at Craighead, Dunblane, in 1748 (or 1758) as he had worked at Alloa. This machine had revolving wooden "scutchers" (beaters) of a type already used in flax-preparing lint mills. Their prototype machine, erected at Knowes Mill, used short scutchers mounted on a revolving drum. When, in 1786, George Meikle installed the first complete machine for James Stein at Kilbagie, Clackmannanshire, he added a pair of fluted feed-rollers, another feature of lint mills. The patent incorporated all of these elements but could not apply in Scotland as the machine had already been publicly used there. Andrew likely worked with George on this thresher as the patent (No. 1645) was granted to both brothers in 1788.

Andrew had previously invented two devices in 1750 for use with windmills, the major source of mechanical power in processing grain. These devices were the fantail gear that kept windmill sails facing into the wind and the spring sail to mitigate the damaging effects of sudden wind gusts on windmill sails. Englishman Edmund Lee had pre-empted Meikle on the fantail gear five years earlier, although it is unlikely that Meikle was aware of Lee's invention.

The principle of Meikle's machine has been retained in all threshing machines up to and including the modern self-propelled combines.[1] In his machine the loosened sheaves were fed, ears first, from a feeding board between two fluted revolving rollers to the beating cylinder. This cylinder had, parallel to its axle, four iron-shod spars of wood that thrashed the ears of corn as they protruded from the rollers. The drum revolved between 200 and 250 times a minute and carried the loose grain and straw onto a concave sieve beneath a revolving drum with pegs, then the drum pushed the straw against the sieve and the grain and chaff fell through. Another revolving drum threw the straw under a peg drum where it was rubbed and tossed to separate the grain and chaff, allowing both to fall to the ground ready for winnowing. Meikle's machine was so successful that it led to the so-called Captain Swing Riots of agricultural labourers in England's south and east during 1830.[2]

Image 3 – Horse-Powered Threshing Machine

A patent was applied for, but in the intervening time Meikle further developed his thresher by a modification that stripped off the corn from the ear by a comparatively sharp edge, or, as termed by him, "scutching out the grain" instead of beating it by a flat surface. The difference may be partially illustrated by supposing a handful of straw with the corn in the ear to be held in the hand, while with the flat sides of a thin strip of wood the ears should be struck or beaten; this is the operation of the common beater. If, instead of striking the ears with the flat side, a sharp blow be given with the thin edge in the direction of the ear, it will strip the corn from such parts as the edge touches with less labour and with greater certainty.

Professor David Low wrote "the invention of Andrew Meikle, an ingenious mechanic of Scotland, to whom, beyond a question, belongs the honour of having perfected the thrashing-machine. Changes and improvements have indeed been made on certain parts of the original machine; but, in all its essential parts, and in the principle of its construction, it remains as it came from the hands of its inventor."[3]

Robert Melville 1723-1809 was lieutenant-governor of Guadeloupe in 1759 and governor from 1763-1770, and he established the famous botanical gardens at St Vincent, in the Caribbean. In 1759, he invented the carronade – a piece of light ordinance very destructive against timber. Named for its place of manufacture, it was first produced for the Royal Navy in 1779 and continued to be in use until the mid-nineteenth century.[1]

The carronade was placed on a naval gun carriage without trunnions. It was a short seven-calibre (177.8 mm) weapon that delivered a slow-moving, heavy shot which, upon impact with timber, caused a large irregular hole and massive splintering. Initially nicknamed "the smasher", the weapon was first made in 1779 at the Carron Iron Works, Falkirk, and was renamed the carronade. Although the larger version, the melvillade, was rarely used, the carronade became one of the most important innovations in naval warfare in the second part of the 18th century. The gun, whose elevation and angle of fire were governed by a screw on its gun carriage, suited the British style of close-in fighting and by 1781 over 600 guns had been mounted by the Royal Navy. The carronade proved decisive in Admiral Rodney's victory over the French at the Battle of The Saints on 12 April 1782.[2]

Image 4 – 68-pounder carronade, with slider carriage, on the deck of HMS *Victory* at Portsmouth

Adam Smith 1723-1790 is remembered as the founder of modern economics.[1] He was "the leading expositor of economic thought. Currents of Adam Smith run through the works published by David Ricardo and Karl Marx in the nineteenth century, and by John Maynard Keynes and Milton Friedman in the twentieth".[2]

The three most important economists were Adam Smith, Karl Marx, and John Maynard Keynes. Each was a highly original thinker who developed economic theories that were put into practice and affected the world's economies for generations.[3] Smith saw economics as a branch of moral philosophy, and he saw capitalism as an ethical project whose success required political commitment to justice and freedom, not merely an understanding of economic logistics.[4]

His *Inquiry into the Nature and Causes of the Wealth of Nations* is one of the most influential books ever written[5] and was one of the earliest attempts to study the historical development of industry and commerce in Europe. That work helped to create the modern academic discipline of economics.[6]

The Wealth of Nations is, in fact, the first comprehensive effort to study the nature of capital, the development of industry and the effects of large-scale commerce. While John Locke, a century earlier, made inroads into showing how rights are moral, Smith made inroads into showing how rights, at least in the economic realm, are practical in that they lead to economic progress. His ideas overall represented a substantial leap forward and were critical in putting capitalism and industrialisation on an intellectual footing. Without Smith's ideas, the economic progress of the past 200 years, progress that is far and away unequalled in human history, would have been greatly diminished.[7]

The Wealth of Nations documented industrial development in Europe. It is a massive work consisting of two volumes divided into five books. The ideas it promoted generated international attention and helped drive the move from land-based wealth to wealth created by assembly-line production methods driven by division of labour. While critics note that Smith didn't invent many of the ideas that he wrote about, he was the first person to compile and publish them in a format designed to explain them to the average reader of the day. As a result, he is responsible for popularising many of the ideas that underpin the school of thought that became known as classical economics. Other economists built on Smith's work to solidify classical economic theory.[8]

Smith is often identified as the father of modern capitalism. While accurate to some extent, this description is both overly simplistic and dangerously misleading. On the one hand, it is true that very few individual books have had as much impact as his *An Inquiry into the Nature and Causes of the Wealth of Nations*. His accounts of the division of labour and free trade, self-interest in exchange, the limits on government intervention, price, and the general structure of the market, all signify the moment when economics transitions to the "modern." On the other hand, *The Wealth of Nations* is not a book on economics. Its subject is "political economy," a much more expansive mixture of philosophy, political science, history, economics, anthropology, and sociology. The role of the free market and the *laissez-faire* structures that support it are but two components of a larger theory of human interaction and social history. Smith was not an economist; he was a philosopher.[9]

Smith's other great, and earlier, work was *Theory of Moral Sentiment* in which he developed the foundation for a general system of morals. It is a very important text in the history of moral and political thought. It provides the ethical, philosophical, psychological and methodological underpinnings to Smith's later works. In *Theory of Moral Sentiment* Smith states that man is self-interested and self-commanded. Individual freedom, according to Smith, is rooted in self-reliance, the ability of an individual to pursue his self-interest while commanding himself based on the principles of natural law.[10]

According to Smith, man is self-interested and self-commanding, and seeks to further his own ambitions. But through these intentions, unknowingly to the individual, he also benefits society as he must produce something others value in the marketplace. This is despite their actions having no benevolent intentions. Smith called this "the invisible hand of the market" and is the foundation of a *laissez-faire* economy unimpeded by government intervention. Smith proposed that a nation's wealth should be judged not by its store of bullion, as was the case under the mercantile system at the time of his writing, but by the total of its production and commerce, and to increase production and commerce a nation must specialise. He explored theories of the division of labour and the improvements it brings to the skill of the individual, its ability to save time and the impact this had on productivity and with it, prosperity. A nation's wealth is therefore the result of extensive division of labour.

Another key idea of Smith's is his canons of taxation. These are four principles that should be considered before setting up a tax:

*Economic – a tax should be simple and cheap to collect so that the revenue is maximised compared to the cost of collection.

*Equity – a tax should be fair; based on the ability to pay (vertical equity) and people of the same income pay the same amount of tax (horizontal equity).

*Certainty – taxpayers should understand how the system works, what to pay and when.

*Convenience – payment and timing of tax should be suited to the taxpayer.[11]

Anyone who cares to read Smith's *The Wealth of Nations* for themselves will find an economics discussed and justified in explicitly moral terms, in which markets, and the division of labour they allow, are shown to both depend upon and produce not only prosperity but also justice and freedom, particularly for the poor. With those concerns in mind, it should not be surprising that Smith was a staunch and vehement critic of those particularly grotesque sins associated with early capitalism: European empires and the slave trade.

Smith's defence of capitalism (or, in his terminology, "commercial society") is unambiguous but qualified. There is no inconsistency here. Smith's commitment to a realistic liberalism led him to endorse commercial society over any previous socio-economic system as a social order in which the most people possible could live decent lives. But he was not the blind zealot for the market he is now portrayed as. Smith was acutely aware of the possible ethical shortcomings of commercial society, and, for example, carefully read and responded to Rousseau's powerful critiques of its materialism, inequality, and inauthenticity. While the structural features of commercial society set the terms of its main opportunities and challenges, they did not determine the outcome. Commercial society was for Smith an ethical project whose greatest potential benefits had to be struggled for, and which could and should be much better than it was. He was in favour of government interventions and regulations properly justified by the public interest.[12]

He also realised that slave owners would not give up their "possessions" easily. "The late resolution of the Quakers [to free] their Negro slaves may satisfy us that their number cannot be very great."[13]

The ideas that became associated with Smith not only became the foundation of the classical school of economics, but also gained him a place in history as the "Father of Economics". His work served as the basis for other lines of inquiry into the economics field, including ideas that built on his work and those that differed.[14]

Smith's economic analysis was thoroughly entangled with a deeply humanistic ethical perspective. The picture of the real Adam Smith that this reveals is of a true "friend of commerce", supporting the project because of its achievements and its even greater potential, but constructively critical about both the shortcomings of the mercantilist society he lived in and commerce in general. He justified commercial society for its tremendous contribution to the prosperity, justice, and freedom of its members, and most particularly for the poor and powerless in society. But he was no naïve ideologue for free markets and profits. He criticised the political machinations and moral character of the very merchants and manufacturers who, he acknowledged, were driving economic development, and not only told them they should act better, but also argued for institutional measures to restrict their worst proclivities (particularly by getting government out of the business of economic micro-management).[15]

Smith did advocate a role for the government in areas such as public education of poor adults, a judiciary, and a standing army. However, Smith vigorously attacked antiquated government regulations which he thought were hindering industrial expansion. In fact, he attacked most forms of government interference in the economic process, including tariffs, by arguing that tariffs create inefficiency and high prices in the long run. Adam Smith may be credited by economists as one of the first advocates of a progressive tax system. "It is not very unreasonable that the rich should contribute to the public expense, not only in proportion to their revenue, but something more in proportion." However, he might also be interpreted as being a proponent of a proportional tax system in the following way: "The subjects of every state ought to contribute towards the support of the government, as nearly as possible, in proportion to their respective abilities; that is, in proportion to the revenue which they respectively enjoy under the protection of the state. The expense of government to the individuals of a great nation is like the expense of management to the joint tenants of a great estate, who are all obliged to contribute in proportion to their respective interests in the estate. In the observation or neglect of this maxim consists what is called the equality or inequality of taxation."[16]

Smith's *The Wealth of Nations* represents the first serious attempt in the history of economic thought to divorce the study of political economy from the related fields of political science, ethics, and jurisprudence. It embodies a penetrating analysis of the processes whereby economic wealth is produced and distributed and demonstrates that the fundamental sources of all income, that is, the basic forms in which wealth is distributed, are rent, wages, and profits. The central thesis of *The Wealth of Nations* is that capital is best employed for the production and distribution of wealth under conditions of governmental non-interference, or *laissez-faire*, and free trade. In Smith's view, the production and exchange of goods can be stimulated, and a consequent rise in the general standard of living attained, only through the efficient operations of private industrial and commercial entrepreneurs acting with a minimum of regulation and control by governments. To explain this concept of government maintaining a *laissez-faire* attitude towards commercial endeavours, Smith proclaimed the principle of the "invisible hand": Every individual in pursuing his or her own good is led, as if by an invisible hand, to achieve the best good for all. Therefore, any interference with free competition by government is almost certain to be injurious. Although this view has undergone considerable modification by economists in the light of historical developments since Smith's time, many sections of *The Wealth of Nations*, notably those relating to the sources of income and the nature of capital, have continued to form the basis for theoretical study in the field of political economy. *The Wealth of Nations* has also served, perhaps more than any other single work in its field, as a guide to the formulation of governmental economic policies.[17] *The Wealth of Nations* is, without a doubt, one of the most important books of all time. And the ideas it contained played a powerful role in shaping the development of American economic thought. Adam Smith's metaphor of the invisible hand remains one of the most important and influential ideas in economics, even today.[18]

In time, *The Wealth of Nations* won Smith a far-reaching reputation, and the work, considered a foundational work of classical economics, is one of the most influential books ever written.[19] So profound was the impact of *The Wealth of Nations* that it is generally considered the most important economic work ever written. Terms that are commonly used today, such as "invisible hand" and "division of labour," had their genesis in Smith's treatise.[20] (Actually, Smith's particular contribution was that he was the first to develop a theory that the division of labour was **the** principle cause of the growth in capitalism rather than being the first to describe the division of labour.)

English politicians, landed gentry, and the nobility paid little attention and enacted none of Smith's suggested reforms in the immediate aftermath of his book's publication. The American colonies, however, began their existence as an independent nation in 1781 with no money, no industry, no banks, and deep in debt. The United States' founding fathers, particularly Alexander Hamilton, James Madison, and Benjamin Franklin, turned to the ideas of Adam Smith to create an economic system for America with both immediate and long-sustained results.[21]

Smith showed that it was possible to study the workings of the mind and the process of socialisation by means of a study of the sentiments and the different strands of the sensibility in which the human personality was embodied. He explored the processes by which we acquire the senses of propriety, justice, political obligation and beauty on which our skills in the arts of social intercourse and our character depend. In doing so, he had introduced into his analysis a simple observation about the principles of human nature that had been ignored by modern philosophy; that man's natural indigence had somehow gone hand in hand with a love of improvement which he would exercise whenever he felt secure enough to do so. It was he [Smith] who had developed the stadial model of civilisation's progress that was to be one of the lasting legacies of his exploration of the science of man to philosophy, history and the social sciences. [22]

Smith strongly opposed slavery on both moral and economic grounds. The "invisible hand" in societies which allow slavery, operates in such a way that increases in the wealth of the rich, leads to increased misery for the poor free citizen as well as for the slaves themselves. It seems that the beneficial workings of the "'invisible hand' are dependent upon commercial societies which are not based upon the institution of slavery." [23]

The publication of *The Wealth of Nations* had immediate effects, including a tax on inhabited houses, a tax on manservants, a tax on property sold at auction, and a tax on malt, used in making beer. These taxes, especially the one on making beer, were unpopular, but Smith's arguments also had effects that were viewed more positively, "such as the entire modern free world". His arguments helped shape the Treaty of Paris which ended the American Revolutionary War when Lord Shelbourne, Britain's Prime Minister, claimed that "a peace was good in the exact proportion that it recognised that principle [free trade]". Prime Minister William Pitt the Younger used Smith's principles when he reformed Britain's customs and excise laws in his Consolidation Bill, and Pitt made the first move to a constitutional union with Ireland based on Smith's ideas. The first mention of *The Wealth of Nations* in the British Parliament was by Charles James Fox, and it is as poignantly true today as it has always been – "that the only way to become rich was to manage matters so as to make one's income exceed one's expenses. This maxim applied equally to an individual and to a nation." [24]

Charles Van Doren, in his *A History of Knowledge*, states that Smith was the first to describe the labour market. This was a monumental observation. "In a sense, before he named it and how it worked, the labour market did not exist." Smith realised that things were changing rapidly with industrialisation (which was still in its infancy when he wrote *The Wealth of Nations*). He saw that labour was a commodity like any other, and as such it was for sale. "In fact, everything was for sale … and money was the lifeblood of the market. … Furthermore, the happiness of humankind lay in efficient buying and selling. The sign of efficiency was profit, which was measured in money. Thus, money was the goal of all striving. And thus, the modern world came about." [25]

William Green 1725-1811 was a military engineer who had been wounded in the head when Quebec fell to the British army in 1759. The defences of Gibraltar were enhanced in 1770 to make it impregnable on the basis of his report and recommendations. "Green not only oversaw the modification of the Line Wall defences and building of barracks, bomb-proofs, store-houses, hospitals and magazines, but also proposed and designed a large bastion in the centre of the Line Wall which would help defend it. This would eventually be called the King's Bastion and it would play a vital role in the defence of Gibraltar during the Great Siege."[1] He also supervised the building of the numerous and extensive tunnels in the upper Rock which were conceived by a Cornish sergeant in Green's unit.

"Green's experience during the reconstruction of the defences of Gibraltar convinced him that the best workmen for military engineering tasks came not from among civilian hired labour but from mechanics in army regiments, particularly the artillery. He proposed, through Governor Edward Cornwallis, that a corps of military artificers should be formed to work exclusively on engineering tasks. The royal warrant for the soldier-artificer company, as it was called, was issued on 6 March 1772; the new company, headed by Green, evolved into the Royal Sappers and Miners (1815) who in 1856 were incorporated into the non-commissioned ranks of the Royal Engineers."[2]

James Hutton 1726-1797 is regarded as the founder of geology as a modern science. He formulated controversial theories of the origin of the Earth and of atmospheric changes known as "uniformitarianism". This paved the way for modern geological science.[1] The uniformitarian principle proposed that the Earth was very old and that the features of the Earth's surface were caused by natural processes that took place over a long period. This theory was contrary to the beliefs of the time, which corresponded to the biblical Creation and considered the Earth to be only a few thousand years old. Hutton's ideas thus advanced the field of geology and permanently altered the way the Earth was viewed.[2]

The uniformitarian principle was Hutton's main contribution to science. Geological observations regarding rocks, fossils, and strata had been made and documented by the late 18th century, but a general scientific theory regarding the formation and features of the Earth had yet to be postulated. Many subscribed to the belief inferred in the biblical book of Genesis that the

Earth had been created some 6,000 years earlier. Hutton proposed, however, that the Earth was immeasurably old and that observable processes could explain geologic phenomena. For instance, Hutton believed that continental topographic features were caused in large part by the erosive action of rivers, and that sedimentation in the ocean collected and formed new rocks through geothermal heat. These processes of erosion, sedimentation, deposition, and upthrusting, Hutton claimed, were cyclical and had been taking place with uniformity over long periods. These tremendously long cycles suggested that the Earth must be ancient. Hutton also stated that these geologic processes scientifically accounted for landforms all over the world; biblical explanations were not needed to justify their existence. Hutton announced his beliefs in papers he presented to The Royal Society of Edinburgh in 1785.

The uniformitarian principle that Hutton proposed provided the foundation for the science of geology and provided a scientific explanation for the features of the Earth's crust. Though Hutton's theories gained popularity, his 1795 *Theory of the Earth*, which explained his views and provided evidence for his conclusions, was not widely read because Hutton's writing style was hard to understand. In 1802, Hutton's friend John Playfair provided a more easily understandable version with *Illustrations of the Huttonian Theory of the Earth*.[3]

Hutton proposed that at its core, the Earth was hot, and that this heat caused new rock to be created: land was eroded by air and water and deposited as layers in the sea; heat then consolidated the sediment and then drove it upwards to create new landscapes.[4]

Hutton's philosophical reflections, particularly concerning time, causation, heat and the immensity of natural forces required, were central to his revolutionary geological claims. He maintained that the observable physical agencies of erosion, deposition, uplift, folding and volcanic activity suffice to explain all the observed phenomena, and can be presumed to operate in an indefinite future, as in an indefinite past. The surface of the globe must therefore have been destroyed and remade an indefinite number of times, and such a cyclical process will continue. Today, Hutton's views on heat and elevation have been accepted, along with the claim that many minerals were formerly fluid. Some metamorphic rocks, however, such as marble, flow and recrystallise as solids not fluids, and the consolidation of sedimentary rocks occurs mainly through compaction and chemical changes.

Hutton also demonstrated that igneous rocks were once molten. Through his study of Salisbury Crags, a Carboniferous igneous intrusion (sill) in Edinburgh, he demonstrated how the molten rock had forced its way between layers of sandstone before cooling to form rock. He published the results of his studies in his *Theory of the Earth* in 1795.[5]

Hutton was also the first person to propose a mechanism of natural selection to account for evolutionary change over time. In his book, *Investigation of the Principles of Knowledge* (1794), he lays out a clear argument for a process of transmutation by natural selection, and does so through analogy with the process of artificial selection. Hutton argues that members of species vary, and that when the environment changes over time, those individuals best adapted to the new environment will survive, while those poorly adapted will perish. Thus, a process of natural selection (Hutton did not use this term) inevitably leads to change within species over time.[6]

The idea that the Earth is alive is probably as old as humankind, but the first public expression of it as a fact of science was by Hutton. In 1785, he stated that the Earth was a superorganism and that its proper study should be physiology. Hutton is rightly remembered as the father of geology, but his idea of a living Earth was forgotten in the intense reductionism of the 19th century. The Gaia hypothesis, originally proposed in the 1960s by scientist James Lovelock, explores the idea that the life on Earth functions as a single organism which actually defines and maintains environmental conditions necessary for its survival.[7]

In 1784, Hutton presented his *Theory of Rain* to The Royal Society of Edinburgh. He proposed the idea that warmer air holds more water vapour and the cooling of air can lead to rain. He studied rainfall and climate data on different regions of the world and concluded that rainfall everywhere is regulated by humidity of the air and other causes which promote mixtures of different aerial currents in the higher atmosphere. Hutton also studied the decrease in temperature, linking it with height.[8]

Thomas Melville [Melvill] 1726-1753, with Alexander Wilson, made the first recorded use of kites in meteorology. They measured air temperature at various levels above the ground simultaneously with a train of kites.

In 1752, Melville discovered that putting different substances in flames and passing the light through a prism gave differently patterned spectra. Ordinary table salt, for example, generated a "bright yellow". Furthermore, not all the colours of the rainbow appeared – there were dark gaps in the spectrum – in fact, for some materials there were just a few patches of light.[1]

Melville published, posthumously in 1756, his observation of what we term today an emission spectrum: "I examined the constitution of these different lights (from the flames of spirit lamps fuelled by alcohol containing dissolved salts) with a prism and found that all sorts of rays were emitted, but not in equal quantities; the yellow being vastly more copious than all the rest put together".[2]

That different substances, when suitably "excited" in a flame or by an electric discharge, emit light that was characteristic of the substance "was first observed by the Scottish physicist Thomas Melvill (1726-1753), who mixed various salts with 'burning spirits' and examined the light through a prism. He found the spectrum of hot gas (the vaporised salt) to be markedly different from that of an incandescent solid or liquid."[3]

Melville's 1752 study of the colour of flames using a prism showed that the spectrum is not continuous like the spectrum of the sun or the radiation emitted by a blackbody. From this historical perspective came the awareness that the interaction of radiation with certain gases produces not a continuous spectrum like the emission spectrum, but a discrete spectrum. The realisation that the bright line spectra of vaporised elements match the dark lines in the solar spectra was the key to understanding the quantum nature of matter.[4]

Joseph Black 1728-1799 discovered carbon dioxide, which he called "fixed air". His experiments involved the very first careful gravimetric (weight) measurements on changes brought about when heating magnesia Alba (with release of CO_2) and reacting the products with acids or alkalis. This foreshadowed the work of French chemist Antoine-Laurent de Lavoisier and laid the foundation for modern chemistry.[1]

Black studied fixed air and found that a candle would not burn in it, that it would not support animal life, and that it was a product of respiration. He showed for the first time that reactions involving air conserved weight. In his experiments, Black made consistent use of quantitative weight measurements. He also discovered latent heat of vaporisation and latent heat of fusion. In addition, he found that the same amount of heat produced different temperature changes in different bodies. The change in temperature for a given amount of heat is now known as specific heat.[2]

Black's research into latent heat was carried out while at Glasgow and, in 1761, he was able to show that when a quantity of water froze, it gave up an amount of heat equal to the amount absorbed or rendered latent during liquefaction of the ice. The results of this brilliant investigation not only formed the basis of modern thermal science, but also gave the first impulse to James Watt's improvements in the steam-engine, and thereby to modern industrial developments. Black taught the doctrine of latent heat in his lectures from 1761 and he read an account of his successful experiments before a literary society in Glasgow on 23 April 1762. In 1767, Black also successfully inflated a balloon with hydrogen, the first time such a thing had been attempted.[3]

Black's lasting accomplishments were: 1. establishing for the first time that a gas could combine with a solid, previously believed to be impossible. 2. Recognising that there were various types of airs (air had been considered an element). "Fixed air" was a definite chemical entity different from air. This completely changed the understanding of the chemical nature of gases and ushered in the era of pneumatic chemistry. 3. Founding the study of calometry. His pioneering work with latent heats of fusion and evaporation and with what is now call specific heat and heat capacity proved invaluable to James Watt who used the information to improve the steam engine. (In Black's time, heat was considered a kind of matter). 4. He explained his observations without reference to the phlogiston theory. This impressed Lavoisier and provided him with an important clue as he formulated his oxygen theory.[4]

Charles Morrison (dates unknown) is an enigma and, despite partisan support for various candidates, his true identity is still unknown. The very first suggestion anywhere in the world for building an electric telegraph was published on 17 February 1753 in the *Scots Magazine*, 37 years before Chappe's optical telegraph (the letter was actually dated Renfrew, 1 February 1753).[1] It suggested using an array of 26 wires, one for each letter of the alphabet, to send messages over long distances. Unfortunately, the author only signed his letter C.M. and ever since he has been the subject of controversy. The two most likely contenders are named as Charles Morrison of Greenock and Charles Marshall of Aberdeen, but this is speculation. C.M.'s recommended device was for 26 insulated wires between two locations, each wire being charged individually by electricity depending on the letter being represented. At the receiving end, the wire that was charged would attract a disc of paper that was marked with the relevant letter. When C.M. made his proposal, there were no batteries (invented in 1800), relying instead on an electrostatic machine, but scientists did not see any use for electricity in communications. In 1782 Georges-Louis Le Sage developed a prototype telegraph based on C.M.'s telegraph, and in 1787 in Paris, Milan Lomond gave a demonstration of a practical experiment of an electric telegraph using static electricity which was a refinement of C.M.'s specifications (*The Telegraph: How Technology Innovation Caused Social Change*, by Annteresa Lubrano, 1997, p 8 – ISBN 0-8153-3001-4).

Not content with the suggestion for an electric telegraph, C.M. also suggested an acoustic telegraph using bells that were struck by a spark from a charged wire. Other people had done work with electricity before this, including French cleric Abbe Jean-Antoine Nollet, who actually gave a mild electric shock to a number of Carthusian monks in 1746 using a wire that was 1.5 kilometres long; and in 1747 William Watson, Bishop of Llandaff, had transmitted a signal across London's River Thames, but neither of these two actually suggested that electricity could be used as a means of communication such as would be achieved almost a century later by the electric telegraph, invented by Englishmen William Cooke and Charles Fothergill Wheatstone, and further improved by American Samuel Finley Breese Morse (there were earlier versions of the electric telegraph but it was Cooke and Wheatstone who made it commercially viable).

Cuthbert Gordon 1730-1810 was an industrial chemist who, in 1758, first produced cudbear, a dye extracted from orchil lichens that produce colours in the purple range. It can be used to dye wool and silk, without the use of mordant (a reagent, such as tannic acid, that fixes dyes to cells, tissues, textiles or other materials). Cudbear was the first dye to be invented in modern times, and one of the few dyes to be credited to a named individual (Cudbear was a corruption of Cuthbert).[1] "Gordon was a merchant who teamed up with his coppersmith brother to sell cudbear to printers and dyers throughout Britain. In 1765, their firm offered a colour sample card that included 78 cudbear colours, ranging through all the red-purples to the violet-blues.

The timing of the development and use of this new colouring process makes it fitting, and perhaps not coincidental, that cudbear could be used to produce pompadour, a fashionable colour that first appeared in Britain in the mid-1750s".[2] "As a source to make pompadour colours, Cuthbert Gordon's cudbear demonstrates the close links that could exist between fashion and production innovations."[3] Production of the lichen in Britain alone exceeded 227 tonnes and there was a need to supplement supplies from Scandinavia, and over 7,500 litres of urine were collected and tested using [William] Twaddell's hydrometer to ensure that the natural product had not been diluted with water.[4] The new product produced tones of blue and purple on cotton and linen, reducing the need to import indigo and cochineal.

Alexander Cumming 1731-1814 was a mathematician, mechanic and horologist and was sufficiently expert at the latter to be one of the examiners of the chronometer of Englishman John Harrison, the device that, with John Campbell's sextant, allowed mariners to determine longitude accurately.

Cumming made a continuously recording barograph – a device that records changes in atmospheric pressure – for King George III and it is still in the collection of the Royal Family. Cumming's barograph came at a price of £1,178 with King George paying Cumming £187.10s a year for Cumming to maintain it.[1] It was built in 1765 and predates by many decades the later claims for inventing the barograph attributed to Frenchman Lucien Vidie (1843) and Englishman Alfred King (1853).

Various people also vied for recognition as inventor of the microtome, an instrument for cutting very thin slices of specimens to be viewed under a microscope. Claimants included Englishman John Hill in 1770, German Benedikt Stilling in 1824, and Czech Jan Evangelista Purkinje in 1837. Frenchman Charles Chevalier is said to have perfected it around 1825.

Englishman George Adams seemingly has priority in the invention of the microtome which he made around 1770. Cumming either invented it independently or improved it shortly afterwards as one of his microtomes, known to be made in 1770, is still in existence[2] and it is known that John Hill used this model for his research into the structure of timber. The specimen to be examined was put in the hole and was pressed upwards by a screw. The blade sliced the top of the specimen, which was then pushed up the required amount by the screw.

Image 5 – A diagram of a microtome drawn by Cumming in 1770

It is, however, for the water closet that Cumming is best known, although overshadowed by Joseph Bramah. The flush toilet was possibly the single most important innovation to improve the quality of life in the home, particularly in cities. For most of history, towns and cities stank with the smell of human and animal excrement, and rampant disease caused by excreta periodically decimated city populations. Hygiene was abysmal and the wealthy often moved to other homes while the sewage pits were emptied out or when there was an epidemic, such as plague, typhoid or typhus. A number of innovations greatly improved urban hygiene – sewage pipes and tunnels to remove excrement; automobiles replaced horses that littered streets with dung; and homes began to install water closets.

Although flush toilets were known in the ancient world, these were mostly seats with a hole placed above running water and they were outside the home, not inside. In 1596, Englishman Sir John Harington, godson of Queen Elizabeth, made a privy, or *jakes* as it was known colloquially, and in the same year published a *New Discourse of a Stale Subject, called the Metamorphosis of Ajax* (a pun on *a jakes*). It was technically successful but didn't catch on in England. Harington went on "travels" due to mockery over his invention, despite Elizabethans having an earthy language as shown when Harington's cousin, Edward Sheldon, wrote to him requesting an account of his invention. Sheldon asked Harington "to employ 'homely' words in his descriptions by christening the new device 'in plaine English a shyting place'", but that is about the sum of the obscenity, despite such apocryphal tales as John Aubrey's concerning how the earl of Oxford, "making of his low obeisance to Queen Elizabeth, happened to let a Fart, at which he was so abashed and ashamed that he went to Travell, 7 yeares,"[3] Harington's flush toilet was more popular in France but was still rare as it lacked the crucial component to prevent evil odours permeating the privy and nearby rooms – the sliding valve, which provided a stink trap similar to the later S-bend. This is what Cumming patented in 1775. The pan held fresh water both before and after use, and a lever was pulled to slide open the valve and drop the contents into a sewage trap while simultaneously releasing fresh water into the pan. The valve was then shut off and about seven centimetres of water remained in the pan to make a seal and prevent the smell of the cesspit coming back through the toilet. This was the true birth of the modern flush toilet although it was later improved by other engineers such as Englishman Joseph Bramah, who added the ball valve and S-bend. Cumming's invention of the modern flush toilet, and its later improvements, allowed toilets to move indoors in the workplace, on long distance passenger transport and, above all, into the home.

Robert Macpherson 1731-1791 invented both the New Water-mill (1766) and Foot Machine in 1763 "for dressing flax and hemp which is much less wasteful of the flax; as much so, it is presumed, as water machinery can possibly be. It not only yields more flax from the scutch, but the flax dressed by it yields still more from the heckle. It is fitter for dressing long hemp and is no way dangerous nor unhealthy to the workmen. It requires a less expensive millhouse, less annual repair, and much less water. The parts of its machinery which dress the flax or hemp, may be joined to the movement of a cornmill, or any other mill, by a small iron axle, or by rope and pulley, through any wall or partition, at a side, above, or below."[1]

The expense of breaking and scutching the £940,000 worth of flax and hemp produced in Britain annually in 1777 was around £150,000; one half of which (£75,000 per annum), "must come in time to be saved by the use of the new machines; for the new scutcher does more than double the work of the old hand-scutch in the same time."[2]

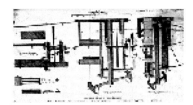

Image 7 – The Foot Machine for Breaking and Beating Flax and Hemp
Invented by Robert Macpherson (1766) Published in the *Scots Magazine* in February 1766

Patrick Miller 1731-1815 built, in 1786, a 235-tonne five-masted, double-hulled boat (catamaran), which was propelled on the Firth of Forth by men working a capstan which drove paddles on each side. The following year he made an 18-metre, triple-hulled boat (trimaran) with three masts,[1] the "first boat with three hulls, derived from the Polynesian latakois ..."[2] He helped sponsor and design a cannon called the carronade, which the British navy adopted for use in 1779.[3]

John Broadwood 1732-1812 was considered the finest maker of harpsichords in the world by 1793 when the instrument started to rapidly give ground to the new pianoforte. The grand piano was co-invented by Broadwood with a fellow Scot, Robert Stodart and a Dutchman, Americus

Backers. Their first attempt to design a grand piano was made in 1777 when they built a piano in a harpsichord case. They were successful by 1781, using the soft pedals and added damper. Broadwood's company went on to be the dominant piano producer in the world throughout the 19th century and the company is still in existence, making it the oldest piano manufacturer in the world.

The wrestpins were placed at the back of the case, not at the right-hand side of the soundboard as was customary on other makers' pianos. The dampers took the form of brass levers beneath the strings (hence termed "under dampers"), each having a little pad of red wool cloth at the tip, to silence the strings. Broadwood pianos also differed from their contemporaries in having no hand stops at the left. At that time, most square pianos had at least two hand stops to disengage the bass and treble dampers, and often a third to produce the "Harp" tone, that sounded rather like gut strings. But hardly any of Broadwood's early square pianos had any means of modifying the tone quality: the pedal for a sustained tone (by disengaging the dampers) was fitted only if the buyer requested it, at a fee of two guineas extra, and surviving instruments show that this was very rarely fitted. Less rare, but still very uncommon, was a pedal to lift part of the lid, the so-called "swell".

Broadwood developed techniques to mass produce his pianos, which were well made, from good quality materials. His two sons became partners and by the 1840s around 2,500 pianos a year were being made at the factory leased in 1823 in Horseferry Road, Westminster. Broadwood's were now among the largest employers of labour in London.[1]

Charles Irving c1734-1794 invented a marine chair designed to compensate for the motion of ships so that telescopes could be used to calculate celestial measurements. By 1770, he had developed an apparatus for distilling seawater and turning it into drinking water, which was subsequently tested and recommended for adoption on ships of the Royal Navy. Earlier, in 1761, Scottish physician James Lind, famous for his scurvy experiment, had discovered that sea-water, distilled without the addition of any ingredients, yielded pure freshwater; and, in 1762, an account of this was read to The Royal Society, and soon after published by authority of the Lords Commissioners of the Admiralty. "Although the principle of distilling freshwater from seawater had long been known, earlier attempts to produce potable water at sea involved bulky equipment, great amounts of fuel, and chemical additives that left nasty aftertastes. Irving's method basically relied on a 'simple addition to the common ship's kettles' used for cooking so that only one source of heat was needed to both boil provisions and distill seawater to produce freshwater through collected condensation."[1]

"Irving, in 1770, by whom distillation was generally introduced into the British navy, obtained a parliamentary reward of £5,000; his invention consisted of a tea-kettle made without a spout, with a hole in the lid in the place of a knob; when filled with sea-water, the fresh vapour will arise as it boils and issue through the hole in the lid; into which the mouth of a tobacco-pipe is fitted, letting the stem incline a little downwards, and the vapour of fresh-water will take its course through the steam of the tube, and may be collected by fitting a proper vessel to its end. He also adapted a tin, iron, or copper tube, of suitable dimensions, to the lid of the common kettle used for boiling the provisions on ship-board; the fresh vapour, arising from boiling the sea-water in the kettle, passes through this tube into a hogshead, which serves as a receiver; and that the vapour may be readily condensed, the tube is kept cool by constantly wetting it with a mop dipped in a tub of cold water."[2]

James Keir 1735-1820 was one of the founders of the British chemical industry, and probably the first successful manufacturer of caustic soda by a fully synthetic route. He worked out how to mass-produce soap, eventually building a 20-acre (8 hectares) soap works in Staffordshire, with compatriot Alexander Blair. The factory produced a million pounds (453,592 kg) of soap a year[1] and, as the first soap factory in the world, it became the second most popular showplace in Britain after the Soho Foundry of Matthew Boulton and James Watt at Smethwick, near Birmingham. This was Keir's greatest accomplishment; he designed the factory, developed the chemical engineering, and trained the workers for their new industry.[2]

In 1779, he patented a metal alloy made of copper, zinc and iron (called tutenag) which could be forged hot or cold (he did not invent it as it was already in use by the Chinese). Window frames made from this metal may still be found at Boulton's home, Soho House.[3] Keir played a significant part in the development of chemistry as writer, experimenter, and, most importantly, industrialist, having developed the first commercially successful process for making synthetic caustic soda. In 1780, he founded the Tipton Chemical Works for the manufacture of alkalis.[4]

"The fall in the mortality rate towards the end of the century has often been put down partly to increased hygiene; it could be that Keir's soap did as much for public health as [Erasmus] Darwin's medicine."[5]

James Lind 1736-1812 proposed, in 1775, a pressure-tube anemometer, which measured wind speed by the movement of water in a U-tube when the wind was blown down one side. This led to the development of more precise and standardised methods of measurement. The use of a U-tube to measure wind speed had been suggested previously by Leon Battista Alberti, Robert Hooke and Pierre Daniel Huet. It was, however, Lind who made the "first satisfactory syphon wind gauge, or manometer ... in 1775. A U-shaped glass tube was blocked at one end, except for a vent hole, the other end having an elbow joint that faces into the wind. The tube is half filled with water to a central zero mark, and the air forced into one end of the tube will push the water up towards the other end. The difference from zero in both arms of the tube is added to give a measure of the force of the wind."[1]

Lind was almost certainly the scientific influence behind Mary Shelley's *Frankenstein*. He also influenced Percy Shelley's own works, including "the likely effect of Lind's interest in forensic medicine as the inspiration for Percy Shelley's creation of perhaps the earliest example of ratiocinative (i.e. the process of logical reasoning) detective drama in his play *The Cenci*. Notwithstanding Mary Shelley's own literary talent, and her night of inspiration in 1816, we might now give some credit to the time spent six years previously by her husband-to-be in the study of a retired Scots physician in Windsor."[2]

James Watt 1736-1819 provided a key innovation of the Industrial Revolution when he improved Englishman Thomas Newcomen's steam engine by adding a separate condenser. It was this innovation more than any other that started the Industrial Revolution and changed the world forever. A number of Englishmen had already set the scene by inventing machines for increasing the production of textiles, but these depended on power from water or wind, or the physical exertion of humans or animals. Watt changed all that. Although various steam engines, including those of Thomas Newcomen, were already in use to pump water out of mines, it was Watt who developed, for the first time in history, a truly effective means of applying power to manufacturing that didn't depend on human labour, wind, water or animals.

In late 1763, Professor John Anderson of Glasgow University sent Watt a model of a Newcomen steam engine that needed repair. This was "not only a turning point in Watt's career but also an important event in the history of civilisation."[1] On inspecting the engine, Watt concluded that it couldn't run efficiently unless it maintained a vacuum, which would require the condensed steam to be no greater than 37C with the cylinder being as hot as the incoming steam.[2] These were incompatible requirements with the single-cylinder Newcomen engine and Watt's flash of ingenuity was to create a separate condenser so that these conditions could be met.

He made several other important changes to Newcomen's engine and in January 1769 patented his own steam engine which needed only a quarter of the fuel consumed by the Newcomen engine to perform the same work.[3] He went into partnership with John Roebuck but couldn't spend much time in refining his steam engine as he undertook surveying work for canals and made plans for harbours and a bridge. Roebuck went bankrupt and James Watt moved to Birmingham in 1774 to join Matthew Boulton in a partnership, with Watt on the engineering side and Boulton on the business end.

Watt took out a second steam engine patent in 1781 in which he described five ways to convert the piston's reciprocating motion into rotating movement, including the method that was eventually adopted – the crank and fly-wheel. However, Englishmen James Pickard and Matthew Wasbrough had patented the crank and fly-wheel on 23 August 1780, so Watt – or perhaps his assistant, William Murdock – developed the so-called sun-and-planet gear to generate rotary motion. It was in 1780 that Watt first applied steam power to a flour mill – the first in the world and the first time that steam power had been used for work other than pumping water out of mines.

In 1788, Watt devised the fly ball, or centrifugal, governor to control the speed of his engines by using negative feedback. Although this is sometimes claimed as the first use of a machine feedback device, governors had been developed earlier, such as those to control windmills, and Englishman Sutton Thomas Wood used a float valve regulator in 1784 to control a steam engine in his brewery; but Watt's governor was the first to become widespread in machinery outside of windmills. Watt initiated classical control theory on which proportional-integral-derivative method is based. This method "controls a system by reading the input sensors and applying a mathematical equation to the inputs to produce the output."[4] Although feedback control has come a long way since James Watt, the basic approach and system elements have not changed.[5]

In a 1784 steam engine patent, Watt introduced the concept of change-speed, or variable velocity, gearing. "Motion [from a steam engine] is communicated to the axle-tree of one or more wheels of the carriage by means of the 'circulating rotative to machinery' formerly patented by the inventor. Two or more loose wheels of different diameters are placed to be locked on the axle and impart extra power for bad roads or steep ascents."[6] Watt didn't build the steam locomotive described in this 1784 patent of his, although its design was more advanced than the first locomotive actually built by Cornishman Richard Trevithick in 1802, as its two-speed transmission gear changer would assist uphill travel. Interestingly, Watt is rarely credited for his role in the history of the locomotive because it wasn't actually built, yet Charles Babbage is usually given the honour of "father of the first computer" (albeit mechanical) although his Analytical Engine has never been built, and his Difference Engine (a sophisticated calculator) wasn't built until 1991 – 120 years after his death.

A possible reason Watt didn't proceed with his locomotive was that, although he was certainly aware of the advantages of high pressure engines, particularly after his work on expansive power, he actively opposed their development because he believed they were unsafe (which was true then and for some time to come until technology advanced to the stage where boilers could effectively handle high pressures). Another reason may have been that Watt spent much of his time in patent battles and he could have been reticent to open up a new field of costly litigation, such as illustrated in one bill for nearly £7,000 (a huge sum at that time) in legal costs from Boulton and Watt's solicitor, Ambrose Weston. By comparison, wages of ordinary employees at Boulton and Watt's Soho Works varied from boys at 2s. 6d (30 pence) to about £1 (240 pence) per week for skilled adult employees. The engine erectors were paid from ten shillings (120 pence) upwards, while Watt's top employee, William Murdock, was paid two guineas weekly (504 pence). For workers earning less than £1 a week Boulton and Watt established an Insurance Society to provide sickness benefit and funeral expenses, with the premium ranging from ½ penny to 4 pence depending on the weekly wage earned.[7] This was one of the world's pioneering work insurance schemes and although the starting date of the Soho scheme is uncertain, "it was definitely before 1782".[8] This was 66 years before the Railway Passengers Assurance Company, which was formed in 1848, first offered accident insurance, an event that is usually considered to be the first accident insurance provided by an employer.

In 1782, with William Murdock, Watt's third patent introduced the double-acting engine, whereby one of the two pistons is always being pushed, effectively doubling the power of the engine. This patent also included: the coupled steam engine – two engines that could work in unison or separately as required; a rotary engine; and a rack on the piston rod to ensure its perfect rectilinear motion. To produce the straight-line motion needed for the cylinder rod and pump, Watt invented the parallel motion/three-bar linkage which he patented on 28 April 1784, and by now he had an engine that was five times more powerful than his first 1769 engine (or 20 times as efficient as Newcomen's engine). Watt and Murdock also patented the vibrating, or oscillating, cylinder whereby power is transferred directly to the crank from the steam piston. He perfected the throttle valve in 1788 and made a machine for duplicating statues that could make identical or smaller copies. Steel magnate Andrew Carnegie wrote a biography on Watt in which he stated that German-born statistician Ernst Engel estimated by 1888 there was hardly a major industry that did not rely on steam, and the value of world industries dependent on steam was, at that time $32 billion – a staggering sum equivalent to a figure between $388 and $940 billion in 2014 (depending on method of calculation), and this at a time when industry constituted only a small fraction of what it is today.[9]

In a 1770 letter Watt included a drawing of a propeller, which he called a spiral oar, for the purpose of propelling canal boats, but he didn't pursue its development, although he did attach a propeller to a steam engine in 1770 (the idea for using a screw propeller for moving boats had been suggested as early as 1752 by Swiss physicist Daniel Bernoulli). In 1784, Watt patented a steam hammer and trunk engine that was more compact and had a large pipe forming the piston rod, being of sufficient diameter to allow one end of the connecting rod to be attached to the crank, and the other end to pass within the pipe directly to the piston.

Also in 1784, Watt developed steam radiator heating for buildings although this needed later refinement by Neil Snodgrass in 1790. "The steam heater was able to carry heat further and more surely than the hot-air system. The first known model was the one installed by James Watt ... in his factory on the outskirts of Birmingham."[10] Watt made instruments to measure temperatures in his steam engines, and in 1790 he invented a mercury gauge to determine the steam pressure of an engine and invented the first revolution counter for machinery. He developed pressure volume diagrams, originally called indicator diagrams, to describe corresponding changes in volume and pressure in a system.[11] These are commonly used in thermodynamics, cardiovascular physiology, and respiratory physiology.

He was the first person to state that water was a compound, notifying Matthew Boulton by letter in December 1782 and a further letter to Joseph Priestley to be read to The Royal Society in April 1783. Its public reading was delayed by a year and he lost priority to Henry Cavendish and Antoine Lavoisier. However, "Sir Humphrey Davy, [Joseph] Henry, [Francois] Arago, [Justus von] Liebig, and many others of the highest authority acknowledged and established Watt's claims."[12] While Watt and Cavendish remained on good terms and hardly entered into any debate on the issue of priority, later in the 19th century supporters of both, now dead, men sought to establish priority for one or the other. In 1875, Hermann Kopp, a German chemist and historian of chemistry, concluded, "'Cavendish was the first to establish the fact from which the knowledge of the composition of water proceeded' but did not state the components of water; Watt 'first concluded from these facts that water was a compound, but without reaching a true knowledge of the components'; Lavoisier, from the same facts 'and with the recognition of the compound nature of water, first gave the correct determination and the exact statement of the components.'"[13]

Watt and Englishman Thomas Beddoes devised breathing bags and face masks, made of oiled silk and attached to a wooden valve box fitted with inspiratory and expiratory check valves. Watt's interest in this technique arose from the fact that his youngest son Gregory suffered from tuberculosis, or consumption as it was then known, eventually dying from the disease in 1804. In 1794, Watt and Beddoes wrote the very first book on the medical application of oxygen – *Considerations on the Medicinal Use of Factitious Airs, and the Manner of Obtaining them in Large Quantities*. Watt built the equipment, which he continued to improve, and he devised means of containing and delivering gases (including oxygen, nitrogen, carbon dioxide, hydrogen) in measured amounts.[14] This was the first time that such a device had been made for inhalation, but it was Beddoes rather than Watt who became known as "The father of inhalation therapy".

In 1772, Watt invented a screw micrometer that would provide greater accuracy in measuring distances, having previously built a simple micrometer in 1767 by placing two parallel hairs in the focus of a telescope. Note: The first micrometer was invented by Englishman William Gascoigne in the 17th century. In 1786, Watt introduced to Britain the use of chlorine for bleaching cloth after having been given a demonstration of it in France by Claude Louis Berthollet.

The earliest form of mechanical copier was patented by James Watt in 1780. It used ink mixed with gum arabic pressed on a sheet of damp tissue paper against the manuscript to obtain a mirror image that could be read from the reverse side of the tissue. Watt further adapted it to make unlimited copies and this was the first true office copier, invented 158 years before American Chester Carlson invented xerography (photocopying).

In 1816, at the age of 80, Watt gave one final display of his innate genius when he was returning from Rothesay in a steamboat. "At that time, the engineer did not reverse his engines, but merely stopped them some time before the vessel reached her mooring-place, and let her gradually slow down. James Watt, then an old man of eighty, tackled the engineer of the boat, and showed him how the engine could be reversed. He tried to explain this with the aid of a foot rule, but not being successful in doing it to the complete satisfaction of the engineer, he is said to have thrown off his overcoat and given a practical demonstration. Although Watt never took up the subject of steam navigation and never made a marine engine, still he was in reality its originator, because he discovered and provided the means by which it could be applied with advantage to the propulsion of ships. Each of his great improvements upon the old engine that worked by atmospheric pressure and condensed its steam in the cylinder – such as the separate condenser; the working by steam pressure as well as by pressure obtained by vacuum; the double action of the steam in the cylinder on both sides of the piston; working the steam expansively; the centrifugal governor for automatically regulating the speed of the engine; and many others – was a direct adaptation for marine purposes."[15]

In autumn 1997, *Life* magazine published a list of the 100 top events of the past 1,000 years. James Watt's patent for improvement to the steam engine was fourth on the list, after Gutenberg's printing, Columbus' voyage to America and Martin Luther's 95 theses. To honour Watt, the British government, via Sir Joseph Banks, proffered a baronetcy but he declined it, [16] although he was later honoured by naming a unit of energy after him because he had scientifically determined the value of one horsepower – the energy expended by a horse in lifting 33,000 pounds (15 tonnes) over the distance of one foot (30.48 cm) in one minute. Horsepower was called *watt*.

Image 6 – James Watt & Co. copying press, in Thinktank, Birmingham Science Museum
Made in 1815, to James Watt's original design of 1780

"In the technology ranking of Human Accomplishment, the instrument maker and mechanical engineer James Watt (1736-1819) of Scotland and the prolific inventor Thomas Alva Edison (1847-1931) of the USA, who created an early research laboratory, are tied for the maximum score of 100. There is a large gap from them down to Leonardo da Vinci (1452-1519), who is then followed by Christiaan Huygens (1629-1695) from the Netherlands, one of the greatest polymaths in all history; Archimedes of Syracuse (ca. 290-212 BC); [and] the Italian radio pioneer Guglielmo Marconi (1874-1937)."[17]

Alexander Dalrymple 1737-1808 became, in 1795, the first ever hydrographer to the British Admiralty. He is credited with the creation and design of the Admiralty Charts, which provided a guide to the safe navigation of the world's oceans. Dalrymple's work meant that the Royal Navy had the most accurate sea charts in the world, paving the way for the rapid growth of the British Empire.[1] During his lifetime he produced thousands of nautical charts, mapping a remarkable number of seas and oceans for the first time and contributing significantly to the safety of shipping.[2]

Dalrymple is correctly credited with the concept and design in 1800 of the Admiralty Chart, developed through the following two hundred years to constitute an ongoing body of over 4,000 charts, guaranteeing safe navigation of the oceans by navies and merchant shipping alike.[3] He advocated, first privately and then officially, a complex form of chronometer log-keeping with tables of the gradations of wind and weather. He derived the wind scale from John Smeaton's calibration of windmill sails, and he later transmitted it to the young Francis Beaufort, who adopted it and by whose name it is now known.[4] Dalrymple's *Practical Navigation* (1789) includes his own "wind scale", which is of particular importance as it predates Beaufort's scheme of 1806, and upon which the latter had heavily drawn.[5]

Dalrymple was responsible for much of the successful voyages of James Cook to the South Pacific. He was convinced that a huge, populous continent existed in the South Pacific, which he called "the Great South Land." Working from manuscripts and original data in archives across the world, Dalrymple had prepared a summary of maritime discoveries made in the Pacific region up to 1764, and his work was of considerable significance to the success of Cook's voyage.

He hoped to personally find this land on the expedition of 1769, but command was given to Cook who found no evidence of its existence. Cook did find evidence of a so-called "Terra Australia," however, by his discovery of New Zealand and the southeast coast of Australia. When Dalrymple published his *Historical Collection of the Several Voyages and Discoveries in the South Pacific Ocean* in 1770-1771, the widespread interest aroused by his continued claim of the existence of the unknown continent led Cook, now promoted to Captain, to undertake yet another voyage into the South Pacific, adding more knowledge of that part of the world and charting many new coasts.[6]

James Anderson 1739-1808 built, in 1784, the so-called Scotch plough, a small two-horse plough which was suited to heavy soils and which replaced the four-horse plough. Anderson published works relating to agriculture and weather, having written an article on monsoons in the 1773 edition of *Encyclopaedia Britannica* in which he made predictions concerning the discoveries of explorer James Cook before he had returned to England to confirm them[1] – namely that New Holland (Australia) was the only large land mass that existed in the unexplored southern hemisphere, in contrast to the common belief that there had to be sufficient southern land mass to counterbalance the northern hemisphere's land mass.

In 1777, Anderson expounded in *Observations and the Enquiry* the differential theory of rent based on the extensive margin, [2] a theory that was subsequently taken up by early English economists David Ricardo, Thomas Robert Malthus, Edward West, and Irishman Robert Torrens. His *Inquiry into the Nature of the Corn Laws, with a View to the new Corn Bill proposed for Scotland*, (Edinburgh, 1777) formulated more specifically what came to be later known as the Ricardian theory of rent, which asserts that rent arises because of the differences in the fertility or location of agricultural land. No rent is paid on the worst land and the total amount of rent increases as the margin of cultivation is extended. Austrian economist Joseph Schumpeter said that Anderson "had to an unusual degree what so many economists lack, vision." Anderson, at the behest of the government of William Pitt, undertook a survey of western Scotland's fisheries.[3]

John Schank 1740-1823 was in command of the 18-gun HMS *Inflexible* which played a major role in the defeat of the American fleet on Lake Champlain in October 1776. He invented the "sliding keel", a form of centreboard that allowed for the building of vessels of very shallow-draught which sailed faster, steered more easily and could tack and wear quicker than conventional craft. A number of vessels were built with sliding keels, notably the sloop *Cynthia* in 1795. All forty-three of the Acute class of gunboat in 1797-1799 had sliding keels as did the *Lady Nelson*, which sailed with Matthew Flinders to the coast of New South Wales between 1800 and 1802. His expertise in the design of shallow-draught vessels led to Schank's being commissioned by the Duke of Bridgewater to design, for use on his canal, a steam tug, *Buonaparte*, which was built at Worsley between 1796 and 1799. In 1800, Schank designed the first of the two paddle steamers named *Charlotte Dundas* for Thomas, Lord Dundas, and the Forth and Clyde Navigation Company.[1]

James Small 1740-1793, a Berwickshire farmer, experimented with changing the shape of the mouldboard and plough. The plough had changed little since medieval times, and its redesign was to be one of the major agricultural developments in Europe. Around the middle of the 17th century the Dutch slightly modified it and this was further developed in England with the advent of the Rotherham swing plough (invented in 1730 by Englishmen Joseph Foljambe and Disney Stanyforth), with its wooden mouldboard, a share covered with an iron plate and a coulter made completely of iron.

By 1780, Small had produced the curved cast-iron mouldboard and wrought-iron share. His plough was sufficiently light and maneuverable to be worked by a man with one or two horses instead of oxen, and it was designed to completely invert the sod, as Small believed that it was important to kill all the weeds. Small is generally thought to have made the critical changes to the plough that helped kick-start the Agricultural Revolution, although the ancient Chinese had manufactured iron ploughs that were similar. "James Small enunciated the following principles of scientific plough design: 'The back of the sock [share] and mould-board shall make one continued fair surface without any interruption or sudden change.' Chinese ploughs, from the Third Century BC, already met these requirements. They had a cast-iron mould-board, which was a curved device that shifted the soil with the minimum of drag. The European plough simply had a wooden board coming off to the side which turned the soil that had been cut."[1] There is, however, no evidence the Chinese plough, via the Netherlands, influenced the design of either the Rotherham plough or the one designed by James Small. If, indeed, the Dutch had copied the Chinese plough, they would have been far in advance of any other European country in this respect, given that the Dutch were inventive and quick to adopt new technology.

Clearly, the developments of Small and others were independent of the Chinese plough, although very much later. In 1784, to underscore that Small wasn't an imitator, he published *A treatise on ploughs and wheel-carriages*, the first publication to set out the scientific principles of the plough. It was to be the main reference on ploughs for more than half a century.[2] Bob Powell, writing for The Professional Interest Group, stated it was James Small ... who scientifically developed the plough. Influenced by the Rotherham model, he focused on the wooden mouldboard profile that he later produced in cast iron. The principles of plough-making that Small incorporated into his "Swing" or "Chain Plough" by 1765 were key to the Agricultural Revolution and by the 1780s were widely adopted in Europe and North America.[3]

Patrick Ferguson 1744-1780 patented what is often claimed as the first practical military breech-loading rifle – patent number 1139 dated 2 December 1776. "Although a French engineer is generally given credit for the development of this successful system, its origins date back to the late 16th century in Spain. The system utilised a screw-threaded plug which, by being screwed and unscrewed vertically at the rear of the barrel, sealed and unsealed the breech for loading with powder and ball. Throughout the 17th century this system was experimented with in Germany, England, and Denmark but was finally developed with success by Isaac de la Chaumette in France in 1704. The inventor was a Huguenot, however, and fled to England subsequently where, in 1721, he took out an English patent to protect his invention.

For the next 50 years screw-plug breech-loading muskets and rifles were made in England as sporting guns but, in 1776, Captain Patrick Ferguson took out a patent for an improved version which he intended for military use. Subsequent trials of his rifle impressed British military authorities and it was made in a small quantity to equip a corps of riflemen to be led by him on campaign in America. Although successful at Brandywine in 1777, Ferguson's corps was broken up after he was wounded there, and his subsequent death at King's Mountain in 1780 ended Britain's experiment with military breech-loaders for the next half-century."[1] Note: "Much has been written about how the American War of Independence might have evolved if a weapon such as Ferguson's breech-loader had been the standard British weapon. In fact, the design of Ferguson's rifle made it useless as a military weapon. The moving part of the breech mechanism, which rendered it supposedly rapid-loading and reloadable from cover, was completely exposed to the deposits created by the burning of the gunpowder and became inoperable after fewer than ten shots. Deposits also accumulated at the front of the area in which the ball and powder were contained, which progressively prevented the ball from seating in the same position as for the previous shot: therefore the point of impact of the bullet would vary with each shot, and the shooting become increasingly inaccurate. The mechanism was mounted in the stock such that much wood was removed and the stock was made very fragile for a military weapon. All of the known surviving examples of the military rifle are broken and crudely repaired at this point. Finally, and by no means least, there would have had to be a complete revolution in military attitudes towards weapons technology and the need for a weapon with the supposed attributes of the Ferguson rifle.

That revolution did not take place until after the self-contained metallic cartridge had been successfully introduced during the last quarter of the nineteenth century."[2]

William Cruickshank c1745-1810 designed, in 1802, the first electric battery capable of mass production by joining zinc and copper plates in a wooden box filled with electrolyte. He also performed experiments leading to electroplating when he showed that metals are deposited on the negative pole, while acids (anions) are deposited on the positive pole.[1] He also discovered the element strontium in 1787, although others also lay claim to this discovery – Adair Crawford (1790), Thomas Charles Hope (1791), Martin Heinrich Klaproth (1793), Richard Kirwan (1794), and Humphrey Davy (1808).[2] Cruickshank and Adair Crawford identified strontium carbonate and published their findings in 1790, this being the first time a strontium compound had been distinguished from barium.[3]

In the last years of the 1790s, Cruickshank was extensively analysing the chemical components of urine in health and disease. In 1797, he produced urea nitrate by adding concentrated nitric acid to evaporated urine.[4] He "can claim to be the first to demonstrate that heavy proteinuria causing dropsy was due to kidney disease."[5] Cruickshank is credited with being first to notice that in some types of dropsy (swelling of soft tissue due to excess water accumulation) the coagulation of urine in a greater or less degree of heat, must be due to the presence of albumin.[6] "The Scots ordnance chemist … was the first to make the distinction, later also emphasised by [William Thomas] Brande in 1806, between dropsy from liver disease (morbid viscera) in which the urine did not coagulate and the 'general' then supposed inflammatory dropsy, in which the urine coagulated with heat or threw a precipitate with several chemical agents."[7]

Cruickshank's description of the electrolysis of brine in 1800 was a landmark in chemistry. "Electrolysis became an extremely important method of transforming materials and especially for the production of inorganic chemicals and compounds, either for use in their own right (or) as a source of feedstocks for the manufacture of other compounds, including organics. For example, the chlorine by-product from the electrolysis of brine was the starting point for the manufacture of organic compounds including solvents, pesticides and plastics."[8]

Cruickshank must have been one of the first analytical chemists to investigate the composition of organic compounds and was particularly interested in sugars. He prepared carbon monoxide by passing carbon dioxide over heated iron. He called it "gaseous oxide of carbone" and described it as "heavy, inflammable air" and correctly proposed its composition as carbon monoxide. Dalton's theory of 1803 that matter consisted of "atoms" was in part inspired by Cruickshank's accurate description of carbon monoxide. The famous chemist Joseph Priestley refused to believe Cruickshank's work, and subsequently there was a robust exchange of correspondence between Priestley and Cruickshank, which continued after Priestley moved to North America.[9]

Cruickshank was the first to observe that hydrogen and chlorine combine under the influence of light, and he also observed that the volume of a mixture of these gases over chlorine water did not begin to diminish until the light had exerted its influence for several seconds – that is, no hydrochloric acid is formed in a freshly prepared mixture of hydrogen and chlorine until the gases have been subjected to the influence of light for a measurable period of time, but that after interaction starts the rate of formation of hydrogen chloride increases and ultimately becomes constant.[10]

Cruickshank modified the Voltaic Pile (a primitive battery) into the trough battery in 1800. This was the first electric battery capable of mass production.[11] Cruickshank had arranged square sheets of copper, which he soldered at their ends, together with sheets of zinc of equal size. These sheets were placed into a long rectangular wooden box that was sealed with cement. Grooves in the box held the metal plates in position. The box was then filled with an electrolyte of brine, or watered-down acid. This flooded design had the advantage of not drying out with use and provided more energy than Volta's disc arrangement.

With this battery, Cruickshank was able to extract metals out of their solutions, thereby establishing the art of electroplating. Although the new arrangement was an important improvement, the cells still leaked and were untidy. Cruickshank decomposed the chlorides of magnesia, soda and ammonia and he was able to precipitate pure copper and silver from their salt solutions – a process that led to the beginnings of the great metal refineries of today.

Additional discoveries showed that the liquid around the poles connected with the positive wire of the battery proved to be alkaline, and the liquid around the negative wire was shown to be acid. Finally, the common term "cell" associated with the elements of an electric battery was derived from Cruickshank's arrangement of elements in his trough battery.[12]

Cruickshank's battery was adopted in the construction of the powerful battery of 600 pairs, which Napoleon Bonaparte presented to the Ecole Polytechnique and upon which Louis Gay-Lussac and Louis Jacques Thenard made their important experiments during the year 1808.

Cruickshank also recommended electrolytic deposition of the metal as a qualitative analysis test and described it as a test for copper. This was how, for example, Davy finally purified strontium.[13]

Cruickshank, once again in 1800, was the first to use chlorine to purify water – demonstrating "that small doses of chlorine would kill germs in water" (it should be noted at this time it was not known that germs caused disease).[14] "Possibly more lives have been saved and more disease prevented by this contribution to sanitation and public hygiene than by any other single achievement in medicine and public health."[15]

James Clark 1747-1829 and his brother **Patrick Clark born 1742** revolutionised the manufacture of sewing thread and, ultimately, turned their company into, not only the largest thread manufacturer in the world, but one of the largest companies in the world. For centuries wool had been the pre-eminent cloth in Britain. Linen and cotton rose to prominence in the 18th century, but a fourth product, silk, was also an important textile in Britain with an estimated 207,300 people employed in the silk industry in 1836 and some 4,340,000 lbs (1,967 tonnes) consumed with a total value of £10,483,245.[1]

During the Napoleonic War, the price of silk rose dramatically as supplies dwindled. The French Emperor, Napoleon, in retaliation for Britain's blockade of continental ports, issued the Berlin Decree on 21 November 1806 prohibiting France, her allies, and even neutral European nations, from trading with Britain. Silk was one of the British imports affected by this decree. Patrick Clark, seeking a substitute for silk, invented a method of twisting cotton threads together to produce a silk substitute. "At one time nobody ever thought of making sewing thread from anything else but linen or silk. Then Napoleon, in those days the tyrant of Europe, struck a blow at the silk industry of Hamburg and caused the stocks of silk to be destroyed. Whence now were the thread-makers of Paisley to procure their raw material? It was, of course, impossible to get it from France while England was at war with that country. At that time [1812] there were living in Paisley two brothers, who in a small way made linen thread. Their names were James and Patrick Clark; Patrick it was who first saw the possibilities of cotton thread. Before his time, it is true, cotton had been spun into thread, but only into the sort of thread suitable for being worked up into cloth. The new Paisley thread was the first cotton sewing thread ever made. At first it was sold in skeins, then the more convenient form of balls. When reels (or spools) were introduced the customer had to pay a half penny for the reel, and if he took the reel back the half penny was returned to him. The new industry flourished, and now the famous firm of Coats turns out in the course of one year enough cotton thread to reach from the earth to the sun."[2]

It is possible that an American from Rhode Island, Hannah Wilkinson Slater, was making and selling cotton suitable for sewing at the start of the 19th century, but information on this is unclear and it was certainly from the Clark Company that the use of cotton sewing thread took hold. The Clarks produced thread that had three cords (3 ply) twisted together and three of these twisted threads were then twisted together (giving nine filaments of thread in one) to give a cotton thread that was strong enough for sewing. To deal with the extra strength required for use in sewing machines Clark's opened a factory in New Jersey to make "Our New Thread" which was "six yarns twisted into three sets of two, and then the three branches were twisted, resulting in a more satisfactory thread that could be used for hand or machine sewing."[3]

Flags made prior to Patrick Clark's innovation were made from linen, silk or wool bunting, but most flags are now made from cotton. In 1896, his company amalgamated with J & P Coats and became the largest thread manufacturers in the world, a position they still retain more than 100 years later, as well as being the world's second largest manufacturers of zippers. They have more than 20,000 employees and manufacture and/or distribute in more than 70 countries.

Robert Blair 1748-1828 invented the aplanatic lens which reduced the aberration in telescopes and microscopes. In 1786, he wrote an unpublished paper – later printed as *Light and Relativity, a Previously Unknown Eighteenth Century Manuscript* "that gave a systematic treatment of the Newtonian kinematics of light, taking into account in the absolute space of Newton the motion of the light source, that of the observer, and the velocity of the corpuscles of light. He wrote an important paper on the classical relativistic optics of moving bodies. The manuscript was never published, but it provides an essential demonstration of the application of Newton's dynamics to light and a most interesting foreword to Einstein's relativity. In this context, after John Michell (on whose work he based his efforts), he discovered what sixty years later would be named the Doppler Effect."[1]

Blair had, in fact, pre-empted the Doppler Effect in his unpublished manuscript and he also proposed an experiment to determine the absolute motion of the Earth more than 100 years before Americans Albert Abraham Michelson and Edward Morley undertook their famous experiment in 1887. Michelson was awarded the Nobel Prize in 1907 for his and Morley's observations that discounted the Earth moving through a luminiferous aether, the commonly held view at that time. Blair's 1786 manuscript apparently deals with questions that relate to light relativity and spectroscopy and showed brilliant thinking in dealing with known issues in science. Unfortunately, despite being the first professor of astronomy at Edinburgh University, Blair was not much of a publicist and his manuscript had no bearing on the future development of science. (In this context, however, it should be noted that the work of Gregor Johann Mendel also had no future bearing on the science of genetics as his writings had been ignored and forgotten. The basic elements of heredity – genes – had been later discovered by others, yet Mendel is today hailed as the Father of Genetics).

Blair investigated ways in which to reduce aberrations and secondary spectra found in lenses of the time. He developed a hollow lens and investigated the effects of using different liquids in them, and in comparison to the flint (lead) glass used at the time. His research into the effectiveness of reflecting telescopes led him to invent (and name) the aplanatic telescope. The aplanatic lens, which maintains a very small focused spot, and allows for much higher energies at the focal point, does not suffer from spherical aberration.[2]

Later, Blair's fluid object-glasses consisted of a biconcave lens of hydrochloric acid combined with a metal and placed next to a plano-convex lens of crown glass. The liquid was introduced between the convex surface of the solid glass lens and a meniscus-plane or zero-power lens, the plane side of the crown lens facing the object. His 3" (7.62 cm) telescope with 17" (43.2 cm) focus was "manifestly superior to one of [famous lens maker] Mr [John] Dolland's of 42" [106.7 cm] focal length."[3]

Archibald Cochrane 1748-1831, 9th Lord Dundonald, took out a patent on coal tar production in 1781, making it possible to manufacture on a commercial scale – there had been several earlier attempts which produced coal tar, but the cost was prohibitive. This had potentially enormous economic benefits for Britain's navy as it could prevent infestations of the Teredo worm (*Teredo navalis)*, which caused great damage to wooden ships in tropical waters, as well as protecting nuts and bolts and providing a means of preventing rust in cast and hammered iron, and particularly on the inside of cannon. Cochrane developed coal tar after having first experimented on a boat at the port of Nore when he was only fifteen, and by 1782 he had lit both his own house and Culross Abbey with coal tar gas.[1] He was granted seven patents for making various substances from coal tar, such as aluminium sulphate (alum) – an important industrial chemical, mainly used as a mordant for dyes.

In 1783, Cochrane was selling his coal tar and by-products as fast as they could be made – 56 barrels a week – and exporting it to Norway and Russia. By 1787, he had been able to use tar water, a waste product, as a fertiliser. Smoke emitted in the process of obtaining tar from coal accounted for 80% of the coal and Cochrane introduced aftercooling which greatly reduced smoke waste by condensation. But Cochrane soon found enemies in both the coal mine owners and in the naval dockyards. Scottish coal miners at that time were virtually serfs who were bound to a mine for life and could be bought and sold by mine owners. It was common for women and children to work in mines and Cochrane was one of the first coal pit-owners in Britain to stop the employment of women and children in mines.[2] It was partly his outspokenness in this matter that turned coal mine owners against him.

At the same time, the Royal Navy was coating its ships with copper, which was more effective but much more expensive than coal tar. This process started back in 1761 when HMS

Alarm was fully clad with copper. Cochrane met resistance to using coal tar because it reduced repairs and many of the shipyards, which made illicit payments to navy and treasury bosses, opposed the wider implementation of coal tar as it reduced their profits, even though many ships simply fell apart at sea from the effects of the Teredo worm, with great loss of life. As a shipbuilder in Limehouse (London) explained it: "We live by repairing ships as well as by building them, and the worm is our best friend. Rather than use your preparation, I would cover ships' bottoms with honey to attract worms."[3] Although many others involved with Cochrane made small fortunes, Cochrane himself had taken out large loans to invest some £22,500 in expanding his coal tar industry and he was unable to make sufficient personal profit from his otherwise very successful enterprise.

He was an early advocate of using chemicals in agriculture and in 1795 wrote *A treatise showing the intimate connection between Agriculture and Chemistry* that explained how fertilisers acted on the soil and put great emphasis on methods of making manure. In the booklet, Cochrane encouraged farmers to better understand the chemical reactions when manure was used on farmland and to increase soil fertility by improving the methods of preparing manure.

Cochrane was a humanitarian and attempted to find cheap, nutritious food sources for the poor and he produced dried, starched potato mix to feed them in times of need. Ironically, Cochrane himself died poor in 1831 in Paris, where he had gone to escape debtors. He had been an early pioneer of an industry that now produces thousands of by-products, including dyes, benzene, naphtha, drugs, toluene, xylene, creosote, waterproofing for roofs, kerosene, paraffin, explosives, paints, varnishes and synthetic resins, and which produced the first plastics.

Robert Stodart 1748-1831 took out a patent in 1777 for a grand forte piano, the first time this term had been used. His patent was a "grand forte piano, with an octave swell, and to produce various fine tones, together or separate, at the option of the performer."[1] The modern grand piano has a total tension of 40,000 pounds (18,144 kg) or more from the wires stretched across the piano. Prior to 1800, pianos were built without the benefit of an iron plate. This greatly limited the total tension that could be placed on the wires. A publication from around 1808 by the piano makers of Wachtl & Bleyer stated that their pianos had a tension of 9,000 pounds (4,082 kg).[2]

Daniel Rutherford 1749-1819 was first to isolate "phlogisticated air", now known as nitrogen.[1] In studying the properties of carbon dioxide, Joseph Black found that a candle would not burn in it. A candle burning in a closed container of ordinary air would go out eventually, and the air that was left would then no longer support a flame. This behaviour certainly seemed reasonable, since the burning candle had formed carbon dioxide. But when the carbon dioxide in the trapped air was absorbed by chemicals, some air remained unabsorbed. This air that was left, and that was not carbon dioxide, would still not support a flame.

Black turned this problem over to one of his students, the Scottish chemist Daniel Rutherford. Rutherford kept a mouse in a confined quantity of air till it died. He then burned a candle in what was left until the candle went out. He then burned phosphorus in what was left after that, until the phosphorus would no longer burn. Next, the air was passed through a solution that had the ability to absorb carbon dioxide. The air remaining now would not support combustion; a mouse would not live in it and a candle would not burn.

Rutherford reported this experiment in 1772. Since Rutherford and Black were both convinced of the validity of the phlogiston theory, they tried to explain their results in terms of this theory. As mice breathed and as candles and phosphorus burned, phlogiston was given off and entered the air, along with the carbon dioxide that was formed. When the carbon dioxide was later absorbed, the air left behind still contained much phlogiston. In fact, it contained so much phlogiston as to be saturated with it; it would accept no more. That was why objects no longer burned in it.[2]

It is claimed that Rutherford also designed the first maximum-minimum thermometer (1793)[3], but Englishman James Six had designed this thermometer in 1782.

CHAPTER 2

1750-1799

After what seemed an agonisingly long time, Scotland began to experience signs of revitalisation some decades after the union of the parliaments of Scotland and England (1 May 1707). The second half of the 18th century saw Jacobinism (i.e. support for the Stuart claimants to the British crown) disappear altogether in the aftermath of the battle of Culloden in 1746, and Scotland produced such a surfeit of truly remarkable men that this period has often been referred to as the Scottish Enlightenment. These men included: Francis Hutcheson, David Hume, Adam Smith, Dugald Stewart, Thomas Reid, Robert Burns, Adam Ferguson, John Playfair, James Watt, Joseph Black, James Hutton, Robert Adam, Henry Home (Lord Kames), Allan Ramsay, William Smellie, William Robertson, and many others.

More than anything else, it was education that gave Scots the competitive edge in many fields of endeavour and underlay their remarkable achievements in technology and other fields. Around 1790, Scotland had 3.3 universities per million inhabitants, the highest ratio in the world. In the same period England, Wales and Ireland had 0.2 and France 0.9 universities per million inhabitants (the USA had about 2.4 universities per million white inhabitants in 1790). In medicine, Oxford and Cambridge (the only two universities in England at that time) produced 246 of the medical graduates in Britain in the second half of the 18th century. In the same period, continental universities produced 194 medical graduates who practiced in Britain, while Scotland produced 2,594 – an astonishing number! Indeed, Scotland exported to countries beyond Britain as many as 6,000 trained doctors during the 18th century.[1] Within Britain, the number of medical practitioners who had graduated from university showed an astounding preponderance coming from Scotland. From 1600-1650 there were 599 medical graduates in Britain who had graduated from Oxford or Cambridge (Oxbridge) universities and 36 from a European university. There were no Scottish medical graduates practicing in Britain during this period. The figures started to rise in the 18th century and in the period 1700-1750 there were 617 from Oxbridge, 385 from Europe and 406 from Scotland. The figures for the next 50 years are shown above and then from 1800-1850 the number of medical graduates working in Britain comprised 273 (Oxbridge), 29 (Europe) and 7,989 from Scottish universities![2] It should also be noted that a great many more Scottish medical graduates were working in other parts of the world, particularly North America and the Caribbean.

Elsewhere, industries such as the Carron Ironworks near Falkirk, in Stirlingshire, gave momentum to technological enquiry and trade expanded rapidly with Europe, the American colonies and Asia, encouraging deep thinkers to ponder on ways to operate more efficiently. Educated Scots were in an advantageous position to capitalise on the demand for skilled people to come to the fore in promoting technological improvement and many Scots born in this period provided a noticeable surge in the number of innovators who gave impetus to what would later be described as the Industrial Revolution. This event irrevocably transformed the world, and Scots played a notable part in this momentous and pivotal period in history.

Charles Abercrombie 1750-1817 was a road surveyor and engineer who was somewhere between Thomas Telford and John Loudon McAdam in the quality of his roads. He built more mileage of roads "and with more satisfaction to the public in general, than any engineer in the United Kingdom."[1] Near the end of the 18th century, the city of Aberdeen commenced major road improvements and, in 1796, Abercrombie suggested the levelling of the top of St Katherine's Hill to build a huge viaduct over the valley. This ambitious project began in 1801 and was finished in 1805, with the resulting 60-foot (18 m) wide viaduct considered one of the engineering feats of its time.[2] His roads were engineered to lines and levels which facilitated horse traction, similar to the build of Telford, "which formed the basis of modern design."[3]

John Austin 1752-1830 invented a power-loom capable of being driven by water or steam. In 1796, the Glasgow Chamber of Commerce issued a favourable report on his invention, and in 1798 it was successfully employed at James Monteith's spinning-works at Pollokshaws, four miles from Glasgow. Monteith erected a building to hold 30 looms and afterwards another to hold 200. The power-loom, in a further improved state, was submitted in 1806 for inspection to the Society for the Encouragement of Arts, Manufactures, and Commerce and won a silver medal. Austin's letter to the society, enumerating 22 advantages of his power-loom over traditional looms, was published in 1807 in William Nicolson's *Journal of Natural Philosophy, Chemistry, and the Arts* (new series, 17, pp. 175-177). Austin entered a caveat for a patent but abandoned the idea of obtaining one.[1]

Charles Stanhope 1753-1816 built a new style of printing press made of cast iron, which permitted the printing area to be doubled while also reducing by 90% the physical force needed to apply the ink to paper. This press was not only stronger and more durable, by reason of the material used in its construction, but a much larger forme (printing blocks assembled in a chase and ready for printing) could be impressed at a time, the platen being made considerably larger than in the old presses.

Hitherto, printing presses used a flat table, called a type-bed or bed, on which the forme rests, and the flat plane or platen which gives the impression. But if the platen was above the type forme, the inking of the latter and the laying on of the paper would be cumbersome. Hence provision was made, even in the early presses, for withdrawing the bed from under the platen after each impression so as to leave the type free to be inked and to receive the paper. In the Stanhope press, and other modern hand-printing presses, the bed is mounted on an iron carriage, which is run in and out on rails or runners by means of a handle, and an endless band. When the handle is turned one way, the carriage moves towards the platen, and passes under it until it reaches the position in which the type should receive the impression. When the handle is turned the reverse way, the carriage recedes, and goes to the far end of the rails or runners. Again, it is very desirable to have some arrangement whereby the sheet may be very accurately laid on the type. For this purpose, a kind of leaf or flap is hinged to one end of the bed, and the paper is fixed upon it to certain marks when it is in an upright position. It is then turned down, and the paper comes upon the type in the exact position in which it is wanted.

The platen must, of course, be large enough to take the forme, and the larger it is the more pressure is required for the impression, so early printing platens were small, and when the forme was large, only a section at a time was brought under the platen; which could require two pulls for the forme. Stanhope not only strengthened the platen by ribbing it but, by devising a system of levers, enabled a man with one pull to give a sufficient impression to a forme of considerable size. By this arrangement, the levers were, at the time of impressing the sheet, in the position when most power is given out, and when most power is wanted. In the descent of the platen, at first merely motion is required; after that, power.

The wooden screw press, manually operated by two men, produced around 200 impressions an hour. The Stanhope press produced 250 better quality impressions in an hour. Its weight doubled the printing surface of each impression, effectively doubling the rate of production.[1]

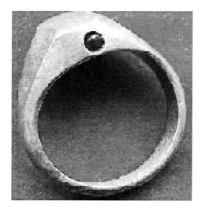

Image 8 – Stanhope Lens in Finger Ring

Stanhope invented the eponymous Stanhope lens, which is also sometimes referred to as a "peep" or "peeper". It is a tiny rod-shaped lens, generally with one convex end and one flat end, and with a microphotograph attached to the flat end. More specifically, the microphotograph resides on a tiny glass plate adhered to the flat end of the rod-shaped lens with a clear adhesive called Canada balsam. The side of the glass plate that hosts the photo is the side that is glued to the lens so the image is well protected since it is essentially encased in glass. Together, the glass lens with the attached glass plate form a cylinder that is about a quarter inch in length and an eighth of an inch in diameter (6.3 mm and 3.175 mm). Once assembled, the cylinder is inserted into another item frequently referred to, not very creatively, as the "holder." A magnification of 4,096 may be obtained, so revealing the detail of microorganisms. Commonly found holders include pens, pencils, letter openers, tape measures, jewellery, charms, thimbles, miniature binoculars or monoculars, which look like they belong in a doll house, and other trinkets such as the lead pigs that were used to hold images of American presidential candidates.[2]

William Murdock 1754-1839 pioneered gas lighting. He changed his name from Murdoch as the Cornishmen he worked with had trouble pronouncing his name. Probably the most famous innovation he is connected with is the application of gas to light up his house. In 1798, he built a large-scale gas-making plant in Birmingham to light the famous Soho factory of his employers Matthew Boulton and James Watt.[1] By 1802, he had lit the outside of the factory as well. He is reported to have commenced experiments with gas much earlier, having lit his own home at Redruth, Cornwall, in 1792 and certainly by 1799 he, along with other employees of Boulton & Watt, had perfected methods for making, storing and purifying gas.[2] By 1806, he had built a gas works with 90 burners to light the large cotton spinning factory of Phillips and Lee in Manchester. In the same year, Murdock presented to The Royal Society a paper entitled *Account of the Application of Gas from Coal to Economical Purposes* in which he described his work at Phillips and Lee. For this paper, he was awarded the Count Rumford gold medal, awarded by The Royal Society every alternating year for an outstandingly important recent discovery in the field of thermal or optical properties of matter made by a scientist working in Europe. "It is probable that this paper led to important consequences: for, at the same time that Mr [Frederick Albert] Winsor was alarming the world with his quackery, Mr Murdoch, by his simple, minute, and perspicuous detail of particulars, demonstrated the utility and practicability of the invention. Mr Murdoch's statements threw great light on the comparative advantages of gas and candles, and contained much useful information on the expenses of production and management."[3]

Winsor, in 1807, started a gasworks and lit one side of London's Pall Mall with gas lamps but did little else until a decade later. In the meantime, various factories in Britain, including the Manchester firm McConnell Kennedy; Wormald, Gott and Wormald of Leeds (two the largest factories in the world); Gillespie and Co. in Glasgow; and another Manchester factory Birley and Co., had all been fitted with gas lighting by the firm of Boulton and Watt. Gas lighting quickly spread around the world although Murdock and his employers had gradually wound back their small but successful gas lighting (the company's income from gas lighting in 1811 was £3,126) by 1815 to concentrate on their main business – steam engines.

Image 9 – Murdoch's model steam carriage

Murdock went on to invent the steam-driven compressed-air gun, and, around 1784, made a model steam locomotive which had: a high pressure, non-condensing steam engine; copper boiler; fire-box and flue; spirit lamp; one double-action cylinder; two driving wheels; and a steering wheel. It could move at 10-12 km an hour and was later converted to use gas.

In 1785, he invented the oscillating steam engine using the cylinder as the steam valve, operating on the same principle as the locomotive steam engine – 43 years before Joseph Maudslay made his oscillating machine in 1827. He invented and patented the long D-slide valve, allowing two valves to do the work of four in rotative steam engines.

Murdock also patented processes for making: dyes and paints from coal; sulphuric acid; and sulphate of iron – the main white pigment in paint, plastics and paper. He invented cast-iron cement (small iron pieces mixed with ammonium chloride and used to repair or join steel and iron surfaces) and a means of preserving wooden ship hulls with a chemical paint. He made: a gas lantern; an apparatus for extracting coal gas; the endless screw for boring steam cylinders; and a lift that worked using compressed air.[4]

In 1799, Murdock built his first bell crank engine that enabled a change in direction of reciprocating movement by varying the angle of the crank piece. It got its name because a crank was often used in large houses to ring a bell for servants. This engine was able to operate at 2-3 horsepower and was the first self-supporting engine to be made available commercially.

He invented pressurised air (pneumatic) tubes to move letters and packages and which were later introduced into department stores in 1880 by American John Wanamaker.[5] They were used in London, Berlin, Paris, Vienna, New York, Philadelphia, Rio de Janeiro, Rome, Munich, Hamburg, Naples, Marseilles, Boston, Chicago and St Louis, where they remained popular into the 20th century. Paris continued with its air tube system until 1984 and Prague until 2002. They can still be found in many large businesses such as Coles and Woolworths in Australia – two of the top 20 retailers by size in the world. Some historians credit Murdock with the invention of the "sun and planet" motion which was patented in 1781 by James Watt. It was Murdock who supplied Robert Fulton with the steam engine that he used on the *Clermont* in 1807 and for two more of Fulton's steamships.

John Loudon McAdam 1756-1836 arrived at the right time to improve roads, so essential to building the infrastructure that would support the British-led Industrial Revolution. The economic progress that arose from the Industrial Revolution depended on steam power, mechanisation of manufacturing, and improved transport for moving goods to markets. Roads were in a sorry state as no decent highway system had been developed in Europe since the fall of the Roman Empire. France had started to make improvements under the French engineer Pierre-Marie-Jérôme Trésaguet (1716-1796) who pioneered the first modern road building when he was about 50 years old. To build his roads, Trésaguet used a foundation of large stones overlaid with a thin layer of smaller stones. Under the pressure of traffic, the smaller stones compacted and provided a firm well-wearing surface. His methods spread across France and were used by English road-makers, such as John Smeaton (who was of distant Scottish ancestry). In France, Trésaguet's method of road building remained in use for almost half a century until they were superseded by the man whose name is forever linked with road building – John Loudon McAdam.

McAdam came late to that occupation, having first made his fortune as an agent who received a commission from the British for the on-sale of goods taken as prizes of war during the American Revolution. McAdam went to New York in 1770 following the death of his father, who had opened the first bank in Ayr in 1763. He worked with his uncle who was a merchant, but during the war he became "agent for prizes", made his fortune and returned to his birth county of

Ayrshire in 1783. He bought an estate at Sauhrie, a village between the county town of Ayr and the small town of Maybole, and began repairing roads around his estate. His experiments led him to develop a method of road building that would first spread through Britain, then right around the world. He used graded layers of small stones, with the very smallest on top forming a convex camber laid over a raised foundation of large stones, usually granite or greenstone, that were placed in tight, symmetrical patterns, allowing rainfall to run off the road without affecting the foundations. He was particular about the size of the small stones, which were graded to pack down tightly, and their "uniformity was secured at first by gauges supplied to the road makers. Rings were used through which the stones must pass before they could be used on the road. Directions were sometime given that no stone should be put aside from the hammer which was not small enough to go into a man's mouth."[1] The top layer was some 5 cm thick, using stone of around 2 cm to fill surface voids between the large stones. Continuing maintenance was essential.

McAdam argued that as long as the soil under the road remained dry, it could carry the weight of all known traffic, which would pack down the surface of the road. In 1816, when he was 60, he became surveyor with the Bristol Turnpike Trust in south-west England. He published two books on his research in 1819 and 1820 and his manner of road-making was adopted by government authorities who appointed him general surveyor of roads in 1827. McAdam's method soon replaced those used since the days of Imperial Rome to make quality roads, which were rare by the 19th century. The Roman method involved making a carefully laid foundation dug into the soil using heavy stone slabs that required skilled workers to lay them correctly. This made road building expensive and, as a result, they were usually only built for military reasons, and even then, contractors did shoddy work to save money so the roads soon fell into disrepair. Other engineers added stone dust mixed with water to provide a smoother surface although McAdam argued that this was unnecessary as his layers packed down smoothly, nor was there any need for the masonry constructions of his predecessors and contemporaries.

Although McAdam drew on the successes and failures of others, his total structural reliance on broken stone represented the largest paradigm shift in the history of road pavements. The principles of the "macadam" road are still used today. McAdam's success was also due to his efficient administration and his strong view that road managers needed skill and motivation.[2]

The use of tar, hence tarmacadam, came long after McAdam's death when, in 1901, Englishman Edgar Purnell Hooley noticed that a particular stretch of road had no ruts (even though McAdam's roads were a big improvement on previous roads, ruts could still form). On investigation, he found that a barrel of tar had fallen over the road and that nearby slag had been used to cover it. In 1902, he patented tar macadam, in honour of John Loudon McAdam, and patented the trademark *macadam* (with an extra "a") the following year. These roads are sometimes known as metalled roads because of the iron slag used in their construction.[3] McAdam's road-making methods quickly spread throughout Europe and, in 1830, the first macadam road was built in America.

Thomas Telford 1757-1834 is often regarded as the greatest civil engineer of the early 19th century, his only serious rival for that honour being Englishman Isambard Kingdom Brunel. Telford was first president of the Institution of Civil Engineers (1820-1834) and was responsible for getting its Royal Charter in 1828 and making it the premier organisation for civil engineers.

He was followed in the role of president by two other Scots, James Walker (1781-1862), who was president from 1835 to 1845, and then by John Rennie (1822-1887) until 1848.

Telford built more than 1,200 bridges and 1,600 km of road in Britain, earning him the soubriquet "Colossus of Roads" from the English poet Robert Southey. He built 32 churches and was consulted on many of the major civil engineering projects in Britain, including St Katharine's Docks in London, the water supply for Liverpool, and the new London Bridge in 1800 (his design wasn't accepted and it was John Rennie who eventually built the replacement London Bridge).

Telford's road-making technique involved digging a foundation, levelling it, then putting down a base of cobblestone-sized rock, covered with 18 cms of broken stone, on top of which 7 or 8 cms of fine stone were laid. This method was more expensive than McAdam's, but it gave a high-quality road that was smooth and durable.

Telford did much work on building and improving harbours, and building canals, including the Caledonian and Ellesmere canals, and he drained around 20,000 hectares of England's fenlands. He provided a detailed plan for building the Standedge Tunnel, the longest (5,029 m), deepest (194 m) and highest (196 m above sea level) canal tunnel in Britain. Telford's report covered every expenditure to the last bucket; it was followed to the letter and the canal finally opened in 1811.[1]

He built the London to Holyhead Road for which he constructed the Menai Suspension Bridge (1819-1826), having earlier put a bridge over the River Severn in 1790. In building the Shropshire Union Canal, he erected the Pontcysyllte Aqueduct, the longest and highest navigable cast-iron aqueduct in the world, rising almost 37 m and being 307 m long. "Just one life was lost during the construction which, for that time, was as impressive as the engineering feat itself."[2]

Telford designed and built the Caledonian Canal. "This 60-mile [96.5 km] long 110 ft [33.5 m] wide ship canal across Scotland between the North Sea and Irish Sea was constructed between 1804 and 1822 using state-of-the-art technology on an unprecedented scale. ... Telford, working with consulting engineer William Jessop and contractors John Simpson, John Wilson and John Cargill, built the canal with 28 locks 170 ft or 180 ft [51-55 m] long, 40 ft [12 m] wide, and 25 ft [7.6 m] deep. At the time, it was the largest series of locks ever built. The canal significantly advanced Highland development and engineering knowledge."[3]

His Menai Bridge was the longest suspension bridge in the world, linking mainland Wales to the Island of Anglesey. It was almost matched by the Conwy Suspension Bridge built by him in 1826, and Telford's use of this type of bridge popularised them internationally. His work wasn't confined to Britain – he was responsible for the plans to build Sweden's 240 km Göta Canal with its 58 locks. He supervised some of the early stages although it was Sweden's Baltzar von Platen who was the architect in charge of construction. Sweden's King Karl XIII knighted Telford in recognition of his work on the canal (some sources say it was King Gustav who knighted Telford. It was Gustav IV Adolf who appointed Telford in 1806 but he died in 1809. Telford was knighted in 1810 by Gustav's successor, Karl).

Telford designed the Gloucester and Sharpness Canal and built the 46 m Galton Bridge in 1829; at that time, the longest single suspension bridge in the world.[4] Two years earlier, he completed the second Harecastle Tunnel on the Trent and Mersey Canal, which was the longest tunnel in the world at 2.67 kilometres. He built Craigellachie Bridge in Scotland and the Waterloo Bridge in Wales from cast iron. The first cast-iron bridge in the world was built by Englishman

Abraham Darby III at Coalbrookdale in 1781, but it was Telford who refined its design by using half as much iron in his Buildwas Bridge, which had a span 10 m wider than Darby's bridge. As a result, iron bridges became much more common.

Thomas Bell (dates unknown) mechanised the printing of fabrics, particularly calico. One of the cheaper cotton textiles, calico was unbleached, so printing on the fabric helped to improve its appearance. Calico was named for Calicut in Kerala State on the Indian Ocean coast of southwest India. It was the pre-eminent producer of calico but, as early as 1700, Calicut's ascendancy was first challenged when Britain introduced ineffective laws prohibiting its import, mainly to protect its native silk weaving industry. Two decades later, this time at the petitioning of the English wool manufacturers, even tougher laws were introduced. "The laws prohibiting the trade in printed textiles could have prevented the lower classes from mimicking the fashions of their social and political superiors. However printed textile manufacturers were not so easily put off. It was not illegal to print for export and as a consequence the domestic source did not entirely dry up, although the penalty was £5 for wearing printed calico, £20 for using it as a home furnishing and £20 for selling the cloth. Printers devised legal loopholes, such as printing on calico/linen blends (fustian) which was not explicitly prohibited by the 1721 statute."[1] Eventually the Lancashire mills made that county the pre-eminent cotton manufacturing site in the world, and new techniques to replace the hand-printing of calico were introduced. Irishman Francis Nixon used copper plates to replace the traditional wooden blocks used for printing patterns onto calico, giving a very high degree of precision in printing. This process spread rapidly through Europe and created an increased demand for calico which was met by the invention of the rotary printing machine by Thomas Bell, a Scottish engraver working for Thomas Livesey in Walton-le-Dale in Lancashire. "Bell realised that the copperplate could be curved around a roller, an invention that enabled printers to decorate a continuous roll of fabric. Bell's process gradually came to dominate the Western textile printing industry."[2]

Bell patented a continuously running engraved roller printing machine for calicoes, which could take the place of the earlier and extremely laborious method of printing by hand with engraved wooden blocks. This machine made possible the production of the most accurate work at relatively great speed, and at a labour cost with which handwork could never have competed. "Bell rolled sheets of copper one eighth of an inch (3 mm) thick into cylinders, and filled them with cement which was held in place by cast iron ends. After being turned true and polished, the cylinders were engraved; they cost about £10 each. The printing machines were driven by a water-wheel."[3]

This important machine was introduced into Lancashire in 1785 and although displacement of hand-block printing was slow, and not nearly completed a century after Bell's patent, the demand for the new machine increased rapidly. The invention was aptly timed, for the rollers were easily driven first by water and then by steam. The advantages of its use were obvious, for one roller machine could produce as much as 100 block printers. England led the Continent in the development of the printing machine and Bell's wooden-framed prototype gave way to a more durable roller printing machine with cast-iron sides, central "bowl" and radially placed printing rollers – which has altered little in its main features to this day.[4]

The machine, which he patented on 17 July 1783, could print six colours at high speed while maintaining high detail and definition. Bell used a sharp steel blade called a "doctor" to remove excess colour from the roller's surface while leaving dye in the recessed areas that had been etched with the pattern. Production of simple patterns on calico using blocks was about six pieces a day but this rose dramatically to 500 pieces for a similar piece of work done by Bell's rotary printer. The output of printed calico produced in England alone rose from around 27 million metres in 1796 to 540 million metres in 1851.[5] Strangely, considering the major impact Thomas Bell had on the cotton industry, his date and place of birth and death are not recorded, but all sources agree that he was Scottish. Note: One possible collateral descendant commented, "I'm frankly amazed that there's so little biographical material available on Thomas Bell. His invention was clearly one of the mainsprings of the Industrial Revolution, particularly in Britain, leading to huge exports of cotton to England, Scotland and Ireland and the rest of Europe from the US Deep South. His invention was the prototype of all the rotary presses now in use around the world, printing newspapers, magazines and anything else that will accept ink, as well as calico, cloth and cotton."[6]

Alexander Nasmyth 1758-1840 invented, in 1794, the bow and string bridge and arch, used for spanning rivers or the roofs of factories and railway stations. In 1816, he invented compression riveting. However, he never sought to patent his inventions.[1] "The first bow-and-string bridge was erected in the island of St. Helena over a deep ravine. … The bow-and-string bridge has since been largely employed in spanning wide spaces over which suburban and other railways pass, and in roofing over such stations as those at Birmingham, Charing Cross, and other Great Metropolitan centres, as well as in bow-and-string bridges over rivers now practiced in every part of the civilised world".[2]

Image 10 – Sydney Harbour Bridge – a bow string arch bridge

Nasmyth's invention of compression riveting "originated in a slight circumstance [when] there were some slight mechanical repairs to be performed upon a beautiful little stove of his own construction. To repair it iron rivets were necessary to make it serviceable. But as the hammering of the hot rivets would annoy his neighbours he solved the difficulty by using the jaws of his bench vice to squeeze in the hot rivets when put into their places. This was, perhaps, the first occasion on which a squeeze or compressive action was substituted for the percussive action of the hammer, in closing red-hot rivets, for combining together pieces of stout sheet or plate iron. This system of riveting was long afterwards patented by [James] Smith of Deanston [Stirlingshire] in combination with William Fairbairn of Manchester; and it was employed in riveting the plates used in the construction of the bridges over the River Conway and the Menai Straits. It is also universally used in boiler and girder making, and in all other wrought-iron structures in which thorough sound riveting is absolutely essential."[3]

James Jeffray 1759-1848 and **John Aitken died 1790** independently invented the chain saw. Aitken first described and illustrated his "flexible saw" (also "flexible knife") in 1785 although he first made it two years earlier. "The prototype of the chain saw familiar today in the timber industry was pioneered in the late 18th century by two Scottish doctors, John Aitken and James Jeffray, for symphysiotomy and excision of diseased bone respectively. The chain hand saw, a fine serrated link chain which cut on the concave side, was invented around 1783-1785. It was illustrated in Aitken's *Principles of Midwifery or Puerperal Medicine* (1785) and used by him in his dissecting room. Jeffray claimed to have conceived the idea of the chain saw independently about that time, but it was 1790 before he was able to have it produced. In 1806, Jeffray published *Cases of the Excision of Carious Joints by H. Park and P.F. Moreau with Observations by James Jeffray M.D.*"[1]

Being primarily an obstetrician, Aitken was familiar with obstructed labour when the mother's pelvis was too small for passage of the baby's head. In such instances, Aitken knew of three procedures employed with differing results: hysterotomy (caesarean section) which at that time commonly resulted in the death of the mother, embryotomy (craniotomy) which ended the life of the child; and pelviotomy (symphysiotomy). For the last of these methods, Aitken invented the chain saw to divide the pubic symphysis and thus increase the pelvic diameter for passage of the child. Previously a scalpel was used which risked damage to the urinary bladder and urethra, and failed if the joint had calcified.

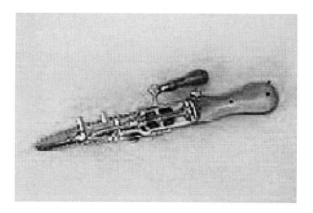

Image 11 – Medical Bone Saw

Jeffray's reasons for inventing the chain saw were entirely different from those of Aitken. After reading an article by a Liverpool surgeon, Henry Park, Jeffray became interested in the method by which diseased joints might be excised. Park's operation was directed at knees and elbows infected by tuberculosis or damaged on the battlefield. It involved cutting through the bone with an amputation saw, on each side of the defective joint, to remove diseased tissues. In the case of the knee, the cut surfaces united through callus formation and the final result was a stiff but usable limb. In the case of the elbow, the bone ends did not unite and scar tissue formed which connected the cut ends and, fortunately, permitted a degree of mobility. Jeffray stated he made a drawing of his idea for a chain saw, and some years later, about 1790, he had it manufactured by a London jeweller, Richards of Brick Lane. It was in 1790 that Jeffray was appointed to the Regius Chair of Anatomy and Botany in Glasgow and maybe it was only then that he could afford the expense of having the chain saw produced.

William Playfair 1759-1823 invented the most common statistical charts to graphically display data – the line graph and bar chart of economic data (both in 1786), and in 1801 the pie chart and circle graph, used to show part-whole relations. Playfair, who "argued that charts communicated better than tables of data, has been credited with inventing the line, bar, and pie charts. His time-series plots are still presented as models of clarity. Playfair first published *The Commercial and Political Atlas* in London in 1786. It contained 43 time-series plots and one bar chart, a form apparently introduced in this work. It has been described as the first major work to contain statistical graphs. Playfair's *Statistical Breviary*, published in London in 1801, contains what is generally credited as the first pie chart."[1]

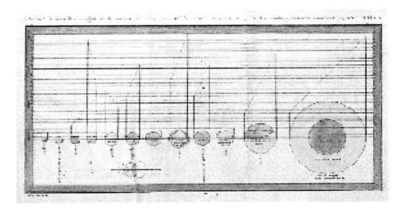

Image 12 – Pie charts from William Playfair's "Statistical Breviary", 1801

Playfair's invention of fundamental forms of statistical graph – the time-series line graph, the bar chart, and the pie chart – was done without significant precursors. Hence, he is the creator of all the basic styles of graph with the exception of the scatterplot, which did not appear until the end of the 19th century. A few examples of line graphs precede Playfair, but these are mostly representations of theoretical functions with data superimposed and are conspicuous by their isolation. His contributions to the development of statistical graphics remain his life's signal accomplishment. Although this work was received with indifference, he rightly never faltered in his conviction that he had found the best way to display empirical data. In the two centuries since, there has been no appreciable improvement on his designs.[2]

Alexander Tilloch 1759-1825 and Andrew Foulis, printer for Glasgow University, revived stereotyping that had earlier been invented by William Ged. Seemingly with no prior knowledge of Ged's work, Tilloch developed stereotyping in 1781 and patented the process on 28 April 1784. Tilloch's method was, once the page was set up in type, to take off "an impression in some soft substance, in its comparatively fluid state, that would harden when exposed to the action of fire, and thus become a mould to receive the metal when in a state of fusion, and form a plate every way correspondent to the page whence the first impression was received. This with him laid the foundation of the stereotype mode of printing, now brought into general use."[1]

The use of stereotyping lapsed when Tilloch moved to London where he became part proprietor of the *Sun*, a daily newspaper and, in 1797, he founded the *Philosophical Magazine* to "diffuse Philosophical Knowledge among every Class of Society, and to give the Public as early an Account as possible of everything new or curious in the Scientific World, both at Home and on the Continent".[2] It became the leading science journal of the day and is still published more than two centuries after it was founded, being one of the oldest scientific journals in the English language. Charles Mahon, Earl of Stanhope, paid £800 to Tilloch and Foulis for the patent rights and to receive training from Foulis in the use of stereotyping, and by the first decade of the 19th century it had become commercially viable. French printer Firmin Didot, who named the process, further improved it in 1795.

Alexander Hall 1760-1849 developed the Aberdeen, or Clipper, bow, in 1839. The New Hull Shape was to influence a whole generation of fast sailing ships. The ships of this design were very fast and yielded tax advantages in respect of the new dimensioning ruling in 1836. New Measurement legislation came into effect on 1 January 1836 when the method of recording the measurements of tonnage and other dimensions of British merchant ships was changed to ensure that the government gained maximum revenue from port taxes etc. The new 1836 regulations measured depth and breadth with length measured at half midship depth. Extra length above this level was tax-free and became a feature of clippers. To reduce tax on ships, Hall tested various hulls in a water tank and found the clipper design most effective. *Scottish Maid*, a schooner of 1839, was the first to have the forward curving Aberdeen bow. It proved swift – regularly making the journey from Aberdeen to London in 49 hours – and reliable, and the design was widely copied.[1] This ship continued sailing until 1941.

Hall's company was also concerned with employee welfare. The Hall's Dockyard Sick and Medical Fund began in 1846. For a weekly contribution, workers received sick pay, medical attendance and medicine. If the worst happened, the fund also provided funeral expenses.[2]

Three schooners of the same model and tonnage, the *Fairy*, *Rapid*, and *Monarch*, were built by Hall's firm in 1842. With *Scottish Maid*, these four were the first Aberdeen clippers. The earliest competition between American and British clippers was in the China seas. As early as 1831, three small English schooners, the *Jamesina*, *Lord Amherst*, and *Sylph*, were engaged in the opium trade, which proved exceedingly lucrative. In 1833, the *Jamesina* sold opium from India to the value of £330,000 at Poo Chow, Amoy, Ningpo, and other ports in China. In 1846, Alexander Hall & Co. built the clipper schooner *Torrington* for Jardine, Matheson & Co., to compete with the American opium clippers in China. This schooner, the first British clipper in the China seas, was followed by the *Wanderer*, *Gaselle*, *Rose*, the brig *Lanark*, and others, until almost every British and American firm in China owned one or more of these smart vessels.[3]

James Hall 1761-1832 succeeded in devising experiments which reproduced in miniature the processes which, according to James Hutton, are responsible for the formation of rock strata under the conditions prevailing in the Earth's crust. Because of his work, Hall became known as the "Father of Experimental Geology". His fusion and cooling experiments demonstrated that lavas and whinstones, when melted and cooled rapidly, gave glasses and, when re-melted and cooled slowly, gave crystallites. He then fused limestone under pressure and crystallised it into a substance resembling marble showing that, heated under pressure, calcium carbonate does not dissociate. He also conducted experiments on the folding of strata by compression.[1]

Sometimes also called the "Father of Experimental Petrology", Hall's experiments on the melting and crystallisation of basalt were decisive in resolving the debate between the Plutonist and Neptunist schools of geologists in the late eighteenth and early nineteenth centuries. However, it was the twentieth century that saw the establishment of the discipline as an integral part of the Earth Sciences. The publication of Norman Levi Bowen's book *The Evolution of the Igneous Rocks* in 1928, which was largely based on his laboratory melting experiments on simple model silicate systems, proved the power of experimentation for understanding the diversity of igneous rocks.[2]

Hall was the first geologist to directly apply the test of laboratory experiment to geological hypotheses. Between 1798 and 1805, Hall conducted more than 500 experiments using a trial-and-error method; finally, he was able to prove that limestone, when heated under pressure, does not decompose during cooling but instead turns to marble. He saw that he could obtain different kinds of rocks by melting minerals and cooling them at a controlled rate. Later, he produced a rock that closely resembled natural marble by heating calcium carbonate under pressure. He experimented extensively with igneous rocks from Scotland and showed that they had been produced by intense heat.[3] Hall's findings refuted many geological beliefs of his time.

Hall's final paper, *On the Consolidation of the Strata of the Earth*, published in 1826, outlined his experimental attempts to prove that loose sand would turn into a firm sandstone when heated in concentrated brine.[4]

George Murray 1761-1803 was an improver of the pre-electrical telegraph. The first real improvement on traditional mail was the development of the telegraph. In 1790, Frenchman Claude Chappe invented the optical telegraph, although it had been earlier described by Englishman Robert Hooke in 1684 and trialled in 1767 by another Englishman, Richard Lovell Edgeworth, in Ireland. Chappe's telegraph was based on semaphore, but Murray greatly simplified it by using six pivoting boards to encode messages one character at a time.

Murray's shutter telegraph was similar to methods used by the English-born Reverend John Gamble in 1795 and Abraham Clewberg (Baron Edelcrantz) a Finnish-born Swede who published a similar method in *Treatise on Telegraphs* in 1796. In Murray's device, characters were sent by opening and closing various combinations of six shutters. This system rapidly caught on in England and in the United States, where a number of sites bearing the name Telegraph Hill or Signal Hill can still be found, particularly in coastal regions.[1] Murray's apparatus was able to send a message, in 1796, over 96 kms in 15 minutes, and from London to Deal on the Kentish coast in one minute. By 1808, there were 65 telegraph stations in Britain. Murray's system was closed down shortly after Napoleon's defeat at Waterloo, but Murray was awarded £2,000 for his shutter telegraph by the British Parliament.

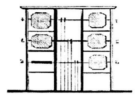

Image 13 – Murray's Shutter Telegraph System

John Rennie 1761–1821 was probably the most famous Scottish-born canal builder. In his youth, he often spent time in the workshop of Andrew Meikle, inventor of the threshing machine. Rennie drained large tracts of marshland in the Norfolk Broads and Solway Firth and built numerous canals, including: Lancaster Canal in Lancashire (66 km); the Crinan Canal in Argyll (14 km); the Kennet and Avon Canal in southern England (92 km); Chelmer and Blackwater Navigation in Essex (22 km); and the Royal Military Canal in Kent (45km).

He was one of the first engineers to manufacture machine tools for sale and in the late 18th century he made a rolling mill, drilling and boring machines for the Soho business of Boulton and Watt, as well as machinery for government mints, printing presses, roperies and mills, such as London's Albion Mills, the largest flour mill in Britain, which was well equipped with Rennie's machinery. He designed many bridges, including three famous bridges in London: Waterloo Bridge; Southwark Bridge; and London Bridge (now relocated to Lake Havasu City in Arizona) – and bridges at Leeds and many other locations.

The Waterloo and Leeds bridges were ground-breaking with their very low, wide elliptical arches. His largest projects were docks, particularly those built for the Royal Navy. Plymouth breakwater was a massive work with more than 3.6 million tonnes of stone placed on the harbour floor. Its base is 61 m wide narrowing to 12 m at the top. In London, he designed, or was consultant on, the West India Dock, London Dock, and Blackwall Dock.

"Among his bridges, those of Kelso, Leeds, Musselburgh, Newton-Stewart, Boston [Lincolnshire], and New Galloway, are to be specially commended. The first of these, which consists of a level roadway, resting upon five elliptical arches, has always been greatly admired, not only for architectural strength and beauty, but for a peculiar harmony in the design with the character of the surrounding scenery. The Aberdeen canal, the Great Western, the Kennet and Avon, the Portsmouth, the Birmingham, and the Worcester canals, are the most important of the works of this nature which he executed. He also erected the docks of Hull, Leith, Greenock, Liverpool, and Dublin; the modern harbours of Berwick, Kingstown, Howth, Newhaven, and Queensferry. He was instrumental also in effecting great improvements in the national dockyards at Portsmouth, Chatham, and other places; the new naval arsenal at Pembroke was constructed from his designs; and he likewise furnished the plan of the Bellrock lighthouse, executed by Mr [Robert] Stevenson."[1]

He designed other docks in Donaghadee, Wick, Torquay, Grimsby, Holyhead, and in other seaports. He was consulted on steam-powered dredgers and diving bells and, such was his reputation, when the British Parliament commissioned the Bell Rock lighthouse, one of the technological wonders of the time, Rennie was appointed Chief Engineer.

William Maclure 1763-1840 compiled the very first true geological map of any part of North America and one of the earliest such maps compiled.[1]

In 1807, he commenced the self-imposed task of making a geological survey of the United States. Almost every state in the Union was traversed and mapped by him, the Allegheny Mountains being crossed and recrossed some fifty times. The results of his unaided labours were submitted to the American Philosophical Society in a memoir entitled *Observations on the Geology of the United States explanatory of a Geological Map*, and published in the Society's Transactions (vol. iv. 1809, p 91) together with the first geological map of that country. This predates William Smith's famous geological map of England by six years. In 1817, Maclure brought before the same society a revised edition of his map, and his great geological memoir was issued separately, with some additional matter, under the title *Observations on the Geology of the United States of America*. Subsequent survey has corroborated the general accuracy of Maclure's observations.[2]

William Symington 1764-1831 was a pioneer in the development of steamships. Steam was the energy that powered the Industrial Revolution, and when it was applied to shipping, it transformed marine transport in a way that could not have been foreseen by a world weaned on sail. The steamship played a vital role in changing the world. It provided a faster, safer and more reliable mode of travel than sail and enabled the mass movement of passengers and cargo on a scale not possible with sailing ships. The steamship had many innovators who contributed to its development, and the Scots played a major role in this process.

The development of the steamboat – like many other inventions – was a staggered process with many claimants to its invention, including Englishman Jonathan Hulls (1736), Frenchman Claude de Jouffroy (1774), Americans William Henry (1763), John Fitch (22 August 1787) and James Rumsey (3 December 1787), whose grandmother was a Scottish-born Douglas. The first person to actually design a boat with the intention of powering it with steam – as opposed to the earlier method of using a steam engine on an existing sailboat or barge – was William Symington, who had been exposed to steam engines since 1785 when he built one to a design of James Watt. The next year he built a working model of a steam-powered carriage, and in 1787 he patented his "improved atmospheric engine", which was a hybrid between James Watt's engine and the earlier steam engine of Thomas Newcomen. Symington was financed by compatriot Patrick Miller, a pioneer of the trimaran.

Symington's first trial for a steamboat was in late 1789, but the paddle wheels were damaged when the boat picked up speed. Further trials on 26th and 27th December were more successful with the 18m boat travelling at 11 km an hour. With the expiry of James Watt's patents in 1800, Symington designed a boat – called *Charlotte Dundas* after the daughter of his sponsor, Thomas Dundas – that successfully travelled on the Carron River in June 1801, yet it didn't do well when tested in canals. The engine on this boat was horizontal, the first steam engine so designed and one that was to become commonplace after 1825. "Symington's design would be, far more than the products of his Cornish contemporary Richard Trevithick (whose pioneer railway locomotive was built and demonstrated in South Wales the following February), the prototype of thousands of such compact power units: on railways, and in ships, factories and mines."[1]

Two years later Symington tested another boat, also called *Charlotte Dundas*, which was over 17 m long, 5.5 m wide and 2.4 m deep. He made two runs, the first on 4 January 1803 and the second on 28 March of the same year. In the second trip, the *Charlotte Dundas* towed the two sloops *Active* and *Euphemia*, weighing a total of 127 tonnes for 30 km over 9½ hours into a headwind gale that was so strong that no other vessels on the canal moved windward.[2] This was the first time in history that a steamboat had moved anything except itself and it was also the first time a boat had been designed specifically to be driven by a steam engine rather than having a steam engine placed on a sailboat or barge.

Symington, before 1819, developed the direct-acting pump, which he called a Lifting Engine, yet this invention is usually credited to American Henry Worthington in 1850, more than three decades later. The first successful steamboat is often attributed to American Robert Fulton, who was of Irish ancestry and not Scottish as is sometimes claimed. Fulton did, indeed, build the first *commercially* successful steamboat, *Clermont*, in 1807 (the ship's name was actually *North River Steamboat*. The name *Clermont* was erroneously used in a biography of Fulton by Cadwallader David Colden in 1817).[3]

Others also claim it was John Fitch who built the first commercially successful steamboat, but that doesn't negate Symington's achievements any more than the Wright brothers should lose credit for sustained, controlled, heavier-than-air, powered, manned flight because that particular aircraft, *Wright Flyer*, didn't become commercially successful. Likewise, Richard Trevithick built the first steam locomotive to run on rails – the Pen-y-darren – but it, too, was not commercially successful. There is no doubt that *Charlotte Dundas*, either the 1801 or 1803 model, is the first boat built anywhere in the world to have been designed as a steamboat, *ab initio*, and within the next half century steamships changed ocean travel forever.

William Kelly c1765-1840 had "outstanding inventive ability, in particular, his achievement of being 'the first to turn the mule by water power'."[1] The "mule" referred to was Samuel Crompton's spinning mule, a machine designed around 1779 which spun yarn suitable for use in the manufacture of muslin (the mule was originally called the Muslin Wheel). The mule's use "spread rapidly as British manufacturers began to produce high-quality yarn [fine muslin] to rival those of Indian craftsmen."[2]

"The mule as first invented was only partially automatic in its action, the attendant, called the spinner, being required to bring out and push back the carriage, and guide other portions of the machine as well. In 1792, William Kelly of Glasgow, Scotland, improved the machine so that it could be moved to a much greater extent by power, and the spinner only had to guide the carriage on its inward trip. The success of converting the spinning phase on the mule to a power drive – though winding on was still done by hand – meant that one worker could look after two mules with up to 400 spindles. While one mule was drafting and spinning, he pushed the carriage of the other inwards, thus winding on the yarns."[3]

Kelly's self-acting, or semi-automatic, mule became quite popular and was exported to America in 1803.[4] He continued to make improvements to his machine but was dismissed by Robert Owen, the son-in-law of the mill owner, David Dale, in 1800 as Owen wanted no competition in the management of the mill. One unfortunate consequence of Kelly's invention was that the heavy lifting previously required was no longer necessary, so children, who were less expensive to employ, soon replaced adults at the loom.

Kelly also "developed various machines that were used in New Lanark such as the different heating and ventilation systems used in the mill buildings. The heating system used in Mill 3 was similar to that in Mill 2 but instead of the hot air being passed from a stove at the lower level up through compartments built into the thickness of the wall and separated by thin iron plates, it passed in this case through external chambers built into the gables."[5]

Charles Baird 1766-1843 played an important part in the industrial and business life of 19th century St Petersburg. His company specialised in steam-driven machinery and was responsible for Russia's first steamboat, the *Elizaveta*, which operated on the route from Kronstadt to St Petersburg. He arrived in Russia in 1786 and in the following three years he reorganised the Alexandrovskii gun works and the Konchezersk iron foundry. He established the Baird ironworks, which operated so well that there is still a phrase used in the city to describe something running smoothly – "kak u Berda na zavode" (like at Baird works). Baird became the leader in machine building and metallurgy and he trained many Russian mining and metallurgical experts. He built the Admiralty's Izhova works and in 1804 restored the Kolpino works founded by Peter the Great.[1]

His Baird Works specialised in steam-driven machinery and supplied machinery for the Imperial Arsenal, Mint, and glassworks, and undertook a range of projects from bridge-building to ornamental metalwork, and by 1825 he had produced 141 steam engines of all kinds. Baird's company supplied the ironwork for several bridges, for which he designed a hydraulic chain-testing machine, his factory providing the material for the first cast-iron arch bridge in Russia (1805). Baird also built a sugar refinery and he developed a new method for purifying the sugar, using non-animal substances, and helped him corner a large share of the city's sugar supply.[2] As he didn't use bullock's blood in the refining process he could sell his sugar during Lent, giving him a commercial advantage.

Thomas Charles Hope 1766-1844 is credited with the discovery of the element strontium (1793), naming it after the place where it was found, Strontian in Argyllshire. He described the characteristic red colour when its compounds are introduced into a flame. Hope was also the first to show that water expands when frozen and that it attains its maximum density a few degrees above its freezing point (3.98C). He published these results in his paper, *Experiment on the contraction of water by heat* (1805).[1]

The peculiar expansion of water had been noted in the 17th century, but a number of scientists were sceptical of the reality of the phenomenon. In a series of carefully devised experiments, Hope proved that water does have a temperature of maximum density which he determined as being between 39.5F and 40F (4.17C and 4.4C). The value accepted today is 39.2F (4C).

Hope was an excellent lecturer and at Edinburgh became the most popular ever teacher of chemistry in Britain. The attendance at Hope's lectures increased from 293 in 1799 to a peak of 559 in 1823 and then gradually declined to 118 in 1842. During his tenure of the Chair, he taught chemistry to over 15,000 students and thus was uniquely influential in Britain in the dissemination of chemical knowledge during the first 40 years of the 19th century. His success as a lecturer was due to his clarity of exposition and the illustration of his material by numerous well-contrived lecture demonstrations.

John Leslie 1766-1832 was an inventive physicist whose work covered heat, glaciation, capillary action, weather and static electricity. He was a pioneer of the experimental studies of radiant heat that provided French mathematician Jean Baptiste Joseph Fourier with the evidence necessary for its mathematisation. Prominent Irish physicist John Tyndall also considered Leslie and American Count Rumford's work as having been the most significant for the progress of the science of radiant heat. Leslie's work was recognised in 1804 by the award of both Royal Society Rumford Medals, one for his contributions to the science of heat and a separate one for his contributions to the science of light (despite an early scepticism that had delayed publication in the *Philosophical Transactions*).[1]

"His systematic study, begun in 1793, of temperature density relations in gases allowed him to propose a widely discussed formula for the decrease of temperature with increasing height in the atmosphere. In 1800, he announced the discovery of the wet – and dry – bulb hygrometer and provided an essentially correct theory of how the instrument operates. In 1802, he presented the first correct interpretation of capillary action, thus stimulating the work of Thomas Young and James Ivory. Finally, in 1810, Leslie showed that it was possible to attain very low temperatures by evaporating water in the presence of a desiccant in an evacuated receiver, thus providing the principle exploited by Ferdinand Carré in creating the first laboratory ice machines."[2]

Although many people had touched on capillary action, it was Leslie who, in 1802, "gave the first correct explanation of the rise of a liquid in a tube by considering the effect of the attraction of the solid on the very thin stratum of the liquid in contact with it. He did not, like the earlier speculators, suppose this attraction to act in an upward direction so as to support the fluid directly. He showed that the attraction is everywhere normal to the surface of the solid. The direct effect of the attraction is to increase the pressure of the stratum of the fluid in contact with the solid, so as to make it greater than the pressure in the interior of the fluid. The result of this pressure if unopposed is to cause this stratum to spread itself over the surface of the solid as a drop of water is observed to do when placed on a clean horizontal glass plate, and this even when gravity opposes the action, as when the drop is placed on the under surface of the plate. Hence a glass tube plunged into water would become wet all over were it not that the ascending liquid film carries up a quantity of other liquid which coheres to it, so that when it has ascended to a certain height the weight of the column balances the force by which the film spreads itself over the glass."[3]

In 1800, Leslie improved the psychrometer, which is a modified hygrometer. A hygrometer gauges atmospheric humidity by measuring the reaction of certain substances to changes in the amount of water vapour present in the air. Hygrometers are used in meteorology and to regulate humidity in buildings and industrial processes. The hygroscopic hygrometer was first built in the early 1400s by Cardinal Nicholas de Cusa, a German mathematician. Swiss mathematician Johann Heinrich Lambert is credited with inventing the first practical hygrometer in 1755. The sling psychrometer was developed by Scotsman James Hutton in 1792.[4] This type of hygrometer used the change in the weight, length, or twist (as with twine) of a moisture-absorbing substance to determine humidity. Sling psychrometers have two thermometers next to each other and one has water to make it wet. Both thermometers are then swung by holding onto the handles. The water evaporates and the amount of evaporation can help scientists find the amount of humidity. In 1800, John Leslie announced his creation of a simpler psychrometer that consisted of two thermometers mounted and attached to a handle.

"Leslie's hygrometer, which is an adaptation of his differential thermometer, is formed by uniting two tubes having a ball blown on the end of each, into which some coloured sulphuric ether has been previously introduced. When both bulbs are at the same temperature, the fluid stands at the zero of the scale, but when one of them is covered with wetted paper or muslin the instrument shows the depression of temperature of the wetted bulb. In order to ascertain the quantity of moisture corresponding to the reading of a Leslie's hygrometer, we must deduct from the total quantity of moisture which the air of the temperature at the time of observation is capable of holding the deficiency due to the degree of cooling shown by the hygrometer."[5]

In 1804, Leslie established the proportionality between the total emission and absorption of two bodies,[6] when he observed that a matte black surface radiates heat more effectively than a polished surface, suggesting the importance of black body radiation. He ascertained this with a device, now known as Leslie's cube, in which the four lateral sides are covered with materials that are different colours and different finishes: white, matte black, glossy black, and shiny tin. The cube is hollow and is filled with air. When a light is shone on each side of the cube, the heat radiated from each surface can be measured to determine which type of surface radiates most heat.

Leslie's 1804 publication, *An Experimental Inquiry Into the Nature and Propagation of Heat*, "established several fundamental laws of heat radiation: that the emissivity and absorptivity for any surface are equal, that the emissivity of a surface increases with the decrease of reflectivity, and that the intensity of heat radiated from a surface is proportional to the sine of the angle of the rays to the surface. The book also played a major role in the early nineteenth-century argument about whether heat was a form of matter or a mode of motion. Leslie's experiments showed that heat, unlike light, was not directly transmitted through transparent solids."[7]

Leslie supported his concept of climate change with geological evidence. In company with pioneer English photographer Thomas Wedgwood, he had gone to the continent in 1796 and travelled by coach over Grimsel Pass in the Swiss Alps, from the headwaters of the Rhône to those of the Aar. Leslie recognised that the innumerable ridges of loose angular stones, vegetated in proportion to their distance from active glaciers, mark the former extents of those glaciers at a colder time. He noted that "this remarkable fact is known to every tourist". He concluded that the glacier must have descended at least 2,000 feet [610 m] lower than it is at present and that in the remote past the lake that now feeds the Aar was probably a glacier.[8]

It would be decades before the same conclusions were reached by Ignaz Venetz (1822), Johann von Charpentier (1835) and Jean Louis Rodolphe Agassiz (1837). Two Scots, James Hutton (1795) and John Playfair (1802), had earlier attributed the granite erratics on the Jura to glacial action, but neither had ever seen a glacier and they were working within the paradigm of slow-acting erosion. Both attributed the former extent of Swiss glaciers to a greater elevation of the Alps (as did Charpentier), not to climatic change. Leslie had the advantage over later geologists that he was not encumbered with the (false) assumption, subsequent to Fourier (1824), that Earth's surface temperature is steadily in decline due to secular dimming of the sun. Leslie's prescient interpretation of Swiss moraines was noted by Gavin de Beer (1932) and Frank F. Cunningham (1990).[9]

In 1810, Leslie produced ice by means of an air pump and sulphuric acid. He obtained very low temperatures by evaporating water in a bell jar containing sulphuric acid as a drying agent and reduced the air pressure with an air-pump. He had been preceded in this by fellow Scot William Cullen some 55 years earlier, but Leslie used a different method that was more efficient and could produce much more ice.

Leslie wrote a paper in 1791 which examined the leakage of static electricity from charged bodies through different conducting paths and, in his analysis, he pre-empted many of Georg Ohm's findings on voltaic electricity.[10]

Leslie independently invented the atmometer, or evaporimeter, which is also credited to Pieter van Musschenbroek of Holland. Atmometers are instruments for measuring the potential evaporation of water with unlimited water supply. "John Leslie was the first known person to use a hollow, porous-porcelain sphere to study evaporation in 1813."[11] Remarkably, in a pre-nuclear scientific world, he presciently argued from observations with his photometer that bodies are, or matter is, so diffuse that the ultimate particles "may bear no sensible proportion" to the space which they occupy.[12] Leslie invented the aethrioscope, an instrument consisting in part of a differential thermometer, and used it for measuring changes of temperature produced by different conditions of the sky, such as when clear or cloudy. He is sometimes credited with the invention of the photometer, pyrometer and differential thermometer, but each of these had been invented earlier. The photometer originated with Johann Heinrich Lambert (born in Alsace), the pyrometer with Josiah Wedgewood in 1782, and the differential thermometer with John Christopher Sturmius, although Jan Baptist van Helmont may have anticipated it. Leslie did, however, make his own variations to each of these instruments to help him in his research into heat.

John Macarthur 1766-1834 was a pioneer of the Australian wool industry. Australia is the largest wool-producing country in the world with annual production consistently accounting for over one quarter of the world's wool and is often valued at well over $2 billion each year. Australia is also recognised as producing the world's highest quality woollen fibre – Australian merino wool. All of this has been achieved in just over 200 years and began with the hard work of one family – the Macarthurs.[1]

Sheep came to Australia with the First Fleet in 1788, but by the end of that year, all but one had been slaughtered for food or had otherwise died. These had been brought over by Governor Phillip from the Cape of Good Hope in southern Africa. They had fat, long tails and their wool was like hair. The first white people wanted sheep for their meat and not their wool. In 1797, two naval officers named Henry Waterhouse and William Kent bought 26 merino sheep at the Cape of Good Hope. Some of the sheep died on the voyage, but the others were brought to Sydney. Merinos have been bred in Spain for more than 2,000 years and were famous for their heavy fleece and very fine wool. Waterhouse and Kent sold merinos to John Macarthur, William Cox, Thomas Rowlet and Samuel Marsden. Most of them crossed their merinos with their other sheep, producing sheep with coarse wool and large bodies. Macarthur wanted fine wool so he bought more merinos and bred from them. He sent one bale of wool to England in 1807. Today (2015), three out of four Australian sheep are merinos and most other sheep in Australia are crossed with merinos.[2]

Though the Australian Merino derives its name and basic appearance from the famed royal flocks of Spain, it is in every way a distinct breed, adapted to the specific conditions of Australia. In 1804, Macarthur made a further very important purchase of seven Spanish fine wool Merino rams and one ewe from King George III, who had been able to obtain these sheep from Spain in exchange for some Flemish horses. By skilful breeding and selection, he evolved the first Australian-bred pure Merino sheep. Within four decades of Macarthur exporting his first bale of wool in 1807, Australia had become the world's biggest producer, and its production grew in step with the industrialisation of leading European nations and also the USA. At the end of the 1980s, the Australian sheep flock numbered 172 million head. Difficult economic conditions and severe drought caused the sheep numbers to fall to a low of 98 million head in 2004.[3] Numbers of pure merino sheep fell to 20.5 million out of a breeding population of 38.7 million sheep in Australia in 2011, but even with this reduced flock, Australia is still the largest individual producing country, accounting for 80% by volume of the merino used in textiles.[4]

Due to business and other reasons, Macarthur was overseas for eight years during which time his wife, Elizabeth, managed the farm and she is sometimes given credit for the success of the merino sheep in Australia. There is no doubt that John Macarthur needed a successful manager to run his sheep station in his absence but it was, unequivocally, his vision and action which were the genesis of Australia's great merino sheep business.

Charles Macintosh 1766-1843 made the first true waterproof fabric. He had his own chemical works by 1786 where he made ammonium chloride, used in various finishing processes such as stained or leaded glass, and also used in making metal ingots to prevent porosity. He was also the first in Scotland to make both Prussian blue and Turkey red for dyeing cloth. He built the first alum works in Scotland at Hurlet, Renfrewshire. Charles' father operated a factory making cudbear, which was patented in 1766 by fellow Scot Cuthbert Gordon. Cudbear was the first dye to be invented since the classical period, being a purple dye that was much cheaper than Tyrian purple and it soon became very popular. It was "prepared from a variety of lichens. Only one of two natural dyes ever credited to an individual."[1] (The other is Bancroft's Mordant, which is not actually a dye, named for American Edward Bancroft).

When Charles' father died, he inherited the factory and it was from this time that he started experimenting with naphtha derived from coal tar. In 1818, he dissolved India rubber – caoutchouc – a latex that comes from the milky sap of some tropical South American plants. He brushed it over one side of two sheets of woollen cloth which he then stuck together, and when it dried, he found that the material was waterproof. He patented the process in 1823 and it became known as the mackintosh (with a "k"). In the early days of raincoat manufacture there were production difficulties as the oils in wool weakened the latex, stitching made holes in the seams which leaked, and in hot weather the latex became sticky – while cold weather made it stiff.

Macintosh also invented a waterproof life preserver which was mocked in a cartoon in 1825 in the *Northern Looking Glass*. "Summer Amusements: Waterproof Life Preserver" is an interpretation of a report in the *Scots Mechanics Magazine* about an inflatable rubber life saver invented by MacIntosh. It was designed to be strapped around the chest under the arms.

Macintosh manufactured other items from latex, including rubber shoes – a forerunner of the more famous gum boots, known in Britain as Wellington boots or wellies. Although based in Edinburgh, the North British Rubber Company that first mass-produced gum-boots was founded in 1856 by American Henry Lee Norris, who actually had to import tradesmen from his homeland to make the rubber boots as there were none to be found in Scotland.

Macintosh worked with James Beaumont Neilson to develop the hot blast method for the production of high grade cast iron. In 1825, he found a way of using gaseous carbon to provide a faster way of making steel from malleable iron, which is a heat-treated iron-carbon alloy, but it wasn't commercially successful because of technical problems in keeping the furnace gas-tight. He was the first in Britain to manufacture aluminium acetate, which is used in the manufacture of antiseptics, and he brought in new dyeing techniques which enabled him to produce various shades of colour from cudbear, ranging from blue to pink.

MacIntosh is probably the inventor of the Twaddell Scale, possibly named after a Glasgow glass-blower, William Twaddell. Whatever its origins, the Twaddell scale was devised at the beginning of 19th century and was popular with industry for determining the strength or concentration of liquids.[2] It was used for liquids with specific gravity greater than water.

Alexander Wilson 1766-1813 is regarded as the "Father of American Ornithology" and the greatest American ornithologist prior to John James Audubon.[1] It was his meeting with Audubon in Louisville, Kentucky, in 1810 which probably inspired the younger man to produce a book of his own bird illustrations. Wilson travelled widely, watching and painting birds and collecting subscribers for his book. The result was the nine-volume *American Ornithology* (1808-1814), illustrating 268 species of birds, 26 of which had not previously been described.[2]

Wilson also conducted the first breeding-bird census (in John Bartram's garden – the oldest surviving botanic garden in North America), corrected earlier errors of taxonomy, and published many observations of natural history.[3] There probably has never been an American treatise on zoology so thoroughly exploited and out of which so many composite works have been fashioned... as Wilson's *Ornithology*.[4] Before leaving Scotland for the newly created United States, Wilson had been a poet whose work may have sold 100,000 copies.[5]

Henry Bell 1767-1830 built a 23-tonne steamship, *Comet*, which travelled on the River Clyde at more than 11 km/h in January 1812 with its 3 hp engine. It was originally some 14 m long but was later lengthened to almost 20 m. Bell was only one in a long line of prior innovators in this field, but his *Comet* was the first commercially successful steamship in Europe, commuting between Glasgow and Greenock on a regular basis, sailing (or steaming) to Greenock at noon on Tuesdays, Thursdays and Saturdays and returning to Glasgow on Mondays, Wednesdays and Fridays, depending on the tide. There were no trips on Sunday, being the Sabbath. The *Comet* continued to ply its trade until it was caught in strong currents near Oban and wrecked on 13 December 1820. The *Comet* had been preceded by American Robert Fulton's *Clermont* which had steamed up the Hudson River on 11 August 1807 on a 32-hour trip. There was a Scottish connection with Fulton as he had been in Scotland aboard the *Charlotte Dundas* in July 1801, when it steamed some 13 km in 85 minutes. William Symington gave him sketches and an explanation of the workings of the steamboat. Fulton was also in regular contact with Henry Bell, who gave Fulton advice and provided him with a working model of a steamboat.[1] Bell's *Comet* heralded the start of Glasgow's River Clyde becoming the largest shipbuilding centre in the world in terms of tonnage. Trade in Glasgow went from £6,676 in 1810 – the year before Bell commenced the construction of the *Comet* – to £76,000 in 1852.[2]

Peter Ewart 1767-1842 published *On the measure of moving force* (1813) – a defence of John Smeaton's ideas on energy. It was a major influence on English physicists John Dalton and James Prescott Joule, whose work led to the theory of conservation of energy. The publication was "remarkable for the extensive knowledge of the subject which the author displays, and for the great perspicuity of his reasoning, which is the consequence of this extensive knowledge."[1]

Ewart initiated the use of cast and wrought iron in building wharfs and dams and, in 1796, he became a partner in a textile mill owned by Englishman Samuel Greg. "Ewart's technical expertise was considered to be so important that Greg was willing to offer him a quarter of the spinning profits in return for an investment of £400 in the company. By 1816 Quarry Bank employed 252 people and was producing 342,578 pounds [155 tonnes] of cloth. Ten years later, the mill was employing 380 and output had reached 699,223 pounds [317 tonnes]. As well as taking a large share of the home market, Samuel Greg was also selling cloth to Italy, France, North America, Russia, Germany and South America."[2]

"Continuing developments in engine technology put pressure on manufacturers to keep up with the changes in order to remain competitive in the market, and trained engineers like Ewart became key players, working side-by-side with local manufacturers, installing new engines and training the manufacturers to maintain and make efficient use of them"[3]

In 1822, he patented a method of using interlocking sheet piles for cofferdams – watertight enclosures placed or constructed in waterlogged soil or under water and pumped dry so that construction or repairs can proceed under normal conditions. Iron piles had first been used in 1820 by Englishman David Matthews at Bridlington Harbour's North Pier, but Ewart's design was different and a considerable improvement on that of Matthews as he used interlocking sheet pile walls which were both strong and watertight. Ewart was an important figure in developing turbines and thermodynamic theory, and he strongly supported education and training. To this end, Ewart, with seven others in 1824, including fellow Scot William Fairbairn, founded the Mechanics' Institute in Manchester (which later merged with Victoria University to become the University of Manchester) to train engineers and improve the level of professionalism. Also on the board of directors were textile manufacturers and compatriots James McConnel and John Kennedy.

Although there were some 600 mechanics' institutes in Britain, the board of directors at Manchester Mechanics' Institute ensured its educational mission "embodied the importance they themselves had come to ascribe to mechanical knowledge and formal learning. In effect, the Institute also elevated the status of practical knowledge to that of natural science in general, both by including topics of practical importance in courses on natural science and by offering independent courses devoted to practical skills like mechanical drawing and machine operation. The Manchester Mechanics' Institute for labouring men proved to be a resounding success for several decades."[4] Note: the world's first Mechanics' Institute (although it didn't use that name) was created in 1821 in Edinburgh as the School of Arts of Edinburgh, with the educational remit to "address societal needs by incorporating fundamental scientific thinking and research into engineering solutions". It also enrolled women from 1869, twenty years in advance of other institutions.[5] The Anderson Institute was founded in 1796 and was the first technical college to provide scientific instruction with the opportunity for practical application of ideas. The institution was the first in the world to provide evening classes in science and the first to admit women on the same terms as men.[6] The Glasgow Mechanics' Institution, inspired by lectures given by Englishman George Birkbeck as early as 1799, was founded in 1823. By the middle of the century there were more than 700 Mechanics' Institutes in Britain, with many others opened overseas. "The early developments and successes associated with the mechanics' institute movement were therefore Scottish, with several mechanics' institutes being established around both Glasgow and Edinburgh".[7] Their early influences quickly spread south of the border to London and then to the provinces.

Image 14 – The wreckage of the USS Maine in Havana harbour surrounded by a cofferdam, on 16 June 1911

Alexander John Forsyth 1768-1843 invented the first successful percussion lock for guns. "During his spare time, he experimented with explosives and in 1805 he succeeded in developing mercury fulminate as a percussion cap for use in small-arms ammunition, thus paving the way for the eventual design of the self-contained metallic cartridge and contact fuse. This he did by rolling the compound into small pellets, which he placed in a nipple at the breech end of the barrel, where they could be detonated by the falling hammer of the gun."[1]

"The lighted match which soldiers originally carried for igniting their guns gave way to the flint and steel; and in 1807 a Scotch clergyman named Forsyth obtained a patent which led to the invention of the percussion cap. This improvement revolutionised the mechanism of firearms."[2]

Encyclopedia Britannica states "the percussion lock revolutionised firearms theory and opened the way to the development of self-contained metal cartridges and contact fuses in artillery shells. Forsyth found that potassium chlorate would explode when given a sharp blow. He made his first percussion lock with it by packing potassium chlorate in the port in the breech of the gun through which the flash of the primer ordinarily travelled. When the compound was struck smartly by the hammer, it exploded with a strong flash that ignited the main charge in the barrel."[3]

The British government lost interest early on and Forsyth was awarded £100 in lieu of the work he had performed, with another £1,000 being given after he had died, this being divided among his surviving relatives, yet such was the importance of this invention that Napoleon Bonaparte offered Forsyth £20,000 for details of his invention. However, being a true patriot, the pious clergyman turned them down flat.[4]

Hugh McIntosh 1768-1840 "was one of the key individuals in developing the British civil engineering industry."[1] He undertook construction contracts for parts of the Grand Trunk Canal. Later he built or made major alterations to canals, including: Thames and Severn; Gloucester and Berkeley; Great Western; Grand Junction; Aire and Calder; Thames and Medway; Kennet and Avon; Stainforth and Keadby; Croydon; and Regents. In all, he undertook over 120 contracts in his lifetime, far more than any of his contemporaries, and these included the British Museum, Hampton Court and Brighton Pavilion. He was also the first to build a railway into any capital city in the world, with London Bridge Station opening on 14 December 1836.[2]

He built, or made major renovations to, docks and harbours, including: Sharpness Dock, the East India Company's Import and Export Docks (London), Eastern Dock (London), Lavender Pond Dock (London), Pembroke Dock, Plymouth Dock (the Royal William Victualling Yard at a cost of £2 million pounds and involving the movement of 300,000 tons [272,151 tonnes] of rock), Junction Dock (Hull), Portsmouth Dock, Shoreham Harbour, Whitstable Harbour, Dover Harbour; and he built sea defences at Dymchurch and Gillingham.[3]

His bridges, new or extension, included: Clopton Bridge at Stratford-on-Avon (widened), Folly Bridge at Oxford, South Bridge in Northampton, Tewkesbury over the Severn River, Rochester Bridge (repairs). His railways include: Grand Junction Railway (Birmingham to Warrington), North Midland Railway, Midland Counties Railway, London and Southampton Railway, Manchester and Leeds Railway, Northern and Eastern Railway, and London and Greenwich Railway, which was the first railway in London and for which there were 878 arches in the viaduct and bridges that he built. His roads include: Vauxhall Bridge Road and Highgate Archway, as well as roads in Manchester and Brighton.[4]

Image 15 – The original London and Greenwich Railway station December 1836

He built sewers in Rotherhithe, Deptford and Southall between 1835 and 1837; a bridge at Brentford over the River Brent, and undertook major works on Blackfriars Bridge. He laid water pipes for Windsor Castle, Hampton Court Palace, Kensington Palace, and Brighton Pavilion. He built gas mains for Bristol and Shrewsbury and a gas works at Carlisle.[5] John Nash, the Prince Regent's favourite architect, gave the best insight into how esteemed McIntosh was when, as architect responsible for the refurbishment of Buckingham Palace, he ensured the work was not put out to tender because, in his view, McIntosh would be the best person to take the contract due to his *known probity* and *great means* of performing the works. In other words, McIntosh was an upright and honest man who had sufficient capital, plant and equipment to see the job through to the end.[6]

"McIntosh would appear to have been the first contractor who had a national organisation and was possibly the first to operate overseas."[7] The reference to working overseas refers to his being sent in December 1809 to dismantle the fortifications at Flushing in Flanders during the evacuation that followed the failed Walcheren Expedition.

"It was his achievement to be amongst the first civil engineering contractors to have created a national organisation that could operate efficiently and, if necessary, simultaneously in several branches or skills of the profession. … While many contractors in the latter half of the 19th century exceeded him in the value of the work they performed 'few equalled him in the diversity and geographical range of the construction operations within Britain.'"[8]

Charles Tennant 1768-1838 introduced a much faster method of bleaching than hitherto had been available. Unlike more expensive cotton textiles, calico wasn't bleached – only the better quality cloth was given this treatment as bleaching was slow, laborious and costly. Traditionally, cloth was bleached by exposure to the sun by laying hectares of material out on open ground, usually after having been soaked in stale urine. Such was the demand for urine that it was collected from army barracks and transported to the bleaching grounds. Sometime in the 18th century, Holland and France started using chemicals, such as dilute sulphuric acid, to bleach cloth, and Frenchman Claude Berthollet discovered the bleaching properties of chlorine in 1785. The really big change in bleaching came when Charles Tennant, in association with Charles Macintosh of raincoat fame, created bleaching powder made from the reaction of chlorine gas on calcium hydroxide. This invention had a threefold effect. First, it launched the chemical industry, and Tennant's factory at St Rollox, then outside Glasgow, became the largest chemical factory in the world, eventually becoming part of the United Alkali Company, which itself formed part of the merger that created ICI in 1926.

The second effect was to release large tracts of land to agriculture as they were no longer required for bleaching. Lastly, there was a correspondingly large increase in the speed of the bleaching process, which now took days rather than months, and a significant reduction in the cost. In Ireland alone, in 1797, where Tennant's powder was used to bleach linen, it saved £168,000 annually.[1] Tennant had more than just skills in chemistry; he was also a good businessman who understood economics and his product changed forever the method of preparing cloth for dyeing.

William Wallace 1768-1843 invented an instrument called the eidograph in 1801, used for the purpose of copying plans or other drawings on the same, or on different, scales. It was an improvement on the simpler pantograph. The eidograph enabled any ratio to be taken between the limits of one to three.[1]

Wallace, a mathematician, was also the inventor of the chorograph, an instrument for describing on paper any triangle having one side and all its angles given, and also for constructing two similar triangles on two given straight lines, having the angles given.

John Kennedy 1769-1855 invented the Jack Frame[1] and he was one of the two main promoters of the Liverpool to Manchester Railway, the world's first intercity passenger railway. It was in the factories, particularly in the cotton mills of Manchester, that the Industrial Revolution was most evident. Britain dominated cotton and other textile manufacturing through a number of technical innovations, including the Flying Shuttle, Spinning Jenny, Water Frame, Spinning Mule (it was called a mule as it was a hybrid between the Water Frame and the Spinning Jenny) and Power Loom, all invented by Englishmen between 1733 and 1785. The two major non-British inventions in textile production were the Jacquard Loom in France and the Cotton Gin (i.e. engine) in America.

Kennedy's Jack Frame was designed for preparing cotton slivers into a fine roving – slivers of cotton, or other material, formed into slightly twisted strands in readiness for spinning. Manchester was the world's major cotton spinning centre during much of the 19th century – it is usually considered the first industrial city in the world – and Kennedy, in partnership with **James McConnel 1762-1831**, produced cotton sufficiently fine to meet the needs of the highest quality garments. They introduced the first steam-driven spinning mules and, in 1793, the double-speed mule for spinning fine yarn, an improvement on Samuel Crompton's spinning mule of 1780.[2] The development of the steam-powered "common mule" [i.e. a power-assisted mule as distinct from the hand mule or the self-acting mule] by McConnel and Kennedy in 1795 eventually produced a machine that could spin a wider range of yarn counts to uniform quality than could either the spinning jenny or water frame. Common mules also were more energy-efficient than water frames, and saved labour by allowing a single worker to operate two mules.[3] They also negotiated with employees to "devote time to machine maintenance by setting aside a portion of each workday for regular machine cleaning".[4]

Kennedy and McConnel donated £600 (a very generous sum) to the foundation of Manchester Mechanics' Institute in 1825 which, with Owens College, formed the embryo of Manchester University. By 1810, they had increased the number of their spindles from 7,464 in 1797 to 78,792 [5] and employed over 1,000 workers. This was the largest cotton spinning company in Britain[6] (and, hence, the world). Their cotton mill was eight levels high and may have been the tallest cast-iron building in the world during its time, having overtaken another Scottish-owned cotton mill – Murrays' Mills at Ancoats. This mill, which operated for over 150 years, was owned by Adam and George Murray and had 1,215 employees, gas lighting (when it was a rarity), and the mill attracted visitors from Europe and America. Such was the importance of cotton it provided about half of Britain's exports well into the 19th century. Murrays' spindleage increased from 7,464 in 1797 to 124,848 in 1824, while their workforce peaked at 1,590 in 1836. In 1819, mills owned by Scots such as the Murrays, Peter Ewart, and Kennedy & McConnel, employed 2,956 of the 8,060 employees (37%) in the Manchester region cotton mills (as compiled from factory inspector lists of 21 factories).

Alexander Anderson Seton 1769-1850 (he added the Seton name in 1812) reported observations on the common pea on both the dominance of certain traits over others and the segregation of these traits in second generations of the hybrids. For example, after crossing green and white peas, Seton noted that the hybrids "were all completely one colour or the other, none of them having an intermediate tint".[1] When Gregor Mendel started his experiments in the mid-1850s, the idea that some characteristics were dominant over others was common knowledge amongst botanists. In the early years of the century, British botanists Thomas Andrew Knight, John Goss (both English), and Alexander Seton had written extensively on the subject.[2]

On 20 August 1822, the then Secretary of the Horticultural Society stated that "Mr Alexander Seton crossed the flowers of *Dwarf Imperial*, a well-known green variety of the Pea, with the pollen of a white free-growing variety. Four hybrid seeds were obtained, which did not differ in appearance from the others of the female parent. These seeds therefore did not obey the law of dominance, or if the statement be preferred, greenness became dominant in this case. The seeds were sown, and produced plants bearing "green" and "white" seeds side by side in the same pod.[3] Note: his son, Alexander Seton 1814-1852 drowned in the *Birkenhead* disaster. He was responsible for the tradition of allowing women and children to leave a sinking ship before able-bodied men – ironically, he could not swim, himself.

James Watt 1769-1848, son of the famous steam engine pioneer, designed the engines for *Caledonia*. In 1817, James Watt junior purchased Henry Bell's steamship *Caledonia* and refitted her with two 14 hp Boulton & Watt engines. He took her across to the Dutch coast and travelled up the Rhine as far as Koblenz. This was probably the first steam crossing of the English Channel. On the way home, the ship visited Antwerp and Rotterdam, returning to the Thames in the spring of 1818. This successful trip brought the firm good publicity and the manufacture of marine engines went from strength to strength.[1]

William Nicol 1770-1851 invented, in 1828, the polarising light microscope, one of the key tools for identification of geological materials. While Nicol was not involved in any criminal cases, the descendants of his microscope are found in crime laboratories around the world.[1]

Nicol is associated with two inventions of considerable significance, both of which helped to lay the foundations of the modern sciences of mineralogy and petrology. The first was the abovementioned prism which bears his name, a sophisticated optical filter designed to polarise light. Used in pairs as a polariser and an analyser, the Nicol prism was a pioneering device which enabled minerals to be identified through optical characteristics which derive from their crystal structures. This was published in 1829, in the *Edinburgh New Philosophical Journal* (issue 6, 1829, pp 83-84). However, the theory and usefulness of this device was not immediately appreciated, and it was not until five years later that William Henry Fox Talbot (1800-1879), the pioneer of photography, announced that he had read about the device in a German journal and realised that the Nicol prism could be effectively applied to the microscope. Even more mysteriously, a paper explaining the mathematics of the Nicol prism written in 1837 by Edward Sang, whose mother was a distant relation of William Nicol, was inexplicably "neglected and left lying in a drawer till rescued from oblivion by [Peter Guthrie] Tait fifty-four years later". The Nicol prism consists of a piece of calcite, rhombohedral in shape, and cut at 68°. The crystal is then bisected; one half inverted and glued back onto the first half. Canada balsam was used originally to glue the two halves together. When non-polarised light impinges on the crystal, the resulting slow ray bends at an angle that results in total reflection at the interface between the two halves. The faster, less refracted ray passes through the interface and exits the opposite end of the crystal as a beam of plane polarised light. Nicol prisms were common in the second half of the 19th century.[2]

Image 16 – Nicol Prism

The second device, which involved Nicol in some fierce controversy, was that of the preparation of thin slices or "sections" of fossils or minerals for viewing through the microscope.[3] Nicol developed new techniques of preparing thin slices of minerals and fossil wood for microscopic examination. These techniques allowed the samples to be viewed through the microscope by transmitted light, rather than reflected light, which only revealed surface features."[4] The origins of making thin slices of rocks are probably obscured in the misty beginnings of the lapidarist's art. Despite Robert Hooke's and David Brewster's preparation of slices of petrified wood and large mineral crystals, respectively, Nicol is commonly credited with the development of the rock thin section by perfecting a method of making slices that he learned from George Sanderson, an Edinburgh lapidary.[5]

James Paterson 1770-1854 mechanised net manufacturing in the first quarter of the 19th century. Although flax was used to make fishing nets, the preferred cord was hemp and, later, cotton. Fishing was, and still is, a key industry for most littoral nations, but much labour was used in hand-making and repairing fishing nets. Joseph Marie Jacquard, who invented the eponymous loom that involved the first use of punch cards, made a machine in 1802 to manufacture nets and was awarded 10,000 francs by Napoleon Bonaparte. Jacquard wasn't the first to do this as four Britons – William Ross, William Horton, Thomas Davies and John Golby – had patented such a machine in 1778. James Paterson patented a loom for making fishing nets in 1812, the first machine that effectively tied knots for making fishing nets.[1] It had taken numerous attempts, working with an unknown local mechanic, as Paterson didn't have the technical training, before he had a machine that worked to their satisfaction and in the early hours of one morning he "had the pleasure of seeing that the idea which he had nursed for so many years was not an impracticable thing after all. There was the machine turning off row after row of meshes at a rate which would leave a dozen hand-workers far behind.[2]

He started a net factory at Musselburgh in East Lothian and built a net-making machine in 1820, but the early results were unsatisfactory as the knots slipped easily. Another Scot, Walter Ritchie, would modify Paterson's design and make it even more successful.

Robert Miller (dates unknown) made important improvements to the power loom in 1796 when he took out a patent for an improved protector which stopped the loom altogether when the shuttle failed to enter its box, thus preventing breakage of the warp threads. The same patent contained the specification for his "wiper" loom. The wipers, or cams, worked the picking stick to drive the shuttle across, a feature found on most later looms. He also moved the sley by a cam in one direction and by springs in the other. His looms were still working in 1808 and may have formed the basis for power looms built in Lowell in the USA.[1] "Yet the honour due to Robert Miller, who introduced power-looms of the same construction as this old loom in 1796, is perhaps greater than to those who have produced the improvements, because his was the beginning."[2]

The "first commercially successful power-weaving mill in Britain appears to have been John Monteith's, at Pollokshaws near Glasgow, set up in 1801 with 200 power-looms designed and built by Robert Miller of Glasgow. The power loom does not appear … to have been introduced in Scotland with a view to overcoming any bottleneck in production at the weaving stage, indeed there are indications that there was an oversupply of labour in handloom weaving in Scotland from an early date. Its initial purpose appears to have been to introduce a type of fabric not previously woven in the Glasgow area, but the economies it permitted by increasing per capita output of cloth apparently led to its being developed to perform processes normally carried out by handloom weavers of even the finest fancy-work." Although the earliest spinning and weaving machinery had been developed in England, the Scots were, by 1790, developing and putting into use machines which were technically superior to English machines, such as William Kelly's self-acting and water-powered mules and Robert Miller's power-looms.[3]

Until 1820 or thereabouts, "the power-loom, owing to its numerous defects, had only made little progress. In 1813, there were only 2,400 in all of Great Britain, and a rather large proportion of these were Robert Miller's 'wiper-loom', as it was called."[4]

John Baildon 1772-1846 went to Prussian Silesia in 1793 where he lived until his death in 1846. Baildon designed and built, at Gliwice, the first coke-fired blast furnaces in continental Europe; he produced the first pig iron – on 21 September 1796 – and, in the same year, built the first iron bridge in continental Europe – the Silesian bridge over the River Striegau at Lassau, near Breslau. He built several more blast furnaces in the period to 1820 and made the first cylinder-boring machine in Europe and the first steam engine to be built in Prussia and, also in Moravia. He expanded his steel production by building works in Moravia and Bohemia. His iron works included those he built at Stepanovo, Benezovo, Polnieska, Zeladna and Bytkow. He also built the 46 km Kłodnicki Canal along the Kłodnica River in Upper Silesia, Poland, between the Oder River and Gliwice, between 1792 and 1812.[1]

Baildon modernised the Mała Panew Steelworks in Ozimek. A foundry of gun-barrels designed by him was the most modern and efficient in Prussia. In January 1798, he was appointed a state technical adviser of the steelworks industry on the Upper Silesia which, at this time, was the biggest industrial enterprise in Europe. Under the management of Fryderyk Reden, and in cooperation with Jan Wedding, Baildon turned the Royal Steelworks in Chorzów into the biggest and the most modern metallurgical works in Europe.[2]

David Mushet 1772-1847 found that the quality of iron and steel could be improved with manganese oxide, and that he could make steel by adding carbon to iron, a process he patented in 1800. He discovered blackband ironstone in 1801, but at the time it was thought that, unlike clayband stone, it was unsuitable for producing quality iron. Mushet argued that non-phosphoric oxide of iron, plentiful in Britain, made better quality wrought iron. He was also important in developing mines and tramroads in the Forest of Dean in the English county of Gloucestershire, and his 1824 survey of coal strata was important in British mining.

Mushet was critical of coal mine owners who obliged children to work in cramped conditions, stating, "that there is no necessity for boys being ever obliged to work in such contracted ways as compel them to go on their hands and knees. In all cases the rubbish might be so removed from the narrow workings as to give sufficient headway: and the only reason it is not done is the increased expense to the proprietor, and consequent deduction from his profits."[1]

Mushet also identified that the "excellence of the Dan[n]emora and other irons is due to the presence in the iron of a small proportion of the metal titanium."[2] Samuel Smiles wrote, "Among the other important results of Mr Mushet's lifelong labours, the following may be summarily mentioned: The preparation of steel from bar-iron by a direct process, combining the iron with carbon; the discovery of the beneficial effects of oxide of manganese on iron and steel; the use of oxides of iron in the puddling-furnace in various modes of appliance; the production of pig-iron from the blast-furnace, suitable for puddling, without the intervention of the refinery; and the application of the hot blast to anthracite coal in iron-smelting. For the process of combining iron with carbon for the production of steel, Mr Mushet took out a patent in November 1800; and many years after, when he had discovered the beneficial effects of oxide of manganese on steel, Mr Josiah Heath founded upon it his celebrated patent for the making of cast-steel, which had the effect of raising the annual production of that metal in Sheffield from 3,000 to 100,000 tons [2,721 – 90,718 tonnes]. His application of the hot blast to anthracite coal, after a process invented by him and adopted by the Messrs. Hill of the Plymouth Iron Works, South Wales, had the effect of producing savings equal to about £20,000 a year at those works; and yet, strange to say, Mr Mushet himself never received any consideration for his invention."[3] Note: Samuel Smiles wasn't an unbiased authority as he tended to selectively quote in order to create a more positive impression of his subjects, however, there is no reason to doubt the accuracy of the quotation provided here.

The aforementioned Josiah Marshall Heath was an Englishman who patented an improved method of making cast steel by adding oxide of manganese in the manufacturing process, following which the number of cast-steel furnaces in the Sheffield district rose from 554 in 1835 to 1,495 in 1853.[4] Heath patented his process in 1839, ten years after David Mushet first experimented with spiegeleisen (literally "mirror iron") – a compound of iron, manganese and carbon - resulting in smoother and stronger tinplate (sheet steel covered with a thin layer of tin). The ferromanganese now used in the production of steel contains around 80% manganese content and about 4 million tonnes is consumed each year to make steel[5] – a testament to Mushet's inventiveness.

Adam Ramage 1772-1850 was a pioneer printer in the United States. He crossed the Atlantic to America in 1794 and within two years he had used a triple-thread screw to replace the Gutenberg spindle screw in printing presses. He laid a line of type in rows – usually six – and locked them into place with wedges; then hand-inked a paper sheet by pulling a handle to press the paper onto the inked type. The Ramage Press gave a better consistency of printed text and it was lighter than the traditional Gutenberg press, with a maximum output around 250 pages an hour. It was also less expensive, usually costing under $800, and it quickly became the most common in America.

Later, Ramage put springs onto his wooden presses to return the bar to rest and raise the platen above the carriage after each impression. "Ramage's wooden press improvements were only a small part of his achievement. His numerous inventions for the improvement of the iron press established his fame as one of the great press builders of the first half of the nineteenth century."[1]

With the emergence of the iron hand presses in the 1820s, Ramage began to incorporate iron into his designs, later making presses completely of iron, most notably the Ruthven in 1817, the Philadelphia in 1833, and the American in 1845, which was the invention of Sheldon Graves. By 1837, Ramage was reported to have manufactured over 1,250 presses of all kinds. These presses were never able to compete with the emerging Stanhope and Columbian presses, but Ramage continued manufacturing them until his death at the age of 78.[2]

William Wilson 1772-1860, with his son **George Fergusson Wilson 1822-1902**, invented a process for making and producing candles that made his company the largest producer of candles in the world and created the modern candle. It had been discovered that, if natural fats (from plants or animals) are mixed with strong alkalis, they separate into liquid and solid components. The Wilsons used this technique, and added a further distillation, to produce stearine – a harder, pure-white fat. Stearine candles burn brightly without smoke or smell.[1]

Tallow, a purified form of beef or mutton fat, was the only available cheap alternative to beeswax for making candles at this time. Candle manufacture had barely progressed since the Middle Ages. The wealthy and the Church burned beeswax candles, while everyone else used the cheaper tallow lights which smoked, smelled and guttered. The poor either made their own tallow dips from hoarded animal fat with rush wicks – known as "rushlights" – or lived in darkness. To make matters worse, there had been a heavy government tax on candles.

In the 1820s, a French chemist, Michel Eugene Chevreuil, had published his researches into fatty acids. By mixing a strong alkali with vegetable or animal fats, he discovered that the solution separated into liquid and solid components. Known as "saponification", this technique was already used by soap makers, but nobody had employed it for candle manufacture.

William Wilson's son, George, experimented with this process; by adding a further distillation using a vacuum or high-pressure steam, he improved Chevreuil's basic chemistry. Wilson adopted and patented the introduction of superheated steam into the still or vat containing the fat acids, which excluded atmospheric air, and carried over the fatty vapours into the receiver in a more perfect condition than they had before been able to obtain them. The same chemistry could also be applied to a range of unsavoury raw materials that had previously been unusable – skin fat, bone fat, fish oil, and industrial waste greases could all be rendered into hard white candles. Wilson also found a way to use palm oil to make candles by treating it with sulphuric acid.[2]

Wilson's company – Price's Patent Candle Company – acquired a reputation for innovation and it generally had first refusal to work any newly patented inventions. As well as industrial chemistry, there was the development of mass production processes. In 1849, they installed a system that moved candle moulds round the factory on a railway. By 1864, a new method of ejecting candles from moulds using compressed air pushed candle production to 14 tons (12.7 tonnes) a day. A decade later increased mechanisation enabled Price's to produce 32 million nightlights a year and dominate that market.

One of the products separated out by saponification was "sweet water", subsequently called glycerine, which had originally been discovered in 1779 by Swedish chemist Karl Wilhelm Scheele. This was a non-flammable liquid and its separation was the reason that stearine candles burned better than tallow. George Wilson manufactured chemically pure glycerine by distillation and then actively promoted his new by-product. Previously, even glycerine sold at a high price was so impure as to be comparatively useless for most purposes.[3] By 1870, it was being used as a treatment for burns and skin disease, as a food preservative, an additive to paints, a photographic emulsion, a suspension for vaccines, and as a base for soaps – which Price's started to manufacture at Battersea in 1856.

George Wilson was elected a Fellow of The Royal Society for his pioneering development of glycerine. The Wilsons "applied glycerine with great success to the preservation of vegetable and animal substances. Another useful employment of glycerine is its substitution for water in gasometers, where the evaporation of the latter is a source of serious loss. Its addition to a soap solution increases the facility of forming soap bubbles to an extraordinary degree."[4]

Another by-product, a liquid fat called oleine, could be used as a light lubricating oil and was successfully marketed to woollen and cotton manufacturers as a "cloth oil" for mechanical looms where it quickly replaced olive oil. This was the first of a whole new range of lubricating oils.[5]

George Cayley 1773-1857 was known as the "Father of Aviation" and he succeeded in launching a manned glider in 1849, being the first heavier-than-air manned aircraft that made a controlled flight – or *potentially* controlled flight as the "pilot", who was a coachman in the employ of Cayley, was scared witless and probably wouldn't have been controlling the aircraft in the way that Cayley himself would have preferred.

Cayley is one of the most significant people in the history of aeronautics. "His most important discoveries included the advantages of streamlining, the means of obtaining longitudinal and lateral stability, elements of wing design, thoughts on biplane and multiplane wings, and the use of rudders and elevators for control."[1] His studies in the principles of lift, drag and thrust founded the science of aerodynamics from which he discovered stabilising flying craft required both vertical and horizontal tail rudders, that concave wings produced more lift than flat surfaces, and that swept-back wings provided greater stability.[2]

"Many consider him the first true scientific aerial researcher and the first person to understand the underlying principles and forces of flight. He built his first aerial device in 1796, a model helicopter with contra-rotating propellers. He also defined the four forces that act on any airborne vehicle: lift, thrust, drag, and gravity. For controlled flight to be possible, he reasoned, humans would need 'to make a surface support a given weight by the application of power to the resistance of the air.' In 1804, he constructed a model with a kite-like wing, adjustable cruciform tail surfaces, and a balancing weight that could be moved back and forth along the fuselage to vary the centre of gravity. The following year Cayley discovered that dihedral wings [i.e. wings set lower at their centre and higher at their outer ends] improved lateral stability. He continued his research using models and by 1807 had come to understand that a curved lifting surface would generate more lift than a flat surface of equal area. By 1810 Cayley had published his now-classic three-part treatise *On Aerial Navigation* which stated that lift, propulsion and control were the three requisite elements to successful flight, apparently the first person to so realise and so state. It is at once the first and the greatest classic of aviation history, and laid the foundations of the science of aerodynamics."[3]

By 1816, Cayley had turned his attention to lighter-than-air machines and designed a streamlined airship with a semi-rigid structure. He also suggested using separate gas bags to limit an airship's loss of gas due to damage. In 1837, Cayley designed a streamlined airship to be powered by a steam engine. In 1849, he built a large gliding machine, along the lines of his 1799 design, and tested the device with a 10-year-old boy aboard. The gliding machine carried the boy aloft on at least one short flight. Soon thereafter, in 1853, Cayley built an even larger gliding machine and had his coachman (possibly John Appleby) aboard when he tested the device that same year. His triplane glider carried his coachman 275 m across Brompton Dale in the north of England before crashing (Orville Wright's first flight in 1903 was 36.5 m). It was the first recorded flight by an adult in an aircraft.[4] (The coachman's thoughts are not recorded but could perhaps be deduced from his reaction immediately after the flight – he quit!) Cayley invented the wire spokewheel now mostly found in bicycles and motorbikes but originally made for the aircraft undercarriage. He also suggested using light tubular beam construction for aircraft, based on the structure and lightness of bamboo, to facilitate flight.

Although Cayley is seen as, perhaps, the single most important aerial researcher and theoretician of his time[5], he was innovative in many other areas. "A man of many talents, Cayley also invented a new type of telescope, artificial limbs and other medical equipment, streamlined artillery shells, railway safety devices, and a caterpillar tractor."[6] His caterpillar track, which he called the Universal Railway, was designed "to facilitate transport over rough ground, and [he] also designed artificial limbs for those who had suffered amputation. He made several proposals for improving the safety of railway travel;"[7] He designed the first seat belt – although it was used in his glider trials rather than in automobiles – and, in 1838, made the first workable open-cycle furnace gas engine (hot air engine) that could power a road vehicle. The caterpillar track had been envisaged earlier by Richard Lovell Edgeworth, but he never actually got around to having a successful one built, just as he had recommended safety curtains for theatres to reduce the risk of fire. In 1794, the Drury Lane Theatre in London introduced the first iron safety curtain, which is sometimes attributed to Cayley. "That the construction of theatres is a matter of public concern has already been very justly observed by Mr Edgeworth, in his paper on this subject, where too the use of iron and incombustible materials is strongly inculcated. Sir George Cayley likewise, in his paper, recommends the use of iron, but not to the same extent."[8]

Cayley designed artificial hands, such as the one that he made in 1847, which is described as follows: "there is a case or sheath, into which the stump of the arm is introduced. A spiral spring is fixed at one end to this sheath, and at the other to a bent lever; while the middle of the lever is connected with the mechanism of rods which move the artificial thumb and fingers. In this arrangement, the wearer uses his sound hand to work his artificial hand. He presses a little button which is connected with the bent lever; by pressing this towards the wrist, the fingers and thumb open to receive any object they may be intended to grasp; and when this pressure from the other hand is taken off, the grasp takes effect, without further effort, till released by a contrary movement. The mechanism is very simple, and is attached wholly to the lower arm, near the stump. But as the sound hand must be taken from anything else it has to perform, at the time the artificial hand is thus put to work; and as it may on other accounts be inconvenient to work the apparatus in this way, Sir George invented a very ingenious means of working the hand by the movement of the upper arm or shoulder-joint."[9]

Cayley also "became a co-founder of the British Association for the Advancement of Science (1831); was elected Whig M.P. for Scarborough (1832); made a speech on land drainage (on which he was a leading authority) to the Institution of Civil Engineers in London (1838); founded the Regent Street Polytechnic Institution (1839) which became the 'Polytechnic' of today [it is now the University of Westminster]; published papers on optics, and on railway safety devices – the first of several (1840); and wrote one of the most moving human appeals of the time, supported by cash from his pocket, for the relief of the widespread industrial distress in Yorkshire (1842)."[10]

Walter Ritchie 1773-1849 took James Paterson's fishing net design in 1835 and modified it to make an ordinary hank-knot on the nets. From this time, it became a commercially viable machine, although it is not clear if this was as a result of Ritchie's patented modification or some other reason. Further improvements were made in Britain and in France, where Onesiphore Pecqueur patented a different method in 1840.

Musselburgh, where both Paterson and Ritchie lived, became the location for the world's first large-scale mechanised production of fishing nets, and the world's largest manufacturer for many decades. The largest net manufacturer was J & W Stuart, with over 800 employees, including workers in cotton processing and rope-making, and the company had sales and repair outposts in Europe, North America and as far away as Australia. Such was the dominance of Scotland in world production that the generic name for machine-made fishing nets was Scotch weave.[1]

Thomas Brunton 1774-1833 invented the broad inserted stud marine chain cable in 1813 to replace cables made from hemp. The studs prevented the cable from kinking and Brunton's invention was in use for more than a century in navies around the world. "He patented this invention as number 3,671 on 26 March 1813 and, in association with his brother William, set up a factory in Stepney where he produced this patent chain cable. Brunton received considerable support from ship owners in England and from the French government, for its navy. This undoubtedly also helped him to get orders for cables for French merchant vessels."[1] Brunton, in co-operation with Samuel Brown (1776-1852), set up machinery at Millwall in London to test these chains for which Brunton had designed the first ever hydraulic machine in 1813. Thomas Telford used this machine to test the chains used in the Menai Straits Bridge in 1826. Brown made a mechanical machine the following year. Brunton also patented an improved ship's anchor on 12 February 1822.

Thomas Burnett 1774-1824 worked on the Lachine Canal to bypass the Lachine Rapids, linking Lake St Louis to Montreal. Over 13 km in length, it had seven stone locks and was much larger than the traditional English canals on which Burnett had been trained. Due to his death in 1824, the canal was completed the following year by his son, John Burnett who later designed the Rideau Canal.[1] The Lachine Canal, at its peak, had more than 15,000 vessels pass through annually. The impact of the Lachine Canal on Montreal during the mid to late 19th century can be seen through the emergence of new working-class neighbourhoods such as Griffintown, St Henri, and Pointe St Charles.

Half a century after Burnett's death, the canal was widened further to cope with the increasing size of ships, allowing for a significant increase in maritime traffic. The adjoining areas also became more industrialised and urbanised. Nearly 600 industrial firms were established in the Lachine Canal corridor between 1840 and 1950, employing nearly a quarter of all the artisans and factory workers of Montreal's manufacturing sector. In 1959, following the opening of the present-day Saint Lawrence Seaway, the authorities gradually abandoned the Lachine Canal and the other Saint Lawrence canals. In 1924, it was recognised for its national significance and was declared a National Historic Site of Canada in 1996 because of its value as a visible and tangible testament to the industrial history of Canada.[2]

David Gordon 1774-1829 invented the portable gas bottle for which he took out a patent at Clerkenwell, London in 1819. William Murdock had previously stored gas in animal bladders and even tin containers, but Gordon's copper container was the true ancestor of the gas bottle as we know it. He established a company to operate mail coaches using steam or vacuum power, or pneumatic engines, with his "portable gas". Gordon "proposed to render gas portable by condensing a number of atmospheres in strong metallic vessels. So long as no gas but that from coal could be obtained the method promised but little success. On the introduction of oil gas however, the plan was resumed and carried into successful operation. By this method ships, steamboats, railroad and other carriages may be furnished with the beautiful and safe light given by oil gas; and if it was compelled to give way before the immense capital vested in coal gas manufactures in the British capital, there is little doubt that it might be applied to advantage in a new and open field; particularly in countries where coal bears as high a price as it does in most of our Atlantic cities."[1]

Neil Snodgrass 1774-1818 designed, in 1797, a scutching machine (called a picker in America) which opened and cleaned cotton.[1] Snodgrass also installed the first practical steam heating system. This was at a Dornoch textile factory in 1799 although an earlier, but impractical heating system, based on James Watt's steam heating method, was patented for use in buildings by Englishman John Hoyle of Halifax in 1791, and in Manchester, George Augustus Lee installed a heating system in the same year as Snodgrass, both unaware of each other's work. "It is cited that the first factory in which steam was used for heating was a cotton mill belonging to a Mr Neil Snodgrass, in which a steam heating system was installed in 1799. This was doubtless about the first instance of the employment of steam primarily and systematically for the purpose of heating."[2]

His scutching machine, according to James Montgomery's *The Theory and Practice of Cotton Spinning* (1836) had by 1836, "become so popular, as to be generally used in most of the spinning factories of this country [UK]."

Robert Thom 1774-1847 made sand-filtered water available to all of Paisley and Glasgow. In 1804, the world's first municipal water treatment plant, designed by Robert Thom, was built in Scotland. The water treatment was based on slow sand filtration, and the water produced was distributed by horse and cart. Some three years later, the first water pipes were installed. The suggestion was made that every person should have access to safe drinking water, but it would take somewhat longer before this was actually brought to practice in most countries.[1] It was Thom's "success in designing a municipal water treatment plant, added to the scientific evidence that had proven decreases in waterborne diseases as a result of filtered water, which led to the passage of the *Metropolis Water Act* of 1852. This law, the first of its kind, required that all water supplied to London be treated by slow sand filtration. Thom provided a revolutionary water filtration design that would change the face of water treatment history."[2]

Paris introduced water filtration in 1806, but this was not a system that connected the fresh water to homes. In 1807, Thom had water piped to houses in Glasgow, which became the first major urban area in the world to have filtered water piped into homes. In 1997, *Life* magazine's special double edition listed 100 events that changed the world in the last one thousand years. Event No. 46 was headed "1829 Water Purification" and said, "But before 1829, when the Chelsea Water Works of London installed its landmark slow sand filter on the Thames River, no one had effectively cleaned it."[3]

This was a tribute to the pioneering concept of filtration of river water through sand for public supply, by the London-born water engineer James Simpson. His reasoning was that water that had percolated underground became clear and sparkling when taken from wells, or emerging from springs. Thom's filters were cleaned by backwash, while Simpson's required scraping. The Simpson design eventually became the English model throughout the world.[4]

In 1827, Thom created a reservoir based on Shaw's Water, now Loch Thom, almost 2½ km in length, to provide fresh water for Greenock's domestic and industrial use via his 9½ km long aqueduct known as The Cut. Thom built Shaw's Waterwheel at Greenock in 1841. It weighed 163 tonnes, was over 21 m in diameter, and could generate 200 horsepower. It was second only in size to Robert Casement's waterwheel at Laxey on the Isle of Man, which was the world's largest.[5]

In 1835, Thom provided a new water supply to a rapidly expanding Paisley from the Harelaw reservoir for which he patented self-acting compensating sluices to ensure a uniform delivery of water which was then purified using Thom's filtration system. His development of the slow sand filter – a simple, cheap, electricity and chemical-free device that could remove up to 99% of bacteria from water – was a notable achievement in the advance of hygiene and health. The filter works by making use of a naturally occurring barrier of fungi, bacteria and protozoa to collect any impurities in the water. This was such a success that other cities soon followed suit and, after dirty water supplies were finally identified as the principal means by which diseases such as cholera and typhoid spread, municipal water filtration was finally made obligatory across Britain in 1852. Today, over 200 years since Thom's innovation, slow sand filters are still used as an effective method of providing clean water. A significant proportion of the London metropolis is served by a filter largely based on Thom's principles. Furthermore, the relative simplicity of its design, its minimal environmental impact and low cost of installation made the device ideal for poorer communities.[6]

Alexander Adie 1775-1858 was a scientific instrument maker who designed a marine barometer that he called the sympiesometer or the Tendency Barometer. It was a compact and lightweight barometer that was widely used on ships in the 19th century. It was similar to the common weather glass but Adie's use of highly compressible hydrogen in a long, thin tube allowed much more accurate measurements, as changes in pressure resulted in much more movement of the liquid. It was particularly useful as a marine barometer, as its sensitivity provided early warning of weather changes at sea, and its construction meant that it was less likely to break in storms.[1]

Unlike Evangelista Torricelli's original barometer, it was more portable, didn't use mercury, and had a scale 2½ times larger. Its ability to handle adverse weather conditions and extreme temperature gave it a popularity which lasted from 1820 to 1870, when it was replaced by the aneroid barometer, which handled rough conditions even better but was less accurate than the sympiesometer. During that half century, more than 2,500 were made and it was used in Antarctic expeditions of 1902-1904 for weather forecasting, as well as on the famous Beagle voyage of Charles Darwin. Adie also made a polarising microscope.

Image 17 – Sympiesometer

When the fluid levels are the same, the weather is changing. When the red fluid level is below the blue fluid level, the weather is fair (high pressure pushes the red fluid down in the tube). When the red fluid level is above the blue, stormy weather is predicted (low pressure allows the red fluid to move up the tube). By measuring the amount of difference between the red and blue fluids on the tendency dial, you get the local weather forecast for the next 12-24 hours.

Thomas Cochrane 1775-1860 was a seaman extraordinaire, inventor, politician and 10th Lord Dundonald. He patented the tunnelling shield which provided temporary support for the Thames Tunnel during excavation and prior to lining it with concrete. The Thames Tunnel, between Rotherhithe and Wapping, was the first tunnel known to have been successfully constructed underneath a navigable river. It was 11 m wide, 6 m high, 396 m long and 23 m below the water of the Thames. It was built by French-born Marc Isambard Brunel and his English-born son Isambard Kingdom Brunel. In 1818, Cochrane and Marc Brunel patented the tunnelling shield to enable excavation through soft or unstable soil. The Brunels started work on the tunnel in 1825 and it was opened in 1843.

Cochrane was responsible for the commission of the PS *Rising Star*, a 388-tonne paddle steamer (hence PS) warship, in 1821-1822. It was the first British steam warship to cross the Atlantic from east to west.

He was also the first to suggest chemical warfare in modern times (the Byzantines had used Greek fire, but this acted much like a flame thrower). "The earliest suggestion for chemical warfare came from the British naval officer Thomas Cochrane in 1811. Cochrane worked out a plan to force Napoleon's troops from Toulon, Flushing, and other ports by means of sulphur dioxide and sent the plan to the Prince Regent in 1812. He suggested that the admiralty load several vessels with alternate layers of sulphur and coal, convoy the ships to the enemy harbours, wait until the wind was blowing in the direction of the French fortifications, then anchor the ships close to shore and set them on fire. When the sulphur dioxide gas had driven the French troops off, the British would send troops ashore to take over the abandoned positions."[1] The British Admiralty rejected Cochrane's plan. He tried several more times to get his idea adopted and, at his last attempt during the Crimean War, he also proposed to use a smoke screen to protect his ships carrying the sulphur. This appears to be the first time that a smoke screen was suggested, although it probably wouldn't have been noticed in battlefields (except at the start of battle) at the time as cannon created great amounts of smoke until smokeless cordite was used to replace gunpowder. Note: One of the earliest documented uses of smoke screen in combat was the burning of green vegetation by the Romans and later the burning of peat moss by the Vikings, but these were opportunistic actions rather than a technique that could be used as part of a planned strategy well in advance of the conflict occurring.

Image 18 – Diagram of the tunnelling shield used to construct the Thames Tunnel

Cochrane also patented compressed-air caissons for constructing foundations on marshy ground. "The idea was quite simple really. An air lock that enabled workers to get in and out of a sealed chamber filled with compressed air had been devised as early as 1831 by Lord Thomas Cochrane, the controversial British admiral.[2] The essence of the system was the pumping of compressed air into a working-chamber at the bottom of a caisson, the pressure being raised to correspond with that of the water outside as the cutting-edge of iron or steel reached greater depths. The workers themselves, and the spoil that they were removing from the river bed, were brought out through an air-lock in the roof of the working chamber."[3] These caissons were important in building many structures, particularly bridges, such as the brilliant engineering construction of the Brooklyn Bridge by German-born John Augustus Roebling and his American-born son Washington Roebling, as well as the pioneering 1852 circular cross-section tubular steel girder bridge at Chepstow on the Anglo-Welsh border, built by Isambard Kingdom Brunel.

Cochrane was one of the most remarkable of all naval sea captains. He was the inspiration for both C.S. Forester's *Horatio Hornblower* and Patrick O'Brian's *Jack Aubrey* novels. (The 2003 film: *Master and Commander: The Far Side of the World* is based on O'Brian's novels).[4]

In August 1806, in command of HMS *Impererieuse*, he terrorised the French coast during the war against Napoleon, and earned the nickname "Sea Wolf" from the enemy. Becoming a master of coastal warfare, Cochrane frequently led cutting-out missions to seize enemy ships and captured French coastal installations. In 1808, his men occupied the fortress of Mongat in Spain which delayed the advance of General Guillaume Duhesme's army for a month.

He was named vice admiral and commander-in-chief upon arriving in Chile in November 1818. Immediately restructuring the fleet along British lines, Cochrane commanded from the frigate *O'Higgins*. Quickly showing the daring that had made him famous in Europe, Cochrane raided the coast of Peru and captured the town of Valdivia in February 1820. After convoying General Jose de San Martin's army to Peru, Cochrane blockaded the coast and later cut out the Spanish frigate *Esmeralda*. With Peruvian independence secured, Cochrane soon fell out with his superiors over monetary compensation and claims that he was treated with contempt.

Departing Chile, he was given command of the Brazilian Navy in 1823. Conducting a successful campaign against the Portuguese, he was made Marquis of Maranhão by Emperor Pedro I. After putting down a rebellion the following year, he made claims that a large amount of prize money was owed to him and the fleet. When this was not forthcoming, he and his men seized the public funds in São Luís do Maranhão and looted the ships in the harbour before leaving for Britain. Reaching Europe, he briefly led Greek naval forces in 1827-1828 during their struggle for independence from the Ottoman Empire.[5]

Samuel Brown 1776-1852 built the first vehicular suspension bridge in Britain – the Union Bridge over the River Tweed between Scotland and England. This bridge, built in 1820, was the world's longest wrought-iron suspension bridge at 137 m. He designed the third, and most famous, pleasure pier in Britain at Brighton in 1823. Of the two pleasure piers that preceded Brighton, Ryde Pier (1814) and Leith Trinity Chain Pier (1821), Brown built the latter. Originally known as The Royal Suspension Chain Pier, Brighton Pier was primarily intended as a landing stage for packet boats to Dieppe, but it also featured a small number of attractions including a camera obscura, a bandstand, shower baths and kiosks. An esplanade with an entrance toll-booth controlled access to the pier.

Brown introduced wrought-iron chain cables to the Royal Navy and, in 1808, he took out patents for twisted open chain links, joining shackles and swivels. His shackle and swivel designs were scarcely improved on for the next 100 years. The conversion from hemp to chain now proceeded quickly. His Newbridge Chain Works became the sole supplier to the Royal Navy for anchor chains. In 1816, Samuel Brown's 2¼ inch (5.7 cm) iron stud link chains were installed on the USS *Constitution* and the USS *Guerriere* and were considered a great success. In the same year, the Royal Navy standardised on iron chain instead of hemp for all new vessels of war. Also in 1816, Walker of Philadelphia wrought the first American-made stud link anchor chains for the US Navy.[1]

Image 19 – Isambard Kingdom Brunel in front of the iron stud link chains made at Brown's Pontypridd Ironworks for the SS *Great Eastern* in 1857. Photo by Robert Howlett (1831-1858)

In 1823, Brown patented the first internal combustion engine to be applied industrially for which he has been called the "Father of the Gas Engine". "The commercial development of gas engines began in 1823 based on Samuel Brown's idea about vacuum and atmospheric pressure."[2] He designed another engine in 1826 that used hydrogen and oxygen. Similar to a Newcomen steam engine, it had separate combustion and working cylinders, but water was circulated around the cylinder using a pump, and this water was cooled by contact with the outside air much like a modern water-cooled engine. This massive engine had a displacement of 8,800 cc. Another source states the three cylinders had a bore of 12 inches (30.5 cm) and a stroke of 24 inches (61 cm), but delivered only 4 hp. He mounted this on a four-wheeled vehicle and, in front of a small crowd, drove it up Shooter's Hill in Greenwich on the morning of 27 May 1826.[3]

James Jardine 1776-1858 was the first to determine, by observations of the tides over a great extent of coast, the mean level of the sea and to show the symmetry of the undisturbed tidal wave above and below that level and the effect of a river current in disturbing that symmetry. These were deemed to be "discoveries of high importance, both scientific and practical".[1] Jardine was also the first to establish a test to determine "where a river ends and a firth [estuary] begins".[2] Jardine surveyed the route for the train line between Glasgow and Edinburgh and, with Thomas Telford, provided Edinburgh's water supply.

William Stodart 1776-1831, son of Robert, took out a patent for his "upright grand pianoforte of the form of a bookcase" on 29 January 1795. He placed the action behind the soundboard and thus the strings were struck from behind.[1] "His instruments were so famous that no less a luminary than Josef Haydn visited the workshop and wrote his three last 'English' fortepiano sonatas, dedicated to the virtuosa Teresa Jansen-Bartolozzi."[2]

William Brunton 1777-1851 designed a calciner that greatly aided the tin industry. Tin mining was a major industry in Cornwall and tin miners, from the time of King John (1199-1216), were legally excused from normal tax and military service, and the tin-mining community was governed by the Stannary Parliament. Tin ores often have sulphur and arsenic impurities and the traditional manner of removing them was by oxidisation through burning, with the toxic fumes going into the atmosphere. "By the 1860s a more sophisticated form of burning house, the Brunton Calciner, became common. It had an enclosed revolving hearth, connected to a complex system of flues in which the arsenious oxide was trapped as a soot, later to be dug out and sold. A tall stack, designed to assist the draught as well as to disperse the sulphur fumes, marked the end of the flue. Vertical metal straps on the outside of the Calciner helped the building to withstand the immense heat of the furnace."[1] This calciner was patented on 21 February 1828 by Brunton and, unlike other calciners, it operated on a continuous basis. The calciner both purified the tin and provided a means of producing white arsenic commercially by roasting arsenical pyrites. The calciners were also used in copper production by reducing copper sulphides to copper oxides.

On 22 May 1813, Brunton patented a four-wheel steam locomotive which used levers to impel two walking feet, as he didn't think locomotives would adhere well to rails when on a steep gradient. At 4½ tonnes, Brunton's *Mechanical Traveller* handled a gradient of 1:36 at 6½ km/h and pulled twelve wagons each weighing 2¼ tonnes (total 27 tonnes) over 3.2 km. The boiler was made longer and the locomotive altered with the intention of pulling 24 wagons. While on trial, the new boiler exploded on 31 July 1815 at Philadelphia in County Durham, killing 16 people in the world's first railway disaster and first boiler explosion (the death toll varies with different sources).[2] Brunton wasn't to blame as the driver had weighted down the safety valve.

Brunton "went on to make some of the original steamship engines which were used in vessels on the Humber and the Trent. He also constructed the steam engine which powered the first Liverpool ferry. Ten years later, whilst a partner in the Eagle Foundry, Birmingham, he designed and constructed a marine engine for the *Sir Francis Drake*, which vessel he fitted at Plymouth".[3] Brunton also made engines for other ferries operating on the Mersey, Humber and Trent, and patented a method of making cast-iron pipes in a rotating mould, only to find a similar patent had earlier been granted for casting terracotta pipes. In 1835, Brunton joined the Cwm Avon tin works as a partner in the Port Talbot firm of Vigurs & Co. He worked on improvements to air ventilation in the mines, building rolling mills and copper furnaces, and making improvements to iron foundry.

William Spence 1777-1815 wrote on "logarithmic transcendents" giving the first detailed account of polylogarithms and related functions. *A theory of algebraic equation*s was published just after his early death; and further essays, edited by John Herschel, were published posthumously. The most substantial of these concern an extension of his work on "logarithmic transcendents", and the general solution of linear differential and difference equations. But awareness of Spence's works was long delayed by their supposed unavailability.[1] Spence had worked in a direction which was to dominate the scene of British mathematics in the first half of the nineteenth century.[2]

James Pillans 1778-1864 invented the blackboard, now ubiquitous in school classrooms, colleges and universities around the world. The blackboard revolutionised education. In our present age of continually evolving desktop, laptop and palm computers, photocopy equipment, PowerPoint presentations, video displays, whiteboards, interactive whiteboards, and internet access, it is startling to realise that the "technology" to first influence education was the invention of the blackboard (aka chalkboard). Blackboards soon became equally important in business organisations, as well as in the fields of maths and science, long before the materials were even invented from which whiteboards could be manufactured. Thanks to the blackboard, not only were large numbers of people in the same room able to be presented with the same material all at once, but these boards also became a method of working out long strings of problems and "brain storming" new concepts among several people at once.[1]

Few people actually realise that the classroom blackboard is one of the most revolutionary educational tools ever invented. And it may be hard to fathom that blackboards as we know them today were unknown until relatively recent times. The invention of the blackboard had an enormous impact on classroom efficiency. Due to its simplicity, effectiveness, economy and ease of use, the simple blackboard, and its cousin the whiteboard, have substantial advantages over any number of more-complex modern technologies. It is unlikely they will ever become obsolete.

At the end of the 18th century, students in Europe and America were still using individual slates made of actual slate or pieces of wood coated with paint and grit and framed with wood. Paper and ink were expensive, but slate and wood were plentiful and cheap, making them the economical option. Unfortunately, they were also highly inefficient. Teachers had no way to present a lesson or a problem to the class as a whole; instead they had to go to each individual student and write a problem or assignment on each one's slate.

"In 1801, the rather obvious solution to the problem made its debut. James Pillans, headmaster and geography teacher at the Old High School in Edinburgh, Scotland, is credited with inventing the first modern blackboard when he hung a large piece of slate on the classroom wall".[2] From our contemporary vantage point, the now common blackboard may not seem like a noteworthy technological innovation. Yet, the blackboard introduced dramatic changes that rippled through society, altering the fundamental nature of education. The technological shift from individual slates to a wall-mounted chalkboard revolutionised education, but not without considerable debate among educators.

Some dismissed it as a fleeting fad; others held that it would completely transform education. Pessimists predicted that the innovation would soon fail because teachers were not skilled enough in its use and pragmatists perceived the economic benefits that would accrue when teachers instructed groups of students rather than painstakingly repeating lessons on each student's individual slate.[3]

Pillans also invented coloured chalk as an aid to teaching geography and to make it more interesting to his students. He made these by "grinding up chalk, adding dye, and binding the powder with porridge."[4]

Pillans encountered serious disciplinary problems at the Old High School in Edinburgh when he first faced his class of 144 boys, predisposed to defiance by their role in opposing his election. In his first year, he frequently resorted to corporal punishment as a means of keeping order. A pupil in this period remembered an occasion when Pillans beat one of the biggest boys "in spite of his most piteous deprecations", employing a strong janitor to hold him down. Perhaps because of such experiences, Pillans came to reject corporal punishment as degrading to the boy who suffered it and the master who inflicted it alike, and to consider its use evidence of the master's failure to employ effective discipline. After his first year, he was able to discontinue the practice altogether, an innovation both by Scottish standards and by those of his preceptors at Eton.[5]

Pillans was an advocate of compulsory education, and in 1834 he gave evidence to a House of Commons committee on education. His publications include *Letters on the principles of elementary teaching* (1827), *Outlines of geography* (1847), *The rationale of discipline* (1852), and *Contributions to the cause of education* (1856).[6]

Francis Watt 1778-1823 invented the jib-crane to assist in the building of the Bell Rock Lighthouse, built 1807-1811 and described as "one of the finest lighthouses ever built."[1] For the same task he also invented the world's first iron counter-balance tower crane used for erecting the upper part of the lighthouse above the range of the jib-cranes. The Bell Rock Lighthouse was included as one of the *Seven Wonders of the Industrial World*, a BBC documentary made in 2003, as it was constructed on a rock which "at high water during spring tides, the part of the rock on which the lighthouse is built, is on average about 12 feet (3.65 m) below water level; and at low water of spring tides, where the lighthouse is built, the rock is about 4 feet (1.22 m) above sea level. Higher parts of the rock may be two to three feet higher above that again. At low water during neap tides hardly any part of the rock is visible."[2]

Two Scots were in charge of its construction – John Rennie (1781-1821) as Chief Engineer and Robert Stevenson (1772-1850) as Resident Engineer. "To achieve construction at this hazardous location in four summer working seasons a narrow-gauge cast iron railway 'about 800 ft [243.8 m] long altogether' was built connecting the site of the lighthouse with wharves at the rock edge. This enabled dressed stones from Arbroath Work-yard weighing up to 1½ tons [1.36 tonnes] to be transported across the rugged rock surface." The railway was built by Watt.

Sometime in 1810, Watt built his "remarkable jib-crane with its optional mechanical advantage of either 20:1 or 98:1. Completion of this reach 'had involved an immense effort in boring the rock, inserting iron-batts and operations, accessible only at the lowest tides.'"[3]

Watt's jib-crane "possesses many advantages over those [cranes] commonly in use, from the complete command it has over every inch of space within the range of the jib. The common building crane, with a fixed jib and moveable track, commands, indeed, the same angular range; but then the truck cannot, without an additional power, be removed farther from the shaft, after the crane is loaded, and thus its operation is confined. The common crane is also much less portable, and cannot be moved even for the shortest distance, without being taken down – an operation which costs a good deal of time and labour. Indeed, in as far as portability, power, and the complete command of a given space are concerned, this crane is decidedly superior to every other."[4]

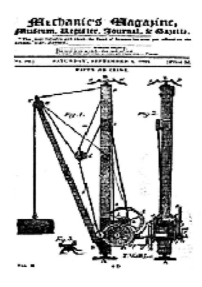

Image 20 – Francis Watt's Jib-Crane
Mechanic's Magazine 4 September 1824

Watt also invented the iron balance crane (forerunner of the modern tower crane).[5] The balance and movable jib-cranes were for the first time used at the Bell Rock. The latter is now in universal use. Ball-bearings were also introduced into the cranes at the Bell Rock for the first time.[6]

George Forrester c1780-after 1841 built, for the Dublin & Kingstown Railway and the Liverpool & Manchester Railway, the first locomotives to have outside horizontal cylinders and the first to have four fixed eccentrics to operate the valves, instead of two loose eccentrics. Two locomotives, *Victoria* and *Comet*, built by Forrester in 1835 for the Dublin & Kingstown Railway, were the first tank locomotives to run regularly on a public railway, and two more supplied in 1836 to the London & Greenwich Railway were the first such locomotives in England.[1] "Forrester's ideas inspired the choice of engines for the Grand Junction Railway … We have got rid of a very great deal of complexity in the machinery itself, and the complexity which remains is on the outside of the engine and not under the boiler."[2]

Charles William Pasley 1780-1861 developed an optical telegraph. He was an engineer in the Royal Artillery who served in a number of actions during the French Revolutionary/ Napoleonic

War. He established a school at his own expense to improve the knowledge of non-commissioned officers on fortifications and fieldworks. The government made this a permanent school, initially known as the Royal Engineer Establishment but changed in 1868 to the School of Military Engineering and then to the Royal School of Military Engineering in 1962. It was given the royal warrant on 23 April 1812 and established at Chatham with Pasley as director, a post he held for 29 years, followed by 16 years as public examiner at the Addiscombe military college. Under Pasley, the Royal Engineer Establishment became the leading scientific military school in Europe.

Pasley wrote the defining text on the role of the post-American Revolution British Empire: *An Essay on the Military Policy and Institutions of the British Empire*, published in 1810. This text changed how Britons thought their empire should relate to the rest of the world. He warned that Britain could not keep its Empire by its "splendid isolation". Britain would need military power to fight for and expand its empire. By using its colonies as a resource for soldiers and sailors. the British Empire grew by an average of 100,000 square miles (260,000km^2) per year between the Battle of Waterloo and the American Civil War. Pasley had created modern geopolitics.[1]

He developed a cement in 1836 that was good by contemporary standards and his 1838 *Observations on Limes, Calcareous Cements, Mortars, Stuccos and Concrete* was the standard text on those subjects current for most of the 19th century, giving a "historical account of cementitious materials unequalled in the nineteenth century".[2] He was commissioned to remove a number of wrecked ships from the Thames, Spithead and St Helens.

In 1804, he designed his Universal Telegraph that was much simpler than earlier telegraphs as it was meant for civilian as well as military use. It used a short arm at right angles to the upright as a reference position and it was less likely to be misinterpreted than other extant telegraphs.

Pasley also used oil lamps on the arms, permitting his telegraph to be used in darkness and light fog, which is probably the first time that lights were successfully used on a telegraph. In Pasley's *Observations on Nocturnal Signals in General* he states that "Many attempts have been made from time to time to use coloured lights for night signals, all of which have failed, for the colour of a luminous point or line cannot be distinguished at any distance."[3]

Pasley was Inspector General of Railways from 1841 to 1846 and he suggested to Charles Hutton Gregory that the Universal Telegraph should be used to inform locomotive drivers on what action they should take on approach, rather than the less reliable and less visible method of using a flag, especially as Pasley's telegraph could be seen at a distance. Gregory followed up on the suggestion, making some modifications to use lights for signalling in darkness or poor light and the system spread world-wide.

David Brewster 1781-1868 invented the kaleidoscope. He was a prodigious writer who published over 2,000 scientific papers and undertook a biography of Sir Isaac Newton. He was the instigator of the British Association for the Advancement of Science as well as being one of the few who created its constitution. He helped establish, in 1819, the *Edinburgh Philosophical Journal* with Robert Jameson, and in 1824 he founded the *Edinburgh Journal of Science*. Like Robert Blair, he was interested in lens and he discovered what is now termed Brewster's angle, or the polarisation angle, which concerns the relationship of light waves and is used to determine the refractive index of an object. Normal light is a multitude of light waves vibrating in all directions, but when light passes through or is reflected by an object, the light waves tend to vibrate in a single direction – it has been polarised. Brewster discovered how to calculate the angle at which light must strike a substance for maximum polarisation. Brewster's angle is used to adjust radio signals, make microscopes for studying molecular structures, and it is fundamental to the progress of laser technology, fibre optics, meteorology and cosmology.

Brewster and Augustin Jean Fresnel, a brilliant French physicist, worked separately on dioptric lens, also called Fresnel or polyzonal lens, although Brewster had described and constructed this lens in 1812, two years before Fresnel had even started to study lens. It was in 1811, while writing an article on Burning Instruments, Brewster investigated Buffon's Needle theory (considered to be the first problem in geometric probability). Brewster did not consider Buffon's proposal practical. However, it sparked an idea that produced awesome scientific results. In the course of his investigation Brewster constructed a lens of great diameter out of one piece of glass by cutting out the central parts in successive ridges like stair steps. Thus was born an apparatus of then-unequalled power – the polyzonal lens – a lens constructed by building it on several circular segments. This useful discovery, which created light-stabs of brilliance that could pierce far into the night, was later perfected and named after Fresnel, and resulted in the lighthouse as we know it today.[1]

Brewster was instrumental in having these lens, with their superior light reflection, installed in British lighthouses, having first suggested their use in 1820, two years before Fresnel, although Fresnel was first to have them installed in (French) lighthouses. These lens prompted taller lighthouses to be built as the light could now be shone much further than previously (over 22 km) with a smaller consumption of energy resulting in greatly improved coastal navigation.

In 1831, Brewster noted in his *Treatise On Optics* that images could be formed using a film of skimmed milk that had dried on a plate of glass. He independently invented the stereoscope, priority for which went to Charles Wheatstone of telegraph fame, whose device was called the Reflecting Mirror Stereoscope used for viewing drawings in 3D. The first patented stereo viewer was Wheatstone's reflecting stereoscope in 1838. The device was a bulky and complicated contraption that utilised a system of mirrors to view a series of pairs of crude drawings. In 1844, a technique for taking stereoscopic photographs was demonstrated in Germany, and a much smaller and simpler viewer that utilised prismatic lenses was developed in Scotland by Brewster.[2] The latter's adaptations to the stereoscope, replacing Wheatstone's mirrors with lenses, turned it into the lenticular stereoscope – the world's first portable, 3D viewing device. Like a pair of binoculars, these could be easily wielded by viewers to see eye-popping 3D images.[3]

In 1849, Brewster invented the two-lensed binocular camera from which stereoscopic photographs developed – previously such photographs had been taken using two successive exposures with a single lens. A stereoscope constructed by French optician, Jules Duboscq, but based on Brewster's design, was displayed at the 1851 Great Exhibition and within five years over half a million units had been sold. Brewster's stereoscope was ultimately developed into the View-Master, invented in 1938 by American William Gruber, with over 100 million viewers sold and over one billion reels of images.[4] The stereoscope was also the ancestor of the modern head-mounted video display devices whereby images are directly displayed before the eyes. Unlike Brewster's other famous invention, the kaleidoscope, the lenticular telescope had more than entertainment value as it was used by Ordnance Survey to make stereoscopic aerial pictures for creating highly accurate topographic maps. In 1850, Brewster followed up on his binocular camera by taking the first photograph using a pinhole camera.

Brewster was a pioneer of the study of minerals by measuring their optical properties, a method of study founded by fellow Scot, William Nicol, who used optical mineralogy to study petrified plants, whereas Brewster studied crystals in transmitted polarised light and distinguished between isotropic, uniaxial, and biaxial crystals.

Another field pioneered by Brewster is photoelasticity and the *brewster*, named for him, is used as a unit to measure the susceptibility of a material to photoelasticity, which is an experimental method to determine stress distribution in a material. Photoelasticity was developed further by Englishman Ernest George Coker and Frenchman Louis Napoleon George Filon in the early 1900s, and they are nowadays generally considered to be its main founders. Brewster was awarded the three major medals of The Royal Society – Copley (1815), Rumford (1818) and the Royal (1830). He is sometimes credited with the invention of the polarimeter, but that was created by Frenchman Francois Arago, a contemporary of Brewster.

In 1832, Brewster showed that some of the dark lines in the solar spectrum are due to absorption in the Earth's atmosphere but that most of them are intrinsic to the sun. Four years later he found that some lines varied in strength with the Earth's seasons and with the elevation of the sun. Brewster, with other scientists such as Robert Bunsen, Gustav Kirchhoff and Anders Jonas Angstrom, turned spectroscopy into a scientific discipline.[5]

Image 21 – Brewster Lenticular Stereoscope

In 1834, Brewster was the first to note the red emission of chlorophyll and "[Pierre-Joseph] Pelletier and [Joseph Bienaimé] Caventou (1818) and Govindjee [Asthana] (1995) considered it likely that this was not only the discovery of Chlorophyll fluorescence, but also of the phenomenon of reabsorption of fluorescence in thick samples."[6]

One of Brewster's most illustrious moments came in 1849. He was nominated as one of a panel of eight foreign associates to the National Institute of France. So great were Brewster's achievements in comparison to all others that, after examination, the Institute struck the names of all other candidates and Sir David Brewster stood in splendid isolation as the sole remaining candidate. His discoveries of the physical laws of metallic reflection and light absorption, the optical properties of crystals, and the law of the angle of polarisation, along with his improvement of the stereoscope and lighthouse apparatus, surpassed most scientific achievements of that era.[7]

Hamilton Fulton 1781-1834 designed the Roanoke Canal Aqueduct over Chockoyotte Creek in Halifax County, North Carolina, a 110-foot (34 m) long structure with a 30-foot (9.1 m) arch, which edifice still stands despite a century of neglect. It is on the National Register of Historic Places. The Roanoke Canal routed river vessels around the rapids, thus opening the upper reaches of the Roanoke River to commercial navigation. An even more impressive structure, designed by Fulton over the Dan River at Milton in Caswell County consisting of eight elliptical stone arches, has been lost. He recommended a network of state roads, classified, financed and maintained in the manner now current in North Carolina.[1]

John Gibb 1781-1851 initiated a system of water filtration that undoubtedly saved countless lives, although he would not have been aware of it. The quest for pure water entered a new phase when Gibb decided to supply filtered water to his bleachery at Paisley and cart it to "almost every door" in town. His is the first known filter for city-wide supply installed anywhere in the world.[1]

The claim for the first sand-filtered water system is generally given to the water supply of Paisley in 1804, although the Italian physician Lucas Antonius Portius detailed a multiple sand filtration method in his 1685 publication *Vade Mecum* (literally, "go with me") which was a 17th century ready reckoner. There is no evidence it was used in an urban situation and Portius' excellent advice was for soldiers fighting in the Austro-Turkish War rather than living in an urban environment.[2] Another pioneer thinker along the same lines was Frenchman Philippe de La Hire who, very early in the 18th century, presented a plan to the French Academy of Sciences, proposing that every household have a sand filter and rainwater cistern.[3] Nothing came of it. Thus, it was in Paisley, Scotland, that the sand-filtered water system first went into use in an urban system. In 1804, John Gibb, who owned a cotton factory with a bleachery, was having trouble getting suitably clean water supplies – for manufacturing, not drinking.

Gibb constructed a circular filter to supply his bleachery as well as private residences because the source of the town's water, the River Cart, was often fouled by mud and industrial waste. In operation from about 1804 to 1861, Gibb's filter consisted of a central well surrounded by concentric rings with walls of masonry. Water flowed from the river to a pump well, then through a "roughing filter" measuring 75' (22.8 m) long. At the end of the filter was a well with a steam engine above to lift the water up to an "air chest" located 16' (4.8 m) above the river. From the "air chest," the water flowed to a settling chamber and then through 200' (61 m) of 3" (7.62 cm) diameter pipe built of Scots fir to the filter, which was made up concentric rings. The exterior ring contained a coarse gravel filtering medium, while the middle ring contained a filtering medium consisting of fine gravel and sand. The central well held the 23½" (7 m) diameter clear water basin. A pipe extended from the clear water basin one-eighth of a mile (201 m) to a cask that could hold 480 wine gallons (2,182 litres). A cart then delivered the filtered water throughout town.[4]

He also had water piped to homes in Paisley, as well as providing water for sale by horse-drawn cart. The surplus water was sold at half a penny a gallon (3.8 litres).

"John Gibb's slow sand filter, built in 1804 in Scotland, was the first filter used for treating potable water in large quantities."[5] The method that Gibb used was the slow sand filtration technique, which is now regarded as the earliest type of municipal water filtration. In the slow sand filter, water passes first through some 90 cm of sand, then through a layer of gravel, before entering the underdrain. The sand removes particles from the water through adsorption and straining.

"Unlike other filters, slow sand filters also remove a great deal of turbidity from water using biological action. A layer of dirt, debris, and micro-organisms builds up on the top of the sand. This layer is known as schmutzdecke, which is German for 'dirty skin.' The schmutzdecke breaks down organic particles in the water biologically, and is also very effective in straining out even very small inorganic particles from water. Maintenance of a slow sand filter consists of raking the sand periodically and cleaning the filter by removing the top two inches [5 cm] of sand from the filter surface. After a few cleanings, new sand must be added to replace the removed sand. Cleaning the filter removes the schmutzdecke layer, without which the filter does not produce potable water. After a cleaning, the filter must be operated for two weeks, with the filtered water sent to waste, to allow the schmutzdecke layer to rebuild. As a result, a treatment plant must have two slow sand filters for continuous operation. Slow sand filters are very reliable filters which do not usually require coagulation/flocculation before filtration."[6]

It was not known until around the third quarter of the 19th century that disease was caused by specific microbes and the purpose of the sand filtration systems was to provide water free from turbidity, but the serendipitous outcome was that in those areas using sand filtration water-borne disease dropped dramatically. "The most convincing proof of the effectiveness of water filtration was provided in 1892 by the experience gained in two neighbouring cities, Hamburg and Altona, which drew their drinking-water from the River Elbe, the former delivering it untreated except for settlement, while the latter filtered the whole of its supply. When the river became infected from a camp of immigrants, Hamburg suffered from a cholera epidemic that infected one in thirty of its population and caused more than 7,500 deaths, while Altona escaped almost unscathed. Subsequent waterborne epidemics in many parts of the world have confirmed this experience; in every case infection has been almost entirely confined to people drinking unfiltered water."[7] The actual number of cholera infections, as distinct from deaths, is even more striking. In Hamburg, there were 19,891 cholera cases from a population of 580,000, a rate of 34.3 per 1,000, while in Altona there were 572 cases from 143,000 residents, a rate of 3.9 per 1,000.[8]

Thomas Morton 1781-1832 invented the patent slip in 1818. Whether a ship used propellers, paddlewheels, steam or sail, maintenance was essential and this was often done in a dry dock. A cheaper alternative to this was the patent slip, costing about 10% of the dry dock as it was easier to effect maintenance of ships.[1] Morton's slip had a cradle to pull a boat up an inclined slipway so that it stood clear of the water, allowing repairs to be more easily carried out. Many ships could have their required maintenance completed between tides or be inspected for insurance purposes much faster than in a dry dock.

The patent slip could even be carried on board a ship so that it could do inspections or repairs in locations where there were no fixed facilities. Unlike dry docks it could accommodate more than one vessel provided the length of the incline was sufficient, and it was easier for repairmen to access the hull on a patent slipway than in a dry dock. Boats could be hauled onto the slipway with an engine or even by manual labour, as six men could haul 90 tonnes at almost a metre per minute. In 1832, a British House of Commons Select Committee reported that it cost £170 to dry dock a ship and £3 to use the patent slip – a savings of 98% (this was for small boats).

Image 22 – Patent Slip at Arbroath

In the same year, the cost of a patent slip compared to the dry dock for larger boats of 90-725 tonnes was only 10%. By the end of 1832, Morton had 44 patent slips built in Britain with others being constructed in America, France and Russia.[2]

George Stephenson 1781-1848 "is considered to be the inventor of the first steam locomotive engine for railways. Richard Trevithick's invention is considered the first tramway locomotive; however, it was a road locomotive, designed for a road and not for a railroad."[1] Stephenson's *Blücher*, built in 1814 and named after the Prussian commander at Waterloo, had the first successful flanged-wheels, the weight of the locomotive gave it traction and kept it on the tracks, and it also had cylinder rods directly connected to the wheels. When *Blücher* was trialled, it was able to move 27 tonnes of coal.

The steam locomotive transformed land travel around the world and opened up large inland regions to world markets. Nicolas-Joseph Cugnot of France built a model steam wagon in 1763 and a full-sized one in 1769, and two years later caused the first automobile accident when his wagon ran into a brick wall. Cugnot left France for Belgium following the French Revolution and nothing further came of his work. American Oliver Evans made a steam wagon in 1772 and William Symington made a model locomotive in 1784. In the same year, James Watt designed a locomotive that had a gear changer for going uphill and William Murdock built a model based on Watt's design which travelled at nearly 13 km per hour. The first steam locomotive that ran on railway tracks was built in 1802 by Englishman Richard Trevithick, a former pupil and next door neighbour of Murdock.

Following on from *Blücher*, Stephenson built *Locomotion* in 1825 for the Stockton to Darlington Railway, the world's first locomotive railway line, which was used for transporting coal. *Locomotion* carried 72.5 tonnes of cargo over 15 km at 39 km per hour. In 1826, he built

Experiment, which was the first purpose-built passenger car. It was Stephenson who researched the effect of gradients on the ability of locomotives to operate effectively and he promoted the building of level, or near level, railway lines after observing that even a 1:200 gradient cut the carrying capacity of locomotives by 50% compared to a level track. He made a number of locomotives, but his most famous was the *Rocket*, built in 1829 with his son Robert, ushering in the period of rapid railway expansion.

When George Stephenson built the Stockton and Darlington Railway he made the rail gauge 4 ft 8½ inches (1.44m) because that was the width of the wagonway at Killingworth Colliery. "It was at Killingworth that he [Stephenson] devised his miner's safety lamp, first put to practical tests in the autumn of 1815, at the same time that Sir Humphrey Davy was producing his lamp. His design was one which used small tubes to allow the entry of air to support combustion and passage of gases. This lamp design was arrived at by trial and error and the prototype was tested at Killingworth on 21 October 1815. An improved version was tested again on the 4 November 1815 and 30 November 1815."[2] There was considerable controversy as to which of the two men was entitled to the honour of having first made an invention which was probably worked out independently, though simultaneously, by both, and when the admirers of Davy in 1817 presented him with a service of plate, those of Stephenson countered with an address and £1,000 early in 1818.

"The Stephensons, genius father George and his brilliant son [Robert], made a remarkable contribution to the development of railways. George did not invent the steam locomotive, but he did ensure that something which was beginning to come together from a variety of sources was engineered into a practical machine. In this respect, a man of relatively humble origins became one of the world's greatest engineers and he was brilliantly astute in ensuring that his son, Robert, lacked for nothing in assisting the engineering of the early railways."[3] Note: There is doubt as to whether George Stephenson's father came from Scotland, but certainly his father's father did. "George Stephenson's father, 'Old Bob', possibly came from Scotland, while his mother Mabel came from Ovingham, a village in the Tyne Valley, near to Wylam, Northumberland."[4] George's "father, Robert, a Scot, was employed as engine fireman at Wylam Colliery, with a wage of 12s. (60p) per week. His mother, Mabel, was the daughter of an Ovingham dyer, George Carr."[5] "A gentleman of high attainments, residing in the neighbourhood of Newcastle, in answer to enquiries for ancestors in the male line of George Stephenson, stated that George Stephenson on a certain occasion said that his family were natives of Castleton, in Liddisdale, and that his grandfather came into England in the service of a Scotch gentleman."[6] Certainly, his paternal grandfather moved from Scotland to become a "gentleman's manservant" and "when Robert Stephenson applied in 1834 for a Coat of Arms he stated that by family tradition they were descended from Hugh Stephenson of Mount Grenan, but it could not be ascertained with the certainty required by the College of Arms. There is a Hugh Stephenson of Mount Grenan who was 'Clerk Deput to His Majesties most honourable privy council', and who died between 1696 and 1700."[7] Another source states that George's father, Robert, was born in Antrim around 1723 where his surname was spelt "Stinson". He and his father then returned to Roxburghshire in 1772 and went south the following year to Northumberland seeking work.[8]

James Walker 1781-1862 was an important civil engineer who worked on canals, railways, docks, bridges and lighthouses. His work included London's Greenland Dock, St Catherine's Harbour in Jersey, the Alderney breakwater, also in the Channel Islands, Regents Bridge at Vauxhall in London, completion of the Caledonian Canal, and improvements to the River Tyne navigation. He designed and built the Wolf Rock Lighthouse which is 17 km east of St Mary's, Isles of Scilly. It stands 41 m high and took nine years to construct due to the difficulty of the weather and rough seas.

Walker was an adviser on the Liverpool to Manchester railway, the first designated passenger train line in the world. It was Walker who suggested a locomotive trial to determine whether fixed steam engines or locomotive engines were best for transporting freight (and passengers) along a railway line. The result was the Rainhill Trials that led to George and Robert Stephensons' *Rocket* winning the prize of £500 and settling the question of the type of motive power to be used not only on the Liverpool & Manchester but also on all future world railways. Walker also designed and surveyed similar routes for railways in Britain, notably the Leeds to Selby line in Yorkshire, which adopted his principles of flat, low operating cost routes.[1]

In 1835, he undertook the survey for the first locomotive railway line (as distinct from horse-drawn rails) in Saxony, which was the first German state to introduce locomotives. Walker chose a flatter route than had previously been envisaged by the German sponsors of the line.[2]

Thomas Bell 1782-1866 was a military engineer who worked from 1818 in Tasmania, where he built numerous roads and bridges, including Australia's oldest existing bridge, the Richmond Bridge, completed in January 1825. He was responsible for public buildings in Hobart, and roads at Macquarie Plains, and Constitution and Spring Hills in the Midlands. He was also responsible for the completion of the Wellington Bridge, Hobart; the construction of the sandstone causeway to Hunter Island; and a new brick bridge across the Hobart Rivulet in Argyle Street."[1] "Bell constructed a road from the Derwent River to St. Peter's Pass near Oatlands, now known as Bell's Line of Road – 'it would ultimately become part of the finest highways in the Australian colonies.'"[2]

Thomas Buchanan 1782-1853 was one of the first to recommend the use of artificial light to better inspect the eardrum.[1] Buchanan invented an auriscope that he called *Inspector Auris*, consisting of a lantern-like apparatus by means of which the light is reflected from a concave mirror, and falls into the meatus through a tube provided with two lenses. Its components were a globular lantern of block tin, with a large door on one side, an iron tube, inside polished and secured to the lantern, a shorter tube made to screw on the end of the iron tube, a double convex lens, about 3 inches (7.62 cm) focus and 3 inches diameter, concave lens to collect rays emitted by a candle and transmit them to the globular lantern, and double convex lens of less diameter than the globular lantern.

Buchanan was a surgeon based at the Hull Dispensary of the Diseases of the Eye and Ear. He wrote extensively about the practice of the "Aurist" and the causes of hearing loss, or, as he described it, the "diminution of hearing". His research was limited to the outer and middle ear as the technology of the day did not enable him to see further than the tympanic membrane (eardrum). In his 1825 publication, *Illustrations of Acoustic Surgery*, he described his own invention, the *Inspector Auris*, an early version of the Otoscope Specula used by clinicians today to look into the ear.[2]

The story of the otoscope has its roots in the tong-shaped specula. This device was first described and illustrated in France in 1363 by Guy de Chauliac. Its primary use included the examination of aural and nasal passages. Because of the similar problems posed by inspecting conical cavities, early otoscopy and rhinoscopy instruments were similar in design, although they diverged over the years. In Italy in 1838, Ignaz Gruber invented the first funnel-shaped speculum, although he didn't publish his findings. In Germany in 1864, Emil Siegle invented a pneumatic otoscope, a model that allows the user to administer air pressure.[3]

Buchanan was also perceptive enough to notice the effect of distance upon harmony. He noted that "the Highland bagpipe, which at a little distance on a wide and blooming heath had a melody and sweetness particularly agreeable to the Scottish ear, may produce a stunning effect when played in a small apartment".[4]

James Chalmers 1782-1853 was a pivotal figure in the development of postage stamps, producing the forerunner of modern adhesive stamps. Stamps became the key to the first major change in distance communication in the mailing of letters. Historically, mail delivery tended to be ad hoc, expensive and slow. The Penny Postage was a revolutionary concept that opened up cheap communication throughout the British Empire and, eventually, the world. Before 1840, mail was usually paid for by the receiver and it was often costly, especially if long distances were involved. It was also not unusual for the recipient to reject receipt of the letter because of the cost involved. In 1833, **Robert Wallace 1773-1855**, the local Member of Parliament for the Scottish seat of Greenock, "began campaigning in Parliament for a more streamlined, cheaper, and more uniform postal system."[1] Wallace had been highly critical of the postal system and, joined by Scottish economist **John Ramsay McCulloch 1789-1864**, from Whithorn, and English politician Richard Cobden, he lobbied Parliament for change resulting in the establishment of the Select Committee on Postage, headed by Wallace.

Englishman Rowland Hill appeared before the Committee in 1837 and, in a later pamphlet, proposed a fee of one penny for posting mail, irrespective of the distance, paid for by the sender in a prepaid envelope or using an adhesive postage stamp. In the report of 14 August 1838 "which was the final *Report of the Wallace Committee* and the one that concluded (vitally for the Postal Reform Campaign and only thanks to the casting vote of Wallace as Chairman) that 'A low and uniform rate of postage' (actually proposed at 2d for the first prepaid half ounce and 1d for each additional half ounce) be introduced as soon as possible. This was the publication that directly led to the start of Cheap Postage and the Introduction of the Penny Black."

Wallace drafted a bill which included Hill's recommendations and it was passed as the *Penny Postage Act* by the British Parliament on 27 August 1839, coming into effect on 10 January 1840. Of Wallace's role, it was said "It is undeniable that he paved the way for Mr Rowland Hill's great measure of the penny postage, and no one admits this more readily than Mr Hill himself."[3]

However, this wasn't the first instance of prepaid postage. As early as 18 July 1653, Frenchman Jean-Jacques Renouard de Villayer von Ludwig XIV (a name that doesn't readily spring to mind!) had established a fixed rate, cheap postal system within Paris. This was taken over by the Government but was dropped in 1662 due to lack of business. Later, in 1680 William

Dockwra, a London merchant, established a London Penny Post to collect and deliver letters within the city. The delivery was not to homes but to identified locations such as inns or shops. Unfortunately for Dockwra it was too successful and the Post Office had it closed down, although it was promptly reinstated as an official service belonging to the Post Office.[4]

In 1814, Sardinia, at that time a separate nation, also used a similar postal service but, like the French one, it disappeared after a few years. None of these systems used adhesive stamps like the 1840 British system, which also went further than the earlier systems because it covered much greater distances for the same fixed price. Adhesive postage stamps were used in Greece for a short time when the Lepta 40 stamp was issued around 1831, thus predating the British use, although it seems these were charity stamps rather than official government stamps, being used to help Greek refugees from Crete. The Smithsonian National Postal Museum states "The 1831 Greek 40-lepta charity tax stamp – the first adhesive stamp ever issued – is rarely found on cover. Only four instances are recorded. The Museum now has one. It is a fragile folded letter with a Piraeus, June 17, 1848, cancel and a handwritten rate of '40' to be collected from the recipient at Chalkis. The stamp is on the back flap. Recent research led to speculation that it is really either a postage-due stamp or a local issue."[5]

In Sweden, Curry Gabriel Treffenberg suggested in 1823 that his homeland should issue postage stamps but, despite local support the Swedish riksdag (parliament) vetoed the idea. In the Austro-Hungarian Empire, Slovenian-born Lovrenc Kosir suggested the use of adhesive stamps in 1836 but, as in Sweden, the government was cool on his proposal. On 3 November 1838, the Government Gazette of the British colony of New South Wales authorised postage stamps as pre-payment for letters and this is probably the first true stamp system for mail delivery. They were embossed stamps for delivery only within the colony's capital of Sydney and cost 15 pence for a dozen but they had three drawbacks, namely "they could be obtained only at the GPO; the embossing was a time-consuming process, having to be done in a letter press; and people often folded the letter sheets incorrectly, with the embossing folded out of sight, resulting in the addressee having to pay full postage."[6]

One other person is often claimed as the "inventor" of the adhesive stamp. "A bookseller and printer from Dundee, James Chalmers, holds a strong claim to be the actual inventor of the adhesive postage stamp. He is said to have been interested in postal reform from about 1822, and to have printed samples of his idea for printed gummed labels in August 1834. It seems that, although Hill also presented the idea of adhesive stamps, he was probably keener on the use of standard prepaid letter folders or lettersheets or envelopes, such as were issued in 1840 using a design by Irish artist William Mulready."[7] "Whether or not the advocates who support Chalmers are correct in attributing priority to his invention, the cancelled essays he submitted to the Treasury Competition in 1840 more closely resembled later postage than the Penny Black does, and reflected his deeper insight into the overlapping requirements of security and mail processing. … If Chalmers had done no more than to join postmarks and cancellations into a unified concept, he would merit higher standing than history has bestowed upon him."[8]

Irrespective of who actually was first with the idea of an adhesive stamp, it was Chalmers who recommended cancelling stamps with postmarks so that they could not be re-used. This concept was critical if abuse of the postal system was to be stopped (de Villayer used a system of prepaid postage tickets which were removed from the wrapper to prevent further use, but without being destroyed or cancelled in some way, there was always the possibility that they could be re-used). The effect of the 1840 *Penny Postage Act* can be seen when comparison is made between the United Kingdom and the United States, which did not introduce uniform postage rates irrespective of distance until 1863. In 1860, the number of letters written in Britain was 564 million for a population of 28 million (20 letters per person) whereas in the United States there were 184 million letters written in a population of 32 million (5.75 letters per person).[9] This difference cannot be ascribed to literacy levels as the United States, around 1850, had an adult literacy level of 85-90% in its white population, while England and Wales had 67-70% literacy and Scotland 80%.[10] There can be no doubt that the changes wrought to the British postal service in 1840 had important repercussions throughout the world and, although many people have contributed to the concept of low cost, fixed-rate, prepaid postage, there is no doubt that a seminal role was played by Scotsmen James Chalmers, Robert Wallace and John Ramsey McCulloch.

Thomas Morton 1783-1862 invented a barrel loom which revolutionised carpet making. The idea for this invention came to him after he was asked to mend a barrel organ and he recognised that the principle of the barrel with pins could be used to produce a pattern in the making of carpets.[1]

His invention allowed for the manufacture of improved Kidderminster carpets by permitting the triple or three-ply fabric composed of three distinct webs, which, by interchanging their threads, produce the pattern on both sides, permitting at the same time much greater variety of colour, with a corresponding increase of thickness and durability in the texture.[2] The *Edinburgh Encyclopedia* states, "Among other benefits, the machine enables the weaver to dispense with the assistance of the draw-boy, who was formerly an inseparable attendant of every carpet loom; and it saves all the tacks, or lashes used in throwing up the figure, which amounted to 40,000 yards, and five-sixths of the time consumed in changing the pattern, which frequently amounted to a fortnight." (D. Brewster, Vol XII, printed by William Blackwood, 1830, page 455). Morton also manufactured quality telescopes for sale.

Alexander Nimmo 1783-1832 worked in Ireland from 1811 until he died in 1832, conducting surveys for the pragmatically – if unfortunately – named Bog Commission in counties Kerry and Galway, following which he was involved in land reclamation. He surveyed about two-thirds of the coastline and organised the building of more than forty piers and some 400 km of road on Ireland's west coast as engineer for the Commission of Irish Fisheries.

Recognised as one of Ireland's pioneering engineers, Nimmo's appointment to the Bog Commission "made him the first of the engineers to attain that position by learning rather than practical experience. ... Exuding energy in both body and mind, he left his mark on almost every county [in Ireland]."[1]

In Wales, he supervised the harbour at Perth Cawl and was employed in surveying and submitting proposals for building railways from Leeds to Liverpool, and from Waterford to Limerick, in which city he designed the docks and Wellesley (now Sarsfield) Bridge.

William Sturgeon 1783-1850 invented the first electromagnet capable of supporting more than its own weight. This device led to the invention of the telegraph, the electric motor, and numerous other devices basic to modern technology. The 7-ounce (200 gram) magnet was able to support 9 pounds (4 kg) of iron using the current from a single cell.[1]

Sturgeon filled the core of a solenoid with a soft iron piece and found that the strength of magnetism increased 100 times.[2] He also learned that when the current was cut off, the iron immediately lost its magnetism (in contrast to steel, which became a permanent magnet after passing through the solenoid). Taking advantage of these effects, Sturgeon incorporated an iron core into many ingenious devices of his own design.[3]

Sturgeon built an electric motor in 1832 and invented the commutator, an integral part of most modern electric motors. In 1836, the year he founded the monthly journal *Annals of Electricity*, he invented the first suspended coil galvanometer, a device for measuring current. He also improved the voltaic battery and worked on the theory of thermoelectricity. From more than 500 kite observations, he established that in serene weather the atmosphere is invariably charged positively with respect to the Earth, becoming more positive with increasing altitude.[4]

James Bremner 1784-1856 salvaged Brunel's SS *Great Britain*, at that time the world's largest ship, when it ran aground on the beach in Ireland's Dundrum Bay. Although Bremner designed or built 19 harbours in Scotland, and 56 ships, his fame rested on being the world's most noted salvage expert, refloating 236 sunken or stranded ships. He was consulted by the contractor for building a harbour at Pultneytown after difficulty in laying the foundation stones of the pier. Bremner designed a crane to operate simultaneously on both sides of the barge.[1] He was also consulted on Dover Harbour and the Thames Tunnel.

He raised the *Unicorn* of Sunderland, which had lain under eleven fathoms of water (198 m) and had been embedded in sand for over two years. She was laden with 700 tons (635 tonnes) of coal and the gross weight of ship and cargo reached nearly 1,100 tons (998 tonnes). Another major salvage feat was that of the *Orion* of Pillau (now Baltiysk, Russia), at Watersound, Orkney, in 1825. The *Orion*'s cargo consisted of 40,000 feet (12,192 m) of timber which, with the wreck of the ship, Bremner constructed into a raft 450-feet long, 22 ft broad and 16 ft deep (137 m x 6.7 m x 4.9 m). With the aid of manually worked paddlers and sails erected on poles, he safely brought the raft to Pultneytown Harbour, after twice being driven through the Pentland Firth.[2]

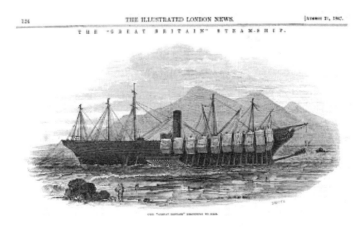

Image 23 – *Great Britain* aground at Dundrum Bay, 1st January 1847

Samuel Hunter Christie 1784-1865 made many contributions to magnetic science, including the effects of temperature upon magnetic forces, the effect of solar rays upon the magnetic needle and terrestrial magnetism. He constantly worked towards the improvement and construction of the magnetic compass. In 1833, he first described his "diamond" in his paper on the magneto-electric conductivity of various metals.[1] Its intrinsic brilliance has captivated many of the greatest minds from then to now. Sir Charles Wheatstone, Lord Kelvin, Cromwell Varley and a host of present-day scientists and engineers have reacted to its sparkling rays and in doing so have enriched mankind. Far outshining any diamond that nature has produced, Christie's diamond was produced by a flash of genius. With the strokes of a master he outlined his diamond in a form that has not basically changed since 1833.

But it is not a diamond in the way we usually think of diamonds, not mounted in a ring, a brooch, nor a pendant. Still, it assumes this form when it is drawn or sketched. Capable of infinite variations, it is blazing new frontiers even in this modern age we live in. The diamond is basically a method for measuring the unknown, whether that unknown be a resistance, impedance, frequency, temperature, weight, gas, or even an abstract mathematical quantity. In an electrical circuit, the unknown is combined with three other known values until no voltage difference, a null, is between adjacent midpoints of the diamond configuration. The configuration is then balanced, and the precise value of the unknown can readily be determined as a proportion. A DC or AC applied voltage is used to operate the circuit.[2]

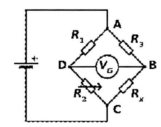

Image 24 – "Wheatstone" bridge circuit diagram

For a decade, few people knew of the bridge. Then another British scientist, Wheatstone, came across Christie's description of the instrument, which Wheatstone referred to as a "differential resistance measurer." A prominent member of The Royal Society of London, Wheatstone was well-positioned to give the tool a popularity boost. He gave an account of Christie's invention at an 1843 lecture, and soon after it came to be called the Wheatstone Bridge and was used in telegraphy and other applications. Wheatstone himself, however, gave full credit for its invention to Christie.[3]

At first, the Wheatstone Bridge was used in telegraphy to measure the resistance of telegraph wires and coils. To accomplish this, the conductor of unknown resistance was made part of the bridge circuit with three known resistors completing the configuration and a galvanometer used as a detector. Thus, the telegraphers possessed an invaluable tool with which to check their equipment and to locate faulty spots.

In 1865, Cyrus Field was busily engaged in his attempt to lay the first Atlantic cable on the ocean floor from Ireland to Newfoundland. On board the giant steamer *Great Eastern* was a veritable brains trust of scientists, including Professor William Thomson of Glasgow University, designer of the 2,300-mile (3,703 km) cable, and electrical superintendent Cromwell Varley of the Varley Loop, a method for determining faults in long lines. Using a modified Wheatstone Bridge, every inch of the cable was tested before it dropped to the ocean floor. Thomson was later titled Lord Kelvin, and his modified Wheatstone Bridge, now known as the Kelvin Bridge for the measurement of extremely low resistances, did much to ensure his prestige. Over the years, many other variations and applications of the Wheatstone Bridge have appeared.[4]

In his early magnetic work, Christie observed that the rotation of iron altered its magnetic properties. He did not immediately publish this phenomenon, with the result that Dominique François Jean Arago was credited with the discovery when he published his observations in 1825. Christie also showed experimentally the relations between temperature and magnetic intensity, and the magnetic influence of sunlight. More significantly, he showed in 1831 that there was a relationship between the aurora borealis and terrestrial magnetism; the idea of a magnetic relationship between the sun and the earth was something upon which he had previously speculated. Christie's knowledge of magnetism led to his being asked to write the report on current knowledge of terrestrial magnetism for the 1833 meeting of the British Association. At the conclusion of this report, he called for the establishment of a national magnetic observatory in Britain. This proposal resulted in a magnetic survey of Britain and ultimately led to the establishment of the Kew Magnetic Observatory.[5]

Richard Barnett Whytock 1784-1857 invented and patented a machine in 1832 for making tapestry carpets. Through the use of printing and weaving, Whytock managed to produce a pile similar to Brussels carpet with only one thread in the texture rather than many threads. Whytock reversed the process from one where the carpet is printed after it is woven, to one where a single thread, often kilometres in length, is printed in coloured stages of one or two centimetres. "When these threads have been all parti-coloured in this manner, they form the elements, as it were, of the intended design or fabric. Singly, they exhibit no regular figure or pattern; but when arranged in their proper order, ready for the weaver's beam, the figure comes into view, much elongated of course, inasmuch as 18 feet [5.5 m] of the warp will sometimes be gathered into 4 feet [1.2 m] of cloth, in order to secure the due proportions of the intended object. The two combined arts of printing and weaving are simplified by this contrivance. Not only can the pile of Brussels carpets be readily imitated by the process of Mr Whytock, but a velvet pile can also be produced by simply cutting the loops as practised for Wilton or Moquette carpets."[1]

Peter Crerar 1785-1856 designed the first railway – and the first standard gauge railway – in North America, at Stellarton, near Pictou, Nova Scotia. "In 1836 the General Mining Association of London, England, owners of the Albion Mines, now Stellarton, decided to build a railway from the Albion Mines to its loading grounds on the East River. At that time, there were few construction engineers in the area. Peter Crerar, a government land surveyor, was given the task. The plans were sent to the head office of the Mining Association in London, with the request that an engineer be sent out to execute them. When the plans were submitted to George Stephenson, builder of the locomotive who had engineered the construction of the Stockton and Darlington, the world's first passenger railway, he reported to the Mining Association that, in his opinion, the person who prepared the drawings was capable of executing them. The railway was then built under the supervision of Crerar. The building of the Albion Mines Railway began in 1836 and the road was opened for traffic in 1839. The line, 10 km in length, was so nearly straight that the least radius of its curves was 1:3,600.[1]

Daniel Fraser 1786-1849 was the technical leader of the Trölhatte Canal Company which built Sweden's Göta Canal between Goteborg and Stockholm under the direction of Baltzar von Platen. To build the canal, a foundry and machine shop – Motala Verkstad – was built at Motala in 1822, with Fraser as its first manager from its inception to 1843. Motala Verkstad was one of the first mechanical workshops in Sweden, and of dominant importance for the development of marine steam engines and shipbuilding of the 19th century.[1] It produced around 400 ships, 800 bridges, 1,300 locomotives, and over 1,100 boilers. The company trained many of Sweden's future technicians and engineers. It is still in existence and during the 1970s was the world's largest exporter of kitchen sinks – a far cry from building canals.

Charles John Napier 1786-1860 proposed, co-designed and prefabricated with English father-and-son engineers Aaron and Charles Manby the 36.6 metre, 116-ton *Aaron Manby* in 1821 (in these pioneering days a ton was not the weight or displacement of a ship, but interior space, calculated differently depending on country and even shipping company. Around 1840 it was approximately forty cubic feet or 1.13 cubic metres). Their steamship sailed from London to Paris, down the Thames, across the English Channel under Napier's command and up the Seine on 10 June 1822 at an average speed of 14 km an hour. As well as being the first iron steamship, it was also the world's first ocean-going iron steamship.[1]

Neil Arnott 1788-1874 invented the therapeutic water bed, as well as a smokeless and highly-efficient stove called Arnott's Stove, and a ventilating chimney-valve. In 1833, he wrote a very astute description of pressure-sore pathogenesis and suggested using a hydrostatic water bed.[1] He promoted its therapeutic value through improved patient comfort and preventing bed-sores. This was later developed into a water-filled chair intended to prevent sea-sickness. The soporific benefits of waterbeds have been known for thousands of years, since Persian nomads first slumbered on sun-warmed goatskin waterbags. Cleopatra is said to have slept on a waterbed, and Leonardo da Vinci sketched designs for their construction. Their therapeutic value was championed in 1833 by Arnott, who visualised the ideal state of "repose on the surface of the water, like a swan on its plumage, without sensible pressure anywhere".[2]

The first volume of his successful book on medicine, *Elements of Physics*, was published in 1827. He expressed his concern about what he called the four necessities of life: Air, Warmth, Aliment (nutrition) and Exercise. All these factors must have created his interest in heating and ventilating which started with his involvement in matters related to public health and the need for improved ventilation in buildings. This led in 1838 to his publishing of the book titled *Warming and Ventilating* which explained the principles used in the Arnott slow combustion stove. The Royal Society awarded him the Rumford medal on 30 November 1854. The medal citation read "For the successful construction of the smokeless firegrate lately introduced by him and for other valuable improvements in the application of heat to warming and ventilating of apartments". In 1855, he published another book on the smokeless fireplace.[3]

Arnott built circular and oblong bronzed corrugated stoves for warming buildings. By the corrugation of the body of the stove, the heating surface becomes multiplied nearly three times and by means of the self-regulating valve the admission of air to the fire is so regulated that it only needs replenishing with fuel once every 12 to 18 hours. The stove needs to be lighted only once in the season, and to be supplied with fuel only once, or twice if desired, in twenty-four hours, consumes its fuel as uniformly as an hour-glass lets fall its sand, and can be adjusted to burn permanently at any wished-for rate. It also facilitates perfect ventilation.[4]

If it could be established that the Arnott slow combustion stove was first installed in the late 1830s, and a letter to *The Times* newspaper in 1841 would seem to confirm this fact, then it becomes one of the first, if not the first, stand-alone warm-air stove to have been invented. The corrugated outer surface of the stove which increased the heating surface area by a factor of three was an innovative design concept which appears to have been adopted in principle in the later designs and patent applications of similar stand-alone stoves invented and patented by Sir Goldsworthy Gurney 1856, and John Grundy 1864.[5]

Arnott declined to patent any of his inventions, and was never happier than when he could devise or apply any means of lessening human suffering, or extending man's dominion over nature. For his various inventions, he was awarded a gold medal by the jurors of the Paris Exhibition of 1855, and Napoleon III gave him the cross of the Legion of Honour. He was one of the founders of the University of London in 1836, and an original member of the senate. In the following year, he was appointed one of the physicians extraordinary to the newly enthroned Queen Victoria.[6]

William Bald 1788-1857 was a civil engineer surveying and building in Ireland, completing the first survey of County Mayo. "His first and most spectacular project in this period was the new Antrim coast road of 1832-1837, which involved much blasting and tunnelling in the cliffs between Larne and Ballycastle. Another road design of the same period, which included Ireland's first suspension bridge, was from Kenmare to Bantry, in the south-west."[1] It was the proving ground for innovative techniques, such as the blasting of complete headlands and the use of the resultant rock to create sea defences. He was responsible for "several hundred miles of roads and associated bridges in Ireland."[2]

In 1809, at age 20, he was appointed director of the Trigonometrical Survey of County Mayo, where he proved to be an exceptional cartographer, mapping large swathes of Ireland, particularly County Mayo. He mapped much of Scotland's Western Isles and also did work in France, Holland and Italy, although it was in Ireland where much of his work was done, building or improving harbours, railways and roads, including the 112 km Grand Coast Road from Antrim to Kenmore.

John Howell 1788-1863 invented the bookbinder's "plough" for cutting edges of paper pages in preparation for book binding.[1] Howell's invention was described as "an instrument now in universal use by bookbinders for cutting the leaves of books."[2]

David Napier 1788-1873 improved the cylinder press used in printing. This press was first conceived in 1790 by Englishman William Nicholson; then German Friedrich Koenig made a steam-driven version in 1811. Note: the first rotating cylinder press for printing was invented by Thomas Bell in 1783, but this was for printing ink on calico, not paper.

In 1819, Napier constructed the steam-operated flat-bed cylinder for printing. It was designed to print simultaneously on both sides of a sheet of paper. His machines were described as "delicate as any clock could be", and his printing press in particular earned praise by Thomas Curson Hansard.[1]

In 1824, Napier invented the automatic paper feed – common on photocopiers and printers today – that used grippers to pick up the sheet of paper from the table and hold it against the cylinder for imprinting. His "press printed 2,000 impressions, or 1,000 copies an hour, six to eight times the capacity of current handpresses."[2] By 1830, Napier had introduced "the most popular press, an improved form of bed and platen press"[3] and it was from this machine of Napier's that American Richard March Hoe patented his *Improvement in Rotary Printing-Presses* on 24 July 1847 (No 5199), with a machine that could print up to 4,000 double-sided pages an hour.[4] Hoe fastened lead type around the circumference of a very large cylinder in the centre of the press and, by rotating the cylinder, he made a press that turned constantly in one direction, unlike the earlier presses that oscillated. The number of pages printed per hour now depended on how fast this large cylinder turned – and on how many impression cylinders were fitted around its circumference.

Napier continued his contributions to the printing industry, inventing an automatic inking device and making printing machines that produced currency notes for the Bank of England until well into the 20th century. It was machines designed by Napier that made the first perforated stamps in January 1854, with five of Napier's machines perforating some 90 million sheets of stamps in the following 26 years. Earlier, in May 1852, a stamp perforating machine was made to the specifications of Henry Archer and was constructed by David Napier and Sons. It was installed at Somerset House for regular operation. Napier later improved the perforating design by fitting a line of pinheads in place of the rotary disc. The new perforator had perfect round holes punched right through the paper and came into use from 28 January 1854. The gauge of perforator at that time was 16 holes per linear inch.[5]

With his son, James Murdoch Napier, he developed a bullet stamping machine which was quickly ordered by Woolwich arsenal and later by foreign governments. "By careful inspection, David discovered that cast bullets tended to contain irregularly spaced air bubbles which made their flight path curve. He designed a machine which produced lead bullets through a cold process making them much more accurate, i.e. they travelled in a straight line! By 1835 David was manufacturing bullet-making machines for Board of Ordnance at Woolwich Arsenal and the Enfield Small Arms Co. In 1839, he received an order for 300,000 'Nay-Peer' rifle balls for the British Army. … He also developed a range of other equipment for minting and sorting coins for the Royal Mint and Bank of England. The design of the new automatic coin weighing machine came from the design of William Cotton, Deputy Governor of the Bank of England. It was David's ingenuity and skill that brought the delicate design to reality and the fact that the specified accuracy of 1/50th of a grain became 1/100th. The success of this balance led to further orders for bigger machines for weighing bullion."[6]

During the 1840s, he also constructed several large hydraulic presses and lifts for Isambard Kingdom Brunel's Great Western Railway. His last invention, in 1848, in collaboration with his cousin Robert, was a registering compass to trace the course and distance covered; these were installed in vessels for the Royal Mail Steam Packet Company and P&O as well as those built at his cousin's Govan yard in Scotland.

Francis Ronalds 1788-1873 erected an experimental telegraph system in 1816 in the grounds of his house in Hammersmith, London. It used clockwork-driven rotating dials, engraved with letters of the alphabet and numbers, synchronised with each other, at both ends of the circuit. They were connected with 12.9 km of electrically-charged iron wire, hung on two strong wooden frames, each with 19 horizontal bars. Ronalds successfully transmitted and received letters; he believed his telegraph would work over distances of 800 km. The British Admiralty was informed of his success but rejected his invention; they felt that the telegraph was not needed in peacetime and that the existing semaphore system was adequate. Since the apparatus used high-voltage electricity, it would probably have failed over long distances, but it embodied principles of construction and maintenance which were followed in later telegraph systems. In 1871, Ronalds received a belated knighthood for his pathfinding work.[1] One person, however, did benefit from this work – Charles Wheatstone. He saw the telegraph as a boy, and later patented the first working electric telegraph with William Cooke.

In 1843, Ronalds was appointed the first Honorary Director and Superintendent of the Observatory at Kew. He began work on a system for registering meteorological data using photography and this time was awarded a grant to continue his work. A similar system was developed independently by Charles Brooke, but the British Association confirmed Ronalds' priority. This was the beginning of automatic, accurate recording of meteorological data and remained in use for some years after Ronalds' death.[2]

Robert Wauchope 1788-1862 was, in 1824, the "inventor of the 'time ball' – a signal hoisted daily at Greenwich to enable nineteenth century sailors to synchronise their ships' chronometers."[1] It was essential for the calculation of longitude that a ship's chronometer be accurate, but astronomical calculations that could ensure accuracy could only conveniently be made in observatories. In 1818, Wauchope became interested in developing a method of signalling the exact time from an observatory to ships so that the chronometers on board could be rated. In 1824, he advised the Admiralty of his Plan for ascertaining the rates of chronometers by signal, which described his "time ball", a large hollow metal sphere rigged on a pole and attached to a mechanism so that it might be dropped at an exact time each day. In 1829, a test was made of his device at Portsmouth. In 1833, time balls were constructed at Greenwich, St Helena and, in 1836, at Cape Town. At the time of his death, time balls were in use on every inhabited continent, being eventually rendered obsolete on the introduction of radio time signals from 1924 onwards. Greenwich Observatory has operated its time ball since 1833. The famous time ball used at New Year in New York is not a maritime time ball but is based on it, the main difference being that the exact time for the Times Square ball is taken when it stops at the bottom, whereas those used for synchronising ships' times were taken from the moment is started to drop from the top of the mast.

William Fairbairn 1789-1874 built iron bridges in large numbers, including the prototype of the plate-girder bridge that came into world-wide use. While working with Robert Stephenson, Fairbairn pioneered the use of rectangular tube steel from which he made the world-renowned Britannia Bridge from Anglesey to mainland Wales. The steel box girders were lighter and stronger than solid steel and became an industry standard in construction. Fairbairn built over 100 such bridges in his lifetime and he designed a hydraulic riveter for use in their construction. In 1864, he built a bridge to cross the Connecticut River at Warehouse Point, between Hartford and Springfield in Connecticut. Its length was 1,525 feet (465 m), it had 17 spans, and it weighed some 800 tons (725.75 tonnes). As the United States was well into its Civil War, the bridge was built in England and shipped from Liverpool in time to erect the bridge in June 1865.[1]

Metal fatigue was a major problem and, in America, iron truss bridges and iron railway axles suffered numerous failures. "Fairbairn undertook repeated load tests on tubular beams which led to the appreciation of the significance of stress range and the concept of endurance limit."[2] He was the first to use wrought iron for the hulls of ships, bridges, structural beams and mill shafting, and he designed a riveter to improve efficiency in boiler manufacturing, in which Fairbairn proved to be an innovator.[3] In 1844, he developed the Lancashire boiler, which has two flues that contain the furnace and extend through the boiler from one end to the other. This was a big improvement on the contemporary Cornish boiler in both efficiency and safety and, as a result, it could also be made smaller, giving even further fuel efficiencies.

Fairbairn built many locomotives, including 69 for the Manchester and Leeds Railway alone. He pioneered construction of ships from wrought iron, and in 1830 he built *Lord Dundas*, the first ever iron-hulled steamship. He was a prolific shipbuilder, with several hundred to his credit, and he also conducted early research into metal fatigue, raising and lowering a three-tonne mass onto a wrought-iron cylinder three million times before it fractured, showing that a static load of 12 tonnes was needed for such an effect.

In 1850, he patented a steam crane with a curved jib constructed of riveted wrought-iron platework to form a square section box girder which could more easily access the holds of ships. Fairbairn was one of the leaders in developing and introducing mechanised manufacturing processes during the Industrial Revolution, and he built watermills in Zurich, Switzerland, that overcame the difficulties caused from irregular water flow on rivers of changing heights. Fairbairn "received medals or other marks of recognition for his services to science from most of the crowned heads of Europe."[4]

Image 25 – Britannia Bridge from Anglesey circa 1860

James Smith 1789-1850, of Deanston in Stirlingshire, designed bridges, a salmon ladder, and in 1811 invented a rotary reaping machine; but his greatest achievement was in 1823 when he devised the method of thorough drainage of soil, eventually publishing the details in *Remarks on Thorough Draining and Deep Ploughing* (1831). This involved a heavy plough making a deep furrow, followed by another plough which cut through the topsoil to a depth of around 25 centimetres with all stones being removed. Drainage was, of course, an ancient art, but after the demise of the Roman Empire, it became neglected. Englishman Walter Blith, who supported Oliver Cromwell in the English Civil War, recommended effective drainage as far back as 1649, and compatriot Joseph Elkington developed the sink-hole drainage system. However, it wasn't until James Smith took up Blith's proposals, or something akin to them, that the so-called Deanston – or thorough – drainage system was put into widespread use. Smith advocated parallel subterranean channels running in line to areas of the field with the steepest inclines, but sufficiently close together to ensure that even when there was heavy rain the water would quickly run away into a main drain that was deeper than the run-off channels. The parallel drains, or channels, were placed around 5-7 metres apart and cut to a depth of 76 cm, then filled with stones to a height of 30 cm with the stones being no larger than 7 cm in diameter. Where such stones were difficult to obtain, tiles or earthenware were used and cylindrical pipes replaced the horseshoe tiles. "The system introduced by Smith of Deanston has now been virtually adopted by all drainers. Variations in matters of detail (having respect chiefly to the depth and distance apart of the parallel drains) have indeed been introduced; but the distinctive features of his system are recognised and acted upon."[1]

Those who wandered too far from Smith's specifications, however, usually encountered lower efficacy or greater cost. In 1843, Royal Agricultural Society engineer Josiah Parkes "Thinking that Smith's trenches were too shallow, advocated a depth of four feet [122 cm], which would give a sufficient layer of warm mellow surface earth. On these principles millions of acres were drained, and thousands of pounds [sterling] wasted where drains were laid too deep."[2]

Smith made changes in weaving machinery and the building for housing it, using soil on the cupola roof of the building to help insulate it. Over 1,000 employees worked on the estate producing curtain lace, cotton stylised sheets and towelling on jacquard looms. Smith devised a salmon ladder and designed a reaping machine, but it was improvement to drainage where his greatest legacy lies. Better drainage increased the time available to work the land, improved the efficacy of manure, enabled seed to be sown earlier, and advanced harvesting time for crops; the cost of labour was reduced, crop output increased, and millions of hectares in Britain were drained.[3] In 1834, he patented an improved version of Archibald Buchanan's self-stripping card used in spinning by fixing the flat cards on an endless chain so that they could be cleaned regularly.[4]

John Fletcher Macfarlan 1790-1861 developed sterile dressings for surgeon Robert Lister in Scotland. His company, along with the brothers Thomas and Henry Smith, also of Edinburgh, laid the foundations of modern pharmacology. Both companies were among the first to master the large-scale manufacture of morphine, and Macfarlan was the first to produce sterile bandages.[1]

In 1832, the company began the manufacture of morphine acetate (the medicinal version of heroin), and hydrochloride, which led to the development and manufacture of the anaesthetics ether and chloroform, and

William Monteith 1790-1864 was a military engineer and surveyor who was involved with British diplomatic and military assistance to Persia (Iran) in several campaigns against Russia, for example, in Georgia, in 1810-1813. Other work included defining the Turkish-Persian border in 1821 and he remained in Persia until the Russian-Persian border was settled in 1828.[1]

David Napier 1790-1869 was one of the most inventive of the pioneering Clyde engineers and in 1812 made the boiler and produced the castings for the engines for the first ocean-going steamboat, *Comet*. His first marine engine, for the *Marion*, was delivered in 1816 and the following year he began operating her on his own account on Loch Lomond. In 1818, he was contemplating starting his own fleet of ocean-going steamers. After conducting the first experiments using a model and observations of a steamer in heavy seas to achieve an optimum hull design, he built *Rob Roy* to provide services between Greenock and Liverpool, and Holyhead and Howth. His firm constructed a succession of vessels, some incorporating novel features, notably a rotary engine, which he developed.[1] In 1826, he designed the SS *United Kingdom*, the largest paddle steamship in the world to that date and the first designed to cross the Atlantic (due to bankruptcy of the firm that commissioned her she never made a crossing).[2] It was 160 feet (48.7 m) long with a beam of 26½ feet (8 m) and her engines generated a tremendous 200 nominal horse-power. In 1827, he designed and built the *Aglaia*, the world's first iron steamship.

Napier made numerous innovations to marine engineering and in the early 1830s built a compact steam engine for use with paddle boats. It was a vertical tandem compound engine that became known as the steeple engine as its piston rod extension resembled a church steeple, and it became very common on American paddle boats. In 1837, Napier designed and built *Fire-King*, a steam yacht of 635 tonnes and the fastest ship afloat, sailing at 24 km an hour. Napier also designed feathered paddlewheel blades that increased the power of ships. He "was the first to combine engineering and shipbuilding in one firm".[3]

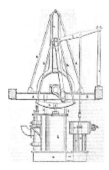

Image 26 – Steeple Engine

Along with his more famous cousin, Robert Napier, he was responsible for the development of marine engineering on the River Clyde, the river that made more than half the steamship tonnage in the world in the second half of the 19th century, and by early 20th century one fifth of all the ships in the world – during that period more than 30,000 ships were built on the Clyde.[4]

Robert Stirling 1790-1878 invented a steam engine that he called the Heat Economiser but which was subsequently named after him. It was built in an attempt to reduce the risk of high-pressure steam causing boilers to explode. The need to generate electricity in space has NASA interested in the Stirling Engine that he invented in 1816. Although it failed to become popular at the time it is now making a resurgence.[1] The Stirling Engine, which now includes any closed cycle regenerative gas engine, has a sealed cylinder with two parts, one hot and one cold. It contains gas such as helium or hydrogen, but usually air, which moves between the hot and cold sides of the cylinder. The gas on the hot side is expanded and pushes up against a piston and when it returns to the cool side the gas contracts. It is a very smooth-running engine, but it has four drawbacks: it needs a much higher level of accuracy in the manufacturing process; it is more costly to make because of the higher precision required; it is larger than traditional engines in relation to power output; and it takes longer to get it started. The use of Bessemer steel made boilers safer and the arrival of the petrol-driven internal combustion engine seemed to consign the Stirling Engine to obscurity, but it is now being made in increasing numbers and some of its advantages are being recognised. It needs no valves; it has more accurate control over the consumption of air-fuel mixture; it has virtually no emissions; it needs much less servicing or lubricants (simple maintenance can be done at 10,000-hour intervals); it is simple to maintain and operate; and it is safer due to lower pressure – its original *raison d'être*.

Image 27 – A desktop alpha Stirling Engine

One function to which it is particularly appropriate is powering submarines, where the higher initial costs are more than offset by its advantages. Compared to using diesel engines, submarines can stay underwater much longer and, because it needs no explosion to drive the pistons, the Stirling Engine runs silently, a critical requirement for submarines. Stirling Engines have a theoretical efficiency almost equal to the Carnot cycle, which is the most efficient a heat engine cycle can be. As it can run on almost any combustible fuel, it is being considered by some countries as a substitute for more expensive oil and gas to run pumps for irrigation and agricultural work. NASA is investigating the Stirling Engine for generating electricity in space and a test unit gave a 10-Watt continuous output for over 87,600 hours without needing maintenance and with no reduction in performance.[2]

George Rodney Blane 1791-1821 was the first British engineer to build canals in India. In 1817, he commenced restoration of the Mughal Canal on the west bank of the Jumna River after it had

134

fallen into disuse around 1750, enabling the 296 km canal to carry water to Delhi on its completion in 1820. "To Blane must be given the credit for the first success in canal engineering by the British in India in this period in which there was little knowledge and certainly no training in the hydraulics flow in open channels."[1]

He was then appointed to "the restoration of another called the canal of Feroze, running from the main canal through a great tract of arid territory towards Hansi and Hissar. When the last accounts arrived from India, not only were the districts on both sides of the great canal cheered and enriched by the abundant water; but the country on each side of that of Feroze, so lately desolate and sterile, was covered with sheets of wheat of two miles (3.2 km) in breadth, and that in succession to other crops of grain. By recent and authentic accounts from Delhi also, it appears that this city had greatly improved in salubrity since the people had the fine water of the canal to drink, and that several families who had been formerly resident were returning on that account."[2]

Henry Burden 1791-1871 invented the first farm cultivator. Arriving in America in his late twenties, he took employment in Troy, New York. His success enabled him to buy the company, which he renamed H. Burden & Sons, and which, at one time, had 1,500 employees. Burden was "technically innovative, and became indeed one of the principal inventors in nineteenth century America."[1]

In 1820, he invented the first farm cultivator,[2] a farm implement that stirred macerated soil to a greater depth than the harrow. Cultivators could be used prior to planting to loosen and aerate the soil and cull weeds amongst the growing crop – an important innovation in both agriculture and horticulture.

Long after the advent of the railway, horses were still indispensable for transport and travel and remained so until well into the age of the automobile. Indeed, during World War II, horses were often used for hauling gun carriages, and in the first decade of the 21st century they were still commonplace in Romania. Horseshoes were essential to prevent the animals going lame and Burden devised a machine capable of mass producing them, which he patented on 23 November 1835, with additional patents in 1843, 1857 and 1862. Burden's "horseshoe machine was acclaimed as one of the technical marvels of the age, capable of turning out thirty-six hundred horseshoes per hour, complete from the iron bar to the finished shoe without the touch of a hand or external process".[3]

"The fame and use of this machine spread to Europe and, unhappily, machine-made horseshoes facilitated the conduct of large-scale wars in Europe and America during the 19th century, from the Crimean and the Austro-Italian wars in the 1850s on, and particularly the American Civil War, in which the North enjoyed a great industrial advantage over the South with Burden's ironworks supplying the Union Army. Indeed, one of the principal objectives of Confederate Army raids was the seizure of Burden-made horse and mule shoes in Union supply stocks. Towards the end of the war there was even a plot to secure designs of the horseshoe machine in Burden's factory in order to set up a factory in Atlanta, but Sherman's capture of that city frustrated the attempt."[4] Not long afterwards, Burden's company was making more than 50 million horseshoes a year, causing a great reduction in price.

In 1839, he made a self-acting machine for rolling puddled iron into cylindrical bars, his so-called Burden's Rotary Concentric Squeezer, which removed impurities (slag) from wrought iron and came into use worldwide. This was probably his most significant contribution to the iron industry. It "substituted mechanical squeezing for the forge hammer in converting the ball of puddled iron into blooms. It was acclaimed by the US Commissioner of Patents as the first truly original American invention in iron-making. It also caught the fancy of British observers, who reported to Parliament in 1854 on the merits of the process."[5]

Image 28 – Henry Burden's Water Wheel

On 26 May 1825, he patented a machine for making wrought-iron nails that were previously made by hand, thus making nails cheap, plentiful and standardised. To provide power for his nail factory, Burden built a water wheel of 18 m in diameter and nearly 7 m in width, the world's most powerful wheel, and apparently the third largest after those in Laxey, Isle of Man, and Greenock, Scotland.[6]

From 1833, Burden was building steamboats, commencing with the 91.4 m *Helen*, which reached 29 km/h in July 1834. He was "the first advocate of the plans at present adopted by English and American ship-builders in the construction of long vessels for ocean navigation. As early as 1825 he laid before the Troy Steamboat Association certain original plans whereby the construction of steamboats for inland navigation could be greatly improved, and which some years later were adopted in the building of the steamer *Hendrick Hudson*. Besides increasing the length of the boats, he wisely suggested, for the convenience and accommodation of passengers, the erection of sleeping-berth-rooms on the upper decks, being a decided change from the holds of vessels, where they had previously been placed. In 1846, he conceived the gigantic plan of a transatlantic steam-ferry company. His prophetic ideas again were shown in the prospectus of Burden's Atlantic Steam-Ferry Company. Although the company was never organised, the salient points advanced by Mr Burden were subsequently copied by the Cunard and other ocean lines. He was also among the first to suggest the use of plates for iron-clad sea-going vessels, and sent specimen plates of his own manufacture to Glasgow for examination."

Among Burden's many inventions was a machine to make wrought-iron countersunk spikes for securing railroad tracks. By 1836, he modified this machine to make hook-headed spikes to suit the newer shape of railway lines, taking out a patent on 2 September 1840. This metal hook greatly helped in the rapid expansion of railroads in North America and elsewhere, and it is still used to fasten railway lines.

John Johnston 1791-1880 lived in the Finger Lakes region of New York and helped open up large areas of land for agriculture by effective drainage. The most common form of drainage in America was the use of clay tiles, which were introduced to the United States from Scotland in December 1835 by Johnston.[1] By 1856, he had laid 82 km of drain tile on his farm, enabling wheat yields to be doubled.[2]

In Illinois alone some 2,832,800 hectares of wetland was made available to agriculture by the use of tile drainage.[3] "The tiles were round and horseshoe shaped, about 15 inches [38cm] long. They were laid end to end and often buried two feet [61 cm] in the ground. As the water rose from below it entered the tiles and was carried to a nearby creek. Today, plastic piping is used to accomplish the same results. Johnston died November 24, 1880 in his ninetieth year, having changed the course of agriculture in the United States."[4]

Robert Napier 1791-1876, more than any other person, was responsible for the incredible rise of shipbuilding on the River Clyde, making it the world's premier shipbuilding site. He first started with marine engines when he built one for James Lang's *Leven* in 1823, then in 1827 he built and installed the engines for the *Clarence* and *Helensburgh*, the two fastest ships in the August Regatta of the Northern Yacht Club, where competition among steamboats was high. In 1835, the East India Company started a steam packet service from Bombay to Suez with the Thames-built *Atlanta* and the Clyde-built *Berenice*, which had a Napier engine. The latter ship proved to be faster by 18 days on the journey and the *Berenice* reduced the average travel time between Britain and India from six months to two months, an incredible achievement. In 1838, Napier built the engines for the world's largest ship, *British Queen* at 1,863 tons, built in London by Curling, Young and Co. In the same year, he managed to win the Royal Navy contract to install marine steam engines for the paddle sloops *Vesuvius* and *Stromboli* but got no further orders for some years due to the Admiralty following its traditional methods of placing contracts close to London. Following a parliamentary enquiry that found Napier's engines were better and needed less maintenance than the Thames-built engines hitherto preferred by the Admiralty, more orders came his way. By 1843, he was building ships as well as their engines, commencing with *Vanguard* and, for the Royal Navy, *Jackall*, *Lizard* and *Bloodhound*.

By this time, he was closely involved with The British and North American Royal Mail Steam Packet Company (Cunard), a company which he had been instrumental in establishing with Samuel Cunard. Four ships were built for Cunard which had won the mail contract from the British government, and Napier's powerful and reliable engines were critical to the success of the company. The four ships, all Scottish-built, were: *Acadia* by John Wood; *Caledonia* by Charles Wood; *Columbia* by Robert Steele; and *Britannia*, built by Robert Duncan. "The names of the ships made careful, portioned reference to Nova Scotia, Scotland, the United States and Great Britain, the four places that had launched and would then sustain the Cunard line."[1] Soon others were added to the fleet, including *Hibernia, Cambria, United Kingdom, America, Niagara* and *Canada* – all constructed by Robert Steele; and *Europa* by John Wood. All of these ships had engines designed and built by Robert Napier.

On 3 July 1855, the *Persia* was launched and completed trials on 8 January – at 110 m she was the longest vessel afloat. She was also the first iron-hulled transatlantic liner and by far the most luxurious at 3,300 tons (2,994 tonnes), and on the first voyage from Greenock to Liverpool averaged just under 30 km/h.[2]

Other ships of Napier for Cunard included *China* and the *Scotia*, the latter being the last paddle wheel vessel built for the transatlantic business. "Along with the *Persia*, the *Scotia* introduced the first real express service for passengers across the Atlantic."[3]

Of the ships which held the record for the fastest westbound Atlantic crossing, six had engines built by Napier: *Columbia* (held 1841-1843); *Cambria* (1845-1848); *America* (1848); *Europa* (1848-1850); *Persia* (1856-1863) and *Scotia* (1863-1872). Eastbound records held by ships with Napier engines were: *Britannia* (1840-1842); *Columbia* (1843); *Hibernia* (1843-1849); *Canada* (1849-1851); *Persia* (1856-1863); and *Scotia* (1863-1869). In the 36 years from the crossing of *Britannia* to his death in 1876, ships with Napier engines held the speed record for traversing the Atlantic for 24 years in either direction – this at a time of intense competition when the fastest Atlantic crossing was seen as highly important to shipping lines.

Napier's company built 270 vessels in the 19th century, of which 107 had been completed or commenced by the time he retired in 1861. As well, he made the engines of 11 other steamboats between 1821 and 1843. Of the vessels built by Napier 42 were paddle steamers, 15 steamships, 1 battleship (*Black Prince*), 2 frigates, 3 gunboats, 13 passenger cargo vessels, 5 passenger ships, brigs, yachts, train ferries, and other vessels. He built the *Rolf Krake* which was the British-built, armour-clad turret-ship (monitor), the first all-iron warship in Denmark. In action during the Danish-Prussian War at Egernsund in 1864, it received 150 hits from Prussian artillery, none of which penetrated its 11.4 cm iron hull.[4]

Napier's company went on to provide engines or ships for the imperial navies of France, Russia, Holland and Turkey, as well as the Royal Navy, for which he built HMS *Black Prince* in 1861. This ship was the second ocean-going iron-hulled armoured battleship built, the first being its sister ship HMS *Warrior,* which was designed by Glasgow-born naval architect John Scott Russell. These two ships were the most powerful warships in the world at the time, with the *Black Prince* having a displacement of 9,250 tons (8,391 tonnes), making it the largest and most powerful warship afloat – 40 tons (36.3 tonnes) heavier than *Warrior*. Around 1900, when output was at its zenith, there were 39 shipyards on the Clyde between Greenock and Glasgow. Then, half of all the steamships in the world were Clyde-built."[5]

In the 75 years before Queen Elizabeth's coronation in 1953, the Clyde built 30.6 million tons (27,760,000 tonnes) of merchant shipping. "By his pioneering efforts, his noted insistence on quality and good workmanship, his technical innovation, and his encouragement of many of the leading shipbuilders and engineers of his day and of the next generation, Robert Napier did more than any other to establish the Clyde's world-wide reputation and may indeed with justice be called 'the father of Clyde shipbuilding.'"[6] This is no empty accolade given that it has been estimated that the Clyde produced over 30,000 vessels in 200 years.[7] "In the peak year of 1913 the Clyde built and launched almost three-quarters of a million tons of shipping, some 756,973 tons [686,714 tonnes]; a feat never to be equalled. This represented not only one-third of British tonnage, but almost 18 per cent of world output".[8] "From 1870 until the start of World War I, Glasgow produced an estimated 20 per cent of the world's ships."[9] In the 150 years from the end of the Napoleonic War in 1814 around 21,000 vessels were built on the Clyde. Of these at least 1,679 were for the Royal Navy, including 454 destroyers, 57 frigates (with another 40 built after 1964), 4 aircraft carriers, 26 battleships/battlecruisers, 81 gunboats, 76 submarines, 201 minesweepers, 273 landing craft, 8 monitors, and another 182 simply described as warships, with the balance being other naval vessels such as troopships, torpedo boats, hospital ships, corvettes, etc. In the same period the Clyde also built more than 2,470 sailing ships, including 37 of the famous clippers such as *Cutty Sark*, over 3,100 passenger liners and ships, 5,168 steamships and paddle steamers, which carried cargo and passengers, with another 2,715 cargo ships, 1,400 barges, 800 tugs, 770 dredgers, 538 tankers, as well as many sundry exploration vessels, research vessels, ferries, pilgrim vessels, pilot boats, rockcutters, icebreakers, cable ships, crane ships, floating cranes, floating docks, oil drilling rigs, lighters, colliers, fishing boats, launches and many yachts, including royal and presidential craft.[10]

While the Clyde is but a shadow of its former glory days, it is still active in shipbuilding, particularly warships. In February 2006, the 7,350 tonne Type 45 destroyer HMS *Daring* was launched, the first of six in this class being built on the Clyde, followed in 2007 by HMS *Dauntless*, then HMS *Diamond*, HMS *Dragon*, HMS *Defender* and HMS *Duncan*, which was launched in 2010. The 150 m long vessels were the most powerful, advanced and deadly warships in the world when they came into service in 2009. Also on the Clyde, in conjunction with Rosyth dockyard, planning and development is underway for the two largest warships in British history, the aircraft carriers HMS *Queen Elizabeth* and HMS *Prince of Wales*, both of 65,000 tonnes, which are both due to be commissioned in 2020, keeping alive the Clyde tradition founded by Napier and others.

Robert Napier and Sons fitted the first, simple, mass-market triple expansion engine on the *Aberdeen*. Powerful and fuel efficient, it was the driving force for the full change from sail to steam, and ushered in a half century of tramp steamers on the world's sea lanes.[11]

In 1849, Napier built the world's first train ferry, the *Leviathan*, (designed by Scotsman Thomas Grainger) which took Edinburgh and Northern Railway trains across the Firth of Forth from Granton to Burntisland. The actual idea for the roll-on/roll-off ferry is claimed for Englishman Thomas Bouch in 1850. Bouch was more famous for his first Tay Bridge, which disastrously collapsed in a storm in 1879, but the world's first roll-on/roll-off service actually started in 1833, some 17 years before that of Bouch. It was operated by the Monkland and Kirkintilloch Railway, which operated a wagon ferry on the Forth and Clyde Canal in Scotland. The *Leviathan* ferry-boat was used only for goods wagons except on its opening day when it transported a railway carriage with passengers. In 1862, the North British Railway took over the ferry from the Edinburgh, Perth & Dundee Railway. The ferry continued in use until the opening of the Forth Bridge in 1890.[12]

George Rennie 1791-1866 was a civil engineer, son of the Scottish engineer John Rennie (1761-1821) and the brother of Sir John Rennie (1794-1874). George, in 1839, built the engines for SS *Archimedes* which was the ship that tested the first effective screw propeller designed by

Englishman Francis Petit Smith and the first steamship ever to be driven by a screw propeller. Such a propeller was fitted to a small iron steamer of 98 tons (88.9 tonnes) displacement, called *Mermaid*, and in May 1843 it achieved a speed of 10.5 knots (19.3 km/h) and, as a result of this trial, it was renamed HMS *Dwarf* and became the first iron screw steamer the British Government possessed.[1]

During the 1820s, Rennie designed the bridge over the Serpentine in Hyde Park and materially improved Thomas Harrison's design for Grosvenor Bridge over the Dee in Chester.[2] With his more famous brother, John, he planned and built the railway to connect Liverpool and Manchester, opened in 1830. It was on this 50 km track that the famous *Rocket* locomotive, built by George Stephenson, was chosen over competitors, thus founding modern rail transport. In 1846, he was appointed Chief Engineer for the railway between Namur and Liege in Belgium and planned the railway from Mons to Manege. He built the Grosvenor Bridge at Chester. He invented the first biscuit-making machinery.[3]

Image 29 – Serpentine Bridge, Hyde Park, London

Roderick Impey Murchison 1792-1871 was the most politically powerful geologist of the 19th century. He developed the modern classification of the Palaeozoic, which previously consisted only of the Greywacke and Coal Measures (Carboniferous). He first defined the Silurian system to distinguish his Welsh rocks from Sedgwick's older, Cambrian "territory"; he then defined the Devonian to resolve a stratigraphic dispute with Henry de la Beche, and finally defined the Permian as an intermediate between the Carboniferous and Triassic. His emphasis on biostratigraphy eventually brought him into a lifelong dispute with Adam Sedgwick over the placement of the Cambrian-Silurian boundary (the two are now separated by the Ordovician), but also modernised geological thinking about time scales.[1]

A founding father of geological science and geographical exploration, he was both President of the Royal Geographical Society and Director-General of the Geological Survey. His identification of the Silurian system in geology – and subsequent prediction of the location of economic riches – is as notable as is his patronage of David Livingstone and other figures of Victorian exploration. More than any contemporary, Murchison emerged as the eminent Victorian who "sold" science to the imperial government, on the grounds of utility as much as prestige.[2]

With Sedgwick, he attacked the difficult problem of the geological structure of the Alps, and their joint paper giving the results of their study is one of the classics in the literature of Alpine geology. During the later years of his life a large part of his time was devoted to the affairs of the Royal Geographical Society, of which he was in 1830 one of the founders, and he was president 1843-1845, 1851-1853, 1856-1859 and 1862-1871.[3]

He was founder of the British Association in 1831 with David Brewster and James David Forbes (both Scots). The learned societies of his own country bestowed their highest rewards upon him: The Royal Society gave him the Copley medal, the Geological Society its Wollaston medal, and The Royal Society of Edinburgh its Brisbane medal. There was hardly a foreign scientific society of note which had not his name enrolled among its honorary members. The French Academy of Sciences awarded him the prix Cuvier, and elected him one of its eight foreign members in succession to Michael Faraday.[4]

James Beaumont Neilson 1792-1865 made a major improvement to the steel industry with his hot blast process. Iron production increased considerably with the advent of the hot blast process in which air blown into a blast furnace was preheated. This greatly reduced the amount of fuel required and the process, patented in 1828 by Neilson, was soon being used in every furnace in Scotland except, as at October 1845, one at the Carron Works.[1] Before long more than half of Britain's furnaces were of this type and its popularity quickly spread to America and Europe, greatly increasing productivity and reducing costs. Use of the hot blast tripled iron output per tonne of coal and permitted the profitable recovery of iron from lower-grade ores. It also made possible the efficient use of raw coal and lower grades of coal instead of coke and permitted the construction of larger smelting furnaces. "Without question, it was the development of the iron industry – employing anthracite coal as fuel – which propelled the United States into a world power for more than a century. The vast iron and steel industry was born; fortunes were made, hundreds of thousands of workers gained employment and the product was used in the building of railroads, ships, skyscrapers and munitions. This evolution – begun in the late 1830s – was made possible by the development of the Pennsylvania anthracite coal fields and the harnessing of the powers of the Lehigh, Schuylkill and other rivers for transportation and power. The real key to the use of anthracite was employment of what is known as the 'hot blast'. Here, the air that is blown into the base of the furnace is heated to a temperature of at least 300F [149C] prior to injection into furnace through pipes known as tuyeres. Credit for the first implementation of this hot-blast process is given to Scotsman James B. Neilson."[2]

The use of a blast of air to increase the heat smelting of iron in a furnace goes back to ancient times, but this air blast was cool, not hot. Indeed, it was accepted wisdom of ironworkers and others that the colder the air, the more effective would be the furnace. Neilson turned this convention on its head through keen observation and repeated experiment. By using a hot air blast, Neilson revolutionised the iron industry. With the pre-Neilson practice, the coal found in Scotland had to be coked before it could be used for smelting and even then, it performed poorly. The hot air blast permitted this coal to be used unprocessed, making available vast quantities of coal not only in Scotland but throughout Britain, particularly the inferior and harder anthracite or non-bituminous coal of South Wales.[3] Neilson's method spread throughout Europe, North America and India, permitting iron output to be tripled and larger blast furnaces to be built in time for the greatly increased demand brought on by the coming of the railways and steamships.

Neilson invented the smokeless swallow-tail jet for use with gas lamps, providing such an improvement in gas lighting that it became universally used. He was also the first to remove oil and tar from gas by passing it through charcoal.

James Dunlop 1793-1848 made about 40,000 observations which form the basis of the *Catalogue of 7385 Stars from Observations Made at the Observatory at Parramatta* and, with an instrument built by himself, made the observations for his catalogues of nebulae and star clusters, and double stars. In June 1822, Dunlop was the first to see the reappearance of Encke's comet. This was only the second case of the predicted return of a comet being verified, the first being that of Halley in 1758. He prepared a catalogue of 621 nebulae, published in *Philosophical Transactions* in 1828, and for his list of double stars, published in *Memoirs of the Royal Astronomical Society* in 1829.[1]

Dunlop compiled the second-ever catalogue of southern star clusters, nebulae and galaxies from Parramatta (NSW, Australia) using a 23 cm reflecting telescope. Initially acclaimed, the catalogue and author were later criticised and condemned by others – including Sir John Herschel – and both the catalogue and author are now largely unknown. The criticism of the catalogue centred on the large number of fictitious or "missing" objects, yet detailed analysis reveals the remarkable completeness of the catalogue, despite its inherent errors. In 2010, astronomers Glen Cozens, Andrew Walsh and Wayne Orchiston stated in the *Journal of Astronomical History and Heritage*, "We believe that James Dunlop was an important early Australian astronomer, and his catalogue should be esteemed as the southern equivalent of Charles Messier's famous northern catalogue."[2]

The most spectacular original discovery of Dunlop is perhaps that of peculiar radio galaxy NGC 5128 in Centaurus (also called Centaurus A) – his Dunlop 482. Also, included in his original discoveries are Sculptor Group galaxies NGC 55 (Dun 507), 300 (Dun 530), and 7793 (Dun 608), and a considerable number of further southern galaxies, open and globular clusters, diffuse nebulae, and 4 planetary nebulae (NGC 2818=Dun 564, NGC 5189=Dun 252, NGC 5882=Dun 447, and NGC 6563=Dun 606). Dunlop has included 6 Messier objects in his list: M54=Dun 624, M55=Dun 620, M62=Dun 627, M69=Dun 613, M70=Dun 614, and M83=Dun 628.[3]

William Handyside 1793-1850 was a civil engineer working mostly in St Petersburg in the early 19th century. Handyside designed a machine to test the chains being built by Charles Baird for Russian suspension bridges in the 1820s. With Auguste de Montferrand, he worked on the Alexander Column and St. Isaac's Cathedral. Handyside worked on the ground level colonnade of pillars and the columns supporting the dome and devised special machinery to help with construction. This included a colonnade of forty-eight granite pillars, each of 2.4 m diameter and 17 m high, and a circle of thirty-six monolithic pillars, each 12.8 m high, raised 61 m off the ground, and surmounted by an iron dome 40 m in diameter.

He developed machinery to assist in its construction and helped with the design of the iron dome, its gilding, and with casting its decorative bronze work.[1] He worked on, but didn't design, the *Elizaveta* steamship, launched in 1815 in St Petersburg, and went on to design and build another ten vessels.[2]

Image 30 – St. Isaac's Cathedral, St. Petersburg, Russia

Thomas Grainger 1794-1852 was a railway engineer whose work was mostly in Scotland, but he built East Yorkshire Junction Railway; West Yorkshire Junction Railway; and the Leeds, Dewsbury, and Manchester Railway. He was the engineer in charge of the Leeds to Thirsk line, which opened in 1849 and included some remarkable achievements with four major viaducts and the Bramhope Tunnel, the construction of which required the solution of considerable drainage problems. Grainger also built the great viaduct at Yarm over the Tees, completed in 1849, which was 695 m long.[1]

Probably his most remembered innovation was the design of a train ferry in 1849. Earlier, in 1833, the Monkland and Kirkintilloch Railway operated a wagon ferry on the Forth and Clyde Canal in Scotland. In April 1836, the first railroad car ferry in the USA, the *Susquehanna* entered service on the Susquehanna River between Havre de Grace and Perryville, Maryland. The first "modern" train ferry, the *Leviathan*, was designed in 1849 by Thomas Grainger for the Edinburgh, Perth and Dundee Railway to cross the Firth of Forth between Granton and Burntisland. "In 1850 the harbour had the distinction of being the Fife terminal of the world's first public train ferry from Granton designed by Thomas Grainger, but with an ingenious loading mechanism accommodating the state of the tide designed by Thomas Bouch."[2]

"The ferries operated successfully from 1850 onwards, generally without any problems, although the crossings were suspended in very rough weather. This was the first roll-on/roll-off train ferry in the world and was withdrawn only in 1890 when the Forth Bridge, further upstream, was completed along with substantial new railway lines to connect it to the rest of the railway network. The vessels themselves and the shore installations were dependent on each other, and purpose-designed. Both at Granton and Burntisland, the slipways were constructed to allow the vessels to be loaded and unloaded at all states of the tide. This was accomplished in two ways – firstly the gantry structures could be moved up and down the slipways, and secondly there were ramps, which could themselves be moved, to connect the shore side to the vessels. Stationary steam engines powered ropes on pulley wheels between the rails to pull wagons on and off the ferries." The *Leviathan* had a capacity of 20 wagons.[3]

William Mackenzie 1794-1851 was the world's first international railway contractor and "one of the most important figures in the civil engineering world of the second quarter of the nineteenth century – a period when British civil engineering, building on the technological lead of the Industrial Revolution, spread beyond the shores of the British Isles, and began developing the infrastructure of much of the rest of the world."[1]

Mackenzie had been the resident engineer for the 52 m long, 7.3 m wide Mythe Bridge at Tewkesbury, which was built in 1826, but his involvement with canals and bridges gave way to railways with his first commission being the Lime Street tunnel underneath Liverpool for the Liverpool and Manchester Railway. Built in 1836, the tunnel was 1.8 km in length. This was followed by other contracts such as the Leicester-Nottingham-Derby line, Glasgow and Greenock line, the London and Birmingham, the Trent Valley, the Lancaster and Carlisle, the North Union, the Ormskirk, the Caledonian railway, and the 20-arch, 457 m Dutton Viaduct on the Grand Junction Railway in 1836.[2]

By 1840, Mackenzie had become one of the leading railway contractors in Britain with considerable financial resources. At this time, the French railway system was being planned, but considerable problems were being experienced in obtaining the necessary capital and expertise to construct the system. The interest of British capitalists and engineers was aroused. When tenders for the Paris-Rouen line were invited, Mackenzie and Englishman Thomas Brassey joined forces to create the company of Mackenzie & Brassey. Over the next ten years they emerged as the largest contracting firm in the world, building much of the French railway network as well as fulfilling other contracts in Britain, France, Belgium and Spain.[3]

Mackenzie, in partnership with Brassey, built the Paris-Rouen railway (131 km) in 1841. "By the end of 1843, Mackenzie & Brassey were a major force on the French scene and British methods of large-scale railway construction and financing under the direction of contractors had been successfully, if temporarily, reconciled with the bureaucratic and highly centralised conventions prevailing on French civil engineering projects of national importance."[4] The two partners went on to finish the 97 km Rouen-Le Havre line in 1847, and Boulogne and Amiens, and built or advised on several other railways in France (including an extension to Dieppe from Le Havre), Belgium, and Spain, notably Barcelona to Mataro (the first railway in Spain built in 1848 and being 90 km), and the railway between the Franco-Spanish border and Madrid via Bilbao.

Within the next three years they had laid 703 km of line, including the Orleans and Bordeaux Railway which alone was 473 km. Mackenzie went on to advise upon or build more railways in Belgium, Spain and the Italian peninsula as well as throughout Britain – Colchester to Ipswich, the Buckinghamshire line, Kings Cross (London) to Peterborough, Rugby to Stafford, Chester to Holyhead, Lancaster and Carlisle, and Carlisle to Glasgow, and Liverpool-Ormskirk-Preston. Altogether, alone or in partnership, he was responsible for nearly 1,000 km of line in Britain and some 830 km of track in France.[5]

In their work in France, Mackenzie and Brassey sought to apply the methods of construction that had already succeeded in Britain. The challenge was to adapt these to foreign circumstances.

Both at home and abroad, Mackenzie first toured the route of a proposed line, usually in the company of one of its engineers. He then assessed the ability of the area around the line to supply him with the materials that would be required in great volume and, if obtained outside that area, would incur severe transport costs.[6]

During his early years as a contractor, Mackenzie worked on his own, but as the scale of the enterprise increased he brought in other members of his family, notably his brother Edward. As William's health declined, Edward played an increasingly important role in the firm. Following William's death in 1851 and the dissolution of the partnership with Brassey, Edward completed the work on the French lines. Brassey went on to become the best known of railway contractors, while the name of William Mackenzie faded into obscurity and never received the recognition it deserved. Edward retired from railway work in the mid-1850s, and other younger members of the family died while working on some of the major railway contracts around the world.[7]

The French, above all, were impressed by the speed at which both Mackenzie and Brassey worked and their ability to take on assignments extending over an entire line. They would not have disputed the claim that Mackenzie was the senior partner in "the first conspicuous effort of British [railway] construction enterprise abroad".[8]

John Rennie 1794-1874, son of the famous civil engineer of the same name, continued the work of his father in removing excess water from the Lincolnshire fens and Norfolk Broads. In fact, John Rennie junior spent a good part of his career completing or extending work started by his father, who died in 1821. He was also one of the pioneers of floating foundations (aka slab foundation) for buildings, using this idea for a warehouse in the West Indian Docks of London.[1] (The word "floating" is used in its literal sense. When a body floats in water, it displaces a volume of water, the weight of which is equal to the weight of the floating body. In just the same way, a building can be floated on soil, the weight of the building and its loads—being equal to the weight of the "displaced" soil, i.e., the soil that must be excavated to provide for the foundation structure of the building. … Construction requirements may modify this desirable state slightly, but the basic idea is sound).[2] Rennie junior built London Bridge, which had been designed by his father, and he also completed the Admiralty dock works at Sheerness, Woolwich, Ramsgate, and the breakwater at Plymouth, as well as undertaking work on other harbours in England and Ireland.

William Allen (Allan) c1795-1840 and James Thom introduced the metal compensation frame in the piano to compensate for string tunings due to atmospheric changes. In respect of pianos, "the first notable European patent or invention produced, after [John Isaac] Hawkins' 'portable upright iron frame grands,' was Allen & Thom's system of metal tube and plate bracing patented in 1820. William Allen was the theoretical inventor of the idea, but James Thom, or Thorns, the foreman at Stodart's, put the invention into practical shape. Allen was a tuner engaged in this concern meanwhile. Like Thom he, too, was a Scotchman."[1]

The metal compensation frame consisted of nine metal tubes of brass in the bass and iron in the treble. Allen, who was employed by Robert Stodart, originally intended his metal system of framing to be primarily for compensation, but it soon became, in other hands, a framing for resistance. Allen's idea was to meet the divergence in tuning caused in brass and iron strings by atmospheric changes by compensating tubes and plates of the same metals, guaranteeing their stability by a cross batoning of stout wooden bars and a metal bar across the wrest-plank. Allen, being simply a tuner, had not the full practical knowledge for carrying out the idea. He had to ally himself with Stodart's foreman, Thom; and Allen and Thom patented the invention on 15 January 1820. The firm of Stodart at once acquired the patent.[2] "The truly successful patented inventions were those that became a makers' hallmark: Robert Wornum's Albion square, Erards' double escarpment action, Thom and Allen's compensation frame in the pianos of William Stodart."[3]

James Braid 1795-1860 is one of the giants in the history of hypnosis. He became interested in mesmerism (named after German physician Franz Anton Mesmer) as a result of watching a demonstration by Charles Lafontaine, whose personality and exhibitions were very similar to those of a stage hypnotist of the present day. Lafontaine came from a theatrical family, was very self-confident and would demonstrate the more dramatic hypnotic phenomena on a particularly susceptible member of the audience or a "good" subject he had brought with him. Braid's personality was quite opposite. He was calm, rational and well-balanced. After watching the demonstration in November 1841, he began to experiment for himself, and quickly dismissed the mistaken theories of the time that mesmeric trances were due to some form of magnetism. He began demonstrating and lecturing and encouraging open discussion and criticism. He was attacked on both flanks. On the one hand, the Mesmerists were naturally incensed at his undermining of the belief in some magnetic power they possessed. On the other, there were the average men and women who were incredulous of the effects of hypnosis and believed that some trickery was involved.[1]

By 1844, Braid had discovered that the practice had been used for centuries in the East. The analogy with yogic meditation soon became obvious to Braid and he wrote, "The Fakirs and Yogins have caused ecstatic trance in themselves for 2,400 years, for religious purpose, by a process quite similar to that which I taught my patients so they could hypnotise themselves using continual fixation upon the end of the nose or another part of the body or an imaginary object, and with intense attention and while holding or slowing down their breath."[2]

It was due to the researches of Braid that hypnosis was placed on a scientific basis.[3] Braid, as well as introducing the concept of hypnotism, also coined the term "self-hypnotism" to refer to the fact that one could hypnotise oneself, and he recounts, in a memorable passage, how he used self-hypnotism to manage his own severe attacks of rheumatic pain. Indeed, as Braid defined hypnotism as being a state of focused attention upon a single dominant idea or mental image, accompanied by expectation of a response, hypnotism and self-hypnotism were never really two distinct activities.[4]

Unlike Mesmer, he maintained a good professional standing in his community during his entire lifetime, and was not only noted as an excellent hypnotist, but also was widely acclaimed for his operating cases of clubbed foot and other deformities. Having concluded that the phenomenon was a form of sleep, Braid named it after Hypnos, the Greek god of sleep and master of dreams, but by 1847, he discovered that all the major phenomena of hypnotism, such as catalepsy, anaesthesia and amnesia, could be induced without sleep. Realising his choice of the term hypnosis had been a mistake; he tried to rename it to monoideism. It was too late. By then

Braid's terms of *Hypnosis* and *Hypnotism* had already become widely adopted as part of all the major European languages.[5]

Although Braid is best known for his renaming Mesmer's art "hypnotism", he also was responsible for a number of ideas that still persist until the present day. They are as follows: 1: That hypnosis is a powerful tool which should be limited entirely to medical and dental professions. 2: That although hypnotism was capable of curing many diseases for which there had formally been no remedy, it nevertheless was no panacea and was only a medical tool which should be used in combination with other medical information, drugs, remedies, etc in order to properly treat the patient. 3: That in skilled hands there is no great danger associated with hypnotic treatment and neither was there pain or discomfort. 4: That a good deal more study and research would be necessary to thoroughly understand a number of theoretical concepts regarding hypnosis.[6]

David Tod 1795-1859 and **John MacGregor 1802-1858** launched, in 1834, the paddle steamer *Rob Roy* from their newly-founded shipbuilding firm of Tod & MacGregor. The following year they launched *Vale of Leven*, which was the first iron ship actually built on the Clyde (other sources say this ship was built in 1837). In 1853, the SS *Bengal* was fitted with a speaking tube between the bridge and the engine room, possibly the first time this form of communication was used in a steamship, although speaking tubes had been noted as far back as 1780 in sailing ships, usually to communicate from the mast top to the bridge. Also in 1853, Tod and McGregor had built two sheds 18 m high and wide, with one 103 m long and the other 85 m, both having a corrugated glass roof. "These sheds had been another pioneering achievement for the two engineers and they are believed to have been the first of their kind in the world. Gas lighting inside permitted work to be carried on at all hours and the cranes also accelerated production. John Macgregor recalled them in his speech at the opening of the new dry dock, saying '…we put up a castle in the air – it was an ornament to the River Clyde; but one windy night threw it all down' (they were not replaced)."[1] The "windy night" was a severe gale in 1856 which caused more than £15,000 damage and delayed its completion. The dry dock mentioned was the first on the Clyde and was constructed by Tod and McGregor at a cost in excess of £100,000, opening on 28 January 1858.

Earlier, in 1850, they had launched the *City of Glasgow*, the first ship designed specifically for carrying steerage passengers (what would now be termed "economy" passengers). With an eye to cashing in on the huge numbers of people crossing the Atlantic to America, especially in the wake of the Irish potato famine, the *City of Glasgow* could carry 85 first class, 130 second class, and 400 third (steerage) class passengers. After a number of successful voyages, it disappeared without trace in January 1854. Their *City of Paris* held the westbound Blue Riband from 1889 to 1891 and again from 1892 to 1893. Eastbound their *City of Brussels* held it from 1869 to 1873.

Nicol Hugh Baird 1796-1849 was the nephew of St Petersburg industrialist Charles Baird, with whom Hugh worked for some four years. He was then employed in Scotland with his father, also Hugh, until the latter's death in 1828 when he proceeded to Canada, where he became Clerk of Works on the Rideau Canal, then Chief Engineer on the Chambly Canal. He was engineer on the

Welland Canal and the Trent Severn Waterway. "The records of his work in setting up and running the early work on the Trent Severn Waterway are models not only of professional design skills but also of the application of the principles of Project Management which we attempt to apply to todays' projects and are inclined to believe are 'modern' applications."[1] He built a sweeping paddle wheel to make canal locks more easily traversed by steamships. "Each of his two side-mounted paddle wheels was narrower than normal, thus reducing the vessel's width, and each had a deeper stroke, thereby imparting greater speed and stability". In 1845, the Admiralty authorised the alteration of the Mohawk River at Penetanguishene to utilise Baird's paddle-wheels. With them the vessel was able to come down through the Welland Canal and so "supervise the whole of the Lakes."[2]

In June 1845, he was re-employed by the board, possibly through the influence of Irish-born civil engineer Hamilton Hartley Killaly, to lay out and superintend the construction of the Arthabaska Road, joining Quebec and Melbourne. He was also to undertake the improvement of the Kennebec Road, from Quebec to the Maine border. Baird completed the surveys by the end of the year and until the summer of 1848 supervised construction of the roads.[3]

He devised a plan for a "suspension wooden bridge," for which he received a patent in 1831. His most significant contribution lies in the development of early canal and road systems in Upper and Lower Canada. In September 1832, he was commissioned by the government to survey the mouth of the Trent River and design a bridge to span it. In 1836, Baird was given the opportunity to carry out his plans when he was employed as superintending engineer by both the commissioners for the improvement of the Trent River and the commissioners for the inland waters of the Newcastle District. With the exception of a brief period in 1842, he was employed continuously on the Trent works until October 1843.

"The outstanding contributor to the construction of the TSW [Trent Severn Waterway] was … Nichol [sic] Hugh Baird. It was his route and plan that prevailed. Without his exertions and exhortations, the beautiful waterway which has given pleasure and recreation to millions during the last 60-odd years might never have been. Like many of Canada's other fine engineers who designed and built the canals, the railways, the bridges, the public buildings, the whole physical fabric of the country, Baird has been ignored by history."[4]

John Condie 1796-1860 invented the water-cooled tuyere in 1834 (a tuyere is a nozzle through which an air blast is delivered to a forge or blast furnace). Condie's tuyere, often called the Scotch tuyere, consisted of a coil of wrought-iron pipe embedded in a mass of cast iron, with a hole in the centre in which the tuyere nozzle rests. One year earlier, in 1833, Scottish pig iron sold at 628 pence per tonne, but by 1844 it had dropped to 371 pence. Scottish iron production had risen from 32,600 tonnes in 1827 to 362,800 tonnes in 1845, in which year Scotland was producing about one third of Britain's total output. By 1884, it had risen to 900,000 tonnes and the cost, compared to the immediate period before the hot blast, had fallen by one third.[1] Much of this increase came about from the hot air blast of James Beaumont Neilson coupled with Condie's tuyere. Note: In 1833, the year before Condie's invention, metallurgist David Mushet attributed an increased productivity of 33% to the hot blast process, a massive improvement in efficiency. The *North British Review* of November 1845 stated that for 400,000 tons (362,870 tonnes) of pig iron produced there was a saving of £650,000 based on a reduction of 2,000,000 tons (1,814,400 tonnes) of coal and 200,000 tons (181,437 tonnes) of limestone. That is a saving of £1.62 per ton of pig iron produced.

In 1840, Condie took out a patent for improvements in applying springs to carriages, both road and rail, and he patented improvements to James Nasmyth's steam hammer on 15 October 1846. In Nasmyth's original design, the steam hammer was guided vertically and operated by a vertical steam cylinder located directly over an anvil. His cylinder was fixed, with the hammer attached to the piston rod. In Condie's adaptation, the hammer had the piston fixed and the hammer was attached to the lower end of the cylinder, providing more power and control.

Robert Foulis 1796-1866 invented the foghorn. Robert was the son of renowned publisher Andrew Foulis. He migrated to Canada and established New Brunswick's first iron works, built early steamships and founded a school of arts. He was an artist, inventor and surveyor of part of the St John River for the New Brunswick government. One of his inventions, installed in 1859, was a foghorn operated by steam. This device was particularly powerful and produced a loud blast followed by a shorter "grunt". Given that in some parts of North America's Atlantic coast fogs could last weeks, and around St John had been known to last more than two months, it greatly improved safety as its sound carried many kilometres – a sound that was to become very familiar a century later to movie-goers worldwide. His automated steam foghorn was the first anywhere in the world when it was installed in 1859 on New Brunswick's Partridge Island, replacing a less effective cannon and bell system.

Captain Winchester of the steamer, *Eastern City*, was typical of the respect this new invention was gaining from seamen; "On the whole coast of America there is not another alarm equal to the one spoken of". Foulis' invention of the steam-powered fog alarm saved the lives of literally thousands of seamen. His revolutionary concept worked by piping high-pressure steam through a nozzle, emitting a loud, deep tone which could be heard for miles. He further refined his idea so that the repetition of the tones would be timed and each alarm would have a distinct frequency, so ships' captains would be able to determine which alarm they were hearing simply by timing the sound. [1]

John McDowall 1796-1857 improved, in 1836, the planing machine for the production of tongue-and-groove floorboards.[1] He began his career as a mechanic in the cotton mills of Johnston, Renfrewshire, and founded his own general engineering business in the town in 1823. By 1834, he had developed and patented a saw frame and a wood-planing machine which were the basis for specialisation in a wide range of woodworking machinery, much of which was exported. In 1836, McDowall invented the first practicable planing machine for the production of tongue-and-groove floorboards.[2]

"About the year 1836 Mr John McDowall, of the Walkinshaw Foundry, Johnstone, near Glasgow, came prominently forward with some most ingenious novelties and improvements in sawing and planing machinery; previously, however, to 1836 he had erected several planing and other machines, in Manchester and elsewhere. These planing machines were made from the designs of Mr Malcolm Muir, of Glasgow, to whom a patent was granted in the year 1827. Some years later Mr McDowall patented a high-speed tension sawing machine, and he also invented and erected a number of cross-cutting and other machines for the Government at Woolwich

Arsenal. One of these [was] a traversing cross-cut circular saw bench. The saw itself was about 7 feet [2.1 m] in diameter, the largest yet made from one solid piece of cast steel.

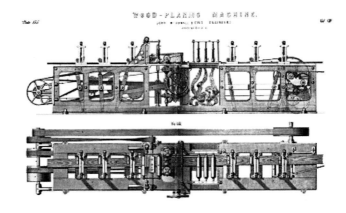

Image 31 – McDowall's Wood-Planing Machine
The Practical Mechanics Journal, Volume 8, October 1855

The driving gear was a great novelty, the saw spindle being totally unconnected with the actuating power; the motion was communicated to the saw through two frictional cones of buff leather embracing the saw on either side, and running at a high speed. With this arrangement, the whole of the saw up to the cones was available for cutting, there being no pulleys in the way of the timber, as there are when saws for cross-cutting are driven in the usual way. The saw ran at 300 revolutions per minute, and by a very ingenious arrangement could be made to travel the whole length of the mill, some 70 feet; and being placed below the ground could also be raised above or depressed below the floor line at pleasure. In fact, the whole machine did infinite credit to its designer."[3]

John Paterson Reid (1796-1854) and **Thomas Johnson died after 1846** took out a patent for an automatic weft-replenishing device for looms. "Oct. 9 [1833] To John Paterson Reid, of the city of Glasgow, merchant and power-loom manufacturer, and Thomas Johnson, of the said city of Glasgow, mechanic, in the employment of John and Archibald Reid, of the said city of Glasgow, power-loom manufacturers, for an invention of certain improvements applicable to certain looms for weaving different sorts of cloth."[1]

"From a research of the earliest published records of patents relating to weaving, which records date from 15th July, 1620, it would appear that the credit for the first patent for an automatic weft-replenishing device for looms is due to Messrs. John Paterson Reid and Thomas Johnson, both of Glasgow, who are the joint patentees of an invention of such a device described in the Patent Specification, dated 20th March, 1834, No. 6579. This is a large document of 69 pages of text comprising over 35,000 words and 12 sheets of diagrams. It describes in a very lucid manner several improvements in power-looms, of which that relating to the automatic replenishing of weft is treated almost as if it were regarded, by the inventors, as of only secondary importance to the other improvements which they describe.

In view of the great progress which has been made within recent years in the development of these looms, and also in consideration of the fact that a patent, which was granted to Charles Parker nearly seven years subsequently, and is described in the Specification dated 22nd October, 1840, No. 8664, has been frequently cited as the first patent relating to the automatic supply of weft in looms, the first-named document acquires a special interest, not only as a record of what is probably the first attempt in that direction, but also because it establishes, beyond refutation, the date and rightful title to the first patent granted for such an invention."[2]

"Owing to an error in the index of the official British publication of *Abridgements of the Specifications relating to Weaving*, [author's italics] it was only recently that we discovered the first patent in which the idea of changing shuttles automatically is referred to. Such a reference occurs in that granted John Patterson [sic] Reid and Thomas Johnson, No 6579 in the British Patent Office. The specification refers to a number of different inventions, contemplating the weaving of four webs of cloth at one vertical loom. It shows a mechanism designed to change the shuttles when any one weft thread breaks, or fails, the substitution occurring by an instantaneous movement, without any act of the attendant, and without stopping the loom, the mechanism being brought into action by a weft stopper annexed to the shuttle. The specification also refers to changing shuttle boxes to bring different coloured weft into action. It also contains a jacquard mechanism. Both Reid and Johnson were prolific inventors, Johnson having taken out a patent as early as 1803, for a dressing machine, and Reid as early as 1827, for a lay motion."[3] Note: Thomas Johnson may have been born in England, although described as being from Glasgow.

Alexander Buchanan (dates unknown) developed a technique, in 1822, of weaving chenille, which had hitherto been made by hand in France, and he used it to create fuzzy shawls for women's wear. His chenille shawls were reversible; an arrangement to bring all the velvet to one side suggested the carpet patent which was the beginning of the great Templeton manufactures.

"Chenille" is French for "caterpillar." It's an appropriate name, since chenille is a fuzzy fabric that had a metamorphic development. Three distinct "chenille" products emerged between 1754 and 1895 in France, Scotland and the United States. The first was an embroidery-like fabric intended as an appliqué for hand embroidery work. The second was a mass-produced shawl that inspired a machine-manufactured technique. The third was a hand-needlework technique for cotton bedspreads that was brought into factory bedspread production.[1]

Chenille fabric is made by forming a tightly wound core for the yarn. Piles, which are short lengths of yarn, are wrapped around this core, causing its edges to stand on right angles from the centre of the fabric. It is this that gives chenille fabric its unique look, softness, and change of colour dependent on how light shines on the fabric from each direction. The yarn is commonly manufactured from cotton, but can also be made using acrylic, rayon and olefin.

Buchanan, of Paisley, created a way of mass producing chenille fabric that he sold as fuzzy shawls. The way he made these fuzzy shawls was from tufts of coloured woollen yarn, woven on a blanket fabric that was then cut into thin strips and fizzed on rollers that were heated. Buchanan's technique was developed further by another shawl manufacturer; James Templeton. Templeton refined the technique so he could machine manufacture tufted carpets, replicating the quality and appearance of hand-woven oriental carpets.[2]

Maxwell Dick 1797-1870 patented the safety rail for use with the monorail. He is also associated with the invention of the screw propeller – one of many such inventors. Dick promoted the monorail for crossing rough terrain. The *Engineers and Mechanics Encyclopedia* of 1839 states, "A suspension railway, combining the characteristic features of H[enry] R[obinson] Palmer and J.G. Fisher … was patented by Maxwell Dick, of Irving, in Ayrshire, on the 21st of May, 1829; doubtless, in ignorance of those precedents. ... Mr Dick has, however, added, what he denominates 'safety rails,' one on each side of the track, against which anti-friction wheels, attached to the carriages, are made to act, in case of the carriages receiving from any cause an impulse upwards. The patent likewise embraces a curious combination of wheel-work, for communicating a high velocity to the carriages."[1]

An article published in *The British Magazine* of 1830 states, "Mr Maxwell Dick, an Ayrshire gentleman, has been recently exhibiting in a room at Charing-cross, the model of a railway on the principle of suspension, with models also of carriages adapted to it. He claims for himself the merit of originality in the conception of this project, and though there is some reason to dispute his pretensions in this respect, it is impossible to refuse him the praise of ardent and persevering ingenuity. He has distinctly shown the plausibility of what others have theoretically suggested. A Mr H. Palmer, four or five years back, proposed by means of a railway of this kind to convey goods and passengers in a couple of hours from London to Brighton; but we are not aware that he proceeded farther than mere suggestion. Mr Dick, however, by (as we judge) a process of independent reflection, has devised and elaborated the present model, which very clearly shows on a small scale, the practicability of that scheme which he proposes for unlimited public adoption."[2]

Thomas Drummond 1797-1840 was surveying near Belfast in 1825, two years before Nicéphore Niépce created his first photograph. Limelight produced a very brilliant light that could be concentrated to illuminate the subject better. Drummond initially used limelight in Ireland during the trigonometrical survey to make distant surveying stations visible – in 1825 one of these lights on Davis' Mountain in Belfast could be seen 105 km away at Slieve Snaught in Donegal. He also used limelight in lighthouses and greatly improved the heliostat which had been invented by Dutchman Willem Jacob s' Gravesende. He spent the latter years of his life in Ireland, commencing "as a military engineer with the Ordnance Survey that would forever change the namescape and historical memory of the country. He stayed on to serve in various capacities – as a railway developer, the director of the Boundary Commission set up to apportion parliamentary seats, and eventually as Under-Secretary for Ireland going on to be one of the most successful Under-Secretaries for Ireland (1835-1840), telling landlords 'Property,' says Mr Drummond, has its duties, as well as its rights;' thereby broadly intimating that the neglect of the one it was which caused the violation of the other."[1]

Drummond was in charge of the Boundary Commission established after the 1832 Reform Act to create fairer parliamentary constituencies with Englishman and fellow Royal Engineer, Robert Kearsley Dawson. In their work on the Commission common considerations were the number of inhabitants and dwellings, amount and use of land, taxes raised from the area, industrial activity (if any) and some idea of how many people were thereafter entitled to vote based on the changes introduced in the Reform Act. The lessons learnt from this first boundary commission were put to good use around the world where members of the Royal Engineer Corps have determined boundaries on behalf of the British as well as foreign governments; some notable boundary commissions include: 1839: Canada-United States; 1858: Canada-United States; 1856 and 1857: Russo-Turkish; 1857: Russo-Turkish; 1878: Turkish-Bulgarian; 1880: Greco-Turkish; 1884: Russo-Afghan; 1894: India-Afghanistan; 1902: Chile-Argentine; and 1911: Peru-Bolivia.

Drummond also greatly improved the heliostat, which was described in a paper published in 1826 by the Royal Society. His heliostat consisted of a mirror connected with two telescopes; the one, forming the axis of the instrument, for looking towards the station of observation, the other, for looking at the sun. The former telescope being turned on the station, and brought, along with the mirror, to a position of horizontality by means of screws and spirit-levels, the mirror was so connected with the latter telescope, that, as the telescope was turned to the sun, the mirror, moving with it, went into position to reflect the sun's rays to the station of observation. It was a problem of geometrical construction prettily solved. Drummond's solution proved of the highest practical importance. He made improvements on the instrument afterwards. The heliostat and the apparatus for exhibiting the light in survey operations, are fully described in the *Philosophical Transactions.*[2]

Despite his considerable achievements, Drummond seems to be best remembered for his limelight, or Drummond light as it was known for a while, which Englishman John Benjamin Dancer applied to optical projectors and, although never popular, some photographs were taken using Drummond light on sensitive paper. "By these two inventions [limelight and heliostat] Drummond armed the Survey officers with the most powerful means of overcoming the difficulties of observation by day and night."[3] Note: the invention of the heliostat is credited to several other people including Willem s'Gravesende, Giovanni Alonso Borelli, and Daniel Gabriel Fahrenheit. Carl Friedrich Gauss also developed one that used the sun's rays to illuminate a distant station. Drummond, who read about this, adapted it so it could be attached to a theodolite rather than a telescope, while also making it smaller, lighter, more portable and easier to adjust.[4]

Joseph Henry 1797-1878 "was acknowledged as the inventor of the electric motor, the father of daily weather forecasts, and the preserver of the Smithsonian".[1] Born to Scottish parents in New York State, he became one of the greatest American scientists of the 19th century. He improved on William Sturgeon's electromagnet, making it the most powerful known at that time, capable of lifting in excess of a tonne.

Henry discovered the property of self-inductance, where the magnetic field created by a changing current in a circuit itself induces a voltage in the same circuit. He was the first to tightly coil insulated wire around a ferrous core to make an extremely powerful electromagnet, improving on Sturgeon's electromagnet which used loosely coiled uninsulated wire. With this method, he built for Yale University the most powerful electromagnet of its day. He also showed that, when making an electromagnet using just two electrodes attached to a battery, it is best to wind several coils of wire in parallel but, when using a setup with multiple batteries, there should be only one single, long coil used.[2]

In his work – which made the electromagnetic telegraph possible over long distances – Henry demonstrated that a battery's electro-motive force needs to be proportional to the length of the conductor for effective transmission of electricity over long distances, a discovery that led to the creation of the *intensity magnet*, so called because it got the greatest magnetic force from an *intensity battery*, a type of battery that has high voltage and low current. Indeed, Henry suggested the intensity magnet be used for an electric telegraph and he solved the problem of power loss in long distance telegraphy when he invented the electromechanical relay in 1835. A coil of wire wound round a metal core carries a small amount of power that magnetises and pulls in a lever, closing a switch which can carry a large amount of power, (sometimes called an amplifier). If placed at regular intervals along the wire, it is possible to send a signal around the globe. Using the natural resistance of Earth as one path for the signal, only one wire is needed.[3]

A wire that he used for sending signals to his wife employed a remote electromagnet to close a switch for a stronger local circuit – the first magnetic relay. He discovered mutual inductance whereby the current through one inductor can induce a voltage in another nearby inductor, the means by which transformers operate. Credit for this discovery is given to English physicist Michael Faraday, but Henry discovered the phenomenon independently.

In 1831, he created one of the first machines to use electromagnetism for motion – one of the earliest ancestors of the modern DC motor. It didn't make use of rotating motion but was simply an electromagnet perched on a pole, rocking back and forth. The rocking motion was caused by one of the two leads on both ends of the magnet rocker touching one of the two battery cells, causing a polarity change, and rocking the opposite direction until the other two leads hit the other battery.[4]

In the *Philosophical Magazine* in August 1835, Francis Watkins wrote "We are indebted to Professor Joseph Henry, New Jersey College, Princeton, for the first hint, and for the first contrivance wherein electro-magnetic power is made to produce continuous motion."[5]

Henry's interests included acoustics and he identified the occurrence of *direct sound, early reflections* and *reverberation* in room acoustics, all of which form the critical link between one person talking and another listening. The level of direct sound, the reverberation time of the room, and the early/late reflections, all determine sound character and speech intelligibility in a room.

He went on to demonstrate that solids and liquids have similar levels of cohesion and he discovered with his brother-in-law and cousin, Stephen Alexander, that sunspots radiate less heat than the average of the general solar surface. He was the first to gather meteorological information and have it displayed on a map. He used observers stationed throughout North America to telegraph local weather conditions to a central location in New York.

In 1846, Henry became the first secretary of the Smithsonian Institution, Washington, DC, where he organised and supported a corps of volunteer weather observers. The success of the Smithsonian meteorological work led to the creation of the US Weather Bureau (later US Weather Service). One of Lincoln's chief technical advisers during the US Civil War, Henry was a primary organiser of the National Academy of Science and its second president (1868-1878).[6] He was secretary of the Smithsonian Institute from 1846 to his death in 1878. He was President of the *American Association for the Advancement of Science* from 1849 to 1850, and was a founder of the *Philosophical Society of Washington* in 1871, being its first President. Such was Henry's reputation and value as a scientist that the International System of Units (SI) uses the *henry* as a unit of inductance.

James Kennedy 1797-1886 was appointed manager of George Stephenson's locomotive works at Newcastle-on-Tyne in 1824. While in this position, he constructed two pairs of winding engines for use on the Stockton and Darlington Railway, and planned the first three (some sources say four) locomotives for the opening of the railway in 1825.[1] Later, in 1830, one of his locomotives, *Liverpool*, was the first built in Britain to have horizontal cylinders linked directly to the crank axle. The *Liverpool* was the pioneer of inside cylinders, practically horizontal, driving a crank-axle."[2] Kennedy moved on to shipping where he introduced the use of iron deck beams for vessels requiring exceptional strength, which soon became universally applied.

Thomas Kennedy 1797-1874 patented, in 1852, a major improvement in the water meter that gave it accuracy for the first time. The inspiration apparently came from fellow clockmaker John Cameron who was "doodling on the fly leaf of a bible" when he came up with a workable idea that was taken to fruition by Kennedy. "If it is desired to record the rate of flow with the piston and cylinder type of meter ... it becomes necessary to introduce a clock and drum, by means of which the number of operations in unit time are recorded or shown. This is effected in the Kennedy meter as follows: The recording arrangement consists of a crank, driven from the index gearing, and connected by means of a connecting rod to a vertical sliding bar. The gearing is so arranged that the crank, and therefore the sliding bar, makes one complete up and down motion for, say, 200 gallons [757 litres], and a line is thus drawn on the diagram, which is wound round the drum of the clock, a pencil being mounted on the lower end of the sliding bar."[1] Going into business with partners his company, Glenfield & Kennedy, eventually sold around the world and at its peak his factory covered 26 acres (10.5 hectares) and employed 2,600 people.

Charles Lyell 1797-1875 conclusively showed that the Earth was very old and had changed its form slowly, mainly from conditions such as erosion. Lyell was able to date the ages of rocks by using fossils embedded in the stone as time indicators. Charles Darwin made use of Lyell's data on fossils for his theory of evolution.[1]

Lyell studied the marine remains of the Italian Tertiary Strata and then conceived the idea of dividing this geological system into three or four groups, characterised by the proportion of recent to extinct species of shells.

In his *Principles of Geology* (1829), Lyell built a synthesis on the methodological limitation that the past could be studied only by analogy to what natural agencies, given enough time, could accomplish in the present. His opinion that there was uniformity in the causes of change – rather than catastrophic floods – "implied that they must forever produce an endless variety of effects, both in the animate and inanimate world". In Thomas Huxley's opinion, Lyell's work bore the primary responsibility for smoothing Charles Darwin's path. Alfred Russell Wallace credits Lyell's idea that the surface of the earth was in a continual state of slow modification for making obvious to him that life must be continually adjusting to these changed conditions.[2]

In August 1838, Lyell published the *Elements of Geology* which, from being originally an expansion of one section of the *Principles*, became a standard work on stratigraphical and paleontological geology.

His third great work, *The Antiquity of Man*, appeared in 1863, and ran through three editions in one year. In this, he gave a general survey of the arguments for man's early appearance on the

Earth, derived from the discoveries of flint implements in post-Pliocene strata in the Somme valley and elsewhere; he discussed also the deposits of the Glacial Epoch, and in the same volume he first gave his support to Darwin's theory of the origin of species.[3]

Lyell's *Principles of Geology* revolved around a variety of interests including geological surveys, uniformitarianism, volcanoes and geological dynamics, glaciers, stratigraphy, and evolution. He felt that geological surveys had the potential to provide information about mapping a country's natural resources. Because Lyell endorsed geological surveys, he helped to propel the oil, coal and other modern extractive industries.

Uniformitarianism is simply defined as the philosophy of naturalism. Lyell proposed four different ideas and these include uniformity of law, uniformity of kind, uniformity of methodology, and uniformity of degree. Because of Charles Lyell's work, the geological dynamics were understood by the destruction they produced. One of his contributions was explaining what caused earthquakes to occur. He also concluded that volcanoes were gradually built as opposed to being up-heaved as was previously thought. Lyell proposed that erratics could have been transported by glaciers. During times of global warming, the Polar Regions' ice would break off and float across the continents submerged in water carrying debris along with it.

The field of stratigraphy contained Lyell's most important work. During his time travelling from the south of France to Italy, with Roderick Impey Murchison, he concluded that current rock layers (strata) could be classified by the proportion and number of marine shells secured within.[4] To these groups, after consulting William Whewell as to the best nomenclature, he gave the names now universally adopted – Eocene (dawn of recent), Miocene (less of recent), and Pliocene (more of recent); and with the assistance of Gerard Paul Deshayes, he drew up a table of shells in illustration of this classification.

Thomas James Alan Henderson 1798-1844 was the first to measure the parallax of the bright double star Alpha Centauri. He performed a series of observations after its large proper motion had been pointed out to him by Manuel Johnson at St Helena. Between April 1832 and May 1833, he made many observations, and came to the conclusion that the brightest star in the southern constellation of Centaurus, Alpha Centauri, might be relatively close to Earth (compared to most other stars) because it had a large "proper motion", i.e. it seemed to move over time relative to the more static stellar background. This led to the thought that it might be possible to measure the distance to Alpha Centauri using parallax, the star's apparent change of location as the Earth moved through its orbit around the sun.[1] A residual error of about one second of arc was, after further observations of its right ascension by Thomas Maclear at the Cape, concluded to be the star's parallax (later estimates gave 0.75 seconds of arc), but was not announced as such to the Royal Astronomical Society (RAS) until January 1839. This, however, was two months after the announcement by Friedrich Wilhelm Bessel of Königsberg of the parallax of 61 Cygni, for which he was given the RAS gold medal. Henderson had been over-cautious because there had been spurious parallaxes before. As the first Astronomer Royal for Scotland, from 18 August 1834, Henderson measured the positions of stars and planets with the Fraunhofer transit circle and the Troughton mural circle and, aided by Alexander Wallace, made some 60,000 observations in 10 years.[2]

Henderson also observed Mars and the moon with a view to deducing solar and lunar parallaxes, and he computed several planetary orbits. From observations at Greenwich, Cambridge, Altona, and the Cape at the opposition of Mars (November 1832), Henderson deduced a solar parallax of 9.125". This figure was not as good as Jean Baptiste Joseph Delambre's or Thomas Hornsby's values, but of course it was appreciated that the Mars method was inferior to that using Venus (the currently accepted solar parallax of 8.80"). From simultaneous lunar observations at Greenwich, Cambridge, and the Cape, he deduced a lunar equatorial horizontal parallax of 57'1.8" – of the many determinations made in the early century, this figure was marginally better than the others.[3]

William Edmond Logan 1798-1875 outlined to the Geological Society of London in 1840 his concept of the origin of coal. The rock succession, including the coal seams, in South Wales suggested that coal had accumulated in situ: below every bed, he found, there occurred persistently an underclay with numerous fossil tree stumps (*Stigmaria*). He was further convinced of the theory's validity by finding later the same association of underclay and stumps at the bottom of coal beds in Pennsylvania, Nova Scotia, and Scotland. Logan's concept of the *in situ* formation of coal is still considered to be generally valid.[1]

During the earlier years of the survey, he had many difficulties to surmount and privations to undergo, but the work was carried on with great tact and energy, and he spared no pains to make his reports trustworthy. He described the Laurentian rocks of the Laurentian mountains in Canada and of the Adirondacks in the state of New York, pointing out that they comprised an immense series of crystalline rocks, gneiss, mica-schist, quartzite and limestone, more than 30,000 ft (9,144 m) in thickness. The series was rightly recognised as representing the oldest type of rock on the globe, but it is now known to be a complex of highly altered sedimentary and intrusive rocks; and the supposed oldest known fossil, the Eozoon, described by Sir John William Dawson is now regarded as a mineral structure. In 1851, Logan was awarded the Wollaston medal by the Geological Society of London for his researches on the coal-strata, and for his excellent geological map of Canada.[2]

In 1842, when the Geological Survey of Canada was formed, Logan was made its director, and he served in this capacity until 1869. His chief work for the Geological Survey was his monumental *Report on the Geology of Canada* (1863), a compilation of 20 years of research. Another of Logan's important achievements was his recognition that the Palaeozoic (from 542 million to 251 million years ago) rocks of north-eastern North America were divided by a prominent zone of thrust faulting running along the valley of the St. Lawrence River and then trending south along the Hudson River valley and southwest across Pennsylvania. This line is known as Logan's Line. The Palaeozoic strata west of Logan's Line are relatively undisturbed, while those lying east of the line have been greatly deformed.[3]

Patrick Bell 1799-1869 brought a revolution to agriculture with the invention of an efficient reaper. Surprisingly, there was an apparently efficient reaper used in Roman Gaul around the first century, but it had disappeared by the end of the 4th century as Roman influence declined following barbarian depredations. In the early 19th century there were many reapers developed in Britain and America, but the first that was truly effective was designed in 1826 by Bell. "He had worked at the making of it when a young man on his father's farm, and the principle he adopted, that of a series of scissors fastened on the 'knife-board,' was followed for a long time. There had been many trials during the thirty or forty years before his time both in this country [Britain] and in America, but his invention was the first practical success."[1]

Bell's reaper, which became the most successful, could cut over four hectares a day, although the blades needed to be sharpened every fifth day. The reaper was pushed by horses rather than pulled so that the crop wasn't crushed by hooves before it was cut. Around twelve pairs of shears were used and an inclined rotating canvas cylinder collected the cut grain and dropped it well to the side of the horses, where it was then sheaved by hand. It was the earliest effective mechanisation of agriculture in the world and it changed farming forever.

Image 32 – Patrick Bell's Reaper – 1851

Americans Obed Hussey and Cyrus McCormick improved upon Bell's design although it is not clear whether they started from a Bell reaper or one of the many other less effective reapers that abounded in both Britain and America. McCormick certainly popularised the reaper in America whereas Bell's machine became popular in the British Empire after 1853 with the production of the so-called Beverley reaper. Bell, Hussey and McCormick were key figures in expediting the process by which agriculture shifted from being labour intensive to highly mechanised and productive. In 1831, Scotland's agriculture employed half of all workers, but 60 years later this had fallen to 25% of the country's workforce. This change came about in large part through the introduction of reapers and threshers.

Peter Fairbairn 1799-1861 improved flax-spinning machinery by applying differential motion to the roving-frame, and the introduction of screw and rotary gills. He invented the revolving tube between drafting rollers to give false twist in machines for spinning flax. "The longer fibres of wool and flax need to have some form of support and control between the rollers when they are being drawn out, and inserting a little twist helps. However, if the roving is too tightly twisted before passing through the first pair of rollers, it cannot be drawn out, while if there is insufficient twist, the fibres do not receive enough support in the drafting zone. One solution is to twist the

158

fibres together while they are actually in the drafting zone between the rollers. In 1834, Fairbairn patented an arrangement consisting of a revolving tube placed between the drawing rollers. The tube inserted a 'middle' or 'false' twist in the material."[1] He wasn't the first to do this but was the most successful.

Fairbairn also increased flax spinning frames from 40 to 80 spindles. "Fairbairn's designs were praised for their classical neatness, and they revolutionised flax and hemp preparation, enabling spinners to produce a far superior yarn at lower cost."[2] Fairbairn founded the Wellington Foundry in 1828 in Leeds. By 1926, it covered 11 acres (4.45 hectares) with 3,000 employees. It also owned works at Lille in France.[3]

James Bowman Lindsay 1799-1862 gave the first ever public display of an electric light bulb in 1835 – 43 years before Joseph Wilson Swan produced one in 1878 and 44 years before Thomas Alva Edison produced his incandescent lamp in 1879. "Among his technological innovations, which were not developed until long after his death, are the incandescent light bulb, submarine telegraphy and arc welding. Unfortunately, his claims are not well documented."[1]

Lindsay, a teacher of prisoners in Dundee Gaol, demonstrated wireless telegraphy underwater in 1853, but his method required laying a landline exceeding the breadth of the water to be crossed so it was clearly not suitable for ocean telegraphy, although it could have been used across the Irish Sea or English Channel. Much of his time was spent writing a philological work known as the *Pentecostaglossal Dictionary* which gave synonyms for words in up to fifty languages and with which Lindsay hoped to clarify mankind's origins and provide proof of the Bible's accuracy.

His greatest feat was to succeed in creating an electric light on 25 July 1835 in which "The light in beauty surpasses all others, has no smell, emits no smoke, is incapable of explosion, and not requiring air for combustion can be kept in sealed glass jars. It ignites without the aid of a taper, and seems peculiarly calculated for flax houses, spinning mills, and other places containing combustible materials. It can be sent to any convenient distance, and the apparatus for producing it can be contained in a common chest."[2]

He gave a public demonstration of his electric light in Thistle Hall, Dundee on 31 July 1835, and another demonstration of his light in the same place in 1836. He claimed he could read a book at night at a distance of around half a metre. In July 1858, Queen Victoria, on the recommendation of the Prime Minister, Edward Stanley-Smith, Earl of Derby, granted Lindsay an annual pension of £100 a year, "in recognition of his great learning and extraordinary attainments."[3]

Aware that the difficulties in laying transatlantic cable had not yet been solved, Lindsay took a great interest in the debate, with the revolutionary suggestion of using electric arc welding to join cables, and sacrificial anodes to prevent corrosion. These ideas, though not entirely new, were not to see widespread practical application for many years to come.[4]

Although Lindsay took no further interest in its development, he forecast that electricity would replace both coal and steam for heating and for moving machinery, and he predicted that cities would be lit by electric light.

Patrick McFarlane born 1799 invented, in 1857, "what appears to have been the first cop changing mechanism, in which mule spun cops placed in special containers were inserted into the shuttle, by means of a transfer hammer"[1] (a cop is a conical mass of thread, yarn, etc., wound on a spindle). McFarlane patented an automatic weft-replenishing device which marks a distinctly new departure from the previous inventions for the same object, and one, moreover, which has the distinction of constituting the prototype of cop – or bobbin – changing devices, of which type a modification had been successfully adopted in the construction of Northrop automatic looms.

McFarlane's invention is described in the Patent Specification dated 13 April 1857, No. 1046, which states that "the first part of the invention consists in means or arrangements by which a loom is made to supply its shuttle or shuttles with fresh weft when the weft last placed in the shuttle or shuttles has become broken or exhausted. The cop or bobbin of weft was placed in a case which fitted inside the shuttle in which it was held securely during weaving, but from which it could be easily rejected and replaced by another weft-case containing a fresh supply of weft whilst the loom continued weaving. Any practicable number of these weft-cases were conveniently stored and retained in a suitable receptacle or hopper, so that the successive weft-cases could take the place of those removed, as they were each in turn inserted in the shuttle. The chamber containing the reserve supply of weft-cases was attached to the framing of the loom opposite the shuttle-box or boxes, so that when the absence of weft was detected by the weft-fork, this put into operation the weft-changing mechanism which forced a weft-case from the hopper into the shuttle, and thereby displaced the previous weft-case which fell into a box or basket."[2]

Andrew Smith born 1799 developed wire ropes which were eventually used in industry, on ships, and for the cable car. Wilhelm Albert, a German engineer, made wire ropes for cable cars in the 1830s, with wire twisted around a hemp core. Albert's rope was inflexible and the humid atmosphere in the mines caused the material to rapidly deteriorate. Smith made further improvements to wire cable for haulage on the Blackwall Railway, and for use on ships' rigging, which he termed metal cordage. It was first used on the schooner *Marshall* in 1836 and then in 1840 on the *John Garrow*, which was the first ocean-going ship to use metal cordage.

He originally used wire rope in 1828 as a replacement for catgut cordage which was vulnerable to rats. Following years of experiments to test the strength of various permutations, he patented his wire rope-making machinery on 12 January 1835 and within a few years had a total of five patents. He claimed that, compared to hemp ropes, there was a saving of 25% in cost and his wire ropes were used for mining, sailing ships and submarine cables.[1]

James Syme 1799-1870 was a surgeon who invented the technique for dissolving rubber in a coal-tar naphtha solution and using it for making a fabric into waterproof laminates. Syme submitted his discovery to the editor of the *Annals of Philosophy*, but for various reasons publication was delayed. During the interim, the Scottish chemist Charles Macintosh learned of the method, elaborated on it, developed it further, and patented it for commercial purposes. As a result, the Mackintosh (with the addition of the letter "k") raincoat was born and Syme, who took little interest in commercial matters, lost an inestimable fortune.[1]

In 1828, Syme performed one of the most remarkable operations carried out in the Royal Infirmary of Edinburgh during the early decades of the 19th century. The patient was Robert Penman, who had an enormous tumour, which weighed two kilograms and was believed to be an osteosarcoma of the lower jaw that produced severe disfigurement of his face. Three years earlier, Robert Liston had seen the patient and judged the tumour to be inoperable. Syme carefully examined the patient, and the operation to remove the tumour was carried out on 7 July by Syme with the assistance of George Ballingall. The operation was performed with the patient sitting in an ordinary chair, and in all took twenty-four minutes, "but all this time was not employed in cutting, as I frequently allowed a little respite, to prevent exhaustion from continued suffering. The patient bore it well, and did not lose more than seven or eight ounces [207-236 ml] of blood. His breathing was never in the slightest degree affected". He recovered well, and the dressings were removed on the third day. During this period, he was fed through a funnel with a curved tube directly into the pharynx. Five weeks later he was seriously thinking of resuming his occupation. Penman lived for another thirty years after the operation.[2]

In a period before anaesthetics, he managed to reduce the time needed to amputate a leg to 90 seconds. He also explored alternatives to amputation, but where these were necessary, he tried to minimise the damage caused by removing as little diseased tissue as possible and even experimented with reconstruction through what is today known as "plastic surgery". In 1842, he introduced an amputation at the ankle now known as Syme's Amputation.[3]

Syme was the last and greatest of the pre-Listerian surgeons, renowned in his day as the most eminent surgeon in the English-speaking world. He developed and perfected many new surgical procedures. Time has outmoded them all save one – his disarticulation amputation through the ankle joint with preservation of the heel flap to permit weight-bearing on the end of the stump. Syme's favourable impression of the merit of Parisian François Chopart's amputation at the midtarsal joint led him to apply the same principle to the ankle joint when caries or compound injury involved the astragalus or calcaneus, problems for which Chopart's amputation was inadequate.

Amputation at the ankle joint might prove as effective as Chopart's amputation in saving the patient's life, but the long stump would prove an intolerable nuisance unless the patient could walk upon it. In Chopart's amputation, walking upon the stump presented no problem since the whole of the posterior half of the sole of the foot remained intact, and upon this the patient walked almost as easily as upon a normal foot. Amputation at a higher level (a hand's breadth below the tibial tubercle) permitted weight-bearing by applying the flexed knee to the padded cleft in the upper end of a crude prosthesis. This was "amputation at the site of election," a useful operation if the patient survived, but the mortality rate was 50 percent.[4]

To make amputation at the ankle joint a functional success, some procedure was needed which would permit all the body weight to be borne upon the end of the stump in a manner similar to Chopart's stump. Other surgeons had attempted to solve this problem without success. Syme's solution was to detach from the underlying tarsal bones the whole thickness of the posterior half of the sole of the foot, disarticulate the astragalus from the mortise of the ankle joint, remove the malleoli (the bony prominence on each side of the ankle), and then reapply the heel flap to the lower ends of the tibia (shinbone) and fibula (calf bone). This proved to be the technique necessary for a satisfactory end-bearing stump at the level of the ankle joint, for it provided a thick and bulky covering for the end of the stump composed of tissue adapted to weight-bearing.

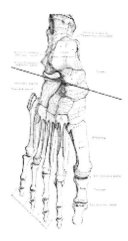

Image 33 – Midtarsal joint on right foot (diagonal line)

The first merit which Syme claimed for his new procedure was "that the risk to life will be smaller." That indeed was the case in his day, when it spared the patient the dangerous amputation at the upper end of the tibia. By 1861, this argument in favour of Syme's operation was no longer valid, since the nature of infection was now known, but his amputation at the ankle joint still has the other merits he claimed for it – "a more comfortable stump, more seemly and useful for support and progressive motion." When circumstances permitted it to be performed, Syme's amputation provided indeed the most useful of all amputation stumps of the lower extremity. The perfection of a new type of Syme prosthesis eliminated the ankle-joint problem and minimised the bulbous appearance of the perfect Syme stump. Seldom in the history of surgery has it been necessary to adhere rigidly to the technique of an operation developed and perfected in pre-antiseptic days. Yet such is the case with Syme's amputation. The simple technique devised by Syme to spare his patients the risks of amputation at the site of election and to give them an end-bearing stump still provides the best end-bearing stump of the lower extremity.[5]

He showed independent thinking as he spoke out against the belief that haemorrhoidal bleeding was beneficial and against the fashionable belief that rectal strictures were a common cause of constipation. Following the precepts of French surgeon Alexis Boyer, Syme regarded a fissure as an ulcer, described the symptoms so accurately that they could be used for teaching medical students as recently as 1970, and called attention to the sentinel pile. He modified Boyer's treatment of the fissure; Syme did not cut the muscles as Boyer did. He advocated the ligature treatment of internal haemorrhoids and excision of external haemorrhoids. Syme's management of anal fistulae was sound by current standards.[6]

A less known pioneering effort of James Syme was the Burn-House at the Royal Infirmary, Surgeons Square, the first ever hospital for burns. This made possible a strict isolation of patients with heavily infected burn wounds.[7] When Syme assumed charge of wards in the Edinburgh Royal Infirmary, he bent all his energy towards improving sanitation by providing adequate space between beds, by better ventilation, and by more cleanliness. An interesting outcome of this activity was his insistence that the Governors establish a separate hospital for the treatment of burns. Syme's purpose was not so much to improve the treatment of burns as to remove the unfortunate burn victims, with their offensive wounds and filthy dressings, from his surgical wards to avoid contamination of his operative cases.[8] Working at the world's first burns hospital in Edinburgh, Syme emphasised that dressings for burns should be applied with firm pressure[9] although, he acknowledged, that the method came from America – "In treating burns, it is necessary to consider whether the injury is so severe as to destroy the vitality of the part affected, or merely sufficient to induce inflammation of it. In the latter case cold applications afford great relief, and if employed immediately after the accident occurs, may prevent the inflammation and vesication altogether. Another mode of treatment which answers extremely well, though it is difficult to say on what principle, consists in enveloping the burned part with cotton. This practice was introduced from America not many years ago, and is now in very general use. It appears that its good effects are most conspicuous when pressure is conjoined with it; and a bandage, therefore, ought to be applied with moderate firmness."[10]

Robert Christison, with James Syme and Thomas Traill, produced the standard work on post-mortem procedure in Scotland, *The Medico-Legal Examination of Dead Bodies*, published in 1839 at the request of the Lord Advocate.[11]

In 1849, Syme broached the subject of medical reform in a letter to the Lord Advocate; in 1854 and 1857 he addressed open letters on the same subject to Lord Palmerston; and in 1858 a Medical Act was passed which largely followed the lines laid down by himself.[12] In June and July of 1858, oppressed by one of the hottest summers on record – a summer which, among other things, required parliamentary staff to hang lime-soaked cloths across the riverside windows of the Houses of Parliament to filter out the stench of a 20% concentration of sewage in the Thames – the United Kingdom Parliament agreed to the passage of a Medical Act. The Act gave statutory recognition for the first time to a distinct occupational category of "legally qualified Medical Practitioner" "entitled according to his Qualification to practise … in any Part of Her Majesty's Dominions". It also set up a general medical council with powers to monitor standards of professional training, to register qualified practitioners, and to de-register practitioners found guilty of criminal acts or of "infamous conduct in any professional respect". The Act fell far short of the hopes of some of its medical promoters, especially those who had campaigned for the criminalisation of "quackery". Yet it was also the first major bill for medical reform to be passed, after sixteen unsuccessful attempts over the previous eighteen years.[13]

CHAPTER 3

1800-1824

The 18th century closed with Great Britain a world power – in fact, the world's greatest power; but now, in the midst of the epic Napoleonic War, it was fighting for its very existence against a resurgent, and republican, France and its allies, not only in Europe but scattered around the world – a world that had grown with discoveries in the Pacific, including Australia and New Zealand, and even the Antarctic. Scots had settled in large numbers in North America but, after the American colonies won their War of Independence in 1783, most New World Scots were concentrated in Canada and the Caribbean, although their numbers in the embryonic United States soon started to increase again. The people born at the start of this period also experienced the unstoppable rise of technology as the Industrial Revolution continued unabated. Following on from James Watt's considerable improvement to the steam engine, industrialisation garnered inexorable momentum that, from the outset, was to invigorate Western Europe and North America. The epicentre of this industrialisation was in Great Britain, where the world's first truly industrial city, Manchester, and other cities such as Glasgow, Liverpool, Birmingham, and parts of London, started on an exponential growth. Scots were to be found at the heart of this frenetic activity, improving steam engines, agricultural equipment, steamships, railways, and much other infrastructure.

John Aird 1801-1876 and his son **John Aird 1833-1911** were civil engineers whose company became the largest contracting company in Britain, employing 30,000 men in December 1874, and, 20 years later, as many as 20,000 men on the Aswan Dam alone.[1] The Airds were involved in numerous projects, including reservoirs at Hampton and Staines in Middlesex, the Beckton plant of the Gas Light and Coke Company, and Brighton's sewerage system, parts of London Underground's Metropolitan and District Lines, the Royal Albert Dock, Millwall Dock in London (with Sir John Kirk), Royal Edward Dock at Avonmouth, Tilbury Docks, East and West India Docks extension, Millom Harbour in Cumbria, and the West Highland railway line. Docks were also built at Portsmouth, Southampton, Newport, and Newhaven.

Outside of Britain, Aird built – alone or with other contractors – waterworks at: Copenhagen, Berlin and Calcutta; gasworks in Denmark, France, Italy, Brazil, and several places in Russia, including Moscow; civil engineering works in Sardinia; the Suakin to Berber railway in Sudan; Singapore docks; and completed the Manchester Ship Canal. Building on mains-laying experience for the east London waterworks in the previous decade, the Airds obtained contracts for the new waterworks of the Southwark and Vauxhall, Grand Junction, and West Middlesex water companies near Hampton in the 1850s. On the continent, where British-owned utility companies were often involved, the Airds began mains-laying in the Netherlands, before building waterworks in Rotterdam, Amsterdam, Hamburg, Altona, Schiedam, Brunswick, Riga,

Archangel, and Moscow. In Copenhagen, in addition to the waterworks, John Aird senior built the first major outfall sewer, which nearly bankrupted the firm. The Airds formed a partnership with Charles Fox and Thomas Crompton to establish the Berlin Water Company.[2]

The project for which Aird junior became most noted was building the first Aswan Dam in Egypt, and later increasing the height of the dam even further (1907-1912). In February 1898, Aird offered to construct dams at Aswan on the first cataract of the Nile and at Assyût some 400 km south of Cairo. Work started in April 1898 and finished in 1902, a year before the stipulated time. Designed by Sir William Willcocks, it was too short and this was why it required to be increased in height twice (the second time in 1929-1933) and eventually replaced by the High Aswan Dam, although both the dams built by Aird are still functioning and are the oldest dams on the Nile in Upper Egypt. "Preliminary operations were commenced at the site of the dam in April, 1898, and in the early summer of 1899 the number of men employed on the undertaking reached a total of 13,000. The dam has a length of about 2,200 yards [2,012 m]; it has 180 sluice-gates, and its maximum height from the foundation is about 130 feet [39.6 m]. The total amount of granite masonry its construction involved was about one million tons [907,185 tonnes]. The effect of the dam is to convert the River Nile above Assuan into an immense reservoir, which, when full, contains about 38,000 million cubic feet [1,076 million cubic metres] of water. Its construction took about 4 years only."[3]

Thomas Clark 1801-1867 patented a process in 1841 for softening water using calcium hydroxide, often referred to as Lime Process or Clark's Process. The advantage of Clark's process over other softening processes is that no derivative compounds remain behind in the water. "This character," says Clark, "is as fortunate as it is rare in chemical processes." Another advantage is that the quantity of organic matter in the water is greatly reduced by the precipitation of the chalk, the water in large bulk having the natural pure blue colour of uncontaminated water, the process is somewhat expensive, from the number of reservoirs required; but the cost of the caustic lime is more than balanced by the high price paid for the chalk obtained by the process. Water so softened requires only one-third the quantity of soap to make a lather; also, there is no fur on the surface of boilers.[1]

The softening agent used by Clark was lime water, the action of which depends on a very simple principle. In contact with lime water, the soluble calcium bicarbonate in hard water is changed to insoluble calcium carbonate and precipitated, the hardening constituent, calcium, being removed simultaneously from the hard water and from the softening agent. This process of improving the quality of water at once acquired wide popularity.[2]

Clark's most important work in pure chemistry was his discovery of sodium pyrophosphate (phosphate of soda), which is used as a buffering agent, an emulsifier, a dispersing agent, and a thickening agent, and is often used as a food additive. Common foods containing sodium pyrophosphate include chicken nuggets, marshmallows, pudding, crab meat, imitation crab, canned tuna, and soy-based meat alternatives and cat foods and cat treats where it is used as a palatability enhancer. It is also used in some common baking powders. In toothpaste and dental floss, sodium pyrophosphate acts as a tartar control agent, serving to remove calcium and magnesium from saliva and thus preventing them from being deposited on teeth. It is also used in commercial dental rinses before brushing to aid in plaque reduction.

John Dalziel born 1801 developed the tank respirator (iron lung) in 1838.[1] The earliest non-invasive ventilators were the "body" ventilators, so called because they assist ventilation by applying negative or positive pressure to various regions of the body. The earliest description of a body ventilator was that of a tank-type negative pressure device by the Scottish physician John Dalziel in 1838. It was Belgian anatomist Andreas Vesalius who made the first report of mechanical ventilation, but Dalziel was the one who made the first respirator to use negative pressure. His invention consisted of a hermetic tank where the patient left only the head and the neck on the outside; the negative pressure within the tank was obtained by means of bellows driven from outside by a piston and a unidirectional valve.[2]

Dalziel described a negative pressure device which augmented respiration in his paper *On sleep, and an Apparatus for Promoting Artificial Respiration* (1838).[3] This apparatus was actually in use at least by 1831 as attested to in a letter to the editor of the *Railway Magazine*: "In 1831, Dr John Dalziel, when practicing in the neighbourhood of Dumfries, started the idea, and had an apparatus constructed for the purpose. It consisted of a large air-tight wooden vessel, containing a pair of bellows, and room for a person to sit in conveniently. The lid consisted of two parts, with a semi-circular notch in each, so as to embrace the neck of the patient. When the patient was to be operated on, he took his seat in the vessel, and, the lid being applied, he was wholely [sic] enclosed, excepting the head; and any aperture between the lid and the neck was made air-tight by means of dough. The nozle [sic] of the bellows passed through the side of the vessel, and terminated in a valve opening outwards. The rarefaction might be produced either by the patient working the bellows himself, or by another person working them on the outside, by means of a rod passing through an air-tight collar in the lid. On inflating the bellows, air was taken into them from the vessel, and on compressing them it was expelled through the valve on the nozle, which permitted its escape but prevented its return. Thus each stroke rarefied the air in the interior of the vessel."[4]

In 1832, Dr Robert Lewins of Leith was able to produce breathing motions when a "drowned man" was placed in Dalziel's respirator.[5]

William Gibbs McNeill 1801-1853 designed the Canton Viaduct, the oldest railroad bridge of its kind in the world and, when it was built in 1835, the longest and tallest railroad bridge in the world. It is the only blind arcade cavity wall bridge in the western hemisphere and it now carries high-speed passenger and freight rail service. This unique stone railroad bridge in Canton, Massachusetts, was erected in 1835 by the Boston and Providence Railroad Corporation.

McNeill led the team that surveyed the route that was taken by the Baltimore and Ohio Railroad – the first important railroad undertaken in America and the first designed for general transportation purposes. From 1830 to 1836, McNeill was Chief Engineer of the Baltimore and Susquehanna Railroad. He superintended the survey and construction of many roads, the chief of which were the Paterson and Hudson River, now the southern terminus of the Erie Railroad (1831-1834); Boston and Providence (1832-1835); Providence and Stonington (1832-1837); Taunton and New Bedford (1835); Fayetteville and Yadkin (1835); Long Island (1835-1836); Western, of Massachusetts, now Boston and Albany (1836-1837).

In 1837, he was appointed Chief Engineer of Georgia and had responsibility for the Cincinnati to Charleston Road before moving on to become President of the Chesapeake and

Ohio Canal from 1842-1843. In 1844, he became Chief Engineer of the Dry Docks at the Brooklyn Navy Yard in New York, which he planned and began construction.[1]

Image 34 – Canton Viaduct

Mungo Ponton 1801-1880 discovered, in 1839, that potassium dichromate in solution made paper light-sensitive. The origin of the modern photoengraving process rests on his report that year "of the light-sensitive properties of certain chromium compounds. But Ponton, who demonstrated the chemical change that occurs when glue containing a compound of chromium is acted upon by light, was not concerned with preparation of printing plates, and it remained for William Henry Fox Talbot, an English pioneer in photography, to propose the use of chromium-treated colloids such as albumin as an etchant-resistant for preparation of intaglio printing surfaces."[1]

This sensitivity had already been noted seven years earlier by Gustav Suckow, a German professor of mineralogy, but he took no action on his discovery. Ponton found that dichromates added to gelatin make a coating that is insoluble when exposed to light. Gum dichromate is a contact printing process which combines gum arabic, water colour pigments and light sensitive dichromate compounds to form the image. The dichromate hardens relative to its exposure to ultraviolet light through a negative. Development takes over half an hour with the paper containing the image being placed in water during that time to wash away unhardened gum. The residual hardened gum that had been exposed creates a sepia positive image of chromium dioxide to give a very striking print that fades a little after several months. Potassium dichromate was cheaper than using a coating of silver salts and it was eventually used in photographic printing processes.

Ponton called his process Pontontype and it was the direct forerunner of the next important step in photography in 1855 when Frenchman Alphonse Louis Poitevin realised the possibilities of adding carbon as a pigment to dichromated gelatine. Although Ponton's role in the development of photography was small, it was an important step.

Alexander Shanks 1801-1845 is most closely associated with the development of the lawnmower, but as early as 1834, he patented a process for preparing and dressing hemp and other fibrous substances. In 1842, he took out a patent for a lawnmower that both cut and rolled the grass in one action. His lawnmower was horse-drawn, the driver walking behind, guiding the machine and controlling the horse's reins.

"Alexander Shanks has been widely regarded as the originator of the first successful lawnmower. Note: Edwin Beard Budding invented the lawn mower in 1830 but Shanks' model was a big improvement. His claim to fame merits some revision. Firstly, there is controversy about who actually invented the first lawnmower, though he undoubtedly designed the first efficient machine. Secondly, the role played by his son James in the subsequent technical development and popularisation of the lawnmower should be recognised."[1]

He created a company, Alexander Shanks and Co of Arbroath, which "produced the first horse drawn mowers in the mid-19th century and they were immediately popular, especially on the growing number of golf courses and other sports grounds that were being built at the time. Some people believe that this is the origin of the term 'Shanks's Pony', meaning to walk, but no definitive source of the phrase is known. It certainly makes sense if one takes the phrase to mean "having a pony but still having to walk".[2]

Francis Baird 1802-1864 took over control of the St Petersburg ironworks run by his father, Charles Baird in 1843. By 1860, the Baird Works was flourishing with between 1,200 and 1,500 employees, and was producing half a million rubles worth of goods per year.[1] Amongst the public works undertaken by Francis was the share taken in the construction of the column erected to the memory of the Emperor Alexander I in the centre of the square of the Winter Palace, and also of the St Isaac's Cathedral, at St Petersburg: the former higher than the Napoleon column at Paris, or the pillars of Trajan and Antonine at Rome, or of Pompey at Alexandria; the latter intended to rank with the cathedral of St Paul in London, St Peter at Rome, St Sophia at Constantinople (Istanbul), and other similar grand temples in Europe. The four bas-reliefs on the base of the Alexander column, the four eagles at the angles of the pedestal, the four candelabra at the corners of – and the bronze railing around – the monument, and the colossal figure of the angel holding a cross, upwards of twenty feet in height at its summit, were all executed at the Baird Works by a then novel process, and in a foundry specially erected for the purpose.

The bas-reliefs in the four fronts of this cathedral, weighing 800,000 lbs. (362,874 kgs), the figures in bronze, each 15 feet 2 inches high (4.6 m), representing the Twelve Apostles, the statues in bronze round the exterior colonnade of the dome, the construction in iron, covered with plates of polished copper, of the gilded dome, 130 feet (39.7 m) in diameter, and the Oases and capitals in bronze, both in the interior and the exterior of the cathedral, were all made at the Baird Works, and so well were they executed as to elicit the warmest encomiums from the architect. Amongst other works of a public nature may be named the Blagavetchari (usually called the St Nicholas) bridge, which was the first permanent bridge of the kind across the Neva. This last was the work of Francis Baird alone and he increased the family business to such an extent that many marine engines of 800 hp were made at his works.[2]

James Baird 1802-1876, with his brother William, in 1828, "began to erect the Gartsherrie Ironworks at Gartsherrie, North Lanarkshire, Scotland, and within 15 years the works had grown to be the largest in the country with 16 furnaces. In 1830, William and James took over all the coal leases and formed the partnership William Baird & Co. In around 1843, William and James

Baird were involved in the establishment of the Eglinton Iron Company that managed the Gartsherrie Ironworks, building furnaces at Kilwinning, North Ayrshire, Scotland, and purchasing those at Blair and Dalry, North Ayrshire, in 1852; Lugar, East Ayrshire, in 1856; and Portland in 1864. Bairds, therefore, became responsible for 25 per cent of Scotland's output making them the largest producers of pig iron in the world."[1]

The work of James Baird, with James Beaumont Neilson and William Dixon, raised the temperature of the hot air blast from 115C to 315C, approaching the melting point of lead (327C). At this heat, it was necessary to protect the nozzle of the air pipe when it was put into the furnace and this was achieved by James Baird by means of a stream of cold water being pushed through a spiral tube to keep the tuyere relatively cool while protecting the nozzle of the air pipe.

Hugh Miller 1802-1856 identified Old Red Sandstone as a fossil-rich rock, contrary to common belief, bringing him eminence in scientific circles.[1] Miller simultaneously pursued his research in geology and palaeontology and made important contributions to the pre-Darwinian debate on evolution.[2]

When Miller dealt with wider issues of God in creation and the truths of geology, he deployed his fossils, as in *Footprints of the Creator* (1849) which attacked the reheated Lamarckian evolutionism of *Vestiges of the Natural History of Creation* (1844). But, contrary to the common misconception that he was driven to suicide by a conflict between science and religion, Miller simply saw these as different facets of the same truth. Indeed, he notably defended geology against religious literalists.[3]

His fossil collection of over 6,000 specimens became the founding core of what is today's Scottish national collection in the Royal Scottish Museum in Edinburgh. His books, such as *The Old Red Sandstone*, *The Cruise of the Betsey*, *Footprints of the Creator*, *Testimony of the Rocks*, *Scenes and Legends of the North of Scotland*, and *My Schools and Schoolmasters* (autobiography) became bestsellers in many editions.[4]

Miller was considered one of the finest geological writers of the 19th century and his writings were widely successful in arousing public interest in geologic history. He also wrote a brilliant geological series for it, part of which was published in book form as *The Old Red Sandstone* (1841). In this work he described his discoveries, in Cromarty, of fossils found in formations of the Devonian strata (approximately 416 to 359 million years ago).

Of his remaining works on geology, *Footprints of the Creator* (1849) was the most nearly original. The book recorded Miller's reconstruction of the extinct fishes he had discovered in the Old Red Sandstone and contended, on theological grounds, that their perfection of development disproved the theory of evolution. He also discovered the fish species subsequently known as *Pterichthyodes milleri*. It was largely from Miller's writings that the Devonian Period became known as the Age of Fishes.[5]

In the mid-1850s, Hugh Miller was one of a half-dozen palaeontologists writing for popular audiences. He illustrated his work with accurate – sometimes coloured – etchings of the fishes and their skeletal components. We are accustomed to thinking that paleontological art of that time was fanciful. What usually comes to mind is the surreal landscape seen in William Buckland's famous Victorian representation of a battle between a plesiosaur and an ichthyosaur in a lagoon of the Lias (Jurassic). Hugh Miller's art was far different. He had the eye of a serious investigator and the mind of a novelist. He not only excavated new fossil fishes from strata dismissed by geologists as non-fossiliferous, he wrote about them and their geologic context in a readable style. Unlike most contemporary work, Miller's writing was dramatic without being wordy.

Miller died in 1856. For most of that year, the brilliant researcher and speaker had been bothered by terrible headaches that seemed to burn inside his head. Had he lived in the 20th century, Miller's doctors could have diagnosed the problem. Perhaps it was a tumour that caused the headaches, and, later, the awful hallucinations, but Victorian-era medicine could not help. He feared that he might harm his wife or children during his delusions in which he pursued imaginary robbers with his gun. Miller committed suicide the night he finished checking printers' proofs for his book on Scottish fossil plants and vertebrates, *The Testimony of the Rocks*.[6]

John Milne 1802-1877 had worked on harbours such as Leith and Inverkeithing in his home country before migrating to Natal on the *Dreadnought* in 1849. He was Durban's first Harbour Engineer from 1850 to 1858 and in that city, he built the first railway that operated in South Africa, consisting of a 1.6 km stretch of wooden timber rails carrying ox-pulled rail trucks. It was constructed to transport stone from the Bluff quarry to Durban Harbour where it was used in the construction of two breakwaters designed to deepen the harbour waters.

Following his own observations, Milne decided that the tidal velocity into and out of the bay would be increased by reducing the size of the mouth, thereby causing the tides to scour the sandbanks and remove the problem. He proposed building a north pier from the Point and a south pier from the end of the Bluff, and estimated that this would result in a permanent depth of 30 feet (9 metres) at the harbour entrance.

Among his various problems, which included gross underfunding, was the lack of suitable stone within reasonable distance of the harbour. A quarry existed at Cato Manor, on the other side of the Berea ridge, and other stone could be obtained to the north of the Berea at the Umgeni, both of which would have required considerable effort to collect and transport. On the south side of the harbour mouth, sandstone existed at the base of the Bluff, and this offered a practicable source. The Bluff sandstone was very calcareous with fossil shells, but Milne, after discussing the matter with William Stanger, Natal's Surveyor-General, decided that once submerged, the stone would prove durable enough for the building of the north pier.

Long drills and gunpowder were used to blast the rock loose. To convey it from this new position to a quiet place in the bay, from where it could be ferried across the channel, Milne elected to build a railway. It is interesting to note that Milne always insisted that his new railway, the first in South Africa, was not to be called a tramway. He argued that the industrial tramways of Britain consisted of flanged tracks between which unflanged wheels ran, whereas he had designed and built flanged wheels to run on wooden rails.

In all the costly later attempts to overcome the problem of the sandbar at the entrance to Durban Harbour, Milne's ideas were very close to being vindicated, certainly in respect of where he commenced building the north pier. His railway, albeit of wooden construction and drawn by oxen, proved highly successful, and introduced to the young colony a new method of transport which it was shortly to develop even further.[1]

Although this work wasn't finished in Milne's time, it was completed later in line with the original plan to remove a sandbar across the harbour entrance. Milne had his critics (including the influential George Cato) and by 1858 he was no longer harbour engineer at Durban. Two of the three Harbour Engineers who followed Milne were also Scots – Cathcart William Methven and James Buchanan Pentland Smith.

Malcolm Muir (dates unknown) invented the first wood-planing machine in 1827. The planer's purpose was specifically for the milling of tongue and groove flooring. It included a cutter head to smooth both faces of the board and to run the tongue and groove joinery in the board's edges.[1] It had for its object, the preparation of complete flooring boards. The operations of sawing, planing, tongueing, and grooving were all combined, and a number of the machines were put into operation.[2] At the same time as Muir invented his planing machine, William Thomson of Fountainbridge, Edinburgh, came up with the same idea and produced a machine that was "found to be so much alike, that they agreed to take the patent jointly, in the name of both, and to share its privileges."[3]

James Templeton 1802-1885 was a carpet manufacturer who made quality carpets available to the masses. One of his employees, William Quigley (a weaver) came up with a method of weaving chenille and Templeton took out a joint patent with Quigley. Realising it could also be applied to carpet manufacture, Templeton bought Quigley's patent share and from 1839 began to produce chenille carpets. His object was to provide a cheaper substitute for the traditional hand-tufted Axminster carpets which, together with imported oriental or Turkey carpets, catered for the top end of the market. The pile yarn for the surface of the chenille carpet was woven in a weft loom, in a manner similar to the weaving of a piece of cloth, and then cut into narrow strips which resembled striped caterpillars in appearance. The strips, each one of which constituted a line of pile, were then woven in a setting loom to the warp threads forming the base of the carpet. This was more efficient than the time-consuming process used in Axminster production, where pieces of yarn constituting the pile had to be tied to each pair of warp threads by hand. The Glasgow factory produced both seamless carpets to fit a particular room, and strips of carpeting woven on looms less than a yard wide which were subsequently sewn together to make a whole carpet. A wide range of colours was employed in the pattern and the carpet surface had a rich appearance closely resembling a traditional Axminster. By the eve of the First World War, the Templeton enterprise had become the largest in the British carpet industry, rivalled only by John Crossley & Sons of Halifax.[1] Note: another source states that Quigley's role in developing Axminster was that his "addition to carpet-making technology came through his discovery that he could steam and press the tufted chenille fabric to make a smooth surface."[2]

Like many other innovations, it was developed independently by another person, Alexander Buchanan of Paisley, in 1822. Buchanan had earlier, in 1796, "experimented with the self-acting mule which he only perfected in conjunction with his nephew, Mr James Smith of Deanston, in 1826."[3] Buchanan was employed as a foreman in a fabric mill in Paisley and developed a method of weaving to produce fuzzy shawls. Tufts of coloured wool were woven into a blanket. The blanket was cut into strips and the resulting strips were treated by heating rollers to frizz the material and set the wool. The result was a very soft and fuzzy fabric that Buchanan thought would enhance shawls.[4] James Templeton invested several years developing Buchanan's technique into the machine manufacture of tufted-pile carpets of a quality that successfully imitated expensive hand-woven Oriental carpets.[5]

George Wilson c1802-1878 invented the sheep dip. Wilson was a pharmacist in Coldstream on the Scottish side of the border with England. The dip was a mixture of arsenic and water to treat sheep for parasites, mainly mites, ticks and lice but would also treat sheep strike caused by *Lucilia sericata* blowfly. Wilson's Sheep Dip was manufactured in High Street, Coldstream and sold nationally. From Coldstream, it was transported by horse and cart to the nearby port of Berwick upon Tweed, from where it was distributed to all points south by package steamer.[1]

John Gorrie 1803-1855 was one of several refrigeration pioneers in America, along with Oliver Evans and Jacob Perkins. There is some doubt as to where John Gorrie was born. Some sources say it was on 3 October 1803 in Nevis, West Indies, while others state he was born in Charleston, South Carolina. In either event, he had a Scottish father, Ian, from Logiealmond in Perthshire, who married a Spaniard and moved from the West Indies to Charleston, South Carolina. John qualified as a physician and moved in 1833 to Apalachicola in Florida. The mosquitoes there spread yellow fever and malaria, although the actual cause was not known until much later. Gorrie noted that fevers abated in milder weather and felt that keeping patients cool would help their recovery. Initially, he used ice to cool the rooms where the patients lay, but then he experimented with making artificial ice as natural ice had to be brought in by boat. Gorrie gave up his medical practice and concentrated on his ice-making machine, sufficiently developing one to patent it in London on 22 August 1850 and then, on 6 May 1851, in the United States.

Earlier, in 1805, Oliver Evans had designed a vapour refrigerator but didn't build it, and fellow American Jacob Perkins, in 1834, had made a closed-cycle compression refrigerator in Britain. With a steam engine providing the power source, Gorrie moved a piston inside a cylinder submerged in salt water. The piston's action drew the heat out of the water which was then used for either cooling air or making ice. It worked, but its performance was erratic and it leaked a lot. Spending more and more time on trying to improve his cooler, Gorrie became poor and, when his funding partner died, Gorrie was unable to obtain the finance to further develop his device and he died broke and alone in 1855.

Gorrie is also credited with the invention of the ice cube tray used in refrigerators. Due to his work, he is considered one of the founders of refrigeration, having invented the first practical mechanical refrigeration,[1] and his efforts were an important milestone in the development of refrigeration, especially as later pioneers, such as Scottish-born James Harrison in Australia, were acquainted with his work.

William Gregory 1803-1858 devised a procedure for making pure morphine from opium ('Gregory's salt'), as a result of which Edinburgh became an important centre for the commercial preparation and sale of alkaloid drugs. From the time of its discovery by Friedrich Wilhelm Adam Sertürner, morphine was manufactured and used in an oral form, morphine acetate, which was a difficult and expensive salt to prepare. In 1831, Gregory discovered a cheap method of isolating and purifying morphine salts.[1]

Gregory's process for isolating morphine hydrochloride in a high state of purity cost no more than that of an equivalent dose of laudanum. An Edinburgh pharmaceutical firm, owned by John Macfarlan and his partner Rennie Brown, had an established trade in laudanum and was thus in a strategic position to follow up Gregory's paper as soon as it was published. Work on the manufacture of morphine hydrochloride began in 1832 and the salt was commercially available in 1833, and was included in the *Edinburgh Pharmacopoeia* of 1839. Another Edinburgh firm, T. and H. Smith, commenced the manufacture of opium alkaloids in 1837. At the time, morphine was administered orally and because of the similar costs, it showed little advantage over laudanum. The fundamental importance of Gregory's work did not become clear until 1855 when Alexander Wood introduced hypodermic injection into general practice and the future of pure morphine salts, which were essential to the technique, was secured. A great demand for opium alkaloids grew up and the production of them by the two Edinburgh companies reached very high levels in the second half of the 19th century, and Macfarlan Smith Ltd., formed by the combination of the two original companies, is still the world's leading manufacturer of opiate alkaloids (as at 2015).

Other significant work by Gregory included the purification of chloroform, the discovery of nitrogen sulphide (uses include: as a detonator, as an ignition promoter in diesel fuel, a component in pesticides and fungicides, and as an accelerator in rubber vulcanisation), work on meconic acid (an analytical marker for the presence of opium), methyl mercaptan (used to produce methionine, which is used as a dietary component in poultry and animal feed; in the plastics industry; as a precursor in the manufacture of pesticides, for alerting mine workers of an emergency by releasing it through the ventilation system, and as an additive to make it easy to detect a gas leak) and the derivatives of uric acid, the preparation of potassium permanganate, and the distillation of rubber, in which he must have discovered isoprene (used in the production of synthetic rubber). He also contributed to practical science, improving processes for the preparation of hydrochloric acid and silver oxide.[2]

John Hastie 1803-1894 patented the first self-holding steering gear in 1853. He used "opposing screws to hold the helm steady. Improved steering gear was essential in the more powerful steamships, which previously required up to 100 men to manage the helm in rough weather."[1]

Hastie went on to produce hand-steering gears of the right and left-hand screw principle and, in 1870, his firm commenced making steam steering gears. From 1903 (nine years after his death), Hastie's company devoted itself to the production of steering gear and was a pioneer in the 1910s in the use of electric hydraulic steering gear.[2]

Joseph Mitchell 1803-1883 was the first engineer to build concrete roads, with three successful trials in Britain being undertaken in 1865-1866. Comparable to asphalt technology, cement roads have been used since Roman days. Modern concrete roads were largely developed around the turn of the 20th century, being limited more by the availability of appropriate application machinery than by the cement material itself. Technical issues were experienced in constructing a surface that could compare with that of hot roller-compacted asphalt. Concrete and asphalt have continued in competition, both offering a similar product at a similar cost, and there has always been little evidence that one would move far in front of the other as gradual technological improvements were made.[1] Mitchell also constructed the first successful paved cement concrete sidewalk (pavement), which was built at Inverness in northern Scotland in 1865.[2] He built many miles of railway in Scotland and connected Inverness directly with Perth against advice that this could not be achieved.

Robert Wilson 1803-1882 was one of many people who designed a screw propeller. Early steamships used paddle wheels, but the form of propulsion that gained later supremacy was the screw propeller, which was invented and re-invented by a number of people: James Watt, Joseph Ressell, Joseph Bramah, John Swan, Richard Trevithick, David Bushnell, Richard Gatling of machine gun fame, and Robert Wilson. All of these men designed or made screw propellers prior to the two men usually credited with its invention, John Ericsson of Sweden and Francis Petit Smith of England. James Watt seems to be the first to have designed one in 1770 for use with a steam engine.

Robert Wilson's screw propeller was designed in 1827, as was one by Austrian Joseph Ressell. In July of that year Wilson's propeller was used in a trial and "The experiment was a great success, and the various members of the [Dunbar Mechanic's] institute who were present 'expressed themselves as delighted with the results.'" Edwyn Gray, an Englishman who specialises in naval writing, investigated the development of the screw propeller by Wilson, Francis Petit Smith and John Ericsson. He states, "Based upon the evidence so far adduced in this chapter, it seems reasonable to submit that Robert Wilson was the true inventor of the modern screw propeller but Francis Pettit Smith was accorded the honour because he was the first to patent the idea."[1]Another Scot who devised an early propeller was **James Steedman** or Steadman **1790-1865** of Irvine who made one around 1830 with fellow Scot **William McCririck born 1788**.

Wilson went on to patent double-action (contra-rotating) screw propellers which were used in fish torpedoes and, in 1880, the British War Office granted him £500 in respect of this invention. Again, Edwyn Gray states "Ericsson's 1836 patent proves beyond question that he was the originator of the contra-rotating propeller concept. ... The credit [for this invention] probably belongs to David Bushnell, although it is equally possible that the manually operated propeller was already in existence when he adopted it for use in the *Turtle*. At the time of writing [2004], its true origins remain unrecorded and unknown."[2]

More importantly, Wilson invented the double-acting steam hammer in 1861, sometimes claimed for the Mckiernan-Terry Company in America, which first made theirs in 1893. Wilson's hammer was an improvement on that of James Nasmyth whose single-acting steam hammer was raised by steam but dropped using only gravity. Wilson applied steam to both raise and drop the hammer, giving it more power. It is used mainly for sheet pile driving and ~~are~~ is designed to impart a rapid succession of blows to the pile. The rate of driving ranges from 300 blows per minute for the light types, to 100 blows per minute for the heaviest types. The mass of the ram is generally on the order of 90-2,300 kg, imparting a driving energy of 165-2,700 m/kg per blow. A piling frame is not required with this type of hammer, which can be attached to the top of the pile by leg-guides, the pile being guided for instance by a timber or steel framework. When used with a pile rig, back guides are bolted to the hammer to engage with the leaders. Heavy-duty hammers can drive under water to depths of 25 m.[3]

Robert Davidson 1804-1894 built the first full-size electric locomotive in 1837. He was an early pioneer in the use of electrical power on appliances, having exhibited "in the early 1840s a lathe, a saw, and a small printing machine, all electrically operated, and a model electric locomotive that would carry two people on a railway."[1] Davidson's electric saw was also built in 1837 and exhibited in 1842 at Piccadilly, London, and was built independently of the one patented on 1 October 1840 by English photography pioneer William Henry Fox Talbot.

Davidson first attracted public attention soon after the news filtered through to Aberdeen on the feat by a Prussian-born Russian inventor, Moritz von Jacobi, in propelling a ship by electric power on the River Neva in 1838. This prompted Davidson to put his own achievements on show at an exhibition in Aberdeen. The exhibition ran for about three weeks in the hall at 36 Union Street.

During 1841-1842, Davidson spent a lot of his time in Edinburgh, seeking help and financial assistance while demonstrating the capabilities of electro-magnetic traction. He built what was to be his historic locomotive, the *Galvani*, which ran on the railway between Glasgow and Edinburgh on 22 September 1842. Although it worked, it didn't generate sufficient power from its four primitive, switched-field reluctance motors to raise interest in it. The locomotive weighed 4½ tonnes and reached a speed of 6½ km/h over 2½ kilometres. Effective electric trains didn't run until the 20th century as they couldn't compete with the power of steam and diesel engines.

Davidson pioneered the switched reluctance motor based on iron rotor elements driven by pulses from electromagnets in the stator. These motors are less complex to construct than DC motors, have a high efficiency, have high reliability as there is no brush wear, and other benefits. On the downside, they are noisy and costlier than DC motors. The switched reluctance motor is robust, has dynamic bandwidth and fault tolerance, and has found many uses since semiconductor technology made electronic commutation possible.[2] "Switched reluctance motors (SRMs) have recently been gaining attention as contenders in the drives industry. The recent advances in power electronics technology have made SRMs an attractive candidate for electric vehicle (EV) applications."[3]

David Alexander Fife 1805-1877 developed Red Fife wheat, which he first grew in 1842 and then distributed in 1849. Fife used a grain from east-central Europe (Ukraine) and by the early 1900s it was grown in Canada and the United States from Maine to Utah. It wasn't until the use of steel roller mills that hard wheat became marketable and began to replace Red Fife. Hard wheat did not mill well with stone grinders. Red Fife was crossed with Hard Red Calcutta to give us Marquis, which matures earlier than Red Fife and has a better bread baking quality.[1]

By the 1860s, Red Fife was distributed and grown across Canada. Renowned for being a fine milling and baking wheat, it set Canadian wheat standards for more than 40 years (1860 to 1900). Its offspring, Marquis, replaced it as the number-one wheat in the early 1900s.

Red Fife wheat was gradually replaced, as "new and improved" varieties of wheat resistant to new fungal diseases and pests came onto the market. Nevertheless, most of the bread wheats in Canada owe part of their genetic lineage to Red Fife wheat. Canadian wheats are some of the finest bread wheats in the world.

Although Red Fife wheat is not now a significant part of the Canadian agriculture industry and is not exported, farmers coast to coast throughout Canada are now growing it, mostly organically. In fact, Red Fife wheat is the newest taste sensation in the Canadian artisan bread world, described by bakers as "full of aroma and golden reddish colour crust."[2]

The value to Canada of this wheat may be summed up as follows:

1. Thousands of institutions, industries, provinces, towns, factories, cereal farmers, and large businesses have benefited from the harvest of Red Fife wheat and of its derivative varieties.

2. In 1842, a small area of David Fife's field was Canada's first experimental farm.

3. Bountiful harvests over the next few years multiplied the amount of grain. Red Fife wheat made Ontario a wheat-producing province.

4. The settlement of the Prairies would likely not have succeeded as well, and the Sifton immigration may not have taken place. The year 1908 would not have seen towns such as Winnipeg, Regina, Saskatoon, and Edmonton built where they are now. At best, the Prairies would have been cattle-ranching country.

5. Ontario Red Fife wheat found its way west, where it became the most important factor in pushing back the prairie grass and establishing thousands of prosperous farmers.

6. This was the first and greatest contribution to the economic wealth of western Canada and other parts of Canada. It pushed the borders of the Prairies hundreds of miles to the north and opened up vast expanses of new land.

7. Up until 1905, the wheat from the Otonabee farmer retained its dominance over all other Canadian varieties.

8. Halychanka (Red Fife) was the wheat that gave Canada the proud title of "Granary of the Empire".

9. Red Fife wheat was the prime factor not only in the development of the West and in making Canada one of the world's grain producers, but also in the establishment and expansion of numerous towns and in the development of this relatively young country into a rich, economically strong, industrial nation.[3]

Thomas Graham 1805-1869 laid the foundations of physical chemistry (the branch of chemistry concerned with changes in energy during a chemical transformation) by his work on the diffusion of gases and liquids.[1]

He published, in 1829, *A Short Account of Experimental Researches on the Diffusion of Gases Through Each Other, and Their Separation by Mechanical Means*, which contained the essentials of what became known as Graham's Law: that the diffusion rate of gases is inversely as the square root of their density. "The diffusion or spontaneous intermixture of two gases in contact is effected by an interchange in position of indefinitely minute volumes of gases, which volumes are not necessarily of equal magnitude, being, in the case of each gas, inversely proportional to the square root of the density of that gas, diffusion takes place between the ultimate particles of gases, and not between sensible masses".[2]

In 1857, Robert Bunsen disputed Graham's diffusion law. Belatedly, in 1863, the latter showed that Bunsen was mistaken. Graham now used graphite instead of stucco for diffusion and emphasised the essential differences between the three modes of gas motion – diffusion, effusion, and transpiration. He also developed atmolysis to separate gaseous mixtures through rubber, clay, and metals, which led to his discovery of the occlusion of gases.[3]

Graham is known as the "father of colloid chemistry." In 1829, his first important paper dealt with the diffusion of gases. Graham's Law showed the rate of diffusion as well as the comparison of the effusion and diffusion of various gases. Graham divided particles into two classes: crystalloids, such as common salt (which has a high diffusibility) and colloids, such as gum arabic (with low diffusibility). He also invented many of the terms used in colloid chemistry.[4] He was the first to use the terms *gel, sol, colloid, osmose, osmotic force*, and *osmometer*. He explained that osmosis was liquid diffusion accompanied by osmose, or water, flowing in the opposite direction through a membrane.

His three major areas of contribution are in the diffusion of gases, colloid, and the determination of the formulas of the P_xO_y (phosphorus oxide) polyatomic ions. In addition, Graham's work with the absorption of hydrogen gas by palladium metal has taken on more significance in light of the cold fusion controversy.[5]

Graham was also the first to observe that palladium metal is able to absorb large amounts of hydrogen gas, especially at lower temperatures. In addition, he observed that when the palladium with hydrogen dissolved in it is exposed to the atmosphere, then the metal is likely to become hot and suddenly discharge the gas. This mechanism was offered as a possible explanation for the energy released during the "cold fusion" controversy several years ago.[6]

Graham's research also pointed out that a "mixture of gases could be separated by diffusion, a process employed during World War II [in making the atomic bomb] … to separate the fissionable isotope uranium 235 from the non-fissionable isotope uranium 238".[7]

Graham's study of the forms of phosphoric acid led to the development of the concept of polybasic acids. His other work included descriptions of the properties of the water of crystallisation in hydrated salts and the obtaining of definite compounds of salts and alcohol. Graham's final paper described the first known instance of a solid compound formed from a metal and a gas: palladium hydride.[8]

Graham invented dialysis (in its modern meaning) in chemistry as a process for separating colloidal and crystalline substances. He found that solutions could be divided into two classes according to their action upon a porous diaphragm such as parchment. If a solution, say of salt, be placed in a drum provided with a parchment bottom, termed a "dialyser," and the drum and its contents placed in a larger vessel of water, the salt will pass through the membrane. If the salt solution is replaced by a solution of glue, gelatin, or gum, it will be found that the membrane is impermeable to these solutes. To the first-class Graham gave the name "crystalloids," and to the second "colloids." This method is particularly effective in the preparation of silicic acid.[9]

His work on the diffusion of gases was used in 1868 to discover the chemical formula for ozone, O_3. Graham's investigations of the behaviour of crystallised compounds passing through membranes, as a method of separating large molecules from similar compounds, led to the technique of dialysis. The human kidney uses the same principle to extract nitrogenous waste and Graham's method is still in use in hospitals today, for purifying the blood of patients with kidney failure.[10]

William Rowan Hamilton 1805-1865 made important contributions to the development of optics, dynamics, and algebra. His discovery of quaternions is perhaps his best-known investigation. Hamilton's work in dynamics was later significant in the development of quantum mechanics, where a fundamental concept called the Hamiltonian bears his name.[1]

In 1835, Hamilton made his greatest contribution – his general theory of dynamics. He rewrote Newton's Laws of Motion in a powerful general way by expressing the energy of mechanical systems as special variables. The energy when written in this way is called the Hamiltonian. Hamiltonians were crucial to the 20th century development of quantum mechanics.[2]

Hamilton had long been working on how to represent rotations in space in the same way that rotations in the two-dimensional plane are represented by the multiplication of complex numbers. What he jotted down in his notebook on that day were the multiplication rules for the four base units, i, j, k, and 1, for a new number system, the quaternions: i2 = j2 = k2 = ijk = -1. Hamilton's detailed description of the circumstances and of the justification of his discovery has provided substantial material for sociological and philosophical case studies in mathematical discovery. Mathematically, it marked a milestone in the development of modern algebra and he spent most of the rest of his life publicising its implications. He published 109 papers on quaternions alone and, in 1853, a large compilation, *Lectures on Quaternions*.[3]

The quaternion involved abandoning commutativity, a radical step for the time. Not only this, but Hamilton had in a sense invented the cross and dot products of vector algebra. Hamilton also described a quaternion as an ordered four-element multiple of real numbers, and described the first element as the "scalar" part, and the remaining three as the "vector" part.[4]

In 1832, he made the daring mathematical prediction that a ray of light passed through a biaxial crystal would be refracted into the shape of a cone.[5] The theory of the characteristic function of an optical system was further developed in three supplements. In the third of these, the characteristic function depends on the Cartesian coordinates of two points (initial and final) and measures the time taken for light to travel through the optical system from one to the other. If the form of this function is known, then basic properties of the optical system (such as the directions of the emergent rays) can easily be obtained. In applying his methods, in 1832, to the study of the propagation of light in anisotropic media, in which the speed of light is dependent on the direction and polarisation of the ray, Hamilton was led to a remarkable prediction: if a single ray of light is incident at certain angles on a face of a biaxial crystal (such as aragonite), then the refracted light will form a hollow cone. In 1856, Hamilton investigated closed paths along the edges of a dodecahedron (one of the Platonic solids) that visit each vertex exactly once. In graph theory, such paths are known today as Hamiltonian circuits.[6]

Andrew Handyside 1805-1887 took over the Britannia Foundry in Derby in 1848 and produced a variety of cast-iron lamp posts, garden ornaments, railway bridges and the ubiquitous red Post Office letterboxes. In the period from 1840 to 1846, his small company made more than 400 bridges for the London, Brighton and South Coast Railway. It manufactured arched structures, such as the train sheds for railway stations, including, in 1854, Bradford Adolphus Street, Middlesbrough, and St. Enoch in Glasgow. In the 1870s, the company's prefabricated market halls, built from standardised components, were exported all over the world. In 1871, it built the Trent Bridge at Nottingham and, in 1872, the Albert Suspension Bridge in London. Other bridges and structures were built in Russia, Japan, Africa, South America, Canada and India. More than two thousand window frames were also produced by his company.

In 1876, Handyside also created a business first when he defeated the English taxation office in court over the right to claim depreciation of buildings, plant and machinery as an offset against net profits. He later lost at the appeal which went to the High Court (Exchequer) in England. A similar case in Scotland in 1875 by Addie and Sons had also been defeated by the High Court (Exchequer) in Scotland.

Image 35 – Victorian era Post Office letterbox

In 1877, the Great Northern Railway came to Derby, with Handyside building a long viaduct from the east across the Derwent Valley, slicing through the northern part of the city, including Friar Gate – a very well-to-do area. To placate the residents, a graceful bridge was built across the road. This, though initially reviled, is now much prized by the citizens of the city, who have successfully resisted several attempts by the modernisers to replace it with a bypass. Handyside also provided a bridge across the River Derwent which was tested by running six locomotives across it.

Also in 1877, the Cheshire Lines Committee opened its new line and Handyside provided the structures of the Central Station in Manchester and of Liverpool Central. Another Handyside structure that still exists is the Outwood Viaduct on the Bury to Rawtenstall line, converted from a timber superstructure in 1881. Although the line closed in 1996, there are plans to preserve it as a cycleway

The largest structure built by Handyside, said to be the largest hall in the United Kingdom covered by one span of iron and glass, was the 1886 National Agricultural Hall in London, now known as Olympia.[1]

Kenneth Treasurer Kemp 1805-1842 invented the earth battery in 1828, and he designed an electrode that was the first to use zinc amalgam, in 1826.[1] An earth battery is a pair of electrodes made of two dissimilar metals, such as iron and copper, which are buried in the soil or immersed in the sea. Earth batteries act as water-activated batteries and, if the plates are sufficiently far apart, they can tap telluric currents (a natural electrical current in the Earth's crust). Earth batteries are sometimes referred to as telluric power sources and telluric generators. Kemp gave a description of his "New Kind of Galvanic Pile" in the *Edinburgh New Philosophical Journal*, Volume 6, October 1828-March 1829, pp 70-77.

John Laird 1805-1874, who had been co-founder of the Birkenhead Iron Works in 1824, moved into building iron ships, the first builder in the world to consistently do so. Starting with the 54.5-tonne *Wye* in 1829, Laird then built *Lady Lansdowne*, an iron paddle steamer, in 1833, followed next year by *John Randolph*, the first iron steamer to operate in American waters. It was shipped in segments and reassembled at Savannah, Georgia, where she became a great commercial success.[1]

In the same year, along with his younger brother, McGregor Laird, he built the 272-tonne *Gary Owen*, the first vessel with transverse bulkheads dividing the hull into separate watertight compartments. Bulkheads became a standard feature of his ships, with *Rainbow*, the longest iron steamship to date at 65 m, having six compartments.[2]

The first screw propelled ship, *Robert F. Stockton*, was launched by Laird on 7 July 1838 and on 12 January 1839 attained a speed of 17.7 knots – 32.8 km/h. Named for the American captain who commissioned the ship, it became the first screw propeller ship in America and was renamed *New Jersey*, and it was also the first iron screw steamship to cross the Atlantic, mostly under sail, in 1839. Also in 1839, John Laird built *Nemesis* for the East India Company, the first gun-carrying iron ship and, with its flat bottom and shallow draught (1.83 m), it was admirably suited as the pioneer of British gunboat diplomacy during the first Opium War. "She first saw action on 7 January 1841 when, having landed a force of 600 Sepoys of the 37th Regiment near the Chuenpi forts, *Nemesis* bombarded the city's watchtower while three seventy-fours remained on station off Boat Island. While the Chinese gunnery proved inaccurate, every round from *Nemesis* found its mark, and the fortress fell shortly afterward. Her finest hour was undoubtedly in late May 1841, in the top of the Macao Passage when her maneuverability, steam power, and pivot-guns made her invincible against Chinese fire-boats and shore batteries. Her master's scouting a safe landing shortly thereafter enabled the British commander, [General Sir Hugh] Gough, to put his men where they needed to be to take Canton, upriver from the city. Thus, the British force had the remarkable luck of combining a redoubtable and highly adaptable vessel with a remarkably resourceful captain."[3] After serving as Britain's secret weapon in the first Opium War, *Nemesis* was last noted in Burmese waters in the early 1850s.

Laird also built *Birkenhead* (originally called *Vulcan*), the Royal Navy's first iron-hulled frigate, which was launched in 1845 and converted to a troopship. During the Kaffir War (or Cape Frontier War as it is now known) in South Africa it was transporting troops to fight against the Xhosa. In all, there were 643 passengers and crew, most of them from Scotland, including 25 women and 31 children, relatives of the officers on board. In the early hours of the morning, they woke with a start when the *Birkenhead* struck a hidden reef off the aptly named Danger Point, sustaining a fatal gash along its iron hull. Water quickly flooded the lower decks, drowning dozens of soldiers in their hammocks.[4] The ship's captain, Robert Salmond, ordered the women and children into the lifeboats. Scotsman Lieutenant-Colonel Alexander Seton (some sources call him Major Seton) gathered his officers and told them, "Gentlemen would you please be kind enough to preserve order and silence amongst the men and ensure that any orders given by Captain Salmond are instantly obeyed?" He then drew his sword in case any men tried to jump aboard. None did." [The two regiments involved were 74th (Highland) Regiment of Foot and The Queen's Royal Regiment (West Surrey)]. When the cutter was launched, and only 15 minutes after the collision, Lt-Col Seton ordered troops to line up on the poop deck, regiment by regiment. They stood to attention, staring silently into the night sky as the lifeboats sailed for the safety of the shore. Suddenly there was a horrific crash as rocks tore open the ship and it began to sink. Captain Salmond climbed the rigging and urged all who could swim to abandon ship. But Lt-Col Seton, his sword still drawn, raised his hands above his head and told his men, "You will swamp the cutter containing the women and children. I implore you not to do this thing and I ask you all to stand fast."[5] Seconds later the *Birkenhead* broke her back, not a man disobeyed Lt-Col Seton's orders and they shook hands and said goodbye as the water closed in over their heads. This was the start of the *Birkenhead Drill* – women and children first – which requires a ship's crew to show complete disregard for their own safety; to remain calm; to give priority to the rescue of any women, children and civilians aboard, and to display endurance and courage beyond the call of duty. This became standard maritime practice around the world and "As a splendid lesson in discipline to his army, the King of Prussia ordered the glorious story to be read on parade at the head of every regiment in his service."[6] Seton, who could not swim, was among the fatalities.

When the *Birkenhead* sank, English-born Irishman Captain Ralph MacGeough Bond Shelton saved himself by getting to shore two kilometres away through using a Mackintosh life preserver, but it's not clear if this was an 1825 model by Charles Macintosh, of raincoat fame, or one patented on 11 November 1837 by John Macintosh of New York.

Image 36 – "The Wreck of the *Birkenhead*" by Thomas M. Hemy

Another famous steamship built by Laird was the steel hulled *Ma Robert* (1858) for David Livingstone's expedition to the Zambezi River. It was transported to Africa in three prefabricated sections and assembled on the Zambezi. Laird also built two 998-tonne iron screw steamers, *Brasileira* and *Lusitania*, and a wooden paddle steamer, *Argentina*, to operate in South America. These were delivered in 1852 to the newly founded Liverpool-based company, the South American & General Steam Navigation Company, which also purchased the *Olinda* from Port Glasgow shipbuilder, John Reid & Company.

Laird, and his father William, virtually created modern Birkenhead, with William instigating Hamilton Square, one of Britain's best Georgian Squares, which was laid out by Scottish architect James Gillespie Graham. John Laird funded the Borough Hospital and the Laird School of Art – the first British public school of art outside London.

John Laird retired in 1861 with three of his sons running the company as John Laird & Sons, which merged with Englishman Charles Cammell's company to create Cammell Laird in 1903. The company launched *Auris* in 1959, the first petroleum tanker powered by gas turbines and three years earlier had launched the 27,216-tonne ore carrier *Leader*, the largest of its type in the world.[7] From the inception of both companies through the merger to 1947, over 1,100 vessels were constructed, including 106 warships during World War II.

Shortly after his sons took over, they built a turret ship, *Huascar*, in 1865 for the Peruvian Navy. This was an armoured, iron-hulled warship with two 300-pounder guns on a revolving turret and, after being seized by rebels, it fought two British ships on 29 May 1877 (during which HMS *Shah* fired the first modern "locomotive" torpedo in action although it missed its target) but, after nightfall, *Huascar* managed to escape. In 1879, back under control of the Peruvian government, its depredations constrained the Chilean army and navy for nearly six months from invading Peru. *Huascar* sank 16 Chilean ships, damaged four others, captured six vessels, recaptured two Peruvian ships, cut the Valparaiso-Antofagasta telegraph cable, damaged ten Chilean ports and destroyed the artillery batteries of Antofagasta, before being captured on 8 October 1879 by two Chilean battleships, three corvettes and a transport, which had been specifically sent out to entrap the small Peruvian turret ship.

John Lamont 1805-1879 (aka Johann von Lamont) produced a catalogue of 80,000 stars, of which 12,000 had been previously undiscovered. Lamont was also the first in Europe to devise a chronometer for recording the transit time of stars across the meridian (1850).

He became interested in the study of weather and proposed a network of meteorological stations. In an effort to co-ordinate measurements, he founded a meteorological association in 1842, and published the *Annalen für Meteorologie und Erdmagnetismus* from 1842 to 1844. His work, though remaining fragmentary due to lack of funding, laid the foundation for meteorological science in Bavaria and introduced new meteorological measuring and recording devices.[1]

With Alexander von Humboldt, he was a member of the Gottingen Magnet Union and they used this organisation to build a global network of geomagnetic observatories with standardised equipment for absolute measurements and for the observation of temporal variations in declination, inclination and horizontal intensity.[2]

He invented a portable theodolite for magnetic measurements and with it he established the constants of the Earth's magnetic force for a number of places through Middle Europe, from Spain to Denmark. Among his contributions to astronomy may be noted his eleven zone-catalogues of 34,674 stars, his measurements, in 1836-1837, of nebulae and clusters, and his determination of the mass of Uranus from observations of its satellites. A magnetic observatory was equipped at Bogenlausen in 1840 through his initiative. He discovered a magnetic decennial period, and the electric current in the Earth closing the electric "circuit" creating the magnetic field in 1850; he executed comprehensive magnetic surveys in 1849-1858, and he discovered Earth-currents in 1862. [3]

He determined the differences of longitude of Vienna, Munich, Geneva, and Strasburg, and completed the astronomical triangulation of Bavaria.[4] In the 1850s, Lamont started making regional magnetic surveys in the kingdom of Bavaria, later extended to other states in south Germany, France, Holland, Belgium, Spain, Portugal, Prussia and Denmark.[5]

Robert McConnell 1805-1867 developed patent beams (1855) with wrought-iron flanges and cast-iron webs which could readily be assembled to whatever length was required and were less susceptible to sudden failure in the event of overloading or casting defects.[1]

Image 37 – Gardner's Warehouse, Jamaica Street Glasgow

"Gardner's Warehouse [36 Jamaica Street, Glasgow] is one of the great landmarks of Western architectural history, being the first [building] in which the lessons of the Crystal Palace's [Hyde Park, London, 1851] prefabricated structure were applied successfully to everyday building. The structural frame was designed by R. McConnell, who held the patent for its wrought and cast-iron beams."[2]

William Muir 1805-1888 was a mechanical engineer who, with Joseph Whitworth, was instrumental in standardising tools. He invented the radial drill which "is a large geared head drill press in which the head can be moved along an arm that radiates from the machine's column. As it is possible to swing the arm relative to the machine's base, a radial arm drill press is able to operate over a large area without having to reposition the workpiece. This saves considerable time because it is much faster to reposition the drill head than it is to unclamp, move, and then re-clamp the workpiece to the table. The size of work that can be handled may be considerable, as the arm can swing out of the way of the table, allowing an overhead crane or derrick to place a bulky workpiece on the table or base."[1]

In 1841, he made what was probably the first mechanical road sweeping machine in model form. He was probably the main technical champion in standardising screw pitch, an achievement usually attributed to Joseph Whitworth, his employer, from whom it became universally known as Whitworth thread. "Long before the connection between Muir and Whitworth was formed, the manifold and serious disadvantages resulting from the varieties of screw pitch in use was universally admitted. We do not know upon what terms he undertook the work, but we believe when at Mr Whitworth's place Mr Muir collected from the principal mechanical engineers, at home and abroad, a collection of the various pitches in existence, and after a series of elaborate experiments arrived at a mean pitch, for ordinary or common threads, which was, after public exposition, adopted as 'Whitworth pitch.' On this subject, it may be interesting to note that Mr Muir's sketch-book for 1841 contains, inter alia, notes of 'experiments with ¾ in. bolts, the nuts in all cases being screwed to the bottom or ends of the screw.' The breaking strains are given for 'Fine V Thread,' 'Square Thread,' 'Common V Thread,' and 'Deep V Thread.' Numerous 'remarks' accompany the statement of results, in the evidently searching, patient, and careful inquiry. Afterwards Mr Muir, when in business for himself, developed on his own account a mean pitch for fine threads for the use of Opticians, Electricians, and Makers of Scientific Instruments. This improvement was before its time. Now, however, the development of Electricity practically applied, and the more sensitive delicacy required in scientific instruments employed for various purposes, have led to a more full appreciation of its value and importance."[2] "It seems that Muir should be given a good deal of the credit for his work on the standardisation of screw threads, the development of various machine tools, and the invention or development of the 'Whitworth' street-sweeping and knitting machines".[3]

"In 1853 [Muir] was granted patents on lathes and machines for grinding edge tools and for cutting out garment pieces. These were followed by two further patents on lathes (1856, 1859); two relating to letter-copying presses (1858, 1864); and a patent on planing machines (1867). His cutting machine for making sugar cubes (1863) eventually became widely used, and a labour-saving machine, which could wind cotton balls and bobbins and label them as well, was universally purchased by those in the trade."[4]

David Boswell Reid 1805-1863 was a chemist from Edinburgh who invented air conditioning, a claim that is usually attributed, wrongly, to American Willis Haviland Carrier, who developed *electrically* powered air conditioning. Reid was asked to better ventilate the temporary House of Commons in London in 1835 following a fire the previous year that had destroyed the original Palace of Westminster. The fire had been caused by thousands of wooden tally sticks used to record Treasury transactions. These had been discontinued in 1724 but were stored in the buildings until it was decided to burn them in a stove in the House of Lords. Putting too many tally sticks in the stove all at once caused the wall panelling to burn and both houses of Parliament were reduced to ashes. Contemporaneously, the River Thames, which flowed beside the House of Commons, was an open sewer and the stench was often oppressive. Reid installed his ventilation system and Lord Sudeley, Chairman of the Commissioners who selected the design for the new Houses of Parliament, said in the House of Lords, "The ventilation of the [Temporary] House of Commons was complete and perfect – and the first plan of systematic ventilation ever carried out in this or any other country."[1]

This system worked until the new House of Commons was opened in 1852. Reid did the same for the House of Lords. In 1842, he managed the implementation of improved ventilation and sewerage technology throughout Britain as a belated reaction to the cholera epidemic of 1831-1832, and Reid realised the inter-relationships between poor health, poor sanitation, poor hygiene and poor ventilation. In the 1830s, he systematically studied room ventilation and its effects on respiration by having five rooms near his lecture room built to his own specifications for the purpose of determining the amount of air required for health and comfort. Reid's system included a means of filtering, heating and moistening air; the capacity to adjust the temperature via a recirculation duct; air speed controls; and cooling and dehumidification features. The air supply could be varied not just for temperature, but in response to the number of people in the room, and Reid could vary the supply of air to different parts of the room to cater for the Speaker of the House, who was present at all times, and the public gallery which could vary in the number of spectators and who sat close to the gas heating. Horace Mann, an American education reformer, described the ventilated House of Commons "as the only edifice he saw in Europe in which a complete system was established that gave members every luxury and comfort that ventilation could afford."[2]

Although Reid's recommendations were never fully implemented in the new House of Commons, because of disagreements with architect Charles Barry, his recommendations on acoustics were agreed to and the ceiling of the main speaking chamber was lowered. Reid was eventually compensated with a payment of £3,700 plus an amount equal to six years' salary to cover lost wages, and Parliament empowered him to make changes as set out in 35 recommendations. It has been suggested that this was the first case of an individual successfully suing a government for wrongful dismissal, although it wasn't couched in those terms at the time.[3]

In 1845, Reid designed the ventilation system for the city of Liverpool's St George's Hall. This was essentially the first air conditioning system to be installed in a public building in Britain or, indeed, the world, as it used fans to cool air as well as hot water to heat pipes, a system that anticipated not only air conditioning but reverse cycle heating. Its major drawback was that it involved a lot of manual labour. Reid went on to build similar ventilation systems in Brighton Pavilion; Windsor Castle; St James' Palace (Chapel Royal); Buckingham Palace; The Old Bailey; London Opera House; The Tuileries, and the Palais Royal in Paris; the Chemistry Academy in Alexandroski (near the Russian capital of St Petersburg); hospitals in London, Chicago, New York and Copenhagen; Queen Victoria's Royal Yacht (*Victoria and Albert*); British gaols; and the steamships of Scottish-born African explorer William Balfour Baikie during the Niger expedition in 1841.

Reid was one of thirteen commissioners of the Health of Towns Commission, which included two other Scots – Lyon Playfair and Chairman Walter Francis Montagu-Douglas-Scott, 5th Duke of Buccleuch. The commissioners were appointed in 1843 to inquire into the state of large towns and populous districts in England and Wales with reference to the causes of disease among the inhabitants, and into the best means of promoting and securing public health.[4] This report was in response to lobbying by Englishman Edwin Chadwick, who worked closely with the commissioners. American Elisha Harris, superintendent and physician-in-chief of the Staten Island quarantine station and President of the American Public Health Association (in 1878), noted in respect of the commission that, "Probably no other attempt at Sanitary reform has produced results at all comparable with this."[5]

Reid, who wrote *Illustrations of the Theory and Practice of Ventilation* in 1844, defined architecture as the act of enclosing and servicing an interior atmosphere, long before this was generally accepted as a concept.[6] He emigrated to America and, in 1858, published *Ventilation in American Dwellings* in which he stressed the benefits of good ventilation and sanitation. Reid's experiments showed how to calculate the amount of fresh air that was needed in relation to the number of occupants, and that humidification of the air was essential in winter for comfort. He advised that the maximum wet bulb depression in occupied rooms should be in the vicinity of 2.2C (dry bulb temperature is the actual temperature while the wet bulb temperature is the temperature air will cool to when water is evaporated into unsaturated air).

There is no doubt that Reid was the true founder of air conditioning, both on a theoretical and practical basis. "The term air-conditioning originated in the United States and it is usually assumed that the first air-conditioned buildings appeared there after the introduction of mechanical refrigeration into building services. However, it is clear that air-conditioned buildings first appeared in the United Kingdom in the middle of the Nineteenth century under the supervision of David Boswell Reid."[7] He died 13 years before the currently accepted "Father of air conditioning", American Willis Haviland Carrier, was born in 1876.

Peter Spence 1806-1883 developed a process in 1845 for the production of alum (potassium aluminium sulphate) based on treating coal-shale with sulphuric acid. Alum was used in dyeing textiles, tanning leather and in paper manufacture. Spence became responsible for the majority of the world's production. Up until Spence introduced his new process, potassium alum was used; after Spence's firm went into production, it was rapidly replaced by the ammonium variety. The old method was a laborious and time-consuming process which involved the roasting of alum shale, lixiviation (water treatment), evaporation, precipitation of the alum by the addition of alkaline salts, washing and crystallisation. It involved considerable labour and waste: an entire year was required for the conversion of the raw materials into alum for the market. Spence's process consisted in the calcinations of shale obtained from Lancashire collieries; it was then treated with sulphuric acid and ammonia, mixed, drained, washed, steamed, and finally precipitated. The entire process was completed within a single month. By the late 1850s, Spence produced over 28 tonnes of alum per week, and by 1865 production had been stepped up to over 6,350 tonnes per year.[1]

James Davidson Wallace 1806-1874 was the engineer who made the Sydney to Parramatta railway happen with technical innovations, new plans and new specifications. He changed the Sydney terminus from Haymarket to Devonshire Street, the bridges from timber to stone, the track from single to double, the rails from timber to wrought-iron Barlow-type and added a branch line to Darling Harbour. For all his achievements, Wallace's most lasting change from broad gauge to standard gauge track ironically led to the great Australian gauge debacle.[1]

"The Act of Council, incorporating the Sydney Railway Company, was finally assented to by his Excellency in November, 1849. Shortly after, surveys were taken of the proposed line, and a commencement was made at excavating and raising embankments at different portions of the distance, together with the building of a few timber bridges. These attempts, although considered as very extensive undertakings by those who executed them, and indeed positively important when regarded as the initiation of a grand enterprise, yet both in imperfectness of execution, and in slowness of procedure, they were ludicrously inadequate to the vastness of the work. Nor is this to be wondered at, when it is known, that the gentlemen who engaged in the undertaking had little or no practical knowledge of railway operations. With the appointment of Mr James Wallace, as engineer to the line, and the subsequent acceptance of the contracts by Mr William Randle, a new era in the history of these enterprises has commenced. Both these gentlemen have brought to bear upon the project the capacity and energy acquired from engaging in those gigantic engineering works in England, which are the wonders of this as they will be of future time, and compared with which the construction of fifteen miles of railway in a level country is a mere bagatelle."[2]

Wallace was consulting engineer on the Great Northern Railway of The Hunter River Railway Company. Bridges were built of timber and small culverts used brickwork, of which some remains. He did pioneering work across the Hexham Swamp using brushwood matting over the soft ground. Governor Dennison opened the line between Honeysuckle Point and East Maitland, by then taken over by government, on 30 March 1857, proclaiming it the Great Northern Railway.

The above-mentioned Australian gauge debacle is often attributed to Wallace who suggested the British standard gauge of 4'8½" (143.5 cm) be used. This was in accord with the 1848 recommendation by Lord Grey, the Colonial Secretary, and had been agreed to by both New South Wales and South Australia as rolling stock would have to be imported. The first engineer for the Sydney Railway Company was Irishman Francis Webb Shields, who recommended the Irish gauge of 5' 3" (160 cm), and three states, New South Wales, Victoria and South Australia agreed. Shields then resigned and, following his appointment and while still in England, Wallace suggested returning to the British standard gauge and this was accepted by the New South Wales government, while the other two states stayed with the Irish gauge as they had already ordered stock for the wider gauge rail. Queensland and Western Australia later chose 42" (106.6 cm) narrow track, while Tasmania started with broad gauge and then changed to narrow gauge.[3] Given the attitudes of the various state governments, and the fact that they determined the gauges within their own states, it seems grossly unfair to attribute any of the so-called "gauge debacle" to Wallace or even to Shields.

Isaac Holden 1807-1897 was born to English parents in the Renfrew village of Hurlet. He had an inventive flair having developed a Lucifer match using sulphur in 1829, but John Walker of England had already invented matches – or Congreves – in 1827, using antimony sulphide, potassium chlorate, gum and starch. Holden turned his attention to the textile industry, which had been important in Britain for centuries. Wool was such a major revenue earner in England that, from the 14th century onwards, the Speaker in the House of Lords sat on a woolsack. Holden patented a square motion wool-comber (combing is the process that precedes spinning) and a process for making genappe, a very smooth worsted yarn used for braids and fringes. He went into partnership in Paris with Englishman Samuel Cunliffe Lister, who retired in 1850, with Holden continuing in what had become the largest wool-combing business in the world with around 4,000 employees in Yorkshire and another factory in Paris.[1]

The square motion was one of 169 combing techniques patented in the peak of the 1840s and 1850s, yet it was one of only a handful that achieved long-term commercial success. It possessed special features and was unique in its ability to comb all grades and thicknesses of wool, but its position among the leaders was also the result of Lister's manipulation of the patent system. Through the practice of purchasing patents on inventions which competed with their own designs, the partners achieved a technical near-monopoly, and Holden created a machine that removed potential competitors by producing the finest combed wool. Holden's activities took the

French industry by storm: between 1865 and 1895 his two factories produced 25% of the industry's requirement of combed wool.[2]

James Pugh Kirkwood 1807-1877 was an authority on hydraulics and built, or was consultant for, municipal waterworks at Brooklyn, St Louis, Cincinnati, Albany, Pittsburgh, Boston, Lowell, and Poughkeepsie (NY) from the years 1868-1876. In 1869, his *Report on the Filtration of River Waters, for the Supply of Cities, as Practiced in Europe* made to the Board of Water Commissioners of the City of St. Louis became a widely-used textbook on water filtration. Because of this book, the water filters he constructed for Poughkeepsie, New York, and his recommendations for St. Louis' water filtration, he became known as the "Father of Slow Sand filtration". He also introduced the coating of cast-iron water pipes with coal tar in order to prevent corrosion.[1]

He was resident engineer for the Stonington & Providence Railroad, followed by resident engineer for the Long Island Railroad in 1837. From 1840 to 1843, he was resident engineer, mountain division of the Western Railroad of Massachusetts. In 1847, he temporarily went from railroad engineering to being the engineer in charge of construction of the docks, hospitals, and workshop for the naval depot at Pensacola, Florida. He then became General Superintendent of the New York & Erie Railroad and introduced the running of trains by using telegraph signals. In 1850, he moved to Missouri to become the Chief Engineer for the Missouri Pacific Railroad from 1850-1855. He perfected the surveys, studied the possible routes, and managed the construction of the railroad. Kirkwood decided to use the broad 5-foot 6-inch (1,676.4 mm) gauge rather than the narrower gauge to allow for more powerful locomotives.[2]

He took charge of the work of lowering and moving horizontally into a rock-cut the great water-main on Eighth Avenue, New York City. From 1856 to 1860, he was Chief Engineer of the Nassau Water Works in Brooklyn. He built the road from St. Louis to Pacific, Missouri. He also built the Springfield and Northampton railroad.

In 1848, in north-eastern Pennsylvania, he built the stone-arched Starrucca Viaduct, then the most costly railroad bridge in the world and the largest stone viaduct, with one of the first significant uses of concrete for the main piers. With three other engineers, including fellow Scot James Laurie, he founded the American Society of Civil Engineers in 1852.[3]

David Dale Owen 1807-1860 performed some of the first and most important geological surveys of the American Midwest.[1] He was a leading American geologist who headed two federal geological surveys and the first official state geological surveys of Indiana, Kentucky, and Arkansas.[2]

In the summer of 1848, while making a geological survey of Wisconsin, Iowa and Minnesota for the United States government, he descended the Red River to Lake Winnipeg, and ascended the Winnipeg River to Lake of the Woods and thence to Lake Superior. He described the character of the country around Upper Fort Garry (Winnipeg) and the rock exposures at Lower Fort Garry, giving a list of fossils and analyses of two specimens of rock. The beds he stated to be of the same age as the Upper Magnesian Limestone of Wisconsin. He also described the exposures on Lake Winnipeg, and those in a small bay near Big Swamp Point.[3]

He obtained what was sometimes seen as more than his fair share of survey work, and completing that work with amazing speed and efficiency. He was an immigrant in an increasingly native-born scientific community, and a westerner in a scientific community periodically divided by regional jealousies. Perhaps most importantly, Owen mastered the quintessential challenge of doing science in the American context: how to produce utilitarian results, on time and within budget while generating and disseminating new scientific knowledge as well.[4]

Alexander James Adie 1808-1879 designed a pyrometer that was used by Charles Babbage in important experimental work on the heat expansion of stone. The experiments involved heating various kinds of stones in an open furnace and recording minute expansions of the stone in different increments of increased heat. With Adie's pyrometer, temperature was more easily controlled and more exact measurements could be determined. In experiments with Adie's pyrometer on different kinds of stone, as well as iron, brick, porcelain and other artificial substances, it was found that "ordinary building materials of stone expand but very little differently from cast iron, and that, consequently, the mixture of those materials in edifices is not injurious to their durability."[1]

William Erskine Baker 1808-1881 "was successively superintendent of the Delhi canals, superintendent of canals and forests in Sind, director of the Ganges Canal project, consulting engineer to the government of India for railways, and secretary to the government of India in the public works department. His services as a civil engineer were considerable, and he was widely regarded as the greatest authority of his time on irrigation."[1] He was instrumental in creating the Civil Engineering College at Roorkee, now The Indian Institute of Technology, Roorkee, founded by Englishman Sir James Thomason. On returning from a trip to England, he was made Consulting Engineer for Railways and, with Sir Rowland Macdonald Stephenson and fellow Scot, George Turnbull, he constructed the East Indian Railway. He was appointed as the first ever Secretary to the Indian Government Public Works Department in 1855. "The great irrigation works which he carried out there have rendered Sir Charles Napier's conquest of real value, and, according to Captain Burton, have made 'the desert flourish like the rose.'"[2]

David Rennie Brown 1808-1875 developed the manufacture of morphine and the isolation of a number of alkaloids and salts. His work resulted in creating apomorphine and ethylmorphine.[1] Brown made the important discovery of how to prevent chloroform's tendency to decompose and yield the poison gas phosgene, by adding a small amount of ethyl alcohol.[2] He independently developed a process for morphine hydrochloride and he converted an existing ether plant to produce chloroform.[3]

James Freeburn 1808-1876 invented shell fuses in 1846, which were set to explode by either concussion (on hitting an object) or length of time. "The evolution of fuses was just as important as the art of gunnery. An explosive shell could not be detonated in the same way as its propellant. ... The first English concussion fuse was invented in 1846 by an Artilleryman, Quartermaster Freeburn ..."[1] The fuse was wooden, about 15 cm long, and used shear wire to hold blocks between the fuse magazine and a burning match. The match was ignited by propellant flash, and the shear wire broke on impact.

James Hall Nasmyth 1808-1890 invented the steam hammer in 1837 and he became one of the most renowned names of the steam era. He originally designed the steam hammer for forging the gigantic paddle shaft of the *Great Britain*, but Brunel altered the ship's original design from using paddlewheels to a screw propeller, so the steam hammer wasn't constructed until later, in France. This was done without Nasmyth's knowledge, but the French conceded they used his designs. The steam hammer became an icon of the Victorian period as it permitted massive machines to be built, symbolising this era of major technical advancement. The steam hammer obviated the need to make large objects of iron in the piecemeal manner whereby each of the separate parts was joined together. While it could exert many tonnes of pressure, the steam hammer was sensitive enough to crack an egg without splattering it.

Many of the steamships, large factory engines and armaments at this time depended on the steam hammer for their manufacture. Using the same principle, in 1843, Nasmyth patented a steam pile driver which was commonly used in construction work, and he designed a hydraulic mattress press in 1839. Englishman Joseph Bramah had invented the hydraulic press in 1795, but the Nasmyth machine was exponentially larger, being able to exert a pressure of 18,150 tonnes over an area of more than 4.5 square metres.[1]

In 1826, Nasmyth devised a steel-arm filing machine that replaced cold chisel work as a method of obtaining a fine finished cut and, in the same year, he designed the expansometer to measure total or relative expansion in solid bodies. Three years later he invented a flexible shaft drill to reach otherwise inaccessible areas, and another machine for square or hexagonal cutting of bolt heads or nuts. In 1836, he designed several machines: one for cutting key-grooves of any diameter in metal wheels and belt pulleys; an instrument for finding and marking the centre of cylinders and bolts that were to be turned on a lathe; a machine for planing flat or cylindrical metal shapes; and a method of cutting a template for making curves in objects such as pottery or glass during manufacture. The following year he designed a means to reverse the motion of a slide lathe, and in 1838 he invented self-adjusting bearings for machine shafts which are supported in such a way that they can tilt to contain movement of the actual shaft, keeping it steady. Also in 1838, he designed a safety foundry ladle that could be worked safely by one man, replacing a crew of twelve men who had to empty the ladle of molten metal by means of cross handles being manually maneuvered, involving high risk of injury or death to the crew.[2] Seven years later, in 1845, Nasmyth devised a disc-grinding machine.

He made a watertight universal flexible joint for water and steam pipes, a suction fan for ventilating coal mines, improvements to methods of welding iron and making chain cables, and a new style of safety valve for steam boilers. He invented a steam ram that was fired from a cradle using pneumatic pressure created by a steam engine. These rams, used in warfare, were typically 12 m long by 3 m wide and could inflict severe damage if sufficiently propelled.

Nasmyth improved telescopes and built a half-metre reflecting telescope along the principles of those developed by Isaac Newton and Frenchman Laurent Cassegrain. His telescope had no hole drilled in the primary mirror, utilising instead a third mirror to reflect light to the side. This telescope could be set in a large azimuthal mount which moved the telescope along two perpendicular axes of motion. Nasmyth had two telescopes built – 38 cm in 1835 for Armagh Observatory in Ireland, and 51 cm in 1845 that was the first successful convex Cassegrain secondary mirror for a major telescope. Nasmyth's telescope is the direct precursor of modern telescopes such as the Very Large Telescope (VLT) – which in 2005 produced some of the first infrared images of extrasolar planets – and the Thirty Meter Telescope being built in Hawaii and which will be the largest in the world (construction of the telescope began on 28 July 2014). This telescope will later be replaced as the world's largest by the European Extremely Large Telescope (49% larger than the Thirty Meter Telescope), which also uses a Nasmyth platform.[3] Many other telescopes, such as the 10 m telescopes at Keck Observatory in Hawaii, use a Nasmyth platform. Nasmyth's telescope design is also used by European Southern Observatory's 3.6 m New Technology Telescope built in 1989.

When Nasmyth first built his own half metre reflecting telescope, he made detailed observations of the moon, making plaster models which he photographed at a time when photography was too primitive to get acceptable pictures of the moon. In 1874, with astronomer James Carpenter, he published, *The Moon: Considered as a Planet, a World, and a Satellite*, in which the authors provided both a physical description and an explanation as to how the moon's features originated. It was one of the first publications with photo-mechanical prints, allowing photographs to be printed by the usual commercial printing method of permanent carbon-based inks.[4]

Nasmyth patented many other inventions, such as turning segmented work pieces on a lathe, and inventing the *V* anvil used for testing round parts of tools or equipment, ensuring that they were always centred. He devised suction fans for ventilating coal mines, improved the method of welding iron, and of punching large holes in iron bars.

Frenchman Pierre Fauchard, sometimes called the "Father of modern dentistry", described an improved drill in 1728. Its rotary movement was powered by catgut twisted around a cylinder, or by jewellers' bowstrings. A hand-cranked dental drill bit was patented by John Lewis in 1838. George Washington's dentist, John Greenwood, invented the first known "dental foot engine" in 1790. He adapted his mother's foot-treadle spinning wheel to rotate a drill. Greenwood's dentist son continued to use the drill, but the idea went no further. James Nasmyth used a coiled wire spring to drive a drill in 1829. Charles Merry of St. Louis, Missouri, adapted Nasmyth's drill, adding a flexible cable, in 1858.[5]

In 1854, Nasmyth invented the reversible rolling mill for moving bars of metal to be progressively flattened and, in 1862, he proposed replacing hardened steel with chilled cast-iron shot for action against armoured plate. He didn't patent it, and Nasmyth's method was adopted by William Palliser in 1867 and used in the British army until 1909 and in warships and forts until 1921.

Nasmyth patented a method of puddling iron with steam to replace the rabbling bar which was used to agitate the molten iron to expose it to oxygen, thus removing carbon. This was arduous work and usually went on for an hour. Nasmyth introduced a small pipe to feed in steam which agitated the iron and did the same job as the manual labour. Puddling had originally been invented in 1784 by Englishman Henry Cort when most blast furnaces produced less than 18 tonnes a week, but by 1855 the output had increased tenfold and the Cort process was a bottleneck on production. In that year, Henry Bessemer invented his hot blast process to drive air into the iron to remove impurities, although his process needed further refinement by Robert Forester Mushet before it became a success. Bessemer's priority was challenged by American Angier March Perkins, who had patented the use of highly heated steam in place of the hot or cold air blast in 1843. "In the [1856] *London Mining Journal*, p. 600, Mr A.M. Perkins claims precedence of Nasmyth in inventing the dry steam puddling blast, having patented it in 1843, and used it in 1850."[6] However, Nasmyth himself recognised that Bessemer's process was superior in using hot dry air instead of steam and supported Bessemer during his presentation at the autumn meeting of the British Association in 1856. This was simply an instance of a very good idea germinating another very good idea, which is the very process that fuels innovation.

Image 38 – Nasmyth with his 51 cm Telescope
Image 39 – Keck Observatory 10 metre telescope

Undoubtedly, Nasmyth was one of the great engineers of the Victorian era who had a major impact on modern telescope design, the standardisation of tool manufacturing and, above all, a profound effect on the hallmark of the Industrial Revolution – industrial manufacturing.

John Scott Russell 1808-1882 was riding alongside the Union Canal when he discovered the soliton – a self-reinforcing solitary wave that holds its shape while moving at a constant speed. Following his discovery, Russell built a 10 m wave tank in his back garden and made further important observations on the properties of the solitary wave. His experimental work helped to re-ignite British interest in theoretical hydrodynamics, but Russell's work was not fully appreciated until the 1960s when applied scientists used computers to study nonlinear wave propagation. Russell viewed the solitary wave as a self-sufficient dynamic entity that exhibited many properties of a particle. Solitons are now a major field of science with research across such diverse areas as plasmas, hydrodynamics, shock waves, tornados, nonlinear optics, elementary particles, and even Jupiter's Great Red Spot.[1]

"The studies of John Scott Russell triggered a lot of controversy in the scientific community of his time, which assumed that nonlinear effects were of secondary importance. Many debates were raised, which highlights how surprising the properties of solitons are."[2]

Russell's discovery of the soliton was one of a number of mechanical phenomena which he described at the meetings of the British Association. Others included wave motion, tidal phenomena and the design of sea-walls and embankments.[3] Russell designed ships, boats, yachts and barges and he created the "wave line" system of hull construction which revolutionised 19th century naval architecture. This system, or theory, involved designing the lines of a vessel to take into consideration the length and shape of a wave travelling at a certain speed. Russell's work provided the basis for plating the skins of vessels and the "longitudinal system", whereby lengthwise girders were used for building ships to give them greater strength.

He was partner to Franco-Englishman Isambard Kingdom Brunel on the construction of the pioneering iron ship *Great Eastern*, the largest ship in the world and the first to have a cellular double-bottom, cellular double upper deck, and longitudinal bulkheads. Unlike previous ships, it was not built on the principles of wooden shipbuilding, but was from the start designed on principles to suit its iron structure. The *Great Eastern* "was designed to carry goods and people to India and Australia, without stopping for fuel. It would be the biggest ship the world had ever seen. Twice the length and five times the weight of any previous ship, it would be the largest moveable object man had ever created".[4] It measured 211 m long, 25 m wide, with a draft of 6.1 m unloaded and 9.1 m fully laden, and displaced 29,030 tonnes fully loaded. Scott Russell was responsible for its hull form, structure and machinery. Brunel meddled in these details, but ignored Scott Russell's advice on launching the heavy hull.[5] Two people were killed in the difficult sideways-launch of the *Great Eastern*, and it became known to some as the unlucky ship. Initially, she only wanted to move some three feet and then stopped and refused to go any further. Almost three months went by until she was pushed into the sea, but on 30 January 1858 the colossus was at last afloat.[6]

Russell designed the first ocean-going iron-hulled armoured warship, *Warrior*, which was also the largest and most powerful warship built at that time, launched in 1860 and capable of 17½ knots (32.7 km/h). Its guns sat in an armoured box 11½ cm thick with 2½ cm thick armour plating which no contemporary guns could penetrate, even at point blank range. It set the standard for future building of warships by the great powers which resulted in *Warrior* and its even more powerful Scottish-built sister ship, *Black Prince*, becoming redundant within a decade. In 1834, Russell started a steam-carriage service between Glasgow and Paisley and, as a result of his familiarity with locomotives, he made the first experimental observation of the Doppler shift of sound frequency as a train passes, and gave an independent explanation of the theory. The Doppler Effect was first described by the Austrian physicist Christian Doppler in 1842.[7]

In 1865, he published *The Modern System of Naval Architecture* which has been called "possibly the most important work on naval architecture of its time".[8] He was a founding member of the Institution of Naval Architects (now Royal Institution of Naval Architects) to study the science of shipbuilding, the forerunner of many similar organisations throughout the world. He wrote books on education including *Technical Education a National Want* (1868) and in his 1869 publication *Systematic Technical Education for the English People* "he advocated a Minister for Public Instruction, a central technical university in London, 15 technical colleges in industrial centres and 1,000 trade schools, with teachers supplied through a technical teacher training scheme."[9]

Russell developed a curriculum for technical education in Britain and played an active role as Joint Secretary in the success of the Great Exhibition at Crystal Palace in London, the genesis of World Expo. He was a promoter and the "indefatigable Secretary" to the Great Exhibition of 1851. Scott Russell recruited the ambitious Henry Cole to help with the venture. In October 1851, both Scott Russell and Henry Cole received letters hand-written by Prince Albert in appreciation of the incredible success of the Great Exhibition.[10]

The French had commenced a series of national industrial expositions with eleven being held from 1844 to 1849, but the 1851 Exhibition truly upstaged these events by having an international display of the world's best on offer. "The Great Exhibition was in good part Russell's doing. When Henry Cole – the man who invented Christmas cards – told him about the wonders of the Paris Exhibition of 1849, Russell saw the possibilities of a British fair of engineering and manufacturing arts. He discussed it with the Prince Consort, the unpopular Albert. The intelligent and catholically educated German was having a bad time in England. The upper classes were suspicious of his erudition and the lower classes abhorred his stiff manners. The Queen, however, wanted Albert to be a success. Russell weighed these factors and sprang his coup one night in 1850. In the course of handing out medals at an art school exercise, Russell remarked cryptically, 'There is now every hope of carrying out His Royal Highness Prince Albert's plans for 1851.' Albert summoned Russell to the Palace and they plotted the Great Exhibition. The Queen blessed Albert's hobby."[11] And thus the Great Exhibition was born.

Russell designed an innovative shallow draught train ferry for Lake Constance. In 1871, his suggestion for a riveted iron-plate cone, stiffened by tapering radial ribs and concentric iron rings, was chosen by the Imperial Commission of the 1873 International Exhibition of the Austrian Empire for the Vienna Rotunda – the largest roof in the world for a decade.[12] The Rotunda had "4,000 tons [3,628 tonnes] of iron. Including its topmost crown which was 60 feet tall [18 m], its height reached to 284 feet [86.5 m]. The diameter of the dome itself was 440 feet [134 m], with a circumference of 1,080 feet [329 m] and peak of 284 feet [86.5 m]. Its structure consisted of 32 pairs of columns of iron each 80 feet tall [24.3 m]. It is estimated that these columns, which had been reinforced with iron plating, each individually bore the weight of 109 tons [99 tonnes]. These iron columns provided the only physical support for the dome. The supporting columns were connected by an iron circular girder riveted together on the site. In a display of modern technology, this ring was then raised by hydraulic lift, with the columns placed under it as it was elevated. Radial girders 200 feet long [61 m] were bolted to the girder at its top and bottom. These measurements place the Vienna Rotunda as the largest of its kind. By comparison, it was 3.17 times larger than the dome of St. Paul's cathedral in London, 2.26 times larger than that of St. Peter's in Rome, and 2.22 larger than the Crystal Palace in London."[13] Note: Other sources provide different dimensions for the Rotunda e.g. 107 metres (352 ft) for the diameter of the dome in *Designing the Centennial: A History of the 1876 International Exhibition in Philadelphia,* Bruno Giberti, The University Press of Kentucky, Lexington, 2002. Wikipedia has a list of buildings that have held the title of the largest dome in the world and, from 128AD -1881 this was the Pantheon in Rome with a diameter of 43.4 metres (142 ft).

Russell was undoubtedly one of the great British Victorian engineers and was certainly in the same rank as Brunel, his erstwhile business partner. On the centenary of the Royal Institution of Naval Architects in 1960, its historian wrote: "It seems to have become a fashion to belittle and malign Scott Russell with the apparent object of increasing the fame of that very eccentric genius Isambard Brunel."[14]

Image 40 – Rotunda, Vienna

Alexander Reed Allan 1809-1891 invented the straight-link valve motion in 1855 to provide better steam distribution and higher efficiency at low speed for locomotives. Allan combined the ideas of the Robert Stephenson and Daniel Gooch gears and used them with a straight link, which he claimed was easier to machine up than a curved one.

The weighbar or reverse shaft had two arms for each set of gears; one arm had a "drop" or lifting-link connected to the straight expansion link, and the other arm was similarly connected to the valve rod, so that when the driver operated his reversing lever the link would move up or down as required, and at the same time the valve rod would move in the opposite direction to meet it.[1] The Allan gear became common in Europe, although less so in Britain.

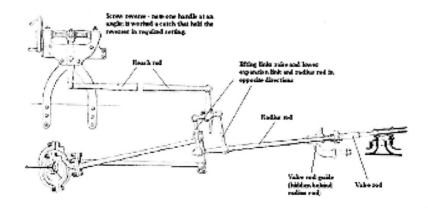

Image 41 – The straight link of Allan's valve gear is moved upwards to reverse the direction of travel, and at the same time the valve-rod die block is moved downwards in the link. This arrangement reduces the vertical height required to accommodate the gear on the locomotive.

James Dowie born 1809 was the first to successfully use elastication in footwear, which he patented in 1838. As early as 1832, there was an American patent for rubber soles on footwear, but the rubber became sticky in the hot summer weather and the concept faded from public view. Dowie, in 1839, read a paper on footwear before the Society of Arts for Scotland.[1]

There was widespread evidence of the harm caused by rigid, tight-fitting shoes and boots. Shoe manufacturers who exhibited at the Great Exhibition stressed the importance of the health and comfort of the foot. Joseph Sparkes Hall and James Dowie wrote publicity material on how their supple shoes and boots corresponded to the anatomical form of the foot, allowing it to move freely without constraint. Small cotton loops were often attached inside ankle boots to help with pulling them on.[2]

"The effects of the boot on the anatomy and function of the foot were already well recognised by the time that Darwin, Huxley and Tylor were writing. In 1839 a paper was read before the Society of Arts for Scotland entitled 'Observations on Boots and Shoes, with reference to the Structure and Action of the Human Foot'. The author, a certain James Dowie, presented himself to the Society as the inventor, patentee and manufacturer of boots and shoes with elastic soles. Explaining the advantages of his invention, Dowie drew attention to some remarks of Sir Charles Bell, the Edinburgh surgeon … in which he compares the Irish agricultural labourer, travelling to harvest barefoot, and the English peasant whose foot and ankle are tightly laced in a shoe with a wooden sole. Look at the way the Englishman lifts his legs, observed Bell, and you will perceive 'that the play of the ankle, foot, and toes, is lost, as much as if he went on stilts, and therefore are his legs small and shapeless'. Indeed, Bell was much in favour of James Dowie's patent elastic boots and shoes, going so far as to provide a public testimonial in which he not only affirmed the correctness of Dowie's understanding of the anatomical details, but also declared himself a highly satisfied user."[3]

James David Forbes 1809-1868 created the first seismometer, an instrument capable of keeping a continuous record of seismic activity, in 1844. "The interest in seismic instruments generated by the Calabrian earthquakes [1783] was not sustained in succeeding years. In 1839, however, a series of small earthquakes began near Comrie, in Perthshire, Scotland. Scores of shocks were felt over a period of several years. A direct result of the Comrie earthquakes was the establishment of a Special Committee of the British Association for the Advancement of Science, the purpose of the committee being to obtain 'instruments and registers to record shocks in Great Britain'. The most significant instrument resulting from the committee's work was an inverted-pendulum 'seismometer', designed by James Forbes." Note: the abovementioned committee's full title was the Committee for the Investigation of Scottish and Irish Earthquakes and its members first discovered how to evaluate the epicentre of an earthquake.[1]

Forbes was probably the first to attempt explicitly to give a seismological instrument a "long" period (around five seconds). He was also the first to try to avoid the clumsiness of a long common pendulum in obtaining long periods. His method of approaching neutral equilibrium was similar to that used by Emil Wiechert in 1900. Forbes desired a long period in order that the pendulum remain stationary as the Earth moved beneath it. He clearly wanted to measure ground displacement in an earthquake with his seismometer. A mathematical theory of the instrument accompanies its description. Forbes was the first to describe mathematically the behaviour of a seismic instrument in an "earthquake". The assumed earthquake, again, is a single motion of uniform velocity, starting and stopping abruptly.[2]

Forbes did important experimental work on the polarisation and refraction of radiant heat, thereby indicating its similarity to visible light and promoting the idea of a continuous spectrum of radiation.[3] After his discovery of the polarisation of radiant heat, he later demonstrated the double refraction of thermal radiation and, in 1836, he found that heat could be circularly polarised. He thus demonstrated the identity of the laws that regulate the phenomena of radiant heat and light, making an important contribution to the development of the concept of a continuous radiation spectrum.[4] His investigations of interference phenomena with thermal radiation established its wave nature, and he built the so-called Forbes bar to measure thermal conductivity of metals.[5]

Forbes also measured the temperature gradient in Earth's surface – i.e. that its temperature increases with depth – and he was among the first to recognise that glaciers move like very viscous liquids, even though they're made of brittle ice. At first, Forbes didn't say how they did; but another scientist, John Tyndall, said that glacial ice constantly breaks up, then freezes back together – creating an illusion of fluid motion. The modern view of glaciers is closer to that of Forbes than to that of Tyndall, and later experiments have shown that ice does display that genuine molecular plasticity or continuous deformation under stress ascribed to it by Forbes. However, as fracture and regelation undoubtedly occur in glacier flow, and other factors also contribute to glacier motion, neither man was wholly right or wrong.[6]

Forbes' work with heat radiation was a first step on the way to Max Planck setting the basis of quantum physics. And the viscoplastic movement of glaciers is like the movement within Earth's mantle. Lord Kelvin's estimate of Earth's age, based on Forbes' data, was defeated by those glacial movements below Earth's surface. Forbes' work continued to echo in so much that followed it.[7]

William Ewart Gladstone 1809-1898 initiated major reforms of public finance and parliamentary accountability. "The true father of the modern company was Gladstone."[1]

"The first modern Act [relating to company law] was the Joint Stock Companies Act 1844, introduced by one of the great statesmen of the nineteenth century, William Gladstone, when he was President of the Board of Trade. This Act ushered in the crucial principle that citizens should be empowered to form companies by going through a relatively simple bureaucratic procedure, presided over by a state official, the Registrar of Companies. Previously, incorporation had been available only by following the cumbersome routes of obtaining a private Act of Parliament or a Royal Charter."[2]

In 1837, Gladstone chaired a Parliamentary Committee to examine the issue relating to corporate law reform. Its recommendations led to the enactment of the Joint Stock Companies Act in 1844, which signalled the merging of the joint stock fund as a form of economic activity with the idea of incorporation. The development of company law thus became separate from that of partnership. Drawing on the Gladstone Committee's recommendations, the 1844 Act was based upon two elements that continue to underpin modern corporate regulation: public registration and public financial accountability.[3]

The recommendations of the Gladstone Committee were in large part adopted in the Joint Stock Companies Act of 1844. "They set an important milestone in the development of the corporation in England. They also provided benchmarks regarding the type and quality of information which should be made available to the public in regard to corporations formed under general statutory provisions. The legislation introduced the notion that publicity might constitute an effective regulatory protection for investors. It also established as a principle that incorporation should be available to any group of intending incorporators so long as they satisfied the statutory requirements of the registration system. General availability of incorporation subsequently became a cornerstone of English company legislation.[4]

Gladstone's committee was established because fraudulent promotion and other abuses were frequently revealed during the cyclical slumps that followed economic booms in the 19th century. Gladstone undoubtedly had a strong influence on the eventual report. This seminal report resulted in what is still referred to as "Gladstone's Act" – the Joint Stock Companies Act 1844. It is this piece of legislation that laid the foundation of the modern registered company; but modern company law still owes very much to those principles of partnership and trust law that the courts had already developed to cope with the unincorporated joint-stock company. However, "Gladstone's Act" set company law on what is still its modern course by conferring ready access to incorporation by a process of registration. It set up the office of Registrar of Companies who had not only to supervise the original registration, but had to keep up-to-date information about each company's constitution, directors and annual returns and make it available on "public file".[5]

Gladstone's 1866 Exchequer and Audit Departments Act required all departments, for the first time, to produce annual accounts, known as appropriation accounts. The Act also established the position of Comptroller and Auditor General (C&AG) and an Exchequer and Audit Department (E&AD) to provide supporting staff from within the civil service. The C&AG was given two main functions – to authorise the issue of public money to government from the Bank of England, having satisfied himself that this was within the limits Parliament had voted – and to audit the accounts of all Government departments and report to Parliament accordingly. The 1866 Act established a cycle of accountability for public funds. The House of Commons authorised expenditure, the Comptroller and Auditor General controlled the issue of funds, and accounts were produced by departments and audited by the Comptroller and Auditor General. The results of the C&AG's investigations were considered by a dedicated Parliamentary Committee, the Committee of Public Accounts (PAC), which had been established in 1861, also by Gladstone. From the 1870s, the PAC took evidence from senior officials, normally Heads of Departments, who were designated as Accounting Officers by the Treasury.[6]

Gladstone went on to be a four-time prime minister of Britain and it was said (in 1892) he "contributed, more than any single man with a pen and a voice has done, to create Italy and to destroy the dominion of the Turk in Europe. As Prime Minister or Plenipotentiary, he has enlarged Greece, transferred Corfu, and established British influence in Egypt. He has familiarised the public with the idea of the European concert, not merely for debate but for action, and has maintained in times of the greatest storm and stress that Russia was not outside the pale of human civilisation or of Liberal sympathy. In Imperial politics, he has constantly condemned the strong creed of the swashbuckler. He has annexed New Guinea, North Borneo, and Bechuanaland, but he has sedulously condemned every extension of the empire that was not forced upon us by inexorable necessity. He has cleared out of Afghanistan and retreated from the Transvaal. He established the great precedent of the Alabama arbitration, and was the first British statesman to recognise that in the future the United States will supersede Great Britain as the most powerful of the English-speaking communities. If he has not exactly belittled the Colonies, he has never cracked them up, and he has always and everywhere preached the doctrine of allowing them to go their own way. He is a housekeeping Scot, whose sympathies have never really strayed far beyond these islands except in the case of those nations struggling and rightly struggling to be free.

At home [UK] his chief exploits have been the reform of the tariff, the establishment of Free Trade, and the repeal of the paper duty. He was the real author of the extension of the franchise to the workmen of the towns, and the actual author of the enfranchisement of the rural house holder. He established secret voting, and agreed to give effect to the Tory demand for single-member constituencies. It was in his administration that the first Education Act was passed, and that purchase in the Army was abolished. He has done his share in the liberation of labour from the Combination Laws, in the emancipation of the Jews, and in the repeal of University Tests. He first taught the democracy, by the great object lesson of his Irish Land Act, that the so-called cast-iron laws of political economy could be banished to Saturn, and that the whole power and resources of the Imperial State could be employed to set poor men up in business on their own account. He was the first to disestablish and disendow a National Church, and to compel the British public to consider the feasibility of establishing subordinate and statutory parliaments within the British Isles".[7]

John Stenhouse 1809-1880 was the first to synthesise Chloropicrin (trichloronitromethane), which is used as a fumigant, fungicide, insecticide, rat poison and a steriliser for soil and seeds. It is also widely used in organic synthesis – the building of organic molecules using chemical processes – a major branch of scientific research. Chloropicrin was also used as a toxic gas in World War I and today is used as a tear gas.

Stenhouse had been working on filtering noxious fumes for three decades before he made his filtration systems, and in 1854 he made one of the earliest practical gas masks to filter toxic fumes. Many other people, before and after Stenhouse, were involved in filtering air using some form of mask. Stenhouse, a trained chemist who published over 100 papers – mainly on organic chemistry – had found that charcoal would remove chlorine, hydrogen sulphide and ammonia from air. This was long before gas attacks in warfare became common and Stenhouse was looking at it from a general safety aspect, such as protecting painters from the fumes of leaded paint and people living near miasmas, which were then believed to be the cause of disease. His copper mask, with soft lead edges lined with velvet, contained charcoal placed between two layers of wire gauze tied to the wearer's head by two bands.

Stenhouse went on to design air filtration systems for homes and workplaces. In 1881, he designed a large-scale filter made of two wire gauze sheets with a layer of charcoal in the middle, to screen out obnoxious odours. He fitted this filtration system to some notable London buildings, such as Mansion House and Guildhall, to filter out the stench from the Thames. Air filtration had been around for personal use since 1823 when Englishmen John and Charles Deane designed a filter for fire-fighters, but Stenhouse seems to have been the first to use it for filtering air in rooms. IQAir, a major air purification company, claim that they introduced the world's first home air cleaner in 1963, so it would appear that Stenhouse was well ahead of his time – by 82 years!

George Turnbull 1809-1889 was the resident engineer for the construction of the Bute Docks in Cardiff, and built Middlesbrough Dock in 1842. In 1845, he was the engineer in Birkenhead for the complex Seacombe Wall sea defence that helped drain the marshes behind the town of Seacombe, as well as the Folkestone and Dover Harbour Works, and the Shakespeare Tunnel and Viaduct at Dover. He completed 15 miles (24 km) of the Great Northern Railway at the London end.[1]

In 1846-1849, he was the resident engineer for the Great Northern Railway making cuttings and the South Mimms in Hertfordshire, and three other tunnels for the first 20 miles (32 km) out of London, and making the first plans for Kings Cross station.

In 1850, he became Chief Engineer of the East Indian Railway, and was responsible for the construction, from 1851 to 1863, of the first railway line from Calcutta (the commercial capital of India at that time) to Benares (now Varanasi) en route to Delhi. It was 541 miles (870 km) from Calcutta to Benares (on the route to Delhi), 601 miles (967 km) including branches. He designed Calcutta's terminus at Howrah which now has 23 platforms. Turnbull was acclaimed in the Indian Government's Official Gazette of 7 February 1863, paragraph 5, as the "First railway engineer of India".[2]

The monsoon-ravaged Ganges tributaries such as the Son River were particularly challenging to bridge: a major constraint for Turnbull was the lack of both quality clay and brick-building skills resulting in the change to importing much ironwork from England for the many bridges and other structures (all rails were imported from England as no Indian steel works existed). Another constraint was the difficulty of moving enormous volumes of materials from Calcutta up the Ganges on its primitive "country boats", particularly during the period of the Indian Mutiny when many boats were sunk and materials stolen. Cholera killed thousands.

In 1851, "Turnbull and other British engineers began detailed surveys of the line. They chose the critical crossing point on the 5,000-foot [1,524 m] wide Son River (the largest Ganges tributary) on 17 February. The best route to Raniganj was determined in the heat of May and June by riding and in palkees. The plans for Howrah station were submitted on 16 June. Tenders for 11 contracts arrived on 31 October 1851. In December Turnbull continued his survey: he took levels and defined the line from Burdwan to Rajmahal. All permanent way, rolling-stock and other stores were transported from England in sailing ships via the Cape of Good Hope (the Suez Canal did not then exist). By 1859, there were 77 engines, 228 coaches and 848 freight wagons. The 541 miles [870 km] of line from Howrah to Benares were opened to Hooghly [37 km] for passenger traffic on 15 August 1854."[3]

John West 1809-1888 invented an automated can-filling machine and was the first on the lower Columbia River to make use of salmon waste for oil and fishmeal by-products. He also experimented with canning beef, mutton, and blackberries to keep the machinery and workers busy during the salmon off-season. His company still produces canned foods under the name of John West Foods Ltd of Liverpool, England. The first fish West processed were salted, packed in barrels, then shipped to California, where they were loaded on sailing ships and sent around Cape Horn to East Coast ports, and then on to Great Britain. In 1868, West entered into partnership with several others to found the Westport Cannery, the first on the Oregon shore of the Columbia River.

West also pioneered in another canning activity that commanded the attention of a few of the salmon canners for a short period. The surplus of meat animals in the Pacific Northwest, the knowledge of packing, and the presence of idle equipment in the salmon canneries for a part of the year, stimulated experiments in the canning of meat products. West, whose salmon canning season lasted only from April to August, utilised the autumn months of 1874 for the canning of mutton and beef, employing a "considerable force of Chinese" in the cannery. A high-quality product resulted as only the best meat was canned, the remainder being combined with vegetables and canned as soup. In September 1874, twenty cases were brought to Portland and shipped east. The experiment was short-lived as there is no evidence of meat canning in the following year. However, interest was revived in 1876 and several canneries on the Columbia from Astoria to The Dalles packed a total of 24,000 cases of which John West packed 1,500 cases. In the fall of 1874, West sent specimens of his canned mutton and beef as well as salmon to the Board of Managers of the Oregon State Fair. The previous year his exhibit of canned and packed salmon received an award. The announcement read "John West & Co., Westport, best exhibit of Oregon salmon, 1st prize, gold medal."[1]

William Wilson 1809-1862 was a locomotive engineer and driver. On 7 December 1835, he drove the *Adler* on the 7.45 km of new railway track between Nuremberg and Fürth, the construction of which had been supervised by Wilson, who also accompanied the locomotive from Newcastle to Nuremberg. This was the first commercially successful locomotive operated in what is now Germany. Note: modern Germany did not exist in 1835 and the *Adler* ran in western Bavaria (or Middle Franconia) but the *Adler* was still the first locomotive to run anywhere in the area now encompassed by modern Germany.

Image 42 – The *Adler* (May 2008)

The second locomotive ordered for the German rail company was *Pfeil* (*Arrow*), and Wilson was put in charge of the locomotives, trains, railway line, workshop and the company's ironworks. Wilson earned 1,500 guilders per annum and earned more as a specialist than the Director of the Ludwigsbahn-Gesellschaft, whose pay was 1,200 guilders.[1]

The German newspaper *Stuttgarter Morgenblatt* described the debut run of the first German train on 7 December 1835 from Nuremberg to Fürth. It was a straight stretch of line 7 km between the two cities, virtually flat, and running parallel to a very busy high street, the Fürther Strasse. The train managed it in twelve minutes. This mini-train that had been started on the initiative of some business people and local politicians of the region was Germany's first steam-propelled train and, despite its modest proportions, caused a great sensation. Bavarian soldiers who had been summoned for the occasion had difficulty in trying to bridle the large crowds who came to witness an event that had caught the attention of the entire country.

Alexander Bain 1810-1877 was the first person to scan a document in linear segments and transmit the images to a receiver, where they were reassembled to make a facsimile copy of the original image. By the time he died on 2 January 1877, Bain had patented an electromagnetic telegraph, single-needle telegraph, printing telegraph, punch-tapes for the telegraph (ticker-tape), as well as other innovations such as an earth battery, electric fire alarm, an improved fountain pen, electric sounding-equipment for ships, insulation for electric cables, fax machine, and the electric clock.

Image 43 – Bain's improved facsimile 1850

Bain's electric clock was patented on 10 October 1840 some 27 years before American Samuel Kennedy – of the Kennedy Electric Clock Company – patented the first electric clock in the United States on 3 December 1867 (Patent No 71,624), which is often claimed as the first ever electric clock. On 11 January 1841, Bain and English clockmaker John Barwise patented another clock in which an electric current and an electromagnetic pendulum were used to work the clock rather than springs or weights.

Bain's earth battery was also built in 1841 and as well as powering early telegraphic transmissions, it amplified signals over long distances, but it wasn't reliable as it was affected by drought and plate polarisation. Two German innovators, Carl Friedrich Gauss and Carl August von Steinheil, had earlier devised an earth battery and Steinheil had also built a clock in 1839 that used electric signals to synchronise other clocks, but his master clock was mechanical, not electric. It was Bain's fully electric model that became the basis for regulating clocks using a standard astronomical clock. This was developed by Englishman Robert Jones in 1857 and again in 1872 by Edinburgh clockmaker Frederick James Ritchie (1825-1906), who designed, with Italian-born Englishman Charles Piazzi Smyth, the one o'clock time ball in Edinburgh's Nelson Monument. In his patent No. 8783 of 1841, Bain anticipated most applications of electricity to horology, such as: the use of electro-magnets to store energy in a weight or spring; the use of electro-magnets to drive secondary clocks; the pendulum to operate contacts to wind-up other clocks; the use of a master clock to regulate the pendulums of other clocks; and the use of a master clock to synchronise other clocks. At the end of his patent, Bain envisaged uniform distribution of time throughout the country.[1]

"In May 1846 Bain demonstrated his system for distributing time signals when he transmitted, telegraphically, time signals from one of his clocks, placed in Edinburgh railway station, so as to synchronise a timepiece situated at the Glasgow terminus of the Edinburgh and Glasgow railway. A contemporary account describes the invention 'as being one of the greatest importance as by its introduction the great evil of variation of time, in distant situations, will be entirely avoided.' Bain's enterprise was not immediately progressed but in 1864 the Magnetic Telegraph Company initiated the control of public clocks by electric time signals transmitted from the Glasgow Observatory."[2]

Bain's electric clock was the first to use an electromagnetic pendulum and electric current instead of springs or weights, so his invention was a true electric clock, unlike those of Steinheil, Francis Ronalds, Giuseppe Zamboni, Charles Wheatstone and many others who had worked on electrostatic and electromechanical clocks. Bain was also interested in the railway and used electricity to move train signals, print reports, and turn off the steam in railway engines to permit idling.

Image 44 – Electric clock, Alexander Bain, London, ca.1845
(Deutsches Uhrenmuseum, Inv. 2004-162)

On 27 May 1843, Bain patented his fax machine, or electrochemical telegraph, in which clocks were exactly synchronised – a considerable technological feat at that time – and produced images that could be sent via the telegraph and reproduced at the other end, including drawings and handwriting. The famous New York ticker tape parade had its genesis in Bain's invention of the punched paper tape, patented in 1846. This made telegraph transmissions faster, and repeatable if there was a line dropout. It was later applied to feeding information into computers, although the original concept of punched cards was used for textile looms by Frenchman Joseph Marie Jacquard back in 1801.

The principle of Bain's punched card was used by Charles Wheatstone, co-inventor of the electric telegraph, to automate the transmission of telegrams. Bain's chemical telegraph was capable of some 244 words per minute compared to 40 words a minute for Samuel Morse's electro-magnetic telegraph, yet Morse – with whom Bain had actually worked in developing Morse code – was able to repress Bain's superior technology by claiming patent infringement. The Kentucky courts ruled that there were sufficient differences between the two methods and Bain's telegraph system was taken up by the Vermont and Boston Telegraph Company which soon had some 3,200 km of telegraph. This was, however, only one tenth the distance covered by Morse, and Bain's patent was eventually purchased in 1866 by Western Union.

Bain's equipment clocked 1,057 words in 57 seconds (1,112 words per minute) at the 1876 Centennial Exhibition in Philadelphia compared to 40-50 words per minute for Morse,[3] but Morse successfully claimed his patent covered the alphabet and continuous paper used by Bain's apparatus. Bain's method for reproducing a facsimile involved a chemical telegraph with paper saturated with a solution of nitrate of ammonia and prussiate of potash. This process was much faster, although requiring greater maintenance rigour, than that of either Morse or Wheatstone, but the greater speed created an additional problem in that hand signallers could not keep pace, so Bain automated it by using paper with punched holes, a method later used by Wheatstone for his automatic sender.

Bain's other inventions included automatically playing wind instruments by controlling the supply of air through the use of perforated paper, and the inked typewriter ribbon, which he invented in 1841 although this development is usually credited to George Kerr Anderson of Memphis, Tennessee, who patented it 45 years later than Bain on 14 September 1886.[4] Unlike Morse, who became wealthy through his eponymous code (Morse did not actually invent the telegraph), Bain died in poverty with the considerable income from his patents spent on litigation defending his priority.

William Hamilton 1810-1880 is seen in Canada as the inventor of the fish-plate bolt which reduced railway accidents caused by rails shaking loose from their ties.[1] Hamilton certainly manufactured the fish-plate bolt but the original fishplate was wedge-shaped and was actually invented by Englishman William Bridges Adams who collaborated with Robert Richardson to patent one in 1847. The modern fish plate – also known as a splice bar or joint bar – is a metal bar that is bolted to the ends of two rails to join them together in a track for railway lines. This version was invented by James Samuel of Glasgow. It is unclear why Hamilton is seen as the inventor of the fishplate – perhaps the patent of Samuel did not extend to North America. Hamilton did, however, obtain the first ever national Canadian patent, granted on 18 August 1869, for a machine that he called the Eureka Fluid Meter, which could measure liquids.

Alexander Murray 1810-1884 was responsible for the preparation of the first complete geological map of Newfoundland and when, in 1873, the Newfoundland government declined to cover the cost of printing it, Murray financed its publication out of his own pocket. In 1875, a further activity for him resulted from the ambitious continental transportation plans of Sandford Fleming which included a railway link in Newfoundland. Murray was assigned the task of overseeing the logistics of a survey of the proposed trans-island route. In Canada, Murray was so overshadowed by William Edmond Logan that his accomplishment of mapping the geology of Canada West almost single-handedly has never been given the recognition it deserves. In 1864, when Murray first arrived in Newfoundland, it was almost *terra incognita* except for the coast. Within 20 years, his survey led to the opening of the interior by showing that mineral, timber, and agricultural resources were present and that Newfoundlanders need no longer depend only on the fisheries.[1]

Murray is credited with recognising that the Canadian Shield near Severn Bridge just north of the Narrows at Lake Couchiching is dominated by metamorphic rocks such as gneiss, an observation that was to unlock the origin of the Shield. He undertook the first geologic exploration of the fossil-rich rocks of the Bruce Peninsula and was shipwrecked in a fierce squall in Georgian Bay in 1861. He was one of the first to recognise the mineral potential of the Sudbury area, the oil deposits of south-western Ontario, and discovered the famous "kettle rocks" at Kettle Point.[2]

Murray investigated the area west of the Ottawa River, including the north shore of Lake Huron, where he mapped the gossan-stained ridge adjacent to which the Creighton nickel mine would be located. He also mapped the synclinal structure near Blind River, with its thick section of quartzite, slate and conglomerate, where uranium was found in the 1950s, and he mapped the great east-west-trending structure now known as the Murray fault.[3]

John Cochran Yule 1810-1877 designed and built the first motorised lorry (truck) at his Hutchestown Engine Works, Rutherglen, in 1870. It was powered by a steam engine. He built the first motor truck, in the sense of a practical self-propelled goods wagon capable of carrying (as opposed to drawing) freight, for transporting large marine boilers from his works at Rutherglen Loan to the Glasgow docks, a distance of 2 miles (3.2km). The vehicle was powered by a 250 rpm twin-cylinder steam engine mounted on a 26 ft (7 m) chassis of red pine, and fully loaded, was capable of moving at ¾ mph (1.2 km/h). Even at this slow speed Yule considered his six-wheeled steam wagon an economic proposition. The cost of employing 400 men to drag a 40 ton (36.3 tonnes) marine boiler to the docks worked out at about £60; a single journey by the wagon incurred a fuel bill of £10.[1]

Adam Clark 1811-1866 built the first permanent bridge across the Danube in Hungary.[1] The 375 m long and 16 m wide Széchenyi Chain Bridge connected the two cities of Buda and Pest in 1836. "The bridge ignited the economic revival that would lead to the golden century and it was one of the factors that made the provincial towns of Pest and Buda into a fast-growing metropolis. In 1989, people demonstrated on the chain bridge for freedom and independence. Since then, the bridge has become a symbol of Hungarian liberty."[2] Built over ten years, the Chain Bridge rests on just two huge pillars and, in its entirety, is 380 m long. To put this in perspective, the first Elizabeth Bridge, built in 1903 was only 290 m, while the Liberty Bridge which still stands today, is only 333 metres. The bridge is an unusual suspension bridge because there are no cables used.

Instead, the roadway is suspended from a chain, which has links very similar to those of a bicycle chain. This is where the bridge obtained its nickname of chain bridge, and over the years, the nickname has stuck. The chain is hung between the two triumphal arch-style structures and the overall effect is of a light yet dignified classical edifice. In 1857, Clark dug a 350 m long tunnel to connect the Chain Bridge with the hinterland of Buda. The central square near the bridge is named after Clark.

At the time of its construction, the Chain Bridge was the suspension bridge with the second-largest span in the world. The portals are decorated with lionhead-shaped capstones and the coat of arms of Hungary with the crown and a wreath of leaves. István, Gróf (Count) Széchenyi made Clark technical adviser to the National Transport Commission, and in the following year, as Minister of Public Works, Széchenyi made him technical adviser to the ministry. Clark twice saved the bridge: first, from the Austrian general who, during the revolution of 1849, wanted to blow up the bridge and, second, from the commander of the Hungarian army, who gave orders to destroy it as his troops retreated. Following the completion of the Buda Tunnel in 1857, Clark worked on several smaller commissions.[3]

At the end of World War II, retreating German troops blew up all bridges in Budapest including, on 18 January 1945, the Chain Bridge. The bridge was destroyed nearly completely, only its pillars remained intact. The decision to rebuild it was made in the spring of 1947. The construction work was started: pillar portals were being extended, abutments broadened, custom-houses pulled down, a pedestrian subway installed at the Buda end and the tram subway completed on the Pest side. The inhabitants of Budapest were finally able to repossess one of the most renowned buildings of the city on 20 November 1949, exactly a hundred years after its initial inauguration.[4]

Image 45 – Széchenyi Chain Bridge, Budapest

David Davidson 1811-1900 invented the telescopic sight for rifles. This invention is often attributed to Morgan James of New York who made one to the design of Englishman John Ratcliffe Chapman, who wrote about it in 1844, but "Davidson was a keen early advocate of optical sights and he wrote in his memoirs that he had introduced 'the telescope sight' to India for hunting use in the late 1830s."[1]

"It was in 1832, when stationed as a lieutenant with his infantry company at Fort Asseergurh, that Davidson first applied a telescopic sight to a firearm. He acquired a single-barrelled, flint-action rifle made by Samuel Staudenmeyer, a Swiss-born gunmaker, of Cockspur Street in London from the regimental adjutant and had a simple draw telescope attached to the barrel. Little else is known about this first piece, not the calibre nor the method of securing the telescope."[2]

Davidson placed an order with "James Purdey of 314½ Oxford Street, London, commissioning him to make a heavy-barrelled 'small-bore' percussion rifle and fit it with a telescopic sight. It should be said that 'small-bore' in that period meant a barrel firing a lead ball of a half-ounce (14 grams) weight!"[3]

"He also, in the 1830s, added a telescopic sight to an 'air-cane'. This was a slightly sinister weapon, formed in the manner of a walking cane, but with a removable small-bore rifled barrel lining a larger smooth-bored barrel in the stem, a high-pressure cylindrical air reservoir at the grip end, and a tiny valve cocked by a key and worked by a 'pop-out' trigger. It fired ball for game, shot for birds and 'harpoons' for fish. Davidson used his for killing cobras and other snakes. In the 1840s, he possessed a single-barrelled, rifled percussion pistol fitted with 'a minute telescope' that he took a shot at a shark with when at sea."[4]

It is worth noting Davidson's other work in relation to sporting firearms and ordnance. During 1833, he had an article published in the *Bombay Sporting Magazine* in which he described the experiments that he had made with elongated bullets for rifles in place of the then normal round ball. He perfected a pointed-nosed, round-based lead bullet with a cannelure or flute around its middle that proved a major advance in accuracy and range. Sportsmen in India and in Scotland used Davidson's cannelured bullet widely, pestering him and his gunmaker in Edinburgh for moulds to cast their own. It was to be another fifteen years before a similar bullet was adopted for military use in rifled arms. Note: Captain John Norton, while based in India, developed a cylindrical bullet with a hollow base in 1832. His design was improved on in 1836 by a London gunsmith named William Greener, who created an oval-shaped bullet, one end of which had a flat surface with a small hole drilled into it. This hole travelled through most of the length of the bullet and was covered by a conical plug with a round, wooden base. Upon firing, the plug would expand to prevent gases from escaping – essentially the same principle as the blowgun dart. The design of Norton and Greener was taken a step further by two French army captains, Claude-Etienne Minié and Henri-Gustave Delvigne, who in 1849 created the conical, soft-lead bullet with four rings and a rifle with a grooved barrel to go with it.[5]

"Davidson also engaged in research into projectiles for ordnance. His paper, *Rifled Cannon*, was presented in 1839 to The Royal Society in Edinburgh by Professor William Piazzi Smyth, the astronomer-royal for Scotland. In this, Davidson advocated rifling the ordinary brass and iron muzzle-loading field guns with four deep grooves and using elongated iron bolts and shells fitted with copper flanges to fit the rifling, to improve range and accuracy. It was to be another 20 years before this invention was to be adopted by the military and naval forces. But it was to be with the telescopic sight that Davidson's name was to be firmly identified. He improved the sight and its mounting for over thirty years before he patented his 'Military Telescopic Sight' in 1862. The sight was used by sportsmen in India for large and small game throughout his period with the East India Company."[6]

At the Great Exhibition of 1851 at the Crystal Palace in London's Hyde Park, he showed the range of telescopic-sighted weapons that he had developed to the public for the first time. They were all made for his personal use by the small gunmaker, John Robertson, from his home town of Haddington in Scotland. The display comprised double and single barrelled rifles; double and single barrelled 10 inch [25.4 cm] rifled pistols; and a single barrel 6-inch [15.24 cm] pistol; all with telescopic sights. Davidson's telescopic sights were focusing, adjustable in windage and elevation, robust in manufacture, small and light in dimensions, and easily removable from its mounts for safekeeping.

During the Crimean War, at the siege of Sebastopol, Davidson invented the collimator for sighting guns. "The siege soon revealed the weaknesses in the British batteries bombarding the city, in particular the lack of any method of accurately targeting shot at night. Once fired the pieces of ordnance recoiled backwards and also had to have their barrels lowered for muzzle-loading. In daylight, they could easily be aimed once again at their targets, at night this was impossible. To overcome this on January 17, 1855, David Davidson, clearly utilising his sporting experiences and pre-existing thoughts and experiments, patented the 'Detached Collimator', an 'Improved apparatus for pointing ordnance and restoring the aim of the piece either by day or night when it is once obtained.' The piece of ordnance is to be correctly sighted and laid by the gunner upon a given object. A moveable telescope is then placed in grooves or studs attached to it at the breech, and its cross wires are made to bear upon and coincide with a given detached object, by preference a collimator, placed behind the piece. The exact adjustment of the telescope is then noted. In order to lay the gun again in the same position as before, the telescope is replaced upon the gun, and the gun is adjusted until the cross wires of the telescope coincide with the same detached object or collimator as before; the axis of the gun will then be in the same line as when aim was first taken by the gunner."[7] The collimator permitted the cannon to be accurately fired again without having to replace it in its original position before it had been fired.

In an unpublished 102-page typed manuscript entitled *The Shot*, written by amateur historian Dale Martin, there is "a drawing of the famous Whitworth sniper rifle, along with a battle line map of Spotsylvania Courthouse, Virginia. The manuscript was researched intermittently over a period of nearly 40 years and details the history of the most celebrated long-range sniper shot of the American Civil War. Confederate sergeant Charles D. Grace takes aim at Union general John Sedgwick through his Davidson telescopic sight at a distance of over half a mile [805 m], and squeezes off the shot that is still talked about today in military history circles as the beginning of long range sniper technology in warfare."[8] Note: General Sedgwick is reputed to have admonished a soldier who told him to take cover and, as he was saying, 'They couldn't hit an elephant at this dist...' he was shot dead. It is a good story but not quite accurate. General McMahon, who was at Sedgwick's side at his untimely death, made the following report on the incident: "I gave the necessary order to move the troops to the right, and as they rose to execute the movement the enemy opened a sprinkling fire, partly from sharp-shooters." As the bullets whistled by, some of the men dodged. The general [Sedgwick] said laughingly, "What! what! men, dodging this way for single bullets! What will you do when they open fire along the whole line? I am ashamed of you. They couldn't hit an elephant at this distance." A few seconds after, a man who had been separated from his regiment passed directly in front of the general, and at the same moment a sharp-shooter's bullet passed with a long shrill whistle very close, and the soldier, who was then just in front of the general, dodged to the ground. The general touched him gently with his foot, and said, "Why, my man, I am ashamed of you, dodging that way," and repeated the remark, "They couldn't hit an elephant at this distance." The man rose and saluted and said good-naturedly, "General, I dodged a shell once, and if I hadn't, it would have taken my head off. I believe in dodging." The general laughed and replied, "All right, my man; go to your place." Those were Sedgwick's last words – but the other story of his last words is more amusing.[9]

John Henderson 1811-1858 brought to the construction of Crystal Palace a wealth of practical experience in production engineering, project and site management and was the man who ensured that things got done, both by the various sub-contractors supplying goods and on the construction site itself. His (metaphorical) descendants are still to be found on every major construction site today. Contrary to designer Joseph Paxton's wishes, Henderson added a transept with a flat roof in order to provide better lateral stability to the building.[1]

Colonel Charles Sibthorp, MP, attacked the idea of building the Crystal Palace (he was opposed entirely to the concept of the Great Exhibition) in 1850 claiming that a clump of young elms would have to be cut down. Paxton acknowledged in a lecture to the Society of Arts in November 1885 that it was Henderson who developed the concept of the great transept which solved the problem of preserving the giant elms in Hyde Park, although the smaller ones were removed, and that he also suggested the semi-circular shape. The building committee finally unanimously approved the plan on 16 July 1850. The engineering partnership of Charles Fox and John Henderson was a great Victorian success story. They built the roof of the former Birmingham New Street Station, Liverpool Tithebarn Street, Bradford Exchange, Paddington Station, Oxford Station, Birkenhead Market, and accepted commissions as far afield as India and Russia.[2] Note: Henderson may have been born in Middlesex although most sources, including the *International Journal of Space Structures* Volume 21, No 1, 2006, p 18, say he is Scottish.

James Laurie 1811-1875 helped to found, in July 1848, the Boston Society of Civil Engineers, the oldest existing engineering society in the USA. He also helped create, and became the first President (1853-1867) of, the American Society of Civil Engineers. He became Chief Engineer in charge of the construction of the Norwich & Worcester Railroad, and later of the New Jersey Central Railroad, and was employed on surveys of railroads in Nova Scotia, and as consulting engineer for the state of Massachusetts on the Hoosac tunnel. He then turned his attention to bridge-construction, and built the wrought-iron bridge across the Connecticut River at Windsor Locks, and designed the major lattice, riveted wrought-iron bridge across the Connecticut River at Warehouse Point, Connecticut, one of the first of its kind in the United States. As the Chief Engineer for the New York, New Haven, & Hartford Railroad, he had the iron work for the bridge's structure imported from England, creating a notable American example of riveted bridge work whose span was more than 177-feet-long [54 m]. He was Chief Engineer on the New Jersey Central Railroad, [and was] consulting engineer in connection with the Housatonic Tunnel. Laurie strove to embody the ethics of the engineering profession. He believed that engineers had a responsibility to the public, and that the ASCE should represent the public interest in affairs of national concern. He supported the advancement of the engineering profession through higher education, and insisted that the requirements for admission into the Society include graduation from a "school of recognised standing."[1]

Lauchlan McKay 1811-1895 invented the ubiquitous cast-iron capstan for ships and was an important figure in shipbuilding during the 1840s. Alongside his brother Donald, Lauchlan played a key role in the innovative design of the American clipper ship. He wrote the first comprehensive American text on shipbuilding, *The Practical Ship-Builder*, which was published in New York by Collins, Keese and Co in 1839. The book provided mechanical and philosophical information on constructing different types of vessels. The famous clippers *Flying Cloud* and *Flying Fish* were considered among the finest clippers of their day, with the latter making the Boston to San Francisco trip in 100 days, 6 hours, although beaten by her rival *Sword Fish* (built by William Henry Webb who had been apprenticed to Scottish-born shipbuilder Henry Eckford). In all, eleven clippers entered San Francisco Harbour inside of four months, in passages of less than 110 days or less around the Cape Horn. Donald McKay's *Sovereign of the Seas* made a run of 103 days in the height of the unfavourable season, largely due to the determination of Captain Lauchlan McKay.[1]

Robert Forester Mushet 1811-1891, son of David Mushet, used manganese to improve steel production. The more famous Bessemer process for "air blowing the carbon out of pig iron" wasn't patented until 1855, and even then it could only be used on a tiny fraction of Britain's iron ores. In fact, Bessemer was unable to get his process underway until he used a method to produce steel invented by Gloucestershire-born Mushet, so the credit for the world-wide expansion of the steel industry belongs to Mushet rather than Bessemer. Mushet added manganese that allowed Bessemer steel to be rolled and forged at high temperatures. He patented his process in 1856 and it was only from then that the Bessemer process started to become commercially viable. In 1857, Mushet developed the first steel to be used on railway lines (at Derby Station),[1] an innovation that had a major impact on the development of railroads worldwide and would later lead to Scottish-born American industrialist Andrew Carnegie becoming the richest private citizen on the planet.

Mushet's so-called spiegeleisen had around 15% manganese with very small quantities of carbon and silicon, and this was added to the blown metal during the melting process. Prior to his discovery, steel was cast in a mould and, where this wasn't practicable due to the shape required, ironmasters either softened the metal before cutting it or used a hardened steel tool to do the cutting. The latter option was the more popular, but in hardening the steel by plunging it into water, the steel often cracked. In 1868, Mushet added tungsten to steel, making it very much harder. "The steel was self-hardening in air. Harder metals could be cut at faster speed and the lifetime of the tools was prolonged by a factor of 5 to 6. Soon it became known as Robert Mushet's Special Steel (R.M.S.). The product was the first real tool steel and the forerunner of modern high-speed steels. Its commercial production began in Sheffield after 1870."[2] Tungsten steel was used in the manufacture of tool bits such as drills, taps, milling cutters, gear cutters and saw blades.

"In 1876 the Bessemer Medal of the Iron and Steel Institute was awarded to Mushet, with the full approval of the founder. In making the presentation, the president, Mr Menelaus, said that the application of spiegeleisen was one of the most elegant, as it was one of the most beautiful, processes in metallurgy, and that it was worthy of being associated with Mr Bessemer's process. ... He is usually regarded as the first important pioneer of alloy steels."[3]

James Young Simpson 1811-1870 was an early pioneer of anaesthesia, particularly the use of chloroform during childbirth. On 16 October 1846, in Massachusetts General Hospital, a patient had a vascular tumour removed from his neck under ether anaesthetic applied by William Thomas Green Morton. News of this momentous event crossed the Atlantic and Simpson was present when Robert Liston performed the first public operation in Britain using ether anaesthetic on 21 December. Note: On 19 December 1846 in both Dumfries and London, ether anaesthetics were given. Few details are available about the Dumfries anaesthetic, but it is believed that the patient had been run over by a cart and required an amputation of his leg; it is also believed that the patient died. In London, at 52 Gower Street, the home of an American botanist Francis Boott, a dentist named James Robinson removed a tooth of a Miss Lonsdale under ether anaesthesia. Two days later at University College Hospital, Robert Liston amputated the leg of a chauffeur, Frederick Churchill, while a medical student called William Squires gave an ether anaesthetic.[1]

Greatly impressed, Simpson began to use ether in his midwifery practice, starting on 19 January 1847, only four months after Morton first used it in America. His patient had a severely contracted pelvis and Simpson used ether to accomplish version and breech extraction. Although the baby died soon after birth, the actual delivery provided effective pain relief to the mother. However, much as Simpson liked ether, he knew the pungent smell, irritation of the bronchi and the tendency to make people sick, along with the large amounts and length of time required to induce and sustain anaesthesia stimulated him to seek an alternative."[2] Note: Simpson is usually credited with being the first medical practitioner to use anaesthetic for childbirth, but on 27 December 1845 American Crawford Williamson Long, a pioneer in anaesthetics, used ether in delivering his own second child, born at Jefferson, Georgia. This date is attested by the family bible record that was in the possession of Eugenia Long Harper, sole surviving child of Crawford Long.[3]

Searching for something better, Simpson tried different anaesthetic agents with his colleagues by inhaling their vapours around the dinner table at his home. Following up on a suggestion by pharmacist David Waldie, Simpson tried chloroform. Waldie's company supplied chloric ether to local physicians for inhalation by patients with respiratory disorders. This was made by dissolving chloroform in alcohol, so Waldie knew that chloroform was safe to inhale.[4]

Chloroform had been hitherto used solely for internal administration. On 4 November 1847, Simpson and two doctors, Matthew Duncan and George Keith, inhaled the vapours of chloroform and subsequently became unconscious. On 8 November, Simpson administered chloroform with excellent results to a colleague's wife who was in labour, except that the unfortunate child was christened "Anaesthesia". On 10 November, he reported his work to the Edinburgh Medical and Surgical Society. On the 15 November, a public demonstration was held at the Royal Infirmary of Edinburgh at which time chloroform's property as an anaesthetic was again proven to be successful. On 17 November, the first preliminary report appeared in the *London Medical Gazette*, followed soon after by the first full report.

Chloroform did many of the things Simpson had wanted: its odour wasn't persistent, a lesser amount could be used to cause unconsciousness, it was cheaper, and its effects on the body occurred more rapidly than ether. Due to its lower volatility, cost, and the amount needed for dosage, chloroform was the preferred anaesthetic for surgeons in the American Civil War; over a million pounds (453,592 kg) of the chemical was used in this conflict.[5]

The most influential endorsement came from Queen Victoria, who received chloroform for her eighth confinement on 7 April 1853. This was administered by the anaesthetist John Snow, who gave it for 53 minutes using a pocket handkerchief in the manner advised by Simpson. The Queen described it as: "Blessed chloroform, soothing, quieting and delightful beyond measure". Both the Queen and her husband, Prince Albert, were very impressed with the benefits of chloroform in labour. Four years later when the Queen gave birth to Princess Beatrice, Prince Albert started the administration of chloroform before the Queen's physicians arrived. At the time of her confinement, Queen Victoria's first physician was an Edinburgh-trained Scot, Sir James Clark. He arranged for John Snow to give the Queen chloroform during her labour. Sir James later wrote to Simpson telling him: 'The Queen had chloroform exhibited to her during her late confinement ... her majesty was greatly pleased with the effect, and she certainly has never had a better recovery'. Realising the importance of this influential event he added: "I know this information will please you, and I have little doubt it will lead to a more general use of chloroform in midwifery practice in this quarter than has hitherto prevailed".[6]

However, there was a fly in the ointment – chloroform was not as benign as first believed. The first fatality was a 15-year-old girl called Hannah Greener, who died on 28 January 1848. The opponents and supporters of chloroform were mainly at odds with the question of whether the complications were solely due to respiratory disturbance or whether chloroform had a specific effect on the heart. Between 1864 and 1910 numerous commissions in UK studied chloroform but failed to come to any clear conclusions. It was only in 1911 that Alfred Goodman Levy proved in experiments with animals that chloroform can cause cardiac fibrillation. The reservations about chloroform could not halt its soaring popularity. Between 1865 and 1920, chloroform was used in 80% to 95% of all narcoses performed in UK, and in German-speaking countries.[7]

Investigation of the effects of chloroform revealed that its prolonged administration as an anaesthetic can cause toxaemia. Acute poisoning is associated with headache, altered consciousness, convulsions, respiratory paralysis and disturbances of the autonomic nervous system: dizziness, nausea, and vomiting are common. Chloroform may also cause delayed-onset damage to the liver, heart and kidneys.[8] Today, chloroform is seldom used as an anaesthetic. It has been found that its effects on the body can be serious, resulting in damage to both the liver and the kidneys.

Simpson's arguments for obstetric anaesthesia contained very little science. His initial paper described only six patients. His method for administering anaesthesia was crude, unmodified from the technique first used for surgery. He simply poured ether, or chloroform, onto a cloth draped over the patient's face. He initiated the anaesthetic during the first stage of labour and kept his patients unresponsive until after delivery of the placenta. He paid little attention to dosage and discounted the possibility of any harmful effect on uterine contractions or the newborn. Thus, he neither acknowledged nor resolved any of the medical issues that concerned his colleagues. Furthermore, he did not persist with this work. After an initial flurry of papers and letters, Simpson turned from obstetric anaesthesia to other issues.[9]

The influence of Queen Victoria on the acceptance of obstetric anaesthesia has been overstated, and the role of John Snow has been somewhat overlooked. It was his meticulous, careful approach and his clinical skills that influenced many of his colleagues, such as William Tyler-Smith and Francis Ramsbotham, and the Queen's own physicians. The fact that the Queen received anaesthesia was a manifestation that the conversion of Snow's colleagues had already taken place. This is not to say that this precipitated a revolution in practice. Medical theory may have changed, but practice did not, and the actual number of women anaesthetised for childbirth remained quite low. This, however, was a reflection of economic and logistical problems – too few women were delivered of newborn infants during the care of physicians or in hospitals. Conversely, it is important to recognise that John Snow succeeded in lifting theoretical restrictions on the use of anaesthesia.[10]

Simpson's reputation soared after the introduction of chloroform in childbirth, although it was John Snow who rendered it safer to use. Honours were showered on Simpson, starting in 1847 when he was appointed one of her majesty's physicians for Scotland. He became a foreign associate of the Academy of Medicine, Paris, the members firmly insisting on his election against the rules of the commission which had omitted his name. In 1856, he was awarded by the French Academy of Sciences the Monthyon Prize of two thousand francs for "most important benefits done to humanity." He received the order of St. Olaf from the king of Sweden, and became a member of nearly every medical society in Europe and America. In 1866, he was made a Doctor of Civil Law at Oxford, and on 3 February of the same year, he received a baronetcy, the first given to a doctor practicing in Scotland. In 1835, long before his use of anaesthetics, he was made senior president of the Royal Medical Society of Edinburgh and in 1841 he was elected president of the Edinburgh Obstetric Society. Post anaesthesia, he was president of the Royal College of Physicians (1849) and in 1852 he was elected president of The Royal Society of Edinburgh.

Simpson made many important contributions to obstetrics. In 1849, he invented the first practical vacuum extractor for childbirth. Modern obstetric vacuum extraction originated in cupping, a therapeutic technique that predates Hippocrates. Applications of cupping to assist in deliveries began early in the 18th century, including one proposed by a Doctor Saemann in Jena, and Neil Arnott in Scotland. Saemann, in a report, described a dream he had of using an air pump to help deliver a baby. He ended by saying, "This is a dream which might come true." There is no evidence that this dream did come true in Saemann's lifetime. There is also no evidence to suggest Arnott clinically applied a pneumatic tractor, although he did argue that the use of the vacuum would require less training and skill than the forceps to be used with safety.[11] Notwithstanding Arnott, the use of vacuum for obstetric use proved difficult and the technique was soon abandoned. It remained to Simpson to first introduce a successful obstetric vacuum extractor in 1849. He advocated the use of a "suction tractor" or "air tractor" as a substitute for forceps, inspired by the analogy of the limpet, anticipating the arrival of the ventouse by some decades. This device was constructed of a metal syringe that had probably been derived from a breast pump attached to a soft rubber cup. This extractor did prove successful in a number of deliveries, but technical problems existed. Vacuum replenishment was impossible after the initial evacuation of the syringe and the device lacked a pelvic curve. These difficulties limited its effectiveness. Simpson's interest in his extractor waned and he moved on to other obstetric interests.[12] Since the advent of the vacuum extractor, many of the earlier high forceps applications have become obsolete.[13] Although the immediate antecedent to modern extractors is the stainless-steel cup vacuum device introduced by Tage Malmström of Sweden in 1956, it is "almost identical" with Simpson's design.

Simpson invented a cranioclast for fracturing the foetal skull base, and a uterine sound and sponge for dilating the cervix to provide access to the uterus for removal of endometrial polyps. He supported the concept of hand washing advocated by Ignaz Philipp Semmelweis but was slow to realise the contribution of Joseph Lister who was his contemporary in Edinburgh.[14]

Aside from chloroform anaesthetic, he was equally famous for his long obstetric forceps. He advocated pelvic applications of the forceps to minimise maternal trauma. His forceps were commonly used for outlet and low pelvic rotational delivery. For nearly a century, this was the most commonly used forceps technique throughout the world.[15] Writing in 1937, Harold Speert said "For fully a century now the vast majority of forceps deliveries has been carried out by means of an instrument popularised by Sir James Young Simpson and usually known as the Simpson forceps, although models embodying minor changes continue to bear the names of their new inventors. Simpson demonstrated his forceps for the first time on 10 May 1848 at a meeting of the Edinburgh Obstetrical Society. The forceps were used in the management of uterine inertia, haemorrhage during labour, and other complications."[16]

Simpson also contributed to the study of hermaphroditism, a subject considered taboo at the time. Until the late 19th century there were two systems of classifying hermaphrodites. In France, they followed Isidore Geoffroy Saint-Hilaire, and in Britain it was Simpson's system that was generally followed. His article *Hermaphroditism, or Hermaphrodism* was written in the 1830s, but was less rigorous and philosophical than Saint-Hilaire's.[17]

Simpson, in 1850, was probably the first to stress the importance of bimanual examination in gynaecological practice – that is, a physical examination of the female pelvic organs.[18] He wrote extensively on pelvic inflammatory disease, and first used the terms pelvic cellulitis and puerperal sub-involution. He was an early supporter of the surgical removal of ovarian tumours (ovariotomy).[19] Diagnostic dilatation of the cervix uteri (neck of the uterus) is often attributed to Simpson but it was "Charles Mackintosh of Edinburgh who, in 1830, earns the credit of having first directed the attention of the profession to the mechanical cause of certain cases of dysmenorrhœa, and the suggestion of mechanical means for its relief, consisting of gradual dilatation of the cervical canal by means of flexible bougies, or by metallic rods of gradually increasing volume."[20] Note: It wasn't Charles, but John Mackintosh (died 1837), Lecturer in Midwifery, who published *Case of Calculus extracted from the Female Bladder, by Dilatation of the Urethra*.[21] With John Lever, Simpson shared credit for pointing out the association of albuminuria and eclampsia. "Of the fact of the concurrence of albuminuria with certain affections of the nervous system during pregnancy and childbed, there can be no doubt whatever. Both Drs. Lever and Simpson have detected it in cases of convulsions during pregnancy and labour".[22]

Simpson's discovery of the means of investigating disease, notably the uterine sound and the sponge tent, gave a power to diagnosis previously wanting. He designed and promoted a uterine sound – a slender flexible metal rod used to calibrate or dilate the cervical canal, or to hold the uterus in various positions during gynaecologic surgery. "Joseph-Claude-Anthelme Récamier used a probe, to study the deeper-seated diseases of the womb, and a curette, to remove from its internal surface small polypi and fungoid granulations; but it was Simpson who made us fully aware of the great value of the uterine sound, as a means of diagnosis".[23]

Until Simpson suggested the use of sponge tents for dilating the cervix and the os (external or internal orifice of the uterus), surgeons were often obliged to look on, quite helpless, while women bled to death from polypi in the cavity of the body of the uterus, where they lay with the os completely closed, and often apparently healthy. Often, as Simpson showed, they "were generally considered to be beyond the pale of any certain means of detection, or any possible means of operative removal."[24] Simpson, in 1843, also advocated and practiced cutting through the walls of the cervix to gain access space without dilatation.[25] He advocated monitoring the foetal heart rate and, in 1855, was perhaps one of the first to point out that foetal death was frequently preceded by slowing of the foetal heart rate.[26]

Simpson is often said to have introduced acupressure to obstetrics, but the actual use of acupressure is one of the oldest known forms of treatment for haemorrhage. He did describe a method of acupressure in 1860 and he was the first to use that particular term. He referred to it as "a new haemostatic process – founded on the principle of the temporary metallic compression of arteries." He used at least three different methods, one of which was to use "a long glass-headed pin passed subcutaneously to cross and compress an artery, much in the same way as a flower stem is held by pin in a coat lapel."[27]

As with acupressure, Simpson is said to have introduced iron wire sutures to arrest haemorrhage, but Italian anatomist Hieronymus Fabricius, in 1647, wrote at length on the use of iron wire sutures, limiting their use, however, to the soft parts.[28]

Simpson was a pioneer of medical statistics – for example, he used them to prove that the male foetus tended to be larger than the female and was associated with a higher foetal and maternal mortality. To confirm that hospital size and overcrowding influenced mortality, he conducted an extensive postal survey of death after traumatic and non-traumatic limb amputation in all major and cottage hospitals in the UK. Over a 10-year period, he confirmed that mortality in major hospitals was greater than in smaller units and proposed that hospitals be designed with this in mind.[29]

He wrote many medical publications including some on archaeology – *Archaeological Essays*, in two volumes, and *Archaic sculpturings of cups, circles, &c. upon stones and rocks in Scotland, England, & other countries*. One of his stranger publications was a 23-page pamphlet in December 1847, immediately following his first use of chloroform anaesthetic – *Answer to the religious objections advanced against the employment of anaesthetic agents in midwifery and surgery*. It is one of the great myths of medical history that Simpson was beset by religious leaders yet, to cite one example, "In 1847 James Young Simpson, a Scotch physician, who afterward rose to the highest eminence in his profession, having advocated the use of anaesthetics in obstetrical cases, was immediately met by a storm of opposition. This hostility flowed from an ancient and time-honoured belief in Scotland. … From pulpit after pulpit Simpson's use of chloroform was denounced as impious and contrary to the Holy Writ; texts were cited abundantly, the ordinary declaration being that to use chloroform was 'to avoid one part of the primeval curse on woman'. Simpson wrote pamphlet after pamphlet to defend the blessing which he brought into use".[30]

Fortunately, Professor Simpson knew his Old Testament. He contended that the Biblical "sorrow" was better translated as "toil", an allusion to the muscular effort a woman exerted against the anatomical forces of her pelvis in expelling her child at birth. Moreover, he cited Genesis 2:21: "And the Lord God caused a deep sleep to fall upon Adam, and he slept: and he took one of his ribs, and closed up the flesh instead thereof". Casting God in the role of The Great Anaesthetist might seem at variance with the historical record; and not everyone was convinced. A Dr Ashwell (*The Lancet* 1848:1, p 291) replied that "Dr Simpson surely forgets that the deep sleep of Adam took place before the introduction of pain into the world, during his state of innocence." Yet the suggestion that God Himself employed anaesthesia helped carry the day.[31]

When chloroform was first used by Simpson, most doctors approached the new practice with caution. The gas had been used for a few minutes during amputations, but the effects when used for a long period were unknown. Many doctors were concerned that they would lose the information normally provided by mothers during a birth. Others were worried that the gas would stop contractions. These doubts were soon overcome and within a few years the gas was being widely used, at least in difficult cases. It is often said that public opinion was changed when Queen Victoria made use of the gas during the birth of Prince Leopold in 1853, but modern historians hold that it had become widely accepted before this date.[32] In fact, examination of contemporaneous publications suggests that the use of chloroform by Queen Victoria in 1853 did not result in the major breakthrough in the acceptability of obstetric anaesthesia with which the event has been credited by some later writers.[33]

Nevertheless, as Alfred Derek Farr points out, documented evidence of the opposition which fuelled Simpson's efforts is thin. In fact, rather than condemning, prominent leaders from across the established religious spectrum agreed with the pro-anaesthesia argument. Dr Protheroe Smith (Anglican obstetrician), Rev. Thomas Chalmers (Moderator of the Free Church of Scotland), and Rabbi Abraham De Sola (Canada's first Rabbi) were in written agreement with anaesthesia. Queen Victoria, the Defender of the Faith, gave implicit endorsement by allowing John Snow to administer chloroform at the delivery of her son, Prince Leopold in April 1853. (Farr AD, 1980). The Most Rev. John Bird Sumner, Archbishop of Canterbury (1848-1862) records no condemnation of anaesthesia, whose daughter had obstetric anaesthesia in the year following Queen Victoria's. Early military opposition to the use of volatile agents was initially based on the anecdotes and bias of military surgeons. John B. Porter was an example. Concern centred on fears of haemorrhage and poor wound healing.[34] In response, Simpson wrote to remind a Dr Charles D. Meigs of Philadelphia, one of his critics, that the fact is "the contractions of the uterus, and not pain, is the essential to the progress of labour."[35]

Scottish papers at the time gave detailed reports of religious synods, meetings and discussions. There is no mention of the issue being raised at any church gathering of importance in Scotland. A detailed study has been made of eighty-four published items (35 of literature and 49 of general magazines and reviews) for the period October 1846 – December 1849. The survey covered Britain and America. Only seven references were made in connection with anaesthesia. None was critical of Simpson's procedure and five of them (including the two theological journals) positively supported Simpson's stand on the use of chloroform in childbirth. This survey of the evidence confirms the findings of A.D. Farr: "On examination, this particular 'conflict' appears to be an artefact of historiography based upon a contemporary defence prepared against an attack which never materialised."[36]

Like many innovators, Simpson seemed to be prescient in some areas and resistant to change in others. He opposed Joseph Lister with his carbolic spray to fight infection, yet he advocated the hygiene regime first mooted by Ignaz Semmelweis before physically checking pregnant women or those who had just given birth. As early as 1863, he thought that light or electricity could be used to inspect the insides of the human body – "in this great line of discovery new victories are certain to be won. Do you search out other additional physical means of diagnosis for these and other viscera? Possibly even, by the concentration of electrical or other lights, we may yet render many parts of the body, if not the whole body, sufficiently diaphanous for the inspection of the practised eye of the Physician and Surgeon."[37]

When he died, Simpson's family was offered burial in Westminster Abbey, but they had him buried closer to home at Warriston Cemetery. A bust was placed in Westminster Abbey, and on it is recorded: "To whose genius and benevolence the world owes the blessings derived from the use of chloroform for the relief of suffering. Laus Deo." Note: Simpson's name at birth was "James Simpson", as recorded at his baptism. It is unknown why he formally adopted the middle name "Young". One theory is that, as a very young professor, he was flaunting his youth in front of his older peers or alternatively that he was known by the affectionate nickname of "Young Simpson" and decided to incorporate it into his name.

John James Waterston 1811-1883 presented a short paper in 1851 on his kinetic theory at the annual meeting of the British Association for the Advancement of Science. The published abstract of that paper clearly states that in gas mixtures, the average kinetic energy of each kind of molecule is the same; thus, he established his priority for the first statement of the equipartition theorem. He also indicated in this abstract that Avogadro's hypothesis follows from the kinetic theory.

Waterston was interested in the problem of explaining gravity by impacts of particles, and his efforts on this problem led him to develop a kinetic theory of gases. Waterston was employed as a Naval Instructor to the East India Company's cadets at Bombay, India. In 1843, he published a book that included some of his early results on the kinetic theory of gases. His most significant conclusion was that "equilibrium of temperature depends on molecules, however different in size" having the same kinetic energy. This was a special case of what later became known as the "equipartition theorem". There is no evidence that any physical scientist read the book; perhaps it was overlooked because of its misleading title, *Thoughts on the Mental Functions*.

Two years later Waterston submitted a long manuscript, presenting a detailed account of the kinetic theory of gases, to The Royal Society of London. Two members of the Society, asked to review the paper, recommended that it should not be published – primarily because they disagreed with its fundamental premises. But no one had told Waterston, still far away in India, that once his paper had been officially "read" to the Society (i.e. presented by title or abstract, not read word for word) it would not be returned to him; and Waterston had not retained a copy for himself. Thus, he could not easily follow John Herapath's course of publishing the original paper in an independent journal, although he did try to call attention to his theory by circulating shorter versions, and by mentioning it when he published papers on related subjects.

The kinetic theory of gases was rejected for more than a century. The kinetic theory relates the independent motion of molecules to the mechanical and thermal properties of gases – namely, their pressure, volume, temperature, viscosity, and heat conductivity. Daniel Bernoulli in 1738, John Herapath in 1820, and John James Waterston in 1845 independently developed the theory. The kinetic theory of gases, like the theory of diatomic molecules, was a simple physical idea that chemists ignored in favour of an elaborate explanation of the properties of gases.

Waterston made the first statement of the law of equipartition of energy, according to which all kinds of particles have equal amounts of thermal energy. He derived practically all the consequences of the fact that pressure exerted by a gas is related to the number of molecules per cubic centimetre, their mass, and their mean squared velocity. He derived the basic equation of kinetic theory, which reads $P = NMV^2$. Here P is the pressure of a volume of gas, N is the number of molecules per unit volume, M is the mass of the molecule, and V^2 is the average velocity squared of the molecules. Recognising that the kinetic energy of a molecule is proportional to MV^2 and that the heat energy of a gas is proportional to the temperature, Waterston expressed the law as PV/T = a constant.[1]

The German chemist and physicist August Karl Kroenig, who published a short paper proposing a kinetic theory of gases in 1856, was probably familiar with the published abstract of Waterston's 1851 paper and may have been influenced by it. In the case of the kinetic theory of gases, the net result of The Royal Society's refusal to publish the works of Herapath and Waterston was to retard the progress of molecular physics by a decade or two, thus permitting Kroenig and Rudolf Clausius to gain the major share of credit as founders of the theory and damaging the Society's own reputation.[2]

James Young 1811-1883 is the person most associated with the rise of the shale oil industry. In 1850, his Bathgate Chemical Works was arguably the first in the world to refine mineral oil on a commercial scale.[1]

By far the most important development as far as the oil industry in Britain was concerned occurred in the year 1847 when Professor Lyon Playfair, whilst visiting one of James Oakes' coal pits at Alfreton, Derbyshire, discovered a black oily substance oozing from the walls of the mine. Thinking that this substance might be of use once chemically treated, he sent a sample to his old friend, James Young. What Young discovered was to lead to the development of one of Britain's greatest industries and, in the process, make him very rich.[2]

Young was the original driving force behind the creation of the oil refinery industry, setting the world to work on his paraffin oil and refined fuel innovations. He was employed at the giant chemical factory of Tennant's when Playfair told him of a natural oil spring in a Derbyshire mine. Young managed to take the oil and tease from it paraffin wax, naphtha, light oil and lubricating oil. It was the beginning of oil refinery, and the beginning of his James "Paraffin" Young nickname. He headed back north to Bathgate to set up what the town claims to have been the world's first oil refinery. Aware that oil from mines was a scarce resource, James worked with the waxy, smokeless cannel coal, submitting it to a destructive distillation process that yielded the desired results. Nine whole years before the first oil well was drilled in the USA, Young was demonstrating the oil and paraffin he had created at the 1851 Great Exhibition. In the midst of the industrial activity of an expanding empire, his fuel was an instant hit, generating profits of up to 98%.[3]

Young also made an important contribution to the rustproofing of ships. He suggested that quicklime could be used to slow down corrosion from the acidic bilge water, and this idea was adopted by the Royal Navy.[4] He also devised a method of making stannate (compounds of tin) direct from tin-stone in 1844, and investigated potato disease and suggested means of overcoming it.

His first scientific paper, dated 4 January 1837 and published in the *Philosophical Magazine*, described a miniature voltaic battery, a modification of Faraday's invention.[5]

Today he is widely regarded as the "Father of the Modern Petrochemical Industry" and a pioneering Chemical Engineer. The company that Young set up in 1866 moved on to pioneer the exploitation of shale oil and by the 1900s was employing 4,000 people and extracting nearly two million tons (1.8 million tonnes) of shale annually. It has since been integrated into one of the world's largest companies, BP.[6] With the advent of oil wells, shale declined, but by 2013 it was estimated that there are "technically recoverable resources of 345 billion barrels of world shale oil resources and 7,299 trillion cubic feet of world shale gas resources ... which represents 10% of the world's crude oil and 32% of the world's technically recoverable natural gas resources."[7] Even greater reserves than this have been mooted. A moderate estimate of 800 billion barrels of recoverable oil from oil shale in the Green River Formation in the USA is three times greater than the proven oil reserves of Saudi Arabia. Present US demand for petroleum products is about 20 million barrels per day. If oil shale could be used to meet a quarter of that demand, the estimated 800 billion barrels of recoverable oil from the Green River Formation would last for more than 400 years.[8] Clearly, the work in oil started by "Paraffin" Young still has a long way to run.

Robert Dunbar 1812-1890, a Scottish-born engineer, and Joseph Dart, an American-born merchant, built a steam-powered elevator for moving grain in 1842. Notwithstanding riots, one of the consequences of agricultural mechanisation was the ability to more effectively plant and harvest grain. America's grain production started to expand as the railroad opened up the prairie that became the country's breadbasket. Such was the volume of grain being harvested that new methods of transporting, storage and handling had to be employed. Canal barges, steamboats and railroads were adapted to move grain; huge silos were built, and technology was also applied to the elevators used to shift grain between transporters and silos. American Oliver Evans devised an automated grist mill that used bucket elevators and conveyor belts, but the first steam-powered grain elevator was built in Buffalo by American Joseph Dart and his engineer, Robert Dunbar.

By 1843, Dunbar's technical skills had turned it into a success as it could unload grain from ships' holds ten times faster than teams of labourers. Although Dunbar is often described as Dart's mechanic, it is highly probable that Dunbar was the main designer as he went on to further improve grain elevators and by 1880 most of those on the busy Buffalo River were of his later design. In its report to the (US) National Register of Historic Places in 2002, the Buffalo Grain Elevator Multiple Property Submission noted, "In 1843, when the schooner *Philadelphia* unloaded the first bulk shipment of grain at the Dart Elevator, it took only hours to lift the wheat from the hold. The man who made it possible was thirty-year-old engineer, Robert Dunbar, the unsung pioneer of grain elevator construction."[1]

Dunbar's elevators could also dry grain by blasting it with hot air through a large metal plate with very small holes, and then fanning it with cool air prior to going into storage. He also constructed elevators for Canadian, British and European ports, including one in Odessa, Ukraine – the largest grain port in the Russian Empire, which itself was the largest exporter of grain in the world. The steam grain elevator made Buffalo the world's largest grain port with some 1.4 million tonnes moved annually. By 1863, Buffalo had 27 grain elevators in operation with a total capacity of 5,855,000 bushels (159,350 tonnes) and a transfer capacity of 2,700,900 bushels (73,500 tonnes) per day and an annual throughput peaking at 70 million bushels (1,905,120 tonnes).[2]

William Fisken 1812-1883 was an innovator who improved the steam plough to the point where it was the first effective plough that didn't rely on human or animal muscles. In 1832, Englishman John Heathcote obtained a patent for a steam plough, but it wasn't very effective. It was improved by Fisken, John Fowler and others, but it wasn't until the 1850s that the steam engine was first effectively used for ploughing in Europe. "The steam plough, although able to plough ten times the area that horses could plough in a day, was cumbersome and costly, and had only a limited impact on farming in either Europe or the United States. Thus, the horse remained the main source of power until the early twentieth century."[1]

Fisken also invented a machine for sowing potatoes, a safety steam boiler, a propeller, and an apparatus for heating churches, but it was his "steam tackle", patented in July 1855, which helped to make the steam plough practicable. Fisken and his brothers Thomas, George and Alfred, patented numerous machines for use in agriculture and elsewhere. The man often credited with the invention of the ploughing engine was John Fowler of Leeds. Fowler contested William and Thomas Fisken on priority, but the Fiskens won the ensuing case.[2]

The Committee on Machinery of the Highland and Agricultural Society of Scotland (the first agricultural society in Europe – and probably in the world – founded in 1723 as the Society of Improvers in the Knowledge of Agriculture in Scotland), on testing a later model of Fisken's steam tractor, commented "a general expression of opinion that the apparatus was admirably suited to perform the work required of it. Since 1871 Messrs. Fisken have improved their apparatus so much as to warrant them in applying to the Judicial Committee of the Privy Council for an extension of their patent, which was granted in March, 1876, for a period of six years."[3] Note: The Highland and Agricultural Society of Scotland was founded in 1723 as the Society of Improvers in the Knowledge of Agriculture in Scotland, mainly through the work of Robert Maxwell 1695-1765 and was concerned with the spread of knowledge to allow farmers to better their agricultural practices. It was dissolved in 1745 at the time of the Jacobite rebellion and resurrected in 1784 as the Highland Society of Edinburgh, becoming the Highland and Agricultural Society of Scotland in 1834. It became the Royal Highland and Agricultural Society of Scotland in 1848 and introduced examinations in 1856 leading to a diploma in scientific and practical agriculture.

Fowler went on to acquire the patent rights of the Fisken brothers although the Fiskens still continued their family business. The Fisken brothers, William and Thomas, patented the concept of the balance plough although it was fellow countryman, David Greig, who made the improvements that made it practicable.[4]

John Haswell 1812-1897 was the first locomotive builder in the Austrian Empire (which covered all or parts of modern-day Austria, Croatia, Czech Republic, Hungary, Italy – Venetia and Lombardy – Poland, Romania, Serbia, Slovakia, Slovenia, and Ukraine) when, in 1837, he drew up and executed plans for the repair shop of the Wien-Raab railway, which later became the Lokomotivfabrik der StEG. This was the first locomotive engineering factory in the empire, where Haswell was in control from 1840 to 1882, undertaking not just repair work, but also the construction of new rolling stock for the railway. The manufacture of railway vehicles was difficult because at that time in Austria there were still no iron foundries and none of the workers had the training for this type of work.

The Lokomotivfabrik der StEG became operational in 1839 and it produced many influential locomotive designs, including the Haswell-built *Wien* in 1841, the first Austrian-made locomotive.[1]

In 1851, he produced *Vindobona* to participate in the trials for the Semmering Alpine railway, where he competed against three other locomotives. His entry was unsuccessful, but *Vindobona* was the first eight-coupled engine on the Continent and a model for the subsequent mountain locomotives designed by Wilhelm Engerth. The *Vindobona* incorporated Robert Stephenson's valve gear, but Haswell brought innovations of his own, including rudimentary forms of the Belpaire firebox, thermic syphons and counter-pressure braking.

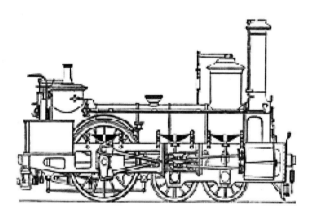

Image 46 – "Duplex", Austria, 1861

In 1872, the Resita factory in Romania manufactured the first railway locomotive in that country called *Resita 2* with a gauge of 948 mm. It was designed and built by Haswell in Vienna for internal transport in the Resita factory.

"By 1855 the various German rail administrations (including that of Austria) were operating over 2,000 locomotives built by forty-six different firms, of which the most important were Borsig in Berlin [with 630 locomotives], [and] Wien-Raab in Vienna [207] ..."[2]

Of the trail-blazing locomotives that Lokomotivfabrik der StEG produced, the following are notable: the first six-coupled locomotive in Austria, the *Fahrafeld*; the Semmering competition engine, *Vindobona*; and the first eight-coupled locomotive, *Wien-Raab*. "The *Wien-Raab* of 1855, a large long-boiler 0-8-0 with all parts accessible, was the pattern for the continental heavy freight locomotive for many years. The *Duplex* of 1861 was the first four-cylinder locomotive although the arrangement was unorthodox."[3]

"At least two designers appreciated that a good way to obtain good balance for both the rotating and reciprocating masses was to fit two pistons on each side, driving crank-pins set at 180 degrees so that one piston would move forward as the other moved back. The only real difficulty was fitting two cylinders where one had grown [gone?] before. John Haswell solved the problem by fitting one cylinder above the other, set at a slight angle. This remarkable locomotive [*Duplex*] had two cylinders on each side, angled slightly so that both piston rods aligned with the centre of the driving wheel. It was designed by John Haswell of the Austrian State Railway Works at Vienna and was exhibited in the International Exhibition of 1862."[4]

Haswell designed a steam brake in 1861 which he used on the *Steyerdorf*. Although claimed as the first steam brake, one had been designed by George Stephenson in 1833. In 1872, Haswell designed the corrugated iron firebox.

Among many of his technical innovations, the hydraulic forging press was the first to enable the forging of heavy machine components in dies, which opened many new opportunities in mechanical engineering. The great hydraulic forging press, constructed by Haswell in 1862, was one of the sensations at the Great London Exposition (1862). The model from the early 1870s is today located at the Vienna Museum of Technology.

"The practice of making axle boxes of cast iron has long since been given up. At one time, they were forged under a steam hammer; but about 1862 the late Mr John Haswell, locomotive superintendent of the Austrian State Railways, invented and constructed a very powerful hydraulic forging press in which axle boxes, cross heads, and such like were pressed out of white hot steel billets, at the rate of about half a minute for each."[5]

Kirkpatrick MacMillan 1812-1878 played a part in the development of the bicycle although his role is disputed and his influence on how bikes developed is questioned. The *Oxford Dictionary of National Biography*, though, refers to him as the "inventor of the pedal bicycle". The advent of automobiles resulted in several ancillary industries arising, one of which was the massive rubber industry to supply tyres. The early industry provided the economic backbone of several countries, particularly Malaya (now part of Malaysia), the former Belgian Congo (now the Democratic Republic of the Congo), and Liberia. But rubber tyres were not originally invented for automobiles – they were first used on bicycles.

The bicycle traces its ancestry to the hobby horse built in 1818 by German-born Karl Friedrich Christian Ludwig, Freiherr Drais von Sauerbronn (better known as Baron Drais), although there are claims it was invented much earlier by English scientist Robert Hooke. With a steerable front wheel, the rider sat on a frame between two inline wheels and used his feet to push on the ground and so propel the "pushbike" forward. The next important step was taken in Scotland, but there is controversy as to which of four contenders added pedals linked by a crank shaft to the rear wheel. This setup provided much greater mobility although it was still not a popular means of transport as it was uncomfortable and heavy to steer, and the state of most roads was so poor as to make riding a bicycle a feat of endurance. The four Scottish contenders were Kirkpatrick MacMillan, James Charteris, **Gavin Dalzell c1812-1863** and **Thomas McCall 1834-1904**. McMillan reputedly added a mechanical crank drive to the rear wheel and pedals to the front wheel in 1839. "This first pedal bicycle was propelled by a horizontal reciprocating movement of the rider's feet on the pedals. This movement was transmitted to cranks on the rear wheel by connecting rods; the machine weighed almost exactly half a hundredweight [25.4 kg] and the physical effort required to ride it must have been very considerable."[1]

Most references credit MacMillan as the person who invented the pedal-driven bike. A newspaper report in 1842 stated that a "gentleman" was fined five shillings for speeding at 8 mph (13 km/h) and knocking down a girl who ran into the road.

Gavin Dalzell lived in Lesmahagow and built bikes from about 1846, but he can be ruled out as he wrote a letter to *Bicycling News* on 12 January 1892 which states, "At the outset I may say that I lay no claim to being the inventor of bicycles or as they were first named, but perhaps have had something to do in improving and introducing them." Dalzell goes on to refer to improvements by Peter (sic) McMillan.

Some historians, such as American David Herlihy and two Scots, Alastair Dodds and Nicholas Oddy, have cast doubt on MacMillan's role in bicycle development.[2] James Johnston, a wealthy relative of MacMillan, went on what seems to be a personal crusade in the 1890s to have MacMillan credited with the invention of the pedal driven bicycle, rather than Dalzell who was generally believed by Scots at the time to be the inventor. Herlihy claimed that there was no evidence of cranks being attached to bicycles, only tricycles and quadricycles. Dodds states that the documents concerning the fine of five shillings don't state that it was a two-wheeled vehicle and that it describes the cyclist as a "gentleman", a description that would not have been used in the mid-19th century to describe a blacksmith such as Kirkpatrick MacMillan.

Supporters of Thomas McCall have not been able to conclusively prove he made the critical improvements that changed the hobby horse to a bicycle. "McCall must have been about six or seven when MacMillan invented the bicycle and he first saw the local blacksmith riding around the country lanes on his fancy contraption about 1845. He never forgot it.

When McCall became an apprentice to a joiner, he bought an old hobbyhorse and soon set about adding pedals, connecting rods and cranks, just as he had seen on MacMillan's bicycle. His machine worked fine and he rode it from Sanquhar to Kilmarnock and back. From about 1869 McCall was making bicycles on a commercial basis and seems to have been the first person to do this (in the UK), though, like MacMillan, McCall never patented any of his innovations. "He built, in 1869, two versions of a two-wheeled velocipede with levers and rods tossing a crank on the rear wheel, as published in the *English Mechanic* of the same year. This was a reaction to the French velocipedes, of the mid-1860s, with their front-wheel pedal cranks. In fact, this rear-wheel idea occupied five more inventors in that year. In 1869, he advertised his bicycle in the *Kilmarnock Standard*."[3]

It was, however, Kilmarnock which had the world's first bicycle factory. There are two McCall bicycles on public display. One is at the London Science Museum. The other is in the Observatory Museum in Dumfries. And as a footnote, it seems that in later years one of McCall's workers later left Kilmarnock for Coventry, where he set up his own bicycle factory, thus starting what became a key industry in that city.[4] Note: credit for establishing Coventry as a bicycle manufacturing centre is usually given to James Starley and, without proof and a name of the Kilmarnock employee Starley must retain that credit.

MacMillan's improvements, if indeed it was him, included two equally-sized wheels with the rider sitting between them, already a feature of the hobby horse, and two new elements – a rear-wheel drive and a front wheel that was steered and was independent of the transmission. However, the bicycle never became truly popular until changes were made by Englishmen James Starley, who designed the penny-farthing, and Henry Lawson, who patented a rear wheel, chain-driven bicycle. Credit is also given to Frenchman Pierre Michaux who, in 1863, made the velocipede, nicknamed the "boneshaker", which was the first mass-produced bicycle.

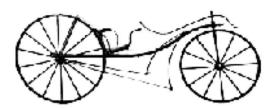

Image 47 – Macmillan Bicycle

Alastair Dodds, Curator of Transport, National Museums of Scotland, states, "It may seem strange that the south west of Scotland during the 19th century provided such a centre for invention and activity, but at the time Glasgow was known as the 'Workshop of the Empire' and many skilled engineers worked in the city and surrounding region. Macmillan [sic] himself had been an apprentice at Napier's, a major shipbuilding and engineering company on the Clyde. A snowball effect may have come into play, with one velocipede, maybe that of Macmillan [sic] or Charteris, being observed and copied, setting off a chain of copycat models being made. Sadly, this Scottish innovation reached an impasse, as, despite the correct assumption that a bicycle should be driven by the rear wheel (unlike a French front-wheel driven invention of the time), the Scottish inventors did not progress from the use of levers and cranks to using a chain. We can, however, be confident that this wonderful invention was the fruit of Scottish innovation." [5]

Whether pedals were first put on a bicycle by MacMillan, Dalzell, Michaux or someone else, it clearly wasn't a leap of the imagination if they already had crank-driven tricycles and quadricycles. Despite the findings of some bicycle historians, the Scots will continue to believe that it was a fellow countryman who "invented" the bicycle, just as Italians and Germans believe one of their compatriots "invented" the telephone.

Colin Mather 1812-1864 and **William Mather 1838-1920** managed the cotton manufacturing company of Mather & Platt and were inventors of textile finishing equipment. Bleaching had become a chemical proposition after Charles Tennant's exploitation of the use of chlorine as hypochlorite (bleaching powder) about 1799. Lancashire soon followed Scotland and by mid-century, Mather & Platt at Salford was largely occupied in providing machinery for all bleaching

224

processes and doing much to develop the technology of the central process of "kiering" or scouring. The bleaching kier is a large cylindrical vessel in which grey cotton – loose yarn or cloth – is boiled with alkaline liquor. The two main technical problems involved in kiering were those of heating and of securing an efficient circulation of scouring liquor inside the kier. In the early years of the Industrial Revolution, kiers were heated by direct furnaces; later on, steam from a central boiler installation was substituted; and, in 1853, Colin Mather patented a device which employed the injector principle in the heating and circulation of the liquor by steam. Finally, in 1885, the Mather kier was invented, and patented by William Mather. It treated the yarn or fabric in wagons, within a horizontal cylindrical vessel, and utilised a sluice valve door, which allowed for the change of the contents of the kier in a few minutes instead of several hours.

By means of a centrifugal pump, the circulation was maintained more efficiently than before and the heating in the later models was provided by a multi-tubular heater, which prevented the weakening of the liquor by the condensation of steam and made for economy in the use of chemicals. These improvements marked a big advance on the previous system, and Mather kiers have since been supplied to more than 300 of the principle bleaching, printing and dyeing works in various parts of the world.

Cotton fabrics are "singed" before scouring in order to burn off fibre ends projecting from the surface of the fabric. Mather & Platt produced both plate-singeing and gas-singeing machines. In singeing techniques, the firm was a pioneer, manufacturing internally heated revolving roller machines, plate machines with oil firing and traversing motion for the cloth, and gas-singeing machines with exhaust suction chambers drawing the flame round the threads of the cloth.

Mather & Platt contributed to this process, before and after 1914. For instance, in addition to improving the design and technique of finishing machinery the firm patented in 1907 an automatic warp-stop motion, a device that, as the name implies, automatically stopped a loom upon the breaking of a warp thread. In days of depression in the cotton industry, it was important that operatives should be enabled to attend a greater number of looms, and such devices contributed to the "more looms per weaver" arrangements. As well as saving labour, they improved the quality of the cloth by minimising the risk of broken threads and by making good work less dependent on the attention of the individual weaver. The Mather & Platt motion was simple, cheap and easy to attach to existing looms.

In warm climates bleaching-powder (essential in cotton bleaching) is not stable, and when exported to the tropics often loses a large part of its strength in transit. Mather & Platt met this difficulty by introducing their electrolyser and perfected a process based on the production of sodium hypochlorite (an equally effective and in some ways preferable bleaching agent) by electrolysis of a solution of common salt (sodium chloride).

These electrolysers have also other uses outside the textile industry. In the worst days of the First World War, medical officers in the Near East demanded large supplies of a powerful disinfectant, and it was suggested by Dr Henry Drysdale Dakin that hypochlorite might be obtainable from seawater. This project was presented to Mather & Platt Ltd and with the utmost urgency, electrolysers adapted for this purpose were produced and installed in the hospital ship *Aquitania*. "Dakin's solution", as it was known, proved of immense value and greatly reduced the loss of life in the Near East campaigns.

From the earliest days of calico printing, fixation of many colours depended upon "ageing" – long exposure to moist air – for which large hanging rooms and much time and labour were required. In 1879, Mather & Platt introduced their "Rapid Ager", an enclosed metal steaming chamber with rollers for continuous running. It revolutionised the processing of prints and long outlived the types of colour (mordants and vegetable colourings) for which it was first devised. Indeed, it has been of the greatest importance throughout the synthetic dyestuffs period. In the literature of printing in all languages it is referred to familiarly as the "Matherplatt", and several languages have verb forms derived from it such as "Matherplattieren" (German) and "Plattning" (Swedish) which meant "Steaming in a Matherplatt". Mather & Platt have manufactured more machines for printing textiles than any other firm in the world.[1]

During the late 19th century some then very important classes of printing colours – the alizarins, chrome mordant and basic types required a much longer steaming time than the "Matherplatt" afforded. For those, the "Festoon" continuous steamer was invented. In this machine, the prints, hung over poles, travelled slowly along a very large steam-filled chamber.

This replaced the inconvenient "Cottage" batch steamer and became standard equipment of large print works in many countries. In the early 20th century it was re-designed to suit the conditions required for the very important "vat" colours and it is today the most advanced form of print steaming equipment and still chiefly a Mather & Platt production.[2] Note: there is confusion as to which Colin Mather (father or son) was the inventor of the injector principle. *Grace's Guide* has the inventor born around 1812 but, according to *The Jubilee Book 1958 – A History of Mather & Platt*, the inventor was a cabinetmaker in 1817, which would make him only five years old. Either way, there is still a Scottish link as Colin senior was born in Montrose in 1788, with Colin junior being born in Durham, England in 1812.

Thomas Meik 1812-1896 undertook construction of the Hendon Dock in Sunderland and was consulting engineer on nearby Blyth Harbour. He designed the Hilton, Southwick and Monkwearmouth Railway for carrying coal and then built a number of railways in Scotland, mainly in Fife, and designed ports for Ayr, Burntisland and Bo'ness. He developed (but was not the inventor of) a self-registering tidal water gauge that was installed at Sunderland Harbour,[1] and in 1868 he founded a company which his two sons inherited. Later, they went into partnership with Sir William Halcrow and had commissions in every continent and in over 70 countries.

Robert Stirling Newall 1812-1889 created a novel method to make wire rope in 1841 while he was working at Washington Chemical Works in Sunderland, England. Newall made his wire ropes using a machine known as a strander, rather than the hand twisted cables of German mining engineer Willhelm Albert. Each of Newall's cables had six strands of wire with each strand having its own fibre core, all being twisted around a central fibre core. The central core of hemp ensured that individual wires and strands were held equidistant from their respective centres to ensure equal stress on each wire.

"The history of telegraphic cable development has been subject to a number of conflicting claims. Newall may have been the person who came up with the idea of a cable within a wire rope."[1] Newall went on to manufacture the transatlantic submarine cable, which was laid using machinery designed and built by him, particularly the cone which had a 1½ metre diameter with a cable-carrying capacity of 2,302 cubic metres. In August 1850, Newall proposed gutta-percha as an insulator for under-ocean cables. Other trans-oceanic cables were laid around the world by Newall's company, starting with ones connecting Britain, Denmark and Norway, as well as across the English Channel in 1851.

Half a century before Frenchman Louis Renault developed the drum brake for cars, Newall had invented it to aid in laying ocean cables. By the time Newall died in 1889, he was far and away the biggest manufacturer of wire rope in Britain, his company having earlier merged with that of Andrew Smith, who promptly afterwards left for California with his son, also Andrew. The junior Andrew went on to create the San Francisco cable car (having added Hallidie to his name).

Alexander Milne Ogilvie 1812-1886 was a railway builder, working mostly in equal partnership with the more famous Thomas Brassey. "The English railway contracts undertaken by Brassey & Ogilvie, in partnership with other contractors, were mainly in the various systems now grouped under the Great Eastern, and London and South-Western Railways; amongst the former may be named the Colchester and Ipswich, the Ipswich and Bury, the Haughley and Norwich, the Sudbury, Bury St. Edmunds and Cambridge, the Epping, and Dunmow Railways; amongst the latter the North Devon, the Portsmouth direct, and the Salisbury and Yeovil Railways. Outside of these, the Runcorn Branch Railway, on the London and North-Western system, with its important bridge over the Mersey, a portion of the Thames Embankment, and the Metropolitan Mid-level sewer, may be mentioned."

The chief foreign works undertaken by Ogilvie were the Mauritius, the Central Argentine, and the Buenos Aires and Ensenada Railways, and the Rio de Janeiro drainage. "It may be of interest to state that Mr Ogilvie executed over £10,000,000 worth of work, out of a total of over £30,000,000 tendered for, and that the actual practical control in the various partnerships fell very largely into his hands.[1]

William McNaught 1813-1881 took the steam engine to a new level of efficiency with his compound steam engine. "One development crucial in the development of steam ships was the compound engine of McNaught. In 1854 the first compound engine was installed on a steam ship, and by 1864 they dominated power supply for large ocean-going steamers."[1]

McNaught was the son of an inventive father, John, who invented the revolving cylinder as an attachment to the steam engine indicator in 1830, receiving a silver medal from the Society of Arts.[2] The low-pressure engines of Watt and others were not robust enough to be converted to use high pressure. "William McNaught avoided this problem by installing a small high-pressure cylinder at the opposite end of the beam to the original low-pressure cylinder. This was cheaper than buying a completely new engine and avoided overstressing the beam. The combination of high pressure steam and compound operation allowed the use of steam in industry to grow at an unparalleled rate during the nineteenth century."[3]

McNaught had sufficient confidence in his design that he even pioneered insurance for steam engines but, just as Watt had not invented the atmospheric steam engine, as is sometimes purported, McNaught did not invent the compound steam engine. Englishman Jonathan Hornblower built one in 1781 and compatriot Arthur Woolf improved on that in 1804, but neither of these were very efficient at the time, so the Watt steam engine remained by far the most popular machine. Then, "almost unnoticed in the great world of marine steam engineering, then mainly centred in Scotland, an obscure New Brunswicker had played a part in the improvements which made possible these long voyage steamers, and heralded an age of increased thermal efficiency in the crude machinery of the early nineteenth century. More than a decade before Robert Napier had built the sister ships *Queen Victoria* and *Napoleon III* with two oscillating simple cylinders, Benjamin Franklin Tibbets had built and installed the first compound steam engine to be employed afloat, in the steamer *Reindeer* at Devon, N.B., in 1845."[4]

McNaught improved on Tibbets' engine with a compound engine that had a second, smaller, low-pressure cylinder which captured the exhausted energy from the high-pressure primary cylinder, returning it to the engine as low-pressure energy. This modification greatly improved efficiency and gave the world the first commercially successful compound steam engine, which became the dominant engine in industry and shipping, although it was unsuitable for use in locomotives. His design was influential in developing the triple-expansion steam engine and "three types of new engine were to emerge using McNaught's principle. The first used cylinders mounted side by side, the second had cylinders in a line (a tandem compound), and the third and rarest type had the high-pressure cylinder enclosed by the low-pressure one."[5] McNaught took out at least five further patents, including ones for a steam generator, improved slide valves, and a design of a diagonal engine, but it was his compound engine that was his greatest legacy, saving up to 40% on the cost of fuel.[6]

James Newlands 1813-1871 was appointed as Britain's first municipal engineer (in Liverpool) to be concerned with comprehensively improving the health, amenity, and efficiency of the city. By 1848, he had drawn plans for the world's first integrated sewerage system which was built in Liverpool, and the same report pioneered both the regulation of housing and the provision of new public housing, as well as the provision of baths, wash-houses, and swimming baths.[1]

In 1848, Newlands drew attention to the type of boulder paving then existing in all but the most important thoroughfares (of Liverpool) and urged the reconstruction of those streets as an essential factor towards their thorough cleansing.[2]

Newlands' sewage system was "deliberately designed in its entirety to take water closets, and to drain foundation subsoil. He placed the small-diameter pipes in back passages where they were accessible should the problems reported elsewhere occur, and connected these to ovoid sewers designed to carry a combined flow. This was not a system based on an *ad hoc* basis, or a case of connecting WC's to unsuitable existing storm sewers, nor was it a system based upon wrong engineering principles. ... It can nevertheless be argued that Newlands, the first Borough Engineer, designed, built and commissioned the first comprehensive purpose-designed system for foul and storm waste in Britain."[3]

In Hansard (the verbatim report of the UK Parliament) the following comment was made in respect of Newlands' work on the sewer system, "The significance of that development cannot be overrated. During his years in office, Newlands succeeded in doubling the average life expectancy [in Liverpool] from 19 to 38."[4]

James Abernethy 1814-1896 was a marine engineer and bridge builder who became Engineer-in-Chief when only 28 years old. He built the South Dock (1858), Prince of Wales Dock (1858) and Half Tide Basin of Swansea Marina, Tennant Canal, Aire and Calder Navigation, New Junction Canal, and many bridges in Scotland. From 1851 to 1855 he was Engineer-in-Chief to the Birkenhead Dock Trustees where he undertook major works including graving (dry) docks and river walls. "He worked on the piers and dock at Silloth in the Solway Firth, Watchet Harbour, Falmouth Piers and Graving Dock, and the Harbours of Stranraer and Port Patrick." In 1862, he accepted the position of Chief Engineer to the Turin and Savona Railway, a line 120 miles (193 km) in length, through difficult country. About this time, he became Consulting Engineer to the Grand Canal Cavour, designed to irrigate some 300,000 acres (121,406 hectares) adjoining the banks of the River Po in Italy.

In 1870, he was appointed a member of an International Commission for the regulation of the River Danube at Vienna. Among other works of importance upon which he was engaged are the Alexandra Docks, Newport, opened in 1868; the Alexandra Dock at Hull, 1881; the reclamation of Lake Aboukir, Egypt, 1888-1889; Torquay Pier, 1890-1894; Bute Docks, Cardiff, 1877-1891. He also prepared designs for Port Victoria, 1888-1889; a reservoir at Merthyr Tydfil; and a dock at Tranmere, 1893. He served on the Royal Commissions on Metropolitan Sewage Discharge (1882) and Irish Public Works (1889) and on a Belgian Royal Commission, which issued a report upon the construction of harbours on sandy coasts. He was Consulting Engineer to the Manchester Ship Canal Company from 1887 to 1892, having been previously connected with the project from its inception in 1880.[1] He was president of the Institute of Civil Engineers between December 1880 and December 1881, at which time presidents were elected for one year only.

John Anderson 1814-1886 was the first Chief Mechanical Engineer to the Royal Arsenal at Woolwich, which produced much of the armaments required by Britain during the growth of its empire and through two World Wars. Along with Marc Isambard Brunel and Samuel Bentham, Anderson put the Arsenal at the very forefront of weapons research and engineering. "Sir John Anderson, the Arsenal's first Chief Mechanical Engineer and Vice President of the Institution of Mechanical Engineers, was one of the most overlooked yet most important of all the Arsenal engineers. The inventor of a new method for mass-producing rifles and bullets, Anderson's innovations became decisive during the Crimean War".[1]

The arsenal had been largely ignored since the end of the Napoleonic Wars, so Anderson became responsible for the design and installation of many machine tools and the recruitment and training of a large workforce to use them. Such was the scope of his work that author Gwilym Roberts entitled his 2008 book *Sir John Anderson, 1814–86: The Unknown Engineer Who Made the British Empire Possible*. In 1855, during the Crimean War, he equipped a 600-ton (544 tonnes) steamship as a floating factory containing a cupola, forges, twenty-eight heavy machines, a saw-mill, a brass and iron foundry. Based off Balaklava, power for the machines was provided by the ship's main engines. When he retired in 1872, he had a staff of over 3,000 and had been responsible for the manufacture of armaments costing over £3,000,000. He was remarkable for his inventions, and for his ability to achieve the tight deadlines often required to put new armaments into service. In addition, he was responsible for designing the new Small Arms

Factory at Enfield and he was involved with the mechanisation of the Royal Gunpowder Mills at Waltham Abbey.[2]

"His impact on the Royal Arsenal, and on British warfare, was remarkable. He oversaw the complete mechanisation of the factories and the laboratory, often designing the machinery himself. After his modernising process was complete, a part which once took a day to produce would take just half an hour. He also invented processes to mass-produce bullets, bayonets and muskets, feeding the huge demand coming from the Empire."[3]

During the first eight years of his service, he devised no fewer than sixteen new and valuable machines for executing different processes in the manufacture of guns, bullets, percussion caps, &c. One bullet machine turned out 40,000 bullets per hour; and another of his inventions was a machine for automatically granulating gunpowder.[4]

Andrew Barclay 1814-1900 invented the steam derrick crane at the suggestion of John Fyfe, a granite quarrier in Aberdeen. Often, in many quarries, derrick cranes provide the only means of removing blocks from the quarry or introducing machinery or tools.[1]

Barclay also pioneered a safety fireless locomotive that did not produce sparks and therefore could be used in areas where fire was a risk. By 1907, after Barclay's death, the order book was well filled with fireless locomotives and between 1912 and 1961 a total of 114 of this type were produced. An average of 28 locomotives per year was turned out in 1908 to 1910 and a total of 247 steam locomotives were constructed during World War I.[2] Note: French-born Emile Lamm built the first fireless engine in 1872 in the USA, which was for a tramway rather than the railway.

Henry Duncan Preston Cunningham 1814-1875 invented a system for reefing sails from the deck of a ship without the need for sailors to clamber up the masts. It was fitted to many thousands of ships, lessening the dangers to seamen in furling and unfurling topsails in bad weather. In 1862, it was fitted to the ram-ship *Resistance*. It allowed the crew of a ship to operate the topsails from the deck of the ship, without going aloft.[1]

The *R. H. Rae*, the first Canadian ship to use "Cunningham's Patent Self-Reefing Topsails, for Reefing from the Deck without sending Men Aloft" had one of the topsails deployed and reefed in a span of three minutes with no men going aloft. This was a major step forward, as men falling or being thrown into the sea, or vessels being damaged when forced to carry too much sail, had always been major concerns.[2]

Cunningham also invented or patented other contraptions, some of which do not seem to have been successful: eccentric paddle wheels with entire shafts; four-way port steam valves; the reefing paddle wheels; a lifeboat; and a lifeboat carriage (for which in 1849 he was awarded a medal by the Society of Arts). For the military, he designed: overhead shot railways; chain traversing gear; atmospheric gun carriages; sling shots; and racks (for naval use).

"In 1873 the Cunningham shot rack was fitted to HMS *Thunderer*. It had previously been employed in *Monarch*, *Devastation* and *Glatton*. The previous method of manipulating projectiles required a powerful tackle and six men to lift a 700lb [317 kg] projectile onto the rack, the operation needing two minutes and taking out the projectile required about half that time. With the Cunningham rack, two men could lift and place the same projectile in five seconds, and remove it in the same time. The Cunningham shot carriage could convey the projectile to the turret loading port in 10 seconds.[3]

Robert Dick 1814-1890 obtained the first patent for a mailing machine. Once letters became commonplace, businesses looked at means of streamlining mailing processes, such as addressing envelopes quickly. In 1859, the first patent for an addressing machine was given in Canada to Dick. The patent explains that his addressing machine involves using a printing press to print columns of names and addresses on sheets of paper. The individual columns of names and addresses were then cut apart and glued together end-to-end to form a roll.

The roll was put on a spool in the back end of the addressing machine and paper was fed through a number of rollers, which moved the paper through a tank containing liquid adhesive, and then to a cutter at the front of the machine which was placed on a stack of envelopes, newspapers, or other items to be addressed. When the first name and address came out of the machine, it was cut off the roll and at the same time pressed onto the top envelope, which was then removed and the process continued. The patent claimed that two people with one machine could address 4,000 items an hour and Dick also advised that the same technology could be used to produce account statements that could be attached to cards and mailed.[1]

John Goodsir 1814-1867 is believed to be the first recorded person to recognise *and* cure a bacterial infection. In 1842, Goodsir realised that microbes make people sick – nearly 20 years before Louis Pasteur's breakthroughs in microbiology. Milton Wainwright of Sheffield University argues that Goodsir "was the first to attempt to kill bacteria". He examined the vomit of a sick boy under a microscope, and saw tiny organisms that he named *Sarcina*. Goodsir treated his patient with antiseptics: sodium hyposulphite and weak carbolic acid. The infection cleared up. Goodsir published his results in the *Edinburgh Medical and Surgical Journal*, and other British pathologists of the period did similar work on the role of microbes in disease. But their ideas failed to become mainstream science. "The forces of conservatism are very powerful," says Wainwright. It was left to Pasteur – a formidable self-publicist, as well as a brilliant scientist – to popularise the link between germs and disease. Historian Anne Crowther counters that "it's risky to anoint him as the first to treat bacterial infection. It's never as straightforward as all that – it's quite likely that several people were pursuing similar work."[1]

Goodsir also investigated matters in marine zoology, human anatomy, pathology and morphology. He was a pioneer in the techniques of preparing anatomical specimens for study and display, such as his revelation of the circulatory system of adult sea-squirts.[2]

Before 1870, only two notable studies in bacteriology occurred in Britain. John Goodsir discovered and named the genus *Sarcina* (1842) when bacteria were virtually inexplicable entities. The other Briton was John Snow on London's waterborne cholera epidemic of 1854.[3] Goodsir made many important observations on the normal and pathological functions of cells at a time when the role of cells in health and disease was not generally appreciated.[4]

In 1845, Goodsir had shown that the cell nucleus divides, although he had been preceded by both Martin Barry and Robert Remak in 1841. More significantly, he also showed that the nucleus is the germinal centre of the cell, He "insisted on the importance of the cell as the centre of nutrition and declared that the cell is divided into a number of departments. He was described as 'one of the earliest and most acute observers of cell life' by the noted physiologist Rudolf Virchow, who dedicated his *Cellularpathologie* (English Translation 1858) to him."[5]

William Low 1814-1886 worked with Sir John Hawkshaw on plans for a tunnel under the English Channel connecting Britain and France, but disagreed with Hawkshaw's proposals for a single-bore tunnel with a double-track railway, arguing that a twin-bore tunnel with a single track in each would be cheaper to construct and could be better ventilated. His suggestions are considered to be the first practical proposals for a Channel tunnel, and the present tunnel under the English Channel was constructed on similar principles. He and a colleague, George Thomas, submitted plans to Napoleon III in 1867, and Low played an important role in subsequent Anglo-French investigations and reports in favour of the scheme. Unfortunately, in 1883, British military authorities vetoed construction on the grounds of national security, but he did manage to tunnel one kilometre out from Shakespeare Cliff in Dover.[1]

Andrew Crombie Ramsay 1814-1891 explained how certain mountain valleys and lakes were formed by the glaciers that once flowed through them. His work on denudation was based on his study of South Wales, in which he proved, from study of strata, that the area had experienced substantial denudation in the distant past.[1]

Ramsay's most important fieldwork was undertaken in Wales in the years 1848-1851. There, his systematic work provided empirical information that eventually helped close the bitter controversy between Roderick Impey Murchison and the Cambridge professor, Adam Sedgwick, concerning the Cambrian-Silurian boundary. Besides having responsibility for the map work, Ramsay was responsible for the geological sections of Wales. Lakes had long troubled proponents of the origin of valleys by river action; and although the glacial theory of Louis Agassiz (which had been presented to the British Association in Glasgow in 1840) accounted for many surface phenomena observable in northern lands, the origin of lakes was still problematic. Could glaciers "scoop" the hollows now occupied by lakes? In 1862, Ramsay presented his view to the Geological Society that glaciers could indeed hollow out lake-basins, without requiring Earth movements to produce areas of weakness. His paper was controversial and led to numerous discussions over several decades. Ramsay's view eventually prevailed, though it is thought that Earth movements may indeed play a part in basin formation. Ramsay also proposed (in 1854) that glacial conditions had existed in the Permian era, as well as in the geologically recent Pleistocene; and subsequently he contemplated other Palaeozoic glaciations.[2]

Edward Samuel Ritchie 1814-1895 was the most innovative instrument maker in 19th century America, making important contributions to both science and navigation. Ritchie began making compasses for the US Navy soon after the start of the Civil War, and within a few years he had developed the first successful liquid compass – a feat that has been described as the first major improvement in compass technology in several hundred years. Ritchie compasses soon became Navy standard. They were also widely used by American merchant mariners.[1]

With the damping provided by the liquid, together with a gimbal mounting, the floating indicator or card of the Ritchie compass remained relatively stable even when a ship's deck pitched and rolled during periods of severe weather. In Ritchie's third patent application (No.

38,126, dated 7 April 1863), several features that contributed to the success of his compass are revealed, including a floating card of nearly the same specific gravity as the liquid, an air-tight metallic case, and an elastic chamber that served as a diaphragm, compensating for temperature changes and resultant unequal expansion of the liquid and the bowl.

He also constructed (but did not invent) another instrument which was a great help to the American Navy, the theodolite, fastened to a pendulum hanging in a tank of water, which enabled surveys to be taken of the harbours on the Atlantic and Gulf coasts.[2]

Augusta Ada Byron 1815-1852 was introduced to Mary Somerville, a Scottish-born mathematician and astronomer. Mary encouraged Ada in her mathematical studies while seeking to put mathematics and technology into an appropriate human context. It was at a dinner party at Mary Somerville's home in November 1834 that Ada heard Charles Babbage's ideas for a new calculating engine, the Analytical Engine. Babbage conjectured: what if a calculating engine could not only foresee but could act on that foresight? Ada was touched by the "universality of his ideas".[1]

"In 1843 she published a translation from the French of an article on the Analytical Engine by an Italian engineer, Luigi Menabrea, to which Ada added extensive notes of her own. The Notes included the first published description of a stepwise sequence of operations for solving certain mathematical problems and Ada is often referred to as 'the first programmer'. Perhaps more importantly, the article contained statements by Ada that from a modern perspective are visionary. She speculated that the Engine 'might act upon other things besides number ... the Engine might compose elaborate and scientific pieces of music of any degree of complexity or extent'. The idea of a machine that could manipulate symbols in accordance with rules, and that number could represent entities other than quantity, mark the fundamental transition from calculation to computation. Ada was the first to explicitly articulate this notion and in this she appears to have seen further than Babbage. She has been referred to as 'prophet of the computer age'. Certainly, she was the first to express the potential for computers outside mathematics".[2]

James Brunlees 1816-1892 was a railway engineer who built the Mersey Railway, Bolton and Preston Railway, the Londonderry to Coleraine Railway, Ulverston and Lancaster Railway (1853), Solway Junction Railway (1869), and was the consultant engineer for the Sao Paulo Railway in Brazil connecting Sao Paulo with Port de Santos (114 km). This railway crossed the steep slopes of the Serra do Mar for which Brunlees used a system of inclined planes and stationary engines. "Other lines in Brazil designed by Brunlees were the Porto Allegre and New Hamburg, and Minas and Rio. In 1873, he was appointed to the Imperial Order of the Rose of Brazil for his railway work. Other work in South America included the Central Uruguay and Hyugentas Railway, the Bolivar mineral line in Venezuela, and a 400 ft [122 m] long iron pier in the River Plate."[1]

During the construction of the Ulverston and Lancaster Railway, Brunlees made civil engineering history: for the very first time, strong jets of water were used to loosen the sand so that supporting piles could be hammered in firmly. "The jetting method of sinking piles is used when the ground is sandy as a pile hammer would be impractical. Air or water (or both) is used under pressure to help the driving process."[2] Brunlees also built a rack railway over the alpine

Mount Cenis Pass which was in use from 1868 to 1871 when the new rail tunnel was opened. In Spain, he designed the Alcoy and Gandia Railway and harbour.

James Harrison 1816-1893 was the first person to make artificial refrigeration commercially successful. He was born in Dunbartonshire and migrated to Australia in 1837. He was employed by Londoner John Pascoe Fawkner who was living in Melbourne, now the capital of Victoria but at that time still part of the founding state of New South Wales. Fawkner funded Harrison to establish the *Geelong Advertiser* in 1840, a newspaper still in existence, being the second oldest continuously printed newspaper in Victoria. Harrison was its first editor, going to press on 21 November. In 1842, Harrison bought the paper and also published the *Geelong Almanac* and then the *Intelligencer* and *Geelong Register*. He was the editor, from 1867, of the *Melbourne Age*, founded in 1854 and was still Victoria's premier broadsheet newspaper until it was printed in Compact (tabloid) format in March 2013. It was while he was with the *Geelong Advertiser* that he noticed cleaning ether cooled the metal of the print typeface as it evaporated. He made his first mechanical ice-making machine in 1851 and by 1854 was producing commercial quantities in Geelong.

American Alexander Catlin Twining developed a commercial ice-production machine using sulphuric ether in 1856, the year Harrison went to London to lodge his patent (he had a local patent granted in 1854). Twining had started on his discovery as early as 1848 and had built a prototype freezing machine in 1850, a year before Harrison. Twining eventually established a commercial ice-making plant in 1856, two years after Harrison designed and built Australia's first plant to produce ice. Harrison's was the world's first commercial scale mechanical refrigeration plant, and was making 3,000 kg of ice each day for Glasgow & Co., a brewery in Bendigo, Victoria.[1]

Harrison's greatest achievement and much of his financial failure stemmed from his inventions: he was a pioneer in all kinds of refrigeration. At Geelong, he designed and built the plant for the first Australian manufacture of ice and began production at Rocky Point, taking out a local patent in 1854. The Bendigo brewers, Glasgow & Co., soon adopted his principles in a pioneer mechanical refrigerator. In 1856, Harrison went to London where he patented both his process (No. 747 of 1856) and his apparatus (No. 2362 of 1857). Finding ice unnecessary for many industrial purposes, Harrison designed a revolutionary refrigerator, and patented it in 1860. It was used next year in Scotland to distil paraffin, about the same time as Alexander Catlin Twining's machine in the United States. Before 1870, as his finances recovered, Harrison began pioneering work on the refrigeration of ships for the export of meat, while competitors were still thinking only of direct freezing. In 1873, he won a gold medal at the Melbourne Exhibition by proving that meat kept frozen for months remained perfectly edible and that it might be shipped to England for 7 shillings a ton (32 pence/ tonne). As a result, he was given £2,500 for an experiment: in July, the *Norfolk* sailed with 25 tons (22.7 tonnes) of beef and mutton. Unfortunately lack of funds for adequate machinery, rough handling and ignorance made the cargo unusable.[2]

A ship designed by Frenchman Charles Albert Abel Tellier, using three methyl ether refrigeration machines, first took meat from Buenos Aires, Argentina to Rouen, France, in 1876 in *Le Frigorifique* – the first successful intercontinental shipment of refrigerated meat – but the results were unsatisfactory. The following year the *SS Paraguay*, travelling from San Nicholas,

Argentina to Le Havre, France, used an ammonia/water refrigeration system designed by compatriot Ferdinand Carre, whose brother Edmond had designed the first absorption machine in 1850 using water and sulphuric acid. The 136 tonnes of meat, after 50 days at sea, arrived in excellent condition. The first successful refrigerated shipment from Australia to Britain was due to Andrew McIlwraith, a major businessman in Australia. His brother was Sir Thomas McIlwraith, Premier of Queensland, both of whom were born in Ayr, Scotland. In 1879, McIlwraith successfully transported 36 tonnes of beef and mutton, as well as butter, on the *SS Strathleven*, which arrived in London on 2 February 1880 after a voyage of 58 days.

Henry Robertson 1816-1888 projected the North Wales Mineral Line, which runs from Wrexham to Chester, with a branch to Brymbo. This line was afterwards extended to Ruabon, and later still to Shrewsbury, and has now become a portion of the Great Western main line to Birkenhead and Liverpool. He was mainly instrumental in carrying out the whole of the extensions of the Great Western Railway in the North Wales district, and he originated and completed the Shrewsbury and Hereford line for the Great Western Company; and for the London and North Western Railway, the Central Wales Railway from Craven Arms to Llandovery.

He then projected and constructed the branch line to Coalbrookdale, Horsehays, and other parts of the district in that locality. He started and successfully completed the railway from Ruabon to Dolgelly, and then he constructed the line from Bala to Blaenau Festiniog, which did so much to bring North Wales nearer important markets. Robertson designed and erected the viaducts which carried the Great Western Railway over the valleys at Cefn and Chirk. "Few viaducts have been constructed which from an engineering point of view, no less than from an artistic standpoint, have been so universally admired".

Robertson also designed and erected the Kingsland Bridge over the Severn at Shrewsbury, which was one of the largest single-span iron bridges in the country at the time it was built. He constructed a line from Shrewsbury to Hereford that formed a connection between South Wales and the markets at Birkenhead, Liverpool, and the North, and he contributed still more to the development of the country by the projection of the Central Wales Line.

Robertson was the proprietor of the Brymbo Ironworks and estate, which he transformed into the largest steelworks in North Wales.[1]

Archibald Sturrock 1816-1909 promoted and standardised high pressure boilers with a working pressure of 172 kg/cm^2 compared to a maximum of 115 kg/cm^2 for other locomotive boilers. In 1863, he invented the steam tender, the forerunner of the locomotive booster, an auxiliary engine designed to boost power at low speeds or when starting up. They made it possible for trains of over 400 tonnes to travel on a gradient of 1:178. Unfortunately for Sturrock, the steam tenders were unpopular with the crews, who had to handle two engines. As a consequence, maintenance was a problem and costs higher than expected. The sidings could not cope with the larger number of trucks needed to achieve the required economies and shunting was difficult. The imaginative idea was abandoned and Sturrock never made the additional income he expected from the steam tender patent.[1]

He designed the prototype of the first articulated locomotive which, at the time, was known as a powered steam tender and which was later developed by Robert Francis Fairlie.

As locomotive engineer for the third largest railway in the United Kingdom, Sturrock was well placed to take advantage of remunerative consultancy opportunities. In 1853, when Sturrock had been in the role for three years, the Great Northern Railway (GNR) had 228 locomotives. Only the London & North Western Railway (LNWR) and the Midland were larger with 629 and 331 locomotives respectively. Sturrock's former employer, the Great Western Railway (GWR), was ranked sixth with 193 locomotives.

In 1850, when Sturrock joined the GNR, there were 340 employees in the Locomotive Department and the locomotive mileage was 609,092 (975,410 km). When he retired in 1866, the employees numbered 3,834 and the mileage was 4,873,113 (7,842,515 km). He designed the locomotives and carriages which established East Coast main line's reputation for comfort and punctuality. He later played a lead role in establishing the Yorkshire Engine Company.[2]

Daniel Wilson 1816-1892 was an anthropologist whose *Prehistoric Man* (1862) marks, with John Lubbock's *Pre-historic Times* (1865), the emergence of a new discipline – prehistoric archaeology – and the use of the term "prehistory" in English. The parallels between the native peoples of the Americas and those of prehistoric Europe had long intrigued Wilson, and became the subject of his next major publication, *Prehistoric Man: Researches into the Origin of Civilisation in the Old and the New World*. This study has been described as "one of the most important works of anthropological synthesis produced in the nineteenth century". It was informed by the tenets of the Scottish enlightenment, in whose shadow Wilson had grown up, which saw all human groups as sharing a common origin and being equally capable of intellectual progress. It thus set him apart from the dominant anthropological current of his day in North America, polygenism, which argued for the separate – and unequal – creation of the races.[1]

He is usually described as the first professional scholar in Canadian archaeology and ethnography, and his examinations on "ethnology", in 1855, appear to mark the first courses on this subject in the English-speaking world.[2]

Wilson adopted the three-tiered division established by Danish antiquaries and arranged Scottish artefacts in terms of the stone, bronze, and iron ages. By connecting these ages to the Christian era, moreover, he drew links between archaeology and written history and thereby extended enormously the chronological depth of the country's past. Through the examination of skeletal remains and the measurement of skulls, Wilson showed that other peoples had lived in Scotland before the Celts. His book also constituted a protest against the tendency to attribute relics that showed skill of workmanship and invention to Roman or Scandinavian influences and to assign all that was rude to Britons. He also pleaded that archaeology, in order to assume the status of a science, be closely associated with ethnology and that data on Scotland be compared with material from other parts of the world.[3]

A group of American writers, including Philadelphia physician Samuel George Morton, an acquaintance of Wilson's, ascribed mental and moral qualities to races on the basis of the shapes of heads, argued that races were distinct species, and contended that a single head type was to be found among all North American native peoples other than the Inuit. The implications of polygenesis, and its association with justifications of Negro servitude, offended Wilson's moral sense as well as his scientific instincts. He had grown up in a family of pronounced anti-slavery views, and in 1853 in Philadelphia, he was surprised and hurt to find that people dismissed as ridiculous the idea that "the black man is sprung from the same stock as the white." All his life Wilson remained true to the cardinal doctrine of the philosophers of the late 18th century Scottish Enlightenment that humankind was everywhere and in all ages the same and that variations of culture and attainments were due to the circumstances in which people were placed, not innate racial character. In a series of articles, Wilson challenged the view that a single head type characterised the North American Indian race by pointing out how varied specimens actually were and how difficult it was to generalise about skulls that had been altered by diet, deliberate deformation, and burial rites.[4]

John Allan Broun 1817-1879 discovered that the Earth loses or gains magnetic intensity not locally, but as a whole. He also found that solar activity causes magnetic disturbances.[1] He published a paper in 1858 containing several pioneering and remarkable ideas in solar-terrestrial physics. He could anticipate more or less correctly the nature and origin of solar wind, solar magnetic fields, sunspot activity and geomagnetic storms in the middle of the 19th century. Broun applied the experimental results of the behaviour of ionised gases in discharge tubes for the first time to space physics, which may be considered as the beginning of astrophysical plasma physics. In this context, he attempted to explain the plasma interactions of solar wind with the comet tails and Earth's magnetosphere. Most of the postulates or hypotheses put forward by Broun in 1858, and later, in 1874, were rediscovered during the 20th century, after the advent of Space Age.[2]

He discovered semi-annual variations in geomagnetic activity (1848) and solar sources of recurrent geomagnetic storms. Broun proposed some new ideas about sunspot activity and solar magnetic fields with some physical insight in his *Philosophical Magazine* paper (1858). He posited that the origin of solar magnetic fields is due to an electromagnetic induction process involving an electromagnet and currents flowing in the solar atmosphere. This can be considered as an early anticipation of dynamo models of astrophysical magnetic fields by Broun.

Broun had a remarkable and intuitive perception of the nature of large-scale solar magnetic fields. During sunspot minimum and declining phases of the sunspot cycles, large-scale solar magnetic fields often resemble a tilted dipole configuration. North-South asymmetry in the strength of solar polar magnetic fields and differences in the epochs of reversals in northern and southern helio hemispheres are well documented in the solar-terrestrial literature of recent times. Broun's idea of inferring properties of solar magnetic fields from geomagnetic data is also acceptable in the modern context.

Scientists prior to Broun suggested a polar force probably of electrical nature from the sun acted on the comet tails during its passage towards the sun. Broun proposed that the observed changes in the tail of comets may be due to the action of extended solar magnetic fields in the interplanetary space.

Scientists of the 18th century like Jean-Jacques d'Ortous de Mairan (1754) and early 19th century like Giovanni Cassini suggested that interplanetary space is filled with matter of solar origin and Zodiacal light (now understood to be an optical phenomenon in Earth's atmosphere) is a visible manifestation of the same. Broun (1858) provided a physical basis to these ideas by proposing that "magnetic gases" are continuously flowing outward from the solar atmosphere to the interplanetary medium by the repulsive action of solar magnetic fields on these gases. Later, in 1874, he proposed a thermodynamical mechanism of coronal expansion to account for the solar wind outflow from the sun.[3]

Alexander Henry 1817-1895 was a gunsmith in Edinburgh who produced a gun which consisted of a seven-groove polygonal rifling, with one twist in 56 cm. The barrel length was 84.2 cm. The Henry rifling system was found superior in all trials. The basis of the rifling was in reality a modernisation of the Whitworth system, which was developed in 1854. The bore was .450" calibre, across the lands of the rifling. "The Third pattern Mk1 P1874 Martini Henry [rifle] was to form the backbone of the British infantry small arms between 1874-1880." During the Martini-Henry period in service, the British army was involved in a large number of colonial wars, most notably the Anglo-Zulu War in 1879. The rifle was used by the company of the 2nd Battalion, 24th Regiment of Foot present at Rorke's Drift. During the battle, 139 British soldiers successfully defended themselves against several thousand Zulus. The weapon was not completely phased out until 1904.[1]

The Martini-Henry Rifle was a weapon of Empire. Unlike the Snider-Enfield it replaced, it was Britain's "first service rifle designed from the ground up as a breechloading metallic cartridge firearm. It protected and served the British Empire and her colonies for over 30 years. This robust weapon utilised a falling block, self-cocking, lever operated, single-shot action designed by Friedrich von Martini of Switzerland. The barrel used the Henry Rifling System, designed by Alexander Henry."[2]

Walter McQueen 1817-1893 did much to develop the American 4-4-0 Jupiter locomotive, and in 1848 introduced the smokebox saddle. The latter, in the form of a plate, was primitive compared with William Mason's later box form saddle, but nevertheless may be regarded as the forerunner of this component.

During his 41 years at the works, McQueen gained a reputation as an outstanding designer and builder of locomotives. By 1880, Schenectady had produced more than 1,200 locomotives and ranked third in number of locomotives built in America. McQueen built his first locomotive in 1840; a 4-2-0 seven-ton (6.35 tonnes) engine made in Albany for the Ithaca and Oswego Railroad. In 1850, he was with the Hudson River Railroad where he built most of their high-speed locomotives. Although he cannot be credited specifically with any major locomotive improvement, "he does appear to have been the earliest user of the cylinder saddle and was the first to apply the air dome to feed pumps. However, his locomotives were regarded as first-class machines and his reputation was founded upon careful construction along conventional lines."[1]

George David Pollock 1817-1897 introduced the idea of using skin grafts to treat burn wounds in 1870. He donated small pieces of his own skin, which he used in conjunction with a burn victim's skin to cover a large denuded area. The idea was brilliant and paved the way for one of the most important modern functions of skin grafts – the treatment of burn victims.

"Pollock experimented with various donor sources, including an unspecified human donor and then himself. He went on to describe one of the earliest accounts of transplant rejection."[1]

The term *allograft* denotes a graft from the same species and is also referred to as homograft. Pollock first described them. He donated pieces of his own skin in conjunction with a patient's autograft (a tissue graft transferred from one part of the patient's body to another part) for treatment of burn wounds. Pollock documented both grafts as taking; however, he noted that the skin he contributed eventually disappeared from the healing wound.[2]

In 1869, Jacques Reverdin, in a report to the Société Imperiale de Chirurgie, described the use of a small epidermal graft, which became known as the pinch graft. This technique did not, however, gain wide recognition until 1870, when successful experiments in skin grafting for the treatment of burn patients were performed by Pollock.[3]

Pollock convinced the world of the efficacy of skin autografting and homografting.[4] At St George's Hospital Pollock "soon became known as a daring and dexterous operator. He was especially fond of plastic operations, particularly those for fissured palate, a malformation which he had studied profoundly and in the cure of which he was peculiarly successful. ... The cure of that most distressing lesion, vesico-vaginal fistula, was another development of plastic surgery which owed much to his patience and his dexterity". The reason for Pollock's preference for constructive surgery over destructive (i.e., ablative) surgery is readily sensed from his frustration over the lack of knowledge about cancer.

It was probably due to the high regard in which he was held that Pollock was able to convince the medical world of the utility of skin grafting burns. On 11 November 1870, he read a paper before the Clinical Society of London entitled *Cases of skin grafting and skin transplantation.* "He describes his first case of skin grafting a burn by saying: On May 5, I removed two small pieces of skin from the lower portion of the abdomen, and implanted them in the middle of the lower part of the ulcer, about 1½ inches [38 mm] apart, and about ¼ of an inch [6.25 mm] from either edge of the sore. June 16 (6 weeks). Both of the transplanted portions were considerably grown; the lower one had bridged across the sore and divided it in two. Two more pieces were now inserted from the abdomen towards the broadest extremity of the ulcer; also, two minute pieces taken from the shoulder of a black man."

Thus, in May 1870, Pollock performed his first autograft of a burn wound. Six weeks later, being stimulated by his initial success and the suggestion of Dr (John) William Ogle, Pollock performed his first homograft of a burn wound. By the end of the century, John Reissberg Wolfe had introduced full-thickness skin grafts into clinical practice to treat ectropion, and John Harvey Girdner had published the first report of skin grafting with human cadaveric skin.

Who deserves credit for the treatment of burns by skin autografting and homografting? Remembering William Osler's quotation of Darwin, "in science the credit goes to the man who convinces the world, not to the man to whom the idea first occurs," one concludes that Pollock deserves credit, for he first made the operation known.

Over a century of progress in the care of burned patients confirms the pertinence of Pollock's principles: the use of skin autografts, the value of skin homografts, and the importance of applying skin grafts early when the wound is healthy to relieve suffering, prevent contractures, and avoid deformity.

Sir Richard Owen wrote in his *Archetype and Homologies of the Vertebrata Skeleton*: "He becomes the true discoverer who establishes the truth; and the sign of the proof is the general acceptance". Pollock established the true value of the use of skin grafts, especially in the treatment of burn patients. This was an advance of great importance in medical science.[5]

Robert Sinclair 1817-1898 was a railway engineer who introduced a completely new design of 2-4-0 passenger engine with stovepipe chimney. He provided cabs of unprecedented protectiveness, against which his enginemen strongly protested. As consultant engineer to the Great Luxemburg Railway, he sponsored the introduction of the fast 2-4-2 locomotive, a type that became popular on the continent and that Sinclair adapted to a 2-4-2 tank locomotive for the Great Eastern's commuter services. As consulting engineer for the East Indian Railway, he designed an outside cylinder 2-4-0 which was built in some numbers.[1]

Robert Angus Smith 1817-1884 discovered acid rain in 1852. He analysed rain water throughout the British Isles in the 19th century and found high levels of acidity in rain water in manufacturing cities and towns, with the highest level being found in Glasgow, Scotland. Smith described three zones of air pollution: carbonate and ammonia in fields and open country; ammonium sulphate in suburbs; and acid sulphate and sulphuric acid in town. The reported value (representing an average of several individual samples) was 109.16 grains (7,073 mg) of sulphuric anhydride per gallon (4.5 litres) of rain water.[1]

Smith was most active, and probably the first to campaign, for the introduction of smokeless fuels. He worked from his laboratory near All Saints Church in Rusholme and was appointed in 1863 as Manchester's first Alkali Inspector. Manchester and Salford were the first in Britain to have smokeless zones, thanks largely to Smith's pioneering work. Salford first introduced smokeless zoning to the Fairhope and Ladywell Districts in 1949, while the Manchester Corporation Act of 1946 led directly to the first controlled zones in 1952, followed by 105 acres (42.5 hectares) of central Manchester in 1956. In July 1972, Salford declared itself to be the world's first fully smoke-free zone.[2]

Smith's most important work is in *Disinfectants and Disinfection* (1869), in which he recognises the quite different chemical effects of the variety of substances proposed as disinfectants, antiseptics, or deodorisers, and *Air and Rain: The Beginnings of a Chemical Climatology* (1872), which presents the vast body of data Smith had accumulated on the composition of urban atmospheres.[3]

Alexander Wood 1817-1884 pioneered the hypodermic syringe for drug administration, having first injected a patient with morphine in 1853. He gave a description of his innovation in a paper entitled *A New Method for Treating Neuralgia by the Direct Application of Opiates to Painful Points*, published in the *Edinburgh Medical and Surgical Journal* (1855). He used a modified model of a syringe developed by Daniel Ferguson to treat one of his lady patients who could not take opium orally. A few years later Wood introduced a graduated scale on the barrel and a better needle. Thus, Wood is generally credited with the idea of using a hypodermic syringe for the first time.[1]

The prototype of the modern-day piston syringe was improvised sometime late in the 15th century and gradually became popular in clinical use mainly for giving enemas. In his textbook, *Chirurgia*, published in 1497, an Alsatian surgeon Hieronymus Brunschwig showed a piston syringe as a surgical tool. In 1580, French surgeon Ambroise Pare mentioned the syringe as a common surgical tool. Its use in modern medical purposes like intravenous, intramuscular and subcutaneous injections began rather recently, around the second half of the 17th century. In 1628,

William Harvey published his book describing the circulation of blood – *Exercitatio Anatomica de Motu Cordis Sanguinia Animalibus* (An Anatomical Exercise on the Motion of the Heart and Blood in Animals). Christopher Wren, who was Professor of Astronomy at Oxford, understood that blood circulation could be used to carry liquid medicine to different parts of the body, thus giving rise to a revolutionary idea of injecting medicine towards systemic level rather than simply at the local level. Wren is probably the first person recorded to have used intravenous injection in Britain.[2]

French physician, Dominique Anel, is usually credited with the invention of the kind of syringe used today. Anel was a surgeon in the army of French King Louis XIV and he created his instrument to clean wounds with suction. It is often claimed that the "first true hypodermic syringe was created by French physician Charles Gabriel Pravaz in 1853".[3] This is a fallacy and, to do him justice, Pravaz never made any such claim. He was interested in the possibility of coagulation of blood in arterial aneurysms by the injection of perchloride of mercury. He conducted experiments in sheep to that end, using a silver syringe screwed to a cannula, which was first introduced into an artery with the aid of a trocar. The confusion may have arisen because Louis Jules Félix Behier, another Frenchman, reported the use of the same equipment for subcutaneous medication with acknowledgements to Pravaz in 1859, the year after publication of Wood's second paper. The syringe used by Pravaz and Behier had a screw mechanism for advancing the plunger, which was cumbersome but useful in estimating dosage when the barrel was made of opaque metal. It is of less practical value when the plunger is visible through glass.[4]

Around the same time, Alexander Wood devised a subcutaneous injection method. This allowed physicians to administer intravenous anaesthesia for the first time. In 1853, Daniel Ferguson developed a syringe and hollow platinum trocar with an oblique opening on one side encased in an outer tubing, also with an oblique opening. His syringe was made partially of glass and this important change permitted visual monitoring of injections. In 1869, the all-glass syringe was developed by Jeanne Wülfing-Lüer who, with her husband, Hermann, operated as surgical instrument makers. The ease with which this syringe could be sterilised further reduced the risk of infection.[5]

Morphia, the alkaloid derivative of opium, was isolated in the early 19th century and was commercially available from the 1820s. But as long as it had to be taken orally, there was little to recommend it over opium. The isolation of morphine was part of a general systematisation of remedies and discovery of alkaloids in line with the growth of toxicology as a science. Quinine, caffeine and strychnine were all isolated shortly after morphine. Other opium alkaloids were also discovered – narceine by Pierre-Joseph Pelletier in 1832, and codeine by Pierre Jean Robiquet in 1821 while examining a new process for obtaining morphine suggested by William Gregory of Edinburgh. Macfarlan and Company of Edinburgh began to manufacture the alkaloid in the early 1830s, when Gregory (the son of James Gregory, of Gregory's Powder) devised a process for the production of morphia muriate. British opium collected by **George Young 1692-1757** in his initial experiments was used. In his 1753 publication, *A treatise on opium, founded upon practical observations*, Young remarked that opium is a poison by which great numbers are daily destroyed. In 41 chapters, he gave a comprehensive account of the indications for the drug, including its complications. The drug was later purified and more exact processes devised. In the early years of morphine production, Macfarlan's received opium from the London wholesale houses and returned the muriate to them. The drug was still brown and formed a brown solution, for the process then used did not abstract the resin of colouring matter. When Macfarlan's produced a purer white substance, they had difficulty in persuading purchasers to accept it. There was little difficulty, however, in persuading medical men to use the new drug.[6]

Morphia did not come into widespread use until the 1860s, a few years after Alexander Wood perfected the hypodermic syringe – a modified model of a Ferguson-type syringe – which made possible an entirely new mode of administering medication. Wood and Doctor Charles Hunter publicised the use of hypodermic injections of morphia for the relief of neuralgia. Wood's paper, delivered before the British Medical Association, and then published in the *British Medical Journal*, was particularly important in making ordinary practitioners aware of the new therapy. Within a few years, it was being applied to a variety of problems, including inflammations of the eye, acute rheumatism, uterine pain, and delirium tremens.

Wood however believed that the action of the opiate given subcutaneously was principally local and he therefore was very careful in delivering the medicine near to a nerve so that effective relief of pain could be given to the patient. Hunter, however, remarked that it also demonstrated systemic action. There is some evidence that this difference in opinion led to an "acrimonious debate" between Wood and Hunter. It has been suggested that Wood's fundamental mistake that the effect of hypodermic injection of a substance was primarily local implicating that drug dependence was very unlikely by hypodermic injection of opiates actually paved the path for emergence of a huge number of patients morbidly dependent upon morphine, the so-called "morphinists" of the 19th century.[7]

The first recorded fatality from a hypodermic syringe-induced overdose was Dr Wood's wife. The tragedy arose because she was injecting morphine to excess. Later, in the American Civil War (1861-1865), an estimated 400,000 soldiers became addicted to opiates after liberal use of morphine injections as well as opium pills: "The returning veteran could be ... identified because he had a leather thong around his neck and a leather bag (with) Morphine Sulphate tablets, along with a syringe and a needle issued to the soldier on his discharge...This was called the 'Soldier's Disease'." [8]

Alexander Gordon 1818-1895 was responsible for the design of many cast-iron railway bridges, buildings of different types and several lighthouses. Gordon built the first cast-iron lighthouse in the western hemisphere at Morant Point in Jamaica in 1841, which is the tallest lighthouse built of cast iron, standing at 40.8 m. He also built Gibbs Hill lighthouse in Bermuda (1846), Cape Pine in Newfoundland (1850), and South Point lighthouse in Barbados (1852). Gordon developed a system of interlocking cast-iron plates which, when assembled, would provide an effective, economical approach to the problem of building lighthouses on inaccessible sites.[1]

William Menelaus 1818-1882 was appointed manager of Dowlais Iron Company in Wales and, through innovation and good management, made it the largest coal producer in Britain in the second half of the 19th century. The success derived from innovation as well as organisation. Menelaus invented several mechanical handling devices and designed the massive new two-directional Goat Mill for iron rolling – the world's most powerful rolling mill. He shifted from iron to steel production, replaced blast furnaces much sooner than his competitors due to their higher running cost, and in 1870 he was first to use the waste gas from the coking ovens to fuel the furnaces.[1]

The owner of Dowlais was keen to adopt new methods and it became the first British company to acquire a licence to produce steel using the Bessemer process in 1856. "However, it was to take the best part of a decade of experimentation at Dowlais, under the guidance of William Menelaus, before a truly industrialised method for the production of steel was perfected.

Prior to its introduction, steel had been around 10 times more expensive than iron – making it far too expensive for use in railways, bridges or the frameworks of buildings. After the industrialisation of the Bessemer process, steel and wrought iron soon became similarly priced and most manufacturers quickly turned to steel. In 1871, Dowlais produced almost 26,000 tons of Bessemer steel; by 1884, it was producing more than 118,000 tons.

With steel production supplanting iron, Dowlais continued to grow through the second half of the century and, in 1888, built a second steelworks in South Wales, this time in Cardiff. The company had successfully evolved its business and entered the 20th century as one of the largest ironworks in the world."[2]

Thomas Stevenson 1818-1887 developed the work of his brother Alan and of Augustin-Jean Fresnel, a French physicist who studied light. In 1849, at Peterhead North Harbour lighthouse, Thomas installed a catadioptric fixed holophote (a lamp with lenses or reflectors to collect the rays of light and throw them in a given direction) which was the first to combine the whole sphere of rays diverging from a light source into a single beam of parallel rays. He then further developed this system by introducing the first dioptric holophotal revolving light which was installed at Horsburgh Rock near Singapore in 1850. The holophotal system, which proved a great improvement in lighthouse illumination, was then adopted on a larger scale by the Northern Lighthouse Board at North Ronaldsay lighthouse in 1851 and afterwards came into universal use. Stevenson also developed the concept of creating an "apparent" light on dangerous reefs by indirect illumination and reflection from a parent lighthouse and installed a "beautiful and ingenious contrivance" at Stornoway in 1851. Stevenson's crowning achievement was his "azimuthal condensing system", which reduced the available light in some sectors of azimuth and optimised it in others. It was introduced at Isle Ornsay lighthouse, Skye, in 1857 to service Sleat Sound.[1] He co-built 31 lighthouses with his other famous Stevenson relatives and was father to the famous author, Robert Louis (Lewis) Stevenson.

In 1864, he created the now ubiquitous instrument shelter – also known as a Stevenson screen – which is an enclosure designed to shield meteorological instruments against precipitation and direct heat radiation from outside sources, while still allowing air to circulate freely around them. It forms part of a standard weather station. The Stevenson screen holds instruments that may include thermometers (ordinary, maximum/minimum), a hygrometer, a psychrometer, a dewcell, a barometer and a thermograph. Its purpose is to provide a standardised environment in which to measure temperature, humidity, dewpoint and atmospheric pressure.

William Swan 1818-1894 was the first to study spectral analysis of radical carbon C_2 in 1856. Swan bands are a characteristic of the spectra of carbon stars, comets and of burning hydrocarbon fuels.[1]

In early 19th century, Joseph von Fraunhofer, a German optician, was looking for a pure source of coloured light to test the properties of various types of glass. When he looked at light from coloured flames through his prisms, he noticed it did not split into the rainbow sunlight does but, rather, into narrow coloured lines. In particular, he noticed that all of his flames produced a bright double band in the yellowish region of the spectrum. Later, when Fraunhofer split sunlight through his prisms, he saw that its rainbow spectrum was not a smooth continuum, but was, in actuality, superimposed by many dark lines. Fraunhofer was interested to note that there were two particularly dark lines in the yellow-orange part of the spectrum coinciding with the bright yellow-orange lines he had seen in the flame spectra. He constructed a map of 576 lines in the Sun's spectrum, labelling the most prominent A-H. The double lines that coincided with the bright lines in the flame he labelled "D". To this day, we call these lines "Fraunhofer lines." Fraunhofer saw the D lines in all of his flame spectra because he was using a sodium flame. Today, low-pressure sodium lamps are sometimes used as outdoor streetlights – they are recognisable by the yellowish light they emit.

It was William Swan in 1857, however, who realised how useful these absorption and emission lines might be. He noted that a Bunsen flame turned bright yellow when he introduced only the tiniest grain of sodium into it and arrived at the realisation that spectrum analysis, or spectroscopy, could provide a tool "of fantastic sensitivity" to detect the presence of various compounds. Because all compounds emit and absorb light at unique, specific frequencies, if an astronomer were to examine the spectrum of, say, a star like the Sun, and see that it has the double D lines, he or she could conclude that there is sodium in the atmosphere of that star. Astronomers can, in fact, infer the presence of any compound if they find its spectral signature. Spectroscopic lines are like the fingerprints of different atoms and molecules.[2]

Spectral bands of the carbon radical C_2, which are a characteristic of the spectra of carbon stars and of comets, were first investigated in 1856 by Swan. Thirty years earlier, William Henry Fox Talbot wrote on the use of spectra for chemical analysis, but it was Swan in Scotland who realised that samples of an unprecedented purity were needed for analysis, which was the step needed for spectral analysis to begin. The Swan absorption bands of molecular carbon in cool stars are named after him.[3]

Thomas Anderson 1819-1874 discovered picoline (an isomer of aniline) and the base pyridine in a series of experiments carried out between 1848-1868 in which he distilled bone oil and investigated the concentrated fractions of organic bases created.[1] Pyridines are used as powerful and versatile solvents capable of dissolving fats, mineral oils and rubber. Anderson also investigated codeine and other opium derivatives and discovered the structure of anthracene, a compound derived from coal tar, and which has a variety of industrial uses.[2]

He devised a method of polymerisation using a platinum salt which came to be known as Anderson's salt. His paper, entitled *The crystalline constituents of opium* (Transactions of The Royal Society of Edinburgh, Volume 20, 1853, pp 347-375), was the first to give correct formulae to codeine and other alkaloids, and it earned him the Keith medal of The Royal Society of Edinburgh in 1853.

Anderson's study of decomposition made him an expert on sewage disposal, and in particular on the manurial use of sewage combined with carbolic as a deodorant. In 1869, with Joseph

Bazalgette, he reported on sewage disposal for the city of Glasgow. He made himself familiar with the work of Louis Pasteur, particularly his germ theory, on which he was able to inform his colleague, Joseph Lister, professor of surgery at Glasgow. He also advised Lister on the use of carbolic as an antiseptic.[3]

Hugh McColl 1819-1885 consistently lobbied for water resources and was, indisputably, the irrigation prophet of colonial Australia. He advocated town water supply, the irrigation of northern Victoria, and the government ownership of all watercourses, with the result that Victoria's irrigation developed a generation earlier than any other large-scale irrigation in Australia.[1]

He greatly contributed to "the construction of Goulburn Weir, Waranga Basin and Waranga Western Channel. The Goulburn Weir was the first major diversion structure built for irrigation in Australia and its design was advanced for its time. The Waranga Basin was described as the largest project of its kind in the world, with an embankment height of 8.8 metres and a length of seven kilometres."[2]

Allan Pinkerton 1819-1884 was perhaps the most celebrated and innovative criminal investigator of the mid to late 19th century in America. By 1869, with offices across the country, the Pinkerton National Detective Agency (originally the North-Western Police Agency), forty years before the creation of the FBI, was the country's first national investigative force. Its motto, "We Never Sleep," and its logo of the unblinking eye, became part of American culture and the symbol of professional crime fighting.

Pinkerton was one of the first in America to understand the value of criminal record keeping, and as such began collecting and recording information of individual criminals in the era before Alphonse Bertillon's body measurements and the science of fingerprinting. Whenever a Pinkerton man took an offender into custody, he took note of scars, tattoos, moles and other notable physical characteristics that distinguished this person from everyone else. Pinkerton also amassed the nation's largest rogues' gallery. As early as the 1850s, he began accumulating photographs of miscreants; this rogues' gallery was imitated by other police forces.[1] The photographs were initially daguerreotypes, then tintypes, and when the wet-plate process was developed after the Civil War, the agency mounted their prints on paper. The reverse sides of these paper-mounted photographs bore detailed physical descriptions of subjects, including notes regarding the offenders' criminal specialty.[2]

Pinkerton came to America in 1842 and was made deputy sheriff of Kane County in 1846 after catching a gang of counterfeiters. He was subsequently deputy sheriff of Cook County, and in 1850 was appointed the first detective for Chicago. He also established Pinkerton's detective agency in that year, and from that date until their emancipation, he was largely engaged in assisting the escape of slaves. He was the first special US mail agent for northern Illinois and Indiana and southern Wisconsin. On the suggestion of General George Brinton McClellan, he organised a system of obtaining military information in the Southern states. From this system, he developed the US Secret Service, of which he was in charge throughout the war, under the assumed name of Major E.J. Allen.[3]

He organised the United States Secret Service division of the national army in 1861, was its first chief, and subsequently organised and was at the head of the Secret Service Department of the Gulf till the close of the Civil War. He added to his detective agency in Chicago in 1860 a corps of night-watchmen, called Pinkerton's preventive watch, established offices of both agencies in several other cities, and was signally successful in the discovery and suppression of crime.

While in the employment of the Wilmington and Baltimore Railroad Company in 1861, he discovered a plan to assassinate Abraham Lincoln on his way to his inauguration in Washington. Among the cases in which he successfully traced thieves and recovered money are the robbery of $40,000 from a bank in Carbondale, Pennsylvania, and that of the Adams express company of $700,000, on 6 January 1866, from a train on the New York, New Haven & Hartford Railroad, and the taking of $300,000 from an express-car on the Hudson River railroad. He also broke up gangs of thieves at Seymour, Indiana, and the "Mollie Maguires" in Pennsylvania.[4]

Alexander Weir Robertson 1819-1879 initiated the founding of the first professional accounting body outside of Italy. In 1853, Robertson, a 34-year-old accountant who had been in public practice for ten years, convened the first meeting of Edinburgh accountants that would lead to the formation of the Society of Accountants in Edinburgh. The Society went on to gain its Royal Charter as the first recognised professional body for accountants on 11 December 1854 (other sources say it was 23 October 1854).[1] Public accountants were well established by this time, associated closely with the practice of law (bankruptcy in particular) in Edinburgh and merchants and stockbrokers in Glasgow. Edinburgh had become a world-renowned city for intellectual inquiry and innovation through the period of the Scottish Enlightenment over the previous century. The resulting growth in trade, wealth and the middle classes helped create demand for accountants. There were 61 original members of the Society of Accountants of Edinburgh, all of whom are named in the Royal Charter. The Society of Accountants in Edinburgh went on to become the Institute of Chartered Accountants of Scotland.[2]

Very little is known of the origin of accountancy as a profession, although its antecedents are ancient, with evidence of some form of "accounting" practice being found in Babylon and pharaonic Egypt. In the modern acceptation of the word, however, a professional man is one who places his skill and learning at the disposal of all and sundry for a reward, as distinct from one who serves a single employer. Accordingly, while there are several references in mediaeval and even classic times to stewards and auditors, these references do not throw much light upon the origin of professional accountancy, as the people referred to were manifestly in the whole-time employment of a single individual or body. The first association of accountants of which there is any record is the Collegio dei Raxonati, which was founded in Venice in 1581, but it is by no means certain that the members of this body were professional or public accountants, or whether they were not rather employees of public bodies. At Milan, however, in 1742, the government established a scale of charges for accountants, so it may be assumed that then, if not earlier, professional accountancy actually existed in that city. It has been said that the first Scottish professional accountant was one George Watson, born in Edinburgh in 1645; but whether he was really able to carry on a practice as a professional accountant in addition to his "large private banking business" seems somewhat doubtful.[3]

Friar Luca Pacioli's 1494 publication in Venice of *Everything about Arithmetic, Geometry, and Proportion* is the first time accounting principles were first expounded. While Friar Luca is often called the "Father of Accounting", he did not invent the system. Instead, he simply described a method used by merchants in Venice during the Italian Renaissance period. His system included most of the accounting cycle as we know it today. For example, he described the use of journals and ledgers, and he warned that a person should not go to sleep at night until the debits equalled the credits. His ledger included assets (including receivables and inventories), liabilities, capital, income, and expense accounts. Friar Luca demonstrated year-end closing entries and proposed that a trial balance be used to prove a balanced ledger. Also, his treatise alludes to a wide range of topics from accounting ethics to cost accounting.[4]

Although the first association of accountants was the Collegio dei Raxonati, nowadays Scotland and England are considered the leading countries in the early development of the auditing profession.[5] In Scotland, the Society of Accountants in Edinburgh received a Royal Charter in 1854. In England, the first professional organisation, the Incorporated Society of Liverpool Accountants, was formed in 1870, with Glasgow-born Anthony Wigham Chalmers as its first secretary and second president. Ten years later the organisation received a Royal Charter under the name the Institute of Chartered Accountants in England and Wales (ICAEW).[6]

"It is not unfitting that when we come to deal with the modern profession of accountant, Scotland should occupy the place of priority. It is there that the Chartered Accountant originated, and in Scotland we find the oldest existing societies of public accountants. We are not unmindful of the claims of Italy, to which country we are indebted for so much in connection with the profession, but however important a position accountants occupied there during the seventeenth and eighteenth centuries, their influence undoubtedly diminished and the old Gilds [sic] and Colleges became either dormant or extinct. Directly after its formation the Edinburgh Society deliberated upon a distinctive title for its members, and resolved to adopt the name of 'Chartered Accountant', indicated by the letters 'C.A.' The same course was followed by the Glasgow Institute as well as by the Aberdeen Society when they were incorporated later. It naturally took some time before the new name became familiar to the public or even in the mouths of the members themselves, but ere long it acquired a definite signification throughout Scotland, and when in 1880 the same designation was adopted by the English Institute, incorporated in that year, it soon became a recognised term wherever the English language is spoken."[7]

The formation process of the first accounting body of modern times was completed within 19 days, from the time that Robertson sent out his invitation to his accounting colleagues in Edinburgh on 17 January 1853, with The Society of Accountants of Edinburgh being formed on 4 February. The following year an application for a royal charter was filed and this was granted on 23 October 1854. "Scots played a significant role in the creation of the accounting professions in Canada and the USA". Three of the so-called "Big Six" international accounting firms can count Scots amongst their original founders – Ernst & Young, KPMG Peat Marwick, and Touche Ross.[8]

The Institute of Chartered Accountants of Scotland (ICAS) has (in 2016) more than 20,000 members and students worldwide. ICAS members play leading roles in 80% of the FTSE 100 companies (The FTSE 100 Index is a share index of the 100 companies listed on the London Stock Exchange with the highest market capitalisation).[9]

John Baird 1820-1891 built New York's elevated railroads on Second and Sixth Avenues. He had been manager of the Burden Iron Works in Troy, New York, in the 1840s and then in 1850 he became general manager of Delamater Iron Works in New York then Chief Engineer and designer for the Cromwell Steamship Line commuting between New York and New Orleans. He was Vice President and Manager of the Metropolitan Elevated Railroad Company in New York City. He had at least 15 patents for machine design, iron vessels and valves for steam engines.[1] The *New Orleans* (1871), the *Knickerbocker* (1873) and the *Hudson* (1874) were all fitted with engines from designs of John Baird, construction engineer of the Cromwell Steamship Line. In 1880, the *Louisiana* steamship was fitted with a pair of compound beam engines, "built by the Delamater Iron Works from designs of John Baird, that were certainly a novelty in design".[2] Baird built the first propeller "that went out upon the sea past Sandy Hook. Prior to this venture propellers were used only on Long Island Sound. When the elevated railroad was projected, it commended itself to him, and he took an interest in it. To obtain $10,000 in ready money for investment in it he mortgaged his house in Lexington Avenue. He became General Manager, Vice-President and Construction Engineer of the Sixth Avenue line."[3]

John William Dawson 1820-1899 investigated the geology and mineral deposits of Nova Scotia, providing data for his *Acadian Geology* (1855; 4th edition 1891), which was the most complete treatment of maritime geology of its day and only slightly modified by the findings of the geological survey of Canada years later. Dawson made his reputation as a geologist of the first rank. He unearthed a fragment of a skeleton of the earliest North American reptile or batrachian (*Dendrerpeton acadianum*), the oldest land snail (*Pupa vetusta*), and the oldest millipede (*Xylobius sigillariae*). He successfully lobbied for the formation of a national scientific organisation, resulting in the creation of The Royal Society of Canada in 1882, for which he served as the first president.[1] (There have been 8 Scottish-born presidents of this Society, with many others who had Scottish parents or grandparents).

From 1850 to 1853, Dawson served as Nova Scotia's first superintendent of education, laying the foundation for the colony's educational system. Then in 1855, he was invited to become principal of McGill College at a time when cows still roamed parts of the campus. Over the next four decades, he would transform McGill from a small but ambitious college into a full-fledged (and widely respected) institution of higher learning. In fact, at the time of Dawson's death in 1899, *The Times* of London wrote "the progress of that institution under his guidance was marvellous. McGill has grown into a richly, though not too richly, endowed University with about 1,300 students and a prestige only excelled in America by that of Harvard."[2]

His paper *On fossil plants from the Devonian rocks of Canada*, published in the *Quarterly Journal of the Geological Society of London* in 1859, is considered a landmark in the history of palaeobotany. Of equal importance was his work on fossil plants of the Devonian and Upper Silurian formations of Canada published by the Geological Survey of Canada in 1871. Dawson discovered a puzzling fossil in 1864, a fragment that appeared to be a foraminifer. The fossil, named by Dawson *Eozoon canadense* (dawn animal of Canada), was presented formally in papers published in the *Quarterly Journal of the Geological Society of London* for February 1865 by Dawson, William Edmond Logan, William Benjamin Carpenter, and Thomas Sterry Hunt. The carefully documented discovery was acclaimed throughout the scientific world as epoch-making. Dawson's *Eozoic Age* would come to rank with others such as the Paleozoic.[3] Since then it has been reclassified and is not now considered to be a biological fossil.

Robert Dick 1820-1891 and James Dick 1823-1902 created artificial soles for shoes when they discovered that the gummy substance known as gutta-percha (latex gum), derived from an equatorial tree, could produce an inexpensive commercial substitute for the leather soles of footwear which could be sold for five shillings. The term "Guttys" originally referred to any type of rubber-soled shoes. For 35 years, they enjoyed great prosperity and created a new industry for Scotland with a record week of sales reaching 34,000 pairs, and total weekly sales never dropping below 20,000 pairs a week. The shoe market declined, but gutta-percha was discovered to be good insulation for electrical cables, and the firm's product was used in the laying of transatlantic cables. Note: James Dowie had used rubber soles as early as 1839.

Robert Dick also used balata, another form of latex, to produce the "Dickbelt", an industrial-strength belting used around the world.[1] The Dick Belt was the original and remains the standard of this type of conveyor belting. It is stronger and tougher than any other belting made and it is unaffected by moisture and does not overly deteriorate with age.[2]

The Dick brothers produced many vulcanisable compounds of gutta-percha of great value, including rubber for tyres, belts, pulley coverings, horseshoes, soles and heels of shoes, wringer rolls, springs, playing balls, and mats. These goods are mixed in the usual way, and vulcanised in the masticator, but not enough to take away the plastic qualities of the gutta-percha. For treating this compound, a special masticator was devised by Dick, the rolling cylinders being hollow, and a Bunsen gas-burner inserted through one end of the hollow axle, while the gases pass off at the other, thus heating both roller and mixture.[3] A Dick Belt made of balata was used on an armoured Goliath-type fighting machine built in India in 1944 and may have been used on the Vezdekhod, which was the first true tank to be developed by Imperial Russia and claimed by Russians as the first tank ever built. Balata was used on the British prototype tank, Little Willie, but discarded in favour of cast flat steel plates.[4]

Image 48 – Dick Balata Belting Advertisement 1926

The Dick Belt produced in 1885 was responsible – by 1946 – "for a trading organisation which encircled the globe". The largest belt ever made was a Dickbelt of 3,000 feet (914 m) for the potash mines of Alsace. There were Dickbelts in every climate, on tea estates in Ceylon, in wheat mills in Chile, in the goldfields of Australia, the jute plants of India, in the rice mills of Burma, in a ropery in New Zealand, carrying wet shale in South Wales, and conveying merchandise in Amsterdam.[5] Note: Thomas Robins in 1892 and Richard Sutcliffe in 1905 are considered inventors of the conveyor belt (for coal), but these were subsequent to the invention of Robert Dick in 1885.

Charles Drummond 1820-1866 printed Season's Greetings cards bearing the message "Compliments of the season". Greeting cards, or their equivalent, have been around for many centuries, and the Chinese exchanged messages of goodwill to celebrate the New Year, as did the Germans from around 1400 AD.[1] But the widespread commercial usage of the modern pictorial greeting card can be traced back to Charles Drummond of Edinburgh, who placed New Year cards in his shop window on 17 December 1841. The cards were sent in envelopes; a one-penny stamp was pasted on the envelope for local Scottish destinations, a two-pence stamp for England and abroad."[2] They proved so popular that the notion of sending seasonal cards took off. Drummond's card, the idea of which he attributed to his photographer friend, **Thomas Sturrock 1820-1907** of Trinity, published in 1841, displayed a fat disembodied face laughing and bearing the legend "A Guid New Year An' Mony o' Them". Note: Drummond's card was two years prior to the Christmas Card of Henry Cole, first created in 1843. Cole's cards were specifically produced to be sent to friends rather than sold to customers but, as he had 1,000 cards made the ones left over after he had mailed his friends were sold in the art shop of Felix Summerly in London's Bond Street.

The design, by Sturrock, was reproduced on copper plate by an Edinburgh engraver, Alexander Aikman, and the finished article was printed and published by Drummond. The card was described later in the Edinburgh *Evening News* in the 1930s thus: "the card showed the curly head of a boy, open-mouthed (minus a tooth in the upper row) with fat, chubby cheeks, merry twinkling eyes and an expression of such hearty laughter that the happy combination, by the natural infectious process, produced the desired result on the onlooker, who was greeted with the wish of 'many happy years.'"[3]

Peter Alexander Halkett 1820-1885 was an amateur inventor and, while serving in the navy, he worked on solving the problem of how to design a boat that would be small and light enough to transport easily on foot through wilderness, but robust enough to carry people in safety across wide bodies of water. His solution was to design a boat in which all components would double as items of clothing or accessories that Halkett assumed the user would be carrying in any event.

He developed two types of inflatable boat intended for use by Arctic explorers. These were the earliest inflatable boats using synthetic material rather than animal skins. Both Halkett's inflatable boats were made of rubber-impregnated "Mackintosh cloth." The "boat cloak" served as a waterproof poncho or cloak until inflated, when it became a one-man boat. A special pocket held bellows for inflation and a blade to turn a walking stick into a paddle. A special umbrella could double as a sail. Halkett also developed a two-man boat which was carried in a knapsack, and could also serve as a waterproof groundsheet. Halkett's boats were used extensively for Arctic exploration, including several of the expeditions mounted to search for Sir John Franklin's lost expedition. John Rae, the famous Arctic explorer, took a Halkett boat on his first expedition in 1846, finding it of great use. Rae maintained his enthusiasm for Peter Halkett's invention through several expeditions. A Halkett boat was left for him at Sault Ste Marie in 1845 and in the record of his first Arctic voyage in 1846-1847 he referred to it in glowing terms. Rae described Peter Halkett as "the ingenious inventor of the portable air-boat, which ought to be the travelling companion of every explorer."[1]

Image 49 – A Halkett boat-cloak in use

Image 50 – A deflated and stowed two-man Halkett boat, oars and umbrella-sail

David Kirkaldy 1820-1897 pioneered the standarised testing of materials used in big civil engineering projects.[1] Robert Woolston Hunt established, in August 1860, the first chemical laboratory associated with an iron and steel firm in America, at Cambria Iron Co. in Johnstown,

Pennsylvania.[2] Early testing for strength and durability goes back to, at least, the Dutch physicist Petrus van Musschenbroek (1692-1791) who developed a machine for the systematic measurement of tensile strength in metal. George Rennie junior also made a significant contribution to the understanding of the strength of materials and some of his correspondence with Thomas Young was published in the *Philosophical Transactions* of The Royal Society in 1818. This included details of a lever testing machine which was used to test a variety of materials, including cast and wrought alloys, wood, and stone (marble, limestone, granite, etc.) in compression and under tension. William Fairbairn also made a significant contribution to the systematic assessment of the strength of materials at high temperatures as early as 1842. The sample could be heated up to "red heat" in a liquid bath heated by a fire grate, which would be removed when the desired temperature had been achieved. Loads up to 446 kilonewtons could be applied to the test pieces by the lever system.[3]

It was, however, Kirkaldy, who expanded testing to include all kinds of materials. He first became involved in testing when he worked for Robert Napier's shipbuilding yard which was building HMS *Black Prince* (launched in 1861), the most powerful warship in the world along with its sister ship HMS *Warrior*. Following on from his three years of research, he published *Results of an Experimental Inquiry into the Comparative Tensile Strength and other properties of various kinds of Wrought-Iron and Steel* (1862). "For the next two and a half years Kirkaldy worked on the design of a massive testing machine that was manufactured in Leeds and installed in premises in London, at The Grove, Southwark." The testing machine was built during 1864/65 by Greenwood & Batley of Leeds. It is 47 ft 6 inches [14.5 m] long, 4 ft 3.5 inches [1.3 m] wide and weighs almost 116 tons [105 tonnes]. It was designed "for the purpose of testing all kinds of constructive materials" by putting these materials "under various stresses, namely, Pulling, Thrusting, Bending, Twisting, Shearing, Punching and Bulging."[4]

"The works was open for trade in January 1866 and engineers soon began to bring him specimens for testing on the great machine: In the years that followed, Kirkaldy gained a worldwide reputation for rigorous and meticulous testing and recording of results, coupled with the highest integrity."[5]

He developed ways of examining the microstructures of materials using a simple optical microscope after polishing and etching specimens taken from components. "Among its many achievements, the machine performed tests for Blackfriars road bridge [opened 1869], the St. Louis Bridge over the Mississippi [built 1867-1874], the Hammersmith Suspension Bridge [opened 1887], the Sydney Harbour Bridge, and the cables used to suspend 'The Skylon' at the 1951 Festival of Britain. The machine was also used in accident investigations, such as the 1879 Tay Bridge disaster and the crash of Britain's Comet airliner in the 1950s."

In 1862, Kirkaldy identified the role of strain rate despite using equipment which would be considered primitive by today's standards. In the context of testing rate, he asserted that "It is absolutely necessary to correctly know the exact conditions under which any tests are made before we can equitably compare results from different quarters".[6]

Abram Lyle 1820-1891 developed Golden Syrup in 1882. One of Britain's most instantly recognisable grocery brands, Lyle's Golden Syrup has been Britain's favourite golden syrup for over a century. Lyle started his working life as a cooper, making barrels for a living, and bought into a sugar refinery – where he learnt how to make sugar (and the syrup we are acquainted with today). He became financially well off, and later adopted the lifestyle of being a provost and a benefactor of many institutions in Greenock, where he grew up.

Lyle realised that money could be made in vast amounts in London and in 1881 he sent two of his sons to Plaistow with one mission – to create and run a sugar refinery. Abram Lyle & Sons started working in 1883, but was soon threatened by closure as the firm came across problems with their cargoes. Lyle was determined that his sons should continue, and knew that during the sugar refining process a thick, gooey, treacly, substance could be made by taking half of the sugar, separating it into its constituent parts (leaving fructose and glucose), then reuniting these with the other half, resulting in golden-coloured syrup (bar a few "secret" processes). This substance usually went to waste, but it could equally be used as a preservative and sweetener in cooking.[1] Thus, in 1883, Lyle's Golden Syrup was created. What had been a by-product of sugar refining – a non-crystallisable syrup – was normally thrown away. Mindful of cost efficiencies, Lyle decided to refine it and obtained a delicious product, which he initially sold to the refinery staff. It proved so popular that a year later, Lyle began selling it commercially. Wooden casks soon gave way to large Lyle's Golden Syrup dispensers that were placed on the shelves of grocery stores. Lyle's Golden Syrup was first filled into tins in 1885 with, today, more than a million tins produced each month.[2]

When the First World War broke out, the gold liquid substance was sold in thick cardboard packaging – but the oozing syrup returned to being sold in tins soon afterwards. The tins themselves, first created in 1885 to replace the shop dispensers, are manufactured using flat sheets of steel that are fused together to make a cylinder shape, before the bottom and top are securely put on. Then the syrup is added, the production process speeding along at a rate of 240 tins per minute.

Research has concluded that over 85% of British people instantly recognise the product, but few would perhaps know that the trademark of a dead lion surrounded by bees arose from Lyle's reading of the Old Testament, with the slogan "Out of the strong came forth sweetness" derived from the biblical character Samson's saying, "Out of the eater came forth meat, and out of the strong came forth sweetness." – Book of Judges, 14:14[3]

Unlike many products that change with time, Lyle's Golden Syrup (and the tins that contain the velvety elixir which often lasts longer than a good bottle of wine), have not altered during the years the syrup has been in production. This is a fact that was duly recognised by Guinness World Records in 2006. "The oldest branding (packaging) for a brand is Tate and Lyle's Golden Syrup (UK). The same packaging has been maintained since 1885 with only slight technical changes during the war due to shortages of materials."[4] The only other change is showing the weight of the contents in grams rather than pounds.

William Lockhart Morton 1820-1898 patented the sheep dip and swing gate. The sheep dip was an important advance in treating scab in sheep, "which is without a doubt the best-known, most dangerous, most destructive, and most dreaded condition."[1]

The treatment in vogue for scab on the station at that time was corrosive sublimate (mercuric chloride) solution and the result of its frequent use was to make the skin of the backs of many of the sheep hard and board-like. The method of treatment consisted of catching the sheep by the hind legs in folds or yards, tying up their legs, then dipping them into the mercuric chloride solution and lifting them on to a grating to drain. The sheep's back was then scraped with an iron hoop before they were released. Due to the constant contact with mercuric chloride, most of the men were affected to some extent with mercury poisoning. At this time, Morton developed the "Dip" (plunge dip) for treating sheep, describing it in *The Geelong Advertiser*. This innovation meant that the rate of dressing sheep could be increased from one or two hundred in a day to over 10,000. Without the "plunge dip" it would have been almost impossible to eradicate sheep scab.[2]

Morton also invented the swing gate and race "by which the sheep followed one another rapidly through a passage too narrow to permit of their turning round; and finally they slide down a slide which terminated the race, and plunged head over ears into the steaming and sulphurous pool, to emerge saturated and staggering upon the battens of the draining-yard, there to stand until the great part of the costly liquid poured from them and flowed back by conduits, duly arranged, into the dip. No handling, no catching, no delay was necessary in this rapid and efficient mode of treatment. The flock ran through almost as fast as if crossing a river, and several thousands a day could be treated thus even more thoroughly than by the old manual system."[3] Note: Although Morton certainly invented the sheep race and patented the sheep dip, he was not the first to invent the dip, as a sheep dip based on using an arsenic powder had already been invented by George Wilson (c1802-1872) of Coldstream, Berwickshire in 1830.

Morton was also an explorer and in July 1859 he "invited twenty businessmen to invest in a Queensland expedition to the Burdekin in hope of a government reward for finding a good port and harbour. This scheme fell through but later that year Morton and two others explored country north of Rockhampton. His account of the trip was given to the Philosophical Institute of Victoria and published in 1860 as *Notes of a recent personal visit to the unoccupied portions of Northern Queensland*. To the Royal Society of Victoria, he proposed the settlement of the Victoria River district in North Australia, claiming that conditions were suitable though labour would have to be imported."[4]

William John Macquorn Rankine 1820-1872 was a founder of the science of thermodynamics, particularly in reference to steam-engine theory. One of Rankine's first scientific works, a paper on fatigue in metals of railway axles (1843), led to new methods of construction. His *Manual of Applied Mechanics* (1858) was of considerable help to designing engineers and architects. His classic *Manual of the Steam Engine and Other Prime Movers* (1859) was the first attempt at a systematic treatment of steam-engine theory. Rankine worked out a thermodynamic cycle of events (the so-called Rankine cycle) used as a standard for the performance of steam-power installations in which a condensable vapour provides the working fluid.[1]

Rankine was the first to formally publish scientific results in thermodynamics. As Professor, Rankine worked closely with Glasgow shipbuilders on radical improvements to the design of vessels and their engines. He introduced the famous "sandwich courses" that required students to work with local engineering firms during their vacations, and he campaigned vigorously for the recognition of Engineering as a degree subject. Largely through his efforts, a Certificate of Proficiency in Engineering Science was introduced in 1863, and in 1872, the degree of BSc was offered for science subjects including Engineering.

Rankine conducted pioneering research in the fields of railway engineering, molecular physics and thermodynamics. He wrote more than 150 scientific papers and manuals as well as textbooks which became standard works of reference for students.[2]

He was awarded the Gold Medal for his essay *The Undulatory Theory of Light* and a prize for his essay *Methods of Physical Investigation*. In 1848, he started a series of researches on molecular physics and on thermodynamics. His paper *Mechanical Action of Heat*, (1850) was read at The Royal Society of Edinburgh. This was followed by *On the General Law of Transformation of Energy*, (1853) and he published his four great textbooks, all of which went to multiple editions: *Manual of Applied Mechanics*, (1858), *Manual of the Steam-engine and Other Prime Movers*, (1859); M*anual of Civil Engineering*, (1861) and *Machinery and Millwork*, (1869). He jointly authored *Treatise on Shipbuilding, Theoretical and Practical*, (1866); undertook consultancy work and devised, in 1859, the Rankine Temperature Scale for scientific experiments.[3]

Rankine examined the rolling, dipping, and heaving motion of ships in waves. His two-dimensional analysis of the flow of water around circular and oval bodies enabled him to determine the waterlines of a ship that would create a minimum of friction as it moved through the sea; he also calculated the efficiency of propellers. A number of his papers were devoted to the exposition of elementary ways of solving hydrodynamical problems. He devised a simple method for obtaining a graphical representation of streamlines to demonstrate propositions in hydrodynamics. [4]

Rankine defined the entropy function and its implications for the theory of thermodynamics which he developed. Rankine's work was extended by James Clerk Maxwell. Rankine wrote on earth pressures in soil mechanics, and the stability of walls. He also developed methods to solve the force distribution in frame structures and worked on hydrodynamics and the design of ships.[5]

With physicists Rudolf Clausius and William Thomson, Rankine is one of the founders of "theoretical thermodynamics". Rankine introduced the term "potential energy" in 1853, and during his apprenticeship to John Macneill, surveyor to the Irish Railway Commission, he developed a technique, later known as Rankine's method, for laying out railway curves, fully exploiting the theodolite and making a substantial improvement in accuracy and productivity over existing methods.[6]

Alexander John Skene 1820-1894 was a land surveyor in Australia at a time when many people in Victoria in the sixth decade of the 19th century were pressuring the colonial government to release more land and Skene was appointed to investigate what suitable, surveyed land was available. His "final report provided a simple but contentious regional evaluation that influenced the drafting and administration of Victoria's first [land] selection Acts in 1860, 1862 and 1865" and he was "a prime mover in the compilation of the first comprehensive and reliable map of Victoria, produced in 1876 on a scale of eight miles to the inch, and also one of the most accurate of the early maps of Australia, first published in 1880."[1]

Patrick Stirling 1820-1895 was a locomotive designer who produced a 2-2-2 type of passenger locomotive with outside cylinders and inside bearings to all axles for the Glasgow and South Western Railway around 1855. He then became locomotive superintendent of the Great Northern

Railway at Doncaster, and in 1867 produced the 0-4-2 type mixed-traffic (passengers and freight) locomotive with this design lasting 28 years. When he joined the Great Northern Railway, he designed two versions of 2-2-2. The outcome, in 1870, was a locomotive with 8-feet 1-inch (2.5 m) drivers, designed specifically for high speed expresses between York and London. The norm in those days was inside cylinders, but these had frequent failures of the cranked axle shafts, and with such large drivers they would have set the boiler too high. He therefore used outside cylinders with a four-wheeled bogie for lateral stability at the front end.[1]

Image 51 – Great Northern Railway – Stirling Single "Eight-Footer"

Stirling's most famous construction was the 4-2-2 steam locomotive Stirling single called "eight-footer" because of the 8 ft (2.4 m) diameter driving wheel. That engine type set speed records during the race to the north with the average train speed between engine-changing of more than 60 mph (96.5 km/h) in 1895.[2] A total of 53 were built at Doncaster between 1870 and 1895. They were able to haul 275-ton (250-tonne) trains at an average of 50 mph (80 km/h), with a top speed, on lighter trains, of 85 mph (122 km/h), taking part in the 1895 Race to the North. GNR Stirling No 775 made the 82 miles (132 km) to York in 1 hour 16 minutes at an average speed of 64.7 mph (108 km/h).[3]

Thomas Taylor 1820-1910 is credited with the introduction of plant pathology into US federal agricultural research and was responsible for the first USDA publications on microscopic plant pathogens.[1] As microscopist to the US Department of Agriculture, he suggested that markings of the palms of the hands and the tips of the fingers could be used for identification in criminal cases. Although reported in 1877 in the *American Journal of Microscopy* and *Popular Science and Scientific American*, the idea was apparently never pursued from this source. This was at least one year before Henry Faulds published his comments on fingerprints in Japan. In 1823, John Evangelist Purkinji, a professor of anatomy at the University of Breslau, Prussia (now Wroclaw in Poland), published the first paper on the nature of fingerprints and suggested a classification system based on nine major types. However, he failed to recognise their individualising potential. By 1856, William Herschel began to use thumbprints on documents both as a substitute for written signatures for illiterates and to verify document signatures.[2]

James Croll 1821–1890 was the first to suggest that changes in the shape of the Earth's orbit from elliptical to nearly circular to elliptical again might explain the onset and retreat of ice ages. His theory received support in the 1970s when rhythmic shifts in the Earth's angle of orientation to the Sun and changes in orbit were recognised as creating cool summers, which in turn have been identified as key triggers of ice ages.[1]

Croll's many works included *The Philosophy of Theism* (1857), *Climate and Time, in their Geological Relations* (1875), *Climate and Cosmology* (1885) and *The Philosophic Basis of Evolution* (1890). His work which linked climate to orbital variations was well ahead of it time. Now called "Milankovitch Cycles", credit went to a Serbian scientist born four years after Croll's book was published and more than fifteen years after Croll began developing these ideas.[2]

Croll proposed that changes in the orbit of Earth would result in changes in the severity of winters, which would generate appropriate changes in snowfall, and then feedback from whitening by reflection of sunlight during the rest of the year. All these various ideas introduced important new concepts to the understanding of climate change. And all of them were insufficient or wrong, at least as far as explaining the sequence of the ice ages, which had not yet been well established. For instance, Croll's explanations lacked the data that they were aiming to explain. Another problem was that Croll's scheme made the last ice age much older than observed. Croll's approach was too far ahead of the evidence, and he gave an explanation for climate cycles before such cycles were known or suspected.[3]

Croll noted how the ice sheets themselves would influence climate. When snow and ice had covered a region, they would reflect most of the sunlight back into space. Sunlight would warm bare, dark soil and trees, but a snowy region would tend to remain cool. If a large land mass, such as India, was covered with ice (or anything white), its summers would be colder than those of England. Croll further argued that when a region became cooler, the pattern of winds would change, which would in turn change ocean currents, perhaps removing more heat from the region. Once something started an Ice Age, the pattern could become self-sustaining. "The Ice Age cycles correspond to changes in the Earth's relation to the Sun. In the mid-1800s, this idea received its earliest compelling formulation by the self-taught Scottish scientist James Croll". However, it was discovered that the geologic records do not match Croll's theory well enough to verify it. In the 1930s, the idea that astronomical factors explained ice ages was refined by Serbian mathematician, Milutin Milankovich.[4]

Croll believed that wind was the primary factor in ocean currents. This is only partly true. The deep water currents are not affected but the surface currents, which comprise about 10% of the water in the ocean are, indeed, affected by wind, but they are also influenced by solar heating, gravity and the coriolis force caused by the Earth's rotation.[5] Notwithstanding that his calculations of ice ages were in error, "since his death, Croll's contributions to the development of geology have attracted attention, particularly after the revival in the 1970s of interest in astronomical causes of glaciations."[6]

Richard Dudgeon 1821-1899 made a major improvement on the commonly used screw jack and it found ready use in railway construction and maintenance. The first hydraulic press had been designed by Englishman Joseph Bramah in 1795 and was one of the great innovations of the Industrial Revolution. Dudgeon patented a portable version in 1851 and it soon found widespread use in the railroad industry, as well as in shipbuilding. It could be operated with water, whale oil or even, so it was claimed, whisky (a decidedly Scottish fuel option).

Dudgeon also built one of America's earliest self-propelled road vehicles. His original model was a steam wagon that was built prior to 1857 and it was said to have been destroyed in May of that year when fire consumed the New York Crystal Palace, an exhibition centre built to emulate the more famous Exhibition at London's Crystal Palace of 1851. In 1866, Dudgeon built a similar steam carriage which is still on display in the Smithsonian Institution. It used coal as fuel and could travel up to 48 km/h[1] but, although the machine ran for hundreds of kilometres, it didn't catch on as a mode of popular travel. Dudgeon was an inveterate innovator, and his engineering works became noted for improving and making various types of jacks, steam forging hammers, lifting equipment, hydraulic hole punches for use on heavy plate sheet metal, and tube expanders for roller boilers.

Charles Meldrum 1821-1901 founded the Mauritius Meteorological Society, which he served as secretary for many years and, in 1861, he was appointed government observer. In 1862, he had charge of the small meteorological observatory at Port Louis from where he continued work he had done for the Meteorological Society, collecting and analysing meteorological observations extracted from the logs of all ships using the harbour. By 1865, he had over 160,000 records.

At that time, the relationship between wind and the distribution of atmospheric pressure was only just being clarified in the northern hemisphere. From his outpost, Meldrum produced the first recognisably modern weather maps for the Southern Ocean at about the same time as Alexander Buchan in Edinburgh was doing so for the Atlantic. Meldrum determined the frequency and behaviour of cyclones in the Indian Ocean. Thus, he confirmed earlier hypotheses that the Earth's rotation causes winds around weather systems to flow in opposite directions in the two hemispheres. When sailing ships carried the world's trade and had no communication with the land, his work was of immeasurable practical benefit. He also detected the curving low level inflow which leads to the ascent of air, and consequent formation of clouds and rain. Meldrum exploited his remote situation and made a defining contribution to meteorology.[1]

James Robert Napier 1821-1879 was a marine engineer, but one of his most memorable inventions was an improvement to the vacuum brewer, used in making coffee, first invented in Prussia in the 1830s by Loeff. This was improved by Mme Jeanne Richard of France in 1838, which was further improved by another Frenchwoman, Mme Vassieux and was called the French Balloon design. Later, the design of the vacuum pot changed and the two glass containers were placed side-by-side and connected via a siphon tube (similar to Cona). Britain's James Napier, in particular, is well known for this design. His coffee brewing system was very similar to the Balancing Siphon, which was used in Paris, but it appears to have been developed independently by Napier.

His 1840 prototype coffee maker was composed of standard laboratory equipment, giving it a rather clinical look. The layout is nearly identical to that of the Balancing Siphon, except that there is no balancing mechanism to extinguish the lamp, and the brewing process was subtly different. Ground coffee and boiling water were combined in the jar, and only a small amount of water was placed in the globe. The water in the globe was heated by a spirit heater creating a small amount of steam which was forced through the siphon tube to agitate the coffee and water mixture in the jar. When the flame was extinguished, a vacuum formed which siphoned the brewed coffee though a filter and back into the globe, from which it was served. The Napierian brewer was much preferred in England, and stunningly beautiful silver-plated versions continued to be made into the early part of the 20th century.[1]

Image 52 – Vacuum coffee pot

He also invented the Napier diagram in 1851, on which compass deviation is plotted for various headings and the points are connected by a smooth curve permitting deviation problems to be solved quickly without interpolation; it consists of a vertical line, usually in two parts, each part being graduated for 180° of heading, and two additional sets of lines at an angle of 60° to each other and to the vertical lines. The diagram was a means of correcting compass error on iron ships. The simple nature of this chart belies its advantages in obtaining a fast and reliable correction. Napier's diagrams could be directly plotted from data obtained as a ship was swung, and much was made of the then-new method of least squares in drawing the curves.[2]

Thomas Nelson 1822-1892 made various improvements to the printing process in 1850, and his modified printer was shown at London's Great Exhibition in 1851. His father, also Thomas, founded a publishing company that still exists today and was, in the first decade of the 20th century, one of the world's largest publishers. In 1854, it was also the first British publisher to establish a branch in the United States. Thomas junior made improvements to the printing process, such as: using monotype keyboards; a device that could put hard covers on books at 900 per hour; and standardising books to 6½" x 4¼" (16.5 cm x 10.8 cm) which became known as the Nelson Size. His rotary stereo press used a continuous sheet of paper and could print on both sides simultaneously, using curved stereotypes to enable them to fit against a cylinder, a process that lasted until hot metal was discontinued in printing.

American Richard March Hoe's initial improvement did not include stereo printing and he did not achieve simultaneous printing of both sides of paper until 1870, seven years after compatriot William Bullock's machine and 20 years after Nelson's. It should be noted that neither Hoe nor Nelson invented the rotary printing press, although this is commonly claimed for both of them. Like Bullock, they improved upon the original paper printing rotary press of David Napier, making it more efficient and although Napier's press could produce 2,000 newspapers an hour, the later improvements to output meant it was a much better commercial option for printers as the early Napier rotary printers cost between $4,000 and $5,000 each.[1]

James Thomson 1822-1892 invented the Vortex turbine in 1850. The Vortex had the great advantage that it could work on any head of water from 3-300 feet (1-91 m), it was relatively small, and had an efficiency of 70% to 75%. If fitted with movable guide blades, it would maintain a reasonable efficiency with a low flow of water. The first Vortex turbine in England was supplied to James Cropper who owned paper mills in Burneside near Kendal.[1]

Thomson became best known for his work on the improvement of water wheels, pumps and turbines and his research into the effect of pressure on the freezing point of water.[2] He was an inventor and contributed to the knowledge of centrifugal and jet pumps, paddleboats and water wheels. He published in scientific journals on such subjects as plasticity of ice, crystallisation, liquefaction and air and water currents.[3]

Thomson also invented the integrator, a vital component in the analog computer. "Thomson's invention is an important chronological landmark, marking the beginning of integrator-based analog computers, which were developed by his younger brother, Lord Kelvin, some ten years later. Integrators were used for continuous calculating devices and had many uses such as determining the speed of propellers. They eventually became "embedded in real-time calculation systems, initiating the class of technology known today as control systems."[4]

Robert William Thomson 1822-1873 – not John Boyd Dunlop – invented the pneumatic tyre. He patented the invention, so important to the popularity of the bicycle, in 1845. Thomson was an inveterate inventor who patented a self-filling pen, a road steamer, a steam omnibus, machinery to improve sugar production, steam gauge improvements, steam tractors and steam boilers. None of these were original inventions, only modifications, nor did he invent the fountain pen as is sometimes claimed, and even the self-filling pen had been first patented in 1831 by American John Jacob Parker. He took out 14 patents between 1845 and 1873 and made a number of other innovations that he didn't patent. His road steamers could pull four coal wagons with a total weight of over 36 tonnes up steep hills in Edinburgh and they used solid India rubber tyres that he had patented in 1867. One of his first inventions was the reversible mangle for pressing water out of washed clothes.

Thomson is credited with inventing the ribbon saw, the first portable steam crane, a prototype elliptical rotary engine and the hydraulic dry dock (it is not stated when the latter was made by Thomson but in America Nathaniel Griswold had a petition referred to the Committee on Naval Affairs on 24 June 1841 concerning a hydraulic dry dock). Thomson was the first person to detonate explosives by using an electrical charge and became supervisor for the construction of the South Eastern Railway where he had to blast chalk cliffs.[1]

Thomson's Aerial Wheels were inflated hollow belts of India rubber with air enclosed within a strong outer casing of leather which was bolted to the wheel. He demonstrated them in London in 1847 by attaching them to horse-drawn carriages and they apparently improved comfort and reduced noise. Although a set of his tyres covered some 2,000 km without exhibiting any great wear and tear, Thomson wanted strong thin rubber to use for the inner tubes. The main producer, North British Rubber Company, was unable to meet his needs so further development on his tyres ceased. In 1847, the tyres on Thomson's steamers cost £42 each, but by the time Dunlop reinvented the pneumatic tyre, the price had dropped considerably. "Mechanical road transport in England was limited to the agricultural traction engines, which were allowed, as a favour, to clank along the high roads at the speed of the man who walked in front with a red flag, and even at those low speeds their hauling capacity was very poor. Thomson, by his invention of rubber tyres of great cross-section which flattened themselves under the weight of the engine, at once doubled the hauling power and allowed his engines to be run at speeds up to ten miles an hour [16 km/h] whenever the Red Flag Act permitted it."[2]

George Aitken Clark 1823-1873 developed a six-cord, soft finished thread around 1866. "This thread, the first ever suitable for machine use, revolutionised the sewing industry, and therefore he called it 'Our New Thread.'"[1] Before Elias Howe's invention of the sewing machine in 1846, thread was usually made of three cords and was used for hand sewing. The thread had a glazed finish and was too wiry and uneven for machine use.

In 1856, Clark went to the United States, where the thread used in machine-made garments, particularly uniforms, was seen to be very unsatisfactory. To avoid the high duty charged on imports, the firm resolved in 1864 to establish a branch factory at Newark, New Jersey, to produce six-cord cable thread. This superior product solved the machine-thread problem and enhanced public reception of ready-made clothes after the American Civil War.

Henry Eckford 1823-1905 was the most famous breeder of sweet peas, transforming the plant from a minor horticultural subject into the queen of annuals. Liberty Hyde Bailey called him "the prince of specialists". In 1888, he moved to the village of Wem in Shropshire where he perfected the breeding of his *Grandiflora* sweet peas, which in size of bloom and general performance were a great improvement over previous varieties.[1]

Thomas Login 1823-1874 was an engineer involved in the Darjeeling and Roorkee roads in India, and worked on the Ganges Canal and other irrigation canals. "One able Civil Engineer, Mr Thomas Login, proved conclusively that protective works, at a comparatively small expense, would ensure the safety of the Canal. He raised the crests of the falls in some places by planking, and crib-work filled with bowlders [sic] was placed below them in the bed of the canal. By these means water-cushions were formed below the falls, which materially reduced the destructive effect of the falling water".[1] It was mainly due to Login's sound judgment, sturdy independence, and having practically proved what could be done at comparatively small expense, that overtaxed India was saved from the great expense that was proposed to be incurred in remodelling the canal, and another serious matter, the closing of the canal for one or two years.

He took a leading part in establishing the works at Roorkee in the Department of Public Works, North-Western Provinces of India, from the end of 1847 to April 1854. He "was employed during the whole of this time on most important works connected with mountain torrents situated between Roorkee and Hurdwar. Under his management the works at Dhunowri in connection with the Rutmoo torrent, and those for the passage of the Puttri torrent over the canal channel, were begun and completed – the latter, as connected with springs in which the flowings of the canal channel had to be laid 17 feet [5 m] below their surface, was a work of extraordinary difficulty and engineering skill – the whole of the details having been carried out by Mr Login with great success."

Login then worked in Burma till 1856, then was appointed successively Executive Engineer of the Ganges and Darjeeling Road, and of the Roorkee and Dehra roads. After this, he had charge of the Northern Division of the Ganges Canal (described above). After again being engaged on road works, and in charge of saltworks, he went to Sealkote in 1864, and made the surveys for a projected canal in the Rechna Doab. In 1865, he was transferred to Umballa, as Executive Engineer of the 7th division of Grand Trunk Road In passing through Egypt, he was much impressed with the mode of cotton cultivation practiced there, which he considered had many advantages over that customary in India, and on his arrival at Umballa, he carried out some experiments on the ridge and furrow system, which apparently produced a much larger yield than the native broadcast system.[2]

William Malcolm 1823-1890 established the first rifle telescope manufacturing business in the USA in 1855. He produced the best telescopic rifle sight up to that time and it was considered superior to any other telescopic sights made for many years. Malcolm did not copy the Chapman-James design; while working for a telescope maker, he had learned optical principles, how to make lenses, the importance of precise lens adjustment and to fabricate the metal tubes to hold lenses.

Malcolm also was the first to use achromatic lenses, which are a combination of lenses that limit colour refraction in an optical piece. Achromatic lenses gave a much better definition of the target, a flatter field of view and a clear definition at the edge of any object. He also made the windage and elevation adjustments more precise than the Chapman-James sight. All of these design improvements were due to his telescope-making experience. The telescopic rifle sights he produced were between 3x and 20x power and considered to be the best available at that time; they had lenses ground for the "normal eye" or were custom ground for the person purchasing the telescopic sight.[1]

James Oliver 1823-1908 developed the chilled plough, a type of plough with a very hard surface that could more readily turn over heavy soil and, due to its hard outer skin, required less maintenance than other contemporary ploughs. Americans had for long been actively improving ploughs, such as William Ashmead's wrought-iron mouldboard and the cast-steel plough of John Deere in 1837. Oliver's 1868 design of the chilled plough was a salient event in the evolution of the plough. Scottish-born Oliver, who had come to America in 1834, became part owner and manager of a plough factory in South Bend, Indiana, and through experiments, he found that quickly cooling the cast iron of the plough in a stream of water left the share hard and shiny, making it easier to plough as the soil was less likely to stick to the share compared to other metal ploughs. He also discovered how to anneal the plough castings so that the softer parts became sufficiently pliable to "work out their strains from shrinkage in cooling without affecting the hardness of the chilled faces."[1] Oliver started manufacturing his ploughs in mid-1868 at the South Bend Iron Works and went on to register 45 patents. His plough became the most popular in the world, originally selling for $6.50 each, rising a dollar in 1863. Some 10% of his production was patented steel ploughs, sold at $17.50 each. In 1878, he sold 62,799 ploughs rising to 200,000 ploughs annually, with sales to all parts of North and South America, the British Empire, Europe and Japan. Oliver's ploughs were popular because of their quality; they could plough heavy soil more easily, and they were made with numbered detachable parts for easy replacement.

By the turn of the century, Oliver employed more than 1,000 men and boys at one of the nation's largest agricultural equipment factories. In prosperous years, it could turn out as many as 300,000 ploughs, with specialised models for every purpose from breaking the thick prairie sod of Nebraska to cultivating the cotton fields of Alabama or the sugar plantations of Cuba. There was even a model for use in the steep hillside vineyards of the Rhineland, designed to throw the earth to the uphill side whichever direction the plough was moving. The Oliver Chilled Plow was one of the most successful agricultural implements of the 19th century, and the firm remained an important manufacturer of farm equipment into the 1970s.[2]

John Elder 1824-1869 added an extra cylinder that provided 30%-40% greater fuel efficiency over existing engines and opened the way to longer and faster sea voyages by steamships as they could go much further without refuelling. The compound engine used both high and low-pressure steam and became the most common steam engine worldwide. John Elder had fourteen patents relating to enhancements of the steam engine, improving both efficiency and efficacy. In July 1854, the first trial of the compound engine was undertaken in the screw steamer *Brandon* and reduced to 1.47 kilograms per indicated horse-power per hour (indicated horsepower is the theoretical power of a reciprocating engine assuming that it is completely efficient in converting the energy contained in the expanding gases in the cylinders). Previously, the best result had been 1.8 - 2.0 kgs/ihp.[1]

Elder, with his partner Charles Randolph, moved into shipbuilding in 1858, and in 1861 completed their first ship, mundanely named *No14*. When he died in 1869, his Fairfield Yard had built ships totalling 22,893 tonnes, while its nearest rival, also on the River Clyde, built 12,179 tonnes. The company also built gear machinery for factories and exported three giant iron floating docks to the Dutch East Indies (Indonesia), Vietnam and Peru. Elder was interested in the well-being of his workers and matched £ for £ their cash contributions to an accident fund. John Elder died prematurely at 45 years of age when he was still engaged in innovative designs for ships and in planning houses and education for his workers and their families.

Alexander Fraser 1824-1898 transformed Yangon (Rangoon) into the commercial and political hub of British Burma. His design for the new city was based mostly on that of William Montgomerie and was constructed on a grid plan on delta land, bounded to the east by the Pazundaung Creek and to the south and west by the Yangon River. Fraser's career is notable for his direction of public works in India, especially railways and lighthouses, and his service in the British government in India.[1]

From 1873 to 1879, he acted as Chief Engineer to the Public Works Department in the North West Provinces. The lighthouses he built were based on designs used by Alan Stevenson.[2] Fraser arranged for the purchase of the design from the Stevensons, who oversaw the designs for the other lights in the series and who, not least, supervised their entire building. There is no evidence that any of the Stevensons (lighthouse engineers) travelled to India or Burma. "We must regard Fraser – the British Army Officer from the Royal Engineers – as the first great Imperial Lighthouse engineer."[3]

Fraser was given the task of building a lighthouse on the Alguada Reef, at the mouth of the Irrawaddy River, in Burma. The 120ft (36.5 m) lighthouse became one of the most important in India and even survived the onslaught of the 2004 Boxing Day tsunami. "General Fraser persuaded the Governor of India the Alguada should be built of stone, rather than iron, which was the favoured construction material of the time.[4]

"The railways of India are Alexander Fraser's first memorial; the lighthouses which he surveyed and built – on Alguada Reef, Galle in Ceylon, and the Oyster Reef, Krishna Shoal, Akyab and the Rangoon River estuary in Burma – are the second. Last but not least came his layouts for wharfs, docks and cantonments at Moulmein and above all at Rangoon, the latter being a truly pukka street plan where Fraser Street still keeps his name in remembrance".[5]

John Kerr 1824-1907 discovered, in 1875, the Kerr Effect – the differential refraction of light by some materials when they are in a strong electric field. The Kerr Effect was the first electro-optic effect to be discoved.[1] A strong electric potential, applied in a direction normal to a beam of light, causes a difference in refractive index for light polarised in the plane of the field and light polarised normal to it, an effect known as birefringence. This causes the resultant polarisation of the light to change.

The effect is exploited in the Kerr cell which is used in applications such as shutters in high-speed photography, with shutter-speeds as fast as 100 nanoseconds. In 1928, August Karolus and Otto Mittelstaedt used a Kerr cell to modulate a beam of light in order to measure its speed. Earlier measurements had used mechanical means of modulation achieving frequencies of around 10 kHz while the Kerr cell allows frequencies of 10 MHz and greater precision of measurement.

Kerr's original glass, induction coil, and crossed polariser set-up is considered the first Kerr cell. Modern Kerr cells usually consist of a transparent shell containing nitrobenzene or some other liquid, rather than being composed of glass. The principle upon which they are based is still the same, however, and exposure to an electric potential allows light to pass through the analyser, which is positioned so that it blocks all light under ordinary conditions. Pulses of light can be controlled so quickly with a modern Kerr cell that the devices are often used as high-speed shutter systems for photography and are sometimes alternatively known as Kerr electro-optical shutters. In addition: Kerr cells have been used to measure the speed of light; are incorporated in some lasers; and are becoming increasingly common in telecommunications devices. The invention of lasers has led to the discovery of a special case of the Kerr effect, known as the AC Kerr effect, which is induced when the electric field in a material is exposed to stems from light itself.

A year after his studies of the electro-optic Kerr effect, Kerr observed a similar phenomenon related to magnetic fields, which is now called the Kerr magneto-optic effect. To demonstrate this effect, he reflected a plane-polarised light from the polished pole of an electromagnet. When Kerr turned the magnet on, the light became elliptically polarised. As he showed, the extent of the effect depends upon the position of the surface from which the light is reflected with respect to the magnetisation direction as well as to the plane of the light's incidence.[2]

James Samuel 1824-1874 patented, in 1844, the bolted fishplate used on railway lines and which was successful in reducing accidents caused by rails shaking loose their ties. Early in 1858 he made, in conjunction with Irishman John Pitt Kennedy, of the Institute of Civil Engineering, the plans and estimates for the line of railway from Smyrna to Cassaba, and thence to Ushak, in Asia Minor. In 1861, he went to the United States to report on and estimate for the completion of the Grand Rapids & Indiana Railroad for the State of Michigan. He was then continuously engaged in inspecting and reporting upon various railways in Austria, France, Germany, and Russia. In May 1863, he accompanied a party of engineers to examine and report upon the feasibility of constructing a ship canal from the port of Greytown, on the Atlantic, up the River San Juan, and through the lakes of Nicaragua and Managua, to the bay of Tamarindo, on the Pacific Ocean; but, after a careful examination, he found that the cost of this route, as laid down by the French engineers – from whose preliminary surveys the scheme originated – would be far in excess of that contemplated by the promoters, and the project was abandoned.

In the beginning of 1864, he was appointed, together with Colonel George Talcott, joint Engineer-in-Chief of the Mexican railway from the port of Vera Cruz to the cities of Puebla and Mexico City. Talcott retired from his connection with the line at the latter end of 1866. In 1871 and 1873 Samuel built a railway of three feet gauge in Cape Breton for developing the extensive coal mines in that region. In 1860, he exchanged the appointment of Chief Engineer to the Mexican railway for that of consulting engineer, a post he held till his death.[1]

Alexander Kennedy Smith 1824-1881 was responsible for many of the major gasworks in the state of Victoria, Australia. In 1853, he moved to Australia to build the gas works for the Melbourne Gas and Coke Company, which commenced supplies to the public on New Year's Day, 1856 – a remarkable achievement despite the effects of flooding and the Bendigo gold rush, which impacted labour supplies. Smith became a consultant but continued building gasworks in Victoria (Ballarat, Castlemaine, and Sandhurst) and New South Wales (Newcastle). As a consultant, he designed detailed plans for the provision of gas supplies to other Australian locations (Sydney, Portland, Warrnambool, and Stawell) as well as internationally to Shanghai, Yokohama, and, in New Zealand, to Auckland, Dunedin and Nelson. He was consulting engineer for the Melbourne and Suburban Railway Company, and he designed and built mining machinery and sawmills as well as the water supplies for Sydney, Bendigo, and South Yarra (Melbourne).[1]

William Thomson 1824-1907 (Lord Kelvin) is rated as one of the world's great physicists. His achievements were many and diverse. He formulated the dissipation of energy principle that is summarised in the Second Law of Thermodynamics. His knowledge of engineering made it possible to lay the first telegraph cable across the Atlantic Ocean. He invented: a temperature scale; instruments for receiving cable signals; a mariner's compass; and a deep-sea sounding apparatus; and he made significant contributions to the theories of elasticity, magnetism, vortex motion, and electricity.[1] During his lifetime, Thomson published more than 600 scientific papers on various subjects ranging from navigation at sea to the laws of thermodynamics. He was also a brilliant inventor, capable of finding practical solutions to highly complicated problems.

In 1845, Thomson mathematically analysed Michael Faraday's magnetic lines of force and wrote a letter to him in August of that year explaining how his calculations predicted that magnetic fields should affect the plane of polarised light. Faraday had, many years before, experimented with light and magnetism, but without observing any connection between the two. Encouraged by Thomson's prediction, Faraday decided to readdress the problem and began a new series of experiments in his laboratory. By mid-September he had proven that magnetism and light are related, discovering what has come to be known as the Faraday Effect.[2]

In 1846, when only twenty-two years of age, he accepted the chair of natural philosophy in the University of Glasgow, which he filled for fifty-three years, attaining universal recognition as one of the greatest physicists of his time. The Glasgow chair was a source of inspiration to scientific men for more than half a century, and many of the most advanced researches of other physicists grew out of the suggestions which Thomson scattered as sparks from his anvil. One of his earliest papers dealt with the age of the Earth, and brought him into collision with the geologists of the Uniformitarian school, who were claiming thousands of millions of years for the formation of the stratified portions of the Earth's crust.

Thomson's calculations on the conduction of heat showed that at some time between twenty million and four hundred million, probably about one hundred million, years ago, the physical conditions of the Earth must have been entirely different from those which now obtain. This led to a long controversy, in which the physical principles held their ground.

"Thomson's speculations as to the age of the Earth and the Sun were inaccurate, but he did succeed in pressing his contention that biological and geologic theory had to conform to the well-established theories of physics".[3] Importantly, although he was wrong about the age of the Sun and Earth, he showed that the age of the Earth isn't infinite (a common thesis at the time), and he also demonstrated that the age of the Earth can be calculated using physical principles.

In 1848, Thomson devised the Kelvin temperature scale (in 1892, Thomson was created Baron Kelvin of Largs in the County of Ayr. The title derives from the River Kelvin, which runs by the grounds of the University of Glasgow, where he was Professor of Natural Philosophy – i.e. Physics). Unlike the Celsius and Fahrenheit scales, both of which are used in daily life, the Kelvin scale is more often used by scientists today. The zero point on the Kelvin scale is equal to -273.15 degrees on the Celsius scale. Thomson noted that molecules stop moving at absolute zero. "This zero point is considered the lowest possible temperature of anything in the universe".[4]

In 1851, Thomson proposed the extension of Johann Carl Friedrich Gauss' system of absolute units to electromagnetism. He applied the principles of energy, calculated the absolute electromotive force of a Daniell cell, and determined the absolute measure of the resistance of a wire from the heat produced in it by a known current. In the same year, he was able to give public recognition to James Prescott Joule's theory, along with a cautious endorsement in a major mathematical treatise, *On the Dynamical Theory of Heat*. Thomson's essay contained his version of the Second Law of Thermodynamics, which was a major step toward the unification of scientific theories.[5]

Following on from the work of Joule, his investigations into the nature of heat led other scientists to the first successful liquefaction of gases, such as hydrogen and helium, and later to the science of low-temperature physics. Thomson's definition of the absolute temperature scale is especially important in the field of superconductivity. Superconductors are materials which are particularly efficient at conducting electricity, but usually only at extremely low temperatures. This phenomenon was only discovered after Thomson's death.

Also in 1851, prompted by the competing investigations of William John Macquorn Rankine and Rudolf Clausius, Thomson finally laid down two propositions: the first a statement of Joule's mutual equivalence of work and heat; and the second a statement of Nicolas Léonard Sadi Carnot's criterion for a perfect engine. His long-delayed acceptance of Joule's proposition rested on a resolution of the problem of the irrecoverability of mechanical effect lost as heat. He now believed that work "is lost to man irrecoverably though not lost in the material world". Therefore, no destruction of energy can take place in the material world without an act of power possessed only by the supreme ruler, yet transformations take place which remove irrecoverably from the control of man sources of power which … might have been rendered available. In other words, God alone could create or destroy energy (i.e. energy was conserved in total quantity), but human beings could make use of transformations of energy, for example in water-wheels or heat-engines. In a private draft, Thomson referred these transformations to a universal statement that "Everything in the material world is progressive".[6]

On the one hand, this statement expressed the geological directionalism of Cambridge dons such as William Hopkins and Adam Sedgwick in opposition to the steady-state uniformitarianism of Charles Lyell; but on the other, it could be read as agreeing with the radical evolutionary doctrines of the subversive *Vestiges of Creation* written anonymously by Scotsman Robert Chambers of *Chambers Encyclopedia* fame (1844). In his published statement, Thomson opted instead for universal dissipation of energy, a doctrine which reflected the Presbyterian (Calvinist) views of a transitory visible creation rather than a universe of ever-upwards progression. Work dissipated as heat would be irrecoverable to human beings, for to deny this principle would be to imply that they could produce mechanical effect by cooling the material world with no limit except the total loss of heat from the world.

This reasoning crystallised in what later became the canonical "Kelvin" statement of the second law of thermodynamics, first enunciated by Thomson in 1851: "it is impossible, by means of inanimate material agency, to derive mechanical effect from any portion of matter by cooling it below the temperature of the coldest of the surrounding objects". This statement provided Thomson with a new demonstration of Carnot's criterion of a perfect engine. Having resolved the recoverability issue, he also quickly adopted a dynamical theory of heat, making it the basis of Joule's proposition of mutual equivalence and abandoning the Carnot–Clapeyron notion of heat as a state function (with the corollary that in any cyclic process the change in heat content is zero).[7]

In 1852, Thomson described the theoretical basis for the heat pump. His key theoretical advance was to overturn the notion that heat could only flow "downhill" – from the hot to the cold. A heat pump collects low-grade heat and can deliver it at a higher temperature, but needs some imported energy to do so. He foresaw its first application in buildings for cooling, and millions of air conditioners, chillers and refrigerators (i.e. heat pumps) are now manufactured and installed every year. "Credit for having thought of the process goes to Lord Kelvin. In 1852, he had already set down the principles of a thermodynamic machine that produced heat as well as cold."[8]

Also in 1852, Thomson argued that the key issue in the interpretation of the Second Law of Thermodynamics was the explanation of irreversible processes. He noted that if entropy always increased, the universe would eventually reach a state of uniform temperature and maximum entropy from which it would not be possible to extract any work. He called this the Heat Death of the Universe. With Rankine, he proposed a thermodynamical theory based on the primacy of the energy concept, on which he believed all physics should be based. He said the two laws of thermodynamics expressed the indestructibility and dissipation of energy. He also tried to demonstrate that the equipartition theorem was invalid.[9]

In 1853, Thomson investigated the oscillatory character of the discharge of the Leyden jar – the foundation of the work of Heinrich Hertz and of wireless telegraphy.

From 1855, Thomson developed earlier work done by Sadi Carnot and James Prescott Joule on the two thermodynamic laws of equivalence and transformation, as well as producing the doctrine of available energy.[10]

His acquaintance with Hermann Ludwig Ferdinand von Helmholtz laid the basis for developing the mathematical theory of electrical oscillation. This in turn led to his work on wireless telegraphy. His 1856 paper, *Dynamical illustrations of the magnetic and helicoidal rotary effects of transparent bodies on polarised light*, laid the groundwork for James Clerk Maxwell's subsequent theories on electromagnetism, while the mirror galvanometer that he designed was crucial in the successful laying of the first transatlantic submarine cable in 1865.[11] By reducing the stresses on the telegraph cable while increasing the speed of transmission from two to 20 words a minute, the galvanometer made the transatlantic telegraph possible.[12]

In 1858, Thomson patented improvements to the mirror galvanometer – a mechanical meter that senses electric current, except that instead of moving a needle, it moves a mirror. The mirror reflects a beam of light, which projects onto a meter, and acts as a long, weightless, massless pointer. It had been invented in 1826 by German physicist Johann Christian Poggendorff, but Thomson's improvements were far more sensitive than any which preceded it, enabling the detection of the slightest defect in the core of a cable during its manufacture and submersion. Moreover, it proved the best apparatus for receiving messages through a long cable.

The Atlantic Cable Expedition of 1857 was an attempt to lay a telegraph cable across the Atlantic Ocean. The expedition was initially unsuccessful, but Thomson's mirror galvanometer helped to get the project back on track. The invention was designed to measure electric current flowing through the newly laid cables, a vital indicator of successful installation. The project was completed in 1866, and the first transatlantic telegraph cable had been laid. The effect was dramatic! Contemporary accounts tell of the fascination of the operators that messages would actually be received hours before they were sent (due to the time differences at the two ends of the cable). Due to the time taken for ships to cross the Atlantic, people did not think much about the time difference – the cable brought it home to them with a start! As with the overland cables, undersea cables were laid rapidly. Within 20 years there were 107,000 miles (172,200 km) of undersea cables linking all parts of the world. The original two cables ceased to work in 1872 and 1877, but by this time four other cables were in operation. It was not until the 1960s that the first communication satellites offered a serious alternative to the cable.[13]

Also in 1858, Thomson invented the siphon recorder which was the first recording device to use electrostatic forces. It was used to automatically record the receipt of a telegraph message, as a wiggling ink line on a roll of paper tape. "Thomson's highly sensitive siphon recorder could both detect [the weak telegraphic signals] and record them. A small electrical charge was introduced into the ink and a continuous fine stream of ink was jetted out onto a moving paper strip, printing a straight line if there was no communication signal received from the telegraph cable. The signal record was a line that wavered from left to right according to the differing pulses and could be translated into standard alphabetic text by a trained operator. As the printing mechanism did not touch the paper, it did not impede the delicate movement resulting from the faint signal that it was designed to record. Listed as patent GB2147 in 1867, it is generally considered to be the first ink jet printer." [14]

Cable telegraphy gave an impetus to the scientific measurement of electrical quantities, and for many years Thomson was a member of the British Association for Advancement of Science formed in 1861 to consider electrical standards and to develop units; these are still in use. Thomson first became Scientific Adviser to the Atlantic Telegraph Company in 1857, sailing on the *Agamemnon* and *Great Eastern* during the cable-laying expeditions. He laid down the design parameters of long submarine cables and discovered that the conductivity of copper was greatly affected by its purity. A major part of the success of the Atlantic cable in 1866 was due to Thomson, who received a knighthood for his contribution. Note: The British Association for Advancement of Science was founded in 1831 following a suggestion by James Dewar. Its founders included fellow Scot James Finlay Weir Johnston.

In 1867, Thomson invented the Kelvin water dropper, which is a type of electrostatic generator. Kelvin referred to the device as his water-dropping condenser. The device uses falling water drops to generate voltage differences by using positive feedback and the electrostatic induction occurring between interconnected, oppositely charged systems. [15]

In and from 1867, Thomson invented new depth sounders and, also, a series of tidal meters, analysers and predictors which allowed the prediction of the tide in any port in the world. He devised the method of reduction of tides by harmonic analysis, his system being based on the fact that any periodic motion or oscillation can always be resolved into the sum of a series of simple harmonic motions. This theory was built upon several other important developments beforehand. For example, Eudoxas (356 BC) explained the irregular motions of the planets by combinations of uniform circular motions. Also, in the early 19th century, Frenchman Pierre-Simon, marquis de Laplace, recognised the "existence of partial tides that might be expressed by the cosine of an angle increasing uniformly with the time, and also applied the essential principles of the harmonic analysis to the reduction of high and low waters." However, Thomson is the one associated with taking this information and moving it into a practical realm. Thus, as an expert, he prepared for the British Association for the Advancement of Science advice for the purpose of the extension, improvement, and harmonic analysis of tidal observations.

The methods for the prediction of the tides are defined as either harmonic or non-harmonic. By the harmonic method, "the elementary constituent tides, represented by harmonic constants, are combined in to a composite tide. By the non-harmonic method, the predictions are made by applying to the times of the moon's transits and to the mean height of the tide systems of differences to take account of average conditions and various inequalities due to changes in the phase of the moon and in the declination and parallax of the moon and sun."[16]

Thomson's device "effectively mechanised the operation of the planimeter, making it possible to automatically evaluate the integrals required for harmonic analysis". He compared his machine to Charles Babbage's difference engine, the great failed attempt to mechanise the labour of computation. Thomson's "analog" computer succeeded, however; and he built several others following the tidal analyser, with potential applications to a broad range of harmonic phenomena.[17] As a technology, it ushered in a new genre of calculating instrument, the continuous calculating machine[18] (that is, an analog computer – one that is not programmable).

In 1869, Thomson constructed his astronomical clock, which has a number of different dials, showing the relative positions of the sun, stars and planets. Construction of an astronomical clock requires determination of the motion of various celestial bodies in relation to each other. Even for the Earth alone, this is not straightforward. The Earth does not take exactly 24 hours to go around the Sun. Also, it "wobbles" a little on its axis. Thomson's talent as a physicist, and interest in navigation, prompted him to create and patent his own version of an astronomical clock which was said to be as accurate as any in existence at the time.[19]

In 1872, Thomson invented an operational wireline sounding machine. Modifications of this machine ultimately replaced hemp-rope sounding methods. The new wireline machines were faster and more accurate, making it much easier for researchers to survey the ocean depths.[20]

In 1874, he patented the modern form of the mariner's compass (these were made in their thousands by the firm of James White, in which he later became a partner). Three years earlier he had become interested in the possible improvement of the mariner's compass. He found that ordinary compasses suffered from many – and grave – defects, which he promptly set out to rectify. He designed a new compass of his own, which was immune from all outside magnetic disturbances, and also steadier and more sensitive than those in use. He mounted a shorter needle on a lighter card and used a shield to protect the compass from the magnetism of a ship's metal hull. His improved compass was an instant success and, "was used almost universally until the advent of the gyrocompass",[21] and his original compass card design remains in use virtually unchanged today.

In April 1874, he presented a paper to the Society of Telegraph Engineers on *Deep Sea Sounding by Pianoforte Wire*. In this paper, he described his success in sounding to a depth of 2,700 fathoms (just over three miles or 4.8 km). Two years later, after the voyage of HMS *Challenger*, he stated that the old system of sounding by hemp ropes was outmoded.[22] Existing sounding equipment was very basic and time-consuming. A weighted rope was manually lowered to the ocean floor before being hauled back up and measured. Thomson's system used piano wire, which could be raised and lowered mechanically, to lower a small glass tube into the water. The glass tube contained a chemical-based system for recording the depth of water, and the measurements taken could be quickly read once the tube had been brought back to the surface. His depth sounder put Britain decades ahead of other countries in underwater sound technology.

Other instruments he designed included a quadrant electrostatic voltmeter to measure high voltages, and his "multi-cellular" instrument for low voltages. They could be used on alternating or direct current and were free from temperature errors. His balances for precision current measurement were widely used in standardising laboratories.[23] He discovered how to determine the unit of current in both the volt and the ampere and established the measuring unit known as the standard ohm by applying to his measurements of the volt and ampere the consequences of Ohm's Law.[24]

In 1880, Thomson proposed a gyrostat for use by the Royal Navy. He designed the gyrostat to illustrate the more complicated state of motion of a spinning body when free to wander about on a horizontal plane, like a top spun on the pavement, or a hoop or bicycle on the road. It consists essentially of a massive fly-wheel concealed in a metal casing, and its behaviour on a table, or with various modes of suspension or support, serves to illustrate the curious reversal of the ordinary laws of statical equilibrium due to the gyrostatic domination of the interior invisible flywheel, when rotated rapidly. Thomson attempted to formulate mechanical models of the elasticity of matter and the ether, using lattices of linked gyrostats.[25]

Thomson brought together disparate areas of physics – heat, thermodynamics, mechanics, hydrodynamics, magnetism, and electricity – and thus played a principal role in the great and final synthesis of 19th century science, which viewed all physical change as energy-related phenomena. Thomson was also the first to suggest that there were mathematical analogies between kinds of energy. His success as a synthesiser of theories about energy places him in the same position in 19th century physics as Sir Isaac Newton in 17th century physics or Albert Einstein in 20th century physics. All of these great synthesisers prepared the ground for the next grand leap forward in science.[26]

In 1887, Thomson proposed that the tetrakaidecahedron was the best shape for packing equal-sized objects together to fill space with minimal surface area. He thought about this problem in the context of the bubbles which make up a foam. His proposed tetrakaidecahedron actually had some slightly curved faces which improved upon the typical flat-faced polyhedron. Scientists still use packed tetrakaidecahedra as a model for regular, monodisperse foam and the tetrakaidecahedron remained the best contender for a minimal surface area, space-filling shape from 1887 until 1994, when Denis Weaire and Robert Phelan presented a counter-example of a space-filling geometry with even less surface area.

The scale and scope of Lord Kelvin's achievements and their lasting legacy bear full testament to an outstanding scientist, ingenious inventor, and successful business man. Author of 661 scientific papers, and 75 patents, he pioneered the field of thermodynamics, the science and development of refrigeration and of electric light. He set down the foundations for modern communication through the successful laying of the transatlantic telegraph cable. His maxim "To measure is to know" drove him to refine the accuracy of electrical units of measurement, to develop the compass for use in iron ships, and calculating engines for the prediction of the tides, and made him the first to apply mathematics to the question of the ages of the Earth and sun.[27]

In 1924, Albert Einstein described William Thomson, Lord Kelvin, in the Introduction to his paper, *On the Centenary of Kelvin's birth*, "as one of the greatest and most productive thinkers of the nineteenth century."[28]

CHAPTER 4

1825-1849

By the end of the first quarter of the 19th century the Napoleonic War was over and the United Kingdom of Great Britain and Ireland (as the British Isles became following the political union of Ireland with Great Britain on New Year's Day, 1801) was the pre-eminent power in the world – in empire, in trade, in naval control of the oceans and, above all, in industrial output. Two of the most important technical innovations in this period were the development of railways and steamships, both of which permitted faster, safer, more comfortable and more affordable travel for passengers, and faster, cheaper, easier and more reliable shipment of goods.

Those born in the second quarter of the 19th century would go on to play a part in the development of electrical communications, refrigeration, and in the increased production of iron and steel and its use in construction of bridges, buildings, railroads, locomotives and ships, as well as industrial, agricultural and domestic implements. Improved methods of production gave the United Kingdom a major advantage over its competitors and, again, Scots were represented out of all proportion to their population in many of these groundbreaking developments.

Andrew Brown 1825-1907 improved the steam hopper dredger. Dredgers had been around for centuries and a steam dredger was invented in England in 1798 and the first practicable one was designed by Scotsman John Rennie. Andrew Brown took dredging to new levels and built a steam dredging plant. "He is credited as being the 'father of the steam dredger', one of the main types of machinery that kept the world ports in business. Simons together with the neighbouring Lobnitz yard and Fleming & Ferguson's on the Cart at Paisley built hundreds of steam dredgers which spread over the globe."[1]

"He was the inventor of the 'hopper' type of dredger, now extensively used, combining the properties of a dredger and barge in one hull. Although giving much time and study to the design and construction of many different types of dredger-plant, Mr Brown never entirely confined himself to this particular branch of engineering. Thus, in 1861, he designed and constructed the Clyde passenger paddle-steamer *Rothesay Castle*, which obtained the then exceptional speed of 20 miles per hour [32 km/h], and which 40 years later, under a different name, was still in employment on the Canadian lakes. In the years 1867-1868 he built and engined the Anchor liner *India*, the first steamer on the North Atlantic route fitted with four-cylinder compound surface-condensing engines. He also achieved considerable success in the design of ferry-steamers."[2]

Charles Augustus Hartley 1825-1915 was appointed Chief Engineer to improve the navigation on the lower Danube River. In 1856, being familiar with the Danube, he was placed in charge of technical and administrative command of the European Danube Commission, a role that he would effectively carry out, on the Galatzi-Sulina, until 1872. He "advised that provisional works should be undertaken to improve the harbour at the Sulina mouth by utilising the natural scour of the river. These works consisted of two piers forming a seaward prolongation of the fluvial channel. They were begun in April 1858 and completed in July 1861, having the effect of doubling the depth of the channel to 16 feet [4.9 m] or more. Hartley was appointed to the order of the Mejidiye, but under British regulations was obliged to decline; he was given a knighthood in 1862. The provisional piers were replaced by permanent solid structures in 1871, making the Sulina, formerly known as 'the grave of sailors', into one of the best harbours on the Black Sea."[1] He completed further similar work above the Sulina estuary and in 1880 a new entrance was built to his plans at the Toulcha Channel after which he turned to the St George branch of the Danube. In total, the displacement of vessels navigating the Danube River at the estuary increased tenfold from 400 tons to 4,000 tons (394 - 3,937 tonnes).

Hartley was dubbed "the Father of the Danube" by the German Chancellor Otto von Bismarck. He carried out expert works on the Suez Canal, the Panama Canal and on the discharge of the Mississippi stream, and he set up projects for ports development of Constanța, Varna, Durban, and Madras. In 1884, the British government nominated him a member of the international technical commission for widening the Suez Canal. In addition, he was consulted by the British and other governments in connection with many other river and harbour works, including the improvement of the navigation of the Scheldt, Hooghly, Don, and Dnieper, and of the ports of Odessa, Trieste, and Burgas.[2]

John Shanks 1825-1895 took out numerous patents for the improvement of water closets, cisterns, baths and sinks. He became a leading sanitaryware manufacturer and was known for good quality merchandise at a sensible price, with no unnecessary frills or decoration. By 1894, he had taken out 100 patents for closets, fittings and other sanitaryware.[1]

His first patent, in 1863, was for a water closet with a plunger valve to release the waste and a ball cock to refill the basin. The plunger valve consisted of an India rubber ball that was contained in a cylinder at the rear and connected to the basin by a short, inclined pipe. It was known as the "patent flexible valve closet", although within the works it was simply called the Number 4. In 1871, he obtained a patent for a combined supply, waste, and overflow fitting for a bath. Before 1870, fixed baths with connections to hot and cold water and a waste outlet had been something of a luxury, but from the 1870s most new middle-class houses were built with bathrooms fitted with a bath, lavatory, washbasin, and water closet.

The same year Shanks took out his first patent for another sanitary appliance with which the firm was to become closely associated: this was the overhead water closet cistern or "water waste preventer", which was developed by many sanitary engineers from the 1850s in an effort to stop the flow of mains water into the tank while the closet was being flushed. In 1877, he patented a cast-iron bath made with a shelf incorporating the waste and overflow. This was marketed as the *Imperial* bath and it enjoyed considerable success.

Before the 1870s most domestic baths were made of sheet iron or copper and required the support of a wooden enclosure. From the early 1880s, the use of wooden cabinet work in bathrooms was widely condemned as unhygienic as it harboured dirt and germs. Cast-iron baths won the approval of health reformers as they were free-standing and therefore easier to clean around; they were also cheap and affordable. They had appeared as early as the 1850s – so Shanks cannot be credited with their introduction – but when they rose to popularity in the 1880s, he was closely involved in their development and production, manufacturing well-designed, free-standing, enamelled cast-iron baths with a comfortable rolled edge.

Shanks introduced a washbasin that replaced the projecting nozzles of ordinary taps with side inlets or slits near the rim. He soon introduced a similar arrangement which was used on his *Citizen* washbasin and *Imperial* baths. Only the spindle and knobs of the tap were visible and the water entered the basin through small perforations in the earthenware. This, the firm claimed in 1886, provided the "maximum of cleanliness".

In 1881, he patented a bath tap with a flexible tube and perforated rose for providing a shower or spray bath and then the following year he patented a mixer tap for baths and washbasins: this had a mixing chamber that received the water from the hot and cold inlet valves, which was then discharged through a single outlet. He also catered for the luxury end of the market with such products as the *Independent* combined shower, spray, and full-length bath, which he exhibited at the Edinburgh International Exhibition in 1886. By then he had introduced another luxury article, a pedestal bidet with hot and cold water and an ascending spray.[2]

Shanks also extended his range of water closets, again taking out patent protection. In 1880, he took out his first patent for a wash-out closet – an all-ceramic water closet basin and trap containing water in the basin separate from the trap – and in 1881 his first for a syphonic water closet cistern, which employed an inverted cast-iron bell to raise the water over the syphon pipe (the syphonic closet was first patented by John Gray in 1855, but his models were not commercially successful). By the early 1880s, support was growing for the free-standing pedestal water closet, free of any wooden enclosure, and Shanks responded with an "encased washing-out closet" in which the earthenware basin and trap were enclosed in an iron shell filled with concrete. In January 1884, Shanks claimed to have sold "many hundreds" to hospitals and private customers, but this device did not remain in production for long. In 1885, he patented a valve closet with two discharge valves for use on ships. Shanks supplied many of the great liners built in the first half of the 20th century, including the *Titanic*. Shanks took out three patents for urinals between 1884 and 1892. Shanks manufactured huge quantities of this type of cistern – many for export – including the well-known model *The Levern*.

In 1892, Shanks took out a patent for a water closet cistern close-coupled to the closet basin. This was arguably his most important and original contribution to the development of the water closet. Some 30 years earlier, Shanks had gone some way towards developing a low-level reserve of flush water with his Number 4 plunger closet, but the 1892 patent described a closet that appeared in full-coloured glory in an illustrated catalogue published about a year later as the "patent combination closet". The cistern was made of cast iron and coupled to a wash-down closet, which was the first of a long line of close-coupled water closets used worldwide in the 20th century. In March 1894, Shanks patented a jet syphon closet that flushed the closet using a jet to charge a syphon that drew the waste from the basin instead of relying on the sheer force of the flush. The syphonic closet had originated in the United States in the 1870s, but Shanks was just ahead of two chief main rivals with his patent: Thomas William Twyford and George Jennings patented their versions a few months later.[3]

John P. Laird 1826-1882 devised a two-wheel equaliser leading truck in 1857 for which he later received a patent. In 1862, he was made superintendent of motive power for the Pennsylvania Railroad (PRR) and rebuilt much of their old power in succeeding years.[1] Laird was also paid $3,000 in 1866 in lieu of his patent for improved locomotive fire boxes.[2] The first locomotive with a 2-8-0-wheel arrangement was likely built by the Pennsylvania Railroad (PRR), but like the first 2-6-0s, this first 2-8-0 had a leading axle that was rigidly attached to the locomotive's frame. To create this 2-8-0 Laird, the PRR's master mechanic, modified an existing 0-8-0, the Bedford, between 1864 and 1865. Only a few railroads purchased this locomotive type upon its introduction by Baldwin Locomotive Works. The 2-8-0 design was given a major boost in 1875 when the PRR made it the railroad's standard freight locomotive. The railroads found that the 2-8-0 could move trains twice as heavy for half the cost of their earlier brethren. From a financial standpoint, the choice of freight locomotives was clear. Total US production of the class totalled "more than 33,000" locomotives of which "12,000 export versions" went to the rest of the world.[3] In Britain the 2-8-0 became the standard heavy freight steam locomotive type in the 20th century and it saw extensive use in Australia.

Image 53 – Victorian Railways J class No 515
Based on John P Laird's design for PRR

Thomas Ormiston 1826-1882 was a civil engineer who erected The Needles lighthouse on the Isle of Wight and worked on the design of docks and harbours on the Isle of Man, the River Mersey, and Cardiff. As Chief Engineer of Bombay Port Trust, he was responsible for creating Prince's Dock and Prong's Lighthouse in Bombay (Mumbai). At the time the Governor of Bombay, Sir Richard Temple, stated that "in no other part of Asia has a wet dock of large proportion been constructed."[1] By 1870, 328 acres (134 hectares) had been reclaimed and converted into a valuable estate, 10,000,000 tons (9,071,800 tonnes) of material having been absorbed, the average depth of filling being 16½ feet (5m); 9 miles (14.5 km) of roads from 40 feet to 80 feet wide (12-24 m); 10 miles (16 km) of drains and 3 miles (4.8 km) of permanent sea walls had been constructed, affording basins for the native craft, with 70 acres (28 hectares) of wharf space and extensive shed and warehouse accommodation.[2]

Alexander Black 1827-1897 was a surveyor in northern and eastern Victoria, Australia, which included surveying the border between that state and New South Wales. Black was Surveyor-General of Victoria from 1886 to 1892 and President of the Victorian Institute of Surveyors in 1879-1880.[1] Black, with George Gordon, surveyed much of northern Victoria and prepared fourteen reports. "The fifth report, which marked an important step in water conservation and distribution in Victoria, was a suggestion for the constitution of water trusts which were to be given authority to carry out water supply projects. These reports led to the *Water Conservation and Distribution Act 1881* which was amended in 1883. This was the first Victorian legislation in which express provision was made for the construction of irrigation works."[2]

Sandford Fleming 1827-1915 "was one of the many Scottish-born engineers who contributed to the British Empire's technological dominance and success."[1] From 1852 onwards, Fleming took a prominent part in the railway development of Upper Canada (Ontario), and from 1855 to 1863 he was Chief Engineer of the Northern Railway. In 1864, he was appointed chief railway engineer by the government of Nova Scotia, and charged with the construction of a line from Truro to Pictou.[2] Earlier, in 1862, Fleming had placed before the Canadian government the first thoroughly thought-out plan for building a Pacific railway. He was appointed surveyor of the first portion of a proposed railway from Quebec City to Halifax and Saint John which became the Intercolonial Railway. "When the construction of the Intercolonial became a federal project, a board of railway commissioners was appointed in 1868 to oversee the work. In disputes with it, Fleming appealed to Ottawa, which usually decided in his favour. A prime case was the construction of bridges, several of them technically challenging. Fleming wished to use stone and iron, while the commissioners, trained to turn a profit, preferred timber. His view prevailed and his structures lasted, not only because of superior materials but also because of the engineering techniques he pioneered, in soil sampling and the prestressing of piers."[3] Fleming was responsible for surveying the route to be taken by the Canadian Pacific Railway, and he had 800 men working in 21 divisions surveying a total of 73,600 km of line.

From 1876, he took a prominent part in forcing the adoption of standard time, which greatly simplified travel in British North America and throughout the world.[4] In 1876, after missing a train in Ireland because its printed schedule listed p.m. instead of a.m., Fleming proposed a single 24-hour clock for the entire world, located at the centre of the Earth and not linked to any surface meridian. At a meeting of the Royal Canadian Institute on 8 February 1879, he linked it to the anti-meridian of Greenwich (now 180°). He suggested that standard time zones could be used locally, but they were subordinate to his single world time, which he called Cosmic Time. He continued to promote his system at major international conferences including the International Meridian Conference of 1884. That conference accepted a different version of Universal Time, but refused to accept his zones, stating that they were a local issue outside its purview. Nevertheless, by 1929 all of the major countries of the world had accepted time zones.[5]

Fleming was the father of the idea of an intra-imperial system of cable communication via a state-owned system of telegraphs throughout the British Empire. In 1879, Fleming broached the idea of linking the trans-Canada telegraph system with a cable across the Pacific. When such a project failed to materialise under free enterprise, he sent an unremitting barrage of memoranda to Ottawa and, via periodic colonial conferences, to London until an imperial cable committee was appointed to steer the project. Opposition from the established private interests that controlled the Atlantic cable was intense. But by mid-1899 it was clear that the proposal would work because the governments of Australia, Canada, and New Zealand were prepared to support it even if London turned it down. After years of labour, he saw the first link forged in the chain, in the opening in 1902 of the Pacific Cable between Vancouver and New Zealand.[6]

He designed Canada's first postage stamp – the three-penny beaver – in 1851, and co-founded the Royal Canadian Institute in 1849. With Collingwood Schreiber, he was co-designer of Canada's first permanent exhibition hall which was built in Toronto in 1858. He was also a major player in moving Queens University in Ontario from being run by the Presbyterian Church to secular control in 1912 and designed an early in-line skate in 1850 (some sources say 1848).[7]

David Greig 1827-1891 is credited with the development of the balance plough. The idea had been originally patented by the Fisken brothers, in 1885, but Greig suggested a frame mounted as a 'see-saw' carried on a two-wheeled axle, one side carrying the right-hand plough bodies and the other side the left hand, thus enabling the plough to turn all the furrows in the same direction by alternating the bodies. Between 1862 and 1880 alone, Greig took out nine patents for improvements to agricultural equipment and eight other equipment patents. He also took out patents shared with others, including 24 for improvements to agricultural equipment and 15 other equipment patents, plus two of his brothers had an additional seven patents between them.

Image 54 – Balance Plough.
The left-turning set of shares have just completed a pass,
and the right-turning shares are about to enter the ground to return across the field.

The foundation of John Fowler and Company, apart from the necessary financial support and business acumen, lay in its steam cultivation patents, many of them in the names of John Fowler and his associates David Greig and Robert Burton.[2]

William Stuart Watson born 1827 was Chief Engineer of the Baltimore & Pittsburgh Railroad (1853) then became Chief Engineer, respectively, of the Placer Canal Company, California; the

Frenchtown Canal Company; California Northern & Sacramento Valley Railroad; California Central Railroad; Yuba Railroad; San Francisco & Central Pacific Railroad; San Francisco & Humboldt Bay Railroad; and Stockton & Copperopolis Railroad – all during the period 1854 to 1868, while concurrently he had charge, as Chief or Consulting Engineer, of nearly all the large mining canals, aggregating several thousand kilometres in length, and costing many millions of dollars, in the northern part of California.

The works of the North Fork Hydraulic Company, 8 km long, were constructed by him in 1857. About 3 km of this construction is of wrought-iron pipe half a metre in diameter, carried through a mountain gap 278 m deep, and conveying 635,000 cubic metres of water in 24 hours. The Cascade Canal Company's works, another of his successful engineering enterprises, is 19.3 km in length, with 9.6 km of flumes. This canal is carried through one of the most formidable canyons in California and portions of the aqueduct and some of the flumes are suspended along the rocky sides of the stream, 91.5 m above the water.

In 1858, working for the California Fluming Company, he had to empty the bed of Feather River, 1.6 km in length, 37 m wide at low water, and 14 m deep, by the means of dams and flumes. The main dam was 95 m long on top, and 30 m long on the bed of the stream. It was constructed of a crib work of timber filled with stone and a flume was built 1.6 km in length, 14 m wide and 3 m deep, and contained 762 km of lumber, and discharged for a period of 94 days, 843,250 m^3 of water per hour. The portion of the river, the bed of which was to be mined (1.6 km long), was pumped dry by chain pumps worked by undershot wheels 9 m in diameter, driven by the water in the main flume, the current of which moved at the rate of 19.3 km/h. The time occupied in removing the water was 14½ days. The "working out" of this portion of the bed of the river required the labour of 600 men for 31 days. The total cost of this project was $316,000.[1]

Duncan Hector Campbell 1828-1894 improved the shoe-stitching machine. It had been first designed by American Lyman Reed Blake in 1860, and this was modified and patented by Massachusetts businessman Gordon McKay (of distant Scottish ancestry through both parents), making a fortune for McKay who was soon producing about half of America's shoes – some 120 million pairs a year. The stitch of this machine caused a ridge on the inside that wore away socks, so it never caught on with the quality end of the market.

Campbell designed an even more effective shoe-stitching machine than McKay's and made a number of innovations in stitching leather that were instrumental in mechanising an industry that relied heavily on manual labour. The Campbell Lockstitch Sewing Machine was designed in the 1880s and "this machine revolutionised the industry and established the standard for other leather machines to follow. It was the first needle and awl machine successfully produced".[1]

Campbell's Lockstitch Machine could quickly stitch cavalry boots and his business expanded, ultimately laying the foundations of the New England dominance in the footwear industry. He invented a machine for using waxed threads which made leather stitching easier and his lockstitch machine gave his company pre-eminence in the footwear manufacturing industry. He also created a machine that could manufacture cloth-covered buttons automatically.

The Campbell Machine Company was established in 1880 with a capital of $500,000 raised on the basis of Campbell's invention, which was not only better than other machines but also superior to slower and costlier hand stitching. Besides footwear, Campbell's machine stitched saddles and harnessing gear, travel bags and the tops of some horse-drawn carriages. No other stitching machinery came close to the dominance of Campbell's and, by 1898, the company – now called Campbell Bosworth Machinery Company, after Campbell teamed up with American Charles Frederick Bosworth – aligned itself with the Goodyear Shoe Machinery Company which, in 1900, became the United Shoe Machinery Company. This company came to dominate footwear production and had affiliated companies in Britain, France, Canada, Germany, and in the continents of Asia and South America. Its factory at Beverly, Massachusetts, appropriately nicknamed "The Shoe", was the largest reinforced concrete structure in the world until 1937, with 34 acres (13.75 hectares) of interior space.[2]

Charles Gordon O'Neill 1828-1900 was surveyor to the Otago provincial government in New Zealand's South Island. As district engineer at Clutha, he laid out the town of Milton and supervised the construction of a bridge over the Clyde River in 1865. He became provincial engineer at Wellington and helped to survey a railway route between Wellington and Wairarapa. He planned and supervised the construction of Wellington's tramway system, and reported on water-supply systems for the Otago and Thames goldfields and for Auckland. A bill he put forward was rejected on the Speaker's casting vote, but the *Plans of Towns Regulation Act 1875* incorporated his main proposals. His evidence at a commission of inquiry into an explosion on the Thames goldfield had helped to create an Inspection of Machinery Department in 1874. In Wellington, he was active in the Society of St Vincent de Paul and, in 1876, founded its first conference to be aggregated in New Zealand. In 1881, O'Neill moved to Sydney and, with aid from the Marist Fathers, founded on 24 July the first conference of the Society of St Vincent de Paul in Australia to be firmly established at St Patrick's, Church Hill.[1]

Frederick James Ritchie 1828-1906 specialised in large-scale public clocks and he not only made the mechanical portion of the floral cuckoo clock in Princes Street Gardens – the first of its kind in the world to be put on public display – but also made the clocks of the Royal Scottish Museum and St Giles' Cathedral. Ritchie further developed the inventions of Alexander Bain and Charles Wheatstone in the field of electric timekeeping. Dispensing with the weight or spring, he realised that only small electric pulses were required to keep one or more clocks synchronised – the master clock sent impulses to each slave clock in place and propelled as well as synchronised the sympathetic pendulum by impulses from each arm of his clock's gravity escapement. He received a patent for this invention and the clocks he made were so successful in trials that a number of clocks were located around Edinburgh in 1873, forming the so-called "Edinburgh Ring".

Ritchie's clocks were connected through the telegraph lines directly to the Edinburgh Royal Observatory and had the advantage of continuously providing the correct time to the citizens of Edinburgh.[1] Ritchie supplied many observatories with pairs and triplets of sympathetic pendulums. In 1873, Ritchie carried it a step further. Realising that only a very small expenditure of electrical energy was required to keep two tuned pendulums in phase, he was tempted to dispense with the spring or weight-driven maintenance with its merit of independent life, and drove the hands from the pendulum as Bain had done in his earliest earth-driven clocks, by an improved method which may be described as a reversed gravity escapement.[2]

Balfour Stewart 1828-1887 was noted for his studies of terrestrial magnetism and radiant heat which contributed to the foundation of spectrum analysis. He essentially established, in a purely empirical and almost intuitive manner, the Radiation Laws later obtained by Gustav Robert Kirchhoff. Stewart also held a life-long fascination with the possible link between terrestrial magnetism and meteorological phenomena. He first postulated the existence of a high, electrically conducting atmospheric layer which he aptly named "ionosphere", and was the primary driver behind the study of possible planetary influences on sunspots carried out during his directorship at Kew.[1] In his work on radiant heat, Stewart was the first to discover that bodies radiate and absorb energy of the same wavelength and, in his studies of terrestrial magnetism, Stewart discovered that daily variation in the magnetic field could be explained by air currents in the upper atmosphere, which act as conductors and generate electrical currents as they pass through the Earth's magnetic field.[2]

He proposed that solar radiation caused tidal effects, making the atmosphere swing back and forth as day follows night, and these would cause a dynamo effect as the conducting layer moved through the Earth's magnetic field, then itself causing diurnal swings in this field. It is no coincidence that, at the time that Stewart made this proposal, experiments were being done which showed that under some conditions currents could flow through gases provided the pressure was low.[3]

John Waddell 1828-1888 built the Mersey Railway, an underground railway running from Liverpool to Birkenhead which involved building the first tunnel under the River Mersey, with a length of just over five kilometres. James Brunlees was joint engineer on the project with Charles Douglas Fox.

Waddell constructed the harbours or docks at Kings Lynn in Norfolk, Bristol, Avonmouth and Whitehaven; and the Llandudno, New Brighton, Southport and Southend piers, the latter being the first iron leisure pier, originally 1,097 m in length but extended to 1,335 m, the longest in Britain. Other examples of his work are: the rebuilding of Putney Bridge in London (1882), the Scarborough & Whitby Railway, completion of the Whitby Redcar and Middlesbrough Union Railway and the Mersey Railway tunnel. His company also built part of the approaches to the Forth Bridge.[1]

James Browne 1829-1896 commanded the Indian engineer contingent during the Egyptian battle of Tel el-Kebir, but it was in British India that he was to make his mark. He had been superintendent of works for the building of the Indus Bridge in 1875 and he later became involved in building railways as Engineer-in-Chief for the Sind-Pishin railway. Commenced in 1884, this line was 360 km long, crossing desert and mountains under tough weather in a politically volatile region. The country was a wilderness of rocks and stones – a land of barrenness and desolation, where there was no timber, no fuel, scarcely a blade of grass, and, in places, for stretches of several miles, no water. It was a land, too, almost devoid of inhabitants, while those who did dwell there were described as "a savage and blood-thirsty race of robbers", continually engaged in plunder and inter-tribal warfare, and not growing sufficient food even for their own consumption.

Almost everything that was wanted – including supplies for some 15,000 to 30,000 workers and materials for the line – had to be imported from a distance. The Nari Gorge, about 23 km in length, beginning just beyond Sibi, has been described as "one of the most weird tracks through which a railway has ever been carried. The hills, absolutely bare, rise above the valley for many thousands of feet in fantastic pinnacles and cliffs. It is a scene of the wildest desolation." The Nari River, running through the gorge, is formed by a combination of three streams having but little water on ordinary occasions, but becoming, in time of flood, a raging torrent which fills up the whole gorge for miles, attains a depth of 10 feet (3 m), and has a velocity of five feet per second. Over this river, the railway had to be carried in five different places. Not just bridges, but heavy embankments, cuttings and tunnels were needed.

Such was the energy which had been shown, in spite of all these difficulties and drawbacks, that the work was completed within the 2½ years fixed by the Engineer-in-Chief and, on 27 March 1887, an engine ran over the line all the way from Sibi to Quetta, and the Hurnai Railway was formally declared open for traffic.[1] Browne became quartermaster-general for British India (1888-1892) then agent to the governor-general of Baluchistan in Asia.

Alexander Buchan 1829-1907 began the use of weather maps for forecasting in 1868, with the publication of a map showing the movement of a cyclonic depression across North America, the Atlantic and northern Europe. In the judgment of English meteorologist Sir Napier Shaw, Buchan's study marks the entry of modern meteorology, with "the weather map as its main feature and forecasting its avowed object."[1]

Buchan realised that the European weather is determined by pressure conditions over Iceland.[2] He published his *Handy Book of Meteorology* (1867), which became a standard textbook and remained in use for many years. In 1869, Buchan produced the first weather maps showing the average monthly and annual air pressure for the world. He statistically noted that the British climate undergoes a series of cold and warm periods which fall approximately between certain dates each year. These are now known as "Buchan spells". Nine periods were put forward by Buchan in 1867 on the basis of 50 years of observations (though some texts quote only 1857-1866), constituting fairly reliable periods of unseasonal cold (6 cases) or warmth (3 cases). Buchan himself did not claim these as "singularities" and it is widely accepted that they have little real predictive merit.[3]

Under Buchan's guidance, the science of meteorology made huge strides, and it is not too much of an exaggeration when he is described as "the father of meteorology", which is often. Until the 1860s, for example, the concept of isobars was little understood, certainly as a tool to predict the weather. A common practice until then was to plot an observation of pressure as the difference from its average, but Buchan realised that it would be far more useful to calculate the sea-level pressure from all of his observations then "join the dots" to create isobars. These are, of course, the lines connecting points of equal pressure that we see every day on weather charts, and which reveal the positions of areas of high and low pressure.

In the autumn and early winter of 1863, Buchan constructed a series of 18 charts through which he could follow the development and movement of weather systems across Europe. As these charts also included observations of wind speed and direction, he was further able to formulate the simple but utterly fundamental rules that winds blow anti-clockwise around an area of low pressure in the Northern Hemisphere, and that wind speed is proportional to the closeness of the isobars (the "barometric gradient").

These discoveries allowed Buchan to be the first to attempt to forecast future weather conditions, and were published in his *Handy Book of Meteorology* in 1868, alongside his investigations into the trajectory and speed of movement of depressions and their relative temperatures-patterns. Later, he produced some of his most influential work: *The Mean Pressure of the Atmosphere and the Prevailing Winds over the Globe for the Months and for the Year*, thus portraying atmospheric circulations on charts that have changed little since.[4]

William Robert Galbraith 1829-1914 was appointed, in 1862, as engineer for new works on the London and South Western Railway (LSWR) where, over the next 40 years, he built most of that railway company's rail lines in Middlesex, Surrey, Hampshire, Dorset, Devon and Cornwall and, with Richard F. Church, branches promoted independently and later acquired by the LSWR, to Swanage, Chard, Seaton, Sidmouth, Ilfracombe and the extensions from Exeter to Okehampton, Plymouth and Devonport, Holsworthy and the North Cornwall Railway to Bodmin and Padstow. In 1892, the LSWR became owners of Southampton Docks which were greatly extended under Galbraith's supervision. He laid out and built the North British Railway Inverkeithing & Burntisland and Glenfarg lines in continuation northwards from the Forth Bridge and he prepared and carried out parliamentary plans for the alteration and enlargement of Waverley station at Edinburgh. From 1892, he was engineer with James Henry Greathead and, later, Alexander Kennedy on the Waterloo & City Railway and with Benjamin Baker and Richard F. Church on the Bakerloo line, and with Douglas Fox on the Charing Cross, Euston & Hampstead Railway, altogether 14 miles (22.5 km) of tube railways.[1]

George Gordon 1829-1907 was a hydraulic engineer who was Chief Engineer of the Amsterdam Water Company in the Netherlands for four years before spending a decade as chief district engineer of the Madras Irrigation and Canal Company. In 1872, he became Chief Engineer of the Lands and Works Board in Victoria, Australia, and three years later he was Chief Engineer of Water Supply in the Department of Mines, still in Victoria. He designed the Lower Stony Creek dam which was built in 1873-1874 in the Brisbane Ranges, 33 km north of Geelong. It "is notable as a very early example of concrete gravity dam, and was the first dam in Australia built with mass concrete, using Portland cement."[1]

The drought years of the late 1870s, and the ongoing struggle of farmers on their new selections, raised concerns about how to best irrigate the dry northern plains of Victoria. To investigate this problem, the Government appointed a Water Conservancy Board in 1880 with two members: George Gordon, formerly Chief Engineer of Water Supply, and fellow Scot, Alexander Black, Assistant Surveyor-General. Following recommendations in their report of 1880, a number of weirs were constructed on major waterways in north-central Victoria, including the Broken River, the Loddon River, and the Avoca River. The 12 reports produced by these two engineers regarding the provision of water to the northern plains of the state for agricultural and domestic usage resulted in the *Water Conservation and Distribution Act 1881*.[2]

Thomas Francis Jamieson 1829-1913 carried out notable research in Quaternary geology and the geomorphology of Scotland, realising that sea-levels had dropped since the time of the glaciers and developing what we now know as the Theory of Isostasy. This suggests that the Earth's crust flexes under the weight of glacial ice, and that after the ice melts, a process of rebound occurs, such that areas which experience the most significant fall in sea-level were subject to the thickest layers of ice. As evidence, he cited the existence of recent marine fossils, and the skeleton of a 9,000-year-old whale, on what is now dry land in the Carse of Stirling.[1]

In his important 1865 paper on the *History of the Last Geological Changes in Scotland*, he referred to evidence of the mammoth having inhabited Scotland before the Glacial period. He noted the enormous thickness of the land-ice, Schiehallion (1,067 m high) being glaciated near to the top as well as on its flanks. He considered that the ice was developed as a thick cake and flowed off "not so much on account of the inclination of the bed on which it rested", but "in the way that a heap of grain flows off when poured down on the floor of a granary . . . given a floor of infinite extension, and a pile of grain of sufficient amount, the mass would move outward to any distance". He concluded that "the want of much inclination in the surface of a country, and the absence of great Alpine heights, are therefore objections of no moment to the movement of land-ice, provided we have snow enough".[2]

Alexander Moncrieff 1829-1906 invented the disappearing gun. In the 1860s, with the rise of the ironclad ship and the general improvement in shipboard armament, the coast defences of the world had been extensively overhauled in an attempt to keep pace. At the beginning of this period, the standard method of deploying coast guns was in open batteries, but the advent of armour and powerful guns on ships led to the adoption of armoured forts in which guns were protected by casements with enormous thickness of iron and granite to protect them. This was a very expensive method of construction; a single armoured casemate for one gun, together with its necessary magazine arrangements, cost over £3,800 without the cost of the gun being considered. Further, the slowness of the rate of fire of the heavy Rifled Muzzle-Loading guns demanded the development and construction of large fortifications with numerous guns to swamp the enemy with gunfire. Picklecombe Fort in Plymouth Sound, for example, was prepared with 42 armoured casements, an expense of £160,000, before the guns were installed. By way of comparison, the Moncrieff carriage and its pit cost a mere £1,345, a considerable saving.[1]

Moncrieff's disappearing gun, invented in 1868, was designed for heavy guns placed in coastal batteries. These would disappear into a pit when the gun had been fired by using the impetus in the gun's recoil. The two main gun mountings at that time were barbette and casemate. In the former, the gun fires over a field of view to the gun-layer, and a larger field of fire for the gun, with, however, more exposure for the detachment. The latter gives a restricted view and greater safety to the layer, but unless the casemate takes the form of a revolving turret, the arc of fire is very limited. An important advantage of the barbette system is its cheapness, and thus in order to obtain with it concealment, suggestions were made for various forms of mounting which would allow the gun, under the shock of recoil, to disappear behind the parapet to emerge only when loaded and ready for the next round. A mounting of this description for muzzle-loading guns, designed by Colonel Moncrieff, was actually in use in the defences of Alexandria and in HMS *Temeraire*. But with the increased charges and length of breech-loading guns, a further change was desirable, and after some trials a system of disappearing mountings was adopted into the British service. Moncrieff developed two types of disappearing gun – the counterweight carriage and the hydropneumatic, which is a disappearing gun carriage in which the recoil is checked by cylinders containing liquid and air, the air when compressed furnishing the power for restoring the gun to the firing position. It was used with some British and European heavy guns. Disappearing guns became obsolete with the use of long range breech-loading guns.

Image 55 – Disappearing Guns – Hawaii Army Museum Society
The gun on left has "disappeared" below the casement wall while the one
on the right is ready to fire.

George Pigot Moodie 1829-1891 built the first railway in Transvaal in 1890, running more than 25 km between Johannesburg and the Boksburg coal mine. He was Surveyor-General of Transvaal from 1881 to 1884. Earlier, in 1870, Moodie had worked with General Petrus (Piet) Joubert on a new boundary between the South African Republic and the Orange Free State. During the early seventies, Moodie explored the route to Lourenco Marques (now Maputo) in Mozambique.

Moodie's *Map of the South African Republic on a large scale including the Diamond Fields and the Tati Gold Fields* was published in 1875 and was one of the first of its kind, pointing to the potential of the Republic in the new era of mineral exploitation. In 1876, Moodie leased mining rights to other companies. For a time *Moodie's* was the focal point of the gold rush that led to the founding of Barberton. Other companies, Moodie's Golden Hill Goldmining Co., and Moodie's Kentish Quarry Goldmining Co., also bore his name.[1]

Lauchlan Rose 1829-1885 invented the world's first concentrated fruit drink.[1] Rose had inherited the family firm at Leith, just outside of Edinburgh, and decided in 1865 to enter the business of growing limes in Dominica, in the West Indies. At the time, lime juice was provided to ships to reduce the risk of scurvy. Indeed, Rose's cordial, which is the forerunner to today's thriving fruit juice market and still sold today, was simply a natural progression from a discovery made many years earlier by another Edinburgh citizen, James Lind.[2]

To make it more palatable, Rose sweetened the juice with sugar for public consumption, while lime juice in the large jars destined for ships was laced with rum as a (largely ineffective) preservative. Rose, however, soon discovered that fumigating casks with the smoke of burning sulphur was much more effective, and a little later, he took out a patent on sulphur dioxide (transformed into sulphurous acid when dissolved in water, and sodium sulphite when then neutralised) as an excellent preservative. Rose's Lime Juice Cordial became the first soft drink to be marketed in Britain, and endures to this day, along with Rose's lime marmalade, its popularity still undimmed.[3]

Rose's lime juice was first patented in 1867, the same year that the *Merchant Shipping Act* required all ships of the Royal Navy and Merchant Navy to provide a daily lime ration to sailors to prevent scurvy. Paragraph 4(4) stated: "The Master or Owner of every such Foreign-going Ship ... shall provide and cause to be kept on board such Ship a sufficient Quantity of Lime or Lemon Juice from the Warehouse duly labelled as aforesaid, such Labels to remain intact until Twenty-four Hours at least after such Ship shall have left her Port of Departure on her Foreign Voyage, or a sufficient Quantity of such other Anti-scorbutics, if any, of such Quality, and composed of such Materials, and packed and kept in such Manner, as Her Majesty by Order in Council may from Time to Time direct."

At this time, lime juice was used solely for medicinal purposes but, as an astute businessman, Rose decided to make it more suitable for popular consumption. He sweetened the juice and put it in bottles, turning it into a new and attractive beverage. And so "Rose's Lime Juice" with its distinctive bottle bearing the lime leaves and fruit emblem was born.[4]

Limes were cheaper than lemons in the Caribbean and the fruit, or its juice, became so ubiquitous in the Royal Navy that Americans called British sailors "Limeys". L. Rose and Lime Company was one of the most successful agricultural companies ever based in Dominica (West Indies). It contributed to the most prosperous period that the island experienced at the height of the green lime trade from 1903 to the mid-1920s and continued to operate there until 1980. L. Rose & Co purchased Bath and Elmshall estates in Dominica from William Davies in 1891 and converted the old sugar factory to the processing of limes. In 1906, the company started the manufacture of calcium citrate, and, in 1921, a factory was erected at Bath Estate for the production of citric acid crystals. Rose and Co was the main buyer of limes and lime products from across the island.[5]

The brand was introduced to the United States in 1901. The first factory producing lime juice was set up by Rose on Commercial Street in Leith in 1868. After World War II, the company saw its UK market share grow. In 1957, Schweppes acquired the company and operated it in the UK until it purchased Mott's in 1982. Cadbury Schweppes merged the operations of the two brands and Rose's operations were transferred to the United States. When Cadbury divested its beverage operations in 2008, Rose's was transferred to the newly formed Dr Pepper Snapple Group.[6]

John Richardson Wigham 1829-1906 made several inventions that enhanced lighthouses. However, before his involvement with lighthouses he had, in 1861, patented the first successful lighted buoy, which was placed in the River Clyde. Initially, buoys only had bells to warn mariners. The difficulty was in designing an oil-lamp which could burn while unattended and not be extinguished by waves and storms.[1]

His design, which required little maintenance, involved a pulley system which delivered a continuous fresh wick to the burner and thus avoided the need for trimming. This allowed the lights to run initially for 31 days without attention, with this later being extended to 90 days. These Wigham buoys and tower lamps and beacons were adopted throughout the world and were particularly successful in the Pacific Ocean where some were in service to the mid-20th century.

In June 1865, while working in Ireland, he installed a gas light, known as a crocus burner – for the shape of the flame – for the Baily Lighthouse near Dublin, the first ever use of gas to provide the lighting for a lighthouse. The gas was manufactured on the spot and the system's main advantages were that it dispensed with the lamp glass essential to the four-wick Fresnel oil lamp of 240 candle-power, in use from 1835, and that the power of the light could readily be increased or decreased. A 28-jet flame, which gave sufficient light for clear weather, could be increased successively to a 48-jet, 68-jet, 88-jet, or 108-jet flame – 2,923-candle-power – on foggy nights. This light was fitted in 1868 and was four times more powerful than the standard oil lights of the time with a new, modified light which John Tyndall, Scientific Adviser to Trinity House, reported was 13 times more powerful than the most brilliant light then known.

Image 56 – Wigham's 31-day Lamp
National Maritime Museum of Ireland

In 1871, Wigham invented the first of the many group-flashing arrangements which enabled mariners to distinguish between different lighthouses. Rockabill Lighthouse was fitted with a combination of revolving flashing lens and intermittent flashing burner to produce the world's first group flashing lighthouse. His arrangement was adopted at Galley Head, Mew Head, and Tory Island off the Irish coast. In 1872, he proposed superimposing lenses, called biform, and later triform and quadriform lenses, adding power according to need. A quadriform system was used at Galley Head, County Cork, which at over one million candlepower was the most powerful light in the world when installed in 1879.

Wigham's other inventions included: a device for fog signals, a gas-driven siren, a "sky-flashing arrangement", and a "continuous pulsating light" in connection with his system of gas illumination for lighthouses.[2]

William Buchanan 1830-1910 was a railway engineer who designed the New York Central and Hudson River Railroad 4-4-0 locomotive No. 999, the first locomotive that passed a speed of 100 mph (160 km/h). From experience, Buchanan knew that only "a crew with gentle skill and terrific nerve could be relied upon to safely drive a high-speed train over great distance without tearing up the sharply-tuned machinery propelling them. And the railroad hoped to best not only its own unofficial speed record, but the world record of 55.4 mph over 400 miles [644 km] set in England in 1888."[1]

Designed by William Buchanan and manufactured by the New York Central Railroad in West Albany, New York in 1893, the 999 was commissioned to haul the Empire State Express, which ran from Syracuse to Buffalo. This relatively smooth run and the 999's cutting-edge design gave the new locomotive an opportunity to make history.

Image 57 – William Buchanan's 999 Steam Locomotive
Museum of Science and Industry in Chicago

"The 999 Steam Locomotive was a new concept in speed locomotives. Engine 999 was assigned to haul the New York Central Railroad's brilliant new passenger train, the Empire State Express. On 10 May 1893, the 999 became the fastest land vehicle when it reached a record speed of 112.5 mph [181 km/h]. The 999 maintained the record for a decade. Following its record-setting run, 'The World's Fastest Locomotive' toured the country and was displayed at the 1893 World's Columbian Exposition in Chicago. After the Exposition, the 999 continued to provide passenger and freight service for many years. The famous locomotive returned to Chicago in 1933 for the A Century of Progress World's Fair and again from 1948-1949 for the Chicago Railroad Fair. Eventually, technological innovation in the railroad industry limited the 999's use. In May of 1952, following a re-enactment of its record-breaking run, the 999 was retired from service."[2]

Robert Francis Fairlie 1830-1885 designed the double-bogie articulated locomotive which he patented in 1864. This locomotive went into operation in Wales on the Neath & Brecon Railway, where it pioneered the way for the use of narrow gauge railways around the world in places where it wasn't suitable to use standard gauge. The Fairlie bogie, as it came to be known, had two pivoting bogies with two boilers that were back to back and a single firebox in the centre with the cabin. Fairlie's concept of double-ended locomotives (ones that could run in either direction) really came into its own with the advent of diesel locomotives, although steam ones were very successfully used in the Russian Empire and Mexico. His idea of mounting them on independent bogies also became widespread with electric and diesel trains, although the principle was used on both freight and passenger steam trains from 1873.[1]

Image 58 – Fairlie Bogie, Mason Janus Locomotive 1877

John Fyfe 1830-1906 designed a mechanism in 1872 to transport granite cut from the deep Kemnay quarry. He apparently got his inspiration from the simple ropeway system that carried the mail to Abergeldie Castle.[1] Known as a "blondin ropeway", other quarries in Aberdeen were using them by 1886, in conjunction with derrick cranes. The blondin had a lifting capacity of three tonnes. Also known as Henderson Aerial Cableways, they were made in 1896 by John M. Henderson & Company at the King's Engineering Works in Aberdeen using a patented form of blondin cableway which quickly became popular in Gwynedd, Wales, and elsewhere and which made use of the newly-available light steel ropes, in place of heavy iron ropes or chains. There were differences in detail between those used in the granite quarries of Scotland, in Gwynedd slate quarries and at Delabole in Cornwall, but all made use of the same principle.

John Fyfe was a very inventive and shrewd businessman who was the first to install Andrew Barclay's steam derrick crane. Fyfe went on to become the largest granite producer in the world, supplying much of Aberdeen as well as work on the Thames Embankment, piers, docks, viaducts, lighthouses, sea defences, and bridges. Indeed, John Fyfe played a major part in giving Aberdeen its Silver City title.[2]

Image 59 – Blondin Ropeway near to Dinorwig, Gwynedd, in Great Britain

Charles George Hood Kinnear 1830-1894 invented the bellows camera using a tapered bellows which enabled it to fold into a very compact form because each pleat nested into the next, larger pleat. The newly designed wood body was also innovative. A lens panel was mounted on the front of a sliding base that could be extended or retracted (for focusing) by an endless screw. A handle at the back of the base was used to focus the camera. To ensure portability, Kinnear designed the camera so it could be completely disassembled and stored inside the rear standard.

Collapsing the camera for storage was relatively straight forward. The front of the bellows was removed from the lensboard and pushed into the rear standard. The rear standard was then unbolted from the base. Supporting rods locking the lensboard were unlocked, which allowed the lensboard to be folded flat against the camera base. The entire camera base (including lensboard) was flipped over and put on top of the rear standard. Small sliding brass latches would lock the base to the rear standard. In a sense, the Kinnear pattern camera could be considered the first "self-casing" camera.[1]

Kinnear was a successful architect with most of his many dozens of commissions being executed in Scotland in association with John Dick Peddie, and Windleston Hall's Chapel Tomb for Sir William Eden (ancestor of British PM Sir Anthony Eden) in County Durham.

Image 60 – Kinnear pattern folding camera, 1907

Alexander Carnegie Kirk 1830-1892 further modified the steam engine so that steam was expanded in three consecutive stages – hence triple-expansion engine. Kirk designed the *Parisian* in 1881 for the Allan Line, the very first steel steamship to make a transatlantic voyage and the first with bilge keels, which mitigate the ship's rolling motion. The triple-expansion engine soon became the world's most common marine engine, allowing steamships to travel farther and faster than ever before. "The compound-engine became obsolete and the triple-expansion engine took its place, effecting a reduction of quite 25% in the consumption of coal and giving great impetus to shipbuilding and marine engineering."[1]

In 1860, based on the Stirling Engine, Kirk developed an effective air-cycle compressor with a closed cycle to make ice (it could make four kilograms of ice for every kilogram of coal used). It became a commercial success and could reduce temperatures to -13C,[2] and it was this system that was primarily used during the next three decades for refrigeration in hospitals and steamships. His refrigeration device, invented in 1856 for separating the solid paraffin in shale oil, was the first practical air-compression refrigerator, which was made under licence by the Norman Co. of Glasgow, and sold all over the world for ice making.[3]

Thomas George Montgomerie 1830-1878 sighted a group of high peaks in the Karakoram from more than 200 km away while he was participating in the Great Trigonometric Survey of India. He named five of these peaks K1, K2, K3, K4, and K5 – where the K denotes Karakoram. Today, K1 is known as Masherbrum, K3 as Broad Peak, K4 as Gasherbrum II, and K5 as Gasherbrum I. Only K2 has kept Montgomerie's name.[1]

K2, the second highest mountain in the world at 8,611 metres (28,251 ft), is part of the Karakoram Range, located on the border between Gilgit and the Taxkorgan Tajik Autonomous County of Xinjiang, China.

Montgomerie had joined the Great Trigonometrical Survey in 1852 and had been on triangulation in the Punjab and on the measurement of two base-lines. His immediate task was to set out a chain of triangles starting from the main series about 20 miles (32 km) east of Jammu, and to work it across the Pir Panjal range to the Kashmir valley. The peaks of the Pir Panjal rise to over 15,000 ft (4,572 m) and carry a heavy crown of snow well into June. Fresh falls of snow were frequent, and the surveyors had to work in wintry conditions right through March and April. They had to camp several days at a time on each summit, building platforms and masonry pillars, and huts for the signal parties, and waiting for clear views.

After selecting the first stations himself, Montgomerie sent Johnson ahead to lay out the advance triangles whilst he and Douglas, who had only joined the survey within the past year, went back to start theodolite observations. Montgomerie decided to dump the large two-foot (61 cm) theodolite as being too cumbersome for work on the mountains, and he worked with a reliable 14-inch (35.5 cm). Observations were taken to heliotropes worked by the signal squads camped on the surrounding peaks, and Montgomerie writes of the thrill of spotting "the bright point of light shining from the apex of a noble snowy cone". When clouds prevented the use of heliotropes by day, observations had to be made to lamps at night. He made a point of keeping his observations and angle-books with the most meticulous refinement, up to the highest geodetic standards.[2]

Neither Montgomerie nor his assistants were mountaineers in the conventional sense of the term. They carried no ice axes, they wore no crampons, they knew nothing of the alpine rope, nor points of belay. Even so, for the purposes of the Kashmir survey, they lugged their theodolites and heliotropes and plane tables and signal poles to very considerable heights, to the 15,000-foot and to the 20,000-foot (4,572-6,096 m) summits, even, of the outer mountains, where they would sometimes camp for weeks – cold, exhausted, and hungry – waiting for the clear line of sight on which all their intricate trigonometrical calculations depended. It was indisputably from the 16,872-foot (5,142 m) summit of Haramukh, above the vale of Kashmir, that Montgomerie, in 1856, first saw at a distance of 140 miles (225 m) "two fine peaks standing very high above the general range" – designated K1 and K2.[3]

Montgomerie's papers in the publications of the Royal Geographical Society remain an important record of discovery in Trans-Himalaya, and the activities of his pandits (native born explorers – also "pundits") continue to capture the imagination, being the inspiration for Rudyard Kipling's *Kim*, in which book Montgomerie was the model for Colonel Creighton, the spymaster and coordinator, and for later travel books.[4]

Robert Adams Paterson 1830-1904 made the first "Gutta" golf ball in 1848 from gutta-percha packing material as he was too poor to buy pigskin balls.[1] Gutta-percha is the evaporated milky juice or latex produced from a tree most commonly found in Malaysia. It is hard and non-brittle and becomes soft and impressible at the temperature of boiling water. Gutta balls were handmade by rolling the softened material on a board. The new durability of the Gutta, together with its much lower cost, resistance to water, and improved run, provided rejuvenation to the game of golf. Not without some resistance from traditionalists, the Gutta gradually replaced the Feathery.[2]

Thomas Pringle 1830-1911 was a hydraulic engineer who developed a particular interest in the exploitation of the hydraulic power provided by the Lachine Canal in Canada. It seems that he was responsible for installing two-thirds of the 76 turbines emplaced along the canal. Pringle operated as a consultant out of the Caledonia Iron Works at Lachine and seems archetypical of the pioneer engineer in Canada, especially as he was highly adaptive in the use of hydraulic power to generate electricity. His Lachine Rapids Hydraulic and Land Company was among the first to use St. Lawrence water for that purpose. In 1892, he established T. Pringle and Son, the oldest full-scale firm of consulting engineers in Canada, designing hydroelectric installations at Shawinigan Falls; at Chaudiere Falls south of Quebec City; and at the Long Sault in Ontario.[1]

Pringle provided advice on using water and steam power to various Canadian companies in Ontario and Quebec, including the Montmorency Cotton Manufacturing Company, the Magog Textile and Print Company (the first calico printing company in Canada), the Hochelaga Cotton Manufacturing Company, and the Compagnie de Filature Sainte-Anne. He advised these mills on the use of water and steam power and on the layout of their machinery. He was also an agent for the highly efficient Hercules turbines – which had a maximum efficiency of 89.2% – and had installed this type of turbine in numerous mills, particularly textile ones.[2]

Archibald Scott Couper 1831-1892 had revolutionary ideas about the way atoms joined to form molecules. He was the first person to form a concrete idea of molecular structure, proposing that atoms joined to each other like *Tinkertoys* in specific three-dimensional structures. He postulated rings of atoms as the structures of some molecules, and straight chains for others. Also of importance was his idea that each carbon atom could be joined to exactly four other atoms in the structure of a molecule. Couper was the first person to draw molecular structures using elemental symbols for atoms and with lines drawn between the atoms to indicate the bonds between them.[1]

Couper wrote three papers which are his main claim to fame. The first, *Some derivatives of benzene*, was a straightforward account of the preparation of two new bromine derivatives of benzene. The second was more theoretical, dealing with the constitution of salicylic acid. This was of interest to the eminent German chemist Friedrich August Kekulé, but he failed to repeat Couper's experiment: many years later Couper was proved perfectly correct. In the third paper, *On a new chemical theory*, Couper clearly enunciated a new theory of the linking of carbon atoms which marked a transition from the prevailing type theory to the modern structure theory. He deduced that carbon had a combining power (valency) of four or two and a unique capacity for joining itself to other atoms of its own kind – the secret of the existence of millions of organic (carbon) compounds. All three papers were published in *Comptes rendus de l'Académie des Sciences*.[2]

John McFarlane Gray 1831-1893 was a maritime engineer who, in 1863, patented a portable steam riveter which could also be used for caulking and chipping. It was particularly suitable for riveting ships' frames lying horizontally on the ground with the riveting cylinder below and the dolly at top. To shift the machine when the rivet is completed, the dolly is compressed by a jerk as before, and the compression is retained by the detent until the machine has been removed to the next hole and the rivet inserted, when the detent is withdrawn, and the dolly holds up the rivet against the blows of the riveter.

Gray also built and installed the first ever steam engine with a powered steering gear. This was a steam-powered mechanical amplifier used to drive the rudder position to match the wheel position. It was installed on Isambard Kingdom Brunel's *Great Eastern*, by far the largest ship of its day, which made power steering a necessity. "In order to turn a rudder a force is applied to a tiller. As ships became larger the rudders also increased in size and the manpower necessary to turn the rudder increased. Brunel's large steamship *Great Eastern* was the first ship fitted with a powered steering gear; this was a steam engine-driven system developed by John McFarlane Gray and it was installed in 1867 during a refit."[1]

Gray was also first to identify that an iron ship could break in two by repeated compression and straightening. "Mr John McFarlane Gray, of the Board of Trade, wrote a most valuable report upon the breaking in two, at sea, of the paddle-wheel steamer *Mary*, built on the Clyde, and he demonstrated that the upper works gave way in compression and not in tension; but, at the same time, he showed that this was not by crushing in the iron, but by repeated bulging and straightening, whereby the honest iron was ultimately obliged to yield."[2]

James Paris Lee 1831-1904 designed the Lee magazine rifle in 1878, capable of firing 30 shots per minute. It was the first rifle from which the spent cartridge could be expelled as part of the loading action. The weapon was adopted first by the American Navy and then by China. In 1888, the British Army approved the Lee-Metford rifle for extensive field tests. This rifle combined Lee's quick firing design with a barrel rifling method developed by William Ellis Metford. When the rifling in the gun proved inadequate, the British Army went back to the old Enfield rifling method and approved the Lee-Enfield for general use for its forces throughout the world.[1]

"The patents granted to the Lee rifle cited its breech-loading mechanism, the bolt action and the detachable magazine in front of the trigger guard. The Lee bolt locked into place by a natural downward movement, tightly sealing the chamber. Almost every sporting arm since has used James Lee's simple and reliable mechanism, the number of moving parts reduced to an absolute minimum, the action reliable and fool-proof despite an army's best effort to prove otherwise. Unlike other designs a soldier in the field could reload the magazine without difficulty, its mechanical function little altered by cold, dampness and dirt. The bolt sealed so tight the cartridge size and propellant were reduced while maintaining both velocity and accuracy."[2]

It had a ten-bullet magazine and a high rate of fire at 12 shots per minute to a trained soldier. The version that was in use by the British Army at the outbreak of the First World War was the Lee Enfield SMLE No.1 Mk.III. The first shots that the British fired in World War I were at Malplaquet. The Germans were pulled up short near Mons as the withering rifle fire of the British caused them heavy casualties. Two days later, on the 25 August 1914 at Le Cateau, the story of Mons was repeated only on a bloodier scale. Once again, the Germans attacked in tightly bunched waves and again they were met with rifle fire so intense that they thought the British were equipped with machine guns. It is most likely one of the most "soldier proof" rifles ever designed. It was also preferred for its reliability under the most adverse conditions, as well as its speed of operation. In 1912, trials conducted at Hythe against the German Service rifle, it was found that about 14-15 rounds a minute could be fired from the Mauser, compared with 28 for the SMLE.[3]

How many Lee-Enfields were produced is open to conjecture. The Stevens Arms Company manufactured more than a million between 1941 and 1945. Australian companies made 650,000 during the same period. Other factories in Toronto and three near Birmingham, England, manufactured huge numbers also. In all, something like sixteen million Lee-Enfields found a role in the theatres of the 20th century, not including unlicensed copies.[4]

James Clerk Maxwell 1831-1879 is known for his four equations that, together, form a complete description of the production and interrelation of electric and magnetic fields.[1]

While only 18, and still a student in Edinburgh, he contributed a paper to the *Transactions* of The Royal Society – *On the Equilibrium of Elastic Solids*, which is remarkable, not only on account of its intrinsic power and the youth of its author, but also because in it he laid the foundation of one of the most singular discoveries of his later life, the temporary double refraction produced in viscous liquids by shearing stress.[2] Maxwell was appointed professor of natural philosophy at Marischal College, Aberdeen, in 1856 before moving to King's College, London in 1860. He later became the first highly prestigious Cavendish Professor of Physics at Cambridge. Maxwell also introduced the terms "vector" and "scalar potential".

He formulated the unified theory of electromagnetism, the kinetic theory of gases and a theory of colour. Maxwell worked towards a theory to explain electrical and magnetic phenomena in mathematical terms, culminating in 1864 with the formulation of the fundamental equations of electromagnetism (Maxwell's equations). These equations also described the propagation of light, for he had shown that light consists of transverse electromagnetic waves in a hypothetical medium, the "ether". This great synthesis of theories uniting a wide range of phenomena is worthy to set beside those of Isaac Newton and Albert Einstein. Like all such syntheses, it led on to further discoveries.

Of more direct technological application was Maxwell's work on colour vision, begun in 1849, showing that all colours could be derived from the three primary colours: red, yellow and blue. This enabled him, in 1861, to produce a colour image of a tartan. Maxwell's discoveries about colour vision were quickly taken up and led to the development of colour printing and photography.[3]

The claim is often made that Maxwell was the first to take a colour photograph, in 1861. This is not true, since Sir John Herschel and Edmond Becquerel took coloured photographs of spectra in 1842 and 1843 respectively; examples of their work are still in existence. Maxwell may have been the first person to produce a coloured image of an object, which is more challenging than photographing a spectrum. But he did not really take a coloured photograph at all; he produced three black and white positive transparencies, and by projecting them simultaneously on a screen, using red, green and blue light, he created a fairly good image of a "bow made of ribbon, striped with various colours". The ribbon, which had red, green and blue stripes, had been tied into a rosette. Maxwell's three-colour system provided the basis for modern colour photography, but it took about 90 years for it to become commercially feasible. In 1935, Eastman Kodak introduced its *Kodachrome* materials, involving three layers containing organic dyes of the three primary colours. Coloured prints were not available until 1942, and not commercially available until the 1950s.[4]

In 1855, he presented to The Royal Society of Edinburgh a paper entitled *Experiments on color, as perceived by the eye, with remarks on color-blindness*. He demonstrated to the audience his favourite colour-experiment device: a specially designed colour top which had a flat surface to which he could attach coloured sectors of various sizes. Maxwell's article, largely experimental, is a model of thoroughness, and marks the beginning of the science of quantitative colorimetry. Maxwell showed that red, green and blue make a better set of primary colours than red, yellow and blue. He distinguished clearly, for the first time, between hue (spectral colour, defined by its wavelength), tint (degree of saturation of colour), and shade (intensity of illumination).

His procedure was to obtain matches between various mixtures of colours, and to relate the compound colours to the primary ones by means of equations. He constructed colour diagrams consisting of equilateral triangles, with the primary colours at the angular points. Any colour produced from a mixture of only two primaries was represented by a point on the side of the triangle. If three primary colours were involved the point was within the diagram.

In 1858, Maxwell abandoned the colour top and arranged for the construction of a colour box with which he could combine colours. He later constructed other colour boxes based on the same principle. His wife and several others assisted him in making observations with these devices. In 1860, he presented a major paper to The Royal Society, *On the theory of compound colors, and the relations of the colors of the spectrum*, which was later published in the *Philosophical Transactions*. In it he established which colours had to be added or subtracted to produce any compound colour.[5]

In 1860, in *Illustrations of the dynamical theory of gases*, Maxwell showed that viscosity is independent of density, or pressure.[6]

In 1861, in *On Physical Lines of Force*, Maxwell announced his discovery that some of the properties of the vibrations in the magnetic medium are identical with those of light: "The velocity of transverse undulations in our hypothetical medium ... agrees so exactly with the velocity of light ... that we can scarcely avoid the inference that *light consists in the transverse undulations of the same medium which is the cause of electric and magnetic phenomena*".[7]

In 1868, Maxwell published *On Governors*, a mathematical analysis of governors, the first significant paper on feedback mechanisms.[8]

In 1871, in *Theory of Heat*, Maxwell proposed the idea that an intelligent being, named "Maxwell's Demon" by William Thomson (Lord Kelvin), could by simple inspection of molecules (i.e., without doing work) violate the second law. "The demon points to ... the problem of reconciling the irreversible increase in entropy of the universe demanded by thermodynamics with the dynamical laws governing the motion of molecules, which are reversible with respect to time".[9] In this book, Maxwell gave a particularly clear account of thermodynamics. It included some fundamental equations which have come to be known as the "Maxwell relations".

In 1873, in *A Treatise on Electricity and Magnetism*, Maxwell tried to finish off the notion of action-at-a-distance and wrote a summary of his equations in terms of symmetry and vector structure. This relational Lagrangian method enabled him to forego any mention of mechanical ether, supposed by many physicists of the time to be the fundamental electromagnetic substance. Maxwell perceived that these equations had wave solutions and that electromagnetic waves of all frequencies were generated by accelerating electric charges and travelled at the same speed. Moreover, based on his electromagnetic theory, he established that light exerts a radiation pressure. This conclusion had many implications. He also proposed that these waves could be generated in the laboratory by creating a quickly oscillating current.

In popular accounts of the theory of relativity, Einstein is usually depicted as the only person responsible for that theory. However, Maxwell's electromagnetism, together with the ether concept, played a central role in Einstein's theory that led to a new dynamic where mass increased with velocity, and energy changes were accompanied by mass changes. Maxwell's *Treatise on Electricity and Magnetism* was published in 1873, containing the theoretical prediction that light should produce pressure. When Maxwell developed the theory of electromagnetic waves, he proved that the speed of those waves should have a speed equal to (or close to) the measured speed of light and concluded that light was an electromagnetic wave. When, in 1887, Heinrich Hertz produced short wavelength electromagnetic waves in the laboratory and showed that they had indeed the speed of light, Maxwell's theory was strongly confirmed.[10]

In 1877, in *On Boltzmann's Theorem on the Average Distribution of Energy in a System of Material Points*, Maxwell proved that the densities of the constituent components in a rotating mixture of gases would be the same as if each gas were present by itself. Hence, gaseous mixtures could be separated by means of a centrifuge.

In 1878, in *On Stresses in Rarefied Gases Arising From Inequalities of Temperature*, explaining the action of a radiometer, Maxwell noted that "when a viscous fluid moves past a solid body, it generates tangential stresses by sliding [i.e., 'slip' effects] over the surface with a finite velocity". Independently, Osbourne Reynolds came to a similar conclusion at about the same time.[11]

Maxwell's work on the rings of the planet Saturn is of particular interest since it led to his later more important work on the kinetic theory of gases. At the time, astronomers had observed three concentric rings about Saturn, all in the same plane. It was known that at least some regions of the rings must be quite thin, since in some areas the planet can be plainly seen through them. Maxwell carried out a careful theoretical treatment, and concluded that the rings could not be solid or liquid, since the mechanical forces acting upon rings of such immense size would break them up. He suggested that instead the rings are composed of a vast number of individual solid particles rotating in separate concentric orbits at different speeds. His final article on the subject, *On the stability of the motion of Saturn's rings*, published in the *Proceedings of The Royal Society of Edinburgh* in 1859, ran to 90 pages and is a monumental, meticulous and lucid analysis of the problem.

Later studies, including observations from Voyager spacecraft, have confirmed Maxwell's conclusions. The particulate nature of the rings is confirmed by observations of stars seen through portions of the rings. Spectroscopic studies have shown that the particles are composed of impure ice, or at least are ice-covered. Radar observations making use of the Doppler Effect have confirmed the range of speeds predicted by Maxwell. It appears that the particles have diameters ranging from a few centimetres to a hundred metres.[12]

Maxwell developed his kinetic theory of gases from 1859 onwards, in which year he presented a theory of the viscosity of gases based on kinetic theory to the British Association for the Advancement of Science. He concluded that gas viscosities are independent of pressure, and that they increase approximately with the square root of the absolute temperature. At the same meeting, he also announced his famous theory of the distribution of molecular speeds. This work was published in the *Philosophical Magazine* in 1860. In 1862, Rudolph Clausius pointed out certain errors in Maxwell's 1860 paper, and Maxwell agreed that the criticisms were valid. Clausius put forward a treatment himself, but it also had unsatisfactory features. Maxwell had to grapple with the problem for some years before he was satisfied. In 1867, he published a much-improved version of his kinetic theory, including a better derivation of his distribution law. Maxwell's work on the distribution of speeds was extended in 1868 by Ludwig Boltzmann in terms of the distribution of energy among the particles. The whole field of statistical mechanics was based on these treatments.[13]

Albert Einstein said of him: "The work of James Clerk Maxwell changed the world forever."[14] The special theory of relativity owes its origins to Maxwell's equations of the electromagnetic field. Einstein also said: "Since Maxwell's time, physical reality has been thought of as represented by continuous fields, and not capable of any mechanical interpretation. This change in the conception of reality is the most profound and the most fruitful that physics has experienced since the time of Newton." [15]

Maxwell is considered a father of modern physics. His ideas had far-ranging impacts in the fields of electricity and electronics, including radio, television, radar and communications; they also helped to make wide-scale industrialisation possible. Maxwell's broader legacy is that he demonstrated the beautiful power of human reason to make intelligible the seemingly unintelligible complexity of the universe.[16]

"The triumph of Clerk Maxwell was the triumph of a new kind of mathematics. It established the authority of mathematicians in a way that nothing ever had, not even the discoveries of Newton." [17]

"James Clerk Maxwell opened the doors of science farther than anyone ever had or possibly ever will." [18]

Andrew Noble 1831-1915 is often considered a founder of the science of ballistics. During the 1850s, while studying the relative merits of smoothbore and rifled cannon, he devised a method of comparing their accuracy of fire. About 1862, he applied his invention, the chronoscope (a device for measuring very small time intervals), to determine the velocity of shot in gun barrels.[1]

Swedish inventor Alfred Nobel, who set up works to produce nitroglycerine at Ardeer, Ayrshire in 1871, is world famous for his bequest of the Nobel Peace Prize, yet he was a manufacturer of gunpowder. The name of Andrew Noble is not as well known, yet he is considered the father of the science of ballistics, by which gunpowder could be put to its most effective and deadly use. With English chemist Frederick Abel, he contributed greatly to the progress of gunnery, making it an exact science instead of a hit-or-miss affair. After leaving Edinburgh Academy, Noble studied at the Royal Military Academy, Woolwich. He entered the Royal Artillery in 1849, and devised a method to compare the accuracy of fire from each gun. After joining an engineering firm, he applied his chronoscope to determine the velocity of shot in gun barrels by measuring very small time intervals. He thus established the science of ballistics. In addition, his invention led to new types of gunpowder, a redesign of guns and new, faster and safer methods of loading.[2]

Noble's chronoscope is so well adapted to the measurement of very small intervals of time that it is usually inside the gun. A series of "cutting plugs" is screwed into the sides of the gun at measured intervals, and in each is inserted a loop of wire which forms part of the primary circuit of an induction coil. On the passage of a shot this wire is severed by means of a small knife which projects into the bore and is actuated by the shot as it passes; the circuit being thus broken, a spark passes between the terminals of the secondary of the coil. There is a separate coil and circuit for each plug. The recording arrangement consists of a series of discs, one for each plug, mounted on one axle and rotating at a high angular velocity. The edges of these discs are covered with a coating of lamp-black, and the secondaries of the coils are caused to discharge against them, so that a minute spot burnt in the lamp-black of each disc indicates the moment of the cutting of the wire in the corresponding plug. Hence measurement of the distance between two successive spots gives the time occupied by the shot in moving over the portion of the bore between two successive plugs. By the aid of a vernier, readings are made to thousandths of an inch, and the peripheral velocity of the discs being 1,100 inches a second (2,794 cm/s), the machine indicates portions of time rather less than one-millionth of a second; it is, in fact, practically correct to hundred-thousandths of a second.[3]

Peter Guthrie Tait 1831-1901 helped develop quaternions, an advanced algebra that gave rise to vector analysis and was instrumental in the development of modern mathematical physics. He made fundamental contributions to the theory of quaternions, as evident in *Elementary Treatise on Quaternions* (1867), which went through three editions. Later he wrote *Introduction to Quaternions* (1873) with Philip Kelland. In collaboration with William Thomson (Lord Kelvin), Tait produced *Treatise on Natural Philosophy* (1867), which traced the concept of conservation of energy to the work of Sir Isaac Newton. Their efforts were vital to the newly emerging concept of energy and its properties.

After the publication of the *Treatise*, Tait concentrated on studies of thermoelectricity and thermal conductivity (the capacity for heat flow). He wrote a pioneering study in the topology of knots (1876-1884), an important series of papers on the kinetic theory of gases (1886-1892), and classic papers on the trajectory of the golf ball (1890-1893).[1]

In a fantastic experiment involving smoke rings, Tait and William Thomson came up with a new atomic theory based around the idea of knots and links. This took on a mathematical life of its own, with Tait becoming one of the world's first topologists and inventing conjectures which remained unproven for over a hundred years.[2] Following up on Kelvin's suggestion that atoms were composed of tiny strings knotted in various configurations, Tait made the first systematic study of knots and their properties.[3]

He conducted important investigations in thermodynamics and experiments to determine the density of the ozone and the effects of passing electrical charges through oxygen and other gases. He was the first to attempt to classify knots of any number of crossings. He established a new vocabulary and gave exact descriptions of terms such as knottiness, beknottedness, plait, link, lock, and a Scottish word flype, which has no English equivalent, the nearest interpretation being "turn-out-side-in."

Tait was the first to raise the question of why a well-driven ball carries so far and remains in the air as long as it does. Most golfers know that a well-struck ball is not the result of mere muscle, but is largely due to skill in making a swing. Tait was the first to realise the question was a dynamical problem that could be precisely stated and approximately solved. He recalled, "We fastened one end of a long, untwisted tape to the ball and the other to the ground and induced a good player [Freddie] to drive the ball into a stiff clay face a yard or two off … the tape is always twisted no doubt to different amounts by different players – say from 40 to 120 or so turns per second. The fact is indisputable."

Early golfers thought all spin was detrimental to distance, but Tait discovered that a ball driven with a "backspin" actually produced lift. He found that a ball driven about a horizontal axis with the top of the ball coming towards the golfer has a lifting force on it that keeps the ball in the air much longer than would be possible without spin. What actually happens is that the backspin imparted by the club on impact at thousands of revolutions per minute causes the ball to behave like the wing of an airplane. Air flows more quickly over the top of the ball than the bottom. As Tait put it, "in topping, the upper part of the ball is made to move forward faster than does the centre, consequently the front of the ball descends in virtue of the rotation, and the ball itself skews in that direction. When a ball is undercut it gets the opposite spin to the last, and, in consequence, it tends to deviate upwards instead of downwards. The upward tendency often makes the path of a ball … concave upwards in spite of the effects of gravity." Tait published several scholarly articles describing his experiments and findings.

He was also the first to experiment with furrowing the face of a club with a number of parallel grooves to improve their driving power by affording a better grip on the ball. Later research has shown that a larger spin produces a larger drag, which makes the ball slow down more rapidly and thus decreases the distance it travels. On the other hand, a larger spin produces more lift, which keeps the ball in the air for a longer time and thus allows it to fly farther. The appropriate ratio of lift to drag depends upon the individual player. Physicist Raymond Penner of Malaspina University College in British Columbia, Canada, established that harder hitters get better results with clubs of lower loft.[4]

James Howden 1832-1913 played a major part in the history of Clyde shipbuilding at a time when it was the dominant shipbuilding river in the world. In 1882, he patented the Howden System of Forced Draught which greatly improved efficiency in steam engines by combining mechanical draught with the transfer of heat from the flue gases to the combustion air. This system used waste gases to heat the air in the combustion chamber of a boiler and was one of dozens of patents granted to Howden. This invention made it much more economical for steam-powered ships and greatly helped the transatlantic and Asian trade. When it was first tested in 1884 on the *New York City*, the engine horsepower was improved by 3% and the fuel consumption reduced by 35%. Within the next 12 years more than 1,000 of these marine boilers were installed in ships and Howden's "system" lasted for more than six decades, saving an estimated 13.6 million tonnes of coal.[1]

"Among Howden's many achievements were the devising of air surface condensers; a scheme for utilising the waste heat from the boiler fire gases; [and] forms of water-tube boilers for high pressure."[2] He founded a company in 1854 and by the time he died it was building the largest reciprocating engine in the world, installed in the year following his death at Woolwich Arsenal in London. That company is, in 2014, the world market leader in air and gas handling equipment with over 4,000 employees. Howden also developed high speed turbines and engines, mainly for generating electricity.

John S. Maxwell 1832-1916 was a Scots-born Confederate Army agent credited with the invention of the time bomb, which he called a "horological torpedo". He used a clockwork mechanism to detonate a bomb on 9 August 1864 on the docks at City Point (now Hopewell), a small village in Virginia which had become Union Army General Grant's headquarters and, as such, the centre of a major war effort. Maxwell and another agent, R.K. Dillard, managed to get through Union security undetected with the Maxwell-designed time bomb. When the bomb exploded about 11.40 AM, the nearby barge *J. E. Kendrick* "was totally vaporised" and another barge exploded, as did a building on the wharf. It was estimated that damage of around $2 million was incurred with at least 43 people killed and 126 injured, although it is believed that the number was much higher, particularly as some of the casualties, like the barge, would have vaporised.[1]

Patrick Stewart 1832-1865 organised and laid the first telegraph cable between Karachi (now Pakistan) and Constantinople (Istanbul, Turkey). The first attempt to lay a cable between Karachi and Aden, via the Red Sea, in 1859, had been a failure and Stewart was determined to avoid its mistakes, particularly to ensure effective insulation and protection of the cable. His remarkable submarine cable was constructed in London in four sections: a total length of 1,250 miles [2,011 km], weighing 4 tons [3.6 tonnes] per nautical mile.

Despite the logistical problems and difficulties with local rulers, the whole submarine cable-laying operation from Bushire to Fao was completed in a mere 2½ months in 1864 without a hitch – a triumph of meticulous organisation and engineering. The tiny Telegraph Island off the Musandam Coast (Oman) was the essential relay station, re-transmitting messages yet ensuring that it took only an average of 45 minutes for messages to reach London. Stewart died of fever in Istanbul, aged only 32. The news of his death was one of the first messages sent over the telegraph cable which he had supervised throughout its length.[1]

John Harper 1833-1906 patented a device in 1863 "for 'straining the wire' in fence-making which was to become crucial in the development of suspension bridges which the firm subsequently began to design."[1] The wire was wound up within the post using a tool rather like an Allen key. Once the desired tension was generated, the spindle was locked by the insertion of a peg into the opposing notches, one on the spindle and the other on the casing.

Henry Charles Fleeming Jenkin 1833-1885 urged an alliance of standardised practice with theory in dealing with the laying of telegraph cables under the ocean. Jenkin experienced seasickness from his first telegraph cruise in 1858 to his last in 1873, during which time he advised British governments on telegraph nationalisation, and served Reuters, the French

Atlantic, and the German Union telegraph companies. In 1861, the *Encyclopaedia Britannica* (8th edition) published Jenkin's Birkenhead investigations, the first measurements in absolute units of the specific resistance of the insulator gutta-percha.

Image 61 – First telpherage, in Glynde, UK, 1885

In 1882, Jenkin filed the first of some dozen patents for telpherage, a system for the economical overhead electrical conveyance of bulky materials.[1] In 1870, he published an essay called *On the Graphical Representation of Supply and Demand*, in which he becomes the first person to draw the supply and demand graphic, indisputably the most famous graphic in economics (popularised through Alfred Marshall).

John Lee 1833-1907 co-invented a prototype bolt action rifle with his brother James Paris Lee. The rifle they made led to the Lee-Metford and Lee-Enfield series of rifles. In 1878, Lee and his brother, James Paris Lee, perfected a rifle with a box magazine. The gun was tested successfully in Wallaceburg, in Ontario. Bullets were fired from the Lee Brothers Foundry across the Sydenham River into an oak tree hundreds of yards away. Ten thousand of these rifles were sold to the US Navy, and they also became the standard issue for the British Army for over 60 years. The patent rights were purchased by England for £50,000 plus 50 pence for each magazine. The rifle was produced in Enfield, England in 1888, thus the "Lee Enfield" name.[1]

John Brunton 1835-1899 invented, in 1862, what he termed the New Otoscope – actually an auriscope. Brunton, Arnold & Sons of England and Husar of Germany were the only companies to manufacture this amazing device which was used to examine ears and also perform surgery on the ear. The early otoscope cone-shaped tube or specula tube was placed in the ear canal. The direct rays of the sun were necessary to reflect into the large reflective tube or if an assistant was available to hold a lantern or candle so the doctor could examine the ear and/or perform surgery. Brunton's otoscope consisted of a tube with a funnel-shaped reflector for collecting and concentrating rays of light, set at a right angle to the tube, and a specula fitted at one end of the tube. At the other end of the tube there is an eye-piece for the observer. Inside the body of the auriscope, a concave mirror with a hole in the centre lies at an angle of 45°. Rays of light are let in at the side of the tube, through the funnel reflector. These rays then fall onto the mirror, are reflected into the ear, and then are carried back to the eye of the observer through the hole in the mirror, being magnified by the lens of the eye-piece.[1]

Brunton devised his own instrument because he had experienced difficulties when examining patients' ears with ordinary aural instruments. Such difficulties included the problems of the observer's head obstructing the light source and the observer's eye being unable to get close enough to the object of study to permit minute examination. Brunton believed that his auriscope improved upon previous aural instruments and he counted among its advantages its simplicity of construction and ease of use.

In the 19th century, it was this rather than an otoscope that was used to diagnose ear problems, including infections. Brunton first described it in *The Lancet*. Retired physician Dr John North, who is an expert on the Royal Australian College of General Practitioners' archive and the college's honorary curator, describes a Lauder Brunton Auriscope in their collection: "As an instrument it is a masterpiece," he says. "It was a great step forward. It is a gem." He explains that it works by the light from a candle or lamp being placed under the circular element of the contraption. It is reflected onto a plane mirror and this enabled the doctor to see inside the patient's ear canal. Other types of auriscope also emerged on the market after the 1862 invention, but none of them ever achieved the popularity of Brunton's invention.[2]

Archibald Campbell 1835-1908 was an amateur astronomer who observed, in 1874, a white halo around Venus, proving it has an atmosphere. He designed a speed indicator, which was fitted to ships in the Royal Navy, and carried out studies into the efficiency of aerial propellers some years before the Wright Brothers first powered flight in 1903.[1]

Archibald Geikie 1835-1924 showed that rivers play a major role in soil erosion and established him as the foremost advocate of the fluvial theories of erosion.[1] He is regarded as a pioneer historian of geology and enhanced its study in Britain through his many readable and popular textbooks, and speaking tours.[2]

Geikie found that in the "immense Mississippi River basin ... erosion removes one centimetre of rock in 200 years. At this rate, North America would be flattened in 4½ million years. In the small Po River basin, the rate of removing one centimetre of rock is only 24 years. At this rate, Europe could be levelled in less than 500,000 years." Geikie pointed out that, although these were only orders of magnitude, they still demonstrated the rapidity of geological action."[3]

Geikie's career was outstandingly successful. He served as president of the Geological Society (1890-1892 and 1906-1908), and as president of the British Association (1892). Elected fellow of The Royal Society in 1865, he served as foreign secretary (1889-1893), secretary (1903-1908), and president (1908-1912), the only geologist ever to have occupied this position. He was also active in the work of the early international geological congresses.[4]

Imrie Bell 1836-1906 made useful changes to concreting, such as soaping the inside of planed formwork to stop it sticking to the concrete. He was the engineer who built the Channel Islands' St Helier Harbour works and breakwater in 1867, and the La Corbiere lighthouse, the first one built in Britain of Portland cement (concrete).[1] He introduced the use of sand pumping during the sinking of wells in 1870 while working on the East Indian Railway, where he had responsibility for the southern end of the large railway bridge over the Jumna River at Allahabad.

Walter Brock 1836-1907 developed the quadruple-expansion steam engine which further improved the consumption of coal. "The economy of fuel which resulted from the introduction of high-pressure steam, and the compound engine with surface condensation for steamships, was very remarkable. Between 1860 and 1870, when the pressure of steam used for marine engines was about 30 lbs [13.6 kg], by boiler gauge, and the steam expanded in a single cylinder, the amount of coal consumed by the best engines was about 4 lbs [1.8 kg] per IHP [indicated horsepower] per hour. On the introduction of the compound engine, the consumption fell to a little over 2 lbs [0.9 kg] per IHP per hour. The triple expansion engine reduced this to as low as 1.4 lbs [0.6 kg] per IHP per hour, and the quadruple expansion engine further reduced the consumption by about 10 per cent."[1] Brock took charge of Denny's Clyde shipyards in 1887 and under his direction the firm "developed into one of the largest and best-equipped marine engineering establishments on the Clyde."[2]

John Carruthers 1836-1914 was appointed Engineer-in-Chief and surveyed and built more than 1,600 km of railway line, bridges and tunnels in New Zealand between 1871 and 1878. He supervised the survey and design of one of the most remarkable engineering achievements in New Zealand, the Rimutaka Incline. Carruthers made the decision that an incline system should be used, and he chose the Fell centre-rail system to combat the problem of steep grades. His was the only really successful implementation of the Fell technology anywhere in the world. He also designed and built the Rakaia Gorge Bridge, a unique piece of invention that is still in use today (2016). From his base in London, Carruthers supervised work in Venezuela and Argentina, and was consulting engineer to the government of Western Australia.[1]

Andrew Smith Hallidie 1836-1900 was responsible for the famous San Francisco streetcar. He was born on 16 March 1836, but there is doubt as to his actual place of birth, with some sources stating he was born in London and others in Dunfermline. Both his parents were from Dumfries-shire – his father, Andrew, born 1798 in Kirkpatrick Fleming and his mother, Julia Johnstone, came from Lockerbie. Hallidie's original name was simply Andrew Smith to which he later added the extra name in honour of his uncle, Sir Andrew Hallidie, physician to King William IV and then to Queen Victoria. Both father and son sailed to California in 1852 where Andrew junior learned the wire rope business, quickly graduating to constructing rigid suspension bridges to a design that he patented in 1867. "Starting in the early 1860s, he built a bridge across the American River at Folsom, and spanned the Bear, Trinity, Stanislaus, and Tuolumne Rivers."[1]

Following the discovery of the Comstock Lode, he concentrated on wire rope production to supply silver mines in Nevada, and by 1871 he had designed plans for streetcars in San Francisco. The streetcars had a connector called a "grip" that could seize a rotating loop of wire rope to propel it forward, or the grip could be released to bring the cars to a standstill (the same system used by ski lifts today). Hallidie was stimulated by a humanitarian desire to help horses after seeing five of them dragged to a terrible death when the brakes on a heavily laden cart failed on the steep roads of San Francisco. Ironically, he came near to death on a number of occasions:

once a bank under which he was working caved in; in Mokelumne Hill he was attacked by a band of Mexicans; once he was caught in the midst of a forest fire; he barely escaped when a blast exploded prematurely in a shaft at the end of a 600-foot (183 m) tunnel; at another time he fell twenty-five feet (7.6 m) from a suspension bridge; at Gray Eagle Bar, on the Middle Fork of the American River, he was carried on a piece of timber over the rapids for half a mile; and the four horses pulling a Concord stagecoach in which he was riding from Nevada City to Lincoln ran away with him when the driver left them standing in front of a hotel.[2]

He raised the funds necessary to build the cable car system, using $20,000 of his own money, which was his total wealth. Although there had been other attempts to build cable cars, Hallidie's was the first to be a success. The Hallidie Ropeway opened for business on 1 September 1873, covering a distance of 853 m and rising more than 93 m in hilly San Francisco. It was a great commercial success and Hallidie's patents were used to build cable cars around America and the world, including London and in Sydney, Australia.

In the decade from 1868, he served as president of the Mechanics' Institute of San Francisco, paying off thousands of dollars of its debt and leaving it both in credit and improved reputation. During that time, he was the leading mover behind the *Rogers Act* of 1878 which paved the way for Californian municipalities to build public libraries using the old social membership libraries as a hub. The Mechanics' Institute contributed to the establishment of the University of California, Berkeley. Hallidie wanted to ensure the positive impact the Institute was having on San Francisco continued indefinitely. With the future of the Institute in mind, Hallidie presented to the board a change in structure from that of a stockholders' company into that of a non-profit trust. Hallidie's restructuring of the Institute, coupled with the earnings generated from the industrial fairs, prevented the Institute from the doom faced by the Mercantile Library, which in time wasted away from want of public support.[3] His streetcars are an internationally renowned tourist attraction while still serving a utilitarian function in the transport system of San Francisco.

Image 62 – San Francisco cable car

James Lyall 1836-1901 made improvements to the textile industry in 1868 when he designed a loom that had a positive-motion shuttle. This type of loom has a series of wheels with the first one being a ratchet that can transfer motion to a beam that draws the cloth forward. These looms spread throughout the world because they increased the width of the fabric that could be woven, and removed the need for picking sticks. They could also process a wider range of fabric, from silk to carpet, and needed less power for the operation of the looms. It became the most common type of loom in Lancashire, the major cotton manufacturing region in the world, as well as being used in the largest mills of the United States, Europe, China and Japan.[1] For his invention, Lyall received the very first gold medal, in 1869, from the American Institute of New York which, along with the Franklin Institute, was the first American organisation to hold exhibitions of scientific developments.

Image 63 – Lyall Positive Motion Loom
Engineering Weekly, 3 September 1869

Colin Campbell Scott-Moncrieff 1836-1916 is inseparably associated with irrigation, and pre-eminently with Egyptian irrigation. As Under-Secretary of State Public Works in Egypt, he restored the Nile barrage (dam) and irrigation works of Lower Egypt. He found the existing irrigation in a state of almost hopeless ruin and decay, and by dint of indefatigable exertions and unremitting toil restored it to a position of efficiency and importance far exceeding anything in its previous history. He said "It is like mending a watch and never stopping the works. ... But he carried through the work, and soon the produce of the fertile delta land was doubled."[1] His appointment was seen as the beginning of Anglo-Indian control over Egyptian hydraulics.[2] Other irrigation and canal projects included the Ganges Canal, where he acted as the Chief Engineer and made modifications to the original work.

He headed a delegation appointed in 1901 by George Nathaniel Curzon, the British viceroy of India, to draw up a comprehensive irrigation plan for India. This was a result of Lord Curzon's observation of famine conditions soon after his arrival in 1899. In 1903, Scott-Moncrieff recommended measures for the irrigation of an additional 10,200 square miles (26,400 square km) beyond the roughly 30,000 square miles (78,000 square km) already irrigated. The acceptance of these proposals by Lord Curzon's government in 1905 was a landmark in the government of India's irrigation policy.[3]

So much water was saved by this reconstruction that it was possible to build new branch canals. This was all to the good of famine prevention, but Scott-Moncrieff was surprised to learn that much of the water saved went to increase the acreage irrigated by farmers who had been irrigating for decades: there was simply too much political pressure to resist these fortunate headenders.[4] He was president of the Indian Irrigation Commission (1901-1903) and his report is said to be the most valuable survey ever written of Indian irrigation.[5]

David Boyle 1837-1891 was one of the American pioneers of refrigeration. He migrated to America and settled in Jefferson, Texas, where he built an ammonia compression plant in 1873 to make ice to cool lemonade. This was based on a patent the previous year – four years before Karl von Linde, the German engineer generally recognised as the designer of the first successful ammonia compression system.

Boyle moved to Chicago when his plant burned down in 1874 and his refrigerators were used to cool beer at the brewery of Ferdinand Heim junior in St Louis. He also had his machines manufactured by Crane and Company of Chicago and one of the first two made was bought by American Richard King, the owner of the King Ranch, the largest ranch in the USA.[1] With the advent of refrigeration, new markets opened up worldwide as the quality of transported meat could be maintained for far longer periods.

William Harkness 1837-1903 and, independently, American Charles Augustus Young discovered, in 1869, a new bright (emission) line in the spectrum of the Sun's corona, never before observed on Earth; they ascribed it to a new element which was named "coronium". In 1941, this green line was identified by Bengt Edlén (Sweden) as iron that has lost 13 electrons.[1]

Harkness articulated, in 1879, the theory of the focal curve of achromatic telescopes, and he designed most of the large instruments at the US Naval Observatory used during the latter part of the nineteenth and early part of twentieth centuries. After the Civil War, he studied the new problem of the behaviour of the magnetic compass under the influence of the heavy iron on ironclad ships using the US ironclad *Monadnock*.[2]

Harkness was one of the founders of the Philosophical Society of Washington and, in 1893, served as president of the American Association for the Advancement of Science.[3]

Frank McClean 1837-1904 identified stars with neutral helium absorption lines, deduced they were early in the stellar sequence, and was the first to show the coincidence of "helium stars" lying in regions of gaseous nebulae. Not least, in 1897, by recognising oxygen absorption in Beta Crucis, he first detected direct evidence of oxygen beyond our planet. McClean thus contributed to disputed schemes of stellar evolution by temperature classification, which were plagued by determining which stars were actually hottest. Spectroscopists before 1914 lacked the advances in nuclear theory that could make interpretation significant. McClean's high-detail spectra compelled reclassification of some stars, and the quality and completeness of the research justified the award to McClean in 1899 of the Royal Astronomical Society's gold medal.[1]

McClean developed a new design of spectroscope, which was named after him. Existing spectroscopes were difficult to use because it was necessary to align the star with a tiny slit. McClean's innovation was to use a concave cylindrical lens to overcome this. In practice, this meant that once a star was lined up with a telescope, the eyepiece could be removed and the spectroscope inserted. This allowed the device to be used on a wider range of telescopes, and became instantly popular with amateur and professional astronomers.[2]

Stuart Murray 1837-1919 championed the Goulburn Weir in Australia and "is regarded by many as the pioneer engineer of Victorian irrigation who turned the dreams of his contemporaries into reality. As engineer of the United Echuca and Waranga Waterworks Trust he played a key role in pressing for the construction of the Goulburn Weir. In 1884, he became Engineer in Chief of the Water Supply Department and helped design Goulburn Weir and Laanecoorie Reservoir and played a significant part in drafting water legislation. He was the first Chairman of the Victorian State Rivers and Water Supply Commission."[1]

John Alexander Reina Newlands 1837-1898 prepared, in 1863, the first periodic table of the elements arranged in order of relative atomic weight, and pointed out in 1865 the "law of octaves" whereby every eighth element has similar properties. He was ridiculed at the time, but five years later Russian chemist Dmitri Mendeleev published – independent of Newlands' work – a more developed form of the table, also based on atomic masses, which forms the basis of the one used today (arranged by atomic number).[1]

No.		No.		No.		No.		No.		No.		No.		No.
H	1	F	8	Cl	15	Co & Ni	22	Br	29	Pd	36	I	42	Pt & Ir	50
Li	2	Na	9	K	16	Cu	23	Rb	30	Ag	37	Cs	44	Os	51
G	3	Mg	10	Ca	17	Zn	24	Sr	31	Cd	38	Ba & V	45	Hg	52
Bo	4	Al	11	Cr	19	Y	25	Ce & La	33	U	40	Ta	46	Tl	53
C	5	Si	12	Ti	18	In	26	Zr	32	Sn	39	W	47	Pb	54
N	6	P	13	Mn	20	As	27	Di & Mo	34	Sb	41	Nb	48	Bi	55
O	7	S	14	Fe	21	Se	28	Ro & Ru	35	Te	43	Au	49	Th	56

Image 64 – Newlands' table of the elements

Just four years before Mendeleev announced his Periodic Table, Newlands wrote in *Chemical News*: "If the elements are arranged in order of their equivalents [i.e. relative atomic masses in today's terminology] with a few transpositions, it will be seen that elements belonging to the same group appear in the same horizontal line. Also, the numbers of similar elements differ by seven or multiples of seven. Members stand to each other in the same relation as the extremities of one or more octaves of music. Thus, in the nitrogen group phosphorus is the seventh element after nitrogen and arsenic is the fourteenth elements after phosphorus as is antimony after arsenic. This peculiar relationship I propose to call 'The Law of Octaves'." Newlands thought that patterns were connected with the relative weights of atoms (we would now call them relative atomic masses – they were then called atomic weights) of different elements.

H	F	Cl	Co/Ni	Br	Pd	I	Pt/Ir
Li	Na	K	Cu	Rb	Ag	Cs	Tl
G	Mg	Ca	Zn	Sr	Cd	Ba/V	Pb
Bo	Al	Cr	Y	Ce/La	U	Ta	Th
C	Si	Ti	In	Zr	Sn	W	Hg
N	P	Mn	As	Di/Mo	Sb	Nb	Bi
O	Si	Fe	Se	Ro/Ru	Te	Au	Os

Image 65 – Newlands' Table of Octaves

On 1 March 1865, he described his ideas at a lecture at the Chemical Society (a forerunner of The Royal Society of Chemistry). The lack of spaces for undiscovered elements and the placing of two elements in one box were justifiably criticised, but an unfair suggestion from Professor George Carey Foster was that he might have equally well listed the elements alphabetically. Foster was on the Publication Committee which refused to publish his paper, supposedly because it was of a purely theoretical nature. Humiliated, Newlands went back to his work as chief chemist at a sugar factory.

Four years later, Mendeleev, unaware of Newlands' ideas, formulated an improved Periodic Table which gained acceptance, particularly because he left spaces for undiscovered elements, some of which were soon found with properties he predicted. As the Periodic Table became accepted, Newlands, understandably, claimed its first publication. However, the Chemical Society did not back his claims. Indeed, the final years of his working life were spent running a family chemical business with his brother.

The Chemical Society made some amends for discrediting him by asking him in 1884 to give a lecture on the Periodic Law. However, its full recognition of his discovery waited until 1998, the centenary of his death, when The Royal Society of Chemistry oversaw the placing of a blue commemorative plaque on the wall of his birthplace.[2] The inscription reads "J.A.R. NEWLANDS, 1837-1898, CHEMIST and discoverer of the Periodic Law for the chemical elements WAS BORN AND RAISED HERE, ROYAL SOCIETY OF CHEMISTRY".

Alexander Crum Brown 1838-1922 proposed a new way to represent chemical constitution – each atom was to be indicated by the chemical symbol for the element concerned, bonds between atoms being symbolised by lines. Essentially this was the system of notation later employed universally. His M.D. thesis was entitled *On the Theory of Chemical Combination* and showed him to be a pioneer in scientific thought. In it he developed a system of graphic formulation of compounds which is essentially identical with that used today. His formulae were the first to show clearly both the valency and the linking of atoms in organic compounds. Some chemists quickly adopted Crum Brown's graphic formulae, e.g. four years later Edward Frankland used them throughout his entire course, considering that they had several important advantages over Friedrich August Kekule's.[1]

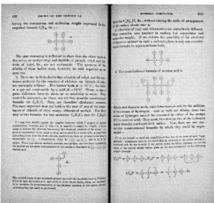

Image 66 – Extract from Alexander Crum Brown's influential paper, 1864

This simple device was of untold value and greatly facilitated the emergence of the theory of structure upon which later chemistry was predicated. It transformed the teaching of organic chemistry, particularly in the hands of Frankland, becoming known, somewhat unfairly, as "Frankland's notation".[2]

In 1892, with Edinburgh-born John Gibson, Brown published the well-known rule for determining the position in the benzene nucleus taken up by an entering radical with respect to one already present. He also, correctly, related vertigo to the motion of fluid in channels of the inner ear.

Thomas Blake Glover 1838-1911 was a merchant whose company, Glover & Co., became the biggest Western firm in Nagasaki, opening branches in Shanghai and Yokohama in 1864. Nicknamed the "Scottish samurai", he brought the first locomotive to Japan in 1865, and in the period 1871-1911 some 1,023 locomotives were exported from Britain to Japan. Of these, 626 came from Glasgow, and of the English-built locomotives fully 334 came from companies founded, or part-founded, by Scottish engineers. Glover acted as a consultant for Mitsubishi in various ways, playing a crucial role in the founding of what became the Kirin Brewery Company.[1] He later participated in establishing businesses that would become pillars of Mitsubishi's early growth and diversification. Demand for coal surged as steamships multiplied in Japanese waters. Glover, in partnership with the Hizen Clan, invested in developing the Takashima coal mine on an island near Nagasaki in 1868. Their mine was the first in Japan to employ Western methods of mining. Financial troubles later forced Glover to sell his stake, but he stayed on as manager of the mine for several more years. Mitsubishi acquired the mine in 1881 in the organisation's first main diversification beyond shipping.

Another enterprise Glover played a role in that later became part of Mitsubishi is the Nagasaki Shipyard. Japan lacked modern facilities for repairing ships, so Glover imported the necessary equipment for a slip dock in Nagasaki in 1868. He later sold his share to the government, which leased the dock to Mitsubishi as part of the shipyard in 1884.[2] For his services, he was the first non-Japanese to be honoured with the Order of the Rising Sun by the Emperor.[3]

Glover would be an important "pro-Japan" lobbyist, most notably through the British courtier and politician Lord Charles Spencer, adding to the impetus behind the 1902 Anglo-Japanese Alliance, which headed off potential problems for Britain during World War I.

By that time, however, and even more so after the victory over Russia in 1905, Glover – while publicly supporting Japan's imperial ambitions – was becoming privately ambivalent about the speed of the military build-up. Indeed, it was to lead to an expansion which would eventually set the new Empire of Japan against the old Western trading powers and end in the suicide of his own son in post-bombing Nagasaki.

Much of what was taken as axiomatic following the Meiji Restoration originally belonged to the Scottish Enlightenment, and was transmitted at a time when imperial free trade had given Scotland a means of expression within the British state. As such, the globalising choices faced by Glover's Japan had been faced by Scotland around a century before, and both countries in their turn came to see that they had to compete aggressively within, or through, empire to avoid being swallowed up by a new order.

In the case of what historians term the First Scottish Enlightenment, Adam Smith and David Hume brought philosophical scepticism and free-trade ideals; in the case of the Second Scottish

Enlightenment, Thomas Carlyle and John Stuart Mill added individual responsibility, heroism, and freedom. Both were imported enthusiastically around the time of the Meiji Restoration, and both fed into the heroic, ethnic, trade-based empire-building Japan embarked upon.[4]

Thomas John Maclagan 1838-1903 was the first person to specifically use salicin to cure acute articular rheumatism.[1] Aspirin – acetylsalicylic acid – in one form or another has been used in everyday life for millennia. About 3,500 years ago, several plants containing salicylate were first used to relieve pain and fever, and willow bark was also used by Hottentot tribesmen in southern Africa to treat rheumatic fever. Influenced by the herbalists' belief that antidotes were to be found in the vicinity of poisons, Maclagan is credited with the first clinical trial of aspirin – on himself. He started with two grams of salicin, increasing gradually to 30 grams. Finding no deleterious effects, he went on to treat a human patient suffering from rheumatic fever.[2]

Maclagan worked in France and Germany before taking a position as medical superintendent in Dundee in February 1864. A year later he was faced with a typhus epidemic through 1865-1866 that killed 23 city doctors and nurses. Maclagan enforced a "basic and rigorous health policy – quarantining patients and their relatives, destroying contaminated clothing and bedding" and, gradually, brought the epidemic under control.[3]

Returning to private practice, he experimented with salicin as a possible treatment for rheumatic fever which was rife in Dundee. Until then, the extensive investigations into the chemical make-up of salicin and the search for an artificial synthesis of salicylic acid had taken place in the closed world of the laboratory and little of this knowledge had yet been exploited. In 1874, even the idea of a trial was a novel one. The significance of Maclagan's experiments was that they tested for the first time – in a scientific framework – the claims made by those who believed in the therapeutic benefits of the salicylates, including their use as an anti-rheumatic treatment.

Maclagan's trials were rigorous – some patients were given drugs and others not, so establishing a simple control process that validated his results – and he was meticulous in insisting on regular doses until he was satisfied that the patient's pain had subsided and his temperature had become normal. Note: the person credited with the introduction of blind, controlled, randomised experiments is American Charles Sanders Peirce in 1884.

Maclagan was "quite aware that cases of acute rheumatism do sometimes unexpectedly improve without treatment and he had no surety that this was not a case in point." Maclagan also noted that the more acute the case, the more effective the therapy appeared to be, a fact that we know today to be true in rheumatoid arthritis."[4]

Maclagan published his results in *The Lancet* on 4 March 1876 with the effect that salicin, already expensive at two shillings an ounce, increased to twelve shillings an ounce within a year. Also, others – mostly German – declared that they had had similar results with the cheaper salicylic acid (aspirin). Until this time there were still few *proven* treatments that physicians could rely on aside from quinine, opiates and digitalis. By taking the salicylates seriously, Maclagan helped create the climate in which they would finally be developed into one of the most significant medicines of the modern era.[5]

For many years, salicylic acid was acclaimed as unique because it was a non-toxic antiseptic and therefore could be administered orally to reduce fevers. In addition to its antipyretic properties, salicylic acid was also found to have anti-inflammatory effects relieving stiffness and pain in rheumatic fever patients, as well as being used as a pharmaceutical and food preservative. Due to later reports that salicin was less efficacious than sodium salicylate and often produced skin rashes, salicin last appeared in the *British Pharmaceutical Codex* in 1954.

Maclagan also pioneered the clinical thermometer. His paper on *Thermometrical Observations* was based on observations made on hundreds of fever patients when he was Resident Medical Superintendent in Dundee. He showed how charting changes in temperature was associated with clinical worsening or lessening of fever, whatever the underlying pathology. Following Maclagan, Professor Thomas Clifford Allbutt, Regius Professor of Physic at the University of Cambridge, brought the size of clinical thermometers down to a manageable five inches, and the time needed to gauge the temperature to only five minutes. Predictably, Allbutt became known as the inventor of the modern clinical thermometer. [6]

John Muir 1838-1914 was America's most famous and influential naturalist and conservationist. He is one of California's most important historical personalities. He has been called "The Father of our National Parks", "Wilderness Prophet", and "Citizen of the Universe."[1] He was one of the earliest advocates of the national park idea, and its most eloquent spokesman.[2]

As a wilderness explorer, he is renowned for his exciting adventures in California's Sierra Nevada, among Alaska's glaciers, and worldwide travels in search of nature's beauty. As a writer, he taught the people of his time and ours the importance of experiencing and protecting our natural heritage. His writings contributed greatly to the creation of the National Parks of Yosemite, Sequoia, Mount Rainier, Petrified Forest, General Grant, and Grand Canyon. Dozens of places are named after John Muir, including the Muir Woods National Monument, the John Muir Trail, Muir College (UCSD), and many schools.

His words and deeds helped inspire President Theodore Roosevelt's innovative conservation programs, including establishing the first National Monuments by Presidential Proclamation, and Yosemite National Park by congressional action. In 1892, John Muir and other supporters formed the Sierra Club "to make the mountains glad." Muir was the Club's first president, an office he held until his death in 1914. Muir's Sierra Club has gone on to help establish a series of new National Parks and a National Wilderness Preservation System.[3]

Pursuit of his love of science, especially geology, often occupied his free time and he soon became convinced that glaciers had sculpted many of the features of the Yosemite Valley and surrounding area. This notion was in stark contradiction to the accepted theory of the day, promulgated by Josiah Whitney (head of the California Geological Survey), which attributed the formation of the valley to a catastrophic earthquake. As Muir's ideas spread, Whitney would try to discredit Muir by branding him as an amateur and even an ignoramus. The premier geologist of the day, Louis Agassiz, however, saw merit in Muir's ideas, and lauded him as "the first man who has any adequate conception of glacial action."

In 1871, Muir discovered an active cirque glacier below Merced Peak, which further helped his theories to gain acceptance. He was also a highly productive writer and had many of his accounts and papers published as far away as New York. Also, that year, one of Muir's heroes, Ralph Waldo Emerson, arrived in Yosemite and sought Muir out.

A large earthquake centred near Lone Pine, California, in Owens Valley, was felt very strongly in Yosemite Valley in March 1872. The quake woke Muir in the early morning and he ran out of his cabin without fear exclaiming, "A noble earthquake!" Other valley settlers, who still adhered to Whitney's ideas, feared that the quake was a prelude to a cataclysmic deepening of the valley. Muir had no such fear and promptly made a moonlit survey of new talus piles created by earthquake-triggered rockslides. This event led more people to believe in Muir's ideas about the formation of the valley.

In addition to his geologic studies, Muir also investigated the living Yosemite area. He made two field studies along the western flank of the Sierra of the distribution and ecology of isolated groves of Giant Sequoia in 1873 and 1874. In 1876, the American Association for the Advancement of Science published a paper Muir wrote about the trees' ecology and distribution.[4]

Although initially finding common ground in the ideas of forest protection put forth by Gifford Pinchot, a pioneer of US forestry and conservation, Muir's views ultimately diverged. Whereas Pinchot supported the sustainable use of resources within national forests, Muir believed that national parks and forests should be preserved in their entirety, meaning that their resources should be rendered off-limits to industrial interests. Muir's enduring contributions to the conservation and preservation of America's wilderness have been far-reaching. His conviction that wilderness areas should be federally protected as national parks has given generations of US citizens an opportunity to appreciate America's landscapes as they exist naturally, in the absence of human industrial influence.[5]

Michael Barker Nairn 1838-1915 is often thought of by Scots as the man who invented linoleum – he didn't. It was Englishman Frederick Walton who first made linoleum, in 1860, by using solidified linseed oil mixed with wood flour, or cork dust, attached to a jute backing. Nairn's father, also Michael, opened Scotland's first floorcloth (made from paint on canvas) factory in 1847 in Kirkcaldy. Michael junior took over the factory in 1861, three years after his father's death and, as part of the floorcloth business, produced linoleum from 1877. He reduced the drying time for floorcloth from twelve to three months and this innovation allowed other firms to be launched. When Walton invented linoleum, it soon replaced floorcloth.[1]

It was Nairn who made linoleum famous by introducing inlaid patterning, and his factory – with five other local producers – soon made Kirkcaldy the largest producer of linoleum in the world. It is still made there today, with Forbo-Nairn being the oldest resilient floor-covering manufacturer in the world. Linoleum wasn't just a poor man's floor covering either for, in 1880, it was used on the yacht of the richest man on the planet, Tsar Nicholas II of Russia.

From 1881, Nairn's was able to make seamless linoleum four yards wide and, in 1895, began to manufacture inlaid linoleum. World sales grew: "I have seen our floorcloth and linoleum beyond the first cataract of the Nile and in the mosques of Constantinople", Nairn recorded.[2]

John Aitken 1839-1919 invented the koniscope for counting "the number of dust particles [by which he meant condensation nuclei] in a closed sample of saturated air. Aitken expanded the air slightly using an air pump, thereby causing cooling and consequent condensation onto the dust particles, and so forming water droplets. The droplets then fell onto a silvered surface which had been ruled into squares, and the number of the droplets could easily be counted. He developed the instrument into a final portable form that was capable of considerable precision in the hands of a skillful operator."[1]

Aitken also invented the chromomictor "for the purpose of mixing lights of different colours for experiments in physiological optics."[2] He made significant contributions to the study of dew formation, showing that the vapour which condenses as dew on cold surfaces comes from the ground below as well as from the air above, and that the "dewdrop" on leaves of plants is actually exuded sap. Through a series of experiments and observations in which he used apparatus of his own design, he elucidated the crucial role that microscopic particles, now called Aitken nuclei, play in the condensation of atmospheric water vapour in clouds and fogs.[3]

Modern quantitative measurements of atmospheric aerosol concentrations began with the work of Aitken. In a long and careful series of studies, Aitken (1884, 1885, 1888, and 1891) had observed that on cloudy days, the nuclei count remained low. The number increased with sunshine, in proportion to the amount of sunshine. Aitken noted that "sunshine may produce some change in the (photochemically active) constituents of the atmosphere which gives rise to nuclei formation in saturated air". He also observed that the high nuclei days were not hazy, which suggested to him that the nuclei were of "molecular dimensions".

Aitken was the first to use the concept of chemical mass budget to support his reasoning. He states that densely inhabited areas "lose their purity", in other words they accumulate particulate matter. "Purifying areas of the world are those regions that lose more impurity than they gain". Without knowing of Constantine Samuel Rafinesque-Schmaltz's theories, Aitken states that "the deposition of vapour on these particles seems to be the method adopted by nature for cleansing them away. Hence cloudy and rainy regions [of the world] are the most purifying." It is ironic, that in the second decade of the 21st century, we still do not have a clear understanding of which are the cleansing regions of the world.

Aitken developed an elegant and still valid method of analysing the relationship between the particle concentration and visibility. He proposed that visibility should be defined as the limit at which objects are visible; observations on rainy days should be discarded and the data were to be classified according to humidity. From his long-term observations, Aitken found that the amount of haze was proportional to the number of particles and that the product of nuclei concentration × visual range was a constant. This corresponds to the modern observations that the horizontal aerosol extinction coefficient is generally proportional to fine particle mass concentration. Finally, Aitken found that the aerosol extinction in moist air is twice the value in dry air.[4]

William Arrol 1839-1913 invented the hydraulic spade to speed the process of digging when the Forth Rail Bridge was being constructed by him in 1890. He also invented the hydraulic riveter for the 6,500,000 rivets used in its construction. "During the building of the Forth Bridges, all sorts of new tricks were learned. ... The builders invented a new riveting machine and a new hydraulic spade for digging the river bed."[1] One of these "new tricks" was an "adjustable work platform that climbed up the towers, as they were constructed, by means of hydraulic rams. On these self-climbing platforms were positioned a series of derricks, hoists and cranes that could raise materials directly from the base of the towers or barges on the water. The inventive Arrol continued to expedite the work with his pipe riveting cages which also functioned in a self-climbing manner." His hydraulic drill could make 20 rivet holes simultaneously.[2]

As well as building (but not designing) the Forth Rail Bridge, which was considered the eighth wonder of the world at the time, he was the builder of the new Tay Rail Bridge in 1887, to replace the one which disastrously collapsed in 1879. These two were among the largest bridges in the world at the time at 2,528 m and 3,264 m respectively. Arrol also built, in London, the Tower Bridge (1894), and the Bankside Power Station (now the Tate Modern Art Gallery). In Lincolnshire, he built the King George V Bridge (Keadby Bridge) 1912-1916, with a 50 m powered lifting span which, at the time, was the largest in Europe, and he also built the innovative Warrington Transporter Bridge.

When he built the railway bridge over the Clyde River near Bothwell, "Not only did William complete it successfully but he was also innovative by eliminating the scaffolding which was previously an essential part of bridge building. It was at this site that he put into practice his idea of building the bridge on land and then rolling it out over the water. Formerly bridges were riveted piece to piece in their place. "In 1875, he obtained the contract to build the first of the two great Caledonian bridges over the Clyde at the Broomielaw in Glasgow. For this project, he devised a new mechanical driller that saved immense labour. Another of his inventions was a hydraulic riveter that did a far superior job than the prior hand method. Shortly thereafter his growing firm built the South Esk railway bridge in Montrose which enhanced his reputation and resulted in contracts to build bridges overseas – especially in Brazil."[3]

Image 67 – Launch of RMS *Titanic* showing Arrol gantry

Internationally, he built the Nile Bridge at Cairo in 1908 and the Hawkesbury River Railway Bridge (1886) in New South Wales, Australia. He designed a new type of gantry to permit Harland and Wolff to build RMS *Titanic* in Belfast. He was co-owner of the pioneering Arrol-Johnston automobile company which lasted from 1895 to the depression year of 1931.

Alexander Richardson Binnie 1839-1917 designed the Blackwall Tunnel and the Vauxhall Bridge, both on the Thames. In the 1870s, Binnie had been executive engineer at Nagpur for the India Department's Public Works where, at Ambajheri, he built a water supply which was important for the subsequent building of a railway to exploit the coal deposits in the area. While employed by London City Council, he built the Barking Road Bridge, widened The Strand, the 1.11 km Greenwich Foot Tunnel from the Isle of Dogs to Greenwich, and built the Aldwych-Kingsway connection with Holborn.[1]

Binnie's Vauxhall Bridge is 231.6 m long and 24.4 m wide, made mostly of concrete and steel and it was the first bridge in London to carry a tramway. When Binnie constructed the Blackwall Tunnel, it was the longest underwater tunnel in the world at 1,344 m. English engineer Joseph Bazalgette was responsible for initiating the London drainage works following the Great Stink of 1858 on the Thames and the realisation that cholera was a water-borne disease. Binnie, with English engineer John Baker, made major extensions to the sewerage system and in 1891, with Englishman William Dibdin – who came up with the idea – introduced treatment through chemical precipitation at Barking. Binnie also built the sewage treatment works at London's Crossness, now one of the largest in Europe, but at the time, its steam-powered pumping station redirected waste so that it entered the Thames down river from London.

James Blyth 1839-1906 demonstrated the world's first wind turbine to generate electricity in July 1887. It was a 12kW turbine having a 17 m rotor. The device was 18 m tall. He provided electricity for some 27 years to the Montrose Lunatic Asylum with his wind turbine generating 10 hp to storage cells capable of lighting the asylum. Blyth's own house at Marykirk in Kincardineshire was powered by wind-generated electricity for 25 years. His turbine was designed to work irrespective of the direction of the wind.[2] Blyth's machine was a cloth-sailed, horizontal wind turbine as distinct from the universally vertical wind turbines of today. His turbine was built several months before the American Charles Francis Brush installed his first wind turbine, though Brush's was larger and featured an automatic brake to prevent damage in high winds. Blyth's design was 33 ft (10 m) in diameter and stored the electricity generated in batteries.

Image 68 – Blyth's Windmill at his cottage in Marykirk in 1891
Note the woman standing in front of the shed bottom right for scale.

James Murdoch Geikie 1839-1915 was the leading British authority on Pleistocene geology. He developed the theory, through observations in Scotland and Continental Europe, that during ice ages, mild inter-glacial periods interrupted the glacial period as a whole. He originated the current belief that human habitation continued in Europe throughout the glacial period.[1]

He joined the Geological Survey of Scotland and was noted for his contribution to mapping the geology of the country. He wrote the standard work of the day on the glacial period, *The Great Ice Age and its Relation to the Antiquity of Man* (1874).[2]

During his mapping activities of drift deposits, he found evidence of warmer, inter-glacial periods. He suggested that the existence of river terraces at different levels might indicate climatic cycles during the Pleistocene, as opposed to Louis Agassiz's theory of a single great Ice Age.[3]

John Lawson Johnston 1839-1900 invented Bovril in 1874. Johnston had won a contract to supply the French army with a million cans of beef after their war with Prussia in 1870-1871. "After the siege and surrender of Paris, the French army sought ways to supply their forces with more nourishing food in the belief that this played a part in the fall of Paris."[1]

Britain didn't contain sufficient beef on the hoof to fill the millions of kilo tins stipulated by the French, and so, in 1873 Johnston formed a company and built a factory in Quebec, Canada. While there he also worked on his liquid beef and re-invented it as a concentrate. A concentrated version would be cheaper to ship as a consumer product. He made it from beef parts left over from the tinned beef for the French government's order.[2] It was originally known as Johnston's Fluid Beef.

In 1879, production moved to Montreal and in 1884 he returned to London and set up a small factory in London and Bovril was first sold in Britain at the 1886 Colonial and Continental Exhibition in London. In 1887, Johnston registered the name "Bovril" as he had decided that Bovril would not only be a more appealing name than "fluid beef", but that it would also be more accurate, now that the fluid was concentrated.[3] The name comes (partially) from the subfamily classification for cattle – *Bovinae*. The "vril" component of the name comes from Edward Bulwer-Lytton's once-popular novel, *Vril: The Power of the Coming Race* (1871), in which a subterranean humanoid race have mental control over, and devastating powers from, an energy fluid named "Vril."[4]

In 1888, the now-iconically-shaped Bovril brown-glass bottles were introduced, by which year there were over 3,000 pubs, grocers, and even chemists serving Bovril. In 1889, the Bovril Company was formed and by the time of Johnston's death Bovril was trading as far as South Africa and South America.[5]

"Johnston was a canny promoter and he organised a stunt for a launch of Bovril at the 1887 [sic – it was 1886] Colonial and Continental Exhibition in London by recreating a Montreal Ice Palace in frosted glass to encourage sales of Bovril from the chilly location."[6]

Bovril was "promoted as a national asset and a form of 'liquid life' during the Boer War, when Rudyard Kipling lent his name to a chorus of praise for the product. An advertisement in the *Daily Mail* in 1900 asserted: 'Doctors, nurses, officers, soldiers and newspaper correspondents unite in bearing testimony to the great popularity of Bovril at the Front as an Invigorating and Nourishing Food, preparing the soldier for battle and aiding him in recovery when weakened by wounds and disease.'"[7]

David Proudfoot 1839-1891 built the Port Chalmers railway in New Zealand in 1872, selling it to the government for a substantial profit. In addition to several large sections of the South Island main trunk line, Proudfoot was responsible for the branch lines to Orepuki, Otautau, Tapanui and Awamoko, and for the Peninsula and Ocean Beach railway. The latter route linked Dunedin with the neighbouring borough of St Kilda, where Proudfoot owned land and where he had built his imposing Grand Pacific Hotel (later known as Onslow House).

Proudfoot operated trams between the inner city and northern suburbs in 1879 as well as to Caversham and St Kilda. The tram service gave Dunedin the most advanced urban transport system in the colony. He widened streets in Dunedin, built roads and bridges in both islands, supplied sleepers for the Waimea Plains railway, erected the Invercargill Waterworks, and performed contracts for dredging and reclamations in Otago Harbour. So extensive were his feats of engineering that he was once described as the "New Zealand Brunel". He won a £500,000 contract for the Uralla to Glen Innes line in New South Wales. He even negotiated for the building of railways in Japan. Proudfoot was said to have employed 1,000 New Zealand workmen in Australia, a measure of the vast scale of his operations.[1]

Dugald Drummond 1840-1912 was a locomotive designer and engineer who worked at various times for the North British Railway; London, Brighton & South Coast Railway; Caledonian Railway; and the London & South Western Railway. For North British he designed seven locomotives including NBR 165 class 0-6-0T, later LNER class J82 and NBR 100 class 0-6-0, later LNER class J32. At Caledonian, he designed nine locomotives including 264 Class 0-4-0ST, later LMS class 0F, which was a 0-4-0 saddle tank locomotive; and the 123, 4-2-2, later LMS 14010, class 1P. For the London and South Western Railway, he designed 20 locomotives and two railcars including the LSWR M7 class 0-4-4 tank engines known as "Motor Tanks" for use on the rail company's the intensive London network.

Among the most important of his innovations was his cross-tube fire-box, which gave improved circulation and greatly increased working-life. In smoke-box design, feed arrangements, spark-arresting and other details, he also introduced many improvements. Drummond was one of the pioneers of the four-cylinder non-compound type of locomotive, and he also designed a new type of very powerful engine intended for express traffic. Another direction in which his skill found full scope was in the design and construction of steam rail-motors, which he succeeded in making powerful and commodious.[1]

John Boyd Dunlop 1840-1921 is synonymous with pneumatic tyres even though it was compatriot Robert William Thomson who first invented them. Dunlop, who was unaware of Thomson's earlier invention, designed the tyre that was eventually to be found on cars, cycles and aircraft around the world. He was born in Dreghorn, Ayrshire, and qualified as a veterinary surgeon, opening a practice in Belfast, Northern Ireland. He obtained a disc of wood and, being skilled at working in rubber, constructed an air tube and laid it round the periphery, fastening it down by a covering of linen tacked to the wood. He tested this arrangement against one of the tricycle wheels by throwing the two along the cobbles of a long courtyard, and the enormously greater resilience and liveliness of the air-tyred disc was at once obvious. Developing the idea further, Dunlop made two rims of wood, fastened air tubes and covers to them, and fixed them over the existing tyres of the rear wheels of his son's machine. A trial of this device in February 1888 having proved eminently successful, a new tricycle frame was ordered, for which wheels with pneumatic tyres were built and fitted. A demonstration before several Belfast businessmen met with approval, and on 23 July 1888, Dunlop lodged his first application for a provisional patent. The patent was finally granted on 7 December.[1]

By the time he patented his tyre in 1888, Dunlop was using wire to hold the tyre to the rim of the wheel. Two years afterwards he sold the patent rights to Irish-born William Harvey du Cros, who went on to found the Dunlop Rubber Company. Although Thomson had died in 1873, the company had a legal fight on the patent rights, but Dunlop Rubber Company won the case and went on to become a major worldwide organisation. Dunlop probably succeeded where Thomson failed because bicycles were becoming more popular and automobiles were starting to appear on the roads, which themselves were being rapidly improved. Dunlop's invention revolutionised cycling and made possible the development of the motor road vehicle, as it greatly increased the speed and comfort of motor travel.[2]

Peter Jack Ferguson 1840-1911 was a marine engineer and pioneer of multiple-expansion steam reciprocating machinery. Ferguson designed several new types of engines, and in 1872 he was responsible for the construction of what is claimed to be the world's first triple-expansion engine, predating the machinery on SS *Propontis* by two years and Napier's masterpiece, the SS *Aberdeen*, by nine years. In 1885, along with others, he founded the shipyard of Fleming and Ferguson, of Paisley, which in the subsequent 85 years was to build nearly 700 ships. From the outset, they built advanced steam reciprocating machinery as well as dredging and other types of plant.[1]

William Galloway 1840-1927 was a mining engineer who proved that fire-damp (flammable gases in mines, usually methane) was not the sole cause of explosions in coal mines. In a series of papers published in the *Proceedings of The Royal Society* between 1875 and 1887, Galloway contended that floating coal dust was the means of extending the area of explosions. From an analysis of the evidence afforded by actual explosions, he demonstrated that fire-damp could not have been present in appreciable quantities along most of the track in the cases examined. He also conducted experiments in galleries specially constructed for the purpose in a south Wales colliery, in which he was able to get ignition and very violent explosions from coal dust without the presence of fire-damp. He showed that an initial explosion raised dust elsewhere in the mine, causing further explosions. As a preventive of such explosions, Galloway first recommended the wetting of the roads in mines, a method which was not found to be wholly effective; later, in 1896, he advocated the spreading of stone dust. This method, which was independently initiated and developed by William Garforth, proved very successful and was generally adopted from 1908, with the result that the death-rate resulting from colliery explosions was considered to have been lowered to 10% of the figure prevailing when Galloway began his investigations.[1] He patented safety devices, including twin guide ropes for sinking pits, and improved counterbalanced doors to cover the shaft top.

David Neilson Melvin 1840-1914 worked in the appropriately named Linoleumville (now Travis), on Staten Island, New York. He patented a method of producing straight-line inlaid linoleum that eliminated the jagged edges between different blocks of colour on the linoleum. Melvin also designed fireproof sugar-refining factories while in Scotland and machinery for the sugar business in Cuba and West Indies. He built some of the largest lumber mills in Michigan and built the Staten Island linoleum factory in 1873.[1]

John Bryson Orr 1840-1933 was a chemist who, in 1874, patented a way to make paint pigment by applying heat to the basic chemicals of zinc and barium, a process that he had worked on since 1861. In his patent, he referred to it as "Orr's permanent white enamel paint" and it was marketed first as Charlton White, then as Orr's Zinc White, and is now most commonly called lithopone – a pigment with a high degree of opacity and a pure white colour. Its hiding capacity equates to covering 4.5 square metres for a kilogram of lithopone compared to 2.7 square metres for white lead or 4.12 square metres for zinc oxide. It has greater resistance to abrasion than other white pigments and it is stable, easily wetted, and insoluble in water, varnish, oils, alcohol and paraffin."[1]

Orr made not only the first washable paint, but the first washable whitewash, Duresco, which could be applied to both internal and external walls. This achievement deserves to rank equally with his pioneering of lithopone, and certainly it is in washable water paint that lithopone was to become most familiar in the home and elsewhere. Indeed, it is no exaggeration to say that the washable distempers (or oil emulsion water paints, as they were called) were made possible by lithopone as no other white pigment was really satisfactory as an ingredient in such paints.[2]

Orr adapted his product for use in linoleum and in the manufacture of damasks, leather cloth, tablecloths, paper and washable wallpaper, as well as in the vulcanisation of rubber where it made the product more elastic and gave it a higher breaking strain. It was widely used in the manufacture of cable for the telegraph and it paved the way for the rise in popularity of rubber products, including car tyres – where the use of lithopone reduced the frequency of burst tyres – and for rubber valves, washers and other component parts. Orr's product revolutionised the paint, pigment and rubber industries and his invention became the basic pigment for the production of paint around the world, with some 230,000 tonnes being produced annually by 1928, with the largest British factory, and one of the world's largest, being at Widnes in Lancashire.

Henry Charles Stanley 1840-1921 designed and built the 75 Miles Dam at Warwick, Queensland in the north-east of Australia in 1880. It was a thick concrete arch dam and is the oldest concrete arch dam in the world.[1]

He joined his older brother, architect Francis Drummond Greville Stanley, in Brisbane around this time. Henry was an assistant engineer on the first railway line, became a railway engineer in 1866, and then Chief Engineer for Railways in 1872, by which time older brother Francis had been appointed Colonial Architect on the retirement of Charles Tiffin.

In 1875, the first railway bridge across the river between Indooroopilly and Chelmer was constructed, but it was destroyed in the mammoth 1893 floods. A new bridge was designed by Henry Stanley, and it opened in 1895. This bridge had only a central pier rather than the multiple piers of the earlier bridge, thereby reducing the risk of damage from floodwaters and debris.[2]

William Tait 1840-1921 predicted, in 1908, that oil reserves lay beneath the Atlantic seabed off the Scottish coast. At the time, his bold forecast was ridiculed by so-called experts and it made him the butt of jokes in his native Caithness. Tait, a veteran of major late Victorian gold rushes in two continents, also foretold the existence of oil beneath the North Sea at the same time. Tait's predictions came shortly after he retired to his native Caithness, fresh from participating in the birth of the oil industry in North America. Tait spent his entire career in the minerals industries, including being involved in the drilling of Alaska's first two oil wells at the dawn of the 20th century. The key to Tait's predictions was that he was absolutely convinced that oil and gas could exist in reservoirs in rocks dating back 400 million years, the same time as the layers of Caithness flagstones were created. Not so, said the experts, insisting that oil could be found only in rocks of half that age or less, starting from the 180 million-year-old Jurassic Age. However, the discovery in 1977 of the vast but complex Clair oilfield, west of Shetland, the biggest yet found in Britain's offshore waters, has changed all that. It provided geologists with the first direct proof of British oil being present in vast quantities in rocks formed at exactly the same time as the Caithness flagstones, during the Devonian era. It was just as Tait had said all those decades earlier.[1]

William Newsham Blair 1841-1891 was engineer and surveyor in Otago in the South Island of New Zealand from 1869. "Until 1878 he was responsible for the construction of all Otago and Southland's railways, and many of their roads and bridges. In 1872, he constructed the long Rangitata Bridge in Canterbury. He was consultant to the Dunedin City Council for various matters, including, between 1876 and 1881, the Silverstream Waterworks – the city's mainstay for 75 years. … He advocated with masterly argument and detailed supporting evidence the value to the national economy of import substitution, tourism, and even the hydroelectric energy potential of the country's rivers. Later he wrote articles on the southern lakes, and one on the adverse effects of mining and deforestation on the landscape and coasts. The latter article was an example of his foresight, keen observation during explorations, and intimate knowledge of New Zealand's natural environment. While assistant engineer-in-chief, Blair carried through the construction of the Otago Central Railway, which he had earlier surveyed. This involved heavy constructions such as the Wingatui viaduct and other much-admired structures. He also explored the King Country to report on the proposed North Island main trunk railway."[1]

Richard Henry Brunton 1841-1901 was, in 1868, employed as Chief Engineer of the Lighthouse Department of the Government of Japan and was the first of a number of so-called *o-yatoi-gaijin* (foreign employees) contracted to the Meiji government, which was seeking to quickly modernise Japan by introducing foreign technology. He built 28 lighthouses (some sources say over 50) in less than eight years and two lightships, and he founded Japan's modern lighthouse service. With advice from David Stevenson, under whom he trained in Scotland, Brunton used stabilising bars to help lighthouses resist earthquakes, and even built complete metal lighthouses. He created a training school modelled on the Northern Lighthouse Board in Scotland and this became the first centre of modern engineering in Japan. "Brunton's great contribution was training Japan's first modern mechanics and insisting on the necessity of scientific training in a country where technical labour was despised and skilled trades barely existed."[1]

Brunton was asked to provide plans for the creation of modern harbours for Osaka, Niigata and Yokohama and, in the latter, his public works resulted in the modernising of what is now Japan's second city and one of the world's great international ports. Modern sewers were built in

Yokohama, using clay pipes rather than traditional bamboo; and macadam roads were laid out, including the Nihon Odori, a 36 m wide boulevard. He designed and built Japan's first truss bridge – the Yoshida Bridge – which was also the second steel bridge in the country, as well as designing Yokohama Park, the first Western-style gardens in Japan. He was instrumental in the 1872 building of the first Japanese railway from Yokohama to Shimbashi following his recommendation to the government.

When the Japanese sought to undertake marine surveying themselves, Brunton convinced them that they needed to have some training in mathematics and related subjects to effectively use theodolites, quadrants and other surveying equipment. A School of Mathematics was built in Yokohama in 1870 and this evolved into Yokohama University in 1949. Stonehaven Heritage Society author Archibald Watt summarised Brunton's work thus "[he] instigated the Japanese lifeboat service in the same period, now the Japanese Maritime Safety Agency. … That was not to be the end of Brunton's achievements in Japan. He also played a major role in the development of the railway system, advised on, and set up, the new-fangled telegraph, becoming the first to establish the telegraph in the Far East, … He drew up probably the first urban planning blueprint in the Far East [Yokohama] and laid out its harbour and port installations. Brunton 'helped develop the harbour of Yokohama into the modern commercial port today.'"[2]

He also compiled the first ordnance survey map of the Japanese Empire, which came to be considered a standard work.[3] Brunton was part of a small group of foreigners who were permitted into Japan. Going well beyond his original commission to build lighthouses, Brunton played a key role in starting the modernisation of Japan and was known as the "Father of Modern Engineering in Japan".[4]

Thomas Richard Fraser 1841-1920 discovered that extracts of the Calabar bean (*Physostigma venenosum)* introduced into the eye caused the contraction of the pupil. He counteracted this effect by use of atropine. In 1872, he published *The antagonism between the actions of active substances* in the *British Medical Journal*. In 1885, Fraser first isolated strophanthinic acid, a cardio-active glycoside. The acid comes from the strophanthus plant and is used by various African tribes in the making of poisonous arrows.[1] Fraser published many papers in practical medicine, particularly on the action and therapeutic uses of medicinal substances, and also on serpent's venom. In addition to his academic work, he was President of the Indian Plague Commission, 1898-1901.

In the 1860s, Fraser and compatriot Alexander Crum Brown worked on the relation between chemical structure and biological activity. They discovered that when alkaloids such as atropine, brucine, codeine, morphine and nicotine had their nitrogen atoms changed from the tertiary to the quaternary form, they acquired curare-like activity. This was the precursor to much of the work on neuromuscular blocking drugs that took place after the Second World War.[2]

The Calabar bean is a violent poison, but did not attract attention on the part of the medical profession until its power of contracting the pupil of the eye was discovered by Fraser. There is no known antidote to poisoning by Calabar bean except atropine. Unfortunately, the antagonism between the active ingredient of Calabar bean, physostigmine, and atropine is not perfect, so that atropine will save life after three and a half times the fatal dose of physostigmine has been taken, but will hasten the end if four or more times the fatal dose has been ingested.[3] Fraser reigned supreme in the study of antagonism between physostigmine and atropine. By the 1870s, the concept of antagonism between therapeutic agents was not new, but it had little, if any, reliable scientific foundation. Fraser's firm belief that physostigmine and atropine were mutually antagonistic at a physiological level was contrary to the conventional wisdom of his contemporaries. This alone would earn him a place in history, but his contribution goes much, much further.

Unlike any other at the time, Fraser investigated it with scientific rigour, experimenting on only one species, ensuring as best he could the animals were the same weight, adjusting the doses of drugs he gave them for bodyweight, determining the minimum lethal dose of each drug before assessing their antagonistic effects, adopting a single, incontrovertible endpoint for efficacy and carrying out sufficient numbers of experiments to appear convincing in a later era where the statistical power of studies is all-important. To crown it all, he presented his results graphically. It is salutary to realise that the doses and dosage frequency of atropine together with the endpoints that define they are adequate were formulated by Fraser and others a century and a half ago.[4]

David Henderson Houston 1841-1906 invented the mechanism that American George Eastman used to transport his new flexible roll film past the lens. Presciently, Houston patented his invention on 11 October 1881 (patent number 248,179), six years before transparent roll film was invented by Hannibal Goodwin of Newark, New Jersey in 1887, and three years before Eastman had patented paper-backed roll film in 1884. Houston simply anticipated that it would eventually be developed to replace the gelatin dry plates which had been invented by Eastman in 1878 – these dry plates had themselves only started to replace wet glass plate photography. Houston's roll film mechanism remained almost unchanged throughout the history of celluloid film cameras, although now basically redundant due to digital photography.

Two reels were positioned internally on each end of the camera. One held the unexposed film and the other, with no film, was wound using a lever or wheel so that the unexposed film was transported past the lens towards the empty reel. When a photograph was taken, the film was wound on, moving more unexposed film behind the lens ready for the next shot. Eventually all the exposed film would be on the originally empty reel while the reel that first held the unexposed film would be empty.

Houston ultimately went on to be a successful farmer in North Dakota, where he patented a disc plough as well as helping to develop bluestem seed wheat, but it was in photography that he made his most important mark, not only with the roll film mechanism but also with camera design. In 1879, Houston patented the first portable camera, to which Eastman bought the patent rights for $5,000 plus monthly royalties, [1] indicative of the importance Eastman placed on the new hand-held camera patent. Houston was a prolific inventor and patented a self-loading magnesia flash lamp and 21 different cameras, including: a magazine camera (patent 639,730 issued 26 December 1899); a folding panoramic camera (670,233 on 19 March 1901); a panoramic camera (694,923); roll holding camera (694,924); folding roll-holding camera (694,925); and a daylight-loading photographic-roll holder (694,926) – all issued on 4 March 1902. Many of these patents were bought by Eastman so Houston is quite unknown to the public at large for the role he played in facilitating the use of roll film and in popularising the camera itself.

Alexander McKay 1841-1917 invented the telephoto lens but he isn't generally recognised for this contribution to photography, partly because he was far away in New Zealand working as a geologist. McKay was born in Carsphairn, Kirkcudbrightshire, and emigrated from there to New Zealand in 1863 where he undertook geological work in Otago, Canterbury and Kaikoura and, eventually, became the New Zealand government geologist. He collected tens of thousands of fossils throughout New Zealand, and he was the first person in the world to document a transcurrent fault – a large-scale geological fault in which the fault surface is steeply inclined. Probably the most well-known and well-studied fault is the transcurrent (strike-slip) fault known as the San Andreas Fault of California.[1]

"McKay's prime discovery, of world importance, was made through his acute observations of earthquake damage. ... He investigated a series of earthquakes in Marlborough in 1888 and reported that at the Glenwye sheep station fence lines were broken and laterally displaced by 8 ft and 9 ft [243-274 cm]. Contemporary theory allowed only for vertical movement along fault lines; here was irrefutable evidence for horizontal shearing traceable for some miles. McKays original theory was not accepted widely; in fact, the significance of transcurrent fault movement was not generally acknowledged until the 1940s."[2]

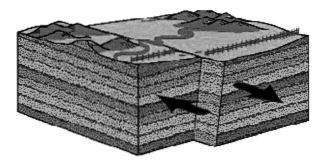

Image 69 – Transcurrent (or strike-slip) Fault

The world's largest faults, such as the Alpine Fault of New Zealand, are now known to be transcurrent: adjacent sections of the earth's crust are horizontally displaced, sometimes by hundreds of kilometres. McKay estimated that New Zealand's mountains were young, only some 15 million years old, but other geologists were sceptical. One of McKay's disadvantages was that he had never been formally trained as a geologist, being wholly self-taught. He pre-empted the modern discipline of neotectonics (the study of geologically recent motions of the Earth's crust) by concluding from his observations of small fault movements caused by earthquakes that New Zealand's mountains were formed from repeated small uplifts along the fault lines.[3]

McKay, correctly, identified the moa hunters as Maori and not prehistoric peoples and, related to this, also re-evaluated the arrival of the Maori in New Zealand. McKay's "final verdict, therefore, was that either the Moa was exterminated by the people of a migration prior to that of 'the [Maori] fleet,' or that this traditional migration must be considered to have taken place not 350 years but 1,350 years ago."[4]

McKay became a keen photographer and made many of his own lenses, inventing the telephoto lens before 1886. It was also independently invented by German Thomas Rudolphus

Dallmeyer in 1891, but neither Dallmeyer nor his compatriot, Adolf Miethe, were the first to use the telephoto lens. McKay had presented his photographs and described his lenses in a paper presented to the New Zealand Institute before either Dallmeyer or Miethe applied for patents and at that time McKay had already printed dozens of telephoto photographs demonstrating his lens' effectiveness.

Image 70 – Believed to be McKay's photograph of *Vjestnik* taken with telephoto lens in 1886 from 2.5 km distance

One of McKay's photographs, taken in 1886, shows the Russian warship *Vjestnik* anchored in Wellington Harbour. The photograph was taken from a spot about two and a half kilometres away from the ship, but its rigging lines and gun ports are clearly visible.[5] The telephoto lens became, and still is, an indispensable part of a professional photographer's camera equipment, both for still shots and motion pictures and, unlike celluloid film, it has not been displaced by digital cameras.

John Gray McKendrick 1841-1926 was in the forefront of the use of graphic methods in recording physiological observations, which he used to demonstrate the links between nerve and muscle. Perhaps his most telling contributions were in the field of the special senses, with his seminal observation that light produced electrical changes in the retina,[1] which work he undertook with James Dewar – a contribution of the highest value to physiology. He was also one of the earliest workers on the relationship of chemical constitution to physiological action, which had a most important bearing on the development of pharmacology.[2] With Dewar, McKendrick's work on chinoline and pyridine bases laid the foundations for antipyrine therapy.[3] (Antipyrines [phenazone] have an analgesic and antipyretic effect).

John Murray 1841-1914 is considered to be, particularly in the USA, the founder of modern oceanography.[1] Murray joined the crew of naturalists aboard HMS *Challenger*, a steam-assisted corvette, which sailed from Portsmouth in December 1872 for a three-year expedition to explore the world's deep oceans. At the end of the voyage, expedition leader Charles Wyville Thomson appointed him assistant in drawing up the scientific results, which were to lay the foundations of almost every branch of modern oceanography. Murray took over from his colleague when the stress of producing the report became too great, and went on to edit and publish more than 50 volumes, completed in 1896.

The survey set out to answer many of the basic questions about the physical and biological characteristics of the open oceans – indeed Murray coined the term "oceanography". Depth soundings mapped the shape of the ocean floor, revealing the existence of the Mid-Atlantic Ridge and of oceanic trenches. Evidence was also obtained of a rich and varied fauna in the very deepest regions, and samples taken led to the discovery of 4,000 new animal species.[2]

The contribution of Murray's research in oceanography is immense and his many research achievements included his study of ocean depths, especially from the *Challenger* Expedition. He was first to observe the Mid-Atlantic Ridge and the existence of marine trenches. He attempted with Glasgow-born John Young Buchanan to construct from temperature and salinity observations a qualitative theory of water movement in the world's oceans. Only in the 1900s was this superseded by the Germans. His work with Pierre Renard of mapping the marine deposits of the world's oceans was monumental. He identified the importance of Aeolian dust and volcanic constituents in the makeup of red clays. His maps on the distribution of carbonates, siliceous deposits and manganese nodules form the basis of understanding oceanic sedimentology.

He investigated and experimented on the dissolution of calcium carbonate and was first to identify the carbonate compensation depth in oceans. He, with Alexander Emmanuel Rodolphe Agassiz, put forward a modified hypothesis for coral reef development, arguing against Darwin's hypothesis and suggesting that subsidence was not always a controlling mechanism. He was first to identify marine sediment diagenesis from observations in sediments off Scotland, particularly with respect to manganese and other metal recycling. From his Granton experiments, he established that organic matter respiration was the dominant control on this, and that organic matter in sediments dictated the speciation of dissolved carbon in sediment pore waters. This work was superseded only in 1960 and is fundamental in the understanding of organic carbon cycling on the planet.[3]

James Dewar 1842-1923 invented the Dewar (vacuum) flask to keep liquids at a cold temperature during his investigations in liquefying helium and hydrogen. It consisted of two flasks, one inside the other, separated by a vacuum. The vacuum greatly reduced the transfer of heat, preventing a temperature change. The walls are usually made of glass because it is a poor conductor of heat; its surfaces are usually lined with a reflective metal to reduce the transfer of heat by radiation. Dewar used silver. The whole fragile flask rests on a shock-absorbing spring within a metal or plastic container, and the air between the flask and the container provides further insulation.[1] Dewar did not patent his invention and a German company produced it under the name of *Thermos* flask.

Dewar also was co-inventor, in 1889, with Frederick Abel, of cordite, a smokeless propellant for guns, although this wasn't, as is sometimes claimed, the first smokeless propellant, which was first obtained in 1884 by Frenchman Paul Vieille and followed by Alfred Nobel's ballistite in 1887.[2] The original cordite formula was soon adjusted as it was found to corrode the inside of the gun barrel. During World War I, a single factory at Gretna, in the south of Scotland, was producing well over 42,000 tonnes per annum and it was the detonating material for the

Hiroshima atomic bomb in 1945. Cordite production ceased at the end of the 20th century as it was superseded by other propellants.

Dewar did wide-ranging work on areas such as organic chemistry, light, heat, electrophotometry, spectroscopy and non-organic chemistry. Dewar's interest was in keeping gases cold in the laboratory as his studies related to the effects of absolute zero. He succeeded in liquefying oxygen in 1877, a year after a small quantity was first liquefied by Frenchman Louis-Paul Cailletet and, separately, Swiss Raoul Pictet. They each used different processes and only liquefied a few drops whereas Dewar could produce it in industrial quantities. In 1898, he was first to liquefy hydrogen and, within a year, the first to solidify it. He did this through lowering the temperature by a cascade method using chloromethane to liquefy ethylene, then ethylene to liquefy oxygen, and finally, oxygen to liquefy hydrogen. This formed a clear liquid hydrogen and Dewar placed a tube of liquefied oxygen into this liquid and the oxygen solidified and turned blue. Finally, in 1905, he discovered that cooled charcoal can help in creating a high vacuum, and this knowledge was used in the research relating to atomic physics. His work was used to help create vapour-cooled radiation shields and multilayer insulations.[3]

Alan Macdougall 1842-1897 was a leading promoter of the Canadian Society of Civil Engineers (CSCE), becoming vice president in 1894, seven years after it was founded. He had conducted meetings in Ottawa, Montreal and Toronto and it was in the Montreal assembly, chaired by Macdougall, where the resolution was passed to form a society of engineers, with 162 elected in January 1887 and another 126 in late February. Macdougall had been an engineer for North British Rail as well as the divisional engineer for part of the Canadian Pacific Railway. He also improved harbours and rivers on the Great Lakes and St Lawrence River, and he developed a large practice advising on waterworks and sewerage to local municipalities in Canada, including Toronto. He was secretary of the Canadian Institute for ten years but it was due to his tireless work in the CSCE that in 1896 the province of Manitoba passed North America's first engineering licensing law, with Quebec following a year later. "Macdougall may be regarded as one of the fathers of Canadian engineering professionalism, and as a consequence an important figure in the development of the professions in Canada."[1]

John Rennie 1842-1918 designed the sails for the clipper *Cutty Sark*. The sails had an area of $20,000^2$ feet (1,858 m^2) making her capable of attaining a speed of over 17 knots, equivalent to an engine of 3,000 hp. In the 1870s, Rennie was Naval Constructor and Instructor for the Chinese Government at the Kiangnan Arsenal in Shanghai for eight years, where two of his sons were born in 1872 and 1875. He completed some wooden ships at the Arsenal at Shanghai, and afterwards laid out what is now the steel shipbuilding yard of the Kiangnan Dock and Engineering Works. Prior to Rennie's arrival at Kiangnan, the site had mainly been used as a peach orchard. Machinery of the best and most powerful kind had been imported from Britain for the purpose of building ironclads. Money for the building of these costly vessels, however, not being forthcoming, only repair work to the already existing fleet of two frigates and several gunboats, and the building of some small iron gunboats comprised the work done during Rennie's term of engagement.[1]

Walter Mucarsay Smith 1842-1906 from Ferry Port-on-Craig (Tayport) was one of the earliest foreign engineers in Japan. He became the Locomotive, Carriage, and Wagon Superintendent for the Imperial Government Railways in 1874, where he was responsible for establishing locomotive workshops, machinery, and running sheds. He became Chief Draughtsman at the North Eastern Railway following his return to Britain in 1883 and he developed a three-cylinder compound system for his locomotives which was perhaps the only successful compound system used in British locomotive design.[1]

James Weir 1842-1920 invented devices for ships at the time when Glasgow was the pre-eminent shipbuilding city in the world. His 1874 hydrokineter used nozzle injectors to promote circulation in ship engine boilers, reducing the time taken to raise steam. It continued in use for about sixty years. Between 1880 and 1886, he produced three more major inventions that laid the foundation of both the new company's success and Weir's fortune. The first was a device to use excess steam to heat the feed water before it entered a steam boiler, so removing the air and limescale that caused boiler corrosion and scaling. The concept of "regenerative feed heating" is still applied in steam plants of the 21st century to improve the thermal economy of the system.

Feed heating was indispensable at a time in Glasgow when, with the greater use of steel in construction and the adoption of triple-expansion engines, the shipbuilding industry was growing fast. While other inventors had proposed components of the feed system, Weir was the first to combine his own inventions into a unified solution to the feed water problem. His pump for the hot feed water was produced with few design changes into the 1960s, and his evaporator for distilling sea water into the fresh water needed for the boiler helped make the great passenger liners possible by increasing the range that ships could travel before taking on extra water.[1]

Weir patented the direct-acting feed pump embodying his principle of regenerative feed heating, which some authorities consider as important to the economy of the steam cycle as James Watt's separate condenser.[2]

James Edgar 1843-1909, much to the delight of children everywhere, introduced the department store Santa Claus in 1890. Edgar opened a department store in Brockton, Massachusetts and, during the Christmas season of 1890, he went to the store in costume and played the part of Santa. Within days of his original appearance, trains were bringing children from far away. Within a few years, Santa was appearing in stores all over the USA, just as he does today.

Santa had actually made his first appearance at J. W. Parkinson's dry-goods store in Philadelphia in 1841. The owner of the store put out a pamphlet proclaiming "Bring the little ones to J.W. Parkinson's, 100 North Donovan Street, at noon exactly on December 18. Mr Kringle himself will meet with the tots while Father and Mother take advantage of our store's unmatched selection of holiday toys. See him arrive down our chimney! Don't be late!"[1] But on-site Santas didn't catch on until 1890, when James Edgar, the jolly, bearded owner of The Boston Store in Brockton, Mass., began dressing in a Santa suit. Eager families from as far away as Providence, Rhode Island, came by train to line up for a visit with Santa.[2]

"James Edgar was an immigrant from Edinburgh [sic – he was born in Longformacus, Duns, Berwickshire], Scotland who opened Edgar's Department Store on Main Street in Brockton. In December of 1890, he dressed up as Santa Claus based on a popular illustration of a jolly Santa drawn in 1863 by the famous cartoonist Thomas Nast. Edgar did not intend for this to be a commercial attraction. He did it for the enjoyment of the children and to promote Christmas. It began the tradition of the department store Santa Claus. The idea quickly transferred to department stores around the country and continues to this day."[3]

To Edgar, whose dry goods store became a landmark in downtown Brockton, every day was about children. "I have never been able to understand why the great gentleman lives at the North Pole. He is so far away, only able to see the children one day a year. He should live closer to them," Edgar once said, according to Jamie Kageleiry's account of "The First Department Store Santa," that appeared in the December 1990 issue of *Yankee Magazine*.

Edgar practiced what he preached, becoming "Uncle Jim" to the children he entertained in his store and at annual 4th July extravaganzas – renting trolleys to carry thousands of Brockton youths to holiday outings where he would dress in costume to delight them. "I love children and they love me," he said in a 1902 interview in *The Enterprise*. "James Edgar was a born showman," Brocktonian Robert A. Kane wrote in his late 20th century biography of the person who would become the man behind the costume, "the P.T. Barnum of Brockton."

Image 71 – Edgar's Children's Day parade lined up outside his Boston Store on Main Street in Brockton in this undated file photo

Through the years, "Colonel Jim," as he was known, was photographed in a variety of costumes, from the historic – George Washington – to the sportsman – a cricket uniform – and even as an Indian – "Big Chief", for one of his annual outings for children. At Christmas time, Edgar would dress as a clown and walk through the store, visiting with children. Then, in 1890, he brought Thomas Nast's 1862 drawing of Santa Claus – jolly and round and dressed in a red suit – to life. In a custom-made red suit, the tall, ample-bodied and bearded Edgar became the first department store Santa Claus, a designation widely recognised today and now memorialised in a plaque in downtown Brockton.[4]

David Ferrier 1843-1928 proved the existence of the localisation of the cerebral functions, a fact hitherto disputed. He was the first to map the cerebral cortex from what had been an unknown area, demonstrating that the combined areas of excitable points on the brain's surface were more extensive, and that more movements throughout the body could be elicited, in an ape than in animals less like human beings. He further inferred, through his research on monkeys, that conditions of disease in the brain could be effectively dealt with surgically, to a far greater extent than had been done previously.[1]

He was one of the founders and editors of the journal *Brain* when it started in 1878, and in 1894 he was president of the Neurological Society. He succeeded in demonstrating, in a spectacular manner, that the low-intensity faradic stimulation of the cortex indicated a rather precise and specific map for motor functions. The same areas, upon being lesioned, caused the loss of the functions which were elicited by stimulation. Ferrier was also able to demonstrate that the high-intensity stimulation of motor cortical areas caused repetitive movements in the neck, face and members which were highly evocative of epileptic fits seen by neurologists in human beings and animals, which probably were due to a spread of the focus of stimulation. These, and other investigations in the same line, gave international fame to Ferrier and assured his permanent place in the pantheon of the greatest neurophysiologists and experimental neurologists of all times.[2]

Where Gustav Theodor Fritsch and Eduard Hitzig had found five motor centres, Ferrier found fifteen and went on to specify areas for each of the five senses. In the obituary notice of Ferrier for The Royal Society, Charles Scott Sherrington pointed out that Ferrier had done the most important research in proving cerebral localisation, in placing it at the centre of neurological interest. The significance of Ferrier's work was quickly appreciated. Accounts from the British Association, the President's Address to The Royal Society, and the 1901 supplement to the *Encyclopedia Britannica*, as well as contemporary reviews of his works, all confirm that it made as much a stir as the Bell-Magendie law had fifty years earlier. Even physiologist William Carpenter was moved to rank Ferrier's localisations among the greatest advances in the physiology of the nervous system which had been made in the last fifty years, and he acknowledged the existence of the missing fibres connecting the cortex and lower centres.[3]

In 1876, Ferrier published *The Functions of the Brain*, which describes his experimental results and in which he remarks, "We may succeed in determining the exact nature of the molecular changes that occur in the brain cells when a sensation is experienced, but this will not bring us one whit nearer the explanation of the ultimate nature of that which constitutes the sensation."[4]

By using faradic current stimulation, Ferrier investigated even further the cortical functioning of many different animals, including primates. He constructed one of the first detailed cortical maps and confirmed many of the principles set forth by Hughlings Jackson. Ferrier firmly established the location of the motor cortex, stating that it extended along the rolandic fissure medially to the interhemispheric area.[5]

Within a few years, renowned surgeon William Macewen had used the cortical maps to undertake operations on the brain. "Thanks to Ferrier, as well as Fritsch and Hitzig, the concept of specialised motor, sensor, and association areas of the brain would now serve as a foundation from many future developments in the brain sciences and medicine.[6]

David Gill 1843-1914 perfected the use of the heliometer, a telescope that uses a split image to measure the angular separation of celestial bodies. Astronomer Gill measured the solar and stellar parallax that show the distances of the Sun and other stars from Earth. He was also a pioneer in the use of photography in mapping the solar system. He photographed the southern sky and helped initiate the international Carte du Ciel project to chart the entire sky. Gill and Jacobus Cornelius Kapteyn, who measured Gill's photographs in the Netherlands, initiated the separation of observation from reduction. Gill also made geodetic surveys of South Africa. In fact, he carried out all of the observations to measure the distances to stars in terms of the standard metre.[1]

In 1901, he determined the first accurate measurement of the solar parallax: 8.80". Gill's measurement was used in all almanacs until 1968, when it was recalculated as 8.794 by observations made with a Mariner space probe using the radar echo method. He also determined the distances, using the heliometer, of twenty of the brighter and nearer Southern stars. In 1882, it was the bright comet (now called the Great Comet) that was of great interest to astronomers. When Gill saw a photograph of the comet, he realised that it would be possible to chart and measure the positions of a star using photography. He immediately started an extensive project, with the aid of other observatories, to produce the Cape Durchmusterung, which locates the positions and brightness of more than 450,000 Southern stars. It was the first important astronomical project to use photography.[2]

Thomas Lauder Brunton 1844-1916 played a major role in establishing pharmacology as a rigorous science. He is best known for his discovery that amyl nitrite relieves the pain of angina pectoris.[1]

In the late 1700s, several English physicians correlated the angina suffered by living patients with the obstruction of heart blood vessels found in post-mortems of the same patients. Despite these early insights, many leading physicians through much of the following century blamed the chest pain on indigestion and treated angina with soda or chalk to relieve stomach acidity. Even the acceptance that the heart was the centre of the problem did not help matters much: an article by Brunton in *The Lancet* on 27 July 1867 listed brandy, ether, ammonia, and chloroform as possible treatments for angina. Patients treated with chloroform stopped reporting pain temporarily, Brunton noted, but resumed when they had recovered from the "partial stupefaction" induced by the chloroform.[2]

Brunton's real discovery in this paper was that a substance called amyl nitrite reduced both angina pain and blood pressure. A number of clues had prompted him to test amyl nitrite. Eight years earlier, a chemist who had inhaled it while doing a routine series of chemical experiments had reported that it made him flushed and caused his arteries and heart to pound. Brunton also knew that amyl nitrite dilated blood vessels in a frog's foot and had heard from others that it reduced blood pressure in humans. Although Brunton was on the right track, he mistakenly believed that amyl nitrite worked by relaxing blood vessels throughout the body. In fact, however, the important site of amyl nitrite action is on heart blood vessels at the site of a blockage.[3]

Brunton suspected that amyl nitrite might also relieve angina by increasing blood flow to the heart. He was right, as he found when he tried the drug on some of his patients. It wasn't long before nitroglycerin, which is chemically similar to amyl nitrite, was discovered to have a similar effect, relaxing the smooth muscles that make up your veins and arteries and allowing them to dilate. Both drugs are still used for treatment of angina, but nitroglycerin is by far the more common, because it is more easily administered and has fewer side effects.[4]

Brunton identified the relationship between high blood pressure and angina pectoris, further discovering that amyl nitrate relieved the angina. He was the first to suggest use of operations for the treatment of mitral stenosis – a narrowing of the outflow path from the heart's left ventricle. He proposed surgical intervention and suggested that a suitable instrument might be passed blindly through the wall of the left ventricle and "by sense of touch" into the mitral valve orifice.[5]

The introduction of amyl nitrite as a remedy for angina was heralded, along with the discovery of bacteria and the germ theory of disease, as an example of the benefits of research to practical medicine and therefore to mankind. An editor of the *Medical News* wrote in 1883, "In few maladies are the improvements in our therapeutical resources more conspicuous. In the use of the most effective remedy for the relief of the paroxysm, an admirable illustration is given of the remarkable value of the contributions made to therapeutics by physiological investigations. We refer to the use of amyl nitrite in this affection – an addition to scientific medicine which we owe to Dr Lauder Brunton."

Brunton's understanding of the pathophysiology of congestive heart failure was advanced for his time. His suggestion that long-acting vasodilators might be efficacious in preventing or treating congestive heart failure has been forgotten. Contemporary writers generally credit George Burch and John Johnson with advocating this approach; but their papers appeared in the 1950s, 70 years after Brunton made his claims about the potential value of vasodilators for the treatment of hypertension and left ventricular failure.[6] Note: Vasodilation refers to the widening of blood vessels resulting from relaxation of smooth muscle cells within the vessel walls, particularly in the large arteries, smaller arterioles and large veins.

As a result of this work by many physicians and scientists, Brunton's proposal that vasodilators should be useful in the treatment of angina pectoris, hypertension, and congestive heart failure has been supported and agents of this class are now in widespread use for these clinical problems.[7]

Brunton was a prolific author; during the first 20 years of his career he published nearly fifty papers, most based on his own research. He also published several books, including a classic textbook of pharmacology and therapeutics considered by one reviewer "the first to consider pharmacology as a scientific study of the physiological action of drugs." His most important work is *A Textbook of Pharmacology, Therapeutics, and Materia Medica* (1885), which was the first comprehensive treatise on pharmacology, emphasising the physiological actions of pure drugs.[8] Note: It is said that Thomas Lauder Brunton also invented the otoscope, an instrument used for inspecting the ear canal, but the Brunton in question is John Brunton (1836-1899).

John Young Buchanan 1844-1925 discovered the Equatorial Undercurrent during 1885-1886, on a cruise off the coast of West Africa in the cable vessel *Buccaneer*, but his results were largely disregarded until the Pacific version of the phenomenon was discovered in 1952 and that in the Atlantic was "rediscovered" in 1959.

As chemist on the HMS *Challenger* expedition, Buchanan took 77 water samples throughout the oceans, deriving data from these that formed the foundation of chemical oceanography.

Buchanan's chief contribution to the cruise was the debunking of a theory that had been put forward by the German scientist Ernst Haeckel, namely that the floor of the ocean was covered in a primordial slime that was even awarded a Latin name, *Bathybius huxleyii*. Huxley himself was a great proponent of the existence of this mythical creature, but it was Buchanan who proved that it was merely sulphate of lime that precipitated in preserving jars when seawater was mixed with the preserving fluid.

Buchanan was also the first to describe the oxygen minimum at intermediate depths around 600 m, and he published a series of papers on the specific gravity of sea water, from which he inferred the distribution of salinity. His charts and vertical sections showed the global distribution of surface salinity for the first time and revealed such features as Antarctic intermediate water penetrating into the North Atlantic. He analysed the chemical composition of newly discovered manganese nodules in 1891, and he demonstrated that increasing pressure enhanced the solubility of calcareous planktonic skeletal debris raining down from the euphotic zone.[1]

Robert Hunter 1844-1913 was co-founder of the National Trust (full name: National Trust for Places of Historic Interest or Natural Beauty). The role of Hunter, a leading member of the Commons Preservation Society (CPS), in the founding of the Trust was absolutely crucial; Hunter turned Octavia Hill's passion and commitment to the protection of open spaces into hard legal reality. In effect, Hunter "invented" the National Trust. He was the first person to come up with the idea of a property-owning charity, operating for the benefit of the nation. It appears that he also came up with the name "National Trust" (Hill – another leading member of the CPS – had wanted to call the organisation the "Commons and Gardens Trust"). Hunter was the organisation's first chairman, and single-handedly wrote the *National Trust Act (1907)*.

He was active in a great many causes in addition to the National Trust. He was chairman of Hampstead Garden Suburb, chairman of an early version of the Ramblers' Association, vice-Chairman of the Leighton House Trust, and campaigned for a great many places and buildings: the Geffrye Almshouses, Lincoln's Inn Fields, and the many commons around his home in Haslemere, including Devil's Punch Bowl. He was also active in pressing for legislative protection for monuments. He wrote *The Ancient Monuments Act 1900* and played a key role in pressing for *The Ancient Monuments Consolidation and Amendment Act 1913*.[1]

In September 1884, in Birmingham, Hunter gave a speech at the National Association for the Promotion of Social Science in which he talked about the formation of a society to protect land. He said, "The central idea is that of a Land Company, formed not for the promotion of thrift or the spread of political principles, and not primarily for profit, but with a view to the protection of the public interest in open spaces in the country". The functions should include, "the acquisition and holding of properties to which common rights are attached; the acquisition of manors ... and the maintenance and management of gardens in towns as such, and the maintenance and management of any buildings connected with them as places of resort for recreation and instruction."[2]

Hunter fought many legal battles, leading to the protection of Epping Forest, Hampstead Heath and Ashdown Forest, among many other commons. Hunter was a meticulous researcher and tireless worker for the cause. He soon became the country's leading expert on the law of commons. In 1882, Henry Fawcett MP, who was Postmaster General in Gladstone's second government, appointed Hunter as solicitor to the General Post Office, where "The whole of the Post Office regulations, again were drafted by Sir Robert Hunter, some of them two or three times to meet alterations. He spent much time and trouble on the details of the Post Office Savings Bank, the practice which he greatly simplified and assisted."[3] In 1905, Hunter chaired a committee formed to buy at auction 750 acres (303.5 hectares) of nearby common land, which included Hindhead Common and the Devil's Punch Bowl. The committee paid £3,260 for the land which it later gave to the National Trust.

The following February, Octavia Hill wrote to Hunter suggesting names for the company. At the head of this letter Hunter pencilled "? National Trust". However, it was to be another ten years before the trust was founded jointly by Hunter, Octavia Hill and Canon Hardwicke Rawnsley.[4] In 2007, an International National Trusts Organisation was launched with 24 full member Trusts, and more than 40 National Trusts throughout the world.[5]

Hugh David Lumsden 1844-1896 was, from 1870, a civil engineer who had a long and successful career in the location and construction of railways across Canada. He was involved as Chief Engineer with the Toronto & Nipissing Railway; the Credit Valley Railway; the Toronto, Grey & Bruce Railway; the Northern Railway; the Georgian Bay Branch of the Canadian Pacific Railway (CPR); The Ontario & Quebec Railway; various eastern extensions of the CPR; and the Crows Nest Pass Railway to name a few. From 1904 to 1909, Lumsden was the Chief Engineer of the Eastern Division of the Transcontinental Railway. He was president of the Canadian Society of Civil Engineers in 1907.[1]

Patrick Manson 1844-1922 founded the field of tropical medicine. He was the first to discover (1877-1879) that an insect (mosquito) can be host to a developing parasite (the worm *Filaria bancrofti*) that is the cause of a human disease – filariasis, which occurs when the worms invade body tissues.[1] While in China, he discovered that mosquitoes carry filariasis and that the embryonic *filariae* only appear in the patient's peripheral blood stream at night when mosquitoes feed. He founded the first western-style medical school in China, and another in Hong Kong after moving there in 1883, and in 1899 the London School of Tropical Medicine, which Manson founded, was opened.[2]

Manson's theories about the mosquito and its contribution to the spread of disease were significant. Under observation, Manson theorised that the mosquito activated the life cycle of the worm, *Filaria*, which causes elephantiasis. These observations, made during his time as medical officer for the Chinese Imperial Maritime Customs, also led to the conclusion that mosquitoes are in fact the carriers of *plasmodium*, a parasite which causes malaria. Under his supervision, Sir Ronald Ross described the life cycle of *plasmodium* and, in 1902, won the Nobel Prize after he proved Manson's theory.[3]

Manson was fascinated by the filarial embryos seen in the blood of some of his Chinese patients, and his studies showed the remarkable phenomenon of nocturnal periodicity of the embryos in the blood. He showed how an insect could harbour the larval parasites which underwent changes to prepare them for re-entry into a subject to carry disease. He also made observations on *Paragonimiasis* but, while still busy with these researches, he was treating patients for smallpox, cholera and leprosy.[4]

During his researches, Manson discovered that many tropical infectious diseases need a warm climate vector for person-to-person transmission. Besides demonstrating the abovementioned nocturnal periodicity of *microfilariae* in the blood of patients with elephantiasis, Manson revealed the linkage between the lung fluke and endemic hemoptysis by finding operculated (lid-like) eggs in the sputum of patients. He predicted that the *miracidium* from hatched eggs used crustaceans, such as fresh-water snails found in tropical conditions, as the intermediate hosts in the life cycle of many trematodes.

In 1877, he excised one tonne of tissue from patients with elephantiasis, with only two deaths out of 61 operations done under chloroform anesthesia and without support by blood transfusions and antibiotics. Many of these patients could not find a job because of their grotesquely disfigured and enlarged lower limbs and scrotums. They were abandoned by their families because of the financial burden or the superstition about demon possession. In one instance, he encountered a 19-year-old man badly affected by a huge elephantoid tumour who attempted suicide by swallowing arsenic but failed because the excessive dose of poison caused gastric irritation leading to vomiting of the poison. He agreed to be operated by Manson because he did not care if he died. This successful operation by Manson earned him reputation and the gradual acceptance of Western medicine by the local Chinese. Besides elephantiasis, he relieved many patients suffering from the distressing colics due to renal, ureteric and bladder stones by surgical lithotomies. Despite these achievements, he was modest in describing himself as a good carpenter but an indifferent surgeon.

Manson was, in fact, a daring and accurate surgeon who tried to tackle liver abscess which was almost invariably fatal in his era with no organ imaging facilities and antibiotics. He designed the Manson trocar and Manson cannula for the single-handed blind exploration and treatment of deep seated liver abscess. The trocar and cannula produced at a local ironsmith in Amoy could be fitted to a stylet and perforated drainage tube which could be used for the exploration of hidden liver abscess in the absence of organ imaging and many other surgical conditions.

The groundwork of Manson has laid a solid foundation for many clinical practices and epidemiological programs in modern tropical medicine. Global programs in vector control remain the mainstay in the control and eradication of malaria, filariasis and dracunculiasis (Guinea worm disease); 22.8% of emerging infectious diseases since 1940 are vector-borne diseases. Control of arthropod vector-borne diseases includes chemical and biological means, as well as by reducing contact between human and vectors. The best example is the control of mosquitoes, which includes the reduction of the mosquito population by environmental modifications, larvicides and adulticides, and the prevention of mosquito-human contact with medicated bed-nets and insect repellants. Alternative biological control strategies under investigation to reduce insecticide resistance and ecological side effects include the use of a bacterial endosymbiont *Wolbachia* to inhibit the replication of the *Plasmodium* in mosquitoes, entomopathogenic fungi and genetically-modified mosquitoes.[5]

Manson set the personal example of excellence in clinical service, medical education and microbial research. His scientific contributions on the importance of vector control to interrupt the life cycle of many tropical disease agents make him well deserved of the title of "Father of Tropical Medicine". In the year 2000, the World Health Organization launched a global campaign for eliminating lymphatic filariasis (elephantiasis) which would not have been possible without the firm foundation laid down by Manson. The task is immense as over 120 million people are currently infected, with about 40 million disfigured and incapacitated by the disease (World Health Organization Fact Sheet N°102, updated March 2014).

His contribution to China did not end after departing that country. Before leaving, he established the Alice Memorial Hospital, the Hong Kong College of Medicine for Chinese (the forerunner of the University of Hong Kong), and the Hong Kong Medical Society for medical service and education.[6] He also incepted the Hong Kong Dairy Farm for supplying hygienic milk affordable by pregnant women, children and patients. In 1896, he helped Dr James Cantlie in saving Dr Sun Yat-Sen from the kidnap and imprisonment by secret agents of the Ching Dynasty in London. If not for their effort, Dr Sun might have been executed, and China may not have been liberated from the feudal Ching Dynasty in 1911.[7]

After Ronald Ross completed the picture of the life cycle of malaria in mosquitoes in 1898, he wrote to Manson, "What a beautiful discovery this is. I venture to praise it because it belongs to you, not to me".[8]

Manson founded the London School of Tropical Medicine and Hygiene in 1899 despite opposition from the War Office, Admiralty and the medical establishment. Manson thus completed his hat-trick of founding medical schools. [9]

Alexander Ogston 1844-1929 showed that by meticulous antiseptic treatment of everything that touched the surgical wound, the incidence of suppuration, and hence patient mortality, was greatly reduced. Operations that were previously thought to be very dangerous were now shown to be safe. These operations included the correction of knock-knee (*genu valgum*) – which became widely known as "Ogston's operation", operations performed on the ovary, uterus ectopic pregnancies, and obstructed bowel. Two additional operating theatres were built in the hospital, this time scrub-in sinks, an autoclave and glass-topped metal trolleys for instruments were introduced.

Ogston often pondered on the cause of acute suppuration and, in 1880, through his own research, he discovered the cause to be an organism he called *Staphylococcus pyogenes aureus* (aka "golden staph"). Its name is derived from its perceived similarity in appearance to a bunch of grapes. Staphylococcus is a gram-positive bacterium that is able to invade host cells. This is the bacterium that the media has dubbed the "superbug", MRSA – *Methicillin resistant Staphylococcus aureus* – that is causing concern as patients are succumbing to infection in hospitals.

When the brilliant German microbiologist Robert Heinrich Herman Koch published *Investigations into the Etiology of Traumatic Infective Diseases* in 1878, it created "something of a sensation". Koch's twofold monumental contributions were the staining of organisms in septic material with aniline dyes, and the use of the microscope for descriptive purposes. But the medical profession was bewildered by his findings. It remained for Ogston to clarify Koch's report by employing the latter's techniques in studies on abscesses. Ogston was the first to grow bacteria in abundance in chicken eggs and to produce abscesses in animals by inoculating them with these cultures. Ogston concluded that suppurating wounds contain micrococci and Listerian dressings prevent micro-organisms from gaining access to wounds. Micrococci in wounds withstand most antiseptic applications. Where no micrococci are present in wounds, no pus is produced; the discharge is serous. Ogston designated the micrococci that occurred in chains as *Streptococcus*, and those that appeared like bunches of grapes as *Staphylococcus*.[1]

George Edward Ormiston 1844-1913 was Chief Engineer of Bombay from 1882 to 1892. He was responsible for the Victoria and Prince's docks, Merewether dry dock, the Apollo Bunder extension, and many other important works.[1]

Walter Scott 1844-1907 received his first patent in 1874 for the first press for printing from a continuous roll of paper, and to cut, paste, fold, and deliver in packs of fifty. He also made the first web machine in America to print in five colours and to deliver in book form. "In 1900 the United States Commissioner of Patents in his report, mentioned Mr Scott as one of thirty-nine inventors who had been granted over one hundred patents each in twenty-six years. Mr Scott led the list with one hundred and fifty-six patents in twenty years. Up to this time, his patents number over two hundred and sixty. They cover the whole range of printing machinery, stereotype, electrotype, and others.[1] He developed the straight-line printing and folding machine in 1890 and, in 1900, he built the first folding machine to be combined with a rotary printing press for the Chicago Inter-Ocean.[2]

Two of his 1879 patents were for a machine that combined the operations of trimming (cutting the rough edges) and shaving (cutting down the back ribs) of curved stereotype plates for rotary printing and another for improvements to a web perfecting rotary press, with cutters and folding apparatus. He designed the small, two-revolution "pony" presses, which were the work-horses of printers of the period, especially in the USA. They were fast, light running and could be changed over to different paper sizes relatively smartly.[3]

In 1889, Paul Cox produced a reel-fed flatbed perfecting press called the Duplex, but this was upstaged two years later when Scott produced a machine that printed a four, six or eight-page newspaper and delivered folded copies at a rate of 3,000 to 4,000 per hour.[4]

Charles Smith 1844-1882 designed "a novel bridge" to replace the "dilatory and dangerous ferry" that carried his men across the harbour at Hartlepool. "It is very much like a travelling crane, with a basket or omnibus suspended, which allows the freest navigation of the channel, combined with safe and rapid transit to passengers and carriages," said the *Echo*, describing for the first time a transporter bridge – or "bridge ferry", as Smith called it. The concept of building a Transporter Bridge was down to one man, Scottish-born Hartlepool engineer Charles Smith. His design had a span of 650 feet (198 m), and a height under the span of 150 feet (45.7 m); the gondola suspended from the structure had to dodge ships passing up and down the Tees. It was estimated to have cost £31,136. He presented it to Hartlepool, Middlesbrough and Glasgow councils, but all said no and, like so many great British inventions, it was turned into reality by foreigners. In 1887, having studied Smith's plans, French bridge builder Ferdinand Arnodin and Spanish engineer Alberto Palacio patented the "transbordeur" concept and set to work building the first one near Bilbao, northern Spain.[1]

The Transporter Bridge is "a European monument – in its daring and finesse, it is a thrill to see from anywhere," according to the famous architecture critic Nikolaus Pevsner.[2]

Image 72 – Middlesbrough Transporter Bridge

Smith's concept was taken up later and, long after his death, the Transporter was opened in 1911 – it "is without doubt the most iconic structure on Teesside and its image has come to represent the region in advertising and is even incorporated into the logo of Middlesbrough Council."

Allan Stirling 1844-1927 invented a commercially successful four-drum boiler in 1892. Making reliable, efficient boilers was, and is, important for the generation of steam to drive locomotives, steamships, turbines and other steam machinery. Stirling's boiler allowed for a large surface heat transfer area, as well as promoting natural water circulation. Because it required less water, it responded more quickly to load change and heat input and could tolerate higher pressures. After designing the four-drum boiler, he built a machine for bending pipes which enabled bent tubes to be used for the first time in boiler construction.

Image 73 – Cable Conveyor
"Hangline Wood Finish" by PaclineConveyor

By 1906, Stirling had a 26-hectare factory in Ohio mass-producing his bent-tube boilers. These differed from standard shell boilers inasmuch as the water is circulated inside tubes with the heat source surrounding them, allowing much higher pressure for the same stress and giving them greater resistance to thermal shock. This design had particular value in installations in low headroom conditions. The continuous and economical production of clean, dry steam, even when using poor feedwater, and the ability to meet sudden load swings, also characterise the Stirling type boilers. By 1906, Stirling boilers had been built in sizes up to 823 horsepower and 300 pounds pressure. They were sixteen times more powerful than the Babcock & Wilcox boiler of 1867.[1] They found particular favour when cotton mill owners started to shift from waterwheel power to steam power. Coal mines also favoured Stirling's boilers which continued to be mass produced by Babcock and Willcox after they bought his Ohio plant in 1906.

It wasn't just boilers that Stirling designed, for as early as 1880 he had designed a cable conveyor, possibly the first ever.[2] These are now commonplace in manufacturing warehouses and factories.

Rookes Evelyn Bell Crompton 1845-1940 invented, in 1878, an arc lamp with an overhead support mechanism to reduce shadow. Previous lamps had been constructed with the support mechanism below the electrodes, producing noticeable shadows.[1] "About Christmas, 1879, Crompton lighted up his own house in Porchester Gardens. At first, he used primary cells, but they were not a success, so he brought one of his portable sets into the mews at the back of his house and gave special parties, using small arc lights fixed in his drawing-room and dining-room. This was probably the first instance of effective electric lighting in a private house, although there had previously been exhibitions of arc lighting at the Royal Institution and elsewhere."[2]

The success of this installation led to numerous orders for similar systems worldwide. Crompton supplied equipment throughout the British Empire, with power stations being built as far away as Australia, which received its first Crompton lighting plant in 1887. In 1899, the company installed a generator set in a Calcutta hotel, producing India's first ever electricity supply. Crompton designed and manufactured dynamos, switchgear, circuit breakers, motors and electric meters, as well as lamps."

His arc lamps started to be used as military searchlights. This was not his only contribution to military technology. During the First World War, he was asked to submit designs for "landships" that could cross trenches. These became the blueprint for the modern military tank. In 1880, he published one of the first lighting manuals, *The Electric Light for Industrial Uses*, and he produced one of the first electric cookers.[3]

The success of his British projects, led to a number of commissions in mainland Europe between 1885 and 1889. One such project was the Viennese Opera House, the first large theatre to be lit electrically anywhere.[4]

"Crompton was the major pioneer of the electrical industry in the late nineteenth and early twentieth century." He was the first major British manufacturer of generators, and his power station at Kensington Court, which began supply in 1887, represented one of the first practical supply schemes. He was also a champion of international electrical standardisation, and was instrumental in the formation of the International Electrotechnical Commission in 1906. He was twice President of the Institution of Engineering and Technology (1895 and 1908), the largest multidisciplinary professional engineering institution in the world.[5]

Alexander McDougall 1845-1923 was a pioneer in a design that influenced both monitors and other ship designs. He arrived in America from Islay to settle in Duluth on the Great Lakes, and in 1881 he invented a new design for a ship – the whaleback, which was designed so that most of it was underwater when moving, reducing the effects of wave and wind action. It was cone-shaped fore and aft with a cigar-shaped body and the main deck had turrets on top of which stood the superstructure.

McDougall's whaleback, also known as a pigboat, had an influence on the design of other ships on the Great Lakes, such as monitors, straightbacks and turtlebacks. "From the whaleback influence, there developed a number of short departures that were more successful in shaping future marine architecture than in extending the prototypes into long-term production. One of these variations was the "turtleback", a vessel with a rounded forecastle that was superseded on the cutting edge of vessel design because masters complained of poor visibility and other problems impacting navigation. Another was the "monitor", a vessel with a conventional bow and sides that sloped from deck to waterline at a forty-five-degree angle. A different variation confined to package freighters was the "straightback", a design that carried a high forecastle, a straight deck line, and the pilot house about a third of the way back from the bow."[1] The whaleback was also influential in the design of modern submarines.

Image 74 – McDougall Whaleback

Joseph L. Colby, built 1890, scrapped 1935, was the second whaleback built by McDougall

In 1889, McDougall founded the American Steel Barge Company to produce whalebacks, and he built the first steamship in north-western America, the *Charles W. Wetmore*. The whaleback design for freight movement went into decline when it was found unsuitable for use with changes to cargo handling machinery, but in England, Doxford & Sons built a whaleback in June 1893 with a slightly modified design to minimise the fees charged for using the Suez Canal. This design, the Doxford turret ship, became popular and the company constructed 176 of these steamships.

John McTammany 1845-1915 invented the mechanical piano (conceived in 1863) and the pneumatic registering voting machine (1892).[1] His mechanical piano, also known as the player piano, used narrow sheets of perforated flexible paper which triggered the notes.

Although Thomas Edison is often credited with the invention of the voting machine, his device tallied votes for small numbers of electors, such as legislators' casting votes within a single chamber. New Yorker, Jacob Hiram Myers invented a voting machine that was authorised for the election of New York town officers in 1892.

McTammany was, however, the inventor of the first voting machine for popular elections. His machine was devised to "avoid … the incidental risk of irregular and fraudulent voting." While Edison's invention was a simple tabulator, McTammany's innovation was a complicated mechanism adaptable to an American political system with a long ballot and electoral rules that change from one locality to another. McTammany's equipment was specified in the first voting-machine laws of the states of Massachusetts, Rhode Island and Connecticut.

The next generation of voting machines depended upon what John McTammany alluded to in one of his patents as "the Australian system of voting, so called." These included the first voting machines actually put into general practice. Australian elections used voting with a municipally prepared ballot instead of a party ticket. Every voter got a copy of the same printed ballot and could exercise his franchise without the intrusion or surveillance of party agents. Massachusetts adopted an Australian ballot in 1889, and the other states followed suit over the next two decades. It was a justly celebrated reform, though results were far from uniform. Note: Australia wasn't the first country to adopt secret ballots – the 1795 French Constitution permitted such voting – but Australia, or more specifically, the state of Victoria, was the first to combine it with other factors, such as municipal voting sheets that did not reveal political party affiliations and, as such, the Australian ballot is the true origin of modern voting in elections around the world. Recent research shows that the state of Tasmania actually legislated for secret ballots in 1856, five weeks before Victoria, but Victoria was first to actually put it into practice.

In 1893, McTammany patented a voting machine that recorded votes on a continuous paper roll. He recognised a shortcoming in this method inasmuch that by recording votes on a continuous roll, "it is possible to identify a man's vote, by counting voters as they go in and afterward counting the rows of marks on the sheet." McTammany's proposed solution was to stagger the rows of marks corresponding to each voter's ballot so that marks corresponding to different voters would be interleaved on the paper roll, making it difficult to reconstruct any particular voter's ballot. This scheme might be considered the first application of cryptography (albeit in rudimentary form) to the problem of ballot secrecy, but McTammany eventually abandoned this staggering scheme.[2] The introduction of voting machines and concurrent reforms also changed the nature of political parties and elections in the United States.

James Manson 1845-1935 improved safety with his new tablet exchange whereby trains could collect and set down single-line tablets while travelling at 80 km/h.

Tablets were tokens that could be inserted or removed from instruments placed at either end of a single-line section of rail that was connected by telegraph wire. Provided no other train was on the line, a tablet could be removed from either instrument and handed to a train driver as authorisation to travel on the line. A second tablet could not be issued until the missing tablet was returned to an instrument at either end of the single line.

Manson also designed the 4-4-0 No 11, the first four-cylinder simple locomotive in Britain, and designed some impressive double-bogie tenders for his large 4-6-0 engines.[1]

Image 75 – Manson 4-4-0 Great North of Scotland Railway No17

Alexander Alan Arthur 1846-1912 played a primary role in the development of the Cumberland Gap area in the United States, and he established the cities of Middlesboro, Kentucky and Harrogate, Tennessee, with the community of Arthur, Tennessee being named for him. In the early 1880s, Arthur identified a rich stand of timber in the upper Blue Ridge Mountains along the Tennessee-North Carolina border, and devised a boom system to extract the timber from the difficult mountain terrain, with the harvested logs to be floated down the Pigeon River in a controlled fashion using a series of logging booms. In Harrogate, Tennessee, he built the *Four Seasons*, a 700-room resort hotel believed to have been the largest hotel in the United States at the time of its completion.

Later, in the same decade, Arthur identified the abundant iron ore deposits in the Cumberland Gap region, and established a multimillion dollar iron production operation in hopes of making Middlesboro the "Pittsburgh of the South". While he never experienced great financial success, Arthur's endeavours were a harbinger of the great logging and mining operations that became major economic forces in Southern Appalachia in the early 20th century. Arthur understood the great wealth that could be obtained from extracting the abundant natural resources of the Southern Appalachian Mountains, but even with million-dollar financing, the lack of technology and inaccessibility of the region proved too much to overcome. It was not until the invention of the Shay locomotive and the steam-powered skidder that large-scale logging of the mountains' timber became profitable. In the early 1900s, firms such as the Little River Lumber Company and Champion Fiber saw enormous returns logging the timber stands Arthur had attempted to reach decades earlier. Likewise, by the time of Arthur's death, the mountains north of Middlesboro had become one of the world's great coal mining regions.[1]

William McGregor 1846-1911 is known as the "Father of the League" for his work in founding the Association Football League. In 1888, he wrote to the strongest football (soccer) clubs, suggesting that the league be formed. His suggestion was accepted and 12 clubs made up the original football league for the 1888-1889 season.

McGregor first became interested in football as a young man in Scotland while he was serving his apprenticeship as a draper. He ended up in Aston when he followed his brother Peter down to Birmingham in 1870 with a view to setting up his own drapery business in the area. Initially, he became involved with a local football club, Calthorpe, on his arrival in the Midlands. However, McGregor must have found out there was a strong Scottish contingent in the Aston Villa side of the time which persuaded him to become a member of the club in 1877. McGregor's organisational skills and passion for the fledgling football club soon helped Aston Villa become a better team than Calthorpe resulting in them winning their first trophy, the Birmingham Senior Cup in 1880. By 1887, they had won the FA (Football Association) Cup for the first time becoming only the 9th club in the history of the competition to do so. It was the success of Aston Villa and the high attendances to their matches that convinced McGregor the public were hungry for more competition. So, in early 1888, three years after football had become professional and one year after Villa's first FA Cup, McGregor wrote to a number of clubs – initially, Blackburn Rovers, Bolton Wanderers, Preston North End, West Bromwich Albion, and Aston Villa.

His letter was "tentative in tone, politely throwing out a suggestion. But the letter which William McGregor posted to five clubs on 2 March 1888 proved the catalyst for the formation of the global game's original and most durable league competition, The [English] Football League. An enduring, worldwide example of his legacy is the use of the League tables; having the tabulated positions of the teams in the press was his idea. He turned Aston Villa club into a limited company in the face of hostility from devotees who viewed it as rampant commercialism".[1]

McGregor decided to act after a fellow director, Joe Tillotson, was so enraged when Villa's opponents pulled out one Saturday that he stormed into McGregor's drapers' shop – "Football Jerseys Always In Stock" – to vent his annoyance at another example of the shambolic state of the fixtures. Football needed structuring, with more monies guaranteed to clubs. McGregor had always been forward-thinking, demanding that the more ale-obsessed members of the Villa squad join him at a coffee house in Aston High Street every Monday, encouraging sobriety. Now he applied his formidable intelligence and energy to rescuing Villa's livelihood as well as their livers.

"Clubs were not then exempt from the preliminary rounds of local and national cup competitions, and it was not edifying to see a strong club beat a minor team by 26 goals to nil,'' McGregor recalled in one of his later newspaper columns. "You could not expect people to take interest in such fixtures, but the professionals' wage bill was there, and it had to be met."

He contacted the five clubs, pointing out "cup-tie interference", and the prevalence of fixtures that failed to attract the public's interest. "I beg to tender the following suggestion as a means of getting over the difficulty: that 10 or 12 of the most prominent clubs in England combine to arrange home-and-away fixtures each season. Of course, this is in no way to interfere with the National Association [the FA]; even the suggested matches might be played under cup-tie rules. However, this is a detail." A rather large "detail". The League was on a collision course with the FA and it had not even been formed yet.

McGregor added that they should invite others and to meet on Friday 23 March 1888 at Anderton's Hotel, off Fleet Street. The "friendly conference" went well, they convened again on April 17, at the Royal Hotel, Manchester, and called themselves the Football League. Clubs agreed that visitors (i.e. the "away" team) should receive £15 per game, always to field full-strength teams and not allow league games "to be cancelled on account of any cup competition or other matches". League football was to be paramount. "The McGregor letter is the point at which professional football decides it has to get organised or be strangled at birth,'' said John Nagle, the Football League's head of communications. "Fixtures previously were sporadic with clubs sometimes going weeks between matches when they needed the certainty, as they still do today, of regular matches and regular income. McGregor's idea perfectly met the needs of clubs and the paying public whilst being utterly simple in its inception. The fact that 125 years [2013] later the Football League continues to thrive and that league football has become a sporting phenomenon across the globe is the greatest possible tribute to McGregor's foresight."[2]

After coming up with the idea to play competitive matches rather than friendlies, McGregor was appointed the first chairman of the Football League, becoming President four years later. In 1894, he was elected the League's first Life President.[3]

John Farquharson McIntosh 1846-1918 designed the Dunalastair 4-4-0 series locomotive, in which he set the fashion for larger boilers, widely regarded as one of the major developments in British locomotive engineering.[1] He was well-qualified to design locomotives that would please both men and management, for he had been fireman, driver, locomotive inspector, and locomotive depot foreman. He also designed 4-6-0 locomotives, including the famous Cardean, and the only eight-coupled locomotive (0-8-0) to be built for Scottish railways. Following the display of one of his locomotives at the Brussels Exhibition, the Belgian State Railway ordered many 4-4-0 and 0-6-0 locomotives of the McIntosh type; these outnumbered his machines built for the Caledonian. From 1895, as Locomotive Superintendent "McIntosh rapidly increased in stature and was capable of mixing as an equal with the greatest locomotive engineers of the late Victorian/Edwardian period, such as Francis Webb and Dugald Drummond."[2]

John Hays McLaren 1846-1943 was the creator of one of the world's most magnificent botanical gardens, Golden Gate Park, in San Francisco. Two men with distinctly different styles share the credit for the creation of Golden Gate Park: US engineer William Hammond Hall, for the park's framework and initial landscaping; and horticulturist John McLaren, who made the park his personal mission until his death. McLaren's long tenure often overshadows Hall's expertise, but the determined efforts of both men led to what exists today.

McLaren became superintendent in 1890, overseeing 40 gardeners whose ranks would swell to 400 during his long tenure. Using experience and direct observation, the shrewd and aggressive superintendent worked diligently to keep politics and commercialism out of the park. He was held in great esteem but was also considered difficult by some who had to work with him. "Wild game is coming" was the muffled cry when McLaren came to inspect his workers. McLaren's landscaping philosophy was similar to Hall's in that he wanted to create a natural look by working with nature, not against it. He was an experienced horticulturist and forester who studied the local climate and what would thrive in it. Still a dynamo when he reached his 70th birthday in 1916, he was granted a special honour. With McLaren's mandatory retirement at hand, the board of supervisors passed special ordinances giving him lifetime tenure over the park. Blind at the end of his life, he relied on protégé Julius Girod to be his eyes.

McLaren's work was not limited to Golden Gate Park but also included other emerging city parks and special events. He did landscaping for the 1915 Panama Pacific International Exposition and for the 1939 Golden Gate Exposition on Treasure Island.[1]

McLaren, having apprenticed as a landscape gardener in Scotland, spent the next fifty years improving Golden Gate Park. One of his stipulations before taking the job was, "There will be no 'Keep off the Grass' signs." By corresponding with gardeners and botanists all over the world, McLaren was able to gather plants, and particularly trees, from every land but one, Bolivia.[2]

Reginald Augustus Frederick Murray 1846-1925 was active in the Bendigo and Ballarat fields of Victoria, Australia, but from 1873 his main attention was devoted to extensive reconnaissance surveys of the rugged country of eastern and south-eastern Victoria in the course of which he suffered much hardship, once having to travel for six days without food. In Gippsland, he worked partly with Englishman Alfred William Howitt. Their reports are models of careful observation and probably the earliest accounts of regional geological studies in Australia to be supported by the techniques of microscopic petrography.

In May 1878 he became, in effect, government geologist of Victoria, though not officially accorded that title for some years. The impressive list of publications issued by the Geological Survey in the following years testifies to a high state of activity despite Murray having the help of only one geological surveyor. He investigated the brown coal deposits that later proved important to Victoria's economy. Murray was a notable pioneer of systematic geological exploration in Australia with a pragmatic attitude to geology. Although his experience was confined largely to Victoria, he recognised the need for particular geological attention to be directed to the study of mineral deposits of economic importance throughout Australia.[1]

William Dundas Scott-Moncrieff 1846-1924 was, in 1891, the founder of the modern practice of biological treatment of sewage in which anaerobic bacteria were used to liquefy the organic matter, and then aerobic bacteria to nitrify and mineralise the products.

He was also the first to use compressed air to propel a tram. This was done on a mile of railway near Govan station in Glasgow in 1880 and was subsequently used on the Vale of Clyde Tramway. With Hercule Linton and John Rennie, he was the senior partner in the firm that built the famous tea clipper *Cutty Sark*. His most important innovation, however, was in improving sewage systems.

Digestion tanks perform their action on sewage by the aid of anaerobic bacteria while aerobic bacteria act most vigorously in contact and trickling filter beds. Imhoff tanks, patented in 1906 by German engineer Karl Imhoff, work through the separation and digestion of the solid particles in the incoming sewage, and the digested particles form a fine mud which is drawn off on sand beds to dry. The sprinkling filter is designed to change the putrescible organic matter of the sewage into stable forms, so that the effluent does not putrefy. Scott-Moncrieff first achieved this in 1891 when he built a closed tank where anaerobic putrefaction was to take place with a series of trays containing coke for the second stage of nitrification.[1]

Full-scale application of the anaerobic process was first conducted in about 1860 for the treatment of domestic wastewater by Jean-Louis Mouras and Abbé Moigno in France, more than 50 years before the invention of aerobic activated sludge process. The first biological treatment of wastewater process was patented by Scott-Moncrieff in 1891 in Great Britain, in which organic matters were first degraded anaerobically and the products were then further degraded and mineralised aerobically, producing a clear effluent and inoffensive gases. Since that time the anaerobic process has been continually improved and applied in many cities in Europe and the United States.[2]

Alexander Graham Bell 1847-1922 invented the telephone, which was but one of his many achievements. He was a prolific inventor and, like his father and grandfather, a tutor for deaf people. After two of Bell's brothers died of tuberculosis, his family moved from Scotland to Canada in August 1870, where they settled in Brantford, Ontario, and by 1873 Bell was a professor of vocal physiology across the border in Boston, Massachusetts.

He teamed up with American Thomas Augustus Watson, and by 6 April 1875 he had a patent for a harmonic, or multiple, telegraph. "Bell believed it was possible to convey several notes simultaneously, each at a different pitch, along a telegraph wire. His harmonic telegraph consisted of a series of metallic reeds, vibrating at different frequencies through an armature (protective covering). The arrangement was placed near an electromagnet with the coil attached to a transmission line. At the receiving end, a series of tuned reeds was placed near a set of electromagnets, each hooked to the line. During experiments with three harmonic telegraphs, Bell concluded that the harmonic telegraphy was too feeble to be useful for speech transmission."[1]

This was followed on 14 February 1876 with a patent application described as "Improvement in Telegraphy" which was granted on 7 March 1876 as US patent number 174,465, destined to become the most lucrative and most litigated patent in world history. Three days later, on 10 March, Watson, who was in another room, clearly heard Bell's voice over the telephone. Bell had, so the story goes, spilt some battery acid that he was using as a transmitting liquid and, later, Bell claimed he uttered the words "Mr Watson, come here, I want to see you.", which are probably not the precise words of someone who has just tipped acid over himself but, nevertheless, this was a historic occasion – the first time coherent words were transmitted electronically. On 3 August – in Ontario, Canada – he made the world's first long distance telephone call over the 6½ kms from Mount Pleasant to Tutelo Heights. Bell was a visionary who envisaged a network of cables, underground or overhead, connecting homes and businesses. This was only two years after he had patented the telephone and when many people still saw it as a novelty that would never replace the telegraph.

On 25 June 1876, on the very same day that General George Armstrong Custer led 265 men of the US 7th Cavalry to annihilation at the Little Big Horn in Montana, the Brazilian Emperor, Dom Pedro II, was attending the Centennial Exhibition in Philadelphia, held to commemorate 100 years of American independence. Alexander Graham Bell had only agreed to attend the Exhibition at the last moment and had to locate his booth in the educational section as he couldn't get one in the electrical section – where Alexander Bain, inventor of the fax, was displaying a telegraph that could process over 1,000 words a minute. With the weather being hot, few VIPs ventured down to where Bell's booth was located, but one who did was Dom Pedro who was promptly given a demonstration of Bell's telephone. On hearing "To be or not to be, that is the question", he exclaimed, "My God! It talks".[2] The Emperor's reaction caused a stir and Bell received considerable publicity thereafter. The actual phone at the Exhibition still suffered from shortcomings, and Bell was astute in using such a well-known piece as Hamlet's soliloquy, for when the sound occasionally dropped out the listener's memory filled in the missing words.

Bell's telephone had a system composed of a microphone and a loudspeaker. "The loudspeaker he invented has the same structure as today's loudspeakers: an iron core attached to a membrane is vibrated by a varying electric current in a coil wrapped around it [this is essentially the principle of electric motors]. The membrane's vibration makes sound waves in the air. The microphone was a more difficult problem. Bell tried the inverse process: a membrane vibrated by sound moves a magnet through a coil of wire, in which it induces a current [this is essentially the principle of the dynamo or generator]. Bell's problem was that this type of microphone produces very weak currents and these were insufficient to drive the loudspeaker; and no means of amplification of electric current then existed. But he serendipitously encountered a better method: having the sound vary the resistance of a wire through which a battery-driven current was flowing. This he did by dipping a wire into a conducting solution and having a sound-driven membrane lift and dip the wire, changing its resistance.

The microphone was like a funnel; one end open, the other end pointing to a membrane connected to a rotor that had to follow the vibrations of the membrane. This vibrating rotor was connected to a coil to induce a voltage with the same frequency of the voice sent into the funnel. Bell's microphone changed sound waves into a pulsating voltage which is faster and easier to transmit than sound waves. The speaker was made similarly to the microphone."[3]

The invention of the microphone has been ascribed to Charles Wheatstone in 1827, Emile Berliner in 1877 (after seeing Bell's telephone at the Centennial Exhibition), Thomas Edison, Francis Blake, David Edward Hughes, Johann Philipp Reis and Henry Hunning. "The word 'microphone' was first coined by Wheatstone around 1827 and was used to describe a purely acoustic device, like a stethoscope, which he had developed to amplify weak sounds."[4] Bob Paquette, of the Microphone Museum, Milwaukee, Wisconsin, states that microphones as we know them started with the first articulate telephone transmitter, developed almost simultaneously by Elisha Gray and Alexander Graham Bell. This was the liquid transmitter of 1876. This transmitter would be classified as a variable-resistance device.

Image 76 – Bell centennial double pole telephone 1876
Popular Science Monthly Volume 69

Western Union entered the telephone business late in 1877. Now, with two companies trying to develop a better transmitter, other experimenters began to appear and offer their devices. Emile Berliner with his loose-contact metal-to-metal transmitter, Edison with his many forms of carbon transmitters and an electrostatic (condenser) design, Hughes' carbon rods, Blake's carbon block, and Hunnings' carbon-granule type were a few of the new names and devices to appear. Both Berliner and Hughes used the term "microphone" to describe their transmitters. This was due to the high sensitivity of both of their devices compared to the others. However, added sensitivity in these units resulted in more erratic behaviour and reduced dependability.

There is no doubt that Emile Berliner designed a better microphone – based on the Reis' model – for Bell's company paid $50,000 to acquire the patent rights, but several eminent organisations nominate Bell (or Bell *and* Elisha Gray) as the inventor of the microphone, including The American Institute of Physics, the Hochschule Esslingen University of Applied Sciences, Germany, the (USA) Institute of Electrical and Electronics Engineers, Inc., The Franklin Institute Resources for Science Learning, and Bloomfield Science Museum, Jerusalem, Israel.[5] John Eargle, in his *The Microphone Book*, starts the history of the microphone from Bell.[6] Undoubtedly Bell's microphone needed to be greatly improved if the telephone was to be a commercial success, but so did Edison's phonograph, yet no-one seeks to challenge his priority due to that machine's primitive state.

Bell not only invented the telephone, he had also conceived of a system to make a business out of it. He outlined his plan in a letter to his father on the same day that he uttered the first sentence to Watson: "I feel that I have at last struck the solution of a great problem – and the day is coming when telegraph wires will be laid on to houses just like water or gas – and friends converse with each other without leaving home." He elaborated on his vision in a remarkable prospectus for British financiers on 5 March 1878: "It is conceivable that cables of Telephonic wires could be laid under-ground or suspended overhead communicating by branch wires with private dwellings, counting houses, shops, manufactories, etc. establishing direct communication between any two places in the City. I believe that in the future wires will unite the head offices of Telephone Companies in different cities and a man in one part of the Country may communicate by word of mouth with another in a distant place."[7]

On 9 July 1878, the Bell Telephone Company of Boston was created and Emperor Dom Pedro became the first person to buy shares in it. Shortly afterwards, the first of some 600 challenges to Bell's patent commenced. His most serious competitor, Elisha Gray, had earlier acknowledged Bell's priority and also seemed not to comprehend the importance of the telephone. In a letter written on 29 October 1875 to his lawyer, Alex L. Hayes, Gray wrote, "Bell seems to be spending all his energies on the talking telegraph. While this is very interesting scientifically it has no commercial value at present, for they can do much more business over a line by methods already in use than by that [Bell's telephone] system. I don't want at present to spend my time and money for that which will bring no return. I thought it would be impossible to make a practical working speaking telephone on the principle shown by Professor Bell, to wit: generating electric currents with the power of the voice, as it seemed to me then that the vibrations were so slight in amplitude and the inductor necessarily so light that the currents thus generated would be too feeble for practical purposes."[8]

Although frequently called to give testimony in these court hearings, Bell's interests lay in new research and he developed, alone or with others, an amazing range of products. He did much research on the tetrahedron and built kites, towers, bridges and other buildings on this design. One of the towers overlooked Bras d'Or Lakes at his Canadian home and stood more than 23 m high, predating the Geodesic Dome of Buckminster Fuller by more than forty years. When asked if Bell's domes were like his geodesic structure, Fuller replied, "Exactly the same. His notebooks are almost like the Leonardo books".[9]

Much of Bell's energy in later life was spent on aerial innovation and he pioneered the first controlled power flight in Canada. His aeroplane, *Red Wing*, first flew on 12 March 1908, piloted by Canadian Frederick Walker "Casey" Baldwin and, after it crashed on 17 March, Bell devised and patented the aileron, although unknown to him it had already been independently invented by Cornishman Richard Pearse in New Zealand in 1902. Bell had actually conceived the aileron while in Scotland, where he had drawn a flying machine with one on 23 September 1877. This device superseded the wing warping which had been used by the Wright brothers to control their pioneering flights at Kitty Hawk. Bell also patented the tricycle undercarriage which aided take-off and permitted the Glenn Curtiss-designed *June Bug* to win the *Scientific American* trophy for the first flight over one kilometre on 21 May 1908. The Wright Brothers by this time had made flights of some 38 kilometres, but their aircraft relied on wind or other assistance for take-off. The *June Bug* was built by the Aerial Experiment Association, which had been founded by Bell for aeronautical research in 1907 at the instigation of his deaf wife Mabel. Bell, with Curtiss, Baldwin, Thomas Selfridge, and John Alexander Douglas McCurdy, formed the Aerial Experiment Association in Hammondsport, New York, and began to build aeroplanes of each members' design, sharing features borrowed from both Gabriel Voison and the Wright's designs. Their third plane, the *June Bug*, attracted far more attention and acclaim then the Wright Brothers had ever received, especially with Alexander Graham Bell's notoriety and influence.[10]

Image 77 – Bell's early design of the tetrahedron kite
Image 78 – Bell's Hydrofoil – Bell HD-4 on a test run ca. 1919

Bell also worked on water desalinisation, sheep breeding and artificial respiration. He invented a forerunner of the iron lung, called the vacuum jacket, after his son Edward died from respiratory failure following his birth on 15 August 1881. It was in the year after the death of Edward that Bell designed the "vacuum jacket" which was pumped by a separate large bellows.

"Apparently this was not used clinically, but was tried on healthy volunteers, who attested to its effectiveness. The original pump and two-part shell are on display at the Alexander Graham Bell Museum in Baddeck, Nova Scotia." [11]

In the same year Bell, with American Charles Sumner Tainter, developed a probe at very short notice to try to save US President James Garfield, who had been shot on 2 July 1881. The probe was an induction-balance electrical device which, essentially, acted as a metal detector. It didn't detect the fatal bullet (there were two bullet wounds) because Garfield was lying on a metal bed and, iron beds being relatively rare at the time, it wasn't realised that it was causing the instrument to deviate. The President died on 19 September 1881 "because of infection produced by the unsterile fingers and probes repeatedly inserted into the wound." [12] The Bell and Tainter metal detector was the first such instrument to be used and was based on the induction balance system invented by Heinrich Dove, a German physicist. The device was further improved by Bell and, now called a telephone probe, it would make a telephone receiver click when it touched metal. This device was eventually superseded by X-rays for medical use, but it found continuing application elsewhere with amateur treasure hunters and for locating electrical wires in the walls of buildings.

Bell and Tainter also patented the photophone, alternatively called the radiophone, on 14 December 1880 (US Patent 235,496). Earlier, on 3 June 1880, they transmitted sounds over 213 metres through most of the range of the visible light spectrum (it didn't work in the extreme violet light wavelengths). Some of these transmissions went through a bar of rubber that was more than 2½ centimetres thick and were obviously radio transmissions that didn't rely on a direct line of sight between transmitter and receiver. "'Professor Bell,' Tainter called into the mouthpiece, 'if you understand what I say, come to the window and wave your hat.' Anxious seconds and then there was Bell in the window, Tainter related, frantically waving his hat. That day, in 1880 the human voice was sent through free space.'" [13] This was the first time the human voice had been sent by artificial means over a considerable distance and it was achieved thirteen years before the generally accepted first public radio transmission in 1894 by Englishman Oliver Lodge (Marconi's first radio transmissions were in 1896 and didn't involve the human voice). The photophone was the precursor of fibre optics and lasers, although the technology wasn't available at that time to fully utilise the implications of the photophone development.

Bell worked with his cousin, **Chichester Alexander Bell 1848-1924**, and Tainter to invent the graphophone and wax cylinders for recording sound. American Thomas Alva Edison had already patented his phonograph on 19 February 1878, but this device used cylinders with tin foil, whereas the graphophone used lines engraved into wax, the forerunner of the vinyl record invented by German-born Emile Berliner. It also had a sideways motion for the stylus, the method that is still used today. Bell and Tainter were interrupted in their graphophone development in 1881 when President Garfield was shot and they designed their metal detector to look for the bullet still lodged in his body. Their work on the graphophone was influential in the development of the Dictaphone, and the Dictaphone Corporation "can trace its history back to 1881, when Alexander Graham Bell and two associates, took on their first team project – finding a practical way of recording sound for the newly invented telephone. [They] produced the first recording device that used a rotating cylinder on whose wax coating a steel stylus would cut up-and-down grooves." In 1888, Bell and Tainter formed the Volta Graphophone Company in Bridgeport,

Connecticut, and began to manufacture machines for the recording and reproduction of sound by businesses in office settings. In 1907, the patent was sold to the American Graphophone Company, which eventually became the Columbia Graphophone Company, and the Dictaphone was trademarked by Columbia.[14] For a brief period, Bell investigated reproducing sound by impressing a magnetic field onto a wax record, but this was unsuccessful and it was left to others to develop this concept into tape recorders and computer discs.

Electric heating of oil and water was investigated by Bell and in a letter to his wife, Mabel, on 11 January 1892, he wrote that a 7½ cm wire with an electric current had heated a volume of oil to 124C. The container was a glass tube 30 cm long and 2½ cm in diameter. It was hoped by Bell that pollution from coal would be eliminated by the use of electric heaters.

Bell was an early advocate of recycling and he composted toilet waste and captured atmospheric moisture. In a paper in 1917, on the depletion of natural resources, he stated that the unchecked burning of fossil fuels would lead to a "sort of greenhouse effect" and global warming.[15] Bell believed that methane and alcohol could be used as alternative, renewable fuels which he said, "can be manufactured from corn stalks, and in fact from almost any vegetable matter capable of fermentation. Our growing crops and even weeds can be used. The waste products of our farms are available for this purpose and even the garbage of our cities. We need never fear the exhaustion of our present fuel supplies so long as we can produce an annual crop of alcohol to any extent desired."[16]

Bell also took a keen interest in the development of the hydrofoil which was invented by Englishman Thomas Moy in 1861. Frenchman Emmanuel Denis Farcot obtained a British patent in 1869 for hydrofoils which were used to give lift to a boat, but it was Italian Enrico Forlanini who built the first effective hydrofoil, one which used propellers and ladder struts that enabled him to reach a speed of more than 68 km/h.[17] An article on hydrofoils by William E. Meacham in *Scientific American* (March 1906) came to the attention of Bell and, with "Casey" Baldwin, he built four hydrofoils, culminating in *Hydrodome 4*, which travelled on 9 September 1919 at 114 km/h and lifted more than 6,350 kg, a world water speed record which stood until it was surpassed on 15 September 1920 by Gar Wood in *Miss America*.

In 1879, he invented an audiometer to detect minor hearing problems in schoolchildren who may have hearing impairment. Other people have also been credited with this invention, including Swiss Marsiglio Landriani, Hungarian Georg von Békésy, and London-born David Edward Hughes. Bell also continued with his teaching of the deaf and lived to see a remarkable change in their treatment within society. At the time, Bell first started teaching deaf American children, only some 40% of them were taught to speak. When he died in 1922, this figure had risen to around 80% due, in very large part, to his influence, and it was Bell who undertook the first census of deaf people in 1890.[18] In the same year he founded and endowed the American Association to Promote the Teaching of Speech to the Deaf (later renamed the Alexander Graham Bell Association for the Deaf). The endowment was from the Volta Prize of 50,000 francs (=$US10,000), which was awarded to him in 1880 by the French government for his invention of the telephone. Bell first established the Volta Bureau in Washington DC with the money from the Volta Prize, plus additional funds from his father. From this endowment, an extensive library of books and other materials relating to the deaf was created and Bell became the Association's first president in 1890.[19]

Bell's "insights into separating the speech signal into different frequency components and rendering those components as visible traces were not successfully implemented until [Ralph Kimball] Potter, [George Adams] Kopp, and [Harriet] Green designed the spectrogram and [Jean] Dreyfus-Graf developed the steno-sonograph in the late 1940s. These devices generated interest in the possibility of automatically recognising speech because they made the invariant features of speech visible for all to see."[20] At the same time, as "an off-shoot of Bell's work in the deaf community, the first speech-recogniser (was) developed by [Kingsbury] Davis, [Rulon] Biddulph, and [Stephen] Balashek of Bell Labs. With training, it was reported, the machine achieved 97 percent accuracy on the spoken forms of ten digits" (i.e. fingers used in sign language).[21]

The unit of sound, the Bel, was named after him and was used to express the magnitude of change in level of power, voltage, current or sound intensity, but it was too large for most measurements in everyday life and the decibel, one-tenth of a Bel, became the more common measuring base.

An invention credited to both Elisha Gray and Bell is the telautograph, an analogue fax machine. Gray patented his in 1888, and Bell applied for a patent in 1875. The true progenitor of the modern fax was Alexander Bain, who patented it back in 1843, but the later patents illustrate that Bell and Gray were both very innovative.

Bell made a phonautograph, which records sound in graphic form but does not replay it. The first such machine was built in 1857 by Frenchman Edouard-Leon Scott de Martinville, who actually made a ten-second recording of the French song "Au Clair de Lune", on 19 April 1860, some 17 years before Edison's first sound recording of "Mary had a little lamb". Bell's phonautograph had a real human ear still attached to the skull of a deceased man. Bell used glycerin to moisten the dry bones, muscles and membrane, and when he shouted into the ear, his voice was recorded on glass by a stylus. Not unexpectedly this form of phonautograph didn't catch on but it was, nevertheless, another display of Bell's ingenuity, which he had shown since his first invention of a device for cleaning wheat when he was just 11 years old. This apparatus removed wheat husks by using a nail brush and paddle to make a rotary brushing wheel. Later in life, Bell predicted a world that would use solar-powered heating and communications akin to fibre optics. His inventive mind never seemed to rest.

Bell pioneered photoacoustic spectroscopy[22] in 1880, by showing that when a rapidly-rotating slotted disc interrupted sunrays, it caused thin discs to emit sound. Bell later found this was also true of the non-visible spectrum. The photoacoustic effect is used to study solids, liquids and gases, with the latter being detectable in parts per trillion. It is used to detect changes in the ozone layer around the Earth and track leakages of gases, particularly toxic or flammable gases – an important safety device.

Just four months after German Wilhelm Roentgen discovered X-rays in December 1895, Bell, with American associate William Ellis, took a radiograph in June 1896 of coins inside a purse (a true Scot!). Just six months after the discovery of X-rays he wrote: "Stereo Radiography. Try to produce a stereoscopic picture. Two radiographs of the same object placed side by side at the same time. Now combine stereoscopically! Good idea. Skeleton in three dimensions! Viscera etc. in place etc., etc."[23] Three dimensional scans using X-rays came to fruition with the CAT scan, which was first publicly announced by Englishman Godfrey Hounsfield in 1972, fifty years after the death of Bell.

In 1903, Bell made a prescient suggestion in a letter to the editor of *Roentgen Ray: and Allied Phenomenon* that radium implants could be used to treat tumours – a current procedure now referred to as brachytherapy. He wrote, "Roentgen rays and the rays emitted by radium have been found to have a marked effect on external cancers, but the effects upon deep-seated cancers have not thus far proved satisfactory. It has occurred to me that one reason for the unsatisfactory nature of these latter experiments arises from the fact that the rays have been applied externally, thus having to pass through healthy tissues of various depths in order to reach the cancerous matter. The Crooke's tube [X-ray tube] from which the Roentgen rays are emitted is of course too bulky to be admitted into the middle of a mass of cancer, but there is no reason why a tiny fragment of radium sealed in a fine glass tube should not be inserted into the very heart of the cancer, thus acting directly upon the diseased material." Some two years earlier, Frenchman Pierre Curie had suggested to compatriot Henri-Alexandre Danlos in Paris that radium should be inserted in a tube into a tumour. Danlos, with Eugene Bloch, used radium to treat a skin lesion caused by tuberculosis, but Bell was unaware of Curie's suggestion, which was in a personal letter to Danlos.[24]

Bell helped others undertake research and to this end he funded the work of Albert Abraham Michelson and Edward Morley to measure the speed of light. They successfully did this and proved there was no ether through which the Earth moved – a commonly held belief at that time (1885). Michelson was awarded the Nobel Prize for this work.

In 1898, Bell's father-in-law, Gardiner Greene Hubbard, died and Bell replaced him as president of the National Geographic Society, which the two men had founded in January 1888 and which is now one of the largest non-profit educational and scientific organisations in the world. Bell always had an interest in photography and geography and he combined the two of these in *National Geographic* magazine to create its modern format with the help of Gilbert Grosvenor, his future son-in-law. The *National Geographic* now has a worldwide circulation of nearly 6,685,684[25] and through "various media vehicles, including its official journal, *National Geographic* magazine, and other publications, its films, television programs, cable channel, radio, music, books, videos, maps and interactive media, the National Geographic Society reaches more than 450 million people a month."[26]

Bell conducted sheep-breeding experiments in an attempt to increase the number of lambs born per ewe, specifically to increase multiple births. He wrote of his studies on human heredity which was published in 1895 by Edward A. Fay, editor of *American Annals of the Deaf*. Historian Robert Bruce remarked, "Bell's paper [*An Inquiry Concerning the Results of Marriages of the Deaf in America*], along with Fay's follow-up, stands as the soundest, and most useful study of human heredity proposed in nineteenth-century America. By that token, it may also be reasonably counted as Bell's most notable contribution to basic science, as distinct from invention."[27]

Bell gave 75% of the Canadian rights for the telephone to his father with the rest going to his equipment maker, Charles Williams.[28] He also set up a trust through his father with the $100,000 from the sale of his graphophone rights, the money to be used for deaf research. His most famous pupil, Helen Keller (both deaf and blind), who first met Bell when she was six years old, later remarked in her autobiography, "Child as I was, I at once felt the tenderness and sympathy which endeared Dr Bell to so many hearts, as his wonderful achievements enlist their admiration. He held me on his knee while I examined his watch, and he made it strike for me. He understood my signs, and I knew it and loved him at once. But I did not dream that that interview would be the door through which I should pass from darkness into light, from isolation to friendship, companionship, knowledge, love."[29]

He spent much of his time and money defending his patents in 587 lawsuits, of which five went to the Supreme Court in Washington DC. Bell won every one of them bar two minor contract suits which had no bearing on the patent. The main challenges to Bell came from Elisha Gray, Thomas Alva Edison, and Amos Dolbear but none of these, nor any of the other many litigants, such as Daniel Drawbaugh, succeeded in overturning Bell's priority. This was not, as is sometimes claimed, because Bell was wealthy and opposed by poor litigants. The value of the shares of the companies contesting Bell exceeded $500 million – a fantastic sum of money in the late 19th century (equivalent in 2015 purchasing power to $11,780,000,000). Western Union alone was valued at $41 million in 1867.

Many famous scientists, including Joseph Henry and William Thomson (Lord Kelvin), had seen Bell's telephone and they agreed that his concept was novel. Despite the publicity that surrounded Bell's telephone at the 1876 Exhibition and afterwards, none of the future litigants promptly came forward to claim priority. It took 17 months before that happened and this was likely due to the fact that the early telephone wasn't particularly successful beyond a local range of some 40-50 km – indeed, it wasn't until 1915 that a transcontinental service was established. During the 17 years of the patent, more than 1,730 companies, including Western Union, set up their own services without offering royalties to Bell in legal compliance with his patent.

Elisha Gray and Bell filed with the patent office on the same day, 14 February 1876. Bell was the fifth entry of that day, while Elisha Gray was 39th. Bell's attorney filed for a patent, whereas Gray's attorney filed for a patent caveat, which prevents "anyone else that filed an application on the same or similar invention from having their application processed for ninety days, while the caveat holder was given an opportunity to file a full patent application first. Caveats are no longer issued."[30] Note: Some sources state caveats were actually valid for one year and could be renewed. The US Patent Office awarded Bell with the first patent for a telephone rather than consider Gray's caveat. On 12 September 1878, lengthy patent litigation involving the Bell Telephone Company against Western Union Telegraph Company and Elisha Gray began.

The Western Union Telegraph Company was one of the largest companies in the world and controlled about 90% of the United States telegraph activity by 1866, and was probably only exceeded in size by some railway companies. Ironically, Bell offered to sell his patent to Western Union in 1877 for $100,000 but they refused the offer, which really underscores the fact that most people, including William Orton of Western Union, Thomas Edison and Elisha Gray, did not realise the potential of the telephone and, in the case of the earlier litigants, their primary interest was in protecting the telegraph (one person who did realise the potential as early as 1877 was German-born Ernst Werner von Siemens who took out a patent for it in Germany where it wasn't yet covered by Bell's patent).

The Western Union case was settled out of court with the telegraph business going to Western Union and the telephone industry being left to Bell, and Western Union's telephone patents being transferred to Bell, with the latter also giving Western Union a 20% royalty of the rental income from every Bell telephone leased in the United States.[31] Significantly, Western Union acknowledged Bell's priority in the invention of the telephone. Elisha Gray had not seen a future for the telephone – he was more interested in improving the telegraph – and did not contest Bell's patent until much later. Gray's phone did not transmit voices – only sounds – and Gray, in a letter to Bell dated 5 March 1877, wrote, "I do not, however, claim even the credit of inventing it, as I do not believe a mere description of an idea that has never been reduced to practice in the strict sense of that phrase should be dignified with the name invention."[32]

A week earlier, in a Chicago lecture on 27 February 1877, Gray said, "Professor Bell, in his investigation, has gone a step beyond composite tones, although they were embraced in it, and developed the transmission of vocal sounds." Even Edison conceded in a letter to George Prescott's *Electricity and Electric Telegraph*, "I can, however, lay no claim to having discovered that conversation could be carried on between one receiver and the other, upon the magneto principle, by causing the voice to vibrate the diaphragm."[33]

Aside from Gray and Edison, the other main claimant to inventing the telephone was Johann Philipp Reis from Germany. His phone, built in 1860, produced sounds such as music and even occasional words, but not continuous coherent speech. Reis' telephone was based on the wrong principle and, during a patent case against Bell by Amos Emerson Dolbear, who based his claim on a modification of the Reis' model, experts could not get it to work. Incidentally, in 1877, well before the court hearing, Dolbear wrote to Bell in recognition of Bell's patent, saying, "I congratulate you, sir, upon your very great invention, and I hope to see it supplant all forms of existing telegraphs, and that you will be successful in obtaining the wealth and honour which is your due."[34] In respect of the patent lawsuit brought by Dolbear, the presiding judge Lowell remarked, "A century of Reis would never have produced a speaking telephone by mere improvement of construction. It was left for Bell to discover that the failure was due not to workmanship but to the principle which was adopted as the basis of what had to be done. ... Bell discovered a new art – that of transmitting speech by electricity, and his claim is not as broad as his invention. To follow Reis is to fail; but to follow Bell is to succeed. The difference between the two is just the difference between failure and success."[35] When Reis first revealed his apparatus in Germany, there was much acclaim, but when it failed to deliver on its promise, German scientists lost interest and even the Free German Institute of Frankfurt described it as a "philosophical toy". Clearly the Germans, who were in the very forefront of scientific discovery, were not impressed by Reis' telephone.

One of the many other telephone litigants was an Italian immigrant to America, Antonio Santi Giuseppe Meucci, who claimed to have invented in 1856 a communication device which he later called the *teletrofono*, but his claim was not in the same league as Gray, Reis, Edison or even Dolbear. Meucci would have remained an obscure footnote in the history of the telephone (outside of his compatriot supporters) but for a resolution first submitted to the United States Congress as House Resolution 269 IH on 17 October 2001 and passed by Congress on 6 November 2002. It was initiated by Representative Vito Fossella, a congressman from New York, a city that has a large electorate of Italian heritage, as did Fossella (note the comment in the Introduction to this book about the attachment of people to their ancestral homeland).

Congressional declarations such as this one normally make positive comments in relation to the subject, such as was done by Senate Resolution 155 of 20 March 1998, which declared 6 April to be National Tartan Day in America in recognition of the contribution to the United States of Scots, and those of Scottish descent. Generally, such resolutions pass unopposed because, by their very nature, they are not contentious nor do they usually require allocation of Treasury funds. The resolution honouring Meucci was different in that it implied Alexander Graham Bell had been other than honest. The resolution also contained errors of fact, although that is also true of the Tartan Day resolution, which stated (incorrectly) that the 1776 American Declaration of Independence was based on the 1320 Scottish Declaration of Arbroath – it wasn't.

It is worth quoting the Meucci Congressional declaration in full (paragraphs are numbered for easier reference):

1. Expressing the sense of the House of Representatives to honour the life and achievements of 19th century Italian-American inventor Antonio Meucci, and his work in the invention of the telephone.

2. Whereas Antonio Meucci, the great Italian inventor, had a career that was both extraordinary and tragic;

3. Whereas, upon immigrating to New York, Meucci continued to work with ceaseless vigour on a project he had begun in Havana, Cuba, an invention he later called the "teletrofono", involving electronic communications;

4. Whereas Meucci set up a rudimentary communications link in his Staten Island home that connected the basement with the first floor, and later, when his wife began to suffer from crippling arthritis, he created a permanent link between his lab and his wife's second floor bedroom;

5. Whereas, having exhausted most of his life's savings in pursuing his work, Meucci was unable to commercialise his invention, though he demonstrated his invention in 1860 and had a description of it published in New York's Italian language newspaper;

6. Whereas Meucci never learned English well enough to navigate the complex American business community;

7. Whereas Meucci was unable to raise sufficient funds to pay his way through the patent application process, and thus had to settle for a caveat, a one-year renewable notice of an impending patent, which was first filed on December 28, 1871;

8. Whereas Meucci later learned that the Western Union affiliate laboratory reportedly lost his working models, and Meucci, who at this point was living on public assistance, was unable to renew the caveat after 1874;

9. Whereas in March 1876, Alexander Graham Bell, who conducted experiments in the same laboratory where Meucci's materials had been stored, was granted a patent and was thereafter credited with inventing the telephone;

10. Whereas on January 13, 1887, the Government of the United States moved to annul the patent issued to Bell on the grounds of fraud and misrepresentation, a case that the Supreme Court found viable and remanded for trial;

11. Whereas Meucci died in October 1889, the Bell patent expired in January 1893, and the case was discontinued as moot without ever reaching the underlying issue of the true inventor of the telephone entitled to the patent; and

12. Whereas if Meucci had been able to pay the $10 fee to maintain the caveat after 1874, no patent could have been issued to Bell: Now, therefore, be it

13. Resolved, That it is the sense of the House of Representatives that the life and achievements of Antonio Meucci should be recognised, and his work in the invention of the telephone should be acknowledged.

The first point to note here is that nowhere does it categorically state Meucci invented the telephone, only that "his work in the invention of the telephone should be acknowledged".

Paragraph 3 states that Meucci "continued to work with ceaseless vigour on a project he had begun" in respect of the telephone after migrating to New York from Cuba in 1850. However, Meucci, from the time he arrived in America to the date of Bell's 1876 patent, spent considerable time on other activities, including:

> 1858-60 two patents on candle moulds
> 1860 The use of dry batteries in electrical traction and other industrial applications
> 1860 A process to turn red corals into a pink colour
> 1862 Patent on a kerosene lamp that generates a very bright flame, without smoke
> 1862-63 Patents for treating and bleaching oil or kerosene to obtain oils for paint
> 1864 Destructive ammunition for guns and cannons
> 1864-65 Patents to obtain paper pulp from wood or other vegetable substances
> 1865 Patent for making wicks out of vegetable fibre
> 1871 Patent for making effervescent drinks from fruits
> 1873 Patent for macaroni sauce
> 1873 Conception of a screw steamer suitable for navigation in canals
> 1874 Caveat with US Patent Office for process for refining crude oil
> 1875 Filter for tea or coffee
> 1875 Household utensil "combining usefulness to cheapness that will find a ready sale"
> 1875 Patent for a lactometer for chemically detecting adulterations of milk
> 1875 Developing and manufacturing several aneroid barometers of various shapes
> 1876 Patent for a hygrometer

For a man who "continued to work with ceaseless vigour" on the invention of the telephone, he certainly spent a considerable time on candle moulds, macaroni sauces, household utensils, kerosene oil, paper pulp, candle wicks, effervescent drinks, explosive ammunition, changing red coral to pink, and many other activities that have no connection whatsoever to the telephone or its development or, indeed, to any other electrically operated device, except the 1860 work on the use of "dry batteries in electrical traction and other industrial applications", which came to nothing.

Paragraph 4 states Meucci set up a communication link with his wife's bedroom, which was reputedly the first electro-magnetic telephone in history, but there is no description of this device that tells how the communication was achieved. Before leaving Italy, Meucci worked in Florence at the Teatro della Pergola in 1834 where he had constructed a communication device which is still in existence.[36] This is a tube which works as an acoustic communicator, much in the same way as officers on the bridge of a steamship would communicate with the engine room. In all probability, he used the same, or similar, device to talk to his wife, Esther, who was bedridden with arthritis. "It was quite the novelty in the small immigrant community, with neighbours and friends vying to speak over the teletrofono. By 1852, by which time Meucci had arrived in New York from Havana, he had several acoustic telephonic systems serving his home and factory. In time, the early telephone system serviced the entire neighbourhood, as Garibaldi, who lived with Meucci between 1850 and 1854, and other contemporary witnesses affirmed."[37] It is quite clear from this description that it could not have been electronic for if it had, it would immediately have excited international attention as electric telegraphy was in its infancy and the human voice had never before been transmitted. When this was first achieved publicly, by Bell at the 1876 Exhibition, it immediately caught the world's imagination even in its embryonic state, yet we are expected to believe that Meucci had an electronic telephone system that "serviced his home and factory" and even the "entire neighbourhood". It is inconceivable that any communication that could service a neighbourhood in a city like New York – where the many capitalists and financiers were eminently predisposed to funding, developing and supporting new technology – would have gone unnoticed by the thousands of entrepreneurs who were heavily investing in telegraphs, railways, steamships and canals, all to improve communications. Americans, particularly New Yorkers, were quick to pick up on any new device that showed promise and there was plentiful cash available for investment.

The web page of "The Garibaldi Meucci Museum On Staten Island, New York", states "Meucci methodically explored vibrating electrical current with speech between 1850 and 1862, developing more than 30 distinct telephonic models. He experimented with copper loops, paper cones in tin cylinders, and thin animal membranes until the model resembled the form of telephone we are familiar with today."[38] This begs the question that for the ten years between 1850 and 1860 he made no attempt to patent such a marvellous invention that had his neighbours "vying to speak" over it. Clearly, the two full US patents he took out between 1858 and 1860 for candle moulds held greater prospects of financial return than his teletrofono.

Paragraph 5 states he gave a public demonstration of his invention in 1860 and described it in an Italian newspaper, but he was too poor to commercialise it – apparently, he had lost the equivalent of half a million dollars in today's money by that date. The public demonstration consisted of a singer's voice which was heard "by spectators at a considerable distance away". The description in the Italian newspaper L'Eco d'Italia is no longer available as no copies of that edition are extant. This is seen by the conspiracy theorists as something sinister, especially as the newspaper offices burned down in a "mysterious" fire that also destroyed Meucci's "personal file". Notwithstanding that, some 26 years later during the Globe/Bell trial in 1886, Meucci was able to mentally reconstruct what he had written. He said, "It is about what I have written; I don't remember the precise words, because it is many years; but the meaning is that: – 'Antonio Meucci living at Staten Island has invented the way to transmit the human word by means of the electricity through an electric conductor. He was since a long time experimenting on it and has obtained an excellent result. His method consists in using two instruments, one to transmit the word and the other to receive it. These instruments are quite easy to make. In their interior, they have a spool of metallic wire, with a bar of tempered and strongly magnetised steel in the centre, and a diaphragm above. These instruments being put in connection with a battery of Bunsen or some other, transmit the human word exact, as it is spoken by the two persons that are in communication by means of the insulated metallic conducting wire.'" The foregoing is quoted from web page *http://www.chezbasilio.org/meucci_faq.htm* by Basilio Catania (2004).

Catania is described as "The Vindicator of Antonio Meucci's rightful place in the forgotten pages of American history" in a statement by Hon. Dominic R. Massaro, Justice, New York Supreme Court, New York, NY, 10 October 2000.[39] Note that Meucci states "the instruments are quite easy to make". This relates to his article published in 1860, yet none of the other luminaries of telephone history – Bourseil, Reis, Gray, Bell, nor the highly inventive Edison – found that the telephone was easy to make.

More important is the claim that Meucci was too poor to register a full patent on his device that "could transmit the human voice exact". This will be addressed in Paragraph 12. It should also be remembered that this description given in court was ten years after the telephone was patented and it would be quite easy to give a contemporary description when referring to his *teletrofono* of 26 years earlier. Also, if he could remember how his *telefotrono* worked some 26 years after the event, then surely the loss of his models and personal files would not have been a problem as, with his wonderful memory, he would have been able to reconstruct his *telefotrono* at any time after their loss – after all these "instruments are quite easy to make".

Paragraph 6 states his English was too poor to navigate "the complex American business community". Besides his native Italian, Meucci spoke French and Spanish well; he had lived in America since 1850 and ran a candle factory in Clifton, New York, where he then set up a lager beer factory in 1856. In 1860, he started a paraffin candle factory in Clifton, later moving it to Stapleton, New York. He sent proposals to the US Army in 1864 for the use of his "new, more destructive ammunition for guns and cannons". In 1867, he established the Perth Amboy Fiber Company in New York and he had successfully lodged eleven full US patents since 1850 – none of which related to the telephone – and a patent caveat in 1874 for refining crude oil, as well as his *teletrofono* caveat of 1871, twice renewed. This hardly reveals a person who had difficulty navigating the "complex American business community". He also had support from Italian/American businessmen (see Paragraph 7) and from American businessman William E. Ryder (or Rider), so he was hardly a babe in the woods.

Paragraph 7 states Meucci had to settle for a caveat in 1871 as he had insufficient funds for a full patent. This caveat was lodged on 28 December 1871 yet just five days later, on 2 January 1872, Meucci was granted a full US patent, No 122,478, for "Improvement in the Manufacture of Effervescent Drinks from Fruits". He obviously had more faith in putting bubbles into fruit drink than he did in his *teletrofono* that "could transmit the human voice exact" since 1860 or earlier. More importantly, on 12 December 1871, Meucci formed the Telettrofono Company with three partners, Angelo Zilio Grandi, Secretary of the Italian Consulate in New York, Angelo Antonio Tremeschin, a contractor for civil constructions, and Sereno Breguglia, lessee of the cigar stand of the Hoffmann Café in New Street, opposite the New York Stock Exchange.[40] It seems incongruous to create a company to promote an exciting new technology when you can't scrape up more than $20 to pay the $10 for a patent caveat plus $10 for the lawyer's fee – hardly a fortune, especially for someone starting up a new company. It is inconceivable that, with their connections in the Italian and New York business communities, they could not have found the $20 for the caveat and legal fees if they had tried, especially when they could find this amount for a fizzy drink just five days later. Note: filing for a patent in 1871 cost $15 and was valid for

17 years – when the patent was issued, there was another fee of $20. Perhaps Meucci couldn't find backers for his *teletrofono* as his caveat "disclosed a mouthpiece and an earpiece connected by a taut wire that transmitted vibrations of sounds mechanically [not electrically] over the wire." Also, "the Meucci caveat, and indeed his 'invention', does not describe or suggest any of the elements of electrical communication of voice, or the principle of undulating current that is set forth even in the broadest claim of the Bell patent."[41] Interestingly, "it [the caveat] was renewed in December 1882, and again in December 1883. During that time, Mr Meucci did not make any improvements on the device that was disclosed in his 1871 caveat".[42] This was more than six years after Bell's patent had been granted and was obviously done to (unsuccessfully) challenge the priority of Bell.

"The *Scientific American* gives a good drawing of this and subsequent phones. In the 1849 model [of Meucci's *teletrofono*] a paper cone contains a copper spatula soldered to a loose coil of fine wire which is insulated in cork. In the 1852 version the cone is made of metal and the wire is wrapped around it. The copper spatula does not appear to serve any purpose in the circuit, and in fact it is hard to see how the circuit could function at a useable level, if at all. By the time of the 1853 model the spatula was dropped and the first diaphragm of sheet iron was introduced. This followed an unsuccessful attempt using an animal membrane diaphragm. The iron diaphragm affected a crude magnet and coil built into the handle. This is coming very close to Bell's patented design. By 1865, the horseshoe magnet was introduced and the *Teletrofono* looked more than ever like the later Bell receiver.

Unfortunately, these drawings were made well after the event, and the early models no longer exist, so it is not possible to corroborate any of the designs apart from the crude drawing included with the Caveat application. No explanation is given for the change from the spatula-in-the-mouth to the coil and magnet assembly, and this lack of documentation must have cost Meucci some credibility. In his summary of the evidence presented in the Globe case the Judge's description of the original *Teletrofono* shows it was a 'string telephone', a well-known device that transmitted sound along a tensioned wire or string [a well-known toy used by generations of schoolchildren]. Meucci apparently tried to electrify this in some way to improve its efficiency, but the only real effect would be to produce the signalling 'tick' when the circuit was broken."[43]

Paragraph 8 mentions the loss of Meucci's working models and his inability, through poverty, to renew his caveat after 1874. Meucci allegedly deposited a model or models with the American District Telegraph Company in 1871, possibly with Edward Grant, who was Vice President of the company. Three years later it is claimed Grant stated that the model was lost after he had handed it on to Henry W. Pope. The Italian Historical Society of America states on its website that Meucci "took recourse in the caveat or notice of intent, which was registered on December 28, 1871 and renewed in 1872 and 1873 [making it current until December 1874] but, fatefully, not thereafter." If this was, indeed, true, why would Grant or anyone else with Western Union want the model, for the caveat – still current at the time it is claimed the model was lost – would have given priority to Meucci. If Western Union had thought the model was valuable, wouldn't they have tried to buy the rights from Meucci as they would have known he still had a current caveat? If, indeed, Meucci did take his model to the American District Telegraph Company, it is likely it was regarded as insignificant and discarded. It should also be noted that the American District Telegraph Company was only created in 1874, from an amalgamation of 57 district telegraph delivery companies so the model, if it existed at all, may possibly have been lost when these 57 companies merged.

However, the website statement is actually incorrect in stating that his caveat was not renewed after 1873, as Meucci did, indeed, renew the caveat not once, but twice more, in 1882 and 1883, well after Bell's patent had been granted.[44] Meucci reportedly could not afford to renew the caveat beyond December 1874 yet, in the three years since first lodging it in 1871, he successfully obtained two full patents, costing $20 each plus legal costs – one for effervescent drinks and the other for macaroni sauce – in addition to a caveat for refining crude oil in 1874. The telephone obviously did not loom large in his thoughts yet we are told in Paragraph 3 that he "continued to work with ceaseless vigour" in pursuit of its development.

Paragraph 9 implies that Bell got hold of Meucci's materials by subterfuge. In 1989, Marco Nese, an Italian author, claimed Bell had worked at a laboratory run by Western Union where Meucci's materials had been stored. Giovanni Schiavo, another Italian writer, claims that *both* Bell and Elisha Gray obtained information on Meucci's invention and that their subsequent patent or caveat was inspired by that information. In 1871, Meucci claimed that he lodged his model with one of 57 telegraph delivery companies (if, in fact, it actually was lodged) which, in 1874, merged to become the American District Telegraph Company, which was an independent organisation until it was incorporated in Western Union as a subsidiary in 1901. There is not one shred of evidence that Bell ever worked where Meucci's materials were claimed to have been stored. In fact, there is no evidence to identify where Meucci's materials actually were stored or, indeed, if they were ever lodged with any company, let alone one that merged into the future Western Union. If they were with Western Union or an allied company, we can be sure that Bell wasn't in the vicinity as his chief sponsor, Gardiner Greene Hubbard, detested Western Union and would never have let Bell work in any place where Bell's own notes or experiments could have been copied. Bell was a prodigious writer and note-keeper who mentioned competitor Elisha Gray in his correspondence – and, tellingly, acknowledged Reis' earlier work – but Meucci is absent from Bell's correspondence.

There is an inference, too, that there is something sinister in Bell's patent and Gray's caveat being lodged on the same day in 1876 (Bell's patent was the 5th entry and Gray's was 39th), but there is nothing unusual in such coincidences. Isaac Newton and Justus von Liebig developed calculus at the same time; Englishman John Hadley and American Thomas Godfrey independently invented almost identical octants in 1731; Archibald Scott Couper and August Kekule von Stradonitz concurrently and independently recognised carbon atoms can link to form chains; three chemists – Frenchman Eugene Soubieran, American Samuel Guthrie and German Justus von Liebig – independently, and in different countries, made chloroform in 1831; Leo Hendrik Baekeland and James Swinburn patented the plastic now known as Bakelite one day apart; Walter Hunt in America was granted a patent for the safety pin one day before Charles Rowley in England filed his patent for one in 1849; Vladimir Zworykin applied for a US patent for an electronic television camera tube, later called the iconoscope, on the exact same day as John Logie Baird applied for a British patent for a spiral scanning disc for use in a television system; German Heinrich Caro lodged a patent for synthetic alizarin (the active component of a natural red dye – famously used for dyeing maraschino cherries) one day before England's William Henry Perkin in 1869; also in 1869 on the very same day – 7 May – Frenchmen Charles

Cros and Louis Ducos du Hauron, who were entirely unaware of each other's work, presented papers to the same organisation – the French Photographic Society – on their independent discovery of trichromatic synthesis; and even Meucci wrote in 1865 to both *L'Eco d'Italia* of New York and *Il Commercio* of Genoa, Italy, "I cannot deny to Signor [Innocenzo] Manzetti his invention [also a "telephone"], but I only wish to remark that two minds may arrive at the same discovery, and that by uniting both ideas one can more easily reach a certainty about a thing so important."[45] Manzetti's device could only transmit simple tones, not coherent sounds like a human voice, although his supporters also claim him as the inventor of the telephone.

Author Tom Farley wrote: "Like Gray, Meucci claims Bell stole his ideas. To be true Bell must have falsified every notebook and letter he wrote about coming to his conclusions. That is, it is not enough to steal, you must provide a false story about how you came along on the path to discovery. You must falsify each step toward invention. Nothing in Bell's writing, character, or his life after 1876 suggests he did so, indeed, in the more than 600 lawsuits which involved him, no one else was credited for inventing the telephone." Farley continues, "Nearly every scholar agrees that Bell and Watson were the first to transmit intelligible speech by electrical means. Others transmitted a sound or a click or a buzz but our boys [Bell and Watson] were the first to transmit speech one could understand."[46]

Paragraph 10 mentions the court case where the US Government moved to annul Bell's patent on the grounds of fraud and misrepresentation, but it fails to state the outcome of the trial or the background to it. James Harris Rogers was manager of the Pan-Electric Telephone Company. He gave a tenth of the company's shares to Senator Augustus Hill Garland, who was also Attorney-General. Garland was asked, and refused, to bring a suit to invalidate the Bell patent. He then went on vacation to Arkansas and his Solicitor-General, John Cooke, authorised the suit against Bell. It is hard to believe Cooke would have done so without the approval of his boss, Garland, or that of President Grover Cleveland. Other companies joined in the suit, including Globe Telephone Company. The Bell Telephone Company countered with a suit against Globe, Antonio Meucci and others, including Amos Rogers, secretary of Globe. The case did not proceed as, on 30 November 1897, a new Attorney-General, Joseph McKenna, under newly-elected President William McKinley, closed it down as it manifestly should never have been instigated in the first place.

Paragraph 11 contends that because of Meucci's death, the matter of who invented the telephone and who was therefore entitled to the patent rights was not determined. Determining patent priority is not the same as identifying the inventor of something, as shown by the classic example of American Andrew Jackson Moyer who patented penicillin, although the major work had earlier been done by Howard Florey, Ernst Chain, James Bertram Collip and Alexander Fleming in Britain, with three of them being awarded the Nobel Prize for their work (Collip didn't get the Nobel, but his work was crucial in the development of penicillin). Moyer's important contribution was to find a means to mass produce penicillin, but the fundamental work had been done by the other four, who had not tried to patent penicillin as they thought it was immoral to patent such a lifesaving discovery. Also, as mentioned earlier, Werner von Siemens obtained the German patent to the telephone, as Bell's patent did not cover Germany – does this mean that the Germans believe he was the inventor of the telephone? As it was, Judge William J. Wallace stated, "The experiments and invention of one Antonio Meucci, relating to the transmission of speech by an electrical apparatus, for which invention a caveat was filed in the United States patent office, December 28, 1871, renewed in December, 1882, and again in December, 1883, do not contain any such elements of an electric speaking telephone as would give the same priority over or interfere with the said Bell patent." In the American Bell Telephone Co. v. Globe Telephone Co and others, the judge was scathing in his criticism of Meucci's claims and his behaviour, and concluded that Meucci was deliberately involved in attempts to defraud investors.[47]

Paragraph 12 claims that if Meucci could have maintained his caveat after 1874, no patent could have been issued to Bell. This is incorrect as any patent application that may have interfered with the caveator's rights in an invention resulted in the caveator being notified by the Patent Office and asked if he wished to act upon the caveat and, if so, he was given three months to provide specifications, drawings and models – which were not required for the original caveat application. A determination on who would be awarded the patent rights was then established in accordance with rules set down in the Patent Act in force at that time.[48]

What drove Meucci and all the others to challenge Bell was the financial reward that became apparent well after Bell's 1876 patent. More importantly, Meucci could have maintained his caveat, but he clearly had other priorities, such as macaroni sauce, so the only reasonable conclusion that can be drawn is that even Meucci saw his *teletrofono* as a toy of little value until he was mesmerised by the possibility of making his fortune, something he had been striving to do ever since he lost his first fortune – made from galvanising metals in Cuba – on a scheme to make statues from human cadavers! [49]

Between the times that Meucci's caveat lapsed and Bell was granted his patent, Meucci had lodged two full patent applications which cost the standard fee of $15, plus legal costs. He filed an application for a patent on 17 July 1875, and was granted patent number 168,273 on 28 September, for a lactometer for chemically detecting adulterations of milk. He also filed another patent on 27 November 1875; patent number 183,062 granted on 10 October 1876 for a hygrometer, "which was a marked improvement over the popular hair-hygrometer of the time". On the eve of Bell's triumphant discovery, Meucci doesn't appear to be too concerned about his *teletrofono* yet the website of Antonio Meucci Lodge #213 states, in relation to Meucci's discovery of the *teletrofono*, many years before Bell's 1876 patent approval, "The inventor [Meucci] realised immediately that he held in his hand something much more important than any other discovery he had ever made, and he spent the next ten years bringing the principle to a practical stage. The following ten years were to be spent perfecting the original device and trying to promote its commercialisation."[50]

This referred to an event in Cuba where Meucci heard a voice over a copper wire, well before he left for America in 1850 and while he was very wealthy, yet Meucci let this "much more important than any other discovery" lapse at the patent office for want of a total $10 for a caveat or $15 for a full patent. His poverty was exacerbated on 30 July 1871, when a "dramatic event", in which Meucci was severely burned in the explosion of the steamship *Westfield* returning from New York, brought things to an even more tragic state. While Meucci lay in hospital, miraculously alive after the disaster, his wife sold many of his working models (including the telephone prototype) and other materials to a secondhand dealer for six dollars. When Meucci sought to buy these precious objects back, he was told that they had been resold to an "unknown young man" whose identity remains a mystery to this day.[51] So, we have a "mystery man" buying Meucci's prototype in 1871 – but wasn't that the same year as Meucci lodged his model with a telegraphic company from whence Bell purloined the design (and the model?) for his own benefit? Which conspiracy theory are we meant to believe? Perhaps the "mystery man" also caused the fire at *L'Eco d'Italia* which destroyed the newspaper description of his 1860 public demonstration, although how he managed to destroy all the extant copies of this newspaper edition held in the homes of Italian/American New Yorkers, not to mention libraries, is rather problematic.

Surprisingly, considering how badly burned and impoverished Meucci was after the ferry disaster in July 1871, just five months later he was granted a full patent for "Improvement in the Manufacture of Effervescent Drinks from Fruits". In fact, from the time that his house was sold on 13 November 1861,[52] due to his destitution (although he could still find the means to establish the Perth Amboy Fiber Company in 1867), and 1876, the year that Bell's patent was granted, Meucci was granted the following full patents at $15 registration plus legal costs:

Patent No	Patent Issued	Description
36,192	12 Aug 1862	Lamp Burner (kerosene)
36,419	9 Sep 1862	Process for treating and bleaching oil or kerosene to obtain siccative (i.e. drying) oils for paint
38,714	26 May 1863	Improvement in Preparing Hydrocarbon Liquids to serve as Vehicles for Paints
44,735	18 Oct 1864	Process for Removing the Mineral, Gummy, and Resinous Substances from Vegetable Material
46,607	28 Feb 1865	Improved Mode of Making Wicks
47,068	28 Mar 1865	Process for Removing the Mineral, Gummy, and Resinous Substances from Vegetable Fibre
53,165	13 Mar 1866	Improved Process for Making Paper-Pulp from Wood
122,478	2 Jan 1872	Improvement in the Manufacture of Effervescent Drinks from Fruits
142,071	26 Aug 1873	Improvements in Sauces for Food
168,273	28 Sep 1875	Method of Testing Milk
183,062	10 Oct 1876	Hygrometers (application filed 27 November 1875)

"When Meucci filed his caveat [for his *teletrofono* on 28 December 1871], he got $20 from Mr Breguglia, one of the partners of the Telettrofono Company, and [Frederick] Bachmann gave him the money to buy the ticket 'to cross on the ferry to New York'. He lived on the generosity of his friends and was helped by the county's Overseer of the Poor."[53] Yet just five days later he was granted a full patent – at $15 plus legal costs – for improved manufacture of effervescent drinks from fruits. He also lodged a caveat in 1874 for refining crude oil.

Interestingly, the above patents, at a total registration cost of $165 plus legal fees of similar magnitude or more, and $20 to be paid on issuance of each of the 11 patents (total $220), did not include any item that was remotely linked to his telephone – an invention "much more important than any other discovery he had ever made" and is "quite easy to make" and which, as far back as 1860, "could transmit the human voice exact". It should also be noted that "during the years 1859, 1860, and 1861 he was in close business and social relations with William E. Ryder, who was interested in his inventions, paid the expenses of his experiments, and, in connection with others whom he introduced to Meucci, invested a considerable amount of money in Meucci's inventions, and their use in business enterprises. He was a constant visitor at Meucci's house, lived near him, and seems to have been his closest personal friend and business adviser. Their intimate relations continued until 1867, when Ryder became satisfied that Meucci's inventions were not sufficiently practical or profitable to devote more time and money to them, and their intimacy ceased, although as late as 1871 he interested himself for Meucci to dispose of some of his inventions. During all these years, according to the testimony of Mr Ryder, he never heard from Meucci, or anybody else, of Meucci's telephone. In 1864 and 1865 David H. Craig was a partner with Meucci and Ryder in the paper manufacture. He [Craig] had been intimately associated with other telegraph inventions and patents, and his interest in such matters must have been known by Meucci. He never heard, from Meucci or otherwise, that Meucci had invented or was experimenting with the telephone."[54]

As Meucci himself declared at the Globe/Bell trial he had made no substantial improvements to his telephonic device since 1865 (why would you if it "could transmit the human voice exact"?) so it is strange that Ryder, who was willing to finance candle moulds and wicks, was not so enthused with Meucci's telephone as to provide him with the necessary funding if the 1865 *teletrofono* had shown the slightest potential. Furthermore, Meucci's supporters claim that he discovered electrical transmission of speech while he was in Havana in 1849, and that he had constructed the first electromagnetic telephone in 1856. Why then did he not patent it at that time? Money was not an obstacle as Meucci arrived in New York in 1850 with the equivalent of $500,000 in today's currency and he did not lose his fortune until 1860, five years after his "invention" (yet he was able to establish a paper manufacturing company – the Perth Amboy Fiber Company – in 1867. How broke was he?). It can't be said that he didn't understand the importance of patent laws because in the period 1858-1860, before he went broke, he took out two full US patents on candle moulds.

Meucci's poverty was mentioned in the Globe/Bell trial where he was cross-examined by Bell lawyer James Jackson Storrow, particularly in respect of Meucci transferring his "Sound Telegraph" rights on 22 September 1883 "for $14, to a Syndicate made up by Alfred P. Willoughby of Chicago and by Messrs. William W. Goodwin, James Work and Robert R. Dearden of Philadelphia. A few weeks later, Meucci's lawyer Carlo Bertolino relinquished to the Syndicate all the telephone prototypes created by Meucci and all the affidavits sworn in his favour up to that time."[55]

Storrow queried why Meucci would sell such rights for so little. "On this low remuneration, Meucci was extensively cross-examined by lawyer James Jackson Storrow, counsel for American Bell. In fact, according to confidential reports of the Pinkerton's Detective Agency, it was rumoured that Meucci received from the Syndicate a remuneration of $200 a month. Meucci, however, refused to answer, because he maintained that he was not compelled to disclose such information in that trial".[56]

To believe Meucci's supporters we must accept that:

1. the US Supreme Court and many state jurisdictions got it wrong on nearly 600 occasions in patent suits brought by many individuals and companies, including the extremely wealthy Western Union which could hire the best lawyers;

2. Bell fabricated his many letters and notes which he meticulously kept over many years prior to his 1876 telephone patent;

3. the US Patent Office staff conspired to pass secrets on to Bell and Gray;

4. Bell and Gray – who were competitors – colluded to prevent Meucci being given due recognition as the telephone's inventor;

5. Western Union and Bell Telephone colluded during their first court case to divide the telephone and telegraph industry between them, yet Western Union turned down the offer from Bell to transfer to them the telephone patent rights for $100,000, an insignificant sum to Western Union, one of the world's richest companies, and probably less than their legal fees paid in trying to defeat Bell's priority;

6. Meucci was too poor to renew his $10 caveat (but could still take out two full patents unrelated to the telephone during the currency of the caveat).

7. Meucci had developed by the early 1850s an electronic telephone system that "serviced the neighbourhood" but which he failed to patent when he was wealthy and which was ignored by the multitude of entrepreneurs with available capital looking to invest in various means of improving communication in this period.

Repeatedly, the supporters of Meucci's claim to have invented the telephone resort to conspiracy theories for, aside from the above seven points, there is the loss of all copies of *L'Eco d'Italia* in which he described his invention (Bell must have had a lot of clout in the New York Italian community to pull that one off!); the mystery fire at the newspaper offices which destroyed his "personal file"; and the "mystery man" who bought his *teletrofono* model from John Fleming's second-hand shop where his wife had sold them (unsurprisingly, Fleming is also described as a "junk dealer").[57] Tellingly, the supporters of other claimants to the invention of the telephone – Bourseil, Reis, Edison and Gray – do not resort to conspiracy theories or mysterious happenings in support of their priority claims.

Between 6 March 1875 and 7 May 1920, Bell was granted 30 patents, of which 18 were in his name alone and, by himself or with others, he invented, greatly improved or was noted for the: telephone, loudspeaker, microphone, photophone, graphophone, metal detector, hydrofoil, aileron, aircraft tricycle undercarriage, telautograph, tetrahedron (geodesic dome), wax cylinders for recording sound, electric oil heaters, audiometer, photoacoustic spectroscopy, suggesting use of radium in treating internal tumours, suggesting use of 3-D X-rays, and his pioneering work with *National Geographic*.

Meucci's efforts were spent, aside from his *teletrofono*, on: transforming red coral to pink; effervescing fruit drinks; making candle moulds and wicks; devising destructive ammunition; making tea and coffee filters; improving aneroid barometers, lactometers and a hygrometer; bleaching oil for use in paint; refining crude oil; obtaining paper pulp from wood; and patenting improved macaroni sauce; – almost every one a dismal failure.

Sadly, the erroneous belief that Meucci was the inventor of the telephone has now spread widely due to House Resolution 269 IH of the United States Congress. For example, the claim that Meucci invented the telephone (or a proto-telephone), and that Bell had "stolen" his design while working in a laboratory where Meucci had sent his appliance, and that Meucci was too poor to patent his invention, appeared in Jheni Osman's *100 Ideas that Changed the World* (page 26), and in *The Noticeably Stouter QI Book of General Ignorance* (pp 30-31) which sold millions of copies and was based on the BBC television show *QI*, the particular episode on Bell and Meucci being broadcast on 20 November 2003 (in Britain).

The comparison between the works of Bell and Meucci speaks for itself. The Italians have made a major contribution to the advancement of science and technology and, indeed, Galileo Galilei is one of the founders of modern science, but Meucci is not in these hallowed ranks. Bob Estreich, a former employee of Telstra Australia, and a telephone hobbyist and researcher made a summary of some salient points regarding Meucci's claim to the invention of the telephone:

"1. In 1871 Meucci was not granted a patent, but a caveat, a kind of provisional patent. Anybody could get a caveat, even if the invention was worthless.

2. Meucci's caveat does not describe any kind of a diaphragm – none whatever.

3. There is no United States Supreme Court decision either in favour or against Meucci, and the reference in the October Term of the 1888 US Reports (or in any other volume), exists only in the imagination of some irresponsible people.

4. In the thousands of pages of manuscript and printed records dealing with Meucci consulted by me [Estreich], there is no such description of the telephone as given in the Italian Encyclopaedia. Least of all, is there any reference to any substance 'capable of inductive action' precisely defined. We have, of course, documentary evidence that Meucci constructed an electric telephone with material capable of inductive action, such as iron, as well as Meucci's description of the effect of the diaphragm on the magnet, but Meucci never used the precise scientific definition quoted in the Treccani article. Least of all in the caveat.

5. The various detailed articles on the Meucci telephone which appeared in the 1880s in American and British journals, such as the *Telegraphic Journal* and *Electrical Review* of London and the *Electrical World* of New York, with accurate drawings of the various instruments constructed by Meucci, have no legal value whatsoever [they happened well after the 1876 Bell telephone patent was lodged].

6. The only court decision about Meucci's telephone in existence was rendered by Judge Wallace of the US Circuit Court in 1887 in the case of the Bell Telephone Company against the Globe Telephone Co., Meucci et al. That decision was against Meucci declaring his telephones as not being 'electrical' but 'acoustical'."[58]

Finally, if the published pontifications of politicians determine who invented what, then the US Congressional declaration was surely neutralised or reversed by the later, and therefore more current, Canadian House of Representatives affirmation on 21 June 2002, in which the Honourable Sheila Copps, Minister of Canadian Heritage, moved, "This House affirms that Alexander Graham Bell of Brantford, Ontario and Baddeck, Nova Scotia is the inventor of the telephone". Not only was this motion carried unanimously, but it was unequivocal about Bell being the inventor of the telephone. It isn't surprising that the Canadian government should pass such a motion, for Bell, although born in Scotland and a naturalised American, lived in Canada for much of his life and undoubtedly regarded it as his spiritual home.

William Denny 1847-1887 was responsible for building the first experimental nautical test tank in any commercial shipyard in the world. Denny's tank was "built on specifications provided by William Froude, an Oxford-trained mathematician and one-time collaborator with Isambard Kingdom Brunel. Froude designed the first private test tank to provide the British Admiralty with an accurate guide to how full-sized ships would perform at sea."[1] Denny's water tank was over 91 m long by 6.7 m wide and 2.7 m deep, and had clay moulding beds for casting wax-model ship hulls and machinery for shaping models.

Denny led his firm through a series of major shipbuilding reforms based on the use of experiments and rigorous sea trials to develop a working knowledge of efficient hull shapes. Denny's proposals for standard cross curves of stability for all ships "had far-reaching effects and are now accepted worldwide."[2]

He instigated the practice of progressive trials to examine the relationship between engine powers, speed and hull resistance in different ships; in the mid-1870s he began to closely work with Froude on the analysis of hull resistance; and in 1884, he finished work overseeing the construction of the test tank. The Denny-built *Rotomahana* (1878) was the first ocean-going steel-hulled steamship and the first to be fitted with twin bilge keels.[3] In 1879, *Buenos Ayrean* was the first Atlantic steamship to be constructed of steel.[4]

Denny's shipbuilding firm "held an uncontested reputation for the quality of its ships which traded in most seas and rivers of the empire. But it was the third William Denny who gave the shipbuilder the reputation for *scientific* shipbuilding with a practical rather than theoretical emphasis. Under William Denny the firm introduced two principal 'scientific' practices into Clyde shipbuilding. First, he was an advocate of progressive speed trials for new ships, a practice which entailed the accurate measurement of engine and hull performance during measured mile trials at *various* speeds rather than simply at the maximum speed as previous theory and practice had seemed to require. ... Second, William Denny introduced the first commercial experimental tank at the Dumbarton yard in 1883. Complementing data obtained from full-size vessels during progressive speed trials, the tank allowed the performance of models with a range of hull forms to be recorded and evaluated."[5]

Alexander Blackie William Kennedy 1847-1928 was a civil and electrical engineer who brought in major changes to the way engineers were educated. While working for the Central Electric Company and the St James and Pall Mall Electric Light Company, he designed and built the first electric generating stations for many cities and towns, including: Belfast, Carlisle, Croydon, Edinburgh, Glasgow, Hartlepool, Kirkcaldy, Manchester, Rotherham, Westminster, Weymouth and York. Kennedy was contracted to build two hydroelectric stations for the British Aluminium Company, their first at the Falls of Foyers in 1896 and a second at Kinlochleven in 1909. As consulting engineer to the Great Western Railway, he prepared the plans for the work of electrification west of Paddington on the Great Western, and Hammersmith & City railways.

His firm was consulting electrical engineers to the London & North Western, and London & South Western railways for their schemes of suburban electrification round London, and later on he carried out similar work for the South Eastern & Chatham railway. He was consulting engineer to the Calcutta Electric Supply Corporation until 1928, and to the Corporation of Edinburgh.

Kennedy designed the steel arch pier at Trouville-sur-Mer, France, and the steel and concrete internal structure of the Hotel Cecil and of the Alhambra Theatre, the latter being probably the first building in which concrete slabs were used on a large scale to carry heavy weights.[1]

In the academic sphere, he achieved a world-wide reputation, and his name will long be remembered in the history of research and for the valuable work he did on the strength and elasticity of materials. In the theory of construction, and as a civil engineer, he was in the first rank, while in the latter part of his life he became one of the foremost electrical consulting engineers in the world. Kennedy's contributions to the development of research in Britain were important. His establishment of the Engineering Laboratory at University College set an example that was quickly followed by many others, and there is no doubt that it was largely responsible for the movement which later brought into being the National Physical Laboratory, the Engineering Standards Association, and the Department of Scientific and Industrial Research. The Westminster Electric Supply Corporation was his first large undertaking. He planned their whole system and works and was their engineer for the remainder of his life.[2]

James MacRitchie 1847-1895 was a civil engineer who did much of his work in Singapore. His name and that of his parents is spelt McRitchie in the 1851 census of England (which also shows his date of birth as 1846) although most records seem to spell it MacRitchie. Born in Southampton, he grew up in Scotland where he was trained. He went to India in 1867 as assistant engineer for the Calcutta Waterworks but had to return to Scotland due to ill health and while there was appointed resident engineer on the reconstruction of the Glasgow Suspension Bridges, completing this work in 1871. In June of that year he became assistant engineer in the Lighthouse Department of the Imperial Government in China, and the year after, he took an identical position and title with the Japanese government, becoming Engineer in Chief from 1876 until 1880. While in Japan, he was instrumental in creating a training establishment which included two lightships, built and fitted out, 22 buoys, and iron and wooden lighthouses built on site for practical training.[1]

"MacRitchie proceeded to Brazil as Resident Engineer, under Mr Alfred Bumball, to the City of Santos Improvements Company. In that capacity, he designed and constructed a complete system of water-supply, new gasworks, and a line of tramway from the city to the Barra, a resort on the coast. These works he carried out with great skill and ability, although suffering from repeated severe attacks of fever which considerably impaired his health." In May 1883, he was Municipal Engineer in Singapore, remaining in that position until he died.

When he arrived in Singapore there were only two iron bridges – Singapore-Cavanagh Bridge and Elgin Bridge – both of which he repaired. He constructed many more with, at least, 23 being major structures including Coleman Bridge and Keppel Road Bridge No. 1. By 1893, he had completed several new markets in iron – shipped out from Glasgow – including Teluk Ayer Market (also called Lau Pa Sat) built on reclaimed land and being one of the largest and best in the East. He built two modern abattoirs – Pulau Saigon and Jalan Besar – in 1893 and ensured regular water supply by improving the existing reservoir and increasing its size considerably to 1,760,000 litres by 1894.[2]

Robert Gibson Eccles 1848-1934 discovered the properties of benzoic acid and benzoate as a food preservative.[1] Microbial spoilage of food causes losses of up to 40% of all food grown for human consumption worldwide. Yeast growth is a major factor in the spoilage of foods and beverages that are characterised by a high sugar content, low pH, and low water activity, and it is a significant economic problem.

Both benzoic acid and sodium benzoate, its salt form, have inhibitory effects on the growth of yeast, a major cause of food spoilage. A study published in 1991 in *Applied and Environmental Microbiology* described the metabolic disruption benzoic acid wreaks upon yeast cells. By slowing the yeast's ability to ferment sugars, benzoic acid starves the yeast of energy and prevents its growth. Benzoic acid is an important precursor for the synthesis of many other organic substances.

In pharmacy, benzoic acid is used as an anti-microbial and anti-fungal agent to preserve drugs, as an intermediate reactive agent to prepare drugs, and it is also combined with alcohol and water to be used as a cleaning agent in pharmacies.

Alexander Muirhead 1848-1920 improved the fax machine that had been invented in 1843 by Alexander Bain. Muirhead Ltd. (now Muirhead Aerospace) is considered Europe's premier manufacturer of, amongst other technological equipment, precision-wound servo components, position sensors, electrical control systems, worldwide news agency wirephoto service, and even fax machines for police vehicles. The firm was founded in 1846 by East Lothian electrical engineer Alexander Muirhead, a pioneer of wireless telegraphy. "The first experimental model was developed in collaboration with the press agency Associated Newspapers. In 1949, Muirhead Ltd installed the first fax system in Japan for the newspaper *Asaha Times*. The system became enormously successful in Japan, where it was manufactured on a large scale, facilitating the transmission of ideograms. It took much longer for the system to be adopted elsewhere. However, since the mid-1970s the market has expanded rapidly."[1]

While Muirhead was studying for his science doctorate, he reportedly obtained a recording of a patient's heartbeat at London's St. Bartholomew's Hospital in 1872, but this has been questioned as he didn't publish his work on what would be the first ever electrocardiogram. In a biography by his widow, published in 1926, she states he didn't publish for fear of misleading others.[2] His descendant, Patrick Muirhead wrote, "Muirhead believed strongly in the doctrine of the mathematician Augustus De Morgan, that absolute accuracy was essential and that it was a crime to mislead future generations if your work contained errors."[3]

Bengt Johansson, of the Department of Oncology, University Hospital, Malmo, Sweden, appears to have no doubts on the matter as he states, "Muirhead in London recorded the first electrocardiogram (ECG) in man in 1869 or 1870 with a siphon instrument".[4] Likewise, Moises Rivera-Ruiz *et al* state: "The first successful recording of electrical rhythm in the human heart was likely achieved by Alexander Muirhead in 1869. He used a Thomson siphon recorder (available at St. Bartholomew's Hospital in London) that had been designed to record transatlantic signals."[5]

In 1875, Muirhead patented duplexing for the trans-Atlantic telegram cable and improved on Lord Kelvin's siphon recorder, an ink-fed glass tube driven by variations in the cable current in which a transversely moving siphon forced electrified ink particles onto a moving paper tape. This anticipated the process used by modern inkjet printers to print on paper. If Muirhead did indeed record an electrocardiogram, it would have been done by the siphon recorder as stated above by Moises Rivera-Ruiz *et al*.

Image 79 – Muirhead Siphon Recorder

Muirhead teamed up with English scientist Oliver Lodge and undertook pioneering work in radio transmissions. Many websites state that Lodge and Muirhead made their first public display of radio signalling before the British Association on 19 August 1894 at Oxford (with Croatian Nikola Tesla having done the same in 1893 at a meeting of the Franklin Institute in Philadelphia, and others such as David Edward Hughes, who transmitted Morse code using radio waves in 1878). However, Lodge and Muirhead had earlier demonstrated radio signalling for The Royal Society's annual "Ladies Conversazione" on 13 June 1894, with Lodge foregoing the headphones for a "sensitive mirror galvanometer – lent him by Muirhead – so that his audience could observe the effects which he wished to demonstrate."[6]

Muirhead had started work with his father, John, at the latter's electrical manufacturing partnership, Latimer Clark, Muirhead and Co., and in 1895 he founded the Instrument & Telegraph Company that evolved over time into a company now involved in aerospace, defence, space and high-tech industrial design and manufacture.

Like Alexander Bain, inventor of the fax, Muirhead was involved in patent disputes and in 1904, both he and Oliver Lodge sold their patent rights to Guglielmo Marconi, the Italian pioneer of radio. It was also an Italian, Giovanni Caselli, who first made the fax commercially viable by linking several French cities to the capital after transmitting over the 112 km distance between Paris and Amiens with a modified Bain fax. In his first year of business, Caselli transmitted nearly 5,000 faxes, with the images scanned line by line during transmission. Caselli made some changes to the equipment but it was fundamentally the same as the original fax machine by Bain, whose scanning principle is used in modern television having been pioneered by him 83 years before John Logie Baird's first public television transmission in 1926.

James Porteous 1848-1922 invented the Fresno scraper. He emigrated from Scotland to America in 1873 and settled in Fresno, California. "Fresno farmers badly needed better earth-moving equipment for their sandy soil. Farmers experimented with horse-drawn earth-mover designs. The problem was harder to solve than it seemed. Yet Porteous solved it. His series of patents reveal a subtle thread of real inventive genius. Fresno farmers had been using something called a buck scraper to move earth. It scraped up dirt and pushed it along in front. It was hard to pull and hard to unload. Porteous' C-shaped scraper had a blade along the bottom. It scooped dirt as it was pulled along. That much was like the buck scraper, but this machine rode on runners and could be tilted. An operator walking behind it could change the angle. When it was full, he tilted it back and let it glide on the runners. He could dump dirt as he passed over low spots and smooth out terrain. He could vary the angle of attack to match the soil. Porteous called it the 'Fresno Scraper,' and he formed the Fresno Agricultural Works to build it. It was soon being used all over the world. It was one of the most important agricultural and civil engineering machines ever made."[1]

"The Fresno Scraper transformed the backbreaking labour of land levelling, ditch digging and road and railroad building. It helped to change the way that earth could be scraped, moved, dumped and levelled. The 'Fresno' and its variants made possible the early-day irrigation canals, ditches, and level fields in the Central Valley of California, as well as the construction of dams, roads and railroad rights-of-way. It indeed was the forerunner and provided the basis for the development of the modern-day earth-moving scraper."[2]

Image 80 – Fresno Scraper
Building the Miocene Ditch near Nome, Alaska

Porteous had more than 200 patents under his name including patents for dirt scrapers (1885, 1887, 1891), raisin stemmers (1887, 1913), a vineyard weed cutter (1887), ploughs (1888, 1898, 1912, 1917), raisin graders (1890, 1894), a raisin/fig press (1891), rotary harrows (1901, 1911), a combined plough and seeder (1896), a fruit-packing press (1895), a steam generator (1904), a brush chopper (1909), tractor wheels (1914) and many others, but by far his most important invention was the Fresno Scraper from which "today's bulldozer blades are its direct offspring. The gigantic scraper-carryall earth mover is its grandchild."[3]

George John Romanes 1848-1894 laid the foundation of what he called comparative psychology, postulating a similarity of cognitive processes and mechanisms between humans and animals.

He was the youngest of Charles Darwin's academic friends, and his views on evolution are historically important. He invented the term Neo-Darwinism, which is still often used today to indicate an updated form of Darwinism. Romanes' own solution to this was called "physiological selection". His idea was that variation in reproductive ability caused mainly by the prevention of intercrossing with parental forms was the primary driving force in the production of new species. The majority view then and now was for geographical separation to be the primary force in species splitting (allopatry) and increased sterility of crosses between incipient species as secondary.[1]

Romanes first demonstrated that animals could show intelligence in *Animal Intelligence*. Then Romanes tried to show that an animal that acts more advanced and humanlike was higher on the evolutionary scale. Finally, he argued that language could have appeared naturally, by natural selection.

Romanes helped clear up some problems faced with Darwin's theories. He was able to clear up the ideas on physiological selection. One of the most significant barriers between closely related species would be the sterility barrier. Romanes used the example of height and eye colour and how no one knew what caused the different or same variations. Romanes explained that a variation could happen and would make some organisms more sterile with other members of the species, but may not affect the somatic characteristics. This showed that from generation to generation the cross of generations would result in a less fertile relationship. Romanes pointed out that successful variations seemed rare, but possible. This type of evolution was call polytypic.[2]

Even though Romanes work does not match with modern science, Romanes is respected for his pioneering efforts in helping and stimulating the development of comparative psychology and helping to prepare the path for experimental studies of animal behaviour. It was Romanes who first leaped into the giant step of observational stages of comparative psychology.[3]

Benjamin Hall Blyth 1849-1917 was a civil engineer who worked mostly on building railway stations, such as the Citadel Station at Carlisle, involving the reconstruction of the lines of four railway companies entering from the south, and three from the north, so as to entirely separate the passenger and goods traffic and avoid several dangerous railway level crossings. The whole works cost nearly £400,000. At the same time, his firm was constructing for the Caledonian Railway Company, the Central Station in Glasgow with its connecting lines, including a large viaduct, with four lines of rails, over the Clyde, the total cost of the works being about £500,000; and also a large new dock at Grangemouth at a cost of over £300,000. Other stations which have been built or re-constructed by his firm include the General Station at Perth, the Joint Station at Paisley, Bridge Street Station in Glasgow, Princes Street and Waverley Stations in Edinburgh, and the Central Station at Leith.

Among many bridges designed and built by his firm, may be mentioned the new Broomielaw Bridge over the Clyde at Glasgow, the new North Bridge connecting the old and new towns of Edinburgh, the Victoria Bridge over the Dee at Aberdeen, the Victoria Bridge over the Tay at Perth, besides bridges over the Tweed, the Spey, the Ayr, the Gala, and other rivers, and three bridges under the Forth and Clyde Canal for roads leading out of Glasgow. One of the last works on which he was engaged was a large new dock at Methil, mainly for the shipment of coal from the extensive coalfields in Fife. He was Vice President of the Institution of Civil Engineers in 1911 and President for the year 1914-1915.[1]

David William Brunton 1849-1927 designed, in 1894, a hand-held surveying compass that could also measure horizontal angles. Unlike most modern compasses, the Brunton Pocket Transit utilised magnetic induction damping rather than fluid to damp needle oscillation. Because "modern surveying is now done with a range of electronic instruments that are fast and precise, you wouldn't think there would still be a need for geologists to use a Brunton pocket transit. The reason for its survival in the electronic age, is that in addition to its rugged field compass, the Brunton contains an accurate inclinometer mechanism. The compass and inclinometer are the tools by which measurements of strike and dip of geologic structures are made. So, no matter how many advances are made with laser surveying instruments or GPS systems, there are some measurements that a field geologist will always need to do using judgment and skill, with a Brunton Pocket Transit."[1]

"The Brunton compass can be clipped to your belt or carried in a large pocket. With its clever mirror, it can be attached to a tripod and plumb bob, replacing a costly and unwieldy surveyor's transit, while producing fairly accurate surveys. The instrument also has a built-in level that allows users to measure the vertical angles ... Surveys of many Aspen [Colorado] mines were accomplished using solely a Brunton compass, as was the first survey of Aspen's lift lines in the 1940s."[2] Sales of the Brunton had surpassed 150,000 by 2010.

Image 81 – A standard Brunton Geo, used commonly by geologists

Brunton also invented practical process-sampling devices and "ran a 600-ton [544-tonnes] per day sampling works in Aspen. His partner F.M. Taylor, and W.S. Copeland, his nephew and manager, joined him in purchasing ore from local mines. They used Brunton's patented process to sample and accurately mix ore before selling and shipping it to smelters. A sampler measures an exact quantity of material passing through the device; 1/25th of that amount is then assayed for mineral content, ascribing a value for the entire quantity. Brunton and Taylor operated similar samplers in Cripple Creek and Salt Lake City."[3]

William Clarke Cowie 1849-1910 was an adventurer and engineer who had aided the Sultan of Sulu (North Borneo) against the Spanish, founded Sandakan, the second city of the Malaysian state of Sabah and the former capital of British North Borneo. Cowie managed to persuade the Sultan to cede sovereignty to a British syndicate which, in August 1881, became the British North

Borneo Company (BNBC) with Cowie as Managing Director.[1] In 1894, he instigated the building of the first railway in Borneo from Kimanis Bay to Beaufort, built by English engineer Arthur West. The railway was helped by a boom in rubber – and helped supply the demand – with exports rising from 2.3 tonnes in 1907 to 2,500 tonnes ten years later. The railway also helped the opening of land for producing sago, sugar, tapioca, silk, soya, pineapples and rice. The BNBC ruled Sabah until World War II when Borneo was invaded by Japan.

John Ambrose Fleming 1849-1945 invented the oscillation two-electrode vacuum-tube rectifier, which he called the oscillation valve. It would become better known as the thermionic valve or vacuum tube. "This was the first Electron Tube device and signified the birth of electronic devices. This device, patented on 16 November 1904, was the first electronic rectifier of radio waves, and enabled the widespread introduction of commercial radio services."[1]

Fleming recognised that the major problem preventing vast improvements being made in wireless transmission was that of detecting the signals themselves. In these early days, the coherer was the main form of detector and it was very insensitive. Fleming devoted his mind to this and, in his quest to make improvements, he tried a large number of new approaches to bring the required enhancements. In October 1904, he had what he later described as a "sudden very happy thought". He instructed G.B. Dyke, his assistant, to set up an experiment with one of his evacuated bulbs with the additional element, to put his new idea to the test. It worked. One month later, on 16 November 1904, a former colleague saw him "scudding" down Gower Street in Central London on his way to patent what he termed his "oscillation valve". He called it a valve because it worked in the same way as a fluid valve, allowing a flow only in one direction. The invention of the diode valve, or vacuum tube, was a revolutionary idea, and put down the foundations for many further inventions.[2]

"This invention is often considered to have been the beginning of electronics, for this was the first vacuum tube. Fleming's diode was used in radio receivers and radars for many decades afterwards, until it was superseded by solid state electronic technology more than 50 years later. ... Fleming's vacuum tube essentially consisted of an incandescent light bulb with an extra electrode inside. When the bulb's filament is heated white-hot, electrons are boiled off its surface and into the vacuum inside the bulb. If the extra electrode (also called a 'plate' or 'anode') is made more positive than the hot filament, a direct current flows through the vacuum. And since the extra electrode is cold and the filament is hot, this current can only flow from the filament to the electrode, not the other way. So, AC signals can be converted into DC."[3]

In 1885, he was appointed the first Professor of Electrical Engineering at University College, London. In 1896, he experimented with methods of focusing cathode rays and three years later he was appointed scientific adviser to the Marconi Wireless Telegraph Company. In this role, he helped to design the transmitter that Marconi used in his successful 1901 trans-Atlantic broadcast and, in 1904, Fleming designed a vastly improved radio receiver for Marconi. In December 1903, Fleming was informed that "his scientific advisory to the Marconi Company would not be renewed. Between 1899 and 1903, Marconi needed Fleming as an expert on patent and as a credible witness of Marconi's secret demonstration. Besides, Fleming played the role of a bridge between Marconi and the British scientific and engineering communities. Fleming also helped Marconi design a high-powered transmitting station at Poldhu for the first transatlantic experiment in 1901. The transatlantic transmission of wireless signals was a huge success, but Fleming was deeply hurt by Marconi's apparent attempt to monopolise credit for the success. Marconi was then much disturbed by Fleming's request to share it."[4]

Fleming even helped design and build much of the equipment that makes wireless communications possible. For example, he contributed greatly to the development of electrical generator stations and distribution networks, helping to usher in the electronic age by allowing long-distance transmission of telephone signals. He even made significant contributions to radar, which were of vital importance in helping the Allies to prevail in World War II.[5]

Fleming also contributed in the fields of photometry, electronics, wireless telegraphy (radio), and electrical measurements. He coined the term Power Factor to describe the true power flowing in an AC power system, and also invented the cymometer – an instrument for measuring the frequency of electric waves.

George Forbes 1849-1936 was the son of distinguished scientist James David Forbes. While he was manager of the British Electric Light Company, the younger Forbes found that replacing the wire brushes with carbon in electric motors greatly improved them. He took out a patent for this in 1885 and sold it to Westinghouse for £2,000 ($8,000). Forbes and Westinghouse again crossed paths in the period 1891-1895 when Forbes appeared before the International Niagara Commission as an advocate of AC electrical supply in preference to the, then, more popular DC which was supported by Thomas Edison, while George Westinghouse recommended using compressed air. Initially the Commission was against AC current, but Forbes supported American financier Edward Dean Adams in his assertion that AC power was the best solution and the Commission eventually concurred. Forbes was appointed as the consulting electrical engineer for the Cataract Construction Company that was building the Niagara Falls hydroelectric scheme – the first major hydro-electric power plant in the world.[1] Note: The world's first hydroelectric power supply was used in 1870 to provide power to the Rothbury home of English industrialist William George Armstrong in England. A hydro-electric plant began generating power on the Fox River in Appleton, Wisconsin on 30 September 1882, but this was a small operation.

Forbes' consulting work was international, covering major schemes in Egypt, New Zealand, India and South Africa. Forbes had an interest in astronomy, and in 1874, he led the British expedition to Hawaii to observe the Transit of Venus to determine the solar parallax and the distance of the sun from Earth. He returned overland by himself, travelling more than 8,000 kilometres through China, across the Gobi Desert and into the Russian Empire where, during the 1877 war between Turkey and Russia, he was Britain's sole war correspondent. He became involved in the action and Tsar Alexander II awarded him the Russian Order of St George for bravery. He went into partnership with James Young in 1880 to determine the speed of light and their calculation of 301,382 km/second was only 1,590 km/s over the currently accepted speed of light, an error of around half of one percent, although their methodology was flawed and discussions by senior scientists concluded "that not the phase velocity but the group velocity was being measured, and that there was no theoretical foundation for Young and Forbes's result."[2] In the same year, Forbes predicted, on the basis of comet behaviour, that there was a planet beyond Neptune, the furthest known planet at that time. "Noting that some short period comets have orbits which are associated with one or other of the large planets of the outer Solar System, George Forbes of Edinburgh proposed in 1880 that a statistical survey of cometary orbits might indicate the existence of an undiscovered remote planet."[3] This was Pluto, which was finally discovered in 1930 by American Clyde Tombaugh, and was later downgraded from planetary status to dwarf planet status in 2006.

Forbes developed a range finder in 1901 that was used by infantry from the time of the Boer War through to World War II, and he devised a method for submarines to communicate using beams of light. "During his time at Anderson's College, Professor Forbes advocated in his lectures the use of electric traction. In 1879, Forbes [was] commissioned to report on how the City and South London Railway should be powered. Forbes recommended electrification. The London Underground (tube) might have been operated by cables had it not been for the suggestions of Prof. Forbes."[4]

Forbes took out patents on dynamos, invented a meter for measuring alternating current and a damposcope to detect firedamp in coal mines, and he made improvements to arc lamps, which are used in searchlights, floodlights, large film projectors and other photography.

William Edmund Garstin 1849-1925 was a civil engineer posted to Egypt where he became inspector-general of irrigation in Egypt in May 1892, then Under-Secretary of State in the Ministry of Public Works. "Garstin's first task was to transform the traditional system of basin irrigation, in which water and silt were trapped in the flood season only, into one of perennial irrigation in which water would be available all year round and larger areas could be brought under cultivation. This work had already begun, but many installations were so poorly designed and constructed that they were of little use. Garstin carried out extensive works on the Nile which, when completed after his retirement, formed an integrated system of water storage and control. This in turn allowed a great increase in crop yields per acre, particularly in cotton, the main cash crop."[1] Between 1898 and 1902, Garstin superintended the construction of the Asyut barrage (dam) halfway between Cairo and Aswan; between 1901 and 1902, he constructed the Zifta barrage on the lower Nile, and between 1906 and 1908, built another barrage across the Nile immediately north of Esna town, all for the purpose of regulating flow and improving irrigation.

Garstin was the first to realise that, although the White Nile was clearly the main supply source of water in Egypt, the Blue Nile played an important role as they "automatically compensate one another, so that, at the time when one system is passing on a large volume of water, the other is storing up its discharge, and when the former begins to decrease in volume, the stored water takes its place and makes good the deficiency."[2] These magisterial works, unequalled in the history of Nile hydrography, reveal the Olympian sweep of Garstin's imagination, combining as they do a firm grasp on the scientific questions and the imperial aspirations of the British.

Cathcart William Methven 1849-1925 was "Durban's harbour engineer in 1888 with the specific task of removing the sandbar at the harbour entrance in order to make the Bay safe for shipping. During his tenure, Durban Bay was transformed from a tranquil stretch of open water to a commercial harbour with a forest of masts alongside the Point Wharves. By 1890, seven acres [2.8 hectares] of land had been reclaimed and electricity was introduced to the Point. In

1892 hydraulic cranes increased the handling capacity of the harbour and in 1893 timber wharves were replaced and extended. Methven designed Durban's first dredgers, the *Octopus* and the *Beaver*."[1] Following removal of the sandbar, "Durban went on to rapidly become Africa's busiest general cargo port and home to one of the largest and busiest container terminals in the Southern Hemisphere", and it also handles the greatest volume of sea-going traffic of any port in southern Africa with the continent's busiest container terminal.[2]

Image 82 – William Cathcart Methven (1849-1925)
Village of Howick and Umgeni Falls

Methven served as President of the Natal Institute of Architects (1905-1908) and on 9 June 1902 was appointed Government Surveyor of Natal. He was a noted artist, as well as architect and musician, with at least 144 paintings of South Africa and was regarded as the foremost landscape artist in Natal before the First World War. In 1892, he donated one of his paintings to the Durban Town Council, and this became the genesis for the founding of the Durban Art Gallery in the same year. Following his tenure as harbour engineer, Methven went into private practice as surveyor, and between 1897 and 1911, he surveyed every harbour on the south-eastern seaboard between Richards Bay, which was developed as a second harbour for Natal on his recommendation, and Cape Town, his surveying work ranging from the Indian Ocean to the Atlantic Ocean.

CHAPTER 5

1850-1874

The second half of the 19th century was ushered in by the Great Exhibition of 1851, more properly called the Great Exhibition of the Works of Industry of all Nations. It was an ostentatious display of Victorian Britain's power and wealth but, more significantly, it was a celebration of British technological achievement. Those born in this period grew up in an environment of rapid change in all spheres of life – in medicine, anaesthesia became the norm for operations and nursing became a profession. Transport became much faster with improved roads, steam locomotives and steamships carrying more people in greater comfort and for less cost. Gas provided light for many at home, in factories and in the streets. Sewerage and clean drinking water became more accessible to urban dwellers. Postage was standardised. Darkest Africa was being explored. The telegraph provided rapid communication overland. Photography captured images for posterity and refrigeration opened up vast markets for meat producers in Australia, New Zealand, Argentina and North America. The rich became unbelievably wealthy; the poor lived in abject poverty but could escape by joining the armed forces or via emigration – Scotland lost between 10% and 47% of its natural population increase every decade in the latter part of the 19th century. In large part, emigration resulted in greater numbers of Scottish inventors and engineers coming to the fore around the world, taking an ever-increasing role in the development and application of technology.

George Thomas Beilby 1850-1924 developed the process of manufacturing potassium cyanide by passing ammonia over a heated mixture of charcoal and potassium carbonate. This process helped meet the increased demand for cyanide for use in extracting gold from low-grade ores.

In 1869, his work in recovering paraffin oil from shale greatly increased yields, breathing new life into this area of the energy industry.[1] Working with William Young, from 1872 they were able to increase the yield of oil, ammonia and other useful materials from the shale by retorting and fractional distillation improvements, and the Young and Beilby patent retort of 1882 was the result. Their methods dominated the oil shale industry for decades to come.

Beilby's membership of the Royal Commission on Oil Fuel from 1912, and his knowledge of Scottish techniques and investments in oil production at home and abroad led indirectly to Winston Churchill, as First Lord of the Admiralty, taking a major government shareholding in the Glasgow-based Burmah Oil Company's substantial Anglo-Persian interests in 1913. This, by bringing together all the Scottish oil-shale businesses and refining expertise, was to form the basis for the semi-nationalised company that became BP.[2]

Beilby's attempts to standardise town gas supplies efficiently resulted in the establishment of the "therm" as the basis for the charging of town gas to consumers. He studied the destruction of metals by ammonia at high temperatures, particularly on the flow of solids. He inferred that when a solid is caused to flow, as in polishing, the crystalline surface is broken down to a harder and denser layer. Although much criticised, this theory explained the hardening of metals under cold working and gave valuable stimulus to further research. Beilby was director of the Fuel Research Board from 1917 to 1923. He was president of the Institute of Chemistry from 1909 to 1912, and of the Institute of Metals from 1916 to 1918.[3]

John Bell 1850-1929 and **Henry Bell 1848-1931**, in partnership with Englishman Joseph James Coleman founded the firm of Bell and Coleman. They designed a dense-air refrigeration machine that was installed in 1879 on the SS *Circassia*, which then transported a cargo of beef to London from America. Later that year, the SS *Strathleven* sailed from Melbourne to London in some 63 days with a cargo of beef, butter and mutton with a Bell-Coleman machine. The patent was sold in 1881 after the SS *Orient* had been fitted out with a Bell-Coleman refrigerator, following which it was installed in some 400 ships and industrial plants.[1] "The invention of the Bell-Coleman steam driven air-cycle refrigerator, in 1877, was the breakthrough which enabled ship-borne refrigeration to develop for transporting frozen meat from Australia, New Zealand and South America to Europe. The Bell-Coleman machine led directly to the domination of the frozen meat trade by British ships for the next 100 years or more."[2]

By 1900, Great Britain imported 360,000 tonnes of refrigerated meat from New Zealand, Australia and Argentina, greatly impacting the economies of those countries and the cost of meat in Britain and, indeed, the world's food production industry was changed forever by refrigeration, greatly aided by the Bell-Coleman refrigerator.

John Benton 1850-1927 worked on canals in Punjab from 1885 to 1892. He was in charge of heavy constructional work on the First Division of the Bari Doab canal and on the First and Fourth Divisions of the Sirhind canal, and he planned the auxiliary supply channel of the Upper Bari Doab canal.

He went to Burma in 1897 as Superintending Engineer, where "he effected great reforms. On the Mandalay Canal, his first work, opened in 1902, when he found that the standardised 10 foot [3 m] openings could not take the amount of drift brought down by the floods, he substituted 40-foot [12 m] openings, a practice which he followed later in the Shwebo and Ye-u canals, the former of which was opened in 1906. In the Thapaugaing Aqueduct, spanning a flood-swept ravine, he converted the walls into folding shutters, so that the flood water might safely sweep over the whole structure. He remodelled the canals in the Kyaukse district, and improved the Meiktila Lake works."[1]

Back in British India, he completed the Triple Canals scheme which doubled the fertile area in the Punjab by distributing the surplus waters of the Jhelum across the province. The scheme, sanctioned in 1905 and completed in 1917 at a cost of £8 million, was the largest irrigation work hitherto carried out in India and served as an example for subsequent achievements. It "ranks as one of the boldest engineering works in the world. It provides for an aggregate flow of 27,000 cusecs, and irrigates 1.75 million acres, [709,000 hectares] of which 1.57 million acres [635,357 ha] was previously waste land."[2]

He then built the upper Swat Valley Canal at Chakdara by a canal, which he carried in a tunnel more than 2 miles (3.2 km) long, known as the Benton Tunnel, under the Malakand Pass through the mountain barrier above Dargai. This extension more than doubled the area formerly served by the Swat River Canal. The fall of 400 feet [122 m] from the mouth of the tunnel into the Dargai Valley provided power for the electrification of the Nowshera–Dargai railway as well as for local purposes.[3]

James Bennett Forsyth 1850-1909 made a fortune, with his siblings, from manufacturing vulcanised rubber. He made a number of inventions to utilise his treated rubber, including a method of lining textile tubes with rubber so as to fit them for use as hose for conducting water or air. Linen had been used for the first water hose developed by Jan Van der Heiden in Amsterdam around 1672. Later, hand-stitched leather was used. Hose of the kind invented by Forsyth came into general use in fire-departments throughout the world, as well as being used extensively in railway stations and repair shops, public buildings, in mills, factories, on ship-board, and wherever a strong, light-weight and durable hose was required. He also devised rubber-covered rollers, which became indispensable for squeezing, sizing, and calendaring purposes in cotton, woollen, paper, and wool-scouring mills, print and dye works, bleacheries and tanneries.[1]

Thomas Lomar Gray 1850-1908 worked in Japan where he co-developed the first modern seismometers in the period 1880 to 1895. Gray was recruited to come to Japan in 1879 to be Professor of Telegraph Engineering at the College of Engineering. He left in 1888 for the USA to be a professor at Rose Polytechnic Institute of Technology, now Rose-Hulman Institute of Technology. Along with John Milne and James Ewing, Gray worked on the development of improved seismographs while in Japan.[1]

William Morrison c1850-1927 was an early pioneer of electric road transport. He settled in Des Moines, Iowa, in 1880 and trained as a chemist, developing an interest in batteries. He adapted a surrey carriage to operate with a battery for which he eventually received a patent in 1891. It may have been the first land vehicle steered by a wheel and featured his patented rack and pinion steering. Powered by 24 storage cells (48 volts) with 112 ampere-hours capacity, it weighed two tons (1.8 tonnes) and used a spur gear on a four horse-power Siemens trolley car motor that Morrison rewound to work at a lower voltage to make it more practical for battery application.[1]

His vehicle was able to run for 13 hours non-stop at 22.5 km/h although the battery took 10 hours to recharge, and he covered a distance of 293 km on a single charge. It was described as "the first really successful electric automobile"[2] and when it took part in a Des Moines parade in 1888, it attracted worldwide attention. It is also claimed that "William Morrison developed not just the first electric car but perhaps the first station wagon" (1891).[3] By 1900, electric cars accounted for 38% of all American cars, and even by the outbreak of World War I in 1914, around one third of all cars were electric.

William Niven 1850-1937 discovered, in 1889, three new minerals: yttrialite, thorogummite, and nivenite, the last a variety of uraninite. In the early 1890s, Niven's attention turned to the mineralogical exploration of Mexico. In 1891, he discovered the new mineral aguilarite at Guanajuato. He also promoted the development of gold reserves in the state of Guerrero, the navigation of the Balsas River, and the commercial exploitation of rose garnets from Morelos. In 1895-1896, he found new localities for xenotime, monazite, and other rare minerals on Manhattan Island and at West Paterson, New Jersey. On a prospecting tour for the American Museum of Natural History in 1894, he discovered prehistoric ruins (later named Omitlán) northwest of Chilpancingo in the state of Guerrero. He found the celebrated Placeres del Oro sepulchre in 1910. His Guerrero collections are now in the American Museum of Natural History, the Peabody Museum of Harvard University, and elsewhere. In 1911, Niven discovered ancient ruins buried beneath volcanic ash near Azcapotzalco in the Federal District, just north of Mexico City. He devoted the next two decades of his life to archaeological exploration in the Valley of Mexico, and through an arrangement with the Mexican government, was able to fund his digging by the sale of artefacts. Niven established a private museum in Mexico City with more than 20,000 exhibits. It was later moved to Tampico.

He recovered the first in a series of unusual stone tablets bearing pictographs from his digs at San Miguel Amantla, Azcapotzalco, and elsewhere in the Valley of Mexico in 1921. This discovery eventually totalled more than 2,600 tablets and acquired notoriety through the occultist writings of James Churchward, beginning with *The Lost Continent of Mu*, first published in 1926. Niven was a founding member of the New York Mineralogical Club.[1]

Modestly excavating neglected sites in the Valley of Mexico for fun and profit, Niven unearthed relics now housed in major museums worldwide. He contributed materially to the early controversies and discoveries surrounding pre-Columbian cultures. Niven intrepidly survived desert thirst, earthquake, bandit skirmishes, skull-packed caves, arrest in revolutionary Mexico, raging rivers and jungle fever. The God-fearing Scotsman managed to keep safe in a world of violence and intrigue by nothing more (nor less) than an ironclad sense of honour and sober industry.[2]

John Perry 1850-1920, with his colleague William Edward Ayrton, invented the surface-contact system for electric railways (1881), also known as the British absolute block system, and invented and coined the words "Voltmeter" and "Ammeter" (1881). Also in 1881, they invented a "single-passenger electric tricycle automobile, complete with electric headlights."[1]

The principle of the British absolute block system of railway signalling is to ensure the safe operation of a railway by allowing only one train to occupy a defined section of track at a time. This system is used on double or multiple lines where use of each line is assigned a direction of travel. Prior to the introduction of block systems, time-intervals were used to ensure that trains were spaced sufficiently apart; typically, if five minutes had passed since the first train had departed, then a second train was allowed to then proceed; although the driver was warned that there was a train only five minutes ahead.[2]

The electric tricycle, built in 1881, had two large wheels at the rear, with the right one driven, and a small wheel up front (the first electric wheelchair), with electric lights. The electric tricycle used ten of Gaston Planté's lead acid cells in series, providing ½ horsepower. The speed was changed by switching the lead acid batteries on and off one after another.

The trike was capable of a range between 10 and 25 miles (16-40 km) and a maximum speed of 9 mph (14.5 km/h), depending on terrain. Ayrton and Perry's tricycle was the very first vehicle to have electric lighting.[3] This vehicle was built five years before Karl Friedrich Benz took out his patent on the first internal combustion automobile in 1886.

Ayrton and Perry collaborated, until about 1889, in a number of electrical inventions, including the electric tricycle, the ammeter and voltmeter. Together they achieved several patents; worked as consultants for the Faure Accumulator Co.; arranged the lighting of the Grand Hotel at Charing Cross; and, with Fleeming Jenkin, co-founded the Telpherage Co. to exploit their patents for transporting goods by wires, which came to be widely adopted in the USA.[4]

William Thomson (later Lord Kelvin) calculated the age of the Earth from physical principles and adhered for over 50 years to an estimate that was far younger than geologists' estimates, despite the virtually unanimous opposition of the geological community of the time. The prevalent version of this tale alleges that the discovery of radioactivity simultaneously provided the demonstration (through radiometric dating) that Kelvin had greatly underestimated the age of the Earth and the explanation of why he was wrong (radioactivity being a source of heat that invalidated Kelvin's calculation). This is incorrect as introducing the known distribution of radioactivity into Kelvin's calculation does not invalidate its conclusion. In 1895, a year before the discovery of radioactivity, John Perry showed that convection in the Earth's interior would invalidate Kelvin's estimate for the age of the Earth, but Perry's analysis was neglected or forgotten, with the consequence that a powerful argument in favour of mobilism was overlooked.[5]

Image 83 – Ayrton and Perry's 1882 Electric Tricycle

Convective motion inside Earth causes heat to flow a lot more rapidly than Kelvin's solid-body mathematics suggested. Perry, who had been an assistant to Kelvin, had realised something of that sort must be going on, but he hesitated to criticise Kelvin, whom he respected greatly.

The Marquis of Salisbury's 1894 address to the British Association for the Advancement of Science sparked an important development in the debate on the age of the Earth. It led Perry to produce the first mathematical rebuttal of Lord Kelvin's calculations, which had, since 1862, functioned as an argument against the theory of evolution by natural selection. "He guessed the mantle was only 30 miles (48 km) thick, and the molten core was well-stirred. He got an age of two or three billion years. That was close to the 4½ billion years we now accept, even if his model needed a lot of refining. And what about radiation? Well, it's there all right, and it does set the surface gradient. But that gradient has no relation to Earth's age."[6]

Perry wished to affirm the independence of geology from physics, keeping each branch of science to its proper domain. With the support of his mathematical friends, Perry tried privately to induce Kelvin to modify his views. This effort failed, however, and the discussion became public in *Nature*. Perry supported his calculations with Oliver Heaviside's new mathematical methods, and also with empirical data, though these were later undermined by Kelvin's experiments. Perry was uncomfortable with his position as Kelvin's critic, however, because he held his old teacher in great esteem. Although Kelvin never stopped believing that the Earth was too young for natural selection to have taken place, geologists and biologists responded very positively to Perry's results, and no longer felt they had to justify their conclusions to physicists.[7]

If Perry's analysis had been absorbed by the scientific community of the day, then the first radiometric ages for the Earth would have come as confirmation of the convective explanation for the Earth's surface heat flux, and the "fixist" view of the Earth, which exerted such a brake on geological progress in the first half of the 20th century, would have been difficult to sustain. As it was, however, proponents of continental drift and convection needed repeatedly to make arguments in favour of a fluid Earth, against considerable scepticism. As late as the 1960s, geophysical models were being constructed that tried to match the surface heat flux, employing a solid Earth with elaborate distributions of thermal conductivity and heat generation.[8]

Sidney Gilchrist Thomas 1850-1885 was a metallurgist who found a way to remove phosphorous from steel. Towards the end of 1875, he arrived at a theoretical and provisional solution to the problem of dephosphorisation. This called for a substance which was chemically basic and physically able to withstand the high temperature involved in the process, because for commercial working, the durability of the converter's lining was essential.

With his cousin, **Percy Carlyle Gilchrist 1851-1935**, he devised in 1876-1877 a process (thereafter widely used in Europe) of manufacturing in Bessemer converters a kind of low-phosphorus steel known as Thomas steel. In the Thomas-Gilchrist process, the lining used in the converter is basic rather than acidic, and it captures the acidic phosphorus oxides formed upon blowing air through molten iron made from the high-phosphorus iron ore prevalent in Europe.[1] For the material of the new lining, experiments led him to the selection of lime or its congeners magnesia or magnesian limestone, but the practical realisation of such a lining engaged him and his associates until 1879. He foresaw not only that by employing such a lining it would become possible to "fix" the phosphorus from the pig iron in a separate slag, but also that the phosphorus deposited in the basic slag itself represented a material of great potential value for agricultural purposes.

His process first comprised substitution of a durable basic lining for the former siliceous one, and, second, provision of abundant basic material (such as lime) to secure a highly basic slag at an early stage of the blow. The process could also be adapted to the Siemens-Martin system of making steel in open-hearth furnaces. In 1885, the year of Thomas' death, world steel output amounted to some 6.1 million tonnes, of which some one million tonnes, or nearly 17%, was produced using his principles. A century later, in 1985, world steel output exceeded 711 million tonnes, with at least 558 million tonnes, or nearly 80%, being made in the conditions he stipulated.[2] The improved process resulted in much more slag forming in the converter. Thomas discovered this "Basic slag" could be useful and profitable as a phosphate fertiliser.

Janet Walker 1850-1940 began business in 1882 as a dressmaker in Queen Street, Brisbane, Australia, and soon had a thriving dressmaking business employing 120 staff. In July 1904, Walker was granted a patent for an improved dressmaker's stand, known as the "plastic bust", which could be manipulated to produce a replica of a customer's body shape. The design was sold to the House of Worth and Madame Paquin in Paris, and to the House of Redfern, London. In 1905, she successfully floated the Plastic Bust Co. while in London. A talented and skilled costumier, Mrs Walker operated her business until she retired in 1938.[1]

"They seemed in many ways a great improvement of the old hard style of dressmakers' dummy. The chief features of the plastic bust are that one bust can in a few seconds be made to assume the exact proportions of any customer. In proof of this, half a dozen tight fitting linings, which have been fitted on the customers themselves, were produced, and a bust was rapidly made to assume the exact proportions of well-known individuals, whose names were attached to the linings. ... They can be made stouter or thinner, in accordance with any alteration of measurement required. The method is simple in the extreme. The busts covered with linen are lightly stuffed with a soft filling until about as hard as a bolster. In the lower part of the stand is a thumbscrew, which enables the person using the figure to lengthen or shorten it as required. A lining which has been fitted on the living model is then pinned on the dummy, and is softly padded out until the lining fits without a wrinkle of the effigy. No further fitting is required and the attendance of a customer is thus required but once.

The convenience of this arrangement for customers at a distance will be readily understood. Another admirable innovation is the padded arm, made like the limbs of the jointed dolls to be seen in every toy shop. A steel plate, with three bars is affixed to the dummy where the armhole should be, and the pliable arm can be hooked on to any one of the bars so that the proper height of the shoulder can be secured and regulated. The jointed elbow enables the arm to be bent backwards when it is necessary to remove the sleeve. The size and shape of the arms can be regulated in the same manner as the bust."[2]

William McWhirter 1851-1933 (later MacWhirter) was a pioneer of environmental engineering who patented a combined voltmeter and ammeter in 1883. Essentially, this was an early multimeter (the multimeter was invented in 1923 by Donald McAdie). Following further improvements, he assigned its manufacture to the General Electric Company from which time it became the basis for virtually every electricity meter in common use.

His invention was used for measuring and indicating both AC and DC electrical currents in a circuit. He later incorporated magnetic shielding into his invention, and made electrical water-level indicators and recorders.[1] In 1898, he patented improvements in automatic apparatus for indicating and recording at a distance changes of level or position of water or other fluid in reservoirs, tanks, or tide ways, or of gas holders, or other structures.

George Smith Duncan 1852-1930 was the engineer responsible for the cable tramway in Melbourne, constructing over 70 km of tramway – the largest in the world. After travelling overseas, he saw that cable tramways were going to be superseded and on his return to Australia, advised the Queensland government to install electric traction in Brisbane.

He managed to extract gold from water, but it wasn't economically viable. He invented the emergency slot brake for use with the tramway. This brake comprises a steel wedge that can be forced into the slot-rail between the running rails by a strong spring. If a runaway car is moving fast enough that the slot blade is necessary, the friction has been known to weld the blade to the slot rail, disabling the line until it can be extracted with a cutting torch. It is still used on the San Francisco cable cars.[1]

He was the engineer who created the cable tramway system in Dunedin, New Zealand. This was the Roslyn cable tramway, the first cable tramway built outside America. A second line from Dunedin to Mornington was opened in March 1883.

Peter Seton Hay 1852-1907 helped plan most of the important New Zealand railway works of the central North Island section and was responsible for the primary design of the Makohine, Mangaweka, Hapuawhenua, Taonui, Manganui-a-te-ao and Makatote viaducts. The erection of these viaducts was a major undertaking: they were fabricated in steel, which was then a fairly new construction material and, because the sites were isolated – and relatively inaccessible – transport and handling of the steel created special difficulties. By any standards, the viaducts were great works of engineering. "Much of the credit for their construction must be attributed to Peter Hay". One of Hay's major achievements was his investigation and report on the proposed Southern Alps rail crossing by the Midland railway in 1903. Hay's scheme, which was ultimately adopted, avoided expensive grading and track work but required a tunnel over five miles (8 km) long. This tunnel, at Otira, was completed in 1923, long after Hay's death.

Equally important was Hay's contribution to the development of hydroelectric power generation in New Zealand. Pioneering surveys of water power resources were initiated by the government in the late 19th century. The most important report arising from these investigations was written by Hay in September 1904. It was the outcome of many years of patient preparatory work by Hay and officers of the Public Works Department. The report was a wide-ranging discussion of hydroelectric potential, focusing on both North and South Island sites. It anticipated many of the major works that were eventually built. In the North Island, the Waikato, Waikaremoana and Mangawhero-Wanganui catchments were singled out; in the South Island, particular attention was paid to the lake and river systems associated with Lakes Coleridge, Hawea, Te Anau and Manapouri.[1]

Robert Kidston 1852-1924 was arguably the best and most influential palaeobotanist of his day. His collections of slides (deposited in the botany collection of the University of Glasgow), together with the hand specimens and notebooks (deposited in the collections of the British Geological Survey, Nottingham) provide a wealth of important scientific data with modern applications in plant taxonomy, biostratigraphy and palaeoclimatic reconstruction.[1]

Over a 40-year period, he published more than 180 papers on the taxonomy and distribution of floras of the Carboniferous, Permo-Carboniferous and Devonian.

It was with David Gwynne-Vaughan and, later, William Henry Lang, that he perhaps produced his most outstanding work. Early in the 1880s, Kidston was asked by the British

Museum (Natural History) if he would catalogue their Palaeozoic plant collection. He began in February 1883, having been awarded a Royal Society grant, and completed the task in 1886. During that time, he collected about 250 specimens, predominantly from Radstock, Somerset, which were donated to the British Museum (Natural History). Kidston can also claim to be amongst the first to use the microscope in research on fossil spores. He described the two-wall layers in megaspores (exosporium and endosporium); dispelled the idea current at that time that any original cellular structure of the wall would not fossilise; observed that spores were often found attached in tetrads; and used spores to characterise and correlate individual coal beds.

Kidston and Gwynne-Vaughan described fossil *Osmundaceae* in a series of five joint papers; the co-operation of the palaeontologist and the plant anatomist, both masters in their crafts, resulted in the production of what is recognised as a botanical classic. He joined up with Lang between 1917 and 1921, and they produced the most important contributions ever made on the knowledge of the plants of the Devonian period.[2]

The most famous plant fossil assemblage representing early terrestrial ecosystems is that preserved in the so-called Rhynie chert of early Devonian age. It was excavated at Rhynie, Aberdeenshire, Scotland, and was initially studied by Kidston and Lang beginning in 1917. The chert is a silicified matrix of a swampy peat bed that contains not only plant remains but also other organisms such as arthropods and fungi as a fossilised subterranean ecosystem.[3]

In a series of five classic papers, Kidston and Lang described in detail the plants we now know as *Rhynia, Aglaophyton, Horneophyton* and *Asteroxylon*. They also described parts of *Nothia* but included it as part of *Asteroxylon*.[4]

Peter Duncan Malloch 1852-1921 produced the first commercially successful spinning reel for angling, although a pivoting fixed spool "spinning" reel had been conceived by G.R. Holding of Kent, England, and patented on 28 November 1878. The Malloch reel, patented on 3 September 1884, lasted for over 50 years and was made in many sizes and variations. The design allowed the drum to be reversed to eliminate line twist. In 1880, Malloch also patented a reel known as the Sun and Planet due to the relationship of the small cog going around the larger cog, which caused a dragging sensation when playing a fish. "The handle was attached to a small cog, so arranged that when a fish took line, the side plate of the reel didn't revolve – the handle simply spun on its own axis until the angler took hold of it. The design was brilliant; solving in a stroke the problem of a whirling handle catching in clothes or in the line, but it was no match for its rivals and the Sun and Planet never achieved the sales that it should have. It was not quite forgotten, because the design was later to prove the inspiration for the 'anti-reverse' fly reels which began to appear after the Second World War. Strange though the association seems, the Malloch reel is the spiritual ancestor of modern classics such as the Billy Pate, and the Tibor series."[1]

In 1908, Malloch designed the *Kingfisher* silk fly line. It was no accident given Malloch's vast experience in the world of fishing, his undoubted mathematical ability, plus his ability to design. The basis for this new type of fishing line, which would replace horsehair, was set against strict criteria set out by Malloch. It is this which resulted in the *Kingfisher* silk fly line and what made it superior to others was the weight and diameter being built into the line at the time of braiding and not by a coating added to a uniform core. Silk lines enjoyed their heyday and then fell out of favour as new materials became available and cheaper.[2]

William Ramsay 1852-1916 is credited with the discovery of argon, krypton, neon and xenon and was the first to discover helium on Earth (it was previously known to occur in the sun). He also demonstrated that these gases, along with helium and radon, make the noble gases; a family of new elements. Ramsay won the 1904 Nobel Prize in Chemistry for his extraordinary efforts.[1]

John William Strutt (better known as Lord Rayleigh) showed, in 1892, that the atomic weight of nitrogen found in chemical compounds was lower than that of nitrogen found in the atmosphere. He ascribed this discrepancy to a light gas included in chemical compounds of nitrogen, while Ramsay suspected a hitherto undiscovered heavy gas in atmospheric nitrogen. Using two different methods to remove all known gases from air, Ramsay and Rayleigh were able to announce, in 1894, that they had found a monatomic, chemically inert gaseous element that constituted nearly one percent of the atmosphere; they named it argon. The following year, Ramsay liberated another inert gas from a mineral called cleveite; this proved to be helium, previously known only in the solar spectrum. In his book, *The Gases of the Atmosphere* (1896), Ramsay showed that the positions of helium and argon in the periodic table of elements indicated that at least three more noble gases might exist. In 1898, he and the English chemist Morris William Travers isolated these elements – called neon, krypton, and xenon – from air, brought to a liquid state at low temperature and high pressure.

In 1910, using tiny samples of radon, Ramsay proved that it was a sixth noble gas, and he provided further evidence that it was formed by the emission of a helium nucleus from radium. This research demonstrated the high degree of experimental skill that Ramsay had developed, but it also marked his last notable scientific contribution. Intrigued by the new science of radiochemistry, he made many unsuccessful attempts to further explore the phenomenon.[2]

Ramsay, with Frederick Soddy, managed to liberate helium from the mineral cleveite, demonstrating that this gas (the lightest of the inert gases) is continually produced during the radioactive decay of radium. "The explanation of their discovery – that the atom could in fact split – took physics into the hazardous nuclear waters of the 20th century".[3]

Donald Cameron 1853-after 1903 invented the septic tank. In 1895, "Cameron, as City Surveyor of Exeter from 1883 to 1903, had become convinced as a result of experiment that the solid matters in sewage were capable of being dissolved and destroyed by the action of anaerobic micro-organisms, erected an installation intended to treat sewage in that way, the first portion of the work being performed anaerobically in a closed tank and the final purification aerobically in clinker filters made after the Barking pattern. Immediate success followed his efforts and the principle of the Septic Tank was at once established."[1]

"In 1895, [Cameron] gave the septic tank its name. [He] installed a water-tight covered basin for treatment of sewage of a portion of the city by anaerobic putrefaction and gave it the picturesque name of the septic tank, by which it has since been known."[2] "Cameron, the quiet Scotchman introduced to Great Britain, if not to the world, what was probably the first septic tank conceived, constructed and operated on scientific lines."[3]

Cameron also recycled the methane by-product of the septic tank. "Cameron recognised the importance of methane gas, and the septic tank at Exeter [in 1895] was designed to collect methane for heating and lighting."[4] Cameron had identified that a combustible gas containing methane was produced when wastewater solids were liquefied. "He collected and used the gas for lighting in the vicinity of the plant." [5]

James Mackenzie 1853-1925 was a physician and clinical researcher who developed the "ink-writing polygraph in 1906. A tambour (a rubber diaphragm) is placed over a vein in the neck, while another one is placed on the arterial pulse in the wrist. The movements of these vessels vibrate the diaphragms. These transmit the waves through rubber tubing to two recording arms which record the pulse as continuous lines on paper. It detected problems such as an irregular heartbeat. Polygraphs were also used as lie detectors. Physiologists found lying could cause physical changes such as a faster heartbeat or increased sweating. Mackenzie's polygraph measured and recorded these changes."[1]

It was while engaged in the heavy industrial practice in Burnley, Lancashire that Mackenzie developed, with the aid of a local watchmaker, the polygraph apparatus, which by recording vascular pulses permitted analysis of cardiac function and performance. He also investigated the treatment of heart disease with digitalis.[2]

Mackenzie's earliest work was upon *Herpes zoster* (shingles); he made use of the phenomena displayed by this disease to map out areas of the skin supplied by the spinal nerves. Out of these observations in large part grew his later observations upon pain and tenderness, and on referred pain and pain as symptom; these were collected in *Symptoms and their Interpretation* (1909). From the same basal observations, he developed his studies and views of angina pectoris, published in a book of that title in 1923.

His reputation rests on his long-continued researches into the nature of irregularities of the heart's rhythm. He graphically recorded the movements of the jugular veins and used these records in conjunction with others in an elaborate and acute analysis of the movements of the heart's separate chambers. Mackenzie's work and example are of the greatest value today. He was first to identify a large number of irregularities in the heart's beat and to establish which were caused by serious disease and which were of no consequence.

"He did more, perhaps, than any other medical practitioner before him to place upon a rational basis forecasts of the course of heart disease in individual patients, and the treatment of heart disease by digitalis."[3]

Beginning in 1892, he published venous pressure curves associated with the diagnosis of cardiac disease. He was the first to associate the venous and arterial pulses, emphasising the timing relationship of contraction of the various cardiac chambers. He investigated the irregular action of the heart, the action of digitalis, and studied atrial (then called auricular) fibrillation and prognostically distinguished between cardiac irregularity resulting from atrial fibrillation, and ventricular extra systoles. He proposed a hypothesis of referred pain in which a diseased viscus projects pain onto the body surface but not directly over the affected organ, with hyperesthesia skin reflection of diseases of specific organs, and hypothesised that the pathway was via the spinal cord and the sympathetic nervous system. He also described the neural distribution of *Herpes zoster* along an affected nerve. He carefully defined angina pectoris and published what was then the definitive monograph, *Angina Pectoris*, in 1923 and published other clinical and research studies in the *British Medical Journal*, the *Quarterly Journal of Medicine*, *Medical Chronicle* and *The Study of the Pulse* in 1909. His major work, *Diseases of the Heart*, published in 1908 and extensively illustrated with venous and arterial tracings, rapidly became the major cardiology text.[4]

His researches did not depend upon the laboratory, nor upon hospital facilities, but upon that continuous and careful observation of patients which is only possible in general practice. There is no doubt that his work led to the recasting of our views on cardiac disease. Sir Thomas Lewis said of him: "He did more perhaps than any other man before him to place upon a rational basis forecasts of the course of heart disease in individual patients, and the treatment of heart disease by digitalis"[5] and he "was undoubtedly the key figure in shaping British cardiology."[6]

Charles Scott Meik 1853-1923 and **Patrick Walter Meik 1851-1910** were engineering sons of Scottish engineer Thomas Meik. Charles was apprenticed to Englishman Sir Thomas Bouch, the builder of the first Tay Bridge which collapsed in a storm on 28 December 1879, killing 75 train passengers and crew. Following this, Meik went to Japan and wrote about Hokkaido, then, on returning to Britain, he constructed Port Talbot Docks and Llynfi Railway with his brother Patrick. This work was funded by Welsh heiress Emily Charlotte Talbot to attract industry and make it easier to export coal, on which her fortune was founded. In 1923, the year of Meik's death, Port Talbot exported more than 3,000,000 tonnes of coal. It was also to export coal that Charles and Patrick Meik were commissioned to enlarge and deepen Seaham Harbour in Durham.

Patrick Meik supervised the piers and foundations of the Forth Railway Bridge in the early 1880s and the Meik brothers also undertook rail and harbour design to the Indian subcontinent, Burma (the Rangoon River training works), Mozambique, Christmas Island and other locations, but their largest enterprise was the Lochaber Water Power Scheme (commenced in 1924). This was built to Charles' design but wasn't completed until six years after his death and involved making a water-supply tunnel 24 km long with a 4½ m diameter conduit, and a dam 275 m long by 55 m wide which collected water from four rivers. The tunnel was the longest water-supply tunnel in the world at the time[1] and remained so for decades until the construction of Colorado's Harold D. Roberts tunnel in 1962.

Charles Herbert Theophilus Metcalfe 1853-1928 became consulting engineer for all the lines which became the railway system of Rhodesia (now Zimbabwe), linking South Africa northward to the Belgian Congo (now the Democratic Republic of the Congo), westward to Angola, and eastward to northern Mozambique. Metcalfe was Chief Engineer for the rail line from Kimberley to Vryburg. Construction of the link began at Vryburg in 1893, the line reaching Mafeking in October 1894 and Bulawayo in October 1897. In October 1902, the railway via Gwelo reached Salisbury, where it met the line from Beira completed three years earlier. The line was completed to the Victoria Falls and across the Zambezi River in 1904. In January 1906, the line reached the Broken Hill (now Kabwe) zinc and lead mines, then the Rhodesia–Katanga Junction railway, completed in 1909, to the Katanga border and rapidly linked to the rich Katanga copper mines.

Metcalfe and Douglas Fox were the consulting engineers for the Benguela railway across Angola from Lobito Bay, which reached the Congo frontier on 28 August 1928. Metcalfe also contributed to establishing rail communication between Nyasaland (Malawi) and Beira, Mozambique. He was joint consulting engineer for the Shire Highlands Railway from Blantyre to Port Herald, completed in 1908. This line, together with the Central Africa Railway from Port Herald to Chindio on the Zambezi, became the Nyasaland Railways Company in 1931. Metcalfe also supervised the survey of the Trans-Zambesia Railway from Beira to Muracca on the Zambezi, completed only in 1922, eight years after he had left Africa.[1]

William Murchland 1853-1941 of Kilmarnock designed and patented the "first successful commercial milking machine."[1] Primary industry mechanisation wasn't restricted to crop planting, harvesting, processing and making fish nets; it was also applied to dairy farming. Since time immemorial, cows had been hand-milked, but during the 19th century a number of innovators turned their attention to milking machines, causing a gradual shift from hand-milking to the vacuum machine. The first steps involved milking tubes and catheters, but none of these were successful. Early vacuum milkers by Englishmen Hodges and Brockenden, and Americans Anna Baldwin and S.W. Lowe damaged the cows' teats. In 1859, another American, John Kingman, patented a tine teat cup and a year later L.O. Colvin made teat cups for a vacuum milker. These were no great advance on the earlier milkers.

Murchland applied for a patent for his milking machine on 27 September 1889, and it was granted on 9 August 1890. In tests conducted in June-July 1889, there was a gain of 14.8% in milk yield from cows milked by Murchland's mechanical milker compared to cows milked by hand. His vacuum milker was granted a US patent in 1892. This machine also irritated the teats of cows and required four people to operate it although Murchland introduced a teat-cup "so formed as to surround the teat with milk, in this way following up Nature again, and so preventing the possibility of injury to the teat by bringing it in contact with a metal surface as originally done."[2]

Alexander Walker Reid 1853-1938 developed, in 1907, a mechanical milking machine that had a variable speed pulsator. He was involved in the opening of the Waitara Freezing Works in New Zealand – a major employer in the Taranaki region. He promoted electric street lighting, making Stratford only the third town in New Zealand to install it, with the power coming from hydro-electricity supplied by his Stratford Electrical Supply Company in 1898. Commencing in 1903, he built three steam-driven cars and an early pop-up caravan in the late 1920s, quarter of a century before American Clyde Grambsch, the person usually credited with the invention, built his first one in 1954.

In 1907, after seeing various milking machines, most of which would have been modelled on the *Thistle*, Reid went on to develop a mechanical milking machine that had a variable speed pulsator with rubber cups that were partly reinforced to replicate the natural sucking of a calf and, importantly, his machine could be easily cleaned to minimise the possible contamination of the milk. His milker incorporated a patented feature called the "releaser" which was a container that filled up with milk and then discharged it.[1]

Elihu Thomson 1853-1937 co-invented the arc light. He was born in Manchester, England, to a Scottish father and migrated to America in 1858 when he was five years old. His first important invention was the 3-coil dynamo, which, with its automatic regulator and other novel features, was the basis of electric lighting systems.[1] With American born Edwin James Houston, he invented the arc light – used in street lighting – and Thomson took out 696 patents in his lifetime, making him the third most prolific inventor in American history.[2] Note: with thousands of patents registered every week, this statistic is outdated. Australian Kia Silverbrook has 4,665 US patents and 9,874 international patents as at 26 March 2014. Shunpei Yamazaki of Japan has 3,793 US patents and 13,092 international ones. Paul Lapstun of Australia has 1,269 US patents and 3,133 international patents. Thomas Alva Edison is 5th with 1,084 patents, although some of these were co-invented and others were innovations of his employees.

Thomson's patents covered arc lights, generators, electric welding machines, a centrifugal cream separator, stereoscopic X-ray pictures, and X-ray tubes. His recording wattmeter was the first practical method of measuring the amount of electricity used by a home or business. He was co-founder of the American Electric Company in 1880, which became the Thomson-Houston Electric Company three years later, and in 1892 it merged with the Edison General Electric Company and was renamed General Electric Company and is now known as General Electric (GE), the world's third largest company (in 2013) as assessed by Forbes Global 2000 (by 2015 it had slipped to 9th place with five Chinese companies ahead of it). On GE's web page it states, "Elihu Thomson, a founder of the company, summed up the mission of the lab: 'It does seem to me therefore that a Company as large as the General Electric Company, should not fail to continue investing and developing in new fields: there should, in fact, be a research laboratory for commercial applications of new principles, and even for the discovery of those principles.'"[3]

John Thomson 1853-1926 patented the first disc-type water meter in 1887. His two major inventions proved highly popular, with the Thomson Printing Press becoming standard in American printing plants and about 20 million Thomson disc water meters in use around the world. Thomson was granted some 350 patents in all, including those for the refinement of metallic zinc and the manufacture of zinc oxide, for which he founded the Electric Zinc Company in London. He also served as president of the Engineers Club of New York, and was Chief Engineer of the Primary Electrical Subway Commission of New York, which installed the first underground conduit for telegraph and telephone wires.[1] A major problem experienced by water meter manufacturers was that the hard rubber discs broke at fast flows. In 1892, Thomson patented a product in which a thrust roller controlled the circumferential thrust of the disc in its movement and thus prevented jamming of the disc against the diaphragm at the slot. This method continues to be widely used.[2]

David Dunbar Buick 1854-1929 was responsible for the appearance of the modern bathroom as we have come to know it – predominantly brilliant white. Although various colours are now used in the decor of bathrooms, the principal colour of the plumbed fittings is still white. The fashion for white sinks and bathtubs in bathrooms came into being following the invention of a process for heat-binding enamel to cast-iron bathtubs that was invented in 1883 by Buick, who had another 12 patents related to plumbing before he became interested in automobiles. In 1902, he and his partner, American William Sherwood, sold the plumbing business for $100,000 to The Standard Sanitary Manufacturing Company, which made a great commercial success of the enamel and went on to become one of the giants in the business. When it merged with the American Radiator Company in 1929, it was said that products from the new company could be found in half of the homes in America and Europe.[1]

Buick went on to found the Buick Manufacturing Company which would be the embryonic company that was built into General Motors by American businessman William Crapo Durant, who came into the business because he was impressed with Buick's vehicles, although Buick played no part in the later expansion of the company into one of the world's industrial giants. While he was still at the helm of his automobile company, Buick developed the overhead valve internal combustion engine which is widespread today, using pushrod-actuated valves parallel to the pistons. Prior to this, side valves and sleeve valves had been used, but the overhead valve was more powerful, had greater fuel efficiency, and lower exhaust emissions. Buick died in poverty in 1929, aged 74, but his ubiquitous overhead valve and white enamel sinks and bathtubs remain his legacy.

Dugald Clerk 1854-1932 (he spelt his name "Clark" in Scotland) was involved in the early development of internal combustion engines. Although electric cars became popular in many cities, their days were numbered due to reduced petrol prices and the electric starter motor, invented by American Charles Kettering in 1911, which did away with the hand crank required to start petrol-driven cars. Both of these occurrences made the internal combustion engine cheaper and they soon became the dominant variety of road vehicle. Clerk built a hydrocarbon vapour engine in 1876, and in 1881 patented a two-stroke diesel engine. Etienne Lenoir of Belgium had made a two-stroke gas engine in 1860, but it wasn't very efficient and they were mainly used in stationary machines. Sometimes called the Clerk Cycle Engine, it has a higher power-to-weight ratio than four-stroke engines, which is why it is commonly found in small motorcycles, lawnmowers, outboard motors, chainsaws, and both small and large gas engines. Clerk's two-stroke engine was modified by Londoner Joseph Day and it is this model that still exists today.

Clerk did important work on gas heating and lighting, and during World War I, he was employed by the Admiralty as director of engineering research. Clerk proposed the "air standard" in 1882 and by the end of 1905, this was adopted as the standard of efficiency for all internal combustion engines. Clerk also discovered that by raising compression ratios, the efficiency of an internal combustion engine could also be raised, leading to the later development of high compression engines. The compression ratio itself, Clerk stated, would be limited by what is known as "knock", which happens when the air/fuel mixture in the cylinder ignites before the spark plug fires, although this has since been mitigated by the development of anti-knock fuels in internal combustion engines.

He formed a partnership with Englishman George Croydon Marks to found Marks & Clerk, considered one of the leading patent and trademark attorney firms in the world, and still the biggest in the United Kingdom, with 92 partners who are patent and trademark attorneys, and 625 employees (October 2014).[1]

Alexander Dey born 1854 invented a machine for recording employee attendance, particularly in large companies, where keeping records of attendance was necessary so that payroll staff could ensure correct payment. One method of doing this was to use a time clock that registered the start and finish time of employees, including unpaid breaks such as lunch.

The first time clock for this purpose was invented by Alexander Dey, who applied for a British patent in February 1888, with a US patent following in May 1889. The Dey Time Register had time clocks to process up to 200 employees clocking on and off six times daily. They were spring-driven clocks with a cast-iron wheel affixed to the dial side. The rim of the wheel was perforated with numbered holes and workers pressed a rotating pointer, which rang a bell, into the hole at their assigned employee number and the time was entered on a pre-printed sheet. A two-colour ribbon printed all regular time in green and all irregular time, such as absence or overtime, in red.[1] Before the start of the 20th century, over 3,000 of these time clocks were used in Britain, North America and as far away as Australia. Moving to New York, Dey's organisation became one of the foundation companies of IBM.[2]

William Paton Reid 1854-1932 introduced super-heating to the New Brunswick Railway (NBR), but is probably best known for his powerful D30 "Scott" and D34 "Glen" 4-4-0 classes. He built the massive Atlantic locomotives; despite handling heavier loads, his management was averse to the 4-6-0, so Reid chose the 4-4-2 as the next best thing. He also built on the foundations laid by his predecessors Drummond and Holmes to develop the NBR 4-4-0, the well-known Scott and Glen classes surviving into the 1950s, as well as 4-4-2Ts for fast suburban services. For freight, he stayed with the 0-6-0 and 0-6-2T. A locomotive foreman on the NBR for many years, he well understood the virtues of simple and robust construction, as indeed did most Scottish locomotive engineers. His locomotives were long-lived, lasting virtually to the end of steam.[1]

Robert Wallace Urie 1854-1937 was a locomotive engineer who organised the Eastleigh, Hampshire, works to manufacture munitions. His locomotive designs were simple and robust, all with two outside cylinders. There were three classes of 4-6-0, one of which formed the pattern for the King Arthur class; a 4-8-0T and 4-6-2T. He rebuilt the Drummond paddlebox 4-6-0 into a better machine and designed the Eastleigh superheater. All his engines had high footplates, exposing the running gear, and all of them were made largely interchangeable as to parts. His first engines were 4-6-0s with 6ft (1.83 m) driving wheels, which appeared in 1914. They were followed by 20 more, with 6ft 7in (2 m) drivers, built from 1918-1923, which proved to be some of the finest express engines on the South-Western Railway, and were afterwards used as the basis for the King Arthur class, developed extensively by Maunsell. Two impressive types of tank engines, a 4-6-2 with 5ft 7in (1.7 m) wheels and weighing 96 tons 8cwt. (87.5 tonnes), and a 4-8-0 with 5ft 1in (1.55 m) drivers, weight 95 tons 2cwt (86 tonnes), are also to his credit, the latter used at Feltham marshalling yards, ("Hump" engines). An extensively used design of Urie's was the Eastleigh superheater, fitted to over a hundred L & SW engines. All Urie's engines were still at work as late as 1945.[1]

David Isauld Bain 1855-1933 was the first person to introduce electric lighting to railway carriages.[1] He was renowned for his superb sleeping and dining cars and designed a sleeping carriage and the royal compartments for King George V and Queen Mary.[2]

Andrew Barr 1855-1939 invented the stump-jump disc plough, in 1880, independently of Richard Bowyer and Clarence Herbert Smith, who were later given priority.[1] In 1921, he invented a machine for the destruction of mallee, herbage and the prickly pear pest, followed by his "jumping scarifier", a power digging machine, and a solar engine.[2]

Archibald Barr 1855-1931 invented range finders, including the optical range finder, and greatly improved the optophone (invented by Irishman Edmund Edward Fournier d'Albe), an electronic device that scans ordinary printed characters and produces combinations of sounds, enabling a blind reader to recognise the characters. It was Barr's version that was approved for manufacture and use by the Inventions and Research Committee of the National Institute for the Blind in 1921.

With William Stroud, he founded Barr & Stroud and the business was so successful that in 1904, a new, purpose-built factory was opened at Anniesland, Glasgow, with a workforce of 100. By that time, the firm had extended its market into Argentina, Austria, Brazil, China, Germany, Japan, Italy, Russia, Spain and Sweden. The firm supplied range-finders to nearly all of the world's navies, and manufactured smaller, portable instruments which were adopted by the British, French, and other European armies.[1] He later developed a number of other instruments including a torpedo-depth recorder, rangetaker-tester, aircraft bombsights, and submarine periscopes.[2]

James Alfred Ewing 1855-1935 "invented an extensometer (a device for measuring small increases in length of metals), a hysteresis tester, and other apparatus for magnetic testing."[1] Ewing, Thomas Lomar Gray, and John Milne invented the horizontal pendulum seismograph. This sophisticated instrument consisted of a weighted rod that, when disturbed by tremors, shifted a slitted plate. The plate's movement permitted a reflected light to shine through the slit, as well as through another stationary slit below it. Falling onto light-sensitive paper, the light then inscribed a record of the tremor. Today most seismographs still rely on the basic designs introduced by these three men, and scientists continue to evaluate tremors by studying the movement of the earth relative to the movement of a pendulum."[2] "Together, and independently, the three men made a significant contribution to the development of seismographs and, over the following decades, to seismology."[3]

Ewing's first seismograph had a 6.4 m long common pendulum as a sensing element. He predicted that the pendulum's five-second period would be sufficiently long that the bob would remain stationary under the short pulse-like motions of the ground which he believed occurred in earthquakes. He took care to build a rigid frame for the pendulum, so that the motion of the frame would not contribute spurious oscillations on the record.

Ewing's common-pendulum seismograph was constructed in 1879. This seismograph was not operated continuously from its inception. It therefore did not record its first earthquake until over a year later. At that time, a more sophisticated instrument, Ewing's horizontal-pendulum seismograph, was also in operation. The long common pendulum thus did not have a major influence in the development of seismology by the British in Japan, but very long common pendulums were later built by Italian seismologists, and these played a significant role in the history of seismology.

Ewing's was the first successful attempt to use a horizontal pendulum to detect earthquakes. Both of his instruments, the common-pendulum and horizontal-pendulum seismographs, recorded a small earthquake on 3 November 1880, giving the first lengthy seismograph records of earthquake motion as a function of time.

Based on five earthquakes recorded in the same month, Ewing noted the most striking features of these early seismograms. They were: "(1) the very gradual beginning and ending of the disturbance. In none of the observations did the maximum motion occur until after several complete oscillations had taken place. (2) The irregularity of the motion. The successive undulations are widely different both in extent and in periodic time. (3) The large number of undulations in a single earthquake, and the continuous character of the shock. (4) The extreme minuteness of the motion at the Earth's surface". The importance of these observations can be imagined. For the first time, scientists had a representation of earthquake motion, and this representation revealed a much different manner of shaking than that which had been previously thought probable. For the first time, also, seismologists could design their instruments with some knowledge of the phenomena the instruments were to record.[4]

Ewing, in 1882, joined a common pendulum with an inverted pendulum, so that the two would move horizontally together, so that he obtained a system in nearly neutral equilibrium, with the unstable tendency of the inverted pendulum lessening the stability of the common pendulum to which it was attached. This was Ewing's "duplex-pendulum" seismometer.

The duplex-pendulum seismometer is of particular interest because in 1887 and 1888 this type of seismometer was placed at ten sites in Northern California and Nevada. The first seismographic observatories in the Western Hemisphere, at Berkeley and Mount Hamilton, were equipped with the duplex instruments as well as Ewing horizontal-pendulum seismometers and Gray-Ewing vertical seismometers. The duplex seismometers in use here wrote two-dimensional particle-motion diagrams on a stationary, smoked glass plate.

Ewing made a joint for the conical pendulum seismometer invented by Alexander Gerard of Aberdeen in 1851 to lessen the friction at the pivot point. This type of joint has been widely used ever since. With the seismometers of Gray and Ewing available, seismologists in Japan were able to make important advances in the understanding of earthquake motion. John Milne, especially, made extensive use of the new instruments.[5]

It was the need to more precisely measure earthquakes that led to the development of the seismometer, which has an ancient lineage going back to 132 AD when Zhang Heng, a talented Chinese astronomer, mathematician, artist, scholar and poet, invented a seismoscope and the odometer. His seismoscope had bronze balls in the mouths of eight dragons on the outside of a vase-like instrument. When an earthquake occurred, it would dislodge one or more balls, causing it to fall into the mouth of a bronze toad, which gave out a sound, letting observers know that an earthquake had occurred. Depending on which balls fell, and how many, estimates could be made of the strength and direction of the earthquake.

This was where the technology remained until 1875 when Italian Filippo Cecchi invented a seismometer in Moncalieri, which recorded the Bussana earthquake on 23 February 1887.

Meanwhile, independently in Tokyo, three British scientists, two of whom were Scottish, were also working on developing a seismometer. Credit is usually given to John Milne for the invention of the seismometer, which was a damped horizontal pendulum seismograph that could record earthquakes, unlike that of Zhang Heng's device. John Milne is sometimes assumed to be of Scottish descent because of his surname, but his ancestry is totally English, from near Rochdale in Lancashire. The other two were Scots: Thomas Lomar Gray, who hailed from Lochgelly in Fife, and James Alfred Ewing from Dundee. Their seismometer was developed by all three men and, despite the fact that Cecchi established a seismology centre at Osservatorio Ximeniano in Florence, it is generally accepted that it was the trio's work in Japan that was the foundation of modern seismology, so important to the inhabitants of earthquake- and tsunami-prone areas. Perhaps Cecchi was unfortunate in that the other three worked in Japan within the far more geologically active Pacific Rim.

James Ewing's involvement in developing modern seismology started in 1878 when he was appointed Professor of Mechanical Engineering and Physics at the Imperial University of Tokyo. He moved back to Dundee five years later, then on to Cambridge University and, finally, Edinburgh University in 1916. While at Cambridge, he began a training program for naval officers at the behest of the British Admiralty, and he was instrumental in having the Royal Navy adopt the steam turbine to power its warships. Ewing was also responsible for the report into the effectiveness of a proposed steam turbine power station at Cambridge.

His most famous contribution to society, however, took place during the First World War, when he was placed at the head of "Room 40", the British codebreaking operation. Messages decoded by his organisation led to the battles of Jutland and Dogger Bank. They also decoded the "Zimmermann telegram", sent by the German foreign minister to his minister in Mexico, which led to the United States joining the war. The telegram had outlined a policy of encouraging Mexico to join the war in Europe, in return for German assistance in a planned invasion of the United States. Ewing resigned his position in "Room 40" in 1917, because he found it impossible to carry out this job and that of Principal at Edinburgh at the same time.[6]

In experiments on the effect of stress on metals, Ewing found that the thermoelectric effect lagged behind the applied stress. Further investigation showed that the phenomenon, which he termed hysteresis (from Greek, to be late), was general in mechanical and electrical systems where the behaviour of a body during the reversal of stress is different from its behaviour in the corresponding part during the increase of stress. In a careful study of magnetism in 1883, he showed that the work done in a cycle of magnetisation and demagnetisation of iron was proportional to the hysteresis loop. Ewing's work on hysteresis proved fundamental in understanding and preventing energy losses in transformers and electric motors.[7] Hysteresis also has applications in nano-electronics, thermostats and the memory effect of batteries, which was where older style rechargeable batteries that were not fully discharged between charge cycles "remember" the shortened cycle resulting in a reduced recharge.

"The occurrence of fatigue-induced slip bands was noted for the first time, in 1903, by Ewing and J.C.W. Humfrey in their pioneering microscopic study of Swedish iron that had been fatigued in rotating bending."[8] Its effects are of critical importance to manufacturers of products that are subjected to high levels of stress, such as aircraft, rockets, high speed machinery, bridges and tall buildings. Stress and strain result from the application of external forces, with stress being the internal resisting force of an object and strain being the displacement and deformation that results.

James Ballantyne Hannay 1855-1931 created the world's first artificial diamond in 1880. He discovered that supercritical fluids dissolve solids, studied the influence of pressure and temperature, and thus set the stage for the development of the powerful analytical and separation technique of supercritical gas extraction. He proved that the critical state is not the solution of one phase in the other, but that the gas and liquid phases become one, having uniform properties throughout. He invented the time method technique that allows determining the existence and nature of hydrates in simple and complex salts. He was the first to prepare artificial diamonds and studied the toasting of pyrite and how to manufacture lead, its oxides and salts in a state of high purity.[1]

He first sealed a mixture of powdered carbon, bone oil, and paraffin in coiled tubes, and then placed the tubes into a furnace. When the heat and pressure built up sufficiently, the tubes exploded and splattered the furnace walls with white-hot debris. After waiting for the furnace to cool, Hannay carefully scraped a number of minute particles off the surface with tweezers and found that these specks scratched glass – one test of a diamond. Triumphantly, Hannay claimed that he had manufactured diamonds and sent about a dozen specimens to the British Museum of Natural History in London.

At the time, however, most of Hannay's contemporaries doubted that he had, in fact, achieved the synthesis of carbon to diamond crystals. Some scientists argued that he had mis-analysed the crystals that had resulted from his experiments as diamonds, and others openly insinuated that Hannay had himself put the diamonds into the tubes to fraudulently create a reputation for himself. Since the crystals that Hannay claimed were produced through his process were too minute to be used in either jewellery or industrial tools, the issue of whether or not these were authentic diamonds remained a purely academic one.

More than a half century later, however, Hannay's crystals were rediscovered by the British Museum and, under X-ray analysis, proved to be diamonds of an extremely rare variety called "Type II". The fact that Type II diamonds were not generally recovered from mines at the time of Hannay's experiments indicated that he had indeed manufactured them.[2]

George Johnston 1855-1945 began designing his own automobile engine and, with the help of two other engineers, in 1895, he was the first person to build a motor car in Britain.

Image 84 – Arrol-Johnston 20 HP Limousine, Baujahr 1904

Not that anybody would have recognised the name: it was known as either a "Benzoline" or petrol "dog cart" and was driven for the first time in November 1895 at 12 miles an hour (19.3 km/h) on a 20-mile (32 km) trip across Glasgow.[1] An Arrol-Johnston car, driven by John Napier, won the first Isle of Man Tourist Trophy race in 1905. The Company entered a works team at a French Grand Prix meeting, developed the world's first "off-road" vehicle for the Egyptian government, and another vehicle designed to travel on ice and snow for Ernest Shackleton's Nimrod Expedition to the South Pole in 1908-1909, which was also the first vehicle to drive in the Antarctic.

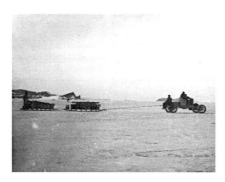

Image 85 – Arrol-Johnston automobile in the Antarctic 1908 Shackleton's Nimrod Expedition

The inclusion of the Arrol-Johnston came not solely due to its air-cooled engine and thus its ability to start and run in extremely cold temperatures. Rather, industrialist Sir William Beardmore (later Lord Invernairn), who financed Shackleton's Nimrod expedition, had recently purchased Arrol-Johnston and sent the car with Shackleton as a sort of publicity stunt. It was a specially built car, featuring a four-cylinder 12-15 hp Simms engine, a coalscuttle hood, and two sets of wheels – one that mounted wooden tyres and another that mounted Dunlop pneumatics. (Other sources mention a third set of wheels fitted with solid rubber tyres, cogged in the back). Its exhaust pipe was routed to travel to the carburettor, under the floor to act as a footwarmer, then through a tank used for melting snow for cooking. Shackleton was quoted as believing that the Arrol-Johnston might make it to the pole, but it proved unable to negotiate the deep snow on either set of tyres and only came within 150 kilometres of the pole.[2]

William McNab 1855-1923 was an engineer in Canada who constructed the International Bridge (Fort Erie to Buffalo), the Lewiston and Auburn Railroad (Maine), Union Station (Toronto), and the ferry docks at Point Edward, Ontario. From 1875-1885, he was exclusively engaged in the Grand Trunk Railway surveys, including those between Scarborough and Toronto; the York Yard; lines in Michigan, Ontario, and Quebec; Terminal Station, Montreal; and the Victoria iron tubular bridge across the St. Lawrence River at Montreal.[1]

Peter Burt 1856-1944 "was very much the Victorian inventor, inventing and manufacturing such things as washing machines, mangles, perambulators, stoves, mincing machines and even ice cream freezers, though it was the Acme clothes wringer that earned the company a deserved reputation. It was called 'the wringer of the age'". The patent files of the Acme Company bulged with every type of invention. Another specialty of note is the "Rustic" baby carriage, made in deal, birch, pine, maple, walnut, and mahogany bodies. The "Acme" perambulator was steel bodied and upholstered.[1]

Burt designed the Acme clothes wringer, a hand-turned device with a pair of reversible rubber rollers used to remove water from household washing before hanging it up to dry. It became ubiquitous until superseded by electric washing machines. He built the first engine to run on blast furnace gas. Unfortunately, steel masters in Britain were not interested in this initiative and it was left to engineers in Belgium and Germany to develop it as a viable proposition. Soon after that, in Belfast, he designed and built one of the first generating stations driven by a gas engine.[2]

John Matthews, head of Argyll Ltd, a Scottish automobile manufacturer, was shown a model of a new engine he had designed, which he hoped would revolutionise the motor car. Argyll, like many other manufacturers, had been testing a number of different types of engine. Their aim was to find a silent, vibrationless engine with sufficient torque to reduce awkward gear changing to the minimum. The Peter Burt engine appeared to be far more advanced and sophisticated than Daimler's and other manufacturers' designs.[3]

Burt's engine used a single sleeve valve that he had patented. It was put into production by Argyll for its cars and was later used in aircraft engines of the 1940s, such as the Napier *Sabre*, Bristol *Hercules* and Bristol *Centaurus*. Mechanically simpler and more rugged, Burt's single sleeve valve had the additional advantage of reducing oil consumption (compared to other sleeve valve designs), while retaining the rational combustion chambers and big, uncluttered, porting area possible in the Knight system.

William Kinninmond Burton 1856-1899, was made Professor of Sanitary Engineering and Lecturer on Rivers, Docks and Harbours in 1877 at the Imperial University of Japan in Tokyo, where he designed a modern water supply and sewage system for the capital and other Japanese cities. He had to overcome the local reliance on the traditional toilet – Benjo – which had a hole going through the outer wall of the house for expelling human excrement that was collected on a regular basis for agricultural fertiliser. Persevering, Burton built sand-filtered water systems in Tokyo and 23 other cities and towns to his plans, and these were instrumental in eradicating cholera from urban areas where some 110,000 people a year died from the disease, plus many more who died of dysentery.

He built the first skyscraper in Japan – Ryounkaku – which stood twelve stories high at 67 m and was octagonally shaped[1] (the building's two electric elevators – Japan's first – were designed by Ichisuke Fujioka, a founder of Toshiba). Burton also recommended that the first floor of buildings should be raised off the ground and this was put into practice both in Japan and Taiwan, which at that time was part of the Japanese Empire.[2]

He was an early promoter of photography and founding member of the Japan Photographic Society, the country's first for amateurs. Ironically, having saved hundreds of thousands of lives from disease, he died at the young age of 43 from a fever. In Scotland, he is virtually unknown, although his childhood pal, Arthur Conan Doyle, dedicated his book *The Firm of Girdlestone* to "my old friend" William K Burton and "in Japan he is revered as the foreign engineer who saved the country from cholera" with his sand-filtered water system.[3]

Cargill Gilston Knott 1856-1922 spent eight years in Japan as a seismologist and was Professor of Physics and Engineering at Tokyo Imperial University for nine years from 1883.

Knott, with Milne, Gray and the Japanese seismologist Fusakichi Omori established a network of recording seismometers across the Japanese Empire. From this, the team was able to locate the time and place where earthquakes occurred, using only the recordings made at remote seismological observatories.

Knott's key contribution to the pioneering group of seismologists in Tokyo was to supplement their skills as instrument makers by his own flair for mathematics and data analysis. One of his innovations was to apply the technique of Fourier analysis to the occurrence of earthquakes. (Fourier analysis seeks to break down a pattern, like the pattern of when earthquakes occur, into components with different recurrence periods). He looked for daily, monthly, seasonal, annual, and astronomical periodicities. Two whole chapters in his 1908 book *The Physics of Earthquake Phenomena* were devoted to this subject, hoping that he would be able to deduce something about the probability of when earthquakes occur. We know now that earthquakes do not recur in regular periods, but Knott's legacy in Japan bore interesting fruit half a century later.

Knott spent more than eight years in Japan busying himself with seismology. But he also expanded his interests to other parts of what we would now call geophysics: he trained local people and introduced geomagnetic surveying to Japan, undertaking a survey of the whole country in only three months. For this, the Emperor awarded him the Order of the Rising Sun in 1891.

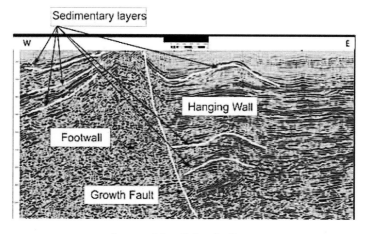

Image 86 – Seismic line
E-W seismic line at Svalbard area showing footwall, hanging wall and the geometry of sedimentary layers around the fault plane. Such images use properties worked out by Knott in 1899 of how strongly seismic waves reflect at the boundary between two different materials.

Fourier analysis is now a very widely used tool, and is applied in analysing all sorts of time-series and even spatial patterns. The Imperial Earthquake Research Institute in Tokyo remained a bastion of civil science in Japan in the middle parts of the 20th century: there, in 1940, Chuji Tsuboi pioneered the use of Fourier analysis to determine the thickness of lithospheric plates, nearly three decades before Plate Tectonics was first described; and, in 1941, Takesi Nagata used Fourier methods to describe the magnetic effect of Mount Fuji. Neither application re-appeared until the 1970s.

In Japan, Knott also began to develop the mathematical description of how seismic vibrations are reflected and transmitted across the boundary between sea-water and the rocks of the sea bed. After returning to become Lecturer in Physics at Edinburgh University in 1892, he was able to extend this description to include the behaviour of earthquake vibrations or waves at the interface between two different rock types. The Knott equations are now the basis for many new developments in seismology, including modern seismic exploration tools for petroleum gas and oil.[1]

Andrew Laing 1856-1931 was a marine engineer who became a director of the Fairfield Shipbuilding and Engineering Company. He was responsible for the engines of a number of Cunard liners, as well as warships, Castle liners, and Norddeutscher Lloyd vessels. Under Laing, the engine and boiler works were redeveloped, and the company he served remained at the forefront of technical innovation. He then removed to Tyneside as the manager of the engine works of the Wallsend Slipway and Engineering Company, in 1896, where his first important design was the machinery for the Russian icebreaker *Ermak*, the first true icebreaker,[1] and in 1900, the company secured its first Admiralty contract. He won the contract for the *Mauretania* – the largest and fastest ship in the world. It was of such a scale that it precipitated a reorganisation of the industry on Tyneside. The merged company of Swan, Hunter, and Wigham Richardson Ltd took a controlling interest in the Wallsend Slipway and Engineering Company, which built the quadruple-screw turbine propelling machinery for the giant liner.

During the First World War, the company engined 68 vessels of all types, including the battleships *Queen Elizabeth* and *Malaya*. The need to improve engine performance led Laing to develop the Wallsend-Howden system of oil firing, which began manufacture in 1909.

Laing eventually became a director of Swan, Hunter as well as of the Newcastle and Gateshead Gas Company. At his death, Laing and his close contemporary Charles Parsons were considered to be on a par, "as being the two greatest marine engineers in the world".[2]

John Stewart MacArthur 1856-1920 introduced the "cyanide process" for the commercial extraction of gold from its ores. By 1888, he was advocating a treatment scheme in which gold was dissolved from crushed rock by a dilute solution of alkali cyanide and then precipitated onto finely divided zinc. During the next few years, with several assistants, he was extremely active in promoting the new gold-extraction technique in various parts of the world.[1]

With the invention of the cyanide process, the use of the mercury amalgamation technique was practically discontinued. The world's gold-mining industry was stagnating, refining only about 45% of metal from complex ores: the new process enabled 98% extraction, and was hailed as the saviour of the industry. However, in 1896, the South African mining bureaucracy took MacArthur through the courts to prove an esoteric weakness in the patent, which allowed them to avoid royalty payments to the man who had rejuvenated their industry. A century later, however, MacArthur was still given credit in South Africa for his contribution to that country's economy. He continued to introduce his process throughout the world, travelling abroad extensively. He also took an interest in cyanide production and in refining processes for copper and antimony.

In 1911, MacArthur concentrated on radium refining on an industrial scale, initially in Runcorn in Cheshire, and from 1915, until his death, in Balloch on Loch Lomond. This pioneering, dangerous, and chemically intensive work was as significant as that on gold, most work on radium being at that time confined to the laboratory. He was the first gold medal winner (1902) of the Institution of Mining and Metallurgy, his obituary in *Nature* noting: "It is given to few men to discover a process which has had such a far-reaching effect in almost every branch of civilised life".[2]

Joseph John Thomson 1856-1940 discovered the electron and his work led to the invention of the mass spectrometer. He was awarded a Nobel Prize in 1906, "in recognition of the great merits of his theoretical and experimental investigations on the conduction of electricity by gases."[1]

In 1897, Thomson demonstrated that cathode rays were actually units of electrical current made up of negatively charged particles of subatomic size. He believed them to be an integral part of all matter and theorised a model of atomic structure in which a quantity of negatively charged electrons was embedded in a sphere of positive electricity, the two charges neutralising each other.[2] Thomson interpreted the deflection of the rays by electrically charged plates and magnets as evidence of "bodies much smaller than atoms" that he calculated as having a very large value for the charge-to-mass ratio. Later he estimated the value of the charge itself.[3]

By the turn of the century, most of the scientific world had fully accepted Thomson's far-reaching discovery. In 1903, he had the opportunity to amplify his views on the behaviour of subatomic particles in natural phenomena when, in his Silliman Lectures at Yale, he suggested a discontinuous theory of light; his hypothesis foreshadowed Einstein's later theory of photons.[4]

Thomson developed a mathematical theory of electricity and magnetism, and discovered a method for separating different kinds of atoms and molecules by the use of positive rays, an idea developed by Francis William Aston, Arthur Jeffrey Dempster and others, towards the discovery of many isotopes.[5] This arose from his investigations into the action of electrostatic and magnetic fields on the nature of so called "anode rays" or "canal rays" and resulted in the invention of the mass spectrometer (then called a parabola spectrograph) by Aston, a tool which allows the determination of the mass-to-charge ratio of ions and which has since become a ubiquitous research tool in chemistry.[6] It was this discovery that, in 1912, helped Thomson prove the existence of isotopes of neon.

Thomson was also responsible for establishing the Cavendish Laboratory as a leading research centre for subatomic physics. His works include *Elements of the Mathematical Theory of Electricity and Magnetism* (1895) and *Conduction of Electricity through Gases* (1903). From 1915 to 1920 he served as president of the Royal Society.[7]

Thomson was foremost a brilliant teacher and he trained seven Nobel Prize winners and 27 Fellows of the Royal Society. His achievements were honoured in numerous ways, and mark him as among the most accomplished physicists of his era.[8]

To a large extent, it was Thomson who made atomic physics a modern science. The studies of nuclear organisation that continue even to this day and the further identification of elementary particles all followed his most outstanding accomplishment – his discovery of the electron in 1897.[9]

Edward Gustavus Campbell Barton 1857-1942 was an electrical engineer who superintended the first commercial electric-lighting system in Britain at Godalming, Surrey. He showed vision and versatility in successfully pioneering the Australian state of Queensland's electricity-supply industry and, in 1901, he installed the first steam turbine in that state.[1]

Williamina Paton Stevens Fleming 1857-1911 was first to discover white dwarf stars. She devised a system of classifying stars according to their spectra, a distinctive pattern produced by each star when its light is passed through a prism.[1] She developed an empirical star classification scheme consisting of 17 categories (a huge advance upon Italian astronomer Angelo Secchi's seminal scheme of five categories) and went on to classify 10,351 stars based on their photographed spectra. Her work, published as a catalogue in 1890, was further refined by Annie Jump Cannon. While engaged in her monumental task, Fleming discovered 10 novae, about 60 new nebulae, and more than 300 variable stars.[2] This work was published in 1890 in a book titled *Draper Catalogue of Stellar Spectra*.[3]

In 1906, she was the first American woman elected to the Royal Astronomical Society. In 1907, she published a study of 222 variable stars she had discovered. A British astronomer made the following observation: "Many astronomers are deservedly proud to have discovered one variable [star] the discovery of 222 is an achievement bordering on the marvellous." Her achievement is especially noteworthy when one takes into account that she had no formal higher education. In 1910, she published her discovery of white dwarfs, stars that are very hot and dense and appear bluish or white in colour. White dwarfs are believed to be stars in a final stage of their existence.[4]

John Charles Barron Jarvis 1857-1935 invented the brace winch in 1890. This machine was used to brace the yards and consisted of two symmetrical cones (made of metal segments), on which the steel braces for the lower yards are rolled (usually main and top gallant). Note: The braces are the ropes used to orientate the yards according to the direction the wind is blowing. A yard is a spar on a mast from which sails are set.

By turning the winch, the braces roll on one side and unroll on the other side at the same time. This allows two or four men to brace the yards (i.e. orientate them), which is much more efficient than having a dozen or so crew members pulling the braces in the previous manner.[1]

Other inventions made by Jarvis are the patent leech lines which checked the sails when furling so that they would not blow back, and the sail furling gaskets secured to double jackstays.[2]

John Lundie 1857-1931 patented the concrete mixer (12 July 1887), stating that his machine deals with four cardinal points: 1st That every motion of the machine should do some useful work. Hitherto box or barrel mixers have gone on the principle of throwing the material about indiscriminately, expecting that somehow or other it would get mixed. 2nd That the sticking of the material anywhere within the mixer should be obviated. 3rd That an easy discharge should be obtained. 4th That the water should be introduced while the mixer revolves.[1] He was also largely responsible for the suburban electrification of the Illinois Central Line.

John Macintyre 1857-1928 set up the first medical X-ray department in the world in Glasgow Royal Infirmary in March 1896.[1] Macintyre was appointed surgeon in charge of the Glasgow Royal Infirmary's ear, nose and throat (ENT) department. He always considered himself to be an ENT surgeon with an interest in X-rays, which meant that the infirmary was in a unique position to exploit the discovery of X-rays by Röntgen in November 1895. After Wilhelm Röntgen announced his discovery of short-wave electro-magnetic radiation, Macintyre and compatriot Archibald Fauld set up X-Ray apparatus in Macintyre's laboratory and succeeded in photographing the bones of Macintyre's hand.[2]

The first report of X-rays of the larynx was published by Macintyre in 1896. In the same year, Macintyre opined that fluoroscopy would likely be more useful in assessing the larynx than radiographs.[3] He subsequently had many other "firsts": an X-ray of a kidney stone, a halfpenny coin in the gullet of a child, and, most spectacular, a "cineradiogram" showing movements of a frog's legs.[4] In April 1897, he showed the motion of a frog's limbs, which he manipulated mechanically and illuminated with a Crookes tube. His camera was protected by lead foil, the lens removed and replaced with a lead diaphragm with a small aperture. He then filmed the X-rays directly as they passed through the frog's body (a subject chosen for its flatness and thin skin, requiring only a low exposure), and showed the film to his audience in loop-form.[5]

On the lead up to this event, Macintyre had been experimenting for some time on the best methods of obtaining rapid exposures with a view to recording movements of organs within the body. A method using an ordinary camera to photograph the images on a fluorescent screen was too slow. The successful method involved a sensitive film passing underneath the aperture in a case of thick lead covering the cinematograph. This opening corresponded to the size of the picture, and was covered with a piece of black paper, upon which the limb of the animal, such as a frog, could be photographed. It was necessary for the movements to be slow and therefore a slow anaesthesia was required. Macintyre was reported at a meeting of the Glasgow Philosophical Society to have moved a film 40 feet (12 m) in length through the cinematograph. The movements of the frog's leg could be clearly seen when demonstrated on a magic lantern screen by means of the cinematograph.[6] He was also one of the first to apply X-rays to diagnosis; in that same month, he took a photograph which located a needle in a woman's hand.

Shortly after Röntgen's discovery of X-rays, this news was flashed around the world. While most read of the discovery in the newspapers, Röntgen sent copies of his scientific paper to only two people in Britain: Lord Kelvin in Glasgow, for whom he had the highest esteem, and Professor Arthur Shuster in Manchester. Kelvin passed his copy to Macintyre, "Medical Electrician" at the Glasgow Royal Infirmary. Like many others – physicists, electrical engineers, and doctors – in those early hectic days, and perhaps the most energetic of all the medical pioneers, Macintyre quickly grasped the significance of this "new light" as it was then known. His X-ray department was up and running by March 1896.[7]

Just five months after X-rays were first discovered, Röntgen wrote to Macintyre for details of his technique for X-raying soft tissues. Macintyre probably did not produce the first medical radiograph in Britain: this is attributed to another Scot, Alan Archibald Campbell Swinton, electrician and photographer in London, who also gave the first public demonstration of X-rays to the Royal Photographic Society in February 1896. "Who did what and where with X-rays from 1896 onwards remains the subject of debate. Macintyre certainly produced among the first, if not the first, radiographs of a bullet, thorax, abdomen, and breast cancer. And the first movie was definitely his."[8]

Those "firsts" included an X-ray of a kidney stone and Macintyre persuaded the Glasgow Royal Infirmary's managers to further expand his electrical department and to include an X-ray unit in February 1896. He then moved his experiments from Bath Street to the hospital. During the first four years after establishment of his department, Macintyre executed more than 3,000 radiological examinations. In addition to the mainly unfavourable working conditions which existed in the cold and humid rooms, this work had to be performed single-handed by a single person; it was only the physician who took the radiograph, developed it, maintained the machinery, and performed the medical evaluation of the X-ray.

Macintyre had published 18 papers on the new field of radiology by the end of 1896, within a year of the discovery of X-rays.[9] He produced the first instantaneous X-ray (with the fluorescent screen cryptoscope which he believed would ultimately replace photographs); the first X-ray: of a renal stone; of the spine; of the interior of the cranium; the heart, lung, and contents of the middle intestine; and of a foreign body in the oesophagus – a halfpenny coin in the gullet of a child.

He was quick to realise the potential harmful effects of exposure and insisted on protection for himself and his staff. By the end of the 19th century, he was using X-rays therapeutically on tumours, and his first published paper on this was in 1902, *Recent electro-therapeutic work in medicine and surgery*.[10]

Macintyre was elected president of the British Laryngological and Rhinological Association for a second time in 1900, and in 1901 he became president of the Röntgen Society.[11]

Robert William Philip 1857-1939 founded the Victoria Dispensary for Consumption, the first of its kind in the world.[1] Tuberculosis, also known as "consumption", "phthisis", or the "white plague", was the cause of more deaths in industrialised countries than any other disease during the 19th and early 20th centuries. By the late 19th century, 70-90% of the urban populations of Europe and North America were infected with the TB bacillus, and about 80% of those individuals who developed active tuberculosis died of it.[2]

Philip graduated MD at Edinburgh in 1882, the year Robert Koch discovered the tubercle bacillus. Originally intending to become a gynaecologist, Philip made a career-changing decision when he saw the possibility of controlling the infection of tuberculosis. Tuberculosis caused one-ninth of all deaths in the UK at the time, heading the mortality tables in 1907 with 77,850 of a total of 678,851.[3] Some estimates placed the figure for tuberculosis mortality at one-seventh of all deaths in Europe and North America.[4]

In 1887, Philip founded the Victoria Dispensary for Consumption in a small flat in Bank Street, Edinburgh. The Dispensary system was to become the keystone in the fight against tuberculosis in the UK, and eventually, throughout the world. Earlier, in 1863, German physician Hermann Brehmer had established the first German sanatorium for the systematic open-air treatment of tuberculosis. This was the *Brehmerschen Heilanstalt für Lungenkranke*, a hospital in Görbersdorf where patients were exposed to plentiful amounts of high-altitude fresh air, and good nutrition. Initially, his sanatorium was based in a small group of cottages, though it would grow to have 300 beds. The results surpassed all previous treatments.[5]

Philip knew that most consumptive patients could not afford the cost or time in a sanatorium which, in any case, did little to help reduce the incidence of the disease. The program Philip initiated included home visiting, health education, and an occupational farm colony for patients. This pioneer endeavour was followed in 1898 by the organisation of the National Association for the Prevention of Consumption and Other Forms of Tuberculosis for the purpose of preventing the ravages of the disease in Great Britain. Its objectives were to educate the public concerning the propagation and prevention of tuberculosis, to influence Parliament and other public bodies in matters relating to the prevention of the disease, and to establish branches of the Association to stimulate action on a local level.[6]

He established the first ever herd of TB-tested cattle on a farm at Gracemount, south-east of Edinburgh. Philip did not wait for the *Milk and Dairies (Scotland) Act 1914* legislation to come into effect – it had been passed but put on hold due to the outbreak of the First World War. He decided to demonstrate in advance to the public and to the farming community alike that tubercle-free milk of the highest grade of purity could be marketed, not as a subsidised project, but as a strictly run commercial proposition. In this he was, as ever, loyally supported by the Royal Victoria Hospital Tuberculosis Trust. The Gracemount Farm Scheme was begun, and in it Philip and the Trust were aided successively by the practical knowledge of Dr J.C. Simpson and of John Johnstone. The plan was a great success, and there can be no doubt that much of the progress made since that time has been due to the bold experiment Philip began in 1922. At that time, half the milk in the country came from cows which were infected with the tubercle bacillus. By 1957, only 2% of the milk produced in registered dairy farms was not guaranteed to be tubercle-free.[7]

His method of treatment became known through the world as the Edinburgh System. He fought hard to make TB a notifiable disease and championed the use of the French-developed drug BCG (Bacillus Calmette-Guérin) for 16 years before Britain took it up. The fact that it is no longer possible to pick up a TB sufferer at random in a British high street is due in large part to Philip.[8]

Philip made his greatest advance in tuberculosis control by making the dispensary the base of operations directed at the patient's home. He pioneered the concept of Tuberculosis Health Visitors when he appointed Miss Craig and Miss McKerrow in 1887. They investigated and supervised the home conditions of the patient, and completed an itemised questionnaire of 40 factors including: Number of windows? Can they open? How is washing of clothes done? And, Approximate income of household?[9]

His revolutionary treatment included putting measures in place to ensure contact tracing for the very first time, whereby the illness could be tracked and measures taken to avoid further contamination. Philip propounded to his teachers a new doctrine. Clinical examination and what then passed for treatment were not enough. All relevant information should be gathered in what he called a "directory of tuberculosis". An account of the patient's environment must be recorded and, where possible, defects corrected. The patient should be taught, since he was the subject of an infective disease, how to prevent the infection spreading to others. All those in contact with the patient should be examined. Advice for the guidance not only of the sufferer but for the whole family should be issued. These new ideas did not commend themselves to his teachers, and he met much passive and even active opposition.[10]

Philip's teaching was that "we cannot wait for patients to present themselves at out-patient departments. We must search them out in their hiding-places" (Philip, 1909). This became the principal burden of dispensary practice, and especially of contact examination. Two special methods of case-finding have, however, been developed, one of which was a method developed by Philip, who recommended regular tuberculin tests from infancy onwards. The child reactor became not only himself the subject of clinical interest but also the index case in the search for tuberculosis among family contacts. Once again, Philip was ahead of his time. That particular method of case-finding could hardly be said to be of practical service in a country where 80% of the children aged 15 showed a positive tuberculin test. The method was more appropriate where there was a lower level of infection. The first major demonstration of this procedure was carried out in Cyprus. It was inspired by Philip and sponsored by the National Association for the Prevention of Tuberculosis, of which Philip was a founder member and for so many years Chairman of Council.[11]

Fifty years later it was said, "The principles thus laid down [by Philip], although based on hardly a vestige of past experience or precedent, have served without essential change as the basis of all effective tuberculosis work since that day."[12]

Philip served as secretary to the Royal College of Physicians of Edinburgh in 1894 and president from 1918 to 1923, president of the British Medical Association in 1927, and president of the Association of Physicians of Great Britain and Ireland in 1937-1938.

Ronald Ross 1857-1932 showed, in 1898, that malaria can be transmitted from infected mosquitoes as they bite healthy hosts. This discovery laid to rest centuries of belief in miasma (the stench from decaying organic matter) as the cause of this debilitating and killing disease.

Earlier, in 1880, Frenchman Charles Louis Alphonse Laveran, then an army doctor in Algeria, observed a motile parasite in blood from a malaria patient. What he saw was the parasite's flagellum form, later identified by others as the male gamete. Despite Laveran's flagellum discovery, how the malaria plasmodium was communicated to humans remained unknown. In 1876, Patrick Manson, working in China, had discovered that the parasite of filariasis, the disease that causes elephantiasis, was taken from human blood by female mosquitoes and continued its growth within the mosquito's abdomen. Manson believed that the infected female mosquito that "nursed" the parasite died quickly after depositing its larvae in standing water. He also conjectured that the parasite was transmitted to humans through drinking water polluted by infected mosquitoes, which he and others at the time believed to be short-lived.[1]

Two decades of research had produced further data on malarial organisms' characteristics, its means of reproduction, and its correlation with disease symptoms, but no one had determined how the disease was transmitted from one person to another. Ross returned to India, where he was frustrated by working conditions, especially the lack of support from his superiors and the primitive equipment available to him, but with Manson's constant letters of support and encouragement, he eventually succeeded. He experimented with birds that were sick with malaria. While in Secunderabad, Ross dissected anopheline mosquitoes which had fed on a malarious patient called Husein Khan on 16 August 1897 ((Khan was paid 1 anna per mosquito he was bitten by; he came away with 10 annas).[2]

Over the next five days, Ross dissected the mosquitoes. On 19 August, he identified some "peculiar vacuolated cells" on the stomach of the mosquito. On the 20th he dissected another mosquito, and found many of these cells on the stomach wall of the mosquito. He concluded that these were the malaria parasite stages in the mosquito (oocysts). The significance of this is that until then, no-one had any idea of how parasites in the blood of malarious patients were transmitted via mosquitoes. There were many theories – for example that infected water carried the parasite from drowned mosquitoes into people when they drank it. Further experiments by Ross showed that the oocysts contained sporozoites, which later on appeared in the salivary glands, and that these salivary gland parasites were able to produce malaria infection (in this case, of birds). This discovery suggested how the disease was transmitted to humans and laid foundations for combating the disease.

Some months later, Ross was able to study the parasite life cycle in caged birds and demonstrate that malaria could be transmitted from infected to healthy birds. This proved beyond doubt that malaria was not contracted from air or water but was an infectious disease transmitted from man to man by mosquito bites. Since Giovanni Battista Grassi and his Italian colleagues had worked on the life cycle of the human malarial parasite, a bitter controversy erupted on the question of who had discovered the cause of malaria first. The award of the Nobel Prize to Ross in 1902 settled much of the debate.[3]

While Ross is remembered for his malaria work, this remarkable man was also a mathematician, epidemiologist, sanitarian, editor, novelist, dramatist, poet, and an amateur musician, composer and artist.

During his active career, Ross's interest lay mainly in the initiation of measures for the prevention of malaria in different countries of the world. He carried out surveys and initiated schemes in many places, including West Africa, the Suez Canal Zone, Greece, Mauritius, Cyprus, and in the areas affected by the 1914-1918 war. He also initiated organisations, which have proved to be well established, for the prevention of malaria within the planting industries of India and Ceylon. He made many contributions to the epidemiology of malaria and to methods of its survey and assessment, but perhaps his greatest was the development of mathematical models for the study of its epidemiology, initiated in his report on Mauritius in 1908, elaborated in his *Prevention of Malaria* in 1911 and further elaborated in a more generalised form in scientific papers published by the Royal Society in 1915 and 1916. These papers represented a profound mathematical interest which was not confined to epidemiology, but led him to make material contributions to both pure and applied mathematics. Those related to "pathometry" are best known and, 40 years later, constitute the basis of much of the epidemiological understanding of insect-borne diseases.[4]

The work of Ross was further developed by **George Macdonald 1903-1967**, and both are credited with developing a mathematical model of mosquito-borne pathogen transmission. A systematic historical review suggests that several mathematicians and scientists contributed to the development of the Ross-Macdonald model over a period of 70 years. Ross developed two different mathematical models, Macdonald a third, and various "Ross-Macdonald" mathematical models exist. Ross-Macdonald models are best defined by a consensus set of assumptions. The mathematical model is just one part of a theory for the dynamics and control of mosquito-transmitted pathogens that also includes epidemiological and entomological concepts and metrics for measuring transmission. All the basic elements of the theory had fallen into place by the end of the Global Malaria Eradication Programme (GMEP, 1955-1969) with the concept of vectorial capacity, methods for measuring key components of transmission by mosquitoes, and a quantitative theory of vector control. The Ross-Macdonald theory has since played a central role in development of research on mosquito-borne pathogen transmission and the development of strategies for mosquito-borne disease prevention.[5]

In 1940, the War Office appointed MacDonald, who had worked with Ross in Ceylon, to form and command successively Nos. 1, 2, and 3 Malaria Field Laboratories in the Middle East and central Mediterranean, and it was claimed that the low incidence of malaria among the British troops was the result of his influence.

By explaining the complex life history of the malarial parasite, Ross made it possible to understand aspects of the problems of malarial fevers that had confounded physicians and scientists for hundreds of years. Millions of people throughout the world suffered from malaria during Ross' time, and many areas were virtually uninhabitable because of malarial fevers. Moreover, his work made it possible for scientists to discover the role of insect vectors in the transmission of many other diseases.

Thomas Stewart 1857-1942 was a hydraulic engineer in Cape Colony, based in Cape Town, where he designed and built the Cradock and Wynberg waterworks. In 1892, he began a private practice in Cape Town designing and constructing five reservoirs on Table Mountain – Woodhead, Hely-Hutchinson, Alexandra, Victoria, and De Villiers.[1]

The Woodhead Reservoir, built on the top of Table Mountain, presented a logistical challenge. He built a cableway up Kasteels Poort from Victoria Road, Camps Bay, to transport to the summit men and materials – including heavy casks of cement imported from Scotland – which were then pulled by mule power along rail tracks to the dam site. Stewart and his workforce lived on the mountain for three years. The dam, completed in 1897, is an elegant structure of rubble masonry faced with dressed stone. It has survived more than 100 years, although it was latterly strengthened as a precautionary measure.

Stewart built reservoirs at Constantia Nek, Silvermine, Simons Town, and a water treatment works at Wynberg, the first municipal sewage treatment works in South Africa. He designed Zuurbekom Waterworks for Johannesburg and water supplies for many small towns including Bloemfontein, Oudtshoorn, Worcester, Stellenbosch, Beira and Riversdale.[2]

Stewart, with W.A. Tait (a Scottish water supply specialist) and David Ernest Lloyd-Davies, formed the Board of Engineers responsible for the design of the Steenbras Dam and delivery pipeline. "The Water Supply Report, submitted to the Suburban Joint Water and Drainage Committee of Cape Town by Mr Thomas Stewart, dated 23 January 1906, indicated the Key Plan for water supply to the southern suburbs. This plan included the Wemmershoek Dam (construction completed in 1957), the Steenbras Dam Water Scheme (inaugurated in 1921) and the Berg River Hoek/Warm Berg water scheme (the Schaufraam Dam), which is part of the Berg Water Project."[3]

John Alexander Brodie 1858-1934 was an engineer and town planner who was appointed City Engineer for Liverpool in 1898. He was one of the first to suggest the installation of an electric tram system for Liverpool and the development of the world's first ring road, Queens Drive, linking the city's outlying districts (the idea came from Scottish engineer James Newlands, who preceded Brodie as City Engineer). Brodie also put forward the scheme for building the East Lancashire Road.

Brodie experimented with using large-panel, reinforced pre-cast concrete as a solution to housing shortages. This led in 1905, in Eldon Street, to the construction of the first tenements made from a prefabricated material. "The world's first prefabricated, pre-cast panelled apartment blocks were pioneered in Liverpool. A process was invented by city engineer John Alexander Brodie, whose inventive genius also had him inventing the football goal net. The tram stables at Walton in Liverpool followed in 1906. The idea was not extensively adopted in Britain; however, it was widely adopted elsewhere, particularly in Eastern Europe."[1] In the same year, he designed and exhibited a pre-cast concrete cottage at the "Cheap Cottages Exhibition" in Letchworth. This was reported in the press worldwide, including in Germany and America. The technique influenced the New York architect Grosvenor Atterbury in particular.

As well as Brodie's new ideas in road building and housing, he became an expert in the field of town planning. International recognition came in 1912 when he was invited to help with the selection of the site and the planning of the new capital of India at Delhi.

Brodie also had a major impact on the most popular team sport in the world – association football – when he invented goal nets. He tested his invention out for the first time at Stanley Park and patented it in 1890, with the Football League agreeing to adopt them in all matches in September 1891.

Archibald Byron Macallum 1858-1934 reported, in 1888, the discovery of the origin of haemoglobin from the nuclear chromatin in embryonic red cells. In 1892, he demonstrated the presence of "masked iron" in the chromatin of every cell, and proposed the generalisation that as haemoglobin is derived from chromatin, the latter must have respiratory powers. Between 1898 and 1908, he demonstrated by microchemical methods the exact localisation in cells, animal and vegetable, of calcium, potassium, chlorine and phosphoric acid, and presented the results he had obtained in communications to The Royal Society of London. This was followed by a demonstration of the relation of potassium to adsorption in the cell. After this, Macallum carried out an investigation on the relation between the inorganic salts of sea water and those in the tissues of jelly fishes, which led to a formulation of the origin of the salts in the blood plasma of vertebrates. In the lower marine invertebrates, which have a circulation not closed off from the sea water, the circulatory fluid is sea water. In those invertebrates with a closed circulation, which have been denizens of the sea since the Silurian period, the circulatory fluid is practically sea water of today.

In vertebrates, the inorganic salts of the blood are in a concentration less than one third of the concentration of those same elements of the sea water of today, but by ranging the concentration of the sodium, potassium, calcium and magnesium in ratios, with sodium as 100, there was revealed a similarity to sea water, with the same elements, except in regard to magnesium. From this followed the generalisation that the salts of the blood plasma in their concentration are those of the sea water of the Cambrian or Silurian period. In that age, the concentration of the salts in the sea must have been less than one-third of what it is in the ocean of the present day, and also the proportion of magnesium was greatly less than it is now. The factor in maintaining this ancient ocean concentration in the blood plasma is to be found in the kidneys of vertebrates which rigidly control the inorganic composition of the blood plasma. The kidneys have rendered it possible for vertebrates to change their environment without changing the inorganic composition of their blood, whereas amongst invertebrates, such a maintenance of uniformity in the blood plasma is not possible, and, consequently, a high degree of evolution amongst invertebrates is possible. This led to a study of the inorganic composition of the living cell, and it was found that the proportions of the elements, sodium, potassium, calcium and magnesium, are utterly unlike those found in the blood plasma.

Hence the conclusion that the organic composition of the cell harks back to a more remote geological age, to a time when the organism was unicellular, and when there diffused into it the salts of its environment. On the other hand, the animal cell represents in its organic composition the sea water of a period much earlier than the Cambrian. Therefore, it may be stated that in the blood plasma, we meet with sea water of the Cambrian period, and in the cell itself a sea water of a date many millions of years earlier.[1]

Academic historian Sandra McRae sees Macallum as exerting "a profound influence on the growth of scientific medicine at Toronto [University], not least through his support for and exemplification of the research ideal." Most consider that the Department of Biochemistry, at the University of Toronto, was "founded in 1908, when Archibald Macallum switched from the chair of physiological chemistry to the chair of biochemistry." Macallum was thus one of the main champions of scientific medicine in Toronto.[2]

James Philip 1858-1911 saved the North American bison from extinction and was one of the first South Dakotans named to the National Cowboy Hall of Fame.[1] At the end of the 1800s, there were only a few dozen buffalo left alive in the United States. After a failed attempt at finding gold in Dakota's Black Hills, Philip left, but not before he had purchased a herd of 57 bison from Fred Dupree, determined that they should be preserved. He enclosed an area at his ranch, near Pierre, South Dakota and brought the total of bison up to 83 in the first years of this century. The herd came to number as many as 900. In 1906, an act of Congress provided Philip with 3,500 acres (1,416 hectares) at nominal rent, the first time the government of the US moved to save a species from extinction. The herds of buffalo (bison) in the American national parks today are the descendants of the breed of "Scotty" Philip, who was also the brother-in-law of the famous Oglala Sioux chief, Crazy Horse.

Hundreds of people came to his funeral in 1911, so many in fact Scotty's friend Alex Johnson, a passenger agent for the Chicago and North Western Railroad, ordered a special free train to haul mourners to the ranch as a compliment to the memory of Scotty. Philip had done so much for so many as a rancher, a freighter, a State Senator, a businessman, and as a neighbour that the funeral was one of the largest ever in the State.[2]

George Edward Mackenzie Skues 1858-1949 discovered that trout in chalk streams feed largely on nymphs, even during hatches, and not on the adult, emerged flies. Skues' place as one of the greats in fly-fishing history centres on this finding. His dressings of artificial nymphs specifically to represent larvae were new and radical. This was extremely controversial and challenged the rigid dry-fly theories of Frederic Michael Halford and his disciples. Halford's greatness lay in his exposition of a method which became universal. Skues' forward-looking theories challenged what had become a rigid aridity with methods that were flexible and thoughtful, and were to become a predominant approach on both sides of the Atlantic. He became probably the finest all-round fly-fisherman and writer on fly-fishing of the 20th century.[1]

James Swinburne 1858-1958 had 15 patents between 1883 and 1907 in respect of incandescent electric lamps, filaments and other related work. Altogether, he had more than one hundred patents, mostly relating to electricity and lighting. While he was working with Crompton & Co, he improved the dynamo and "helped spur the growth of the electric lighting industry."[1]

Swinburne was beaten by one day in lodging a patent for a synthetic resin. The earliest commercially produced synthetic resin, *Bakelite*, came from a base of phenol formaldehyde in 1907. In an echo of the earlier telephone patents lodged on the same day by Alexander Graham Bell and Elijah Gray, Swinburne was beaten to the patent office by Belgian Leo Hendrik Baekeland who was granted a similar patent one day before. Unlike Bell and Gray, who litigated for patent priority, Baekeland joined forces with Swinburne in 1927 to form Damard Lacquer Company, which took its name from a resin created by Swinburne, which set hard and clear to make a lacquer suitable for the protection of brass and other metal surfaces. Damard eventually became Bakelite Limited, with Swinburne as its first Chairman until 1948.

The company ultimately merged into Union Carbide in 1939. This was the start of the plastics industry that has had untold effect on modern life with a multitude of different plastics being developed and eventually making *Bakelite* all but redundant. Swinburne was President of the Institution of Electrical Engineers and, in the field of synthetic resins, he was one of the world's pioneers and was the founder of the modern British plastics industry. He was also one of the leading electrical authorities in the world, and the author of original and authoritative technical books.[2]

Swinburne invented a watt-hour meter and the "hedgehog" transformer, a device for translating medium-voltage alternating current into high-voltage power for transmission over long distances. He reputedly introduced the terms "motor" and "stator" to electrical engineering terminology.[3]

Swinburne was president of the Institution of Electrical Engineers from 1909 to 1911 and was a member of that institution for 73 years.

William Marshall Callender born 1859 discovered a means to insulate electrical cable, originally calling it bitite, but, later, better known as vulcanised bitumen. "Callender used 20 per cent bitumen as an extender milled with cotton seed pitch to produce a material similar to rubber and gutta-percha which could be extruded. Cables comprising a standard copper conductor insulated with v.b. [vulcanised bitumen] and tape and braid overall became popular for LV [low voltage] distribution. They were laid in compound-filled troughing (the 'solid system')." His father founded Callender's Bitumen Telegraph and Waterproof Company Limited with William and his brother, **Thomas Octavius Callender 1855-1938**, as partners. Thomas invented the

Callender solid system, whereby cables were laid in wooden troughs and embedded in bitumen, a development which was later used extensively for the laying of mains cables.[1]

By 1914, the company had 5,000 employees and went on to supply cable to many markets, including the Covent Garden Opera House, underground collieries, tramways, and the first electrified underground railway and, ultimately, Britain's national electricity grid. By 1965, it was the world's largest supplier of cable with 1,300 employees at its 26-hectare plant at Erith in London – just one of its ten plants.

"The success of vulcanised bitumen was such that a number of installations were carried out on the continent. There were large scale installations at Antwerp and at Le Mans, and later in many parts of the British Empire."[2]

In 1943, during World War II, the company would go on to lay the first three-core 132 kV cable in the world – two kilometres of impregnated gas pressure cable used in Oxfordshire. Callenders at Erith and WT Glovers of Trafford Park both played an important role in the manufacture of PLUTO (Pipe Line under the Ocean) which played such a big part in helping the Allies in Europe during the Second World War, supplying fuel from refineries in England to Dungeness and Boulogne. Callenders also supplied cables for the Spitfire fighter and produced a buoyancy cable that deflected enemy magnetic mines.[3]

Harry Fielding Reid 1859-1944 was notable for his contributions to seismology, particularly his theory of elastic rebound that related faults to earthquakes. Reid, in 1890, took a set of measurements that showed how the glaciers were moving and changing, and he proposed a theory for how the front of a glacier maintained the shape that it did. The United States Geological Survey (USGS) would later name one of these glaciers for him.

Geophysics was a new field at that time, and Reid could later fairly claim to be the first American scientist to practice it as a specialty.

Reid published, in 1911, the first comprehensive treatment on seismographs in English. Reid was able to determine that the 1906 San Francisco earthquake was a result of forces he identified as "elastic strain." The principal outcome of Reid's seismological work was the formulation and discussion of the theory which he named *The Elastic Rebound Theory of Earthquakes*, now generally recognised as an important advance in the science of geology.[1] He would call his new theory "Elastic Rebound,", and his report on this phenomenon "is one of the great classics of twentieth-century geology, and the elastic rebound concept developed in it has stood the test of time."[2] "If a stretched rubber band is broken or cut, elastic energy stored in the rubber band during the stretching will suddenly be released. Similarly, the crust of the earth can gradually store elastic stress that is released suddenly during an earthquake. This gradual accumulation and release of stress and strain is now referred to as the 'elastic rebound theory' of earthquakes. Most earthquakes are the result of the sudden elastic rebound of previously stored energy."[3]

William Sutherland 1859-1911 beat Albert Einstein by more than a year to one of his greatest discoveries – the Einstein Diffusion Equation – the most cited of all Einstein's amazing achievements and one that has played a crucial role in a century of industry and manufacturing, as well as having other scientific uses.[1] Sutherland reported his relation linking the diffusion coefficient to the viscosity of a solvent and the diameter of a diffusing molecule. Soon afterwards, in 1905, Einstein published the same equation in his paper on Brownian motion, having arrived at it by exactly the same line of reasoning. Sutherland reported his relation in 1904 at a conference in New Zealand and published it in 1905.[2]

In the field of molecular dynamics, Sutherland's approach was founded on the assumption that the particles of which matter is composed exert an attractive force on each other in addition to gravity. Although his theory contrasted with that of Ludwig Boltzmann and other contemporaries who adopted a purely kinematical outlook, it is now widely accepted. Indeed, in introducing the idea, modern texts usually refer to the "Sutherland model" and characterise the force in terms of the "Sutherland potential". In his early papers Sutherland supposed that the complete law of force between particles is a power series in $1/r2$ of which gravity is but the first term; he believed he had uncovered the second, $1/r4$ term, in his own investigations into the behaviour of matter at the molecular level. (Nowadays this force is usually taken to be $1/r7$ in form.)

In 1893, Sutherland's general approach enabled him to account successfully for one of the more striking difficulties confronting molecular theory at the time – the discrepancy between theory and experiment in regard to the dependence of the viscosity of a gas on its temperature. He showed that the existence of an attractive force between the molecules of the gas would increase the effective diameter of the molecules in the theory that had been worked out for forceless molecules. This research led him to include an extra term C/T in the formula, linking viscosity and temperature, T being the absolute temperature and C a constant for any particular gas that is now called Sutherland's Constant. Sutherland later came to regard his new inter-molecular force as quite separate from gravity and attributable to the existence within all ordinary molecules of polarised electric doublets. Working out the consequences of this notion became a major part of his subsequent research.[3]

Sutherland's principal concern was to understand the properties of matter in bulk in terms of its behaviour at the microscopic level. He worked very much on his own, although he enjoyed cordial relations with the few other physicists working in Australia. He wrote for an international audience, attacking such questions as the surface tension of liquids, diffusion, the rigidity of solids, the properties of solutions (including an influential analysis of the structure of water), the origin of spectra and the source of the earth's magnetic field. His ideas were invariably treated with respect, even when they did not win wide acceptance.[4]

It is remarkable that three papers published in 1905 by Einstein and Sutherland laid such a foundation for science that they lie at the base of our understanding of nanostructures, are useful to biologists, and are essential to professional investors.[5]

William Kennedy Laurie Dickson 1860-1935 pioneered movies. He worked in the laboratories of the Edison Company in West Orange, New Jersey, in 1888. While working for Thomas Alva Edison, Dickson investigated materials for making film strips, finally settling on celluloid photographic film. To expose the film, he developed a method of lighting a drum with a stroboscopic flash triggered by pins at the end of the drum aligned with each picture. By May 1891, he had developed a camera, called the Kinetograph, which used a 19 mm film with a row of sprockets along one side to ensure even motion past the lens. The film was played back through a projector called a Kinetoscope, patented on 24 August 1891, which was the first continuous film projector. On 30 May 1889, Dickson obtained film supplies from Eastman which were 70 mm (2¾ inches) wide and he split this in two for greater control, making the now standard 35 mm film.[1]

He put four holes in each picture frame to keep them equidistant and allowing a more even progression of the film past the lens. The film format, camera transport and film projection have remained much the same until the early 21st century when replaced by digital movie cameras. To make commercial films to show on the Kinetoscope, Dickson made the first purpose-built film studio. "In 1892 construction began on what was said to be the world's first purpose-built film studio on Thomas A. Edison's Laboratory in West Orange, New Jersey. Its accidental architecture prompted the nickname 'Black Maria' after the police patrol wagon used at the time. The tar paper-clad structure was revolving on rails, in order to maximise the daylight required for the Kinetograph camera. Constructed by Edison's assistant William Kennedy Laurie Dickson, this was the centre for development of audiovisual technique at Menlo Park."[2] Around 80 films were produced, each being around 20 seconds in length and the first public demonstration was given at the Brooklyn Institute of Arts and Sciences on 9 May 1892.

Dickson nurtured the embryonic motion picture industry whereas Edison looked on it as a toy for children and he showed little enthusiasm for the innovation, seeing it in the same light as other peep-show devices. "The Edison Company exhibited the first motion pictures in the United States at the Brooklyn Institute of Arts and Sciences on 9 May 1893. Others tried to profit from his breakthrough in the next few years, but it was the American Mutoscope and Biograph Company, popularly known as Biograph, that became Edison's most formidable rival. Although Thomas Edison owned several key motion picture patents that prevented most competitors from developing their own systems, he was powerless to stop Biograph because its hardware simply did not use his technology. The two systems did share one significant connection. They were both invented by the same man, William Dickson."[3]

Some of the greatest stars of the silent movie era were launched on the road to stardom by Dickson's company, American Mutoscope and Biograph Company, including Lillian Gish, Mary Pickford and Mack Sennett.

Dickson produced some of the world's first-ever films and, although he is often credited with the first actual film *Dickson's Monkeyshines*, this honour likely belongs to Frenchman Louis Le Prince who made *Roundhay Garden Scene* in England on 14 October 1888, with film clips of some few seconds. Dickson's next film, *Dickson Greeting*, was shown in 1891, when he filmed himself saying "Good morning, Mr Edison. How do you like this?" He also made the first sound film – originally unnamed but now uninspiringly called *Dickson's Experimental Sound Film* (1894) – when he synchronised it with the phonograph. "This short 35 mm film was a test for Edison's Kinetophone project, the first attempt in history to record sound and moving image in synchronisation. This was an experiment by Dickson to put sound and film together either in 1894 or 1895. Unfortunately, this experiment failed because they didn't understand synchronisation of sound and film."

A broken cylinder labelled "Violin by WKL Dickson with Kineto" was catalogued in the 1964 inventory at the Edison National Historic Site. In 1998, Patrick Loughney, curator of Film and Television at the Library of Congress, retrieved the cylinder and had it repaired and re-recorded at the Rodgers and Hammerstein Archive of Recorded Sound, Lincoln Center, New

York. Since the Library did not possess the necessary synchronising technology, Loughney – at the suggestion of producer Rick Schmidlin – sent multi-Oscar winner Walter Scott Murch a videotape of the 17 seconds of film and an audiocassette of 3 minutes and 20 seconds of sound with a request to marry the two. By digitising the media and using digital editing software, Murch was able to synchronise them and complete the failed experiment 105 years later."[4]

Dickson was possibly the world's first film director (or co-director) having shot a number of movies, some of which were mere seconds long and the earliest were too fuzzy to see any real detail. The films he directed alone or co-directed* with American William Heise were: *Monkeyshines* No 1* and *Monkeyshines* No 2* (both 1889); *Indian Club Swinger*; *Dickson Greeting*: *Newark Athlete* (all 1891); *Blacksmith Scene* (1893); *Barbershop*; *Band Drill*; *Fred Ott's Sneeze*; *Carmencita*; *Buffalo Dance*; *Sioux Ghost Dance*; *Bucking Broncho*; *Annie Oakley*; *Hadj Cheriff* (all 1894); *Chinese Laundry* (1895); *Mounted Police Charge**; *A Morning Alarm* or *Morning Fire Alarm**; *The Morning Alarm**; *Going To The Fire**, *Upper Rapids From Bridge* (all 1896); *Mlle Catharina Bartho* (1899) and *A Nymph Of The Waves* (1900).

Image 87 – Film still from *Dickson Greeting*, the oldest American film shown to a public audience (in 1891)

Dickson went on to film notable people of the era, including Queen Victoria in Britain, Kaiser Wilhelm II in Germany, Pope Leo XIII in Rome and Emperor Franz Josef of Austria, and he was probably the world's first motion picture war correspondent when he took his camera off to the Boer War in southern Africa in 1899.

John Scott Haldane 1860-1936 developed several procedures for studying the physiology of breathing and the physiology of the blood, and for the analysis of gases consumed or produced by the body. In 1898, he published on: the physiological mechanism and toxic effects of carbon monoxide, describing the role of ferricyanide in releasing oxygen from oxyhemoglobin; examined blood gases; and produced a respiratory gas analyser.[1] In 1905, he established that it was the high concentration of carbon dioxide in the blood, not the low concentration of oxygen, which regulated the breathing rate.

Haldane and Thomas Carnelley conducted chemical and bacteriological analyses of the air of schools and slum dwellings. Invited by Henry Roscoe to investigate the source and possible effects of the offensive smells that troubled the House of Commons during warm weather, they went on to examine the constituents of sewer air in Dundee and other cities. Their findings indicated that sewer gas was not the serious source of infection that it was widely supposed to be. In 1889, Haldane and James Lorrain Smith refuted the widely-held view that expired air contained potent organic poisons, and showed that while accumulation of carbon dioxide might cause discomfort, it was unlikely under normal conditions to damage health. They concluded that the current enthusiasm among public health experts for higher standards of ventilation was misguided, and that more beneficial effects would be secured by promoting cleanliness and removing potential sources of infection.[2]

Between 1892 and 1900, Haldane introduced new methods both for investigating the physiology of the respiration and blood and also for gas analysis. Among his inventions, the haemoglobinometer, the apparatus for blood-gas analysis, and the one for the accurate and fast analysis of air or mixtures of gases were the most widely in use.[3]

He became an authority on the effects of pulmonary diseases on industrial workers and was appointed in 1912 as Director of the Mining Research Laboratory in Doncaster. Haldane improved mine safety by demonstrating the toxic effects of carbon monoxide and the use of rescue equipment. He introduced the use of small animals for miners to detect dangerous levels of poison gases underground, using either mice or canaries. The reason for this (aside from their portability) was that they have a faster metabolism which causes them to show symptoms of poisoning before gas levels became critical for workers, giving an early warning sign. Canaries were used until 1986 when the method was replaced by the electronic gas detector.[4]

During the First World War, Haldane was asked to identify the type of gas that the Germans had used in the first poison gas attack of the war (this was on 22 April 1915 at Ypres at 5.00 PM against the French which caused over 5,000 deaths. There was another, earlier, attack on 27 October 1914 at Neuve Chapelle, but the chemical used was non-lethal tear gas). Haldane found the gas used at Ypres was chlorine. Both sides used gas and it was much feared by the soldiers. In order to protect the soldiers, Haldane designed gas masks, which proved better than the urine-soaked handkerchiefs that the soldiers had used at first. In fact, it was a portable oxygen administration apparatus for use in the field.[5] In doing so, he demonstrated the value of oxygen in treating soldiers when they were gassed. Science and medicine worked together to prevent an enormous number of casualties from gas attack on the western front during the First World War.[6] Note: there are many other claimants to the invention of the gas mask.

Haldane demonstrated the effects of altitude and water pressures on respiration and devised a procedure for the decompression of deep-sea divers, permitting their safe return to the surface avoiding "the bends". Using his technique, a valuable cargo of gold was recovered from the wreck of the RMS *Lusitania* between 1917 and 1924.[7] He founded the *Journal of Hygiene*, in which he published, with Arthur Edwin Boycott and Guybon Chesney Castell Damant, the first set of diving decompression tables. *The Prevention of Compressed-Air Illness* (1908) lays the foundation for staged decompression. Decompression tables based on this research were adopted by the British Navy and, later, the United States Navy, saving many divers from the bends.[8] Haldane's basic staged decompression model formed the basis for what all divers (military and civilian) use world-wide for non-saturation type diving.[9] His development of the detailed method of "stage decompression" led to the end of the risks of caisson disease.[10]

D'Arcy Wentworth Thompson 1860-1948 was the first biomathematician, although he followed in the tradition of another great natural historian with mathematical skills, namely Georges-Louis Leclerc, Comte de Buffon. His understanding of mathematics was of the modern subject but based on the firm foundations of an understanding of Greek mathematics.

Although he was to write around 300 scientific articles and books, all Thompson's various skills came together in his most famous book *On Growth and Form* (1917). This book assumes that all science and learning are one, and attempts to reduce biological phenomena to mathematics. He claimed that all animals and plants could only be understood in terms of pure mathematics.[1] For instance, the spicules of sponges adopt a number of characteristic shapes. Thompson argued that these were the consequence of slight differences in the "starting conditions" such as ionic concentrations and other physical parameters. Thus, the initial conditions might well reflect some aspect of natural selection, but the resulting morphology of the spicules did not.

Thompson was one of the most famous scientific personalities of his time – and that time was extensive, for he occupied important University chairs for a total of 64 years. He was greatly admired by many scientists, but his direct influence is hard to trace. In part, this is because some of his ideas have been accepted so entirely that they seem self-evident. Equally, it is because some of his ideas are not yet fully accepted.[2]

One clear demonstration of his notions of the dynamic influence of starting conditions lies in the morphology of shells and horns. These are the permanent, non-living, three-dimensional record of a temporary, two-dimensional living state – the base of the horn, or the mantle of the shellfish. Thompson showed that all horn and shell morphologies could be described in simple mathematical terms readily derived from the incremental nature of growth.

Even if a morphology was plainly functional, this did not imply for Thompson that it was incorporated into the genome by natural selection. For instance, geometrical rules of packing determine cell arrangements. These need not be specified, but can arise spontaneously. Yet the packing arrangement may be "useful" in minimising the space occupied by the cells, by maximising cell-cell contacts, by establishing different categories of cells ("inside" versus "outside"), and so on.

Perhaps the most famous images from *On Growth and Form* are the transformations. Thompson showed that gross variation in form between related species could be modelled by the consistent deformation of a sheet. The consistency of the deformation is the crucial point here: it is obvious that any fish form could be made to look like any other fish form, if it were sketched on a perfectly deformable elastic sheet, and stretched in many directions at once. But Thompson showed that if the sheet were stretched in one particular pattern, then a new species form would be generated. This remarkable and curious observation has not been fully explained even today.[3]

On the concept of allometry, Thompson wrote: "An organism is so complex a thing, and growth so complex a phenomenon, that for growth to be so uniform and constant in all the parts as to keep the whole shape unchanged would indeed be an unlikely and an unusual circumstance. Rates vary, proportions change, and the whole configuration alters accordingly."

Thompson pointed out example after example of correlations between biological forms and mechanical phenomena. He showed the similarity in the forms of jellyfish and the forms of drops of liquid falling into viscous fluid, and between the internal supporting structures in the hollow bones of birds and well-known engineering truss designs. His observations of phyllotaxis (numerical relationships between spiral structures in plants) and the Fibonacci sequence has become a textbook staple.[4]

John Duncan Watson 1860-1946 specialised in sanitation and was regarded as a pioneer in the development of sewage treatment. Watson was engineer to the Birmingham and District Drainage Board and also General Manager to the Birmingham, Tame and Rea District Drainage Board. At Birmingham, he was responsible for the construction of the first large-scale percolating filter plant, a complete departure from the traditional land treatment in use in the city and elsewhere. Other changes that he introduced were the separation of sludge digestion, the introduction of flocculation prior to the percolating filter, and the extraction of methane from sewage for use in power generation.[1] "Methane used for energy – while currently in use and much under discussion as a green (or greener) technology in fact is an early 20th century technology developed by the Scottish civil engineer John Duncan Watson".[2]

Robert Williams 1860-1938 was a Scottish mining engineer who discovered the enormous copper deposits in Katanga Province of the, now, Democratic Republic of Congo, and those of Zambia. By 1929, Williams had completed the 1,344 km Benguela railway from the Angolan town of Lobito (which was founded by Williams as a port for the railway) to Luau in the Congo where it then leads to the Katanga province. This line forms part of a transcontinental railway, via links to Zambia's railways, leading to the Indian Ocean. Williams sponsored the further construction of the railway into Katanga, and the line crossed the border at the close of 1909. Production of copper in the Congo increased steadily thereafter, rising from 1,014 tonnes in 1911 to 86,943 tonnes in 1924.[1]

In colonial days, the railway line was used to shift huge supplies of mineral ore and saved 4,800 km in trans-shipment distance from the Katanga copper mines to Europe. It had an enormous economic impact on this region of central Africa, and even today it is the only railway connection from the Atlantic Ocean to central Africa.

Percy Allan 1861-1930 was a civil engineer working in New South Wales, Australia. He was in charge of designing and building Sydney's sewerage system with ocean outfalls, and from 1908 he was responsible for the works to build the city of Newcastle water supply and drainage system. He became Chief Engineer for national and local government works in mid-1918 and in the next nine years, until his retirement, his department had designed and built 583 bridges. The swing bridges carrying city traffic at Pyrmont and Glebe Island (both in Sydney) are among the structures standing as monuments to his skill.[1]

Edward Alexander Ernest Cullen 1861-1950 made the first survey of the Norman River in 1884 in Queensland, Australia, and was with the discovery team in 1887 that first saw Port Musgrave. He surveyed the northern half of Moreton Bay in 1890-1891, then set about making the 22 km shallow Brisbane River into navigable waterway. He recognised that dredging alone would not work so, in 1897, he suggested that training walls be built to confine the tidal flow. "In 1913, he obtained consent to the reclamation of land at Hamilton and, against considerable opposition, organised the progressive transfer of port facilities downstream. His continuing work on the river made Brisbane one of the few successful river ports of the era. ... In one way or another he was involved in the development of all ports in Queensland, twenty of which were gazetted."[1]

Harley Hugh Dalrymple-Hay 1861-1940 "devised a technique for driving the tunnel [on the Waterloo and City Railway in London] under compressed air, through water-bearing ground, whereby small pockets of ground were excavated by hand up to 2 feet [61 cm] ahead of the hooded cutting edge of the shield, and packed with clay; when the shield was advanced, the hood entered the clay pockets, and provided a seal behind the lining. This system, which he patented in 1896, and other improvements in the methods of constructing tube railways also originated by Dalrymple-Hay, were subsequently widely used, both in Britain, and in the United States of America."

"Dalrymple-Hay's tube-railway works comprised over 60 miles [97 km] of tunnels in London alone, including works on the Bakerloo, Hampstead (Northern), and Piccadilly lines; extensions from Golders Green to Edgware, from Finsbury Park to Cockfosters, and from Highgate to East Finchley; stations at Piccadilly Circus, Leicester Square, Waterloo (Bakerloo Line), King's Cross, Hyde Park Corner, Knightsbridge, Elephant and Castle, and many others; also numerous escalator schemes, among which was the first escalator on the underground system, that at Earls Court, which was completed in 1911. Throughout these works Dalrymple-Hay demonstrated an innovative approach including the application of the [Albert] François cementation process [grouting] of ground-stabilisation to tunnelling."

"Dalrymple-Hay was asked in 1921 to report on a system of tube railways for Calcutta, and later designed a tunnel to carry electricity supply cables under the River Hooghly. This tunnel, completed in 1931, was the first shield-driven iron-lined tunnel under a great tidal river in Asia, and its construction was carried out under high air pressures, in difficult climatic conditions, and with the use of unskilled labour."

He widened and strengthened the 150-year-old Richmond Bridge (Surrey, England) by 3.3 m, without interruption to road or river traffic, and without any alteration to the architectural design; the existing facade stonework and parapet were dismantled, numbered, and later replaced on the widened bridge.

Dalrymple-Hay was consulting engineer for the construction of the Post Office (London) Railway (1927-2003), a system of great ingenuity, which was opened in 1928, and it was for the Post Office that he undertook his last major work. This was a secret system of deep-level tunnels beneath Whitehall designed to allow communication between government offices to continue, despite aerial bombardment.[1]

David Anderson Hendrie 1861-1940 was the very first Chief Mechanical Engineer of the newly formed South African Railways and Harbours following the Union on 31 May 1910. He designed the South African Rail Class 3BR locomotive, now known as the *Inchanga Choo-Choo*, which still takes tourists for recreational trips. It was built by the North British Railway Company in 1912, when William Paton Reid was the company's Chief Mechanical Engineer.

Hendrie had worked for a number of years in Scotland then migrated to Africa where he became locomotive superintendent of the Natal Government Railways for whom he designed 4-6-2 tank engines which were manufactured by Hunslet and Hawthorn Leslie in Britain. He introduced many notable locomotives, including the world's first 4-8-2, and this wheel arrangement became a SAR standard, culminating in the Classes 15, 19 and 23. He was also an innovator, introducing the steam reverser and electric headlamps. His British training did not make him overly conservative and he visited America in 1909, returning with ideas on superheating and the Mallet engine. In 1921, he introduced the GA and GB Garratts. The latter was a success on such lines as the difficult Barkley East branch where they worked for many years.[1]

Image 88 – Natal Government Railways 4-8-0 locomotive – designed by David Anderson Hendrie

"He stunned the locomotive world at the time because the steam locomotives he designed were 50 percent bigger, heavier and more powerful than the average train running in Britain and had many advanced features, which were later adopted as standard."[2]

Robert Thorburn Ayton Innes 1861-1933 discovered Proxima Centauri (1915), the closest star to earth after the Sun. Invited by David Gill to the Cape Observatory, South Africa (1894), he became a successful binary star observer with the 7-inch (17.8 cm) refractor (1,628 discoveries). His most famous discovery, Proxima Centauri, is a faint star near the binary star Alpha Centauri, which is so far south it is not visible from most of the northern hemisphere. He was also the first to see the Daylight Comet of 1910, though this comet was found independently by so many people in the Southern Hemisphere that no single "original'" discoverer could be named.[1]

Arthur Pillans Laurie 1861-1949 specialised in the chemistry of pigmentation in art and was the first to chemically analyse paintings. His work on paintings was, in many ways, ground-breaking. He used chemical analysis to determine the make-up of paint samples of pictures, in order to determine the origin and age of paintings. He also introduced infra-red photography of paintings to see hidden layers of paint, covered under later reworkings. This allowed the identification of the true date of a self-portrait by Rembrandt, the part of the painting with the date inscribed having been painted over.[1]

In the identification of forgeries, Laurie's analytical approach achieved widespread acceptance and is integrated into decision-making today about paintings (in regard to authenticating them).[2]

Andrew Cowper Lawson 1861-1952 was Chairman of the State Earthquake Investigation Commission, which he had asked the State Governor to establish, which undertook a study report of the 1906 California earthquake – the most complete ever made of a major earthquake. A landmark in its field, the study initiated the theory of the elastic rebound of shock waves. Note: Harry Fielding Reid identified elastic rebound in 1890. Lawson's discoveries of Precambrian rock structures led to his revolutionary interpretations of these strata.

While the 1906 earthquake marked a seminal event in the history of California, it can also be remembered as the birth of modern earthquake science in the United States. It was the first time that an earthquake was recognised and documented as the result of a recurring tectonic process of strain accumulation and release. Under the leadership of Lawson, of the University of California-Berkeley, teams of scientists and engineers spread across the state, carefully collecting and documenting physical phenomena related to the quake. Their exhaustive data and thoughtful conclusions, published in landmark volumes two and four years after the earthquake, together with a complementary report published by the US Geological Survey in 1907, led to a number of new discoveries about the cause and effects of earthquakes. These discoveries underlie much of modern seismic hazard analysis.[1]

The Commission Report contains the first integrated description of the San Andreas Fault. Small sections had previously been mapped and described (in 1895, Lawson had mapped and named a few miles of the fault on the San Francisco Peninsula after the San Andreas Valley in which it was contained), but the earthquake rupture demonstrated the continuity of the structure. The location and morphology of the fault zone are described in detail and depicted on numerous large-scale maps along the 220 km onshore portion of the surface rupture. One commission member, Harold Wellman Fairbanks, continued mapping the San Andreas fault southeast of the 1906 rupture all the way to Southern California, southeast of San Bernardino, connecting the 1906 rupture to the same fault as the still relatively fresh rupture from the 1857 magnitude 7.8 earthquake in Southern California. The Commission thus established the San Andreas Fault as a continuous geologic structure extending for over 600 miles (965 km) throughout much of California.[2]

Lawson's leadership in seismology led to University of California, Berkeley, becoming one of the main world centres for earthquake studies. He was one of the founders of the Seismological Society of America.

Duncan Mackenzie 1861-1934 was one of the first professional field archaeologists, and the unsung hero of the famous excavations at Knossos. His relative obscurity was partly due to the fact that he was overshadowed by his more flamboyant and charismatic employer – Arthur Evans – and partly to the fact that, unlike Evans, he was not a prolific or gifted writer. His most important published works are the chapter *The successive settlements at Phylakopi in their Aegeo-Cretan relations* in T.D. Atkinson and others, The *Excavations at Phylakopi in Melos* (1904), 238-272; the two articles *The pottery of Knossos* (*Journal of Hellenic Studies*, 23, 1903,

157-205) and *The Middle Minoan pottery of Knossos* (*The Journal of Hellenic Studies*, 26, 1906, 243-67); the four articles on Cretan palaces in *Annual of the British School at Athens*, 11–14 (1905-8); and his reports on *The excavations at Ain Shems* published in *Palestine Exploration Fund* Annual, 1 and 2 (1911, 1913).

His daybooks of the excavations at Phylakopi, Ain Shems, Dar al-Mek, Saqadi, and especially Knossos, are his most significant contribution to archaeology. They formed the basis of important publications by others, notably Evans. Moreover, they not only contain precious, often unpublished, information on these important sites, but also show a precision in the recording of excavations, and an attention to problems of methodology and interpretation, which are remarkable for the period.[1]

After Mackenzie's death in Italy, some of Evans' system of Minoan dating came into question. It was the meticulous work of Mackenzie that became the key witness in defence of Evans' work. Though conflict existed between Evans and Mackenzie, Evans respected Mackenzie for his contributions to the excavation and paid tribute to his right-hand man in the last volume of *The Palace of Minos*.[2]

George James Foster King 1862-1947 was Chief Surveyor to the British Corporation Register (founded 1890 in Glasgow), which was established in direct competition to Lloyd's Register of Shipping in 1890. He held office in this position from 1903 to 1940, by which time the Register "was a world leader, with hundreds of thousands of tons of shipping on its books; it acted as consultant to many governments and international agencies.

Throughout his working life, King did everything in his power to quantify the risks and problems of ship operation: his contribution to the Load Lines Convention of 1929 was typical, and few major enactments in shipping were designed without his approval. During the inter-war period the performance of the British Corporation outshone that of all rivals, for which King deserved full credit. … His especial understanding was for steel structures, and in this respect he ensured that the British Corporation enabled owners to build ships of strengths equal to any others despite using up to 10 per cent less steel within the structure. In 1949, Lloyd's Register of Shipping and the British Corporation merged to form the largest and most influential ship classification society in the world. "[1] "King will be particularly remembered for introducing commercial reality into ship classification."[2]

Samuel Herd Milne 1862-1943 worked from 1891 for Bertrams Ltd., a paper manufacturing company which also made floor cloth and linoleum machinery, gun cotton plant, rubber machinery, asbestos machinery, artificial silk machinery, machine tools for shipbuilders and structural engineers, and drying machinery for the manufacture of milk powder. Between 1919 and 1943, Milne had, at least, 52 patents credited to him for improvements to machinery and production processes, including: the purifying of paper pulp; digestion of raw fibrous material for paper-making and other purposes; improvements in paper making machines; improvements in the manufacture of paper; improvements in machines for cutting grass, bamboo and cane; improvements in paper pulp-beating engines, washing and bleaching engines; improvements in the manufacture of jars, bottles and like vessels of pottery ware; improved method of removing impurities from paper pulp.[1]

Ernest William Moir 1862-1923 was the contractor's engineer for the Blackwall Tunnel (the contractor was Englishman Weetman Dickinson Pearson). Moir designed a circular tunnelling shield weighing 227 tonnes to dig much of the 1.9 km tunnel (1.3 km under water). Moir had worked on the Forth Rail Bridge, having responsibility for erecting one of the cantilever spans. With English engineer Benjamin Baker, he then worked on the Hudson River Tunnel for which he designed a hydraulic shield – based on an earlier design by American Alfred Ely Beach – which, as he put it, "cut away the bottom of the plum-pudding [a 3.65 metre diameter plug that was put in the tunnel when the original American company ran out of funds and work stopped] and there made a chamber to put together a shield that was imported from Scotland. This was done in December 1889. The erection of the shield began early in 1890, and by July, under a pressure of about 40 pounds per square inch [2.8 kg/cm^2], it had been riveted up and put through the temporary bulkhead. … On first commencing to push the shield there was great difficulty in preventing the tunnel from becoming a shaft. The ground was exceedingly soft, due to the eruptions of air to the river and other disturbances, and the sinking of the shield was very considerable."[1]

A major problem that occurred with the compressed air for the caissons used in tunnelling under the Hudson River Tunnel was "the bends", or compression sickness, which also affected deep sea divers. In 1890, during the construction of the Hudson River Tunnel, Moir built the first medical air lock to decompress workers who were being stricken by the bends while working in underwater caissons.[2] Moir provided valuable case studies to John Scott Haldane when he did his research on compression sickness, resulting in decompression equipment to aid recovery of deep-sea divers. Baker and Moir took one of the twin tunnels to 1.25 km (from both sides) and the south tube had reached 174 m when funding ceased due to a financial crisis and completion of the tunnels was delayed until 1908.

Image 89 – Moir's Hydraulic Shield
Hydraulic tunnel shield installed during construction in the south tube of the North River Tunnels under the Hudson River, 1905

Alan Archibald Campbell Swinton 1863-1930 set out the principles of electronic television in the first decade of the 20th century. The electronic television system that ousted the original mechanical system of John Logie Baird was first described by Swinton in a letter to *Nature* on

18 June 1908 (Baird later developed the first fully electronic system). Three years later *The Times* published a lecture Swinton had given eight days previously to the Roentgen Society of London, in which he propounded using cathode-ray tubes (CRT) to transmit and receive images. He described how the image would be scanned from one CRT, which had a fixed photoelectric pattern, by a beam of electrons that would send an electric signal to a receiving CRT where it would be scanned by another beam of electrons. In 1907, Russian-born Boris Rosing had proposed using a CRT as a receiver, but Campbell-Swinton was first to propose a complete system involving transmission and receiving.

In the *Nature* letter he stated, "Distant electric vision can probably be solved by the employment of two beams of kathode [sic] rays (one at the transmitting and one at the receiving station) synchronously deflected by the varying fields of two electromagnets placed at right angles to one another and energised by two alternating electric currents of widely different frequencies, so that the moving extremities of the two beams are caused to sweep synchronously over the whole of the required surfaces within the one-tenth of a second necessary to take advantage of visual persistence. Indeed, so far as the receiving apparatus is concerned, the moving kathode beam has only to be arranged to impinge on a suitably sensitive fluorescent screen, and given suitable variations in its intensity, to obtain the desired result".[1] Campbell-Swinton's proposed camera was electronic, using only mechanical focusing and would be capable of displaying 25 images a second. Indeed, as far back as 1903, he had used a Braun tube to conduct experiments in television transmission.

After John Logie Baird had given a public demonstration of his mechanical television, Campbell-Swinton wrote to *Modern Wireless* in June 1928, "Surely it would be better policy if those who can afford the time and money would abandon mechanical devices and expend their labours in what appears likely to prove the ultimately more promising method in which the only moving parts are imponderable electrons". Only in 1932 did technology catch up with the theory of Campbell-Swinton when two EMI engineers displayed electronic images on a CRT. Campbell-Swinton opened Britain's first radiographic laboratory to research X-rays for medical uses in March 1896 and was one of the first to explore the medical applications of radiography.[2] He gave Guglielmo Marconi a foot in the door with his introduction to the Chief Engineer of the British Post Office, who then arranged for Marconi to give a demonstration of his "wireless" in July 1896.

James Rennie Barnett 1864-1965 was described as one of the "Fathers of the Modern Lifeboat Fleet". In 1904, Barnett was appointed Consulting Naval Architect to the Royal National Lifeboat Institution (RNLI), a post he held until his retirement in 1947. "During this period, many changes in lifeboat design brought increasing efficiency, better ranges of stability and improvements in operational safety."[1]

Image 90 – *Nahlin* – built by John Brown & Co in 1930
Designed by James Rennie Barnett

In 1904, Barnett succeeded fellow Scot George Lennox Watson as senior partner of the firm G.L. Watson and Co. where his long career covered the development of the modern yacht from *Britannia* onwards and he continued to develop the firm's tradition of handsome yachts. Barnett designed amongst many others; *Nahlin, Blue Bird, Sunbeam II* and *Rainbow*.[2]

Peter Chalmers Mitchell 1864-1945 inaugurated a period of prosperity at the London Zoo, and was responsible for the Mappin Terraces, Monkey Hill, Whipsnade, the Aquarium, and other improvements. Whipsnade Zoo, opened in 1931, was the world's first open zoological park.[1] It is also the UK's biggest zoo, set in 600 acres (243 hectares) of parkland on the Chiltern Hills, north of London. The zoo is home to more than 2,500 animals, many of which are endangered in the wild.[2]

Herbert Akroyd Stuart 1864-1927, was born in England to a Scottish father, Charles, who had founded the Bletchley Iron and Tinplate Works in Buckinghamshire. Herbert took out an early patent for an oil-fired engine in 1886, with Englishman Charles Richard Binney, but it was their patent of May 1890 that described the first compression-ignition (solid injection) engine in the world and which was put into production the following year with the first working engines being sold on 8 May 1892. In 1896, Stuart's engine powered the first oil tractor and first oil locomotive. Some 32,417 of this particular engine were made by Hornsby, who had been contracted to build them.[1]

Hornsby built an experimental high-pressure Stuart engine in 1892, five years before Rudolf Diesel's first high pressure engine. Diesel's original patent in 1893 was for a coal-dust engine, but it exploded when used and he didn't have a working oil engine until 1897, based on a patent filed three years earlier. Diesel eventually used Stuart's injection system, so his only contribution to the hot bulb engine that now bears his name was an increase in pressure using a water-jacketed vaporiser, patented in 1892, to increase compression ratios, but Stuart had already beaten him on this also, so perhaps the so-called Diesel engine should more properly be referred to as the Stuart engine.

Arthur James Arnot 1865-1946 patented the world's first electric drill, with William Blanch Brain, on 20 August 1889. He also installed much of the street lighting in the centre of Melbourne, Australia, in 1891-1892 and, in the same city, the Spencer Street Power Station from which the streets of the central business district were first illuminated on 7 March 1894. He worked on the draft of the Victorian *Electric Light and Power Act* of 1896. Later, he was President of the Electrical Association of New South Wales, and President of the Victorian Institute of Electrical Engineers in 1899.[1]

"The first electric drill didn't look very much like modern hand-held drills. It was big, huge. It wasn't remotely portable, and it was designed to drill through rocks, making it more useful for mining than putting shelves together. Even with this disadvantage though, the invention was superior to other tools of the time. In fact, it was one of the first power tools. Other inventors continued to refine this concept, leading to the invention of the first portable drill in 1895."[2]

Thomas Bell 1865-1952 was director in charge of John Brown and Company, shipbuilders in Clydebank, for which he acquired a [Charles] Parsons' licence in 1903, and had erected a set of experimental engines by 1904, subsequently installed in the Clyde passenger ferry *Atlanta*. Turbines were then quickly installed in the *Carmania* in 1905, Cunard's first such venture, and in the prototype of the quadruple screw machinery of the *Lusitania*, launched the following year.

The *Lusitania*, with her sister ship, *Mauretania*, were built to travel at 25 knots requiring some 70,000 HP, which was double the power of any other ship built at the time. The performance of this innovative machinery was the subject of a paper presented in 1908 by Bell to the Institution of Naval Architects. "In a fast passenger liner such as the *Lusitania*, it is of the utmost importance that the manoeuvring capabilities should leave nothing to be desired, and to demonstrate the possibilities of the ship in this respect, various trials were made, the most important being the following: Stopping Trial. The ship was run on the Skelmorlie measured mile at a speed of 25.6 knots, the average revolutions of the propeller being 194 per minute. On entering the mile, the engine-room telegraphs were rung to 'Full speed astern'; the ship was brought to rest in 3 minutes 55 seconds, the distance run being about three-quarters of a mile, or about six times the length of the ship."[1] This early application to the development of turbine machinery was carried a stage further in the building of the *Aquitania* in 1913.

Among other ships built by Bell were the battle cruiser HMS *Hood*, the *Empress of Britain*, and the *Queen Mary*. The production of turbine machinery for merchant ships under Bell's guidance reached its climax in the *Queen Mary*, launched in 1934. The British Admiralty appointed Bell as deputy controller of dockyards and warship building in 1917 where he remained until the end of the war. His services in that position and his contribution to the development of shipbuilding were recognised in 1917, when he was made a KBE.[2] The Clydebank yard was only saved from closure by Bell's success in landing the Cunard contract in December 1930, for the construction of their new giant transatlantic express liner, yard number 534, ultimately to be launched as the *Queen Mary*. The contract was worth £4 million.[3]

Thomas Duncan 1865-1929 built a watt-hour meter in 1892 to determine how best to charge customers for the use of electricity. Originally customers were charged for electricity usage by lamp hours, but later meters recorded watt-hours. Duncan's watt-hour meter was produced earlier than Croatian Nikola Tesla's patent and two years before American Oliver Blackburn Shallenberger developed a single-phase watt-hour meter. Shallenberger's fellow countrymen made the first known DC meter patented in 1872 (Samuel Gardiner) and the first AC meter in 1878 (J.B. Fuller), both of which measured lamp-hours. Duncan's design in 1892 was the first induction watt-hour meter to use a single disc for driving and braking, but he never took out a patent for it and the commercial advantage went to General Electric and Westinghouse. Several others patented meters, but the first true watt-hour meter to become a commercial success was designed, possibly with the help of Duncan, by Elihu Thomson.[1]

George Keith Buller Elphinstone 1865-1941 was an electrical engineer who designed the first continuous roll strip chart recorder. He improved motor car speedometers, installed the original electric speed recording equipment at Brooklands motor racing circuit, and jointly with Harry Egerton Wimperis, in 1909, designed a very popular accelerometer for testing road and rail transport, which measured acceleration irrespective of the gradient or curvature of the track. Also, in the years preceding the First World War, he jointly patented with Wimperis several early aircraft instruments and bombsights, and, although these were never produced commercially, the relationship resulted in Elliott Brothers manufacturing all Wimperis bombsights and navigation instruments after the war.

Elphinstone is most remembered for his development work in the field of naval fire control equipment. He had been responsible for licensing the Anschutz naval gyrocompass from Germany and was involved with the gunnery calculator of Prince Louis of Battenberg and then, in 1902, with that of Captain John S. Dumaresq. However, as the speed of warships increased and target ranges changed rapidly, these early calculators became obsolete and were replaced by large, complex fire control equipment and plotting tables, specifically that designed by Frederic C. Dreyer in 1911, in which the integrating mechanism, or clock, stretched contemporary electromechanical technology to its limits.

The Elliott equipment with its Dreyer-Elphinstone clock was selected in preference to the Argo equipment of Arthur J. H. Pollen for early installations and was used on many warships throughout the war. Elphinstone's service to the Admiralty was recognised by his O.B.E. in 1917 and his K.B.E. in 1920.[1]

Alexander Gillies 1865-1952 patented, in Australia in 1902, a two-chambered teat cup, and an air admission hole at the top of the teat cup which allowed the milk to clear away efficiently. These were significant advances which are still in universal use. The improved machine became known as the LKG (Lawrence-Kennedy-Gillies) and some 300 of them were said to be in use in Australia and New Zealand by 1905. Gillies also developed a simple tubular "claw" for connecting the milk and air tubes from the four teat cups with the receiver and pulsator, and this design has also survived until the present day.[1]

"The Gillies system generated constant vacuum at the base of the inner teat cup, directly at the teat and intermittent vacuum between the layers. The combination worked brilliantly and became known as double action milking."[2]

"The LKG milking machine is of State significance because it represents a high degree of technical achievement. It demonstrates the innovation developed by a Western District farmer, Alexander Gillies, and enabled dairy farms throughout Victoria to move successfully from hand milking to machine milking, thus contributing to the mechanisation of one of Victoria's major rural industries."[3]

Arthur Harden 1865-1940 shared the Nobel Prize in Chemistry in 1929 with Hans Karl August Simon von Euler-Chelpin for their investigations into the fermentation of sugar and fermentative enzymes.[1] Harden helped establish the modern field of biochemistry with his research on fermentation, which held profound implications for the understanding of the processes of metabolism. Harden relied more on perspiration than inspiration, allowing his meticulous experimentation to guide him to a conclusion instead of hypothesising his intended outcome and then trying to achieve that result.[2]

Harden elucidated the entire process of fermentation, thereby helping establish the field of biochemistry by opening the door to future scientists to further their discoveries and establish the mechanics of metabolism. Among his achievements, Harden first identified the sugar glycogen as the agent that survived the extraction from yeast cells and activated fermentation with Eduard Buchner's zymase (enzymes). Even more significant was the discovery by him and his assistant William Young of a cofactor, which Harden called "coferment" that was necessary for fermentation. Furthermore, Harden and Young discovered the existence of phosphate in the ash of heated coferment, thereby identifying phosphate as an important active agent in the fermentation process.[3]

His more than 20 years of study of sugar fermentation advanced knowledge of metabolic processes in all living forms. He also produced pioneering studies of bacterial enzymes and metabolism.[4]

Harden demonstrated that the activity of yeast enzymes was lost following dialysis (the separation of large from small molecules by diffusion of the smaller molecules through a semipermeable membrane). He went on to show that the small molecules are necessary for the successful action of the yeast enzyme and that, whereas the activity of the large molecules was lost on boiling, the activity of the small molecules remained after boiling. This suggested that the large molecules were proteins, but the small molecules were probably nonprotein. This was the first evidence for the existence of coenzymes – nonprotein molecules that are essential for the activity of enzymes. Harden also discovered that yeast enzymes are not broken down and lost with time, but that the gradual loss of activity with time can be reversed by the addition of phosphates. He found that sugar phosphates are formed during fermentation as intermediates – phosphates are now known to play a vital part in biochemical reactions.[5]

Alexander Cruikshank Houston 1865-1933 was a pioneer of the chlorination of water supplies. He was involved in the investigation of an outbreak of typhoid at Lincoln in England and was instrumental in establishing a chlorination plant of a rudimentary nature there, and also in organising the comprehensive chlorinating system which was then applied to London's water supply. He also advised on water supplies in Egypt and Canada.[1]

Houston may be said to have devoted a large portion of the remainder of his life to perfecting the analysis of water by the application of bacteriology on thoroughly scientific lines with the result that today in respect of pollution from sewage, the purity and safety of water can be guaranteed – provided the methods of analysis elaborated by him are applied.[2]

Alan Alexander MacMasters 1865-1927 invented the first electric bread toaster in 1893, which went on to be developed by Crompton, Stephen J. Cook & Company as the *Eclipse*.[1] MacMasters realised new high-resistance wire could be heated to a high enough temperature to toast bread. The wiring, unfortunately, tended to melt and cause a fire and the bread had to be monitored to stop it from burning or catching fire. Early toasters tended to be open with the heating mechanism exposed. The bread was placed in them and then removed when it was toasted enough.

Donald Murray 1865-1945 invented the 5-unit code multiplex telegraph system. His Type Printing Multiplex System combined the best features of Frenchman Emile Baudot's multiplex system and Murray's own automatic system, which incorporated a number of new features including ones that avoided mutilation of the tape and disconnection of the transmitter.[1] The Murray system, as distinct from that of Baudot, employed an intermediate step, a keyboard perforator, which allowed an operator to punch a paper tape, and a tape transmitter for sending the message from the punched tape. At the receiving end of the line, a printing mechanism would print on a paper tape, and/or a reperforator could be used to make a perforated copy of the message. As there was no longer a direct correlation between the operator's hand movement and the bits transmitted, there was no concern about arranging the code to minimise operator fatigue, and instead Murray designed the code to minimise wear on the machinery, assigning the code combinations with the fewest punched holes to the most frequently used characters. The Murray code also introduced what became known as "format effectors" or "control characters" – the CR (Carriage Return) and LF (Line Feed) codes. Murray's improvements were made in 1901 and became the basis for CCITT Alphabet No. 2 (ITA-2) which was still in use one hundred years later.[2]

Alexander Shiels 1865-1907, assisted by William Elliot of Muirglen, Lanarkshire, made improvements to the milking machine designed by William Murchland. Shiels developed the *Thistle* milking machine that was the first to use the pulsator method (intermittent flow), initially criticised but later found to be the most effective type of milker. Besides emulating the sucking action of a calf, the milk was also piped to churns or tankers ready for distribution or pasteurisation. The *Thistle* used a steam-driven vacuum pump, but it was noisy and the air needed for the sucking action tended to cause contamination of the milk. Shiels' pulsator "alternated suction levels to successfully massage the blood and fluids out of the teat for proper blood circulation. That device, along with the development of a double-chambered teatcup in 1892, led to milking machines replacing hand milking."[1] The *Thistle* was sold around the world, being granted four US patents – two in 1896, and one each in 1899 and 1900. It was said the machine had a soothing effect on the cows being milked during New Zealand trials.

Alexander Smith 1865-1922 and **Alan Wilfrid Cranbrook Menzies 1877-1966** jointly invented the isoteniscope, an apparatus for the exact measurement of vapour pressures. It consists of a submerged manometer and container holding the substance whose vapour pressure is being measured. The open end of the manometer is then connected to a pressure measuring devise. A vacuum pump is used to adjust the pressure of the system and purify the sample.

In physical and inorganic chemistry, Smith's first research of considerable importance was an exhaustive, classical investigation of the forms of sulphur. Many others had preceded him in this field, but he brought to the problem such an insight into the varied and complex factors involved and such an ingenuity in applying the methods of modern physical chemistry that, at the close of his work, the subject might be considered as an almost completed chapter of our chemical knowledge.[1]

His ideas of chemical education were quite unusual for their time and included the thought that instead of solely receiving lectures, students should begin by acquiring the ability to state simple ideas correctly … the conclusions would not be new, but going through the operation of reaching them for themselves would be new to the student.[2]

Smith was Head of the Department of Chemistry at Columbia University from 1911 to 1919. He became President of the American Chemical Society (1911) and published many textbooks, his first being *Laboratory Outline of General Chemistry* (1899) which had sold 66,000 copies by the 6th edition.[3]

Adam Alexander Boyd 1866-1948 was a mining engineer in 1898 at Broken Hill Proprietary (BHP) Ltd in the far west of New South Wales in Australia. "Boyd devised the steel water-curtain, applying coal-mine practice to restrict underground fires, and modernised practice by standardising extraction methods and introducing improved systems of haulage and handling. When he left Broken Hill for the Wallsend Colliery in 1911 he was considered one of the best mining engineers in Australia."[1] He made the Mount Morgan mine in Queensland into a profitable enterprise, producing gold, silver and copper, despite predictions that its ore could not be profitably extracted by open cut methods. He was awarded the Institute Medal in 1942, the highest honour given by the Australian Institute of Mining and Metallurgy.

Robert Broom 1866-1951 became the most successful hominid fossil hunter of all time. He found more hominid fossils than all other field workers combined.[1] With persistence, luck, and superb analytical skills, he produced the "smoking gun" to prove Australian-born Raymond Dart was correct about human origins in Africa. Broom was very successful in finding adult specimens although his work was interrupted for a time by World War II.

In the early part of the 20th century, palaeontologists believed that humankind's origins lay in Asia or Europe. Professor Dart theorised that the Taung Child, found in Africa in 1924, was a human ancestor.

His theory was not well received, but he did, however, have a supporter in Broom, a keen palaeontologist who, until then, had specialised in fossils of mammal-like reptiles found in the Karoo. After the Taung Child was discovered, Broom, determined to find an adult *Australopithecus*, went looking in dolomite caves west of Pretoria. He discovered instead the fossil of a giant baboon, which received considerable press coverage. After reading about the baboon in a newspaper, two students, Harding le Riche and Gerrit Willem Hendrik Schepers, who had visited the Sterkfontein Caves and recovered fossil monkeys, approached Broom and encouraged him to visit the caves with them. At Sterkfontein, Broom met George Barlow, the site manager, who had also worked at Taung. Broom asked Barlow to keep a look out for anything similar to the Taung Skull, and a few days later, Barlow handed him a rare find – a natural brain cast in rock of the world's first adult specimen of *Australopithecus*, later catalogued as TM 1511.[2]

Broom recognised this as a primate with a chimpanzee-sized brain. He looked over the local dumps and discovered parts of the crushed skull matching the breccia cast. The teeth were human-like; it clearly represented an adult *Australopithecus*. In 1938, two years after his discovery, Broom named the specimen *Australopithecus transvaalensis* ("southern ape of the Transvaal"), although it has since been reclassified as *Australopithecus africanus*, the same as the Taung Child. Broom went on to recover many other specimens of *Australopithecus* from the lime miners' dumps.[3]

Broom made one of the most famous discoveries in anthropology at the Sterkfontein excavations. He found a female cranium of the genus *Australopithecus africanus* in 1947, known as "Mrs. Ples", which is a vital link to the history of human evolution. She is believed to be about 2.5 million years old.

Broom also discovered fossils which were thought to be similar in many ways to *Australopithecus africanus*, but which were more "robustly" built. The fossils exhibited larger jaws and teeth and after discovering many more differences, Broom decided to group these discoveries to a new species name of *Australopithecus robustus*.[4]

He made a succession of spectacular finds including fragments from six hominids in Sterkfontien, later classified as an adult australopithecine, as well as more discoveries at sites in Kromdraai and Swartkrans. Broom's 1937 discovery of *Australopithecus robustus* helped support Dart's claims for the Taung species. The remainder of Broom's career was devoted to the exploration of these sites and the interpretation of the many early hominid remains discovered there.[5]

Murdoch MacDonald 1866-1957 did much of his irrigation work on Egypt's Nile, such as increasing the height of the original High Aswan Dam in 1932 when it was found that the original dam was too low. Unfortunately, MacDonald, who also proposed building two dams in Sudan – Sennar and Jabal Auliya – to harness Nile waters, came under attack from the original designer of the Aswan Dam, William Willcocks, and Egyptian nationalists who feared British expansion of power. "Not surprisingly, MacDonald was found guilty by the politicians and the populace and innocent of any impropriety by the commission and the courts. The courts concluded: 'There had been no falsification or intentional suppression of records nor any fraudulent manipulation of data or gauges by Sir Murdoch MacDonald or anyone else'."[1]

"MacDonald's firm was most prominently associated with Nile engineering works over the past half century".[2] He created an engineering company that, with mergers, exists today as Mott MacDonald with over 14,000 employees and operations in 100 countries (as at March 2013).

Long after he died, his company continued to prosper, being involved in designing or other work on the new Wembley Stadium; Channel Tunnel (principal design consultant – second longest tunnel in the world and longest undersea tunnel); Heathrow Airport Terminal 5; Crossrail (new railways under central London); Greenwich Peninsula ICT; Bangkok's Rama VIII and Seoul's Kayang bridges; Taiwan High Speed Rail; and Hong Kong's Lantau Link between the International Airport and the city; Mall of the Emirates; Bahrain City Mall; Brighton Marina; and Dubai Marina where "Mott MacDonald was appointed in 2006 as the lead consultant for the development of Dubai Sports City's mixed use canal hubs, one of the main components within the world's first purpose built sports city." [3]

Henry Gordon Stott 1866-1917 was for many years active in the design, construction, and operation of the power systems supplying subway, elevated, and surface lines of New York City. In 1901, he was appointed superintendent of motive power for the company which later became the Interborough Rapid Transit Company of New York City (IRT). In 1904, he undertook the construction of a power plant for the IRT, and from that time until his death on 15 January 1917, he was in charge of the design, construction, and operation of the power generating stations and the distributing system of the Interborough. [1]

"The Interborough Rapid Transit Subway … was the first subway company in New York City. Even with elevated train lines springing up around the city, the need for an underground rapid transit railroad was obvious as a solution to street congestion and to assist development in outlying areas. On 27 October 1904, the first IRT subway line opened, and the city would never be the same." [2] Stott was President of the American Institute of Electrical Engineers from 1907 to 1908.

James Stevenson-Hamilton 1867-1957 founded Kruger National Park, an internationally renowned wildlife sanctuary covering an area of 19,633 square kilometres in South Africa. The aims of game reserves at that time were to prevent poaching, to eradicate a wide range of "vermin" species (including lion, leopard, cheetah, and wild dog) and to nurture antelope and buffalo herds for the pleasure of sport-hunters. With his innovative leadership, Stevenson-Hamilton's accomplishment was to found an African national park that was both ecologically sound and receptive of visitors. He laid the foundations of South African nature conservation by initiating an effective paramilitary bureaucracy, careful formalised reporting, and a close personal knowledge of the people, landscape, and wildlife of the area. Initially, he evicted all Africans from the game reserve. This earned him the name of Skukuza ("he who sweeps clean"), but he later came to value the labour that the local people could provide. He greatly expanded his area of control northwards by incorporating privately owned land up to the Olifants River and by taking over control of the Singwitsi, a game reserve established in 1903 between the Letaba and Levuvhu Rivers.

Stevenson-Hamilton publicised the value of wildlife protection by writing promotional and educational material in a number of books and journals. *Animal Life in Africa*, published in 1912, is a forerunner of modern animal behavioural ecology. Stevenson-Hamilton brought South

African wildlife protection to international attention. He returned to South Africa in 1926, becoming warden of the Kruger National Park, a position he held until his retirement in 1946. He managed the process of turning the game reserves into a national park that was attractive to tourists. Moreover, he transformed the conservation ethic by emphasising the intrinsic value of the natural world and he ended "vermin" killing.[1]

James Boyce 1868-1935 invented vegetable shortening and formulated *Gold Dust* washing powder, the first all-purpose laundry powder. Hydrogenated vegetable oils were used in its processing and it soon was found in many American homes during the first half of the twentieth century. Boyce's industrial hydrogenation procedure, when applied to cottonseed (and other plant materials), proved successful and was considered a scientific breakthrough. This allowed for its subsequent application (by the likes of French chemist Paul Sabatier and manufacturing giant Procter & Gamble) in the commercial exploitation of vegetable oils and fats, resulting in such products as "Oleomargarine" and "Crisco" shortening. These are in worldwide use today.

Boyce "became one of the chemists most loved by the American housewife, although few ever knew his name. Rather, they knew – and greatly appreciated – the products he developed: detergents. Boyce was involved in formulating the ingredients of washing powder, and in the process studied the hydrogenation process". He found that, by applying the hydrogenation process to plant oils, he could create a material with a consistency closer to the animal fats used in the manufacturing of soap – and the animal fats used in cooking.[1]

Louis Harper 1868-1940 built many bridges in Britain and abroad, using the method of straining wire for cables patented by his father, John. In 1871, he built a 300 ft (91.5m) bridge at Aboyne, Aberdeenshire, and the Hunting Bridge at Shocklach in Cheshire. A unique feature of the Harper bridges was the arched cable supported deck, so designed to give stiffness to the structure. At some stage, he replaced the wooden pylons of certain of these bridges with 'I' section steel beams, topped with his distinctive finials. In the early 1890s, tubular cast-iron pylons were introduced, (e.g. at Trentham, Larbert, and Sellack). Then in the later 1890s came the steel lattice pylon (e.g. Abercynon, Keswick, Newquay, and the Indian and Nepalese bridges, Tsomo, Narva). All these were manufactured at Harpers Limited, Aberdeen, Scotland. At least four are still in use and well maintained in Nepal, where Harpers supplied the first suspension bridge in 1900 and all subsequent ones until 1909.[1]

His bridges include: Water of Tanar (1870); Dundee (1872); Monymusk and Burnhervie (1879-1880); Birkhall and GNR at Holme (1880); Cromdale (1881); Blairgowrie (1886); Nairn and GNR at Offord (1887); Crathorne, GNR at Lincoln, Bandon, Eire (1888-1890); Polhollick (1892), Larbert on the River Carron, Trentham, Banchory (all in 1893); Grimsby (1894); Sellack Boat on the River Wye (1895); Jumna (1895) and Bombay (1896) both in India; Doveridge, Derbyshire, Keswick, Abercynon, all in UK (1898); Tsomo on the River Tsomo, South Africa (1898); Baroda, India (1899); Newquay (1900); Tursoli River in Nepal (1900), Aberlour (1900); Tadi (1901), Sundari (1903) and Chobar Gorge (1903) all in Nepal; Cambus' O'May on the River Dee (1905); Mangaltar, Nepal (1907); Narva on the River Narva, Estonia (1908) and Ballochbuie on the River Dee (1924).

William Wilson Hoy 1868-1930 had become, by 1910, the youngest railway general manager ever and had control of the second largest Government-owned railways in the world – the South African Railways and Harbours – when he became the first general manager of the unified railway system that covered the whole of South Africa. Hoy introduced the first road service of the South African Railways from the railway station at Bot River to Hermanus in 1912. One of Hoy's first tasks as railway manager was the drafting of new legislation. One clause which he is credited with personally was that the railway would be run on business principles. His next great project was in servicing outlying districts. He began building road transport depots which eventually led to the largest road transport operation in Africa. In 1925, he introduced electric traction against great opposition.

He was a legendary South African who affected the outcome of the German South-West African Campaign in 1914-1915, the Rand Revolt in 1922, and was also the first general manager of the unified South African Railways. His influence in South Africa can be gauged by his presence at the Paris Peace Conference with General Smuts and Louis Botha in 1919 and his attendance at the Imperial Conferences in London in the 1920s with the Prime Minister of South Africa, including that of 1926 when South Africa was granted Dominion Status.

When Hoy became the first general manager of the South African Railways in 1910, formed from the Natal Government Railways, Cape Government Railways and Central South African Railways (Imperial Military Railways during the Boer War), the total capital of the organisation was 87,263,366 rand. In 1914, with the rank of Colonel and because of the military action against German South-West Africa, he was appointed director of Military Railways. He superintended the line between Prieska and Upington, which was completed in eighty-two days. He was granted a knighthood for his services and became a C.B. in 1918.[1]

William Ramsay 1868-1914 invented the first modern shoe polish that preserved and restored the colour of leather and made shoeware water resistant. With fellow Scot Hamilton McKellar, Ramsay introduced *Kiwi* boot polish, named after the country of origin of his wife, New Zealand-born Annie Elizabeth Meek. Their first polish had been introduced in October 1906, but it was with *Dark Tan* that modern shoe polish originated in 1908. The Kiwi Polish Company Pty Ltd was created in 1916 with William's father, John, as chairman and his brother James as a director. The company claimed to have made in 1917 the earliest advertising film in existence, a two-hundred foot (61 m), six-minute promotion. *Kiwi's* first brand advertising was screened in the UK showing one of the first *Kiwi* tans. By 1918, *Kiwi* had sold thirty million tins and by 1924 it was distributed in fifty countries. *Kiwi* is still sold (2015) and has more than 50% of the current world-wide shoe polish market.

Ernest Dunlop Swinton 1868-1951 is credited as having an influence on the development of the military tank and for coining the phrase "no-man's land". Swinton recounts in his book *Eyewitness* how he first got the sudden idea to build a tank on 19 October 1914, while driving a car in France. It is known he received a letter in July 1914 from a friend, the South-African engineer Hugh Merriot, asking his attention for the fact that armoured tractors might be very useful in warfare. In November 1914, Swinton, then a Major, suggested the idea of an armoured tracked vehicle to the military authorities. In the same year, he prepared from his own resources a propaganda leaflet and had it dropped from aircraft over German troops. His armoured vehicle proposal was stalled within the British Army, but Colonel Maurice Hankey took it to Winston Churchill, then at the Admiralty, which led to the formation of the Landships Committee, in which Swinton did not initially participate. In 1916, Swinton became Lieutenant Colonel responsible for the training of the first tank units. He created the first tactical instructions for mobile armoured warfare.[1]

Swinton was given the task of recruiting and training the new tank unit, which, he noted regretfully, did not form part of the Royal Engineers. His lack of command experience, however, meant that he would not be chosen to lead the tank force in France. In great secrecy, he created battle training conditions at Elveden, near Thetford, and despite mechanical and logistical problems, a small force of the heavy section, albeit with under-trained men, was available to participate in the renewal of the Somme offensive on 15 September 1916. Swinton had wanted to wait until sufficient tanks were available to make a substantial contribution, backed by the element of surprise, to the battle, but he was overruled. This premature deployment of the new weapon was to form a contentious element in his post-war writings.[2]

William Brownie Garden 1869-1960 invented the Rollerboard in 1911, which he called the Revolving Surface Writing Board. Using the roller-towel principle, and substituting a specially treated fabric for slate, the first of the now internationally known revolving boards was created. The original prototype is still in use today (2015).[1]

Garden also took out patents for improvements in machines for cramping doors (3 May 1934), a variable speed gear box (December 1957), an anti-skid attachment for motor vehicles (November 1930), an improved transmission gear (December 1922), and an apparatus for counting coins in bulk (June 1920), although none of these seem to have gone into commercial production.

Brodie Haldane Henderson 1869-1936 was a railway engineer who worked for many railway companies across South America, Australasia and Africa. He worked extensively on railway contracts abroad, including the Buenos Aires Great Southern and Central Argentine. In Brazil, he worked with the Great Western and the Leopoldina, and in Uruguay, with the Central and North Western. He also designed and built for the Antofagasta (Chile) and Bolivia Railway, the United Railways of Havana, the Midland Railway of Western Australia, and Nyasaland railways. Henderson also supervised the construction of the new docks in Buenos Aires. He was the consultant for the Dona Ana Bridge over the Zambezi River in Mozambique which, when it was built in 1935, was the longest railway bridge in the world with a length of 3.58 km.[1]

Charles Thomson Rees Wilson 1869-1959 was joint recipient of the Nobel Prize for Physics in 1927. Wilson was a meteorologist who began studying clouds in 1895. To aid his studies, Wilson had devised a way of allowing moist air to expand in a closed container – a cloud chamber – that was later to prove indispensable in the study of nuclear physics and would lead to the development of the bubble chamber. When dust-free air was used, the air remained supersaturated and clouds did not form until a critical point of supersaturation was reached. Further experiments, based on his knowledge of the newly discovered X-rays showed Wilson that radiation left a trail of condensed water droplets in the cloud chamber in an experiment which he then worked to perfect.

After the end of World War I, Wilson published his theory of thunderstorm electricity. Wilson's additional work on lightning led to a method of protecting barrage balloons used in World War II to deflect German airplanes during their bombing runs on Britain. [1]

Wilson discovered that X-rays and "uranium rays" could cause large numbers of fog droplets, and concluded that they must have been producing the same nuclei as those occurring spontaneously. He identified these as negatively charged ions, partly explaining the electric field in thunderclouds; as drops formed on negative particles, the law of gravity caused them to fall, separating the charge in the cloud. Therefore, he discovered that condensation could also be caused by an external influence, speculating that radiation from outside earth's atmosphere – cosmic rays – might be the cause.

The greater part of his work on the behaviour of ions as condensation nuclei was thus carried out in the years 1895-1900, whilst after this his other occupations – mainly tutorial – prevented him from dealing sufficiently with the development of the cloud chamber. Early in 1911, however, he was the first person to see and photograph the tracks of individual alpha- and beta-particles and electrons. (The latter were described by him as "little wisps and threads of clouds"). The event aroused great interest as the paths of the alpha-particles were just as William Henry Bragg had drawn them in a publication some years earlier. But it was not until 1923 that the cloud chamber was brought to perfection and led to his two, beautifully illustrated, classic papers on the tracks of electrons. Wilson's technique was promptly followed with startling success in all parts of the world – in Cambridge, by Patrick Maynard Stuart Blackett (who in 1948 received the Nobel Prize on account of his further development of the cloud chamber and his discoveries made therewith) and Pyotr Leonidovich Kapitsa; in Paris, by Irène Curie and Pierre Victor Auger; in Berlin, by Walther Wilhelm Georg Bothe, Lise Meitner, and Philipp von Lenard; in Leningrad, by Dmitri Skobelzyn; in Tokyo, by Hiroshi Kikuchi.[2]

Some of the most important achievements using the Wilson chamber were: the demonstration of the existence of Compton recoil electrons, thus establishing beyond any doubt the reality of the Compton effect (Arthur Holly Compton shared the Nobel Prize with Wilson in 1927); the discovery of the positron by Carl David Anderson (who was awarded the Nobel Prize for Physics in 1936 for this feat); the visual demonstration of the processes of "pair creation" and "annihilation" of electrons and positrons by Blackett and Giuseppe Paolo Stanislao Occhialini; and that of the transmutation of atomic nuclei carried out by John Douglas Cockcroft and Ernest Thomas Sinton Walton. Thus, Ernest Rutherford's remark that the cloud chamber was "the most original and wonderful instrument in scientific history" has been fully justified.[3]

Wallace Rupert Turnbull 1870-1954 is best known as the inventor of the first reliable variable pitch propeller which revolutionised air travel by allowing greater flight control, especially for take-off and landing, and increased engine and fuel efficiency,[1] although others such as Henry Selby Sele-Shaw had patented such propellers. This device adjusts the angle at which propeller blades cut the air and it became as essential to aviation as the gearbox is to the automobile. It provides for safety and efficiency at all engine speeds, for example, maximum power on take-off and landings and economical cruising for long distances. It was independently perfected in several countries, so that Turnbull's work has been overlooked by most historians, perhaps because he licensed its manufacture and went on with other inventions. But his variable-pitch propeller (now in the National Aviation Museum, Ottawa) appears to have been the first to fly successfully.[2]

He was one of the world's first aeronautical engineers and Turnbull did important work on the stability of aircraft and important research into propeller behaviour and the science of aerodynamics, and one of his early contributions to aviation was the construction in 1902 of the first wind tunnel in Canada, and one of the earliest in the world.[3] At his home in Rothesay, New Brunswick, the Canadian engineer built a basic wind tunnel out of an old packing case, and used it to experiment with propellers and various types of engines. "His research strongly influenced the design of aircraft for the next century, concludes Captain Gerry Howe. "General aviation aircraft today are still designed upon the foundational work he did."[4]

Lawrence Ennis 1871-1938 (born Laurence Innes) was the Chief Engineer from 1924 to 1932 for the construction of the Sydney Harbour Bridge; the widest long-span bridge in the world, which opened in 1932. Ennis joined "Dorman Long in 1903, and played a prominent part in the firm's development. During the latter years of the European War [World War I] he laid out the company's huge modern steel works at Warrenby, Redcar. ... Mr Ennis had supervised the work on this bridge [Sydney Harbour] from the preparation of Messrs. Dorman Long's successful tender until the last rivet had been driven in the mammoth structure. He stayed at Sydney for seven years when the bridge was being built. While in Australia he was made a director of the firm."[1] There was controversy over who actually designed the bridge – John Job Crew Bradfield or Sir Ralph Freeman. "The controversy was never finally resolved, but when Bradfield retired in 1933, the director of public works stated that Bradfield was the designer of the bridge and that 'no other person by any stretch of imagination can claim that distinction'.

However, modifications had been made to the design after Freeman's visit in 1926, and in 1932, Dorman Long threatened to sue the government if it erected a plaque naming Bradfield as the designer. One informed view was that the 'detail design was entrusted to Lawrence Ennis who became first Honorary Member of the Institution [of Engineers, Australia] in 1932'. Professor Crawford Munro also considered that Bradfield 'did not design the Sydney Harbour Bridge which we now behold'."[2] "The signatures that appear on the main contract for the Sydney Harbour Bridge were those of Lawrence Ennis for Dorman, Long and Company (as director responsible for the Sydney operations) and the Honourable Richard T. Ball, Minister for Public Works, New South Wales."[3]

Donald Macadie 1871-1955 invented the AVOmeter multimeter, the first multimeter combining the measurement of Amps, Volts and Ohms. The first multimeter was manufactured by The Automatic Coil Winder Company (predecessor to AVO, later Megger) in 1923. By 1965, the company had already created over one million AVOmeters. The meter comprised a galvanometer, voltage and resistance references, and a switch to select the appropriate circuit for the input under test.[1]

Ernest Rutherford 1871-1937 famously "split" the atom and made many other discoveries in physics. He invented a detector for electromagnetic waves, an essential feature being an ingenious magnetising coil containing tiny bundles of magnetised iron wire. He worked jointly with Joseph John Thomson on the behaviour of the ions observed in gases which had been treated with X-rays, and also, in 1897, on the mobility of ions in relation to the strength of the electric field, and on related topics such as the photoelectric effect. In 1898, he reported the existence of alpha and beta rays in uranium radiation and indicated some of their properties. Rutherford and Frederick Soddy proposed that radioactivity results from the disintegration of atoms.[1]

In Montreal, there were ample opportunities for research at McGill University, and his work on radioactive bodies, particularly on the emission of alpha rays, was continued in the Macdonald Laboratory. With Robert Bowie Owens, he studied the "emanation" of thorium and discovered a new noble gas, an isotope of radon, which was later to be known as thoron. Frederick Soddy arrived at McGill in 1900 from Oxford, and he collaborated with Rutherford in creating the "disintegration theory" of radioactivity which regards radioactive phenomena as atomic – not molecular – processes.[2]

In 1909, he began experiments that were to change the face of physics. He discovered the atomic nucleus and developed a model of the atom that was similar to the solar system. Like planets, electrons orbited a central, sun-like nucleus. Acceptance of this model grew after it was modified with quantum theory by Niels Bohr.[3] For his work with radiation and the atomic nucleus, Rutherford received the 1908 Nobel Prize in Chemistry. "He much resented that the prize was in chemistry rather than physics, and his acceptance speech made a remark to the effect that he had seen many transformations in his studies, but never one more rapid than his own from physicist to chemist".[4]

Rutherford continued his research on the properties of the radium emanation and of the alpha rays and, in conjunction with Hans Geiger, a method of detecting a single alpha particle and counting the number emitted from radium was devised. In 1910, his investigations into the scattering of alpha rays and the nature of the inner structure of the atom which caused such scattering led to the postulation of his concept of the "nucleus", his greatest contribution to physics. According to him, practically the whole mass of the atom and at the same time all positive charge of the atom is concentrated in a minute space at the centre.

In 1912, Niels Bohr joined him at Manchester and he adapted Rutherford's nuclear structure to Max Planck's quantum theory and so obtained a theory of atomic structure which, with later improvements, mainly as a result of Werner Karl Heisenberg's concepts, remains valid to this day. In 1913, together with Henry Gwyn Jeffreys Moseley, Rutherford used cathode rays to bombard atoms of various elements and showed that the inner structures correspond with a group of lines which characterise the elements. Each element could then be assigned an atomic number and, more important, the properties of each element could be defined by this number.

In 1919, during his last year at Manchester, he discovered that the nuclei of certain light elements, such as nitrogen, could be "disintegrated" by the impact of energetic alpha particles coming from some radioactive source, and that during this process fast protons were emitted. This was the first artificially induced nuclear reaction. Rutherford had virtually created a new discipline, that of nuclear physics.[5] Patrick Maynard Stuart Blackett later proved, with the cloud chamber, that the nitrogen in this process was actually transformed into an oxygen isotope, so that Rutherford was the first to deliberately transmute one element into another.[6]

George Udny Yule 1871-1951 had great influence on the early development of modern statistics, particularly on experimentation in biology and agriculture, and analysis of vital and industrial statistics. His main contributions in the theoretical field were concerned with regression and correlation, with association, particularly in 2×2 contingency tables, with time-series, with Mendelian inheritance, and with epidemiology.[1]

Yule did not develop any completely new branches of statistical theory, but he took the first steps in many areas which proved important in their further development by later statisticians.[2]

Most of his early lectures focused on topics which led to his first book, which appeared in 1911, *An Introduction to the Theory of Statistics*. This book was essential to the people of the time because it was the only comprehensive textbook on the subject for more than 45 years.[3]

One major contribution Yule made began in 1912, when he worked with Major Greenwood (Major is his name, not his rank) on the foundations of theory of accident distributions. In 1915, Greenwood and Yule published a paper in which they were two of the first people to study anti-typhoid and anti-cholera inoculations. Many of their results and much of their original work are still used today.

Another contribution Yule and Greenwood made was their equation to figure out vaccine efficacy. This was significant in that it helped test vaccines more quickly so they could be used to treat the diseases that were so common in the early 1900s.

Yule was one of the first statisticians to work on unusual correlations. In 1926, Yule gave one of the first cohesive mathematical treatments of spurious correlations. He took a look at two variables which showed a very high correlation. He commented on the high correlation between the fall in proportion of Church of England marriages and the fall in mortality. Both the number of marriages and the mortality rate were affected by the Progress of Science since 1866. Because both variables were influenced by a common factor, it is reasonable to expect that they would be highly correlated. Yule concluded, however, that the correlation between the two is sheer nonsense and its meaning has no significance at all. Therefore, the two variables are not, in any sort of way, causally related to one another. This supports the fact that correlation does not imply causality.

Yule's work on regression was specifically built from Francis Galton's original work. He further developed Galton's ideas about multivariate data. Although his formulation and use of regression analysis was not a full solution, it was a masterly step towards one. Yule was just one of a series of remarkable men who introduced many new ideas into statistical theory. Without Yule's devotion and hard work, the use of probability-based statistical methods in the social sciences as well as in other disciplines would not be as advanced as it is today.[4]

John Anderson 1872-1929 was co-developer, with American Fred Dornbrook, of radiant superheating – a superheater so arranged and located to absorb heat mainly by radiation. He designed and supervised construction of the Lakeside generating plant in 1920, which was one of the first and largest plants in existence to burn pulverised coal. His invention of numerous devices connected with the development of pulverised fuel and high-pressure boilers made low-cost central service possible by more efficiently and economically utilising coal, thereby lowering the principal variable cost of producing electricity.[1] He was Chief Engineer of the Milwaukee Electric Railway & Light Company which became "the first central power station in the United States to be equipped and successfully operated with pulverised fuel."[2]

"Practically every big coal-burning plant built since 1935 has been designed to burn pulverised fuel. As this took place, pressures and temperatures throughout the country went steadily up, while the coal needed to make a unit of power went steadily down".[3]

George Balfour 1872-1941 pioneered the national electricity grid in Britain and designed the first hydro-electric schemes in Scotland. "He was one of the pioneers of electricity-supply development in Great Britain, and through his direction of the Scottish Power Company Limited; the Midland Counties Electricity Supply Co. Ltd.; the Metropolitan Electric Supply Company, Limited; the London Power Company, Limited, and the Lancashire Power Company, Limited; of all which he was Chairman, and in his capacity as a director of many other companies, he had a great influence on such development over very large areas of England and Scotland."[1]

In 1924, he was building hydro-electric schemes in East Africa and two years later in Jerusalem and Bethlehem. In 1926, he commenced the Lochaber Water Power Scheme, which involved building the longest tunnel in the world at 24 km. His activities covered railways, tramways and power stations in Bermuda, Uruguay, Argentina, Malaya (Perak River Hydro Scheme), and the 488 m Kut Barrage across the Tigris River in Iraq at Kut-el-Amara in 1938 involving 248,480 cubic metres of concrete.

The National Grid – initiated by Glasgow-born William Douglas Weir, 1st Viscount Weir – was completed by Balfour in 1939. During World War II, he linked the five major Orkney Islands by a causeway and, long after his death, his company was involved in the Channel Tunnel, working on the British end of the tunnel track work, catenary (i.e. overhead cables and wires) and power supplies.[2]

Alexander Gibb 1872-1958 established a firm of consulting engineers which became one of the largest in the world. Between 1909 and 1916 he was involved in the construction of Rosyth naval dockyard. Owing to administrative delays and various difficulties, it appeared at one time impossible that the dockyard could be completed in time to be of substantial use to the Fleet during the most vital period of the 1914-1918 war. "It was, and this was due to Alexander Gibb who, through his friend Winston Churchill, put forward an accelerated construction program and carried it through with extraordinary courage and persistence."

In 1916, in the middle of World War I, Gibb was appointed Chief Engineer, ports construction, to the British armies in France with responsibility for organising the reconstruction of Belgian ports and railway junctions. In 1918, he became the first civil engineer-in-chief to the Admiralty where, to counter the submarine menace, he developed the "mystery towers" to be sunk in the English Channel. These floating towers could be towed out and sunk in a line across the Channel, forming gun emplacements and bases for mines and nets. Although it came too late for use in the Great War, the principle was applied in the Second World War to provide anti-aircraft gun emplacements in the Thames and Mersey.[1]

He founded a consulting company in 1922 and produced the designs for Barking power station and later the Galloway hydroelectric development, the first major work of its kind to be linked to the national grid. He gave sage advice to the Government of Burma, when he recommended that no work be undertaken to remove a silt bar on the Rangoon River. He undertook tests and concluded that the bar would eventually disappear, thus saving a large amount of money that would have been spent dredging the river.

In 1936, his company designed the Kincardine Bridge over the Firth of Forth, which was at the time the largest road bridge in Britain. He was heavily involved in hydro-electric schemes, bridges, docks, and harbours. He was president of the Institution of Civil Engineers in 1936-1937.

In his lifetime, Gibb advised the governments of at least 17 countries. These included: Canada, for the administration and development of the Canadian National Ports; New Zealand, for the Arapuni hydro-electric station; Australia, for the Captain Cook Graving Dock at Sydney, 1941-1945; Burma, for the Port of Rangoon; Venezuela, for the La Guaira Harbour extension; and Colombia, for the sea walls at the mouth of the Magdalena River and the new port at Barranquilla. He also arranged the purchase, manning, and despatch of two destroyers built in Portugal to British designs. This was Colombia's Navy. Gibb advised on various works for the governments of Persia, India, and Turkey as well, and he was Consulting Engineer to the Admiralty for certain aspects of the Singapore Naval Base.[2]

Arthur Lapworth 1872-1941 discovered the electronic nature of organic chemical reactions in 1909. He was one of the founders of modern physical-organic chemistry. He formulated the electronic theory of organic reactions (independently of English chemist Robert Robinson). The ideas and principles of physical chemistry changed the world's teaching and practice of chemistry and, in particular, changed the way organic chemistry is performed, with enormous practical consequences.[1]

Lapworth was one of the first to emphasise that organic compounds can ionise, and that different parts of an organic molecule behave as though they bear electrical charges, either permanently or at the moment of reaction.

With the development of theories of valency based on the electronic structure of the atom, Lapworth was able to refine some speculations about "alternative polarities" in organic compounds into a classification of reaction centres as either anionoid or cationoid, the changes being determined by the influence of a key atom such as oxygen. He collaborated on these concepts with Robinson in the mid-1920s.[2]

Bertrand Arthur William Russell 1872-1970 made ground-breaking contributions to the foundations of mathematics and to the development of contemporary formal logic, as well as to analytic philosophy. His contributions relating to mathematics include his discovery of Russell's paradox, his defence of logicism (the view that mathematics is, in some significant sense, reducible to formal logic), his introduction of the theory of types, and his refining and popularising of the first-order predicate calculus. Along with Kurt Gödel, he is usually credited with being one of the two most important logicians of the 20th century.[1]

Russell discovered the paradox which bears his name while working on his *The Principles of Mathematics* (1903) which, although immensely complex, had a tremendous impact on the philosophy of mathematics. Russell's "solution", the theory of types, anticipated modern axiomatic set theory.[2] The paradox arose in connection with the set of all sets which are not members of themselves. Such a set, if it exists, will be a member of itself if and only if it is not a member of itself. The significance of the paradox follows since, in classical logic, all sentences are entailed by a contradiction. In the eyes of many mathematicians (including David Hilbert and Luitzen Brouwer), it therefore appeared that no proof could be trusted once it was discovered that the logic apparently underlying all of mathematics was contradictory. A large amount of work throughout the early part of this century in logic, set theory, and the philosophy and foundations of mathematics was thus prompted.[3]

In 1905, Russell published the essay *On Denoting* in which, for the first time, he applies his "theory of descriptions", arguing that it is through an analysis of denoting phrases that thought can be represented. Convinced that ordinary language differs from "logical" forms of expression, he furthermore coins the term "descriptive phrases" to denote incomplete symbols that acquire their meaning only within a given context. Propositions, therefore, ought to be constituted by existing (concrete) entities.[4]

Russell abandoned all vestiges of his earlier idealism and adopted the view, which he was to hold for the rest of his life, that analysis, rather than synthesis, was the surest method of philosophy and that therefore all the grand system building of previous philosophers was misconceived. In arguing for this view with passion and acuity, Russell exerted a profound influence on the entire tradition of English-speaking analytic philosophy, bequeathing to it its characteristic style, method, and tone.

Inspired by the work of the mathematicians whom he so greatly admired, Russell conceived the idea of demonstrating that mathematics not only had logically rigorous foundations, but also that it was in its entirety nothing but logic. The philosophical case for this point of view – subsequently known as logicism – was stated at length in *Principia Mathematica*, his magnum opus, published in three volumes in 1910, 1912 and 1913. The first volume was co-written by Alfred North Whitehead, although the later two were almost all Russell's work. The aspiration of this ambitious work was nothing less than an attempt to derive all of mathematics from purely logical axioms, while avoiding the kinds of paradoxes and contradictions found in the German mathematician Gottlob Frege's earlier work on set theory.[5]

Russell argued that the whole of mathematics could be derived from a few simple axioms that made no use of specifically mathematical notions, such as number and square root, but were rather confined to purely logical notions, such as proposition and class. In this way, not only could the truths of mathematics be shown to be immune from doubt, they could also be freed from any taint of subjectivity, such as the subjectivity involved in Russell's earlier Kantian view that geometry describes the structure of spatial intuition. Near the end of his work on *The Principles of Mathematics*, Russell discovered that he had been anticipated in his logicist philosophy of mathematics by Frege, whose book *The Foundations of Arithmetic* (1884) contained, as Russell put it, "many things…which I believed I had invented." Russell quickly added an appendix to his book that discussed Frege's work, acknowledged Frege's earlier discoveries, and explained the differences in their respective understandings of the nature of logic.[6]

Given his impact in various fields such as logic, mathematics and philosophy, Russell is undoubtedly one of the most important scholars and philosophers of the 20th century. During his lifetime, he published more than two thousand articles and many dozens of books.[7] He was arguably the greatest logician since Aristotle. Analytic philosophy, the dominant philosophy of the 20th century, owes its existence more to Russell than to any other philosopher, and the system of logic developed by Russell and Whitehead, based on earlier work by Richard Dedekind, Georg Ferdinand Ludwig Philipp Cantor, Friedrich Ludwig Gottlob Frege, and Giuseppe Peano, broke logic out of its Aristotelian straitjacket. He was also one of the century's leading public intellectuals and won the Nobel Prize for Literature in 1950 "in recognition of his varied and significant writings in which he champions humanitarian ideals and freedom of thought."[8]

William Cameron 1873-1934 played a major part in the popularisation of canned food. It was the desire to store food for his army that prompted Napoleon Bonaparte to offer 12,000 francs for anyone who could find a way to prevent military supplies from spoiling. Frenchman Nicholas Appert devised a method using glass jars with corked lids sealed with pitch and, by 1804, he was producing food supplies in vacuum packed jars. While Appert's method was successful, moving glass jars around the countryside was problematic with the state of roads, and also hot weather could damage the pitch seal. In England, Peter Durand took out a patent (No 3,372 on 25 August 1810) for preserving food in "vessels of glass, pottery, tin, or other metals or fit materials."[1]

By 1818, the British Navy was using 24,000 large handmade cans per annum containing over 18 tonnes of food, but mass production in the United States during their Civil War saw output rise from 5 million cans a year in 1861 to 30 million by war's end in 1865. In the 1880s, American Edwin Norton increased capacity to 2,500 per hour by mechanically soldering seams on the sides of cans. This, however, presented a problem as there was no easy way to test cans for perforations or incomplete soldering when they were processed at such speed.

Cameron solved this problem in the 1920s and 1930s when, with a series of patents, he was able to test cans at the rate of 18,000 per hour by using an air tester which not only detected faulty cans but separated them from good ones. His first can-testing patent was on 4 December 1922 (No. 1,568,956), although he had filed an earlier patent on 28 March 1919 for applying a composition "to can ends for the purpose of effecting an air tight seal between the ends and the can bodies when these ends are double seamed onto the bodies without the use of solder."[2]

He established the Cameron Can Machinery Company which had offices in New York, London, Paris and Hong Kong, and agents worldwide. His patents were not just for testing cans, but also manufacturing and stacking them. In 1944, Cameron Can Machinery Company became part of Continental Can Company which itself became part of the giant United States Can Company.

Walter Reginald Hume 1873-1943 invented, in or around 1910, a method for making concrete pipes using a centrifugal process. Canals and rivers were important means of transport, water supply and sewage disposal. Gradually the use of piping, particularly concrete pipes, became increasingly important in supplying fresh water and disposing sewage. Hume's invention changed the manufacture of concrete pipes forever by greatly reducing their cost. He greatly facilitated the construction of supply lines to provide fresh water and to remove sewage and improve drainage, and it is his method that is used in the manufacture of concrete water, sewage and drainage pipes worldwide. His company, Hume's Patent Cement Iron Syndicate Ltd, founded in 1911, was the only Australian company prior to the Second World War that pioneered a new technology and exported it worldwide.[1]

William Murray Morrison 1873-1948 made major improvements to the production processes for aluminium, particularly to electrolytic cells, which are used in electro-refining and electrowinning of several non-ferrous metals. Almost all high-purity aluminium, copper, zinc and lead are produced industrially in electrolytic cells. Between 1915 and 1930, Morrison increased the size of individual electrolytic cells by a factor of five, from 8,000 to 40,000 amperes.[1]

As General Manager of British Aluminium Corporation, he expanded production at Kinlochleven, where a 24 km pressure tunnel was bored under the solid rock of Ben Nevis to connect Treig Dam with a steel pipeline dropping 180 metres to the powerhouse just outside Fort William. This was undertaken during the height of World War II. Morrison "stands out in the history of British Aluminium for his engineering brilliance, energy and vision".[2]

David Randall-MacIver 1873-1945 conducted excavations of the Great Zimbabwe ruins in Southern Rhodesia (now Zimbabwe). He wrote *Medieval Rhodesia* (1906), in which he contended that the ruins were not built by an ancient and vanished white civilisation as was currently believed but were of purely African 14th century origin (as confirmed by later archaeological study). Walls at these ruins stood as high as 9.7 m over the surrounding savannah. From 1907 to 1911, he led an expedition into Egypt and the Sudan.[1]

In 1899-1900 he discovered and investigated the mortuary temple of Pharaoh Senwosret III and to him goes the credit for initially identifying its royal owner. With Arthur Weigall and Charles Currelly, Randall-MacIver defined the basic elements of the complex of Senwosret III, providing the foundation for the Penn Museum's excavations at South Abydos.[2]

Randall-MacIver carried out several important field seasons, at the sites of Areika, Karanog, and Buhen, in Nubia (1907-1910) with the Museum's Assistant Curator, Leonard Woolley. At the time, Nubia had been virtually untouched by archaeology, and their work led to the discovery of rich cultural remains that spanned over three millennia, from 3100 BC well into the Roman and Byzantine periods.[3]

Charles Vickery Drysdale 1874-1961 invented, in 1910, the alternating current polar potentiometer, "which is the universal instrument by which currents are determined in terms of a difference of potential between the end of a known resistance ... for the measurement of alternating potentials."[1] The "first sensitive and practical AC potentiometer was devised by Drysdale in 1910 on the principle of balancing two alternating P.D.'s [power distributions], both in magnitude and phase, and using a telephone or vibration galvanometer as the detector".[2] He invented the Torsion Head Dynamometer Polyphase Wattmeter in 1912 for use in laboratories, and the phase-shifting transformer, or quadrature booster (quad booster for short), is a specialised form of transformer used to control the flow of real power on three-phase electricity transmission networks. It became the basis of servo-mechanisms throughout the world.

Another Drysdale invention was non-inductive shunts (1909), and in 1911 Drysdale devised a vibration galvanometer, primarily for use with his AC potentiometer. The control was exercised by a large horizontal permanent magnet, the strength of which could be varied by varying the distance between its pole pieces and by sliding an armature or "magnetic shunt" along it, so that tuning could be effected without touching the moving system. In 1920, he substituted an electromagnet controlled from outside by a battery and rheostat, and this form has since been independently conceived and constructed by the Cambridge Instrument company. Drysdale was a founder of the Family Planning Association in Britain.[3]

He made "several important contributions to technical literature on alternating current measurements, and included his pioneer work on the design of instrument transformers. The regenerative dynamometer, together with the cone stroboscope, was also devised at about this time for the equipment of the laboratories. He also ... had some of the first iron-cored wattmeters built to his design which gave remarkably good performance. The simple phase shifting transformer was also designed and built, being originally intended to facilitate testing the performance of wattmeters at low power factors, and eventually this apparatus made possible his adaptation of the direct current potentiometer to the measurement of alternating potentials. This was the first self-contained instrument for this purpose, and in connection with it he designed the first vibration galvanometer with tuning effected by variation of the magnetic control. He also gave considerable attention to accurate resistance measurement and devised a new form of standardising bridge which was a combination of the Kelvin and Carey Foster principles, and allowed precise comparisons between standards over a wide range of values to be made with great accuracy and rapidity, and in connection with this bridge he developed a novel and accurate ohm standard ingeniously compensated for temperature change. Sometime later he designed low resistance standards with very small time constants for use in alternating current circuits."[4]

John Knight Fotheringham 1874-1936 was noted for his extensive researches on the accelerations of the moon and sun as revealed by the study of ancient astronomical observations. He was the first person to make a reasonably accurate estimate of the apparent solar acceleration, and also considerably refined the adopted value for the lunar acceleration. His most outstanding paper on this subject was published in *Monthly Notices* in 1920. Here he produced an intriguing diagram showing lunar acceleration versus solar acceleration as derived from ancient eclipse observations. During the 1960s and 1970s in particular, this diagram attracted remarkable interest among geophysicists, and Fotheringham's work is still frequently quoted in geophysical literature.[1] Fotheringham's work helped him, Carl Schoch and Stephen Langdon identify the chronology of some Babylonian kings through the use of observations of Venus during the first dynasty.[2] They assigned 1921 BC for the ascension to the throne of King Ammizaduga, fifth king after Hammurabi, although this is now thought too early by some scholars.

William McLellan 1874-1934 was an electrical engineer who went into partnership with Charles Merz. Their company designed the first three-phase electrical supply network in the UK on Tyneside. Opening in 1901, it was the largest integrated power system in Europe by 1912. The

British government, seeking to replace the hodgepodge electricity generating systems in the United Kingdom turned to William Douglas Weir to provide a solution. He turned to Merz & McLellan and the outcome was the *Electricity (Supply) Act 1926*, which created the Central Electricity Board to provide a gridiron transmission system, running at 132 kV, 50 Hz. Commencing supply in 1933, it became truly national by 1938. "As demand for electricity grew so too did the firm continue to flourish and grow over the following decades, not only in the UK but throughout the British Empire, Africa, the Middle and Far East and South America. Most of the biggest power schemes in these places have been influenced in some way by Merz & McLellan."[1]

In 1929, McLellan designed the Galloway Hydro-Electric Power Scheme, the first large-scale hydro-electric power scheme in Scotland. The scheme was made viable by the recent formation of the National Grid which made generation of electricity in remote areas useful. Hydro power was particularly helpful to this grid because of its ability to be turned on and off very quickly to meet peak demands (in contrast to oil and coal stations), and to meet the natural increase during the more energy demanding winter months.

Guglielmo Marconi 1874-1937 shared the 1909 Nobel Prize (with Karl Ferdinand Braun of Germany) "in recognition of their contributions to the development of wireless telegraphy".

Marconi did not discover any new and revolutionary principle in his wireless-telegraph system, but rather he assembled and improved a number of components, unified and adapted them to his system.

In 1896, he was granted the world's first patent for a system of wireless telegraphy. In 1899, he established wireless communication between France and England across the English Channel. He erected permanent wireless stations at: The Needles, Isle of Wight; at Bournemouth; and later at the Haven Hotel, Poole, in Dorset. In 1900, he took out his famous patent No. 7777 for "tuned or syntonic telegraphy" and, on 12 December 1901, determined to prove that wireless waves were not affected by the curvature of the Earth, he used his system for transmitting the first wireless signals across the Atlantic between Poldhu, Cornwall, and St. John's, Newfoundland, a distance of 2,100 miles (3,380 km).

Between 1902 and 1912, he patented several new inventions. In 1902, during a voyage in the American liner *Philadelphia*, he first demonstrated "daylight effect" relative to wireless communication, and in the same year patented his magnetic detector which then became the standard wireless receiver for many years. In December 1902, he transmitted the first complete messages to Poldhu from stations at Glace Bay, Nova Scotia, and later Cape Cod, Massachusetts, these early tests culminating in 1907 in the opening of the first transatlantic commercial service between Glace Bay and Clifden, Ireland, after the first shorter-distance public service of wireless telegraphy had been established between Bari in Italy and Avidari in Montenegro. In 1905, he patented his horizontal directional aerial and in 1912 a "timed spark" system for generating continuous waves.

During his war service in Italy, he returned to his investigation of short waves, which he had used in his first experiments. After further tests by his collaborators in England, an intensive series of trials was conducted in 1923 between experimental installations at the Poldhu Station and in Marconi's yacht *Elettra* cruising in the Atlantic and Mediterranean, and this led to the establishment of the beam system for long-distance communication. Proposals to use this system as a means of Imperial communications were accepted by the British Government and the first beam station, linking England and Canada, was opened in 1926, other stations being added the following year.

In 1931, Marconi began research into the propagation characteristics of still shorter waves, resulting in the opening in 1932 of the world's first microwave radiotelephone link between the Vatican City and the Pope's summer residence at Castel Gandolfo. Two years later at Sestri Levante, he demonstrated his microwave radio beacon for ship navigation and in 1935, again in Italy, gave a practical demonstration of the principles of radar, the coming of which he had first foretold in a lecture to the American Institute of Radio Engineers in New York in 1922.[1] Note: In addition to Marconi, two of his contemporaries, Nikola Tesla and Nathan Stufflefield, took out patents for wireless radio transmitters. Nikola Tesla is now credited with being the first person to patent radio technology; the US Supreme Court overturned Marconi's patent in 1943 in favour of Tesla.[2]

Charles Hesterman Merz 1874-1940 was an electrical engineer who pioneered the use of high-voltage three-phase AC power distribution in the United Kingdom, building a system in the North East of England in the early 20th century that became the model for the country's National Grid.

In 1898, Merz became the first Secretary and Chief Engineer of the Cork Electric Tramways and Lighting Company in Cork, Ireland. This project was followed by the Neptune Bank Power Station in Wallsend near Newcastle. It was the first three-phase electricity supply system in Great Britain, and was opened on 18 June 1901. He was a consultant to a local tramway company on the electrification of their horse-drawn routes and, subsequently, to the Tyneside local lines of the North Eastern Railway, a pioneer of British mainline railway electrification, whose electric systems were turned on in 1904.

Between 1907 and 1913, Merz was hired by Thomas James Tait to electrify the railway system in Melbourne, Australia. The new system began operation in 1919, after World War I.

In recommending the Newmarket (Melbourne) substation for listing as a heritage site it was stated: "The Newmarket substation is scientifically important because it is one of the first group of buildings constructed for the electrified Melbourne suburban railway network, which was the first electric railway system in Australia, had the largest power generating plant in the southern hemisphere, and was the largest electrified suburban train service converted from steam operation in the world. The Melbourne suburban network was the first electric system to employ a 1,500 volt Direct Current overhead system. It became the model for later installations in England, France, Holland, Brazil, Japan, New Zealand and India. The Melbourne electrification scheme was a significant work of engineer Charles Hesterman Merz, who had acquired experience of railway electrification while acting as consulting engineer on the 1904 electrification of the Newcastle suburban system on Britain's North Eastern Railway in 1904. The electric railway system was also important because its central power generating station supplied electricity for suburban domestic and industrial use, thereby replacing a number of small scale power generating plants."[1]

He was also involved in the electrification of suburban railways at Buenos Aires (1909), and Bombay (1913), followed by extension of the electrification of the railway over the Ghats (a mountain range on the western side of India); the Carville "B" power-station and the North-Tees power-station with Scottish-born William McLellan, (1914-1918); and many other power schemes in America and South Africa. During the Great War, he was Director of Experiment and Research at the Admiralty, dealing especially with anti-submarine warfare. In 1919, he advised upon the design of the new large power-station at Barking.[2]

In 1916, Merz pointed out that the UK could use its small size to its advantage, by creating a dense distribution grid to feed its industries efficiently. His findings led to the *Williamson Report* of 1918 (a committee chaired by Scotsman Sir Archibald Williamson, 1st Baronet), which in turn created the *Electricity Supply Bill* of 1919. The bill was the first step towards an integrated system. He also sat on the Weir Committee, which produced the more significant *Electricity (Supply) Act 1926*, leading to the setting up of Britain's National Grid.[3]

William Paterson 1874-1956 made major improvements to the purification of water in bulk, initially for industrial use but then for domestic consumption. Weardale and Consett Water Company undertook "pre-treatment of 2.5 million gallons [11,365,230 litres] of water a day to improve its condition before passing through slow sand filters then in general use. Such pre-treatment greatly prolonged the life of the slow filters and obviated the need for large and costly extensions. In 1910, Paterson designed and installed a plant for the complete purification of 4 million gallons [18.2 million litres] pumped daily from the River Severn for the drinking supply of Cheltenham. It was the first plant in Britain to use chlorine for the routine sterilisation of a water supply to eliminate pathological bacteria.

Paterson was always interested in the prevention of water-borne diseases, and he had extensive researches carried out on the use of chlorine gas for this purpose, either alone or in conjunction with ammonia to form chloramine. This led to important improvements in the method and equipment for applying these reagents for sterilisation, and also in the use of ozone for the same purpose."[1] He then built a demonstration water purification plant in Poona (now Pune), India, following which his techniques were adopted throughout the sub-continent.

He was active during both World Wars, designing several purification plants in the Great War, including the 38 million litres per day plant at Gretna in the borders of Scotland. In the Second World War, he designed a mobile filtration and sterilisation unit "which combined light weight and compactness with high capacity and great efficiency. This type of filter was widely adopted by British, American, and colonial forces and was responsible, to a large degree, for the extremely low incidence of fatal outbreaks of water-borne diseases among allied troops. Paterson's activities resulted in many other important new developments in water treatment. These included the excess lime process of water softening and sterilisation for public supplies in which he collaborated with Sir Alexander Houston, then director of water examination in the Metropolitan Water Board, and the use of chlorine gas for inhibiting algal accumulations in thermal electric power-station condenser systems. This method, originally applied in 1922, was adopted worldwide with important consequent fuel economies, estimated at perhaps half a million tons [453,592 tonnes] of coal a year in Britain alone."[2]

With Oscar Carl Kerrison, he patented the ubiquitous Anderson bomb shelter, named for Edinburgh-born John Anderson M.P. who was in charge of Air Raid Precautions and who commissioned Paterson to design a small and cheap shelter that could be erected in people's gardens. "Within a few months nearly one and a half million of these Anderson Shelters were distributed to people living in areas expected to be bombed by the Luftwaffe. Made from six curved sheets bolted together at the top, with steel plates at either end, and measuring 6ft 6in by 4ft 6in (1.95m by 1.35m) the shelter could accommodate six people. These shelters were half buried in the ground with earth heaped on top. The entrance was protected by a steel shield and an earthen blast wall. Anderson shelters were given free to poor people. Men who earned more than £5 a week could buy one for £7. Soon after the outbreak of the Second World War in September 1939, over 2 million families had shelters in their garden. By the time of the Blitz this had risen to two and a quarter million."[3] "During his career he had taken out more than seventy British patents, many of which presaged improvements only fully developed by the industry years later. The world history of water purification in the first half of the 20th century conforms closely to the pattern of the developments due to his foresight."[4]

CHAPTER 6

1875-1899

By the start of the last quarter of the 19th century, Great Britain, the unrivalled world power since the end of the Napoleonic War, saw a unified Germany and a growing United States – now in full recovery after its Civil War – start to make inroads into its premier position. The telephone, invented in 1876, saw not only cities and nations connected to rapid communication, but continents, too. One of the great technical achievements of this period was the linking of Britain with Europe and North America by the transatlantic cable made possible through inventions of William Thomson (Lord Kelvin). The peak of the railway mania had passed in Western Europe, but feverish activity took place to connect the east and west coasts of both Canada and the United States, as well as major railway building in Australia, New Zealand and parts of Asia, Africa and Latin America. In Africa, a number of European powers claimed much of the continent for themselves, with Britain obtaining the lion's share during the "Scramble for Africa" in the last decade of the century. Electricity began to challenge gas as the preferred means of lighting and power supply. Moving pictures – the flicks – caused a sensation towards the end of the century and petrol-driven automobiles started to appear on roads that still were, almost universally, dirt. Medical operations became safer with the discovery that bacteria and other microbes could cause infection, heralding the dominance of aseptic surgery to replace the inferior, but still useful, antiseptic surgery. James Clerk Maxwell unified magnetism and electricity, and the first radio signals were sent, although Alexander Graham Bell beat all of the radio pioneers in 1880 when he transmitted the human voice by artificial means over a distance with his photophone.

Armaments improved with steel-clad warships, and railways and steamships sped the movement of men, materiel, machine guns and improved rifles to expand or control imperial possessions and, ominously, chemists were discovering powerful toxic gases that would be used on future battlefields. In all of these technological advances, Scots were up amongst the leaders. Scotland, which had a level of education at the higher end of world nations in the 18th century, continued to produce a surfeit of medical doctors, engineers, teachers, missionaries, steamship officers, and railway men, providing a nucleus of technically skilled workers who took their knowledge to the ends of the Earth.

Charles Edward Inglis 1875-1952 invented a precursor of the Bailey bridge. Immediately prior to World War I, he contrived a lightweight, reusable tubular steel bridge of triangular truss sections that was easy to erect and which was successfully used during the Great War and in World War II until replaced by the Bailey bridge. In 1913, he published a seminal paper on stresses in a metal plate due to the presence of cracks and sharp corners.

Inglis and, independently, the Russian mathematician Gury Vasilyevich Kolosov, identified an issue with stresses around an elliptical hole. "Their solution showed that the concentration of stress could become far greater, as the radius of curvature at an end of the hole becomes small compared with the overall length of the hole. These results provided the insight to sensitise engineers to the possibility of dangerous stress concentrations at sharp re-entrant corners, notches, cutouts, keyways, screw threads, and similar openings in structures for which the nominal stresses were at otherwise safe levels. Such stress concentration sites are places from which a crack can nucleate."[1]

Inglis pioneered the use of temporary bridges suitable for tanks in co-operation with Giffard Le Quesne Martel. Inglis convinced his military superiors that the weight of the component parts of these bridges did not prevent their rapid assembly on the battlefield or when making rapid manoeuvres. With Martel, he even developed a tank capable of carrying and laying bridges. Their bridges were the first dry-gap (i.e. not crossing water), prefabricated military bridge in service with any Army. A number of Stock Spans were introduced earlier, but these were used in construction bridging rather than as a self-contained portable bridge. The Inglis Bridge was without a doubt the best military bridge of the time with short construction times and high carrying capacity, but because of its tubular steel construction, it was expensive. After the Great War, the Inglis Mk II continued to be used and developed into assault and floating bridges.

The Inglis Assault Bridge was a 135 foot (41 m) long span with a pair of idler tracks. The concept called for the Royal Engineers Tank to use its jib to push the assembled bridge over the gap. In less than a minute, a 70-foot (21 m) gap could be bridged without exposing any personnel to fire, the first true assault bridge to use a bridge of substantial length, over the standard 30-foot (9 m) assault bridges of the time.[2]

Image 92 – Inglis Bridge over the River Monnow, Herefordshire

Archibald Page 1875-1949 was director and general manager of the County of London Electric Supply Corporation. His period of office was marked by the construction of the Barking generating station (to become one of the largest thermo-electric stations in Europe) and of the associated high-voltage transmission system. The formation of the Central Electricity Board in 1927 brought Page the final opportunity of his career. With fellow Scot Sir Andrew Rae Duncan as chairman, Page, as Chief Engineer and general manager, directed the construction of the National Electricity Grid and the standardisation of frequency of the national system. The enterprise was conducted with promptness, efficiency, and economy, both in construction and in operation.[1]

Robert John Strutt 1875-1947 (Lord Rayleigh) made important contributions with his investigations into the age of minerals and rocks by measurements of their radioactivity and helium content, his studies of the resonance and fluorescence of metallic vapours excited by electric discharges, and his discovery of active nitrogen (active nitrogen is "made" when high voltage is exposed to almost pure nitrogen with an almost non-existent amount of oxygen or other gases. The nitrogen glows with a golden colour).[1]

In 1916, he and his colleague, Alfred Fowler, were the first to prove the existence of ozone in the atmosphere, and Strutt proceeded to show that it was mainly located in the higher regions. A number of other subjects came under his investigation: electrical discharges in vacuo, the Becquerel rays, optical contact, the green flash at sunset, the glow of phosphorus, iridescent colours in nature, the bending of marble and glass, and the formation of pebbles, pallasites, and red sandstones. His work on the helium content of rocks was pioneering research and led to a great extension of Lord Kelvin's estimate of the age of the Earth, and a closer accord with geological evidence.[2]

He was the first to distinguish between two types of light in the night sky, the aurora seen in Polar Regions and the airglow observable all over the earth; his posthumous nickname was "the Airglow Rayleigh". In 1929, he succeeded in measuring the intensity of the light from the night sky, and the photometric unit for sky brightness, the rayleigh, is named after him. Rayleigh was very methodical in his ways, and his papers are a model of lucidity. He was author of one of the earliest books on radioactivity – *The Becquerel Rays and the Properties of Radium* (1904).[3]

Robert James Dickie 1876-1958 patented the world's first stamp vending machine in 1909. As Dickie was working at the front desk of the New Zealand Post Office selling stamps, "it occurred to him that tearing stamps from a large sheet by hand was a waste of time, especially since most of the stamps sold were for the same value. A machine, he thought, could do this job just as well as a person." By 1938, 18,000 had been installed in Britain alone.[1]

William Wallace Gibson 1876-1965 designed and built the first successful Canadian aircraft engine, installed in the Twin-Plane aircraft, which he also designed with wings fore and aft of the pilot, despite have no formal training. His aircraft first flew on 8 September 1910 near Victoria, British Columbia, with a 60 hp gasoline engine flying a distance of 200 feet (61 m) at a height of 20 feet (6.1 m). It was a new six-cylinder, air-cooled, two cycle engine which flew his plane with a tractor screw at one end of the crankshaft and a 1:2 geared lower-pitch pusher propeller running counterwise at the other end.[1]

Herbert Nigel Gresley 1876-1941 designed the *Mallard* A4-class 4-6-2 locomotive which still holds the world speed record for steam traction. He was born in Edinburgh but raised in England to English parents (see Introduction). In 1906, he designed and produced a bogie luggage van with steel underframe, teak body, elliptical roof, bowed ends and buckeye couplings, which became the prototype for East Coast main-line coaches built over the next thirty-five years. In

1921, Gresley introduced the first British restaurant car with electric cooking facilities. He modified the 4-6-2 locomotives to reduce their coal consumption, enabling them to run non-stop from London to Edinburgh. In 1923, he designed the A3 *Flying Scotsman*, which was the first steam locomotive in passenger service to surpass 100 mph (161 km/h).[1]

He continued to develop his designs over the years, and in 1922 completed the first of the famous three cylinder 4-6-2 Pacific engines. Many Pacifics were constructed at the London and North Eastern Railway's centres at Darlington and Doncaster. These were constantly improved with modifications such as increased boiler pressures and a higher degree of superheat.

In 1925, Gresley introduced the *Mikado*, a 2-8-2 locomotive for heavy freight traffic. He adopted the design nine years later for the *Cock o' the North*, a larger wheeled engine for heavy express work. In 1935, the *Silver Link* locomotive was built. It was a streamlined Pacific, and it was put to work on a completely streamlined train, the first in the United Kingdom, known as the *Silver Jubilee*. It made the daily journey from London to Darlington, a distance of 232 miles (373 km), in three hours eighteen minutes, without a stop.

In 1937, another streamlined train was introduced on the 393-mile (632 km) journey from London to Edinburgh, completing the journey in six hours. His streamlined 4-6-2 engine No. 4468, Mallard, broke the record for the highest speed ever reached by a train in the UK, maintaining 120mph (193 km/h) for five miles (8 km), with a short burst at 125 mph (201 km/h).

As well as his pioneering locomotive designs, another major achievement was the establishment of a locomotive testing station in the UK. He had long believed this to be of great importance to locomotive engineering in the country, and his efforts resulted in a national testing centre being constructed jointly by the London and North Eastern and the London, Midland and Scottish Railways, at Rugby. Work had commenced in 1937, but was postponed on the outbreak of war; unfortunately, Gresley did not live to see its completion.[2]

Anderson Gray McKendrick 1876-1943 and **William Ogilvy Kermack 1898-1970** were responsible for the most widely accepted mathematical model to describe the progress of an epidemic, the *General Epidemic Model* (1927). Their model is an "age of infection model", that is, a model in which the infectivity of an individual depends on the time since the individual became infective. It was the "first complete *model* (deterministic general epidemic) for the spread of an infectious disease which received attention in the literature."[1]

McKendrick pioneered the use of mathematical methods in epidemiology as well as many discoveries in stochastic processes (i.e. processes involving chance or probability). Early in his life, he took an active interest in health, including a review of rabies immunisation and trying to minimise dysentery in the local prison, both of which he did in India, and a study on the mode of carriage for infections. He produced 58 publications covering medical, statistical, epidemiological and demographic topics. McKendrick is remarkable for three major contributions to epidemic modelling – he described the Poisson Process, derived equations for the pure birth process, and a particular birth-death process. He also formulated the differential equations for the deterministic general epidemic, where he had anticipated many of the later discoveries in the area of stochastic processes. Second, he concluded that a Poisson distribution in observed cases of illness meant that there was no infectious process involved. Third,

McKendrick, with Kermack, published in 1927 a paper which provided the differential equations for a deterministic general epidemic.[2]

In 1914, he published a paper in which he gave equations for the pure birth process and a particular birth-death process. The earliest study concerned with estimating the incubation period of influenza was published by McKendrick and Morison in the *Indian Journal of Medical Sciences* in 1919. To obtain a precise estimate of the incubation period, appropriate censoring methods with well-defined short periods of exposure are needed, in addition to a large sample size. It is therefore remarkable that McKendrick was able to estimate the incubation period of pandemic influenza considering the unknown time of exposure in the given data. McKendrick was a world expert in rabies and he also made very important strides towards combating malaria by understanding mathematically how the diseases behaved in populations and tailoring preventative methods to respond to that.[3]

His 1926 publication, *Applications of mathematics to medical problems*, was considered ground-breaking. Describing an epidemic of cholera in an Indian village, McKendrick derived a Poisson model for the data, but there were too many 0s for the simple Poisson model to fit. If McKendrick had settled for the simple Poisson model in this situation, it would not have been the earliest citation in the seminal paper on the expectation-maximisation (EM) algorithm by Arthur Dempster, Nan Laird, and Donald Rubin (1977), nor would it have been reprinted in *Breakthroughs in Statistics*, Volume III (Kotz and Johnson 1997).[4] The link of McKendrick's work to the EM algorithm is due to an improvement made by Joseph Oscar Irwin on a novel method McKendrick used for estimating an infection rate when the observed data do not distinguish between those individuals who are not susceptible to the infection and those who are susceptible, but do not develop symptoms.[5]

The Lancet paper by Kermack, McKendrick and Peter Laird McKinlay (1901-1972), in 1934, was a landmark in the discussion of birth cohort influences on adult disease risk. It pre-dated Wade Hampton Frost's paper on cohort influences on tuberculosis mortality, and, whilst it was pre-dated by several demographic analyses highlighting birth cohort influences, was prescient in using these analyses to inform hypotheses regarding early-life exposures and their influence on later disease. As Kermack, McKendrick and McKinlay concluded, the data behaved as if "the expectation of life was determined by the conditions which existed during the child's early years", and concluded, "the health of the child is determined by the environmental conditions existing during the years 0-15, and ... the health of the man is determined preponderantly by the physical constitution which the child has built up".[6]

John James Rickard Macleod 1876-1935 was the co-recipient of the 1923 Nobel Prize for Physiology or Medicine with Canadian Frederick Grant Banting for the discovery of insulin, which has been "hailed as one of the most dramatic events in the history of the treatment of disease".[1]

Immediately, Macleod became the subject of controversy when Banting initially refused to accept the co-nomination as his assistant, Charles Herbert Best, had been omitted from the Prize (he was never nominated and, therefore, not eligible). Ever since, Macleod has been sidelined and "many historians believe that Macleod should not have been awarded the Prize because he had little or nothing to do with the actual work on insulin."[2]

However, one of the Nobel Prize committee, Hans Christian Jacobaeus, noted that "Dr Banting, who undoubtedly was the first to have the idea and who has carried out the investigations, should be the one who in the first place is awarded the Prize." But, he further stated that "it is very likely, that the discovery would never have been made if Macleod had not guided him, at least not as early as it turned out."[3] It is one of the myths of medical history that Macleod may have only received the Nobel Prize because he was the head of the department and did not contribute much to the discovery. This has been proven to be wrong.[4]

Many researchers worked on discovering the cause of diabetes, notably three Germans – Bernhard Naunyn, Joseph von Mering and Oskar Minkowski – and American Eugene Lindsay Opie, who established the association between diabetes and the destruction of the islets of Langerhans. Two Scots – zoologist John Rennie 1865-1928 and physician Thomas Fraser 1872-1951 – working in Aberdeen noted, in 1902, that the islet tissue (responsible for hormone production) of certain fish was anatomically distinct from the acinar pancreas (responsible for digestive enzyme production and secretion). They made extracts of islets of cod and hake, which, unlike those of mammals, are separate from the exocrine pancreas. They studied the effects in five patients with diabetes of giving an extract of "principal islets" – large islets forming separate globular aggregates made up mostly of endocrine pancreatic tissue present in some fishes and snakes – but no convincing benefit was detected.[5] Note: John Rennie discovered the tracheal mite that is implicated in Acarine disease in honey bees. Known to western beekeepers as Acarine disease, but better described as the Honeybee Tracheal Mite or simply the Tracheal Mite, it was first discovered by Rennie and his co-worker Philip Bruce White. The two men were investigating the cause of Isle of Wight disease. The mite was then thought to be the cause of this disease, but that is now believed to be caused by a bee virus and not by the mite. The full scientific name is *Acarapis woodi Rennie*, being first reported (Rennie, 1921) as *Tarsonemus woodi n.s.p.* (Rennie, 1921) and re-named by Hirst (1921). *Acarapis woodi Rennie*, known as the Honeybee Tracheal Mite (H.B.T.M.), reduces the resistance of bees to other parasites and diseases, shortens the life cycle and in heavy infestations can block the tracheae of bees.

Americans Ernest Scott and Israel Kleiner both carried out experiments whereby the pancreas was removed or tied off. One of the most notable of these early researchers was Romanian Nicola Paulesco who showed pancreatic extracts (pancreine) caused hypoglycemia (low blood sugar levels) in dogs when their pancreas was disabled or removed. His method of extraction involved removing the pancreas under conditions as sterile as possible, mincing it, extracting with ice-cold water and then filtering it. Paulesco's detailed description of his experiments provided convincing proof of the hypoglycaemic properties of the pancreatic extracts he had isolated, but the First World War delayed publication until 1921, when his research was reported in a series of short articles in a rather obscure French journal.[6]

In the meantime, Macleod had married and emigrated to work at Western Reserve University in Cleveland, Ohio. In 1905, he became interested in diabetes and began investigating the metabolism of carbohydrates, particularly the physiology of diabetes mellitus. He also investigated air sickness, electric shock, purine bases, carbamates, and the bacterium that causes tuberculosis.[7] He went on to publish thirty-seven papers on carbohydrate metabolism and an additional twelve papers on the experimentally-produced glycosuria (excretion of glucose into the urine). Twelve of his papers were published in the *American Journal of Physiology* between

1907 and 1914. Macleod concluded that impaired utilisation of sugar was probably the major reason for hyperglycaemia (higher than normal blood sugar level) in diabetes. This work came together in 1913 in an important monograph entitled *Diabetes: Its Pathological Physiology*, which established his reputation as an authority in the field. In this he points out that repeated attempts to lower blood glucose by injection of pancreatic extract had been unsuccessful, and speculated that this might be either because the hormone existed as an inactive precursor in the gland or was inactivated by pancreatic enzymes in the preparations that had been used.[8]

Macleod's textbook, *Physiology and Biochemistry in Modern Medicine* (1918), went through seven editions during his lifetime and was unique in its emphasis on the important role of chemistry in physiology.[9]

Macleod was by now the leading physiologist in diabetes,[10] which attracted Banting to him. In late October 1920, Banting read an article on the islets of Langerhans and their relation to diabetes, published in a medical journal he had received earlier that day. Of interest was the finding, during an autopsy, that a rare pancreatic stone had blocked the corpse's main pancreatic duct and that although the acinar cells of the pancreas had atrophied, the islet cells appeared intact. Additionally, the corpse was found not to have suffered from the effects of diabetes. In 1921, Banting came up with the hypothesis that the internal secretion of the pancreas (the protein hormone responsible for metabolism) originated in the cells of that organ. Before this, there was no understanding of how the disease worked.[11]

Banting hit upon the idea of ligating the duct as a way to increase the relative proportion of "internal secretion," which contained insulin, to that of the "external secretion," which emptied into the duodenum to aid digestion and which had nothing to do with the anti-diabetic properties of the pancreas. The story gets complicated soon after when Banting, who seems to have suffered from constant insecurity and possessed a very short-fused temper, looked to secure a small laboratory cum operating space and a few dogs.[12] Encouraged by Professor Frederick Miller from the Department of Physiology at Western University Medical School in London, Ontario, Banting approached Macleod in his office and related his idea about isolating the internal secretion of the pancreas. Macleod was not overly impressed with Banting's presentation. Still, in 1921, he arranged for Banting to come to the University of Toronto.

Banting's idea interested Macleod because he (Macleod) had come to believe that the pancreas was involved in diabetes, but he had been unable to determine its exact role. Ironically, Banting's original idea wasn't entirely correct. He and Best later found they could obtain insulin even from an intact pancreas. Improved technology for testing and detecting sugar in the blood and urine provided information that earlier researchers didn't have, and this encouraged them to pursue a line of thinking that may have looked like a dead end to those working in the decades before them.[13] Macleod assigned Best to work with Banting, and on 17 May Macleod joined them, instructing and assisting in their first pancreatectomy on a dog. They decided to use Eduard Emanuel Hedon's two-stage procedure, leaving a remnant of pancreas under the abdominal wall to be removed one week later.[14]

Shortly afterwards, Macleod left on a planned trip to Scotland. Professor Michael Bliss dispels the notion that Macleod set Banting and Best to work and then left town for his holidays. Macleod had worked for a month before he left, had gone through the technical problems with Banting and Best, had given fairly explicit parting instructions, and corresponded through the summer.[15] When he returned in September, Banting and Best had succeeded in extracting a substance that controlled the level of blood sugar in dogs whose pancreases had been removed. Macleod pointed out that there were flaws with the design of some of the experiments, and advised Banting and Best to repeat the experiments with better laboratory equipment, more dogs, and better control procedures. Macleod then provided better laboratory space for Banting and Best to work in, and began paying Banting a salary out of his research grants. Thus, while Banting's association with Macleod had been unofficial when he made his initial discovery, Macleod's providing a salary to Banting made their relationship official, and equivalent to what would now be considered the relationship between a postdoctoral researcher (Banting) and his supervisor (Macleod).[16]

Banting and Best repeated the experiments, which were conclusive when better equipment and techniques were used. While Banting's original method of isolating the insulin had been successful, it was too labour-intensive for large-scale production of insulin. Best then set about to find a biochemical extraction method for isolating insulin as an alternative to Banting's more labour-intensive method. At the same time, James Bertram Collip, a chemistry professor, joined what was now Macleod's insulin research team. This was apparently at the request of Banting in October 1921.[17] With Collip's help, using fractional precipitation with different concentrations of alcohol and other procedures, extracts of islets were obtained which could be safely injected into humans. This potent, effective and non-toxic material, named "isletin" (later called by Macleod "insulin" from its Latin root), was used in the first effective clinical studies."[18]

On 30 December 1921 Macleod, Banting, and Best presented their findings at the conference of the American Physiological Society, at Yale University. Banting, out of nervousness and inexperience, did a poor job delivering the paper, and the audience was highly critical of the findings presented. Macleod, as the chair of the session, joined the discussion in an attempt to rescue Banting from the scathing commentary, as one audience member recalled, years later: "Banting spoke haltingly, Macleod beautifully." After this fiasco, Banting became convinced that Macleod had stepped in to steal the credit from him and Best, and relations between the two began to deteriorate.[19]

The first human trial involved a patient in January 1922, using an extract made by Banting and Best, which was not effective. Days later, the same patient was injected with Collip's extract with quite different results. Fourteen-year-old Leonard Thompson had been diabetic since 1919, weighed only 65 pounds (29.5 kg), and was about to slip into a coma and die. After receiving Collip's extract, Thompson's symptoms began to disappear; his blood sugar returned to normal and he was brighter and stronger. The results were unequivocal; this extract of pancreas had a significant anti-diabetic effect on humans.[20]

In March 1922, English-born George Henry Alexander Clowes, director of research at Eli Lilly and Company, a large pharmaceutical manufacturer based in Indianapolis, Indiana, approached Macleod with a proposal. Clowes suggested that Eli Lilly help the researchers develop a method of large-scale insulin production. Macleod first rejected the offer; he wanted his team to do it on its own. However, the researchers made little progress in developing a way to mass-produce insulin, and Macleod re-contacted Clowes. In May of 1922, the University of Toronto entered into an agreement with Eli Lilly and Company. Clowes assigned two research chemists to the task of developing a method of mass-production that did not diminish insulin's potency. Lilly chemists George and Eda Bachman added an isoelectric precipitation step that ensured a potent product of standardised purity.[21] By the summer, thanks to the increased amount of insulin now available, more extensive clinical trials involving insulin could be conducted.

This increased activity added to Macleod's administrative responsibilities. During 1921-1922, he was already the President of the American Physiological Society, and from August 1922 to May 1923, Macleod served as official secretary of the insulin committee created by the board of governors of the University of Toronto to deal with patenting and licensing issues. He was also responsible for coordinating the patenting of insulin in Great Britain and the United States, and he was the main contact for both Clowes and Eli Lilly. Proceeds from the patent were given to the British Medical Research Council for the Encouragement of Research. The four researchers gained no profit from their discovery. In 1926, insulin was isolated in pure form by John Jacob Abel, and it eventually became available as a manufactured product.[22]

After Macleod and Banting were awarded the Nobel Prize, relations between them deteriorated, wholly due to Banting who went on an acrimonious campaign to minimise the role played by both Macleod and Collip in the development of insulin. Macleod didn't involve himself in the unseemly diatribe that developed, and he left Canada in 1928 to become Regius Professor of Physiology at the University of Aberdeen in Scotland. Before leaving, he was asked to remain on the board of The American Physiological Society, because APS Council decided it would be valuable to have a British representative. This was the origin of the European Editorial Committee (still in existence in 2015).

Macleod died in 1935, honoured in his native country but not in his adopted one. Contrary to Banting's and Best's later distorted accounts, Macleod was an active, essential supervisor of a research effort that, by the spring of 1922, had resulted in the discovery of insulin. His elaboration of the early crude results, his handling of the clinical trials, and his highly professional presentations of the research particularly impressed the Swedish investigators who rightly recommended that he share the 1923 Nobel Prize for Medicine or Physiology with Banting.[23]

Banting was ferociously assertive of his own role in the discovery, and Macleod, a reserved and modest man, was ill-equipped to stand up to the campaign that was waged against him. "Yet, it was exactly the qualities associated with Macleod – particularly his vast knowledge of the complexities of his subject and his commitment to the scientific vocation – that made it possible for him to play a vital role in the discovery of insulin."[24] This was shown in the years following the Nobel Prize when Macleod continued with an active research program, among other things providing the conclusive demonstration that insulin comes from the pancreatic islets. In some fish, the islets form an organ separate from the exocrine pancreas, and Macleod showed that extracts from these islets produced a hypoglycaemic effect in rabbits, whereas extracts from acinar tissue were inert. His published output was phenomenal and included a leading textbook of physiology, which went through seven editions in his lifetime. Macleod's contributions to the discovery of insulin were largely forgotten following his death.[25]

Banting lacked the scientific background to appreciate the value of the advice and contributions that Macleod and Collip had made to the work, and was convinced to the end of his life that he, with Best's help, had discovered insulin. Macleod was openly accused of stealing credit for work done by his juniors, and this did lasting harm to his reputation. The full story emerged with the publication in 1983 of Michael Bliss's *The Discovery of Insulin*. Macleod's major personal contributions were finally established beyond doubt. Bliss went on to show that Best had made an attempt to rewrite history in his own favour, behaviour that must be contrasted with the dignified silence of Collip and Macleod. Macleod himself was described by a friend as "immodestly modest, unassuming, social, sensitive, a born researcher and teacher", and this perhaps can serve as his epitaph. Insulin is his legacy.[26]

John Burton Cleland 1878-1971 discovered the viral aetiology of dengue fever and its transmission by mosquitoes. Today, dengue ranks as the most important mosquito-borne viral disease in the world. Current estimates report that, at least, 112 countries are endemic for dengue and about 40% of the world's population (2.5 billion people) are at risk in tropics and sub-tropics. Annually, 100 million cases of dengue fever and half a million cases of dengue haemorrhagic fever occur worldwide. Early recognition and prompt initiation of treatment are vital if disease-related morbidity and mortality are to be limited.[1] Cleland made his major contributions to experimental medicine in collaboration with Burton Bradley and W.M. McDonald. The first was the proof in 1916, using human volunteers, that the virus disease dengue is transmitted by the culicine mosquito *Aedes aegypti*. The second was the defining of the newly discovered encephalitis, then called "Australian X disease", and the proof that it was distinct from poliomyelitis, not only by its microscopic characteristics, but also by the experimental transmission of virus strains to monkeys, sheep and other herbivores.[2]

After his return to Adelaide, his interest in fungi expanded and he published two volumes (1934-1935) on the larger fungi of South Australia which included many other Australian records. Today, this is the only general Australian work on the subject. He presented a collection of nearly 30,000 plants to the South Australian Herbarium. His collecting included nearly 60 plant species new to science, described by John McConnell Black and others.

Cleland's biological collecting resulted in perhaps forty species or subspecies among fungi, vascular plants and animals being named after him, as well as a new genus *Clelandia* being erected in both the plant and animal worlds.[3]

Alexander Logie Du Toit 1878-1937 modified Alfred Wegener's theory of continental drifting by suggesting that two continents were present, Laurasia in the north and Gondwana in the south, as opposed to the one continent of Pangea. Du Toit theorised that the two great landmasses were separated by an oceanic area called Tethys. Du Toit helped modify the continental drift theory which was an important precursor to the development of the theory of plate tectonics which incorporates it. The theory of plate tectonics in the late 1960s and early 1970s grew out of observations and ideas of continental drift and seafloor spreading from scientists such as Wegener and Du Toit.[1]

Logie du Toit mapped the entire Karoo System in South Africa through the complete stratigraphy from Dwyka tillite to the basalt of the Drakensberg. In 1921, he wrote on the carboniferous glaciation of South Africa and on former land connections between South Africa and other continents. He expressed the belief that, to the end of Karroo times, the present fragments of Gondwanaland formed a unit landmass around or near a south pole and that this unit had suffered fracture into parts which had drifted away from one another ultimately to occupy their present positions. Assisted by a grant from the Carnegie Institution of Washington, du Toit spent six months of 1924 in South America where, in Argentina, Uruguay, Paraguay, Bolivia and Brazil he made a detailed study of the Palaeozoic and Mesozoic successions, a study whose results appear in the work entitled *A geological comparison of South America with South Africa*, which was published by the Carnegie Institution in 1927.

He wrote, "The concordance between the opposed shores, incidentally pointed out and discussed by others long before Wegener, has consistently been extended by each fresh geological observation until at present the amount of agreement is nothing short of marvellous." Persuasive of a former proximity of the two continents are the discoverable linkages that "cross from coast to coast, not only directly but diagonally as well, and are furthermore of widely different ages." In the map to illustrate this, tectonic and phasal (lateral variation in a formation) comparisons were delineated by du Toit between South America and Africa when separated only by the 300-400-kilometre width of their shelf areas. This brought the two, now separate, continents closer than du Toit had proposed in some of his earlier reconstructions before he had learned that "the mid-Atlantic Rise is ... more probably a recent structure and not a relic of fractured Gondwana."[2]

In this book, he appears as a whole-hearted supporter of the theory of continental drift, considering that it explains more simply than does that of land bridges the close geological, zoological and palaeontological similarities between the southern continents. These similarities, he asserted, are all the more striking in that the fossil remains contained in the Permian and Triassic formations of the various parts of "Gondwanaland" are not marine but entirely terrestrial. Almost identical climatic vicissitudes during these periods can be deduced for the several fragments, while major pre-drift tectonic structures find their homologues across the wide intervening seas.[3] Du Toit tabulated, under seven heads, the criteria for the establishment of continental drift "with any degree of probability". The heads are geodetic, physiographical, stratigraphical, tectonic, volcanic, palaeoclimatic, and palaeontological. He endeavoured, in his book, to consider the evidence available under each of these heads, recognising that earlier protagonists of the theory had been partial in their treatment of the subject.[4]

He was the first South African to be elected as a Fellow of the Royal Society (1943) and was twice President of the Geological Society of South Africa. He was President of the South African Archaeological Society in 1946-1947.

James Graham 1878-1954 took the first film of an eclipse of the sun, but, more importantly, he is remembered as the person who conceived and designed the first aircraft-carrier, the *Argus*, which was launched in 1918.[1]

The first person to take off in an aircraft from a ship was American pilot Eugene Ely in November 1910. He did so from a specially constructed platform on the deck of the cruiser USS *Birmingham*. In the following January, he landed on a platform built on the quarterdeck of the battleship USS *Pennsylvania,* using wires attached to sandbags on the platform as arresting gear; he then took off from the same ship.[2] HMS *Furious* was modified during World War I to take aircraft but it still had a superstructure which forced planes to manoeuvre around it. In 1918, HMS *Argus* was launched and this was the first true aircraft carrier and the model for every aircraft carrier that followed. *Argus* had an unobstructed flight deck 170.7 metres long and a hangar that could accommodate 20 aircraft. It was armed with six four-inch (10 cm) guns and could reach a speed of 20.2 knots (37.4 km/h).[3]

Image 93 – HMS *Argus* at sea during Operation Torch in late 1942
Image 94 – Five Sea Hurricanes and a Seafire in the hangar, c. 1942-44

Its origins go back to 1912 when, as a director of William Beardmore and Co. Ltd., Graham played a considerable part in the design of a 14,682-tonne vessel intended for delivery to the Italian Lloyd Sabaudo Line as the SS *Conte Rosso*. When war broke out in 1914, work on the vessel ceased. Two years later it was resumed; she was to be converted into an aircraft carrier. It is said that Graham – who had served in merchant vessels, and was later to serve in the Auxiliary Naval Service, and eventually in the Royal Naval Volunteer Reserve – was responsible for the conversion plans, which he first laid before the Admiralty in 1912. The conversion work was completed in September 1918 and the vessel was commissioned as HMS *Argus* – the first true "flat top". After modification in 1920 to carry about 20 aircraft, she was re-commissioned in 1921, and remained in service until 1947.[4]

Cluny Macpherson 1879-1966 designed a gas mask during World War I to protect soldiers from gas attacks. Gas masks in primitive form – such as sponges – had been used in ancient times but mainly for working in areas with putrid smells. In 1849, American Lewis Phectic Haslett took out a patent for an inhaler that filtered dust. The first practical gas mask for filtering toxic chemicals was invented by John Stenhouse in 1854 and two decades later, in 1871, another mask was made by John Tyndall. In the year that World War I started, American Garrett Morgan took out a patent for a safety hood and smoke protector. None of these had been used in chemical warfare, although the Stenhouse design would have provided the best protection of those listed. American James Bert Garner designed an effective gas mask in 1915 to counteract the use of chlorine gas and thousands of his masks were used by soldiers and in industry. Also in 1915, Englishman Edward Frank Harrison designed an effective gas mask that was issued to the army.

Canadian-born Cluny MacPherson developed the Hypo Helmet which was a mask made of chemical absorbing fabric and covered the whole head. By August 1916, British and Empire soldiers (and, from 1917, American troops) were issued with an updated version of Edward Harrison's mask, called the Small Box Respirator or canister gas mask. The Russians and French also had effective gas masks, as did the Germans, all developed independently.[1]

Peter Lymburner Robertson 1879-1951 invented the square-drive Robertson screw in 1908. He used an ingenious process he had developed to punch square holes into cold metal, then developed the innovative screw for industrial markets. The design remains popular: 85% of screws sold in Canada and 10% of American screws are Robertsons.[1]

Gladstone Adams 1880-1966 invented the automobile windscreen wiper, which he patented in 1911. He had conceived the idea when he attended the F.A. Cup Final in April 1908 and on his return journey was caught in a blizzard and had to stop the car frequently to wipe the windscreen.

Adams was also an aerial photographer during World War I, and he found the body of the German air ace, Baron Von Richthofen, the "Red Baron", and helped arrange the funeral.[1]

David Anderson 1880-1953 was a civil engineer and lawyer who went into partnership with Basil Mott and David Hay to create the firm of Mott, Hay & Anderson. During this time, he was engaged on design and supervision concerning construction of numerous large and important bridge and tunnel works, including the Mersey Tunnel between Liverpool and Birkenhead. This was the largest sub-aqueous vehicular tunnel in the world. Other works included many miles of London underground, railway tunnels, and numerous escalator tunnels in conjunction with them. Among the bridges were the Tyne Bridge at Newcastle, Wearmouth Bridge, and the Tees (Newport) Vertical Lift Bridge. He was elected president of the Institution of Civil Engineers for the November 1943 to November 1944 session.[1]

John Boyd Orr 1880-1971 was awarded the Nobel Peace Prize because he had used science as a way of "making men healthier and happier so as to secure peace" (Nobel Presentation Speech). He founded and became editor of *Nutrition Abstracts and Reviews* in 1931. Time-consuming as his various administrative duties were, he was still able to direct fundamental research in nutrition, primarily in animal nutrition in these early days of the Institute. His influential *Minerals in Pastures and Their Relation to Animal Nutrition* (1929) was published in this period. During the 1930s, however, after extensive experiments with milk in the diet of mothers, children, and the underprivileged, and after large-scale surveys of nutritional problems in many nations throughout the world, Orr's interests swung to human nutrition, not only as a researcher but also as a propagandist for healthful diets for all peoples everywhere. Orr first gained fame with the publication of *Food, Health and Income* (1936), a report of a dietary survey by income groups made during 1935 that showed that the cost of a diet fulfilling basic nutritional requirements was beyond the means of half the British population and that 10% of the population was undernourished. This and other reports conducted by the Rowett Research Institute (formerly Institute of Animal Nutrition) formed the basis of the British food-rationing system during World War II.[1]

He was instrumental in having free milk provided in British schools and, in his Nobel acceptance speech, he linked nourishment, economic well-being and the removal of hunger as necessary for world peace. Orr was the first scientist to discover the link between low income and nutritional deprivation and the consequent public outcry in the 1930s led to the adoption of his recommendations. These included improvements in agricultural output and increased consumption as consequent on the lowering of food prices. His work on the National Council for the Development of Scotland was later adopted as UK national policy and was amongst the most successful of the Welfare State reforms of the Modernist era. The introduction of free school milk – a simple and practical measure – contributed to the disappearance of rickets from Britain's poor children. This alone demonstrates his ability as a scientist to see the general arising from the particular, and as a humanitarian, his determination that knowledge should benefit ordinary people. Orr saw nutrition, productivity, national regeneration, freedom from class and national conflicts as interdependent and interrelated.

After 1945, his ideas on international food rationing influenced policy in the USA, and crucially prevented famine in Europe. As director-general of the United Nations Food and Agricultural Organisation (FAO), he ensured the mid and late 20th century acceptance of famine as an international responsibility. However, he felt bureaucracy and politics inhibited his work at the FAO and he resigned to promote the cause of world government that, he believed, could mount a two-pronged attack on famine. First, by third-world agricultural development, and second through the World Bank as controller of food prices on the world markets, and by the sale of food surpluses and the accumulation of food reserves. Linked to this was the aim of world peace that he actively pursued through a number of international peace organisations.[2]

Believing that the United Nations Food and Agriculture Organisation could not, at that point, become a spearhead for a movement to achieve world unity and peace, Orr resolved to resign as director-general and to go into business. Within three years he earned a bigger net income from directorships than he had ever had from scientific research and, with capital gains made on the Stock Exchange, he established a comfortable personal estate. It was symbolic of this period of his life that he should have been informed of his Nobel Peace Prize award by his banker. The prize money, however, he donated to the National Peace Council, the World Movement for World Federal Government, and various other such organisations.[3]

Alfred Walter Stewart 1880-1947 isolated the unstable organic compound ketene in 1908. In 1918, he proposed the name 'isobares' (later isobars) to designate elements with the same atomic weights but different atomic numbers. His main research during his second tenure at Queen's University was Tesla luminescence spectra. He developed a new field of emission spectroscopy by using a new method of excitation (the discharge of a high-tension transformer through a gaseous phase) to reveal series of spectra which he correlated with the structure of many organic compounds. His studies on the selective absorption spectra of organic compounds (1906) led to the concept of isorrepsis, which, expressed two decades before the application of electronic theory to organic chemistry, foreshadowed later ideas of resonance.[1]

Preston Albert Watson 1880-1915 was the first Briton to fly in a plane with powered, controlled flight, doing so around 1905. He also designed a new method of control called the "parasol plane". This device was a small second wing placed above the main wing that could be rocked back and forth, causing the plane to bank and turn. Watson incorporated this device into his later gliders as well as powered aircraft. This structurally sound method of control was much simpler than that of the Wrights, who twisted, or warped, the wings on their plane, and later it earned for Watson a French award for improved stability in an aircraft. With his method, he was able to dispense with a movable rudder to correct side-slip. The tail of the plane was fashioned like a box kite, and this also helped to support the machine in the air.[1]

His glider sat in a wooden cradle or on skids, which could slide freely on planks lubricated with lard or graphite. A rope hooked under the glider led forward to a pulley, then back under the plane, round another pulley and finally up and over the branch of a tall tree. On the end of this rope hung two 56 lb (25.4 kg) weights and an anvil borrowed from a nearby smithy. On releasing a catch under his seat, the pilot caused the weights to fall, and so propelled his machine for a short distance into the air. Since he was attempting gliding flight from level ground, Watson had to provide some form of assisted take-off, and his device must have been the first to be used for this purpose.[2]

Watson built two improved versions of his original powered aircraft. His second plane made use of a 30 hp gasoline engine while the third employed a 60 hp engine. It is said that these two machines were flown frequently in the years before World War I. During that conflict, Watson volunteered for the newly formed air wing of the Royal Navy and was killed when his aircraft exploded in flight.[3]

Alexander Fleming 1881-1955 observed, in 1928, that colonies of the bacterium *Staphylococcus aureus* (golden staph) could be destroyed by the mould *Penicillium notatum*, proving that there was an antibacterial agent there in principle. This principle later led to medicines that could kill certain types of disease-causing bacteria inside the body. Many infections can be treated with a shot of penicillin, but it was a different kind of shot that got the discoverer of penicillin started in his bacteriological career. Fleming took top scores in the qualifying examinations, and had his choice of medical schools. He lived equally close to three different schools, and knowing little about them, chose St. Mary's Hospital in Praed Street in London, because he had played water polo against them. In 1905, he found himself specialising as a surgeon for almost as random a reason. His switch to bacteriology was even more surprising; if he took a position as a surgeon, he would have had to leave St. Mary's. The captain of St. Mary's rifle club knew that and was desperate to improve his team. Knowing that Fleming was a great shot, he did all he could to keep him at St. Mary's. He worked in the Inoculation Service and he convinced Fleming to join his department in order to work with its brilliant director, Almwroth Wright – and to join the rifle club. Fleming would stay at St. Mary's for the rest of his career.[1]

In 1921, Fleming discovered lysozyme in human tears and found it to be a natural antibiotic protecting the cornea of eyes by catalysing the breakdown of certain carbohydrates found in the cell walls of particular bacteria such as *Micrococcus lysodeikticus*.[2] Lysozyme (named for lysing, or dissolving, bacteria) was the first natural antibacterial discovered,[3] and it is produced within the body and provides some protection against infection as lysozyme destroys harmful bacteria like *Escherichia coli* by tearing open the cell wall, causing its insides to leak out. Because lysozyme is commonly found in those spots where microorganisms are most likely to enter the body, it is one of the powerful first-line defences against bacterial infection. The enzyme is found in the milk, saliva and tears of all mammals, but human breast milk contains about 3,000 times more than the milk of goats. Human breast milk contains valuable antibacterial enzymes that milk from dairy animals did not – until now.

Researchers report that transgenic goats can successfully produce milk containing the enzyme lysozyme, and that this milk exhibits an antibacterial effect when fed to young goats and pigs. The researchers hope, that in the future, enhanced non-human milk will give an immune boost to children in the developing world where diarrhoea takes more than two million lives each year.[4] Unfortunately, lysozyme is a large molecule that is not particularly useful as a drug. It can be applied topically, but cannot rid the entire body of disease, because it is too large to travel between cells.[5]

Fleming continued to search for other antibiotics, and in September 1928, he found one of his Petri dishes had a mould growing in it which inhibited the growth of *Staphylococcus aureus*. The active mould was found to be *Penicillium notatum* and Fleming published his findings in the *British Journal of Experimental Pathology* in 1929. *Penicillium* mould had been known to have antibacterial properties long before Fleming's 1928 serendipity and, indeed, the use of moulds to treat infection goes back to the ancient world. The first to actually report on *Penicillium*'s antibacterial properties was John Scott Burdon-Sanderson in 1871, and this was later confirmed by Joseph Lister. William Roberts (1874) and John Tyndall (1875) also reported that *Penicillium glaucum* had antibacterial properties, as did Frenchman Ernest Duchesne in 1897. There were further reports from Belgium (1920) and Costa Rica (1923), confirming similar results. So why did Fleming get the accolades? First, the strain he found was *Penicillium notatum*, a more potent mould but, much more importantly, because biochemist Ernst Boris Chain, a refugee Jew from Nazi Germany, came across some of Fleming's earlier work and decided to investigate it further.

Fleming's research proved that the broth – named penicillin by him – would destroy a number of major pathogens and had no detrimental effect on blood cells of laboratory mice, but its toxicity disappeared within minutes, so it was useless in fighting bacterial infection. Two English biochemists, Frederick Ridley and Stuart Craddock, formed a concentrate in alcohol which kept its potency for a few weeks. In further tests, Craddock had shown penicillin disappeared from the blood of a rabbit a mere 30 minutes after injection, so Fleming tried it as a topical application, but it only worked on one patient who had pneumococcal conjunctivitis.[6]

Chain not only accessed Fleming's, reports but he managed to get hold of the actual penicillin strain used by Fleming, who had continued to use it as a reagent in his continuing research into what was incorrectly believed to be the causative agent of influenza, *Bacillus influenzae* (later renamed *Haemophilus influenzae*).

With Australian pathologist Howard Florey, Chain undertook the necessary work to refine the active ingredient in the mould – penicillin – and use it in animal trials, then on humans. However, penicillin proved to be highly unstable and Florey and Chain were making very little headway in isolating it until English biochemist Norman Heatley joined the team. Heatley's first task was to culture sufficient *Penicillium* from which Chain was to extract the active principle – penicillin – and determine its formula. Eventually they produced enough to treat some patients but, clearly, they did not have the ability to mass produce it and, as Britain was in a life or death struggle with Hitler's Germany, the American company Pfizer Incorporated was co-opted.

Biochemist Jasper Herbert Kane worked for Pfizer, which at that time was not a pharmaceutical company but supplied chemicals and ingredients for the food and drink industry. Kane, working with James Currie, developed a technique known as deep fermentation and it was this process that permitted the mass production of penicillin as a drug.

There is no doubt that much of the credit for the eventual successful mass production belongs to others – Chain, Florey, Heatley, Kane, Currie – but as Australian geneticist, Sir Henry Harris, said, "Without Fleming, no Chain or Florey; without Florey, no Heatley; without Heatley, no penicillin."[7]

Fleming has had quite a bit of negative press because he failed to pursue the development of penicillin, but he had gone as far as he could. Certainly, he could have persisted in publicising it, but no-one was listening. Even Florey had encountered penicillin in 1932, when a colleague employed it in three cases of skin infection,[8] and he did not follow up on its potential at that time. Penicillin also proved extremely difficult to produce in a stable condition and to mass produce, and the resources marshalled to get it to market were substantial, and probably only provided as part of the war effort, as it was the armed services who were first to benefit from penicillin. Undoubtedly, Heatley and Kane should have been included in the Nobel Prize that went to Fleming, Florey and Chain, but that was not the fault of Fleming. Nor was it Fleming's fault that he got the bulk of the publicity. His boss, Almwroth Wright, wanted his employee to get as much publicity as possible to benefit St Mary's Hospital in getting additional funding. Florey was reticent about publicity, at least in the early period, and Chain was a German at a time when they were anathema to the British press, even though Chain, as a Jew, was a refugee from Hitler's Nazi Germany.

Irving Langmuir 1881-1957 invented electric lamps in gaseous atmospheres, measured the melting point of refractory solids, and discovered atomic hydrogen (i.e. hydrogen in the form of single atoms, rather than molecules, which makes it extremely reactive). As a result of his research on gaseous reaction, kinetics derived the adsorption isothermic named after him. Langmuir also studied the hypothesis of producing artificial rain (1946).[1]

He investigated the properties of adsorbed films and the nature of electric discharges in high vacuum and in certain gases at low pressures. His work on filaments in gases led directly to the invention of the gas-filled incandescent lamp and to the discovery of atomic hydrogen. He later used the latter in the development of the atomic hydrogen welding process. He was the first to observe the very stable adsorbed monatomic films on tungsten and platinum filaments, and was able, after experiments with oil films on water, to formulate a general theory of adsorbed films (in chemistry adsorption is a process in which a substance, usually a gas, accumulates on the surface of a solid, forming a thin film, often only one molecule thick). He also studied the catalytic properties of such films. Langmuir's work on space charge effects and related phenomena led to many important technical developments which have had a profound effect on later technology.[2]

Langmuir's study of thermionic phenomena produced effects that later became the heart of the electronics industry. His research gave the world the first high-vacuum electron tubes and the first high-emission electron tube cathodes. Not only was the study of heat transfer in gases the scientific source of Langmuir's basic invention of the gas-filled lamp and atomic hydrogen welding, but it also provided the technology for hydrogen-cooled turbines. He made basic contributions to the understanding of gaseous discharge phenomena – he invented the word *plasma* – and his work on surface films, including protein films on water, provided an important new technique in biochemistry.[3] He developed a theory for the catalytic effect of an adsorbing surface which considered the chemical reaction as actually occurring in the adsorbed film and elucidated many features of such reactions which hitherto had been obscure. This theory became the basic approach to surface kinetics.

One of Langmuir's first achievements was in the field of lighting. After William David Coolidge, also of the Research Laboratory, developed the drawn tungsten-filament incandescent lamp, it fell to Langmuir to further develop an improved lamp – a gas-filled one instead of the vacuum type – and thereby make a great gain in lighting efficiency. The gas-filled lamp soon began driving arc lamps from the street lights, greatly increasing the use of electric lighting by increasing efficiency. With the lower cost of lighting came a large increase in the amount of light used, so that electric utility revenues from lighting were soon higher than ever before. They continued to increase steadily as efficiency improved. Further improvements in incandescent lamps were to be made in various laboratories, but Coolidge's tungsten filament and Langmuir's gas filling remain today two basic elements of incandescent lamps.

Langmuir made basic contributions to the understanding of gaseous discharge phenomena and his work on surface films provided an important new technique in biochemistry. He received the Nobel Prize in 1932.[4]

William Hamilton Shortt 1881-1971 devised a system to keep two pendulums in precise sympathy at Edinburgh University, the first successful free-pendulum clock with accuracy of the order of one second per year, which he patented the same year (Patent No. 187814). The clock's performance was far better than that of existing clocks, such as those made by Clemens Riefler, and a slightly modified version was produced commercially by the Synchronome Company. These clocks provided the time standard at Greenwich and many other observatories and scientific institutions across the world until they were supplanted by the quartz clock. The introduction of the Synchronome-Shortt Free Pendulum was a great step forward and about one hundred of these clocks were built, the first Synchronome-Shortt Free Pendulum being installed in the Edinburgh Observatory. Suddenly the accuracy of time measurements was increased to about one millisecond a day and it was not long before astronomical observatories all over the world made use of this system. It is still the most accurate mechanical clock ever made.[1]

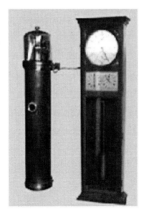

Image 95 – Synchronome-Shortt Free-Pendulum Clock

In the Shortt clock, there are two separate pendulums. The timekeeping pendulum is simply that, a timekeeper. It does no work. The clock mechanism is controlled by a second pendulum which is kept synchronised with the master pendulum electrically. It is important to note that the timekeeping is all done by the mechanical, gravity driven pendulum – hence the Shortt clock remains a mechanical timekeeper despite the use of electricity. The master timekeeping pendulum is kept as free as possible by being enclosed in a sealed, part vacuum tube fixed to a wall. This master pendulum then signals electrically to a slave pendulum which in turn does the actual work of controlling the clock. This ingenious combination of mechanical free-pendulum timekeeping with electrical power was the ultimate mechanical clock. Indeed, it was the Shortt clock that first proved the Earth itself is a far from perfect timekeeper. It could be argued that the Shortt Clock was the first clock more accurate than nature.[2]

James Williamson 1881-1953 was the engineer responsible for: the Barking Power Station, the largest steam power station in Britain; the Gander Valley Water Power and Paper Scheme, Newfoundland; the Uhl River Water Power Scheme, Mandi State, India, for which he prepared reports; the Salt River Steam Power Station, Cape Town, for which he prepared designs and specifications; the new Strand Market Wharf and Transit Sheds, Rangoon, and reconstruction of the Sule Pagoda Wharf; and the Galloway Water Power Scheme, with which he was connected from its very beginnings. He was largely responsible for the design and construction of the Loch Sloy, Tummel-Garry, and Shira power schemes.[1]

Harold Delf Gillies 1882-1960 was a New Zealand-born surgeon who is considered to be the father of plastic surgery (the term "Plastic" was used before plastics as we know them now were invented – the term originally meant "moulding and shaping"). During World War I, Gillies persuaded the army's chief surgeon, William Arbuthnot Lane, that a facial injury ward should be established at the Cambridge Military Hospital, Aldershot. On the 11 January 1916, Gillies was ordered by the War Office to go to that now approved hospital "for special duty in connection with Plastic Surgery". His request for a British unit had been granted; he was to be Britain's first plastic surgeon with full responsibility for getting the Aldershot unit up and running. This rapidly proved inadequate, and a new hospital was developed at Sidcup devoted to facial injury.

The Queen's Hospital opened in June 1917 and with its convalescent units provided over 1,000 beds. There, Gillies and his colleagues developed many techniques of plastic surgery; more than 11,000 operations were performed on over 5,000 men. Instead of stitching the edges of wounds together, Gillies pioneered skin-grafting techniques to rebuild faces using tissue from elsewhere in the body. Many of his methods form the basis of plastic surgery techniques used today. Tens of thousands of people who suffered injuries due to road traffic accidents, facial cancers, assaults, war, acts of terrorism, and a host of other traumas and diseases, have benefited from Gillies' ground-breaking work.[1]

To him, no problem was identical with its predecessor – no patient possessed all the characteristics of another – no surgical procedure could be expected to produce perfection unless it was capable of modification to suit the individual needs. Nothing was standardised. This characteristic of nonconformity was probably the most important weapon in his armoury.[2]

Gillies' work was revolutionary, and yet is little remembered. Most field surgeons, faced with blasted faces, simply stitched together the edges of wounds to stop infection. As wounds healed and scar tissue contracted, the skin of men's faces would become twisted and not only disfiguring, but disabling. Men returned from the horrors of the front terrified to face their loved ones. Gillies' technique used bones and cartilage to reconstruct faces, and pioneered the extraordinary "tubed pedicle" method of skin grafting, in the days before skin grafts were possible. Multiple surgeries were required and the patients were kept in hospital for years at a time.[3]

During World War II, Gillies acted as a consultant to the Ministry of Health, the RAF and the Admiralty. He organised plastic surgery units in various parts of Britain. His own work continued at Rooksdown House, part of the Park Prewett Hospital, Basingstoke. During this period, and after the war, he trained many doctors from Commonwealth nations in plastic surgery. For Gillies, plastic surgery not only involved restoring function but also making the person look normal and sometimes more beautiful than before. He was driven by the idea that the surgeon should be creative, imaginative – in fact an artist.[4]

In addition to making pictorial records, Gillies spent at least an hour before each operation visualising the final outcome. He would pace up and down the hospital in a world of his own, scribbling designs on pieces of paper, cutting them out with scissors, and then fitting them back together again in a jigsaw-like fashion. He sometimes used a lump of wax in order to mould onto the patient's face the features and contours that he hoped to restore to it. But his usual method was to create a plaster model of how he imagined the patients face would eventually look. Gillies was without a doubt the consummate surgeon-artist.[5]

The "epithelial outlay technique" and "pedicle tube" were not his only innovations. Later in his career, Gillies used what he called an "intranasal skin graft" to correct a nose defect caused by leprosy. This established a new principle in the treatment of facial disfigurement from leprosy. Gillies also pioneered a new method for reattaching severed limbs. This involved de-gloving the amputated section of skin and suturing the limb on bone to bone, tendon to tendon, and nerve to nerve. In contrast to surgeons' previous methods, this method proved successful.[6]

Rhinoplasty, skin grafts, and facial reconstructions have been practiced for centuries. However, Gillies standardised these techniques and established the discipline of "plastic surgery". In 1920, his textbook *Plastic Surgery of the Face* was published, setting down the principles of modern plastic surgery; principles which were adopted by surgeons from every part of the world. The *British Medical Journal* described it as "one of the most notable contributions made to surgical literature in our day". *The New York Medical Journal* said that "his are the greatest of all contributions to the advance of this interesting reparative work."[7]

Two of Gillies' major surgical innovations were the tubed pedicle flap – invented independently as it turned out greatly to his disappointment by Vladimir Filatov of Odessa and Hugo Ganzer of Berlin – and the epithelial onlay technique for reconstructing eyelids and lining the mouth.[8] His innovation of the pedicle tube proved extremely successful, and within a few weeks tubes were seen sprouting from scores of his patients. The pedicle tube simplified grafting and made it more certain that a shattered face would be recognisable again. More importantly, the patient could return to society with some semblance of normalcy.[9]

It was Gillies, too, who was largely responsible for establishing a collaborative relationship between the general surgeon and plastic surgeon. In the 1930s, surgeon Gordon Gordon-Taylor requested Gillies treat one of his patients who had malignant tumours, entailing surgery to excise his lower lip, part of his jaw, left cheek, and upper lip. Recalling the incident, Gillies wrote; "Gordon-Taylor had faith that a destruction could be reconstructed". Gillies was successful, although it took four years of grafting to replace the lost tissue. Nevertheless, it was the first recorded instance of collaboration; a collaboration which is now standard practice.[10]

He developed a new technique, still used, which allowed new eyelids to be created for burns patients. He apparently got the idea when he was worrying about a patient without eyelids who had to sleep through air raids with his eyes open. Face lifts were not the only cosmetic changes Gillies helped pioneer. Gillies and his cousin Archibald McIndoe, a fellow plastic surgeon and New Zealander, published a paper in 1938 on their mammoplasty technique; a technique devised for correcting breast abnormalities. In 1941, while on a lecture tour in the United States, Gillies told an audience at Galveston University in Texas how he once operated on the breasts of an amateur golfer; "once because they impeded her swing and the second time at her lover's request". While such operations were normally condemned by society and the medical fraternity, Gillies had an attitude that was ahead of his time; "From the psychological point of view the patient finds herself able to go among her friends with a new-found equanimity". "Those girls ... with a sensitiveness amounting to melancholia regain their self-confidence".[11]

While Gillies played a pioneering wartime role in Britain developing pedicle flap surgery, what is not so well-known is that he was also one of the pioneers of sex change surgery. He later performed surgery on Britain's first male-to-female transsexual, Roberta Cowell. Later, in 1945, Gillies and his colleague Ralph Millard carried out the world's first sex change of a woman into a man on the young aristocrat, Lawrence Michael Dillon, who had been born Laura Maud Dillon. She is also believed to be the first woman to have taken the male hormone testosterone in order to look like a man. Within months of starting testosterone, he had grown a beard and was living as a man. It was the dramatic transition in his appearance that finally persuaded Gillies to operate. Dillon later showed his amended birth certificate to Debrett's Peerage, who agreed to change their entry, thus acknowledging his claim to the baronetcy as the next male in line after his childless brother. The editor assured him that changes in Debrett were automatically followed by Burke's Peerage.[12]

Gillies was first President of the British Association of Plastic Surgeons in 1946. He later became honorary president of the International Society of Plastic Surgeons. Note: George David Pollock 1817-1897 introduced the idea of using skin grafts to treat burn wounds in 1870.

Albert Edward MacColl 1882-1951 invented the "MacColl Protective System". He started building the first of many hydro-electric schemes in Scotland at Falls of Clyde in Lanarkshire in 1919. He created, in Central Scotland, the first regional electricity supply grid in the United Kingdom while working for the Central Electricity Board, a United Kingdom organisation established in 1926 to standardise the country's electricity supply which was at that time supplied by more than 600 companies using different voltages, frequencies and, in some cases, using DC current. It was MacColl's vision to establish a hydro-electric scheme linking Loch Lomond and Loch Sloy, and with the backing of Tom Johnston, often considered Scotland's greatest Secretary of State, MacColl was made Deputy Chairman and Chief Executive of the North of Scotland Hydro-Electric Board when it was created in 1943. It was one of the most successful government agencies of the period[1] and, renamed Scottish & Southern Energy plc, it had nearly 20,000 employees in 2015. MacColl built other hydro-electric schemes including Glen Garry-Glen Moriston, Glen Affric-River Beauly, Loch Sloy-Loch Awe, Breadalbane, Strath Conon and Loch Tummel. MacColl was appointed to the Central Electricity Board in 1927 and immediately began to work on solutions to the problem of long-distance transmission of power – a vital step to allow the accelerated development of the hydro sector in Scotland.

MacColl's invention of the "MacColl Protective System" was the crucial technological breakthrough that provided the basis internationally for long-distance power transmission.[2] Note: The MacColl Protective System is a form of protective system used on electric power networks; it operates on the balanced principle embodying biased beam relays.

Alexander Ogilvie 1882-1962 invented the airspeed indicator in 1909, which he patented on 3 November. It was first fitted to his own Short-Wright biplane at Rye in Surrey. It was used during Ogilvie and Anglo-Irishman Frank McClean's successful flight up the Nile to Khartoum. The Ogilvie air-speed indicator is characterised by extreme simplicity.[1]

Samuel James Shand 1882-1957 developed the first practical instrument for modal analysis, and the modern line integrators are all lineal descendants of the Shand stage. He improved and publicised staining techniques for the feldspathoids. His interest in chemistry, chemical analysis and rock classification, so strongly foreshadowed in the Assynt papers, soon found expression in journal articles devoted to principles upon which a sound chemical mineralogical classification might be constructed. The system he finally developed formed the backbone of his major work, *Eruptive Rocks*, which was first published in 1927 and went through four editions between then and 1951. It continues to exert a powerful and salutary influence on the study and teaching of petrology.[1]

When the University at Stellenbosch was founded in 1918, geology was already well established. Berthault van der Riet served for eight years as head of the Geology Department (1895-1903). He was succeeded by Robert Broom, a Scottish medical doctor who later became famous as a palaeontologist. "The person who contributed most to the reputation of the Department in those early days was Professor Samuel J. Shand, between 1911 and 1937. He also hailed from Scotland and attained worldwide recognition for his research on South African igneous rocks. From Stellenbosch he moved to the USA where he became Professor at Columbia University in New York State. Shand is commonly regarded as the real founder of the Geology Department, and was one of the founding fathers of the University itself". His pronouncements, in a public lecture of 1916, on what constitutes a University are still quoted today: "A university is not a lecture theatre, or a library, or a laboratory; it is not a building or a place at all; its essence is a frame of mind."[2]

Joseph Henry Maclagen Wedderburn 1882-1948 made important advances in the theory of rings, algebras and matrix theory. He published a paper in 1905 that included three claimed proofs of a theorem stating that a noncommutative finite division ring could not exist. The proofs all made clever use of the interplay between the additive group of a finite division algebra A, and the multiplicative group A* = A-{0}. Karen Hunger Parshall (1983) notes that the first of these three proofs had a gap not noticed at the time. Meanwhile, Wedderburn's Chicago colleague, Leonard Eugene Dickson, also found a proof of this result but, believing Wedderburn's first proof to be correct, Dickson acknowledged Wedderburn's priority. But Dickson also noted that Wedderburn constructed his second and third proofs only after having seen Dickson's proof. Parshall concludes that Dickson should be credited with the first correct proof.

In 1907, Wedderburn published what is perhaps his most famous paper on the classification of semisimple algebras. He showed that every semisimple algebra is a direct sum of simple algebras and that a simple algebra was a matrix algebra over a division ring. In total, he published around 40 works mostly on rings and matrices.[1]

John Scoular Buchanan 1883-1966 had a very important impact on the Royal Air Force (RAF) prior to World War II. Writing in the *Journal of the Royal Aeronautical Society*, Volume 30, 1926, pp 434-452, he showed that the United States had surpassed Britain in high speed flying and that there was a need for a British unit within the RAF to counter this. "The outcome was that a RAF high-speed flight was set up; increasing government money was devoted to the development of the design of the seaplanes, and a Rolls Royce engine was specially developed. The subsequent contests at Venice in 1927, Cowes in 1929, and again at Cowes in 1931 were won by Britain and the trophy was finally secured for British possession."[1] Buchanan pressed the British government to mass-produce the R J Michell designed Spitfire fighter which, with the Hurricane, was critical to the success of the Battle of Britain against Hitler's Luftwaffe.

William Thomson Halcrow 1883-1958 constructed the King George V Graving (dry) Dock in Singapore in 1938, the largest dry dock in the world at the time.[1] During World War I, he had responsibility for land and submarine defences at Scapa Flow in the Orkney Islands. In 1919, he was in charge of the construction of the Johor Causeway between Singapore Island and the mainland, a distance of just over one kilometre.

During the Second World War, Halcrow constructed flood gates to prevent the London Underground from being flooded, and designed numerous deep level air raid shelters, including eight beneath London underground stations, the one under Goodge Street becoming the centre from which General Dwight David Eisenhower directed the Normandy Landings in 1944. For the D-Day landings, Halcrow, with other construction companies, designed and built the reinforced concrete caissons for the Mulberry Harbours which were towed across the sea to provide two vast harbours at Arromanches and St. Laurent. On seeing the harbours being towed, King George VI remarked that this was "the greatest combined operation the world has ever seen, perhaps the greatest it will ever see".[2]

In 1924, Halcrow took over the design of the Lochaber hydroelectric scheme in Scotland after the death of his partner, Charles Meik, part of which included building a tunnel that was 24 km long with a 5 m diameter. It was the longest water-carrying tunnel in the world until 1970. Halcrow then worked on the new Victoria line for London Underground and designed and constructed Beyt and Velan Harbour in India (1921) and the port of Beira, Mozambique's second city, from 1927 to 1946.[3]

Muriel Robertson 1883-1973 worked out the sequence of development of the trypanosome and discovered the pathway by which the trypanosomes migrated to the salivary glands of the tsetse fly.[1] She succeeded in elucidating the life cycle of *Trypanosoma gambiense,* both in blood and in its insect vector, the tsetse fly.

This work resulted in several papers, the most important of which appeared in 1913 in the *Philosophical Transactions of The Royal Society* (203, 1913, 161 84). In the papers, the soundness of her scientific observations was matched by the elegance of her illustrations. She noted the undulating parasitaemia associated with trypanosome infections of mammals and predicted that this related to destruction of parasites in waves by blood plasma.

Her work anticipated the modern view that antibodies are raised to trypanosomes that sequentially express a multitude of different variant surface antigens, work pioneered by Professor Keith Vickerman in Glasgow. She also noted how it was only the short stumpy trypanosome that could transmit to the tsetse fly. She went on to develop diagnostic tests for Trichomonas' foetus and also made important contributions to research into Clostridium species. The disease in cattle remains arguably the most important veterinary problem in Sub-Saharan Africa today.[2]

Robert Robison 1883-1941 undertook the identification of the phosphoric esters formed during alcoholic fermentation, his care and skill leading to the discovery of six new hexosephosphoric esters during the next few years. While studying the action of emulsion on certain of these esters, Robison was led to consider whether a similar enzymic hydrolysis was involved in bone ossification and, early in 1923, he extracted the enzyme phosphatase from the bone of young, rapidly growing animals. From this time, his more biological work included the experiments which led to the identification of a mechanism which played an important role in the deposition of the bone salts. His views on this subject were developed steadily and new ideas continually emerged up to the moment of his untimely death, and his work in this field is a rare example of beautifully planned research carried out with eminent skill.[1]

Johnstone Wright 1883-1953 was Chief Engineer of Britain's Central Electricity Board from 1932 to 1944, during the period when the National Grid was created.[1] *The Electricity (Supply) Act 1926* was passed following an inquiry by Glasgow-born Lord (William) Weir to standardise Britain's electricity supply which, at the time, consisted of more than 600 electricity supply companies and local authority undertakings, and different areas operated at different voltages and frequencies (including DC in some places). A Central Electricity Board was formed to construct and operate a large number of high-tension transmission lines called a Grid. The board divided the network into nine schemes covering the whole of Great Britain except northern Scotland. Not only did the construction of the Grid have a beneficial effect upon national employment at a time of acute depression, but also the experience in high voltage construction that it entailed placed British manufacturers in the forefront of technical progress.[2]

The Central Electricity Board established the UK's first synchronised AC grid, running at 132 kilovolts and 50 Hertz, which by 1933 was a collection of local grids, with emergency interlinks, covering most of England. This started operating as a national system, the National Grid, in 1938.

George Ernest Gibson 1884-1959 proved through his work on thallium vapour in 1911 that spectral lines are produced by thermal emission. He spent 1927-1928 with Professor Walter Heinrich Heitler at Goettingen as a Guggenheim Fellow. This led to a publication on the then new quantum statistics. One of the results of this collaboration was a proof that nuclear spin effects do not shift chemical equilibria appreciably at ordinary or higher temperatures. He devised numerous experiments on the band spectra of chlorine, iodine, and iodine monochloride related particularly to predissociation and isotope effects.[1]

James Kenneth MacDougall 1884-1960 designed equipment for wire-drawing for the Austral Nail Co. in 1911 which, in 1921, became part of Ryland Bros (Australia) Ltd. Under MacDougall's direction, the company created the "keyhole" type of self-locking tie for the binding of "dumped" wool, and by 1935, Rylands was drawing equivalent wires twice as fast as the best American mills, making Rylands the world leader in this manufacture.[1]

Thomas Murray MacRobert 1884-1962 won international recognition for his research in a number of fields, most particularly on the hypergeometric function and for his discovery of the *E*-function (exponential function).[1] The *E*-function was a generalisation of the generalised hypergeometric functions, and from 1938 onwards, MacRobert produced a whole series of works on the properties of the *E*-function and integrals with *E*-functions.[2]

Over the years he built up an impressive body of results, including, in particular, a formidable number of integrals with *E*-functions. These results not only serve to unify and express conveniently known facts involving special functions of the hypergeometric type, but also lead to many new formulae.[3]

John Fraser 1885-1947 published, in 1912, his famous work on the relative frequency of bovine and human tubercle bacilli in tuberculous disease of bones and joints in children. This was the start of the process to identify tuberculosis in dairy herds and to create TB-free cattle. Fraser also made important original observations on the path of physiology of traumatic shock, his work on blood transfusion and plasma substitutes and by his work on penetrating wounds of the abdomen.[1] **Alexander Philp Mitchell 1885-1959** published parallel observations on tuberculous cervical glands and, in the *British Medical Journal* of 17 January 1914 advocated wholesale sterilisation of milk. Taken with the work of Sir Robert Philip, it is not surprising, therefore, that a large part of the *Final Report* of the Royal Commission on Tuberculosis (March 1913), which had taken ten years of investigation at a cost of £80,000, dealt with bovine tuberculosis, and that in the following year the *Milk and Dairies Act* was passed into law on 10 August 1914. This legislation aimed at ensuring the purity of milk supplies, but on account of the First World War, the operation of the Act was postponed until 1925 in Scotland, where it was covered by the *Milk and Dairies (Scotland) Act 1914*, though the preparations for the grading of milk were made under an order of June 1923.

Douglas Graham Gilmour 1885-1912 invented an aircraft anchor slip device to enable pilots to run an engine up and take off without assistance. He also demonstrated the vulnerability of naval warships to aerial attack and he demonstrated the possibilities of aircraft in war by bombarding the forts of Portsmouth with oranges.[1]

William Hogarth Robertson Nimmo 1885-1970 investigated the water-supply and flood-mitigation requirements for Brisbane, Australia, completing the investigation almost single-handed in about fifteen months. For the economic assessment, he derived flood-probability data and unit-hydrographs which he used in conjunction with the flood plan of the city. His efforts led to the establishment in 1934 of the Stanley River Works Board to build the Somerset Dam on the upper reaches of the Brisbane River. This was the first major dam project for Brisbane's water supply and flood mitigation.[1]

He was seconded to the Board, initially as Designing Engineer and later as Chief Engineer (1935-1949). Innovations in design and construction included measures to prevent hydraulic uplift on the base of the dam, and hydraulic models to test the performance of the dissipator and sluice-gates. With his staff, he conducted a feasibility study of the Burdekin irrigation, hydro-electric and flood-mitigation scheme. He also designed and took charge of construction of the Tully Falls hydro-electric project.[2]

Maurice Edward Denny 1886-1955 was "the main collaborator in the design of the Denny-Brown ship stabiliser."[1] It was developed, with **William Wallace 1881-1963**, with the first commercial version being installed in 1937 in the Isle of Park. The innovation was widely used by the Royal Navy during the Second World War to help stabilise gun-platforms, and in the post-war period, it came into widespread use in merchant ships. Denny "also developed a 'vane-wheel' system for powering flat-bottomed riverboats, and two types of torsion meters, the Denny-Johnson and the Denny-Edgecumbe."[2]

Ian (Isidor) Morris Heilbron 1886-1959 determined the structure of squalene (from shark liver oil). His research on the relationship between sterols and vitamin D, the field of vitamin A, and polyene synthesis brought him international renown.[1]

This interest led to his opening up the broad topic of the general chemistry of acetylenic derivatives of diverse types to provide the foundation of much industrial development. Heilbron was in turn concerned with numerous other substances of actual or potential therapeutic interest and made important contributions to the chemistry of penicillin, particularly during World War II when the subject was of major national importance. He developed purification methods for the small supplies of crude material that were initially available, and showed that penicillin exists in many forms. He wrote extensively in the scientific field as the author or part-author of about 300 publications dealing with original work.[2] Heilbron also played a major role in the development of DDT and he was the first non-American to be honoured with the Priestley Medal.[3] He was also awarded the Davy Medal (1943) and four years later received the American Medal of Freedom.

Colin Peter Kininmonth 1886-1975 was, with Russian émigré George Gray, the co-inventor in 1937 of *Sellotape*, a brand of transparent, cellulose-based, pressure sensitive adhesive tape, which is the leading brand of clear, pressure-sensitive tape in the United Kingdom. It is made using cellulose film derived from wood pulp. The cellulose film decomposes naturally in soil, and is naturally easy to tear and is non-static.

Kininmonth and Gray coated cellophane film with a natural rubber resin, creating a "sticky tape" product, which had been based on a French patent. They registered their product under the name *Sellotape*. When it was put on sale in 1937, it quickly began to replace string as the method of wrapping parcels and, during WWII, it was seen on just about every window in the land laid in a big X from corner to corner, a basic way of reducing the danger from flying glass in the event of bombs dropping nearby. The choice of name derived from the cellophane material on which they had put rubber glue: they had to change the *cello* prefix to *sello* to avoid trademark conflict.[1]

Wilfrid Thomas Reid 1887-1968 pioneered Canada's aircraft industry. Englishman Reginald Kirshaw Pierson had started a design for an aircraft and Reid developed it into the *Vedette*, the first aircraft specifically designed to meet Canadian conditions, and the first production aircraft designed and built in Canada, marking the true beginning of the Canadian aircraft industry. Reid also designed the *Reid Rambler* used as a training aircraft in Canada. It was purchased by the Curtiss Aeroplane and Motor Company (later Curtiss-Reid Aircraft Company) and renamed the *Curtiss-Reid Rambler*. Reid's design was revolutionary in Canada, with a metal-framed fuselage covered in fabric and wings with Warren truss bracing so that the wings did not require bracing wires. The wings could also be folded so that the aircraft would fit into a small storage space, thereby not requiring a large hangar. The prototype flew on 23 September 1928 with production starting soon thereafter on the *Rambler I* and *II*. The *Rambler III* appeared in April 1931 with major design changes to improve handling and visibility.[1]

Image 96 – Reid-designed Vickers Vedette

John Logie Baird 1888-1946 is often described dismissively as the inventor of "mechanical television". The "invention" of television has been claimed on behalf of nationals of Britain, United States, Italy, Russia, Germany, France, Hungary and Japan (and possibly other nations). Questions such as "Who invented television?" or "Who made the first successful television broadcast?" don't have easy answers. The answers you might get would depend on where in the world you were when you asked. If you ask about television pioneers in the United States, you would likely hear names such as Charles Francis Jenkins, Philo Farnsworth, and/or Vladimir Zworykin mentioned. Corporations such as Westinghouse, AT&T, and GE might come up. In Russia, respondents would most likely say Boris Rosing invented television. Adolf Hitler liked to credit German Paul Nipkow with the invention of television. In Britain, and especially Scotland, you would certainly hear the name John Logie Baird. There are other television "inventors" whose names could be added to the list above. But whether you place the name John Logie Baird at the top of the list as those in the UK would, or a bit further down, his interesting story must be prominent in any history of television.[1]

In truth, television evolved from a series of inventions over many years, but there is no doubt that the first public demonstration, to some 40 members of the Royal Institution, was by John Logie Baird on 26 January 1926. Although he used 30 lines per inch (76 lines/cm) scanning on his *Televisor*, the images had full tonal gradations of light and shade. He had demonstrated his invention earlier that month to a reporter from the *Evening Standard* on 7 January.

If anyone was the Hollywood archetype "mad inventor", it was John Logie Baird. As a child, he had built: a glider that broke in half on being launched from the roof of his house and dumped him on the lawn; home electric lighting; and a telephone exchange that connected his home to that of four friends. As an adult he tried: jam and soap-making in Trinidad; making diamonds from coal; and – the only one that returned a profit – a thermal undersock. Baird suffered from cold feet, and after a number of trials he found that a thin cotton sock sprinkled with borax and worn below regular socks provided warmth. He brilliantly used women with sandwich-boards to advertise his socks – as this role was invariably done by men at the time people took more notice of the women and his billboard message – and he arranged for friends to visit various department stores as pretend purchasers, who then got indignant when they were told the store didn't stock Baird Undersocks. It was a financially successful innovation for Baird, but he fell ill and during his six-week convalescence the business failed.

His "mad inventor" image was neatly summarised in the following comment by Trevor Blake: "Beginning with a personal ad in the *London Times* 'SEEING BY WIRELESS: Inventor of apparatus wishes to hear from someone who will assist (not financially) in making working model', Baird set out to build a working television system using borrowed money and the material he had at hand, which included darning needles, hat boxes, a *Rich Mix* biscuit tin, sealing wax and a bicycle lantern. His Nipkow disc was cut from an old tea chest. In February 1923, he entered the shop of Hastings radio dealer, Victor Mills, and asked for assistance, saying 'I've fitted up an apparatus for transmitting pictures and I can't get it to go.' Mills accompanied Baird back to his laboratory/apartment and waved his hand in front of the neon: when Baird shouted, 'It's here, it's here!' the first real-time electronic moving picture in history occurred. Not long after Baird demonstrated his system to the local press, but was evicted from his apartment."[2]

On 7 April 1927, the American Telephone and Telegraph Company, one of the biggest companies in the world, made the first public transmission of television pictures over telephone lines from New Jersey to Washington DC, a distance of some 322 km – using Baird's system in secret. Six weeks later, on 24 May, Baird did the same between London and Glasgow – 705 km.[3] The following year Baird's English assistant Benjamin Clapp (who, on 7 October 1927, was first to use the abbreviation "TV") demonstrated Baird's equipment in America to massive media acclaim. Returning to Britain on the RMS *Berengaria* Clapp arranged for the ship's wireless operator to view his fiancée, Dora Selvey, live from England on 6 March 1928, still some 1,600 km out in the Atlantic Ocean. The Baird broadcast of her picture commenced at 9.00 PM and lasted an hour.

Image 97 – Advertising Baird Undersocks
Baird Family Archive

Baird continued to make improvements to his system, and on 30 September 1929, he commenced tentative 30-line broadcasts via the BBC, achieving sound and vision synchronisation by 31 March 1930, on which day he installed a *Televisor* receiver at 10 Downing Street, the British prime minister's official London residence. Baird's television company went on to sell 20,000 *Televisors* in Britain and Europe.[4] On 14 July, his studio transmitted Luigi Pirandello's *The Man with a Flower in his Mouth* and less than six months later, he demonstrated multi-channel television (known as Zone TV) which overcame the problem of Baird's narrow vertical screens by using three 30-line scanners to give a single 90-line picture.

On 3 June 1931, using a 120-line mirror-drum camera which sat on a trolley, Baird televised the English Epsom Derby horse race, which was the first outdoor event broadcast. Earlier, on the 8th May, Baird had broadcast the immediate surrounds of the Long Acre studio from a van parked outside – even earlier, in February, the Japanese had broadcast a baseball game, but it was on closed circuit television.

In Paris, on 19 May 1932, Baird exhibited his *Visiophone* – a telephone using visual as well as audio communication. While based in London's Broadcasting House on 8 November 1932, he introduced the Danish film star, Carl Brisson, who was in the Arena Theatre in Copenhagen, 965 km away. In July 1933, Baird's company was filming subjects, then immediately developing the film and scanning the original film as a negative for transmission with a delay of only one minute. On 12 September 1933, he demonstrated 120 lines at 25 frames per second, which soon increased to 180 lines with synchronised audio. In December 1934, Baird's company installed a 10kW VHF transmitter at Crystal Palace – the world's most powerful.[5] On 2 February 1935, the *Daily Express* Radio Correspondent headlined an article "First Televised Pictures Shown – As Clear as a Talkie Film".

By June 1935, American Harry Selfridge, a financial backer of Baird, was selling Baird video discs in his London department store. These 78 rpm (revolutions per minute) *Phonovision* discs played six minutes on each side and could be replayed on Baird's 30-line system. Baird had previously made video recordings on shellac and aluminium gramophone records in the 1920s, the earliest videodiscs ever made, but these were never produced commercially. Also, in 1935, the following article was published in London's *News Chronicle*, "The existence of a fully equipped television broadcasting station in the Crystal Palace, which could act at any moment, was the great surprise which Mr J.L. Baird sprang on the radio world yesterday."[6]

On 4 January 1936, Baird demonstrated 183 cm x 122 cm television at London's Dominion Theatre, and at the same location on 4 February 1938, he showed the first large screen colour television to 3,000 patrons, with the transmission being made 12 km away from Crystal Palace.[7]

In January 1939, his company installed a television projection screen at London's Marble Arch Pavilion cinema, measuring 457 cm x 365 cm.[8] Three more were installed in other cinemas by September and another seven were planned but put on hold due to the outbreak of war with Germany in September 1939.

In December 1940, Baird displayed a 600-line colour television that, at the push of a button, could convert to 425 monochrome lines, which had by this time become the standard. It was from this particular model that the first ever photograph of a colour television was published, showing a clear image of the face, shoulders and red hair of aviatrix Eirane "Paddy" Naismith. "This sequential-frame colour system was not unlike the colour TV system developed by CBS in the United States after the war, but in Baird's case, the image was made up of 600 scanning lines and was of impressive quality.[9] In 1941, he developed an electro-mechanical 600-line, high definition colour television with a 5:4 aspect and a 96.5 cm screen.

The British publication *Electronics*, t*elevision and short-wave world* of April 1941 (in the same year the journal was renamed *Electronic Engineering*) wrote "Reports have appeared recently of colour television demonstrations in the USA. These appear to be of an experimental nature, only coloured lantern slides and coloured films being sent, the difficulty of sending studio scenes not having been overcome in that country. The pictures are of a relatively low number of lines (343). The system they use appears to be on the same principle as that demonstrated to the Press by Mr Baird eighteen months ago. ... Mr Baird's new 600-line television system was shown in operation. Artists in an outdoor studio were transmitted to a receiving set in an adjoining house. ... The screen is 2ft 6in [76 cm] by 2ft 0in [61 cm], the largest screen ever produced for the home." This set included an all-wave radio set, an automatic record changing radiogram, BBC television and colour television. Baird went on to develop *Telechrome*, a fully electronic system that was publicly demonstrated on 16 August 1944 – the world's first demonstration of a fully integrated electronic colour picture tube.[10] In late October of that year, he exhibited the first facsimile television system, using scanned film as the source, with a transmission rate of 25 newspaper pages a second.

What makes Baird's achievement even greater is that he worked with his own funds during the severe restrictions imposed in World War II. By way of comparison, "David Sarnoff of RCA boasted in 1954, that RCA, a huge multi-national company, had spent $75 million to develop colour television and employed hundreds of research scientists in the process. The contrast to John Logie Baird, who developed it ten years earlier for less than $20,000, paid out of his own pocket, with two employed assistants, is quite astounding. If that isn't a demonstration of genius then I do not understand the term. (RCA referred to the *Telechrome* and Baird's patents as prior art in their patent application)."[11] Baird gave his last demonstration – of large-screen television – at London's Classic Cinema on 10 June 1946. Four days later John Logie Baird died.

Image 98 – Eirane "Paddy" Naismith shown on a 1940 Baird 600 line colour TV

Interestingly, and wrongly, Baird's role in the development of television is often disregarded, dismissed or downplayed because he used a "mechanical" scanning system and not the electronic one that later came into general acceptance. It is not uncommon to refer to his work as a blind alley, dead end, or that he backed the wrong horse. But using such a criterion would relegate very many pioneer inventors to the "also ran" category. Thomas Alva Edison reputedly recorded the first human voice on 6 December 1877, but was this a blind alley because he used a tinfoil cylinder to record the voice rather than iPod technology? In fact, his device didn't use electricity at all but was a completely mechanical device. Note: Edouard-Leon Scott de Martinville of France recorded a 10-second clip of a woman singing "Au Clair de la Lune", taken from a so-called phonautogram in 1860, some 17 years before Edison.

Did the early computer pioneers back the wrong horse because they used valves and couldn't produce images of any kind – all data was input and output by punched cards or tape? Is French photography pioneer Joseph Nicéphore Niépce to be written off for having gone up a dead end with his primitive form of photography? Not only was his first camera not digital, but it took some 8 to 20 hours to fix an image and, troglodyte that he was, he didn't even use 35mm film. And, of course, Johannes Gutenberg misled the world for half a millennium with his moveable printing type when really he should have known that electronic word processors were the way to go! The first telegraph was created by Frenchman, Claude Chappe, but it was manual; the first fax by Alexander Bain wasn't electronic, and the Wright brothers' claim to the first manned, controlled, heavier-than-air flight relied on manual wing warping (twisting) to control their plane – clearly a dead end in aviation if ever there was one. All inventions that have a long life will change over time, often radically, from their original manifestation.

Clearly, Baird was first to develop *real* television but, like all inventions, its ongoing development was a continuous process, to which Baird contributed many improvements – far more than any other individual or company even to this day (2015) – despite ill health and great adversity.

He was plagued by ill health from thyroid problems; he was initially opposed by the chief of the BBC, fellow Scot John Reith, who didn't like or understand television and whose hand had to be forced by the Postmaster General; he was sidelined into screening television in cinemas by Gaumont boss Isodore Ostrer; his *Noctovision* was cornered by Britain's military for security reasons; his premises were destroyed in the Crystal Palace fire of 30 November 1936; he was stymied in America by a ruling that foreigners should have no share of their broadcasting; and in 1939 the start of World War II greatly impacted his access to funding and technical resources, especially when many of his staff were conscripted to the war effort because of their technical expertise – such as Englishman Ray Herbert who worked on a project for the French government transmitting television pictures of, and to, the Earth from aircraft and who worked in radar installations for the British military during the war. Ironically, in that same year Baird demonstrated colour television using a cathode ray tube in front of which revolved a disc fitted with colour filters, a technique later adopted by America's CBS and RCA.

Despite these setbacks, Baird took out 177 patents[12] and his inventions forced a more rapid development of television than would otherwise have happened. Baird was the first to:

26 July 1923	File a patent for television. Later, on 29 December he lodged a patent for a spiral scanning disc for use in a television system.
February 1924	Transmit an image of a figure – a Maltese Cross. This was a St John's Ambulance medal belonging to Baird's doctor, George Locke.
February 1924	Transmit a moving silhouette image – human fingers.
2 October 1925	Achieve true television transmission with halftones – when he televised the image of a ventriloquist's dummy followed by images of a youth, William Taynton, at his Frith Street, London residence (some sources say this event was on 30 October).
26 January 1926	Demonstrate television in public. The audience was from the Royal Institution and *The Times* newspaper. The moving images had tone graduation.
15 October 1926	File a patent (British Patent 289,104) for a method of archiving and replaying broadcasts. He first demonstrated his *Phonovision* video disc in September 1927 and the patent, for an improvement called *Phonovisor* (British Patent 324,049), was granted 10 October 1928. The system involved recording 30 line mechanically-derived pictures and sound on conventional 78 rpm gramophone records. Vibrations from the disc were converted into electrical impulses that operated a neon light illuminating openings in a scanning disc synchronised with the turntable. Baird's *Phonovisor* video discs appeared 25 years before video tape came into use. One of the aluminium discs was rediscovered in 1996 and contains the earliest known recording of a television

broadcast, from 21 April 1933, showing the Paramount Astoria Girls dancing. This patent has also been seen as a precursor of fibre optics as it described an array of hollow copper pipes or parallel glass rods to transmit images of television. "By using hollow metal tubes Baird had ready-made waveguides for the control of centimetric or millimetric radio waves. Baird's tube bundles would appear in publications of 1926, as part of the world's first military infra-red night vision units. The 1926 apparatus used an infra-red searchlight to illuminate the target, the reflected rays were dissected, scanned in a desired pattern and then converted into visible images by Baird's TV unit which was called a NOCTOVISOR (night vision). The range of the unit was stated as being 25 miles [40 km]."[13] Danish inventor Holger Møller Hansen was denied a patent on fibre optics in Denmark as late as 1951 on the basis of Baird's priority (and also that of American Clarence Weston Hansell who filed a similar patent on 13 August 1927 based on an earlier description he outlined in his notebook on 30 December 1926).

21 December 1926	File a patent for ultra-short-wave transmission. Baird took out a patent under his and his company's name – *Baird, John Logie, and Television Limited, "Improvements on or relating to Apparatus for Transmitting Views or Images to a Distance"*, which was an early foray into radar. Baird chose to televise a metal cross rather than a person as the latter would not be a good reflector of the ultra-short waves with which he was experimenting. Baird's 1930 US patent 1,699,270 (British patent 292,185) described the system as "extremely valuable in case the invention is used during a war, for instance, where it is desired to view the enemy's position without detection".
24-27 May 1927	Use infrared light to shoot in darkness. Patented in 1926, Baird demonstrated his *Noctovisor* in May the following year. This was a night scope that used infra-red light, but public knowledge of it was constrained by the British defence authorities.
9 February 1928	Broadcast internationally. Baird made the first international television broadcast – which was also the first transatlantic broadcast. It was made from Surrey, England to Hartsdale, New York (it was 8 February in America due to the time difference).
6 March 1928	Transmit television pictures to a ship at sea (it was 5 March on the ship). Moving images of Dora Selvey were sent from the Baird television studio at Motograph House, London, to the RMS *Berengaria* in mid-Atlantic, over 1,600 km away in a transmission that lasted more than 60 minutes.
12 June 1928	Make an outdoor television transmission. This was from the roof of Baird's London studio at 133 Long Acre, Strand. It featured Scottish

	actor Walter John (Jack) Buchanan, who was born in the same town as Baird – Helensburgh – and who provided financial backing for him.
3 July 1928	Transmit colour television pictures. He used sequential scanning through red, green and blue filters. The images included flowers, a policeman's helmet, the end of a lit cigarette, a man sticking out his tongue, coloured scarves, and strawberries.
10 August 1928	Use stereoscopic, or 3-D, television. This was true stereoscopic television.
November 1928	Broadcast a television documentary feature. This featured Geoffrey Holme, editor of *The Studio, A Magazine of Fine and Applied Art*. He discussed various items that he had brought into Baird's studio in London's Long Acre.
November 1928	Publicly schedule a television performance. This was the above broadcast by Geoffrey Holme.
1928-1929	Broadcast a ballet performance – from Baird's Studio in Long Acre, London. It featured Ailsa Bridgewater, sister of one of Baird's engineers. The precise date is not recorded but would have been between 5 December 1928 and 30 September 1929.
30 September 1929	Make an official television broadcast – from Brookmans Park, the world's first television studio, in Hertfordshire, England. It was also in 1929 that Germany and France began broadcasting, using the Baird system in conjunction with local companies. Arrangements had also been made for Baird to work with W.M.C.A. in the United States, but American law was applied to ban Baird's company from involvement.
14 March 1930	Synchronise sound and vision – using 30-line television transmission from Brookmans Park, Hertfordshire, England.
29 April 1930	Broadcast a television interview. American actress Margaret (Peggy) O'Neill (Eaton) was interviewed by a columnist from the *Southern Daily Echo* at the Ideal Home Exhibition in Southampton, England, where Baird had created a temporary studio.
29 April 1930	Demonstrate television using ultra short waves.
14 July 1930	Transmit live drama – Luigi Pirandello's *The Man with a Flower in his Mouth*. It was also the first time make-up was used on television to accentuate the features of the actors. General Electric in America had broadcast *The Queen's Messenger* on 11 September 1928, but it wasn't live and it was on a low definition 24-line mechanical system. Baird followed up shortly afterwards with Gordon Sherry's *Box and Cox* broadcast on 15 December 1928, which was the first time an animal performer had appeared on television – a cat.
28 July 1930	Demonstrate a theatre television system – on a screen 152 cm x 61 cm at the London Coliseum, followed by similar demonstrations of Luigi Pirandello's *The Man with a Flower in his Mouth* in Berlin, Paris and Stockholm. The picture was not shown on the cinema screen but on

one consisting of 2,100 lamps operated by a mechanical commutator switch. The Coliseum trial went for three weeks.

5 November 1930	Televise a commercial – the Eugene Method of permanent hair wave which was broadcast via closed circuit television at the Hairdressing Hair of Fashion held in London's *Olympia* from 5-13 November 1930. (The first commercial broadcast over a television network was for Bulova watches on New York City NBC on 1 July 1941).
8 May 1931	Schedule an outdoor transmission – of the immediate surrounds of the Long Acre studio from a van parked outside.
3 June 1931	The first outdoor broadcast of a public event was the English Epsom Derby horse race on 3 June 1931. Baird used a mirror drum camera mounted in a caravan and with the light modulated by a Kerr cell. The 1932 Derby was also televised by Baird. The 2,000 lamps had by now been superseded by the "flying spot" whereby the picture was traced out in strips by a strong light beam deflected on rotating mirror drum. Earlier, a baseball game had been telecast in Japan on 17 February 1931 at the Tozuka Baseball Ground, but this was shown on closed circuit television.
19 May 1932	Demonstrate the *Visiophone* in Paris. The *Visiophone* was an early telephone capable of transmitting both video and audio.
22 August 1932	Regularly televise broadcasts. This was by the BBC using the Baird system.
4 January 1936	Program live television – shown at London's Dominion Theatre on a screen 244 cm x 183 cm.
August 1936	Commercially produce high definition television receivers. The Baird T5 had a 30 cm x 23 cm screen and was first exhibited at Radiolympia (National Radio Exhibition held at the Earls Court *Olympia* in London).
4 February 1938	Demonstrate high definition colour television – at the Dominion Theatre, to which images were sent 12.8 km from Crystal Palace to be displayed on a 366 cm x 274 cm screen. An earlier demonstration had been given to the press in December 1937. The system was a two-colour process with a 120 line interlace picture shown to some 3,000 patrons.
17 February 1938	Demonstrate live high definition colour television – broadcast from Baird Studios at Crystal Palace, London.
January 1939	Use direct projection television in a theatre – on a 457 cm x 366 cm screen at the 1,190 seat Marble Arch Pavilion in London.
1939	Use aerial television. A Baird television camera was placed on a French Marcel Bloch bomber and broadcast images to a ground station. The System used the intermediate film method by means of which a moving picture of the scenery below the airplane was taken on a 16mm film, which was rapidly processed and transmitted to a

	ground receiving station. This was an early use of radar and it was undertaken by one of Baird's assistants – Ray Herbert, who worked at Hendon Airport, London, and also in France in Orleans and Toulouse.
17 September.1940	Patent colour television at 600 lines.
December 1940	Use 600-line high definition television – it was capable of projecting an image on a screen 76 cm by 61 cm.
23.December 1941	Give the first demonstration of 500-line stereoscopic (electronic) colour television.
16 August 1944	Give the world's first demonstration of a fully electronic colour television display using a 600-line system. Baird's 600-line *Telechrome* colour system had triple interlacing, using six scans to build each picture. The images were good quality and it was the first colour tube in the world to dispense entirely with mechanical devices.
October 1944	Demonstrate the first facsimile television system (the forerunner of Ceefax). Baird used scanned film as the source, with a transmission rate of 25 newspaper pages a second. The English *Daily Telegraph* headlined this apparatus under "5 Novels a Minute" in respect of the high speed of transmission – around 750,000 words per minute. When the British cracked the German cipher machine, Enigma, it permitted the Allies to monitor German communications, but the most advanced radio of the time could only transmit 80 words per minute. Baird's facsimile television could transmit more than 9,000 times faster and, by changing the camera's interlacing, the message could be scrambled for security. Baird had first shown the possibilities of facsimile television as early as 1928 during a public demonstration of his *Televisor* at which it is also claimed the first advertisement was sent by television – the contents bill of England's *Daily Mail*.

The report of the 1943 Television Committee, chaired by Lord (Maurice) Hankey, was presented on 29 December 1944 to the British government. It recommended that 405-line transmission be commenced again when the war ended, but Britain should then develop the 1,000-line stereoscopic colour television transmission recommended by Baird. Such transmission would have provided picture quality comparable with modern HDTV. Baird's vision was never implemented as Britain suffered severe constraints after the war and, more pertinently, Baird died in 1946. Britain languished with monochrome 405 lines until 1964, when 625 lines became the norm, followed by colour television in 1967.

John Logie Baird was instrumental in setting the pace of television development and no-one has come close to achieving the number of "firsts" he attained. Baird recommended using pre-recorded material rather than live broadcasts and today an overwhelming percentage of modern television is pre-recorded. Contemporary television uses film scanning systems, such as that of Rank-Cintel, which absorbed Baird's Cinema Television. Baird's single electronic gun CRT development work in 1945 pre-empted the Sony Trinitron tube.[14]

Andy Finney, a BBC radio and television producer who pioneered interactive media within the BBC, wrote, "There is an ongoing friendly battle between the television and computer-led factions over the development of digital television, particularly over whether the future of television should be interlaced, as it is now, or progressive like computer screens. A representative of Microsoft described their approach to the assembled TV engineers at the 1997 IBC conference in Amsterdam. As part of the presentation, Microsoft showed their 240-line progressive scan suggestion for a possible future format. It was possible that neither the presenter, nor most of his audience, were aware that John Logie Baird was advocating such a standard for broadcasting television throughout Britain as far back as 1936, the same year he lost out to EMI's electronic television."[15]

Considering how Baird has been disparaged for his "mechanical" television, it is telling to note that mechanical imaging still forms much of modern computing systems. The PC mouse operates via a track ball that rotates two slotted discs which are then detected by photo sensors. VCRs (now replaced by DVD recorders) were mechano-electronic, as is radar. High resolution pictures are obtained in mechanical laser printers and scanners, and laser lighting displays use computer-controlled mirrors to create images.

Digital Light Processing technology used in projectors and video projectors is electro-mechanical telecine equipment (that is, technology which permits the transfer of motion picture film into electronic form to be viewed on television, video or cassette – the word *Telecine* being formed from *tele*vision and *cine*ma). It was also pioneered by John Logie Baird, who "is remembered as the inventor of mechanical television, radar and fibre optics." Unveiled with much fanfare in London in early 1926, mechanical television technology was quickly usurped by electronic television, the basis of modern video technology. Nonetheless, Baird's achievements, including making the first trans-Atlantic television transmission, were singular and critical scientific accomplishments. His television research during World War II was highly productive. Although it received little publicity at the time, it was taken up by other companies, including RCA in the United States. Baird's spinning colour wheel (from his *Telechrome*) was part of the design of the special NASA colour camera which televised the moon landing in 1969 and it is also a feature of many digital light projection televisions. Modern 3D television, using polarised glasses, can be traced back to the work of Baird more than 60 years ago.[16]

"Lonely, driven, tireless and often poor, the native Scot defined the pioneering spirit of scientific inquiry. During his long career, John Logie Baird created a host of television technologies. Among them, *Phonovision*, a forerunner of the video recorder (which largely still relies on mechanical scanning); *Noctovision*, an infra-red spotting system for 'seeing' in the dark; open-air television, a theatre-projection system; videophone, which he called *Visiophone*; stereoscopic [3D] colour TV; and the first high definition colour TV. According to present-day TV historians, Baird only pursued mechanical scanning to get a television system working as quickly as possible. He changed to electronic scanning in the early 1930s and refined the system to a high degree. Before he died in 1946, Baird was drafting plans for a television with 1,000 lines of resolution and he had earlier patents for television with up to 1,700 lines of resolution using interlacing technology. The world would not catch up with him until 1990 when the Japanese introduced a TV with 1,125 lines of resolution per frame."[17] Interestingly, Guglielmo Marconi was awarded a Nobel Prize in Physics with Karl Ferdinand Braun "in recognition of their contributions to the development of wireless telegraphy", although he actually invented nothing new in radio technology and his main achievements were the transatlantic broadcast of December 1901 and the synthesis of technologies invented by others. John Logie Baird, on the other hand, was an inveterate inventor who had many well-documented firsts in television technology yet he is largely ignored outside his homeland today, although the Australian television industry awards are known as the Logie Awards in his memory.

William Brown 1888-1975 did experimental work on the mechanism of fungal infection in plants and on the physiology of fungal growth in culture, which was published during the years between 1915 and 1928 in a series of 18 papers. He showed that nutrients diffusing through the cuticle of flower petals and young leaves increased the infectivity of fungal sporelings. He also anticipated the later interest in diffusates from pollen grains as an adjuvant to fungal infection of leaves. He also demonstrated that cuticle penetration by *Botrytis cinerea* is effected by growth pressure of the extending but eventually rigid penetration hypha; fungal deformation of the cuticle is opposed both by the tensile strength of the cuticle and by the turgor pressure of the underlying epidermal cells (the water pressure inside plant cells is called turgor pressure). Brown is also well known for his studies on the variation of growth in culture among species and strains of Fusarium, which revealed serious flaws in the contemporary classification of this genus and led eventually to new taxonomic dispositions.

Brown studied gas storage and cold storage for the control of fungal rots of apple fruits. He found that a combination of the two gave much better control than either method alone. In these experiments on the fungistatic effects of carbon dioxide and low temperature respectively, Brown included a wide series of comparisons between fungal spores sown in water and others sown in nutrient solution (to simulate leakage of nutrients from damaged fruit). Control of spore germination and mycelial growth is always better when the spores are sown in water alone. Brown epitomised his findings in the generalisation that the effect of fungistatic factors is greatest when the fungal energy of growth is least. This is one of the most fundamental and far-reaching generalisations that Brown ever made. Recently, this concept has provided the simplest explanation for repeated observations that general soil fungistasis, which keeps fungal spores dormant in soil, can be overridden both by a glucose solution and by the nutrients present in root exudates.[1]

Archibald Montgomery Low 1888-1956 developed an early forerunner of what was to become television, which he called *TeleVista*, and invented the first electrically-steered rocket. In May 1914, he gave a demonstration of a form of television at the Institute of Automobile Engineers, of which he was a member. His system employed a selenium cell, a semi-conductor, to convert light into electrical impulses, but this proved too slow to adequately handle a moving image, spoiling the effect. Under a headline *Seeing by Wireless*, a leading newspaper commented, "An Inventor, Dr A.M. Low, has discovered a means of transmitting visual images by wire. If all goes well with this invention we shall soon be able, it seems, to see people at a distance, as now we can talk to them at a distance. Whether Dr Low will be regarded in future as a benefactor, or the opposite, depends on something more than the degree to which the business will be mismanaged by the government department that will certainly absorb it as soon as private enterprise and capital have made it a going concern". But then came the war, and so the first Government department to show an interest in Low's work was the War Office. Low volunteered and was commissioned into the army, and was then set to adapting his *TeleVista* system to range finding, and the control of coastal artillery batteries.[1]

During World War I, he was head of Experimental Works, the military organisation in charge of a project to remotely control aircraft. Low supervised a hand-picked team and conducted a test flight of an unmanned craft on 21 March 1917 – known as the *Ruston Proctor Aerial Target* (AT) – this was in essence a precursor of the smart bomb. The AT was launched from the back of a lorry using compressed air (a first) and successfully demonstrated the ability to be remotely controlled before an engine failure led to a crash landing. He improved the test vehicle by adding an electrically driven gyroscope (another of his innovations), but the project was soon abandoned by the British military.[2]

In 1917, Archibald Low and his team also invented the first electrically-steered rocket, a forerunner of a weapon used by the Germans against merchant ships in World War II. Low's inventions during World War I were, for the most part, too advanced to be appreciated by his own government, but he has been called the "Father of radio guidance systems" for his wartime accomplishments. The Germans, however, were well aware of how effective his remote-controlled weapons might be and, in 1915, made two unsuccessful attempts to assassinate him.[3]

Low developed the first data link and solved interference problems caused by the UAV (unmanned aerial vehicle) engine. His first UAVs crashed, but on 3 September 1924 he made the world's first successful radio-controlled flight.[4]

On 7 October 1946, Low thought speedway racing in England could use a little boost and arranged a demonstration at Wembley track, with 90,000 people watching. British motorcycle racer Bill Kitchen was protected by a steel shield over the top of the rocket bodies; the speedway JAP motorcycle used four solid-core rockets, angled downwards to prevent lift-off. Kitchen used switches on the handlebars to ignite the candles, and said "acceleration was absolutely terrific" when the rockets lit off.[5] Note: Fritz von Opel used rockets to power a motorbike in 1928 in Germany, but the government banned it for safety reasons.

Chalmers Jack Mackenzie 1888-1984 "was the single most important figure in the post-war growth of Canadian science". He was trained in civil engineering at Dalhousie and Harvard, served in the Canadian Army in WWI, then became Dean of Engineering at the University of Saskatchewan (1921-1939). During this period, he organised important research in protecting concrete buildings from attack by "alkali salts" in the soil. Mackenzie became the government's chief scientist in WWII and became the right-hand man of Clarence Decatur Howe in planning post-war science policy. His war work included the tenfold expansion of the NRC (National Research Council of Canada) Laboratories, top-secret war gas, aviation, radar and atomic bomb research, membership on the US-British-Canadian Combined Policy Committee, allocating uranium supplies, and even the chore of telling Winston Churchill that "Habakkuk", the British Prime Minister's pet project of an iceberg-aircraft carrier, was impossible.

Mackenzie was NRC president in his own right from 1944-1952, president of Atomic Energy of Canada Ltd from 1953-1954, and president of the Atomic Energy Control Board from 1948-1961. In the post-war years, he and Edgar William Richard Steacie laid the foundations of the

Canadian scientific system as it is today.[1] Note: He was born in Canada of Canadian-born parents: all eight of his great-grandparents were born in Scotland.

James Wright 1888-1952 invented *Silly Putty* in 1943. He was an engineer at General Electric who first made *Bouncy Putty*, later renamed *Silly Putty*. During World War II, the United States couldn't obtain natural rubber from Asian suppliers, who gathered it from rubber trees. General Electric (GE) was trying to find a way to supply rubber for truck tyres and soldiers' boots. James Wright, an engineer at GE, was working with silicone oil – a clear, gooey compound composed of silicon bonded to several other elements. By substituting silicon for carbon, the main element in rubber, Wright hoped to create a new compound with all the flexibility and bounce of rubber. In 1943, Wright made a surprising discovery. He mixed boric acid with silicone oil in a test tube. Instead of forming the hard rubber material he was looking for, the compound remained slightly gooey to the touch. Disappointed with the results, he tossed a gob of the material from the test tube onto the floor. To his surprise, the gob bounced right back at him. The new compound was very bouncy and could be stretched and pulled. However, it wasn't a good rubber substitute, so Wright and other GE scientists continued their search.[1]

Seven years after this event, a toy seller named Peter Hodgson packaged some of Wright's creation in a small plastic egg and presented his new product at the 1950 International Toy Fair in New York. The material was called *Silly Putty*, and it proved to be popular. Millions of eggs containing the starch have been sold to kids of all ages since. Its first name was *Nutty Putty* but changed later due to marketing concerns. By 1987, two million eggs of *Silly Putty* were being produced. In the mid-1990s, production of *Silly Putty* in different colours was begun. In the year 2000, gold *Silly Putty* was created to celebrate 50 years of production, and *Silly Putty* was put on display at the Smithsonian Institute in Washington, DC, as part of an exhibit celebrating 1950s objects that shaped American Culture. Note: Earl L Warrick is also claimed as the inventor of Silly Putty.[2]

Alexander Keiller 1889-1955 is best known for his excavations at Windmill and Avebury and his pioneer flights recording the archaeology of Wessex from the air. In 1922, he approached Osbert Guy Stanhope Crawford of the Ordnance Survey, suggesting an aerial survey of archaeological sites in south-west England. This project culminated in the publication of *Wessex from the Air* (1928), the first book of aerial archaeology to be published in the UK.[1]

One of the sites they photographed was Windmill Hill in Wiltshire, and in 1925, after it was threatened by the construction of radio masts, Keiller bought it and began excavating it. He subsequently bought further land in the area, including much of Avebury and the adjoining West Kennet Avenue. Though much of the work was done in conjunction with the Office of Works, the whole cost of undertaking it was met by Keiller. To provide a base for operations, he established the Morvan Institute of Archaeological Research (named after the Keiller estate in Aberdeenshire) in a small building near Avebury Manor which is now the site museum. The excavations took place between 1925 and 1939, with restoration works thereafter to open the site for public viewing.[2]

The appearance of Avebury today is largely due to the efforts of Keiller, who purchased the monument in the 1930s, his wealth deriving from the family's Dundee-based marmalade business. In a way, it is also due to the fact that a good number of the stones were buried for whatever reason during earlier centuries which was to save many from the predations that were to come later.

Image 99– Avebury

After clearing the parts of the site which nature had re-claimed and emptying the ditches of the accumulation of rubbish they contained, Keiller commenced a careful investigation of the henge. Then, using modern equipment and materials, he excavated and re-erected the surviving stones in their original holes mainly on the western side of the circle and along the West Kennet Avenue. Where stone-holes were found but the stones were missing, he marked them with concrete plinths. World War II caused a halt in further proceedings. Apart from a recent adjustment to the Cove stones, nothing to change the appearance of the henge has been done since.[3]

In re-erecting many of the stones, Keiller uncovered the true wonder of one of the most important megalithic monuments in Europe. His fascinating finds are on display in the Stables Gallery of the Alexander Keiller Museum.[4] One of the most important prehistoric archaeological collections in Britain is housed in the Stables Gallery, including many artefacts from the World Heritage Site (WHS) monuments.

Edwin Howard Armstrong 1890-1954 has been called "the most prolific and influential inventor in radio history".[1] Among Armstrong's 42 patents was one for frequency modulation radio transmission, better known as FM. He invented the regenerative circuit in 1914, the super-regenerative circuit in 1922, and the superheterodyne receiver in 1918.

The regenerative circuit enabled a vacuum tube to amplify an electronic signal many times over and was in widespread use in radios (or wireless as it was then known) for two decades from the 1920s. Even today it still is used for opening and closing garage doors. The super-regenerative circuit was used in more specialist activities, particularly during World War II in weaponry such as the proximity fuse. The principle of Armstrong's superheterodyne receiver underlies almost all modern radio and television receivers. "Armstrong contributed the most to modern electronics technology. His discoveries revolutionised electronic communications. Regeneration or amplification via positive feedback is still in use to this day. He created several of the radio industry's basic technology circuits".[2]

Armstrong's regenerative circuit was revolutionary. "On 30 December 1916, 'the world's first wireless dance' was held at a house in Morristown, New Jersey, United States, reported the *New York Times* newspaper the following day. Couples danced to music from a phonograph that was some 40 miles [65 km] away in New York City. The sound was not only transmitted by radio, but also – astonishingly – amplified so that it 'could be heard all over the house'. Previously, to hear the experimental radio broadcasts that were beginning at this time, listeners had to wear a headset. The revolutionary amplification was due to a local man, Edwin Howard Armstrong."

His device amplified sound up to 1,000 times compared to Lee De Forest's vacuum tube which could amplify 12 to 18 times. In 1936, Armstrong gave a demonstration of a jazz recording that showed the superiority of his FM signal over AM and his invention was described "as one of the most important radio developments since the first earphone crystal sets were introduced". In 1955, Armstrong was recognised by the International Telecommunication Union as one of the greatest figures in the history of telecommunications.[3]

David Miller 1890-1973 initiated research on methods of timber preservation, particularly the control of insect pests. In 1928, Miller succeeded as head of the Cawthron Institute Department of Biology, in Nelson, New Zealand. His work on forest and timber insects continued, leading to his establishment of the Forest Biological Research Station at Nelson in 1929. The success of the New Zealand timber industry is largely due to research initiated by Miller.

During the economic depression of the early 1930s, appreciating the need to have public support and interest in scientific research, Miller campaigned vigorously to obtain backing from primary producer organisations, local bodies and banks to keep the services of the highly skilled staff he had attracted. Because he was successful, New Zealand was able to help lay the foundations of two international institutions: the Commonwealth Institute of Entomology and the Commonwealth Institute of Biological Control, both located in London. Parasites were imported into New Zealand for the biological control of pests such as white butterfly, diamond-backed moth, pear midge, gum-tree weevil, sheep-maggot fly and grass-grub. Plant-feeding insects were imported for the biological control of weeds. New Zealand became a world leader in the field of biological control.[1]

Robert Eric Mortimer Wheeler 1890-1976 was probably the best-known British archaeologist of the 20th century.[1] His notable excavations in Britain were at Verulamium (St Albans) and Maiden Castle. While director-general of archaeology in India (1944-1947), he was most active at Mohenjo-Daro and Harappa. His particular excavation method was the "Wheeler" box trench system – a method of setting out archaeological excavation trenches in a pattern of regular square or rectangular boxes with baulks between.[2] Other excavations were carried out at Charsada and Taxila in north-western India, and at Arikamedu (the Roman-Indian trading post of Poduca) in southern India after identifying Roman pottery in the government museum.[3]

During his career, he performed many major excavations within Britain, such as Stanwick Iron Age Fortifications in Yorkshire and including the abovementioned Roman Verulamium and the late Iron Age hill-fort of Maiden Castle, Dorset. His grid system (later developed further by Kathleen Kenyon and known as the Wheeler-Kenyon method) was a significant advance in archaeological method, although later superseded. The two constant themes in his attempts to improve archaeological excavation were, first, to maintain strict stratigraphic control while excavating (for this purpose, the baulks between his trenches served to retain a record of the strata that had been dug through), and, second, to publish the excavation promptly and in a form that would tell the story of the site to the intelligent reader.[4]

Perhaps the most important of Wheeler's accomplishments were a focus on problem-oriented excavation and the creation of meticulous techniques for excavating sites and recording the materials therein. Highly unusual at the time – archaeologists of his era were generally intent on acquiring beautiful objects rather than resolving questions about the past – his techniques have become de rigueur in the field.[5]

George Bennie 1891-1957 built a monorail train in 1930, but because the test track was too short at 130 m, it only reached speeds of 80 km/h instead of the intended 240 km/h. Patented in 1921 and known as the *George Bennie Airspeed Railway* or *Railplane*. it was propelled by four-bladed propellers at both ends. It was built to deal with steep gradients of 1:25 and it had wing airfoils at either end to give it lift.

Bennie described it in his patent, saying "As the speed of the craft increases, the weight of the same is gradually transferred from the rail to the planes so that any tendency of the craft to rise can be overcome by adjustment of the lifting planes."[1] It received a lot of publicity on its opening day, 8 July 1930, but the onset of the Great Depression stopped it from attracting the necessary investment capital and thus died the *Railplane* project, which was mooted to speed up travel between Glasgow and Edinburgh.

Image 100 – Poster for the Bennie Railplane system from 1929

Henry Lamont Murray 1891-1959 invented, with fellow New Zealander Frank S. Board, the *Vacreator*, which mixes steam with cream to both pasteurise and deodorise the cream. This process is now used throughout the world and is a vital factor in New Zealand's butter export trade. Pasteurisation is necessary to kill microorganisms while deodorisation removes feed taints from the cream. Vacreation deodorises the cream so that butter kept frozen for two years still has an acceptable flavour. This feature was most significant in developing the butter trade with the United Kingdom prior to World War II.[1] The process employs a continuous-type machine and is especially adapted for use on high-viscosity material, although it can even operate on plain fluid milk.[2]

John Burdon Sanderson Haldane 1892-1964 was one of the founders of population genetics and his first major work, *The Causes of Evolution* (1932), of what came to be known as the "modern evolutionary synthesis", re-established natural selection as the premier mechanism of evolution by explaining it in terms of the mathematical consequences of Mendelian genetics.[1]

His greatest achievement – in uniting Darwinian evolution theory with Mendelian genetics – was set out in a series of papers starting in 1924. He used a Mendelian system of heredity to work out, mathematically, the consequences of natural selection. He assigned selective values to genes, and deduced the number of generations required to bring about changes in gene frequency under many alternative assumptions. Haldane's work in developing a quantitative theory of evolution – together with that of Ronald Aylmer Fisher and Sewall Green Wright – re-established Darwin's natural selection as the accepted mechanism of evolutionary change. He did much to encourage the development of human genetics, both through his own work and through discussions with others, particularly during his time at University College. He continued working in this field all his life, but made important contributions in many other areas. His early work in biochemistry laid the foundations of a mathematical theory of enzyme action. His other interests ranged from cosmology to animal behaviour and the origin of life.[2]

Haldane's rule relating to hybrids of species and extending to speciation in evolutionary theory is easily stated: When, in the offspring of two different animal races, one sex is absent, rare, or sterile, that sex is the heterozygous (heterogametic) sex. Haldane's rule has a correspondence with the observation that some negative recessive genes are sex-linked and express themselves more often in men than women, such as colour blindness or haemophilia.[3]

He is also known for an observation from his essay, *On Being the Right Size*, which Jane Jacobs and others have since referred to as Haldane's principle. This is that sheer size very often defines what bodily equipment an animal must have: "Insects, being so small, do not have oxygen-carrying bloodstreams. What little oxygen their cells require can be absorbed by simple diffusion of air through their bodies. But being larger means an animal must take on complicated oxygen pumping and distributing systems to reach all the cells." The conceptual metaphor to animal body complexity has been of use in energy economics and secession ideas.[4]

David Aylmer Scott 1892-1971 was one of Canada's most distinguished biochemists. He played a key role in the development of methods for large-scale preparation and purification of insulin.[1] He discovered, in 1931, the important role zinc chloride played in the crystallisation of insulin. This discovery led to Connaught Laboratories establishing the international standard for insulin. It also facilitated the development of several longer-acting types, such as Protamine Zinc Insulin.[2]

Another of Scott's major contributions was in the development of heparin during the mid-1930s with Charles Best and others.[3] Heparin is used to control the coagulation of blood in veins and arteries, thus allowing more complex surgical operations.

Kenneth Manley Smith 1892-1981 designed methods to improve the health of potatoes during the Second World War. He developed the system of producing nuclear stocks of virus-free tubers, a scheme which is still the main one used in this country (1982). He developed methods for using viruses for the biological control of insect pests. By 1931, he had achieved the separation and identification of the potato virus X and Y complex (X = plant pathogenic virus of the family *Flexiviridae*; Y = a species in the genus *Potyvirus*), and he and the rest of the group quickly recognised and characterised several other potato viruses. Smith studied the relationships between these viruses and their vectors and was among the first to realise that viruses differed in their vector relationships.[1]

Robert Alexander Watson-Watt 1892–1973 designed the first workable radio direction finding device for locating moving objects by bouncing radio waves off them and calculating the range by transmitted pulses. Soon to be known as "radar" (RAdio Detection And Ranging), it was critical in aiding the Royal Air Force detect where German bombing raids were to be concentrated during World War II, thus allowing British fighter aircraft to be deployed more effectively to deal with this threat. As early as 1916 he had proposed the use of cathode ray oscillographs for radio-direction-finding displays and, around 1927, he proposed the name "ionosphere" for the ionised layer in the upper atmosphere. With Edward Victor Appleton and James F. Herd he developed the "squegger" hard-valve transformer-coupled timebase and with the latter devised a direction-finding radio-goniometer.[1]

Asked, in 1933, to investigate the possibility of a death ray against enemy aircraft, he advised that the technology available wasn't capable of such use. In February 1935, Watson-Watt produced a report entitled *The Detection of Aircraft by Radio Methods*. This report intrigued a committee headed by Sir Henry Tizard. His committee was concerned with air defence.

The theory seemed possible, and the committee looked upon the suggestion with great enthusiasm. But, as Harry Egerton Wimperis pointed out to Watson-Watt and Hugh Dowding, who was then Air member for Research and Development, holding the rank then of Air Vice Marshal, that all this was simply just theory as no such instrument had yet been designed or constructed.

Dowding was full of enthusiasm and even more so later when Watson-Watt said that he could get hold of a BBC shortwave transmitter of just ten kilowatts at Daventry. By setting up a receiver and cathode ray tube 20 miles (32 km) distant, it was hoped that the theory would work by using a light bomber as the enemy aircraft. On 26 February 1935, a full test was arranged. A Heyford light bomber flew along a pre-determined line and the scientists stood holding their breath as they had no idea if the theory would work. Then, suddenly, a green line appeared on the screen, it moved from right to left for a while then as the aircraft turned and came towards them, the line got slightly bigger and bigger. They were elated. Without looking for a visual sighting of the aircraft, they watched the cathode ray tube oscillograph that looked something like a small television set. They could track the Heyford bomber without even looking up into the skies. The results were very promising and when word got back to the Department of Research and Development, Dowding was elated with the results saying, "If we can produce such apparatus it would become the 'eyes' of our defence system and the greatest innovation we could dream of".

Over the next three years, and with an allocation of £10,000 to continue with the experiments, the team of Wimperis, Watson-Watt and Albert Percival Rowe concentrated on radio-direction finding. There were a few disappointments, and there were successes in further tests, but slowly it was all coming together. Once it was discovered that they could determine the height and direction of detected aircraft, further work was carried out in getting this information to the various departments so that the RAF could dispatch aircraft quickly and meet the intruders before they reached the British coast. The system became known as radar, although its correct name was Radio Direction Finding (RDF).[2]

From then onwards, guided largely by Robert Watson-Watt, the foundation of the British radar effort – the early warning Chain Home – materialised. The Chain Home began in December 1935, with Treasury approval for a set of five stations to patrol the air approaches to the Thames estuary. Before the end of 1936, and long before the first test of the Thames stations in the autumn of 1937, plans were made to expand it into a network of nineteen stations along the entire east coast; later, an additional six stations were built to cover the south coast. The Chain Home played a crucial role in the Battle of Britain, which began in July 1940. The final turning point was on 15 September, when the Luftwaffe suffered a record number of planes lost in a single day. Never again did Germany attempt a massive daylight raid over Britain. However, if radar won the day, it lost the night. Night-time air raids showed a desperate need for radar improvements.[3]

In 1940, Watson-Watt, assisted by John Randall and Henry Boot of Birmingham University, invented the cavity magnetron.[4] This produced a compact source of short-wave radio waves that could be installed in British aircraft and allowed Fighter Command to detect incoming enemy planes from a much greater distance giving Fighter Command even more time to organise itself in preparation for an attack. The magnetrons were also found to have another use – they could heat up water. Today, magnetrons are used as the source of heat in microwave ovens. Note: Contemporaneously with Watson-Watt, German scientists were developing radar and, although they were working on the more effective VHF and UHF wavelengths, they failed to use their radar effectively, unlike Britain. Also, most sources cite Randall and Boot as the inventors of the cavity magnetron, with no reference to Watson-Watt who was, indeed, their boss as he was in charge of all radar research in Britain. It was known that a multi-cavity resonant magnetron had been developed in 1935 by Hans Hollmann in Berlin, however, the German military considered its frequency drift to be undesirable, and based their radar systems on the klystron instead. It was primarily for this reason that German night fighter radars were never a match for their British counterparts.[5]

The contribution of Radio Detection and Ranging (RADAR) to the defence of Britain during World War II was a major factor in winning the "Battle of Britain" and ultimate victory. In 1952, Watson-Watt was awarded £52,000 tax-free by the UK government's Royal Commission on Awards to Inventors. He was also awarded the US Medal for Merit.

Leslie John Comrie 1893-1950 founded the world's first private computer bureau in 1937 – Scientific Computing Service Limited. During World War II he headed a team of 30 scientists to computerise war work, (e.g., bombing tables for the USAF). Later, he computerised British football pools.

His impact on computational and precision astronomy may perhaps be appreciated only by those engaged in such subjects over the last few decades, but its immensity would soon be discovered if students had to revert to the methods in use before his time. Virtually, he made the discovery that the then existing calculating machines, which were designed for commercial practice, could be adapted to scientific work, and that specialised machines need not be designed. Further, he showed that such machines had the inherent power to perform hitherto difficult tasks with great ease and accuracy. Before his time, at His Majesty's Nautical Almanac Office, all astronomical calculations were performed by hand, using logarithms. The development of machine work wrought a change which is still having its effect today in all branches of astronomy.[1]

Comrie greatly influenced the development of scientific computation in the interwar period[2] and much of the success of modern electronic calculating machines can be credited to the pioneer work of Comrie.[3]

Victoria Alexandrina Drummond 1894-1980 was the first woman marine engineer in Britain and the first female member of the Institute of Marine Engineers. She served her apprenticeship from 1918 to 1922 at the Caledon Ship Yard and then served on 32 ships, from 1922 on SS *Anchises* and, finally, from 1961 on SS *Santagranda*. She was awarded the MBE for exceptional gallantry at sea in time of war while serving on SS *Bonita* in 1940 when she single-handedly kept the ship's engines going during an attack by a German bomber. She was Chief Engineer from 1959 until retiring in 1962, the first British woman to ever hold that position.[1]

Alexander Strang Thom 1894-1985 undertook the project of accurately surveying and carefully measuring megalithic sites throughout Britain, the initial results of which he published in 1955 in the *Journal of the Royal Statistical Society*. Thom also contributed a heightened awareness of the geometry of stone circles, showing there were six types: true circles, ellipses, two sorts of egg-shaped circles, and two sorts of flattened circles. In important ways, Thom's work converged with that of Gerald Hawkins which emphasised the preoccupation of Stonehenge's builders with astronomy and mathematics. Whereas Hawkins focused on Stonehenge, Thom was able to demonstrate that a large number of other megalithic sites were also oriented to the sun and the moon.[1]

Thom's book *Megalithic Sites in Britain*, published in 1967, caused huge controversy within academic archaeology. Thom's premise that Stone Age culture used complex mathematics and applied this to constructing monuments undermined the progressional idea of culture as continually advancing from savagery to civilisation. Glyn Daniel commissioned the eminent astronomer Sir Fred Hoyle to consider Thom's evidence for *Archaeology* magazine. Hoyle found that Thom's theories were essentially accurate.[2]

Thom published the results of his field surveys of over three hundred stone circles, cairns, and standing stones in England, Scotland, Wales, and Ireland. The accuracy of his field measurements, the precision of his analyses, and the quantity of his data set a new standard for the young discipline of archaeoastronomy. Based on his findings, which did not initially include Stonehenge, Thom argued that the megalithic builders made their circles and alignments for the purpose of marking the solstices, the equinoxes, and nineteen-year cycle of the moon, and the rising and setting of sixteen bright (first magnitude) stars.

On the basis of his site surveys and astronomical interpretations, Thom believed that the fundamental motive for the megalithic builders was scientific, not ritualistic. He argued, with impressive mathematical precision, that the megalithic sites were astronomical observatories where alignments were established with an accuracy of a single solar diameter. At these sites, Thom supposed that genuine, practical astronomy was carried out for the purpose of devising an accurate sixteen-month calendar. The precision of Thom's site surveys also led him to claim that the Neolithic builders used a standard unit of measurement, a megalithic yard (2.72 feet), which they employed at every site across the British Isles.

Thom also attempted to demonstrate on the basis of his site surveys that the megalithic builders were interested in exploring the mathematical properties of various geometrical shapes: circles, egg shapes, ellipses, flattened circles, isosceles triangles, Pythagorean triangles, and spirals.

Thom's work created an immediate impact upon astronomers but drew little response from prehistorians. As archaeologist Richard Atkinson pointed out in 1975, this was because "many prehistorians either ignore the implications of Thom's work, because they do not understand them, or resist them because it is more comfortable to do so". Atkinson himself was prepared to accept that Thom's results were not due to chance, and he was willing to raise his estimation of the intellectual and technological abilities of the Neolithic peoples of Britain, in keeping with the implications of calibrated Carbon-14 dating. In recent years, however, Thom's work has been subject to critical examination. Analysis of Thom's data indicates that some of his results were subjectively biased or due to chance or based upon what Thom calls "indicated foresights", which figure significantly in his later work.

The astronomer Clive Ruggles' recent study of 189 megalithic sites in Scotland, which does not make use of indicated foresights, gives little evidence to support Thom's work. There was no evidence of alignments for the summer solstice, equinox, other lunar standstills, or stellar positions, as reported by Thom for Scottish sites. As the evaluation of Thom's work continues and the investigation of other circles and alignments progresses, it is abundantly clear that the study of Stonehenge must be fitted into the developing picture of archaeoastronomy in the British Isles. Astronomers can no longer write about Stonehenge as if it were virtually a unique case. Although Thom pioneered the recent astronomical study of British megalithic sites, he was not responsible for starting the current astronomical investigation of Stonehenge.[3]

Charles Drummond Ellis 1895-1980 was a world authority on the nature and behaviour of P-rays and y-rays. Ellis became recognised as the leading figure in P-radioactivity which already appeared to be a more complex phenomenon (compared to a-radioactivity), involving a continuous and line spectrum of P-rays as well as 7-rays. He was able to establish the existence of energy levels in the nucleus and obtain the main features of the level distribution for radioactive nuclei. At the time he began research work, the only basic particles known were the electron, proton and photon, while wave mechanics was nearly six years in the future.[1]

In the early 1930s, Ellis and Nevill Francis Mott developed the earlier work on the energetics of nuclear processes to explore the energy relations in beta decay in the light of the new wave mechanics. This work was important in developing Wolfgang Ernst Pauli's theory of the neutrino. Indeed, Mott considered later that Ellis had "practically discovered the neutrino".[2] His achievements were very great, and place him among the most accomplished and important experimental physicists of the century.

In 1930, Ernest Rutherford, James Chadwick and Ellis collaborated on *Radiations from Radioactive Substances*, which came to be recognised as a landmark in the field. Ellis and Chadwick were also part of a team that proved that the beta decay spectrum is continuous. In addition, Ellis and colleague William Alfred Wooster established that the emission of alpha and beta particles occurs before the radiation of gamma rays in certain elements.[3]

Like many of Rutherford's students, Ellis was fortunate in being given a research project with the potential of leading to a major advance in physics. He played a key role in founding nuclear spectroscopy by following Rutherford's directions, as he acknowledged at the end of his first paper: "In conclusion I would like to express my indebtedness to Prof. Sir Ernest Rutherford, who suggested the problem and the method of attack, and directed the whole course of the work."

However, he (Ellis) displayed great technical skill in obtaining his results, and determination in following up his crucial insight that the nucleus, like the atom itself, could fruitfully be characterised in terms of discrete energy levels experimentally determined by accurate measurements of photon energies. The circumstances involved in establishing the continuous nature of the spectrum were rather different. With the exception of Chadwick, who had other responsibilities, Ellis was almost alone in his conviction both that the primary spectrum is continuous, and that the phenomenon is of fundamental importance. In the *Biographical Memoir* Nevill Mott is quoted as concluding: "I feel he did not get enough credit for practically discovering the neutrino."[4]

Aubrey Duncan Mackenzie 1895-1962 was Chief Engineer in the Public Works Department in Melbourne, Australia, having already been responsible for construction of the Yarra Boulevard and the Mount Donna Buang, Acheron Way and Ben Cairn roads, and for the surroundings of the Shrine of Remembrance. From 1940 to 1960 he was executive-chairman of the Melbourne Harbor Trust and, under his administration, Melbourne remained the best mechanised Australian port, especially for bulk-loading. Construction of the Appleton Dock in 1956 and introduction of the Tasmanian car-ferry were some of his achievements.[1]

Hugh William Bell Cairns 1896-1952 was a key figure in the development of neurosurgery as a specialty, the formation of the Medical School at Oxford University, and the treatment of head injuries during the Second World War. He was adviser on head injuries to the Ministry of Health and neurosurgeon to the army. A new base hospital for head injuries was established at St Hugh's College, Oxford, where "The Nutcrackers Suite" became a neurological unit of first importance. During World War II, Cairns was swift to stress the advantage of air evacuation of battle casualties and he quickly organised the mobile surgical teams which revolutionised the treatment of wounded in the North African campaigns.[1]

Cairns realised that, in order to save the lives of the greatest number of soldiers suffering from head wounds, they should be treated in the field by specialist neurosurgical teams. He devised and brought about the formation of eight mobile neurosurgical units. These units treated more than 20,000 patients in North Africa, Italy and the other European theatres of war, as well as in India, and their formation was one of Cairn's greatest contributions in the field of military medical care.[2]

Profoundly affected by treating Thomas Edward Lawrence (T.E. Lawrence of Arabia) for head injuries during the six days before the latter died after a motorcycle accident, Cairns began a long study of what he saw as the unnecessary loss of life by motorcycle despatch riders through head injuries. His research led to the use of crash helmets by both military and civilian motorcyclists. As a consequence of treating Lawrence, Sir Hugh Cairns would ultimately save the lives of many motorcyclists.[3]

Alexander Bannatyne Stewart Laidlaw 1896-1968 designed the combustion chamber which made practicable the jet engine designed by Frank Whittle. Writing later, Whittle remarked, "I was fairly confident in the compressor and turbine elements, but felt rather out of my depth with the combustion problem." Most of the oil burner firms considered Whittle's requirements too stringent but although Laidlaw "recognised that we were aiming at something far in advance of previous experience in this field he considered the target possible of attainment, and so it was with his help that we attacked the combustion problem."[1]

Following modifications and rebuilding, the engine was ready for trials again in April 1938. The "new" engine incorporated a number of modifications. The impeller was improved and inlets were added for more air flow, the combustion chamber was redesigned based on Whittle/Laidlaw improvements [2]

Patrick Maynard Stuart Blackett 1897-1974 won the Nobel Prize for Physics in 1948 for his discoveries in the field of cosmic radiation, which he accomplished primarily with cloud-chamber photographs that revealed the way in which a stable atomic nucleus can be disintegrated by bombarding it with alpha particles (helium nuclei). Although such nuclear disintegration had been observed previously, his data explained this phenomenon for the first time and were useful in explaining disintegration by other means.[1]

He improved Charles Thomson Rees Wilson's cloud chamber, redesigning it as a mechanism for automated study of cosmic radiation. By 1924, his cloud chamber photographs showed disintegration of a nitrogen nuclei by alpha particles, the first photographic evidence of nuclear transformation.[2] Blackett had obtained 23,000 photographs showing 415,000 tracks of ionized particles, of which eight tracks were of a strikingly different type. These showed the path of a proton ejected from a recoiling nitrogen nucleus and the capture of the alpha particle by the nitrogen nucleus, creating an isotope of oxygen.[3]

Together with Italian scientist Giuseppe Paolo Stanislao Occhialini, he designed the counter-controlled cloud chamber, a brilliant invention by which they managed to make cosmic rays take their own photographs. By this method, the cloud chamber is brought into function only when the impulses from two Geiger-Muller tubes, placed one above and one below the vertical Wilson chamber, coincide as the result of the passing of an electrically charged particle through both of them.

In the spring of 1933, Blackett and Occhialini not only confirmed Anderson's discovery of the positive electron, but also demonstrated the existence of "showers" of positive and negative electrons, both in approximately equal numbers. This fact and the knowledge that positive particles (positrons) do not normally exist as normal constituents of matter on the Earth, formed the basis of their conception that gamma rays can transform into two material particles (positrons and electrons), plus a certain amount of kinetic energy – a phenomenon usually called pair production. The reverse process – a collision between a positron and an electron in which both are transformed into gamma radiation, so-called annihilation radiation – was also verified experimentally. In the interpretation of these experiments Blackett and Occhialini were guided by Dirac's theory of the electron.[4]

Blackett was one of the most distinguished experimental physicists of the 20th century and is known as the father of operational research, applying the scientific method to the air defence of Great Britain and the anti-U-Boat war in the North Atlantic, and he reduced the average number of shots taken to down an enemy aircraft by anti-aircraft guns from 20,000 to 5,000. He was regarded as being unlucky not to share the Nobel Prize for the discovery of the positron in 1936.[5]

Blackett is widely recognised as having had a significant impact on fields ranging from particle physics to continental drift.[6] A group under his direction studied many aspects of the properties of rocks with the object of finding out the precise history of the Earth's magnetic field, in magnitude and direction back to the earliest geological times. This work, and that of others, showed that the rock magnetism data strongly supported the conclusions of Alfred Lothar Wegener and Alexander Logie Du Toit that the continents have drifted relative to each other markedly in the course of geological history.[7]

Cyril Norman Hinshelwood 1897-1967 worked on reaction rates and reaction mechanisms, particularly those of the combination of hydrogen and oxygen to form water, one of the most fundamental combining reactions in chemistry. For this work, he shared the 1956 Nobel Prize for Chemistry with the Soviet scientist Nikolay Semyonov.[1]

Studying gas reactions and the decomposition of solid substances in the presence and absence of catalysts, Hinshelwood went on to demonstrate that many reactions can be explained in terms of a series – a chain – of interdependent stages. At high temperatures, the chain reactions of some elements accelerate the process to explosion point. He provided experimental evidence for the role of activated molecules in initiating the chain reaction. In his bacterial-growth experiments, too, he considered that all the various chemical reactions that occurred were interconnected and mutually dependent, the product of one reaction becoming the reactant for the next.[2]

His early studies of molecular kinetics led to the publication of *Thermodynamics for Students of Chemistry* and *The Kinetics of Chemical Change* in 1926, the latest (fourth) edition of the latter appearing in 1940, and he subsequently worked on chemical changes in the bacterial cell, producing physicochemical explanations for the biological responses of bacteria to changes in environment. His findings proved to be of great importance in later research work on antibiotics and therapeutic agents, and his book on the topic, *The Chemical Kinetics of the Bacterial Cell*, was published in 1946.[3]

Henry Thomas McLaren 1897-1993 designed the first surf ski with his brother, Jack. They used an early version of the surf ski in 1912 for use around the family's oyster beds on Lake Innes, near Port Macquarie, New South Wales, Australia, and the brothers used them in the surf on Port

Macquarie's beaches. The board was propelled in a sitting position with two small hand blades, which was probably not a highly efficient method to negotiate the surf. The deck was flat with a bung plug at the rear and a nose ring with a leash, possibly originally required for mooring. The rails were square and there was a pronounced rocker. The boards' obvious buoyancy indicated hollow construction, with thin boards of cedar fixed longitudinally down the board.[1]

Arthur Edward Walton 1897-1959 was a physiologist who had an influence on artificial insemination. Prior to the development of artificial insemination, the genes of superior livestock could be shared only by transporting the adult animals from one farm to another in order to mate them with local animals. Thus, the process of breeding better livestock was slow, cumbersome, and risky. An obvious improvement to the process would be to transport not the animals themselves, but only their sperm.

Walton demonstrated that the metabolic activity of ram and bull spermatozoa, particularly their respiration, is directly correlated with motility and that, under certain conditions, respiring spermatozoa produce hydrogen peroxide which, in turn, is responsible for a gradually inhibitory effect on respiration and decline in motility. He then developed an ingenious apparatus to maintain spermatozoa alive for long periods by allowing both continuous feeding and removal of toxic metabolites. This was crucial to the development of artificial insemination, which he first tested just before the Second World War by transporting ram semen to Poland, where it was used successfully to inseminate ewes. He also shipped rabbit and bull semen.[1]

In 1941, Walton and Joseph Edwards proposed to the Agricultural Improvement Council the organisation of a system for the artificial insemination of the British dairy herd. The proposal was opposed at the time, partly due to its commercial orientation, Walton being closely associated with the Cambridge Cattle Breeding Society (a farmers' co-operative which he had helped to organise to take advantage of the new technology). However, after suitable revisions, it won acceptance, and the following year two national centres for artificial insemination were established in Reading and Cambridge.[2]

John Masson Gulland 1898-1947 contributed to the unravelling of the structure of the DNA molecule, but died six years before Francis Crick and James Watson published their seminal work on its double helix structure.

In 1946, Gulland wrote about DNA: "There is at present no indisputable chemical evidence that the nucleotides are arranged in anything other than a random manner in the polynucleotides. It must be realised that the existence of tetranucleotide units, repeated throughout the molecule, would limit the potential number of isomers and hence diminish the possibilities of biological specificity. Thus, the immense numbers of variations presented by a polynucleotide in which the nucleotides occur in random sequence is reduced, in the case of an unbranched polynucleotide, to a single possible structure, varying only in its length, if the same, uniform tetranucleotide unit occurs throughout".[1]

Nearly four decades after Lithuanian-born biochemist Phoebus Aaron Theodore Levene first postulated his "tetranucleotide hypothesis" in 1910, most scientists still believed that DNA was made up of equal numbers of the four nucleotide bases in a repeating tetrameric structure, with each sub-unit containing all four bases.

Then in 1947, John Masson Gulland, together with Dennis Oswald Jordan and their colleagues at University College, Nottingham, perfected a method of extracting DNA from calf thymus glands. Importantly, their protocol avoided the use of acid or alkali, which kept the solution at a constant neutral pH, allowing them to isolate pure, fibrous, nondegraded DNA. When they added strong acids or bases to the sample, however, electrometric titrations showed that hydrogen bonds, rather than covalent bonds, linked the amino and hydroxyl groups of the nucleotide bases.

These results, along with Erwin Chargaff's 1950 discovery that DNA contains equal amounts of adenine and thymine and equal amounts of cytosine and guanine, paved the way for James Watson and Francis Crick's discovery that the molecule is, in fact, a double helix. As Watson put it in *The Double Helix* (1970): "A rereading of J. M. Gulland's and D. O. Jordan's papers made me finally realise the strength of their conclusion that a large fraction, if not all, of the bases formed hydrogen bonds to other bases."[2]

Archibald Milne Hamilton 1898-1972 devised a new type of bridge, which enabled any span or strength of bridge to be erected quickly from standard parts. The War Office adopted this type of bridging for operations in the Second World War and since then it has been used throughout the world for the construction and reconstruction of roads and bridges.[1]

Between 1928 and 1932, he was the principal engineer of the Hamilton Road, through Kurdistan, which he hoped would unite the peoples of the region. During the construction of the road, Hamilton became aware of the need for strong, adaptable bridges with components that could easily be transported and erected in remote and/or difficult terrain. The modern day prefabricated Panel/Floor Beam/Deck system was first patented by Hamilton in 1935. The bridge was used for quick mobilisation to allow military access to remote locations or to replace bridges destroyed in times of conflict.

Image 101 – Callender-Hamilton Bridge, 4th Walton Bridge

The design was centred on a series of gusset plates that allowed the direct attachment of the longitudinal, diagonal, vertical, and cross framing members. The centralising of connection points increased the speed of construction and also allowed identical panels to be fabricated from identical members and then installed on site. This system is known as the Callender-Hamilton System, as they were manufactured by British Insulated Callender's Cables. Since the gusset plate carried the direct attachment of the vertical, diagonal, and cross members, the lateral stiffness carried by the floor beams is isolated and thereby increased. The members and connection points are modular in that many similar components could be erected to meet various applications. Truss panels that are stacked on top of each other can easily be attained by attaching two prefabricated gusset plates together, forming a central location for all connection members. This design was augmented by Sir Donald Bailey in the 1940s and is the predecessor to what is now the most commonly prefabricated truss system produced, known as "The Bailey Bridge".[2]

Hamilton's non-floating military bridge was designed for heavy traffic use in rear areas where ultra-rapid erection was not the first essential. Though not so publicised as the Bailey bridge, it was widely used in all theatres or war and has many civil applications.[3]

George Martin Lees 1898-1955 examined oil prospects and oil company geological methods in many countries, including the United States, Canada, Egypt, Germany, and Australia. Under his geological direction, his company in the Middle East discovered more oil for fewer wells drilled than the world had yet seen. Over 100,000 square miles (259,000 km²) of mountainous Persia (Iran) were also geologically surveyed at appropriate scales. In 1933, he initiated a new program of oil search in England and Scotland which resulted in the discovery of the east midland oilfields in 1939; these explorations added much new information to British geology, discovering the Yorkshire potash deposits as a by-product. Other successful explorations, which he helped to initiate and which came to fruition in post-war years, were those in Nigeria, Libya, and Abu Dhabi (Trucial Coast). In 1954, he was awarded the Sidney Powers memorial medal of the American Association of Petroleum Geologists, their highest distinction, never previously given to a non-American, for service to Middle East geology.[1]

John Wishart 1898-1956 derived, in 1928, the generalised product-moment distribution which is now named the Wishart distribution, described as a fundamental to multivariate statistical analysis.[1] It is any of a family of probability distributions defined over symmetric, nonnegative-definite matrix-valued random variables ("random matrices"). These distributions are of great importance in the estimation of covariance matrices in multivariate statistics.

Frank Macfarlane Burnet 1899-1985 and Peter Medawar were co-recipients of the 1960 Nobel Prize for Physiology or Medicine for demonstrating acquired immune tolerance. This research provided the experimental basis for inducing immune tolerance, the platform for developing methods of transplanting solid organs. Burnet made seminal contributions to bacteriology, virology, and immunology, and produced fundamental advances in several areas of clinical medicine. His experimental work on bacteriophages and animal viruses, especially influenza virus, resulted in major discoveries concerning their nature and replication, and he was a pioneer in the application of ecological principles to viral diseases. He proposed two concepts in immunology – acquired immunological tolerance and the clonal selection theory of antibody production – which proved to be of critical importance in stimulating research and led to a more complete understanding of immune processes.

Early in his career he recognised a rickettsia (later named *Rickettsia burnetii* but now known as *Coxiella burnetii*) to be the cause of Q Fever, a highly infectious disease that is carried by animals and passed to humans. Burnet's principal contribution lay in describing, for the first time, what is now the accepted view of the epidemiology of *Herpes Simplex*, a ubiquitous human disease. After confirming that aphthous stomatitis in infants was usually due to herpes simplex virus, he and his colleagues showed by serial antibody assays that these were primary infections. They suggested that non-specific resistance to primary infection developed in later childhood, except when there was intimate exposure. In adults, there was a sharp distinction between people with high titre antibody and those without any antibody – intermediate levels of antibody were not found. Further, the presence of antibody was correlated with socio-economic status, being lowest among university graduates and highest among public hospital patients. It was clear from the occurrence of recurrent herpes that the virus persisted somewhere in the body, but Burnet was unable to demonstrate this directly.[1]

In 1935, he isolated a strain of influenza-A virus in Australia, and subsequently did much work on serological variations of the influenza virus and on Australian strains of the swine influenza. He also published papers on variations in the virulence of influenza virus and on the mutation rates in it, which he calculated.

In 1947, he discovered, in collaboration with Joyce Stone, the receptor-destroying enzyme present in *Vibrio cholerae*, a discovery which led to the synthesis of neuraminic acid and to the demonstration, by Alfred Gottschalk and John Cornforth, that purified influenza virus will quantitatively split the acetylgalactosamine neuraminic acid compound. Later it was shown that this enzyme, derived from *Vibrio cholerae*, can prevent infection by influenza to a significant degree.[2]

From 1951 to 1956, Burnet himself concentrated on studies of the genetics of influenza virus. His demonstration of high frequency recombination was received with great scepticism by scientists overseas, since it did not accord with what was found with bacteriophages and therefore with conventional wisdom. The soundness of Burnet's experimental work in this field became apparent when it was demonstrated several years later that influenza virus had a segmented genome.

Burnet's first paper on animal virology was the demonstration that the causative agent of a disease of canaries was a poxvirus. It was in studies with ectromelia virus in the developing chick embryo that Burnet introduced into virology the concept that the temperature of incubation influenced viral multiplication, later to be extensively developed in poxvirus research under the designation of "ceiling temperature".

His major contributions to the study of influenza virus began in 1940, with the demonstration that amniotic inoculation of the developing chick embryo provided a method for isolating virus directly from human patients, a method which quickly supplanted intranasal inoculation of ferrets.

In parallel with his work on virology, Burnet had always been interested in the immune response, and in 1941 he had produced a monograph analysing the nature of antibody production. In 1948, he re-examined this topic and propounded a new hypothesis on antibody production based on analogies with adaptive enzymes. More important, however, was his enunciation in this book of the hypothesis of acquired immunological tolerance.

In 1958, Gustav Nossal and Joshua Lederberg showed that one B cell always produces only one antibody, which was the first evidence for clonal selection theory. Burnet wrote further about the theory in his 1959 book, *The Clonal Selection Theory of Acquired Immunity*. His theory predicted almost all of the key features of the immune system as we understand it today, including autoimmune disease, immune tolerance and somatic hypermutation as a mechanism in antibody production. The clonal selection theory became one of the central concepts of immunology and Burnet wrote that he and Niels Kaj Jerne should have received the Nobel for this work. Jerne was recognised for his contributions to the conceptualisation of the immune system when he was a co-recipient of the Nobel Prize in 1984.

In 1957, Burnet decided that henceforth he and all staff in the Institute would abandon virology and concentrate instead on immunology. A few years later, this decision was vindicated by the award of the Nobel Prize not for virology (for which the award would certainly have been merited), but for an immunological discovery – acquired immunological tolerance. By then, Burnet had gone beyond immunological tolerance to formulate what he himself regarded to be his major contribution to science, the clonal selection theory of antibody production.[3] Burnet was President of both the International Association of Microbiological Societies (1953-1957), and the Third International Congress of Immunology (1977).

Archibald Walter Forbes 1899-1996 led a team of specialists who pioneered in Bermuda for the Imperial Government and Cable & Wireless a superior system and station for Air to Ground radio-direction finding for ships. "When, on May 6, 1936 the German Zeppelin Transport Company began its *Hindenburg* air ship from Berlin, Bermuda's Cable and Wireless station, including Mr Forbes, had day and night activity. Via radio telephone, its 36 staff guided aircraft, dirigibles and ships across the Atlantic. This was done with bearings, messages, weather conditions and more."

In 1937, he led point-to point radio direction finding and telegraph services for aircraft, in particular Imperial Airways (now British Airways) and Pan American, which commenced services by flying boats at the same time. Forbes boarded the Royal Navy warship HMS *Dragon* at HM *Dockyard* in Bermuda on 5 January 1937 and, the next day sailed off to circumnavigate Bermuda completely, for a very special purpose. As a radio direction finding engineer, Forbes' task for the Imperial Government was to calculate and log radio direction finding calibrations by sea for ships and aircraft approaching Bermuda, having already done so by land radio direction finding. This very successful special project removed from Bermuda all remaining navigational obstacles for ships and flying boats at sea to find Bermuda and safely navigate its dangerous and extensive ring of outer coral reefs.

From 20 February 1937, Forbes and his team followed this up by beginning and finishing their design at Bermuda's highest point, The Peak in Smith's Parish, of what became the Eagle's Nest – the world's first Adcock shortwave radiodirection finding station, specifically for pilots and navigators of Imperial Airways and Pan American World Airways flying boats and other aircraft to home in to the signal. It was another "first" for Bermuda in aviation support technology. These initiatives established the navigational systems that were used in all weather conditions to safely guide ships and flying boats right into Bermuda. They made Bermuda attractive to Imperial Airways and Pan American. They put Bermuda firmly for the first time into mainstream winter and summer tourism for visitors by air from around the globe.[1]

Charles William Feilden Hamilton 1899-1978 successfully developed water-jet propulsion in the early 1950s that made his name world famous. Known as Bill, he had always dreamed of designing a boat that could go against the flow of rivers too shallow for conventional propeller-driven craft. Hamilton never claimed to have invented the jetboat; the water-jet principle was not new and had already been applied with some success to low-speed displacement craft overseas. His achievement was in designing a jet unit that would propel a planing hull efficiently at high speeds and with the advantages of a shallow draught.[1]

His first jetboat, eponymously known as a Hamilton Jetboat, was a 3.6 m plywood hull with a 100 E Ford engine, and the jet a centrifugal-type pump. This craft was tested on the Irishman Creek dam and water race before successfully, if somewhat slowly, travelling up the Waitaki River in early 1954. Continual improvements in the waterjet design, particularly the shift to a multi-stage axial flow pumping system, allowed boats to travel to places that had never been accessible before. In 1960, Bill's son Jon was a key member of the Colorado River expedition team – the first to travel up through the Grand Canyon. Over the next 20 years other ground-breaking trips were made up the Sun Kosi (Nepal), Sepik (Papua New Guinea), Zaire, Ganges and Amazon Rivers, and jetboats became widely used for flood relief, surveying and recreation.[2]

CHAPTER 7

1900-2015

In a world-wide context, the first half of the 20th century saw events on a level never hitherto seen. World War I was cataclysmic in its scale, with many millions dead, economies seriously distorted and many of the ancient ruling royal households of Europe disappearing, along with the creation of many new nations and re-assigned colonies from the dismemberment of the German, Austro-Hungarian and Ottoman empires. Such was the loss of men through death and injury that women filled positions hitherto excluded. In the 1920s, the major economies of the world went into deep depression which ended only with another World War. The development of aircraft, tanks, gas, radio and telephone communications, plastic surgery, mass vaccination (mainly for typhoid) were all greatly stimulated by the 1914-1918 war effort. Radio broadcasts for entertainment commenced, as did television. Radar was developed to detect aircraft early enough to intercept them and X-rays became commonplace in developed countries for medical treatment.

The first of the "magic bullet" treatments for disease appeared, including penicillin and the sulpha drugs. The universe became bigger with the discovery that the Milky Way is not the only galaxy but one of millions, and that the universe is expanding. The atom was "split", inaugurating the start of the nuclear era, which was also to influence the outcome of the end of World War II with atomic bombs being dropped on two Japanese cities. A stumbling block for the Theory of Evolution was overcome with the discovery of genes, providing a mechanism to pass on undiluted acquired traits. The discovery of genes also gave impetus to understanding how to better grow food crops and to research genetic illness. Insect vectors were found to be part of the chain involved in numerous diseases such as malaria, yellow fever and trypanosomiasis (sleeping sickness). The age of plastics was born with the advent of Bakelite, Nylon, Perspex, Sellotape, PET, and other forms of this ubiquitous material. World War II also stimulated research into aircraft design, with jets emerging as the future of air travel. Rockets were used by Hitler to assail Britain's south and would provide the basis for space exploration later in the century, and the electronic computer first appeared.

The period following World War II saw the start of the Cold War and the spread of communism to many parts of the world. There was massive growth in population due to a better ability to grow more food and to preserve it, as well as the use of mass immunisation programs and improved hygiene and greater access to clean drinking water. Organ transplants, microsurgery, realistic prosthetics, beta-blockers and other drugs, all combined to improve quality of life and extend life expectancy. Starvation, relative to total population, declined dramatically and humans faced a new epidemic – obesity, as well as the arrival of acronymistic ailments such as AIDS, HIV, SARS, ADHD, ARDS, BSE, DVT, HPV, PMS and STDs.

Computing played a major role in: the research of disease; predicting weather; sending satellites – and people – into space and onto the moon; and in replacing many labour-intensive business activities. The Internet and World Wide Web provided a means of making massive amounts of text and images available almost instantly. Digital cameras and smart phones became ubiquitous, as did photocopiers and fax machines. Refrigeration, air-conditioning, central heating, microwave ovens, washing machines, television, personal computers and scanners all became part of everyday life, and the remarkable 3-D scanner is fast becoming common.

Car ownership and better public transport enabled suburbs to sprawl for miles, often taking up productive land. The subatomic world of quarks, leptons, photons and bosons became better understood, while cosmologists were investigating dark matter, black holes, cosmic background radiation and string theory. Electricity was generated by nuclear reactors, solar panels, wind turbines and wave technology; video games saturated the home market; synthetic materials were used in much of our clothing and footwear; affordable international holidays became normal for many people, as did staying in hotels and motels, and eating out in restaurants. Fast food outlets appeared everywhere, even in communist countries, many of which had adopted capitalism while retaining the veneer of Marxism, while the Soviet bloc collapsed and abandoned its extreme brand of socialism altogether. The discovery of DNA led to the mapping of the human genome, animal cloning, and the identification of the cause of a number of genetic diseases, as well as providing the greatest advance in forensic science since the adoption of fingerprints for identifying criminals and victims. LED and plasma technology permitted far higher definition of electronic screens such as those used by computers, televisions and smartphones. Global Positioning System technology was developed with the use of computer and space technology. Plastic "money" became ubiquitous, gradually taking the place of notes and specie and even a virtual currency appeared, in the form of Bitcoin, described as a decentralised digital currency.

The number of burgeoning technologies would fill a book in itself, especially as government-funded research has become commonplace and university student numbers increased dramatically following the need for massive government projects during World War II, such as the Manhattan Project that produced the atom bomb. Although they are not household names like James Watt, Alexander Graham Bell, Lord Kelvin, John Logie Baird, Alexander Fleming or Robert Watson-Watt, there are still many Scots contributing to the technological advances that are continuing to improve the quality of life of many people around the world.

David Kay 1900-1971 and **John Grieve (dates unknown)**, both from Perthshire, Scotland, designed one of the world's early gyroplanes in 1934 – it was also built in Scotland, at Shields Garage in Perth. The Kay Type 33/1 was the first rotorcraft to successfully use variable incidence rotors, a feature that would become standard on all helicopters. The increased lift gained by fitting a four-bladed rotor was another significant feature.[1]

With the Kay Gyroplane, the incidence can be reduced at operational height so that the coning angle is reduced and therefore the drag, and the speed is increased. Thus it would seem that this machine embodies the same effects as a slotted, flapped, variable-area and variable-incidence fixed-wing aircraft. A further point of value in the variable incidence is the braking effect which can be secured at the moment of landing by an increase in incidence, so that extremely gentle landings can be made. Finally, setting the incidence at a negative value immediately on landing precludes any possibility of the machine blowing over in gusty winds.[2] The Kay Autogyro was the first rotorcraft to employ collective pitch control and usher in the development of a truly practical helicopter.[3]

Image 102 – Autogyro built in 1934 by David Kay and John Grieve

John Monteath Robertson 1900-1989 was a pioneer in the field of X-ray crystallography and the founder of organic crystallography. Among many other achievements, he is noted for the development of heavy-atom and isomorphous-replacement methods for solving the phase problem in chemical crystallography, thereby laying the foundations for subsequent determination of the structures of proteins and other biological macromolecules by X-ray diffraction. In 1939 (*Nature*, 143, 75), he predicted that the structure of insulin would be solved in this way – replacing zinc atoms in insulin with mercury atoms.[1] This was finally accomplished by Dorothy Hodgkin and her Oxford Group in 1969.

He established structures for a large number of molecules, including accurate measurements of bond length in naphthalene, anthracene, durene, resorcinol, and many natural products. He also established bond length variations in condensed ring hydrocarbons and was first to suggest a practical method to determine the structure of proteins.[2]

Robertson's analysis of phthalocyanine was much more direct and complete and represented the first direct determination of the structure of a sizeable molecule by X-ray methods. The use of X-rays to determine molecular structures had previously been limited to relatively simple structures due to the inability of scientists to measure the phases of X-ray waves. Robertson solved the "phase problem" by realising that if he could replace one (or more) of the atoms in a molecule with heavier alternatives, without changing the molecular shape (isomorphous replacement), then the enhanced X-ray scattering from the greater electron density in the heavy atoms would allow him to measure the phases directly. This breakthrough signalled the start of a revolution in chemical crystallography and structural biology, leading to the many thousands of structures of natural products, synthetic compounds, proteins and other biological macromolecules that we know today. The 1961 paper is also remarkable as an example of the early use of the newly-developing programmable electronic computers to perform some of the tedious mathematical manipulations required to calculate structures from X-ray diffraction data.[3] In a few years, starting from 1958, Robertson and his students revolutionised structural organic chemistry.

James Martin Stagg 1900-1975 persuaded General Dwight David Eisenhower to change the date of the Allied invasion of Europe in World War II, from 5 June to 6 June 1944. Stagg was the senior staff meteorologist working with input from three separate forecasting teams from the Royal Navy, Meteorological Office and USAAF. He led the British Polar Year Expedition to the Canadian Arctic in 1932–1933, and he served as superintendent of the Kew Gardens Observatory in 1939. In 1943, he was given the rank of group captain and appointed the chief meteorological adviser to Eisenhower, the supreme commander of the projected Allied invasion of northern France.

Stagg headed the committee of meteorologists who forecast weather conditions in the English Channel in the weeks leading up to the D-Day landings. These landings were projected for any day between June 5 and 7, but the first days of June saw low-lying rain clouds, high winds, and stormy seas that would disrupt an amphibious assault across the Channel and ground the Allies' air cover over the invasion beaches. With the invasion forces already having embarked from the Channel ports, the weather was still so poor on the morning of 4 June that Eisenhower postponed the landings from 5 June to the following day. At this point, the prospects for the invasion actually taking place looked as bleak as the weather. On the night of 4 June, however, Stagg informed Eisenhower that a temporary break in the weather might allow the invasion to go ahead on 6 June. The following morning, Eisenhower decided to proceed with the landings on 6 June. As it happened, weather did not seriously disrupt the D-Day landings, though the poor conditions had lulled the German defenders into thinking that an Allied landing was impossible that day.[1]

William Elgin Swinton 1900-1994 was a palaeontologist who popularised dinosaurs in Britain last century. Swinton produced many publications, mostly short, semi-popular or philosophical papers but a few rather more esoteric; one, for example, showed that remains from Nigeria, supposedly of dinosaurs that appeared to have survived the dinosaur extinction some 65 million years ago, were in fact those of gigantic crocodiles. His fame, however, stemmed originally from his popular book, *The Dinosaurs* (1934). It might be compared unfavourably with the plethora of beautifully illustrated dinosaur books now available, but it must be remembered that it was based on a much smaller store of information and lacked the benefits of modern book design and colour printing. At the time, it created a great deal of interest, being the first – for a long time the only – popular book on the subject. It led Swinton to branch out into popular lecturing and public relations, in both of which he excelled. He developed a great interest in the use of the museum in children's education, helping to improve and update the appropriate exhibitions.[1]

Francis Lions 1901-1972 was an organic chemist who is known for working with Francis Dwyer to devise organic compounds capable of bonding with a metal molecule at six separate sites. The research was groundbreaking because the molecules were highly stable.[1]

Lions, Dwyer, and their students synthesised the organic compounds and their metal chelate complexes, and established their properties. These molecules became justly famous because of their design elements and high stabilities. It is a tribute to Lions' knowledge and foresight that he recognised all the ingredients essential for success with such molecules, including the necessary types of binding atoms, the atoms needed to link them, and the spatial requirements of the metal and the binding atoms. It was grand design some 20 years ahead of its time, and a milestone in the chemical literature. Proud of his classical linguistic knowledge, Lions called the molecules "sexidentates" (six-toothed), and was offended when the editor of the *Journal of the American Chemical Society* changed this to "sexadentates" because he thought they would be confused with contraceptives. In the 1950s he toured the USA, informing many inorganic chemists about these important compounds and their variants.[2]

Robert Gregory Henderson 1902-1999 pioneered the introduction of the first ventilator, or "iron lung", in Britain. He bought materials from local firms, including portholes and other items obtained from ships' chandlers. The contraption, built in the evenings and at weekends with the help of Aberdeen City Hospital's engineer, was mounted in a cabinet on the base of a children's cot and became known as the Henderson Respirator. It was Britain's first iron lung. Four weeks after its construction it was used to save the life of a 10-year-old boy from New Deer, Aberdeenshire, who was suffering from infantile paralysis (poliomyelitis).[1]

Henderson's "Respirator" was built in 1933 being an air-tight cabinet, mounted on a child's cot, inside which the patient would lie. A vacuum pump enabled the doctor to expand and contract the patient's lungs, while portholes allowed him to monitor the patient's breathing. Note: the modern ventilator was invented by Philip Drinkwater and Louis Agassiz Shaw at Harvard University in 1927.

John Mackay Murray 1902-1966 was a naval architect who added to the understanding of the structural strength of ships. Starting with plan approval, he worked his way to experimental work on ship structures and was ultimately given the massive task of revising Lloyd's Rules and placing them on a scientific basis. During the Second World War, he acted as liaison officer between Lloyd's and the Admiralty. Throughout his career he presented no fewer than 22 papers on ship design, and of these nearly half dealt with hull longitudinal strength. This work won him considerable acclaim and several awards and was of fundamental importance to the shipping industry.[1]

Alan Rayson Raw 1902-1964 developed new cereal varieties for Australian conditions. He produced the *Insignia*, *Olympic*, *Sherpa*, *Beacon*, *Diadem*, *Stockade* and *Emblem* wheats, *Research*, *Resibee* and *Anabee* barleys, and *Algeribee* and *Orient* oats. All these varieties were extensively planted in Victoria. Raw became Australia's leading authority on barley. By 1964, his *Research* variety comprised 95% of the malting barley grown in southern Victoria, and it was also important in Tasmania, New Zealand and Kenya.

A geneticist as much as a breeder, Raw took a fundamental approach and frequently employed the genetic modification techniques of his day, which involved irradiation and the use of chemical mutagens such as colchicine. He also sought improvements through the introduction of new germ-plasm. Some of this work led to the production of fertile crosses between wheat and the grass *Agropyron*, and to the introduction of high-yielding wheats which produced flour with good baking qualities. While his major interest lay in cereal crops, staff working under his direction followed his methods in developing new varieties of flax, linseed, potatoes, tobacco, tomatoes and onions.[1]

William Black 1903-1975 was one of the world's leading potato breeders and specialised in breeding for resistance to late blight caused by *Phytopthora infestans*, the fungus directly responsible for famine in Ireland in 1845-1847. He had acquired wild potato material that had been collected in Central America, identified resistance genes, and had incorporated the first one (R1) into a new variety called *Craig's Snow-White*. It was never commercialised because the resistance rapidly broke down due to the emergence of a new race of blight, and the same thing happened to *Craig's Bounty*, which incorporated R2. Soon after, he released *Pentland Ace*, which had R3. Unfortunately, new types of blight appeared which affected each of these varieties.[1]

His work was mainly concerned with research in the genetics of the potato, and with the breeding of new varieties. The breeding work has resulted in seven selections being registered as new varieties by the Department of Agriculture for Scotland. They are the *Alness*, *Craig's Defiance*, *Craig's Royal*, *Craig's Snow-White*, *Craig's Alliance*, *Pentland Ace* and *Pentland Beauty*. In addition, *Craig's van Riebeeck* was named and approved in South Africa, while several unnamed blight resistant selections have been grown commercially in Tanganyika (now Tanzania) and Kenya.[2]

Alan Dower Blumlein 1903-1942 "was one of the most innovative of the first generation of electronics engineers."[1] He developed stereophonic sound and was the main driver of the "world's first electronic high definition TV system" in 1936. Blumlein immersed himself in every aspect of the project, from the *Emitron* electronic cameras, to the transmitters at Alexandra Palace. His colleagues argue that Blumlein, more than any other individual, should be considered the true inventor of television. Within six months of the launch of the BBC service, Blumlein had designed the video links which permitted outside broadcasts, and they were used to show the Coronation procession of King George VI, live from Hyde Park Corner in May 1937. Blumlein played a key role in getting the Air Interception (AI) radar, the world's first, to work. From the start of 1941, he helped the RAF to beat back the German night bomber offensive, although the public were told the success of the pilots was due to their diet of carrots which helped them see in the dark.

Blumlein and EMI were then elevated to working on the most important radar project of the war, H2S, a system which enabled the RAF to bomb through thick cloud. In June 1942, he was testing a prototype of H2S on board a Halifax bomber which crashed in the Wye Valley, killing all 11 on board, including Blumlein. News of the crash was suppressed to stop Hitler discovering about the setback to the project. However, using Blumlein's circuit designs, the Air Ministry managed to complete the development of H2S, which proved decisive in turning the war."[2]

"Blumlein made sterling contributions to the realisation of the world's first, public, all-electronic, high-definition television service. His patents on camera tubes, camera mosaics, wide-band amplifiers of all types, modulators, pulse circuits, power supplies, transmission lines, antennas, test equipment, and electronic circuits generally, constitute a set which illustrates the manifold ideas and the intellectual power of Blumlein's genius. With Edward Cecil Cork, he designed the wide-band cable which was utilised during the televising of the 1937 coronation. In 1938, he invented slot antennas, and, with Heinz Kallman and William Spencer Percival, the transversal filter. ... Blumlein's work on the navigation radar H2S and its adaptation, known as air surface vessel (ASV) radar, for locating enemy U-boats, was invaluable. These radars had a dramatic effect on the battle of the Atlantic and on the allies' long-range strategic bombing of Germany. His delay-line circuits, automatic strobe-following concepts, and diverse electronic circuits found application in other types of radar, including GL Mark III – a gun-laying radar which played a significant role in the anti-aircraft gunnery defence of the United Kingdom."[3]

He developed electrical recording techniques so the company wouldn't need to license the related Bell Labs patents. Blumlein approached the task systematically and designed highly linear components, including a microphone, a moving-coil cutter head and amplifiers. These components became EMI standards. And while stereophonic recording equipment was not commercialised until the late 1950s, he also invented a single-groove system for stereophonic recording independently of a similar system invented at about the same time by Arthur Keller at Bell Labs. "From 1934 to 1938, Blumlein worked on EMI's electronic television system. He was responsible for the overall system design (405 scan-lines interlaced two-to-one at 25 frames) as well as many component circuits. In November 1936, the British Broadcasting Company used the EMI system, when it inaugurated the world's first public all-electronic television service."[4] He contributed to airborne interception radar, microwave radar and ground-mapping radar, among other systems and had a total of 128 patents to his name.

James Robbie Farquharson 1903-2005 was pivotal to the growth of rail in Sudan, as well as much of East Africa. Over a period of 35 years, from 1925, he built more than 30,000 km of railway lines in Kenya, Tanganyika (Tanzania), Uganda and Sudan, with many more kilometres of line planned. He held many important posts including: Chief Engineer, Tanganyika Railways 1941-1945, then General Manager from 1945-1948; General Manager of Sudan Railways 1952-1957; and General Manager East African Railways and Harbours 1957-1961. Such was his influence in Sudan that he was among a handful of foreigners asked to remain after independence in 1955, at which time the country was linked by rail to its northern neighbour, Egypt, by a connecting rail link that was built for military reasons by the British.[1]

William Vallance Douglas Hodge 1903-1975 made the discovery of far-reaching topological relations between algebraic geometry and differential geometry – an area now called Hodge theory and pertaining more generally to Kähler manifolds – which has been a major influence on subsequent work in geometry.[1]

The Hodge index theorem was a result on the intersection number theory for curves on an algebraic surface; it determines the signature of the corresponding quadratic form. This result was sought by the Italian school of algebraic geometry, but was proved by the topological methods of Solomon Lefschetz. The *Theory and Applications of Harmonic Integrals* summed up Hodge's development during the 1930s of his general theory. Hodge decomposition has become a fundamental tool. In broad terms, Hodge theory contributes both to the discrete and the continuous classification of algebraic varieties. He published a polished account of his important theory in 1941, marking an important change in direction for the Cambridge school of geometry which, under Henry Frederick Baker's leadership, had become somewhat isolated from other areas of mathematics.[2]

He was also awarded the Copley Medal by The Royal Society in 1974 in recognition of his pioneering work in algebraic geometry, notably in his theory of harmonic integrals.[3]

Charles Francis Dalziel 1904-1986 was a pioneer in understanding electric shock in humans. He studied the effects of electricity on animals and humans. He wrote *The Effects of Electric Shock on Man*, a book in which he explains the effects of different amounts of electricity on human subjects. Dalziel (pronounced dee-ell), using unique methods of persuasion, extreme care and rigorous methods of testing, amassed a large amount of data from a wide range of tests on approximately 200 volunteers of both sexes and a range of ages. These data provided an excellent source of information on the physiological effects of electric shock, and Dalziel soon became a world authority on the subject.[1]

He came to realise that the commonest cause of deaths from electric shock came from ordinary household circuits under the malfunction known as "ground-fault." His research objective then became to create a device which would interrupt a ground-fault current before it became large enough to cause human physiological damage. The sensitivity, speed of action, reliability, small size, and small cost required made the device almost impossible to design. However, in 1965, Dalziel received a patent for a "ground-fault current interrupter" that would interrupt current before it grew to 5 milliamps and that was small, reliable, and inexpensive. The device was based on a magnetic circuit plus a newly developed semiconductor device. Subsequently, the National Electric Code was modified to require that this device be installed in electric circuits in all bathrooms, kitchens, swimming pools, and outdoor electric circuits in all new construction and extensive modifications of older constructions. Dalziel's ground-fault interrupters are now installed in electrical systems all over the world.

Robert Ferguson Legget 1904-1994 was Resident Engineer on the construction of the Upper Notch Hydro Plant, the largest automatic plant in Canada. In 1932, he joined the Canadian Sheet Piling Company Ltd, and as their Engineer was responsible for the design and construction of sheet piling. He worked on many major construction projects across Canada and advised on the design and planning of the Toronto Subway System, construction of which commenced after the Second World War. Legget's contributions to professional societies were many and varied. He was Vice President (North America) of the International Society of Soil Mechanics and Foundation Engineering from 1961 to 1965; President of the American Society for Testing Materials (1965 to 1966); President of the Geological Society of America (1966); President le Counseil International du Batiment (Netherlands) from 1966 to 1969, and the Founding President of the Canadian Academy of Engineering (1987-1989).[1]

Daniel Stewart MacLagan 1904-1991 performed work on theoretical models of insect population densities that led to the development of prediction models on insect infestations and of control techniques for a range of pests, including leather jackets, carrot root fly and cabbage root fly. This work was novel and exceptional in its field and merited his election as a Fellow of The Royal Society of Edinburgh in 1946. He had a unique ability to combine excellent basic research with applied work, which had a significant influence in agricultural practice. A series of studies on ticks (*Ixodes ricinus*) led to methods of control involving the use of insecticidal creams for the protection of young lambs, a technique still in use in a modified form. He also made a major contribution to the development of insecticides and techniques for the control of warble fly in cattle. He showed great vision and perspicacity as he was one of the first, in a series of articles and papers in *Nature*, to draw attention to the problems associated with the use of pesticides in agriculture, notably the organochlorines.

"Despite the remarkable insecticidal and acaricidal [pesticides that kill arachnids such as ticks and mites] properties of those new substances they are not the universal panaceas which was portended in the first flush of enthusiasm. They have their limitations and dangers, and ignorance of their ultimate effects has led to their abuse. ... Some of the original claims made for DDT were exaggerated; but used with discretion, it is possibly the most generally useful insecticide available, being toxic to most insects. A unique feature – not without danger – is its extraordinary persistency ..."[1] This was published in 1951 (*Nature* 168, 360-362, 1 September 1951), eleven years before *Silent Spring*, the seminal work of Rachel Carson, which is seen as the starting point for the American environmental movement.

At the same time (1951), he was also writing popular articles dealing with the residual effects of pesticides and about care in the choice and use of them by farmers and others. In this respect, he was unquestionably a visionary whose concern for the environment was ahead of its time and which created a new approach to pest control that is now widely accepted.[2]

Colin Campbell Mitchell 1904-1969 designed the steam catapult for launching airplanes from aircraft carriers. The aircraft was hooked to a piston in a concealed cylinder below the flight deck and accelerated by releasing high pressure steam from the ships boilers into the cylinder. "The hydraulic catapult had reached its limit, but the demand for power had not. The Grumman F9F Cougar, the standard [US] Navy fighter at the time ... weighed 21,000 pounds [9,526 kg] fully loaded. The Douglas A-3 Skywarrior, which had first flown the year before, would reach a gross weight of 82,000 pounds [37,195 kg], well beyond the capacity of any conceivable hydraulic catapult. Fortunately, the Royal Navy had long recognised the limitations of hydraulic catapults, and by 1950 Commander Colin C. Mitchell had designed and built an entirely new type of launcher, based on one of the Industrial Revolution's oldest motive fluids. Mitchell's steam catapult, as refined over the next five decades, can still be seen aboard today's Navy carriers. Only now, after over half a century is it being superseded by electro-magnetic systems."[1]

The citation when Mitchell was presented with an OBE for this work read: "For exceptionally meritorious conduct in the performance of outstanding services in the invention and development of the catapult for launching aircraft from carrier vessels. With the weight and complexity of the steam catapult only a fraction of that for an equivalent hydraulic device, this invention represents a practical system and a substantial advancement in the art of catapulting aircraft from carriers. Adopted by the United States Navy in 1952 the steam catapult system has become standard equipment on all first-line aircraft carriers. By accepting this system, instead of continuing the development of the hydraulic catapult, the Navy has saved an estimated three years of time and made a comparable savings in cost. In addition, the steam catapult makes possible the operation of high take-off speed and heavy aircraft from practicable sized carriers. Through his outstanding resourcefulness and ingenuity, Mr Mitchell has been directly instrumental in effecting considerable savings and improved carrier operations."

Colin Simson Cadell 1905-1996 was involved in the development of radar, signal interception and intelligence, including involvement with Enigma decoding at Bletchley Park. He rose to become Director of Telecommunications and of Signals in the Air Ministry (1944) and was awarded a CBE in the same year. It is now taken for granted that aircraft should have radio controls throughout flight and an approach under radio control to any airport in the world, but in the late 1940s and early 1950s when Air Commodore Colin Cadell was managing director of International Aeradio, this was far from the situation. Cadell went round the world, supervising the installation of novel systems then at the frontiers of technology. For this internationally important task, he was technically and managerially superbly well qualified. Cadell installed radio signalling and take-off and landing facilities in 30 countries.[1]

William Malcolm Chalmers 1905-1995 was one of a number of people involved in the invention of acrylic glass, known as *Plexiglas* in America and *Perspex* in Britain. Chalmers was born in Edinburgh in 1905 and his family migrated to Vancouver in 1911. He obtained US Patent 2,087,468 on 20 July 1937 for "Polymerisation Products and Process of Making Same", which was a continuation of his first application lodged on 27 February 1930 (serial number 431,982).

Chalmers had discovered that the polymers of methacrylic ethylester and methacrylic nitrile could make a hard, clear material. In 1877, the German chemist Wilhelm Rudolph Fittig co-discovered the polymerisation process that turns methyl methacrylate into polymethyl methacrylates, but took their discovery no further. It was studied by Otto Rohm for his doctorate dissertation in 1901. Joseph A. Schwarcz, professor of chemistry at McGill University (as at 2015), followed the story from there – "in the 1920s, Rohm ... discovered a way to join molecules of methyl methacrylates to make polymethyl methacrylates. The clear sheets of *Plexiglas*, as they named the novel substance, had obvious commercial appeal. They were transparent and strong, and they could be heat-moulded into whatever shape one desired. Dr Rohm was soon sporting the world's first pair of glasses that had acrylic lenses instead of plastic ones. This gave the Luftwaffe an idea. Why not replace glass windows in aircraft with shatter-resistant *Plexiglas*? An excellent proposition – but there was a hitch. It was impossible to produce methyl methacrylates, the required starting material, on an economically viable scale. The answer to this dilemma would come from across the Atlantic, from the chemistry labs at McGill University.

At McGill, William Chalmers had found a way to make methyl methacrylates from acetone and hydrogen cyanide, both of which were readily available. Chalmers knew that **John William Croom Crawford 1901-1989**, a chemist at the laboratories of Explosives Group of ICI at Stevenston in Scotland, was working with acrylic polymers, and he suggested to Crawford that he try the new method for making methyl methacrylates. Crawford successfully scaled up the process, making the mass production of methyl methacrylates possible. ICI called it *Perspex*."[1] "In 1932 J.W.C. Crawford discovered a new route to the monomer using cheap and readily available chemicals – acetone, hydrocyanic acid, methanol and sulphuric acid – and it is his process which has been used, with minor modifications, throughout the world."[2] Crawford had over a dozen patents relating to acrylics, and to improved methods for the production of uranium.

Chalmers sold his patent for it to ICI for $5,000, and then in 1933, ICI licensed DuPont and the Rohm and Haas Company to produce it commercially. The web page for the Rohm and Haas

Company has a timeline of their discoveries and activities. For 1933, it states, "In Germany, Otto Rohm returns to his first love, acrylic chemistry, and discovers *Plexiglas*."[3]

Perspex is tougher than glass although it scratches more easily. It doesn't splinter or smash readily so it became known as shatterproof glass (it is neither shatterproof nor glass). Acrylic glass has since found many applications in products such as: cement to aid prosthetic implants; rebuilding worn areas of lost bone; contact lens; various parts of cars, including external light covers and windows; dentures; acrylic paint; laserdiscs and some DVDs; artificial fingernails; sheets of plastic used in building, such as roofing over patios; furniture; cosmetic surgery; nanotechnology; large commercial aquariums; aircraft cockpits; submarine "bubbles"; motorbike helmet visors; and bullet-proof uses in police vehicles and bank shutters.

This invention is also credited to two chemists, Barker and Skinner, in 1924, and other sources state that *Perspex* was invented in 1933 when it was first polymerised at the Rohm & Haas Laboratories in Darmstadt in Germany. The Boston Museum of Fine Arts unequivocally states, "*Plexiglas* is composed of polymethyl methacrylate. It was invented by William Chalmers in 1930 and called *Plexiglas* because it looked like glass but could be heated and formed into many shapes. It was marketed in Britain as *Perspex* and in the US as *Plexiglas*. It is used for signs, lens, windows, and furniture."[4] The first mention of the term *Plexiglas* in a US patent is for a *Plexiglas* Shaping Machine on 5 April 1949 (filed 20 November 1946) for patent number 2,466,045 and, like many other plastics, it is now omnipresent.

Thomas Angus Lyall Paton 1905-1999 was regarded as a world authority in the field of hydroelectric schemes.[1] He was the civil engineer responsible for the design and construction of the Zambezi River hydro-electric scheme's Kariba Dam, one of the largest dams in the world, being 128 m tall and 579 m long. It included a 128 m high double curvature arch dam – the biggest ever constructed – and a 600 megawatt underground power station in a remote location more than 280 km downstream from the Victoria Falls.

After WWII, Paton undertook an economic survey of Syria and Lebanon, and his report made recommendations for port, water infrastructure, irrigation and hydroelectric improvements, including Latakia Harbour which, although built by another company that managed to put in a bid two weeks after tenders had closed, was still built to Paton's design. He also was responsible for a large irrigation works in Syria to take water from a reservoir to the Euphrates Dam, which had been built earlier by the Russians.

Paton continued with dam building for producing hydro-electricity including the Owen Falls Hydroelectric Scheme in Uganda, the Indus Basin Project, the Aswan High Dam (consulting engineer), the Hendrik Verwoerd Dam, the P.K. Le Roux Dam, and the Spioenkop Dam – all in South Africa – and the Tarbela Dam on the Indus River in Pakistan. This dam is the second largest dam in the world by structural volume being 148 m high and has a water storage area of 14.3 km^2 (as at 2014). The Owen Falls Hydroelectric Scheme comprised a concrete gravity dam 30 m high and a power station of 10 turbines, with total capacity of 150 megawatts, providing power for Uganda and Kenya. When it was opened on 29 April 1954 by Queen Elizabeth, the six control gates were closed for a few hours before she pressed a button and opened them again. This was the first time in history that the White Nile had been stopped. Winston Churchill, who was Prime Minister at the time, observed, "It is possible that nowhere else in the world could so enormous a mass of water be held up by so little masonry".[3]

In Canada, Paton was Senior Consultant on the James Bay Project in Quebec, one of the largest hydroelectric schemes in the world, with an installed capacity of 10.5×106 kilowatts in four main stages. The work included five aerodromes, 1,287 km of access roads and construction camps for 11,000 workers, and comprised 207 dams and dikes of a total length of 122 km to contain the reservoirs. Four powerhouses were constructed, the largest being a kilometre long underground with 16 turbo-alternators, each of 333,000 kilowatts capacity. The work was substantially complete in 1984, including the 1,126 km long transmission lines to Montreal. Paton's role was advisory, but the design and construction closely followed his practice and experience. Paton also managed the team that designed the structural work for the new Royal Mint at Llantrisant in Wales.

Grace Murray Hopper 1906-1992 served on the Mark I computer programming staff headed by Howard Hathaway Aiken, becoming the third person to program the Mark I computer. She received the Naval Ordnance Development Award for her pioneering applications programming success on the Mark I, Mark II, and Mark III computers. Hopper and Aiken co-authored three papers on the Mark I, also known as the Automatic Sequence Controlled Calculator.

A true visionary, Admiral Hopper conceptualised how a much wider audience could use the computer if there were tools that were both programmer-friendly and application-friendly. In pursuit of her vision, she risked her career in 1949 to join the Eckert-Mauchly Computer Corporation and provide businesses with computers. There she began yet another pioneering effort working on UNIVAC I, the first large-scale electronic digital computer. To ease their task, Admiral Hopper encouraged programmers to collect and share common portions of programs. Even though these early shared libraries of code had to be copied by hand, they reduced errors, tedium, and duplication of effort.

By 1949, programs contained mnemonics that were transformed into binary code instructions executable by the computer. Admiral Hopper and her team extended this improvement on binary code with the development of her first compiler, the A-O. The A-O series of compilers translated symbolic mathematical code into machine code, and allowed the specification of call numbers assigned to the collected programming routines stored on magnetic tape. One could then simply specify the call numbers of the desired routines and the computer would "find them on the tape, bring them over and do the additions. This was the first compiler," she declared.

Admiral Hopper believed that the major obstacle to computers in non-scientific and business applications was the dearth of programmers for these far from user-friendly new machines. The key to opening up new worlds to computing, she knew, was the development and refinement of programming languages – languages that could be understood and used by people who were neither mathematicians nor computer experts. It took several years for her to demonstrate that this idea was feasible.

Pursuing her belief that computer programs could be written in English, Admiral Hopper moved forward with the development for UNIVAC of the B-O compiler, later known as FLOW-MATIC. It was designed to translate a language that could be used for typical business tasks like automatic billing and payroll calculation. Using FLOW-MATIC, Admiral Hopper and her staff were able to make the UNIVAC I and II "understand" twenty statements in English. When she recommended that an entire programming language be developed using English words, however, she "was told very quickly that [she] couldn't do this because computers didn't understand English". It was three years before her idea was finally accepted; she published her first compiler paper in 1952.

Hopper devoted much time to convincing business managers that English language compilers such as FLOW-MATIC and COBOL were feasible. She participated in a public demonstration by Sperry Corporation and RCA of COBOL compilers and the machine independence they provided. After her brief retirement from the Navy, Admiral Hopper led an effort to standardise COBOL and to persuade the entire Navy to use this high-level computer language. With her technical skills, she led her team to develop useful COBOL manuals and tools. With her speaking skills, she convinced managers that they should learn to use them.

Another major effort in Admiral Hopper's life was the standardisation of compilers. Under her direction, the Navy developed a set of programs and procedures for validating COBOL compilers. This concept of validation has had widespread impact on other programming languages and organisations; it eventually led to national and international standards and validation facilities for most programming languages.[1]

Owen Finlay Maclaren 1906-1978 invented the lightweight baby buggy with a collapsible support assembly in 1965. "There had been no major innovations in baby transport since the pram was invented in 1733 by English architect William Kent for the family of the 3rd Duke of Devonshire."[1]

Maclaren was a test pilot and aeronautical engineer who had earlier invented the Supermarine Spitfire undercarriage, allowing the aircraft to be steered or swivelled whilst on the ground.[2] During World War II, Maclaren designed what was an entirely new undercarriage for Britain's Spitfire fighter aircraft. The main legs were not only strengthened, but also raked forward at a steeper angle to counter the increased nose weight. The new four-spoked wheel featured a larger tyre. Later, production shifted to a three-spoke wheel which can be seen on many later marks (versions) of the Spitfire. Another new detail of the updated undercarriage leg was a forward-facing scissor link over its oleo part, and the covers differed from the earlier marks, having a distinctly bulged appearance, to accommodate the thicker tyre which could no longer fit into the thin wing when retracted.[3] These modifications enabled aircraft to take off and land in a crosswind.

"In 1943, he saved lives with the invention of the 'Maclaren Radiator,' an innovation which doubled the chances of a Spitfire pilot making a safe return back to base when the plane's radiator had been hit by a bullet."[4] Using two radiators, there were front and side grids made of bakelised linen with electro-deposited copper moulded between the sheets. The grids were connected to the gunsight switch so that when a pilot was about to go into action, and there was the possibility of a radiator suffering damage, the protection scheme would operate. If the radiators were damaged, a red light showed in the cockpit, indicating the grid had been pierced, solenoid relay switches then operated valves which cut off coolant flow through the damaged radiator and switched it to the undamaged unit.[5]

Prior to his innovative buggy design, babies travelled in unwieldy carriages of unattractive proportions with huge hoods that hid the child from the outside world. The Maclaren Baby Buggy was far more practical for both transporting the infant and for storage. Employing lightweight materials such as tubular aluminium, Maclaren's structure could carry a sizable toddler and still fold away into a space not much bigger than that of a rolled umbrella. Its three-dimensional folding mechanism was umbrella-like too. In fact, it is sometimes referred to as the "umbrella stroller". Maclaren also invented the world's first folding aluminium chair – the Gadabout Chair for picnics.[6]

Colin Douglas Buchanan 1907-2001 was consulted by the British government in 1961 on the future of automobile transport in cities, particularly privately-owned vehicles. "The resulting report, *Traffic in Towns*, published in November 1963, presented a new and comprehensive view. Its central premise was that certain environmental standards – maximum allowable levels of noise, pollution, etc. – must be imposed as fixed norms. Beyond that, economic trade-offs were possible and desirable. Thus, if a city was both financially able and willing, it could rebuild to admit more traffic. But if it was either unable or unwilling or both, it would have to restrain traffic, perhaps severely. This was revolutionary; it brought a clash with transport economists, who assumed that everything had its price and that environmental standards could be traded off against other considerations. The report was a bestselling sensation; Buchanan became Britain's most famous planner, the first to receive intensive media attention. But his central message was distorted and even inverted: the media seized upon the images of radical urban surgery, which was almost the reverse of what he was arguing."[1]

Bruce Chalmers 1907-1990 was a world-renowned metallurgist, whose principal contributions were in understanding how to solidify alloys to achieve a smooth, unbranched interface between the solid and the liquid that yields a nearly defect-free structure, providing superior properties in semiconducting and magnetic materials.[1]

Chalmers and his students performed the experiments and analyses that laid the foundations of our present understanding of the origin and nature of the grain and subgrain morphology formed in the crystallisation of liquids. Their analyses took due account of the heat and material transport and interface movement and morphology attending crystallisation. Especially important was their concept of "constitutional undercooling", which accounted for the role of impurities in the development of cellular and dendritic structures.[2]

Alexander Haddow 1907-1976 discovered the first chemical therapy to treat cancer. His work in Edinburgh and London showed that polycyclic hydrocarbons and other compounds that cause cancer also inhibit the growth of tumours. These discoveries led to the development of chemotherapeutic agents that were effective in the clinical treatment of cancer.[1] Based on Paul Ehrlich's pioneering work that resulted in chemical therapy (i.e. chemotherapy) to treat bacterial infections, Haddow investigated the therapeutic potential of numerous polycyclic hydrocarbons to cause tumour regression in experimental animals. Some compounds were effective, but the fact that they were known carcinogens prohibited further exploration in humans. Nevertheless, the triphenylethylene-based oestrogens have a structural similarity to polycyclic hydrocarbons and they were also observed to cause tumour regression in animals. This was the translational basis of Haddow's landmark clinical experiments to evaluate the efficacy of high-dose oestrogen on the growth of breast and prostate cancer.[2]

Haddow reasoned that if these carcinogens were compared to other closely related but non-carcinogenic chemicals, the differences between them would prove significant in explaining the genesis of cancer. He also discovered what is known as the Haddow Effect, in which a carcinogenic chemical can be used to arrest a cancer caused by some other carcinogenic chemical (provided that the two chemicals are not closely related). Clinical trials at the Royal Cancer Hospital led to the adoption of the platinum compound cisplatin as a treatment for cancer of the ovary, and other compounds such as chlorambucil, melphalan and busulphan being used for treatment of breast and ovarian cancer, and malignant blood diseases.[3]

Haddow's 1940s cancer research showed that synthetic estrogens could shrink tumours in animals. He eventually found that one-third of postmenopausal women with metastatic breast cancer responded well to high doses of estrogen and that some patients had an extraordinary regression of their cancers. Under his leadership, the Chester Beatty Research Institute became even more important as a world centre for research into the causes, nature, and treatment of cancer. Many of the therapeutic agents widely used in the treatment of cancer and leukemia were developed at the Institute during Haddow's directorship.[4]

Norman Wingate Pirie 1907-1997 discovered, with Frederick Bawden, that the genetic material found in all viruses is ribonucleic acid (RNA) and thus contradicted the view of Wendell Stanley, who had thought the viruses consisted entirely of protein. Pirie and Bawden accomplished the separation in semi-crystalline or crystalline form of 12 or more viruses, or strains of viruses, including tobacco mosaic virus (TMV), and showed that they all contain nucleic acid of the type now called RNA, the genetic material of viruses.

Bawden and Pirie realised that RNA might be the infective component of viruses, but they were unable to confirm this experimentally, and it was not until 1956 that this was established by others.[1]

Pirie discovered the advantages of freeze-drying non-crystalline substances while working late one Christmas in the poorly heated laboratories. A solution of glutathione that he was drying in a desiccator froze; when it was dried without thawing, it yielded a product of unexpectedly fine, feathery texture. This impressed many colleagues, including David Keilin, and helped to introduce freeze-drying into biochemistry.[2]

Alexander Robertus Todd 1907-1997 received the 1957 Nobel Prize for Chemistry relating to the structure and synthesis of nucleotides, nucleosides, and nucleotide coenzymes. He also synthesised vitamin B_1 and vitamin E, and elucidated the structure of vitamin B_{12}. In 1949, he synthesised adenosine triphosphate (ATP) – the universal energy carrier in the living cell – and flavin adenine dinucleotide (FAD). In 1955, he clarified the structure of vitamin B_{12}, subsequently working on the structure and synthesis of vitamin B_1 and vitamin E, the anthocyanins (the pigments of flowers and fruits) from insects (aphids, beetles) and studied alkaloids found in cannabis.[1]

In 1935 Todd, as well as Adolf Otto Reinhold Windaus in Germany, showed that thiamine was composed of a thiazole (a five-atom ring containing sulphur and nitrogen) linked to a pyrimidine. Although the first complete synthesis of vitamin B_1 was made by the American biochemist Robert Runnels Williams in 1935, Todd (with the help of Franz Bergel) independently developed an industrial synthetic route in 1937 that enabled Hoffmann-La Roche to become a major player in the vitamin manufacturing market.[2]

Todd worked mainly on nucleosides, the compounds that form the structural units of nucleic acids (DNA and RNA). In 1949, he was able to synthesise adenosine triphosphate, a related substance that is vital to the utilisation of energy in living organisms. During that same year, he also synthesised the compounds, flavin adenine dinucleotide (FAD) and, later, uridine triphosphate in 1954. His work greatly contributed to our understanding of the workings of genes. A year later, Todd elucidated the structure of vitamin B_{12}.[3]

Todd began preliminary studies of the structure of vitamin B_{12}, completed at Cambridge with A.W. Johnson and Dorothy Hodgkin in 1955, as well as vitamin E (from which he isolated the active principle, α-tocopherol). He also began the investigation of cannabinol, an inactive constituent of cannabis, showing it to be derived from dibenzopyran. The latter research brought him into brief conflict with the Home Office, which accused him of illegal possession of the drug. Todd came to the realisation that it, as well as other vitamins, acted as co-enzymes (in this case co-carboxylase, or diphosphothiamine) in metabolic processes. By the mid-1930s, work by the Russian-born American biochemist Phoebus Aaron Theodore Levene on the degradation of the nucleic acids by hydrolysis, had revealed them to be composed of a small number of nucleotides that contained sugars and organic bases that were related to well-known purines and pyridines, such as adenine, guanine, uracil (or thymine), and cytosine. Nucleotides themselves could be hydrolysed into nucleosides and phosphoric acid.

Given this existing chemical knowledge, it was Todd's key insight that many of these fragments were related to the B-group vitamins and other intermediate molecules such as adenosine diphosphate and triphosphate (ADP and ATP) that played fundamental roles in metabolism and energy exchanges, and which were themselves clearly products of nucleic acid degradation. To this end, and over a twenty-year period, he and his co-workers developed new methods of synthesising purines and pyrimidines, as well as their sugar derivatives, the glycosides (nucleosides). This enabled deductions to be drawn concerning the structure of nucleosides, and the processes of phosphorylation whereby nucleosides could be built into nucleotides. Such studies demanded deeper understanding of organic phosphate chemistry and of phosphorylation using dibenzyl phosphorochloridate or diesters of phosphorous acid.

Todd's ambitious research program at Cambridge embraced, among many other successes, the synthesis of the energy-providing coenzyme ATP (adenosine triphosphate, 1948), and FAD (flavin–adenine dinucleotide, 1954). The development of pathways for polynucleotide synthesis also had a great bearing on the elucidation of the structures of ribonucleic and deoxyribonucleic acids (RNA and DNA). Todd's synthesis of nucleotides with Don Brown in 1952 established unequivocally that the sugars in both RNA and DNA were linked to specific nitrogen atoms of a purine or pyrimidine ring by a β-glycosidic bond. Further syntheses of nucleotides by phosphorylation of nucleosides confirmed such linkages, as did enzymatic degradation of the nucleic acids, which gave identical nucleotides. Todd's work, using chromatography and ion-exchange methods, therefore confirmed that both RNA and DNA contained 3', 5' linked polynucleotides, the links being made by phosphoric acid residues.[4] Todd was President of The Royal Society from 1975 to 1980.

George Harold Brown 1908-1987 held more than 80 patents and, in 1933, he conducted research into AM broadcasting antennas that became standard throughout the world. In 1935, he followed this with development of the "turnstile" antenna. The turnstile concept offered for the first time an effective combination of high gain and broad bandwidth with a wave propagation pattern which made it possible to broadcast FM radio and television signals over long distances. Brown added an absorbing resistor to the design which resulted in increased bandwidth and permitted the simultaneous radiation of television pictures and sound from the same antenna.[1]

Image 103 – Turnstile antenna 1936

In 1939, he produced a device for enabling high resolution of broadcast television. He named it the "vestigial side-band filter". It was accepted in January 1939 by the Federal Communications Commission for broadcasting throughout the USA, and it is used throughout the world today.

He and his colleagues developed a method for speeding the production of penicillin by means of radio-frequency heating techniques. Using inexpensive vacuum pumps and simple condensers, it was estimated to be about one-tenth of the cost of freeze drying. Radio-frequency heating also became used in the manufacture of plastic raincoats, bags and other products.

He was a participant in the team at RCA Laboratories that developed the dot-sequential colour television system and as the team leader who relentlessly pursued its adoption as the US standard for broadcasting. The principles in that system are incorporated in all present-day systems of colour television, including NTSC (National Television Systems Committee), PAL (Phase-Alternating Line), and SECAM (Sequentiel Couleur avec Memoire).[2]

Kenneth Mellanby 1908-1993 helped create the first university in Nigeria, at Ibadan, becoming its first Principal (1947-1953). When he arrived to take up the position, he found there were no buildings, no staff and no students. His organisational and human qualities were demonstrated in that, by the time he left, in 1953, the college was a going and growing concern with an excellent and carefully chosen staff and several hundred students.[1]

He was appointed Head of the Entomology Department at Rothamsted Experimental Station in 1955. Mellanby founded the Monks Wood Research Station in Huntingdon, Cambridgeshire, in 1961, becoming its Director. Here he led research into the effects of pesticides on the environment, advocating biological control, using predators to eat the pests, as a safer alternative. He wrote the pioneering book *Pesticides and Pollution* (1967) and founded the journal *Environmental Pollution* in 1970.[2]

Mellanby conducted research on head lice. He found that possibly 50% of girls aged up to fourteen were infested with head lice. He correlated the incidence of head lice with poverty and with family size. At the prompting of medical officers, in December 1940, he set up a research unit to study the effects of scabies infestations. He used pacifist volunteers to carry out experiments which showed that all stages of the disease-carrying mite *Sarcoptes scabiei* died quickly at room temperature, so that stored bedding was not the cause of infection as had been falsely assumed. He and the volunteers proved that infection only came from intimate contact and that it could be cured in an hour by a single whole-body treatment with benzyl benzoate. He calculated that this discovery alone freed the equivalent of two divisions of soldiers from hospital.[3]

Robert Louis Waland 1908-1999 was an optical engineer whose work on telescopes at the University of Arizona enabled astronomers to compile an atlas of the moon surface that was used by the first astronauts to land on the moon in 1969.[1]

He developed new techniques for making the optics of Schmidt telescopes. In the 1960s, when he was at the University of Arizona's Lunar and Planetary Laboratory, he made the superb mirrors for the 1.54 m reflector at the Catalina Station.[2]

His breakthrough came in 1945 when his "Dumfries Telescope" was brought to the attention of Professor Erwin Finlay-Freundlich, who had worked with Albert Einstein. The refracting telescope with two attached astro cameras was built in a garage and so impressed the professor that he gave Robbie the job of head technician to the Department of Astronomy at St Andrews University. He went on to construct the revolutionary and world-famous Schmidt-Cassegrain telescope in the university observatory which, for the first time, accurately photographed and recorded stars millions of light years away. In 1962, he moved to Tucson in the United States to become a research associate at the Lunar and Planetary Laboratory in the University of Arizona, and his work was closely linked to the American space program. He designed and constructed the optics for a 61 inch (155 cm) reflecting telescope for planetary research, and this was used to compile an atlas of the moon for the Apollo program, helping the astronauts find their way around the lunar surface after their moon landings. He wrote a book about his research and worked on an electronic telescope scheduled to be used on satellites launched by the Space Shuttle. In 1992, he had an asteroid named after him.[3]

John Tuzo Wilson 1908-1993 achieved worldwide acclaim for his theory of plate tectonics, the assumption that the Earth's crust is comprised of plates floating on magma. In 1963, Wilson developed a concept crucial to the plate-tectonics theory. He suggested that the Hawaiian and other volcanic island chains may have formed due to the movement of a plate over a stationary "hotspot" in the mantle. This theory eliminated an apparent contradiction to the plate-tectonics theory – the occurrence of active volcanoes located many thousands of kilometres from the nearest plate boundary. Hundreds of following studies have proven Wilson right. However, in the early 1960s, his idea was considered so radical that his "hotspot" manuscript was rejected by all the major international scientific journals. This manuscript finally was published in 1963 in a publication called the *Canadian Journal of Physics*, and became a milestone in plate tectonics. Everyone else believed that the continents were not movable and stayed in one place.[1]

Wilson pioneered the use of air photos in geological mapping and was responsible for the first glacial map of Canada. While searching for unknown Arctic islands in 1946, he became the second Canadian to fly over the North Pole. He was internationally respected for his work on glaciers, mountain building, geology of ocean basins and structure of continents, but his greatest contribution lies in his explanation of plate tectonics – the notion that the Earth's crust is made up of a series of floating plates. His 1965 paper, *A New Class of Faults and their Bearing on Continental Drift*, is a classic in geology.[2]

Another of Wilson's important contributions to the development of the plate-tectonics theory was published two years later. He proposed that there must be a third type of plate boundary to connect the oceanic ridges and trenches, which he noted can end abruptly and "transform" into major faults that slip horizontally. A well-known example of such a transform-fault boundary is the San Andreas Fault zone. Unlike ridges and trenches, transform faults offset the crust horizontally, without creating or destroying the crust.[3] Note: Alexander McKay 1841-1917 was the first to discover transverse slip faults in 1888 in New Zealand.

Wilson was first non-American president of the American Geophysical Union, which altered its rules to allow his election.[4]

Alexander King 1909-2007 was responsible for the use of dichlorodiphenyltrichloroethane (DDT) as an effective insecticide. During World War II, King was working for Britain's Ministry of Supply, involved in intercepting communications involving scientific information. An employee of Geigy in Switzerland, Paul Müller, had identified DDT (which was given that name by King) as being useful as a moth-balling agent with no toxicity to humans, but King recognised it had potential as an insecticide, particularly against lice and mosquitoes, which had caused high mortality in the First World War and would again be a menace in the following war. In 1942, he was transferred to the Ministry of Production on its formation, as deputy scientific adviser, and then in 1943 was sent to Washington to share knowledge of DDT's properties with the Americans, who started to mass produce it. In Washington, he was made head of the British scientific mission, and scientific attaché at the British embassy; he was awarded the American Medal of Freedom in 1946.[1]

King was a pioneer of the sustainable development movement and was one of the 17 researchers under Dennis Meadows who commissioned the 1972 *Limits to Growth* report, which triggered the first wave of international concern about the environment. King and Italian industrialist, Aurelio Peccei, were not confident that either the market or technology could function as a way of solving environmental problems. They gathered a group of economists and scientists to discuss problems facing the world, then sought help from a group of computer experts at the Massachusetts Institute of Technology to study the effects of increasing consumption of resources around the world. This study became the basis of the *Limits to Growth* book, which remains the world's largest selling book on the environment, selling over 12 million in 37 languages within a short time (by comparison Rachel Carson's *Silent Spring* had sold two million copies by September 2012, fifty years after it was first published).[3] King then became one of the founders of the international think tank, The Club of Rome, which the Duke of Edinburgh has called the "conscience of the world".[2] He co-founded The Club of Rome with Peccei, inviting a small international group of professionals from the fields of diplomacy, industry, academia and civil society to meet at a quiet villa in Rome in April 1968, to discuss the dilemma of prevailing short-term thinking in international affairs and, in particular, the concerns regarding unlimited resource consumption in an increasingly interdependent world.[4]

DDT, which was the first modern synthetic insecticide, was initially used with great effect to combat malaria, typhus, and the other insect-borne human diseases among both military and civilian populations and for insect control in crop and livestock production, institutions, homes, and gardens.[5] DDT's quick success as a pesticide and broad use in the United States and other countries led to the development of resistance by many insect pest species. Its cumulative toxic effect, especially on birds of prey, was highlighted in Rachel Carson's *Silent Spring* and it was eventually discontinued by the United States and some other nations, although the World Health Organisation (WHO) still approve it for indoor use and the Stockholm Convention on persistent organic pollutants (signed in 2001 and effective from May 2004) includes a limited exemption for the use of DDT to control mosquitoes, which are vectors that carry malaria – a disease that still kills millions of people worldwide. In September 2006, WHO declared its support for the indoor use of DDT in African countries where malaria remains a major health problem, citing that benefits of the pesticide outweigh the health and environmental risks. While DDT is undoubtedly not benign for wildlife, it has saved the lives of millions of people at risk from malaria, yellow fever and typhus. Note: Daniel Stewart MacLagan published a warning in *Nature* about the long-term effects of insecticides, particularly organochlorines, in September 1951, eleven years before Rachel Carson published *Silent Spring*.

King developed many of the concerns raised by The Club of Rome in his own writings, which included *The International Stimulus* (1974), *The State of the Planet* (1980) and, with Bertrand Schneider, *The First Global Revolution* (1991). He also travelled indefatigably on behalf of the Club, which he served as its second president from 1984 to 1991, following the death of Peccei. Before the Reykjavík Summit in October, King, along with Eduard Pestel, sent a memo to both President Ronald Reagan of the USA and Mikhail Gorbachev of the USSR, suggesting that the United States and the USSR might be induced to work together on reducing arms sales to poorer countries. Mr Gorbachev reacted very positively, and this led to crucial contacts during the period of glasnost and perestroika.[6] For a decade from 1974, he was chairman of the International Federation of Institutes of Advanced Study.

Ian Donald 1910-1987 made the first practical medical ultrasonic scanner, then initiated and developed the techniques of pregnancy scanning now in use everywhere. Along with Glasgow-born engineer Thomas Graham Brown, he developed the first contact ultrasound scanner. He pioneered diagnosis using the technique, reporting the developments in *The Lancet* (1958). Donald developed the procedure over succeeding years such that it became standard practice in hospitals, especially used to maintain a check on the health of the developing foetus during pregnancy.

Together with John MacVicar, who joined the department as registrar in 1956, Brown and Donald came up with the world's first compound contact scanner where the transducer can be moved manually over the patient's abdomen with a resultant 2-D image reproduced on an oscilloscope. The transducer was mounted on a frame with linear potentiometers to measure its mean x- and y- positions and a sine/cosine resolving potentiometer to give a measure of the angle at which it was pointing into the patient.[1]

Donald borrowed an industrial ultrasound machine used to detect flaws in metal and tried it out on some tumours, which he had removed previously, using a beefsteak as the control. He discovered that different tumours produced different echoes. Soon Donald was using ultrasound not only for abdominal tumours in women but also on pregnant women.[2] Early results were disappointing and the enterprise was greeted with a mixture of scepticism and ridicule. However, a dramatic case where ultrasound saved a patient's life by diagnosing a huge, easily removable, ovarian cyst in a woman who had been diagnosed as having inoperable cancer of the stomach, made people take the technique seriously.[3]

John Freeman Loutit 1910-1992 demonstrated the immunosuppressive effect of radiation. He used a strain of mouse with a chromosome translocation resulting in a recognisable cell marker and showed that these mice, treated with high doses of X-rays, would accept bone marrow grafts from genetically incompatible donors, and could thus be rescued from the lethal effects of irradiation. This discovery led to major advances in knowledge of the effects of radiation, and also to advances in the treatment of leukaemia and other malignancies, and was relevant to organ transplantation. He also contributed significantly to the development of improved techniques for the storage and transfusion of blood during the Second World War and made many contributions to knowledge of the uptake and retention of radioactive isotopes from the air and the food chain, particularly isotopes of strontium and iodine.[1]

Between 1947 and 1969, Loutit established and ran the Medical Research Council's Radiobiology Unit at Harwell. In 1954, he was made an Officer of the Order of Orange, Nassau. In 1956, he was awarded the Robert Roesler de Villiers Award by the Leukaemia Society for his discovery of a new therapy for the treatment of the disease.[2]

In the early 1950s, he studied the protective effect of splenic extracts and was amongst the very first to demonstrate that the transplantation of haemopoietic cells was responsible, a conclusion of enormous interest to the world of transplantation. With colleagues, he made important observations on radiation chimeras and described secondary disease, soon afterwards identified as a graft versus host reaction. He also made extensive studies on: the versatility of haemopoietic stem cells; on the distribution and toxicity of radioactive strontium; on osteoclasts; on osteopetrosis; and on haematological mutants in mice. He served on many national and international committees on radiation protection and was generally accepted as one of the world's leading radiobiologists

Loutit's own work on survival of transplanted haematopoietic cells in irradiated animals was of major importance in immunology, and in the treatment of leukaemia and other types of malignancy. Although the most dramatic effects of atomic bomb explosions are produced by blast, flash and very high doses of external radiation, important longer-term effects are produced by the ingestion of fission products carried downwind of the explosion. Loutit first wrote about this in a paper given with Scott Russell to the British Veterinary Association in 1955. It was pointed out that long-lived fission products are ingested by grazing animals and thus enter the food chain and that strontium and iodine are the most critical elements. Strontium is important because of the long half-life (29 years) of its isotope strontium-90, because of the energetic beta particle of its daughter, yttrium-90, and because strontium is taken up into bone and retained there for long periods, and thus has great potential for irradiating myeloid cells and of inducing leukaemia. Iodine is important because although iodine-131 has a relatively short half-life (8 days), it is concentrated in the thyroid. Obviously, the danger from iodine-131 diminishes rapidly with the time since the explosion. Cesium-137 has a very long half-life (30 years) and is almost completely absorbed from the gut but it is widely distributed in the body and its main threats are of causing cancer and genetic injury.

In the late 1950s, following various atomic bomb tests worldwide, a survey of bones (femurs) obtained at autopsy showed that peak values of strontium-90, as radioactivity per gram of calcium, rose from 1.0 pCi between 1956 to mid-1958 to 4.3 pCi in 1959, following a period when the rate of fall-out was three times higher than in previous years. After the temporary discontinuation of tests, the level fell to 2.6 pCi g-I Ca in 1961 and increased again when testing was restarted in 1962. It should be added that Loutit was the driving force behind the scheme for collecting bones; he persuaded pathologists all over the country to collaborate, had the bones sent to Harwell where he inspected every one, labelled those suitable for measurement, and passed them on for analysis.

Haemopoietic cells are very sensitive to radiation and failure of haemopoiesis is the principal cause of death after exposure to lethal doses of X-rays or gamma rays. In 1954 Loutit, with David Walter Hugh Barnes, produced highly suggestive evidence that recovery depended on the presence of intact cells in the spleen. Using donor, rather than autologous spleen cells, they showed that recovery depended critically on the dose of radiation to which the cells were exposed.[3]

Hugh Macdonald Sinclair 1910–1990 pioneered and undertook the research that identified diet with chronic degenerative diseases that are common in First World countries. He proposed that EFA (essential polyunsaturated fatty acids) are crucial to nutrition, and that Omega 3 and Omega 6 are equally important and might be related to a number of diseases, including coronary disease and multiple sclerosis. Sinclair also suggested that the low lung cancer rates in high-smoking Spain and Japan (and low areas of coronary disease as well) might be related in some way to a diet high in essential fatty acids. This hypothesis, along with dietary protection from anti-oxidants, is being actively pursued in Japan today.[1]

Sinclair was the Director of the Oxford Nutrition Survey (ONS) from 1942-1947. The ONS carried out surveys for the Government on a wide range of groups in the UK, such as pregnant women, students and manual workers. The surveys were used to help ensure that ration levels were sufficient for maintaining a healthy population. The ONS also carried out survey work in the British occupied areas of Germany and the Netherlands after the war where the people were suffering from malnutrition. The ONS became the Laboratory of Human Nutrition (LHN) in 1946.[2]

By the 1950s, Sinclair was interested in the relative deficiency of essential polyunsaturated fatty acids (EFAs) which he felt was the main cause of various "diseases of civilisation" such as heart disease. Sinclair wrote a long and controversial letter outlining his views to *The Lancet* (6 April 1956, 381). He was widely disagreed with. In 1979, Sinclair took his early research into EFAs further and carried out a self-experimentation on the effect of eating a diet similar to the Eskimos. He ate only seal meat and fish for one hundred days and tested his blood-clotting times to see the influence of the diet. Sinclair's studies on Eskimos and indeed his self-experimentation are of seminal importance to medical history. Not only did they establish the role of dietary n-3 polyunsaturated fatty acids in human cardiovascular health, but they pioneered the more general view that dietary modulation can have an impact on the incidence of the chronic degenerative diseases that are prevalent in modern Western societies.[3]

Yvonne Aitken 1911-2004 made major contributions to the science of plant breeding by increasing our understanding of genetic factors within a species that control reproductive development in different seasons and climates. She first studied the effect of daily temperature and photoperiod on a group of nine well-known agricultural species (three legumes, six cereals and grasses) sown at Melbourne (latitude 38°S) at intervals during the year. Over 30 years, she planted the same varieties at locations all over the world to test extremes of daylight, temperature and altitude, and visited the sites during her holidays. These travels included Central Asia, Patagonia, Alaska and Mexico. Collaborations within Australia combined with these study leave and sabbatical trips in 1955, 1963 and 1975 resulted in Aitken's work covering several continents and 10 distinctly different climates. She became a world authority on predicting geographic and climatic limits for plant varieties.[1]

Alexander Bryce Cameron 1911-2001 was employed for nearly two decades with the Anglo Persian Oil Company (now British Petroleum) exploring the oilfields of Iran, and developing the oil production of Kuwait. He then worked on the offshore fields of Trinidad's Gulf of Paria, then Canada, where he located oil and gas in Alberta and Saskatchewan. He also explored the Canadian Arctic where he predicted, correctly, that oil and gas would be found. He explored the British North Sea oil fields and, in Romania, the Transylvanian foothills.[1]

Alexander George Ogston 1911-1996 specialised in the thermodynamics of biological systems. He was particularly interested in connective tissue and the use of physico-chemical methods to study the size, weight and structure of molecules. He made the "three-point attachment" contribution to stereochemistry.[1]

Ogston was able to solve a theoretical biochemical problem of considerable interest at the time in the 1940s when the metabolic pathways of living organisms were being worked out by Hans Krebs and others.

Several chemical steps had been considered and rejected by other investigators because they required an apparent impossibility – the paradoxical formation of only one of two equally likely asymmetric products from a symmetrical precursor. In the summer of 1948, Ogston convincingly argued in a scientific paper of fewer than 400 words that the paradox disappears if the symmetrical precursor is attached to its relevant enzyme at three points.

This three-point attachment hypothesis was widely accepted (Krebs devoted almost the whole of a chapter of his autobiography to Ogston's "penetrating theoretical analysis" in this matter), and was a factor in Ogston's election to The Royal Society in 1955. Typically, Ogston was somehow slightly embarrassed by the importance others placed on this work, because, as he would diffidently explain, the idea only took him a few moments to conceptualise.[2]

Ogston was a pioneer of the study of large molecules of biological interest, especially proteins and hyaluronic acid, the natural lubricant of joints. He made significant contributions to the early theoretical treatments of sedimentation in the analytical ultracentrifuge and he was a tireless and effective advocate of the application of quantitative physical methods to biological problems and gave this approach a strategically-timed shot in the arm in Australia following his appointment to the John Curtin School.[3]

Ogston and his student, Joseph Percy Johnston, discovered what came to be known as the Johnston-Ogston effect, which is of such generality that the same principles can predict the changes in the spacing of cars as they pass along a road with zones having different speed restrictions.[4] The Johnston-Ogston effect is a phenomenon occurring in sedimentation velocity experiments when two or more solutes are present in a mixture and their sedimentation coefficients are mutually concentration-dependent.

Another of Ogston's elegantly simple solutions to complex problems, in this case related to the strange behaviour of mixtures of proteins and long chain carbohydrates, subsequently proved relevant to the permeability of paper and gels, and even to the growth of roots. He moved to the Australian National University in 1960 as the Professor of Physical Biochemistry – a field which was the precursor of modern molecular biology, in which he was one of the earliest protagonists, in which physical methods are used to study biological processes.[5]

Frederick Malloch Bruce 1912-1997 was an electrical engineer who "published two outstanding seminal papers dealing with precision high voltage measurements using an ellipsoid voltmeter and specially-designed uniform field electrodes. 'Bruce profile' electrodes continue to be used in high voltage research to this day."[1]

These Bruce profile electrodes were a series of electrode shapes that approximated an ideal uniform field. The Bruce profile is a figure of revolution, starting with a flat plane in the centre, with a sine curve used as a transition to a circular section at the edge. The idea is to have a large area of uniform field (2 flat plates) with a gradually increasing radius of curvature to the edge.

Samuel Crowe Curran 1912-1998 co-invented the proximity fuse with William Alan Stewart Butement. It was designed to detonate an explosive device automatically when the distance to target becomes smaller than a predetermined value, or when the target passes through a given plane. It needed to be miniaturised and this was done in the USA under a team led by Merle Anthony Tuve. This was later an important weapon in destroying enemy planes, and was largely responsible for the destruction of over 90% of the V1 rockets launched against southern England in 1944.

By 1944, Curran had been seconded to work on the Manhattan Project (the development of the atomic bomb) and, while in America, he invented the scintillation counter for the detection and counting of radiation sources, which was later used in almost every scientific laboratory in the world.[1] The counter is used for medical imaging, for checking nuclear contamination and for border security.

He was part of the project team that successfully developed Britain's first hydrogen bomb. Curran was appointed head of Glasgow's Royal College of Science and Technology which, in 1962, he took to university status (University of Strathclyde) as the first technological university in Britain.

Robert Lang Lickley 1912-1998 worked under Sydney Camm, the famous English aeronautical engineer who designed the Hawker Hurricane fighter plane. Lickley "made his mark with Roy Chaplin in the mid-Thirties by creating the project design of a single-seat eight-gun monoplane fighter." This project was conceived by the Hawker team as their reaction to the outcome of the Air Ministry specification F5/34 which Sydney Camm dismissed as "just not good enough". The Hawker team incorporated the new Rolls-Royce PV12 engine, a retracting undercarriage and a fabric covered monoplane wing with eight Browning .303" machine guns buried therein. This formidable concept eventually emerged as the Hurricane, which proved a huge advance on its predecessors, very robust, and a good steady gun platform. The Air Ministry was so impressed by the prototype's performance that a production order was placed in 1936 for no fewer than 600 of the type. This enabled the RAF to have quite a number of squadrons in service by the critical early summer of 1940. During the Battle of Britain which followed, Fighter Command used its Hurricanes to great effect, when they shot down more enemy aircraft than all other aircraft and ground forces combined."[1]

During the Second World War, Lickley was appointed as Chief Project Engineer 1941-1946, working on the development of the Typhoon, Tempest, Fury, and the jet-powered Sea Hawk. He was in charge of the development of the Fairey Rotodyne, the first large compound helicopter.[2] Rotodyne, a large, fast rotary-wing aircraft of 33,000lb (15 tonnes) design weight capable of vertical take-off and landing and aimed at the short-haul intercity market. The sole prototype flew several hundred hours, setting a world-speed record of 307 km/h over the 100 km closed circuit in January 1959, a record that stood for many, many years. However, the Rotodyne was cancelled in 1962 on the grounds of budgetary shortage and external noise.[3]

Lickley designed the Fairey Delta 2 or FD2 (internal designation Type V within Fairey), a British supersonic research aircraft produced by the Fairey Aviation Company in response to a specification from the Ministry of Supply for investigation into flight and control at transonic and supersonic speeds. The British-built Fairey Delta 2 research aircraft set a new world airspeed record of 1,132 mph (1,822 km/h), becoming the first plane to exceed 1,000 mph (1,609 km/h) in level flight. The new mark beat the previous record by 300 mph (483 km/h), set a year earlier by a North American F-100 Super Sabre.[4]

The British government decided not to go ahead with production as it believed that guided missiles would make fighters obsolete. The French government used the FD2 design for their very successful Dassault Mirage fighter jets. Lickley returned to Hawker Siddely where he was involved in VTOL development from which arose the Harrier jump jet which was designed by John William Fozard. After the collapse of Rolls Royce in 1971, Lickley was assigned to revive its aero-engine business which he did successfully.[5]

Kenneth Ross MacKenzie 1912-2002 was a co-discoverer of the element astatine – element 85 of the periodic table. Astatine is recognised as the rarest element on the planet by the *Guinness Book of World Records*. At any given time, there is less than one ounce of astatine within Earth's crust, due to its relatively short half-life. Astatine is produced by bombarding bismuth with alpha particles. Once the longer-lived astatine-209 – astatine-211 compounds are obtained, it is distilled by heating it in the presence of air.[1]

MacKenzie joined the UCLA faculty in 1947 and helped install Ernest Orlando Lawrence's original cyclotron, the first atom smasher of its kind in the world, which was shipped from Berkeley to Westwood. In 1955, he directed construction of a 49-inch (124.5 cm) cyclotron for UCLA and formally retired the Lawrence device.

By 1958, MacKenzie and his colleague Byron Wright had developed such expertise in building cyclotrons that they formed MEVA Corp. to build cyclotrons for teaching physics. They also constructed a 7-tonne model magnet and power supply for the Naval Radiological Defense Lab in San Francisco. Their firm was later bought by Hughes Aircraft Co.

When MacKenzie turned to studying plasma gases for use in fusion energy, he founded UCLA's Plasma Physics Laboratory. He focused his research and teaching on fusion technology and studying dark matter. As an emeritus professor, he continued his research long after leaving the classroom.[2]

William Watt 1912-1985 developed, with Leslie N. Phillips and William Johnson, a commercially feasible process for manufacturing high-strength, high-modulus carbon fibres (graphite fibres had been invented in 1958 by US physicist Roger Bacon). Researching polyacrylonitrile (PAN), some Japanese researchers, in 1961, demonstrated high strength and high modulus fibres from PAN precursors. In 1964, while the Japanese were undertaking a pilot test of their discovery, Watt invented a still higher-modulus fibre from PAN which was quickly put into commercial production.[1]

Watt and his team combined carbon fibres with the polymer polyacrylonitrile and exposed it to a unique, multistage heating process. This created a material as strong as steel but considerably lighter. The fibres could be used to reinforce polymers and moulded to create versatile composites that were stiff, light, corrosion-proof, heat-resistant and tear-resistant. Carbon-fibre composite, as it is known, is now used in Formula One racing cars as well as Olympic-level bicycles, sailing boats and hi-tech sports equipment as well as for top-end sports racquets and golf clubs. It is also being increasingly used in aviation.[2]

Better aircraft propellers were the target of Watt and his team at RAE Farnborough when they worked out how to synthesise strong, stiff carbon fibre composite. Its high-flying role continues today as the material for the fuselage of the new Boeing 787 Dreamliner (in operation from October 2011). Designers and architects are also experimenting with it as a building material.[3] Watt's invention was patented in 1964, and was recognised in 1968 by the civil service Wolfe Award for outstanding technical innovation.[4]

Wilfred Gordon Bigelow 1913-2005 introduced the concept and technique of hypothermia that first made open heart surgery possible. He also co-developed the first electronic pacemaker in 1950. In 1956, he was influential in developing the first formal cardiac surgery training program in Canada.[1] He was President of The American Association for Thoracic Surgery 1974-1975, President of the Society for Vascular Surgery 1968-1969, and President of the Canadian Cardiovascular Society from 1970-1972.

During World War II, he served as a surgeon in casualty clearing stations, during which time he grew interested in the ravages of injury brought on by hypothermia, or total body cooling. In 1941, he treated a young Canadian for frostbite, and had to amputate the man's gangrenous fingers. Shocked by how little was known about frostbite, and encouraged by a professor, he started to research frostbite. It was a pivotal moment in his career and life.

After the war, Bigelow studied at Johns Hopkins University, and then at Toronto General Hospital and the University of Toronto, investigating the physiological effects of hypothermia. His key discovery, made in 1950, was recognising how to lower the body's oxygen requirements while lowering the body's core temperature to a point at which safe open heart surgery was possible. The first successful human application of Bigelow's hypothermia research for open heart surgery occurred in 1953. In applying the technique, the patient was anaesthetised and placed on a bed of ice to give surgeons a window of roughly 10 minutes of access to the heart. The hypothermia technique was supplanted by the heart-lung machine in the 1960s, although it is now used on parts of the heart during surgery in tandem with the machine to allow access to the heart for two or more hours. Bigelow's technique was recognised as "an extraordinarily revolutionary concept that allowed an entire field to evolve," said Dr Richard K. Reznick, chairman of the department of surgery at the University of Toronto. [2]

Meanwhile he had pioneered another major advance in the management of heart disease – the pacemaker – which evolved quite unexpectedly out of his hypothermia research. In 1949, during experimental surgery, he found he was able to restart a dog's heart by stimulating it at regular intervals with a probe. The following year he co-developed the first electronic heart pacemaker with Dr John C. Callaghan and electrical engineer John A. Hopps. Their design, as reported in a paper published that year, formed the basis for subsequent technological developments and refinements leading to the modern implantable cardiac pacemaker. Together, these discoveries revolutionised heart surgery and have made a significant difference to the lives of millions of people with heart disease.

Bigelow also established the first Division of Cardiac Surgery in Toronto in 1947. In 1956, he was influential in developing the first formal cardiac surgery training program in Canada and in 1957 set up the first inter-hospital postgraduate cardiovascular surgical training program in Canada. He authored 120 publications, including important historical works on hypothermia and the electric cardiac pacemaker, and on the development of heparin in Toronto. Dr "Bill" Bigelow is one of the most distinguished surgeons Canada has ever produced and stands among the world's titans of medicine.[3]

Douglas Falconer 1913-2004 found that litter size in mice could be increased substantially by successive generations of artificial selection, even though it was apparently a fitness trait subject to natural selection. He undertook a number of very significant selection experiments in mice, each lasting 20 or more generations (or five years), in which he revealed that, contrary to the then animal breeding dogma, selection for increased growth rate in a good environment was not necessarily more effective than in one where food was restricted, a model "poor" environment.[1]

His early work was on linkage and genetic analyses of major Mendelian mutations in mice, including the discovery of the first sex-linked mouse mutation. His major contributions, however, were in the area of genetic analysis of quantitative traits, for which variation is determined by segregating alleles at multiple interacting loci with individually small effects, and whose expression is contingent on the environment. In particular, he is best known for his work on response to artificial selection in mice, the concept of the cross-environment genetic correlation, development of the theory for understanding the genetics of complex human diseases in terms of an underlying continuous liability, and of course, his highly acclaimed textbook, *Introduction to Quantitative Genetics*, first published in 1960. What is remarkable is that this book has lasted over 40 years, with only evolution and not revolution of content, and is still used for courses. He invented the concept of realised heritability, obtained by regressing the cumulated selection response on the cumulated selection differential, the latter weighted by the number of progeny measured.[2]

He also showed how the genetic correlation could be used to define performance across different environments. In his final experiment, he used a very neat molecular technique with the high and low growth selection lines to show that the genetic influence on body size was not controlled through any single organ.

Falconer made a significant direct contribution to human genetics. He developed a simple and elegant method for estimating, from only the incidence in the population and in relatives of affected individuals, the genetic contribution to liability to diseases such as diabetes that have all-or-none expression, but that are affected by many genes.[3]

William George Nicholson Geddes 1913-1993 worked under the direction of **James Arthur Banks 1897-1967** on the construction of the Allt-na-Lairige Dam in Argyllshire in 1957, this being the first concrete dam in Western Europe, and possibly the world, to be prestressed with high tensile steel bars. "A relatively new development in the construction of gravity dams is incorporation of post-tensioned steel into the structure. This helped reduce the cross section of Allt-Na-Lairige Dam in Scotland to only 60 percent of that of a conventional gravity dam of the same height. A series of vertical steel rods near the upstream water face, stressed by jacks and securely anchored into the rock foundation, resists the overturning tendency of this more slender section. This system has also been used to raise existing gravity dams to a higher crest level, economically increasing the storage capacity of a reservoir."[1]

Later, he was in charge of Backwater Dam, the first in the UK to use a chemical grout cut-off. One of his outstanding achievements was the major shipbuilding dock at the head of the Musgrove Channel in Belfast for Harland and Wolff. The dock was the largest in the world when it was completed in 1970, having been designed and constructed scarcely two years after the decision was taken to proceed.[2]

Mary Douglas Leakey 1913-1996 was a noted archaeologist and paleoanthropologist. She quickly established a reputation as a competent excavator of Stone Age sites. Beginning in the 1930s, Mary Leakey and her late husband, Louis, awakened the world to Africa's primary place in human origins with their spectacular discoveries and increasingly pushed back the time of those origins much earlier than had been thought. Until then, many scientists still believed the human birthplace would be found in Asia.[1]

In 1951, she recorded some 1,600 Stone Age rock paintings (believed to be some 1,500 years old) in the Kondoa-Irangi region of central Tanzania, a task she regarded as one of the highlights of her life and work, which were published many years later in *Africa's Vanishing Art: the Rock Paintings of Tanzania* (1983). On 6 October 1948, on Rusinga Island near the west coast of Lake Victoria, Mary discovered part of a skull of *Proconsul africanus*, an 18 million-year-old Miocene ape, in which there was tremendous public interest. Some of her favourite finds – a collection of Miocene fossil insects, fruits, and seeds which she and Louis stumbled upon during a cigarette break – were also made at Rusinga Island.

The site that will always be associated with Mary Leakey is Olduvai Gorge, a canyon in northern Tanzania containing rich collections of fossils and artefacts approximately spanning the last two million years. This became her second home, where she enjoyed fieldwork and research, accompanied by her pack of beloved dalmatian dogs, of which she was a well-known breeder. At Olduvai on 17 July 1959 she made one of the most famous fossil discoveries of all time, the skull of a 1.8 million-year-old early human relative whom Louis named *Zinjanthropus* (now *Australopithecus* or *Paranthropus*) *boisei*.[2] A few years later, the two Leakeys uncovered the fossils of the first known member of the genus *Homo habilis*, or "able man", in recognition of the many stone tools found among the bones.[3]

Television coverage of the find made the Leakeys household names all over the world and brought them desperately needed funding from the National Geographic Society. Mary laboured under the hot sun, meticulously recording scatters of early stone tools and fossil bones, setting new standards for archaeological fieldwork, while Louis concentrated on fund-raising and lecturing. The technical details of her work are published in volumes 3 (1971) and 5 (1994) of the Olduvai Gorge series of Cambridge University Press and a popular account is given in *Olduvai Gorge: my Search for Early Man* (1979).

Perhaps the crowning triumph of Mary Leakey's remarkable career was the discovery and excavation at her dig at Laetoli in northern Tanzania during 1978-1979 of 3.7 million-year-old trails of early hominid footprints, which proved that hominids walked on two legs more than a million years before the earliest known stone tools.[4]

As often happens, the discovery of the prints was made by chance – more Leakey luck. While tossing dried elephant dung in a playful camp fight, one scientist on Mrs. Leakey's expedition fell down and saw in the gray surface some curious indentations. They were imprints of raindrops and animals, now hardened to stone and recently exposed by erosion and weathering. After further exploration, scientists determined that the tracks were made about 3.7 million years ago. The animals had walked over volcanic ash when it was damp from rain, leaving impressions of their feet. The wet ash set like concrete and was later covered over by more ash and silt. There the tracks remained to be found by dung-throwing scientists.

It was two years before a scientist uncovered a heel print that hinted of an even more significant find. It seemed to belong to a hominid. On 2 August 1978, Mary Leakey spent three hours examining one of the clearest of these prints. She cleaned the crevices of the print with a small brush and dental pick. All the important elements were preserved: heel, toes and arch. She appraised the print from every possible angle.

She was at last sure that a hominid had left this print and a trail of prints extending more than 75 feet (23 m) across the plain. Two and possibly three individuals had walked this way 3.7 million years ago: the largest one, presumably a male; the middle-sized one, presumably female, and an even smaller individual, perhaps their child, whose prints are sometimes superimposed on the others.

Somewhere along the way, the female appeared to pause and turn to her left. She might have sensed danger, possibly from a predator or the rumble of a volcanic eruption nearby. Then she resumed her walk to the north. "This motion, so intensely human, transcends time," she wrote in the *National Geographic* magazine. "A remote ancestor – just as you or I – experienced a moment of doubt."

These evocative footprints are the earliest known traces of human behaviour. At the time, the discovery established that human ancestors had begun walking upright much earlier than previously thought, long before the evolution of larger brains. Whether upright walking preceded the larger brain, or vice versa, was still a much-debated issue among scholars.[5]

Ian Martin-Scott 1913-2002 undertook the research and clinical trials into infantile eczema and investigated the properties of *Neutrogena* soap and E45 cream.[1]

In 1960, a medical committee in Britain determined that *Neutrogena* was not a drug and therefore should not have been prescribed freely on the National Health Service. The doctor appealed the case. "In giving their decision, the referees stated that if the patient had washed with ordinary soap its alkaline ingredients would have irritated the skin. If he had not washed at all he would have been predisposed to secondary infection and to the psychological effects of being always dirty. *Neutrogena* soap was not only non-alkaline but it also removed the crusts caused by the dermatitis and had an optimum soothing effect due to the inclusion of triethanolamine and glycerin in its composition. The doctor had studied reports on clinical tests described in the *British Medical Journal* (this was an article by Martin Scott and A.G. Ramsay on 30 June 1956). Cetrimide, which was included in the National Formulary, had somewhat similar properties, but the doctor thought that *Neutrogena* soap was better for the patient, and the referees thought he was entitled to use his judgment. They decided that *Neutrogena* soap was in this case a drug which the executive council was bound to provide".[2]

In his research, Martin-Scott and A.G. Ramsay concluded, after the skin had been washed with the soap [*Neutrogena*], the skin-fat factor showed no change from the normal, and the pH of the skin remained unaltered. Thus, its use did not involve any denaturing of the skin, and its protective acid mantle remained intact. Clinically it was found to be innocuous to persons who found the excessive use of ordinary toilet soap to be detrimental to skin health. Furthermore, about 100 patients suffering from subacute eczema, who would normally be forbidden to wash with soap, were able to enjoy using this neutral soap with impunity.[3] Note: *Neutrogena* was developed by Belgian-born Edmond Fromont. Martin-Smith assisted by A.G. Ramsay undertook independent research into its properties.

Robert Simpson Silver 1913-1997 invented the Multi-stage Flash (MSF) Distillation System. MSF distillation plants produce 64% of all desalinated water in the world.[1] This invention resulted from a careful analysis of the sources of entropy in various systems for water purification. Today the method of analysis he used is called "Second Law Analysis," but when he applied it to seawater demineralisation, it was a novel idea. The first MSF plant was sold in Saudi Arabia. Multistage flash distillation represented an improvement in thermal efficiency of about two and one-half times. It also made practical the design of very large plants, upwards of millions of gallons per day of freshwater production. A 1,000,000 gallon per day plant (4,546,092 litres), based on the same principle, was built in San Diego as a demonstration plant by the US Office of Saline Water, in the early 1950s. That plant was later dismantled and shipped to Guantanamo Bay, where it is still in use. Silver also wrote fundamental papers on the theory of condensation of pure liquids, on combustion, and on explosives.[2]

Mary Isolen Fergusson 1914-1997 became the first female senior partner in a United Kingdom engineering firm on 1 January 1948. She also became the first female full member of the Institution of Civil Engineers in 1957, 21 years after graduating with Honours in Civil Engineering at University of Edinburgh.[1] At the time of her appointment she had "been responsible for the design of over £2 million worth of engineering works, including reinforced concrete bridges, steel-framed buildings, and the River Leven Purification Scheme."[2]

Donald Darnley Reid 1914-1977 studied the tremendous stresses to which the bomber crews were exposed during World War II, and his enduring admiration for these often very young airmen was profound. By bringing together the medical records and the operational records of flights and casualties, he was able to demonstrate that psychological breakdown related to the cumulative effect of multiple dangerous missions. This was the beginning of psychiatric epidemiology.[1] Twenty years later, he wrote on the use of epidemiological methods to study mental disorders.

Reid's most substantive involvement in clinical trials was with the Medical Research Council trials of anticoagulants after myocardial infarction. These highlighted the problem of maintenance of contact with patients. Information about 86% of those lost from the original series was obtained by involving the patients' family physicians and the Ministry of Pensions and National Insurance. After reviewing the quality of similar studies in other countries, he concluded that more than half of the drug trials relating to myocardial infarction reported in North American medical journals were insufficiently well controlled.

Between 1949 and 1952, Reid and C.G. Roberts surveyed the records of disabling illness and premature death in male post office workers. They identified a gross disparity in the rates of retirement on grounds of ill health between workers whose jobs made different physical demands upon them: older manual workers suffered 50% more occupational disability or death before 60 than non-manual workers.

During the 1950s, Reid devised modes of analysis of sickness records to monitor the spread of the common cold among office workers, the incidence of cancer in coking plant workers, and the hazard of tuberculosis in pathology laboratory staff, and he promulgated the use of morbidity data and sickness and disease recording systems to generate data for statistical and epidemiological methods in occupational medicine. His main interest at that time was in associations between respiratory disease and environmental pollution and minor respiratory illnesses. He had a particular interest in chronic bronchitis and reviewed the evidence for the possible aetiological importance of smoke pollution and infections such as the influenza outbreak of 1952.[2]

George Stephen Ritchie 1914-2012 commanded four survey ships. In 1950-1951, he took *Challenger* on a circumnavigation of the world during which, using echo sounding, he measured the Challenger Deep, in the Pacific Ocean. Modern science has not been able to improve on Ritchie's accuracy. From 1953 to 1956, he commanded HMNZS *Lachlan*, and in 1959 he commanded the British Navy's anti-aircraft frigate HMS *Dalrymple* on surveys of the Persian Gulf. His command of HMS *Vidal* (1963-1965) ended with a survey of the western approaches to the Strait of Gibraltar, using temporary radio stations in Spain.

In 1966, Ritchie was promoted rear-admiral and became 19th Hydrographer of the Navy, in a line which stretches back to 1795. As "Droggy", he commanded the Royal Navy's survey squadron and oversaw the publication of the world-renowned Admiralty charts. He also introduced automation in the production of charts instead of engraving, merged his headquarters with the chart printing office at Taunton, and campaigned hard for a new class of survey ships.

The survey methods which Ritchie had used as a young man had barely changed in two centuries, but now he began the widespread introduction of computers and – despite opposition from "The Friends of the Fathom", led by A.P. Herbert – the metrication of charts.[1]

Hamish Nisbet Munro 1915-1994 studied protein metabolism and nutrition's role in the ageing process. In 1980, he became founding director of Tufts University's Human Nutrition Research Center in Aging in Massachusetts. The centre was the first for the study of nutrition and the ageing process in the world.[1]

"As one of the most gifted writers, challenging teachers and incisive scientists of his time, Dr Munro helped redefine the importance of nutrition in human metabolism".[2] For over six decades, Munro's studies of the biochemical effects of nutritional change – particularly protein metabolism – led to a deeper understanding of the role of nutrition in ageing.[3]

In an early series of publications, he demonstrated that it was possible to change loss of protein to gain in an individual by increasing the intake of energy, without changing the intake of protein; an observation of considerable significance for the nutritional care of patients. In 1939, he was a joint author of a paper on the relationship between vitamin C and capillary fragility. With Vernon R. Young, he showed that corticosteroids affected protein metabolism only when present in the levels associated with stress, whereas thyroxine was effective in the physiological range.[4]

Robert Alexander Rankin 1915-2001 was an eminent Scottish number theorist and, for several decades, one of the world's foremost experts in modular forms.[1] He undertook research on the difference between two successive primes, which won him the Rayleigh Prize in 1939.[2]

Rankin worked on the development of rockets. He developed a theory to allow the trajectory of the rocket to be calculated from the initial conditions. The British Government, however, paid little attention to the work of Rankin and his team. He was transferred from Fort Halstead to Wales where he continued to work until the end of the war. During the war, his work on rockets was classified information, but once the war was over, the information was declassified and

Rankin was released early from his war service on the condition that he wrote up the theoretical work which he had done on rockets, which was published as *The mathematical theory of the motion of rotated and unrotated rockets*, and it was published in the *Philosophical Transactions of The Royal Society* in a paper which was longer than any previously published in that journal.[3]

Rankin originated what has become to be known as the "Rankin-Selberg method", which is a technique for directly constructing and analytically continuing several important examples of automorphic L-functions. Some authors reserve the term for a special type of integral representation, namely those that involve an Eisenstein series. It has been one of the most powerful techniques for studying the Langlands program.[4]

James Kerr Grant 1916-2004 played a significant role in working out the pathways of adrenal steroidogenesis and the enzymes that control the process.[1]

Working with his team in the 1950s and 1960s, he carried out autopsies at all hours of the day and night to minimise post-mortem changes, comparing adrenal structure in patients dying suddenly with those in patients at the end of prolonged illnesses. This led him to propose for the first time the functional zonation of the adrenal cortex. Thereafter, using new morphological and chemical techniques, an understanding of the complicated structure emerged, together with an explanation of the role of cells in different zones of the adrenal cortex with respect to the production of the various types of steroid hormones. This research opened up a new era in appreciation of adrenal diseases and he led a group of young investigators whose work based on the functional zonation of the cortex gave a new understanding and classification of the various forms of adrenocortical hyperactivity.[2]

George Gray Macfarlane 1916-2007 worked on radar at the secret Telecommunications Research Establishment (TRE), led by Robert Watson-Watt, in a team that played a pivotal role in British air defence, the bombing of Germany and the destruction of U-boats. At TRE, first in Dorset and then in Malvern, Worcestershire, he worked with the mathematical group on the theory of radio wave propagation and reflection, crucial to the development of microwave radar, TRE's key advance. This hugely increased the range and accuracy of detection equipment, and paved the way for some crucial applications, including a guidance system for fighters tracking German night bombers. Macfarlane also advised on the technology, codenamed *Window*, which was designed to confuse enemy radar by dropping strips of metallised paper.

As the war turned in Britain's favour, TRE shifted its emphasis to guiding RAF bombers to targets over Germany. It produced a grid of radar signals across Europe, which allowed bombers to navigate towards their targets. And its Oboe system allowed controllers on the ground to track and guide bombers with unprecedented accuracy – allowing the devastation of the Ruhr industries. On the night before D-Day, it allowed bombers to silence the defensive coastal batteries.

No less important was TRE's development of a radar system for spotting surfacing U-boats; this rendered them much more vulnerable to detection, and Hitler blamed it for German reverses in the battle of the Atlantic. After the war, Macfarlane initiated a project to develop the UK computer industry and worked on computer programming languages.[1]

His appointment in 1954 to an individual merit post in the scientific civil service gave him the freedom to pursue his research on semiconductors and infra-red detection, which formed the basis for thermal imaging. His 1955 study of the optical properties of germanium and silicon was central to the development of infra-red detectors for medical and defence use.[2]

He designed and developed the first digital computer, RREAC, using transistors instead of valves, worked on new computer languages, and initiated the Advanced Computer Techniques Project, a program of research and development between government and industry to strengthen the British computer industry. [3]

John Alexander Simpson 1916-2000 invented the neutron monitor pile, which became the world standard for cosmic ray research sponsored by the 68 nations participating in the International Geophysical Year in 1957-1958.[1]

In 1939, he designed and constructed a two-stage electron microscope. During World War II, while working on the Manhattan Project to develop the atomic bomb, Simpson invented a gas flow alpha particle (helium nuclei) proportional counter for measuring plutonium yields in the presence of high intensity fission products. Alpha particles emitted in the radioactive decay of plutonium, and other transuranic elements, have but little penetrating power. A sheet of paper stops them. They do not penetrate the thin window of particle counters, so the trick was to pipe the plutonium-bearing gas through the counter itself. Simpson patented the device, which was the first of the 15 patents that now bear his name, ranging from the multiwire proportional counter to a device that assists in improving reading speed and accuracy.[2]

From 1945, he began investigations of the energy spectrum of the primary galactic cosmic ray protons by means of their production of a secondary nucleonic component cascade in the atmosphere. Using the fast neutron production as a tracer of the nucleon cascade, he discovered the existence of the large latitude dependence of the cascade, the production of which was shown to extend to very low primary particle energies. From these studies, Simpson invented, in 1948, the concept and instrumentation called the neutron monitor pile, based on the early nuclear chain reaction at Chicago, which for the first time enabled the investigation of the time-dependent intensity changes of the very low energy primary cosmic ray nucleon component. His studies of the time dependence of the nucleonic component over a wide range of incident particle energies led to the proof that the cosmic ray intensity variations were due to interplanetary electrodynamical processes of solar origin – called the solar modulation of the galactic cosmic rays. In 1950-1951 he established a network of these neutron monitors extending from the geomagnetic equator to high latitudes. It was his neutron monitor network which recorded the flare of 23 February 1956, leading to his demonstration with colleagues Peter Meyer and Eugene Parker that there existed a large-scale heliosphere of magnetic fields surrounding the solar system.[3]

Simpson and his colleagues developed new concepts, including Simpson's invention of polyvinylidene fluoride polymer sensors for detection of super heavy charged particles or mass measurements of dust particles in the coma of Comet Halley (1986). This technology support, plus the sequence of discrete space missions, provided a sustaining level of support for his group in LASR (Laboratory for Advanced Systems Research). The ability of his laboratory to respond rapidly to new opportunities is illustrated by the Vega missions. Simpson invented his dust detector in 1983 and it was incorporated into an instrument in the spacecraft and launched in 1984.

The story of the development of the modern cosmic ray concept is to a large degree the story of Simpson's scientific investigations. Simpson discovered that the latitude effect seen with neutrons is about 20 times greater than observed with ionisation chambers, and it was soon apparent that the time variations are much greater, too. The neutrons are produced mostly by incoming cosmic ray protons of 15 GeV or less, while the mesons are produced mostly by protons above about 15 GeV. Simpson recognised the potential of the neutrons and the lower energy cosmic ray particles for probing the causes of the time variations. That is to say, the strong time variation of the lower energy cosmic rays is a thumbprint of whatever is happening out in space.

A stable ground-based neutron detector was needed, so Simpson invented the neutron monitor. This instrument was bulky, with layers of both lead shielding and paraffin moderator, but it was inexpensive, stable, and could be built large to obtain any desired counting rate. It had the big advantage that the diurnal atmospheric corrections required little more than the local barometric reading. Ionisation chambers, for instance, must include the height (temperature) of the atmosphere in the corrections, as a consequence of the decay of the downward propagating mesons. Simpson recognised the importance of determining the energy dependence of the time variations, so he established neutron monitor stations at Chicago, Illinois; Climax, Colorado; Sacramento Peak, New Mexico; Mexico City, Mexico; and Huancayo, Peru. The Peruvian station responded only to cosmic rays above 15 GeV, while the Chicago station responded to cosmic rays above about 2 GeV, with the other three stations distributed between.

For the International Geophysical Year (IGY) in 1957-1958, Simpson was one of the 12 discipline scientists responsible for organising and coordinating the international program. The neutron monitor was adopted as the standard for cosmic ray measurements worldwide. Indeed, the fundamental role of the neutron monitor is evidenced today by the 23 nations that use them at 51 centres around the world. These centres are part of a network of stations that monitor space weather under the auspices of the National Science Foundation. The IGY was a huge success, with its tightly coordinated worldwide observations providing a general picture that had never before been possible.

Simpson realised the necessity for sending instruments into space and, together with Peter Meyer, he started work immediately on the development and construction of small lightweight particle detectors suitable for going into space; his first particle detector was launched into space on Pioneer 2 in 1958. Rocket failures on the Ranger 1 and 2 launches delayed things momentarily, so the second instrument to go into space was on Pioneer 5 in 1960. It was clear to Simpson that the limited weight and power available on spacecraft made it necessary to invent small detectors that could determine the mass, charge, and energy of the individual energetic particles passing through the instrument. Only with such detailed knowledge of the cosmic ray particles would it be possible to infer their origin. Attention turned first to silicon crystals, and a long program of development in collaboration with Anthony J. Tuzzolino and others ensued. By 1980, the art of particle detection and measurement had advanced to the point where it was possible to resolve the individual isotopes of nuclei, eventually all the way up through Fe and Ni, at the same time measuring their kinetic energy. This technology is now generally employed in the space program for studies of galactic cosmic rays, solar cosmic rays, and energetic particles trapped in planetary magnetic fields.

An offshoot into plastic detectors led to the dust flux monitor instrument (DFMI) developed by Simpson and Tuzzolino in the 1980s. It is a novel pyroelectric scheme involving a thin sheet of plastic that has been polymerised in the presence of a strong electric field perpendicular to the plane of the plastic; the final sheet is electrically polarised and carries a positive electric charge on one surface and a negative charge on the other. A dust particle or heavy nucleus penetrating though the sheet vaporises a small area, thereby releasing the charges. The electrical signal indicates the location and size of the hole in the plastic and can be calibrated to give information on the speed and size of the particle. This device was first carried into space on the Soviet Vega 1 and 2 spacecraft to Comet Halley in 1986. The ability to handle up to 0.5×105 hits per second made the DFMI indispensable for studying the cometary dust cloud close to the comet and using the results of Vega 1 to judge how close to send Vega 2. Simpson was awarded the Gagarin Medal for Space Exploration in 1986 for his contribution to the success of the Vega mission. His instruments were the only ones from the United States to encounter Comet Halley.

A more recent DFMI is carried on the Cassini mission to Saturn, where it will investigate the dust environment of Saturn's gravel rings. DFMIs are flown on the Air Force's unclassified Advanced Research and Global Observation Satellite and on the ARGOS spacecraft in low Earth orbit, where it monitors the space dust of both natural and human origins. It is evident that the DFMI has joined the silicon detectors and the neutron monitor in the stable of scientific workhorses.

It was Simpson's detection of the fixed energetic particle populations around Mercury that first established that the magnetic fields observed at Mercury belong to the planet itself, rather than being carried from the Sun by the impacting solar wind (1974). Then Simpson and others detected a tiny gap in the distribution of energetic particles trapped in the magnetic field of Saturn, indicating the presence of a previously undetected small moon of Saturn orbiting at that position in space and absorbing the particles that would otherwise be found there (1980). The moon was subsequently identified optically.

Another discovery by Simpson eventually led to the realisation that plasma waves can also be efficient accelerators. It began with Simpson's discovery, in 1970, that impulsive flares at the Sun produce energetic particles among which 3He is ten or more times abundant relative to 4He than normal. Subsequently, others observed instances in which 3HE actually outnumbered 4HE. L.A. Fisk showed that this very selective acceleration can be understood in terms of the plasma waves created by current instabilities, and M. Temerin and J. Roth more recently have shown that ion cyclotron waves are another possibility, both processes being remarkably efficient under the right circumstances.[4]

John Alexander Wiseman Strath 1916-2009 headed a team at Weapons Research Establishment in Salisbury, South Australia, which made fundamental contributions to our understanding of the ionosphere, to antenna design, frequency management and computing systems. He investigated the possibility of aircraft detection with "over the horizon radar" (OTHR), using radio reflections from the ionosphere – a layer enveloping the earth at a few hundred kilometres height. This made it possible to develop Jindalee, which could make observations of aircraft at great distances from our coast with great precision and by bouncing signals off the atmospheric layer known as the ionosphere, so they follow the Earth's curvature. That allows a far greater range than conventional line of sight radar.[1]

In 2010, Wing Commander Peter Davies identified the key role John Strath – the "Father of Jindalee" – played in researching the potential defence benefits of high frequency radar with the Defence Science and Technology Organisation. This included his role in leading the team that built Jindalee – the demonstrator technology for today's OTHR.[2]

Douglas Frew Waterhouse 1916-2000 was an entomologist who is best known for the invention of the active ingredient in *Aerogard*, an Australian insect repellent. The formula was also given to the company which makes *Mortein*, a household insecticide. He oversaw the Australian Dung Beetle Project (1965–1985) that saw the introduction of dung beetles to Australia as a fly control measure. While this was a risky decision because of the threat that the dung beetles could themselves become pests or disrupt the delicate ecological balance, it proved very successful and reduced the population of bush flies by 90%. All indications suggest that this has been one of the most valuable and cost-effective programs ever conducted in Australian agriculture.[1]

Waterhouse carried out pioneering studies on the sheep blowfly, a major pest. This work was interrupted by the Second World War where his attention turned to ways of protecting Allied troops from the mosquitoes responsible for malarial transmission. By 1943, the repellent – a product containing about 35% of either dimethyl phthalate or of diethyl phthalate – was widely deployed in the Pacific, and Waterhouse was considered a hero for his development of the repellent, referred to by the troops as "Mary".[2]

However, it took the visit of Queen Elizabeth II to Australia in 1963 for the repellent to become a household name. Although the Queen was meant to be sprayed with the repellent at a garden party held at Government House in Canberra, the aide responsible lost his nerve and the Queen was left madly swatting flies. The next day was a different story, when Government House staff made sure the Queen was liberally sprayed before heading off for a game of golf. Journalists following the Queen noted the absence of flies around the official party, and word about CSIRO's new fly-repellent spread. A few days later, the people at *Mortein* called Doug Waterhouse for his formula, which he passed on freely, as was CSIRO's policy at the time.[3]

Waterhouse played a leading role in establishing the Stored Grain Research Laboratory (SGRL), its research program and in selecting its staff. The Australian Wheat Board accepted, with some hesitation, Waterhouse's suggestion that the SGRL's research staff be recruited from outside the field of stored product entomology in order to encourage highly innovative approaches.

Since its inception, the SGRL has been an outstanding success, and has devised a number of effective ways of marketing insect-free grain that has never been treated with insecticides. On several occasions, its research (particularly that of Jim Des Marchelier) secured Australia's pre-eminence as a leading grain-exporting nation. Successful innovations from SGRL include: emergency bunker storage in good seasons; insect-free grain that has been fumigated without leaving residues (e.g. phosphine using the SIROFLO technology); inert dusts; sealed storage (to suffocate insects); storage under carbon dioxide (as a waste product from industry, e.g. aluminium smelting) and other inert gases; grain aeration (to lower temperature to a level at which insect reproduction ceases and then to a level at which development ceases); and fluidised bed heating (which can be used to provide rapid heat disinfestation of grain during loading on a ship). Outcomes of the research led to the extension of the useful life of many ageing and leaky bulk silos and positioned the industry for deregulation with the inevitable expansion of on-farm grain storage.[4]

Stanley Hay Umphray Bowie 1917-2008 made major contributions in isotope geology, fluid-inclusion studies, trace-element geochemistry (including high-resolution geochemical mapping), ore mineralogy, economic geology and analytical chemistry. He started work on autoradiography studies of uranium and thorium minerals in thin and polished sections and, in collaboration with the Atomic Energy Research Establishment at Harwell, he began a program of instrument development for uranium exploration that helped to develop Geiger-Muller counters for use in uranium exploration, borehole logging and aero-radiometric surveys. He also developed an index of radioactive minerals, which remained classified until 1976.

He developed, with Kenneth Taylor, a new system of opaque-mineral identification based on the measurement of indentation hardness and reflectance. Representing a major advance over the complex system of ore-mineral identification previously developed by Paul Ramdohr, the Bowie-Taylor system gave Britain an important lead in economic geology.

In 1970, he was appointed by NASA as a principal investigator for returned lunar samples. His work with Peter Simpson on the ore mineralogy of these samples, and with Clive Rice on the distribution of uranium using fission-track analysis, made an important contribution to understanding the lunar surface.[1] Bowie was a pioneer of geochemistry who established high quality geochemical mapping, researched radioactivity and radio-elements in the Earth's crust, and applied these studies to the exploration and development of mineral resources and to the improvement of human health.[2]

Thomas Robb Coughtrie 1917-2008 invented the Mole wrench (also known as self-grip, vise-grip, locking grip pliers) in 1955 when he was managing director of M.K. Mole and Son. The first locking pliers were invented in 1921 by a Danish immigrant to the USA, William Petersen. The Mole wrench, with its combined fixed and movable jaws, can be clamped with irresistible force on to an object of any width, shape or diameter, thanks to an easily adjustable bolt device in the handle. At the point where exertions with a normal spanner, or even adjustable spanner, would have to be suspended while the grip of the operator was rested, the Mole could continue to be deployed with impunity. When the job was over, it could be unclamped by a simple quick-release lever. Versions of the Mole wrench are still used in households all over the world more than half a century after Coughtrie patented it.[1]

James Tennant Dickson 1917-1991 was co-inventor of polyethylene terephthalate (PET) with John Rex Whinfield. Also known as *Dacron*, it is a thermoplastic polymer resin of the polyester family and is used in synthetic fibres; beverage, food and other liquid containers; thermoforming applications; and engineering resins often in combination with glass fibre.

Dickson and Whinfield, with C.G. Ritchie, also discovered *Terylene*. Dickson was working under Whinfield at the Calico Printers' Association research laboratory at Broad Oak Print Works in Accrington. He was put onto fibre research and, probably in April, but certainly by 5 July 1941, a murky-looking resin had been synthesised, out of which Dickson successfully drew a filament, which was named *Terylene* by its discoverers. Owing to restrictions imposed in Britain during the Second World War, this fibre was developed initially by the DuPont Company in the USA, where it was marketed under the name *Dacron*. When Imperial Chemical Industries (ICI) were able to manufacture it in Britain, it acquired the brand name *Terylene* and became very popular. The uses of *Terylene* are similar to those of nylon, but it has two advantages. First, it can be heat-set by exposing the fabric to a temperature about 30C higher than is likely to be encountered in everyday use, and therefore can be the basis for "easy-care" clothing such as drip-dry shirts. It can be blended with other fibres such as wool, and when pressed at a high temperature the creases are remarkably durable. It is also remarkably resistant to chemicals, which makes it particularly suitable for industrial purposes under conditions where other textile materials would be degraded rapidly.[1]

The discovery of *Terylene* could have been achieved earlier than 1941. Whinfield, had become increasingly interested in Wallace Carothers' work on synthetic fibres at DuPont (Carothers would eventually invent *Nylon*). In 1935, Whinfield urged Calico Printers' Association (for whom he worked) to likewise enter the field of synthetic fibres. Five years went by, however, before his advice was followed. When Whinfield, assisted by Dickson, was permitted by his employers to re-open the line of inquiry which Carothers had explored but then abandoned, he adopted a different approach from the American chemist. Whereas Carothers had worked with aliphatic acids, which have a long-chain molecular make-up, Whinfield chose one of the so-called aromatic acids, with a different structure including a benzene ring. This was terephthalic acid. As Whinfield suspected, the resulting molecular chain was closely packed and strong, and highly resistant to melting. Terephthalic acid was, however, notoriously difficult to react, being extremely impure. Dickson devised a way to purify it, however, and created a few grams of a polymer which had most of the properties of nylon as well as certain unique ones of its own. The new fibre was less affected by water than nylon and it could be crimped to give the feeling of a woollen yarn. It was also exceptionally resistant to wrinkling and could be heat-set in pleated skirts, which became one of the great early successes of *Terylene*. Unlike rayon or cellulose acetate, it was, moreover, highly resistant to sunlight through glass and made excellent curtains. Net curtaining became one the biggest markets for the new synthetic fibre. *Terylene* was undoubtedly the most influential of the inventions of that period in terms of post-war business for ICI.[2]

William Drummond MacDonald Paton 1917-1993 discovered that many familiar drugs cause the release of histamine (a powerful endogenous chemical mediator) from tissues in the body – an effect which can give rise to unwanted side-effects when such drugs are used clinically. The first effective treatment of high blood pressure, the facilitation of artificial respiration in an intensive care unit, and the exploitation of oil and gas from beneath the North Sea are mostly a result of Paton's research.

In 1949, with Eleanor Zaimis, Paton discovered two different actions of the chemical neurotransmitter acetylcholine that cause muscles to contract and that cause an increase in blood pressure (through activation of sympathetic ganglia), could be separated by means of two antagonist drugs that differed only in the number of carbon atoms in a linear chain. This was decamethonium, the first specific neuromuscular blocking drug and the father of all modern drugs used in surgery as muscle relaxants, and in intensive care to permit artificial ventilation. "The work of Paton and Zaimis on decamethonium iodide showed that it was a very potent substance, and that it was capable of replacing *d*-tubocurarine chloride in medicine. An antidote exists for decamethonium iodide in hexamethonium bromide, and owing to its pharmacological properties this substance has been suggested for use in hypertension and vascular diseases, thereby replacing tetraethylammonium iodide."[1] Hexamethonium was the first drug that specifically and safely lowered blood pressure.

The number of people who have directly benefited from drugs in these two classes must by now run into many millions, and yet the discovery was not driven by the need to develop such drugs, but by intellectual curiosity. Both classes of drug act on receptors for acetylcholine on cells, but, at the time they were discovered, the concept of the drug receptor was not universally accepted – Paton's work provided dramatic evidence of such specific sites where drugs act on cells. It was only with the advent of molecular biology in the 1970s that his concept of the two types of receptor, one in muscle and one in ganglia, was confirmed directly.[2]

During his time at the National Institute for Medical Research, Paton started to work on submarine physiology. Divers were limited to working at depths which did not exceed 200 feet (61 m), below sea level because of changes that happen in their bodies as they go deeper, usually resulting in the so-called "bends". It was thought that the convulsions were caused by the effects of oxygen and helium at high pressure, but Paton found that it was the high pressure itself. He and his colleague, E. Brian Smith, discovered that high pressure was in fact able to reverse the anaesthetic effect of gases. By a complex series of creative thought, this led to experiments on a mixture of oxygen, helium and nitrogen (Tri-mix) enabling divers to work at depths of around 2,000 feet (610 m), which has also enabled the oil industry to plumb the ocean depths for oil.[3]

Paton became interested in the phenomenon of drug dependence, and developed a very simple *in vitro* laboratory preparation, based on an isolated segment of guinea-pig intestine, stimulated to contract by electrical pulses, which allowed many of the phenomena of opiate dependence to be reproduced and analysed in the laboratory. He also devised a new theoretical approach, known as the rate theory of drug action, published in 1961, which explained the way in which drug molecules, acting on specific receptors, can produce a range of stimulant or antagonistic effects, depending on the kinetics of the reaction between the drug and its receptors. Though this theory eventually proved incorrect, it was influential in kindling interest in the molecular mechanisms involved in drug-receptor interactions – a topic which became one of the major themes of pharmacological research from 1970 onwards.[4]

Paton and colleagues discovered that compound 48/80, a phenylethylamine condensation product discovered accidentally as a contaminant in the synthesis of isoquinolines, was a particularly powerful histamine releaser, and this compound is still used as a standard in tests for histamine release.[5]

Paton investigated the actions of morphine, a substance used clinically as a powerful analgesic agent. At this time, although the actions of morphine in animals and humans had been documented in great detail, very little was known about its actions on cells and tissues. Paton found that low concentrations of morphine strongly inhibited the contraction of the tissue produced by electrical stimulation, without affecting the inherent contractility of the smooth muscle, implying that it could inhibit the release of acetylcholine from the nerve plexus. Moreover, if the preparation was exposed continuously to morphine for an hour or more, the contraction tended to return, and when the morphine was washed away, the muscle went into a state of hyperactivity and spasm, events which paralleled the phenomena of morphine tolerance and dependence that were well known clinically. This was the first time that morphine dependence had been observed "in the test-tube", and these studies paved the way for much more detailed analysis of the mechanisms underlying morphine action and morphine dependence. The coaxially stimulated ileum preparation was later taken up and adapted to other tissues by Hans Walter Kosterlitz and his colleagues in Aberdeen, whose studies led to an important re-classification of opiate receptors. The realisation that many of the effects of morphine are attributable to inhibition of neurotransmitter release in the central nervous system stems from Paton's original observations on the guinea-pig ileum.[6]

Michael James Steuart Dewar 1918-1997 was one of the first, if not the first, organic chemists to master molecular orbital theory and to apply it to problems in organic chemistry. His sparkling intellect and theoretical insight introduced many of the fundamental concepts that are now taken for granted, and his ceaseless efforts over four decades produced the semi-empirical methods of computation that are still used the world over.[1]

He wrote his first influential book, *The Electronic Theory of Organic Chemistry* (1949), which represented a landmark, as it was the first treatment of organic chemistry in terms of molecular orbital theory. In 1945, he deduced the correct structure for stipitatic acid, a mould product whose structure had baffled the leading chemists of the day. It involved a new kind of aromatic structure with a seven-membered ring for which Dewar coined the term "tropolone". He then correctly suggested that a similar structure would account for the properties of another problem compound, the alkaloid colchicine. The discovery of the tropolone structure launched the field of non-benzenoid aromaticity, which witnessed feverish activity for several decades and greatly expanded the chemists' understanding of cyclic π-electron systems.

Also in 1945, Dewar devised the then novel notion of a π complex, which he proposed as an intermediate in the benzidine rearrangement. This notion turned out to be extraordinarily fruitful, as it also automatically accounted for the ease of 1, 2-shifts in carbocations, as opposed to radicals and carbanions. It also provided a simple explanation for the structure of "non-classical" carbenium ions for which Saul Winstein was starting to provide experimental evidence at the time, and offered the first correct rationalisation of the electronic structure of complexes of transition metals with olefins, later known as the Dewar-Chatt-Duncanson model.

While at Courtaulds, he measured the first absolute rate constants in a vinyl polymerisation and in an autoxidation, and performed an array of other kinetic and mechanistic studies, coming close to describing the modern concept of photoinduced electron transfer. In this period, Dewar developed the key ideas discussed in T*he Electronic Theory of Organic Chemistry* at nights and on weekends. When this revolutionary book was published, it was the start of the conversion of organic chemists to a new creed. By 1951, Dewar had succeeded in formulating the molecular orbital theory of organic chemistry in a semi-quantitative form, later termed "perturbational molecular orbital theory". This approach was clearly superior to the purely qualitative resonance theory then still in use, but the papers were written in such a condensed manner that the theory was virtually incomprehensible to practicing bench chemists, the intended users.

He elucidated the electronic structure of phosphononitrile chlorides and started a long series of experimental studies of new stable heterocycles, the borazaromatic compounds. He performed the first studies of self-assembled monolayers of thiols on a metal surface, a field that has grown immensely in popularity in recent years. He started a series of investigations of the structure and properties of liquid crystals and developed a novel analysis of substituent effects in aromatic and aliphatic compounds, showing that the classical inductive effect is insignificant. He built an electron paramagnetic resonance spectrometer for use in his research when this kind of spectroscopy was just beginning to be recognised as useful for chemistry applications.[2]

Quentin Howieson Gibson 1918-2011 is best known for his pioneering work on the kinetics of ligand binding to haemoglobins and the development of stopped-flow and flash photolysis instruments.[1]

He discovered methemoglobinemia after studying properties of haemoglobin, the molecule that carries oxygen. It has four globular protein subunits with a heme group. He discovered that in certain people, the haemoglobin molecules could not carry oxygen. This condition was eventually known as Gibson's Syndrome, or methemoglobinemia.[2]

He began close collaborations with Francis John Worsley Roughton who, in 1923, built the first rapid mixing device with Hamilton Hartridge to examine the rates of O_2 and CO binding to haemoglobin and red cells. Gibson, who was a skilled machinist, designed and built a stopped-flow, rapid mixing spectrometer and a flash photolysis apparatus to re-examine these reactions and, with Roughton, showed for the first time that the major increase in iron reactivity during cooperative ligand binding does not occur until roughly three ligands have been bound. Gibson and his colleagues then used these instruments to examine a variety of enzymatic and globin reactions. The stopped-flow spectrometer was commercialised by Durrum (later Dionex) Instruments, Inc. and sold as the "Durrum-Gibson" instrument until approximately 1990.[3]

John Michael Hammersley 1920-2004 was one of the outstanding problem-solvers of 20th century mathematics. He formulated many problems of significance for theoretical and applied science, and made remarkable progress towards their solutions. His work covered percolation theory, subadditive stochastic processes, self-avoiding walks, and Monte Carlo methods.[1] He is famous worldwide as the founder of the mathematical theory of percolation. With David Handscomb, Hammersley developed the basic theory and published the standard work. Their book *Monte Carlo Methods* (1964) – a technique to estimate a quantity through computations involving random numbers – remained for many years the only work available to practitioners, and the techniques therein are used currently in banks and elsewhere throughout the world.[2]

His work on self-avoiding walks and percolation is fundamental to the theory of stochastic Loewner evolutions that is now causing a re-think of the relationship between probability and conformal field theory; his results on the Ulam problem underlie the proof that the relevant weak limit is the Tracy-Widom distribution.[3] Note: a self-avoiding walk is a sequence of moves on a lattice that does not visit the same point more than once. In physics, the Fermi–Pasta–Ulam problem was the apparent paradox in chaos theory that many sufficiently complicated physical systems exhibited almost exactly periodic behaviour.

Lionel Alexander Bethune Pilkington 1920-1995 invented the float glass process for making sheet glass, the greatest technological innovation in glass production in the 20th century. He conceived the idea that molten glass could be formed into a continuous ribbon by pouring it into a bath of tin and "floating" it while it cooled. In this way, neither surface would be marked by the rollers of the plate glass process or the glass distorted by the vertical pull of the sheet glass process. "In 1949, at the Doncaster works, he began a long series of experiments on the interaction of molten glass and tin at high temperatures. The critical success was achieved at St Helens in 1952, when his team first floated a continuous ribbon of molten glass on a bed of molten tin. Tin melted at a temperature less than the hardening point of glass (about 600C), which meant that the surface of the bed was completely flat. If the glass was sufficiently hot it flowed over the tin bed until its surface was also perfectly flat. When the glass had cooled to below 600C it was too hard to mark and could be removed on rollers. Previously the only feasible method of producing flat glass had involved feeding molten glass between rollers, which inevitably left marks on both sides. The necessary grinding and polishing was expensive and consumed about 20% of the glass. Float glass became the standard method for producing high-quality flat glass, both plate and sheet."[1]

"Float is so good that since 1959 it has supplanted all other techniques for forming flat glass. Alastair Pilkington played a leading part in licensing his invention throughout the world. The process has been licensed to 42 manufacturers in 30 countries with more than 170 plants in operation, under construction or planned."[2]

William Morris Russell 1920-2006 designed the world's first automatic coffee percolator in 1952. The coffee was kept hot after it had dripped through by means of a temperature control similar to that on a thermostatic iron, allowing the machine to turn itself off. There was also a device for controlling the strength of the coffee. The coffee percolator was followed by an automatic tea maker, which was switched on by an alarm clock.

Image 104 – A CP1 coffee percolator

With the introduction of electricity at the turn of the 20th century there was naturally a desire to use it to heat water. Initial designs included a plate-shaped heater joined to the underside of a standard design. Later it became usual to have a heating element immersed directly in the water. Recent designs have reverted to the element being underneath again. The most significant development was that of the Russell Hobbs K1 kettle in 1955. On boiling, switching off the power is effected by a vapour controlled thermostat. The copper body is pressed from a circle of copper made to very strict requirements for surface finish, hardness and grain size so that there is no need for an interstage anneal.

The automatic electric kettle K1 (a world first), designed in October 1955, used a bi-metallic strip at the rear of the kettle. Steam was forced through an aperture in the lid of the strip and this knocked the switch, turning the kettle off. In 1960, the K2 kettle was introduced, which was manufactured for the next thirty years, and was possibly its best-known product. Russell also designed the world's first fully programmable kettle, the M2.[1]

Russell was in charge of product development and Hobbs was the sales director. Russell's *de facto* ultimate safety test for any new product was to pour half a pint of boiling gravy on it. The company was always in profit from day one. In the late 1960s, it was chiefly manufacturing automatic electric coffee pots, vapour-controlled electric kettles, and tea makers. Regarded as a classic of British design, the K2 kettle is displayed in the Design Museum, in London, while the CPI coffee percolator and the K1 kettle are on show in the Science Museum.[2]

David Cumming Simpson 1920-2006 was one of the worldwide pioneers of orthopaedic bioengineering – the application of engineering methods and principles to problems in orthopaedic medicine. At the Department of Surgery at Edinburgh University from the early 1950s, Simpson designed monitoring equipment to support the transplant surgery work of the Royal Infirmary of Edinburgh and the Western General Hospital, including a multi-channel recorder for monitoring the condition of patients in the operating theatre and the first successful foetal heart monitors in 1959, for clinical use at the Simpson Memorial Maternity Hospital in Edinburgh, and the first UK system of patient monitoring equipment in 1961, for the Surgical Neurology Department at the Royal Infirmary.[1]

In 1945, while serving in the Highland Light Infantry at the very end of the war, he was wounded by shell shrapnel which entered his neck and left through his shoulder, injuring his lung and causing severe nerve damage to his right arm and shoulder. Sent back to Edinburgh, he was immensely fortunate to have the intense interest of Sir James Learmonth, at that time the leading authority on peripheral nerve injuries. Learmonth himself carried out a series of operations over successive years to restore to Simpson the use of his arm, although he had to teach himself to write left-handed. Simpson always attributed any insights into the design of prosthetic limbs to the three and a half years he spent as a virtual unilateral amputee.

Since the early 1950s, Ernst Marquardt in Heidelberg had been building and fitting pneumatic carbon dioxide-powered limbs to adults. Simpson went over and observed them and on 4 May 1963, Scottish-powered prosthetics and Edinburgh's bioengineering centre was born. Simpson and his co-workers at the then Powered Prosthetic Unit in Edinburgh began to design and fit a series of gas-powered limbs, the legacy of which resonates still.

One such prosthetic device enabled the user to place a spoon in a hook at the end of the powered arm and to take up food, which remained on the spoon until it reached the child's mouth. He was thrilled when a thalidomide child, only one morning after it was introduced to her, started using it.[2]

From a technical perspective, Simpson achieved much in the next 17 years, but in particular he is known in bioengineering for two things. First, his Edinburgh powered-arm prostheses, the bionic limbs of their day, were fitted to over 60 children from Scotland and Northern Ireland, most of whom had bilateral upper limb absence. Simpson's first arm was for when the children were 2-3 years of age, and had an elbow, wrist and hand/hook function. In later years, the arm grew another two functions at the shoulder to give an impressive five functions. Electrical-powered devices did not supersede the functionality of this carbon dioxide device until 30 years later, vindicating Simpson's choice of carbon dioxide as the correct solution for its time.

Second, and perhaps as important, he had reasoned that power without control was largely useless, and if multifunctional limb prostheses were to prosper, then the users needed to be able to control them. In the early days, the perceived wisdom was to have the user operate small gas control valves mounted in the steel harness/girdles worn to support the prostheses. The control valve levers were positioned adjacent to the residual body movements available, and the children operated the limbs by pressing the valves in an open loop time-velocity relationship. Simpson and his team were disappointed to note that despite the lightweight and elegant nature of their prostheses, the children struggled to co-ordinate the movements.

Simpson observed that control was not intuitively learnt, with more than one degree of freedom being difficult to operate in a parallel mode. In typical fashion, Simpson went back to basics and analysed the problem from its root, beginning with a clever analysis of arm movement and choosing an appropriate polar co-ordinate scheme. The result was the simple yet ingenious decision to move the control valve to the actuator itself. This was linked to the user's residual movement via a flexible cable that served as a feedback mechanism in a closed-loop control servomechanism. Simpson had realised that if the output and input of the control loop that linked the user's movement to that of the prosthesis could be linked in a one-to-one unambiguous relationship, then the result would be a position force servo system, which in effect transferred the proprioception of the intact input movement to the movement of the output. He called this extended physiological proprioception (EPP). This property is present in all of us when we swing a golf club, cricket bat or tennis racket, and it acts in a perfectly controlled manner as an extension of ourselves. The results were immediate, with children learning to control three and more movements in an afternoon. In fact, Simpson liked to show off the technique by having the children mark lines on a blackboard with a chalk held in their toes and then repeat the act (unsighted) using the prosthesis. This marked out the Edinburgh work from that of other centres, which often produced similarly actuated prostheses, but lacking the physiologically accurate control of EPP.

He co-designed the Simpson-Edinburgh Low Pressure Airbed and helped prevent pressure sores by supporting the body over a maximum surface area and regulating the pressure to that which kept the capillaries open. The air bed prevented the patient from bottoming out, while the adjustable pressure control ensured that the bed was not overinflated for the patient's weight.[3] Typically, Simpson contrived this from two camping mattresses, an aquarium pump and, as pressure regulator, an old-fashioned confectionery glass jar. Following government sponsored trials of 64 such airbeds to prove clinical effectiveness, the airbed went into commercial production. Much to Simpson's chagrin, it had been refined at this point and the confectionery jar had been replaced, but over the next 20 or so years hundreds of these airbeds were sold and maintained throughout the UK and enhanced the quality of life of users and carers alike. Another of his bio-engineered appliances was an IBM electronic typewriter adapted to operate with a switch activated by a shoulder shrug in 1970. [4]

William Brass 1921-1999 set up the Centre for Overseas Population Studies, which he directed until 1978 which later became the Centre for Population Studies, with Brass as its director until his retirement in 1988. Brass invented a new technique for demography: the "indirect" or "Brass" methods of demographic estimation. Much of what we know about the populations of the developing world stems from the battery of methods that he devised.[1]

With creative mathematical imagination and profound understanding of how populations worked, Brass realised that accurate estimates of mortality, the numbers of births, the spacing of children, and their trends could be derived from information which had little direct relationship to the desired measure. Thus, conventional measures of fertility, normally derived from expensive registration systems in conjunction with censuses, could instead be derived from answers to simple questions in censuses and surveys about the number and survival of children, spouses, and parents. "Such was the importance of his contribution to this field that the techniques were often described as 'Brass methods'. ... But the importance of his work is reflected in the fact that the figures, published regularly by the United Nations and other bodies, of the numbers of people living on this planet have been compiled largely with the help of the methods which he devised."[2]

They included such innovations as the estimation of infant and child mortality from the proportions of children lost to women of given ages. Brass, tending to assume that data were guilty until proven innocent, showed how survey questions on births (suspected of bias) could yield accurate estimates of past fertility. His elegant and parsimonious "model life table" methods employ the regularities in human mortality patterns to convert fragmentary data on deaths into scientifically usable statistics on lifetime risks of dying. Further innovations provided mortality estimates for adults from the proportions of their children who were orphans.[3]

William Piper Brown 1921-2004 had emigrated from Scotland to Australia as a child and in the early 1950s joined EPM Concrete as Chief Engineer where he was responsible for the implementation of a program for the mass production of pre-cast, pre-stressed, concrete flat panels and I-section members for industrial floor systems. In 1953, he established the firm High Strength Concrete Pty Ltd, which specialised in the production of pre-stressed concrete products. This was pioneering work in Australia at that time and was highly successful in providing bridge units for the Country Roads Board and the State Rivers and Water Supply Commission, as well as other commercial enterprises.

His next major engineering career move was to establish the consulting engineering practice of W.P. Brown Consulting Engineer, and he continued to work closely with government departments and entered into a close association with the Victorian State Housing Commission in the development of low cost housing. He advised on the introduction of pre-cast concrete panels for the walls and floors of single and multi storey accommodation units and developed highly successful production and assembly processes. This was very advanced technology for the time and he validated his ideas by comprehensive full scale testing in association with the University of Melbourne. This work is still regarded as an outstanding example of practical research and development and there are many buildings in Melbourne which are readily recognisable as his work.[1]

Keith Dalziel 1921-1994 developed general rules for analysing any two-substrate reaction, and he published these in a seminal paper which appeared in 1957. This work was quickly recognised as being of a fundamental nature in helping our understanding of enzyme reactions, and in predicting the kinetic behaviour of enzymes.[1]

With P.C. Engel and others, Keith undertook an extensive study of the very complex reactions of glutamate dehydrogenase. In seven original papers and four meeting contributions, he provided a clear picture of the different interactions of this enzyme. With two other students, he undertook a detailed investigation of the enzyme6-phosphogluconate dehydrogenase, starting with the purification and crystallisation of the enzyme. Keith regarded the discovery that CO_2, rather than carbonate, is the substrate/product that was the most important finding of this investigation. "Keith was beyond any doubt one of the leading enzymologists of his generation".[2]

Leslie Alexander Geddes 1921-2009 was an electrical engineer and physiologist who conducted research in electromyography, cardiac output, cardiac pacing, ventricular defibrillation, and blood pressure. He discovered and demonstrated precisely the optimal sites on the chest for defibrillation or pacing. He was presented the 2006 National Medal of Technology by President George W. Bush. The citation read: "For his contributions to electrode design and tissue restoration, which have led to the widespread use of a wide variety of clinical devices. His discoveries and inventions have saved and enriched thousands of lives and have formed the cornerstone of much of the modern implantable medical device field."[1]

Many of Geddes' innovations at Baylor University Medical College in Houston, Texas, used electrodes to monitor the human body. For example, he developed the first clinical electromyograph for diagnosing nerve damage. Geddes also invented a respiratory monitoring system for NASA, which was later modified to detect apnea in newborns. Geddes even modernised Baylor's medical pedagogy: he used his "Physiograph" recording device to introduce medical students to cardiology.

In 1982, Geddes and two colleagues patented a device that detects and corrects potentially lethal cardiac arrhythmia. In 1984, Geddes and another team patented a conductivity catheter that measures cardiac output; and in 1986, Geddes co-patented a pocket-sized, personal electrocardiograph. Geddes also won many patents for improvements to the cardiac pacemaker, including the first model to increase its pace automatically when its wearer exercises.

Geddes and yet another team earned three patents in the 1990s for a new biomaterial – small intestine submucosa – which, when grafted onto tissue in need of repair, completely remodels itself to mimic that tissue – be it a blood vessel, tendon, or stomach lining – without provoking an immune response. In total, Geddes has earned over thirty patents for both esoteric and everyday inventions: e.g., a baby pacifier that can deliver medication (1994).

Geddes is no less celebrated for his innovations in medical therapy and theory. He developed "electroventilation", a safer technique of artificial respiration by electrical stimulation of the nerves of the chest and diaphragm. With three colleagues, he propounded the "three laws of defibrillation", which have saved countless patients from myocardial damage. Geddes is estimated to have taught over 2,000 biomedical engineers – about one fifth of those now working in the US.[2]

Alick Isaacs 1921-1967 co-discovered and named interferon in 1957 with his Swiss colleague, Jean Lindenmann. Interferon was an entirely new defence mechanism against viruses. Also in 1957, Isaacs demonstrated that antibiotics act only against bacteria – not against viruses.

Interferon was the first cytokine to be discovered (cytokines are cell signalling molecules that aid cell-to-cell communication in immune responses and stimulate the movement of cells towards sites of inflammation, infection and trauma). There are a number of substances known as cytokines that are secreted by specific cells of the immune system which carry signals locally between cells, and thus have an effect on other cells. There are three basic types, all of which prevent the spread of viral infections and the growth of tumour cells. In addition, one type alters the way the body's immune system responds to infection. Isaacs – director of the World Influenza Centre in London – and Lindenmann injected a small amount of flu virus into chicken embryos. The eggs responded by producing a protein, interferon, that seemed to cling to virus particles and inhibit their replication process. During their investigation, the two scientists found that virus-infected cells secrete a special protein that causes both infected and noninfected cells to produce other proteins that prevent viruses from replicating. They named the protein interferon because it "interferes" with infection. Initially, scientists thought there was only one interferon protein, but subsequent research showed that there are many different interferon proteins.[1]

Interferons can be divided into two main types. Type I (alpha, beta, tau, and omega) interferons are more effective at bolstering cells' ability to resist infection. Type II (gamma) interferon is more important to the normal functioning of the immune system. Alpha interferon may be used to treat some cancers; interferon beta 1b has been found useful in the treatment of multiple sclerosis.

While aiming to develop an improved vaccine for smallpox, two Japanese virologists, Yasuichi Nagano and Yasuhiko Kojima working at the Institute for Infectious Disease at the University of Tokyo, noticed that rabbit skin or testes previously inoculated with UV-inactivated virus exhibited inhibition of viral growth when re-infected at the same site with live virus. They hypothesised that this was due to some "facteur inhibiteur" (inhibitory factor), and began to characterise it by fractionation of the UV-irradiated viral homogenates using an ultracentrifuge. They published these findings in 1954 in the French journal now known as *Journal de la Société de Biologie*. While this paper demonstrated that the activity could be separated from the virus particles, it could not reconcile the antiviral activity demonstrated in the rabbit skin experiments with the observation that the same supernatant led to the production of antiviral antibodies in mice. A further paper in 1958, involving triple-ultracentrifugation of the homogenate demonstrated that the inhibitory factor was distinct from the virus particles, leading to trace contamination being ascribed to the 1954 observations.[2]

In 1947, Isaacs began studying different strains of the influenza virus and the body's response to them. Working with Lindenmann, he eventually found that when a virus invades a cell, the cell produces interferon, which then induces uninfected cells to make a protein that prevents the virus from multiplying. Almost any cell in the body can make interferon, which seems to act as the first line of defence against viral pathogens, because it is produced very quickly and is thought to trigger other defence mechanisms.[3]

Further research showed that interferon was produced within hours of a viral invasion (antibodies take several days to form), and that most living things, including plants, can make the protective protein. As interferon was seen as the cell's first line of defence against viral infections, its discovery was expected to pave the way for successful treatment of viral diseases.[4]

Later experimental evidence pointed also to the potential effectiveness of interferon against malignancies. Interferon and interferon-inducers have been found to alter the course of solid tumours, leukaemia, sarcomas and lymphomas in experimental animals, possibly by stimulating the reticuloendothelial system to produce tumour rejection or by altering the surface of cells to change tumour and host reactions.[5]

Since interferons enhance the immune system in many ways, they are used for many diseases that involve the immune system, including: hairy cell leukemia, AIDS-related Kaposi's sarcoma, chronic myelogenous leukemia, malignant melanoma, condylomata acuminata, chronic hepatitis B, chronic hepatitis C, multiple sclerosis, genital and perianal warts caused by human papillomavirus (HPV), chronic granulomatous disease, and severe, malignant osteopetrosis. [6]

Patrick Joseph Lawther 1921-2008 was a driving force and catalyst for the United Kingdom's *Clean Air Act* of 1956, which was prompted by the great death toll (over 4,000) in the London smog of December 1952. In 1955, the Medical Research Council established the MRC Group for Research on Atmospheric Pollution and made Lawther its director.

Lawther's research showed an association between smoke levels and patients' symptoms of bronchitis, laying the groundwork for the UK Clean Air Acts of 1956 and 1968, as well as the first guidelines on air quality from WHO and air pollution regulations in the USA. Lawther was one of the first people to stress the long-term effects of carbon monoxide and particles, says Maynard. Since Lawther's work, research has linked long-term exposure to particles to heart disease. Throughout his career, Lawther collaborated with Robert Waller to characterise the composition of air pollution as well as its respiratory effects. In one study, they gave diaries to patients with emphysema and bronchitis and asked them to record how they felt each day: better, worse, much worse, or the same as the previous day. They measured the concentration of smoke and sulphur dioxide in the air on each day as well and reported a close association between high concentrations of pollution and poor health of the patients. It was "one of the most elegant experiments done in the air pollution field", says Maynard.

In the years after the Clean Air Acts, smoke slowly disappeared from London, but other pollutants remained. Lawther and his colleagues gassed themselves with sulphur dioxide to determine its effect on respiration and defined a dose-response curve and tolerable level for the gas.[1]

Robert Lewis Fullarton Boyd 1922-2004 pioneered British space science and played an instrumental role in the founding of the European Space Research Organisation and its subsequent incarnation, the European Space Agency (1974/1975). Boyd succeeded Harrie Massey as the chair of the British National Committee for Space Research in 1976. The first international collaborative science mission of the space age, Ariel I, was designed to study the ionosphere, solar X-rays and high-energy cosmic-ray particles. UK/US collaboration in this ground-breaking project established an enduring relationship with NASA that led to many future UK involvements in NASA spacecraft. Boyd and his colleagues played the major part in this hugely successful mission that thus paved the way for a substantial expansion of the British space science effort.

Boyd established the College's Mullard Space Science Laboratory (MSSL) at Holmbury St Mary in Surrey and became its first Director. The laboratory subsequently became a world-leading centre for the space sciences. Under Boyd's leadership, MSSL instruments were launched on orbiting spacecraft at an average rate of one each year. He also initiated a program of Earth studies from space that has grown to become a leading activity in the study of Earth's climate evolution. His role in an early version of the European Space Agency's science advisory structure was crucial in setting the course of the ESA scientific program, which has since become a major European success.[1]

Hugh John Forster Cairns born 1922 succeeded in carrying out genetic mapping of an animal virus for the first time (1959). Among his accomplishments was the discovery, in 1952, that the influenza virus is released from an infected cell in a slow trickle. In contrast, a bacteriophage – a virus that attacks bacteria – is released from an infected cell in a burst. Comparing the rates of replication of DNA in mammals with those in the bacterium *Escherichia coli*, he found that mammalian DNA is replicated more slowly than that of *Escherichia coli*, but is replicated simultaneously at many points. Cairns' later work studied the link between DNA and cancer, some forms of which may be caused by the alkylation of bases in the DNA. He showed that bacteria are able to inhibit the alkylation mechanism in their own cells, and later demonstrated this ability in mammalian cells.[1]

William Cochran 1922-2003 realised that isomorphous replacement was the key to solving protein structures. With Francis Crick, he invented methods for deducing helical patterns from crystallographic data, which ultimately led to the solution of the structure of DNA.

Cochran was part of a team in Cambridge which did much to lay the foundations of modern crystallography. He undertook much pioneering work which underpinned the Nobel prizes won by others: in direct methods in crystallography (Karle and Hauptman); he advised Francis Crick on X-ray crystallography which led to the discovery of the structure of DNA; and assisted Bertram Brockhouse by developing a new model for crystal dynamics while on a sabbatical year in Canada.[1]

Cochran also worked on so-called "direct methods" for determining the arrangement of atoms in crystal structures and on the interpretation of the way atoms vibrate in solids. He was responsible for advances in the theoretical understanding of the way crystalline solids transform from one structure to another at structural phase transitions.[2]

He developed a Geiger-counter diffractometer for the precise measurement of X-ray intensities and with its aid, he showed that an (F_o-F_o) synthesis could accurately detect hydrogen atoms and even excess electron density within covalent bonds.[3]

The work done by Cochran at Penn State arose from his conversations with David Sayre. Three papers, produced by Sayre, Cochran and William Houlder Zachariasen respectively, that appeared in *Acta Crystallographica* in 1952, provided the foundation of modern direct methods that were to have a profound effect on structural crystallography.[4]

His research at Cambridge was in three distinct areas, although all within crystallography. The first was to make accurate electron-density measurements to study hydrogen bonding and covalent bonds. The second was on structural studies of molecules of biochemical interest, and the third area was that of the phase problem. EDSAC, an early and rather primitive digital computer, was available in Cambridge, and Cochran struck up a fruitful collaboration with Sandy Douglas, who knew how best to use EDSAC. Together they produced a program for using sign relationships to give automatic solutions of the phase problem in two dimensions. This was the first program of its kind and the forerunner of more powerful programs that eventually were to revolutionise structural crystallography.

Donald Murdo McCallum 1922-2011 designed a "supersonic airspeed indicator", one of many aircraft innovations he would be involved with. His influence would later be apparent in warplanes including the *Lightning*, *Buccaneer*, *Harrier* and *Tornado*, as well as during the flight trials of *Concorde*. McCallum, jointly with colleagues since he preferred to work as a team, held numerous patents relating to flight control and navigation systems.

In 1982, when he had already been Ferranti Scotland's general manager for 14 years, he oversaw the development of the Seaspray radar system for Skua missiles on board British Lynx helicopters. Although it had barely been through its trials and had not formally been accepted into service, the system proved extremely effective, as did the Ferranti Laser Target Marker to "light up" targets for laser-guided bombs.[1]

Ian Alexander McGregor 1922-2007 provided the first reliable experimental data showing that humans repeatedly exposed to malaria infection could develop an immunity that was capable of restricting clinical illness and the density of parasites in the blood. Since this acquired immunity could be transferred by antibodies from immune serum, vaccination against malaria was at least theoretically possible. Subsequent experiments demonstrated that adult Gambian serum had the same therapeutic effect when used in children from Tanzania who had *Plasmodium falciparum* malaria, suggesting that west and east African strains of the malaria parasite had common features and that a vaccine against parasites from one region of Africa might be effective in protecting against parasites from other regions.[1]

His scientific contributions centred on his detailed epidemiological, clinical and immunological studies. He demonstrated the interactions between malnutrition and disease, and described how parasitic diseases can initiate a downward cycle where infections deplete the body's nutrient reserves, which in turn impairs the host's resistance, allowing further invasion by other infections and an exacerbation of the malnutrition.

His early papers documented the fact that in the 1950s barely more than half the children born in Keneba in Gambia survived to their fifth birthday. He would relate vividly the horrors of a measles outbreak in 1961 that killed a quarter of the children – measles, now eradicated from Keneba, was a devastating disease for malnourished children.

McGregor demonstrated that with repeated exposure to malaria each rainy season, children built up an immunoglobulin-based resistance that decreased parasite intensity and the risk of severe disease. He showed that such immunity was transferable and that it required repeated exposure to parasites to maintain its protection. This began his interest in acquired immunity, leading to major contributions to our understanding. He was the first to show that in pregnancy, the uterus and placenta start off immunologically naïve to malaria, but that these organs, too, develop resistance.

He published widely on how resistance to malaria was influenced by other host factors such as blood group, and genetic variants in haemoglobin, in the heme-sequestering protein haptoglobin, and the enzyme glucose-6-phosphate dehydrogenase. These discoveries laid a solid foundation for our understanding of acquired immunity.[2]

In collaboration with Sidney Cohen, he showed that infusions of serum from adults deemed clinically immune from malaria could protect children from the disease. Brian Greenwood, a professor at the London School of Hygiene and Tropical Medicine, says McGregor's work provided the first indication that it would be possible to develop a malaria vaccine: "Before this study was done, it was known that after repeated exposure to malaria, adults developed some protection against severe forms of the infection but this study showed for the first time that this was mediated, at least in part, by something present in serum, almost certainly antibodies." According to Greenwood, McGregor's greatest contribution was showing the value of painstaking longitudinal studies to tease out the contributions of factors, including climate, nutrition, and infection, to overall health. He believes that McGregor's work in "establishing a site at Keneba where this kind of study could be done was highly innovative and has provided a rich reward in many areas of health that affect African children. This would not have been possible without his foresight."[3]

Many other important contributions followed. McGregor's work at the MRC Laboratories, Gambia, on malaria immunology and epidemiology underpinned the global effort to combat malaria. The quest for an effective vaccine, essentially triggered by McGregor's passive transfer of immune serum, continued at his death. His nutritional studies from Keneba provided demographic and health data that was also still being used by researchers at the time of his death.[4]

John Paul 1922-1994 was one of the first scientists to realise that culture of human and mammalian cells in the laboratory would become a key factor in research into the biology of normal and cancerous cells. He wrote what for many years was the most authoritative textbook on the subject. He was a pioneer, and many people went to him to learn the new techniques and with his help adapted them to their special requirements in cancer research haematology, human genetics, and embryo research.[1]

The rapid and dramatic transformation of the small Research Department of the Glasgow Cancer Hospital to the modern Beatson Institute, with several scientific teams of international repute, is almost entirely due to John Paul.

He also recognised the importance of understanding how genes regulate the synthesis of proteins and, with his colleagues, was the first to demonstrate tissue-specific differences. During his most productive years, his publications were among the 1,000 most-cited scientific papers in the world.[2]

Alexander Mair Smith 1922-2003 was an engineer for Rolls Royce who was responsible for the design of the famous RB211 aircraft engine. He undertook research on new structural materials, on plasmas and high-speed gas dynamics, and on air-lubricated bearings. In 1965, his laboratory set up a facility to produce carbon fibre laminate on a large scale for use in fan blades of the Rolls-Royce RB211 aero engine, of which large-scale production began in 1967. Originally developed for the Lockheed L-1011 (TriStar), it entered service in 1972 and was the only engine to power this aircraft type. Although the costs of development forced Rolls-Royce Limited into bankruptcy and nationalisation by the British government, the company survived and the RB211 became the first true three-spool engine (turbofan engines that have low, intermediate and high pressure compressors running independently on separate shafts), which also turned Rolls-Royce from a small player in the airline industry into a global competitor.[1]

James Arnot Hamilton 1923-2012 designed the wings for the *Concorde* supersonic jet. Earlier, in 1964, he had been appointed Director of Anglo-French Military Aircraft for the Ministry of Aviation where he was project director for the *Jaguar* and *Tornado* aircraft.[1] Between 1966 and 1970, he was the first Director-General of the Anglo-French *Concorde* project at the Ministry of Technology, where his huge experience in wing design culminated in the distinctive shape of the wings of the supersonic airliner.[2] Specifically, Hamilton designed the revolutionary wings of the *Concorde*.

"On a traditional wing there can be well over 50 moveable parts to control and trim the aircraft and complex flaps and leading edge slats to generate extra lift at slower speeds. *Concorde* has none of this. The *Concorde* delta wing only has 6 trailing edge 'elevons' to control the pitch and roll of the aircraft. As flying speeds have increased, more 'sweepback' has been seen in wing designs. The slender delta wing on *Concorde* takes this a step further. Looked at head-on, the *Concorde* wing does not just sweep back by 55 degrees; it twists and droops, apparently simple yet very complex in reality. This design gave *Concorde* lift at low speeds by increasing the angle of attack of the wing. And it gives efficiency at high speeds during the supersonic cruise where the delta wing's long chord, narrow profile and short span generates very little drag. On a traditional aircraft wing a swirling vortex forms only at the wing tips. On a delta wing at low speeds and a high angle of attack, the vortex forms along the entire wing surface, giving the lift required for reliable takeoff and landing. Over 5,000 hours of wind-tunnel testing were carried out to modify camber, droop and twist, to ensure the wing surface vortex would be a stable and dependable source of lift. As the delta wing gets closer to the ground, the downwash of air creates a cushion and landing is made very smooth even though the plane descends at much higher speed."[3]

Donald Michie 1923-2007 became one of the leading pioneers of Artificial Intelligence. His work in machine learning was particularly visionary in its relation to the automatic synthesis of new knowledge. During World War II, Michie worked at Bletchley Park, contributing to the effort to solve "Tunny", a German teleprinter cipher. Predictive text on mobile phones, realistic characters in video games and efficient call-centre systems all rely on the fundamental research done by Professor Donald Michie and his colleagues during his long and distinguished career at Edinburgh and Strathclyde universities. Michie also made a significant contribution to the wartime codebreaking work done at Bletchley Park, where his improvements to the Colossus computer significantly shortened the time needed to crack the so-called "Tunny" intercepts. He should also be remembered for his contribution to embryology research in the early days of molecular biology.[1]

In 1942, he was recruited to Bletchley Park. He was put into Hut F, working to crack the Wehrmacht's "Tunny" machine, which encoded material more sensitive than that carried by the now celebrated "Enigma". The team's success gave the Allies access for the first time to German army situation reports in the run-up to D-Day, with invaluable insights into troop dispositions in France.

Crucial to cracking "Tunny" was "Colossus", the complex electro-mechanical analytical device put together by Alan Turing and others to work out the permutations of positioning for the wheels in German cipher machines. It was capable of performing 10 to the power of 11 Boolean mathematical calculations without a significant error; Michie's greatest contribution was to simplify its working so that it could be operated by Wrens instead of by higher mathematicians without the need to halt it.[2]

With his second wife, Anne McLaren, and fellow geneticists, John Burdon Sanderson Haldane, Peter Medawar and Alex Comfort, he made significant advances in embryology, developing techniques that would later be used for in-vitro fertilisation.

In 1960, he built *Menace*, the Matchbox Educable Noughts and Crosses Engine, a game-playing machine consisting of 300 matchboxes and a collection of glass beads of different colours. Each box had a noughts-and-crosses game position drawn on it, and beads inside to represent possible moves that could be made from that position. Inside each box was a wedge that could trap one bead, and a move was chosen by shaking the matchbox and opening it to show which colour bead had been trapped. *Menace* was able to "learn" from experience, as each time a game was played beads were added to the box to reinforce successful moves.

In the early 1970s, in work that received international attention and helped make Britain a force in advancing artificial intelligence, Michie led a team that produced "Freddy," a computer-directed robotic arm that could choose and assemble parts from a jumbled and potentially confusing array. To demonstrate Freddy's capabilities, Michie programmed the machine to put together the parts of a toy truck. Nils J. Nilsson, an emeritus professor of engineering at Stanford University and a former chairman of the department of computer science there, said the machine was "ahead of its time" and impressed researchers at Stanford and elsewhere as "one of the first automatic assembly systems in the world".

Dr Nilsson added that industry had been slow to see Freddy's potential, and it was not until the 1980s, after industries in Japan began to use robotic machines in manufacturing, that the work of Michie and other scientists was fully appreciated.[3]

He showed the extent of his vision when, at the British Association meeting of 1968, he forecast that householders would one day tap information from computers in the same way that they could draw water, gas or electricity. "Along with question-answering services, which will allow us to inquire about the restaurants in our locality or politics in Paraguay, will come the games opponent, the puzzle setter and the quiz master", he said in an uncanny glimpse of the future.[4]

Michie's primary research involved finding ways for machines to extract rules and behaviours from example data, so that they could learn from experience, and he developed the technique of "standard induction". This was effectively applied in industrial plants, for example at a uranium reprocessing plant in Pennsylvania. Aware of the broader applications of his research, Michie developed a commercial version, *ExpertEase*, to make the process of extracting general rules from human experts more efficient.[5]

Alexander Forbes Moodie born 1923 worked with John Maxwell Cowley to create the first high-resolution electron diffraction camera. Working in Melbourne, Moodie was a key figure in some of the major developments in electron diffraction and electron microscopy. He has been a leader in the development of the theoretical basis for the formulation and application of many-beam dynamical diffraction processes. He has made important contributions to the instrumental techniques and he has demonstrated how the methods may be applied to current problems of solid-state science. His influence on the development of the subject areas has been profound and much broader than may be suggested by a review of his publications.

After developing a proper theoretical description for this phenomenon, based on Moodie's profound knowledge of physical-optics theory, he and Cowley realised that the optics of self-focusing periodic objects could lead to a new, physical-optics approach to the description of the interaction of electron waves with crystals. A particular significance of this "multislice" formulation of the dynamical diffraction theory is that it forms the basis for most of the computer programs used for the simulation of the high-resolution electron-microscope images of crystals. It is also routinely used in the computation of electron diffraction intensities, particularly in the form of convergent-beam electron diffraction patterns.

Moodie's other developments in instrumentation included the first successful high-resolution, high-temperature stage for an electron microscope, used subsequently in studies of the surface structure and reactions of ceramics.[1]

Moodie was greatly involved in the discussions that led to the first attempts by John Sanders and John Allpress to use an electron microscope to form direct images showing the arrangements of atoms in projections of the structure of thin crystals. He was largely instrumental in establishing the use of computer simulations to interpret such images, through his classical paper with Peter Goodman in 1974 and the series of papers with various co-authors that explored and tested the methods. "He was the first ever recipient [co-winner] of the Ewald Prize from the International Union of Applied Crystallography. The prize was awarded to Moodie because of his "outstanding achievements in electron diffraction and microscopy, especially for their fundamental contributions to the theory and technique of direct imaging of crystal structures and structure defects by high resolution electron microscopy".[2]

James Whyte Black 1924-2010 discovered important drugs that treat angina, gastric ulcers, hypertension, migraines, and other health problems. He received the Nobel Prize for Physiology or Medicine in 1988 for his development of two important drugs, propranolol and cimetidine. Black was the discoverer of beta blockers, a milestone in the treatment of high blood pressure and heart disease. He is also the discoverer of H-2 receptor-antagonists used in the treatment of ulcers. Black has contributed to basic scientific and clinical knowledge in cardiology, both as a physician and as a basic scientist. His invention of propranolol, the beta adrenergic receptor antagonist that revolutionised the medical management of angina pectoris, is considered to be one of the most important contributions to clinical medicine and pharmacology of the 20th century. His method of research, his discoveries about adrenergic pharmacology, and his clarification of the mechanisms of cardiac action are all strengths of his work.[1]

The Nobel committee said of beta-blockers: "The greatest breakthrough when it comes to pharmaceuticals against heart illness since the discovery of digitalis 200 years ago".[2] Over a three-year trial, sufferers of heart disease given beta-blockers had four times less fatal heart attacks than similar untreated patients.

Until the invention of propranolol, nitrates were the only pharmacologic tools that physicians could use against angina, and these proved inadequate in the treatment of the condition. Propranolol reduced both morbidity and mortality in ischemic heart disease, and eventually proved useful in other areas of cardiology. Black's accomplishment, however, was not limited to the clinical impact of the drug. His research in cardiovascular pharmacology contributed to the clinical understanding of the etiology of angina pectoris and fostered a deeper knowledge of the basic pharmacology of the autonomic nervous system.

Quite apart from its effects on clinical medicine, propranolol added momentum to the wave of drug discovery that changed the role of the pharmaceutical industry in medicine. Propranolol also served to highlight the difficulties in obtaining international approval of new drugs. Although introduced in 1964, propranolol was not approved in the United States for the treatment of angina until 1973, much later than in most other countries. By the late 1970s, the conservatism of the Food and Drug Administration had delayed the approval of many drugs developed outside the United States, particularly cardiovascular drugs.

Black's second great discovery, a drug used for treating ulcers, was based on the same blocking principle and developed in the early 1970s when he was with the pharmaceutical company Smith, Kline and French. Released in 1975 under the name *Tagamet*, it transformed life for people with ulcers and worked by blocking the absorption of histamine, which irritated the stomach lining.

Black's drug discoveries arose out of his systematic research on the interactions between certain cell receptors in the body and chemicals in the bloodstream that attach to them. Black wanted to find a drug that would relieve angina pectoris, i.e., the spasms of intense pain felt in the chest when the heart is not receiving enough oxygen. It was known that beta receptors in the heart muscle, when stimulated by the hormones epinephrine and norepinephrine, cause the heartbeat to quicken and increase the strength of the heart's contractions, thus increasing its oxygen requirement. Black developed a drug that would block the beta receptor sites, thus preventing epinephrine and norepinephrine from attaching to them. The resulting inhibition of the hormones' excitatory effects reduced the heart's demand for oxygen and could thus help relieve anginal pain. Other beta-blocking agents were subsequently developed to treat heart attacks, hypertension, migraines, and other conditions.[3]

Allan MacLeod Cormack 1924-1998 won a share of the 1979 Nobel Prize for Physiology or Medicine for his work in developing computed axial tomography, commonly known as the CAT or CT scan. At present, this complicated machine gives physicians their best look inside the human body. With Godfrey Hounsfield, he developed the powerful CAT scanning system that is used to capture three-dimensional X-ray images of body organs. The system is particularly useful in generating 3-D images of the brain. In many cases, CAT scanning has eliminated the need for exploratory surgery.

Cormack, in a remarkable paper of 1963, discussed the idea of making measurements of the X-ray transmission "along lines parallel to a large number of different directions" so as to obtain a sequence of X-ray transmission profiles".[1]

The two-dimensional representations of conventional X-ray plates were often unable to distinguish between such tissues. More information could be gained if X-rays of the body were taken from several different directions, but conventional X-ray techniques made this procedure problematic. In the early 1960s, Cormack showed how details of a flat section of soft tissues could be calculated from measurements of the attenuation of X-rays passing through it from many different angles. He thus provided the mathematical technique for the CAT scan, in which an X-ray source and electronic detectors are rotated about the body and the resulting data is analysed by a computer to produce a sharp map of the tissues within a cross section of the body.[2]

In October 1980, the world's first MRI (Magnetic Resonance Imaging) service for patients was launched by Francis Smith at Aberdeen Royal Infirmary.

Robert Donald Bruce Fraser born 1924 made important contributions to ideas about the structure of DNA. Maurice Wilkins, one of a team working to determine the structure of DNA, asked Fraser about making a model of the molecule. Fraser completed it very quickly. It was a simple structure that had what would turn out to be all main features correct except for the number of chains. It had a helical shape, phosphates on the outside, and bases stacked like a pile of pennies, separated by the 3.4Å distance worked out by William Astbury, but his model was never published by King's College, London.

Fraser then settled in Australia, but was contacted by Wilkins, who was aware that Francis Crick and James Watson had realised that their original model of DNA, which also had the phosphates in the middle, was quite untenable. Their thinking had taken a new twist after the Kings group had gone up, at their invitation, to see the structure that had been developed in Cambridge. Rosalind Franklin was very supportive of the idea that phosphates were on the outside, and in 1951 she told Crick and Watson in no uncertain terms that they'd got it all wrong. By 1952, they had a new model in which there were only two chains, and they had put the phosphates on the outside and the bases on the inside and so on. Wilkins' cable was asking Fraser to write up the work he had done (because it was so close to what they had done) in order for the thinking at Kings to get publicity at the same time. Fraser sent Wilkins a draft manuscript with a couple of figures illustrating everything, but unfortunately Wilkins never published it.

It was, however, mentioned in the actual 1953 paper, *Molecular structure of nucleic acids: a structure for deoxyribose nucleic acid* by Watson and Crick. In the introduction, they stated:

"Another three-chain structure has also been suggested by Fraser (in the press). In his model the phosphates are on the outside and the bases on the inside, linked together by hydrogen bonds. This structure as described is rather ill-defined, and for this reason we shall not comment on it."

Fraser later said, "That comment is extraordinary, when their initial model was rubbish. With three chains and the bases down the middle, yes! Also, I had gone to great lengths to try to work out standard patterns of bonding between the bases, which of course was the key to the final model."[1]

Wilkins later wrote about the Fraser model: "It was helical, with the phosphates on the outside and the flat bases stacked inside. The bases on one chain were hydrogen bonded to the bases on the other chains. The model had most of the features of the Double Helix except of course that there were three chains instead of two, and because of that, could not have the very special and unique system of base pairs which was such a staggering feature of the Watson and Crick model. The reason why the Fraser model had three chains was that we at Kings thought that density and water content data on DNA meant that there were three chains. We barely considered that there were only two chains. We were not alone in making that mistake: both Linus Pauling and William Thomas Astbury fell into the same physical chemistry trap."[2]

Over the next 35 years, Fraser would lead the research at the CSIRO Biochemistry Unit in Parkville, Australia, into the 3-D structure of keratins and collagen. Techniques employed included infrared absorption; birefringence of stretched and normal fibres; histology of the wool fibre and enhancement of fibre characteristics by means of shadow casting. With Tom MacRae, he conducted pioneering X-ray diffraction studies on various fibrous proteins.[3]

Ainsley Iggo 1924-2012 was a neurophysiologist whose pioneering study of sensory receptors, particularly in the skin, made a huge contribution to our understanding of pain. His major breakthrough came in 1958, when he became the first scientist to demonstrate electrical recordings from individual C fibres, the thinnest of the body's nerves. He went on to identify and analyse the function of the various sensory receptors in the skin that allow us to detect touch, tickle, heat and pain; one of the receptors he described carries his name. He also studied sensory nerves of the internal organs and the organisation of pain nerve cells in the spinal cord. His findings lent strong support to the "specificity school" of pain interpretation – which sees pain as "a specific sensation, with its own sensory apparatus independent of touch and other senses".[1]

He co-founded and later became president (1981-1984) of the Seattle-based International Association for the Study of Pain (IASP), the world's largest multidisciplinary organisation specialising in pain research, control and treatment – for animals and humans alike.

Iggo made the extraordinary discovery that the Australian duck-billed platypus used receptors in its bill to catch food by detecting the minutest electric currents in the water generated by the muscles of its prey. His findings were published in the magazine *Nature* in 1987.[2]

Iain MacIntyre 1924-2008 discovered that the source of calcitonin – which regulates calcium – was the thyroid gland. MacIntyre and co-workers reported the amino acid structure of human calcitonin in the late 1960s, and work in that decade also identified calcitonin as an inhibitor of bone resorption.[1] MacIntyre was the first to isolate and sequence, with colleagues, the novel human neuropeptide calcitonin gene-related peptide, demonstrating its role as a potent vasodilator.[2]

In a carefully conducted corpus of elegant experiments, MacIntyre showed not only a thyroid origin for calcitonin, later confirmed by Paul Munson from Harvard, but also localised calcitonin to the "C" cell of the thyroid gland using some of the earliest histochemical methods. He then demonstrated that calcitonin prevented the flux of calcium from bone to blood by inhibiting the resorption of bone, thus establishing its existence as a potent calcium regulating hormone.

MacIntyre purified and provided the first chemical sequence of pig calcitonin, and then human calcitonin, which his group isolated from medullary thyroid carcinoma. Importantly, thereafter, he pioneered the use of calcitonin clinically in patients with Paget's disease, and with Howard Morris at Imperial College, isolated and sequenced human calcitonin gene-related peptide (CGRP), which he found was the most potent known vasodilator.

He made the groundbreaking discovery in 1990 that nitric oxide, which was considered solely a vasodilator, regulated bone cell metabolism directly. His work on studying nitric oxide regulation by hormones continued until the last.[3]

In 1967, Iain shared with Harold Copp the Gardner International Award for the co-discovery of the origin and existence of calcitonin. He also acknowledged in the Copp memoir the great contribution of Paul Munson and colleagues at Harvard.[4]

Alastair Graham Walter Cameron 1925-2005 was a founder of modern planetary astrophysics. His work included developing the s-process, the r-process, and statistical equilibrium models for nucleosynthesis, providing elemental abundances and the first numerical models for the physics of the solar nebula, and developing the now widely accepted "giant impact" hypothesis for the origin of the Moon.[1]

Cameron predicted what elements are produced in the sun and in what quantities. He found that, indeed, technetium is produced along the way, explaining Paul Merrill's observation. In order to be found in the atmospheres of the Sun and other stars, and in solid bodies such as planets and meteorites, new elements have to first be ejected from the parent star into space where they contaminate interstellar matter destined to form new generations of stars and planets. Thus, the full understanding of nucleosynthesis involves the formation of stars and planets, as well as the ejection of heavy elements into space by red-giant winds and supernova explosions. Undaunted by the challenge, Cameron plunged into a full range of theoretical astrophysics. His model of the Solar Nebula, a disc of gas and dust formed at the time of the origin of the Sun 4.5 billion years ago, provides quantitative temperatures that theorists use in their studies of planet formation.

Cameron attacked a long-standing theoretical problem in planetary physics: the origin of the Moon. The Apollo Program had found that unlike the Earth, the Moon has no iron core, but is composed solely of the same material as the mantle of the Earth. At the time, theorists could not explain this fact. Cameron proposed that the Moon formed from a disc of debris orbiting the Earth, much as the Solar Nebula orbited the Sun. But where could the debris have come from? Cameron proposed that it was material ejected from Earth's mantle when a Mars-sized body collided with the Earth early in the history of the solar system. That would explain the Moon's composition, but how would the debris reach the distance of the Moon? Cameron attacked this problem head on, acquiring faster computers for his office in order to model the collision event.

He finally succeeded in showing that such a collision would result in a disc of the correct mass, as well as the angular momenta of the Earth and Moon that are observed today. Cameron's theory is now the accepted one for the origin of the Moon.[2]

Alick Edwards Glennie 1925-2003 created the first of several programs called Autocode for the Mark I computer in September 1952 while he was a student at the University of Manchester. Autocode was the first compiler actually to be implemented. (The language that it compiled was called by the same name.)[1] The Ferranti Mark I Star filled a room at least the size of the ground floor of a modern detached house. It had some peculiar number of 36-bit words, maybe 32k. Its storage comprised magnetic drums, which took aeons to rotate. Input was from paper tape and output via a Teletype.[2]

Glennie did computational work for the British atomic bomb, and he introduced inverse differential operators for handling partial differential equations in his morphogenetic theory.[3]

He worked with the legendary genius Alan Turing on several projects and in 1952 he played what is generally considered the first ever game of computer chess against a program devised by Turing. Because the computers of the day were not fast enough to calculate the algorithms, Turing used a pen and paper to decode the program calculations. The match took several weeks to complete at the end of which Alick came out the victor.[4]

James Anderson McFadzean 1925-2002 developed a therapeutic agent called *Flagyl* (Metronidazole) – a drug that has saved the lives of countless thousands across the world. *Flagyl* is used to treat bacterial infections of the vagina, stomach, skin, joints, and respiratory tract. The drug was given the name *Flagyl* because it was produced in the first place to treat a flagellate protozoan parasite, the trichomonad.[1]

Metronidazole is used for the treatment of bacterial vaginosis, pelvic inflammatory disease in conjunction with other antibiotics, anaerobic infections such as peritonitis, diverticulitis, empyema, pneumonia, aspiration pneumonia, lung abscess, diabetic foot ulcer, meningitis and brain abscesses, bone and joint infections, septicaemia, endometritis, or endocarditis, pseudomembranous colitis due to *Clostridium difficile*, *Helicobacter pylori* eradication therapy, as part of a multi-drug regimen in peptic ulcer disease, dental infection of bacterial origin, such as periapical abscess, periodontal abscess, acute pericoronitis of impacted or partially erupted teeth; often used in conjunction with *Amoxicillin*, infections caused by *Entamoeba histolytica*, Giardiasis infection of the small intestine caused by the ingestion of infective cysts of protozoan *Giardia lamblia*, Trichomoniasis infection caused by *Trichomonas vaginalis*, which is a common cause of vaginitis and is the most frequently presenting new infection of the common sexually transmitted diseases.

Further uses for Metronidazole include: non-specific prophylaxis for those undergoing potentially contaminated colorectal surgery or appendectomies and may be combined with neomycin; Crohn's disease with colonic or perianal involvement; rosacea; and in the treatment of malodorous fumigating wounds.

Metronidazole is now widely used as being the drug of choice for the treatment and prophylaxis of anaerobic infections in man. Its action is bactericidal, destruction of the bacterial cell being brought about by the prevention of nucleic acid synthesis.[2]

Marshall Meek 1925-2013 was the chief naval architect and director of Ocean Fleets. He perfected the design of the fast cargo liner, then designed the first ocean-going purpose built containerships that revolutionised shipping.[1] In 1956, American Malcom Purcell McLean developed the metal shipping container revolutionising how cargo is moved by using large containers that were never opened in transit between shipper and consignee and that were transferable on an intermodal basis, among trucks, ships and railcars (of distant Scottish ancestry, he was born Malcolm but changed to Malcom later in life as he is claimed to have thought – incorrectly – that this was the original Scottish spelling of the name).

Meek was employed with the owners of the Blue Funnel Line, where he was both a director and naval architect. "When the company had become Ocean Fleets, it joined with other British ship-owners and looked to Meek for the first purpose-built containership fleet in the world. This required new ship designs, massive worldwide investment in port facilities and marketing to win public acceptance of freight containers, thereby revolutionising dry-cargo shipping. Under the house flag of OCL this pioneer service set the highest standards of service and safety and continues to operate on almost every ocean."[2] Between 1972 and 1973, OCL (Overseas Containers Ltd) introduced container services on all the main Far East routes.

Other factors had to be considered when Meek designed *Priam*, the first purpose-built container ship, and then *Encounter Bay*. The entire concept had to be worked up from scratch – even the standard size for a container had yet to be agreed. Five 282,817-tonne ships were ordered from German yards, and delivered on time in 1969. One was placed with Fairfields, Glasgow; it arrived a year late. Dockers at Tilbury blacked the ships' cargoes and they had to be handled at Rotterdam and Antwerp. But *Encounter Bay* stayed in service for 30 years. Meek next designed the larger Liverpool Bay class – all five built in Germany – for the Far East run. They spent so much more of their time at sea with larger payloads that each replaced six conventional vessels, forcing redundancies among seamen.[3]

Andrew William Morrison 1925-2006 specialised in otolaryngology and led the field in ground-breaking surgery for inner ear conditions, acoustic tumour surgery, and the earliest multi-channel cochlear implantation. He was referred to as the father of neurotology.[1]

He was a pioneer and refiner of surgical technique for stapedectomy operations, which restore hearing to patients suffering from otosclerosis. He was one of the first to study and publish details of the hereditary pattern and to look at the chromosomes of this condition, for which the genes are currently still under investigation. This surgery is very delicate, and risks destroying all hearing permanently. Morrison was, however, a dexterous and highly skilled operator, able to publish outstanding results with hardly any disappointing outcomes in the last 1,000 operations.

In the early 1960s, he was influenced by the House Otologic Institute in California, and at this time he was instrumental in the development of the trans-labyrinthine surgical approach for removal of acoustic nerve tumours. He was the first surgeon in Britain to undertake this operation, which, because of the superior results and much improved recovery for the patient, gained hold, and throughout Europe and America became one of the mainstay operations for removal of acoustic nerve tumours from the posterior fossa of the brain. The legacy of this surgical approach, working through the bone of the ear to reach the brain tumour, has allowed many thousands to benefit from the expertise of following generations of surgeons over the past 40 years.[2]

Heading a national group, Project Ear, in the late 1970s and 1980s, he was at the heart of the earliest developments in cochlear implantation. Before this, only a single electrode placed outside the cochlea had been attempted. The Project Ear group developed its own purpose-built hardware and speech processing, including multi-channel intra-cochlear electrodes, which proved successful.

His other major contribution to deafness and dizziness, extending until his death, was his study and treatment of Meniere's disease. This affliction causes great distress to the sufferer, who can be plagued by unexpected attacks of severe vertigo, with tinnitus and progressive deafness. His observant and innovative mind led to new medical and surgical procedures in the treatment of this condition. In his seventies, he became an expert in genetics, studying the genome in the subgroup of patients who suffer from familial Meniere's disease, and searching for candidate genes.[3]

John Adrian Shepherd-Barron 1925-2010 is credited with inventing the world's first automatic cash machine, popularly known as "the hole in the wall" but more properly the automated teller machine (ATM).[1] It was built by NCR in Dundee and went into operation in Barclays Bank in north London at Ealing Town on 27 June 1967. A forerunner of the ATM, a mechanical dispenser, had been installed as early as 1939 in New York but failed to catch on. Shepherd-Barron's machines used special cheques which had been impregnated with a radioactive compound of carbon-14, which was detected and matched against the personal identification number (PIN), patented by James Goodfellow, entered on a keypad and was the first to be used 24/7. The four-digit PIN subsequently transformed the way people across the world handle financial transactions. According to the ATM Industry Association, there are now more than 2.2 million ATMs (as at 14 March 2014) around the world. In Britain alone a total of £10 billion a month was withdrawn from ATMs in 2013, with an average of a million transactions per hour.[2]

George William Gray 1926-2013 undertook research on liquid crystals, which led to the development of the ubiquitous LCD. The legacy of Professor George Gray, the world's leading authority on the chemistry of liquid crystals, could be measured by the quality of televisions, mobile phones and MP3 players and, at a deeper level, how we communicate with each other, whether through Twitter, Facebook or Skype. After graduation, he spent the next decade laying down the rules on the design and preparation of liquid crystals formed by organic compounds, culminating with the publication, in 1962, of his book, *Molecular Structure and the Properties of Liquid Crystals*, the first English text on the subject.

Gray, with two researchers, Ken Harrison and John Nash, had success – not by designing favourable structures into molecules, but by leaving parts out, and so the stable cyanobiphenyls were born. They became the workhorses in the development of modern flat panel displays and inspired the creation of an international industry, such that now there are more liquid crystal displays in the world than there are people. After the invention of cyanobiphenyls, more developments followed, including materials for colour-change thermometer strips, large screen LCD TVs, and the eyepieces of digital cameras.

In addition to technological developments, Gray made many fundamental contributions on the true nature of matter, including discoveries of new liquid crystal phases and their properties. His original research was published in more than 300 scientific papers and patents, and several textbooks.[1] Gray did not invent the chemicals; nor was he the first to describe their properties. Liquid crystals are a class of substances that defy the normal rules of science by being able to flow like liquids, while maintaining the crystalline structure of solids. Another important feature is that, with the application of a small electric current, the orientation of the crystals can be made to change so that the liquid "flips" from opaque to translucent.

Until Gray began his research, however, liquid crystals were regarded as little more than a scientific curiosity, since the chemicals then available were insufficiently stable at room temperature and could be destroyed when exposed to moisture, air or light. Scientists at Hoffmann-La Roche had developed a liquid crystal display, but the device worked only at very high temperatures, making it useless for all practical purposes.

In 1973, Gray and his colleagues designed and synthesised a new class of liquid crystals, called cyanobiphenyls, which were stable, yet still "flippable", at room temperature. They published a paper describing their work on 22 March 1973. Commercialised by BDH Chemicals (now E Merck), in collaboration with the Ministry of Defence, the first liquid crystal displays in commercial devices appeared the following year.

Before long small LCDs, such as on watches and calculators, had become ubiquitous. Nowadays they are used in everything from calculators to mobile phones and laptop computers. During the 1980s, in collaboration with Merck, Gray and his team synthesised a new class of liquid crystals, called difluoro-terphenyls, which are used in television screens.

In 2012, more than 750 million LCD products, with an estimated value of £56 billion, were manufactured worldwide – all inspired by Gray's breakthrough. Yet outside scientific circles, his name remained largely unknown – apart from, maybe, to a few travellers who use a Hull-bound train named in his honour.[2] Note: the projected revenues for 2014 were estimated to be $US208 billion (£133 billion).[3]

Allen Kerr born 1926 pioneered plant genetic engineering. His research career included fundamental observations which led to the discovery of the tumour-inducing plasmids (Ti plasmids) in Agrobacterium, paving the way for plant genetic engineering, and the discovery and understanding of the most successful example of biological control in plant pathology, the use of strain K84 for control of crown gall disease of stonefruit.[1]

In the 1970s, a closely related natural soil bacterium was identified, referred to as strain K84, which produced an antibiotic antidote to the Crown Gall bacterium. Crown Gall is a plant cancer and one of the most devastating diseases in horticulture, responsible for huge losses in flower, fruit and nut crops. Its name is derived from tumour-like swellings (galls) created at the crown of the host plant, just above the ground. The bacterium transfers part of its DNA to its host, which changes the latter's genome, causing tumours and other malformations.

Kerr was able to recognise this antidote was flawed in one critical respect – the harmful Crown gall bacterial pathogen, *Agrobacterium tumefaciens*, was actually able to develop immunity to K84's antibiotic. Indeed, the very genetic material responsible for reproducing the antibiotic agent was transferred from the K84 strand to pathogenic organisms like the Crown Gall bacterium.

In what was to be the first real application of plant genetic engineering, Kerr decided to remove the piece of K84's DNA that allowed the transfer of the antibiotic gene to the Crown Gall bacterium. This new version of K84 was named K1026, and went on the Australian market as Nogall in the 1980s.

Nogall is used to control Crown Gall by treating disease-free propagation stock. It is applied in an aqueous solution to seeds, seedlings and cuttings before planting and works by protecting wound sites from infection. This new strain is the first genetically engineered micro-organism to be sold live to the public. Its significant commercial potential in major world producers of stone fruits and nuts is highlighted by its user-friendliness, its long shelf-life, and its harmlessness to produce from plants it has treated, as well as to the surrounding environment.[2]

Kerr, in his own words, states: "My most important work has been a study of crown gall, one of the three known plant cancers. It is the only cancer, of either plant or animal, induced by a bacterium." Note: *Helicobacter pylori* is suspected of causing stomach cancer but this has not been proven. His work on this disease began in 1967, as an ecological study of agrobacteria in soil and on the roots of stone-fruit trees. It resulted in significantly improved understanding of the ecology and biology of the pathogen, and a unique and widely adopted biological method for control of the disease. Kerr's findings and scientific leadership facilitated numerous cooperative projects with graduate and postgraduate students and colleagues throughout the world.

Strain K1026, the genetically engineered organism for crown gall control, was the first such organism registered as a pesticide and released for general use. Kerr's research led to the characterisation of the chemistry of Agrocin 84, a new and very potent antibiotic with marked specificity.

Other major contributions by Kerr include fundamental research on the nature of bacterial conjugation, plasmid transfer, and conjugation factors. This work was of crucial importance in demonstrations by others that pathogenicity in Agrobacterium is encoded by the Ti plasmid. In addition to his investigations of crown gall of stone fruit, Kerr has conducted research on the transformation and regeneration of flax, control of cane gall disease of grapes, and annual ryegrass toxicity. During his tenure at the Tea Research Institute in Sri Lanka, he studied the epidemiology of blister blight of tea, developed a model relating disease incidence to weather, and successfully integrated the model with a user-friendly calculating device for implementation of effective control of this disease.[3]

Ian James Mathieson 1927-2010 pioneered methods of surveying and mapping large archaeological sites without the expense or intrusion of excavation, particularly through the use of sound waves and radar to reveal any structures beneath the surface. Initially, he worked with parties from the Egypt Exploration Society and Cambridge University before the Supreme Council of Antiquities of Egypt granted him his own site at Saqqara – the vast complex near Cairo which served as the necropolis for the ancient Egyptian capital, Memphis.

From 1990, Mathieson led the Saqqara Geophysical Survey Project, producing archaeological and geophysical maps of a little-explored area of the site; and in 2001 his survey turned up several large, previously unknown temples, as well as a number of tombs and dwellings.[1]

Mathieson and his team undertook a pioneering remote-sensing program of the Saqqara plateau, employing techniques such as electricity resistivity-meter survey, magnometry, ground-penetrating radar, and sonic and thermal reflection, in combination with global positioning satellite equipment (GPS). The team mapped the whole of the area to the north and east of the Step Pyramid, plus the full length of the Wadi Abusir (stretching from the former lake of Abusir south to the Gisr el-Mudir). These geophysical maps show numerous hitherto unknown structures, as well as others which were seen during the 19th or early 20th centuries but have again disappeared under drift sand. Among the latter is the avenue of sphinxes originally leading up to the entrance of the Serapeum. The former includes several rows of Late Period temple platforms lining the Serapeum enclosure to the west of the Step Pyramid. Some of these were also excavated by the expedition, and limited sondages at the Gisr el-Mudir have been the first to show the impressive construction of its limestone perimeter walls. Among the most recent discoveries is a large mastaba suspected to date to Dynasty 3, possibly the long-lost tomb of the legendary Imhotep, architect of the Step Pyramid.[2]

Thomas Summers West 1927-2010 developed a spectrophotometric technique for the analysis of fluoride, which is still a method of choice; in the fields of flame and atomic absorption spectroscopy and atomic fluorescence spectroscopy, he introduced innovative methodologies which massively reduced detection limits to sub-parts per billion levels; his research also led to notable developments concerning microwave-powered, electrode-less spectral lamps, atom trapping techniques and low luminosity flames.[1]

Alastair Ian Scott 1928-2007 discovered how bacteria produce vitamin B_{12} and other insights that helped revolutionise organic and natural product chemistry.[1] He did revolutionary work on the way in which vitamin B_{12} – the essential life pigments chlorophyll and heme, and the important anti-tumour agent taxol – are produced.[2]

He developed biomimetic syntheses of griseofulvin and tetracycline. Scott worked on the mechanisms leading to vitamin B_{12}, plant alkaloids and antibiotics, and helped develop the area of biological nuclear magnetic resonance. Among the many applications of Scott's work are the control of metabolism at the molecular level in cells and tissues by direct, non-invasive spectroscopy, the development of very sensitive probes of enzyme-substrate interactions and the discovery of short-lived, air-sensitive intermediates in biosynthetic pathways. Scott has also developed the area of genetically engineered synthesis, which involves chemistry, spectroscopy and molecular biology.[3]

He has made a number of unparalleled discoveries in the area of biological nuclear magnetic resonance (NMR), which have revolutionised both practice and theory in this field. As a result of his work, it is now possible to study the control of metabolism at the molecular level in living cells and tissues by direct, non-invasive spectroscopy, to devise extremely sensitive probes of enzyme-substrate interactions and to discover short-lived, air-sensitive intermediates in biosynthetic pathways at the microgram level.[4]

James Dewey Watson born 1928 was one of the co-discoverers of the structure of DNA, with Francis Crick. Watson, Crick and Maurice Wilkins were awarded the 1962 Nobel Prize in Physiology or Medicine "for their discoveries concerning the molecular structure of nucleic acids and its significance for information transfer in living material".

Watson and Crick found they had similar scientific interests and initiated a collaboration to discover the structure of DNA. Crick soon solved the mathematical equations that govern helical diffraction theory; Watson knew all of the key DNA results of the Phage Group. In late 1951, Crick and Watson began a series of informal exchanges with Maurice Wilkins during which Wilkins gave some of Rosalind Franklin's findings to Watson and Crick without her permission or knowledge. In November, Watson attended a seminar by Franklin. She spoke about the X-ray diffraction data she had collected with Raymond Gosling at King's College London. The data indicated that DNA was a helix of some sort. Soon after this seminar, Watson and Crick constructed an incorrect molecular model of DNA in which the phosphate backbones were on the inside of the structure. Franklin asserted that the phosphates almost certainly were on the outside, not the inside. Watson and Crick eventually came to see that she was right and used this information in their final determination of the helical structure. In 1952, the final details of the chemical structure of the DNA backbone were determined by biochemists like Alexander Robertus Todd. Watson's key contribution was in discovering the nucleotide base pairs, the key to the structure and function of DNA. This key discovery was made in the Pauling "tradition", by playing with molecular models.[1]

Watson was at the same time experimentally investigating the structure of tobacco mosaic virus using X-ray diffraction techniques. His object was to see if its chemical sub-units, earlier revealed by the elegant experiments of Gerhard Schramm, were helically arranged. This objective was achieved in late June 1952, when use of the Cavendish laboratory's newly constructed rotating anode X-ray tubes allowed an unambiguous demonstration of the helical construction of the virus.[2]

In 1968, Watson wrote *The Double Helix*, one of the Modern Library's 100 best non-fiction books. The account is the sometimes painful story of not only the discovery of the structure of DNA, but the personalities, conflicts and controversy surrounding their work.[3]

Alexander Brown 1929-1975 was a bandleader and clarinet player who, in the mid-1950s, headed one of the leading groups as the Brown-Fairweather All Stars, but it was his engineering skills in acoustics that had a greater impact. "As the BBC's chief acoustics architect Brown was involved with all major BBC radio and television projects throughout the UK. His collaboration with the BBC research department resulted in the first modular acoustic absorbers; a mobile, stacking acoustic screen used in all BBC and commercial recording studios; and the innovative use of refrigerator magnetic seals in acoustic doors. He left in 1969 to set up his own consultancy practice and in six years of independent practice as Sandy Brown Associates he raised the acoustic design of commercial sound recording studios to an internationally known product, and built studios for the Beatles, Eric Clapton, the Rolling Stones, and others. In 1972, he was invited as acoustic consultant to the Edinburgh opera house project, using a one-eighth-scale physical acoustic model. This technique had been developed by his colleagues at the BBC, subsequently his partners, and this was the first time it had been used in the design of an auditorium. Sandy

Brown Associates was the first major UK buildings acoustics consultancy and his work, and that of the practice, survives him. He has had a major influence on the development of building acoustics both in the UK and throughout the world."[1]

Alexander Gilchrist Frame 1929-1993 was appointed director of the UK Atomic Energy Authority in 1964 and was in charge of building Britain's first prototype fast reactor at Dounreay, where work began in 1966: this was supplying electricity to the national grid from 1975. In 1968, Frame was appointed Chief Engineer of Rio Tinto-Zinc Corporation Ltd (RTZ), in charge of the building of a nuclear power station linked to an aluminium smelter at Holyhead, Anglesey. The smelter was completed on time, and under cost.

Frame's next project was the Channel Tunnel. He was appointed managing director of Rio Tinto-Zinc Development Enterprises Ltd (RTZ-DE), formed by RTZ to be responsible for the planning, financing, and construction of large-scale projects worldwide. RTZ-DE was appointed project manager by the British Channel Tunnel Company, in which RTZ held 20% of the shares, in 1971, and was given the responsibility for carrying out new studies on the feasibility of constructing a tunnel under the English Channel. Frame took expert advice on tunnel design and construction, estimated the cost and time-scale of the project and its economic benefits, and proposed a new route for the tunnel on the British side, which would shorten its length by two miles (3.2 km), save £7 million in construction costs, and reduce the annual operating costs by £300,000.

During the two years of the study, Frame built up a close rapport with his French counterpart, Jean Gabriel, project director of the Société Française du Tunnel sous la Manche. On the basis of his final report to the government in June 1973, the government decided to go ahead. Work began on both sides of the Channel at the end of 1973, with Frame, newly elected to the board of RTZ, in charge of the management of the Channel tunnel project on the English side. Following the defeat of the Conservative government in the February 1974, general election, and the death of the French president, Georges Pompidou, in April of the same year, the Channel Tunnel project was cancelled by the new Labour government, as an unnecessary use of public money, in January 1975. It was revived by the Conservative government in 1982, and the tunnel that opened in 1994 followed the RTZ design. Frame joined the board of Eurotunnel in 1990.[1]

He became chairman of RTZ in 1985 and in 1989 acquired British Petroleum's mineral interests, including Kennecott, the large American copper company. This made RTZ the world's largest mining company.

Robert M. Graham born 1929 participated in the development of MULTICS (Multiplexed Information and Computing Service), a pioneering time-sharing operating system initiated by MIT. This was a major project that took about seven years from the initial planning until the system was in daily use by a large community of users. Graham was one of the principal designers, with particular responsibility for protection, dynamic linking, and other key system kernel areas.[1] It was an important influence on operating system development. MULTICS was conceived as a general-purpose time-sharing utility. It would be a commercial product for GE, which sold time-sharing services. It became a GE and then a Honeywell product. About 85 sites ran MULTICS. However, it had a powerful impact in the computer field, due to its many novel and valuable ideas. Since it was designed to be a utility, such as electricity and telephone services, it had numerous features to provide high availability and security. Both the hardware and software were highly modular so that the system could grow in size by adding more of the appropriate resource even while the service was running. Since services were shared by users who might not trust each other, security was a major feature with file sharing provided at the file level via access controls.[2]

Peter Ware Higgs born 1929 is one of the world's leading theoretical physicists and is best known for his 1960s proposal of broken symmetry in electroweak theory, explaining the origin of mass of elementary particles in general, and of the W and Z bosons in particular. This so-called Higgs mechanism, which was proposed by several physicists besides Higgs at about the same time, predicts the existence of a new particle, the Higgs boson (which was often described as "the most sought-after particle in modern physics".[1]

In 1964, with Robert Brout and Francois Englert, he explained how weak force elementary particles acquire mass, postulating the existence of the Higgs field and the "Higgs boson"; the primary object of enquiry for CERN's Large Hadron Collider in Geneva.[2]

The Higgs boson or Higgs particle is an elementary particle initially theorised in 1964 and tentatively confirmed to exist on 14 March 2013. The discovery has been called "monumental" because it appears to confirm the existence of the Higgs field, which is pivotal to the Standard Model and other theories within particle physics.[3]

Two physicists suggest that the Higgs boson had a key role in the early Universe, producing the observed difference between the number of matter and antimatter particles and determining the density of the mysterious dark matter that makes up five-sixths of the matter in the Universe. In a paper accepted for publication in Physical Review Letters, Sean Tulin of the University of Michigan in Ann Arbor and Geraldine Servant of the Catalan Institute for Research and Advanced Study in Barcelona, Spain, say that there may have been an asymmetry in the early Universe between the Higgs boson and its antimatter counterpart, the anti-Higgs.[4]

In the 1970s, physicists realised that there are very close ties between two of the four fundamental forces – the weak force and the electromagnetic force. The two forces can be described within the same theory, which forms the basis of the Standard Model. This "unification" implies that electricity, magnetism, light and some types of radioactivity are all manifestations of a single underlying force known as the electroweak force.

The basic equations of the unified theory correctly describe the electroweak force and its associated force-carrying particles, namely the photon, and the W and Z bosons, except for a major glitch. All of these particles emerge without a mass. While this is true for the photon, we know that the W and Z have mass, nearly 100 times that of a proton. Fortunately, theorists Robert Brout, François Englert and Peter Higgs made a proposal that was to solve this problem. What we now call the Brout-Englert-Higgs mechanism gives a mass to the W and Z when they interact with an invisible field, now called the "Higgs field", which pervades the universe.[5]

Following the announcement that scientists have discovered a new particle consistent with the Higgs boson, Britain's Prime Minister David Cameron said: "This is a great breakthrough, one that could be profoundly significant to our understanding of the universe and the fundamental laws that govern it."[6]

In 2013, Peter Higgs and Francois Englert of Belgium won the Nobel physics prize for predicting the existence of the Higgs boson that explains how elementary matter attained the mass to form stars and planets (Brout died in 2011 and the Nobel is not awarded posthumously). Half a century after their original work, the new building block of nature was finally detected in 2012 at the European Organisation for Nuclear Research (CERN) centre's giant, underground particle-smasher near Geneva. The discovery was hailed as one of the most important in physics.

To find the elusive particle, scientists at the Large Hadron Collider had to pore over data from the wreckage of trillions of sub-atomic proton collisions. "The awarded theory is a central part of the Standard Model of particle physics that describes how the world is constructed," the Royal Swedish Academy of Sciences said in a statement. "According to the Standard Model, everything, from flowers and people to stars and planets, consists of just a few building blocks: matter particles." The Higgs boson is the last piece of the Standard Model of physics that describes the fundamental make-up of the universe. Some commentators – though not scientists – have called it the "God particle" for its role in turning the Big Bang into an ordered cosmos.[7]

Norman Alexander MacLeod born 1929 invented the Claymore mine, used as an anti-personnel weapon ever since the Korean War (1950-1953). After the People's Republic of China entered the conflict on the side of North Korea a new tactic was unleashed on the United Nations forces. The communist Chinese, short of adequate weapons, mitigated this disadvantage by using wave after human wave of soldiers to attack enemy positions. The slaughter of Chinese troops was horrendous, but they often overran UN forward lines as the defenders often ran out of ammunition during these incessant attacks. "To counter this sort of determined attack, the Allies began looking at new kinds of weapon capable of defending set positions. One such weapon was the Claymore mine."[1]

MacLeod worked for the Explosive Research Corporation and developed what was officially called T-48 but became better known as the Claymore mine. The T-48 got a name change to M18 Claymore and some 10,000 were manufactured and they came into use in the Vietnam War. "The M18 was 235 millimetres long and 83 millimetres high with a plastic case with three folding spike legs on the bottom. An electrical blasting cap for triggering the mine was inserted through a small hole in the side. Internally the mine consisted of a layer of 340 grams of C-3 explosive (the forerunner of C-4 explosive) in front of which was laid an array of ¼" [6.35 mm] steel cubes. In total, the mine weighed about 1.1 kilograms, and could be fitted with an optional peep sight for aiming. It lacked the later version's iconic 'FRONT TOWARD ENEMY' marking. The mine was planted in the ground using its three sharp legs and was aimed in the direction of enemy approach and then fitted with an electrical blasting cap. The mine was then triggered from a safe position, preferably to the side and rear. The mine was barely more than a prototype and was not considered a 'reliable casualty producer' with an effective range like the Phoenix of only 90 feet (30 m)."[2]

There are two versions of the M18 Claymore anti-personnel mine – one with a peep-type sight and the other without. The peep sight was devised to help give a Claymore operator a "field-of-vision" for the semi-circle blast pattern presented by the M18 when detonated. The steel balls packed within the mine are then projected out from just above ground level by the resulting explosion to a height of about two metres with a maximum kill radius of 100 metres and an effective kill range of 50 metres. Wounding has been noted as far away as 260 metres from the blast zone though a range of 50 metres is deemed optimal. The M18 can still be detonated in the electrical or non-electrical fashion which lends it to be used as a dedicated mine or as an "individual weapon".[3]

The Claymore mine "has been used to great effect in battle zones from Vietnam in the 1960s to Afghanistan in the 21st century. During its 60-year lifespan, the Claymore idea has been developed and refined. It has also been copied by the armies of numerous countries around the world…"[4]

Donald Metcalf 1929-2014 is regarded as the "father of modern haematology" for his pioneering research, which saw him identify colony stimulating factors (CSFs) – critical molecules that tell stem cells to multiply and mature to boost the immune system. CSFs are now widely used in clinical medicine, predominantly in the treatment of cancer patients who have undergone chemotherapy. To date, Professor Metcalf's discovery has benefited more than 10 million cancer patients worldwide.[1]

With his colleagues, Metcalf researched for over 20 years to show that the CSFs, when injected into animals, stimulated the formation and activity of white blood cells. After successful testing on humans, the treatment was accepted worldwide and has helped millions of cancer patients in accelerating the regrowth of blood cells following treatment and bone marrow transplants and for increasing resistance to infections. His work on the control of blood cell formation has revolutionised the understanding of many diseases of blood cells and their treatment.[2]

In early studies, he discovered the function of the thymus gland in controlling the formation of lymphocytes and, beginning in 1965, co-developed a series of specialised culture techniques permitting the growth of the various types of blood cells. These cultures led him and his team to the discovery of CSFs and his work, with that of others, led to the successful cloning of the genes for all four mouse and human CSFs, and the mass production of these hormones by bacterial, yeast, and other cells. His work provided the pivotal demonstration that the CSFs, when injected into animals, stimulated the formation and regulated the activity of white blood cells. Exploiting this, his collaborators then documented the effectiveness of GM-CSF and G-CSF (two primary white blood cell regulators) when injected into patients. These blood cell regulators are now in extensive clinical use throughout the world as valuable drugs, which can accelerate the regrowth of blood cells following anti-cancer treatment and bone marrow or peripheral blood transplantation.[3]

John Lennox Monteith 1929-2012 was a leading authority in the related fields of water management for agricultural production, soil physics, micrometeorology, transpiration, and the influence of the natural environment on field crops, horticultural crops, forestry, and animal production.[1]

In evapotranspiration (ETo) Monteith's pioneering work, along with Howard Penman, is applied worldwide as the "Penman-Monteith" equation. The FAO Penman-Monteith method is recommended as the sole ETo method for determining reference evapotranspiration.[2]

In 1954, Monteith moved to Rothamsted Experimental Station as a Scientific Officer and began working under Penman, who was carrying out seminal research into how variation in weather conditions affected soil moisture. Penman had developed a method to predict the rate of evaporation from wet surfaces, but this did not take account of the complicating effects that vegetation imposed on water loss. By harnessing the analogy of electrical resistance, Monteith showed how to account for surface conductance of water, and produced the Penman-Monteith equation that more correctly accounted for wind and surface effects. The approach was subsequently adapted to model the behaviour of any natural system involving mass or energy exchange in fields ranging from animal energetics to pollutant deposition. While at Rothamsted, Monteith also made, in collaboration with Geza Szeicz, some of the world's first measurements of carbon dioxide exchange between the land surface and the atmosphere. The discipline of Environmental Physics as a defined field of study really became established with the publication of Monteith's *Principles of Environmental Physics* in 1973.

Monteith and his colleagues at Nottingham developed diffusion porometers to measure the stomatal conductance of plants and tube solarimeters to measure shortwave solar radiation in collaboration with two major suppliers of state-of-the-art environmental research instrumentation for Britain and Europe, Delta-T Devices, and Campbell Scientific Ltd, for whom Monteith was a co-founder. Much of the progress in environmental physics made in the past 30 years has resulted directly from the availability of good field instrumentation provided by these companies.[3]

June Dalziel Almeida 1930-2007 pioneered new methods for viral imaging and diagnosis. Her skills in electron microscopy enabled her not only to identify viruses whose fine structure had hitherto been unknown, but also to shed light on the pathogenesis of viral infections, and to pioneer and improve methods for viral diagnosis.[1]

She achieved the first visualisation of rubella virus using immune-electronmicroscopy and collaborated with others to show common cold viruses. Among her most important discoveries was that there are two distinct components to the hepatitis B virus.[2]

With David Tyrell, she investigated the characteristics of a new class of viruses, now known as coronaviruses, which includes the SARS virus. She discovered how to better photograph viruses by using antibodies to group them and her novel images included those of HIV.

Malcolm Andrew Ferguson-Smith born 1931 first recognised the potential of flow cytometry for isolating individual chromosomes to address the clinical problems of particular patients. At that time, during the mid-1980s, the conventional wisdom was that chromosomes could only be efficiently sorted using the especially developed and super-expensive high-speed sorters at the Los Alamos and Lawrence Livermore laboratories in the USA. However, Ferguson-Smith demonstrated that commercially available cell sorters could also be successfully used and, with his team, he went on to use sorted chromosomes in reverse painting, i.e. hybridising DNA from sorted aberrant human chromosomes back onto normal metaphases to demonstrate the origin of the aberration.

Ferguson-Smith proceeded to sort the chromosomes of other species to produce chromosome specific paints with the mouse being the most notable. Undoubtedly, one of the most extraordinary developments was the discovery that chromosome-specific paints of one species could be successfully hybridised to the chromosomes of another to demonstrate homology, facilitating widespread evolutionary studies in vertebrates. Ferguson-Smith proposed, in 1966, that the XX male phenotype derives from an unequal meiotic exchange between the X and the Y chromosome resulting in transfer of the male-determining factor from the Y to the X. This was at a time when it was not even known which arms of the X and Y paired with each other or the extent of the pairing segment and predated the use of XX males with differing levels of XY interchange to dissect and map the Y chromosome by some 20 years.[1]

Arthur Richard Ivor Cruickshank 1932-2011 was a palaeontologist who used CT scans to look at the internal structure of the *Rhomaleosaurus* skull; and developed the idea that plesiosaurs (extinct marine reptiles) used their nostrils not to breathe air, but to take in and monitor a flow of water (effectively "tasting" it).

With the Witwatersrand University engineer Beric Skews, he undertook a joint wind tunnel study of the fluid dynamics of nectrideans, bizarre extinct amphibians that look like boomerang-headed newts. The resulting paper, a minor classic, published in the *Proceedings of The Royal Society of London* in 1980, concluded that the animals lurked on the river-bed, lifting their heads to rise rapidly in the current to seize prey when it came overhead.[1]

Cruickshank continued his interest in dicynodonts, publishing on other Triassic species, as well as writing overviews of their evolution and functional morphology. Dicynodonts are of "great importance to understanding the evolution of life on Earth, for dicynodonts comprise the first major group of plant-eating land vertebrates."[2]

He extended his interests to the basal archosaurs – important as the ancestors of crocodiles and dinosaurs, and therefore birds. In the 1970s, he published definitive works on the basal archosaurs *Proterosuchus* and *Erythrosuchus*. This led to wider investigations of terrestrial ecosystems through the Permian and Triassic, in which he collaborated with palaeobotanist John Malcolm Anderson.[3]

Thomas Walter Bannerman Kibble 1932-2016 wrote several papers that were instrumental in leading to the development of a unified theory of weak and electromagnetic interactions, the "electroweak" theory, for which Abdus Salam shared the 1979 Nobel Prize for Physics with Sheldon Glashow and Steven Weinberg. This theory suggests that there is an underlying symmetry between these interactions that is hidden except at very high energy by the phenomenon of spontaneous symmetry breaking. It is now part of the very successful "standard model" of particle physics.[1]

In 1964, Kibble wrote a paper entitled *Global conservation laws and massless particles* in collaboration with two American scientists – National Science Foundation postdoctoral fellow Gerald Guralnik, and Richard Hagen from the University of Rochester, New York. This was one of three papers that appeared in the summer and autumn of that year in the leading journal *Physical Review Letters*, describing a mechanism for giving mass to elementary particles within the context of "gauge theories". In June 2008, these papers were selected by the journal as among the most significant published there in the last 50 years. In 2009, the six authors of these papers were jointly awarded the prestigious J.J. Sakurai Prize by the American Physical Society for this achievement. One feature of this mechanism is the existence of a mass-giving particle now known as the "Higgs boson", which was finally detected in 2012 at the European Organization for Nuclear Research (CERN) centre's giant, underground particle-smasher near Geneva. The discovery was hailed as one of the most important in physics and resulted in the 2013 Nobel Prize for Physics being awarded to Peter Higgs of Britain and Francois Englert of Belgium.

Kibble went on to publish a second influential paper in 1967, in *Physical Review*, entitled *Symmetry breaking in non-Abelian gauge theories*. Kibble has made many other contributions, often related to spontaneous symmetry breaking, including the idea of cosmic strings – hypothetical one-dimensional defects that may have been created in the very early history of the universe. No observational evidence for them has yet been found, but the same mechanism has found application in condensed matter physics.[2]

Charles Smith 1932-1997 and Englishman John King, seeking to improve the quality of meat, undertook research at the Animal Breeding Research Organisation in Edinburgh. Working with John Gibson, their research examined a wide variety of applied problems in animal breeding. Smith teamed up with Frank Nicholas in Australia and pioneered cattle production through multiple ovulation and embryo transfer (MOET), but ways of exploiting this technology had lagged behind. Nicholas came up with a scheme which opened up new possibilities. Others in the scientific community largely neglected this scheme, but Smith saw its promise, and, working in collaboration, showed how much more rapid improvement in dairy cattle might be possible. This involved not only the use of new technology but also consequent changes in herd structure making the change an entirely different proposition. After a great deal of discussion, the first MOET herd was established in Britain by Premier Breeders (later taken over by Genus). Elaboration of the MOET principle led to a most productive phase in the development of thinking about cattle improvement schemes.[1]

Thomas Graham Brown born 1933 invented a computer-linked 3-D electric eye scanner for viewing inside the human body in 1976. Earlier, he worked with Ian Donald on the development of the ultrasound scan, which was originally designed as an ultrasound detector for finding flaws in metal. Together with John MacVicar, who joined the department as registrar in 1956, Brown and Donald came up with the world's first compound contact scanner where the transducer can be moved manually over the patient's abdomen with a resultant 2-D image reproduced on an oscilloscope.[1]

Brown also invented and patented an elaborate and expensive automated compound B-scanner in 1958 which took care of a number of scanning variables of the operator but, due to its expense, it never became popular. He joined Sonicaid Ltd in 1973 and led a team to develop an entirely new 3-dimensional stereoscopic contact compound scanner. "The man who spotted and exploited the 'resolution enhancement' aspect was a radiologist in Edinburgh, Bruce Young, with an honourable record of achievement in other areas of diagnostic medicine, and who used it amongst other things to follow the ripening of follicles in the ovaries of infertile women."[2]

Struther Arnott 1934-2013 discovered tiny creases along the "ladder" structure of DNA molecules. The "wrinkles" were revealed in computer-enhanced X-ray pictures of DNA structures.[1] Arnott developed more systematic methods for analysing X-ray diffraction patterns from fibrous DNA (in nature DNA comes in several different forms including fibrous bundles of DNA helices). These methods made it easier to explore the many different forms of DNA and RNA (a polymer related to DNA) and to solve the structures of complex molecules such as polypeptides, polysaccharides and other carbohydrates.[2]

Stewart Crichton Miller 1934-1999 was a mechanical engineer who spent more than forty years working with Rolls Royce, where he became Director of Engineering and Technology, then became Director of Advanced Engineering in 1984. From 1985 to 1990 he was in charge of all Aero Engine Design and Development. He was a prominent contributor to several of the company's most important development projects, chief among them being the RB211-535 engine project,[1] later produced for variants of the Boeing 747, 757 and 767, as well as the Russian Tupolev Tu-204 airliner. "It is the world's most durable engine, mainly because of Stewart's attention to detail, his insistence on people doing things right from day one, and his ability to follow things through to a conclusion. One engine has recently achieved a world record of 40,000 hours in service, or 24 million miles [38,624,256 km], a distance equivalent to 50 round trips to the moon, with nothing more than routine servicing."[2]

David James Thouless born 1934 won the 2000 Lars Onsager Prize with John Michael Kosterlitz for the introduction of the theory of topological phase transitions, as well as fundamental contributions to our understanding of electron localisation and the behaviour of spin glasses. He has made many theoretical contributions to the understanding of extended systems of atoms and electrons, and of nucleons. He has also won the Howleck Prize for Physics (1980), Wolf Prize for Physics (1990), and the Dirac Prize of the Institute of Physics (1993).[1]

Thouless, Kosterlitz, Bertrand Halperin, David R. Nelson and Allan Peter Young proposed the existence of the hexatic phase in theoretical studies about melting in two dimensions. The hexatic phase is a phase that is between the solid and the isotropic liquid phases in two dimensional systems of particles. It is characterised by two order parameters: a short-range positional and a quasi-long-range orientational (sixfold) order. More generally, a hexatic is any phase that contains sixfold orientational order, in analogy with the nematic phase (with twofold orientational order).

They proposed two phase transitions by binding of topological defects (dislocation and declination). The first transition occurs when the solid (quasi-long-range positional order, long-range orientational order) undergoes a dislocation unbinding transition to the hexatic phase (short-range positional order, quasi-long-range orientational order). The second transition is the disclination unbinding transition which transforms the hexatic phase into an isotropic phase (short-range positional and orientational order).[2]

Frank Matthews Leslie 1935-2000 was a distinguished applied mathematician, who was above all foremost in creating the modern continuum theory of nematic liquid crystals in the late 1960s. This theory is now known as the Ericksen-Leslie theory, and the crucial elements in it are known as Leslie coefficients. After developing the hydrodynamic theory of nematic liquid crystals, he went on to perform a similar task in the 1990s for smectic liquid crystals. He also actively collaborated with experimentalists and engineers involved in liquid crystal applications, and his work has been extremely influential in the development of liquid crystal display (LCD) device technology.[1]

In 1970, in what turned out to be a particularly important paper for the development of liquid crystal devices, he analysed the distorting effect of a magnetic field on twisted orientation patterns. The physical problem was what is called a "hybrid" liquid crystal cell, in which the directors at the (parallel) cell boundaries are oriented in the planes of the boundary, but perpendicular to each other. Inside the cell the director twists around uniformly from one orientation to the other. A magnetic field across the cell, however, interacts with the director, and in Leslie's hypothetical case, favoured director orientation along the magnetic field. The director will thus swing out of the plane of the boundary, but for reasons of symmetry will only do so at a threshold field. Mathematically this required a three-dimensional solution for the director.

The general effect had been observed by Vsevolod Konstantinovich Frederiks (1927) – giving rise to the eponymous Frederiks effect – and explained by Hans Zocher (1933), but only in the case of a "normal" cell in which in the field-free case the director was uniform. Untwisting of twisted liquid crystal textures was observed and understood in principle, though not in any theoretical detail, by Charles Mauguin in 1911. Using an argument due to Jules Henri Poincare, he showed that a twisted structure could, in a suitable limit now known as the Mauguin regime, act as a wave guide, twisting the light polarisation axis with it. Leslie found a specific formula which generalised Zocher's result.

The importance of the result, however, is not its mathematical sophistication (although it was by no means trivial). Rather, it was the presence in the audience at Leslie's Berlin talk of Martin Schadt and Wolfgang Helfrich, who were in the process of patenting the twisted nematic liquid crystal device. This has turned out to be *the* major (flat screen) liquid crystal display technology. Schadt and Helfrich (1971) realised that the mathematics would remain more or less unchanged if an electric field were to be substituted for a magnetic field. Leslie's result thus formed the foundation for the emerging flat screen display industry, although he did not directly benefit financially.[2]

James Hunter Whitelaw 1936-2006 researched the development and application of "universal" calculation methods for turbulent flows. The advent of such computational methods required experimental confirmation, and Whitelaw's groundbreaking research resulted in the development and application of non-intrusive laser-based instrumentation for flow characterisation. The early helium-neon lasers were highly unstable in operation, and difficulties in aligning the different optical components made progress slow. A key development, pursued jointly by Whitelaw and his research assistant, Franz Durst, resulted in a compact integrated system that formed the basis for subsequent commercial instruments.

Further contributions were made in the area of counter-type processors and in the treatment of data through time-averaging. Together with Adrian Melling, Whitelaw and Durst wrote the first, highly influential book on the subject of laser Doppler anemometry (a technique for measuring the direction and speed of fluids). The experimental techniques developed under Whitelaw's leadership found wide application, for example in the study of the dynamics of combustion processes in furnaces and engines. Whitelaw's main research goal was to reveal the nature of aerodynamic and thermo-physical processes rather than simply to develop instrumentation. His research covered fundamental topics, like the anisotropy of turbulent stresses and the extinction/re-ignition of turbulent flames, as well as practical devices, including complex industrial burners, automotive engines, and gas turbines. Further developments followed, such as the phase-Doppler anemometer for spray research and the shadow-Doppler anemometer for irregular particles, the latter in collaboration with colleagues at Keio University in Japan. During thirty-six years at Imperial, Whitelaw published over 300 research papers and successfully supervised eighty-six PhD students.[1]

James Goodfellow born 1937 patented the PIN (Personal Identification Number) concept. As a Development Engineer with Smiths Industries Ltd, Goodfellow was given the project of developing an automatic cash dispenser in 1965. Chubb Lock & Safe Company were to provide the secure physical housing and the mechanical dispenser mechanism. Goodfellow designed a system which accepted a machine-readable encrypted card, to which he added a numerical keypad. UK Patent Number 1,197,183, with a priority date of 2 May 1966, covers this invention, and it is also covered by US Patent No. 3,905,461 and Patents granted by many other countries. These patents list James Goodfellow as inventor, along with the late A.I.O. Davies, the company General Manager. This US Patent still describes the basic ATM function almost 50 years later.[1]

Alan James Duncan 1938-1999 participated in and supervised the design, construction and operation of a metastable atomic hydrogen beam apparatus which was used to observe successfully for the first time the two-photon decay of metastable atomic hydrogen. The apparatus was then used in a practical realisation of the famous Einstein-Podolsky-Rosen thought experiment to test some for the fundamental predictions of quantum theory. The results obtained were novel and unique and brought wide national and international recognition, as evidenced by the numerous invitations Duncan received to speak at scientific conferences.[1]

Duncan, in collaboration with Wilson Sibbett and Miles Padgett, was successful in developing two novel optical instruments with important practical applications. The first was a compact Fourier-transform spectrometer with no moving parts, which can be used, for example, in the detection of atmospheric pollutants. The spectrometer has been granted a full patent and has been successfully marketed. The second instrument was a new type of optical profilometer for recording surface profiles. The profilometer system won joint first prize in the 1998 National Physical Laboratory "Metrology for world class manufacturing awards" competition. It records the profile of surfaces without any mechanical contact, a considerable advantage in the preparation of precision or ultra-clean devices.[2]

Bryan Barnet Molloy 1939-2004 co-invented *Prozac*. He worked with Klaus Schmiegel as head of the chemistry team at Eli Lilly that was searching for an effective antidepressant that was safer than past medications. He co-invented a class of aryloxyphenylpropylamines, which includes the active ingredient – fluoxetine – in *Prozac*, the most widely used antidepressant, which was prescribed on Britain's National Health Service six million times in 2011 and, in the USA, 24.4 million prescriptions for fluoxetine in 2010. Introduced by Eli Lilly & Co. in the USA in 1988, *Prozac* represented a new class of antidepressants called selective serotonin reuptake inhibitors.[1]

Molloy and Schmiegel began by examining aryloxyphenylpropylamines and synthesised many new compounds in their search for a drug with desirable properties. One of these compounds, fluoxetine hydrochloride, was found to be highly selective, affecting only the neurotransmitter serotonin.

In the early 1970s, evidence of the role of serotonin (5-hydroxytryptamine or 5-HT) in depression began to emerge and the hypothesis that enhancing 5-HT neurotransmission would be a viable mechanism to mediate antidepressant response was put forward. On the basis of this hypothesis, efforts to develop agents that inhibit the uptake of 5-HT from the synaptic cleft were initiated. These studies led to the discovery and development of the selective serotonin-reuptake inhibitor fluoxetine hydrochloride (*Prozac*). Two other Eli Lilly researchers, Ray W. Fuller and David T. Wong, worked with Molloy on the development of *Prozac*.

In 1983, Eli Lilly applied to FDA for approval to sell *Prozac* for treatment of depression. Fluoxetine was initially approved for treatment of depression in Belgium in 1986, and then Eli Lilly's *Prozac* was approved by the FDA on 29 December 1987 and introduced in the United States at the beginning of 1988. It was the first of a new class of drugs, called selective serotonin reuptake inhibitors (SSRIs), to be approved for use in the United States.[3] During his 33 years at Lilly, Molloy published over 100 papers and acquired over 30 patents.

Prozac became one of the most prescribed antidepressants, with worldwide annual sales in the $2-3 billion range until the expiration of its patent in 2001 and the rise of competition from other pharmaceutical companies, ultimately including manufacturers of generic drugs. *Prozac* and similar drugs enabled many of the estimated 10 million people in the United States suffering from depression to lead normal lives.[2]

Fluoxetine may be useful for patients who cannot use standard prophylactic agents or if other agents fail. It is also a good choice for people with concomitant depression or other illness treatable with SSRI. Fibromyalgia is the most common rheumatic cause of chronic pain. In a randomised placebo-controlled study, women who received fluoxetine had significant improvement in pain, fatigue and depression compared with those who received a placebo. Fluoxetine has been found to increase the latent period of intravaginal ejaculation and therefore to be beneficial in patients who prematurely ejaculate.[4]

William Napier born 1940 was one of the first astronomers to recognise that the Earth is at risk from its interplanetary and galactic environments, and to put forward the controversial proposition that celestial bombardments may even have been responsible for catastrophe in historical times.

Some 13,000 years ago, the Earth was struck by thousands of Tunguska-sized cometary fragments over the course of an hour, leading to a dramatic cooling of the planet, according to astronomer Bill Napier of the Cardiff University Astrobiology Centre.

The cooling, by as much as 8 degrees Celsius, interrupted the warming which was occurring at the end of the last ice age and caused glaciers to readvance. Evidence has been found that this catastrophic change was associated with some extraordinary extraterrestrial event. The boundary is marked by the occurrence of a "black mat" layer a few centimetres thick found at many sites throughout the United States containing high levels of soot indicative of continental-scale wildfires, as well as microscopic hexagonal diamonds (nanodiamonds) which are produced by shocks and are only found in meteorites or impact craters. These findings led to the suggestion that the catastrophic changes of that time were caused by the impact of an asteroid or comet 4 km across on the Laurentide ice sheet, which at that time covered what would become Canada and the northern part of the United States.

The cooling lasted over a thousand years, and its onset coincides with the rapid extinction of 35 genera of North American mammals, as well as the disruption of the Palaeoindian culture. The chief objection to the idea of a big impact is that the odds against the Earth being struck by an asteroid this large only 13,000 years ago are a thousand to one against. And the heat generated by the rising fireball would be limited by the curvature of the horizon and could not explain the continent-wide occurrence of wildfires.

Napier has now come up with an astronomical model which accounts for the major features of the catastrophe without involving such an improbable event. According to his model, the Earth ran into a dense trail of material from a large disintegrating comet. He points out that there is compelling evidence that such a comet entered the inner planetary system between 20,000 and 30,000 years ago and has been fragmenting ever since, giving rise to a number of closely related meteor streams and co-moving asteroids known as the Taurid Complex.[1]

Gordon Bryce Donaldson 1941-2012 developed a technique to measure minute magnetic fields using gradiometers, which he invented during his time at Berkeley. These instruments are based on SQUIDs (superconducting quantum interference devices), whose usefulness Donaldson developed and championed. The uses of SQUID-based gradiometry are remarkably diverse; for example, non-destructive testing of materials (such as examining aircraft chassis for minute cracks) and medical imaging of heart and brain function (such as in epilepsy patients).[1]

SQUIDs were ingenious devices using quantum effects to detect minute magnetic fields such as those generated in the brain.[2] A SQUID can detect a change of energy some 100 billion times weaker than the electromagnetic energy that moves a compass needle. Donaldson, using SQUID gradiometers, was an independent originator of nondestructive evaluation (NDE) of materials.[3]

Ronald Shade Hamilton born 1941 invented the world's first daily disposable contact lens. Danish ophthalmologist, Michael Bay, considered the problem of cleaning contact lens and decided that the best thing to do with the lenses was to throw them away rather than try to clean them. In 1982, he launched the Danalens in Denmark, a lens to be worn overnight for one week then thrown away. These were the first disposable lenses. Johnson & Johnson bought him out, changed the material he was using, refined his unique manufacturing process and added the packaging and marketing from the pharmaceutical industry. The result was *Acuvue*.

At that time, contact lenses were treated as individual items even when made in sizeable batches because the processes involved gave rise to significant lens-to-lens variation, even when made under so-called identical conditions. Quality control involved intensive inspection to remove unacceptable lens and to assign parameters to each individual good lens. "Process yield was typically 30%. By contrast, making bottles of cleaning solutions relied on strict process control, from the manufacturing environment right through to the selection and mixing process of the various chemicals involved. Process yield was around 100%."[1]

Due to the high wastage and inspection demands, a pair of soft contact lenses retailed at around £150 whereas the cost of cleaning a lens was just a few pence. "In those days if your contact lens went down the plug you'd call an emergency plumber to fish it out."[2]

Hamilton felt that if the moulding technique could be improved even further then a low-cost, daily disposable lens could be achieved. His original approach to his employer at the time was rejected as it would reduce profits from lens cleaning solutions, so Hamilton went out on his own. He worked in a shed in his back garden with the *Award* lens being the result. In 1993, Hamilton opened a factory in Livingston, Scotland, to manufacture the world's first daily-disposable lenses and launched them in early 1995 through Boots Opticians in the UK. Johnson & Johnson launched their one day *Acuvue* lens to the world later in the same year.

In 1996, Hamilton sold the rights to an American company but, by 2001, he had become disillusioned that the price still remained high despite several competitors, so he designed a new contact lens and formed his own company, Provis Daysoft, the only company in the world dedicated to the manufacture and sale of one-day disposable contact lenses. Provis Daysoft supplies about 30 million lenses a year via internet sales to independent opticians in 23 countries including the UK, Egypt, Sri Lanka, Australia, Germany, France, Italy and the Scandinavian nations, with more than 450 million sold to date.[3]

Christopher Andrew Lipinski born 1941 published a seminal paper identifying a series of features commonly found in orally active drugs. These features are referred to as Lipinski's Rule of Five and can be used as a rule of thumb to indicate whether a molecule is likely to be orally bioavailable (bioactive). The "rule of five" is so called because most of the features start with the number five. In general, an orally active drug has: not more than 5 hydrogen bond donors (OH and NH groups), not more than 10 hydrogen bond acceptors (notably N and O), a molecular weight under 500, a LogP under 5. Molecules that possess this rule are not automatically drug-like. For classifying a molecule as drug-like or non-drug-like, a proper cheminformatic approach must still be used, e.g. quantitative structure-activity relationship (QSAR) models. This rule was derived for drugs and not for lead structures, which usually have a lower molecular weight, fewer rings, fewer rotatable bonds, and a lower lipophilicity. The rules have spawned many extensions.[1] The publication of these rules that became known as the Lipinski Rule of Five is one of the most highly cited papers in the field of medicinal chemistry.[2]

Since its publication in 1997, the Lipinski Rule of Five has been a critical filter for drug development programs. A simple algorithm that helps identify successful drug candidates, the principles filter out molecules likely to have poor intestinal permeability or poor aqueous solubility, and hence poor oral absorption. This landmark contribution to drug development has influenced the way that the pharmaceutical industry approaches the development of orally active drugs. Drug discovery programs worldwide use the Rule as a filter in high-throughput screening libraries and the TB Alliance is applying Lipinski's Rule to its go/no-go decision-making process for its projects in the nitroimidazopyran and quinolone classes. Lipinski has authored over 190 publications and invited presentations, and has 17 issued US patents.[3]

Stephen William Hawking born 1942 has been called the most insightful theoretical physicist since Albert Einstein[1] and one of the intellectual giants of the modern world.[2] His work concentrates on the puzzling cosmic bodies called black holes and extends to such specialised fields as particle physics, supersymmetry, and quantum gravity.

In the late 1960s, he and his Cambridge friend and colleague, Roger Penrose, applied a new, complex mathematical model they had created from Albert Einstein's general theory of relativity. This led, in 1971, to Hawking proving the first of many singularity theorems; such theorems provide a set of sufficient conditions for the existence of a singularity in space-time. This work showed that, far from being mathematical curiosities which appear only in special cases, singularities are a fairly generic feature of general relativity.[3]

He supplied a mathematical proof, along with Brandon Carter, Werner Israel and David Robinson, of John Wheeler's "No-Hair Theorem" – namely, that any black hole is fully described by the three properties of mass, angular momentum, and electric charge.

Hawking also suggested that, after the Big Bang, primordial or mini black holes were formed. With James Maxwell Bardeen and Carter, he proposed the four laws of black hole mechanics, drawing an analogy with thermodynamics. In 1974, he calculated that black holes should thermally create and emit subatomic particles, known as Hawking radiation, until they exhaust their energy and evaporate. One of Hawking's most controversial claims is that information can be irretrievably lost when black holes diminish in size and disappear due to Hawking radiation. The law of information conservation is one of the fundamental principles of physics. Information is *never* lost. … "Information, he continued to insist, is truly lost when black holes evaporate, and this means we can predict even less than we thought on the basis of quantum theory."[4]

One proposed solution to the problem of Hawking's lost information is a suggestion "that any information gratuitously destroyed in a black hole *balances out* information that is equally gratuitously *created* elsewhere in the universe – notably out of the "white hole" constituted by the radiation origin, but also out of lesser "white hole" phenomena such as stars and supernova explosions."[5]

In collaboration with Jim Hartle, Hawking developed a model in which the Universe had no boundary in space-time, replacing the initial singularity of the classical Big Bang models with a region akin to the North Pole; while one cannot travel north of the North Pole, there is no boundary there. While originally the no-boundary proposal predicted a closed Universe, discussions with Neil Turok led to the realisation that the no-boundary proposal is also consistent with a Universe which is not closed.[6]

His science book, *A Brief History of Time* (1988), has sold over 10 million copies.[7] It attempts to explain a range of subjects in cosmology, including the Big Bang, black holes and light cones, to the nonspecialist reader. Its main goal is to give an overview of the subject but, unusual for a popular science book, it also attempts to explain some complex mathematics. The 1996 edition of the book and subsequent editions discuss the possibility of time travel and wormholes and explore the possibility of having a universe without a quantum singularity at the beginning of time.[8]

David Irvine-Halliday born 1942 was stuck in Nepal in 1996 due to a cancelled flight and, with a fortnight before the next available flight, he went for a hike in the Annapurna Circuit in the Nepalese Himalayas. "On his way, he encounters a small village with a tiny schoolhouse. Walking by that school, he hears children singing, yet there is no light inside. In that moment,

Irvine-Halliday both wonders at and realises the issues facing poor, rural villages all over the world. Eventually, he went back to his laboratory at the University of Calgary and began experimenting with light-emitting diodes (LEDs). After toying around with pedal power and hydro power, he settled on solar power, which makes a wonderful companion to LEDs because both have excellent longevity. LEDs use 10 times less electricity than conventional incandescent bulbs and last many times longer. What Irvine-Halliday dreamt of was a solar lighting scenario that could last for decades. In the end, he worked out a product that consists of a single white LED light, small battery and solar panel. In 2000, he went back to Nepal and began putting these in homes. Soon his piece of the solar movement was growing, so Irvine-Halliday started the Light Up The World Foundation and expanded his solar-powered relief plan well beyond the borders of Nepal.[1] His revolutionary low-cost lighting system enables each household to have two lamps bright enough to read by, consumes less electricity than is needed to light a single conventional 100 watt light bulb. Affordable for those with annual incomes as low as $US200, the system is powered with batteries that are recharged by a central solar panel and will be effective for about 20 years.[2]

As at 16 March 2014, Light Up the World has installed 31,890 lights into homes sheltering 1,203,787 people in 54 countries across Asia, South America and Africa.[3]

Alastair David Milne born 1942 created Wolfson Microelectronics Ltd. with Jim Reid. The Company designed integrated circuits for clients in emerging applications such as mobile phones, medical instrumentation, industrial monitoring, and toys. In 1995, Wolfson began creating its own products aiming at the growing digital consumer electronics market. Wolfson products have found applications within the digital audio player market, such as in Microsoft's Zune product line, including the Zune 30 and Zune HD, as well as providing the codec functionality for much of the Apple iPod series (with the exception of the iPod shuffle and iPod classic) and Sony's PSP. Wolfson chips have also found a place in the Microsoft Xbox game console, Logitech Squeezebox Duet and the PalmOne Treo smartphone, with the Apple connection continuing with the earlier versions of the iPhone and iPod Touch. Wolfson audio products can also be found in the Samsung Wave S8500 and Samsung i9000 Galaxy S smartphones, as well as a number of LG phones including the LG-LB4400 music phone and the Android-powered LG Optimus GT540 smartphone. In 2011, Wolfson delivered the world's first Audio System-on-a-Chip (SoC), and in 2012, the year it produced its 2 billionth chip, it introduced the world's first quad core HD Audio Processor System-on-a-Chip.[1] The Company experienced phenomenal growth and rapidly became a global brand. In 2006, it achieved over $200 million of revenue with a market value of $1billion, although that had dropped to $156.9 million in 2012.[2] It was sold in April 2014 to Cirrus Logic.

Gordon Robert Bruce Skinner 1942-2013 was a Senior Clinical Lecturer at the Medical School, University of Birmingham and Honorary Consultant at the Queen Elizabeth Hospital, Birmingham for approximately 30 years. At the University, he directed programs to develop vaccines against herpes simplex virus, cytomegalovirus, *varicella zoster* virus, human immunodeficiency virus (HIV) and staphylococci. Skinner has published approximately 100 papers in medical and scientific journals and he has patented 16 viral and bacterial vaccines and various other medical therapies and devices.[1]

He developed a vaccine to treat herpes simplex in the 1980s. It was also trialled to test the efficacy and safety in the modulation of herpes genitalis. The frequency of recurrences was reduced in the vaccinated female patients at both 3 and 6 months following vaccination with an overall reduction in patients of both sexes which did not reach statistical significance. Recurrence severity was reduced as measured by decreased number of lesions and associated symptoms per recurrence. The data suggest that clinical manifestations of latent HSV genital infection may be modified by therapeutic immunisation.[2]

Skinner was asked by colleagues to see patients who were considered to have myalgic encephalopathy or chronic fatigue syndrome or post viral syndrome or post viral fatigue on account of his interest in virus disease. He noted that a number of these patients had clinical features of hypothyroidism but had "normal" levels of thyroid hormones which would lead most workers in the field to reject a diagnosis of hypothyroidism. Skinner treated and returned to health many patients who were clinically hypothyroid but had normal thyroid chemistry.[3]

James Fraser Stoddart born 1942 helped establish the field of molecular nanotechnology.[1] Stoddart is one of the few chemists of the past quarter century to have created a new field of organic chemistry – namely, one in which the mechanical bond is a pre-eminent feature of molecular compounds. He has pioneered the development of the use of molecular recognition and self-assembly processes in template-directed protocols for the syntheses of two-state mechanically interlocked compounds (bistable catenanes and rotaxanes) that have been employed as molecular switches and as motor-molecules in the fabrication of nanoelectronic devices and NanoElectroMechanical Systems.[2]

Stoddart was recognised for his pioneering work in the development of a new field in chemistry dealing with nanoscience and, in particular, his work in molecular recognition and self-assembly. "His introduction of quick and efficient template-directed synthetic routes to mechanically interlocked molecular compounds is of seminal importance. It has changed dramatically the way chemists think about molecular systems and how they can be used in the fabrication of molecular switches and machines such as molecular elevators and shuttles. Stoddart's work was cleverly, elegantly and meticulously done, and carries tremendous creativity, originality and innovation."[3]

Stoddart has given more than 1,000 plenary/invited lectures. During 43 years, more than 390 PhD and postdoctoral students have passed through his laboratories and been inspired by his imagination and creativity, and more than 80 have subsequently embarked upon successful independent academic careers.[4]

Stoddart, the Board of Trustees Professor of Chemistry at Northwestern University in Evanston Illinois, is internationally recognised as one of the most important figures in molecular nanotechnology today (Armes Lecture 2009).[5]

Some measure of the influence and impact of Stoddart's work may be drawn from citation statistics. Two of his more than 1,000 publications have been cited over 1,000 times, 13 over 500, 24 over 300, 137 over 100, and 312 over 50. He has an h-index of 115. Note: The h-index is an index that attempts to measure both the productivity and impact of the published work of a scientist or scholar. The index is based on the set of the scientist's most cited papers and the number of citations that they have received in other publications. For example, if you have an h-index of 20, it means you have 20 papers with at least 20 citations. Jorge Hirsch, who developed the index, reckons that after 20 years of research, an h index of 20 is good, 40 is outstanding 60 is truly exceptional.

Archibald Robin Forrest born 1943 has been at the forefront of many computer graphics programs used today. In 1971, whilst a student at Cambridge, he defined the subject of Computational Geometry and published the first paper in the field. His re-working of Bezier curves can today be found in Adobe Illustrator, PostScript and PDF.[1] He published one of the first papers on scientific visualisation in 1979, on point-based rendering, and he was a pioneer in 3-D computer-aided design (CAD) using curves (e.g. car bodies) and for creating computer-generated imagery for movies and games. In 1965, Forrest and Donald Welbourn began serious research into 3-D modelling CAD software at Cambridge University's Computing Laboratory.[2] In 1968, Forrest published *Curves and surfaces for computer-aided design* and he "realised that the Bezier curves could be expressed in terms of Bernstein polynomials". His article on this was very influential and helped popularise Bezier curves considerably.[3] A practical outcome of this was an improvement in the "crazy way Renault design [car] surfaces"[4] Forrest designed and built Cambridge University's CAD Group's Mark II foam-cutting machine which was used to cut rigid foam, wood and rigid, high-density polyethylene models.[5]

Jonathan Copus born 1944 invented the Dentron *Biogun*, in 1989, an electronic painkiller for dentists, which works by producing specially shaped electronic signals that "switch off" pain messages before they reach the brain at the same time as stimulating the release of endorphins, the body's natural painkillers. In dentistry, it is used to treat: dental caries; lesions being fissure-sealed or remineralised; or when traditional restorative techniques are demanded. The *Biogun* can be used to sterilise the cavity, candidiasis, including angular cheilitis, periodontitis, gingivitis, and mouth ulcers.

His Dentron *Biogun* has been shown to ionise molecular oxygen and generate superoxide radical anions (O_2-) with a bactericidal effect against microorganisms. In vitro studies using the *Biogun* have shown it to be effective against a range of microorganisms, in particular MRSA. "The Dentron *Biogun* might represent a simple, effective, and, because it can be used repeatedly, inexpensive method for eradicating MRSA".[1]

The *Biogun*'s use of ultra-violet light aids in podiatry for verrucae, athlete's foot, infected leg ulcers, infected onychocryptosis, fungal nail infections, diabetic foot ulcers and exudative venous ulcers.[2]

The table-top device produces a concentrated stream of electrically-charged air particles which literally burst the bugs causing an infection. More technically, a mix of particles including the superoxide radical anion de-esterify the fatty acids in the phospholipid bilayer making up the cell membrane of micro-organisms, causing lysis. The practitioner uses a handpiece to aim the particles at the site of infection from a distance of about 6 mm. As the device is fully automatic, treatment can be administered after only a few minutes' training. In laboratory tests and in clinical trials, the *Biogun* has been proved effective against 43 representative micro-organisms responsible for a wide variety of diseases. Experiments in food preservation have also produced positive results, with the method killing both food spoilage and food-poisoning organisms – including the pathogenic *E. Coli* H: 0157 responsible for a number of food-poisoning outbreaks in recent years. Dentron describe the *Biogun* as the world's first "electronic antibiotic".[3]

Peter Mitchell Grant born 1944 had responsibility, in 1970, for the development of an electronic coin recognition system implemented as a metal oxide silicon (MOS) custom integrated circuit. In 1977, he supervised the design of a digital phased array acoustic imaging system. His team's research resulted in new signal processing algorithms for smart antenna base stations and multi-user detection for CDMA systems.[1]

He also supervised studies on the design of digital adaptive filters. This covered the use of linear tapped transversal, lattice, frequency domain "fast convolution" and neural network based nonlinear equaliser techniques. This latter work has investigated both Volterra series and radial basis function (RBF) structures. The work on adaptive RBF structures provides quantifiable and significant performance improvements over linear adaptive filters. His particularly significant 1991 IEEE Trans NN paper on the orthogonal least squares processor design has received almost 1,200 citations, due to its widespread applicability in the training of linear-in-the-parameter neural networks and adoption by researchers in the sparse signal representation community as a computationally efficient method for orthogonal matching pursuit.[2]

In 2007, Grant was one of the first four signal processing researchers to be elevated to EURASIP Fellow, the new most prestigious honour of the European Association for Signal, and in 2005 he was awarded the EURASIP Meritorious Service award for fundamental activities in adaptive signal processing and CDMA. In 2000-2002, he was President of EURASIP.

Richard Henderson born 1945 collaborated with Nigel Unwin to develop electron microscopy into a tool for the direct determination of the structure of proteins, applying it most notably to the light-driven proton pump, bacteriorhodopsin, from Halobacteria. During the next 15 years, he worked to solve a number of the technical and conceptual problems which limited the attainable resolution of electron crystallography, and by 1990, he and his colleagues had succeeded in obtaining the first atomic structure of the membrane protein, bacteriorhodopsin, by using electron microscopy and diffraction. Subsequent analysis of the structure of some of its photochemical intermediates has helped to understand how bacteriorhodopsin and other closely related family members function.[1]

Henderson produced a high-resolution 7 ångström map of the purple membrane from *Halobacterium halobium*, showing the helical structure of bacteriorhodopsin that have led to his detailed proposal for the mechanism of ion pumping, providing the first such view of a membrane-transport protein.[2]

In Cambridge, Henderson and Rekha Subramaniam shock-froze bacteriorhodopsin in its "open state," while it was pumping a proton across the bacterial membrane. They then used the electron beam of an electron microscope to analyse two-dimensional crystals of the protein, in a method called electron crystallography. This resulted in the first study that described the structure of the "open state". "[It] was the first structural description of a proton pump caught in action," Subramaniam says.[3]

Gordon David Plotkin born 1946 is a computer scientist best-known for his introduction of structural operational semantics and his work on denotational semantics. In particular, his notes on *A Structural Approach to Operational Semantics* (1981) were very influential. He is also a winner of The Royal Society Wolfson Research Merit Award and the citation for his SIGPLAN Achievement Award in 2010 reads: "Professor Gordon D. Plotkin has made fundamental advances in almost every area of the theory of programming languages. His contributions have helped to establish the mathematical foundations on which the scientific study of programming languages are based. His 1975 paper *Call-by-name, Call-by-value, and the λ-calculus* exposed the relationship between the reduction semantics of the λ-calculus and its operational semantics, as defined by Landin's SECD machine."[1]

In the process, he defined what it meant for a calculus and a semantics to correspond: this launched the study of operational semantics as it is now understood. He invented Structural Operational Semantics as a technique for specifying the semantics of a wide range of programming languages, concurrent as well as sequential; this form of semantics is now one of the basic working tools of researchers developing new programming languages and type systems.

Plotkin's contributions to the development of the mathematical theory of domains, and its applications to the denotational semantics of programming languages, have been of fundamental importance: they include his powerdomain construction, systematic development of the general theory of the solution of recursive domain equations, and his work on Programming Computable Functions and the full abstraction problem.

Plotkin's work with Glynn Winskel on event structures is the basis for reasoning about distributed systems, process algebras, and reactive systems. Event structures have been enormously influential in the development of models of concurrency. He has also investigated the logical foundations of computer security, including logics for specifying authorisation policies for computer systems. Plotkin continues to make bold and deep contributions, for example, in his current work on the algebraic theory of effects, and on languages and calculi for biochemical modelling. "Taken together, Gordon Plotkin's contributions over the past four decades exhibit a range and depth unmatched in the field."[2]

William Hill 1949-2012 co-invented Microsoft *ClearType*, which improved the ability to read text on PC monitors. "In layman's terms, Mr Hill's visionary concepts helped create what most of us now take for granted – reading comfortably on a computer screen. His colleagues say his work was a major factor in the creation of eBooks, including those on Amazon's *Kindle* or the Apple *iPad*. 'The job of making the screen as comfortable to read as paper is not yet completed,' he wrote in a blog shortly before he died."[1]

Addressing machines were superseded by the advent of computerised word processors and mailing labels, but displaying the printed word on a computer monitor required a different approach to printing. While many of the traditional typefaces could still be used, there was room for improvement with new typefaces, and computer software opened up new possibilities. In 1985, Glasgow-born Bill Hill was asked to write the documentation for *Guide*, the first hypertext authoring and reading application for the Apple Macintosh computer.

In 1994, he moved to Microsoft to lead the typography team. It was Hill who commissioned American type designer Matthew Carter, who then created the Georgia and Verdana type for computer monitors. The transition from reading books to reading PC monitors was problematic because "with the advent of the computer, reading became infinitely more difficult. The biggest problem was resolution – the clarity of words and images on the screen. A big stumbling block in computer evolution was fuzzy letters arranged on glaring screens that left the reader with a blinding headache. Readability is so poor that, according to Microsoft, the average reader hits the print button after just three paragraphs."[2]

Hill decided the "brain works on two levels as we read: it subconsciously recognises words as patterns, which frees the unconscious to concentrate on the words and their meaning. So typographical elements – the shape and thickness of the characters, the space between the letters and words – help us recognise the patterns. If the proportion of those elements is radically different, as it is on a computer screen, it interrupts the reading process. The brain has to make a conscious effort to identify the patterns, which takes away from the comprehension. *ClearType* mathematically manipulates the subpixels, tricking the eye into seeing smooth edges where there is nothing but snaggle-toothed letters. The impact on resolution is immense: it is the equivalent of reading 300 dpi."[3]

In 1998, when Hill first started to investigate the readability of type used in eBooks, resolution was around 88 dpi. He developed software to "unlock the true resolution of the colour LCD screen, which is actually three times better than anyone ever realised, because we've always assumed the pixel was the smallest unit we could effectively address. We were astonished at the quality of what could be achieved with our new technology, which we've called *ClearType*."[4] Before *ClearType*, the smallest level of detail that a computer could display was a single pixel, but with *ClearType* running on an LCD monitor, features of text as small as a fraction of a pixel in width can be displayed. The extra resolution increases the sharpness of the tiny details in text display, making it much easier to read over long durations. With *ClearType* font technology, the words on your computer screen look almost as sharp and clear as those printed on a piece of paper.[5]

Leslie Johnston Browne born 1950 discovered *Fadrozole*, the first marketed non-steroidal aromatase inhibitor for the treatment of oestrogen-dependent breast cancer. He also managed cardiovascular research at Ciba-Geigy Ltd., in Basel, Switzerland, where he helped discover *Diovan*, the second angiotensin II antagonist ever to be marketed.[1] He was closely involved, with Robert Mathews Bowman and Robert Edward Steele, in the discovery of *Femara* (Letrozole), which became a major product for Novartis.[2] The US Food and Drug Administration approved *Femara* in 1997 for the treatment of advanced breast cancer in postmenopausal women with disease progression following antiestrogen therapy. It is currently available in more than 75 countries worldwide. In 2000, the FDA designated *Femara* for priority review based on a supplemental new drug application (sNDA) for use as first-line therapy.[3]

Douglas Crombie Anderson born 1951 developed and commercialised the world's first ultra-wide field retinal imaging system capable of detecting a wide range of sight and life- threatening diseases. The system gives a complete and detailed picture of a patient's retina in a quarter of a second via a non-invasive laser scanning technology. Known as *Optos*, it has also led to a revolution in the way health-care professionals perform routine eye exams today and diagnose non-eye diseases such as diabetes as well. Since 1992, Anderson's company has produced more than 4,000 retinal scanning devices that capture an ultra-wide field image (82%) of the retina without dilating patients' pupils. The device has been used more than 30 million times on patients in 17 countries around the world and earned him the 2008 European Inventor of the Year award.[1]

Patrick Prosser born 1952 was awarded the Association for Constraint Programming's Research Excellence Award on 15 September 2011: he is only the sixth recipient of this award. Prosser invented Conflict Directed Backjumping to help reduce thrashing (in systems that use virtual memory, the resulting condition of a hard drive being used excessively for virtual memory because the physical memory – i.e. RAM – is full. Disc thrashing considerably slows down the performance of a system because data has to be transferred back and forth from the hard drive to the physical memory).[1] Note: The process of moving data into and out of virtual memory also is called swapping pages.

Conflict-directed backjumping is an advanced technique for reducing search in constraint problems by avoiding unnecessary work on backtracking. In the late 1980s, Prosser, Peter Burke and John Costello developed a distributed asynchronous scheduling system (DAS) with a scheduling agent on each factory resource. These scheduling agents viewed the scheduling problem as one of constraint satisfaction. The agents then had to maintain schedules, in a changing environment, and be able to deliver explanations of why schedules could not be produced. This research lead to, amongst other things, new algorithms for constraint satisfaction. Prosser then moved on from factory scheduling to workforce management (with BT) and vehicle routing (with ILOG, Pirelli, Sintef, and TollPoste Globe, resulting in the ILOG product Dispatcher).[2]

Ian Hector Frazer born 1953 has "contributed significantly to the health of mankind by developing a technology which has become the basis of a vaccine to prevent infection with human papillomavirus (HPV) and hence prevent cervical cancer. This vaccine, which has recently been licenced in many countries worldwide, has the potential to save up to 0.25 million lives annually".[1]

Frazer and Chinese-born Dr Jian Zhou developed a vaccine to prevent cervical cancer, which is one of the few human cancers that is known to be directly caused by a viral infection, and which is the second leading cause of cancer amongst women, with more than 500,000 cases diagnosed annually resulting in some 275,000 deaths each year. Marketed as *Gardasil* and *Cervigard*, this was the first preventive vaccine in the world developed to fight cancer, although it has to be administered before cancer appears, preferably before sexual activity had occurred. It was hailed as "the biggest breakthrough in women's health since the contraceptive pill".[2]

Within three years of going on sale, more than 40 million doses of cervical cancer vaccines had been administered to women and girls in more than 90 countries since Frazer personally administered the first publicly available injection of the vaccine in Australia in August 2006. The HPV vaccine has proven to be 100% effective in preventing common cervical cancers caused by the virus types covered by the vaccine.[3] Sales for *Gardasil* in 2012 were $1.6 billion.[4] Note: *Gardasil* may not fully protect everyone, and does not prevent all types of cervical cancer. *Gardasil* is given as 3 injections over 6 months.[5]

Ian Frazer, himself, wrote that the current vaccines, which have been through a 15-year development process and clinical trials involving over 25,000 young women in the developed and developing world, incorporate two high risk HPV types, HPV16 and HPV18, which together are responsible for about 70% of cervical cancers. *Gardasil* also incorporates HPV6 and HPV11 virus-like particles, and can therefore protect against more than 90% of genital warts. In extensive clinical trials, these vaccines have been demonstrated 95% effective at preventing infection with the HPV types they incorporate, and 100% effective at preventing HPV-associated disease over a 5-year follow-up period.[6]

In February 2013, it was announced that Australian teenage boys will become the first in the world to receive the groundbreaking cervical cancer vaccine even though it is a cancer they won't ever develop. Starting in 2014, the HPV vaccine was provided free in schools in Australia as part of the National Immunisation Program. Boys aged 12-13 can be vaccinated with *Gardasil* at schools around the country and boys aged 14-15 will get the jab as part of a catch-up program. More than one million teenage girls aged 12-16 have already been vaccinated under the free program that is expected to reduce the 700 new cases of cervical cancer diagnosed each year. The vaccine fights off 70% of cervical cancers caused by the human papilloma virus, and although boys can't develop the cancer, they still carry the virus and can infect female sexual partners.[7] Note: In 2015, the latest incarnation of the vaccine, *Gardasil 9*, will protect against HPV types 31, 33, 45, 52 and 58 as well as types 6, 11, 16 and 18 which the original *Gardasil* blocked. It is predicted sales of *Gardasil 9* will reach $1.9 billion.[8]

Keith Henry Stockman Campbell 1954-2012 with **William Alexander Ritchie born 1951** succeeded in producing a pair of lambs, Megan and Morag, from embryonic cells. This was followed by Dolly the sheep, a Finn Dorset sheep, born in 1996 and the first clone derived from adult cells. Campbell was in a team headed by Ian Wilmut, but it was Campbell who was "primarily responsible for the scientific breakthrough that led to the birth of the cloned sheep, Dolly."[1]

Campbell played a leading role in making possible the birth of Dolly, the cloned sheep. This discovery opened up revolutionary new opportunities in regenerative medicine by demonstrating that the future of cells is not rigidly fixed, but can be changed from one tissue type to another.

In 1995, Campbell's research at the Roslin Institute, Edinburgh University, led to the birth of Megan and Morag, two Welsh mountain sheep. These were the first mammals to be cloned from cultured cells at an early stage of specialisation, or "differentiation". The following year, these experiments were extended to produce Dolly, the first mammal cloned from a somatic cell – one from a part of the body, in this case the breast – taken from an adult.

The aims of this program were to understand the basic mechanisms underlying cellular differentiation and to provide a means for the precise genetic modification of farm-animal species. The first of Campbell's key insights was that it is necessary to coordinate the cell cycles of the donor cell and recipient egg in order for the cloned embryo to develop normally. These mechanisms regulate replication of DNA and cell division. Second, it seemed that "reprogramming" of gene function in the transferred nucleus is more accurate if the donor cell is induced to hibernate before transfer. This was achieved routinely by depriving the cell of nutrients.[2]

Many considered the possibility of cloning from a differentiated adult cell to be futuristic – straight out of the pages of a sci-fi novel. At the Roslin Institute, it was Campbell's ground-breaking research on cell cycles that paved the way to the cloning of mammals from differentiated cells. He believed that, following fertilisation, egg cells went into a state of suspended animation as they coordinated the DNA acquired from sperm with their own. By synchronising the process, the team successfully cloned two Welsh mountain sheep, named Megan and Morag, in 1995. It was substantially the same technique that the scientists at Roslin used when they cloned Dolly in 1998.[3]

Scientists had long been able to clone animals – and humans – from embryonic cells. In 1993, for example, embryologists in Washington took cells from 17 human embryos. The embryos were formed of just a handful of cells, which the scientists separated before growing each one separately until they were large enough to be implanted in a woman. This did not happen, but if it had, the resultant foetuses would technically have been clones.

The difference between this experiment and that behind Dolly the sheep was that it is relatively simple to make a clone from embryo cells, which are able to develop into any other kind of cell – from a brain cell to shinbone cell. However, once embryonic cells have made this transition into specific adult cells (or become differentiated, as it is known), they are barred by proteins from developing in other ways. Thus, though each differentiated cell carries the genetic blueprint for the whole organism, the information not directly relevant to its task is locked away.

This was the hurdle that Campbell and his colleague Ian Wilmut faced as they worked on cloning animals from a single, differentiated, adult cell: they needed to activate the rest of the genetic information it contained. In Dolly's case, they need the udder cell to develop into an entire sheep, not just more udder cells.

To achieve this, Campbell drew on a method he had used to clone two sheep from embryo cells in 1995 – Megan and Morag. This involved starving the cell of nutrients, making it "quiescent". In this state, all the cell's genetic information has the potential to develop. A sheep egg cell contains proteins that would, he realised, activate this potential for development, "switching on" all the genes in the cell, not just the genes related to its specific, differentiated, role.

A total of 430 eggs were surgically removed from ewes and given to the technicians Bill Ritchie and Karen Mycock. Each egg was then stripped of its DNA and filled with the udder cell. The egg and the cell were then fused with an electric current. This was done successfully in 270 of the 430 cases, and of these 270, 29 grew into the precursors of embryos known as blastocysts. Only one of these 29 developed successfully inside a surrogate mother. Five months later, Dolly was born.

For the scientists, the achievement opened up a new world of positive possibilities, far removed from the nightmarish prospect of hordes of Hitlers imagined by journalists. The researchers' goal was to create sheep and cows whose milk could contain human proteins – such as proteins containing amino acids, or Factors VIII and IX, with therapeutic uses for patients from newborn babies to hemophiliacs. They also hoped that animals could be farmed to develop organs that can be transplanted into people without rejection.[4]

Bruce Fraser 1954-2006 "almost single-handedly shaped the way we work with colour, how we process RAW images in *Photoshop*, and even how we sharpen our photos," National Association of Photoshop Professional (NAPP) president Scott Kelby said in the announcement of Fraser's Lifetime Achievement Award, the first that NAPP had ever awarded. He was a founding member of PixelGenius, LLC, where he designed the PhotoKit Expert Sharpener plug-in toolset and other PhotoKit products.[1]

Fraser is widely regarded as the "Father of digital colour management", and became an industry legend by teaching colour and its importance in the digital workflow. Since the early years, he played an important role in the development of Adobe *Photoshop* as an Alpha and Beta tester for the program. In December 2002, he partnered with five other industry experts to form Pixel Genius LLC – a company dedicated to creating leading-edge products and services for the photographic and digital imaging industries.[2]

"He was the expert's expert and collaborated with virtually every manufacturer and developer of colour imaging products from the earliest days (including Adobe Systems, Inc., Apple Computer, Inc., Epson America Inc., Hewlett-Packard Company, Microsoft Corporation, and X-Rite Inc.). For more than 20 years, Bruce wielded enormous influence in the evolution of digital colour management, and became an industry legend by teaching colour and effective means for its use in digital workflow. Since the early years, he played an important consulting role in the development of Adobe Photoshop, including during the earliest incarnation of the program when it was known as BarneyScan XP. He contributed to the introduction of the very first spectrophotometer targeting the desktop world – the COLORTRON – a product that pointed the way to current instruments deemed essential to successful colour reproduction from the desktop."[3]

David Scott born c1955 is a structural engineer who has worked on long span structures and tall and super-tall towers around the world. Following the terrorist attack on New York's World Trade Center, he was extensively involved in the industry review of design standards and procedures for tall buildings in extreme events. He has authored papers on Fire Induced Progressive Collapse, and was a reviewer of the US Government's (GSA) design requirements to mitigate progressive collapse that were issued in 2002. He also worked extensively with Daniel Libeskind on the WTC master plan and his design for Freedom Tower (now One World Trade Center) in New York.[1]

During his 15 years in Hong Kong, he led the design of many towers in China, South Korea, Indonesia, Philippines and Taiwan. He has worked on many award-winning and innovative projects, such as the following in Hong Kong: the Hong Kong Bank Headquarters, the Biological Sciences Building at Hong Kong University, the International Airport Terminal Building, the 300 m Cheung Kong Center, and the 425 m Landmark Tower and the China Resources Tower.[2] In South Korea he was involved in Songdo Convensia Convention Center and the Northeast Asia Tower in Songdo – the tallest skyscraper in the country, and the 110-storey Hyundai Amco Tower. Elsewhere he worked on the 115 m Orco Tower in Warsaw, a major development in New York's 250 West 55th Street, and in the same city the redevelopment of Penn Station and of the Second Avenue Subway project, which has 16 stations and 8 miles (12.8 km) of track as well several commercial tall building projects – the first major expansion of the subway system in over 50 years.[3]

From 2006 to 2009 he was Chairman of the Council on Tall Buildings and Urban Habitat, a Chicago-based organisation of architects, engineers, planners, developers and contractors, which exists to maximise the international interaction of professionals involved in creating the built environment in urban contexts throughout the world.

Robert Houston McNaught born 1956 ranks among the most prolific all-time discoverers of asteroids and comets – 474 asteroids and 82 comets (as at end of 2014). In recent years he's found them on images taken with the 20-inch (0.5-metre) Uppsala Schmidt telescope at Siding Spring Observatory.[1]

He has his name attached to more than 38 different comets[2] and has discovered numerous asteroids and several comets, including Comet McNaught (C/2006 P1), the brightest comet for 40 years, which he identified on 7 August 2006.[3]

"A new comet, C/2013 A1 (Siding Spring), was discovered on 3 January 2013 by the Scottish-Australian astronomer Robert H. McNaught, a prolific observer of both comets and asteroids who has 74 comet discoveries to his name [now 82 comets]. It is apparently a new or 'virgin' comet, travelling in a parabolic orbit and making its very first visit to the sun". McNaught was a participant in the Siding Spring Survey program that hunts down asteroids that might closely approach the Earth.[4]

David James Gow born 1957 invented the world's first commercially available bionic hand. In the late 1980s, he developed electronic arms, including shoulders, wrists and hands. In 1993, a partial hand system received international publicity and, in 1998, major international profile was achieved through the fitting of the world's first electrically powered shoulder, after which Gow unveiled the world's first fully articulating bionic hand in 2007.

The i-limb hand had been fitted to more than 1,400 patients worldwide within just three years of its release in 2007. Touch Bionics sells 500 units per year, tremendously improving the lives of patients worldwide.[1]

"Initially, Gow pursued the conventional method of using a centralised motor system to control the many different gestures and movements a prosthetic hand has to perform. However, this approach failed to deliver the intricate motion he envisioned, which would allow for the complex articulation of every individual finger. In addition, a centralised motor is difficult to scale down to fit into a prosthetic hand small enough for a child.

The breakthrough came when Gow abandoned the concept of a centralised motor system entirely and instead decided to equip each individual digit with its own motor."[2]

The i-limb ultra-revolution developed by Gow in 2013 is the first prosthetic hand that can be controlled by apps from a mobile device. Using a phone, iPad or iPod, users can touch a screen icon and their hand will move instantly into one of 24 possible grip patterns, including index point, mouse grip, cylindrical, handshake, thumb rotate, custom grip and more. Each hand comes with an iPod with mobile apps. The i-limb is the first prosthetic hand that has five individually-powered articulating digits. "The first generation [of prosthetics] had what I call a pincer grip – the fingers are reflexed so they do not change shape and they move in one plane," explains David Gow, the British inventor and engineer behind i-limb. "Whereas what we produced is something that rotates at the knuckles."[3]

"Made from lightweight plastic usually found in car engine components the hand is attached to the arm via a laminated socket. The socket, which slips over the patient's arm, conceals a rechargeable battery and a pair of electrodes which sit on top of the skin, where they pick up signals destined for the absent hand. The signals are transmitted to a tiny computer housed in the back of the artificial hand and control the motors hidden in the fingers. Small objects such as coins can be picked up between the index finger and thumb, while other grips allow turning a key in a lock, holding a plate and handing over a business card. So flexible are the fingers that they can open the ring-pull of a soft drink can. Best of all, the wearer doesn't have to do the washing up as it's not totally waterproof."[4]

In 2015, Britain's Royal Mail issued eight new stamps as part of its Inventive Britain Special Stamp set – one of these was the i-limb.

Iain Neill Reid born 1957, with New Zealand-born colleague Gerard Francis Gilmore, found evidence that something was missing in the standard picture of the Milky Way. When they counted the galaxy's stars, the pair found that there were far more than the known components of the Milky Way could account for. To explain the discrepancy, the two scientists suggested that the galaxy's disc has a second part – a thicker, diffuse one, extending about 3,000 light-years above and below the familiar flat disc. They calculated that this thick structure contains 5 to 10 percent of our galaxy's stars.[1]

Reid studied globular clusters by focusing on subdwarfs via the *Hipparcos* mission – the very first space mission for measuring the positions, distances, motions, brightness and colours of stars. He discovered that the 15 metal-poor sub-dwarf stars that he studied are more distant, and therefore more luminous, than previously thought, so Reid was able to use these stars as a standard candle for probing cluster distances. Reid found that the distance to metal-poor globular clusters had been underestimated by 2-15% or more.[2]

In 2008, Reid was appointed Head of the Space Telescope Science Institute's Science Mission Office for oversight of science policies and for acting as an interface between the Hubble Space Telescope and the broader user community.[3]

Ian Underwood born 1959 has been a key player in the development of Liquid Crystal on Silicon (LCoS) and Light Emitting Polymer on Silicon (LEPoS). LCoS is a reflective technology that uses liquid crystals instead of individual mirrors. In LCoS, liquid crystals are applied to a reflective mirror substrate. As the liquid crystals open and close, the light is either reflected from the mirror below, or blocked. This modulates the light and creates the image, which is usually very high resolution. LEPoS actually emits light and does not require sunlight or a lamp to illuminate it.

Underwood is recognised as a worldwide authority on microdisplay technology. In 1999, he co-founded MicroEmissive Displays (MED), whose technology achievements include a Guinness World Record in 2004 for the world's smallest colour TV screen. As a MED screen typically uses at least 70% less power than commonly used LCD microdisplay modules, it is anticipated that this development will lead to smaller, lighter cameras with longer battery life. "MED technology can also produce a highly magnified viewable virtual image in space, as is the case in electronic viewfinders of the type found in camcorders or digital cameras and in wearable or headset displays."[1]

Underwood was co-inventor of polymer organic light emitting diode microdisplay technology (P-OLED).[2] "A microdisplay is a very-small active-matrix electronic display that is capable of showing TV-quality pictures. Microdisplays are optically magnified in order to produce a viewable image. Microdisplay-based systems have the unique advantage of being able to produce a viewable image that is much larger than the physical size of the unit that produces the image."[3]

John Duncan Waldron born 1959 discovered the asteroid 3753 Cruithne (pronounced croo-EEN-ya) on 10 October 1986.[1] 3753 Cruithne is an asteroid in a horseshoe orbit around the Sun in 1:1 orbital resonance with the Earth. It is a periodic inclusion planetoid and has been incorrectly called "Earth's second moon"; it is a quasi-satellite, not a moon. Cruithne does not orbit Earth, and at times it is on the other side of the Sun. Its orbit takes it inwards towards the orbit of Mercury, and outside the orbit of Mars. Cruithne orbits the Sun in about one year, but it takes 770 years for the series to complete a horseshoe-shaped movement, with the Earth in the gap of the horseshoe.

Alan Wilson Black born 1962 is a world leader in the area of speech synthesis and is the principal author of the Festival Speech Synthesis System. He is also the author of the FestVox Voice Building tools which have been used to create speech synthesisers in over 40 different languages. He pioneered unit selection speech synthesis, where appropriate sub-word units are automatically selected from large databases of natural speech, helping to move the field of speech synthesis from a rule driven approach to one that is data driven.[1]

Richard John Tait born 1964 co-invented the board game *Cranium* with American Whit Alexander in 1998. Cranium Inc. went on to win over 130 awards and sell over 22 million games and toys. During a vacation with his wife and friends, Tait came up with the idea that evolved into *Cranium*. After Tait and his wife easily defeated the other couple at Pictionary and then lost miserably at *Scrabble*, he began to dream up a board game that would allow everyone to shine and to have a great time. Tait took his idea to Alexander, who at first laughed at it, then came around. Together Tait and Alexander began work on the board game with the goal of getting it into stores by Christmas 1998. Their first step was to embark on research on intellectual aptitudes, including the studies of Harvard University educator and psychologist Howard Gardner, whose theories explain that people learn and perform through a variety of intelligences. According to Gardner, people who excel spatially and verbally may do well at the game of *Scrabble*, but will not necessarily stand out at *Trivial Pursuit*, which rewards a good memory. Alexander and Tait also consulted numerous books about indoor activities, such as parlour games, published before television became commonplace in American households in the 1950s. In so doing, we "were able to get a much richer framework to base the game on than just the left brain/right brain idea," explained Alexander in the 2001 *Arizona Daily Star*. The men spent $100,000 of their own money to build and test the prototype *Cranium* game from 1997 to 1998.[1]

Graeme John Devine born 1966 conceived and, with Rob Landeros, designed the 1992 horror game *The 7th Guest*. Graeme was the lead programmer on the game and also on its sequel *The 11th Hour*. "Using the untapped potential of CD-ROM technology, they planned to incorporate full motion video of live actors into a horror-themed puzzle game. Their intuition proved correct. Upon its release in 1993, *The 7th Guest* was heralded as a technical marvel, selling more than two million copies and pushing sales of CD-ROM drives through the roof. Bill Gates even called it a 'new standard in interactive entertainment.'"[1]

Devine joined id Software to work as a designer on *Quake III Arena* and *Quake III Team Arena*. At id Software he gained recognition in the Mac gaming community for supporting development on the platform. He also worked on the Game Boy advance versions of *Commander Keen* (2001), *Wolfenstein 3-D*, and *Doom 2*, and was a programmer on *Doom 3* until he moved to Ensemble in August 2003.[2]

Devine was also one of the forefathers of file compression. *The 7th Guest* made extensive use of movie footage, which required a great deal of disc space. Most games in the industry at that point were still shipping on floppy discs, which could only hold about 1Mb of data each. *The 7th Guest* used roomier CD technology, but there was still a limit as to how many CDs could practically be used for a single game. File compression technology at the time, especially for videos which could run into hundreds of megabytes, was still in a primitive state. However, Devine innovated a way to compress movie files, so Trilobyte could fit two hours of footage, along with the game itself, onto only two CDs.

Other games credited to Devine as designer or programmer include: *Halo Wars*; *Command and Conquer: Red Alert 3*; *Age of Empires III: The WarChiefs*; *Call of Duty; Commander Keen*; *Kingpin: Life of Crime*; *Clandestiny*; *Overlord*; *Silver Surfer*; *Spot*; *Turbo Champions*; *J.R.R. Tolkien's War in Middle Earth; Metropolis;* and *Xcel*.

Devine held a key role at Apple, a position crucial to helping usher in more robust, more gamer-friendly titles to the successful iPhone, iPad and iPod platforms.[3]

David Jones born 1966 co-founded DMA Design, later Rockstar North, and co-created *Grand Theft Auto*. DMA Design was founded in 1984 by Jones and his first employees were Mike Dailly, Russell Kay and Steve Hammond and their first game was *Menace*.

In 2002, Jones founded Realtime Worlds, which got two BAFTA awards in 2007 for Best Use of Audio and Best Action and Adventure for their Xbox 360 title *Crackdown*.

The first major output from DMA Design/Rockstar North was the video game of *Lemmings* with "stupid little creatures with green hair that you had to save from repeated and grisly doom". The game sold 55,000 on its first day and has, by 2015, sold over 20 million copies.[1] Jones biggest success was with *Grand Theft Auto* which, in all of its incarnations, has sold 143.8 million copies as at May 2015.[2]

Other games for which Jones has design credit include: Director/Creative Director for *APB: All Points Bulletin* (2010), *Crackdown* (2007), *Shadow of the Beast* (1989). He was manager for: *Crackdown* (2007), *Mobile Forces* (2002), *Tanktics* (1999), *Wild Metal Country* (1999), *Body Harvest* (1998), and author for *Blood Money* (1989).[3]

By 2012, Jones was working with Stieg Hedlund on *ChronoBlade*, which was created as a cross-platform action RPG for Facebook, iOS, Android, Smart TVs and even Ouya.

David John Cameron MacKay born 1967 developed Bayesian methods for neural networks, then rediscovered, with Radford M. Neal, low-density parity-check codes, and invented *Dasher*, a software application for communication especially popular with disabled people and which enables efficient communication in any language with any muscle.[1]

Dasher is a computer accessibility tool which enables users to write without using a keyboard, by entering text on a screen using a pointing device such as a mouse, a touchpad, a touch screen, a roller ball, a joystick, a push-button, a Wii remote, or even the mouse being operated by the foot or head. Such instruments could serve as prosthetic devices for disabled people who cannot use standard keyboards, or where the use of one is impractical. You point where you want to go, and the display zooms in wherever you point. The world into which you are zooming is painted with letters, so that any point you zoom in on corresponds to a piece of text. The more you zoom in, the longer the piece of text you have written. You choose what you write by choosing where to zoom.

A big advantage of *Dasher* over other predictive text-entry interfaces that offer word-completions to the user is that it is mode-free: the user does not need to switch from a writing mode to an "accept-model-predictions" mode.[2]

Brian Watson born 1967 has been credited with development/programming/design of the following computer games in conjunction with other developers: Menace Atari ST (1988); Lemmings Atari ST (1990); Lemmings 2 Amiga (small parts) (1991); Lemmings for Lynx (1992); Lemmings for 3DO (1993); Quarterback Club for Genesis & SNES (1994); QBC96 for Genesis/32X (1995); QBC97 for Genesis (1996); QBC98 for N64 (1997); Some Turok QBC99 for N64 (1998); Turok2 (1998); Small parts of Revolt, Shadowman, Allstar Baseball, Turok 3 (all 1999); Tribes: Aerial Assault (PS2) (2002); Medal of Honor: Rising Sun (online component, PS2) (2003).

His games credits include: Ratchet & Clank: All 4 One (2011), Ratchet & Clank Future: A Crack in Time (2009), Sony Computer Entertainment America, Inc.; Area-51 (2005), Midway Home Entertainment, Inc.; Gauntlet: Seven Sorrows (2005), Midway Home Entertainment, Inc.; Ratchet: Deadlocked (2005), Sony Computer Entertainment America, Inc.; Ratchet & Clank: Up Your Arsenal (2004), Sony Computer Entertainment America, Inc.; Batman: Dark Tomorrow (2003), KEMCO USA., INC.; The Hobbit (2003), Sierra Entertainment, Inc., Vivendi Universal Games, Inc.; Medal of Honor: Rising Sun (2003), Electronic Arts, Inc.; Terminator 3: Rise of the Machines (2003), Atari, Inc.; Defender (2002), Midway Home Entertainment, Inc.; Pac-Man Fever (2002), Namco Limited; Tribes: Aerial Assault (2002), Sierra Entertainment, Inc.; All-Star Baseball 2000 (1999), Acclaim Entertainment, Inc.; NFL Quarterback Club 2000 (1999), Acclaim Entertainment, Inc.; Re-Volt (1999), Acclaim Entertainment, Inc.; Shadow Man (1999), Acclaim Entertainment, Inc.; South Park: Chef's Luv Shack (1999), Acclaim Entertainment, Inc.; Star Wars: Episode I – The Gungan Frontier (1999), Lucas Learning Ltd.; Star Wars: Episode I – The Phantom Menace (1999), LucasArts Entertainment Company LLC; Turok: Rage Wars (1999), Acclaim Entertainment, Inc.; All-Star Baseball 99 (1998), Acclaim Entertainment, Inc.; Forsaken (1998), Acclaim Entertainment, Inc.; NHL Breakaway 98 (1998), Acclaim Entertainment, Inc.; Turok 2: Seeds of Evil (1998), Acclaim Entertainment, Inc.; Breath of Fire III (1997), Capcom Co., Ltd.; Turok: Dinosaur Hunter (1997), Acclaim Entertainment, Inc.; NFL

Quarterback Club (1995), Acclaim Entertainment, Inc.; NFL Quarterback Club 96 (1995), Acclaim Entertainment, Inc.; NFL Quarterback Club (1994), Acclaim Entertainment, Inc.; The Pirates of Dark Water (1994), Sun Corporation of America; Hired Guns (1993), Psygnosis Limited; Holiday Lemmings (1993); Lemmings (1993), Psygnosis Limited; Lemmings 2: The Tribes (1993), Psygnosis Limited; Shadow of the Beast (1992), Psygnosis Limited, Turbo Technologies, Inc.; and Menace (1989), Psyclapse.[1]

Colin Robert McInnes born 1968 discovered a practical and relatively cheap way of propelling equipment or a vehicle once it is in space using solar sails. His sails are coated in special charged particles, which allow the force of sunlight to "blow" the ship in a particular direction. The sail can be tilted to steer the object, just as an ordinary sail would.

Solar sails must be of enormous diameter, but small enough to be propelled on a rocket. The trick is to make them thin – two thousandths of a millimetre thick, allowing them to be packed into a space the size of a fridge. Once in space, the craft would start slowly – getting to the moon would take about a year – but with no resistance, a ship would slowly accelerate up to speeds of around 16,000 mph (25,750 km/h), allowing it to sail off into deep space.

He is researching autonomous spacecraft control, principally through the application of artificial potential field methods. This work has been developed for automated rendezvous and docking and for the distributed control of multiple spacecraft for formation-flying missions.[1]

David William MacMillan born 1968 pioneered a new method for creating organic molecules, an area of research called organic synthesis. In organic synthesis, chemists work to create new molecules that have the capacity to bind to different sites in the body. The new molecules must be designed to fit into biological receptor sites like a key in a lock. The research has an enormous impact on pharmacology; these new molecules can be used in the development of new drugs.

MacMillan's research group made its breakthrough searching for a method for organic synthesis that would replace the metals usually used in the process – which were expensive, toxic and unstable – with safer, cheaper, organic compounds. The new process they invented has since been used by researchers all over the world to create hundreds of new molecules.[1]

MacMillan has a distinguished place for his pioneering role in opening up and defining the area of asymmetric organocatalysis. This new field has revolutionised organic reaction methodology and chemical synthesis over the past 10 years. MacMillan has discovered new iminium ion catalysts and has designed over 50 new chemical reaction processes. His work is inventive and creative and has provided considerable insight and leadership that others can only follow. He continues to discover brilliant new processes of molecule activation that include SOMO catalysis (in 2007) and photoredox organocatalysis (in 2008). These discoveries open up vast new opportunities for molecule assembly and have caused a step change in thinking and reaction design. MacMillan has also applied his methods in the most elegant manner in the efficient and truly beautiful syntheses of several complex natural products.[2]

Through his research contributions, MacMillan has become a leader in the currently active area of asymmetric organocatalysis. His numerous accomplishments include the design of a series of chiral amines, available from amino acids, to catalyse the enantioselective cycloaddition reactions of dienes or 1, 3-dipoles and a, b-unsaturated aldehydes by reversible iminium ion formation.

The approach has been admirably applied to the catalytic asymmetric Friedel-Crafts alkylations of pyrroles, indoles, anilines, and furans, which proceed in excellent yields and with high enantiomeric excess. These are the first examples of this reaction in catalysis; no organometallic catalyst has been devised for these transformations.

In addition, using chiral amine catalysts, MacMillan has achieved the first enantioselective cross-aldol condensation of aldehydes, a reaction type which eluded chemists for some time, and could previously only be carried out with the aid of enzymes. This landmark achievement has been improved and extended, and applied to the rapid assembly of natural and non-natural carbohydrates with enantioselectivities approaching 100 %.

Recently, MacMillan and his group devised the first enantioselective transfer hydrogenation reaction for alkenes using organocatalysts.[3]

Stephen Cochran Tweedie born 1969 worked on the Linux ext2 journaling file system and wrote the ext3 file system in 1999. The latter is based on the ext2 file system, yet with a forked code base so that development can proceed with a pristine code base in the same kernel. The addition of the ext3 file system to the development tree was made basic so that compatibility can be addressed. ext3 introduced another virtual layer similar to VFS, called *JFS*. This virtual layer is an application programming interface, responsible for handling the journalising transactions independently of the ext3 layer.[1]

Leslie Benzies born 1971 is a computer games developer noted for Grand Theft Auto and other games produced by Rockstar North, of which he is president. His credits include: Grand Theft Auto V (Video Game) (producer); 2012 Max Payne 3 (Video Game) (executive producer); 2011 L.A. Noire (Video Game) (executive producer); 2010 Red Dead Redemption (Video Game) (executive producer); 2009 Grand Theft Auto: Chinatown Wars (Video Game) (producer: Rockstar North); 2008 Grand Theft Auto IV (Video Game) (producer); 2006 Grand Theft Auto: Vice City Stories (Video Game) (producer: Rockstar North); 2005 Grand Theft Auto: Liberty City Stories (Video Game) (producer); 2004 Grand Theft Auto: San Andreas (Video Game) (producer); 2003 Manhunt (Video Game) (producer); 2002 Grand Theft Auto: Vice City (Video Game) (producer); 2001 Grand Theft Auto III (Video Game) (producer).[1]

Video games don't get much bigger than Take-Two Interactive's Grand Theft Auto (aka GTA). With the release of Grand Theft Auto V on 17 September 2013, the franchise moved beyond just being one of the biggest video game franchises in the world and set its sights on a larger crown; becoming the world's most successful release across all of entertainment. Costing roughly $265 million to develop and market, on its first three days after release Grand Theft Auto V raked in more than $1 billion in sales, compared with sales for the contemporary biggest blockbuster at the box office, Iron Man 3, which brought in "only" $372 million in its first weekend across the globe.[2] "Grand Theft Auto V has sold 2 million copies [as at 11 August 2015], pushing its worldwide total to over 54 million copies shipped (but not sold). There are no officially recognised statistics for the best-selling video games but it's clear that GTA V is the best-selling paid-for, non-bundled video game of all-time."[3]

Michelle Georgina Mone born 1971 invented the *Ultimo* gel bra in 1999 after three years of research. In August 1999, Mone launched *Ultimo* at Selfridge's department store in London. "Selfridges sold the pre-launch estimate of six weeks of stock within 24 hours. It is still known as the biggest ever bra launch in the UK with over 50 photographers present and camera crews from all over the world."[1]

The *Ultimo* bra has tiny pockets filled with silicone gel to imitate the natural movement of a real breast. This was followed in 2003 by the *Ultimo Miracle Body*, a backless and front-less bra. In 2010, Mone released the *Ultimo OMG Extreme Cleavage* bra, bringing together the "lift technology" and silicone gel – adding a minimum of two cup sizes. Another model, the *OMG Plunge Bra*, was famously worn by Julia Roberts in her Oscar-winning portrayal of Erin Brockovich in the eponymous film. Renowned cosmetic surgeon and star of ABC hit series "Extreme Makeover", Dr Garth Fisher, hailed the new bra as the next best thing to having a breast operation.[2]

Gordon Love born 1974 led an international team in 2008-2009 that discovered fossil animal steroids dating back to more than 635 million years ago. This would make the find the oldest evidence for animals in the fossil record. The researchers examined sedimentary rocks in south Oman, and found an anomalously high number of distinctive steroids that date back to 635 million years ago, to around the end of the last immense ice age. The steroids are produced by sponges – one of the simplest forms of multicellular animals.

The researchers argue that the discovery of the sponges is evidence for multicellular animal life beginning 100 million years before the Cambrian explosion, a well-studied and unique episode in Earth history that began about 530 million years ago when, as indicated by the fossil record, animal life diversified rapidly. The discovery can help scientists reconstruct Earth's early ecosystems and explain how animal life may have first evolved on the planet.

"Our findings suggest that the evolution of multicellular animals began earlier than has been thought," said Gordon Love, an assistant professor of Earth sciences, who led the research group. Love began working on the project while he was a postdoctoral researcher at MIT. "Moreover, sponges live on the seafloor, growing initially in shallow waters and spreading, over time, into deeper waters, implying the existence of oceanic environments which contained dissolved oxygen near the shallow seafloor around 635 million years ago."

According to Love, the climatic shock of the extensive glacial episodes of the Neoproterozoic era (1,000-542 million years ago) likely caused a major reorganisation of marine ecosystems, perhaps by irrevocably altering ocean chemistry. "This paved the way for the evolution of animal feeders living on the seafloor," he said. "We believe we are converging on the correct date for the divergence of complex multicellular animal life, on the shallow ocean floor between 635 and 750 million years ago."

The steroids that Love and his colleagues observed in the Omani rocks are essential biochemicals present in the cell membranes of the sponges, and help provide the membranes with structural support. The sponges are a few millimetres in size, immobile, and were filter feeders existing on the seafloor.[1]

Alison May Grieve born 1977 invented the *Safetray*, a revolutionary and proven serving tray solution. *Safetray* is an adapted service tray that provides improved stability and functionality, so reducing the incidence of accidents, providing cost savings to a margin-sensitive industry and improved health and safety.

Image 105 – Inventor Alison Grieve holds a Safetray

Safetray's success is down to a unique adaptation to the underside of trays: a retractable clip slips between the middle fingers of waiting/service staff to offer stability through downward and horizontal traction. The use of these adapted trays provides far greater balance and stability and eradicates instances of the trays becoming unbalanced and/or tipping.[1]

Matthew McGrath born 1977 developed the world's first fully portable video laryngoscope. McGrath's new and refined design led to the birth of a product which has been used on more than 500,000 patients (as at 31 May 2013).[1] Aircraft Medical Ltd., founded by McGrath in 2001, claims, "The McGrath Series 5 is designed for difficult airway management and is the world's first and only laryngoscope to feature a variable length blade to support a variety of patients from children to large adults."[2]

The McGrath Series 5 was introduced in 2006 after years of research by McGrath and his team at Aircraft Medical, and advanced the video laryngoscope in a number of ways, including portability – the world's first fully portable video laryngoscope; a better anterior view; an LCD screen; and battery power. The McGrath laryngoscope has "a super-curved blade to better follow the anatomy," and a camera stick inside the blade – the first of its kind to be guaranteed sterile.[3]

The McGrath Series 5 has continuously been updated since 2006 and the McGrath X-blade for Extreme Airways for the McGrath MAC Video laryngoscopes go "beyond routine and moderately difficult airways towards extreme airways, where a more acute anterior curvature and slimmer blade profile is needed."[4]

CONCLUSION

Over the last half millennium, Scots have achieved more than would be expected from a country that for much of that period had a small, wretchedly poor population. Yet, following the advent of Calvinist-inspired schooling, albeit often rudimentary, Scots became better educated, on average, than most of their contemporary European neighbours, including England and France. "Putting men and women in touch with the word of God was seen by the Scottish authorities and clergy as of paramount importance. To achieve this goal schools paid for by the Church of Scotland and local landowners were established in all rural parishes and burghs by an Act of Parliament [the *Education Act 1696*]. These educational establishments were run by the [Presbyterian] Church and were open to all boys *and girls* [author's italics] regardless of social status. The democratic nature of the Scottish system so impressed the 18th century writer Daniel Defoe that he remarked that while England was a land 'full of ignorance', in Scotland the 'poorest people have their children taught and instructed'. The openness of the Scottish system ran all the way from the schoolroom to the university."[1]

As mentioned in the Introduction, Britain's first chair of engineering had been established at the University of Glasgow in 1840 and soon built a solid reputation so that "the Scottish universities of Glasgow and Edinburgh were perhaps the leading universities in engineering in the world in the 1870s".[2] But the introduction of engineering simply reflected a national predisposition of Scots to "tinker" with machinery, a trait that gathered pace with the invention of the Watt steam engine. Educated Scots took this penchant to the far corners of the world and, in the process, made an indelible mark on the modern world – indeed, much of what is considered intrinsic to our idea of the modern world was fashioned by Scots. The 867 Scots in this book are but a small part of a multitude of Scottish thinkers and innovators who have improved our daily existence and fashioned the way we live. And still the story continues.

ACKNOWLEDGEMENTS

I would like to thank the following people, both private individuals and those who work for organisations, for the information and assistance that they provided in gathering and verifying information provided in this book.

Andy Philpot (descendent of Sir Alexander Ogston), Valerie Mason (Alexander Graham Bell National Historic Site of Canada), Jennifer Sammartino (Garibaldi Meucci Museum), Jim Nelson (Refrigeration Research), Jim Murray (Royal Highland and Agricultural Society of Scotland), Dr Jeff Pan (ChinaCulture.org re: James Small plough), Marta Pardee-King (Curator of Social Sciences, Boston Public Library), James C. Scott (Sacramento Public Library, California), Susan Payne (Perth Museum and Art Gallery, UK), Ronald Morrison, (Borders Family History Society), Onne Vegter (Kruger Parks, South Africa), Richard Elliott (British Association for the Advancement of Science), Claire Cabrie (Local Studies Library, Paisley Central Library), Ceri Thompson (Big Pit: National Coal Museum), Natasha Keatch (Scottish Mining Museum), Lesley Richmond (Glasgow City Archives, Mitchell Library), Henry Sullivan (Archives and Special Collections, Mitchell Library), Craig Statham (Local History Officer, East Lothian Council), McGill University News Staff, Diana Mackie (descendent of William Cameron), Research Center of the Chicago History Museum, Lindsey MacAllister and Robert Spieler (Museum of Science and Industry, Chicago), Chicago Public Library, James Winter (Central Pacific Railroad), Jill Brook (National Coal Mining Museum for England), Chris Graves (Central Pacific Railroad), Emily Malcolm (Museum of Transport, Glasgow), Alice Ford-Smith and Jette Nielsen (Wellcome Library, London), Katrina Presedo (Kensington Central Library), David Kiltie (Maybole.org), Kyle K. Wyatt (California State Railroad Museum), Emma Challinor (Wirral Museum, Birkenhead), Mike Porter (Scottish Maritime Museum), Barbara Miller (National Candle Association), Meredith Hughes and Tom Hughes (foodmuseum@yahoo.com), Morag Fyfe (The National Archives of Scotland), Tom Longden (NewsBank Inc.), Ann Marie Johnson (Morrison County Historical Society, MN), Rory Cook (Science Museum, Kensington, UK), Trevor Dean (Australian Aviation Museum), Val King and Julie Millerick (Dundee Heritage Trust), Christine A Wood (Perth & Kinross Council Archive), Ian Holdsworth (Plastics Historical Society), Alan Walker MBE (University of Edinburgh), Stuart Tyler (Devon Heritage Centre), Ian Brown (National Museum of Flight, East Lothian), Gill Paterson (New Lanark Trust), John Arthur (James Clerk Maxwell Foundation), Malcolm Baird (son of John Logie Baird).

APPENDIX

Place and date of birth, if known, of main entries or of their Scottish-born parent(s) or grandparent(s)

Abercrombie, Charles b. 1750 St Cyrus, Kincardineshire d. 13 August 1817.

Abernethy, James b. 12 June 1814 Aberdeen d. 8 March 1896

Adams, Gladstone b. 16 May 1880 Newcastle, Northumberland, England d. 28 July 1966. Mother: Agnes Mcgregor, was born in Dundee about 1838 (1881 England and Wales census)

Adie, Alexander James b. 16 December 1808 Edinburgh d. 1879

Adie, Alexander James b. 7 January 1775 Edinburgh d. 4 December 1858

Aird, John b. 20 June 1801 Rosemarkie, Ross and Cromarty d. 1876

Aird, John b. 3 December 1833 Greenwich, England d. 6 January 1911. Father: John Aird born Scotland (1841 England census - Greenwich West sub-registration district)

Aitken (or Aitkin), John b.? Scotland d. 22 September 1790 (source Dictionary of National Biography Volume 1, p 206)

Aitken, John b. 18 September 1839 Falkirk, Stirlingshire d. 13 November 1919

Aitken, Yvonne b. 17 October 1911 Horsham, Victoria, Australia d. 29 November 2004. Paternal grandmother Elizabeth Wilson born 30 April 1839 in Erskine, Renfrewshire

Allan, Alexander Reed b. 28 February 1809 Montrose, Angus d. 2 June 1891

Allan, Percy b. 12 July 1861 Sydney, Australia d. 7 May 1930. Father: Maxwell Rennie Allan born 17 October 1827 in Edinburgh

Allen, William b.? Scotland d. 1840 (Ref: The Piano: An Encyclopedia 2nd Edition, edited by Robert Palmieri, Routledge, New York, 2003, p 22) Allen, or Allan, may have come from Aberdeen as he was back there from London in 1807.

Almeida, June Dalziel b. 5 October 1930 Glasgow d. 1 December 2007

Anderson, David b. 1880 Leven, Fife d. 1953

Anderson, Douglas Crombie b. 1951 Elie, Fife Still Living

Anderson, James b. 1739 Hermiston, Midlothian d. 15 October 1808

Anderson, John b. 28 November 1872 Aberdeen d. 1929

Anderson, John b. 9 December 1814 Aberdeen d. 28 July 1886

Anderson, Thomas b. 2 July 1819 Leith, Midlothian 2 November 1874

Armstrong, Edwin Howard b. 18 December 1890 New York, USA d. 31 January 1954. Grandfather: John Armstrong born Scotland (1900 Federal US census)

Arnot, Arthur James b. 26 August 1865 Hamilton, Lanarkshire d. 15 October 1946

Arnott, Neil b. 15 May 1788 Arbroath, Angus d. 2 March 1874

Arnott, Struther b. 25 September 1934 Larkhall, Lanarkshire d. 20 April 2013

Arrol, William b. 13 February 1839 Houston, Renfrewshire d. 20 February 1913

Arthur, Alexander Alan b. 30 August 1846 Glasgow d. 4 March 1912

Austin, John b. 17 April 1752 Craigton, Glasgow d. 1830

Baildon, John b. 11 July 1772 Larbert, Stirlingshire d. 7 August 1846

Bain, Alexander b. 22 November 1810 Watten, Caithness d. 2 January 1877

Bain, David Isauld b. 11 October 1855 Isauld, Caithness d. 18 September 1933

Baird, Charles b. 20 December 1766 Westerton, Bothkennar, Stirlingshire d. 10 December 1843

Baird, Francis b. 16 February 1802 Russia d. 25 March 1864. Father: Charles Baird born 1766 Westerton, Stirlingshire

Baird, James b. 5 December 1802 Kirkwood, Lanarkshire d. 20 June 1876

Baird, John b. 8 March 1820 Kirkintilloch, Dunbartonshire d. 17 October 1891

Baird, John Logie b. 13 August 1888 Helensburgh, Dunbartonshire d. 14 June 1946

Baird, Nicol Hugh b. 26 August 1796 Glasgow d. 18 October 1849

Baker, William Erskine b. 29 November 1808 Leith, Midlothian d. 16 December 1881

Bald, William b. 1788/9 Burntisland, Fife d. 26 March 1857

Balfour, George b. 30 November 1872 Portsmouth d. 26 September 1941. Father: William Balfour born circa 1839 Aberdeenshire (England census 1881)

Banks, James Arthur b. 14 March 1897 Kelvinside, Glasgow d. 1 December 1967

Barclay, Andrew b. 12 August 1814 Dalry, Ayrshire d. 20 April 1900

Barnett, James Rennie b. 6 September 1864 Johnstone, Renfrewshire d. 13 January 1965

Barr, Andrew b. 12 July 1855 Lesmahagow, Lanarkshire d. 9 February 1939

Barr, Archibald b. 18 November 1855 Paisley, Renfrewshire d. 5 August 1931

Barton, Edward Gustavus Campbell b. 11 December 1857 Melbourne, Australia d. 14 June 1942. Mother: Jane Crichton Campbell b. c1829, Kilmarnock (ref: http://www.bartondatabase.com/getperson.php?personID=I22279&tree=gbtree)

Beilby, George Thomas b. 17 November 1850 Edinburgh d. 1 August 1824

Bell, Alexander Graham b. 3 March 1847 Edinburgh d. 2 August 1922

Bell, Chichester Alexander b. 1848 Dublin, Ireland d. 11 March 1924. Father: David Charles Bell b. 12 March 1817, Orkney

Bell, Henry b. 25 May 1848 Gareloch, Argyllshire d. 16 March 1931

Bell, Henry b. 7 April 1767 Torphichen, Linlithgowshire d. 14 March 1830

Bell, Imrie b. 9 April 1836 Edinburgh d. 21 November 1906

Bell, John b. 16 January 1850 Glasgow d. 1929

Bell, Patrick b. 29 April 1799 Auchterhouse, Angus d. 22 April 1869

Bell, Thomas b.? Scotland d.? Ref: History of the Borough of Preston and its Environs, in the County of Lancaster, published 1857 "Mr. Bell, a Scotchman ..." p 376. All other records refer to him as being a Scotsman.

Bell, Thomas b. 14 December 1782 Duns, Berwickshire d. 10 June 1866

Bell, Thomas b. 21 December 1865 Sirsawa, India d. 9 January 1952. Father: Imrie Bell 9 April 1836 Edinburgh Mother: Jane Walker born 1836, Edinburgh

Bennie, George b. 29 August 1891 Auldhouse, Lanarkshire d. 19 November 1957

Benton, John b. 5 August 1850 Sheriffhaugh, Banffshire d. 29 August 1927

Benzies, Leslie b. 17 January 1971 Aberdeen Still Living

Bigelow, Wilfred Gordon b. 18 June 1913 Manitoba, Canada d. 27 March 2005. Mother: Grace Ann Carnegie Gordon, born 1 June 1876 at Montrose

Binnie, Alexander Richardson b. 26 March 1839 London, England d. 18 May 1917. Father: Alexander Binnie born 1801 Edinburgh

Black, Alan Wilson b. 1962 Edinburgh Scotland Still Living

Black, Alexander b. 25 May 1827 Arndilly, Banffshire d. 13 March 1897

Black, James Whyte b. 14 June 1924 Uddingston, Lanarkshire d. 22 March 2010

Black, Joseph b. 16 April 1728 Bordeaux, France d. 6 December 1799. Mother: Margaret Gordon born 1692, Holhead, Aberdeenshire - d. 1747

Black, William b. 1 September 1903 Bathgate, West Lothian d. 16 May 1975

Blackett, Patrick Maynard Stuart b. 18 November 1897, London, England d. 13 July 1974. Mother: Caroline Frances Maynard, born 23 January 1868 in Edinburgh

Blair, Robert b. 1748 Garvald, East Lothian d. 1828

Blair, William Newsham b. 10 August 1841 Islay, Hebrides d. 4 May 1891

Blane, George Rodney b. 7 January 1791 London, England d. 18 May 1821. Father: Gilbert

Blane b. 29 August 1749, Blanefield, Ayr

Blumlein, Alan Dower b. 29 June 1903 London, England d. 7 June 1942. Maternal grandparents: William Dower, born 5 November 1837; Jesse Edward, born 1838. Both born in Banchory Ternan, Kincardineshire

Blyth, Benjamin Hall b. 25 May 1849 Edinburgh d. 13 May 1917

Blyth, James b. 4 April 1839 Marykirk, Kincardineshire d. 15 May 1906

Bowie, Stanley Hay Umphray b. 24 March 1917 Bixter, Shetland d. 3 September 2008

Boyce, James b. 15 November 1868 Illinois, USA d. 2 June 1935. Father: Joseph Boyce born 15 May 1832 Edinburgh

Boyd, Adam Alexander b. 15 April 1866 Eastwood, Renfrewshire d. 16 December 1948

Boyd, Robert Lewis Fullarton b. 19 October 1922 Saltcoats, Ayrshire d. 5 February 2004

Boyle, David b. 31 October 1837 Johnstone, Renfrewshire d. 25 June 1891, Mobile, Alabama

Braid, James b. 19 June 1795 Fife d. 25 March 1860

Brass, William b. 5 September 1921 Edinburgh d. 11 November 1999

Bremner, James b. 25 September 1784 Stain, Caithness d. August 1856

Brewster, David b. 11 December 1781 Jedburgh, Roxburghshire d. 10 February 1868

Broadwood John b. 6 October 1732 St Helen, Cockburnspath, East Lothian d. 17 July 1812

Brock, Walter b. 21 January 1836 Govan, Lanarkshire d. 1907

Brodie, John Alexander b. 5 June 1858 Shropshire, England d. 16 November 1934. Father: James Brodie of Kettins, Forfarshire b. 14 November 1822. Mother: Elizabeth Freeland born 1821, Carluke, Lanarkshire

Broom, Robert b. 30 November 1866 Paisley, Renfrewshire d. 6 April 1951

Broun, John Allan b. 21 September 1817 Dumfries d. 22 November 1879

Brown, Alexander b. 25 February 1929 India d. 15 March 1975. Parents born Scotland. Father: John Brown born 1892, Edinburgh; Mother: Wilhelmina Ward Henderson born 1899

Brown, Alexander Crum b. 26 March 1838 Edinburgh d. 28 October 1922

Brown, Andrew b. 8 October 1825 Glasgow d. 6 May 1907

Brown, David Rannie/Rennie b. 2 December 1808 Edinburgh d.1875

Brown, George Harold b. 14 October 1908 Wisconsin, USA d. 11 December 1987. Paternal grandparents born in Scotland (1910 US census - North Milwaukee)

Brown, Samuel b. 1776 London, England d. 15 March 1852. Father: William Brown, b. 1755

Borland, Galloway: Mother: Hannah Hogg of Roxburgh Ref: http://www.royalsoced.org.uk/cms/files/fellows/biographical_index/fells_indexp1.pdf

Brown, Thomas Graham b. 10 April 1933 Glasgow

Brown, William b. 17 February 1888 Middlebie, Dumfriesshire d. 18 January 1975

Brown, William Piper b. 14 April 1914, Ayrshire d. 21 December 2004

Browne, James b. 12 February 1829 Stewarton, Ayrshire d. 3 June 1896

Browne, Leslie Johnston b. 3 February 1950 Glasgow Still Living

Bruce, Alexander b. 1629 Kincardine d. 9 July 1680

Bruce, Frederick Malloch b. 13 July 1912 Aberdeen d. 23 July 1997

Bruce, George b. circa 1550 Carnock, Fife d. 1625

Brunlees, James b. 5 January 1816 Kelso, Roxburghshire d. 2 June 1892

Brunton, David William b. 11 June 1849 Ontario, Canada d. 20 December 1927. Father: James Russell Brunton born 7 January 1920 in Galashiels; Mother: Agnes Dickie born 24 April 1824, West Kilbride, Ayrshire

Brunton, John b. 16 May 1835 Campbeltown, Argyllshire d. 25 March 1899

Brunton, Richard Henry b. 26 December 1841 Muchalls, Aberdeenshire d. 24 April 1901

Brunton, Thomas Lauder b. 14 March 1844 Hiltonshill, Roxburghshire d. 16 September 1916

Brunton, William b. 26 May 1777 Lochwinnoch, Renfrewshire d. 5 October 1851

Buchan, Alexander b. 11 April 1829 Kinnesswood, Kinross d. 13 May 1907

Buchanan, Alexander b.? Paisley, Renfrewshire d.?

Buchanan, Colin Douglas b. 22 August 1907 Simla, India d. 6 December 2001. Grandfather: George Buchanan, born 8 December 1834 in Edinburgh

Buchanan, John Scoular b. 23 November 1883 Cambuslang, Lanarkshire d. 5 April 1966

Buchanan, John Young b. 20 February 1844 Glasgow d. 16 October 1925

Buchanan, Thomas b. 1782 Edinburgh d. 1853

Buchanan, William b. 6 March 1830 Dumbarton d. 20 January 1910

Buick, David Dunbar b. 17 September 1854 Arbroath, Angus d. 5 March 1929

Burden, Henry b. 22 April 1791 Dunblane, Perthshire d. 19 January 1871

Burnet, Frank Macfarlane b. 3 September 1899 Traralgon, Victoria, Australia d. 31 August 1985. Father: Frank Burnet, born 1856 Langholm. Maternal grandfather: George Gilbert Mackay born in Glasgow

Burnett, Thomas b. 6 March 1773 Aberdeen d. 9 November 1824 (Ref: The Lachine Canal: Riding the Waves of Industrial and Urban Development 1860-1950, by Yvon Desloges, Alain Gelly, Septentrion, Ottowa, 2002, p 56)

Burt, Peter b. 22 December 1856, Glasgow d. January 1944

Burton, William Kinninmond b. 11 May 1856 Edinburgh d. 5 August 1899

Byron, Augusta Ada b. 10 December 1815 London, England d. 27 November 1852. Grandmother: Catherine Gordon born 1764, Castle of Gight, Aberdeenshire

Cadell, Colin Simson b. 7 August 1905 Colinton, Edinburgh d. 29 October 1996

Cairns, Hugh John Forster b. 1922 Oxfordshire, England (Still Living as at 2013). Grandfather: William Cairns born 1868 in Glasgow died 1958 (ref: Australian Dictionary of Biography for Sir Hugh William Bell Cairns 1896-1952)

Cairns, Hugh William Bell b. 26 June 1896 Port Pirie, South Australia d. 18 July 1952. Father: William Cairns born Glasgow in 1868

Callender, Thomas Octavius b. 9 April 1855 Partick, Lanarkshire d. 2 December 1938

Callender, William Marshall b. 23 February 1859 Govan, Lanarkshire d.?

Cameron, Alastair Graham Walter b. 21 June 1925 Winnipeg, Manitoba d. 3 October 2005. Grandfather: Alexander Cameron born circa 1854 Scotland (Ref: 1891 England census - Wimbledon)

Cameron, Alexander Bryce b. 5 November 1911 Rangoon, Burma d.? Father: Hugh Porteous Cameron, born 24 September 1841, Barony, Lanarkshire. Mother: Sarah McKinlay probably born Scotland

Cameron, Donald b. 1853 Scotland d.? (Ref: 1891 England census - Exeter: also "British sewage works and notes on the sewage farms of Paris and on two German works" p 23 "... welcomed by Mr. Cameron, the quiet Scotchman ..."

Cameron, William b. 11 October 1873 Charleston, Nigg, Kincardineshire d. 21 December 1934

Campbell, Archibald b. 22 February 1835 Florence, Italy d. 8 July 1908. Mother: Caroline Agnes Dick christened 9 May 1814, Pitkerro, Fife

Campbell, Duncan Hector b. 1 September 1828 Sutherland d. 2 November 1894

Campbell, John b. 8 February 1719 Kirkbean, Kirkcudbrightshire d. 16 December 1790

Campbell, Keith Henry Stockman b. 23 May 1954 Birmingham, England d. 5 October 2012. Father: Henry Stockman Campbell born Milnathort, Perth & Kinross, 21 May 1929, died November 1990

Carruthers, John b. 21 June 1836 Inverness d. 2 September 1914

Cayley, George b. 27 December 1773 Yorkshire, England d. 15 December 1857. Mother: Isabel Seton, born before 1748, Parbroath, Creich, Fife; d. 30 July 1828

Chalmers, Bruce b. 15 October 1907 London, England d. 25 May 1990. Grandfather: John Chalmers, born 15 May 1850 in Markinch, Fife

Chalmers, James b. 2 February 1782 Arbroath, Angus d. 26 August 1853

Chalmers, William Malcolm b. 16 November 1905 Edinburgh d. 16 October 1995

Christie, Samuel Hunter b. 22 March 1784 London, England d. 24 January 1865. Father: James Christie born 15 November 1730, Forgandenny, Perth

Clark, Adam b. 14 August 1811 Edinburgh d. 23 July 1866

Clark, George Aitken b. 9 August 1823 Paisley, Renfrewshire d. 13 February 1873

Clark, James b. 12 August 1747 Paisley, Renfrewshire d. 1829

Clark, Patrick b. April 1742, Paisley, Renfrewshire d.?

Clark, Thomas b. 31 March 1801 Ayr d. 27 November 1867

Cleland, Archibald b. circa 1700 Scotland d. 1771 (Ref: The Catheter: URL - http://jaivirdi.com/2012/07/25/the-catheter/)

Cleland, John Burton b. 22 June 1878 Norwood, South Australia d. 11 August 1971. Mother: Matilda Lander Burton, born circa 1849 in Edinburgh. Paternal grandfather, John Fullerton **Cleland**, was born in 8 July 1821 in Kilsyth, Stirlingshire

Clerk, Dugald b. 31 March 1854 Glasgow d. 12 November 1932

Cochran, William b. 30 July 1922 Newton Mearns, Kincardineshire d. 28 August 2003

Cochrane Archibald b. 1 January 1748 Ochiltree, Ayrshire d. 1 July 1831

Cochrane, Thomas b. 14 December 1775 Annsfield, Lanarkshire d. 31 October 1860

Comrie, Leslie John b. 15 August 1893 New Zealand d. 11 December 1950. Grandparents: James Comrie born before 27 June 1813 in Fowlis Wester, Perthshire; Helen Young born before 24 October 1824 in Methven, Perthshire

Condie, John b. 1796 Glasgow d. 1860

Copus, Jonathan b. 6 April 1944 Dundee

Cormack, Allan MacLeod b. 23 February 1924 Johannesburg, South Africa d. 9 May 1998. Father: George Cormack, born 21 October 1884, Caithness. Mother: Amelia McKenzie MacLeod born 24 December 1883, Glasgow

Coughtrie, Thomas Robb b. 25 November 1917 Motherwell, Lanarkshire d. 27 August 2008

Couper, Archibald Scott b. 31 March 1831 Kirkintilloch, Dunbartonshire d. 11 March 1892

Cowie, William Clarke b. 8 April 1849 Friockheim, Angus d. 14 September 1910

Crawford, John William Croom b. 13 January 1901 Kelvin, Glasgow d. 1989

Crerar, Peter b. 1785 Breadalbane, Perthshire, d. 5 November 1856

Croll, James b. 2 January 1821 Little Whitefield, Perthshire d. 15 December 1890

Crompton, Rookes Evelyn Bell b. 31 May 1845 Yorkshire, England d. 15 February 1940. Mother: Mary Alexander born 20 October 1806 in Ayrshire

Cruickshank, Arthur Richard Ivor b. 29 February 1932 Kenya d. 4 December 2011. Father: Arthur Alexander MacDonald Cruickshank, born 1901 Elgin, Morayshire

Cruickshank, William b.? Scotland d. circa 1811 (Ref: ODNB - possibly born in north-east Scotland in the 1740s or 1750s)

Cullen, Edward Alexander Ernest b. 21 December 1861 Brisbane, Australia d. 13 April 1950. Father: Edward Boyd Cullen, born 19 March 1827 at Balmaclellan, Kirkcudbrightshire

Cullen, William b. 15 April 1710 Hamilton, Lanarkshire d. 5 February 1790

Cumming, Alexander b. 1731 (or 1732) possibly in Edinburgh. He was the son of James Cumming of the parish of Duthil, Inverness-shire, d. 8 March 1814

Cunningham, Henry Duncan Preston b. 29 June 1814 Hampshire, England d. 19 January 1875. Father: John Cunningham born 1776 Annandale

Curran, Samuel Crowe b. 23 May 1912 Ballymena, Northern Ireland d. 25 February 1998. Father: John Curran, born 1885 Fife

Dalrymple, Alexander b. 24 July 1737 New Hailes, Midlothian d. 9 June 1808

Dalrymple-Hay, Harley Hugh b. 7 October 1861 Rawalpindi, India d. 17 December 1940. Father: George James Dalrymple-Hay born 1828 Old Luce, Wigtownshire; Mother: Amelia Emily Maitland born 1831 in Bengal to Scottish father, James Dalrymple-Hay, from Glenluce, Wigtownshire

Dalzell (or Dalziel), Gavin b. 29 August 1811 Lesmahagow, Lanarkshire d. 14 June 1863

Dalziel, Charles Francis b. 6 June 1904 California, USA d. 15 December 1986. Grandfather: Robert Dalziel, born 8 November 1836 Paisley. Paternal grandmother, Agnes Smith, born Renfrewshire

Dalziel, John b. 21 December 1801 Penpont, Dumfries-shire d.?

Dalziel, Keith b. 24 August 1921 Lancashire, England d. 7 January 1994. Father Gilbert Dalziel, born 1885 Tinwald, Dumfries-shire

Davidson, David b. 18 August 1811 Haddington, East Lothian d. 15 May 1900

Davidson, Robert b. 18 April 1804 Aberdeen d. 16 November 1894

Dawson, John William b. 13 October 1820 Pictou, Nova Scotia, Canada d. 19 November 1899. Father: James Dawson born 1789 Ordiquhill, Banffshire, Mother: Mary Rankine born Stirlingshire

Denny, Maurice Edward b. 11 February 1886 Dumbarton d. 2 February 1955

Denny, William b. 25 May 1847 Dumbarton d. 17 March 1887

Devine, Graeme John b. 1966 Glasgow Still Living

Dewar, James b. 20 September 1842 Kincardine-on-Forth, Kincardineshire d. 27 March 1923

Dewar, Michael James Steuart b. 24 September 1918 Ahmednagar, India d. 10 October 1997. Father: Francis Dewar. Parents born in Scotland (ref National Academy of Sciences http://www.nap.edu/html/biomems/mdewar.html)

Dey, Alexander b. 5 August 1854 Kirkmichael, Banffshire d.?

Dick, James b. July 1823 Kilmarnock, Ayrshire d. 1902

Dick, Maxwell b. 28 June 1798 Irvine, Ayrshire d. 17 May 1870

Dick, Robert b. 12 January 1814 Bathgate, West Lothian d. 9 December 1890

Dick, Robert b. 5 May 1820 Ayr, Ayrshire d. 1 August 1891

Dickie, Robert James b. 30 December 1876 London, England d. 1958. Father: William Dickie born 1 March 1817, Cluny, Aberdeen

Dickson, James Tennant b. 11 February 1917, Tranent, East Lothian d. 1991

Dickson, William Kennedy Laurie b. 3 August 1860 Brittany, France d. 28 September 1935. Father: James [Waite] Dickson born 23 October 1821 Kelso, Roxburgh. Mother: Elizabeth Kennedy Laurie was born 31 December 1821 and baptised 19 February 1822 in Balmaghie, Kirkcudbright. 1880 US Census shows father and mother as born in Scotland

Donald, David b.? Scotland d.? (Ref: The Cambridge Economic History of Europe: The economic organization of early Modern Europe, edited by Edwin Ernest Rich, Michael Moïssey Postan, H. J. Habakkuk, 1977, p 476 – "In 1727 a Scot, David Donald, invented a flax-beating machine ...") A David Donald, hammerman of Carntyne, was admitted to the Glasgow Guild of Hammermen on 7 April 1694. Although a child, his father and grandfather and been hammermen and both were now deceased. It is possible that this is the David Donald described in the article.

Donald, Ian b. 27 December 1910 Liskeard, Cornwall, England d. 19 June 1987. Father: John Donald born 19 July 1872 Paisley, Renfrewshire

Donaldson, Gordon Bryce b. 10 August 1941, Edinburgh d. 28 November 2012

Dowie, James b. 5 February 1809 Midlothian d.? (1841 Scottish census shoes James Dowie, age 30, Shoemaker, St Cuthberts Parish not far from Frederick Street where he was based when he patented his invention. He is the only shoemaker by that name in Edinburgh at that time)

Drummond, Charles b. 23 April 1820 Leith South, Midlothian d. 30 August 1866

Drummond, Dugald b. 1 January 1840 Ardrossan, Ayrshire d. 8 November 1912

Drummond, Thomas b. 10 October 1797 Edinburgh d. 15 April 1840

Drummond, Victoria Alexandrina b. 14 October 1894 Errol, Perthshire d. 25 December 1980

Drysdale, Charles Vickery b. 8 July 1874 France d. 7 February 1961. Father: Charles [Robert] Drysdale born 1829 Edinburgh (1881 England and Wales census)

Du Toit, Alexander Logie b. 14 March 1878 South Africa d. 25 February 1948. Maternal grandfather: Robert Clunie Logie born 22 May 1799 in Bellie, Morayshire

Dudgeon, Richard b. 3 January 1821 Tain, Ross-shire d. 1899

Dunbar, Robert b. 13 December 1812 Carnbee, Fife d. 1890

Duncan, Alan James b. 4 November 1938 Kingston, Berwickshire d. 9 July 1999

Duncan, George Smith b. 11 July 1852 Dunedin, New Zealand d. 4 September 1930. Parents: George Duncan born circa 1827 in Aberdeen and Elspeth Wilson born circa 1829 in Aberdeenshire

Duncan, Thomas b. 26 December 1865 Girvan, Ayrshire d. 22 January 1929

Dunlop, James b. 31 October 1793 Dalry, Ayrshire d. 22 September 1848

Dunlop, John Boyd b. 5 February 1840 Dreghorn, Ayrshire d. 23 October 1921

Eccles, Robert Gibson b. 1 January 1848 Kilmaurs, Ayrshire d. 9 June 1934

Eckford, Henry b. 17 May 1823 Stonehouse, Midlothian d. 5 December 1905

Edgar, James b. 5 March 1843 Longformacus, Duns, Berwickshire d. 20 September 1909

Elder, John b. 8 March 1824 Glasgow d. 17 September 1869

Ellis, Charles Drummond b. 11 August 1895 London, England d. 10 January 1980. Mother: Isabella Flockhart Carswell, born 29 May 1872 Tibbermore, Perthshire

Elphinstone, George Keith Buller b. 11 May 1865 Edinburgh d. 6 July 1941

Ennis, Lawrence b. 31 August 1871 West Calder, West Lothian d. 6 May 1938

Ewart, Peter b. 14 May 1767 Troqueer, Dumfries-shire d. 15 September 1842

Ewing, James Alfred b. 27 March 1855 Dundee, Angus d. 7 January 1935

Fairbairn, Peter b. September 1799 Kelso, Roxburghshire d. 4 January 1861

Fairbairn, William b. 19 February 1789 Kelso, Roxburghshire d. 18 August 1874

Fairlie, Robert Francis b. 5 April 1830 Glasgow d. 31 July 1885

Falconer, Douglas Scott b. 10 March 1913 Old Meldrum, Aberdeenshire d. 23 February 2004

Farquharson, James Robbie b. 1 November 1903 Glen Moy, Angus d. 17 February 2005

Ferguson, Patrick b. 4 June 1744 Edinburgh d. 7 October 1780

Ferguson, Peter Jack b. 21 July 1840 Glasgow d. 17 March 1911

Ferguson-Smith, Malcolm Andrew b. 5 September 1931 Glasgow

Fergusson, Mary Isolen b. 28 April 1914 Plymouth, England d. 30 November 1997. Father: John Newbery Fraser Fergusson, born 1882 Wick, Caithness

Ferrier, David b. 13 January 1843 Woodside, Aberdeenshire d. 19 March 1928

Fife, David Alexander b. 22 August 1805 Kincardine-on-Forth, Kincardineshire d. 9 January 1877

Fisken, William b. 16 September 1812 Crieff, Perthshire d. 28 December 1883

Fleming, Alexander b. 6 August 1881 Lochfield, Ayrshire d. 11 March 1955

Fleming, John Ambrose b. 29 November 1849 Lancashire, England d. 18 April 1945. Father: James Fleming born 8 March 1816 Earlston, Berwickshire

Fleming, Sandford b. 7 July 1827 Kirkcaldy, Fife d. 22 July 1915

Fleming, Williamina Paton Stevens b. 15 May 1857 Dundee, Angus d. 21 May 1911

Forbes, Archibald Walter b. 1 November 1899 Strathdon, Aberdeenshire d. 30 August 1996

Forbes, George b. 5 April 1849 Edinburgh d. 22 October 1936

Forbes, James David b. 20 April 1809 Edinburgh d. 31 December 1868

Forrest, Archibald Robin b. 13 May 1943 Glasgow

Forrester, George b. 7 January 1781 Dunipace, Stirling d. after 1841 (1841 England census)

Forsyth, Alexander John b. 28 December 1768 Belhelvie, Aberdeenshire d. 11 June 1843

Forsyth, James Bennett b. 2 February 1850 Boston, Massachusetts, USA d. circa 1910. Father: William Forsyth born 8 November 1807 in Ayrshire

Fotheringham, John Knight b. 14 August 1874 London, England d. 12 December 1936. Father: David Fotheringham, born 25 June 1830, Dunnichen, Angus

Foulis, Robert b. 5 May 1796 Glasgow d. 28 January 1866

Frame, Alexander Gilchrist b. 3 April 1929 Dalmuir, Dunbartonshire d. 26 December 1993

Fraser, Alexander b. 8 May 1824 Devon, England d. 11 June 1898. Father: James Fraser came from Durris in Kincardineshire

Fraser, Bruce b. 9 January 1954 Edinburgh d. 16 December 2006

Fraser, Daniel b. 5 November 1786 Ancrum, Roxburghshire d. 30 December 1849

Fraser, John b. 1885 Tain, Ross and Cromarty d. 1947

Fraser, Robert Donald Bruce b. 14 August 1924 London, England. Maternal grandparents born Scotland (ref Interview with RDB Fraser, Australian Academy of Science http://www.science.org.au/scientists/interviews/f/bf.html)

Fraser, Thomas Richard, b. 5 February 1841 Calcutta, India d. 4 January 1920. Father: John Richard Fraser born circa 1807 Jedburgh, Roxburghshire. Married in Jedburgh to Mary Palmer on 26 July 1831

Frazer, Ian Hector b. 6 January 1953 Glasgow Still Living

Freeburn, James b. 1808 Edinburgh d. 5 August 1876

Fulton, Hamilton b. 26 May 1781 Paisley, Renfrewshire d. 1834

Fyfe, John b. 26 June 1830 Goodhope, Bucksburn, Aberdeenshire d. 18 July 1906

Galbraith, William Robert b. 7 July 1829 Stirling d. 5 October 1914

Galloway, William b. 12 February 1840 Paisley, Renfrewshire d. 2 November 1927

Garden, William Brownie b. 2 December 1869 Bucksburn, Aberdeen d. 1960

Garstin, William Edmund b. 29 January 1849 India d. 8 January 1925. Mother: Helen Mackenzie born 1 October 1822 in Dingwall

Ged, William b. 1690 Baldridge, Fife d. 19 October 1749. Dictionary of National Biography 1922 has him born in Edinburgh

Geddes, Leslie Alexander b. 24 May 1921 Portgordon, Morayshire d. 25 October 2009

Geddes, William George Nicholson b. 29 July 1913 Oldhamstock, East Lothian d. 10 November 1993

Geikie, Archibald b. 28 December 1835 Edinburgh d. 10 November 1924

Geikie, James Murdoch b. 23 August 1839 Edinburgh d. 1 March 1915

Gibb, Alexander b. 12 February 1872 Dundee, Angus d. 21 January 1958

Gibb, John b. 1781 (possibly 10 January) Paisley d.?

Gibson, George Ernest b. 9 November 1884 Edinburgh d. 26 August 1959

Gibson, Quentin Howieson b. 9 December 1918 Aberdeen d. 16 March 2011

Gibson, William Wallace b. 28 March 1876 Dalmellington, Ayrshire d. 25 November 1965

Gilchrist, Percy Carlyle b. 27 December 1851 Lyme Regis, Dorset d. 16 December 1935. Grandfather: James Gilchrist born 16 March 1783 Kilsyth, Stirlingshire - his father was a farmer in Larbert. He died in 1835

Gill, David b. 12 June 1843 Aberdeen d. 24 January 1914

Gillies, Alexander b. 1 November 1865 Victoria, Australia d. 1952. Father: Donald Gillies born 1822, Portree, Skye; Mother: Catherine McLean born circa 1821 in Raasay, Inverness-shire

Gillies, Harold Delf b. 17 June 1882 Dunedin, New Zealand d. 10 September 1960. Father: Robert Craig Gillies, born 31 July 1835 in Rothesay, Bute

Gilmour, Douglas Graham b. 7 March 1885 Kent, England d. 17 February 1912. Father: David Gilmour, born 5 July 1842 Glasgow; Mother: Margaret Jane Muirhead, born 12 September 1848 Glasgow

Gladstone, William Ewart b. 29 December 1809 Liverpool, England d. 19 May 1898. Father: John Gladstones born 11 December 1764 Leith North, Midlothian; Mother: Anne Mackenzie Robertson born 4 August 1772, Dingwall, Ross-shire

Glennie, Alick Edwards b. 8 April 1925 West Ham, Essex d. 2003. Father: William Glennie, born 1894 Logie Coldstone, Aberdeenshire

Glover, Thomas Blake b. 6 June 1838 Fraserburgh, Aberdeenshire d. 16 December 1911

Goodfellow, James b. 1937 Paisley, Renfrewshire

Goodsir, John b. 20 March 1814 Anstruther, Fife d. 6 March 1867

Gordon, George [Andrew] b. 15 June 1712 Cofforach, Forfarshire d. 22 August 1751

Gordon, Alexander b. 3 January 1818 Glenmuick, Aberdeen d. 1895

Gordon, Cuthbert b. 22 February 1730 Kirkmichael, Banffshire d. 10 July 1810

Gordon, David b. 1774 Castle Douglas, Kirkcudbrightshire d. 1829

Gordon, George b. 1829 Arbroath, Angus d. 25 February 1907

Gorrie, John b. 3 October 1802/3 Nevis, West Indies d. 29 June 1855

Gow, David b. 1957 Dumfries Still Living

Graham, James b. 1 May 1878 London, England d. 20 January 1954. Father: Douglas Graham born 7 November 1852 at Buchanan House, Cowcaddens, Glasgow

Graham, Robert b. 1929 Michigan, USA Still Living. Paternal Grandfather born in Scotland (ref Biographical Sketch by Robert Graham http://people.cs.umass.edu/~bob/bio.html)

Graham, Thomas b. 21 December 1805 Glasgow d. 16 September 1869

Grainger, Thomas b. 12 November 1794 Ratho, Midlothian d. 25 July 1852

Grant, James Kerr b. 21 March 1916 Dundee d. 6 January 2004

Grant, Johannes b. Scotland d. 29 May 1453

Grant, Peter Mitchell b. 20 June 1944 St Andrews, Fife

Gray, George William b. 4 September 1926 Alloway, Ayrshire d. 12 May 2013

Gray, John McFarlane b. 7 April 1831 Tulliallan, Perthshire d. 1893

Gray, Thomas Lomar b. 4 February 1850 Lochgelly, Fife d. 19 December 1908

Green, William b. 4 April 1725 London, England d. 11 January 1811. Mother: Helen Smith, born in Aberdeen (Her parents were Adam Smith and Margaret Douglas)

Gregory, James b. 6 November 1638 Drumoak, Aberdeenshire d. October 1675

Gregory, William b. 25 December 1803 Edinburgh d. 24 April 1858

Greig, David b. 27 October 1827 Kincardineshire d. 28 March 1891

Gresley, Herbert Nigel b. 19 June 1876 Edinburgh d. 5 April 1941

Grieve, Alison May b. March 1977 Bruntsfield, Edinburgh Still Living

Grieve, John b.? Perthshire d.?

Gulland, John Masson b. 1898 Edinburgh d. 26 October 1947

Haddow, Alexander b. 18 January 1907 Leven, Fife d. 21 January 1976

Halcrow, William Thomson b. 4 July 1883 Durham, England d. 31 October 1958. Father: John Andrew Halcrow, born 9 June 1838 Urafirth, Shetland. Mother Jane [nee] Halcrow, born 1848 Lerwick, Shetland

Haldane, John Burdon Sanderson b. 5 November 1892 Edinburgh d. 1 December 1964

Haldane, John Scott b. 3 May 1860 Edinburgh d. 14 March 1936

Halkett, Peter Arthur b. 1820 Gloucestershire, England d. 23 March 1885. Father: John Halkett born John Wedderburn 1768 in Pitfirrane, Fife. Mother: Catherine Douglas, born 1778 in Wigtown

Hall, Alexander b. 1760 (baptised 7 August 1761 Auchterless, Aberdeen) d. 1849

Hall, James b. 17 January 1761 Dunglass, East Lothian d. 23 June 1832

Hallidie, Andrew Smith b. 16 March 1836 London, England d. 24 April 1900. Father: Andrew Smith born 1798 Kirkpatrick Fleming, Dumfries-shire. Mother: Julia Johnstone born Lockerbie, Dumfries-shire. Hallidie surname adopted later in life

Hamilton, Archibald Milne b. 18 November 1898 New Zealand d. 1972. Mother: Janet Smart [Stirling], born 1 July 1858 Edinburgh

Hamilton, Charles William Feilden b. 26 July 1899 Fairlie, New Zealand d. 30 March 1978. Grandfather: Andrew Hamilton born 28 February 1793 Edinburgh

Hamilton, James Arnot b. 2 May 1923 Penicuik, Midlothian d. 24 May 2012

Hamilton, Ronald Shade b. 1 November 1941 Lanarkshire

Hamilton, William b. 9 July 1810 Lasswade, Midlothian d. 28 November 1880

Hamilton, William Rowan b. 4 August 1805 Dublin, Ireland d. 2 September 1865. Paternal grandmother Grace Mcferrand, born 8 May 1743, Kirkmaiden, Wigtownshire

Hammersley, John Michael b. 21 March 1920 Helensburgh, Dunbartonshire d. 2 May 2004

Handyside, Andrew b. 25 July 1805 Edinburgh d. 9 June 1887

Handyside, William b. 25 July 1793 Edinburgh d. 26 May 1850

Hannay, James Ballantyne b. 1 January 1855 Glasgow d. 1931

Harden, Arthur b. 12 October 1865 Manchester, England d. 17 June 1940. Mother: Eliza Macalister born Paisley

Harkness, William b. 7 December 1837 Ecclefechan, Dumfries-shire d. 28 February 1903

Harper, John b. 21 May 1833 Turriff, Aberdeenshire d. 1906

Harper, Louis b. 6 June 1868 Old Machar, Aberdeenshire d. 26 January 1940

Harrison, James b. April 1816 Renton, Dunbartonshire d. 3 September 1893

Hartley, Charles Augustus b. 3 February 1825 Durham, England d. 20 February 1915. Mother: Lillias Todd born 23 December 1788, Bo'ness, West Lothian

Hastie, John b. 10 November 1803 Littlemark, Sanquhar, Dumfries d. 22 September 1894

Haswell, John b. 20 March 1812 Lancefield, Lanarkshire d. 8 June 1897

Hawking, Stephen William b. 8 January 1942 Oxford, England. Mother: Isobel Eileen Walker, born 3 March 1915 Glasgow died 2013

Hay, Peter Seton b. 12 July 1852 Glasgow d. 19 March 1907

Heilbron, Isidor [Ian] Morris b. 6 November 1886 Glasgow d. 14 September 1959

Henderson, Brodie Haldane b. 6 March 1869 Ealing, Middlesex, England d. 28 September 1936 Father: George Henderson of Langholm, Dumfries (Ref: Oxford Dictionary of National Biography)

Henderson, John b. 1811 Scotland d. 4 January 1858 (Note: may have been born in Middlesex although most sources, including the International Journal of Space Structures Volume 21, No 1, 2006, p 18, say he is Scottish)

Henderson, Richard b. 19 July 1945 Edinburgh Still Living

Henderson, Robert Gregory b. 7 April 1902 Aberdeen d. 26 December 1999

Henderson, Thomas James Alan b. 28 December 1798 Dundee, Angus d. 23 November 1844

Hendrie, David Anderson b. 30 May 1861 Inverness d.1940

Henry, Alexander b. 4 June 1818 Edinburgh d. 27 January 1894

Henry, Joseph b. 17 December 1797 Albany, New York, USA d. 13 May 1878. Father: William Henry born 1757 in Scotland; Mother: Ann Alexander born 13 December 1760 (died 1835) probably in Glasgow, Maternal Grandparents Hugh Alexander born 1729 in Glasgow and Abigail/Eufane Stephenson born circa 1730 in Glasgow; paternal grandfather, William James Hendries born Argyllshire

Higgs, Peter Ware b. 29 May 1929 Newcastle upon Tyne, England. Grandfather: James Davidson Mackay Coghill born 2 April 1839 in Edinburgh, died 1909

Hill, William b. 16 September 1949 Glasgow d. 17 October 2012

Hinshelwood, Cyril Norman b. 19 June 1897 London, England d. 9 October 1967. Grandfather: George Frederik Hinshelwood, born 1827 in Glasgow

Hodge, William Vallance Douglas b. 17 June 1903 Edinburgh d. 7 July 1975

Holden, Isaac b. 7 May 1807 Hurlet, Renfrewshire d. 13 August 1897

Hope, Thomas Charles b. 21 July 1766 Edinburgh d. 13 June 1844

Hopper, Grace Brewster Murray b. 9 December 1906 New York, USA d. 1 January 1992. Maternal Grandfather: John W[alter] Murray born 31 October 1834, Kirkcudbright; his wife was New York-born Mary Struthers Davidson, both of whose parents were born in Scotland

Houston, Alexander Cruikshank b. 18 September 1865 Yorkshire, England d. 29 October 1933. Father: John Houston born 1832 Tullochgriban, Strathspey

Houston, David Henderson b. 14 June 1841 Auchterarder, Perthshire d. 6 May 1906

Howden, James b. 29 February 1832 Prestonpans, East Lothian d. 21 November 1913

Howell, John b. 1788 Edinburgh d. 4 April 1863

Hoy, William Wilson b. 11 March 1868 Portmoak, Kinross d. 1930

Hume, Walter Reginald b. 29 November 1873 Melbourne, Australia d. 21 July 1943. Father: James Hill Hume born 22 November 1828, Perthshire [Christened at Errol]

Hunter, Robert b. 27 October 1844 London d. 6 November 1913 F: Robert Lauchlin Hunter born 31 December 1805 Ayr died 30 October 1878. Mother: Anne Lachlan was a cousin of Robert Lauchlin Hunter. She was born around 1806 in Scotland, daughter of Joseph Lachlan

Hutton, James b. 3 June 1726 Edinburgh d. 26 March 1797

Iggo, Ainsley b. 2 August 1924 Napier, New Zealand d. 25 March 2012. Maternal Grandmother born Scotland

Inglis, Charles Edward b. 31 July 1875 Worcester, England d. 19 April 1952. Father: Alexander Inglis, born 1834 Edinburgh (1881 England census)

Innes, Robert Thorburn Ayton b. 10 November 1861 Edinburgh d. 13 March 1933

Irvine-Halliday, David b. 1942 Perth

Irving, Charles b. circa 1734 Dumfries d. 1794

Isaacs, Alick b. 16 July 1921 Glasgow d. 26 January 1967

Jamieson, Thomas Francis b. 1 April 1829 Aberdeenshire d. 1913

Jardine, James b. 13 November 1776 Applegarth, Dumfries-shire d. 20 June 1858

Jarvis, John Charles Barron b. 5 August 1857 Glasgow d. 10 September 1935

Jeffray, James b. 1759 Kilsyth, Lanarkshire d. January 1848

Jenkin, Henry Charles Fleeming b. 25 March 1833 Kent, England d. 12 June 1885. Maternal grandmother: Susan Campbell born circa 1772, Greenock, Renfrewshire

Johnson, Thomas b.? Glasgow d.? (Ref: The Annual Register, Or, A View of the History, Politics, and Literature of the Year 1834, Volume 7, Printed by J G & F Rivington, London, 1835, p 393)

Johnston, George b. 3 August 1855 West Linton, Peeblesshire d. 3 November 1945

Johnston, John b. 11 April 1791 Dalry, Dumfries-shire d. 24 November 1880

Johnston, John Lawson b. 28 September 1839 Roslin, Midlothian d. 24 November 1900

Jones, David b. 1966 Dundee, still living

Kay, David b. 20 July 1899, Blackford, Perthshire d. 1971 Perth

Keiller, Alexander b. 1 December 1889 Dundee d. 29 October 1955

Keir, James b. 29 September 1735 Edinburgh d. 11 October 1820

Kelly, William b.1790s Lanark d. 1840 (Ref: Biographical Dictionary of the History of Technology)

Kemp, Kenneth Treasurer b. 17 April 1805 Edinburgh d. 28 November 1842

Kennedy Alexander Blackie William b. 17 March 1847 London, England d. 1 November 1928. Father: John Kennedy born 1813 in Aberfeldy, Perthshire. Mother: Helen Stodart Blackie born 1821 in Aberdeen

Kennedy, James b. 13 January 1797 Gilmerton, Midlothian d. 25 September 1886

Kennedy, John b. 4 July 1769 Knocknalling, Kirkcudbright d. 31 October 1855

Kennedy, Thomas b. 8 September 1797 Oban, Argyllshire d. 6 September 1874

Kermack, William Ogilvy b. 26 April 1898 Kirriemuir, Angus d. 20 July 1970

Kerr, Allen b. 2 May 1926 Edinburgh

Kerr, John b. 17 December 1824 Ardrossan, Ayrshire d. 15 August 1907

Kibble, Thomas Walter Bannerman b. 1932 Madras, India. Maternal grandparents: William Burney Bannerman, born 6 July 1858 in Edinburgh; Helen Brodie Cowan Watson, born 25 February 1862 in Edinburgh

Kidston, Robert b. 29 June 1852 Bishopston House, Renfrewshire d. 13 July 1924

King, Alexander b. 26 January 1909 Glasgow d. 28 February 2007

King, George James Foster b. 9 May 1862 Erskine, Renfrewshire d. 11 August 1947

Kininmonth, Colin Peter b. 9 November 1886 London, England d. 20 July 1975. Grandfather: Peter Kininmonth, born 2 April 1817, Kirkcaldy, Fife

Kinnear, Charles George Hood b. 30 May 1830 Kinloch, Fife d. 5 November 1894

Kirk, Alexander Carnegie b. 16 July 1830 Barry, Angus d. 5 October 1892

Kirkaldy, David b. 4 April 1820 Mayfield, Angus d. 25 January 1897

Kirkwood, James Pugh b. 27 March 1807 Edinburgh d. 22 April 1877

Knott, Cargill Gilston b. 30 June 1856 Valleyfield, Penicuik, Midlothian d. 26 October 1922

Laidlaw, Alexander Bannatyne Stewart b. 3 August 1896 Kelvin, Glasgow d. 1968 Cockpen, Midlothian

Laing, Andrew b. 31 January 1856 Edinburgh d. 24 January 1931

Laird, John b. 14 June 1805 Greenock, Renfrewshire d. 29 October 1874

Laird, John P. b. 1826 Scotland d. 1882 (1870 USA census Alton, Illinois)

Lamont, John b. 13 December 1805 Braemar, Aberdeenshire d. 6 August 1879

Langmuir, Irving b. 31 January 1881 Brooklyn, New York, USA d. 16 August 1957. Paternal grandparents born Scotland: Charles Langmuir born 16 March 1810 in Glasgow and Margaret McCulloch born 1810 in Glasgow. They were married on 14 December 1833 in Gorbals, Lanarkshire

Lapworth, Arthur b. 10 October 1872 Galashiels, Selkirkshire d. 5 April 1941

Laurie, Arthur Pillans b. 6 November 1861 Edinburgh d. 7 October 1949

Laurie, James b. 9 May 1811 Bell's Mills, Edinburgh d. 16 March 1875

Lawson, Andrew Cowper b. 25 July 1861 Anstruther, Fife d. 16 June 1952

Lawther, Patrick Joseph b. 9 March 1921 Gretna, Dumfries-shire d. 6 June 2008

Leakey, Mary Douglas b. 6 February 1913 London, England d. 9 December 1996. Grandfather: Erskine Nicol born 3 July 1825 in Leith

Lee, James Paris b. 4 October 1831 Harwich, Roxburghshire d. 1904

Lee, John b. 25 June 1833 Hawick, Roxburghshire d. 30 October 1907

Lees, George Martin b. 16 April 1898 Ireland d. 25 January 1955. Father: George Murray Lees, born 22 November 1863 Edinburgh

Legget, Robert Ferguson b. 29 September 1904 Liverpool, Lancashire, England d. 17 April 1994. Grandfather: James Ferguson Legget born 1846, Edinburgh; Grandmother: Lucy MacKay Watson born circa 1843 Inverary, Argyllshire

Leslie, Frank Matthews b. 8 March 1935 Dundee d. 15 June 2000

Leslie, John b. 10 April 1766 Largo, Fife d. 3 November 1832

Lickley, Robert Lang b. 19 January 1912 Dundee, Angus d. 7 July 1998

Lind, James b. 17 May 1736 Edinburgh d. 17 October 1812

Lind, James b. 4 October 1716 Edinburgh d. 13 July 1794

Lindsay, James Bowman b. 8 September 1799 Carmyllie, Angus d. 29 June 1862

Lions, Francis b. 30 November 1901 Perth, Western Australia d. 13 March 1972. Mother: Mary McDonald, born 1 January 1880, Scotland (ref. Australian Dictionary of Biography)

Lipinski, Christopher Andrew b. 1 February 1944 Dundee, Angus

Logan, William Edmond b. 20 April 1798 Montreal, Canada d. 22 June 1875. Father, James Logan, born 1759 Polmont, Stirlingshire; Mother, Janet E Edmond, Conniehill, Stirlingshire

Login, Thomas b. 21 April 1823 Stromness, Orkney d. 5 June 1874

Loutit, John Freeman b. 19 February 1910 Western Australia, Australia d. 11 June 1992. Grandfather: Thomas Flett Loutit, born 19 February 1832, Kirkwall

Love, Gordon b. 1974 Airdrie, Lanarkshire Still Living

Low, Archibald Montgomery b. 17 October 1888 Purley, London d. September 1956. Father: John Smith Low born 18 February 1854 in Dundee

Low, William b. 11 December 1814 Rothesay, Bute d. 10 July 1886

Lumsden, Hugh David b. 7 September 1844 Belhelvie, Aberdeenshire d. 12th of August 1896

Lundie, John b. 14 December 1857 Arbroath, Angus d. 9 February 1931

Lyall, James b. 13 September 1836 Auchterarder, Perthshire d. 23 August 1901

Lyell, Charles b. 14 November 1797 Kinnordy, Forfarshire d. 22 February 1875

Lyle, Abram b. 14 December 1820 Greenock, Renfrewshire d. 30 April 1891

McAdam, John Loudon b. 21 September 1756 Ayr d. 26 November 1836

Macadie, Donald b. 14 August 1871 Olgrinbeg, Halkirk, Caithness d. 13 February 1955

Macallum, Archibald Byron b. 9 June 1858 Westminster, Ontario, Canada d. 5 April 1934. Father: John McCallum born 1817 in Kilmartin, McCallum, Donald Murdo b. 6 August 1922 Edinburgh d. 18 October 2011: Mother: Flora McNichol born 1827 in Argyll

Macarthur, John b. 18 August 1766 Stoke Damerel, Devonshire, England d. 11 April 1834. Father: Alexander Macarthur c1720-1790 in Strachur, Loch Fyne, Argyllshire

MacArthur, John Stewart b. 9 December 1856 Glasgow d. 16 March 1920

McCall, Thomas b. 24 November 1833 Penpont, Dumfriesshire d. 1904

McClean, Frank b. 13 November 1837 Glasgow d. 8 November 1904

MacColl, Albert Edward b. 1882 Dumbarton d. 1951

Macdonald, George b. Yorkshire, England d. 1967. Mother: Katherine Mary Stewart, born circa 1869 Stornoway, Isle of Lewis, Hebrides

McColl, Hugh b. 22 January 1819 Glasgow d. 2 April 1885

McConnel, James baptised 25 June 1762 Kells, Kirkcudbright d. 1831

McConnell, Robert b. 1 July 1805 Glasgow d. 29 November 1867

McCririck, William b. 15 June 1788 Cumnock, Ayrshire d.?

McCulloch, John Ramsay b. 1 March 1789 Whithorn, Dumfries-shire d. 11 November 1864

MacDonald, Murdoch b. 6 May 1866 Inverness d. 24 April 1957

MacDougall, Alan b. 22 May 1842 Madras, India d. 23 April 1897. Father: John Macdougall born 1810, Edinburgh

McDougall, Alexander b. 16 March 1845 Islay, Hebrides d. 23 May 1923 St Louis, Minnesota

MacDougall, James Kenneth b. 25 September 1884 Melbourne, Australia d. 10 February 1960. Father: James MacDougall, born 9 July 1858 in Glasgow; Mother: Elizabeth Brydie **McRobbie** born 30 September 1854, Perth, Perthshire

McDowall, John b. 1796, Renfrewshire d. 14 May 1857

McFadzean, James Anderson b. 21 September 1925 Troon, Ayrshire d. 30 July 2002

Macfarlan, John Fletcher b. 16 December 1790 Edinburgh d. 20 February 1861

Macfarlane, George Gray b. 8 January 1916 Airdrie, Lanarkshire d. 20 May 2007

McFarlane, Patrick b. 23 March 1799 Comrie, Perthshire d.?

McGrath, Matthew b. 1977 Benbecula, Outer Hebrides Still Living

McGregor, Ian Alexander b. 26 August 1922 Cambuslang, Lanarkshire d. 1 February 2007

MacGregor, John b. 24 August 1802 Fintry, Stirlingshire d. 16 September 1858

McGregor, William b. 13 April 1846 Braco, Perthshire d. 20 December 1911

McInnes, Colin Robert b. 1968 Glasgow Still Living

MacIntosh, Charles b. 29 December 1766 Glasgow d. 25 July 1843

McIntosh, Hugh b. 4 December 1768 Kildrummie, Nairn d. 30 August 1840

McIntosh, John Farquharson b. 28 February 1846 Farnell, Brechin, Angus d. 6 February 1918

MacIntyre, Iain b. 30 August 1924 Glasgow d. 18 September 2008

Macintyre, John b. 2 October 1857 Glasgow d. 29 October 1928

McKay, Alexander b. 11 April 1841 Carsphairn, Kirkcudbrightshire d. 8 July 1917

MacKay, David John Cameron b. 22 April 1967 Staffordshire, England Still Living. Father: Donald MacCrimmon MacKay, born 9 August 1922 Lybster, Caithness

MacKay, Hugh b. circa 1640 Scourie, Sutherlandshire d. 1692 (July/Aug)

McKay, Lauchlan b. 16 December 1811 Shelburne, Nova Scotia, Canada d. 5 January 1892. Three grandparents born in Scotland - Donald McKay, 1842 in Tain, Laughlin McPherson, 1766 in Glasgow, Elizabeth Urquhart, 6 August 1767 in Edinburgh. Fourth grandparent was Margaret McGrigor born 1770, died 1870

Mackellar Patrick b. 1 September 1718 Maam, Argyllshire d. 22 October 1778

McKendrick, Anderson Gray b. 8 September 1876 Edinburgh d. 30 May 1943

McKendrick, John Gray b. 9 March 1841 Aberdeen d. 2 January 1926

Mackenzie, Aubrey Duncan b. 3 January 1895 Melbourne, Australia d. 21 March 1962. Father: Duncan A Mackenzie born 1863, Spynie, Morayshire

Mackenzie, Chalmers Jack b. 10 July 1888 St Stephen, New Brunswick d. 26 February 1984. All 8 great grandparents were born in Scotland

Mackenzie, Duncan b. 17 May 1861 Ross-shire d. 25 August 1934

Mackenzie, James b. 12 April 1853 Scone, Perthshire d. 26 January 1925

MacKenzie, Kenneth Ross b. 12 June 1912 Portland, Oregon d. 3 July 2002. Grandfather: William Wood MacKenzie, born 1838, Dornoch, Sutherlandshire. William married Joan Purves 18 October 1867 in Kilmuir-Easter, Ross and Cromarty

Mackenzie, William b. 20 March 1794 Little Marsden, Lancashire, England d. 20 October 1851. Father: Alexander Mackenzie, born 1769, Muirton, Ross-shire

McKinlay, Peter Laird b. 11 June 1901 Old Kilpatrick, Dunbartonshire, d. 8 August 1972 Strachur, Argyllshire

MacLagan, Daniel Stewart b. 3 June 1904 Crieff, Perthshire d. 3 February 1991

Maclagan, Thomas John b. 6 July 1838 Gardiners Lodge, Scone, Perthshire d. 20 March 1903

McLaren, Henry Thomas b. 19 May 1897 New South Wales, Australia d. 3 September 1993. Father: Daniel James McLaren born 15 January 1860 in Braendam, Stirlingshire

McLaren, John Hays b. 20 December 1846 Bannockburn, Stirlingshire d. 1 December 1943

Maclaren, Owen Finlay b. 26 May 1906 Saffron Walden, Essex, England d. 13 April 1978. Father: Andrew Liddell Maclaren, born 23 February 1872 in Govan, Lanarkshire

Maclaurin, Colin b. February 1698 Kilmodan, Argyllshire d. 17 June 1746

McLellan, William b. 1874 Glasgow d. 1934

MacLeod, John James Rickard b. 6 September 1876 Cluny, Perthshire d. 16 March 1935

MacLeod, Norman Alexander b 14 January 1929 Peterhead, Aberdeenshire Still living

Maclure, William b. 27 October 1763 Ayr d. 23 March 1840

MacMasters, Alan Alexander b. 20 March 1865 Edinburgh d. 25 December 1927

MacMillan, David William b. 1968 Bellshill, Lanarkshire Still Living

MacMillan, Kirkpatrick b. 2 September 1812 Keir Mill, Dumfries-shire d. 26 January 1878

McNab, William b. 1855 Scotland d. 23 February 1923 (Ref: Biographical Dictionary of Canadian Engineers)

McNaught, Robert Houston b. 1956 Prestwick, Ayrshire Still Living

McNaught, William b. 27 May 1813 Sneddon, Paisley, Renfrewshire d. 8 January 1881

McNeill, William Gibbs b. 3 October 1801 Bladen, North Carolina, USA d. 16 February 1853. Father: Charles Daniel McNeill born 1760, Kintyre, Argyllshire died 8 December 1828 in North Carolina

Macpherson, Cluny b. 18 March 1879 Newfoundland, Canada d. 16 November 1966. Grandfather: Peter MacPherson, born 10 June 1787, Greenock

Macpherson, Robert b. 19 December 1731 Kingussie and Insh, Inverness-shire, d. March 1791

McQueen, Walter b. 8 October 1817 Kippen, Stirlingshire d. 1893 New York

MacRitchie, James b. 26 September 1847 Southampton, Hampshire, England d. 1895. Father: Alexander MacRitchie born Scotland (1851 census). He was a superintendent engineer for P&O at Greenock; Mother: Mary born in Leith

MacRobert, Thomas Murray b. 4 April 1884 Dreghorn, Ayrshire d. 1 November 1962

McTammany, John b. 26 June 1845 Glasgow d. 26 March 1915

McWhirter, William b. 27 May 1851 Maybole, Ayrshire d. 6 March 1933

Malcolm, William b. 13 October 1823 New York, USA d. 12 July 1890. Father: William Malcolm born Perthshire 1 January 1782; died 9 September 1844

Malloch, Peter Duncan b. 15 July 1852 Almondbank, Perthshire d. 22 May 1921

Manson, James b. 1845 Saltcoats, Ayrshire d. 5 June 1935

Manson, Patrick b. 3 October 1844 Old Meldrum, Aberdeenshire d. 9 April 1922

Marconi, Guglielmo b. 25 April 1874 Bologna, Italy d. 20 July 1937. Grandfather: Andrew Jameson, born 18 August 1783, christened 2 September 1783 in Alloa, Clackmannanshire

Martin-Scott, Ian b. 17 December 1913 Glasgow d. 9 October 2002

Mather, Colin b. 1812 North Shields, Durham d.2 May 1877. Father: Colin Mather born 8 September 1788 Montrose, Angus d. 1864 Salford, Lancashire

Mather, William b. 15 July 1838 Manchester, England d. 18 September 1920. Grandfather: Colin Mather born 8 September 1788 Montrose, Angus d. 1864 Salford, Lancashire

Mathieson, Ian James b. 23 May 1927 Edinburgh d. 24 June 2010

Maxwell, James Clerk b. 13 June 1831 Edinburgh d. 5 November 1879

Maxwell, John S. b. 11 July 1832 Paisley, Renfrewshire d. 21 September 1916

Meek, Marshall b. 22 April 1925 Auchtermuchty, Fife d. 7 August 2013

Meik, Charles Scott b. 21 April 1853 Bishopwearmouth, Durham, England d. 1923. Father: Thomas Meik born 20 January 1812 Duddingston, Midlothian, died 22 April 1896. Mother: Isobella McGregor born 21 March 1812, baptised four days later in Stralachlan, Argyllshire

Meik, Patrick Walter b. 22 March 1851 Bishopwearmouth, Durham, England d. 1910. Father: Thomas Meik born 20 January 1812 Duddingston, Midlothian, died 22 April 1896. Mother: Isobella McGregor born 21 March 1812, baptised four days later in Stralachlan, Argyllshire

Meik, Thomas b. 20 January 1812 Duddingston, Midlothian d. 22 April 1896

Meikle, Andrew b. 26 July 1719 Carriden, West Lothian d. 27 November 1811

Meikle, George born 30 October 1712, baptised 2 November 1712 Carriden, West Lothian d. 29 November 1811

Meldrum, Charles b. 6 November 1821 Kirkmichael, Banffshire d. 28 August 1901

Mellanby, Kenneth b. 26 March 1908 Barrhead, Renfrewshire d. 23 December 1993

Melvill[e], Thomas baptised 14 September 1726 Monimail, Fife d. December 1753

Melville, Robert b. 12 October 1723 Monimail, Fife d. 20 August 1809

Melvin, David Neilson b. 21 July 1840 Glasgow d. 1914

Menelaus, William b. 10 March 1818 East Lothian d. 30 March 1882

Menzies, Alan Wilfrid Cranbrook b. 11 July 1877 Edinburgh d. 8 September 1966

Menzies, Michael b. end of 17th century, Lanarkshire d. 13 December 1766 (Ref: Biographical Dictionary of the History of Technology, edited by Lance Day, Ian McNeil, Routledge, 1998, p 831)

Merz, Charles Hesterman b. 5 October 1874 Newcastle upon Tyne, England d. 15 October 1940. Maternal grandmother: Jane Wigham born 19 March 1808, Edinburgh

Metcalf, Donald b. 26 February 1929 Mittagong, NSW, Australia. Father: Donald Davidson Metcalf born in Scotland (ref Interview with Donald Metcalf http://www.australianbiography.gov.au/subjects/metcalf/interview1.html)

Metcalfe, Charles Herbert Theophilus b. 8 September 1853 Simla, India d. 29 December 1928. Grandfather: John Low born 13 December 1788 in Clatto, Fifeshire

Methven, Cathcart William b. 24 September 1849 Edinburgh d. 30 August 1925

Michie, Donald b. 11 November 1923 Rangoon, Burma d. 7 July 2007. Father: James Kilgour Michie born in Falkland, Fifeshire, 18 September 1887

Miller, David b. 21 February 1890 Glasgow d. 28 April 1973

Miller, Hugh b. 10 October 1802 Cromarty, Ross-shire d. 24 December 1856

Miller, Patrick b. 27 July 1731 Glenlee, Galloway d. 9 December 1815

Miller, Robert b.? Glasgow d.?

Miller, Stewart Crichton b. 2 July 1934 Kirkcaldy, Fife d. 7 August 1999

Milne, Alastair David b. 8 November 1942 Edinburgh

Milne, John b. 11 February 1802 Fordoun, Kincardineshire d. 1877

Milne, Samuel Herd b. 31 July 1862 Newhills, Aberdeenshire d. 1943

Mitchell, Alexander Philp b. 1885 Edinburgh d. 2 September 1959

Mitchell, Colin Campbell b. 12 March 1904 Corstorphine, Midlothian d. 21 January 1969

Mitchell, Joseph b. 3 November 1803 Forres, Moray d. 26 November 1883

Mitchell, Peter Chalmers b. 23 November 1864 Dunfermline, Fife d. 2 July 1945

Moir, Ernest William b. 9 June 1862 London, England d. 14 June 1923. Father: Alexander Mitchell Moir born 19 May 1833 in Marykirk, Kincardineshire; Mother: Mary Isabella Japp, born 2 April 1837 in Montrose

Moir, George b. c1704 d. 27 October 1792. Probably born Leckie, Stirlingshire as he became Laird of Leckie on death of his brother James

Molloy, Bryan Barnet b. 30 March 1939 Broughty Ferry, Angus d. 8 May 2004

Moncrieff, Alexander b. 17 April 1829 Culfargie, Perthshire d. 3 August 1906

Mone, Michelle Georgina b. 8 October 1971 Glasgow Still Living

Monteith, John Lennox b. 3 September 1929 Fairlie, Ayrshire d. 20 July 2012

Monteith, William b. 22 June 1790 Paisley, Renfrewshire d. 18 April 1864

Montgomerie, Thomas George b. 23 April 1830 Ayrshire d. 31 January 1878

Moodie, Alexander Forbes b. 6 August 1923 Kirkcaldy, Fife

Moodie, George Pigot b. 22 January 1829 Grahamstown, Cape of Good Hope, South Africa d. 2 November 1891. Father: Donald Moodie born 25 June 1794 Melsetter, Orkney

Morrison, Andrew William b. 3 December 1925 Huelva, Spain d. 6 January 2006. He was born to Scottish parents (ref BMJ 6 May 2006: http://www.ncbi.nlm.nih.gov/pmc/articles/PMC1458536/)

Morrison, Charles b.? Greenock, Renfrewshire d.?

Morrison, William b. circa 1850 Scotland d. 1927 Des Moines, Iowa (Ref: The Des Moines Register states he was born in Scotland http://data.desmoinesregister.com/famous-iowans/william-morrison as does AmericanAutoHistory.com at http://www.americanautohistory.com/Pioneers/Pioneer450.htm)

Morrison, William Murray b. 7 October 1873 Birchwood, Inverness d. 21 May 1948

Morton, Thomas b. 21 November 1783 Mauchline, Ayrshire d. 1862

Morton, Thomas b. 8 October 1781 Leith, Midlothian d. 24 December 1832

Morton, William Lockhart b. 19 December 1820 Cambusnethan, Lanarkshire d. 10 March 1898

Muir, John b. 21 April 1838 Dunbar, East Lothian d. 24 December 1914

Muir, Malcolm b.? Glasgow d.?

Muir, William b. 17 January 1805 Catrine, Ayrshire d. 15 June 1888

Muirhead, Alexander b. 26 May 1848 Barley Mill, Saltoun, East Lothian d. 13 December 1920

Munro, Hamish Nisbet b. 3 July 1915 Edinburgh d. 28 October 1994

Murchison, Roderick Impey b. 19 February 1792 Tarradale, Ross-shire d. 22 October 1871

Murchland, William b. 28 May 1851 Kilmarnock, Ayrshire d. 19 June 1941

Murdock, William b. 21 August 1754 Auchinleck, Ayrshire d. 15 November 1839

Murray, Alexander b. 2 June 1810 Crieff, Perthshire d. 16 December 1884

Murray, Donald b. 20 September 1865 Invercargill, New Zealand d. 14 July 1945. Father: John Murray born 1835 in Dunbartonshire; Mother: Isabella Simpson born 3 December 1814 in Edinburgh

Murray, George b. 30 January 1761 Dunkeld, Perthshire d. 3 June 1803

Murray, Henry Lamont b. 1891 New Zealand d. 1959. Grandfather: Henry Dundas Murray born 8 April 1818 at Monzievaird, Perthshire

Murray, John b. 3 March 1841 Coburg, Ontario, Canada d. 16 March 1914. Father: Robert Murray born Stirlingshire; Mother: Elizabeth Macfarlane, born Bridge of Allan, Stirlingshire

Murray, John Mackay b. 25 June 1902 Glasgow d. 5 August 1966

Murray, Reginald Augustus Frederick b. 18 February 1846 Surrey, England d. 5 September 1925. Father: Virginius Murray born, 20 Sep 1817; birthplace not recorded but christened four months later in London. Grandfather Alexander Murray, born 12 Oct 1764, Edinburgh

Murray, Robert b. 10 March 1609 Craigie, Ayrshire d. 4 July 1673

Murray, Stuart b. 8 October 1837 Dundee, Angus d. 12 April 1919

Mushet, David b. 2 October 1772 Dalkeith, Midlothian d. 12 June 1847

Mushet, Robert Forester b. 8 April 1811 Coleford, Gloucestershire, England d. 19 January 1891. Father: David Mushet born 2 October 1772 Dalkeith, Midlothian

Nairn, Michael Barker b. 29 May 1838 Kirkcaldy, Fife d. 24 November 1915

Napier, Charles John b. 6 March 1786 Falkirk, Stirlingshire d. 6 November 1860

Napier, David b. 1788 Dumbarton d. 17 June 1873

Napier, David b. 29 October 1790 Dumbarton d. 23 November 1869

Napier, James Robert b. 12 September 1821 Glasgow d. December 1879

Napier, John b. 1550 Merchiston, Midlothian d. 4 April 1617

Napier, Robert b. 21 June 1791 Dumbarton d. 23 June 1876

Napier, William b. 29 June 1940 Perth

Nasmyth James Hall b. 19 August 1808 Edinburgh d. 7 May 1890

Nasmyth, Alexander b. 9 September 1758 Edinburgh d. 10 April 1840

Neilson, James Beaumont b. 22 June 1792 Glasgow d. 18 January 1865

Nelson, Thomas b. 25 December 1822 Edinburgh d. 20 October 1892

Newall, Robert Stirling b. 27 May 1812 Dundee, Angus d. 21 April 1889

Newlands, James b. 28 July 1813 Edinburgh d. 15 July 1871

Newlands, John Alexander Reina b. November 1837 London, England d. 29 July 1898. Father: William Newlands, born Glasgow 1786

Nicol, William b. 18 April 1770 Humbie, Midlothian d. 2 September 1851

Nimmo, Alexander b. 1783 Kirkcaldy, Fife d. 20 January 1832

Nimmo, William Hogarth Robertson b. 10 February 1885 Devon, England d. 7 May 1970. Father: William Henry Nimmo, born 29 October 1861 Logie, Perthshire

Niven, William b. 6 October 1850 Bellshill, Lanarkshire d. 2 June 1937

Noble, Andrew b. 13 September 1831 Greenock, Renfrewshire d. 22 October 1915

Ogilvie, Alexander b. 8 June 1882 London, England d. 18 June 1962. Grandfather: Alexander Milne Ogilvie, born 15 February 1812, at Clocksbriggs, Forfarshire. Maternal Grandmother: Bella Anderson Dalgleish born 14 May 1915 Edinburgh

Ogilvie, Alexander Milne b. 15 February 1812 Clockbriggs, Forfar d. 15 February 1886

Ogston, Alexander b. 19 April 1844 Aberdeen d. 1 February 1929

Ogston, Alexander George b. 30 January 1911 Bombay, India d. 29 June 1996. Father: Walter Henry Ogston, born 29 November 1873 Aberdeen

Oliver, James b. 28 August 1823 Newcastleton, Roxburghshire d. 2 March 1908

O'Neill, Charles Gordon b. 23 March 1828 Glasgow d. 8 November 1900

Ormiston, George Edward b. 8 February 1844 Glasgow d. 3 October 1913

Ormiston, Thomas b. 28 July 1826 Edinburgh d. 9 July 1882

Orr Hugh b. 2 January 1715 Lochwinnoch, Renfrewshire d. 6 December 1798

Orr, John Boyd b. 23 September 1880 Kilmaurs, Ayrshire d. 25 June 1971

Orr, John Bryson b. 1840 Blantyre, Lanarkshire d. 23 September 1933

Owen, David Dale b. 24 June 1807, Lanark, Lanarkshire d. 1860

Page, Archibald b. 5 September 1875 Alloa, Clackmannanshire d. 7 March 1949

Pasley, Charles William b. 8 September 1780 Eskdale Muir, Dumfries-shire d. 19 April 1861

Paterson, James b. 9 February 1771 Musselburgh, Midlothian d. 25 December 1854

Paterson, Robert Adams b. 1829 St Andrews, Fife d. 16 April 1904

Paterson, William b. 5 August 1874 Roslin, Midlothian d. 9 August 1956

Paterson, William b. April 1658 Skipmyre, Dumfries-shire d. 22 January 1719

Paton, Thomas Angus Lyall b. 10 May 1905 Jersey, Channel Islands d. 7 April 1999. Father: Thomas Lyall Paton, born 29 October 1868 Liff Benvie and Invergowrie, Angus. Mother: Janet Gibb, born 1 November 1874, Bo'ness, Linlithgowshire

Paton, William Drummond MacDonald b. 5 May 1917 Middlesex, England d. 17 October 1993. Mother: Grace Mackenzie MacDonald, born 29 June 1887 Edinburgh. Both paternal grandparents born in Scotland: James Paton born 13 October 1860 at Calton, Glasgow and Elizabeth Dunlop born 8 October 1860 in Old Monkland, Lanarkshire

Paul, John b. 1922 Wishaw, Lanarkshire d. 27 June 1994

Perry, John b. 14 February 1850 Garvagh, Ulster d. 4 August 1920. Mother: Agnes Smith born circa 1822 Scotland, died 1 May 1905

Philip, James b. 30 April 1858 Auchness, Morayshire d. 23 July 1911

Philip, Robert William b. 29 December 1857 Govan, Lanarkshire d. 25 January 1939

Pilkington, Lionel Alexander Bethune b. 7 January 1920 India d. 5 May 1995. Maternal grandparents: Alexander Bethune born 21 March 1860 in Kemback, Fife; Elizabeth Constance Carnegie Maitland Heriot, born 20 June 1866 in Edinburgh

Pillans, James b. April 1778 Edinburgh d. 27 March 1864

Pinkerton, Allan b. 25 August 1819 Glasgow d. 1 July 1884

Pirie, Norman Wingate b. 1 July 1907 Sussex, England d. 29 March 1997. Father: George Pirie, born 5 December 1863, Campbeltown, Argyllshire; Mother, Jean Wingate [Smith] born Scotland

Playfair, William b. 22 September 1759 Liff, Angus d. 11 February 1823

Plotkin, Gordon David b. 9 September 1946 Glasgow Still Living

Pollock, George David b. 18 October 1817 India d. 14 February 1897. Mother: Frances Webb Barclay born October 1785 in Tain, Ross & Cromarty

Ponton, Mungo b. 27 November 1801 Edinburgh d. 3 August 1880

Porteous, James b. 12 April 1848 Haddington, East Lothian d. 1922

Pringle, Thomas b. 3 February 1830 Huntingdon, Ontario, Canada d. 7 May 1911. Father: David Pringle, born 8 January 1798, Mother: Janet Murray born 31 January 1793, both born in Haddington, East Lothian

Prosser, Patrick b. 8 September 1952 Glasgow Still Living

Proudfoot, David b. circa 1839 Gilmerton, Midlothian d. 20 March 1891 (age 2 at 1841 Scotland census)

Ramage, Adam b. 1772 Edinburgh d. 24 July 1850

Ramsay, Andrew Crombie b. 31 January 1814 Glasgow d. 9 December 1891

Ramsay, David b. circa 1575 Fife d. 1660

Ramsay, William b. 2 October 1852 Glasgow d. 23 July 1916

Ramsay, William b. 6 June 1868 Glasgow d. 4 September 1914

Randall-MacIver, David b. 31 October 1873 London, England d. 30 April 1945. Grandfather: Charles MacIver, born 8 April 1812, baptised 16 April 1812 in Greenock; Grandmother: Mary Ann Morison, born 3 January 1818 in Glasgow

Rankin, Robert Alexander b. 27 October 1915 Garlieston, Wigtownshire d. 27 January 2001

Rankine, William John Macquorn b. 5 July 1820 Edinburgh d. 24 December 1872

Raw, Alan Rayson b. 24 August 1902 Melbourne, Australia d. 9 September 1964. Father: John Thomas Raw born Scotland (ref Australian Dictionary of Biography)

Reid, Alexander Walker b. 14 September 1853 Glasgow d. 21 November 1938

Reid, David Boswell b. 11 June 1805 Edinburgh d. 5 April 1863

Reid, Donald Darnley b. 6 May 1914 Buckie, Morayshire d. 26 March 1977

Reid, Harry Fielding b. 18 May 1859 Maryland, USA d. 18 June 1944. Grandfather: George Reid born 1760 in Forfarshire; Paternal Grandmother: Elizabeth Taylor born 1777 in Aberdeenshire

Reid, Iain Neill b. 1 April 1957 Helensburgh, Dunbartonshire Still Living

Reid, John Paterson b. 1796 Glasgow d.5 May 1854 Glasgow (**Reid**, Wifrid Thomas b. 4 March 1887 Surrey, England d. 5 April 1968. Father: James Reid born 1848, Scotland

Reid, William Paton b. 8 September 1854 Glasgow d. 2 February 1932

Rennie, George b. 3 September 1791 London, England d. 30 March 1866. Father: born 26 June 1842 Stranraer, Wigtownshire

Rennie, John b. 26 June 1842 Stranraer, Wigtownshire d. 20 September 1918

Rennie, John b. 30 August 1794 London, England d. 3 September 1874. Father: born 7 June 1761, Phantassie, East Lothian

Rennie, John b. 7 June 1761 Phantassie, East Lothian d. 4 October 1821

Ritchie, Edward Samuel b. 18 August 1814 Massachusetts, USA d. 1 June 1895. Grandfather: Andrew Ritchie baptised 26 October 1729, Mearns, Renfrewshire

Ritchie, Frederick James b. 1828 Edinburgh d. 1906

Ritchie, George Stephen b. 30 October 1914 Yorkshire, England d. 8 May 2012. Mother: Margaret Stephen Allan, born 28 April 1891 Methlick, Aberdeen

Ritchie, Walter b. 23 December 1773 Musselburgh, East Lothian d. 13 October 1849

Ritchie, William Alexander b. 1951 Scotland Still Living

Robertson, Alexander Weir b. 7 June 1819 St Cuthbert's Edinburgh d. 1879 St Andrews, Edinburgh

Robertson, Henry b. 11 January 1816 Banff d. 22 March 1888

Robertson, John Monteath b. 24 July 1900 Auchterarder, Perthshire d. 27 December 1989

Robertson, Muriel b. 8 April 1883 Glasgow d. 14 June 1973

Robertson, Peter Lymeburner b. 1879 Ontario, Canada d. 1951. Father: John Robertson born 16 September 1833, Argyllshire. Mother: Isabella Brown born 1797 in Argyllshire, died 7 February 1883 in Ontario

Robison, Robert b. 29 December 1883 Nottingham, England d. 18 June 1941. Mother: Jessie Clark born circa 1843 Maxwelltown, Dumfries (1891 England census Newark, Nottingham)

Romanes George John b. 19 May 1848 Ontario, Canada d. 23 May 1894. Father: George Romanes born 30 November 1806 Edinburgh; Mother: Isobel Cair born 4 January 1809, baptised 31 January 1809 Brechin, Angus

Ronalds, Francis b. 21 February 1788 London, England d. 8 August 1873. Grandfather: Hugh Ronalds born 1725/6 Moidart, Inverness-shire

Rose, Lauchlan b. 1829 Leith, Midlothian d. 9 May 1885 in London (England 1881 census shows his age as 52)

Ross, Ronald b. 13 May 1857 Uttar Pradesh, India d. 16 September 1932. Grandfather: Hugh Ross born 26 April 1788 in Ayr, Ayrshire

Russell, Bertrand Arthur William b. 18 May 1872 Monmouthshire, Wales d. 2 February 1970. Maternal Grandmother: Frances Elliot born 15 November 1815, Minto House, Roxburghshire

Russell, John Scott b. 9 May 1808 Glasgow d. 8 June 1882

Russell, William Morris b. 22 July 1920 London, England d. 16 February 2006. Maternal grandparents: Thomas Henderson Carrick, born 7 February 1863 Lanarkshire; Agnes Charlotte Lang born 4 August 1862 in Calton, Glasgow

Rutherford, Daniel b. 3 November 1749 Edinburgh d. 15 November 1819

Rutherford, Ernest b. 30 August 1871 Nelson, New Zealand d. 19 October 1937. Father: James Rutherford born 24 November 1838, Dundee

Samuel, James b. 21 March 1824 Glasgow d. 25 May 1874

Schank, John b. 1740 Castlerig, Fife. Baptised 23 March 1740 Ceres, Fife d. 6 February 1823

Scott, Alastair Ian b. 2 April 1928 Glasgow d. 18 April 2007

Scott, David Aylmer b. 2 October 1892 Ontario, Canada d. 18 November 1971. Maternal grandfather: Neil Bain McKenzie 2 December 1821, Applecross, Wester Ross

Scott, David Maxwell b. c1955 Glasgow Still Living (Ref: http://www.royalsoced.org.uk/cms/files/press/2010/Election_of_new_fellows.pdf)

Scott, Robert b. after 1568 Balwearie, Fife d.1631 He was the son of Sir William Scott, Baron of Balwearie in Fife and Janet Lindsay, daughter of John Lindsay of Dowhill, Cleish, Kinross-shire

Scott, Walter b. 22 May 1844 Ayr d. 14 September 1907

Scott-Moncrieff, Colin Campbell b. 3 August 1836 Edinburgh d. 6 April 1916

Scott-Moncrieff, William Dundas b. 11 May 1846 Queensferry, Midlothian d. 1924

Seton, Alexander Anderson b. 16 October 1769 Monkshill, Fyvie, Aberdeenshire d. 16 April 1850

Shand, Samuel James b. 1882 Edinburgh d. 19 April 1957

Shanks, Alexander b. 3 September 1801 Milnetown of Bridgetown, Angus d. 16 July 1845

Shanks, John b. 25 December 1825 Paisley, Renfrewshire d. 18 December 1895

Shepherd-Barron, John Adrian b. 23 June 1925 Shillong, Assam, India d. 15 May 2010. Father: Wilfred Philip Shepherd-Barron (born Barron) born 2 May 1888, Caithness

Shiels, Alexander b. 12 September 1865 Lauder, Berwickshire d. 22 October 1907

Short, James b. 10 June 1710 Edinburgh d. 14 June 1768

Shortt, William Hamilton b. 1881 Surrey, England d. 1971. Father: Charles Henry Shortt, born 12 February 1852. Baptised 8 March 1852 Inverness

Silver, Robert Simpson b. 13 March 1913 Montrose, Angus d. 21 April 1997

Simpson, David Cumming b. 24 July 1920 Corstorphine, Midlothian d. 15 May 2006

Simpson, James Young b. 7 June 1811 Bathgate, West Lothian d. 6 May 1870

Simpson, John Alexander b. 3 November 1916 Oregon, USA d. 31 August 2000. Father: John Alexander Simpson, born 15 January 1890 Greenock; Mother: Janet Christie Brand born 7 March 1887, Greenock

Sinclair, Hugh Macdonald b. 4 February 1910 Edinburgh d. 22 July 1990

Sinclair, Robert b. 1 July 1817 Caithness d. 1898

Skene, Alexander John b. 5 April 1820 Peterhead, Aberdeenshire d. 22 August 1894

Skinner, Gordon Robert Bruce b. 21 February 1942 Glasgow d. 26 November 2013

Skues, George Edward Mackenzie b. 13 August 1858 Newfoundland, Canada d. 9 August 1949. Father: William Mackenzie Skues born 15 March 1828 in Aberdeen

Sloane, Hans b. 16 April 1660 Killyleagh, County Down, Ireland d. 11 January 1773. Father: Alexander Sloane b. 1622, Dunlop, Ayrshire

Small, James b. 28 March 1740 Ladykirk, Berwickshire d. 1793

Smellie, William b. 5 February 1697 Lesmahagow, Lanarkshire d. 5 March 1763

Smith, Adam b. 5 June 1723 Kirkcaldy, Fife d. 17 July 1790

Smith, Alexander b. 11 September 1865 Edinburgh d. 1922

Smith, Alexander Kennedy b. 7 July 1824 Cauldmill, Roxburghshire d. 16 January 1881

Smith, Alexander Mair b. 15 October 1922 Lossiemouth, Moray d. 28 February 2003

Smith, Andrew b. 17 November 1799 Kirkpatrick Fleming, Dumfries-shire d.

Smith, Charles B b. 1844 Scotland d. 1882 Lucerne, Switzerland (1881 England census: SMITH, Charles B Head Married M 37 1844 Town Councillor Managing Engineer & Partner at Hartlepool Engine Works (E & M) born Scotland

Smith, Charles b. 1932 Aberdeenshire d. 16 June 1997

Smith, James b. 3 January 1789 Glasgow d. 10 June 1850

Smith, Kenneth Manley b. 13 November 1892 Glasgow d. 11 June 1981

Smith, Robert Angus b. 15 February 1817 Glasgow d. 12 May 1884

Smith, Walter Mucarsay/Mackersie b. 25 December 1842 Ferryport-on-Craig, Montrose, Fife d. 1906

Snodgrass, Neil b. 7 April 1774 Paisley, Renfrewshire d. 1818

Spence, Peter b. 19 February 1806 Brechin, Angus d. 5 July 1883

Spence, William b. 31 July 1777 Greenock, Renfrewshire d. 22 May 1815

Stagg, James Martin b. 30 June 1900 Dalkeith, Midlothian d. 23 June 1975

Stanhope, Charles b. 3 August 1753 London, England d. 15 December 1816. Mother: Grizel Hamilton born 1717 Jerviswood, Lanarkshire died 28 December 1811

Stanley, Henry Charles b. 15 May 1840 Edinburgh d. 23 February 1921

Steedman, James b. 22 March 1790 Clackmannan d. 1865

Stenhouse, John b. 31 October 1809 Glasgow d. 31 December 1880

Stephenson, George b. 9 June 1781 Northumberland, England d. 12 August 1848. Grandfather: Robert Stinson/Stevenson born 1723 in Ricalton, Oxnam, Roxburghshire

Stevenson, Thomas b. 22 July 1818 Edinburgh d. 8 May 1887

Stevenson-Hamilton, James b. 2 October 1867 Dublin, Ireland d. 10 December 1957. Father: James Stevenson born 6 November 1838 in Braidwood, Lanarkshire; Mother: Eliza Hamilton born 1839, Lanarkshire

Stewart, Alfred Walter b. 5 September 1880 Glasgow d. 1 July 1947

Stewart, Balfour b. 1 November 1828 Edinburgh d. 19 December 1887

Stewart, Patrick b. 28 January 1832 Cairnsmore, Kirkcudbrightshire d. 16 January 1865

Stewart, Thomas b. 30 March 1857 Craigend, Perthshire d. 23 October 1942

Stirling, Allan b. 26 July 1844 Rutherglen, Lanarkshire d. 1927

Stirling, James b. May 1692 Garden, Stirlingshire d. 5 December 1770

Stirling, Michael b. 18 February 1708 Gateside, Dunblane, Perthshire d. 1 February 1796

Stirling, Patrick b. 29 June 1820 Kilmarnock, Ayrshire d. 11 November 1895

Stirling, Robert b. 25 October 1790 Gloag, Methven, Perthshire d. 6 June 1878

Stodart, Robert b. 19 July 1748 Walston, Lanarkshire d. 7 March 1831

Stodart, William b. 1776 London, England d. 1831. Father: Robert Stodart born 1748 in Walston, Lanarkshire

Stoddart, James Fraser b. 24 May 1942 Edinburgh

Stott, Henry Gordon b. 13 May 1866 Firth and Stenness, Orkney d. 1917

Strath, John Alexander Wiseman b. 21 September 1916 Forgan, Fife d. 26 February 2009

Strutt, Robert John b. 28 August 1875 Essex, England d. 13 December 1947. Grandfather: James Maitland Balfour, born 5 January 1820, Whittinghame, East Lothian

Stuart, Herbert Akroyd b. 28 January 1864 Halifax, Yorkshire d. 19 February 1927. Father: Charles Stuart born 1824, Paisley

Sturgeon, William b. 22 May 1783 Whittington, Lancashire, England d. 4 December 1850. Father: John Sturgeon, born circa 1751 in Dumfries

Sturock, Thomas b. 15 February 1820 South Leith d. 1907

Sturrock, Archibald b. 30 September 1816 Petruchie, Angus d. 1 January 1909

Sutherland, William b. 24 August 1859 Glasgow d. 5 October 1911

Swan, William b. 13 March 1818 Edinburgh d. 1 March 1894

Swinburne, James b. 28 February 1858 Inverness d. 30 March 1958

Swinton, Alan Archibald Campbell b. 18 October 1863 Edinburgh d. 30 February 1930

Swinton, Ernest Dunlop, b. Bangalore, India 21 October 1868 d. 15 January 1951. Grandfather: William Swinton born 10 February 1874 Scotland

Swinton, William Elgin b. 30 September 1900 Kirkcaldy, Fife d. 12 June 1994

Syme, James b. 7 November 1799 Edinburgh d. 26 June 1870

Symington, William b. October 1764 Leadhills, Lanarkshire d. 22 March 1831

Tait, Peter Guthrie b. 28 April 1831 Dalkeith, Midlothian d. 4 July 1901

Tait, Richard John b. 1964 Broughty Ferry, Angus. Still Living

Tait, William b. 1840 Caithness d. 1921

Taylor, Thomas b. 22 April 1820 Perth d. 22 January 1910

Telford, Thomas b. 9 August 1757 Westerkirk, Dumfries-shire d. 2 September 1834

Templeton, James b. 7 July 1802 Campbeltown, Argyllshire d. 27 August 1885

Tennant, Charles b. 3 May 1768 Ochiltree, Ayrshire d. 1 October 1838

Thom, Alexander Strang b. 26 March 1894 Argyllshire d. 7 November 1985

Thom, Robert b. 26 January 1774 Tarbolton, Ayrshire d. 14 December 1847

Thomas, Sidney Gilchrist b 16 April 1850 Islington, London d. 1 February 1885. Grandfather: James Gilchrist born 16 March 1783 Kilsyth, Stirlingshire - his father was a farmer in Larbert. He died in 1835

Thompson, D'Arcy Wentworth b. 2 May 1860 Edinburgh d. 21 June 1948

Thomson, Elihu b. 29 March 1853 Manchester, England d. 13 March 1937. Father: Daniel Thomson born 1829, Gorbals, Glasgow

Thomson, James b. 16 February 1822 Belfast, Northern Ireland d. 8 May 1892. Mother: Margaret Gardner born 1790 Glasgow died 1830

Thomson, John b. 25 October 1853 Bellie, Morayshire d. 1 June 1926

Thomson, Joseph John b. 18 December 1856, Manchester, England d. 30 August 1940. Paternal grandmother: Margaret Cuthbertson Sword born 22 July 1806 in Westhorn, Glasgow.

Thomson, Robert William b. 29 June 1822 Stonehaven, Aberdeenshire d. 8 March 1873

Thomson, William b. 26 June 1824 Belfast, Northern Ireland d. 17 December 1907. Mother: Margaret Gardner born 1790 Glasgow died 1 May 1830

Thouless, David James b. 21 September 1934 Glasgow

Tilloch, Alexander b. 28 February 1759 Glasgow d. 26 January 1825

Tod, David b. 17 May 1795 Colen, Perthshire d. 24 January 1859

Todd, Alexander Robertus b. 2 October 1907 Glasgow d. 10 January 1997

Turnbull, George b. 2 September 1809 Luncarty, Perthshire d. 26 February 1889

Turnbull, Wallace Rupert b. 16 October 1870 St John, New Brunswick, Canada d. 26 November 1954: Grandparents: George Turnbull born 1774 in Bedrule, Roxburghshire died 1815 and Isabella Baxter born 1779 in Edinburgh died 1846

Tweedie, Stephen Cochran b. 1969 East Kilbride Still Living

Underwood, Ian b. 24 June 1959 Airdrie, Lanarkshire Still living

Urie, Robert Wallace b. 22 October 1854 Ardeer, Ayrshire d. 6 January 1937

Waddell, John b. 16 August 1828 New Monkland, Lanarkshire d. 17 January 1888

Waland, Robert Louis b. 15 September 1908 Dumfries d. 27 February 1999

Waldron, John Duncan b. 1959 East Kilpatrick, Dunbartonshire Still Living

Walker, James b. 14 September 1781 Falkirk, Stirlingshire d. 8 October 1862

Walker, Janet b. 10 June 1850 Neilston, Renfrewshire d. 27 November 1940

Wallace, James Davidson b. 1806 Dundee, Angus d. 16 January 1874 St Leonards, NSW, Australia

Wallace, Robert b. 7 January 1697 Kincardine, Perthshire d. 29 July 1771

Wallace, Robert b. 18 April 1773 Auchinleck, Ayrshire d. 1 April 1855

Wallace, William b. 23 September 1768 Dysart, Fife d. 28 April 1843

Wallace, William b. 25 August 1881 Leicestershire, England d. 27 May 1963 Father: Matthew Wallace born 1845 in Paisley; Mother: born 1843 in Kilmarnock, Ayrshire

Walton, Arthur Edward b. 16 March 1897 London, England d. 6 April 1959. Father: Edward Arthur Walton born 15 April 1860 Glanderston House, Barrhead, Renfrewshire; Mother: Helen Urie Henderson [Law] born 15 April 1859, Paisley, Renfrewshire

Waterhouse, Douglas Frew b. 3 June 1916 Sydney, Australia d. 2000. Mother: Janet Frew Kellie, born 24 August 1885 Ayr, Scotland

Waterston, John James b. 1811 Edinburgh d. 18 June 1883

Watson, Brian b. 1967 Edinburgh Still Living

Watson, James Dewey b. 6 April 1928 Illinois, USA. Maternal Grandfather: Lauchlin Alexander Mitchell, born 8 May 1855 Glasgow

Watson, John Duncan b. 7 March 1860 Dundee d. 1946

Watson, Preston Albert b. 17 October 1880 Dundee, Angus d. 30 June 1915

Watson, William Stuart b. 14 March 1827 Dumfries d.?

Watson-Watt, Robert b. 13 April 1892 Brechin, Angus d. 5 December 1973

Watt, Francis b. 18 July 1778 Newhills, Aberdeen d. before 21 April 1823

Watt, James b. 18 January 1736 Greenock, Renfrewshire d. 25 August 1819

Watt, James b. February 1769 Warwickshire, England d. 2 June 1848. Father: James Watt, born 19 January 1736, Greenock, Renfrewshire

Watt, William b. 14 April 1912 Edinburgh d. 11 August 1985

Wauchope, Robert b. 19 December 1788 Niddrie-Marischall, Midlothian d. 14 June 1862

Webster, Alexander b. 1707 Edinburgh d. 25 January 1784

Wedderburn, Joseph Henry Maclagen b. 2 February 1882 Forfar, Angus d. 9 October 1948

Weir, James b. 1842 Airdrie, Lanarkshire d. 10 July 1920

West, John b. 27 August 1809 Linlithgow, West Lothian d. 21 March 1888

West, Thomas Summers b. 18 November 1927 Peterhead, Aberdeenshire d. 9 January 2010

Wheeler, Robert Eric Mortimer b. 10 September 1890 Glasgow d. 22 July 1976

Whitelaw, James Hunter b. 28 January 1936 Newmains, Lanarkshire d. 16 August 2006

Whytock, Richard Barnett b. 24 March 1784 Dalkeith, Midlothian d. 22 January 1857

Wigham, John Richardson b. 15 January 1829 Edinburgh d. 16 November 1906

Williams, Robert b. 21 January 1860 Aberdeen d. 25 April 1938

Williamson, James b. 5 April 1881 Holytown, Lanarkshire d. 18 August 1953

Wilson, Alexander b. 1714 St Andrews, Fife d. 18 October 1786

Wilson, Alexander b. 6 July 1766 Paisley, Renfrewshire d. 23 August 1813

Wilson, Charles Thomson Rees b. 14 February 1869 Glencorse, Midlothian d. 15 November 1959

Wilson, Daniel b. 5 January 1816 Edinburgh d. 6 August 1892

Wilson, George b. circa 1802 Berwickshire d. 26 April 1878

Wilson, George Fergusson b. 25 March 1822 London, England d. 28 March 1902. Father: **William** Wilson, born 1772 in Lanarkshire. Mother: Margaret Nimmo Dickson, born 1785 in Edinburgh.

Wilson, John Tuzo b. 24 October 1908 Ottawa, Ontario, Canada d. 15 April 1993. Father: John Armistead Wilson, born 2 November 1879 Broughty Ferry, Angus died 10 October 1954 Ottowa

Wilson, Robert b. 1803 Dunbar, East Lothian d. 28 July 1882

Wilson, William b. 1772 Lanarkshire d. 1860

Wilson, William b. 8 May 1809 Aberdeen d. 17 April 1862

Wishart, John b. 28 November 1898 Montrose, Angus d. 14 July 1956

Wood, Alexander b. 10 December 1817 Cupar, Fife d. 26 February 1884

Wright, James b. 22 August 1888 Scotland d. 8 November 1952

Wright, Johnstone b. 22 January 1883 Dunning, Perthshire d. 19 July 1953

Young, George b. 1692 Edinburgh d. 1757

Young, James b. 13 July 1811 Glasgow d. 13 May 1883

Yule, George Udny b. 18 February 1871 Morham, East Lothian d. 26 June 1951

Yule, John Cochran b. 23 December 1810 Inchinnan, Renfrewshire d. 1877

REFERENCES

Note: Birth years in italics indicates estimated year of birth

Chapter 1
1453-1749

1	Introduction			http://news.bbc.co.uk/2/hi/asia-pacific/3701581.stm
2	Introduction			https://edblogs.columbia.edu/histx3570-001-2014-1/timelines/school-of-engineering-1864-2014-a-timeline/
3	Introduction			Biographical dictionary of civil engineers in Great Britain and Ireland, Volume 1, 1500 to 1830, by A. W. Skempton, Thomas Telford Publishing, London, 2002, p xxv
1	Grant, Johannes	*1428*	1453	The Fall of Constantinople, 1453, by Steven Runciman, Cambridge University Press, 2004 p 119
2	Grant, Johannes	*1428*	1453	Ibid. p 84
1	Bruce, George	1550	1625	Oxford Dictionary of National Biography
2	Bruce, George	1550	1625	http://www.undiscoveredscotland.co.uk/usbiography/b/georgebrucecarnock.html
3	Bruce, George	1550	1625	The Juridical Bay by Gayl Shaw Westerman, Oxford University Press, 1987, p 258
4	Bruce, George	1550	1625	http://www.scottishmining.co.uk/492.html
1	Napier, John	1550	1617	http://digital.nls.uk/scientists/biographies/john-napier/discoveries.html
2	Napier, John	1550	1617	http://www.17centurymaths.com/contents/napier/jimsnewstuff/Promptuary/MakingthePromptuary.html
3	Napier, John	1550	1617	http://www.oughtred.org/history.shtml
4	Napier, John	1550	1617	The Book of Inventions, by Ian Harrison, Cassell Illustrated, 2004, p 260
5	Napier, John	1550	1617	Pioneers in Mathematics, The Age of Genius 1300 to 1800, by Michael J Bradley, Chelsea House Publishers, New York, 2006, p 32
6	Napier, John	1550	1617	The Book of Inventions, by Ian Harrison, Cassell Illustrated, 2004, p 260
7	Napier, John	1550	1617	Note on Napier's Rules of Circular Parts, by Professor Edgar Odell Lovett, Bulletin of the American Mathematical Society, 4 July 1898, p 552

8	Napier, John	1550	1617	http://research.microsoft.com/en-us/um/people/gbell/CyberMuseum_files/Bell_Book_Files/books.htm
9	Napier, John	1550	1617	http://www.brown.edu/Facilities/University_Library/exhibits/math/textfr.html
1	Scott, Robert	*1569*	1631	The Army of Gustavus Adolphus (2) Cavalry, by Richard Brzezinski, Osprey Publishing, Oxford, 1993, p 18
2	Scott, Robert	*1569*	1631	Ibid. p 17
3	Scott, Robert	*1569*	1631	The Furie of the Ordnance, Artillery in the English Civil Wars, by Stephen Bull, Boydell Press, Woodbridge, 2008, pp 9-10
4	Scott, Robert	*1569*	1631	A History of Firearms: From Earliest Times to 1914, by W. Y. Carman, Dover Publications, New York, 2004, p 62
5	Scott, Robert	*1569*	1631	The Military Revolution: Military Innovation and the Rise of the West, 1500–1800, by Geoffrey Parker, Cambridge University Press, 1996, pp 33–35
6	Scott, Robert	*1569*	1631	Oxford Dictionary of National Biography
1	Ramsay, David	1575	1660	Oxford Dictionary of National Biography
2	Ramsay, David	1575	1660	http://wiki.vintagemachinery.org/The-History-of-the-Steam-Engine-1890.ashx
3	Ramsay, David	1575	1660	The Scot in England by John Herries McCulloch, Hurst and Blackett, London, 1935, Chapter II
1	Murray, Robert	1609	1673	http://royalsociety.org/about-us/
2	Murray, Robert	1609	1673	http://www.theodora.com/encyclopedia/m2/sir_robert_murray.html
3	Murray, Robert	1609	1673	The Invisible College, by Robert Lomas, Corgi, London, 2009, p 259
4	Murray, Robert	1609	1673	Ibid. p 265
5	Murray, Robert	1609	1673	Ibid. p 276
6	Murray, Robert	1609	1673	Ibid. pp 322-323
1	Bruce, Alexander	1629	1680	http://www.antique-horology.org/Oosterwijck/a-royal-haagse-klok.HTM
2	Bruce, Alexander	1629	1680	http://www.princeton.edu/~hos/Mahoney/articles/huygens/timelong/timelong.html
3	Bruce, Alexander	1629	1680	http://news.bbc.co.uk/2/hi/uk_news/magazine/4950876.stm
4	Bruce, Alexander	1629	1680	http://www.antique-horology.org/piggott/rh/appendix5.pdf
5	Bruce, Alexander	1629	1680	Ibid.
6	Bruce, Alexander	1629	1680	Freemasonry and the birth of modern science, by Robert Lomas, Fair Winds Press, Gloucester, MA, 2003, p 198

7	Bruce, Alexander	1629	1680	http://www.amazon.com/Going-Dutch-England-Plundered-Hollands/dp/0060774096
1	Gregory, James	1638	1675	Oxford Dictionary of National Biography
2	Gregory, James	1638	1675	http://www.nahste.ac.uk/isaar/GB_0237_NAHSTE_P0263.html
1	MacKay, Hugh	1640	1692	50 Weapons That Changed Warfare, by William Weir, Career Press, Franklin Lakes NJ, 2005, p 81
2	MacKay, Hugh	1640	1692	Military antiquities: respecting a history of the English army from the Conquest to the Present Time, Volume 2, by Francis Grose, Nabu Press, 2011 (first published 1801), p 341
1	Paterson, William	1658	1719	Encyclopedia Britannica 2009 Deluxe Edition
2	Paterson, William	1658	1719	http://www.bankofengland.co.uk/about/pages/history/major_developments.aspx#2
3	Paterson, William	1658	1719	Oxford Dictionary of National Biography
4	Paterson, William	1658	1719	The Ascent of Money, by Niall Ferguson, published by Allen Lane, Victoria, Australia, 2008, p 75
5	Paterson, William	1658	1719	http://www.bankofengland.co.uk/about/pages/history/major_developments.aspx
6	Paterson, William	1658	1719	The Scotsman 7 September 2006
7	Paterson, William	1658	1719	http://www.bbc.co.uk/history/british/civil_war_revolution/scotland_darien_01.shtml
1	Sloane, Hans	1660	1753	Sir Hans Sloane and the value of breast milk, by P.M. Dunn, Archives of Disease in Childhood, Fetal Neonatal, BMJ, Volume 85, pp 73-74
2	Sloane, Hans	1660	1753	The scientific revolution: an encyclopedia, by William E. Burns, ABC CLIO, Santa Barbara, 2001, p 241
3	Sloane, Hans	1660	1753	http://www.bbc.co.uk/northernireland/yourplaceandmine/down/A762798.shtml
4	Sloane, Hans	1660	1753	http://royalsociety.org/Science-chocolate-and-the-Royal-Society/
5	Sloane, Hans	1660	1753	Encyclopedia Britannica 1911
6	Sloane, Hans	1660	1753	http://www.naturalhistorymuseum.org.uk/research-curation/research/projects/sloane-herbarium/hanssloane.htm
7	Sloane, Hans	1660	1753	http://www.clas.ufl.edu/users/ufhatch/pages/03-Sci-Rev/SCI-REV-Home/resource-ref-read/major-minor-ind/westfall-dsb/SAM-S.htm
1	Ged, William	1684	1749	http://www.oldandsold.com/articles09/stereotype-7.shtml
1	Stirling, James	1692	1770	http://www-history.mcs.st-andrews.ac.uk/Printonly/Stirling.html

2	Stirling, James	1692	1770	James Stirling's Methodus Differentialis: An Annotated Translation of Stirling's Text, by Ian Tweddle, Springer-Verlag, London, 2003, p 1
1	Smellie, William	1697	1763	http://www.neonatology.org/pdf/dyingtohaveababy.pdf
2	Smellie, William	1697	1763	http://www.britannica.com/EBchecked/topic/549522/William-Smellie
3	Smellie, William	1697	1763	William Smellie, by Gavin Boyd, Royal Maternity Hospital, Belfast. Presidential Address to the Ulster Obstetrical and Gynecological Society, 18th October 1956, p 33
4	Smellie, William	1697	1763	http://www.neonatology.org/pdf/dyingtohaveababy.pdf
5	Smellie, William	1697	1763	http://digitalcommons.library.tmc.edu/cgi/viewcontent.cgi?article=1006&context=homl
6	Smellie, William	1697	1763	http://www.neonatology.org/pdf/dyingtohaveababy.pdf
7	Smellie, William	1697	1763	Clinical obstetrics and gynaecology, by James O. Drife and Brian A. Magowan, Saunders, 2004, p 16
8	Smellie, William	1697	1763	The history of obstetrics and gynaecology, by M. J. O'Dowd and Elliot E. Philipp, Parthenon Publishing Group, Carnforth, 2000, p 651
9	Smellie, William	1697	1763	The Obstetrician's Armamentarium: Historical Obstetric Instruments and Their Inventors, by Elliot E Philipp, Journal of The Royal Society of Medicine, Vol. 94, No 7, July 2001, pp 362-363
10	Smellie, William	1697	1763	The history of obstetrics and gynaecology, by M. J. O'Dowd and Elliot E. Philipp, Parthenon Publishing Group, Carnforth, 2000, p 651
11	Smellie, William	1697	1763	William Smellie, the Master of British Midwifery, by R.W. Johnstone, Edinburgh, 1952, reviewed by James Young, History and Bibliography Reviews, British Medical Bulletin, 1952, p 410
12	Smellie, William	1697	1763	The Journal of the American Medical Association, Volume 187, No 2, 11 January 1964
13	Smellie, William	1697	1763	Dr. William Smellie and his Library at Lanark, Scotland, by Haldane P Tait and Archibald T Wallace, Bulletin of the History of Medicine, Volume 26, No 5, September-October 1925, p 403
14	Smellie, William	1697	1763	William Smellie, by Gavin Boyd, Royal Maternity Hospital, Belfast, Presidential Address to the Ulster Obstetrical and Gynæcological Society, 18th October 1956, p 36

1	Wallace, Robert	1697	1771	The Ascent of Money, by Niall Ferguson, published by Allen Lane, Victoria, Australia, 2008, p 185
2	Wallace, Robert	1697	1771	Ibid. p 195
3	Wallace, Robert	1697	1771	Adam Smith's The Wealth of Nations: A modern-day interpretation of an Economic Classic, by Karen McCreadie, Infinite Ideas Limited, Oxford, 2009, p 51
4	Wallace, Robert	1697	1771	The Nine Pillars of History: ..., by Gunnar Sevelius, Authorhouse, Bloomington, Indiana, 2012, p 295
5	Wallace, Robert	1697	1771	Wallace, Robert (1697-1771), by Thomas Wilson Bayne, Dictionary of National Biography, Volume 59, 1885-1900
6	Wallace, Robert	1697	1771	http://www.academia.edu/8532092/A_Critique_of_Malthusian_Population_Theory
1	Maclaurin, Colin	1698	1746	http://www.robertnowlan.com/pdfs/Maclaurin,%20Colin.pdf
2	Maclaurin, Colin	1698	1746	http://scienceworld.wolfram.com/biography/Maclaurin.html
3	Maclaurin, Colin	1698	1746	http://www-history.mcs.st-and.ac.uk/Extras/Gibson_history_9.html
4	Maclaurin, Colin	1698	1746	http://www-history.mcs.st-andrews.ac.uk/Biographies/Maclaurin.html
5	Maclaurin, Colin	1698	1746	Colin Maclaurin, Complete Dictionary of Scientific Biography by Charles Coulston Gillespie; Frederic Lawrence Holmes; Noretta Koertge; Thomson Gale, Charles Scribner's Sons, Detroit, Michigan, 2008
1	Menzies, Michael	1699	1766	General View of The Agriculture of East Lothian, from the papers of The Late Robert Somerville, Esq., Surgeon in Haddington, printed by W. Bulmer and Co, London, 1805, p 75
2	Menzies, Michael	1699	1766	Biographical Dictionary of the History of Technology, edited by Lance Day, Ian McNeil, Routledge, 1998, p 831
1	Cleland, Archibald	1700	1771	http://laparoscopy.blogs.com/endoscopyhistory/chapter_04/
2	Cleland, Archibald	1700	1771	British Medical Journal, Volume 288, 14 April 1984, p 1132
3	Cleland, Archibald	1700	1771	Offbeat otolaryngology: what they didn't teach you in medical school, by John D. C. Bennett, John R. Young, Thieme, Stuttgart, 2002, p 75
4	Cleland, Archibald	1700	1771	A practical treatise on the diseases of the ear including the anatomy of the organ, by D.B. St

				John Roosa, William Wood & Co., New York, 1885, p 38
1	Donald, David	*1702*	X	The Linen Trade Ancient and Modern, by Alex J. Warden, published by Frank Cass and Company Ltd., Abingdon, Oxon., 1967, No page numbers
2	Donald, David	*1702*	X	The Cambridge Economic History of Europe, by John H. Clapham, Michael M. Postan, Edwin E. Rich, Cambridge University Press, 1977, p 476
1	Moir, George	1704	1792	Scottish Country Life, by Alexander Fenton, Community Life Section, National Museum of Antiquities of Scotland, published by, John Donald Publishers Ltd. Edinburgh, 1976, p 82
1	Stirling, Michael	1708	1796	The London Encyclopaedia: or Universal dictionary of science, art, literature and practical mechanics, Volume 22, printed by Thomas Tegg, London, 1829, p 71
1	Cullen, William	1710	1790	Refrigeration - How it works: Science and Technology by Marshall Cavendish Corporation, 3rd edition, New York, 2003, p 1945
2	Cullen, William	1710	1790	http://www.hsl.virginia.edu/historical/rare_books/classics/
1	Short, James	1710	1768	http://www.antiquetelescopes.org/history.html
2	Short, James	1710	1768	Transits of Venus and the Astronomical Unit, by Donald A. Teets, Mathematics Magazine, Volume 76, No 5, December 2003, p 335
3	Short, James	1710	1768	Science in the British Colonies of America, by Raymond Phineas Stearns, Board of Trustees of the University of Illinois, 1970, p 656
4	Short, James	1710	1768	http://www.rasc.ca/1761-transit
5	Short, James	1710	1768	http://www.antiquetelescopes.org/history.html
6	Short, James	1710	1768	http://fp.optics.arizona.edu/antiques/Telescope/Catalogue/T26/T26.htm
7	Short, James	1710	1768	http://stjarnhimlen.se/bigtel/LargestTelescope.html
1	Gordon, George Andrew	1712	1751	http://encyclopaedic.net/history-science-ii-beginnings-modern-science/xiv-progress-electricity-gilbert-and-von-guericke-frank?page=7
2	Gordon, George Andrew	1712	1751	Bibliographical History of Electricity and Magnetism, compiled by Paul Fleury Mottelay, Charles Griffin and Company, London, 1922, p 168
3	Gordon, George Andrew	1712	1751	Oxford Dictionary of National Biography
4	Gordon, George Andrew	1712	1751	http://www.arcsandsparks.com/franklin.html

1	Wilson, Alexander	1714	1786	http://www.kitehistory.com/Miscellaneous/meteorological_kites.htm
2	Wilson, Alexander	1714	1786	http://www.asahi-net.or.jp/~et3m-tkkw/history5.html
3	Wilson, Alexander	1714	1786	http://www.kitehistory.com/Miscellaneous/meteorological_kites.htm
4	Wilson, Alexander	1714	1786	The Structure of a Sunspot, by P. R. Wilson and C. J. Cannon, Solar Physics, No 4, 1968, p 3
1	Orr, Hugh	1715	1798	http://www.irishlinenmills.com/Flax/fibre.htm
2	Orr, Hugh	1715	1798	The Scot in America by Peter Ross, The Raeburn Book Company, New York, 1896, pp 207
1	Lind, James	1716	1794	Scurvy, Stephen R. Brown, Penguin Books, Australia, 2003, p 9
2	Lind, James	1716	1794	The Naval Review, Volume LV, No 2, April 1967, p 54
3	Lind, James	1716	1794	Scurvy, Stephen R. Brown, Penguin Books, Australia, 2003, p 267
4	Lind, James	1716	1794	http://www.jameslindlibrary.org/pdf/theses/troehler-1978.pdf
5	Lind, James	1716	1794	Ibid.
6	Lind, James	1716	1794	http://www.healthandeverything.org/files/Scurvy%20for%20New%20Journal.pdf
7	Lind, James	1716	1794	James Lind and scurvy: a revaluation, by Michael Bartholomew, Journal for Maritime Research, January 2002
8	Lind, James	1716	1794	Ibid.
9	Lind, James	1716	1794	Lind and scurvy: 1747 to 1795, U Tröhler, JRSM: Journal of the Royal Society of Medicine, Volume 98, No 11, November 2005, pp 519-522
10	Lind, James	1716	1794	Lind at Haslar, Michael Bartholomew, Journal for Maritime Research, 2001
11	Lind, James	1716	1794	Pioneers of public health: the story of some benefactors of the human race, M. E. M. Walker, Oliver and Boyd, Edinburgh, 1930, p 32
12	Lind, James	1716	1794	Ibid. p 33
13	Lind, James	1716	1794	Infectious diseases - prevention and treatment in the 19th and 20th centuries, Wesley W.am Spink, University of Minnesota Press, Minneapolis, 1978, p 11
14	Lind, James	1716	1794	James Lind: Laudatory Address, K.C.B Sheldon Dudley, Proceedings of the Nutrition Society, Volume 12, Issue 3, September 1953, p 202
15	Lind, James	1716	1794	Dates in infectious diseases, Helen S. J. Lee, Parthenon Publishing Group, New York, 2002, p 30

16	Lind, James	1716	1794	James Lind: Laudatory Address, K.C.B Sheldon Dudley, Proceedings of the Nutrition Society, Volume 12, Issue 3, September 1953, p 203
17	Lind, James	1716	1794	The Journal of Nutrition, Willard A. Krehl, Yale Nutrition Laboratory, May 1953, p 10
18	Lind, James	1716	1794	Encyclopedia of Medical History, Roderick E McGrew, McGraw-Hill, New York, 1985, p 312
19	Lind, James	1716	1794	Terrors of the table: the curious history of nutrition, Walter Bruno Gratzer, Oxford University Press, Oxford, 2005, p 24
20	Lind, James	1716	1794	James Lind: Laudatory Address, K.C.B Sheldon Dudley, Proceedings of the Nutrition Society, Volume 12, Issue 3, September 1953, p 204
21	Lind, James	1716	1794	James Lind: founder of nautical medicine, Louis H Roddis, Wm. Heinemann Medical Books Ltd, London, 1950
1	Mackellar, Patrick	1718	1778	Dictionary of Canadian Biography Online
2	Mackellar, Patrick	1718	1778	Oxford Dictionary of National Biography
3	Mackellar, Patrick	1718	1778	Dictionary of Canadian Biography Online
4	Mackellar, Patrick	1718	1778	Oxford Dictionary of National Biography
5	Mackellar, Patrick	1718	1778	The Siege and Capture of Havana, 1762, by David Syrett, Navy Records Society, January 1970, ISBN 9780853540038
1	Campbell, John	1719	1790	Oxford Dictionary of National Biography
1	Meikle, Andrew	1719	1811	http://www.answers.com/topic/threshing
2	Meikle, Andrew	1719	1811	Biographical Dictionary of the History of Technology, edited by Lance Day, Ian McNeil, Routledge, 1998, p 827
3	Meikle, Andrew	1719	1811	Elements of Practical Agriculture: Comprehending the Cultivation of Plants, The Husbandry of the Domestic Animals, and the Economy of the Farm, by David Low, Printed for Bell and Bradfute, Edinburgh, 1834, pp 116-117
1	Melville, Robert	1723	1809	The poetics of empire: a study of James Grainger's The sugar-cane, by John Gilmore, The Athlone Press, New Jersey, 2000, p 287
2	Melville, Robert	1723	1809	Oxford Dictionary of National Biography
1	Smith, Adam	1723	1790	http://www.compilerpress.ca/ElementalEconomics/mic_1_1.htm
2	Smith, Adam	1723	1790	http://www.econlib.org/library/Enc/bios/Smith.html
3	Smith, Adam	1723	1790	The Complete Idiot's Guide to Economics, 2nd Edition, by Tom Gorman, published by Alpha, 2011, Chapter 1 (no page numbers)
4	Smith, Adam	1723	1790	http://www.philosophersbeard.org/2011/10/recovering-adam-smiths-ethical.html

5	Smith, Adam	1723	1790	http://www.adamsmith.org/adam-smith
6	Smith, Adam	1723	1790	Introductory Economics (micro and Macro): A Textbook for Class XII, by Subhendu Dutta, Published by New Age International (P) Ltd, 2006, p 4
7	Smith, Adam	1723	1790	http://www.westerncultureglobal.org/smith.html
8	Smith, Adam	1723	1790	http://www.investopedia.com/articles/economics/08/adam-smith-economics.asp
9	Smith, Adam	1723	1790	http://www.iep.utm.edu/smith/
10	Smith, Adam	1723	1790	http://economics.about.com/od/famouseconomists/a/adamsmith.htm
11	Smith, Adam	1723	1790	http://www.romeconomics.com/adam-smith-1723-1790/
12	Smith, Adam	1723	1790	http://www.philosophersbeard.org/2011/10/recovering-adam-smiths-ethical.html
13	Smith, Adam	1723	1790	Adam Smith's Legacy, Adam Smith Institute, edited by Nicholas Elliott, published by ASI (Research) Limited, London, 1990, p 7
14	Smith, Adam	1723	1790	http://www.investopedia.com/articles/economics/08/adam-smith-economics.asp
15	Smith, Adam	1723	1790	http://www.philosophersbeard.org/2011/10/recovering-adam-smiths-ethical.html
16	Smith, Adam	1723	1790	http://wweb.uta.edu/economics/facpages/wehr/adamsmith.pdf
17	Smith, Adam	1723	1790	http://www-tc.pbs.org/wgbh/commandingheights/shared/pdf/prof_adamsmith.pdf
18	Smith, Adam	1723	1790	http://www.shmoop.com/economic-systems/adam-smith.html
19	Smith, Adam	1723	1790	http://www.biography.com/people/adam-smith-9486480
20	Smith, Adam	1723	1790	http://www.vision.org/visionmedia/biography-adam-smith/868.aspx
21	Smith, Adam	1723	1790	http://www.amazon.com/dp/0312285523?tag=lucidcafe&link_code=as2&creativeASIN=0312285523&creative=374929&camp=211189
22	Smith, Adam	1723	1790	Adam Smith, An Enlightened Life, by Nicholas Phillipson, published by Allen Lane, London, 2010, p 280
23	Smith, Adam	1723	1790	Slavery, Adam Smith's Economic Vision and the Invisible Hand, by Spencer J. Pack, History of Economic Ideas, IV/1996/1-2, p 253
24	Smith, Adam	1723	1790	On The Wealth of Nations, by P.J. O'Rourke, Atlantic Books, 2007, pp 184-187

25	Smith, Adam	1723	1790	A History of Knowledge, Past, Present and Future, by Charles Van Doren, Ballantine Books, New York, April 1992, p253
1	Green, William	1725	1811	The Fortifications of Gibraltar 1068-1945, by Darren Fa, Clive Finlayson, Adam Hook, Osprey Publishing Ltd., Oxford, 2006, p 25
2	Green, William	1725	1811	Oxford Dictionary of National Biography
1	Hutton, James	1726	1797	http://digital.nls.uk/scientists/biographies/james-hutton/discoveries.html
2	Hutton, James	1726	1797	Encyclopedia of World Scientists, Revised Edition, by Elizabeth H. Oakes, Infobase Publishing, New York, 2007, p 359
3	Hutton, James	1726	1797	Ibid. p 360
4	Hutton, James	1726	1797	http://blog.mikerendell.com/?p=836
5	Hutton, James	1726	1797	http://www.scottishgeology.com/geo/famous-scottish-geologists/james-hutton-1726-1797/
6	Hutton, James	1726	1797	http://spot.colorado.edu/~friedmaw/Early_Evoluti on/Hutton.html
7	Hutton, James	1726	1797	Rediscovering Gandhi, Vol. 1, by R. P. Misra, Concept Publishing Company, New Delhi, 2007, p 273
8	Hutton, James	1726	1797	http://digital.nls.uk/scientists/biographies/james-hutton/discoveries.html
1	Melville, Thomas	1726	1753	http://galileo.phys.virginia.edu/classes/252/spectra.html
2	Melville, Thomas	1726	1753	http://www.rsc.org/Education/EiC/issues/2010July/LookWhoDiscoveredCaesium.asp
3	Melville, Thomas	1726	1753	Great Experiments in Physics: Firsthand Accounts from Galileo to Einstein, edited by Morris H. Shamos, Dover Publications, NY, 1987, p 329
4	Melville, Thomas	1726	1753	http://www.heliosat3.de/e-learning/radiative-transfer/rt1/AT622_section8.pdf
1	Black, Joseph	1728	1799	http://www.chem.gla.ac.uk/~alanc/dept/black.htm
2	Black, Joseph	1728	1799	http://scienceworld.wolfram.com/biography/Black.html
3	Black, Joseph	1728	1799	http://www.gashe.ac.uk:443/isaar/P0308.html
4	Black, Joseph	1728	1799	http://mattson.creighton.edu/History_Gas_Chemis try/Black.html
1	Morrison, Charles	*1728*	X	http://people.seas.harvard.edu/~jones/cscie129/im ages/history/lesage.html
1	Cuthbert, Gordon	1730	1810	The Merriam-Webster new book of word histories, Merriam-Webster Inc., Philippines, 1991, p 285

2	Cuthbert, Gordon	1730	1810	http://www.gutenberg-e.org/lowengard/C_Chap31.html
3	Cuthbert, Gordon	1730	1810	Consumers and luxury: consumer culture in Europe 1650-1850, by Maxine Berg, Helen Clifford, Manchester University Press, 1999, p 109
4	Cuthbert, Gordon	1730	1810	Chemistry, society and environment: a new history of the British Chemical Industry, by Colin Archibald Russell, The Royal Society of Chemistry, 2000, p 66
1	Cumming, Alexander	1731	1814	http://www.royalcollection.org.uk/eGallery/object.asp?object=2752&row=0&detail=about
2	Cumming, Alexander	1731	1814	http://www.scienceandsociety.co.uk/results.asp?image=10191188&wwwflag=&imagepos=2
3	Cumming, Alexander	1731	1814	The Privy Politics of Sir John Harington's New Discourse of a Stale Subject, Called the Metamorphosis of Ajax, by Jason Scott-Warren, Studies in Philology, Volume 93, No. 4 (Autumn, 1996), University of North Carolina Press, p 426
1	Macpherson, Robert	1731	1791	The Scots Magazine, Volume 28, James Boswell, Edinburgh, February 1766, p 77
2	Macpherson, Robert	1731	1791	Flax, The Complete Farmer, 3rd edition, by A Society of Gentlemen, Printed for J F and C Rivington, et al, London, 1777
1	Miller, Patrick	1731	1815	Oxford Dictionary of National Biography
2	Miller, Patrick	1731	1815	Sports Trimaran - Inventions and Discoveries, by Valerie-Anne Giscard d'Estaing and Mark Young, Facts on File Inc., New York, 1993, p 129
3	Miller, Patrick	1731	1815	http://founders.archives.gov/documents/Washington/05-12-02-0059
1	Broadwood, John	1732	1812	http://www.surreycc.gov.uk/sccwebsite/sccwspages.nsf/LookupWebPagesByTITLE_RTF/John+Broadwood+and+Sons+Piano+Manufacturers?opendocument
1	Irving, Charles	1734	1794	Equiano, the African: biography of a self-made man, by Vincent Carretta, University of Georgia Press, Athens, Georgia, 2005, p 137
2	Irving, Charles	1734	1794	A New Universal Dictionary of the Marine ... by William Burney, published by T. Caldell and W. Davies, London, 1815
1	Keir, James	1735	1820	Endeavour, New Series, Volume 9, No. 3, 1985, pp 129-130
2	Keir, James	1735	1820	Oxford Dictionary of National Biography
3	Keir, James	1735	1820	http://www.gracesguide.co.uk/James_Keir

4	Keir, James	1735	1820	http://www.chem.ed.ac.uk/about-us/history-school/professors/andrew-plummer
5	Keir, James	1735	1820	The Lunar Men by Jenny Uglow, Faber and Faber, London, 2002, p 165
1	Lind, James	1736	1812	Nineteenth-century scientific instruments, by Gerard L'Estrange Turner, Sotheby Publications, 1983, p 244
2	Lind, James	1736	1812	The real Doctor Frankenstein? By Christopher Goulding, Journal of the Royal Society of Medicine, Volume 95, May 2002, p 259
1	Watt, James	1736	1819	http://www.makingthemodernworld.org.uk/stories/the_age_of_the_engineer/03.ST.02/?scene=4&tv=true
2	Watt, James	1736	1819	http://www.nndb.com/people/531/000050381/
3	Watt, James	1736	1819	Inventors and Inventions, Marshall Cavendish, Volume 4, New York, 2008, p 1147
4	Watt, James	1736	1819	http://www.fuzzysys.com/fuzzyestimationtutorial.htm
5	Watt, James	1736	1819	http://ww1.microchip.com/downloads/en/appnotes/00937a.pdf
6	Watt, James	1736	1819	British patent No1432 Certain New Improvements upon Fire and Steam Engines and upon Machines worked or moved by the same James Watt, 1784
7	Watt, James	1736	1819	Capital and Steam Power 1750-1830, by John Lord, published by P.S. King and Son, Ltd, London, 1923, Chapter 10
8	Watt, James	1736	1819	http://www.search.revolutionaryplayers.org.uk/engine/resource/default.asp?theme=53&originator=%2Fengine%2Fcustom%2Fpeople%2Easp&page=&records=&direction=&pointer=163&text=0&resource=17
9	Watt, James	1736	1819	http://www.measuringworth.com/calculators/exchange/result_exchange.php
10	Watt, James	1736	1819	Central Heating: The Home - Inventions and Discoveries, by Valerie-Anne Giscard d'Estaing and Mark Young, Facts on File Inc., New York, 1993, p 102
11	Watt, James	1736	1819	MacMillan Profiles: Scientists and Inventors, Simon & Schuster Inc., New York, 1998
12	Watt, James	1736	1819	James Watt, by Andrew Carnegie, Doubleday, Page & Company, New York, May 1905, Chapter 7
13	Watt, James	1736	1819	Discovering Water: James Watt, Henry Cavendish, and the Nineteenth century 'Water controversy', by David Philip Miller, Ashgate Publishing Ltd., Aldershot, Hants, 2004, p 43

14	Watt, James	1736	1819	Young Humphry Davy: The Making of an Experimental Chemist, by June Z. Fullmer, Diane Publishing Company, 2000, pp 83-84
15	Watt, James	1736	1819	Nature: International weekly journal of science, 14 March 1895, pp 475-477
16	Watt, James	1736	1819	The Life of James Watt: With Selections from His Correspondence, by James Patrick Muirhead, 2nd Edition, published by John Murray, London, 1859, p 507
17	Watt, James	1736	1819	http://tundratabloids.com/2011/06/the-fjordman-report-human-accomplishment-technology.html
1	Dalrymple, Alexander	1737	1808	http://eandt.theiet.org/magazine/2011/07/one2ten-scottish-heritage.cfm
2	Dalrymple, Alexander	1737	1808	http://www.adelaidebooksellers.com.au/?page=shop/browse&fsb=1&searchby=keyword&keyword=seas
3	Dalrymple, Alexander	1737	1808	http://www.gov-news.org/gov/uk/news/culture_minister_defers_export_rare_portrait/99833.html
4	Dalrymple, Alexander	1737	1808	Oxford Dictionary of National Biography
5	Dalrymple, Alexander	1737	1808	http://pendientedemigracion.ucm.es/info/cliwoc/Dictionary_text.pdf
6	Dalrymple, Alexander	1737	1808	http://www.britannia.com/celtic/scotland/greatscots/d1.html
1	Anderson, James	1739	1808	The Scots Magazine and Edinburgh Literary Miscellany, Volume 71, Part 1, 1809, p 186
2	Anderson, James	1739	1808	Marx's Critique of Political Economy: Intellectual Sources and Evolution. Vol. II: 1861 to 1863, by Allen Oakley, Routledge & Kegan Paul, London, p 108
3	Anderson, James	1739	1808	A History of Economic Analysis, by Joseph Alois Schumpeter, Oxford University Press, 1954, p 263
1	Schank, John	1740	1823	Oxford Dictionary of National Biography
1	Small, James	1740	1793	http://east_west_dialogue.tripod.com/id1.html
2	Small, James	1740	1793	Oxford Dictionary of National Biography
3	Small, James	1740	1793	http://www.alhfam.org/pdfs/FARM_PIG_Info_sheet-1.pdf
1	Macpherson, Robert	*1741*	X	The Scots Magazine, Volume 28, James Boswell, Edinburgh, February 1766, p 77
1	Ferguson, Patrick	1744	1780	The Oxford Companion to Military History, by Stephen Wood, Oxford University Press, 2004
2	Ferguson, Patrick	1744	1780	Oxford Dictionary of National Biography
1	Cruickshank, William	1745	1810	William Cruickshank (FRS - 1802): Clinical chemist, by Guy H. Neild, Nephrology Dialysis

				Transplantation, Volume 11, European Renal Association-European Dialysis and Transplant Association,1996, p 1888
2	Cruickshank, William	1745	1810	http://www.vanderkrogt.net/elements/element.php?sym=Sr
3	Cruickshank, William	1745	1810	Oxford Dictionary of National Biography
4	Cruickshank, William	1745	1810	Four Centuries of Clinical Chemistry, by Louis Rosenfeld, published by Taylor & Francis, New York, 1999, p 40
5	Cruickshank, William	1745	1810	William Cruickshank (FRS - 1802): Clinical chemist, by Guy H. Neild, Nephrology Dialysis Transplantation, Volume 11, European Renal Association-European Dialysis and Transplant Association,1996, pp 1885-1886
6	Cruickshank, William	1745	1810	Four Centuries of Clinical Chemistry, by Louis Rosenfeld, published by Taylor & Francis, New York, 1999, p 89
7	Cruickshank, William	1745	1810	Landmark Papers in Nephrology, edited by John Feehally, Christopher McIntyre, J. Stewart Cameron, Oxford University Press, 2013, p 91
8	Cruickshank, William	1745	1810	The Chemical Element: Chemistry's Contribution to Our Global Future, edited by Javier García-Martínez, Elena Serrano-Torregrosa, Wiley-VCH Verlag & Co, Germany, 2011, p 3
9	Cruickshank, William	1745	1810	William Cruickshank (FRS - 1802): Clinical chemist, by Guy H. Neild, Nephrology, Dialysis, Transplantation, Volume 11, 1996, pp 1888-1889
10	Cruickshank, William	1745	1810	The interaction of Chlorine and Hydrogen, by Charles Hutchens Burgess and David Leonard Chapman, Journal of the Chemical Society, Transactions, Volume 89, 1906, p 1399
11	Cruickshank, William	1745	1810	The Chemical Element: Chemistry's Contribution to Our Global Future, edited by Javier García-Martínez, Elena Serrano-Torregrosa, Wiley-VCH Verlag & Co, Germany, 2011, p 3
12	Cruickshank, William	1745	1810	http://canov.jergym.cz/objevite/objev4/crua.htm
13	Cruickshank, William	1745	1810	William Cruickshank (FRS - 1802): Clinical chemist, by Guy H. Neild, Nephrology, Dialysis, Transplantation, Volume 11, 1996, pp 1888-1889
14	Cruickshank, William	1745	1810	http://www.madehow.com/Volume-4/Water.html
15	Cruickshank, William	1745	1810	Chlorination of Water - 1800: Breverton's Encyclopedia of Inventions, by Terry Breverton,

				Quercus Publishing Plc, London, 2012 (no page numbers shown)
1	Clark, James	1747	1829	A Statistical Account of the British Empire: Exhibiting Its Extent, Physical Capacities, Population, Industry, and Civil and Religious Institutions, 2nd edit, Vol 1, by J. R. McCulloch, Charles Knight & Co., London, 1839, p 682
2	Clark, James	1747	1829	The Canberra Times 6 April 1929 p 6
3	Clark, James	1747	1829	Clues in the Calico, by Barbara Brackman, C& T Publishing Inc, Lafayette, CA., 2009, p 50
1	Blair, Robert	1748	1828	The New Dictionary of Scientific Biography (Robert Blair), edited by Noretta Koertge, Scribner, 2008
2	Blair, Robert	1748	1828	http://www.virtualscotland.co.uk/scotland_articles /famous-scots/robert-blair.htm
3	Blair, Robert	1748	1828	The History of the Telescope, by Henry C. King, published by Charles Griffin & Co. Ltd, Bucks, England, 1955, p 189
1	Cochrane, Archibald	1748	1831	http://www.gasmuseum.co.uk/milestones.htm
2	Cochrane, Archibald	1748	1831	Archibald Cochrane, 9th Earl of Dundonald (1748-1831): Father of the British Tar Industry, by Paul Luter, Journal of Broseley Local History Society, No 28, 2006, p 10
3	Cochrane, Archibald	1748	1831	Mr. Midshipman Cochrane: Cochrane, The Life and Exploits of a Fighting Captain, by Robert Harvey, Carroll & Graf Publishers Inc., 2000, Chapter One
1	Stodart, Robert	1748	1831	The pianoforte, its origin, progress and construction, by Edward F Rimbault, published by Robert Cocks and Co., London, 1860, p 140
2	Stodart, Robert	1748	1831	http://www.oldpianos.com/1818_gibson_&_davis.htm
1	Rutherford, Daniel	1749	1819	The Basics of Chemistry, by Richard Myers, Greenwood Press, Westport, Connecticut, 2003, p 22
2	Rutherford, Daniel	1749	1819	http://acd.ucar.edu/textbook/ch1/box3/Rutherford.html
3	Rutherford, Daniel	1749	1819	http://todayinsci.com/11/11_15.htm

Chapter 2
1750-1799

1	Chapter 2, Introduction	1750	1799	The Most Powerful Idea In The World, by William Rosen, Pimlico, London, 2011, p 91
2	Chapter 2, Introduction	1750	1799	The Healers: A History of Medicine in Scotland, by David Hamilton, Canongate Publishing Ltd, Edinburgh, 1981, p 151
1	Abercrombie, Charles	1750	1817	The literary panorama and national register, by Charles Taylor, printed by Cox, Son, and Baylis, London, 1809, p 7
2	Abercrombie, Charles	1750	1817	http://www.cranntara.org.uk/tourab.htm
3	Abercrombie, Charles	1750	1817	Biographical Dictionary of Civil Engineers, Volume 1 – 1500 to 1830, Edited by Alex Skempton, Thomas Telford Publishing, London, 2002
1	Austin, John	1752	1830	Oxford Dictionary of National Biography
1	Stanhope, Charles	1753	1816	Dictionary of Nineteenth-century Journalism in Great Britain and Ireland, edited by Laurel Brake, Marysa Demoor, Academia Press, 2009, p 508
2	Stanhope, Charles	1753	1816	http://politicalstanhopes.com/Technology___History.html
1	Murdock, William	1754	1839	http://www.glias.org.uk/Chemicals_from_Coal/PART_1.HTM
2	Murdock, William	1754	1839	http://www.britannica.com/EBchecked/topic/398073/William-Murdock
3	Murdock, William	1754	1839	The London Magazine, Volume 9, by John Scott and John Taylor, published by Hunt and Clarke, London, September to December 1827, p 511
4	Murdock, William	1754	1839	Men of Invention and Industry, by Samuel Smiles, Verlag, 2012 (original 1884), p 121
5	Murdock, William	1754	1839	http://www.ids.u-net.com/cash/pneumatictube.htm
1	McAdam, John Loudon	1756	1836	The Steam Engine, Steam Navigation, Roads, and Railways, Explained and Illustrated, 8th Edition, by Dionysius Lardner, published by Taylor, Walton and Maberly, London, 1851, p 331
2	McAdam, John Loudon	1756	1836	http://universalium.academic.ru/285519/roads_and_highways
3	McAdam, John Loudon	1756	1836	The Book of Firsts, by Ian Harrison, Cassell Illustrated, London, 2003
1	Telford, Thomas	1757	1834	http://www.gracesguide.co.uk/Standedge_Tunnels

2	Telford, Thomas	1757	1834	http://www.theheritagetrail.co.uk/industrial/pontcysyllte%20aqueduct.htm
3	Telford, Thomas	1757	1834	http://www.asce.org/history/landmark/projects.cfm?menu=loc
4	Telford, Thomas	1757	1834	Encyclopedia Britannica 1911 edition
1	Bell, Thomas	*1758*	X	http://www.chickenfish.cc/copy/Publications/Goodtaste.pdf
2	Bell, Thomas	*1758*	X	Clues in the Calico, by Barbara Brackman, C& T Publishing Inc., Lafayette, CA., 2009, p 78
3	Bell, Thomas	*1758*	X	Biographical Dictionary of the History of Technology, edited by Lance Day, Ian McNeil, Routledge, 1998, p 97
4	Bell, Thomas	*1758*	X	http://home.zipworld.com.au/~lnbdds/Boschi/book/
5	Bell, Thomas	*1758*	X	Objects of Desire: Desire and Society since 1750, by Adrian Forty, Thames & Hudson, London, 1986, p 47
6	Bell, Thomas	*1758*	X	http://archiver.rootsweb.ancestry.com/th/read/BELL/2007-11/1195606060
1	Nasmyth, Alexander	1758	1840	Oxford Dictionary of National Biography
2	Nasmyth, Alexander	1758	1840	James Nasmyth, Engineer: An Autobiography by James Nasmyth, edited by Samuel Smiles, published by John Murray, London, 1897, p 34
3	Nasmyth, Alexander	1758	1840	Ibid. p 35
1	Jeffray, James	1759	1848	http://www.ncbi.nlm.nih.gov/pubmed/15209147
1	Playfair, William	1759	1823	http://www.readanybook.com/author/playfair-william-1580
2	Playfair, William	1759	1823	Oxford Dictionary of National Biography
1	Tilloch, Alexander	1759	1825	The Imperial Magazine, Or, Compendium of Religious, Moral, & Philosophical Knowledge, Vol. 7, publ. by H. Fisher, Son, & Co. Caxton Press, London, 1825, p 211
2	Tilloch, Alexander	1759	1825	Science in the Making Volume 1: 1798-1850, Edited by E. A. Davis, Taylor & Francis, CRC Press, 1995, p xxii
1	Hall, Alexander	1760	1849	http://www.aberdeenships.com/single.asp?index=100020
2	Hall, Alexander	1760	1849	http://www.aberdeenships.com/sb_alexander_hall.asp
3	Hall, Alexander	1760	1849	Opium Clippers and Early Clipper Ships, 1832-1848 - The Clipper Ship Era, by A. H. Clark, publ. by G. P. Putnam and Sons, NY, 1910, Chapter 4

1	Hall, James	1761	1832	http://www.bbc.co.uk/arts/yourpaintings/paintings/sir-james-hall-of-dunglass-17611832-4th-baronet-frse-186222
2	Hall, James	1761	1832	http://www.springerreference.com/docs/html/chapterdbid/30032.html
3	Hall, James	1761	1832	Encyclopedia of World Scientists, Revised Edition, by Elizabeth H. Oak, Infobase Publishing, 2007, p 301
4	Hall, James	1761	1832	Ibid. p 301
1	Murray, George	1761	1803	http://www.britannica.com/EBchecked/topic/398229/George-Murray
1	Rennie, John	1761	1821	http://todayinsci.com/R/Rennie_John/RennieJohn-BioStPaul(1843).htm
1	Maclure, William	1763	1840	American Geographers, 1784-1812: A Bio-bibliographical Guide, by Ben A. Smith, James W. Vining, Praeger Publishers, 2003, p 129
2	Maclure, William	1763	1840	Encyclopaedia Britannica, 11th edit. Vol. 17, 1911
1	Symington, William	1764	1831	http://www.uni-tuebingen.de/intelligent-mr-toad/html/profharvie/articles/transport/head_of_steam2.pdf
2	Symington, William	1764	1831	A Sketch of the Origin and Progress of Steam Navigation from Authentic Documents, by Bennet Woodcroft, Publisher: Taylor, Walton, and Maberly, London, 1848, p 54
3	Symington, William	1764	1831	http://www.learnnc.org/lp/editions/nchist-newnation/4337
1	Kelly, William	1765	1840	Historic New Lanark: the Dale and Owen industrial community since 1785, by Ian L. Donnachie, George Hewitt, Edinburgh University Press, 1999, p 55
2	Kelly, William	1765	1840	The fashion handbook, by Tim Jackson, David Shaw, Routledge, Oxon, 2006, p 7
3	Kelly, William	1765	1840	Historical Sketches Of Samuel Slater and Other Pioneer Manufacturers, With Notices of Some of the Famous Cotton Men of To-Day, and a Comprehensive Account of the Leading Cotton Manufacturing Centres of New England and the United States, by Robert Grieve and John P. Fernald, published by J. A. & R. A- Reid, Providence, R.I., 1891, p 13
4	Kelly, William	1765	1840	Biographical Dictionary of the History of Technology, Lance Day, Ian McNeil, Routledge, New York, 1996, p 685
5	Kelly, William	1765	1840	http://www.britishlistedbuildings.co.uk/sc-37053-new-lanark-mill-no-3-

1	Baird, Charles	1766	1843	Great Britain and Her World, 1750-1914: Essays in Honour of W. O. Henderson, edited by Barrie M. Ratcliffe, Manchester University Press, 1975, p 13
2	Baird, Charles	1766	1843	Oxford Dictionary of National Biography
1	Hope, Thomas Charles	1766	1844	http://www.scottish-places.info/people/famousfirst1116.html
1	Leslie, John	1766	1832	http://discovery.ucl.ac.uk/1348492/1/1348492.pdf
2	Leslie, John	1766	1832	Complete Dictionary of Scientific Biography, published by Charles Scribner's Sons, 2008
3	Leslie, John	1766	1832	Encyclopedia Britannica, 1911
4	Leslie, John	1766	1832	http://www.dtic.mil/dtic/tr/fulltext/u2/733293.pdf
5	Leslie, John	1766	1832	Encyclopedia Britannica, 9th Edition, 1902
6	Leslie, John	1766	1832	The historical development of quantum theory, Volume 1, Part 1, by Jagdish Mehra, Helmut Rechenberg, Springer-Verlag, New York, 1982, p 25
7	Leslie, John	1766	1832	Complete Dictionary of Scientific Biography, published by Charles Scribner's Sons, 2008
8	Leslie, John	1766	1832	http://gsa.confex.com/gsa/2011AM/finalprogram/abstract_192963.htm
9	Leslie, John	1766	1832	Ibid.
10	Leslie, John	1766	1832	Complete Dictionary of Scientific Biography, published by Charles Scribner's Sons, 2008
11	Leslie, John	1766	1832	A Comparison of Modified Atmometer Estimates of Turfgrass Evapotranspiration with Kimberly-Penman Alfalfa Reference Evapotranspiration, by E. H. Ervin and A. J. Koski, International Turfgrass Society, Research Journal, Volume 8, 1997, p 665
12	Leslie, John	1766	1832	http://www-history.mcs.st-and.ac.uk/Extras/Leslie_works.html
1	Macarthur, John	1766	1834	http://australia.gov.au/about-australia/australian-story/macarthurs-and-the-merino-sheep
2	Macarthur, John	1766	1834	http://www.rochedalss.eq.edu.au/wool.htm
3	Macarthur, John	1766	1834	http://www.bigmerino.com.au/history-of-wool
4	Macarthur, John	1766	1834	http://newmerino.com.au/wp/production/
1	Macintosh, Charles	1766	1843	http://www.straw.com/sig/dyehist.html
2	Macintosh, Charles	1766	1843	What a load of Twaddell, David G Rance, Slide Rule Gazette, Issue 11, Autumn 2010
1	Wilson, Alexander	1766	1813	http://www.pinterest.com/seiurus/wilson-ornithological-society/
2	Wilson, Alexander	1766	1813	http://www.wilsonsociety.org/society/awilsoninfo.html

3	Wilson, Alexander	1766	1813	Ibid.
4	Wilson, Alexander	1766	1813	http://www.christies.com/lotfinder/books-manuscripts/wilson-alexander-american-ornithology-or-the-5670740-details.aspx
5	Wilson, Alexander	1766	1813	http://mith.umd.edu/eada/gateway/wilson_intro.php
1	Bell, Henry	1767	1830	Biographical Dictionary of Civil Engineers, Volume 1 – 1500 to 1830, Edited by Alex Skempton, Thomas Telford Publishing, London, 2002, p 50
2	Bell, Henry	1767	1830	http://deriv.nls.uk/dcn6/7442/74422531.6.pdf
1	Ewart, Peter	1767	1842	Annals of Philosophy, Or, Magazine of Chemistry, Mineralogy, Mechanics, Natural History, Volume I, by Thomas Thomson, published by Robert Baldwin, London, 1813, p 463
2	Ewart, Peter	1767	1842	http://www.spartacus.schoolnet.co.uk/TEXgreg.htm
3	Ewart, Peter	1767	1842	Technical knowledge and the mental universe of Manchester's early cotton manufacturers, by Margaret Jacob and David Reid, Canadian Journal of History, University of Saskatchewan, August 2001, p 6
4	Ewart, Peter	1767	1842	Practical Matter: Newton's Science in the Service of Industry and Empire, 1687-1851, by Margaret C. Jacob, Larry Stewart, Harvard University Press, 2005, p 136
5	Ewart, Peter	1767	1842	http://www.hw.ac.uk/about/reputation/history.htm
6	Ewart, Peter	1767	1842	http://eprints.hud.ac.uk/14051/1/415.pdf
7	Ewart, Peter	1767	1842	Ibid.
1	Forsyth, Alexander John	1768	1843	Biographical Dictionary of the History of Technology, by Lance Day, Ian McNeil, Routledge, London, 1996, p 466
2	Forsyth, Alexander John	1768	1843	Weapons and Gunpowder, Great Inventions and Discoveries, by Willis Duff Piercy, published by Charles E Merrill Company, New York, 1911
3	Forsyth, Alexander John	1768	1843	http://www.britannica.com/EBchecked/topic/451179/percussion-lock
4	Forsyth, Alexander John	1768	1843	Sniping: An Illustrated History, by Pat Farey, Mark Spicer, Compendium Publishing Ltd, London, 2008, p 51
1	McIntosh, Hugh	1768	1840	Oxford Dictionary of National Biography
2	McIntosh, Hugh	1768	1840	http://www.whenlondonbecame.org.uk/page9.html
3	McIntosh, Hugh	1768	1840	A biographical dictionary of civil engineers in Great Britain and Ireland, Volume 1, 1500 to

				1830, by A. W. Skempton, Thomas Telford Publishing, London, 2002, pp 418-420
4	McIntosh, Hugh	1768	1840	Ibid. pp 418-420
5	McIntosh, Hugh	1768	1840	Ibid. p 419
6	McIntosh, Hugh	1768	1840	Ibid. pp 418-420
7	McIntosh, Hugh	1768	1840	http://www.whenlondonbecame.org.uk/page9.html
8	McIntosh, Hugh	1768	1840	http://www.pubs-newcomen.com/tfiles/(/66p175-001s.pdf
1	Tennant, Charles	1768	1838	Fortunes Made in Business or Life Struggles of Successful People, Anonymous, by Kessinger Publishing Company, Montana, 2003, p 343
1	Wallace, William	1768	1843	Nineteenth-century Scientific Instruments, by Gerard L'Estrange Turner, Sotheby Publications, University of California Press, 1983, p 280
1	Kennedy, John	1769	1855	http://www.teonline.com/knowledge-centre/textile-personalities.html
2	Kennedy, John	1769	1855	A biographical dictionary of civil engineers in Great Britain and Ireland, Volume 1, 1500 to 1830, by A. W. Skempton, Thomas Telford Publishing, London, 2002, p 283
3	Kennedy, John	1769	1855	Complementarity and the Rise of the Factory System in English Textiles, 1800-1850, by Thomas M. Geraghty, Gardner Hall, University of North Carolina, Chapel Hill, NC., 2006, p 18
4	Kennedy, John	1769	1855	Ibid. p 24
5	Kennedy, John	1769	1855	http://archives.li.man.ac.uk/ead/search?operation=search&fieldidx1=bath.corporateName&fieldrel1=exact&fieldcont1=fine%20cotton%20spinners%20and%20doublers'%20association%20ltd.
6	Kennedy, John	1769	1855	Britain ascendant: comparative studies in Franco-British economic history, by Francois Crouzet, University of Paris-Sorbonne [translation by Martin Thom], Cambridge University Press, 1991, p73
1	Seton, Alexander Anderson	1769	1850	The Social Basis of Scientific Discoveries, by Augustine Brannigan, Cambridge University Press, 1981, p 104
2	Seton, Alexander Anderson	1769	1850	Fabulous Science: Fact and Fiction in the History of Scientific Discovery, by John Waller, Oxford University Press, 2002, p 144
3	Seton, Alexander Anderson	1769	1850	http://www.esp.org/foundations/genetics/classical/holdings/w/wfrw-02.pdf
1	Watt, James	1769	1848	http://www.ampltd.co.uk/digital_guides/ind-rev-series-1-part-14/publishers-note.aspx

1	Nicol, William	1770	1851	An Introduction to Forensic Geoscience, by Elisa Bergslien, published by Wiley-Blackwell, 2012, p 3
2	Nicol, William	1770	1851	http://microscopy.berkeley.edu/courses/tlm/plm/birefr.html
3	Nicol, William	1770	1851	Oxford Dictionary of National Biography
4	Nicol, William	1770	1851	Biographical Encyclopedia of Scientists, 2nd Edition, Inst. Physics, CRC Press, 1994, p 662
5	Nicol, William	1770	1851	Mind Over Magma: The Story of Igneous Petrology by Davis A. Young, Princeton University Press, 2003, p 145
1	Paterson, James	1770	1854	http://eskmills.com/history/
2	Paterson, James	1770	1854	The Industries of Scotland, Their Rise, Progress and Present Condition, by David Bremner, published by Adam and Charles Black, Edinburgh, 1869, p 314
1	Miller, Robert	*1771*	X	Biographical dictionary of the history of technology, Lance Day, Ian McNeil, Routledge, London, 1996, p 849
2	Miller, Robert	*1771*	X	Hunt's Hand-Book to the Official Catalogues of the Great Exhibition: edited by Robert Hunt, Cambridge Library Collection: Technology, 2011, p 523
3	Miller, Robert	*1771*	X	The Growth of the Cotton Industry and Scottish Economic Development, 1780-1835, by Alexander James Robertson, The University of British Columbia, July 1965, p 34 and p 115
4	Miller, Robert	*1771*	X	Cotton weaving: its development, principles, and practice, by Richard Marsden, printed by George Bell & Sons, Manchester, 1895, p 230
1	Baildon, John	1772	1846	A biographical dictionary of civil engineers in Great Britain and Ireland, Volume 1, 1500 to 1830, by A. W. Skempton, Thomas Telford Publishing, London, 2002, p 30
2	Baildon, John	1772	1846	http://www.gliwiczanie.pl/Biografie/Baildon/Baildon_eng.htm
1	Mushet, David	1772	1847	Minutes of evidence to the Children's Employment Commission. Appendix to First Report of Commissioners (Mines), 1842, No. 37: p. 24, 1. 42
2	Mushet, David	1772	1847	The Annual of Scientific Discovery, by David A. Wells, Charles Robert Cross, John Trowbridge, Samuel Kneeland, George Bliss, published by Gould and Lincoln, Boston, 1861, p 199

3	Mushet, David	1772	1847	Industrial biography; iron-workers and tool-makers, Samuel Smiles, Volume 1, published by Ticknor and Fields, Boston, 1864, p 187
4	Mushet, David	1772	1847	The Genesis of the Common Market, by William Otto Henderson, Routledge, London, 1962, p 8
5	Mushet, David	1772	1847	http://metals.about.com/b/2011/12/28/what-is-spiegeleisen.htm
1	Ramage, Adam	1772	1850	The Colonial Printer, by Lawrence C Wroth, Constable and Company, London, 1994, p 86
2	Ramage, Adam	1772	1850	http://letterpresscommons.com/press/ramage-screw-press/
1	Wilson, William	1772	1860	http://www.vauxhallandkennington.org.uk/candles.shtml
2	Wilson, William	1772	1860	http://www.prices-candles.co.uk/history/historydetail.asp
3	Wilson, William	1772	1860	Dictionary of National Biography, Second Supplement, volume 3
4	Wilson, William	1772	1860	The Technologist, 1 December 1864, p 200
5	Wilson, William	1772	1860	http://www.gracesguide.co.uk/Prices_Patent_Candle_Co
1	Cayley, George	1773	1857	Encyclopedia Britannica, 2009 Deluxe Edition
2	Cayley, George	1773	1857	http://www.todayinsci.com/12/12_27.htm
3	Cayley, George	1773	1857	Sir George Cayley: 'Father of Aerial Navigation' (1773-1857), by Charles H. Gibbs-Smith, Notes and Records of the Royal Society of London, Volume 17, No. 1, May 1962, p 42
4	Cayley, George	1773	1857	http://www.ctie.monash.edu.au/hargrave/cayley.html
5	Cayley, George	1773	1857	http://www.flyingmachines.org/cayl.html
6	Cayley, George	1773	1857	The Facts on File Guide to Good Writing, by Martin H. Manser, Facts on File, Inc., New York, 2006, p 20
7	Cayley, George	1773	1857	Remarkable Engineers: From Riquet to Shannon, by Ioan James, Cambridge University Press, 2010, p 39
8	Cayley, George	1773	1857	On the Construction of Theatres, The Emporium of Arts and Sciences, Volume 2, No 11, March 1813, p 385
9	Cayley, George	1773	1857	Knight's Cyclopaedia of the Industries of all Nations, Charles Knight, printed by Reed and Fardox, London, 1851, p 222
10	Cayley, George	1773	1857	Sir George Cayley: Father of Aerial Navigation (1773-1857), Charles H. Gibbs-Smith, Notes and Records of the Royal Society of London, Volume 17, No. 1, May 1962, p 44

1	Ritchie, Walter	1773	1849	http://eskmills.com/history/
1	Brunton, Thomas	1774	1833	http://collections.rmg.co.uk/collections/objects/13954.html
1	Burnett, Thomas	1774	1824	A biographical dictionary of civil engineers in Great Britain and Ireland, Volume 1, 1500 to 1830, by A. W. Skempton, Thomas Telford Publishing, London, 2002, p 105
2	Burnett, Thomas	1774	1824	http://www.ameriquefrancaise.org/en/article-685/The_Lachine_Canal_and_its_Industrial_Corridor.html
1	Gordon, David	1774	1829	Railway locomotives and cars, American Railroad Journal and Advocate of Internal Improvements, Volume 5, published by D. K. Minor and George C. Schaeffer, New York, 1836, p 623
1	Snodgrass, Neil	1774	1818	The Development of the West of Scotland, 1750-1960, by Anthony Slaven, published by Routledge and Kegan Paul, London, 1975, p 96
2	Snodgrass, Neil	1774	1818	Steam Heating and Ventilation, by William S Monroe, The Engineering Record, New York, 1902, p 7
1	Thom, Robert	1774	1847	http://www.lenntech.com/history-water-treatment.htm
2	Thom, Robert	1774	1847	http://www.historyofwaterfilters.com/water-filter-technology.html
3	Thom, Robert	1774	1847	Cosmic Rays: Essays on Science and Technology from Royal Institution, edited by Richard Catlow, Susan Greenfield, Oxford University Press, 2001, p 42
4	Thom, Robert	1774	1847	On Tap, West Virginia University, Volume 5, Issue 2, Summer 1996, p 8
5	Thom, Robert	1774	1847	http://www.angelfire.com/journal/millbuilder/album3.html
6	Thom, Robert	1774	1847	www.strath.ac.uk/media/ps/comms/itallstartedhere/Thom.pdf
1	Adie, Alexander	1775	1858	Oxford Dictionary of National Biography
1	Cochrane, Thomas	1775	1860	The Idea of Chemical Warfare in Modern Times, by Wyndham D. Miles, Journal of the History of Ideas, Volume 31, No 2, April- June 1970, University of Pennsylvania Press, pp 297-298
2	Cochrane, Thomas	1775	1860	The great bridge: the epic story of the building of the Brooklyn Bridge, by David G. McCullough, published by Simon & Schuster, New York, 2001, pp 169-170

3	Cochrane, Thomas	1775	1860	A Short History of Technology: From the Earliest Times to A.D. 1900, by Thomas Kingston Derry, Trevor Illtyd Williams, Courier Dover Publications, 1993, p 453
4	Cochrane, Thomas	1775	1860	http://www.bbc.co.uk/radio4/history/making_history/makhist10_prog12a.shtml
5	Cochrane, Thomas	1775	1860	http://militaryhistory.about.com/od/naval/p/Napoleonic-Wars-Admiral-Lord-Thomas-Cochrane.htm
1	Brown, Samuel	1776	1852	http://66.241.199.22/baldt_anchor_history.htm
2	Brown, Samuel	1776	1852	http://library.thinkquest.org/22361/internal-combustion.htm
3	Brown, Samuel	1776	1852	http://www.thunderpress.net/motorcycle-touring/a-short-history-of-the-internal-combustion-engine/2009/01/19.htm
1	Jardine, James	1776	1858	http://lists.bcn.mythic-beasts.com/pipermail/bitlist/2009-November/004558.html
2	Jardine, James	1776	1858	The Encyclopaedia Britannica: Or, Dictionary of Arts, Sciences and Volume 9, eighth edition, edited by Thomas Stewart Traill, published by Adam and Charles Black, Edinburgh, 1855, p 600
1	Stodart, William	1776	1831	Encyclopedia of keyboard instruments, Volume 2, by Robert Palmieri, Margaret W. Palmieri, Igor Kipnis, Routledge, New York, 2003, p 152
2	Stodart, William	1776	1831	http://schureckcollection.org/fortepianos-2/fortepianos-english-action/english-compensating-grand-fortepiano-by-william-stodart-london-c-1820/
1	Brunton, William	1777	1851	http://www.chycor.co.uk/tourism/tolgus/
2	Brunton, William	1777	1851	History, Topography, and Directory of the County Palatine of Durham comprising A General Survey of the County and a History of the City and Diocese of Durham, by Francis Whellan, published by Ballantyne, Hanson, Co., London, 1894, p 826
3	Brunton, William	1777	1851	http://www.lordbrunton.com
1	Spence, William	1777	1815	http://www.sciencedirect.com/science/article/pii/S0315086013000426
2	Spence, William	1777	1815	The Development of Newtonian Calculus in Britain, 1700-1800, by Niccol- Guicciardini, Press Syndicate of the University of Cambridge, 1989, p 107
1	Pillans, James	1778	1864	http://www.ergoindemand.com/about_chalkboards.htm

2	Pillans, James	1778	1864	http://education.cu-portland.edu/blog/reference-material/the-history-of-the-classroom-blackboard/
3	Pillans, James	1778	1864	http://www.europeanfinancialreview.com/?p=3324
4	Pillans, James	1778	1864	The History of Britain Companion, by Jo Swinnerton, Robson Books, London, 2005, p 128
5	Pillans, James	1778	1864	Oxford Dictionary of National Biography
6	Pillans, James	1778	1864	http://archiveshub.ac.uk/data/gb237-coll-343
1	Watt, Francis	1778	1823	http://www.bbc.co.uk/history/british/empire_seapower/bell_rock_01.shtml
2	Watt, Francis	1778	1823	http://www.bellrock.org.uk/lighthouse/lighthouse_rock.htm
3	Watt, Francis	1778	1823	Ibid.
4	Watt, Francis	1778	1823	Mechanic's Magazine, No 54, 4 September 1824, pp 404-405
5	Watt, Francis	1778	1823	http://canmore.rcahms.gov.uk/en/site/36215/details/bell+rock+lighthouse/
6	Watt, Francis	1778	1823	http://www.jonathanahill.com/book.php?book_id=1441
1	Forrester, George	1780	X	Biographical Dictionary of the History of Technology edited by Lance Day, Ian McNeil, Routledge, London, 1996, p 463
2	Forrester, George	1780	X	http://www.steamindex.com/people/engrs.htm
1	Pasley, William Charles	1780	1861	The Scottish Enlightenment, Arthur Herman, Fourth Estate, London, 2003, p 330
2	Pasley, William Charles	1780	1861	Biographical Dictionary of Civil Engineers, Volume 1 - 1500 to 1830, edited Professor Sir Alex Skempton, Thomas Telford Publishing, London, 2002, p 514
3	Pasley, William Charles	1780	1861	http://www.du.edu/~jcalvert/railway/semaphor/semhist.htm
1	Brewster, David	1781	1868	http://www.brewstersociety.com/brewster_bio.html
2	Brewster, David	1781	1868	http://urv.nict.go.jp/member/gulliver/papers/vsmm99.pdf
3	Brewster, David	1781	1868	http://www.3dglassesonline.com/blog/?p=51
4	Brewster, David	1781	1868	http://www.stereoscopy.com/news/news-archive-7-2004.html
5	Brewster, David	1781	1868	http://www.hao.ucar.edu/education/TimelineD.php
6	Brewster, David	1781	1868	Chlorophyll a Fluorescence: A Signature of Photosynthesis, edited by George C. Papageorgiou, Govindjee, Springer, The Netherlands, 2004, p 3
7	Brewster, David	1781	1868	http://www.brewstersociety.com/brewster_bio.html

1	Fulton, Hamilton	1781	1834	Dictionary of North Carolina Biography: D-G, Volume 2, edited by William Stevens Powell, the University of North Carolina Press, 1986, p 253
1	Gibb, John	1781	1851	Slow Sand Filtration, L. Huisman and W. E. Wood, World Health organization, Geneva, 1974, ISBN 92 4 154037 0, p 15
2	Gibb, John	1781	1851	http://intro.chem.okstate.edu/ChemSource/Solubility/page17.htm
3	Gibb, John	1781	1851	Evolution of Water Supply Through the Millennia edited by Andreas Nikolaos Angelakis, Larry W. Mays, Demetris Koutsoyiannis, and Nikos Mamassis, IWA Publishing, London, 2012, p 37
4	Gibb, John	1781	1851	http://lcweb2.loc.gov/pnp/habshaer/md/md1700/md1796/data/md1796data.pdf
5	Gibb, John	1781	1851	http://water.me.vccs.edu/concepts/filters.html
6	Gibb, John	1781	1851	http://water.me.vccs.edu/concepts/filters.html
7	Gibb, John	1781	1851	Slow Sand Filtration, L. Huisman and W. E. Wood, World Health Organization, Geneva, 1974, ISBN 92 4 154037 0, pp 15-16
8	Gibb, John	1781	1851	Cholera Studies, by R. Pollitzer, Bulletin of the World Health Organization, No 10, 1954, p 450
1	Morton, Thomas	1781	1832	http://www.clydesite.co.uk/articles/patent.asp
2	Morton, Thomas	1781	1832	http://nla.gov.au/nla.pic-an4828511-v
1	Stephenson, George	1781	1848	http://inventors.about.com/library/inventors/blrailroad.htm
2	Stephenson, George	1781	1848	http://england.prm.ox.ac.uk/englishness-Miners-lamp.html
3	Stephenson, George	1781	1848	http://www.steamindex.com/people/stephen.htm
4	Stephenson, George	1781	1848	http://www.stephensonloco.org.uk/SLSgeorge.htm
5	Stephenson, George	1781	1848	Where Railways Were Born, Philip R B Brooks 2003 ISBN 0 9504646 2 7
6	Stephenson, George	1781	1848	The Life of Robert Stephenson...: With Descriptive Chapters on Some of His Most Important Professional Works, by William Pole, John Cordy Jefferson, publ. by Longmans, 1866, p 1
7	Stephenson, George	1781	1848	http://www.robertstephensontrust.com/page10.html
8	Stephenson, George	1781	1848	http://stephensonfamily.us/robert_stinson_stephenson.htm
1	Walker, James	1781	1862	http://easyweb.easynet.co.uk/~jjlace/part7.html
2	Walker, James	1781	1862	Blood, Iron and Gold, by Christian Wolmar, Atlantic Books, London, 2010, p 28

1	Bell, Thomas	1782	1866	http://www.transport.tas.gov.au/__data/assets/pdf_file/0008/49238/39593_Richmond_Bridge_CMP_Final_Report_-_Jan_2010_Part1of2.pdf
2	Bell, Thomas	1782	1866	http://www.heritagehighway.com.au/history-and-towns
1	Buchanan, Thomas	1782	1853	Offbeat otolaryngology: what they didn't teach you in medical school, by John D. C. Bennett, John R. Young, Gulde Druck, Stuttgart, 2001, p 79
2	Buchanan, Thomas	1782	1853	Tranquility is a State of Mind: Listening Aids for a Listening Impaired Society, by Frances Crow and David Prior, Wellcome Trust, Final Report, June 2010, p 6
3	Buchanan, Thomas	1782	1853	http://www.ehow.com/about_5070327_history-otoscope.html
4	Buchanan, Thomas	1782	1853	Offbeat Otolaryngology: What the Textbooks don't tell you, by John Bennett, John Riddington Young, by Gulde Druck, Tubingen, 2001, pp 67-68
1	Chalmers, James	1782	1853	Great Britain Establishes Penny Postage (Transportation) Great Events from History: The 19th century, Edited by John Powell, Oklahoma Baptist University, November 2006, p 641
2	Chalmers, James	1782	1853	http://www.cavendish-auctions.com/sale694_26apr07/a641_720.html
3	Chalmers, James	1782	1853	The Gentleman's Magazine Volume XLIII, by Sylvanus Urban, published by John Bowyer Nichols and Sons, London, January 1855, p 527
4	Chalmers, James	1782	1853	http://www.postalheritage.org.uk/page/markings-pennypost
5	Chalmers, James	1782	1853	http://www.postalmuseum.si.edu/collection/3a2c_acquis1999.html
6	Chalmers, James	1782	1853	http://www.norbyhus.dk/btpb.html
7	Chalmers, James	1782	1853	http://www.stamp-shop.com/penny-black.html
8	Chalmers, James	1782	1853	http://www.norbyhus.dk/btpb.html
9	Chalmers, James	1782	1853	The Merchants' Magazine and Commercial Review, Volume 46, Editor and Publisher William B. Dana, New York, 1862, p 529
10	Chalmers, James	1782	1853	Literacy and Development in the West, by Carlo M. Cipolla, Penguin Books, London, 1969. (USA data on page 99; British data on page 115)
1	Morton, Thomas	1783	1862	http://www.futuremuseum.co.uk/collections/people/key-people/science-invention/thomas-morton.aspx

2	Morton, Thomas	1783	1862	http://www.libraryindex.com/encyclopedia/pages/cpxlfavrm3/carpet-carpets-pattern-manufacture.html
1	Nimmo, Alexander	1783	1832	http://www.tandfonline.com/doi/abs/10.1080/09670882.2011.541654
1	Sturgeon, William	1783	1850	http://www.britannica.com/EBchecked/topic/570124/William-Sturgeon
2	Sturgeon, William	1783	1850	http://services.indg.in/test/modules/Magnetism/main11.html
3	Sturgeon, William	1783	1850	Power Struggles: Scientific Authority and the Creation of Practical Electricity before Edison, by Michael B. Schiffer, Massachusetts Institute of Technology, 2008, p 28
4	Sturgeon, William	1783	1850	http://www.britannica.com/EBchecked/topic/570124/William-Sturgeon
1	Bremner, James	1784	1856	A biographical dictionary of civil engineers in Great Britain and Ireland, Volume 1, 1500 to 1830, by A. W. Skempton, Thomas Telford Publishing, London, 2002, pp 72-73
2	Bremner, James	1784	1856	http://www.brebner.com/history/james_bremner_centenary.pdf
1	Christie, Samuel Hunter	1784	1865	Oxford Dictionary of National Biography
2	Christie, Samuel Hunter	1784	1865	http://www.creativeplanetnetwork.com/dcp/news/christies-fabulous-diamond-sir-charles-wheatstone-saw-sparkle-samuel-hunter-christies-diamo
3	Christie, Samuel Hunter	1784	1865	http://www.magnet.fsu.edu/education/tutorials/museum/wheatstonebridge.html
4	Christie, Samuel Hunter	1784	1865	http://www.creativeplanetnetwork.com/dcp/news/christies-fabulous-diamond-sir-charles-wheatstone-saw-sparkle-samuel-hunter-christies-diamo
5	Christie, Samuel Hunter	1784	1865	Oxford Dictionary of National Biography
1	Whytock, Richard Barnett	1784	1857	The Encyclopaedia Britannica: a dictionary of arts, sciences, and general literature, 9th edition, Volume 5, edited by Thomas S. Baynes, published by Henry G. Allen, New York, 1838, p 130
1	Crerar, Peter	1785	1856	http://www.barnesandnoble.com/w/scottish-immigrants-to-pre-confederation-nova-scotia-books-llc/1022946284
1	Fraser, Daniel	1786	1849	The Paddle Steamer Eric Nordevall II, 2nd Edition, Association Forsvik Shipyard, 2010, p 2

1	Napier, Charles John	1786	1860	Cruisers and Battle Cruisers: An Illustrated History of Their Impact, by Eric W. Osborne, ABC-Clio Inc., California, 2004, p 18
1	Arnott, Neil	1788	1874	Pressure sores: aetiology, treatment, and prevention, Colin Torrance, Croom Helm, Kent, England, 1983, p 54
2	Arnott, Neil	1788	1874	London Medical and Surgical Journal, Volume 2, Edited by Michael Ryan, published by Renshaw and Rush, London, 1833, p 166
3	Arnott, Neil	1788	1874	http://www.hevac-heritage.org/victorian_engineers/arnott/arnott.htm
4	Arnott, Neil	1788	1874	Ibid.
5	Arnott, Neil	1788	1874	Ibid.
6	Arnott, Neil	1788	1874	http://www.historyhome.co.uk/people/arnott.htm
1	Bald, William	1788	1857	Oxford Dictionary of National Biography
2	Bald, William	1788	1857	A biographical dictionary of civil engineers in Great Britain and Ireland, Volume 1, 1500 to 1830, by A. W. Skempton, Thomas Telford Publishing, London, 2002, p 35
1	Howell, John	1788	1863	The Scotsman, 6 April 1863
2	Howell, John	1788	1863	Daily Southern Cross, [NZ], 30 June 1863, p 3
1	Napier, David	1788	1873	http://lawchuntak.files.wordpress.com/2010/01/history-of-communication-technology-timeline-clement-law.pptx.
2	Napier, David	1788	1873	American Journalism, 1690-1940, by Frederic Hudson, Alfred McClung Lee, Frank Luther Mott, Routledge, 2000, p 116
3	Napier, David	1788	1873	http://www.scienceandsociety.co.uk/results.asp?image=10254414&wwwflag=2&imagepos=1
4	Napier, David	1788	1873	The Golden Age of the Newspaper, by George H. Douglas, Greenwood Press, Westport, Connecticut, USA. 1999, p 15
5	Napier, David	1788	1873	http://www.geocities.ws/paknetmag/A-6.htm
6	Napier, David	1788	1873	http://www.npht.org/david-napier/4579780662
1	Ronalds, Francis	1788	1873	Oxford Dictionary of National Biography
2	Ronalds, Francis	1788	1873	http://www.theiet.org/resources/library/archives/biographies/ronalds.cfm
1	Wauchope, Robert	1788	1862	http://www.eden.gov.uk/leisure-and-culture/museum-penrith-and-eden/museum-collections/vice-admiral-wauchopes-geological-collection/
1	Fairbairn, William	1789	1874	http://www.gracesguide.co.uk/William_Fairbairn_and_Sons

2	Fairbairn, William	1789	1874	Structural Engineering: History and development, by R.J.W. Milne, published by E & FN Spon, London, 1997, p 47
3	Fairbairn, William	1789	1874	Encyclopedia Britannica
4	Fairbairn, William	1789	1874	Eminent Persons, Biographies, Volume 1 1870-1875, Macmillan and Company, London, 1892, p 245
1	Smith, James	1789	1850	Encyclopedia Britannica 1911
2	Smith, James	1789	1850	High Farming 1837-1874 Chapter XVII - English Farming: Past and Present, by Lord Ernle, published by Longmans, Green and Co., London, 5th edition, 1912
3	Smith, James	1789	1850	High Farming 1837-1874 Chapter XVII - English Farming: Past and Present, by Lord Ernle, publ. by Longmans, Green and Co., London, 5th Edit., 1912
4	Smith, James	1789	1850	Biographical Dictionary of the History of Technology, by Lance Day, Ian McNeil, Routledge, London, 1996, p 1128
1	Macfarlan, John Fletcher	1790	1861	The Herald, 27 August 2006
1	Monteith, William	1790	1864	http://www.nls.uk/media/22553/2006_aug_dec_pa.pdf
1	Napier, David	1790	1869	Oxford Dictionary of National Biography
2	Napier, David	1790	1869	Robert Steele and Company: Shipbuilders of Greenock, by Mark Howard, The Northern Mariner/Le Marin du nord, (Canadian Nautical Research Society), Volume II, No. 3, July 1992, p 20
3	Napier, David	1790	1869	The Scottish Nation: A History 1700-2000, by T. M. Devine, Penguin Books, 1999, p 257
4	Napier, David	1790	1869	http://www.educationscotland.gov.uk/Images/ClydeShipbuildingIndustry_tcm4-543994.pdf
1	Stirling, Robert	1790	1878	http://www.grc.nasa.gov/WWW/tmsb/stirling.html
2	Stirling, Robert	1790	1878	Run silent, run long: Power & energy Volume 2, No.1, by Harry Hutchinson, Executive Editor, The American Society of Mechanical Engineers, February 2005
1	Blane, George Rodney	1791	1821	A biographical dictionary of civil engineers in Great Britain and Ireland, Volume 1, 1500 to 1830, by A. W. Skempton, Thomas Telford Publishing, London, 2002, p 61

2	Blane, George Rodney	1791	1821	The Gentleman's Magazine, Volume 91, Part 2, published by John Nichols & Son, London, July-December 1821, p 564
1	Burden, Henry	1791	1871	Burden Iron Works (Burden Iron Company), by Samuel Rezneck, Historic American Engineering Record, Office of Archaeology and Historic Preservation, National Park Service, US Department of the Interior, August 1969, p 4
2	Burden, Henry	1791	1871	History of Rensselaer Co., New York: with illustrations and biographical sketches of its prominent men and pioneers, by Nathaniel B. Sylvester, publ. by Everts & Peck, Phil., 1880
3	Burden, Henry	1791	1871	http://lcweb2.loc.gov/pnp/habshaer/ny/ny0600/ny0671/data/ny0671data.pdf
4	Burden, Henry	1791	1871	Burden Iron Works (Burden Iron Company), by Samuel Rezneck, Historic American Engineering Record, Office of Archaeology and Historic Preservation, National Park Service, U. S. Department of the Interior, August 1969, pp 4-5
5	Burden, Henry	1791	1871	Ibid.
6	Burden, Henry	1791	1871	Henry Burden, History of Rensselaer Co., New York, by Nathaniel Bartlett Sylvester, published by Everts & Peck, Philadelphia,1880
1	Johnston, John	1791	1880	Agricultural Nonpoint Source Pollution: Watershed Management and Hydrology, by Adel Shirmohammadi and William Frederick Ritter, CRC Press, 2000, p 209
2	Johnston, John	1791	1880	http://www.asabe.org/media/127397/asabe_historic_landmark_summary.pdf
3	Johnston, John	1791	1880	Miles of Tile, by Alison Carney Brown, Chicago Wilderness Magazine Inc., Skokie, Illinois, Spring 2004
4	Johnston, John	1791	1880	http://www.genevahistoricalsociety.com/Johnston.htm
1	Napier, Robert	1791	1876	The Ocean Railway, by Stephen Fox, Harper Perennial, London, 2003, p 93
2	Napier, Robert	1791	1876	http://www.merchantnavyofficers.com/cunard2.html
3	Napier, Robert	1791	1876	http://www.norwayheritage.com/p_ship.asp?sh=scotj
4	Napier, Robert	1791	1876	http://www.milhist.dk/vaaben/vands/rolf_krake/rolf_krake_uk.htm
5	Napier, Robert	1791	1876	The Scale of Clyde Shipbuilding, Clyde Breakers, Issue 2, January 2003

6	Napier, Robert	1791	1876	Robert Napier: The Father of Clyde Shipbuilding, by Brian D. Osborne, Dumbarton District Libraries, Dumbarton, Scotland, 1991
7	Napier, Robert	1791	1876	The Tears that Made the Clyde, by Carol Craig, Argyll Publishing, Glendaruel, 2010, [no page numbering but figures are found on page 2 of the chapter "The need for competence"]
8	Napier, Robert	1791	1876	Shipbuilding: The Development of the West of Scotland, 1750-1960, by Anthony Slaven, Routledge, 2006, p 178
9	Napier, Robert	1791	1876	http://www.bbc.co.uk/history/scottishhistory/modern/trails_modern_glasgow.shtml
10	Napier, Robert	1791	1876	Data derived by author from information on individual ships built on Clyde at Shipping Times UK, Fullarton House, Ayr – 6 August 2007 http://www.clydesite.co.uk/clydebuilt/index.asp
11	Napier, Robert	1791	1876	Scottish Firsts, by Elspeth Willis, Mainstream Publishing, Edinburgh, 2006, p120
12	Napier, Robert	1791	1876	The Light in the Glens: The Rise and Fall of the Puffer Trade, by Len Paterson, published by House of Lochar, 2002, p 19
1	Rennie, George	1791	1866	Warships and Their Story, by R. A. Fletcher, Cassell and Co., 1911, p 94
2	Rennie, George	1791	1866	Oxford Dictionary of National Biography
3	Rennie, George	1791	1866	The Smeatonians: The Society of Civil Engineers, by Garth Watson, published by Thomas Telford Ltd, London, 1989, p 56
1	Murchison, Roderick Impey	1792	1871	http://www.nceas.ucsb.edu/~alroy/lefa/Murchison.html
2	Murchison, Roderick Impey	1792	1871	http://www.cambridge.org/at/academic/subjects/history/history-science-and-technology/scientist-empire-sir-roderick-murchison-scientific-exploration-and-victorian-imperialism
3	Murchison, Roderick Impey	1792	1871	Encyclopedia Britannica, 11th Edition, 1911
4	Murchison, Roderick Impey	1792	1871	Encyclopedia Britannica, 1902
1	Neilson, James Beaumont	1792	1865	North British Review Volume IV: The Scottish Iron Manufacture, by Allan Freer, edited by W. P Kennedy, Edinburgh, November 1845, pp 131-132
2	Neilson, James Beaumont	1792	1865	http://himedo.net/TheHopkinThomasProject/TimeLine/IndustrialRevAmerica/Iron/AnthraciteIronIndustry.htm

3	Neilson, James Beaumont	1792	1865	Memoirs and portraits of one hundred Glasgow men who have died during the last thirty years and in their lives did much to make the city what it now is, by James MacLehose, publ. James MacLehose & Sons, Glasgow, 1886, p 246
1	Dunlop, James	1793	1848	Australian Dictionary of Biography, Volume 1, Melbourne University Press, 1966, p. 338
2	Dunlop, James	1793	1848	James Dunlop's Historical Catalogue of Southern Nebulae and Clusters, by Glen Cozens, Andrew Walsh and Wayne Orchiston, Journal of Astronomical History and Heritage, Volume 13, No 1, 2010, p 59
3	Dunlop, James	1793	1848	http://archive-org.com/page/263692/2012-09-02/http://messier.seds.org/xtra/similar/dunlop.html
1	Handyside, William	1793	1850	Oxford Dictionary of National Biography
2	Handyside, William	1793	1850	A biographical dictionary of civil engineers in Great Britain and Ireland, Volume 1, 1500 to 1830, by A. W. Skempton, Thomas Telford Publishing, London, 2002, p 296
1	Grainger, Thomas	1794	1852	Oxford Dictionary of National Biography
2	Grainger, Thomas	1794	1852	http://canmore.rcahms.gov.uk/en/site/52799/details/burntisland+harbour/
3	Grainger, Thomas	1794	1852	http://www.grantonhistory.org/transport/train_ferry.htm
1	Mackenzie, William	1794	1851	The diary of William Mackenzie, the first international railway contractor, by William Mackenzie, David Brooke, Thomas Telford Publishing, London, 2000, p xi
2	Mackenzie, William	1794	1851	http://www.fullbooks.com/History-Of-The-Mackenzies12.html
3	Mackenzie, William	1794	1851	http://www.nationalarchives.gov.uk/a2a/records.aspx?cat=107-mc&cid=0&kw=william%20mackenzie#0
4	Mackenzie, William	1794	1851	The diary of William Mackenzie, the first international railway contractor, William Mackenzie, David Brooke, Thomas Telford Publishing, London, 2000, p 15
5	Mackenzie, William	1794	1851	A biographical dictionary of civil engineers in Great Britain and Ireland, Volume 1, 1500 to 1830, by A. W. Skempton, Thomas Telford Publishing, London, 2002, pp 424-425
6	Mackenzie, William	1794	1851	William Mackenzie and Railways in France, by David Brooke, Construction History, Volume 13, 1997, p 3

7	Mackenzie, William	1794	1851	http://www.nationalarchives.gov.uk/a2a/records.aspx?cat=107-mc&cid=0&kw=william%20mackenzie#0
8	Mackenzie, William	1794	1851	William Mackenzie and Railways in France, David Brooke, Construction History, Volume 13, 1997, p 6
1	Rennie, John	1794	1874	http://reocities.com/yosemite/cabin/6735/gedney/fenareas.html
2	Rennie, John	1794	1874	Buildings Founded on Soil: CBD-81. Selecting the Foundation, by R.F. Legget and C.B. Crawford, Canadian Building Digest, National Research Council of Canada, 1996
1	Allen, William	*1795*	1840	History of the American pianoforte: its technical development, and the trade, by Daniel Spillane, published by D. Spillane, New York, 1890, p 41
2	Allen, William	*1795*	1840	Pianoforte, Encyclopaedia Britannica, 11th Edition, 1911 – also; Makers of the Piano: 1820-1860, Volume 2, by Martha N. Clinkscale, Oxford University Press, 1999, p xi
3	Allen, William	*1795*	1840	http://encyclopedia.jrank.org/INV_JED/JAP.html
1	Braid, James	1795	1860	http://www.durbinhypnosis.com/braid.htm
2	Braid, James	1795	1860	The Discovery of Hypnosis-The Complete Writings of James Braid, the Father of Hypnotherapy, James Braid, edited by Donald Robertson, National Council for Hypnotherapy, 2008, p 66
3	Braid, James	1795	1860	http://societyofclinicalhypnosis.com/clinical_hypnosis
4	Braid, James	1795	1860	http://ukhypnosis.com/category/james-braid-the-founder-of-hypnotherapy/
5	Braid, James	1795	1860	http://www.jamesbraidsociety.com/jamesbraid.htm
6	Braid, James	1795	1860	http://www.medical-library.net/content/view/56/40/
1	Tod, David	1795	1859	http://www.gregormacgregor.com/Tod&Macgregor/
1	Baird, Nicol Hugh	1796	1849	http://www.ryerson.ca/~amackenz/pdf/spring01b.pdf
2	Baird, Nicol Hugh	1796	1849	Dictionary of Canadian Biography Volume VII 1836 to 1850, by George W. Brown, David M. Hayne, Francess G. Halfpenny, Ramsay Cook, University of Toronto Press, Toronto, Canada, p 34
3	Baird, Nicol Hugh	1796	1849	Dictionary of Canadian Biography
4	Baird, Nicol Hugh	1796	1849	Submission to the Panel on the Future of the Trent Severn Waterway, Donald Mackay,

				Professor Emeritus, Trent University and University of Toronto, July 4, 2007
1	Condie, John	1796	1860	North British Review, Volume IV: The Scottish Iron Manufacture, by Allan Freer, Edited by W. P Kennedy, Edinburgh, November 1845, p 135
1	Foulis, Robert	1796	1866	Robert Foulis, Inventor of the Steam Foghorn - Nearly Lost in the Pages of Time, Lighthouse Digest, March 2005
1	McDowall, John	1796	1857	British History 1815-1914, 2nd edition, by Norman McCord, Bill Purdue, A. William Purdue, Oxford University Press, 2007, p 237
2	McDowall, John	1796	1857	Short Oxford History of the Modern World, British History 1815-1914, 2nd edition, by Norman McCord, Bill Purdue, Oxford University Press, 2007, p 237
3	McDowall, John	1796	1857	Woodworking Machinery: Its Rise, Progress, and Construction, with Hints on Management of Saw Mills and the Economical Conversion of Timber, by Manfred Powis Bale
1	Reid, John Paterson	1796	1854	The Edinburgh new philosophical journal: exhibiting a view of the Progressive Discoveries and Improvements in the Sciences and the Arts, Robert Jameson, Vol. 16, by Robert Jameson, Royal Society of Edinburgh, Wernerian Natural History Society, October 1883 to April 1834, Adam & Charles Black publ. Edinburgh, 1834, p 398
2	Reid, John Paterson	1796	1854	Cotton Weaving and Designing, 6th edit, John T Taylor, Longmans, Green and Co., London, 1909, p 12
3	Reid, John Paterson	1796	1854	Labor Saving Looms, First Edition, by George Otis Draper, presented by The Draper Company, Hopedale, Mass., Printed by Cook & Sons, Milford, Mass., 1904, pp 18-19
1	Buchanan, Alexander	*1797*	X	http://www.ehow.com/about_5408400_history-chenille-fabric.html
2	Buchanan, Alexander	*1797*	X	http://www.the-millshop-online.co.uk/blog/what-is-chenille-fabric/
1	Dick, Maxwell	1797	1870	http://www.gracesguide.co.uk/Engineers_and_Mechanics_Encyclopedia_1839:_Railways:_Maxwell_Dick
2	Dick, Maxwell	1797	1870	The British Magazine, Volume 1, published by Frederick Westley and A. H. Davis, London, January to June 1830, p 123

1	Drummond, Thomas	1797	1840	The University Magazine: A Literary and Political Journal Volume XIV July 1839, William Curry Junior and Company, Dublin, 1839, p 252
2	Drummond, Thomas	1797	1840	Thomas Drummond, under-secretary in Ireland, 1835-40: life and letters, by R. Barry O'Brien, published by Kegan Paul, Trench and Co., London, 1889, p 55
3	Drummond, Thomas	1797	1840	http://todayinsci.com/D/Drummond_Thomas/DrummondInventions.htm
4	Drummond, Thomas	1797	1840	Map Of A Nation: A Biography Of The Ordnance Survey, by Rachel Hewitt, Granta Books, 2010
1	Henry, Joseph	1797	1878	http://www.aps.org/programs/outreach/history/historicsites/henry.cfm
2	Henry, Joseph	1797	1878	http://www.edisontechcenter.org/JosephHenry.html
3	Henry, Joseph	1797	1878	http://www.museumoftechnology.org.uk/stories/telegraphy.html
4	Henry, Joseph	1797	1878	http://www.edisontechcenter.org/JosephHenry.html
5	Henry, Joseph	1797	1878	The London and Edinburgh Philosophical Magazine and Journal of Science, Volume XII, January-June 1838, p 90
6	Henry, Joseph	1797	1878	Encyclopædia Britannica 2009 Deluxe Edition
1	Kennedy, James	1797	1886	http://heritage.imeche.org/Biographies/Jameskennedy
2	Kennedy, James	1797	1886	A History of Railway Locomotives Until 1831, by Chapman Frederick Marshall, Hochschulverlag GmbH & Co, Bremen, 2010, p 207
1	Kennedy, Thomas	1797	1874	Engineering instruments & meters, by Edgar A Griffiths, Van Nostrand Co, New York, 1921, p 67
1	Lyell, Charles	1797	1875	http://users.hol.gr/~dilos/prehis/prerm1.htm
2	Lyell, Charles	1797	1875	http://steamline.wikidot.com/tl-1800s
3	Lyell, Charles	1797	1875	Encyclopaedia Britannica, 11th Edition, Vol. 17
4	Lyell, Charles	1797	1875	http://www.brighthub.com/environment/science-environmental/articles/66602.aspx
1	Henderson, Thomas James Alan	1798	1844	http://www.undiscoveredscotland.co.uk/usbiography/h/thomasjameshenderson.html
2	Henderson, Thomas James Alan	1798	1844	Oxford Dictionary of National Biography
3	Henderson, Thomas James Alan	1798	1844	http://www.encyclopedia.com/doc/1G2-2830901931.html

1	Logan, William Edmond	1798	1875	Dictionary of Canadian Biography
2	Logan, William Edmond	1798	1875	http://www.theodora.com/encyclopedia/l2/sir_william_edmond_logan.html
3	Logan, William Edmond	1798	1875	http://www.britannica.com/EBchecked/topic/346135/Sir-William-Edmond-Logan
1	Smith, Andrew	1798	X	The Merchants' Magazine and Commercial Review, Vol. 33, Freeman Hunt, NY, 1855, p 640
1	Bell, Patrick	1799	1869	Reaping, Encyclopedia Britannica 1911
1	Fairbairn, Peter	1799	1861	Biographical Dictionary of the History of Technology, by Lance Day, Ian McNeil, Routledge, London, 1996, p 430
2	Fairbairn, Peter	1799	1861	Oxford Dictionary of National Biography
3	Fairbairn, Peter	1799	1861	The Basic Industries of Great Britain. Coal: Iron: Steel: Engineering: Ships. An Historic and Economic Survey by The Right Honorable Lord Aberconway (Charles McLaren), published by Ernest Benn Ltd, London, 1927
1	Lindsay, James Bowman	1799	1862	http://www.princeton.edu/~achaney/tmve/wiki100k/docs/James_Bowman_Lindsay.html
2	Lindsay, James Bowman	1799	1862	http://dspt.club.fr/LINDSAY.htm
3	Lindsay, James Bowman	1799	1862	James Bowman Lindsay: A History of Wireless Telegraphy (2nd edition, revised), by J. J. Fahie, Dodd, Mead and Co., New York, 1901, pp 13-32
4	Lindsay, James Bowman	1799	1862	http://www.princeton.edu/~achaney/tmve/wiki100k/docs/James_Bowman_Lindsay.html
1	McFarlane, Patrick	1799	X	A Note on the Diffusion of the Automatic Loom Within the British Cotton Industry, by B. Pourdeyhimi and K.C. Jackson, Ars Textrina, Volume 6, Charles Babbage Research Centre, Winnipeg, December 1986, p 101
2	McFarlane, Patrick	1799	X	Cotton weaving and designing, by John T Taylor, Frederick Wilkinson, Harry Nisbet, Longmans, Green, and Co., London 1909, p 205
1	Syme, James	1799	1870	http://www.whonamedit.com/doctor.cfm/2088.html
2	Syme, James	1799	1870	Ibid.
3	Syme, James	1799	1870	http://www.geo.ed.ac.uk/scotgaz/people/famousfirst988.html
4	Syme, James	1799	1870	The History and Development of Syme's Amputation, by R. I. Harris, Artificial Limbs, Volume 6, No 1, p 4
5	Syme, James	1799	1870	Ibid.

6	Syme, James	1799	1870	James Syme (1799–1870), a great surgeon who promoted proctology, by Leon Banov Jr. and Jane Banov, Diseases of the Colon & Rectum, Volume 13, No. 6, November 1970, pp 475-479
7	Syme, James	1799	1870	http://www.whonamedit.com/doctor.cfm/2088.html
8	Syme, James	1799	1870	The History and Development of Syme's Amputation, by R. I. Harris, Digital Resource Foundation for the Orthotics & Prosthetics Community, Volume 6, No. 1, p 4
9	Syme, James	1799	1870	The history of analgesia in burns, by J. F. Murray, Post Graduate Medical Journal, Volume 48, 1972, pp 124-127
10	Syme, James	1799	1870	Principles of Surgery, by James Syme, published by H. Bailliere, London, 1842, pp 139-140
11	Syme, James	1799	1870	http://archives.ucl.ac.uk/DServe/dserve.exe?dsqIni=Dserve.ini&dsqApp=Archive&dsqCmd=Show.tcl&dsqSearch=RefNo=='MS%20ADD%20316'&dsqDb=Catalog
12	Syme, James	1799	1870	Encyclopedia Britannica, 1911 edition
13	Syme, James	1799	1870	The Politics of Professionalization: MPs, Medical Men, and the 1858 Medical Act, by Michael J D Roberts, Medical History, Volume 53, No.1, January 2009, pp 37-56

Chapter 3
1800-1824

1	Aird, John	1801	1876	http://www.steamindex.com/people/civils.htm
2	Aird, John	1801	1876	http://www.thepeerage.com/e144.htm
3	Aird, John	1801	1876	http://www.gracesguide.co.uk/John_Aird_(1834-1911)
1	Clark, Thomas	1801	1867	Dictionary of National Biography, Vol. 10, p 408
2	Clark, Thomas	1801	1867	The geochemical interpretation of water analyses, by Chase Palmer, Government Printing Office, Washington, 1911, p 5
1	Dalziel, John	1801	X	Mechanical Ventilation: A Tutorial for Pharmacists: History of Mechanical Ventilation, by Michael J. Cawley, Pharmacotherapy, Pharmacotherapy Publications, Feb 2007, pp 250-266
2	Dalziel, John	1801	X	Noninvasive Ventilation, by Sangeeta Mehta and Nicholas S. Hill, American Journal of Respiratory

				and Critical Care Medicine, Volume 163, Number 2, February 2001, pp 540-577
3	Dalziel, John	1801	X	Artificial Airways, Part 1, Respiratory Care, Volume 44, No 6, June 1999
4	Dalziel, John	1801	X	The Railway Magazine, Volume 2, by John Herapath, published by Wyld and Son, London, 1837, p 94
5	Dalziel, John	1801	X	The Evolution of Iron Lungs, published by J. H. Emerson Company, Cambridge, Massachusetts, 1978, (supplement)
1	McNeil, William Gibbs	1801	1853	http://penelope.uchicago.edu/Thayer/E/Gazetteer/Places/America/United_States/Army/USMA/Cullums_Register/172*.html
1	Ponton, Mungo	1801	1880	Photoengraving, Encyclopædia Britannica 2009 Deluxe Edition
1	Shanks, Alexander	1801	1845	Oxford Dictionary of National Biography
2	Shanks, Alexander	1801	1845	http://www.oldlawnmowerclub.co.uk/mowers/moms/mp025-shanks-pony-mower
1	Baird, Francis	1802	1864	http://rub.fxexchangerate.com/usd/1860-currency-rates.html
2	Baird, Francis	1802	1864	Minutes of the Proceedings, Institute of Civil Engineering, Volume 30, Issue 1870, 1 January 1870, pp 428-429
1	Baird, James	1802	1876	http://cheshire.cent.gla.ac.uk/ead/search?operation=search&fieldidx1=bath.geographicName&fieldrel1=exact&fieldcont1=gartsherrie%20(scotland)
1	Miller, Hugh	1802	1856	http://www.nahste.ac.uk/isaar/GB_0237_NAHSTE_P0493.html
2	Miller, Hugh	1802	1856	http://www.nationalgalleries.org/collection/artists-a-z/B/4561/artist_name/William%20Brodie/record_id/23378
3	Miller, Hugh	1802	1856	https://lra.le.ac.uk/handle/2381/180
4	Miller, Hugh	1802	1856	http://www.hughmiller.org/who_was_hugh_g.asp
5	Miller, Hugh	1802	1856	http://www.britannica.com/EBchecked/topic/382788/Hugh-Miller
6	Miller, Hugh	1802	1856	http://fossilnews.com/2001/hughmiller/fishstory.html
1	Milne, John	1802	1877	Wooden Railway on Durban's Bluff, by T. Hutson, Natalia, No 26, 1997, pp 74-78
1	Muir, Malcolm	*1802*	X	http://www.bensmill.com/machinery
2	Muir, Malcolm	*1802*	X	http://wiki.vintagemachinery.org/Short%20History%20of%20Woodworking%20Machinery.ashx

3	Muir, Malcolm	*1802*	X	Mechanics Magazine, Volume 6, Knight and Lacey, London, 1827, p 223
1	Templeton, James	1802	1885	Oxford Dictionary of National Biography
2	Templeton, James	1802	1885	http://www.fundinguniverse.com/company-histories/stoddard-international-plc-history/
3	Templeton, James	1802	1885	Local industries of Glasgow and the west of Scotland, (Classic Reprint), edited by Angus McLean, printed by William Hodge and Company, 2012, p 142
4	Templeton, James	1802	1885	http://selbysoftfurnishings.co.uk/blog/category/upholstery-fabric/chenille/page/2/
5	Templeton, James	1802	1885	http://www.ehow.com/about_5408400_history-chenille-fabric.html
1	Wilson, George	1802	1878	http://www.coldstreamhistorysociety.co.uk/index.php/projects/historic_document/howdens-of-coldstream
1	Gorrie, John	1803	1855	Refrigeration, Encyclopaedia Britannica Online 27 July 2007
1	Gregory, William	1803	1858	http://www.medgadget.com/2005/05/may_21_morphine.html
2	Gregory, William	1803	1858	http://www.chem.ed.ac.uk/about-us/history-school/professors/william-gregory
1	Hastie, John	1803	1894	Scottish Firsts by Elspeth Wills, Mainstream Publishing, Edinburgh, 2006, p 119
2	Hastie, John	1803	1894	http://cheshire.cent.gla.ac.uk/ead/search?operation=search&fieldidx1=bath.corporateName&fieldrel1=exact&fieldcont1=john%20hastie%20%26%20co%20ltd,%20steering%20gear%20manufacturers
1	Mitchell, Joseph	1803	1883	http://www.ecopave.com.au/bio_bitumen_asphalt_concrete_research_ecopave_australia_013.htm
2	Mitchell, Joseph	1803	1883	Encyclopedia Britannica Online (roads and highways) 10 December 2011
1	Wilson, Robert	1803	1882	Nineteenth-century torpedoes and their inventors, by Edwyn Gray, Naval Institute Press, Annapolis, Maryland, 2004, p 72
2	Wilson, Robert	1803	1882	Ibid. p 77 and p 84
3	Wilson, Robert	1803	1882	http://www.geoforum.com/info/pileinfo/view_process.asp?ID=17
1	Davidson, Robert	1804	1894	IEEE Magnetics Society Newsletter, Volume 40, No. 1, January 2002
2	Davidson, Robert	1804	1894	http://www.mpoweruk.com/history.htm
3	Davidson, Robert	1804	1894	http://itee.uq.edu.au/~aupec/aupec03/papers/037%20Takau%20full%20paper.pdf

1	Fife, David Alexander	1805	1877	http://www.producer.com/2013/07/red-fife-the-great-grandfather-of-todays-wheat/
2	Fife, David Alexander	1805	1877	http://www.thecanadianencyclopedia.com/articles/red-fife-wheat
3	Fife, David Alexander	1805	1877	http://www.agr.gc.ca/eng/science-and-innovation/science-publications-and-resources/resources/from-a-single-seed-tracing-the-marquis-wheat-success-story-in-canada-to-its-roots-in-the-ukraine-1of11/from-a-single-seed-tracing-the-marquis-wheat-success-story-in-canada-to-its-roots-in-the-ukraine-11-160of-16011/?id=1181318115137
1	Graham, Thomas	1805	1869	http://www.talktalk.co.uk/reference/encyclopaedia/hutchinson/m0018986.html
2	Graham, Thomas	1805	1869	The life and works of Thomas Graham, by Robert Angus Smith, published by John Smith & Sons, Glasgow, 1884, p 72
3	Graham, Thomas	1805	1869	Oxford Dictionary of National Biography
4	Graham, Thomas	1805	1869	http://www.britannia.com/celtic/scotland/greatscots/g1.html
5	Graham, Thomas	1805	1869	http://www.questionhub.com/YahooAnswers/20081124012349AAmWx75
6	Graham, Thomas	1805	1869	http://archive.is/CO8yK
7	Graham, Thomas	1805	1869	http://www.sciencetimeline.net/1651.htm
8	Graham, Thomas	1805	1869	http://www.britannia.com/celtic/scotland/greatscots/g1.html
9	Graham, Thomas	1805	1869	The Encyclopaedia Britannica, 11th edition, Volume 8, Cambridge, 1910, p 157
10	Graham, Thomas	1805	1869	http://scienceonstreets.phys.strath.ac.uk/new/Thomas_Graham.html
1	Hamilton, William Rowan	1805	1865	http://www.shortopedia.com/I/R/Irish_mathematicians
2	Hamilton, William Rowan	1805	1865	http://understandingscience.ucc.ie/pages/sci_williamrowanhamilton.htm
3	Hamilton, William Rowan	1805	1865	Oxford Dictionary of National Biography
4	Hamilton, William Rowan	1805	1865	http://answers.yahoo.com/question/index?qid=20100531195323AAY1VdV
5	Hamilton, William Rowan	1805	1865	http://understandingscience.ucc.ie/pages/sci_williamrowanhamilton.htm
6	Hamilton, William Rowan	1805	1865	http://www.britannica.com/EBchecked/topic/253431/Sir-William-Rowan-Hamilton
1	Handyside, Andrew	1805	1887	http://www.geolocation.ws/v/W/File:Friargate%20Railway%20Bridge%20-%20geograph.org.uk%20-%20356839.jpg/-/en

1	Kemp, Kenneth Treasurer	1805	1842	http://nms.scran.ac.uk/database/record.php?usi=000-180-001-004-C
1	Laird, John	1805	1874	http://www.cviog.uga.edu/Projects/gainfo/gahistmarkers/savannah-randhistmarker.htm
2	Laird, John	1805	1874	http://www.freewebs.com/maritime-history-two/shipbuildersshipyards.htm
3	Laird, John	1805	1874	http://www.victorianweb.org/history/empire/opiumwars/nemesis.html
4	Laird, John	1805	1874	http://www.history.com/news/women-and-children-first-on-sinking-ships-its-every-man-for-himself
5	Laird, John	1805	1874	http://heritage.scotsman.com/greatscots.cfm?id=592282005
6	Laird, John	1805	1874	http://www.queensroyalsurreys.org.uk/1661to1966/birkenhead/birkenhead.html
7	Laird, John	1805	1874	http://blog.liverpoolmuseums.org.uk/MaritimeTalesCammellLairdsFinest.aspx
1	Lamont, John	1805	1879	Oxford Dictionary of National Biography
2	Lamont, John	1805	1879	EOS, Transactions, American Geophysical Union, Volume 87, Issue 25, 20 June 2006, p 247
3	Lamont, John	1805	1879	Encyclopaedia Britannica 1911
4	Lamont, John	1805	1879	http://www.newadvent.org/cathen/08766b.htm
5	Lamont, John	1805	1879	http://www.geophysik.uni-muenchen.de/observatory/geomagnetism/history
1	McConnell, Robert	1805	1867	http://www.scottisharchitects.org.uk/architect_full.php?id=206780
2	McConnell, Robert	1805	1867	http://canmore.rcahms.gov.uk/en/site/44140/details/glasgow+36+jamaica+street+gardner+s+warehouse/
1	Muir, William	1805	1888	https://sites.google.com/site/sainiworks/machines-and-working-of-machines/radial-drilling-machine
2	Muir, William	1805	1888	http://www.gracesguide.co.uk/Brief_Memoir_of_the_late_William_Muir_by_Robert_Smiles
3	Muir, William	1805	1888	Capital, Entrepreneurs and Profits, by Richard Peter Treadwell Davenport-Hines, published by Frank Cass and Company Ltd, London, 1990, p 249
4	Muir, William	1805	1888	Oxford Dictionary of National Biography
1	Reid, David Boswell	1805	1863	http://www.hevac-heritage.org/victorian_engineers/reid/reid.htm
2	Reid, David Boswell	1805	1863	Wisconsin Journal of Education, Volume 4, edited by A. J. Craig, printed by Atwood, Rublee & Reed, Madison, Wisconsin, 1860, p 195

3	Reid, David Boswell	1805	1863	http://www.hevac-heritage.org/victorian_engineers/reid/reid.htm
4	Reid, David Boswell	1805	1863	http://www.british-history.ac.uk/report.asp?compid=16910#s5
5	Reid, David Boswell	1805	1863	Ventilation in American Dwellings: With a Series of Diagrams, Presenting Examples in Different Classes of Habitations, by David Boswell Reid, Wiley & Halstead, New York, 1858, p xv
6	Reid, David Boswell	1805	1863	Abstract of Central Heating and Forced Ventilation: Origins and Effects on Architectural Design, by Robert Bruegmann, The Journal of the Society of Architectural Historians, Volume 37, No.3, October 1978, pp.143-160
7	Reid, David Boswell	1805	1863	http://www.hevac-heritage.org/victorian_engineers/reid/reid.htm
1	Spence, Peter	1806	1883	Science in Victorian Manchester: Enterprise and Expertise, by Robert Hugh Kargon, The John Hopkins University Press, 1977, p 139
1	Wallace, James Davidson	1806	1874	Along Parallel Lines: A History of the Railways of New South Wales 1850-1986, by John Gunn, Melbourne University Press, 1989, p 29
2	Wallace, James Davidson	1806	1874	The Empire, Sydney, Saturday, 10 December 1853, p 6
3	Wallace, James Davidson	1806	1874	Australia in Maps: Great Maps in Australia's History from the National Library's Collection, edited by National Library of Australia, Canberra, reprinted 2008, p 130
1	Holden, Isaac	1807	1897	Sir Isaac Holden, Encyclopedia Britannica, 11th Edition, University Press, Cambridge, New York, 1911
2	Holden, Isaac	1807	1897	Oxford Dictionary of National Biography
1	Kirkwood, James Pugh	1807	1877	http://www.asce.org/PPLContent.aspx?id=2147487352
2	Kirkwood, James Pugh	1807	1877	Ibid.
3	Kirkwood, James Pugh	1807	1877	Environmental and water resources: milestones in engineering history, by Jerry R. Rogers, EWRI National History & Heritage Committee, Environmental and Water Resources Institute (U.S.), Tampa, FLA, 15-19 May 2007, pp 12-16
1	Owen, David Dale	1807	1860	http://www.nlm.nih.gov/exhibition/historicalanatomies/clorion_bio.html
2	Owen, David Dale	1807	1860	http://faculty.evansville.edu/ck6/bstud/owen.html

3	Owen, David Dale	1807	1860	http://www.mhs.mb.ca/docs/people/owen_dd.shtml
4	Owen, David Dale	1807	1860	https://gsa.confex.com/gsa/2008NC/finalprogram/abstract_137585.htm
1	Adie, Alexander James	1808	1879	The Architectural Magazine and Journal, Volume 2, edited by John Claudius Loudon, Longman, Rees, Orme, Brown, Green, & Longman, London, 1835, p 517
1	Baker, William Erskine	1808	1881	Oxford Dictionary of National Biography
2	Baker, William Erskine	1808	1881	Biographical notices of officers of the Royal (Bengal) engineers, by Edward Talbot Thackeray, Smith, Elder & Co., London, 1900, p 163
1	Brown, David Rennie	1808	1875	The History of Anaesthesia Society Proceedings, Volume 29, Proceedings of the meeting in Edinburgh, 29th and 30th June 2001, p 34
2	Brown, David Rennie	1808	1875	Scottish Firsts, by Elspeth Wills, Mainstream Publishing Company, Edinburgh, 2006, page 42
3	Brown, David Rennie	1808	1875	The History of Anaesthesia Society Proceedings, Volume 28, Proceedings of the joint meeting with the Royal Society of Chemistry in London, 4th November 2000, p 40
1	Freeburn, James	1808	1876	History of Firearms: From Earliest Times to 1914, by W. Y. Carman, Dover Publishing, New York, 2004, p 172
1	Nasmyth, James Hall	1808	1890	http://emotional-literacy-education.com/classic-books-online-b/jnasm10.htm
2	Nasmyth, James Hall	1808	1890	http://www3.museumofmaking.org/dbtw-wpd/machine.htm
3	Nasmyth, James Hall	1808	1890	http://www.astro.uva.nl/eltmosws/Talks/ELT_MOS_Padovani.pdf
4	Nasmyth, James Hall	1808	1890	Science and Fiction: James Nasmyth's Photographic Images of the Moon, by Frances Robertson, Victorian Studies, Volume 48, Number 4, Indiana University Press, Summer 2006, pp 595-623
5	Nasmyth, James Hall	1808	1890	http://www.carabelli.com/pages/patient_library/history.htm
6	Nasmyth, James Hall	1808	1890	The Mining Magazine, Volume 7, by William J. Tenney, Publisher John F. Trow, New York, July 1856, p 508
1	Russell, John Scott	1808	1882	http://digi.lib.ttu.ee/archives/2005/2005-10/1130352358.PDF
2	Russell, John Scott	1808	1882	Physics of Solitons, by Thierry Dauxois, Michel Peyrard, Cambridge University Press, 2010, p 9

3	Russell, John Scott	1808	1882	http://www.ice.org.uk/getattachment/9895337a-d8e1-4d17-8f08-72871d1d631f/PHEW-Newsletter-No-118-June-2008.aspx
4	Russell, John Scott	1808	1882	http://www.bbc.co.uk/history/british/victorians/seven_wonders_gallery_01.shtml
5	Russell, John Scott	1808	1882	http://www.ma.hw.ac.uk/solitons/JOHN_SCOTT_RUSSELL_Catalogue_and_Labels.pdf
6	Russell, John Scott	1808	1882	http://telephonecollecting.org/greateastern.html
7	Russell, John Scott	1808	1882	http://www.ma.hw.ac.uk/~chris/doppler.html
8	Russell, John Scott	1808	1882	http://www.tenpound.com/155/76.html
9	Russell, John Scott	1808	1882	Dictionary of British Educationists, by Richard J. Aldrich, Peter Gordon, Routledge, 1989, p 215
10	Russell, John Scott	1808	1882	http://www.ma.hw.ac.uk/solitons/JOHN_SCOTT_RUSSELL_Catalogue_and_Labels.pdf
11	Russell, John Scott	1808	1882	http://www.victorianweb.org/history/1851/engineers.html
12	Russell, John Scott	1808	1882	http://www.ma.hw.ac.uk/solitons/JOHN_SCOTT_RUSSELL_Catalogue_and_Labels.pdf
13	Russell, John Scott	1808	1882	http://digital.lib.umd.edu/worldsfairs/record?pid=umd:992
14	Russell, John Scott	1808	1882	http://www.ma.hw.ac.uk/solitons/JOHN_SCOTT_RUSSELL_Catalogue_and_Labels.pdf
1	Allan, Alexander Reid	1809	1891	http://www.engrailhistory.info/r132.html
1	Dowie, James	1809	X	Being Alive: Essays on Movement, Knowledge and Description, by Tim Ingold, Routledge, New York, 2011, p 37
2	Dowie, James	1809	X	http://collections.vam.ac.uk/item/O11194/ankle-boots-unknown/
3	Dowie, James	1809	X	Culture on the Ground, Tim Ingold, J o u r n a l of Material Culture, Volume 9, No 3, November 2004, p 320
1	Forbes, James David	1809	1868	http://www.strathearn.com/pl/earthquake.htm
2	Forbes, James David	1809	1868	http://earthquake.usgs.gov/learn/topics/seismology/history/part05.php
3	Forbes, James David	1809	1868	The Physical Tourist: A Science Guide for the Traveler, edit. by John S. Rigden, Roger H. Stuewer, publ. by Birkhauser Verlag AG, Berlin, 2009, p 36
4	Forbes, James David	1809	1868	Oxford Dictionary of National Biography

5	Forbes, James David	1809	1868	The Versatile Soliton, by Alexandre R. Filippov, published by Springer, New York, 2010, p 24
6	Forbes, James David	1809	1868	Oxford Dictionary of National Biography
7	Forbes, James David	1809	1868	http://uh.edu/engines/epi2269.htm
1	Gladstone, William Ewart	1809	1898	http://www.hmrc.gov.uk/manuals/intmanual/intm120210.htm
2	Gladstone, William Ewart	1809	1898	Introduction to Company Law 2nd edit., by Paul L. Davies, Oxford University Press, 2010, p 1
3	Gladstone, William Ewart	1809	1898	Corporations Law in Australia 2nd Edition, by Roman Tomasic, Stephen Bottomley, Rob McQueen, The Federation Press, Sydney, Australia, 2002, p 12
4	Gladstone, William Ewart	1809	1898	A Social History of Company Law: Great Britain and the Australian Colonies 1854-1920, by Rob McQueen, Ashgate Publishing Limited, Surrey, 2009, p 46
5	Gladstone, William Ewart	1809	1898	Boyle & Birds Company Law, 8th Edition, Jordans, Bristol, 2011, p 3
6	Gladstone, William Ewart	1809	1898	http://archive.is/5M1rK
7	Gladstone, William Ewart	1809	1898	Mr. Gladstone — Part II, by W. T. Stead, The Review of Reviews, Volume 5, May 1892, p 453
1	Turnbull, George	1809	1889	Oxford Dictionary of National Biography
2	Turnbull, George	1809	1889	Obituary, George Turnbull: Minutes of the Proceedings, Institution of Civil Engineers, Volume 97, Issue 1889, 1 January 1889, p 418
3	Turnbull, George	1809	1889	http://www.gracesguide.co.uk/East_Indian_Railway
1	West, John	1809	1888	Oregon's First Salmon Canner, "Captain" John West, by Glenn Cunningham, Oregon Historical Quarterly, Volume 54, No.3, September 1953, pp 240-248
1	Wilson, William	1809	1862	http://translate.google.com.au/translate?hl=en&sl=de&tl=en&u=http%3A%2F%2Fwww.nuernberginfos.de%2Fbedeutende-nuernberger%2Fwilliam-wilson.html&sandbox=1
1	Bain, Alexander	1810	1877	www.electric-clocks.eu/clocks/en/index.htm
2	Bain, Alexander	1810	1877	Communications: An International History of the Formative Years, by Russell W. Burns, The Institution of Engineering and Technology, London, 2004, p 121
3	Bain, Alexander	1810	1877	The Story of Electricity: Chapter VI, The Telegraph and Telephone, by John Munro, Published by G. Newnes, London, 1896

4	Bain, Alexander	1810	1877	The Office: Business and Commerce - Inventions and Discoveries Valerie-Anne Giscard d'Estaing and Mark Young, Facts on File Inc., New York, 1993, p 109; and also Invention by Design: How Engineers Get from Thought to Thing Henry Petroski, Harvard University Press, 1998, p 106
1	Hamilton, William	1810	1880	Dictionary of Canadian Biography Online
1	Murray, Alexander	1810	1884	Dictionary of Canadian Biography
2	Murray, Alexander	1810	1884	http://planetrocks.ca/c80-alexander-murray-an-overlooked-rock-star/
3	Murray, Alexander	1810	1884	William Edmond Logan (1798-1875), Knighted Canadian Geologist: An Anthology, by C. Gordon Winder, Trafford Publishing, 2004, p 138
1	Yule, John Cochran	1810	1877	The Book of Firsts, by Patrick Robertson, Bramhall House, New York, 1982, p 201
1	Clark, Adam	1811	1866	Encyclopedia Britannica 2009 Deluxe Edition
2	Clark, Adam	1811	1866	http://www.aviewoncities.com/budapest/chainbridge.htm
3	Clark, Adam	1811	1866	Encyclopedia Britannica 2009 Deluxe Edition
4	Clark, Adam	1811	1866	http://www.bridgesofbudapest.com/bridge/chain_bridge
1	Davidson, David	1811	1900	Sniper Rifles: From the 19th to the 21st century, by Martin Pegler, Osprey Publishing, 2010, p 18
2	Davidson, David	1811	1900	http://springfieldarsenal.files.wordpress.com/2010/10/davidson-telescope.pdf
3	Davidson, David	1811	1900	Ibid.
4	Davidson, David	1811	1900	Ibid
5	Davidson, David	1811	1900	http://www.historynet.com/minie-ball
6	Davidson, David	1811	1900	http://springfieldarsenal.files.wordpress.com/2010/10/davidson-telescope.pdf
7	Davidson, David	1811	1900	Ibid
8	Davidson, David	1811	1900	http://www.researchpress.co.uk/longrange/longrangeusa04.htm
9	Davidson, David	1811	1900	http://www.civilwarhome.com/sedgwickdeath.htm
1	Henderson, John	1811	1858	The Crystal Palace and its Place in Structural History, by B. Addis, International Journal of Space Structures, Vol. 21, No. 1, 2006, p 18
2	Henderson, John	1811	1858	Farewell, Cousin to the Crystal Palace, by Richard Morris, British Archaeology, edited by Simon Denison, Issue 38, October 1998
1	Laurie, John	1811	1875	http://www.asce.org/People-and-Projects/People/Bios/Laurie,-James/

1	McKay, Lauchlan	1811	1895	Published by Crosby Lockwood and son, 1894, p 11
1	Mushet, Robert Forrester	1811	1891	People & Industries, by William H. Chaloner, Rutledge, 1963, p 83
2	Mushet, Robert Forrester	1811	1891	The History of Tungsten, by Erik Lassner and Wolf-Dieter Schubert, itia Newsletter (International Tungsten Industry Association), London, December 2005, p 4
3	Mushet, Robert Forrester	1811	1891	Oxford Dictionary of National Biography
1	Simpson, James Young	1811	1870	http://www.rcoa.ac.uk/about-the-college/history-of-anaesthesia
2	Simpson, James Young	1811	1870	Blessed Days of Anaesthesia: How anaesthetics changed the world, by Stephanie J Snow, Oxford University Press, 2008, p 1802
3	Simpson, James Young	1811	1870	Long's Contribution to Discovery of Ether, by F. K. Boland, Journal of the American Medical Association, Volume 107, No 8, 1936, p 605
4	Simpson, James Young	1811	1870	Drug discovery: a history, by Walter Sneader, published by John Wiley & Sons, West Sussex, 2005, p 82
5	Simpson, James Young	1811	1870	http://svmsl.chem.cmu.edu/vmsl/genanes/ga_bg3.htm
6	Simpson, James Young	1811	1870	Sir James Simpson's introduction of chloroform, by Eve Blantyre Simpson, Century Magazine, Volume 47, Issue 3, January 1894, pp 412-421
7	Simpson, James Young	1811	1870	http://www.general-anaesthesia.com/chloroform.html
8	Simpson, James Young	1811	1870	http://www.general-anaesthesia.com/chloroform.html
9	Simpson, James Young	1811	1870	John Snow's Practice of Obstetric Anaesthesia, by Donald Caton, American Society of Anesthesiologists, published by Lippincott Williams & Wilkins, Inc., 2000, p 248
10	Simpson, James Young	1811	1870	ibid p 68
11	Simpson, James Young	1811	1870	Vacuum Assisted Delivery: The History of Vacuum Extraction, by Thomas F. Basket, Aldo Vacca, August 2009, p 2 [Accessed via www.vaccaresearch.com]
12	Simpson, James Young	1811	1870	http://emedicine.medscape.com/article/271175-overview
13	Simpson, James Young	1811	1870	http://www.slideshare.net/drmcbansal/forceps-14991711 (page 6 of slide show)

14	Simpson, James Young	1811	1870	James Young Simpson and the Development of Obstetric Anaesthesia, by Don Todman, The Internet Journal of Gynecology and Obstetrics, Volume 10, No 1, 2008
15	Simpson, James Young	1811	1870	Milestones, Sir James Young Simpson and Obstetric Analgesia, by E Dastur Adi and P.D. Tank, The Journal of Obstetrics and Gynecology of India, Volume 59, No 3, May/June 2009, p 208
16	Simpson, James Young	1811	1870	Obstetrical-Gynaecological Eponyms: James Young Simpson and his Obstetric Forceps, by Harold Street, The Journal of Obstetrics and Gynaecology of the British Empire, 1957, p 232
17	Simpson, James Young	1811	1870	Hermaphrodites and the medical invention of sex, by Alice Domurat Dreger, Harvard University Press, 1998, p 143
18	Simpson, James Young	1811	1870	Milestones, Sir James Young Simpson and Obstetric Analgesia, by E Dastur Adi and P.D. Tank, The Journal of Obstetrics and Gynecology of India, Volume 59, No 3, May/June 2009, p 208
19	Simpson, James Young	1811	1870	A list of the works of Sir James Young Simpson, 1811-1870: A centenary tribute, by K.F. Russell and F.M. Forster, University of Melbourne, 1971, p 2
20	Simpson, James Young	1811	1870	The history of obstetrics and gynaecology, by Michael J. O'Dowd, Elliot Elias Philipp, Parthenon Publishing Group, New York, 2000, p 345
21	Simpson, James Young	1811	1870	Edinburgh medical and surgical journal, Volume 24, Printed by Archibald Constable & Co., Edinburgh, 1825
22	Simpson, James Young	1811	1870	The American journal of the medical sciences, edited by Isaac Hays, Volume 28, Blanchard & Lea, Philadelphia, 1854
23	Simpson, James Young	1811	1870	A Handbook of Uterine Therapeutics and of Diseases of Women, by Edward John Tilt, 3rd edition, printed by John Churchill & Sons, London, 1868, p 25
24	Simpson, James Young	1811	1870	On The Treatment Of Intrauterine Polypi, by George H. Kidd, The British Medical Journal, Volume 1, No. 422, 30 January 1869, p 94
25	Simpson, James Young	1811	1870	American armamentarium chirurgicum, by George Tiemann & Co, James M. Edmonson, F. Terry Hambrecht, Norman Publishing, 1989, p 505

26	Simpson, James Young	1811	1870	Perinatal Lessons from the Past, Sir James Young Simpson (1811–1870) and obstetric anaesthesia, by P. M. Dunn, Archives of Disease in Childhood - Fetal and Neonatal Edition, Volume 86, 2002, pp 207-209
27	Simpson, James Young	1811	1870	The evolution of surgical instruments: An Illustrated History from Ancient Times to the Twentieth Century by John Kirkup, Norman Surgery Series, No 13, USA, 2005, p 320
28	Simpson, James Young	1811	1870	Reaction of Bone to Various Metals, Arthur A Zierold, Archives of Surgery, Volume 9, No 2, 1924, pp 365-412
29	Simpson, James Young	1811	1870	So just who was James "Young" Simpson? by S.M. Rae and J.A.W. Wildsmith, British Journal of Anaesthesia, Volume 79, No 3, September 1997, p 1
30	Simpson, James Young	1811	1870	New Chapters in the Warfare of Science, Andrew Dickson White, ex-President of Cornell University, The Popular Science Monthly, Volume 39, published by D. Appleton and Co., New York, May to October 1891, p 165
31	Simpson, James Young	1811	1870	http://www.general-anaesthesia.com/
32	Simpson, James Young	1811	1870	http://www.churchinhistory.org/pages/booklets/chloroform.htm
33	Simpson, James Young	1811	1870	Did the use of chloroform by Queen Victoria influence its acceptance in obstetric practice? by H. Connor, T. Connor, Anaesthesia, Volume 51, No 10, October 1996, pp 955-957
34	Simpson, James Young	1811	1870	Early opposition to obstetric anaesthesia, by A.D. Farr, Anaesthesia, Volume 35, No 9, 1980, pp 896-907
35	Simpson, James Young	1811	1870	Is the artificial womb inevitable? by Edward Grossman, The Obsolescent Mother, The Atlantic, May 1971
36	Simpson, James Young	1811	1870	http://www.churchinhistory.org/pages/booklets/chloroform.htm
37	Simpson, James Young	1811	1870	Sir J.Y. Simpson's Graduation Address, The Medical Times and Gazette, Volume 2, 8 August 1863, p 144
1	Waterston, John James	1811	1883	Kinetic Theory of Gases, Encyclopaedia Britannica, 2009, Deluxe Edition
2	Waterston, John James	1811	1883	http://www2.math.umd.edu/~lvrmr//History/Neglected.html

1	Young, James	1811	1883	http://www.scottishshale.co.uk/HistoryPages/Biographies/JamesYoung.html
2	Young, James	1811	1883	http://www.cromfordcanal.info/news/portal/Portal26.pdf
3	Young, James	1811	1883	http://www.strath.ac.uk/media/ps/comms/itallstartedhere/Young.pdf
4	Young, James	1811	1883	http://www.engineeringhalloffame.org/profile-young.html
5	Young, James	1811	1883	Dictionary of National Biography, 1885-1900, Vol 63
6	Young, James	1811	1883	http://www.engineeringhalloffame.org/profile-young.html
7	Young, James	1811	1883	http://www.eia.gov/todayinenergy/detail.cfm?id=11611
8	Young, James	1811	1883	RAND Corporation Oil Shale Development in the United States Prospects and Policy Issues. J. T. Bartis, T. LaTourette, L. Dixon, D.J. Peterson, and G. Cecchine, MG-414-NETL, 2005
1	Dunbar, Robert	1812	1890	http://buffaloah.com/h/elev/hist/1/index.html
2	Dunbar, Robert	1812	1890	http://www.buffalohistoryworks.com/grain/history/history.htm
1	Fisken, William	1812	1883	http://historylink101.com/lessons/farm-city/steam-engine.htm
2	Fisken, William	1812	1883	Mataura Ensign, Rōrahi 6, Putanga 338, 11 Poutūterangi, 1884, p 5: also, Harper's New Monthly Magazine, Issue 4, March 1884 – Obituary
3	Fisken, William	1812	1883	http://www.electricscotland.com/agriculture/page26.htm
4	Fisken, William	1812	1883	http://www.steamploughclub.org.uk/history.htm
1	Haswell, John	1812	1897	World railways of the nineteenth century: a pictorial history in Victorian Engravings, by Jim Harter, The Johns Hopkins University Press, Baltimore, 2005, p 160
2	Haswell, John	1812	1897	The Great Train Race: Railways and the Franco-German Rivalry, 1815-1914, by Allan Mitchell, Berghahn books, 2000, p 57
3	Haswell, John	1812	1897	Illustrated Encyclopedia of World Railway Locomotives, by P. Ransome-Wallis, General Publishing Company, Toronto, 2001, p 499
4	Haswell, John	1812	1897	http://www.aqpl43.dsl.pipex.com/MUSEUM/LOCOLOCO/balanced/balanced.htm
5	Haswell, John	1812	1897	The railway locomotive: what it is and why it is what it is, by Vaughn Pendred, A. Constable & co., Ltd., London, 1908, p 2

1	MacMillan, Kirkpatrick	1812	1878	Oxford Dictionary of National Biography
2	MacMillan, Kirkpatrick	1812	1878	Bicycling Science, by David Gordon Wilson, MIT Press, 2004, pp 12-13
3	MacMillan, Kirkpatrick	1812	1878	http://www.gracesguide.co.uk/Thomas_McCall
4	MacMillan, Kirkpatrick	1812	1878	Kilmarnock had first bicycle factory in the world, by Frank Beattie, Kilmarnock Standard, 24 October 2008
5	MacMillan, Kirkpatrick	1812	1878	The Wheel Thing, by Brigid James, Scotland Magazine, Issue 4, September 2002
1	Mather, Colin	1812	1864	The Jubilee Book 1958, A History of Mather & Platt Ltd, by Marcel A Boschi, David Drew-Smythe & John F. Taylor, 1958
2	Mather, Colin	1812	1864	http://home.zipworld.com.au/~lnbdds/Boschi/book/five1.htm
1	Meik, Thomas	1812	1896	http://sine.ncl.ac.uk/view_image.asp?digital_doc_id=3916
1	Newall, Robert Stirling	1812	1889	http://www.gracesguide.co.uk/R._S._Newall_and_Co
1	Ogilvie, Alexander Milne	1812	1886	Obituary: Minutes of the Proceedings – The Institution of Civil Engineers, Volume 86, edited by James Forrest, London, January 1886, p 373
1	McNaught, William	1813	1881	http://www.lclark.edu/~bekar/IR.pdf
2	McNaught, William	1813	1881	http://www.gracesguide.co.uk/William_McNaught
3	McNaught, William	1813	1881	http://www.makingthemodernworld.org.uk/stories/the_age_of_the_engineer/03.ST.02/?scene=7&tv=true
4	McNaught, William	1813	1881	http://www.best-maritime-crewing.info/catalogue_companies_list/company_source_15401_8.html
5	McNaught, William	1813	1881	http://www.cartage.org.lb/en/themes/biographies/MainBiographies/M/McNaught/1.html
6	McNaught, William	1813	1881	Oxford Dictionary of National Biography
1	Newlands, James	1813	1871	Oxford Dictionary of National Biography
2	Newlands, James	1813	1871	Letters and Diaries of A.F.R. Wollaston, edited by Mary Wollaston, December 2013, isbn: 9781107626454, p 179
3	Newlands, James	1813	1871	Liverpool's drainage history: seventeenth century to MEPAS, by G. N. Olsen, Proc. Instn. Civ. Engrs Mun. Engr., September 1998, 127, paper 11356, p 140

4	Newlands, James	1813	1871	http://www.publications.parliament.uk/pa/cm201011/cmhansrd/cm100602/debtext/100602-0016.htm
1	Abernethy, James	1814	1896	Obituary, Minutes of the Proceedings of the Institute of Civil Engineering, Volume 124, Issue 1896, 1 January 1896, pp 406-407
1	Anderson, John	1814	1886	http://www.imeche.org/news/archives/11-06-03/Royal_Arsenal_awarded_top_engineering_honour.aspx
2	Anderson, John	1814	1886	A Floating Factory in the Crimea – the career of Sir John Anderson, superintendent of machinery at the Royal Arsenal, 1842-72 (abstract), by Gwilym Roberts, presented to the Newcomen Society on 12 December 2007 and produced in Transactions of the Newcomen Society, Volume 78, Number 2, July 2008, pp 261-291
3	Anderson, John	1814	1886	http://www.waymarking.com/waymarks/WMFN57_The_Royal_Arsenal_Beresford_Street_Woolwich_London_UK
4	Anderson, John	1814	1886	http://www.gracesguide.co.uk/John_Anderson_(1814-1886)
1	Barclay, Andrew	1814	1900	Stone: Building Stone, Rock Fill and Armourstone in Construction, edited by Mick R. Smith, the Geological Society, Bath, 1999, p 204
2	Barclay, Andrew	1814	1900	http://www.trainweb.org/loggingz/builders_1.html
1	Cunningham, Henry Preston Cunningham	1814	1875	http://www.fortgilkicker.co.uk/cunningham.htm
2	Cunningham, Henry Preston Cunningham	1814	1875	http://www.niagaradivers.com/divesites/rae.html
3	Cunningham, Henry Preston Cunningham	1814	1875	http://gosportsociety.co.uk/smforum/index.php?topic=9.0
1	Dick, Robert	1814	1890	http://www.earlyofficemuseum.com
1	Goodsir, John	1814	1867	http://www.nature.com/news/2003/031009/full/news031006-9.html
2	Goodsir, John	1814	1867	http://www.nhc.ed.ac.uk/index.php?page=24.25.312.326.350
3	Goodsir, John	1814	1867	Victorian Britain (Routledge Revivals): An Encyclopedia, edited by Sally Mitchell, Garland Publishing, 1988, p 59
4	Goodsir, John	1814	1867	A Calendar of the Correspondence of Charles Darwin, 1821-1882, by R. Colp, American Book Review, Volume 61, No.7, edited by Frederick

				Burkhardt and Sydney Smith, Garland Publishing, September 1985, p 686
5	Goodsir, John	1814	1867	http://www.britannica.com/EBchecked/topic/238835/John-Goodsir
1	Low, William	1814	1886	Oxford Dictionary of National Biography
1	Ramsay, Andrew Crombie	1814	1891	http://www.nahste.ac.uk/isaar/GB_0237_NAHSTE_P0220.html
2	Ramsay, Andrew Crombie	1814	1891	Oxford Dictionary of National Biography
1	Ritchie, Edward Samuel	1814	1895	http://amhistory.si.edu/navigation/maker.cfm?makerid=59
2	Ritchie, Edward Samuel	1814	1895	http://archive.org/stream/jstor-20020639/20020639_djvu.txt
1	Byron, Augusta Ada	1815	1852	http://cant.ua.ac.be/resources/lovelace
2	Byron, Augusta Ada	1815	1852	http://www.computerhistory.org/babbage/adalovelace/
1	Brunlees, James	1816	1892	Oxford Dictionary of National Biography
2	Brunlees, James	1816	1892	http://www.engineering-timelines.com/scripts/engineeringItem.asp?id=840
1	Harrison, James	1816	1893	http://www.bookrags.com/research/the-advent-of-mechanical-refrigerat-scit-05123456/;
2	Harrison, James	1816	1893	James Harrison 1816? -1893, by L. G. Bruce-Wallace, Australian Dictionary of Biography, Volume 1, Melbourne University Press, 1966, pp 520-521
1	Robertson, Henry	1816	1888	http://www.gracesguide.co.uk/Henry_Robertson
1	Sturrock, Archibald	1816	1909	http://www.rchs.org.uk/trial/4-3%20Sturrock.pdf
2	Sturrock, Archibald	1816	1909	http://www.bookdepository.co.uk/Archibald-Sturrock-Tony-Vernon/9780752441351
1	Wilson, Daniel	1816	1892	Oxford Dictionary of National Biography
2	Wilson, Daniel	1816	1892	http://www.anthropology.utoronto.ca/about/history
3	Wilson, Daniel	1816	1892	http://www.biographi.ca/en/bio/wilson_daniel_12E.html
4	Wilson, Daniel	1816	1892	Ibid
1	Broun, John Allan	1817	1879	http://books.google.com.au/books/about/John_Allan_Broun.html?id=BVfeXwAACAAJ&redir_esc=y
2	Broun, John Allan	1817	1879	http://arxiv.org/pdf/1301.1971.pdf
3	Broun, John Allan	1817	1879	ibid
1	Henry, Alexander	1817	1895	www.rorkesdriftvc.com/potpourri/martini.doc
2	Henry, Alexander	1817	1895	http://www.martinihenry.com/

1	McQueen, Walter	1817	1893	A history of the American locomotive: its development, 1830-1880, by John H. White, Dover Publications, 1980, pp 444-445
1	Pollock, George David	1817	1897	http://utmj.org/archive/86-2/REV-Skin.pdf
2	Pollock, George David	1817	1897	Cadaveric Allograft as Adjunct Therapy for Nonhealing Ulcers, by Robert J Snyder and David A Simonson, The Journal of Foot and Ankle Surgery, Volume 38, No 2, p 94
3	Pollock, George David	1817	1897	Management of the Burn Wound, by Jose P Sterling, David M Heimbach, and Nicole S Gibran, Trauma and Thermal Injury, Section 7, ACS Surgery: Principles and Practice, Decker Intellectual Properties, August 2010, p 8
4	Pollock, George David	1817	1897	http://www.mendeley.com/research/george-david-pollock-and-the-development-of-skin-grafting/
5	Pollock, George David	1817	1897	George David Pollock and the Development of Skin Grafting, by M. Felix Freshwater, M.D., and Thomas I. Krizek, M.D., Annals of Plastic Surgery, Volume 1, No 1, January 1978, pp 98-101
1	Sinclair, Robert	1817	1898	http://www.lner.info/eng/sinclair.shtml
1	Smith, Robert Angus	1817	1884	http://www.eoearth.org/view/article/156054/
2	Smith, Robert Angus	1817	1884	http://www.icp-forests.org/DocsTFM/26TFMICP0_GregorICPForests25.pdf
3	Smith, Robert Angus	1817	1884	http://www.abebooks.co.uk/Air-rain-beginnings-chemical-climatology-SMITH/4299178614/bd
1	Wood, Alexander	1817	1884	Evolution of Medical Application of Syringe, Indian Journal of Physiology and Pharmacology, Volume 50, No 3, 2006, p 202
2	Wood, Alexander	1817	1884	Evolution of Medical Application of Syringe, Indian Journal of Physiology and Pharmacology, Volume 50, No 3, 2006, p 199
3	Wood, Alexander	1817	1884	http://www.discoveriesinmedicine.com/Ra-Thy/Syringe.html
4	Wood, Alexander	1817	1884	Proceedings of June 1986 Meeting, The History of Anaesthesia Society, Volume 1, published by Abbott Laboratories Ltd., 7 June 1986, p 33
5	Wood, Alexander	1817	1884	http://www.discoveriesinmedicine.com/Ra-Thy/Syringe.html
6	Wood, Alexander	1817	1884	Morphine and Its Hypodermic Use, Opium and the People, Opiate Use in Nineteenth-Century

				England, Virginia Berridge and Griffith Edwards, Chapter 12
7	Wood, Alexander	1817	1884	Evolution of Medical Application of Syringe, Indian Journal of Physiology and Pharmacology, Volume 50, No 3, 2006, p 202
8	Wood, Alexander	1817	1884	http://www.druglibrary.org/schaffer/History/soldis.htm
1	Gordon, Alexander	1818	1895	The First Landfall: Historic Lighthouses of Newfoundland and Labrador, by David John Molloy, Breakwater, St John's, 1994, p 77
1	Menelaus, William	1818	1882	History of the Iron, Steel, Tinplate and Other Trades of Wales, by Charles Wilkins, Cambridge University Press, 1903, p 291
2	Menelaus, William	1818	1882	http://www.gkn250.com/1825.html
1	Stevenson, Thomas	1818	1887	Oxford Dictionary of National Biography
1	Swan, William	1818	1894	http://www.nationmaster.com/encyclopedia/Swan-bands
2	Swan, William	1818	1894	http://newworlds.colorado.edu/objectives/spectroscopy.htm
3	Swan, William	1818	1894	http://www.europa.com/~telscope/histspec.txt
1	Anderson, Thomas	1819	1874	http://www.nahste.ac.uk/isaar/GB_0237_NAHSTE_P0383.html
2	Anderson, Thomas	1819	1874	http://www.scottish-places.info/scotgaz/people/famousfirst931.html
3	Anderson, Thomas	1819	1874	Oxford Dictionary of National Biography
1	McColl, Hugh	1819	1885	Hugh McColl (1819 - 1885), Australian Dictionary of Biography, Volume 5, Melbourne University Press, 1974, pp 131-132
2	McColl, Hugh	1819	1885	http://www.g-mwater.com.au/warangabasin
1	Pinkerton, Allan	1819	1884	Oxford Dictionary of National Biography
2	Pinkerton, Allan	1819	1884	http://jimfisher.edinboro.edu/forensics/vidocq.html
3	Pinkerton, Allan	1819	1884	http://www.nndb.com/people/223/000093941/
4	Pinkerton, Allan	1819	1884	Appleton's Encyclopedia, 2001
1	Robertson, Alexander Weir	1819	1879	The History of Accounting (RLE Accounting): An International Encyclopedia edited by Michael Chatfield, Richard Vangermeersch, Routledge, 1996, p 477
2	Robertson, Alexander Weir	1819	1879	Seekers of truth: the Scottish founders of modern public accountancy, by Thomas Alexander Lee, Elsevier, Oxford, 2006, pp 313-317

3	Robertson, Alexander Weir	1819	1879	http://gluedideas.com/Encyclopedia-Britannica-Volume-01-A-Anno/Accountancy-and-Accountants.html
4	Robertson, Alexander Weir	1819	1879	http://aaahq.org/southwest/pacioli.htm
5	Robertson, Alexander Weir	1819	1879	Revisionens formål og genstand i reguleringshistorisk og reguleringsteoretisk perspektiv, Bind II: Perioden 1900-1920, Köpenhamn: Handelshøjskolan i København, Det Økonomiske Fakultet, Ph.D. serie 2.2000., pp. 8–9
6	Robertson, Alexander Weir	1819	1879	https://www.victoria.ac.nz/sacl/about/events/past-events2/past-conferences/6ahic/publications/6AHIC-95_FINAL_paper.pdf
7	Robertson, Alexander Weir	1819	1879	http://documents.clubexpress.com/documents.ashx?key=7ZPfhrgSH4ej5qOo06gTZ1j%2FWfzYw%2BhpXBNOQ%2BbRiWgYV1UQpbPezRxbi%2FPDVo7X
8	Robertson, Alexander Weir	1819	1879	The History of the German Public Accounting Profession, by Hugh Brian Markus, Taylor & Francis, 1997 pp 18-19
9	Robertson, Alexander Weir	1819	1879	http://www.scottish.parliament.uk/S4_EconomyEnergyandTourismCommittee/Inquiries/institute_of_chartered_accountants_of_scotland.pdf
1	Baird, John	1820	1891	A Biographical Dictionary of People in Engineering: From the Earliest Records to 2000, by Carl W. Hall, Purdue University Press, 2008, p 11
2	Baird, John	1820	1891	History of American steam navigation, by John Harrison Morrison, published by W. F. Sametz and Co., New York, 1903, p 460
3	Baird, John	1820	1891	Telling a Straight Story, The New York Times, 11 September 1886
1	Dawson, John William	1820	1899	Oxford Dictionary of National Biography
2	Dawson, John William	1820	1899	https://aoc.mcgill.ca/greatest-mcgillians/william-dawson
3	Dawson, John William	1820	1899	http://www.biographi.ca/en/bio/dawson_john_william_12E.htm
1	Dick, Robert	1820	1891	http://www.bbc.co.uk/ahistoryoftheworld/objects/adapsA21S_GzMIhHJ0fhEw
2	Dick, Robert	1820	1891	http://archive.org/stream/miningscien103unse/miningscien103unse_djvu.txt

3	Dick, Robert	1820	1891	Crude rubber and compounding ingredients, by Henry Clemens Pearson, India Rubber Publishing Company, 1918, p 34
4	Dick, Robert	1820	1891	http://mailer.fsu.edu/~akirk/tanks/GreatBritain/BritishHeavyTanks.html
5	Dick, Robert	1820	1891	One Hundred Years of Guttapercha R & J. Dick Ltd., by Thomas Chalmers, Published by R & J Dick Ltd, Glasgow, 1946, p 29
1	Drummond, Charles	1820	1866	http://www.greetingcard.org/AbouttheIndustry/History/tabid/72/Default.aspx
2	Drummond, Charles	1820	1866	http://www.old-prague.com/history-of-postcards.php
3	Drummond, Charles	1820	1866	Edinburgh: A cultural and Literary History, by Donald Campbell, Signal Books Limited, Oxford, 2003, p 178
1	Halkett, Peter Alexander	1820	1885	http://www.manitobamuseum.ca/main/hbc_collection/2012/03/05/halkett-boat-to-halkett-collection/
1	Kirkaldy, David	1820	1897	http://www.richarddonkin.com/Archive/x_selecting_for_type.htm
2	Kirkaldy, David	1820	1897	Three Hundred Years of Assaying American Iron and Iron Ores, by Kevin K. Olsen, Wyeth-Ayerst, Bulletin for the History of Chemistry, 17/18, 1995, p 52
3	Kirkaldy, David	1820	1897	http://resource.npl.co.uk/docs/science_technology/materials/measurement_techniques/tenstand/test_method_review.pdf
4	Kirkaldy, David	1820	1897	Oxford Dictionary of National Biography
5	Kirkaldy, David	1820	1897	Biographical Dictionary of the History of Technology, edited by Lance Day, Ian McNeil, Routledge, 1998, p 403
6	Kirkaldy, David	1820	1897	http://resource.npl.co.uk/docs/science_technology/materials/measurement_techniques/tenstand/test_method_review.pdf
1	Lyle, Abram	1820	1891	http://news.bbc.co.uk/dna/ptop/alabaster/A41606976
2	Lyle, Abram	1820	1891	http://www.tateandlyle.com/aboutus/history/pages/abramlyle.aspx
3	Lyle, Abram	1820	1891	http://news.bbc.co.uk/dna/place-lancashire/plain/A41606976
4	Lyle, Abram	1820	1891	http://www.guinnessworldrecords.com/world-records/4000/oldest-branding-(packaging)
1	Morton, William Lockhart	1820	1898	http://www.elsenburg.com/info/els/075/075e.html

2	Morton, William Lockhart	1820	1898	Australian Veterinary History Record, Australian Veterinary History Society, March 2003, No 36, Cheltenham, Victoria, p 12
3	Morton, William Lockhart	1820	1898	Ibid.
4	Morton, William Lockhart	1820	1898	William Lockhart Morton (1820-1898), by J. Ann Hone, Australian Dictionary of Biography, Vol. 5, Melbourne University Press, 1974, pp 302-303
1	Rankine, William John Macquorn	1820	1872	http://www.britannica.com/EBchecked/topic/491239/William-John-Macquorn-Rankine
2	Rankine, William John Macquorn	1820	1872	http://www.universitystory.gla.ac.uk/biography/?id=WH0067&type=P
3	Rankine, William John Macquorn	1820	1872	http://www.nahste.ac.uk/cgi-bin/view_isad.pl?id=GB-0248-DC-320&view=basic
4	Rankine, William John Macquorn	1820	1872	Rankine, William John Macquorn, edited by Noretta Koertge, Complete Dictionary of Scientific Biography, Scribner, 2008
5	Rankine, William John Macquorn	1820	1872	http://www-history.mcs.st-and.ac.uk/Biographies/Rankine.html
6	Rankine, William John Macquorn	1820	1872	http://www.eoht.info/page/William+Rankine
1	Skene, Alexander John	1820	1894	Alexander John Skene (1820 - 1894), by J. M. Powell, Australian Dictionary of Biography, Volume 6, Melbourne University Press, 1976, pp 131-132
1	Stirling, Patrick	1820	1895	http://www.trainworld.com.au/pricelists/ukbook.pdf
2	Stirling, Patrick	1820	1895	http://www.gracesguide.co.uk/Patrick_Stirling
3	Stirling, Patrick	1820	1895	http://www.bookshops.com.au/isbns/0901115746
1	Taylor, Thomas	1820	1910	http://www.huh.harvard.edu/libraries/Amanita_exhibit/Amanita_images.htm
2	Taylor, Thomas	1820	1910	http://piccaver.weebly.com/uploads/1/1/7/5/1175893/forensic_science.pdf
1	Croll, James	1821	1890	http://www.britsattheirbest.com/ingenious/ii_19th_century_1855.htm
2	Croll, James	1821	1890	http://www.trademe.co.nz/books/rare-collectable/first-editions/auction-45746972.htm
3	Croll, James	1821	1890	Ocean: Reflections on a Century of Exploration, by Wolfgang H. Berger, University of California Press, 2009, p 381
4	Croll, James	1821	1890	http://www.aip.org/history/climate/simple.htm
5	Croll, James	1821	1890	http://earth.usc.edu/~stott/Catalina/Oceans.html
6	Croll, James	1821	1890	http://rsnr.royalsocietypublishing.org/content/early/2011/08/16/rsnr.2011.0021.full

1	Dudgeon, Richard	1821	1899	http://americanhistory.si.edu/onthemove/
1	Meldrum, Charles	1821	1901	Oxford Dictionary of National Biography
1	Napier, James Robert	1821	1879	http://baharris.org/coffee/History.htm
2	Napier, James Robert	1821	1879	http://myreckonings.com/wordpress/2009/04/18/magnetic-deviation-comprehension-compensation-and-computation-part-ii/
1	Nelson, Thomas	1822	1892	The Golden Age of the Newspaper, by George H. Douglas, Greenwood Press, Westport, Connecticut, USA. 1999, p 15
1	Thomson, James	1822	1892	http://www.lakelandmuseum.org.uk/williamson-brothers-vortex-turbine-number-one
2	Thomson, James	1822	1892	http://www.victorianweb.org/technology/ir/14.html
3	Thomson, James	1822	1892	http://www.universitystory.gla.ac.uk/biography/?id=WH2192&type=P
4	Thomson, James	1822	1892	http://www.newulsterbiography.co.uk/index.php/home/viewPerson/1632
1	Thomson, Robert William	1822	1873	http://www.historic-uk.com/HistoryUK/Scotland-History/RobertWilliamThomson.htm
2	Thomson, Robert William	1822	1873	http://www.jstor.org/stable/768897 .Accessed: 28/09/2013
1	Clark, George Aitken	1823	1873	http://www.coatsandclark.com/about+coats/history/
2	Clark, George Aitken	1823	1873	http://socialarchive.iath.virginia.edu/ark:/99166/w66r6wnt
1	Eckford, Henry	1823	1905	http://en.academic.ru/dic.nsf/enwiki/6044225
1	Login, Thomas	1823	1874	Irrigation canals and other irrigation works: including the flow of water in irrigation canals and open and closed channels generally, with tables simplifying and facilitating the application of the formulæ of Kutter, D'Arcy and Bazin" by Patrick John Flynn, San Francisco, 1891, pp 186-187
2	Login, Thomas	1823	1874	Obituary: Thomas Login, Minutes of Proceedings Institution of Civil Engineers, Volume 27, Issue 1875, 1 January 1875, pp 270-271
1	Malcolm, William	1823	1890	http://www.berdansharpshooter.org/target_scopes.htm
1	Oliver, James	1823	1908	Biographical Dictionary of American Business Leaders N-U, by John N. Ingham, Greenwood Press, 1983, p 1028
2	Oliver, James	1823	1908	http://www.indianahistory.org/our-collections/reference/notable-hoosiers/james-oliver

1	Elder, John	1824	1869	Memoirs and portraits of one hundred Glasgow men, by James MacLehose, published by Maclure & Macdonald, Glasgow, 1886 http://gdl.cdlr.strath.ac.uk/mlemen/mlemen031.htm 1 June 2011
1	Fraser, Alexander	1824	1898	http://www.victorianresearch.org/atcl/show_author.php?aid=459
2	Fraser, Alexander	1824	1898	Of Planting and Planning: The making of British colonial cities, by Robert K Home, published by E & FN Spon, London, 1997, p 96
3	Fraser, Alexander	1824	1898	http://pharology.eu/Burma.html
4	Fraser, Alexander	1824	1898	http://www.echo-news.co.uk/news/3951213.print/
5	Fraser, Alexander	1824	1898	Fraser of North Cape: The Life of Admiral of the Fleet, Lord Fraser, 1887-1981, by Richard Humble, published by Routledge & Kegan Paul plc, London, 1983, p 5
1	Kerr, John	1824	1907	Light and Matter: Electromagnetism, Optics, Spectroscopy and Lasers, by Yehuda B. Band, John Wiley & Sons Ltd, Chichester, England, 2006, p 143
2	Kerr, John	1824	1907	http://micro.magnet.fsu.edu/optics/timeline/people/kerr.html
1	Samuel, James	1824	1874	Memoirs, Obituary, James Samuel, 1824-1874, Minutes of the Proceedings, Journal of the Institute of Civil Engineers, Volume 39, Issue 1875, 1 January 1875, p 281
1	Smith, Alexander Kennedy	1824	1881	Alexander Kennedy Smith (1824 - 1881), by Jill Eastwood, Australian Dictionary of Biography, Vol. 6, Melbourne University Press, 1976, p. 139
1	Thomson, William	1824	1907	http://todayinsci.com/K/Kelvin_Lord/Kelvin_Lord1.htm
2	Thomson, William	1824	1907	http://www.magnet.fsu.edu/education/tutorials/pioneers/kelvin.html
3	Thomson, William	1824	1907	http://www.britannica.com/EBchecked/topic/314541/William-Thomson-Baron-Kelvin/13896/Later-life
4	Thomson, William	1824	1907	Encyclopedia of Research Design, Volume 1, edited by Neil J. Salkind, SAGE Publications, 2010, p 629
5	Thomson, William	1824	1907	The 100 Most Influential Scientists of All Time, edited by Kara Rogers, Britannica Educational Publishing, 2012, p 193
6	Thomson, William	1824	1907	The Cambridge History of Science: Volume 5, Edited by Mary Jo Nye, Cambridge University Press, 2003, p 299

7	Thomson, William	1824	1907	Oxford Dictionary of National Biography
8	Thomson, William	1824	1907	Inventions and Discoveries, by Valerie-Anne Giscard d'Estaing and Mark Young, Published by Facts on File Inc., New York, 1993, p 38
9	Thomson, William	1824	1907	http://www.eoearth.org/view/article/154011/
10	Thomson, William	1824	1907	http://www.nahste.ac.uk/isaar/GB_0237_NAHSTE_P0385.html
11	Thomson, William	1824	1907	http://www.iec.ch/about/history/beginning/founding_iec.htm
12	Thomson, William	1824	1907	Scottish Firsts, by Elspeth Wills, Mainstream Publishing, Edinburgh, 2006, p 99
13	Thomson, William	1824	1907	http://www.history-magazine.com/cable.html
14	Thomson, William	1824	1907	Ink Jet Textile Printing by Christina Cie, Woodhead Publishing, Cambridge, 2015, p 16
15	Thomson, William	1824	1907	http://encyclopedia.thefreedictionary.com/Kelvin+water+dropper
16	Thomson, William	1824	1907	http://www.public.asu.edu/~gbadams/tides/
17	Thomson, William	1824	1907	http://digital.nls.uk/scientists/biographies/lord-kelvin/discoveries.html
18	Thomson, William	1824	1907	From Energy to Information: Representation in Science and Technology, Art, and Literature, edit. by Bruce Clarke, Linda Dalrymple Henderson, Stanford University Press, California, 2002, p 173
19	Thomson, William	1824	1907	http://www.rutherfordjournal.org/article020106.html
20	Thomson, William	1824	1907	http://todayinsci.com/K/Kelvin_Lord/Kelvin_Lord1.htm
21	Thomson, William	1824	1907	http://digital.nls.uk/scientists/biographies/lord-kelvin/discoveries.html
22	Thomson, William	1824	1907	Biographical Dictionary of the History of Technology, edited by Lance Day, Ian McNeil, Routledge, 1998, p 1216
23	Thomson, William	1824	1907	http://www.seasky.org/ocean-exploration/ocean-timeline-1801-1900.html
24	Thomson, William	1824	1907	http://todayinsci.com/K/Kelvin_Lord/Kelvin_Lord1.htm
25	Thomson, William	1824	1907	http://scitation.aip.org/content/aapt/journal/ajp/77/6/10.1119/1.3095813
26	Thomson, William	1824	1907	Geological Sciences, edited by John P. Rafferty, Britannica Educational Publishing, New York, 2012, p 181

| 27 | Thomson, William | 1824 | 1907 | http://www.gla.ac.uk/news/archiveofnews/2007/december/headline_59629_en.html |
| 28 | Thomson, William | 1824 | 1907 | http://dspace.gla.ac.uk:8080/bitstream/1905/701/1/Kelvin+tribute.pdf |

Chapter 4
1825-1849

1	Brown, Andrew	1825	1907	http://www.panoramio.com/photo/10797526
2	Brown, Andrew	1825	1907	Minutes of the Proceedings, Institution of Civil Engineers, Volume 170, Issue 1907, p 385
1	Hartley, Charles Augustus	1825	1915	Oxford Dictionary of National Biography
2	Hartley, Charles Augustus	1825	1915	Encyclopaedia Britannica 1911
1	Shanks, John	1825	1895	http://www.redoakleaves.com/downloads/The_hidden_room.pdf
2	Shanks, John	1825	1895	http://www.gracesguide.co.uk/Shanks_and_Co
3	Shanks, John	1825	1895	Oxford Dictionary of National Biography
1	Laird, John P	1826	1882	A History of the American Locomotive: Its Development, 1830-1880, by John H White Jnr., Dover Publications Inc., 1968, p 454
2	Laird, John P	1826	1882	Regulating Railroad Innovation: Business, Technology, and Politics in America, 1840-1920, by Steven W Usselman, Cambridge University Press, New York, 2002, p 104
3	Laird, John P	1826	1882	http://railfanning.org/rolling/2-8-0/
1	Ormiston, Thomas	1826	1882	The Sydney Mail, 7 June 1879
2	Ormiston, Thomas	1826	1882	Obituary, Thomas Ormiston, CIE, 1826-1882, Minutes of the Proceedings, Journal of the Institution of Civil Engineers, Volume 71, Issue 1883, 1 January 1883, p 411
1	Black, Alexander	1827	1897	http://www.adb.online.anu.edu.au/biogs/A030158b.htm
2	Black, Alexander	1827	1897	One Hundred Years of Engineering in Victoria, edit. L. R. East, Journal of the Institution of Engineers Australia, Melbourne, 1934, p 390
1	Fleming, Sandford	1827	1915	http://members.kos.net/sdgagnon/grc.html
2	Fleming, Sandford	1827	1915	Oxford Dictionary of National Biography

3	Fleming, Sandford	1827	1915	Dictionary of Canadian Biography Online
4	Fleming, Sandford	1827	1915	Oxford Dictionary of National Biography
5	Fleming, Sandford	1827	1915	http://www.canadafreepress.com/index.php/article/21200
6	Fleming, Sandford	1827	1915	Canadian Dictionary of Biography
7	Fleming, Sandford	1827	1915	http://inventors.about.com/od/fstartinventors/a/SandfordFleming.htm
1	Greig, David	1827	1891	http://www.steamploughclub.org.uk/history.html
2	Greig, David	1827	1891	http://www.nationalarchives.gov.uk/a2a/records.aspx?cat=007-fowler_2&cid=-1#-1
1	Watson, William Stuart	1827	X	Lives and works of civil and military engineers of America, by Charles B. [Beebe] Stuart, published by D. Van Nostrand, New York, 1871, pp 294-300
1	Campbell, Duncan Hector	1828	1894	http://www.campbell-randall.com/machines/sewing-machines/campbell-lockstitch-sewing-machine/
2	Campbell, Duncan Hector	1828	1894	http://www.massofficespace.com/bldgs_mod_awards_apr2000.htm
1	O'Neill, Charles Gordon	1828	1900	Australian Dictionary of Biography
1	Ritchie, Frederick James	1828	1906	http://www.ritchies-edinburgh.co.uk/mainpages/history.html
2	Ritchie, Frederick James	1828	1906	Electric Clocks, by Frank Hope-Jones, N.A.G. Press, London, 1931, p 24
1	Stewart, Balfour	1828	1887	http://www.astro.umontreal.ca/~paulchar/grps/histoire/newsite/bio/stewart_e.html
2	Stewart, Balfour	1828	1887	http://www.britannica.com/EBchecked/topic/566011/Balfour-Stewart
3	Stewart, Balfour	1828	1887	Weather, Volume 57, Issue 4, p 141
1	Waddell, John	1828	1888	http://www.engineering-timelines.com/scripts/engineeringItem.asp?id=840
1	Browne, James	1829	1896	The rise of rail-power in war and conquest, 1833-1914, with a bibliography, by Edwin A Pratt, published by P.S. King & Son Ltd, Westminster, 1915, p 33
1	Buchan, Alexander	1829	1907	http://www.britannica.com/EBchecked/topic/539101/Sir-Napier-Shaw
2	Buchan, Alexander	1829	1907	http://www.scottish-places.info/scotgaz/people/famousfirst412.html
3	Buchan, Alexander	1829	1907	http://weatherfaqs.org.uk/node/179

4	Buchan, Alexander	1829	1907	http://www.weathercast.co.uk/weather-news/news/ch/23ba64ba62807a6e3d649985141b30d3/article/alexander_buchan-1.html
1	Galbraith, William Robert	1829	1914	http://www.steamindex.com/people/civils.htm
1	Gordon, George	1829	1907	Victorian Water Supply Heritage Study, Volume 1: Thematic Environmental History, Final Report, 31 October 2007 - Prepared for Heritage Victoria, p 25
2	Gordon, George	1829	1907	Ibid. p 32
1	Jamieson, Thomas Francis	1829	1913	http://www.scottish-places.info/scotgaz/people/famousfirst2418.html
2	Jamieson, Thomas Francis	1829	1913	http://journals.cambridge.org/download.php?file=%2FGEO%2FGEO5_10_07%2FS00167568001 26913a.pdf&code=0b563742baa284efa467b20ce538f628
1	Moncrieff, Alexander	1829	1906	http://www.navyandmarine.org/ondeck/1880DisappearingGuns.htm
1	Moodie, George Pigot	1829	1891	Pretoriana, Magazine of the Old Pretoria Society, Volume 71 April-December 1973, pp 36-38
1	Rose, Lauchlan	1829	1885	Genius! Deceptively simple ways to become instantly smarter, by James Bannerman, Pearson Education Canada, 2012 (pages not numbered)
2	Rose, Lauchlan	1829	1885	http://tablet.scotsman.com/firsts-city-s-forgotten-1-855468
3	Rose, Lauchlan	1829	1885	Terrors of the Table: The curious history of nutrition, by Walter Gratzer, Oxford University Press, 2005 (No page numbers - Chapter 2: Lime juice for all)
4	Rose, Lauchlan	1829	1885	http://www.leithlocalhistorysociety.org.uk/businesses/roses_lime_juice.htm
5	Rose, Lauchlan	1829	1885	http://www.lennoxhonychurch.com/heritage.cfm?Id=191
6	Rose, Lauchlan	1829	1885	http://thevintagedrink.com/ingredients/lime-juice-cordial-drink-recipes
1	Wigham, John Richardson	1829	1906	http://maritimeinstituteofireland.wordpress.com/history-2/articles/people/john-richardson-wigham/
2	Wigham, John Richardson	1829	1906	Oxford Dictionary of National Biography
1	Buchanan, William	1830	1910	http://softsource.com/999.html
2	Buchanan, William	1830	1910	http://www.msichicago.org/whats-here/exhibits/transportation-gallery/the-exhibit/999-steam-locomotive/

1	Fairlie, Robert Francis	1830	1885	http://www.steamindex.com/people/fairlie.htm
1	Fyfe, John	1830	1906	http://mcjazz.f2s.com/GraniteMasons.htm
2	Fyfe, John	1830	1906	Ibid.
1	Kinnear, Charles George Hood	1830	1894	http://www.antiquewoodcameras.com/ottewill.html
1	Kirkaldy, Alexander Carnegie	1830	1892	Obituary, Alexander Carnegie Kirk, Institution of Civil Engineers, Minutes of the Proceedings, Volume 111, Issue 1893, 1 January 1893, p 382
2	Kirkaldy, Alexander Carnegie	1830	1892	http://www.iifiir.org/en/doc/1037.pdf
3	Kirkaldy, Alexander Carnegie	1830	1892	http://www.gracesguide.co.uk/Alexander_Carnegie_Kirk
1	Montgomerie, Thomas George	1830	1878	http://www.mountainsoftravelphotos.com/Gasherbrum%20I/Main.html
2	Montgomerie, Thomas George	1830	1878	http://www.himalayanclub.org/journal/survey-of-kashmir-and-jammu-1855-to-1865/
3	Montgomerie, Thomas George	1830	1878	Fallen Giants: A History of Himalayan Mountaineering from the Age of Empire to the Age of Extremes, by Maurice Isserman, Stewart Angas Weaver, 2008, p 18
4	Montgomerie, Thomas George	1830	1878	Oxford Dictionary of National Biography
1	Paterson, Robert Adams	1830	1904	First, Last & Only: Golf, by Paul Donnelly, Octopus Publishing Group, London, 2010, p 1875
2	Paterson, Robert Adams	1830	1904	http://www.thedesignshop.com/history.htm
1	Pringle, Thomas	1830	1911	http://qed.econ.queensu.ca/pub/faculty/mcinnis/EngineeringExpertise.pdf
2	Pringle, Thomas	1830	1911	Dictionary of Canadian Biography Online
1	Couper, Archibald Scott	1831	1892	http://www.scottish-enterprise.com/microsites/chemical-sciences-scotland/chemical-sciences-in-scotland/scotlands-heritage-in-chemical-sciences.aspx#barton
2	Couper, Archibald Scott	1831	1892	Robert Burns Woodward: Architect and Artist in the World of Molecules, edited by Otto Theodor Benfey, Peter John Turnbull Morris, The Chemical Heritage Foundation, Philadelphia, 2001, p 440
1	Gray, John McFarlane	1831	1893	http://www.encyclopedia.com/topic/steering_gear.aspx

2	Gray, John McFarlane	1831	1893	North of England Institute of Mining and Mechanical Engineers, Transactions, Volume 29, printed by A. Reid, Newcastle-upon-Tyne, 1880
1	Lee, James Paris	1831	1904	http://www.cambridge.ca/cs_pubaccess/hall_of_fame.php?aid=93&cpid=0&did=0&sid=0&ssid=0&tp=0&grid=0
2	Lee, James Paris	1831	1904	http://www.pchswi.org/archives/bios/jamesparislee.html
3	Lee, James Paris	1831	1904	http://bsamuseum.wordpress.com/1916-lee-enfield-smle-no-1-mk-iii/
4	Lee, James Paris	1831	1904	http://www.pchswi.org/archives/bios/jamesparislee.html
1	Maxwell, James Clerk	1831	1879	http://www.britannica.com/EBchecked/topic/370686/Maxwells-equations
2	Maxwell, James Clerk	1831	1879	http://www.libraryindex.com/encyclopedia/pages/cpxkur1ull/maxwell-james-clerk-theory.html
3	Maxwell, James Clerk	1831	1879	Biographical Dictionary of the History of Technology, by Lance Day, Ian McNeil, Routledge, London, 1998, 2003, p 475
4	Maxwell, James Clerk	1831	1879	http://faculty.wcas.northwestern.edu/~infocom/Ideas/maxwell.html
5	Maxwell, James Clerk	1831	1879	Ibid.
6	Maxwell, James Clerk	1831	1879	http://inst.gov.vn/ispun11/Proceeding/Dang.pdf
7	Maxwell, James Clerk	1831	1879	http://www.sciencetimeline.net/1651.htm
8	Maxwell, James Clerk	1831	1879	http://www.manhattanrarebooks.com/pages/books/958/james-clerk-maxwell/on-governors
9	Maxwell, James Clerk	1831	1879	http://journalofcosmology.com/Consciousness125.html
10	Maxwell, James Clerk	1831	1879	Physics Before and After Einstein, edited by Marco Mamone Capria, University of Perugia, IOS Press, Oxford, 2005, p 32
11	Maxwell, James Clerk	1831	1879	http://www.sciencetimeline.net/1866.htm
12	Maxwell, James Clerk	1831	1879	http://faculty.wcas.northwestern.edu/~infocom/Ideas/maxwell.html
13	Maxwell, James Clerk	1831	1879	Ibid.
14	Maxwell, James Clerk	1831	1879	http://www.biographyonline.net/scientists/james-maxwell.html
15	Maxwell, James Clerk	1831	1879	http://www.clerkmaxwellfoundation.org/html/who_was_maxwell_.html

16	Maxwell, James Clerk	1831	1879	http://www.westerncultureglobal.org/maxwell.html
17	Maxwell, James Clerk	1831	1879	A History of Knowledge, Past, Present, Future by Charles Van Doren, Ballentine Books, New York, April 1992, p 271
18	Maxwell, James Clerk	1831	1879	http://www.geog.ucsb.edu/~jeff/115a/history/jamesclarkemaxwell.html
1	Noble, Andrew	1831	1915	http://www.britannica.com/EBchecked/topic/116333/chronoscope
2	Noble, Andrew	1831	1915	http://www.britannia.com/celtic/scotland/greatscots/n1.html
3	Noble, Andrew	1831	1915	Encyclopaedia Britannica, Volume 6, 1911
1	Tait, Peter Guthrie	1831	1901	http://www.britannica.com/EBchecked/topic/580898/Peter-Guthrie-Tait
2	Tait, Peter Guthrie	1831	1901	http://www.gresham.ac.uk/lectures-and-events/peter-guthrie-tait-a-knots-tale
3	Tait, Peter Guthrie	1831	1901	http://scienceworld.wolfram.com/biography/Tait.html
4	Tait, Peter Guthrie	1831	1901	http://www.robertnowlan.com/pdfs/Tait,%20Peter%20Guthrie.pdf
1	Howden, John	1832	1913	Fact Book, Charter plc, London August 1998, p 29
2	Howden, John	1832	1913	Studies in Scottish Business History, by Peter Lester Payne, Routledge, 2006, p 285
1	Maxwell, John S	1832	1916	http://www.militaryhistoryonline.com/civilwar/articles/citypoint.aspx
1	Stewart, Patrick	1832	1865	http://www.scottish-places.info/people/famousfirst3778.html
1	Harper, John	1833	1906	http://www.scottisharchitects.org.uk/architect_full.php?id=201747
1	Jenkin, Henry Charles Fleeming	1833	1885	Oxford Dictionary of National Biography
1	Lee, John	1833	1907	http://www.geocities.ws/nzsrhc/more-news.html
1	Brunton, John	1835	1899	http://www.rcpsg.ac.uk/en/library/archive-and-heritage/instrument-collection/auroscope-invented-by-john-brunton.aspx
2	Brunton, John	1835	1899	http://issuu.com/racgp/docs/wywjune2009
1	Campbell, Archibald	1835	1908	http://archive.is/TrF1h
1	Geikie, Archibald	1835	1924	http://www.minrec.org/libdetail.asp?id=440
2	Geikie, Archibald	1835	1924	http://www.haslemeremuseum.co.uk/geikie_files/Geikie%20leaflet.pdf
3	Geikie, Archibald	1835	1924	A Natural History of Time by Pascal Richet, The University of Chicago Press, 2012, p 217
4	Geikie, Archibald	1835	1924	Oxford Dictionary of National Biography

1	Bell, Imrie	1836	1906	Biographical Dictionary of the History of Technology, by Lance Day, Ian McNeil, Routledge, London, 1996, p94
1	Brock, Walter	1836	1907	http://www.norwayheritage.com/articles/templates/ships.asp?articleid=87&zoneid=5
2	Brock, Walter	1836	1907	Studies in Scottish Business History, edited by Peter Lester Payne, Published Routledge, 2006, p 282
1	Carruthers, John	1836	1914	Dictionary of New Zealand Biography
1	Hallidie, Andrew Smith	1836	1900	http://www.sierranevadavirtualmuseum.com/docs/specialex/biographies/hallidiea.htm
2	Hallidie, Andrew Smith	1836	1900	http://www.sfmuseum.net/bio/hallidie.html
3	Hallidie, Andrew Smith	1836	1900	http://vr00mf0nd3l.wordpress.com/tag/andrew-s-hallidie/#mechanics
1	Lyall, James	1836	1901	Appleton's Cyclopedia of American Biography, edited by James Grant Wilson, John Fiske and Stanley L. Klos, Publ. D. Appleton and Company, New York, 1887-1889
1	Scott-Moncrieff, Colin Campbell	1836	1916	Growth of the British Empire, by M. B. Synge, published by Yesterday's Classics, Chapel Hill, North Carolina, 2006, p 199
2	Scott-Moncrieff, Colin Campbell	1836	1916	Imperial Rivers: Irrigation and British Visions of Empire, David Gilmartin, North Carolina State University, p 20
3	Scott-Moncrieff, Colin Campbell	1836	1916	http://www.britannica.com/EBchecked/topic/1574304/Scott-Moncrieff-Commission
4	Scott-Moncrieff, Colin Campbell	1836	1916	http://parker.ou.edu/~bwallach/documents/Losing%20Asia%20-%20Ch%204.pdf
5	Scott-Moncrieff, Colin Campbell	1836	1916	Losing Asia: Modernization and the Culture of Development: Chapter 4: Irrigation in British India, Bret Wallach, The Johns Hopkins Press, Baltimore, 1996, p 27
1	Boyle, David	1837	1891	http://www.tshaonline.org/handbook/online/articles/dqr01
1	Harkness, William	1837	1903	http://www.mreclipse.com/Totality2/TotalityApH.html
2	Harkness, William	1837	1903	http://leroy.cc.uregina.ca/~weilds/john.html
3	Harkness, William	1837	1903	Nature, Issue 140, 11 December 1937, p 1004
1	McClean, Frank	1837	1904	Oxford Dictionary of National Biography
2	McClean, Frank	1837	1904	http://arxiv.org/ftp/arxiv/papers/1309/1309.5199.pdf

1	Murray, Stuart	1837	1919	Murray, Stuart (1837-1919) Australian Dictionary of Biography, Online Edition
1	Newlands, John Alexander Reina	1837	1898	http://www.cartage.org.lb/en/themes/Biographies/MainBiographies/N/Newlands/1.html
2	Newlands, John Alexander Reina	1837	1898	http://www.rsc.org/education/teachers/resources/periodictable/pre16/develop/newlands.htm
1	Brown, Alexander Crum	1838	1922	http://www.chem.ed.ac.uk/about-us/history-school/professors/alexander-crum-brown
2	Brown, Alexander Crum	1838	1922	http://link.springer.com/chapter/10.1007%2F978-94-015-9737-1_3#
1	Glover, Thomas Blake	1838	1911	Oxford Dictionary of National Biography
2	Glover, Thomas Blake	1838	1911	http://www.mitsubishi.com/e/history/series/thomas/index.html
3	Glover, Thomas Blake	1838	1911	http://www4.rgu.ac.uk/files/GloverJapaneseSeminarInvite1.pdf
4	Glover, Thomas Blake	1838	1911	The Japan Times, 11 December 2011
1	Maclagan, Thomas John	1838	1903	http://www.biomedsearch.com/nih/Perthshire-pioneer-anti-inflammatory-agents/3327165.html
2	Maclagan, Thomas John	1838	1903	Nonsteroidal anti-inflammatory drug prescribing: past, present, and future, by Roger Jones, The American Journal of Medicine, Volume 110, Issue 1A, January 2001
3	Maclagan, Thomas John	1838	1903	Aspirin: The Remarkable Story of a Wonder Drug, Diarmuid Jeffreys, Bloomsbury Publishing, New York, 2005, p 50
4	Maclagan, Thomas John	1838	1903	Choice of NSAID: Safety Profile, by W. Watson Buchanan and Walter F. Kean, Singapore Medical Journal, Volume 28, 1987, p 478
5	Maclagan, Thomas John	1838	1903	Aspirin: The Remarkable Story of a Wonder Drug, Diarmuid Jeffreys, Bloomsbury Publishing, New York, 2005, pp 52-54
6	Maclagan, Thomas John	1838	1903	http://www.jameslindlibrary.org/illustrating/articles/thomas-john-maclagan-1838-1903
1	Muir, John	1838	1914	http://www.sierraclub.org/john_muir_exhibit/intro.aspx
2	Muir, John	1838	1914	http://www.pbs.org/nationalparks/people/historical/muir/
3	Muir, John	1838	1914	http://www.sierraclub.org/john_muir_exhibit/intro.aspx
4	Muir, John	1838	1914	http://books.google.com.au/books?id=rQG2tdf5n4UC&printsec=frontcover#v=onepage&q&f=false

5	Muir, John	1838	1914	http://www.britannica.com/EBchecked/topic/396596/John-Muir
1	Nairn, Michael Barker	1838	1915	Employer Strategy and the Labour Market, edited by Jill Rubery, Frank Wilkinson, Oxford university Press, 2002, p 207
2	Nairn, Michael Barker	1838	1915	Oxford Dictionary of National Biography
1	Aitken, John	1839	1919	Oxford Dictionary of National Biography
2	Aitken, John	1839	1919	Collected scientific papers of John Aitken, Cambridge University Press, 1923, p 114
3	Aitken, John	1839	1919	http://www.britannica.com/EBchecked/topic/11151/Aitken-nucleus
4	Aitken, John	1839	1919	Atmospheric Aerosol Science Before 1900, Paper presented at the Meeting "History of Aerosol Science", Vienna, Austria, August 31-September 2, 1999, by Rudolf B. Husar, Center for Air Pollution Impact and Trend Analysis, Washington University, St. Louis, pp13-14 - Submitted to Journal of Aerosol Science
1	Arrol, William	1839	1913	Machinations: computational studies of logic, language, and cognition, by Richard Spencer-Smith, Stephen B. Torrance, Ablex Publishing Corporation, Norwood NJ, 1992, p 68
2	Arrol, William	1839	1913	Spans: The Quarterly Newsletter of Inspired Bridge Technologies Volume 7, October 2009, p 3
3	Arrol, William	1839	1913	The Arrol, Arroll and Arrell Families, John Arrol and Robert Arrol, Penn and Ink, Berkeley, California, 1994, p 127
1	Binnie, Alexander Richardson	1839	1917	A Vision for London 1889-1914: Labour, Everyday Life and the LCC Experiment, by Susan Dabney Pennybacker, Routledge, 1995, p 279
1	Blyth, James	1839	1906	http://windsector.tumblr.com/post/4711554356/the-first-wind-turbine-in-america
2	Blyth, James	1839	1906	http://www.strath.ac.uk/archives/iotm/march2012/
1	Geikie, James	1839	1915	http://www.nahste.ac.uk/cgi-bin/view_isad.pl?id=GB-0237-James-Geikie&view=basic
2	Geikie, James	1839	1915	http://www.scottish-places.info/people/famousfirst150.html
3	Geikie, James	1839	1915	http://www.scottishgeology.com/geo/famous-scottish-geologists/james-geikie-1839-1915/

1	Johnston, John Lawson	1839	1900	The Coming Race, by Edward Bulwer-Lytton, edited with an Introduction by David Seed, Wesleyan University Press, 2006, p xli
2	Johnston, John Lawson	1839	1900	http://www.cooksinfo.com/john-lawson-johnston
3	Johnston, John Lawson	1839	1900	Ibid.
4	Johnston, John Lawson	1839	1900	http://www.health24.com/Experts/Question/marmite-20061117
5	Johnston, John Lawson	1839	1900	http://www.cooksinfo.com/john-lawson-johnston
6	Johnston, John Lawson	1839	1900	The Scotsman, 8 June 2010
7	Johnston, John Lawson	1839	1900	The Coming Race, by Edward Bulwer-Lytton, edited with an Introduction by David Seed, Wesleyan university Press, 2006, p xli
1	Proudfoot, David	1839	1891	Dictionary of New Zealand
1	Drummond, Dugald	1840	1912	Obituary, Dugald Drummond, 1840-1912, Minutes of Proceedings, Journal of the Institution of Civil Engineers, Vol. 195, No. 1914, 1 Jan 1914, pp 371-372
1	Dunlop, John Boyd	1840	1921	Oxford Dictionary of National Biography
2	Dunlop, John Boyd	1840	1921	http://www.scotlandspeoplehub.gov.uk/famous/examples/c-d.html
1	Ferguson, Peter Jack	1840	1911	Biographical Dictionary of the History of Technology, edited by Lance Day, Ian McNeil, Routledge, London, 1996, p 442
1	Galloway, William	1840	1927	Oxford Dictionary of National Biography
1	Melvin, David Neilson	1840	1914	Morris's Memorial History of Staten Island, by Ira K Morris, published by Ira K Morris, Staten Island, 1900, p 516
1	Orr, John Bryson	1840	1933	http://www.niir.org/books/book/zb,,19_a_30_0_3e8/Manufacture+of+Paint,+Varnish+&+Allied+Products/index.html
2	Orr, John Bryson	1840	1933	http://patrickbaty.co.uk/2012/04/07/orrs-white/
1	Stanley, Henry Charles	1840	1921	http://espace.library.uq.edu.au/eserv/UQ:9054/ARTI89_2.pdf
2	Stanley, Henry Charles	1840	1921	http://www.yourbrisbanepastandpresent.com/2013/02/tighnabruaich-indooroopilly.html
1	Tait, William	1840	1921	The Herald, 20 March 1997
1	Blair, William Newsham	1841	1891	Dictionary of New Zealand Biography

1	Brunton, Richard Henry	1841	1901	http://search.barnesandnoble.com/booksearch/isbnInquiry.asp?z=y&endeca=1&isbn=0313277958&itm=4
2	Brunton, Richard Henry	1841	1901	http://www.edinburgh.uk.emb-japan.go.jp/speechSDI.htm
3	Brunton, Richard Henry	1841	1901	Richard Henry Brunton 1841-1901, by Archibald Watt, 1996
4	Brunton, Richard Henry	1841	1901	Building Japan, 1868-1876, R. Henry Brunton, Routledge, by Hidenobu Takahide, Doctor Engineering, Mayor, City of Yokohama, 1991, p 2
1	Fraser, Thomas Richard	1841	1920	History of the Disorders of Cardiac Rhythm, by Berndt Lüderitz, 3rd edition, Futura Publishing Company, 2002, p 91
2	Fraser, Thomas Richard	1841	1920	Neuromuscular blocking drugs: discovery and development, by Thandla Raghavendra, Journal of The Royal Society of Medicine, Volume 95, No 7, 2002, p 364
3	Fraser, Thomas Richard	1841	1920	Calabar Bean, Encyclopaedia Britannica, 1911
4	Fraser, Thomas Richard	1841	1920	The Early Toxicology of Physostigmine: A Tale of Beans, Great Men and Egos, by Alex Proudfoot, Toxicological Reviews, Volume 25, Issue 2, pp 99-138
1	Houston, David Henderson	1841	1906	http://inventors.about.com/library/inventors/bl_rolled_film_camera.htm
1	McKay, Alexander	1841	1917	http://www.tinynet.com/faults.html
2	McKay, Alexander	1841	1917	http://www.wcrc.govt.nz/Resources/Documents/NaturalHazardsResourceKit/Appendix1.pdf
3	McKay, Alexander	1841	1917	Dictionary of New Zealand Biography
4	McKay, Alexander	1841	1917	http://www.nzetc.org/tm/scholarly/tei-BuiMoaH-t1-body-d0-d2-d1-d1.html
5	McKay, Alexander	1841	1917	http://www.lensrentals.com/blog/2011/02/who-invented-the-telephoto-lens
1	McKendrick, John Gray	1841	1926	The Glasgow Medical Faculty 1869–1892: From Lister To Macewen, by H. Conway and R.T. Hutcheson, Journal of the Royal College of Physicians of Edinburgh, Volume 32, 2002, p 56
2	McKendrick, John Gray	1841	1926	Obituary, The British Medical Journal, 9 January 1926, pp 72-73
3	McKendrick, John Gray	1841	1926	Oxford Dictionary of National Biography
1	Murray, John	1841	1914	http://www.geos.ed.ac.uk/public/JohnMurray.html

2	Murray, John	1841	1914	http://www.questia.com/library/1G1-135661562/sir-john-murray-1841-1914-the-founder-of-modern
3	Murray, John	1841	1914	http://www.geos.ed.ac.uk/public/JohnMurray.html
1	Dewar, James	1842	1923	http://inventors.about.com/library/inventors/blthermos.htm
2	Dewar, James	1842	1923	Sources of Power: How Energy Forges Human History, by Manfred Weissenbacher, Greenwood Publishing Group, Santa Barbara CA, 2009, p 278
3	Dewar, James	1842	1923	http://www.phys.ufl.edu/courses/phy4550-6555c/spring09/milestones.pdf
1	Macdougall, Alan	1842	1897	Dictionary of Canadian Biography Online
1	Rennie, John	1842	1918	London and Liverpool Journal of Commerce, 7 October 1918
1	Smith, Walter Mucarsay	1842	1906	http://www.lner.info/eng/smith.shtml
1	Weir, James	1842	1920	Oxford Dictionary of National Biography
2	Weir, James	1842	1920	Scottish Firsts by Elspeth Wills, Mainstream Publishing, Edinburgh, 2006, p 120
1	Edgar, James	1843	1909	The Great Santa Search, by Jeff Guinn, Penguin Group, London, 2006, Chapter 1 (no page numbers)
2	Edgar, James	1843	1909	How dreary the world would be without Santa Claus, by Cecelia Goodnow, Seattle Post-Intelligencer, 18 November 2004
3	Edgar, James	1843	1909	http://www.firstdepartmentstoresanta.com/Edgar Award/
4	Edgar, James	1843	1909	http://www.enterprisenews.com/x1013044544/James-Edgar-s-Santa-Claus-the-spirit-of-Christmas?view=pop
1	Ferrier, David	1843	1928	http://www.aim25.ac.uk/cats/8/7194.htm
2	Ferrier, David	1843	1928	http://www.cerebromente.org.br/n18/history/ferrier_i.htm
3	Ferrier, David	1843	1928	The Functions of the Brain: Gall to Ferrier, by Robert M. Young, published by Isis, Volume 59, Part 3, No. 198, 1968, pp. 251-68
4	Ferrier, David	1843	1928	www.dictionaryofneurology.com/search/label/Discovery
5	Ferrier, David	1843	1928	A History of Cerebral Localization, by P. Benjamin Kerr, Anthony J. Caputy, and Norman H. Horwitz, Neurosurgical Focus, Volume 18, No 4, April 2005, pp 1-3
6	Ferrier, David	1843	1928	Minds Behind the Brain: A History of the Pioneers and Their Discoveries, by Stanley Finger, Oxford University Press, 2005, p 175

1	Gill, David	1843	1914	http://www.phys-astro.sonoma.edu/brucemedalists/gill/
2	Gill, David	1843	1914	http://www.lcas-astronomy.org/articles/display.php?filename=david_gill&category=biographies
1	Brunton, Thomas Lauder	1844	1916	http://www.britannica.com/EBchecked/topic/82311/Sir-Thomas-Lauder-Brunton-1st-Baronet
2	Brunton, Thomas Lauder	1844	1916	http://www.biotext.com/NO.pdf
3	Brunton, Thomas Lauder	1844	1916	Ibid.
4	Brunton, Thomas Lauder	1844	1916	http://www.cccgroup.info/drugcdc.asp
5	Brunton, Thomas Lauder	1844	1916	Landmarks in Cardiac Surgery, by Stephen Westaby and Cecil Bosher, Isis Medical Media, Oxford, 1997, p 139
6	Brunton, Thomas Lauder	1844	1916	Preludes and Progress, T. Lauder Brunton and amyl nitrite: a Victorian vasodilator, by W. Bruce Fye, Circulation: journal of the American Heart Association, Volume 74, No. 2, August 1986, pp 222-229
7	Brunton, Thomas Lauder	1844	1916	Ibid.
8	Brunton, Thomas Lauder	1844	1916	http://www.britannica.com/EBchecked/topic/82311/Sir-Thomas-Lauder-Brunton-1st-Baronet
1	Buchanan, John Young	1844	1925	Eos, Volume 67, No 40, 7 October 1986, p 109
1	Hunter, Robert	1844	1913	http://ntplanning.wordpress.com/2013/02/11/remembering-sir-robert-hunter-1844-1913/
2	Hunter, Robert	1844	1913	http://pcwww.liv.ac.uk/~Sinclair/ALGY399_Site/national_trust.html
3	Hunter, Robert	1844	1913	Obituaries, The Times, 7 November 1913, p 9
4	Hunter, Robert	1844	1913	http://www.oss.org.uk/what-we-do/about-us/sir-robert-hunter-1844-1913/
5	Hunter, Robert	1844	1913	http://www.conservationinnovation.com/sites/poci.dl-dev.com/files/Turner%20slides%2010.9.09.pdf
1	Lumsden, Hugh David	1844	1896	http://www.trentu.ca/admin/library/archives/77-001.htm
1	Manson, Patrick	1844	1922	http://www.britannica.com/EBchecked/topic/362832/Sir-Patrick-Manson
2	Manson, Patrick	1844	1922	http://www.lshtm.ac.uk/library/archives/history/frieze/manson.html

3	Manson, Patrick	1844	1922	http://www.sahistory.org.za/dated-event/sir-patrick-manson-scottish-doctor-and-founder-tropical-medicine-born
4	Manson, Patrick	1844	1922	Patrick Manson: The Father of Tropical Medicine, Postgraduate Medical Journal, Volume 39, Issue 453, July 1963, p 440
5	Manson, Patrick	1844	1922	In memory of Patrick Manson, founding father of tropical medicine and the discovery of vector-borne infections, by Kelvin KW To and Kwok-Yung Yuen, Emerging Microbes & Infections, Volume 1, No 31, 2012
6	Manson, Patrick	1844	1922	Constancy of Purpose, by Dafydd Emrys Evans, Hong Kong University Press, 1987, p 29
7	Manson, Patrick	1844	1922	In memory of Patrick Manson, founding father of tropical medicine and the discovery of vector-borne infections, by Kelvin KW To and Kwok-Yung Yuen, Emerging Microbes & Infections, Volume 1, No 31, 2012
8	Manson, Patrick	1844	1922	The Malaria Story, by Philip Manson-Bahr, Section of the History of Medicine, Proceedings of the Royal Society of Medicine, 2 Nov 1960, p 95
9	Manson, Patrick	1844	1922	http://www.lshtm.ac.uk/library/archives/history/frieze/manson.html
1	Ogston, Alexander	1844	1929	Infectious Diseases: Prevention and Treatment in the Nineteenth and Twentieth Centuries, by Wesley William Spink, published by Books on Demand, USA, 1978, pp 266-267
1	Ormiston, George Edward	1844	1913	Obituary, George Edward Ormiston: Minutes of the Proceedings, Institution of Civil Engineers, Volume 196, Issue 1914, 1 January 1914, page 363
1	Scott, Walter	1844	1907	Wairarapa Daily Times, 27 December 1907, p 2
2	Scott, Walter	1844	1907	http://invention.smithsonian.org/Resources/MIND_Repository_Details.aspx?rep_id=1423
3	Scott, Walter	1844	1907	http://letterpressprinting.com.au/page99.htm
4	Scott, Walter	1844	1907	Printing Presses: History and development from the Fifteenth Century to Modern Times, by James Moran, University of California Press, Los Angeles, 1973, p 205
1	Smith, Charles	1844	1882	Transporter Bridge left boats in its wake, Chris Lloyd, The Northern Echo, 12 October 2011
2	Smith, Charles	1844	1882	http://www.thenorthernecho.co.uk/history/9301870.Transporter_Bridge_left_boats_in_its_wake/

1	Stirling, Allan	1844	1927	http://files.asme.org/ASMEORG/Communities/History/Landmarks/5649.pdf
2	Stirling, Allan	1844	1927	Ibid.
1	Crompton, Rookes Evelyn Bell	1845	1940	Encyclopedia Britannica
2	Crompton, Rookes Evelyn Bell	1845	1940	http://www.jstor.org/discover/10.2307/768897?uid=2&uid=4&sid=21103197389511
3	Crompton, Rookes Evelyn Bell	1845	1940	http://www.iec.ch/about/history/figures/colonel_crompton.htm
4	Crompton, Rookes Evelyn Bell	1845	1940	Ibid.
5	Crompton, Rookes Evelyn Bell	1845	1940	http://www.theiet.org/resources/library/archives/biographies/crompton.cfm
1	McDougall, Alexander	1845	1923	Commercial Steam Vessels: Maritime Heritage, Thunder Bay National Marine Sanctuary http://thunderbay.noaa.gov/history/vessels/steamers.html 8 August 2007
1	McTammany, John	1845	1915	A biographical dictionary of people in engineering: from the earliest records to 2000, by Carl W. Hall, Purdue University Press, 2008, p 147
2	McTammany, John	1845	1915	http://www.divms.uiowa.edu/~jones/voting/ReVote09history.pdf
1	Manson, James	1845	1935	http://spellerweb.net/rhindex/UKRH/GandSWR/Manson.html
1	Arthur, Alexander Alan	1846	1912	The Kentucky Encyclopedia, University Press of Kentucky, 1992, p 35
1	McGregor, William	1846	1911	http://www.football-league.co.uk/footballleaguenews/20130227/the-father-of-the-football-league_2293334_3091039
2	McGregor, William	1846	1911	Time to raise a glass to William McGregor, the original godfather and founder of league football, by Henry Winter, The Telegraph 25 February 2013
3	McGregor, William	1846	1911	http://www.avfc.co.uk/page/HistoryMcGregor
1	McIntosh, John Farquharson	1846	1918	http://www.heritagerailway.co.uk/news/caldeonian-828-is-back
2	McIntosh, John Farquharson	1846	1918	http://www.steamindex.com/people/mcintosh.htm

1	McLaren, John Hays	1846	1943	http://www.sfhistoryencyclopedia.com/articles/g/goldenGate-park.html
2	McLaren, John Hays	1846	1943	http://www.plantsgalore.com/gardens/us/US_Golden_Gate_Park.htm
1	Murray, Reginald Augustus Frederick	1846	1925	Australian Dictionary of Biography, Volume 5, Melbourne University Press, 1974, pp 321-322
1	Scott-Moncrieff, William Dundas	1846	1924	Studies on the Biology of Sewage Disposal: A Survey of the Bacteriological Flora of a Sewage Treatment Plant, by Margaret Hotchkiss, Journal of Bacteriology 1924, 9 (5), p 438
2	Scott-Moncrieff, William Dundas	1846	1924	Environmental Anaerobic Technology: Applications and New Developments, edited by Herbert H. P. Fang, Imperial College Press, London, 2010, p xv
1	Bell, Alexander Graham	1847	1922	http://museumvictoria.com.au/discoverycentre/infosheets/bell-telegraph-and-telephone/
2	Bell, Alexander Graham	1847	1922	http://www.pbs.org/wgbh/amex/telephone/peopleevents/mabell.html
3	Bell, Alexander Graham	1847	1922	http://archive.is/kg8IW
4	Bell, Alexander Graham	1847	1922	http://www.coutant.org/12mics/
5	Bell, Alexander Graham	1847	1922	http://www.pbs.org/transistor/album1/addlbios/bellag.html
6	Bell, Alexander Graham	1847	1922	A Short History of the Microphone, Chapter 1, The Microphone Book, by John Eargle Focal Press, 2001, p 1
7	Bell, Alexander Graham	1847	1922	Dictionary of Canadian Biography Online
8	Bell, Alexander Graham	1847	1922	Early Electromagnetic Telephone Receivers, Basilio Catania, Antenna, Newsletter of the Mercurians, (Special Interest Group: Society for the History of Technology) April/June 2006, p 8
9	Bell, Alexander Graham	1847	1922	First 'Radio' Built by San Diego Resident, Partner of Inventor of Telephone Keeps Notebook of Experiences with Bell, San Diego Evening Tribune, 31 July 1937
10	Bell, Alexander Graham	1847	1922	http://www.kitehistory.com/Miscellaneous/Wright_Bros.htm
11	Bell, Alexander Graham	1847	1922	The Evolution of Iron Lungs, published by J. H. Emerson Company, Cambridge, Massachusetts, 1978, (supplement)
12	Bell, Alexander Graham	1847	1922	Death of a President and his Assassin - Errors in their Diagnosis and Autopsies, by George

				Paulson, Journal of the History of the Neurosciences, Volume 15, Number 2, June 2006, pp 77-91
13	Bell, Alexander Graham	1847	1922	First 'Radio' Built by San Diego Resident, Partner of Inventor of Telephone Keeps Notebook of Experiences with Bell, San Diego Evening Tribune, 31 July 1937
14	Bell, Alexander Graham	1847	1922	http://scripophily.net/diconewyo.html
15	Bell, Alexander Graham	1847	1922	Canadian Dictionary of Biography Online
16	Bell, Alexander Graham	1847	1922	Biofuels: Global Impact on Renewable Energy, Production Agriculture, and Technological Advancements, by D. Tomes, P. Lakshmanan, D. Songstad, Springer, NY, 2011, p 2
17	Bell, Alexander Graham	1847	1922	http://www.foils.org/gallery/forlani.htm
18	Bell, Alexander Graham	1847	1922	http://deafness.about.com/cs/featurearticles/a/alexanderbell.htm
19	Bell, Alexander Graham	1847	1922	http://listeningandspokenlanguage.org/The_Volta_Bureau/
20	Bell, Alexander Graham	1847	1922	http://aitopics.org/topic/speech
21	Bell, Alexander Graham	1847	1922	http://www.infinitec.org/learn/learningaboutat/techhistory.htm
22	Bell, Alexander Graham	1847	1922	Air Monitoring by Spectroscopic Techniques, edited by Markus W. Sigrist, published by John Wiley & Sons, 1994, p 163
23	Bell, Alexander Graham	1847	1922	Canadian Medical Association Journal, Volume 131, 15 August 1984, p 376
24	Bell, Alexander Graham	1847	1922	http://www.americanbrachytherapy.org/aboutBrachytherapy/history.cfm
25	Bell, Alexander Graham	1847	1922	http://ngm.nationalgeographic.com/ngm/advertising.html
26	Bell, Alexander Graham	1847	1922	http://press.nationalgeographic.com/about-national-geographic/
27	Bell, Alexander Graham	1847	1922	Perspective: The Bell Family Legacies, W. D. Stansfield, Journal of Heredity, 23 December 2004. The American Genetic Association
28	Bell, Alexander Graham	1847	1922	Dictionary of Canadian Biography Online
29	Bell, Alexander Graham	1847	1922	http://www.afb.org/mylife/book.asp?ch=P1Ch3
30	Bell, Alexander Graham	1847	1922	http://inventors.about.com/od/gstartinventors/a/Elisha_Gray.htm

31	Bell, Alexander Graham	1847	1922	http://faculty.insead.edu/adner/research/Wester%20Union%20case%20sample.pdf
32	Bell, Alexander Graham	1847	1922	http://www.porticus.org/bell/capsule_bell_system.html
33	Bell, Alexander Graham	1847	1922	Bell's Electric Speaking Telephone: Its Invention, Construction, Application, Modification and History, by George B. Prescott, Ayer Publishing, 1972, p 114
34	Bell, Alexander Graham	1847	1922	http://www.telephonetribute.com/telephone_inventors.html
35	Bell, Alexander Graham	1847	1922	U.S. Supreme Court Dolbear v American Bell Tel. Co., 126 U.S. 1 (1888), p 126 U.S. 1, 545 Justia, US Supreme Court Center http://supreme.justia.com/us/126/1/
36	Bell, Alexander Graham	1847	1922	Antonio and the Electric Scream: The Man Who Invented the Telephone, by Sandra Meucci, Branden Books, Boston, 2010, p 100
37	Bell, Alexander Graham	1847	1922	http://wvvv.essortment.com/guiseppegariba_obg.htm
38	Bell, Alexander Graham	1847	1922	Ibid.
39	Bell, Alexander Graham	1847	1922	http://www.chezbasilio.org/vindicator.htm
40	Bell, Alexander Graham	1847	1922	Antonio Meucci: Telephone Pioneer, by Basilio Catania, Bulletin of Science, Technology & Society Volume 21, Sage Publications Inc.,1 February 2001, p 66
41	Bell, Alexander Graham	1847	1922	Intellectual Property Law for Engineers and Scientists, by Howard B. Rockman, Wiley-IEEE, 2004, p 109
42	Bell, Alexander Graham	1847	1922	Ibid. p 108
43	Bell, Alexander Graham	1847	1922	http://www.telephonecollecting.org/Bobs%20phones/Pages/Essays/Meucci/Meucci.htm
44	Bell, Alexander Graham	1847	1922	Ibid.
45	Bell, Alexander Graham	1847	1922	Chapter 15 – Who Stole Meucci's Invention? Antonio Meucci Inventor of the Telephone, Giovanni E. Schiavo, The Vigo Pess, New York, 1958, pp 171-181
46	Bell, Alexander Graham	1847	1922	http://inventors.about.com/library/inventors/bl_Antonio_Meucci.htm
47	Bell, Alexander Graham	1847	1922	http://www.privateline.com/TelephoneHistoryA/refute.htm

48	Bell, Alexander Graham	1847	1922	Section 40, Patent Act of 1870 http://ipmall.info/hosted_resources/lipa/patents/Patent_Act_of_1870.pdf
49	Bell, Alexander Graham	1847	1922	http://www.americanheritage.com/articles/magazine/it/1990/3/1990_3_6.shtml
50	Bell, Alexander Graham	1847	1922	http://telephonecollecting.org/meucci.htm
51	Bell, Alexander Graham	1847	1922	http://www.albany.edu/~scifraud/data/sci_fraud_4944.html
52	Bell, Alexander Graham	1847	1922	http://en.wikipedia.org/wiki/Antonio_Meucci
53	Bell, Alexander Graham	1847	1922	http://www.chezbasilio.org/meucci_poverty.htm
54	Bell, Alexander Graham	1847	1922	http://www.scripophily.net/globtelcom18.html Referring to "31 Federal Reporter 728-735, American Bell Telephone Co. v. Globe Telephone Co. and others"
55	Bell, Alexander Graham	1847	1922	http://www.chezbasilio.org/us_bell.htm
56	Bell, Alexander Graham	1847	1922	Ibid.
57	Bell, Alexander Graham	1847	1922	http://www.interestingamerica.com/2010-12-02_Garibaldi_Meucci_Museum_Grigonis.html
58	Bell, Alexander Graham	1847	1922	The Tangled Web of Patent #174465, by Russell A. Pizer, Author House, Bloomington, Indiana, 2009, p 316
1	Denny, William	1847	1887	http://www.bshs.org.uk/travel-guide/william-denny-brothers-test-tank-dumbarton-scotland
2	Denny, William	1847	1887	Biographical Dictionary of the History of Technology, edited by Lance Day, Ian McNeil, published by Routledge, New York, 1998, p 357
3	Denny, William	1847	1887	Scottish Firsts, by Elspeth Willis, Mainstream Publishing, Edinburgh, 2006, p 120
4	Denny, William	1847	1887	http://www.theodora.com/encyclopedia/s2/steamship_lines.html
5	Denny, William	1847	1887	The Dreadnought and the Edwardian Age, by Andrew David Lambert, Jan Rüger, Robert J. Blyth, Ashgate Publishing Limited, Farnham, Surrey, 2011, pp 145-146
1	Kennedy, Alexander Blackie William	1847	1928	Oxford Dictionary of National Biography
2	Kennedy, Alexander Blackie William	1847	1928	Obituary, Alexander Blackie William Kennedy, by Alexander Gibb, Notices of Fellows of the

				Royal Society, Volume 2, No. 6, January 1938, pp 212-223
1	MacRitchie, James	1847	1895	Building Japan, 1868-1876, Richard Henry Brunton, Japan Library Limited, Folkestone, Kent, 1991, p 248
2	MacRitchie, James	1847	1895	http://www.archive.org/stream/minutesproceedi43britgoog/minutesproceedi43britgoog_djvu.txt
1	Eccles, Robert Gibson	1848	1934	http://plants.jstor.org/person/bm000379807
1	Muirhead, Alexander	1848	1920	Telephone: Media and Communications - Inventions and Discoveries, by Valerie-Anne Giscard d'Estaing and Mark Young, Facts on File Inc., New York, 1993, p 198
2	Muirhead, Alexander	1848	1920	http://www.ecglibrary.com/ecghist.html
3	Muirhead, Alexander	1848	1920	Pipped to the post Michael Vestey, The Spectator, 20 May 2000
4	Muirhead, Alexander	1848	1920	http://www.ncbi.nlm.nih.gov/sites/entrez?cmd=Retrieve&db=PubMed&list_uids=11848076&dopt=Abstract
5	Muirhead, Alexander	1848	1920	Einthoven's String Galvanometer, The First Electrocardiograph, by Moises Rivera-Ruiz, Christian Cajavilca, and Joseph Varon, Texas Heart Institute Journal, Volume 35, Issue 2, 2008, pp 174–178
6	Muirhead, Alexander	1848	1920	Communications: An International History of the Formative Years, Russell W. Burns, (IEE History of Technology Series 32), Institution of Electrical Engineers, London, 2004, p 273
1	Porteous, James	1848	1922	http://www.uh.edu/engines/epi353.htm
2	Porteous, James	1848	1922	http://www.valleyhistory.org/index.php?c=103
3	Porteous, James	1848	1922	http://www.uh.edu/engines/epi353.htm
1	Romanes, George John	1848	1894	http://www.readanybook.com/author/romanes-george-john-844
2	Romanes, George John	1848	1894	http://faculty.frostburg.edu/mbradley/psyography/romanes.html
3	Romanes, George John	1848	1894	Ibid.
1	Blyth, Benjamin Hall	1849	1917	Obituary, Institution of Civil Engineers, Minutes of the Proceedings, Volume 203, Issue 1917, 01 January 1917, pp 415-417
1	Brunton, David William	1849	1927	http://www.kooters.com/sezbrntn.html
2	Brunton, David William	1849	1927	http://www.aspentimes.com/article/20100808/ASPENWEEKLY/100809925

3	Brunton, David William	1849	1927	Ibid.
1	Cowie, William Clarke	1849	1910	South East Asia, Colonial History, by Paul H. Kratoska, Routledge, 2001, p 282
1	Fleming, John Ambrose	1849	1945	http://www.ee.ucl.ac.uk/about/history/fleming
2	Fleming, John Ambrose	1849	1945	http://www.radio-electronics.com/info/radio_history/gtnames/fleming.php
3	Fleming, John Ambrose	1849	1945	http://history-computer.com/ModernComputer/Basis/diode.html
4	Fleming, John Ambrose	1849	1945	Exposing Electronics, edited by Bernard S. Finn, Robert Bud, Helmuth Trischler, published by NMSI Trading Ltd., Science Museum, London, 2003, p 14
5	Fleming, John Ambrose	1849	1945	http://www.icr.org/article/sir-ambrose-fleming-father-modern-electronics/
1	Forbes, George	1849	1936	http://www.teslasociety.com/exhibition.htm
2	Forbes, George	1849	1936	Abstract from Dispersion in the Ether: Light over the Water, by Sir Brian Pippard, Physics in Perspective, Volume 3, No 3, Published by Birkhäuser Basel, September 2001
3	Forbes, George	1849	1936	The Earth in Context: A Guide to the Solar System, by David Michael Harland, Springer, 2001, p 342
4	Forbes, George	1849	1936	http://www.timdawsn.demon.co.uk/duthie_article.htm
1	Garstin, William Edmund	1849	1925	Oxford Dictionary of National Biography
2	Garstin, William Edmund	1849	1925	The River Nile in the age of the British: political ecology and the quest for economic power, by Terje Tvedt, I. B. Tauris & Co. Ltd, London, 2004, p 69
1	Methven, Cathcart William	1849	1925	http://www.lifewithart.com/artists/cathcart-william-methven.html
2	Methven, Cathcart William	1849	1925	http://www.ports.co.za/durban-harbour.php

Chapter 5
1850-1874

1	Beilby, George Thomas	1850	1924	http://www.information-britain.co.uk/famousbrits.php?id=1207
2	Beilby, George Thomas	1850	1924	http://www.kosmoid.net/technology/George%20Beilby
3	Beilby, George Thomas	1850	1924	http://www.britannica.com/EBchecked/topic/58819/Sir-George-Thomas-Beilby
1	Bell, John	1850	1929	http://www.cryogenicsociety.org/resources/cryo_central/history_of_cryogenics/
2	Bell, John	1850	1929	http://www.machine-history.com/Refrigeration%20Machines
1	Benton, John	1850	1927	Oxford Dictionary of National Biography
2	Benton, John	1850	1927	Obituary, Minutes of the Proceedings, Institution of Civil Engineers, Volume 225, Issue 1928, 1 January 1928, p 354
3	Benton, John	1850	1927	Obituary, Minutes of the Proceedings, Institution of Civil Engineers, Volume 225, Issue 1928, 1 January 1928, p 353
1	Forsyth, James Bennett	1850	1909	Memorial of the family of Forsyth de Fronsac, Frederic Gregory Forsyth, Boston Press, 1903, p 79
1	Gray, Thomas Lomar	1850	1908	https://www.eeri.org/site/images/awards/reports/reithermanpart1.pdf
1	Morrison, William	1850	1927	http://www.earlyelectric.com/carcompanies.html
2	Morrison, William	1850	1927	http://www.oocities.org/athens/crete/6111/electcar.htm
3	Morrison, William	1850	1927	http://mikethehistoryguy.blogspot.com.au/2011_09_01_archive.html
1	Niven, William	1850	1937	http://www.tshaonline.org/handbook/online/articles/fni06
2	Niven, William	1850	1937	http://www.blnz.com/news/2008/04/23/Early_Mineral_Dealers_WILLIAM_NIVEN_5391.html
1	Perry, John	1850	1920	Earthquakes and Engineers: An International History by Robert Reitherman, published by American Society of Engineers, 2012, p 130
2	Perry, John	1850	1920	http://www.electricvehiclesnews.com/History/historyearlyIII.htm
3	Perry, John	1850	1920	http://www.gracesguide.co.uk/William_Edward_Ayrton
4	Perry, John	1850	1920	John Perry's neglected critique of Kelvin's age for the Earth: A missed opportunity in

				geodynamics, by Philip England, GSA Today: Volume 17, No. 1, January 2007, pp 4-9
5	Perry, John	1850	1920	http://sp.lyellcollection.org/content/190/1/91.abstract
6	Perry, John	1850	1920	http://www.uh.edu/engines/epi2235.htm
7	Perry, John	1850	1920	http://profs.princeton.edu/leo/journals/Shipley-KelvinPerryNatSelecAgeOfEarth-GeologSocLondSpecialPub2001.pdf
8	Perry, John	1850	1920	John Perry's neglected critique of Kelvin's age for the Earth: A missed opportunity in geodynamics, by Philip England, GSA Today: Volume 17, No. 1, January 2007, pp 4-9
1	Thomas, Sidney Gilchrist	1850	1885	Encyclopedia Britannica 2009 Deluxe Edition
2	Thomas, Sidney Gilchrist	1850	1885	Oxford Dictionary of National Biography
1	Walker, Janet	1850	1940	Australian Dictionary of Biography
2	Walker, Janet	1850	1940	The Brisbane Courier, 2 February 1904, p 6
1	McWhirter, William	1851	1933	Nature, Volume 131, 25 March 1933, p 427
1	Duncan, George Smith	1852	1930	Australian Dictionary of Biography
1	Hay, Peter Seton	1852	1907	Dictionary of New Zealand Biography Volume Two (1870-1900), 1993
1	Kidston, Robert	1852	1924	http://nora.nerc.ac.uk/8399/1/RKidston.pdf
2	Kidston, Robert	1852	1924	Ibid.
3	Kidston, Robert	1852	1924	http://www.phys.kanagawa-u.ac.jp/~usami/2D_Web/Land%20Plants/e-text/06.htm
4	Kidston, Robert	1852	1924	http://www.abdn.ac.uk/rhynie/history.htm
1	Malloch, Peter Duncan	1852	1921	http://www.flyfishinghistory.com/malloch.htm
2	Malloch, Peter Duncan	1852	1921	http://www.herndonrods.com/silk_line_history_and_care.htm
1	Ramsay, William	1852	1916	http://www.famousscientists.org/william-ramsay/
2	Ramsay, William	1852	1916	http://www.britannica.com/EBchecked/topic/490808/Sir-William-Ramsay
3	Ramsay, William	1852	1916	Scottish Firsts, by Elspeth Wills, Mainstream Publishing Company, 2006, p 67
1	Cameron, Donald	1853	X	The bacterial treatment of sewage; a handbook for councillors, engineers, and surveyors, by George Thudichum, the Councillor and Guardian Offices, London, printed by H.R. Grubb, Croydon, Surrey, p 35 (Year of print not stated but probably in 1890s)

2	Cameron, Donald	1853	X	The Septic System Owner's Manual, by Lloyd Kahn, John Hulls, Peter Aschwanden, Lloyd Kahn and Shelter Publications, Bolina, California, 2007, p 152
3	Cameron, Donald	1853	X	British sewage works and notes on the sewage farms of Paris and on two German works, by J Baker, Chapter III, The Engineering News Publishing Co., New York, 1904, p 23
4	Cameron, Donald	1853	X	Anaerobic biotechnology for bioenergy production: principles and applications, by Samir Kumar Khanal, Blackwell Publishing, Ames, Iowa, 2008, p 3
5	Cameron, Donald	1853	X	http://www.curtisengine.com/docs/greenEnergy/ DigesterGas.pdf
1	Mackenzie, James	1853	1925	http://www.sciencemuseum.org.uk/broughttolife/ objects/display.aspx?id=93324
2	Mackenzie, James	1853	1925	Biographical Dictionary of the History of Technology, by Lance Day and Ian McNeil, Routledge, London, 1996, p 457
3	Mackenzie, James	1853	1925	Oxford Dictionary of National Biography
4	Mackenzie, James	1853	1925	http://www.zoominfo.com/p/James-Mackenzie/276253668
5	Mackenzie, James	1853	1925	http://circ.ahajournals.org/content/31/3/374.full.p df
6	Mackenzie, James	1853	1925	http://www.dundee.ac.uk/museum/exhibitions/me dical/cardiology/cardiology1/
1	Meik, Charles Scott	1853	1923	http://www.gracesguide.co.uk/Lochaber_Hydro-Electric_Station
1	Metcalfe, Charles Herbert Theophilus	1853	1928	Oxford Dictionary of National Biography
1	Murchland, William	1853	1941	http://www.uwex.edu/uwmril/pdf/MilkMachine/S cientificLit/05_NMC_HistoryVacuumRegulation. pdf
2	Murchland, William	1853	1941	The Sydney Mail, 31 January 1891, p 4
1	Reid, Alexander Walker	1853	1938	Dictionary of New Zealand Biography
1	Thomson, Elihu	1853	1937	http://www.ieeeghn.org/wiki/index.php/Elihu_Th omson
2	Thomson, Elihu	1853	1937	http://links.jstor.org/sici?sici=0048-7511(199406)22%3A2%3C248%3APIOMIP%3E 2.0.CO%3B2-H
3	Thomson, Elihu	1853	1937	http://www.ge.com/company/history/research.ht ml

1	Thomson, John	1853	1926	Dictionary of American Biography
2	Thomson, John	1853	1926	Water meters-selection, installation, testing, and maintenance, 4th edition, American Water Works Association, Denver, Colorado, 1999, p 17
1	Buick, David Dunbar	1854	1929	http://nyjobsource.com/americanstandard.html
1	Clerk, Dugald	1854	1932	http://www.marks-clerk.com/uk/attorneys/about/keyfacts.html
1	Dey, Alexander	1854	X	http://www.btrs.co.uk/clock-card-history/
2	Dey, Alexander	1854	X	http://www.thebrandingjournal.com/2014/04/9-famous-tech-companies-logo-evolution/
1	Reid, William Paton	1854	1932	http://www.steamindex.com/people/reid.htm
1	Urie, Robert Wallace	1854	1937	http://www.oocities.org/heartland/acres/6884/roburie.html
1	Bain, David Isauld	1855	1933	http://www.steamindex.com/people/engrs.htm
2	Bain, David Isauld	1855	1933	http://www.scottish-places.info/scotgaz/people/famousfirst934.html
1	Barr, Andrew	1855	1939	Australian Dictionary of Biography
2	Barr, Andrew	1855	1939	http://www.slwa.wa.gov.au/pdf/mn/mn1501_2000/mn1533.pdf
1	Barr, Archibald	1855	1931	Oxford Dictionary of National Biography
2	Barr, Archibald	1855	1931	http://worldchanging.gla.ac.uk/article/?id=21
1	Ewing, James Alfred	1855	1935	Encyclopedia Britannica 2009 Deluxe Edition
2	Ewing, James Alfred	1855	1935	http://www.madehow.com/Volume-1/Seismograph.html
3	Ewing, James Alfred	1855	1935	http://www.eoearth.org/article/Seismology?topic=50013
4	Ewing, James Alfred	1855	1935	http://earthquake.usgs.gov/learn/eqmonitoring/eq-mon-6.php
5	Ewing, James Alfred	1855	1935	The Early History of Seismometry (to 1900), by J. Dewey and B. Perry, Bull. of the Seismological Soc. of America, Vol. 59, No. 1 Feb 1969, pp 183-185
6	Ewing, James Alfred	1855	1935	http://www.nahste.ac.uk/isaar/GB_0237_NAHSTE_P1760.html
7	Ewing, James Alfred	1855	1935	Oxford Dictionary of National Biography
8	Ewing, James Alfred	1855	1935	Cyclic Slip Irreversibilities and the Evolution of Fatigue Damage, by Hael Mughrabi, Metallurgical and Materials Transactions A, Vol. 40A, June 2009, p 1260
1	Hannay, James Ballantyne	1855	1931	James Ballantyne Hannay, by Jaime Wisniak, Dept of Chemical Engineering, Ben-Gurion Univ.

				Revista CENIC Ciencias Químicas, Vol. 41, No. 3, pp. 183-192, Septiembre-Diciembre, 2010
2	Hannay, James Ballantyne	1855	1931	James Ballantyne Hannay, Synthetic Diamond Pioneer, by David Harvie, The Highlander, May / June 1999
1	Johnston, George	1855	1945	http://www.driving.co.uk/features/the-heroes-and-harebrained-men-women-who-shaped-motoring/12099
2	Johnston, George	1855	1945	http://blog.hemmings.com/index.php/tag/nimrod-expedition/
1	McNab, William	1855	1923	http://history.uwo.ca/cdneng/mcnab.html
1	Burt, Peter	1856	1944	http://www.glasgowwestaddress.co.uk/1888_Book/Acme_Machine_Co.htm
2	Burt, Peter	1856	1944	http://www.gasenginemagazine.com/tractors/the-glasgow-tractor.aspx#axzz2ijVR3eRc
3	Burt, Peter	1856	1944	http://www.motoringheritage.co.uk/html/argyll_company.html
1	Burton, William Kinninmond	1856	1899	http://www.raeng.org.uk/news/publications/ingenia/issue28/Issue28_In_Brief.pdf
2	Burton, William Kinninmond	1856	1899	Experiences of Establishing Tropical Architecture in Japanese Colonial Taiwan, by Lin Szu-Ling and Fu Chao-Ching, Department of Architecture, National Cheng Kung University, 2005, p 6
3	Burton, William Kinninmond	1856	1899	Japanese to honour Briton who saved them from cholera, Colin Joyce, Daily Telegraph, 8 May 2006
1	Knott, Cargill Gilston	1856	1922	http://www.kosmoid.net/lives/knott
1	Laing, Andrew	1856	1931	http://www.globalsecurity.org/military/world/russia/icebreaker-1.htm
2	Laing, Andrew	1856	1931	http://www.sclews.me.uk/laing.htm
1	MacArthur, John Stewart	1856	1920	Biographical Dictionary of the History of Technology, edited by Lance Day, Ian McNeil, published by Routledge, London, 1996, p 451
2	MacArthur, John Stewart	1856	1920	Oxford Dictionary of National Biography
1	Thomson, Joseph John	1856	1940	Fundamentals of the Physics of Solids: Volume 1: Structure and Dynamics, by A. Piróth, Jenö Sólyom, Springer-Verlag, Berlin, 2007, p 1
2	Thomson, Joseph John	1856	1940	http://www.scribd.com/doc/18237265/Atomic-Theorists
3	Thomson, Joseph John	1856	1940	http://www.chemheritage.org/discover/online-resources/chemistry-in-history/themes/atomic-and-nuclear-structure/thomson.aspx

4	Thomson, Joseph John	1856	1940	Encyclopaedia Britannica 2009 Deluxe Edition
5	Thomson, Joseph John	1856	1940	http://www.nobelprize.org/nobel_prizes/physics/laureates/1906/thomson-bio.html
6	Thomson, Joseph John	1856	1940	http://www.atomicarchive.com/Bios/Thomson.shtml
7	Thomson, Joseph John	1856	1940	http://www.sciencemuseum.org.uk/onlinestuff/people/sir%20joseph%20john%20thomson%2018561940.aspx
8	Thomson, Joseph John	1856	1940	https://www.aip.org/history/electron/jjthomson.htm
9	Thomson, Joseph John	1856	1940	Encyclopaedia Britannica 2009 Deluxe Edition
1	Barton, Edward Gustavus Campbell	1857	1942	Australian Dictionary of Biography
1	Fleming, Williamina Paton Stevens	1857	1911	http://www.distinguishedwomen.com/biographies/flemingw.html
2	Fleming, Williamina Paton Stevens	1857	1911	http://www.daviddarling.info/encyclopedia/F/Fleming.html
3	Fleming, Williamina Paton Stevens	1857	1911	http://space.about.com/od/astronomerbiographies/a/wflemingbio.htm
4	Fleming, Williamina Paton Stevens	1857	1911	http://www.internationalpbi.it/en/index.php?pageLoad=inc/adp_home.php&label=The%20president%20corner&sottosez=3,ADPSTORI&idtext=845&idanno=2011
1	Jarvis, John Charles Barron	1857	1935	http://www.trekearth.com/gallery/Europe/Finland/South/Aland/Mariehamn/photo280332.htm
2	Jarvis, John Charles Barron	1857	1935	http://www.bruzelius.info/Nautica/Biography/GB/Jarvis,_JCB.html
1	Lundie, John	1857	1931	http://www.gutenberg.org/files/16671/16671-h/16671-h.htm
1	Macintyre, John	1857	1928	The History of Radiology, by Adrian M. K. Thomas, Arpan K. Banerjee, Oxford University Press, 2013
2	Macintyre, John	1857	1928	http://www.universitystory.gla.ac.uk/biography/?id=WH3015&type=P
3	Macintyre, John	1857	1928	Neuroradiology Back to the Future: Head and Neck Imaging, E.G. Hoeffner, S.K. Mukherji, A. Srinivasan, D.J. Quint, American Journal of Neuroradiology, December 2012, p 2026

4	Macintyre, John	1857	1928	http://www.encyclopedia.com/doc/1O128-Xrays.html
5	Macintyre, John	1857	1928	http://www.victorian-cinema.net/macintyre.htm
6	Macintyre, John	1857	1928	Historia medicinae: X-rays in 1896-1897, by Richard F Mould, Journal of Oncology, Volume 61, No 6, 2011, p 107e
7	Macintyre, John	1857	1928	Davidson, Tish. "X Rays" Gale Encyclopedia of Children's Health: Infancy through Adolescence. 2006. Encyclopedia.com. 6 Nov. 2013
8	Macintyre, John	1857	1928	http://historycompany.co.uk/2011/07/12/the-man-who-made-the-worlds-first-x-ray-movie/
9	Macintyre, John	1857	1928	Reception of Rontgen's Discovery in Britain and U.S.A., E. Posner, British Medical Journal, 7 November 1970, p 359
10	Macintyre, John	1857	1928	Oxford Dictionary of National Biography
11	Macintyre, John	1857	1928	http://www.universitystory.gla.ac.uk/biography/?id=WH3015&type=P
1	Philip, Robert William	1857	1939	Sir Robert W. Philip (1857-1939)-Pioneer of Tuberculosis Control, American Journal of Public Health, Volume 48, No 1, January 1958, p 82
2	Philip, Robert William	1857	1939	http://ocp.hul.harvard.edu/contagion/tuberculosis.html
3	Philip, Robert William	1857	1939	History of Medicine, Robert W. Philip: Pioneer of the Holistic Approach to Tuberculosis and its Voluntary Movement, by H. Dubovsky, South African Medical Journal, 16 June 1973, p 1007
4	Philip, Robert William	1857	1939	Notable Fellows, Sir Robert William Philip, by Derek Doyle, The Journal of the Royal College of Physicians of Edinburgh, Volume 38, 2008, p 283
5	Philip, Robert William	1857	1939	The key to the sanatoria, by O. R. McCarthy, Journal of the Royal Society of Medicine, Volume 94, No 8, August 2001, pp 413-417
6	Philip, Robert William	1857	1939	A History of Public Health, by George Rosen, The Johns Hopkins University Press, 1993, p 362
7	Philip, Robert William	1857	1939	Sir Robert Philip and the Conquest of Tuberculosis, by Christopher Clayton, British Medical Journal, Volume 2, No 5060, 28 December 1957, p 1504
8	Philip, Robert William	1857	1939	The man who fought TB: Sir Robert Philip, by Alwyn James, The Scotsman, 3 October 2006
9	Philip, Robert William	1857	1939	History of Medicine, Robert W. Philip: Pioneer of the Holistic Approach to Tuberculosis and its Voluntary Movement, by H. Dubovsky, South African Medical Journal, 16 June 1973, p 1008

10	Philip, Robert William	1857	1939	Sir Robert Philip and the Conquest of Tuberculosis, by Christopher Clayton, British Medical Journal, Volume 2, No 5060, 28 December 1957, p 1503
11	Philip, Robert William	1857	1939	Ibid. p 1506
12	Philip, Robert William	1857	1939	Sir Robert W. Philip - World Benefactor, American Journal of Public Health, November 1937, Volume 27, No 11, p 1169
1	Ross, Ronald	1857	1932	Journal of the History of Medicine and Allied Sciences, Volume 57, Number 4, October 2002, pp 385-409
2	Ross, Ronald	1857	1932	http://www.malariasite.com/malaria/ross.htm
3	Ross, Ronald	1857	1932	http://www.banglapedia.org/HT/R_0281.htm
4	Ross, Ronald	1857	1932	http://nobelprize.org/nobel_prizes/medicine/laureates/1902/ross-bio.html
5	Ross, Ronald	1857	1932	Smith DL, Battle KE, Hay SI, Barker CM, Scott TW, et al. (2012) Ross, Macdonald, and a Theory for the Dynamics and Control of Mosquito-Transmitted Pathogens. PLoS Pathog 8(4): e1002588. doi:10.1371/journal.ppat.1002588
1	Stewart, Thomas	1857	1942	http://email.asce.org/international/documents/05.MurrayStewartTWoodhead.pdf
2	Stewart, Thomas	1857	1942	http://email.asce.org/international/documents/05.MurrayStewartTWoodhead.pdf
3	Stewart, Thomas	1857	1942	http://www.ewisa.co.za/misc/WaterHistoryEvents/defaultcccwaters.htm
1	Brodie, John Alexander	1858	1934	http://pebsteelalliance.com/pebsal/prefabricated-building-history/
1	Macallum, Archibald Byron	1858	1934	Obituaries, Archibald Byron Macallum, The Canadian Medical Association Journal, May 1934, p 577
2	Macallum, Archibald Byron	1858	1934	Partnership for Excellence: Medicine at the University of Toronto and Academic Hospitals, by Edward Shorter, University of Toronto Press, 2013, p 428
1	Philip, James	1858	1911	http://genealogytrails.com/sdak/newspaper_index.html
2	Philip, James	1858	1911	http://www.blackhillsvisitor.com/old-west.html?pid=880&sid=916:James-Scotty-Philip-Saving-the-Buffalo
1	Skues, George Edward Mackenzie	1858	1949	Oxford Dictionary of National Biography

1	Swinburne, James	1858	1958	http://www.madehow.com/inventorbios/38/James-Swinburne.html
2	Swinburne, James	1858	1958	Obituary, Sir James Swinburne, 1858-1958, ICE Proceedings, Volume 11, Issue 2, 1 October 1958, p 283
3	Swinburne, James	1858	1958	A to Z of STS Scientists, by Elizabeth H. Oakes, Facts on File Inc., New York, 2002, p 289
1	Callender, William Marshall	1859	X	Oxford Dictionary of National Biography
2	Callender, William Marshall	1859	X	The history of electric wires and cables, by Robert Monro Black, Science Museum (Great Britain), Peter Peregrinus Ltd., London, 1983, p 56
3	Callender, William Marshall	1859	X	National Museums Liverpool Archives Department, Information Sheet 63, British Insulated Callenders Cables Plc
1	Reid, Harry Fielding	1859	1944	http://www.nasonline.org/publications/biographical-memoirs/memoir-pdfs/reid-harry.pdf
2	Reid, Harry Fielding	1859	1944	A Source Book in Geology, 1900-1950, edited by Kirtley F. Mather, Oxford University Press, 1967, p 50
1	Sutherland, William	1859	1911	The Age, 31 July 2005
2	Sutherland, William	1859	1911	Archimedes to Hawking: Laws of Science and the Great Minds Behind Them, by Clifford Pickover, Oxford University Press, 2008, p 472
3	Sutherland, William	1859	1911	Australian Dictionary of Biography
4	Sutherland, William	1859	1911	Australian Dictionary of Biography
5	Sutherland, William	1859	1911	http://www.ph.unimelb.edu.au/html/events/julylectures/handout_150705.pdf
1	Dickson, William Kennedy Laurie	1860	1935	Motion Pictures - Inventions and Discoveries: Scientific American, by Rodney Carlisle, published by John Wiley and Sons, Inc., Hoboken, New Jersey, 2004, p 362
2	Dickson, William Kennedy Laurie	1860	1935	http://www.leeds.ac.uk/cath/ahrc/congress/2005/programme/abs/80.shtml
3	Dickson, William Kennedy Laurie	1860	1935	http://www.silentfilm.org/pages/detail/2267
4	Dickson, William Kennedy Laurie	1860	1935	http://www.suizidal.de/
1	Haldane, John Scott	1860	1936	A Contribution to the Chemistry of Hemoglobin and its Immediate Derivatives, John Haldane, The

				Journal of Physiology, Volume 22, No 4, 17 February 1898, pp 298-306
2	Haldane, John Scott	1860	1936	Oxford Dictionary of National Biography
3	Haldane, John Scott	1860	1936	http://www.giffordlectures.org/Author.asp?AuthorID=73
4	Haldane, John Scott	1860	1936	http://navxdivingu.blogspot.com/2009/10/diving-history-john-scott-haldane.html
5	Haldane, John Scott	1860	1936	http://www.giffordlectures.org/Author.asp?AuthorID=73
6	Haldane, John Scott	1860	1936	http://www.sciencemuseum.org.uk/broughttolife/people/johnscotthaldane.aspx
7	Haldane, John Scott	1860	1936	http://www.scottish-places.info/people/famousfirst1349.html
8	Haldane, John Scott	1860	1936	http://www.divinghistory.com/id28.html
9	Haldane, John Scott	1860	1936	http://navxdivingu.blogspot.com/2009/10/diving-history-john-scott-haldane.html
10	Haldane, John Scott	1860	1936	http://www.giffordlectures.org/Author.asp?AuthorID=73
1	Thompson, D'Arcy Wentworth	1860	1948	http://www-history.mcs.st-andrews.ac.uk/Biographies/Thompson_D'Arcy.html
2	Thompson, D'Arcy Wentworth	1860	1948	http://www.darcythompson.org/about.html
3	Thompson, D'Arcy Wentworth	1860	1948	Ibid.
4	Thompson, D'Arcy Wentworth	1860	1948	http://www-groups.dcs.st-and.ac.uk/~history/Miscellaneous/darcy.html
1	Watson, John Duncan	1860	1946	Minutes of the Proceedings of the Institution of Civil Engineers, Obituaries, Journal of the Institute of Civil Engineers, Volume 27, Issue 4, 1 February 1947, pp 497-498
2	Watson, John Duncan	1860	1946	http://popularlogistics.com/2009/02/methane-from-sewage-used-for-energy/
1	Williams, Robert	1860	1938	Black and White in Southern Zambia: The Tonga Plateau Economy and British Imperialism, 1890-1939, by Kenneth Powers Vickery, published by Praeger and Greenwood, 1986, p 48
1	Allan, Percy	1861	1930	Australian Dictionary of Biography
1	Cullen, Edward Alexander Ernest	1861	1950	Australian Dictionary of Biography

1	Dalrymple-Hay, Harley Hugh	1861	1940	Oxford Dictionary of National Biography
1	Hendrie, David Anderson	1861	1940	http://www.steamindex.com/backtrak/bt24.htm#637-ws
2	Hendrie, David Anderson	1861	1940	http://www.inverness-courier.co.uk/News/Restored-loco-could-honour-unsung-engineering-pioneer-9619.htm
1	Innes, Robert Ayton Innes	1861	1933	http://todayinsci.com/3/3_13.htm
1	Laurie, Arthur Pillans	1861	1949	http://www.nahste.ac.uk/isaar/GB_0237_NAHSTE_P1161.html
2	Laurie, Arthur Pillans	1861	1949	http://www.incorm.eu/journal2009/authenticity.pdf
1	Lawson, Andrew Cowper	1861	1952	ftp://rock.geosociety.org/pub/GSAToday/gt0604-05.pdf
2	Lawson, Andrew Cowper	1861	1952	Ibid.
1	Mackenzie, Duncan	1861	1934	Oxford Dictionary of National Biography
2	Mackenzie, Duncan	1861	1934	http://wiki.phantis.com/index.php/Dr._Duncan_Mackenzie
1	King, George James Foster	1862	1947	Biographical dictionary of the history of technology, by Lance Day, Ian McNeil, Routledge, London, 2005, p 693
2	King, George James Foster	1862	1947	Ships and Shipbuilders: Pioneers of Design and Construction by Fred M Walker, Seaforth Publishing, 2010, p 182
1	Milne, Samuel Hird	1862	1943	http://archiver.rootsweb.ancestry.com/th/read/SCT-EDINBURGH/2004-02/1075826457
1	Moir, Ernest William	1862	1923	http://catskillarchive.com/rrextra/tuhud1.Html
2	Moir, Ernest William	1862	1923	http://www.hyperoxyhealth.com/members.html
1	Campbell-Swinton, Alan Archibald	1863	1930	http://www.terramedia.co.uk/quotations/Quotes_S.htm
2	Campbell-Swinton, Alan Archibald	1863	1930	http://www.nationalmediamuseum.org.uk/collection/photography/royalphotographicsociety/collectionitem.aspx?id=2003-5001/2/20187
1	Barnett, James Rennie	1864	1965	Biographical Dictionary of the History of Technology, edited by Lance Day, Ian McNeil, Routledge, London 1996, p 77
2	Barnett, James Rennie	1864	1965	http://www.glwatson.com/content/History/DirectorsBiographies.aspx

1	Mitchell, Peter Chalmers	1864	1945	http://www.zsl.org/support-us/legacy/whipsnade,1245,AR.html
2	Mitchell, Peter Chalmers	1864	1945	http://www.zsl.org/zsl-whipsnade-zoo//planning-your-visit/how-to-find-us,160,AR.html
1	Stuart, Herbert Akroyd	1864	1927	http://www.enginemuseum.org/eoe.html
1	Arnot, Arthur James	1865	1946	Australian Dictionary of Biography
2	Arnot, Arthur James	1865	1946	http://blogs.howstuffworks.com/transcript/how-arthur-arnot-electrified-the-drill/
1	Bell, Thomas	1865	1952	The electric propulsion of ships, by H. M. Hobart, publ. by Harper, London, 1911 p 25
2	Bell, Thomas	1865	1952	The Glasgow Herald, 10 January 1952, p 3
3	Bell, Thomas	1865	1952	Oxford Dictionary of National Biography
1	Duncan, Thomas	1865	1929	http://www.watthourmeters.com/history.html
1	Elphinstone, George Keith Buller	1865	1941	Oxford Dictionary of National Biography
1	Gillies, Alexander	1865	1952	http://www.austehc.unimelb.edu.au/tia/024.html
2	Gillies, Alexander	1865	1952	Contingent Mechanization: The Case of American Dairying, by Noelle Foster Feliciano, Rensselaer Polytechnic Institute, New York, 2008, p 75
3	Gillies, Alexander	1865	1952	http://victoriancollections.net.au/items/4f72a2c697f83e030860213d
1	Harden, Arthur	1865	1940	http://www.nobelprize.org/nobel_prizes/chemistry/laureates/1929/
2	Harden, Arthur	1865	1940	Encyclopedia of World Scientists, Revised Edition, by Elizabeth H. Oakes, Infobase Publishing, New York, 2002, p 305
3	Harden, Arthur	1865	1940	Ibid.
4	Harden, Arthur	1865	1940	Encyclopedia Britannica, 2013
5	Harden, Arthur	1865	1940	A Dictionary of Scientists, Oxford University Press, 1999
1	Houston, Alexander Cruikshank	1865	1933	Biographical Dictionary of the History of Technology, edited by Lance Day, Ian McNeil, Routledge, London, 1996, p 619
2	Houston, Alexander Cruikshank	1865	1933	www.jstor.org/stable/10.2307/768834
1	MacMasters, Alan	1865	1927	http://historum.com/general-history/39937-empire-british-empire-1900-s-11.html
1	Murray, Donald	1865	1945	http://www.nadcomm.com/fiveunit/fiveunits.htm
2	Murray, Donald	1865	1945	http://www.nadcomm.com/timeline.htm

1	Shiels, Alexander	1865	1907	http://www.madehow.com/Volume-2/Milking-Machine.html
1	Smith, Alexander	1865	1922	Biographical Memoir Alexander Smith, by William A Noyes, Memoirs of the National Academy of Sciences, Volume XXI, Twelfth Memoir, Government Printing Office, Washington, 1927, p 2
2	Smith, Alexander	1865	1922	http://www.acs.org/content/acs/en/about/president/acspresidents/alexander-smith.html
3	Smith, Alexander	1865	1922	http://scalacs.org/magazine/2013-10.pdf
1	Boyd, Adam Alexander	1866	1948	Australian Dictionary of Biography
1	Broom, Robert	1866	1951	http://www.uic.edu/classes/osci/osci590/3_2PersonalitiesInHumanOrigins.htm
2	Broom, Robert	1866	1951	http://www.maropeng.co.za/content/page/the_age_of_emaustralopithecus
3	Broom, Robert	1866	1951	http://www.maropeng.co.za/content/page/mining_and_the_discovery_of_the_sterkfontein_caves
4	Broom, Robert	1866	1951	http://www.oocities.org/palaeoanthropology/Aafricanus.html
5	Broom, Robert	1866	1951	http://www.princeton.edu/~achaney/tmve/wiki100k/docs/Robert_Broom.html
1	MacDonald, Murdoch	1866	1957	The Nile: Histories, Cultures, Myths, by Haggai Erlich and Israel Gershoni, Lynne Rienner Publishers, Boulder, Colorado, USA, 1999, pp 249-250
2	MacDonald, Murdoch	1866	1957	Reining the State Back In: When Capitalists Collide - Business Conflict and the End of Empire in Egypt, by Robert Vitalis, University of California Press, London, 1995
3	MacDonald, Murdoch	1866	1957	http://www.bsee.co.uk/news/archivestory.php/aid/3773/Mott_MacDonald_appointed_lead_consultant_.html
1	Stott, Henry Gordon	1866	1917	http://www.ieeeghn.org/wiki/index.php/Henry_Stott
2	Stott, Henry Gordon	1866	1917	http://www.nycsubway.org/irtsubway.html
1	Stevenson-Hamilton, James	1867	1957	Oxford Dictionary of National Biography
1	Boyce, James	1868	1935	Fat Chemistry: The Science Behind Obesity, by Claire S. Allardyce, RSC Publishing, The Royal Society of Chemistry, 2012, p 170
1	Harper, Louis	1868	1940	http://www.harperbridges.com/index.asp?id=51
1	Hoy, William Wilson	1868	1930	http://www.christies.com/lotfinder/LotDetailsPrintable.aspx?intObjectID=1551283

1	Ramsay, William	1868	1914	http://adb.anu.edu.au/biography/ramsay-william-8152
1	Swinton, Ernest Dunlop	1868	1951	http://www.onread.com/writer/Swinton-Ernest-Dunlop-1962/
2	Swinton, Ernest Dunlop	1868	1951	Oxford Dictionary of National Biography
1	Garden, William Brownie	1869	1960	http://www.spacerighteurope.com/about-spaceright-europe-store
1	Henderson, Brodie Haldane	1869	1936	Oxford Dictionary of National Biography
1	Wilson, Charles Thomson Rees	1869	1959	http://www.britannica.com/EBchecked/topic/644646/CTR-Wilson
2	Wilson, Charles Thomson Rees	1869	1959	http://www.nobelprize.org/nobel_prizes/physics/laureates/1927/wilson-bio.html?print=1
3	Wilson, Charles Thomson Rees	1869	1959	Ibid.
1	Turnbull, Wallace Rupert	1870	1954	http://www.museevirtuel-virtualmuseum.ca/edu/ViewLoitDa.do%3Bjsessionid=3176E9644A2F349A7C45554AA272410D?method=preview&lang=EN&id=4997
2	Turnbull, Wallace Rupert	1870	1954	http://www.thecanadianencyclopedia.com/en/article/wallace-rupert-turnbull/
3	Turnbull, Wallace Rupert	1870	1954	Canadian Scientists and Inventors: Biographies of People Who Shaped Our World, by Harry Black, Pembroke Publishers, Ontario, 2008, p 183
4	Turnbull, Wallace Rupert	1870	1954	http://glosbe.com/en/fr/Wright%20Flyer
1	Ennis, Lawrence	1871	1938	The Glasgow Herald, 7 May 1938, p 13
2	Ennis, Lawrence	1871	1938	Australian Dictionary of Biography
3	Ennis, Lawrence	1871	1938	http://sydney-harbour-bridge.bos.nsw.edu.au/building-the-bridge/agreement.php
1	Macadie, Donald	1871	1955	http://www.vintage-radio.net/forum/showthread.php?t=34040
1	Rutherford, Ernest	1871	1937	http://www.bbc.co.uk/history/historic_figures/rutherford_ernest.shtml
2	Rutherford, Ernest	1871	1937	http://www.nobelprize.org/nobel_prizes/chemistry/laureates/1908/rutherford-bio.html?print=1
3	Rutherford, Ernest	1871	1937	http://www.pbs.org/wgbh/aso/databank/entries/bpruth.html
4	Rutherford, Ernest	1871	1937	http://scienceworld.wolfram.com/biography/Rutherford.html
5	Rutherford, Ernest	1871	1937	http://www.bbc.co.uk/history/historic_figures/rutherford_ernest.shtml

6	Rutherford, Ernest	1871	1937	http://www.nobelprize.org/nobel_prizes/chemistry/laureates/1908/rutherford-bio.html?print=1
1	Yule, George Udny	1871	1951	Oxford Dictionary of National Biography
2	Yule, George Udny	1871	1951	http://www-history.mcs.st-andrews.ac.uk/Biographies/Yule.html
3	Yule, George Udny	1871	1951	http://mnstats.morris.umn.edu/introstat/history/w98/Yule.html
4	Yule, George Udny	1871	1951	Ibid.
1	Anderson, John	1872	1929	Dictionary of Wisconsin Biography
2	Anderson, John	1872	1929	Mechanical Engineering: A Century of Progress edited by Thomas H. Fehring, Society of Mechanical Engineers. Milwaukee Section, 1980, p 4
3	Anderson, John	1872	1929	Popular Science, March 1956, p 165
1	Balfour, George	1872	1941	Obituary, George Balfour, 1872-1941, Journal of the Institution of Civil Engineers, Volume 17, Issue 2, 1 December 1941, p 195
2	Balfour, George	1872	1941	Ibid.
1	Gibb, Alexander	1872	1958	http://www.jstor.org/stable/769278
2	Gibb, Alexander	1872	1958	http://www.icevirtuallibrary.com/content/article/10.1680/iicep.1958.2021
1	Lapworth, Arthur	1872	1941	Biographical Memoirs, by Office of the Home Secretary, National Academy of Sciences, National Academies Press, 1974, p 137
2	Lapworth, Arthur	1872	1941	http://www.cartage.org.lb/en/themes/biographies/MainBiographies/L/Lapworth/1.html
1	Russell, Bertrand Arthur William	1872	1970	http://www-groups.dcs.st-and.ac.uk/~history/Biographies/Russell.html
2	Russell, Bertrand Arthur William	1872	1970	http://www.egs.edu/library/bertrand-russell/biography/
3	Russell, Bertrand Arthur William	1872	1970	http://www.educ.fc.ul.pt/icm/icm2003/icm14/Russell.htm
4	Russell, Bertrand Arthur William	1872	1970	http://www.egs.edu/library/bertrand-russell/biography/
5	Russell, Bertrand Arthur William	1872	1970	http://www.storyofmathematics.com/20th_russell.html
6	Russell, Bertrand Arthur William	1872	1970	http://www.britannica.com/EBchecked/topic/513124/Bertrand-Russell
7	Russell, Bertrand Arthur William	1872	1970	http://www.egs.edu/library/bertrand-russell/biography/
8	Russell, Bertrand Arthur William	1872	1970	http://www.users.drew.edu/~jlenz/brs-about-br.html
1	Cameron, William	1873	1934	http://www.cancentral.com/hist_invention.cfm

2	Cameron, William	1873	1934	Patent No 1,433,673, 31 October 1922 (filed 28 March 1919) Serial No 285,793 - US Patent Office
1	Hume, Walter Reginald	1873	1943	Australian Dictionary of Biography Online Edition
1	Morrison, William Murray	1873	1948	Biographical dictionary of the history of technology, edited by Lance Day, Ian McNeil, Routledge, London, 1996, p 868
2	Morrison, William Murray	1873	1948	http://www.aluminiumville.co.uk/wmm.html
1	Randall-MacIver, David	1873	1945	http://www.britannica.com/EBchecked/topic/491010/David-Randall-MacIver
2	Randall-MacIver, David	1873	1945	http://www.penn.museum/documents/publications/expedition/PDFs/48-2/Houser-Wegner.pdf
3	Randall-MacIver, David	1873	1945	Ibid.
1	Drysdale, Charles Vickery	1874	1961	http://www.computinghistory.org.uk/det/6538/Drysdale-s-Alternating-and-Continuous-Current-Potentiometer-1909/
2	Drysdale, Charles Vickery	1874	1961	Encyclopedia Britannica Volume 12, 14th edition, 1929
3	Drysdale, Charles Vickery	1874	1961	Ibid.
4	Drysdale, Charles Vickery	1874	1961	Nature, volume 133, 10 February 1934, pp 203-204
1	Fotheringham, John Knight	1874	1936	Oxford Dictionary of National Biography
2	Fotheringham, John Knight	1874	1936	The Venus Tablets of Ammizduga, by S. Langdon and J. K. Fotheringham, Oxford University Press, 1928
1	McLellan, William	1874	1934	Underneath the Arches, by Malcolm Kennedy, Newsletter of the N. E. Branch of the Alumni Association, Spring 2009, p 6
1	Marconi, Guglielmo	1874	1937	http://www.nobelprize.org/nobel_prizes/physics/laureates/1909/marconi-bio.html#
2	Marconi, Guglielmo	1874	1937	http://inventors.about.com/od/rstartinventions/a/radio.htm
1	Merz, Charles Hesterman	1874	1940	http://www.onmydoorstep.com.au/heritage-listing/3763/railway-sub-station
2	Merz, Charles Hesterman	1874	1940	Obituary, Charles Hesterman Merz, 1874-1940, Journal of the ICE, Volume 15, Issue 2, 1 December 1940, p 146
3	Merz, Charles Hesterman	1874	1940	http://www.gracesguide.co.uk/Charles_Merz
1	Paterson, William	1874	1956	Oxford Dictionary of National Biography

2	Paterson, William	1874	1956	Ibid.
3	Paterson, William	1874	1956	http://www.spartacus.schoolnet.co.uk/2WWandersonJ.htm
4	Paterson, William	1874	1956	Oxford Dictionary of National Biography

Chapter 6
1875-1899

1	Inglis, Charles Edward	1875	1952	Encyclopedia Britannica, 1995
2	Inglis, Charles Edward	1875	1952	http://www.thinkdefence.co.uk/2014/02/inglis-bridge/
1	Page, Archibald	1875	1949	Oxford Dictionary of National Biography
1	Strutt, Robert John	1875	1947	http://www.energeticforum.com/renewable-energy/2143-allotropic-nitrogen-active-nitrogen.html
2	Strutt, Robert John	1875	1947	Oxford Dictionary of National Biography
3	Strutt, Robert John	1875	1947	Ibid.
1	Dickie, Robert James	1876	1958	http://www.nzedge.com/heroes/dickie.html
1	Gibson, William Wallace	1876	1965	http://earlyaviators.com/egibson.htm
1	Gresley, Herbert Nigel	1876	1941	http://store.steampowered.com/app/208363/
2	Gresley, Herbert Nigel	1876	1941	http://heritage.imeche.org/Biographies/NigelGresley
1	McKendrick, Anderson Gray	1876	1943	Stochastic epidemic models and their statistical analysis, by Håkan Andersson and Tom Britton, published by Springer U.S., New York, January 2000, p 7
2	McKendrick, Anderson Gray	1876	1943	Statisticians of the centuries, by C. C. Heyde, Eugene Seneta, Springer-Verlag, New York, May 2009, pp 325-326
3	McKendrick, Anderson Gray	1876	1943	http://www.universitystory.gla.ac.uk/ww1-biography/?id=4354
4	McKendrick, Anderson Gray	1876	1943	Missing Data: Dial M for ???, Xiao-Li Meng, Journal of the American Statistical Association, Volume 95, No 425, December 2000, p 1325
5	McKendrick, Anderson Gray	1876	1943	The EM algorithm and medical studies: a historical link, by Xiao-Li Meng, Statistical Methods in Medical Research, Volume 6, No 1, 1997, pp 3-23

6	McKendrick, Anderson Gray	1876	1943	Commentary, by Bernard Harris, International Journal of Epidemiology, Volume 30, pp 688-696
1	Macleod, John James Rickard	1876	1935	Insulin: Discovery and Controversy, Louis Rosenfeld, Clinical Chemistry, Volume 48, No 12, pp 2270-2288
2	Macleod, John James Rickard	1876	1935	John J. R. Macleod-Nobel Prize for Discovery of Insulin, Marc A. Shampo and Robert A. Kyle, Mayo Clinic Proceedings, Volume 81, Issue 8, August 2006, p 1006
3	Macleod, John James Rickard	1876	1935	http://www.nobelprize.org/nobel_prizes/themes/medicine/lindsten/
4	Macleod, John James Rickard	1876	1935	The Diabetes Monitor, European Association for the Study of Diabetes, Dr Monika Grüßer, Dusseldorf, November 2005
5	Macleod, John James Rickard	1876	1935	Diabetes, the Biography, Robert Tattersall, Oxford University Press, 2009 [no page numbers are used – it is the 12th page in Chapter II – Unravelling the Role of the Pancreas]
6	Macleod, John James Rickard	1876	1935	http://www.jameslindlibrary.org/illustrating/articles/the-introduction-of-successful-treatment-of-diabetes-mellitus-wi
7	Macleod, John James Rickard	1876	1935	John J. R. Macleod-Nobel Prize for Discovery of Insulin, Marc A. Shampo and Robert A. Kyle, Mayo Clinic Proceedings, Volume 81, Issue 8, August 2006
8	Macleod, John James Rickard	1876	1935	John James Rickard Macleod, Michael Williams, Diabetologia, Journal of the European Association for the Study of Diabetes Volume 48, No 9, September 2005
9	Macleod, John James Rickard	1876	1935	http://www.the-aps.org/fm/presidents/introjjm.html
10	Macleod, John James Rickard	1876	1935	The Diabetes Monitor, European Association for the Study of Diabetes, Dr. Monika Grüßer, Dusseldorf, November 2005
11	Macleod, John James Rickard	1876	1935	http://www.rotaryd9450.wa.inaust.org/html/Public/Newsletter/Newsletter.php?ArticleNo=92
12	Macleod, John James Rickard	1876	1935	Beyond the Bench, Representations of pharmacology and science in the media, John Nelson, American Society for Pharmacology and Experimental Therapeutics, Volume 8, No. 5, October 2008, pp 254-255
13	Macleod, John James Rickard	1876	1935	http://www.pbs.org/wgbh/aso/databank/entries/dm22in.html

14	Macleod, John James Rickard	1876	1935	Clinical diabetes mellitus: a problem-oriented approach, John K. Davidson, Thieme Medical Publishers, New York, 2000, p 5
15	Macleod, John James Rickard	1876	1935	The Tumultuous Discovery of Insulin: Finally, Hidden Story is Told, Lawrence K Altman, The New York Times, 14 September 1982
16	Macleod, John James Rickard	1876	1935	http://en.wikipedia.org/wiki/Nobel_Prize_controversies
17	Macleod, John James Rickard	1876	1935	Clinical diabetes mellitus: a problem-oriented approach, John K. Davidson, Thieme Medical Publishers, New York, 2000, p 5
18	Macleod, John James Rickard	1876	1935	The introduction of successful treatment of diabetes mellitus with insulin, by Charilaos Stylianou and Christopher Kelnar, Journal of The Royal Society of Medicine, Volume 102, No 7, 1 July 2009, p 302
19	Macleod, John James Rickard	1876	1935	Pharmaceutical Achievers: The Human Face of Pharmaceutical Research, by Mary Ellen Bowden, Amy Beth Crow, Tracy Sullivan, Chemical Heritage Foundation, 2003, p 55
20	Macleod, John James Rickard	1876	1935	http://ibox.co.in/insulin.html
21	Macleod, John James Rickard	1876	1935	Pharmaceutical Achievers: The Human Face of Pharmaceutical Research, by Mary Ellen Bowden, Amy Beth Crow, Tracy Sullivan, Chemical Heritage Foundation, 2003, p 57
22	Macleod, John James Rickard	1876	1935	John Macleod, The Nobel Prize in Physiology or Medicine 1923, From Nobel Lectures, Physiology or Medicine 1922-1941, Elsevier Publishing Company, Amsterdam, 1965
23	Macleod, John James Rickard	1876	1935	http://www.thecanadianencyclopedia.com/index.cfm?PgNm=TCE&Params=A1ARTA0004986
24	Macleod, John James Rickard	1876	1935	J.J.R. Macleod and the Discovery of Insulin, Historical Note, The Endocrinologist, March 1994, Volume 4, Issue 2, p 85
25	Macleod, John James Rickard	1876	1935	The Diabetes Monitor, European Association for the Study of Diabetes, Dr. Monika Grüßer, Dusseldorf, November 2005
26	Macleod, John James Rickard	1876	1935	John James Rickard Macleod, Michael Williams, Diabetologia, Journal of the European Association for the Study of Diabetes Volume 48, No 9, September 2005
1	Cleland, John Burton	1878	1971	A Prospective Study of Clinical and Haematological Profile of Dengue Fever in the Tertiary Centre, by Ashish Mehrotra, Amrit

				Kejriwal and Yash Patel, International Journal of Medicine and Allied Health Sciences, Volume 1, Issue 1, 2014, p 1
2	Cleland, John Burton	1878	1971	Australian Dictionary of Biography
3	Cleland, John Burton	1878	1971	http://www.eoas.info/biogs/P000313b.htm
1	Du Toit, Alexander Logie	1878	1937	http://www.learningace.com/doc/1111232/b2b43e95094151de66485f4a60904dcf/history-of-plate-tectonics
2	Du Toit, Alexander Logie	1878	1937	http://geowords.com/histbookpdf/i11.pdf
3	Du Toit, Alexander Logie	1878	1937	Alexander Logie du Toit 1878-1948, by S. H. Haughton, Obituary Notices of Fellows of the Royal Society, Volume 6, No. 18, November 1949, p 387
4	Du Toit, Alexander Logie	1878	1937	Ibid. p 389
1	Graham, James	1878	1954	Oxford Dictionary of National Biography
2	Graham, James	1878	1954	Encyclopedia Britannica 2009 Deluxe Edition
3	Graham, James	1878	1954	Encyclopedia Britannica 2009 Deluxe Edition
4	Graham, James	1878	1954	Flight and Aircraft Engineer, Vol 65, No 2349, 29 January 1954, p 114
1	Macpherson, Cluny	1879	1966	World War I Gas Warfare Tactics and Equipment, by Simon Jones, Osprey Publishing, Oxford, 2007
1	Robertson, Peter Lymburner	1879	1951	http://suite101.com/article/peter-lymburner-robertsons-screwdriver-a58454
1	Adams, Gladstone	1880	1966	http://www.bbc.co.uk/insideout/content/articles/2008/04/08/north_east_wipers_s13_w7_feature.shtml
1	Anderson, David	1880	1966	Institution of Civil Engineers, ICE Proceedings, Volume 2, Issue 3, 01 May 1953, pp 366-367
1	Orr, John Boyd	1880	1971	http://www.britannica.com/EBchecked/topic/76466/John-Boyd-Orr-Baron-Boyd-Orr-of-Brechin-Mearns
2	Orr, John Boyd	1880	1971	http://www.nahste.ac.uk/isaar/GB_0237_NAHSTE_P1868.html
3	Orr, John Boyd	1880	1971	http://nobelprize.org/nobel_prizes/peace/laureates/1949/orr-bio.html
1	Stewart, Alfred Walter	1880	1947	Oxford Dictionary of National Biography
1	Watson, Preston Albert	1880	1915	http://chrisbrady.itgo.com/watson/watson.htm

2	Watson, Preston Albert	1880	1915	The Meccano Magazine, Vol. XLII, No. 6, June 1957, pp 284-285
3	Watson, Preston Albert	1880	1915	http://www.aerospaceweb.org/question/history/q0159.shtml
1	Fleming, Alexander	1881	1955	http://www.pbs.org/wgbh/aso/databank/entries/bmflem.html
2	Fleming, Alexander	1881	1955	http://www.britannica.com/EBchecked/topic/353197/lysozyme
3	Fleming, Alexander	1881	1955	Antimicrobial Peptides: Old Molecules with New Ideas, Teruaki Nakatsuji and Richard L Gallo, Journal of Investigative Dermatology, Volume 132, 2012, pp 887-895
4	Fleming, Alexander	1881	1955	Transgenic Goat's Milk Kicks Up Immunity, Karen Schrock, Scientific American, 4 August 2006
5	Fleming, Alexander	1881	1955	http://www.pdb.org/pdb/static.do?p=education_discussion/molecule_of_the_month/pdb9_1.html
6	Fleming, Alexander	1881	1955	Drug discovery: a history, by Walter Sneader, John Wiley & Sons Ltd, Chichester, 2005, p 290
7	Fleming, Alexander	1881	1955	http://news.bbc.co.uk/local/oxford/hi/people_and_places/history/newsid_8828000/8828836.stm
8	Fleming, Alexander	1881	1955	Drug discovery: a history, by Walter Sneader, John Wiley & Sons Ltd, Chichester, 2005, p 291
1	Langmuir, Irving	1881	1957	http://nautilus.fis.uc.pt/st2.5/scenes-e/biog/b0024.html
2	Langmuir, Irving	1881	1957	http://www.nobelprize.org/nobel_prizes/chemistry/laureates/1932/langmuir-bio.html?print=1
3	Langmuir, Irving	1881	1957	Biographical Memoirs, by Office of the Home Secretary, National Academy of Sciences, National Academies Press, 1974, p 223
4	Langmuir, Irving	1881	1957	http://www.nasonline.org/publications/biographical-memoirs/memoir-pdfs/langmuir-irving.pdf
1	Shortt, William Hamilton	1881	1971	http://www.electric-clocks.nl/clocks/en/page10.htm
2	Shortt, William Hamilton	1881	1971	http://www.jewels-gems-clocks-watches.com/gemdict_en/index.php?le=S&la=E&entry=117103
1	Williamson, James	1881	1953	http://www.icevirtuallibrary.com/content/article/10.1680/iicep.1954.11163
1	Gillies, Harold Delf	1882	1960	http://www.wellcome.ac.uk/Funding/Public-engagement/Funded-projects/Awards-made/Highlights/WTDV030203.htm
2	Gillies, Harold Delf	1882	1960	http://www.ncbi.nlm.nih.gov/pmc/articles/PMC2414003/pdf/annrcse00366-0062.pdf

3	Gillies, Harold Delf	1882	1960	Faces of battle, The Auricle, Royal College of Nursing, Winter 2007/08, p 7
4	Gillies, Harold Delf	1882	1960	http://www.nzedge.com/heroes/gillies.html
5	Gillies, Harold Delf	1882	1960	http://www.nzedge.com/heroes/gillies.html
6	Gillies, Harold Delf	1882	1960	http://www.nzedge.com/heroes/gillies.html
7	Gillies, Harold Delf	1882	1960	http://www.nzedge.com/heroes/gillies.html
8	Gillies, Harold Delf	1882	1960	The Surgeon, Journal of the Royal Colleges of Surgeons of Edinburgh and Ireland, Volume 4, No 5, October 2006
9	Gillies, Harold Delf	1882	1960	http://www.nzedge.com/heroes/gillies.html
10	Gillies, Harold Delf	1882	1960	http://www.nzedge.com/heroes/gillies.html
11	Gillies, Harold Delf	1882	1960	http://www.nzedge.com/heroes/gillies.html
12	Gillies, Harold Delf	1882	1960	http://www.gendercentre.org.au/71article7.htm
1	MacColl, Edward	1882	1951	North of Scotland Hydro-Electric Board, or NSHEB (British agency), Encyclopedia Britannica
2	MacColl, Edward	1882	1951	http://www.historic-scotland.gov.uk/power-to-the-people.pdf
1	Ogilvie, Alexander	1882	1962	http://www.flightglobal.com/pdfarchive/view/1914/1914%20-%200521.html
1	Shand, Samuel James	1882	1957	Memorial of Samuel James Shand, by F. Chayes, The American Mineralogist, Volume 43, March-April 1958, p 319
2	Shand, Samuel James	1882	1957	http://academic.sun.ac.za/earthsci/history_e.htm
1	Wedderburn, Joseph Henry Maclagen	1882	1948	Fundamentals of Cryptology: A Professional Reference and Interactive Tutorial, by Henk C.A. van Tilborg, Kluwer Academic Publishers, New York, 2000, pp 451-452
1	Buchanan, John Scoular	1883	1966	Oxford Dictionary of National Biography
1	Halcrow, William Thomson	1883	1958	Ground warfare: an international encyclopedia, Volume 1, by Stanley Sandler, ABC-CLIO Inc., Santa Barbara, CA, 2002, p 810
2	Halcrow, William Thomson	1883	1958	Sir William Halcrow, edited by Anna Mann, Vox, Issue 1, December 2008, p 42

3	Halcrow, William Thomson	1883	1958	http://www.gracesguide.co.uk/William_Halcrow
1	Robertson, Muriel	1883	1973	International women in science: a biographical dictionary to 1950, by Catharine M. C. Haines, ABC-CLIO Inc., Santa Barbara, CA, 2001, p 264
2	Robertson, Muriel	1883	1973	http://worldchanging.gla.ac.uk/article/?id=83
1	Robison, Robert	1883	1941	Oxford Dictionary of National Biography
1	Wright, Johnstone	1883	1953	ICE Proceedings, Volume 3, Issue 1, 1 January 1954, p 106
2	Wright, Johnstone	1883	1953	The British Grid System, Nature, Volume 140, pp 394-419, 4 September 1937
1	Gibson, George Ernest	1884	1959	http://texts.cdlib.org/view?docId=hb2t1nb146&doc.view=frames&chunk.id=div00013&toc.depth=1&toc.id=
1	Macdougall, James Kenneth	1884	1960	Australian Dictionary of Biography
1	MacRobert, Thomas Murray	1884	1962	http://worldchanging.gla.ac.uk/article/?id=62
2	MacRobert, Thomas Murray	1884	1962	http://www-history.mcs.st-and.ac.uk/Biographies/MacRobert.html
3	MacRobert, Thomas Murray	1884	1962	http://journals.cambridge.org/download.php?file=%2FGMJ%2FGMJ6_02%2FS2040618500034742a.pdf&code=428716ebc9670342329e7a33e0a9df0e
1	Fraser, John	1885	1947	http://www.ed.ac.uk/polopoly_fs/1.55988!/fileManager/History%20of%20the%20Chair%20of%20Clinical%20Surgery.pdf
1	Gilmour, Douglas Graham	1885	1912	http://earlyaviators.com/egilmo4a.htm
1	Nimmo, William Hogarth Robertson	1885	1970	http://www.waterysauces.org.au/history/consolidation/pullarbook/fbh.pdf
2	Nimmo, William Hogarth Robertson	1885	1970	Australian Dictionary of Biography
1	Denny, Maurice Edward	1886	1955	Biographical Dictionary of the History of Technology edited by Lance Day, Ian McNeil, published by Routledge, London, 1996, p 356
2	Denny, Maurice Edward	1886	1955	http://www.gracesguide.co.uk/Maurice_Edward_Denny
1	Heilbron, Ian Morris	1886	1959	1945: Ian Morris Heilbron (1886-1959), C&EN Special Issue, Volume 86, No 14, 7 April 2008
2	Heilbron, Ian Morris	1886	1959	Oxford Dictionary of National Biography

3	Heilbron, Ian Morris	1886	1959	1945: Ian Morris Heilbron (1886-1959), C&EN Special Issue, Volume 86, No 14, 7 April 2008
1	Kininmonth, Colin Peter	1886	1975	http://www.information-britain.co.uk/famdates.php?id=1197
1	Reid, Wilfrid Thomas	1887	1968	http://essexbest.com/history_of_flight.php
1	Baird, John Logie	1888	1946	John Logie Baird – British Television Pioneer, by Brian Belanger, Dials and Channels, The Journal of the Radio & Television Museum, Volume 16, No 3, September 2010, p 1
2	Baird, John Logie	1888	1946	http://www.deadmedia.org/notes/11/119.html
3	Baird, John Logie	1888	1946	http://www.thocp.net/biographies/baird_john.htm
4	Baird, John Logie	1888	1946	http://www.thocp.net/biographies/baird_john.htm
5	Baird, John Logie	1888	1946	http://www.ambisonic.net/bairdcp.html
6	Baird, John Logie	1888	1946	News Chronicle, Saturday 2 February 1935
7	Baird, John Logie	1888	1946	http://www.bairdtelevision.com/crystalpalace.html
8	Baird, John Logie	1888	1946	http://www.terramedia.co.uk/Chronomedia/years/1939.htm
9	Baird, John Logie	1888	1946	http://www.transdiffusion.org/tv/baird/baird_itv
10	Baird, John Logie	1888	1946	http://www.nationalmediamuseum.org.uk/~/media/Files/NMeM/PDF/Collections/Television/ColourTelevisionInBritain.ashx
11	Baird, John Logie	1888	1946	http://www.tvhistory.tv/JLB-MBL.htm
12	Baird, John Logie	1888	1946	http://www.historynet.com/exploration/science_engineering/3033831.html?showAll=y&c=y
13	Baird, John Logie	1888	1946	http://spie.org/x648.html?product_id=960980
14	Baird, John Logie	1888	1946	http://www.thocp.net/biographies/baird_john.htm
15	Baird, John Logie	1888	1946	http://www.atsf.co.uk/ilight/
16	Baird, John Logie	1888	1946	http://www.bairdtelevision.com/war.html
17	Baird, John Logie	1888	1946	http://www.thocp.net/biographies/baird_john.htm
1	Brown, William	1888	1975	William Brown: Pioneer Leader in Pland Pathology, Annual Review Phytopathology, by S. D. Garrett, Botany School, Cambridge University, Annual Reviews Inc., Volume 23, 1985
1	Low, Archibald Montgomery	1888	1956	The Low Flying Bomb, by Paul R. Hare, Cross & Cockade International, Spring 2011, 42.045
2	Low, Archibald Montgomery	1888	1956	http://warnepieces.blogspot.com.au/2012/07/the-predators-ancestors-uavs-in-great.html#!/2012/07/the-predators-ancestors-uavs-in-great.html
3	Low, Archibald Montgomery	1888	1956	http://www.nmspacemuseum.org/halloffame/detail.php?id=20

4	Low, Archibald Montgomery	1888	1956	Introduction to UAV Systems by Paul Gerin Fahlstrom, Thomas James Gleason, published by John Wiley and Sons, Ltd, 2012, p 4
5	Low, Archibald Montgomery	1888	1956	http://thevintagent.blogspot.com.au/2008/08/rocket-cycles-2.html
1	Mackenzie, Chalmers Jack	1888	1984	The Canadian Encyclopedia
1	Wright, James	1888	1952	http://www.science20.com/news_articles/weird_accident_behind_invention_silly_putty-78817
2	Wright, James	1888	1952	http://www.nytimes.com/2002/11/22/business/earl-l-warrick-91-a-dow-corning-creator-of-silly-putty.html
1	Keiller, Alexander	1889	1955	http://aveburymanor.blogspot.com.au/2012/07/alexander-keiller.html
2	Keiller, Alexander	1889	1955	http://www.answers.com/topic/alexander-keiller-1
3	Keiller, Alexander	1889	1955	http://www.avebury-web.co.uk/marmalade_man.html
4	Keiller, Alexander	1889	1955	http://www.nationaltrust.org.uk/avebury/things-to-see-and-do/alexander-keiller-museum/
1	Armstrong, Edwin Howard	1890	1954	http://www.cybercollege.com/frtv/frtv020.htm
2	Armstrong, Edwin Howard	1890	1954	The Monitor, Volume 60, No 16, New Yori (IEEE), June 2013
3	Armstrong, Edwin Howard	1890	1954	http://www.itu.int/itunews/manager/display.asp?lang=en&year=2008&issue=10&ipage=45&ext=html
1	Miller, David	1890	1973	Dictionary of New Zealand Biography
1	Wheeler, Robert Eric Mortimer	1890	1976	Creating Prehistory: Druids, Ley Hunters and Archaeologists in Pre-War Britain, by Adam Stout, Blackwell Publishing, Oxford, 2008, p 27
2	Wheeler, Robert Eric Mortimer	1890	1976	Archaeology: An Introduction, by Kevin Greene, Tom Moore, Routledge, New York, 2010, p 95
3	Wheeler, Robert Eric Mortimer	1890	1976	http://www.talktalk.co.uk/reference/encyclopaedia/hutchinson/m0009115.html
4	Wheeler, Robert Eric Mortimer	1890	1976	http://www.princeton.edu/~achaney/tmve/wiki100k/docs/Mortimer_Wheeler.html
5	Wheeler, Robert Eric Mortimer	1890	1976	http://www.britannica.com/EBchecked/topic/641690/Sir-Mortimer-Wheeler
1	Bennie, George	1891	1957	http://www.gearwheelsmag.co.uk/archive/the_bennie_railplane_feature_13.htm
1	Murray, Henry Lamont	1891	1959	http://www.ipenz.org.nz/heritage/itemdetail.cfm?itemid=113
2	Murray, Henry Lamont	1891	1959	Handbook of food preservation, 2nd edition, by Shafiur Rahman, Taylor and Francis Group, Boca Raton, Florida, 2007, p 578

1	Haldane, John Burdon Sanderson	1892	1964	http://www.princeton.edu/~achaney/tmve/wiki100k/docs/Biostatistics.html
2	Haldane, John Burdon Sanderson	1892	1964	Oxford Dictionary of National Biography
3	Haldane, John Burdon Sanderson	1892	1964	http://books.google.com.au/books/about/Haldane_s_Rule.html?id=tFlOXwAACAAJ&redir_esc=y
4	Haldane, John Burdon Sanderson	1892	1964	http://www.phys.ufl.edu/courses/phy3221/spring10/HaldaneRightSize.pdf
1	Scott, David Aylmer	1892	1971	http://biochemistry.utoronto.ca/graduate_studies/scholarships.html
2	Scott, David Aylmer	1892	1971	https://www.facebook.com/SanofiPasteurCanada100/timeline
3	Scott, David Aylmer	1892	1971	https://www.facebook.com/media/set/?set=a.588569901189103.1073741868.520495177996576&type=1
1	Smith, Kenneth Manley	1892	1981	Obituary, Kenneth Manley Smith, by R Hull, Journal of General Microbiology, Volume 128, 1982, pp 431-432
1	Watson-Watt, Robert Alexander	1892	1973	Biographical Dictionary of the History of Technology, edited by Lance Day, Ian McNeil, Routledge, London, 1996, p 1280
2	Watson-Watt, Robert Alexander	1892	1973	http://www.battleofbritain1940.net/0003.html
3	Watson-Watt, Robert Alexander	1892	1973	http://history.nasa.gov/SP-4218/ch1.htm
4	Watson-Watt, Robert Alexander	1892	1973	http://ceeserver.cee.cornell.edu/wdp2/cee6100/6100_monograph/mono_11_F12_Radar.pdf
5	Watson-Watt, Robert Alexander	1892	1973	http://microwavetubes.iwarp.com/Magnetron.html
1	Comrie, Leslie John	1893	1950	An Encyclopaedia of New Zealand 1966
2	Comrie, Leslie John	1893	1950	http://archives.li.man.ac.uk/ead/search?operation=search&fieldidx1=bath.corporateName&fieldrel1=exact&fieldcont1=scientific%20computing%20service%20ltd
3	Comrie, Leslie John	1893	1950	Popular Astronomy, Volume Lix, No. 3, March 1951, p 116
1	Drummond, Victoria Alexandrina	1894	1980	http://www.nls.uk/learning-zone/science-and-technology/women-scientists/victoria-drummond
1	Thom, Alexander Strang	1894	1985	http://www.britannia.com/wonder/thom.html
2	Thom, Alexander Strang	1894	1985	http://www.bbc.co.uk/archive/chronicle/8604.shtml

3	Thom, Alexander Strang	1894	1985	Stonehenge: A New Theory: History of Religions, by Benjamin C. Ray, The University of Chicago Press Volume 26, No. 3, February 1987, pp. 225-278
1	Ellis, Charles Drummond	1895	1980	Charles Drummond Ellis, 1895-1980, by Kenneth Hutchison, J. A. Gray and Harrie Massey, Biographical Memoirs of Fellows of the Royal Society, Volume 27, November 1981, pp 199-233
2	Ellis, Charles Drummond	1895	1980	Oxford Dictionary of National Biography
3	Ellis, Charles Drummond	1895	1980	http://tobaccodocuments.org/profiles/ellis_sir_charles.html
4	Ellis, Charles Drummond	1895	1980	The Third Man: Charles Drummond Ellis, 1895-1980, by A. R. Mackintosh, Notes and Records of the Royal Society of London, Volume 49, No. 2 (July 1995), pp. 277-293
1	Mackenzie, Aubrey Duncan	1895	1962	The Age, 3 March 1930, p 2
1	Cairns, Hugh William Henry	1896	1952	Australian Dictionary of Biography
2	Cairns, Hugh William Henry	1896	1952	http://www.sofo.org.uk/colleges
3	Cairns, Hugh William Henry	1896	1952	Lawrence of Arabia, Sir Hugh Cairns, and the origin of motorcycle helmets, NF Maartens, AD Wills, CB Adams, Neurosurgery, Volume 50, No 1, January 2002, pp 179-180
1	Laidlaw, Alexander Bannatyne Stewart	1896	1968	http://www.imeche.org/docs/default-source/presidents-choice/jc12_1.pdf
2	Laidlaw, Alexander Bannatyne Stewart	1896	1968	The Jet Race and the Second World War, by Sterling Michael Pavelec, Praeger Security International, 2007, p 51
1	Blackett, Patrick Maynard Stuart	1897	1974	The Britannica Guide to Particle Physics, edited by Erik Gregersen, Britannica Educational Publishing, New York, 2011, p 165
2	Blackett, Patrick Maynard Stuart	1897	1974	http://www.nndb.com/people/756/000099459/
3	Blackett, Patrick Maynard Stuart	1897	1974	Oxford Dictionary of National Biography
4	Blackett, Patrick Maynard Stuart	1897	1974	http://www.nobelprize.org/nobel_prizes/physics/laureates/1948/blackett-bio.html

5	Blackett, Patrick Maynard Stuart	1897	1974	Profiles in Operations Research: Pioneers and Innovators, by Arjang A. Assad, Saul I. Gass, Springer, New York, 2011, pp 1-8
6	Blackett, Patrick Maynard Stuart	1897	1974	Patrick Blackett: Providing 'White Heat' to the British Computing Revolution, by David Anderson, Communications of the ACM, Volume 56, No. 12, pp 26-28
7	Blackett, Patrick Maynard Stuart	1897	1974	Nobel Lectures in Physics 1942-1962, World Scientific Publishing Co. Ltd., Singapore, 1998, p 122
1	Hinshelwood, Cyril Norman	1897	1967	http://www.britannica.com/EBchecked/topic/266508/Sir-Cyril-Norman-Hinshelwood
2	Hinshelwood, Cyril Norman	1897	1967	http://www.cartage.org.lb/en/themes/biographies/MainBiographies/H/Hinshelwood/1.html
3	Hinshelwood, Cyril Norman	1897	1967	http://www.nobelprize.org/nobel_prizes/chemistry/laureates/1956/hinshelwood-bio.html
1	McLaren, Henry Thomas	1897	1993	http://www.nationaltrust.com.au/heritagefestival/nsw/aussieinventions/
1	Walton, Arthur Edward	1897	1959	Biodiversity, by Edward Osborne Wilson, National Academy Press, Washington D.C., 1988, p 303
2	Walton, Arthur Edward	1897	1959	Oxford Dictionary of National Biography
1	Gulland, John Masson	1898	1947	http://www.sebiology.org/publications/Bulletin/July06/Thymus.html
2	Gulland, John Masson	1898	1947	http://www.the-scientist.com/?articles.view/articleNo/27357/title/Hints-of-a-Helix--circa-1947/
1	Hamilton, Archibald Milne	1898	1972	http://www.teara.govt.nz/en/1966/expatriates-biographies/page-32
2	Hamilton, Archibald Milne	1898	1972	http://www.fhwa.dot.gov/bridge/prefab/psbsreport03.cfm
3	Hamilton, Archibald Milne	1898	1972	http://search.informit.com.au/documentSummary;dn=763233377446479;res=IELENG
1	Lees, George Martin	1898	1955	Oxford Dictionary of National Biography
1	Wishart, John	1898	1956	http://www-history.mcs.st-and.ac.uk/Biographies/Wishart.html
1	Burnet, Frank Macfarlane	1899	1985	http://www.asap.unimelb.edu.au/bsparcs/aasmemoirs/burnet.htm
2	Burnet, Frank Macfarlane	1899	1985	http://nobelprize.org/nobel_prizes/medicine/laureates/1960/burnet-bio.html
3	Burnet, Frank Macfarlane	1899	1985	http://www.science.org.au/fellows/memoirs/burnet.html

1	Forbes, Archibald Walter	1899	1996	http://www.bermuda-online.org/aviation.htm
1	Hamilton, Charles William Feilden	1899	1978	http://www.teara.govt.nz/en/biographies/4h10/hamilton-charles-william-feilden
2	Hamilton, Charles William Feilden	1899	1978	http://www.hamjet.co.nz/about_hamiltonjet/sir_william_hamilton

Chapter 7
1900-2015

1	Kay, David	1900	X	E&T Engineering and Technology Magazine, Volume 6, Issue 7, 11 July 2011
2	Kay, David	1900	X	Flight, 27 December 1934, p 1378
3	Kay, David	1900	X	http://www.gyroplanepassion.com/KayType331GyroplaneAutogyro.html
1	Robertson, John Monteath	1900	1989	J. Monteath Robertson,1900-1989, Crystallographers, by G. Sim, Journal of Applied Crystallography, Volume 23, 1990, pp 349-350
2	Robertson, John Monteath	1900	1989	McGraw-Hill Modern Scientists and Engineers; McGraw-Hill, Volume 3, 1980, pp 34-35
3	Robertson, John Monteath	1900	1989	http://worldchanging.gla.ac.uk/article/?id=65
1	Stagg, James Martin	1900	1975	http://www.britannica.com/EBchecked/topic/1056774/James-Martin-Stagg
1	Swinton, William Elgin	1900	1994	The Independent, 28 June 1994
1	Lions, Francis	1901	1972	http://www.eoas.info/biogs/P005102b.htm
2	Lions, Francis	1901	1972	Australian Dictionary of Biography, Volume 15, Melbourne University Press, 2000, pp 101-102
1	Henderson, Robert Gregory	1902	1999	The Herald, 15 February 2000
1	Murray, John Mackay	1902	1966	Biographical Dictionary of the History of Technology, edited by Lance Day, Ian McNeil, Routledge, London, 1996, p 508
1	Raw, Alan Rayson	1902	1964	Australian Dictionary of Biography, Volume 16, Melbourne University Press, 2002, pp 62-63
1	Black, William	1903	1975	http://www.caithness.org/caithnesspotatobreeders/Potato%20Breaders%20Harvest.pdf
2	Black, William	1903	1975	http://potatoassociation.org/About%20the%20PAA/Honorary%20Life%20Members/1957HLMBiogs.htm
1	Blumlein, Alan Dower	1903	1942	http://www.todaysengineer.org/2003/Jun/history.asp

2	Blumlein, Alan Dower	1903	1942	BBC News, 1 August 2008 http://news.bbc.co.uk/2/hi/technology/7538152.stm 4 June 2011
3	Blumlein, Alan Dower	1903	1942	Oxford Dictionary of National Biography
4	Blumlein, Alan Dower	1903	1942	http://www.todaysengineer.org/2003/Jun/history.asp
1	Farquharson, James Robbie	1903	2005	Sir James Farquharson, The Herald (Scotland), 21 April 2005
1	Hodge, William Vallance Douglas	1903	1975	http://www.barnesandnoble.com/w/w-v-d-hodge-lambert-m-surhone/1026277325?ean=9786132990143
2	Hodge, William Vallance Douglas	1903	1975	http://www-history.mcs.st-and.ac.uk/Printonly/Hodge.html
3	Hodge, William Vallance Douglas	1903	1975	http://www-history.mcs.st-andrews.ac.uk/Biographies/Hodge.html
1	Dalziel, Charles Francis	1904	1986	http://texts.cdlib.org/view?docId=hb767nb3z6&doc.view=frames&chunk.id=div00022&toc.depth=1&toc.id=
1	Legget, Robert Ferguson	1904	1994	http://www.royalsoced.org.uk/cms/files/fellows/obits_alpha/Legget_r.pdf
1	MacLagan, Daniel Stewart	1904	1991	Modern Insecticides and the Balance of Nature, by Dr. D. Stewart MacLagan, Nature, Volume 168, 1 September 1951, p 360
2	MacLagan, Daniel Stewart	1904	1991	http://www.royalsoced.org.uk/cms/files/fellows/obits_alpha/maclagan_daniel.pdf
1	Mitchell, Colin Campbell	1904	1969	http://www.eos-strut.org.uk/newsletters/11-05.pdf
1	Cadell, Colin Simson	1905	1996	Obituaries, The Independent, 21 November 1996
1	Chalmers, William Malcolm	1905	1995	That's the way the cookie crumbles: 62 all-new commentaries on the Fascinating Chemistry of Everyday Life, by Joe Schwarcz, Joseph A. Schwarcz, ECW Press, Toronto, 2002, pp 194-195
2	Chalmers, William Malcolm	1905	1995	Plastics Materials 7th edition, by J A Brydson, Butterworth-Heinemann, Oxford, 1999, p 399
3	Chalmers, William Malcolm	1905	1995	http://pubs.acs.org/subscribe/archive/tcaw/09/i12/html/12chemch.html
4	Chalmers, William Malcolm	1905	1995	http://cameo.mfa.org/wiki/Plexiglass
1	Paton, Thomas Angus Lyall	1905	1999	Biographical Memoirs of Fellows of The Royal Society, by F. M. Burdekin, volume 47, 1 November 2001, p 421

2	Paton, Thomas Angus Lyall	1905	1999	Biographical Memoirs of Fellows of The Royal Society, by F. M. Burdekin, volume 47, 1 November 2001, p 423
3	Paton, Thomas Angus Lyall	1905	1999	Ibid. p 422
1	Hopper, Grace Murray	1906	1992	http://cs-www.cs.yale.edu/homes/tap/Files/hopper-story.html
1	Maclaren, Owen Finlay	1906	1978	http://geisscommunications.com/pdf/maclarencorporatebackgrounder.pdf
2	Maclaren, Owen Finlay	1906	1978	http://spitfiresite.com/2009/06/mclaren-spitfire.html
3	Maclaren, Owen Finlay	1906	1978	http://www.ipmsstockholm.org/magazine/2001/12/stuff_eng_detail_spitfire_ix_03.htm
4	Maclaren, Owen Finlay	1906	1978	http://geisscommunications.com/pdf/maclarencorporatebackgrounder.pdf
5	Maclaren, Owen Finlay	1906	1978	http://bbs.hitechcreations.com/smf/index.php?topic=305850.0
6	Maclaren, Owen Finlay	1906	1978	http://geisscommunications.com/pdf/maclarencorporatebackgrounder.pdf
1	Buchanan, Colin Douglas	1907	2001	Oxford Dictionary of National Biography
1	Chalmers, Bruce	1907	1990	http://www.engr.uconn.edu/brody-chalmeraward.php
2	Chalmers, Bruce	1907	1990	Bruce Chalmers 1907-1990; A Biographical Memoir, by David Turnbull, National Academy of Sciences, National Academies Press, Washington D.C., 1999, p 7
1	Haddow, Alexander	1907	1976	Obituary, Professor Sir Alexander Haddow, by E. Boyland and R. J. C. Harris, Cancer Research, Volume 37, p 1586
2	Haddow, Alexander	1907	1976	By looking back we can see the way forward: enhancing the gains achieved with antihormone therapy, by V Craig Jordan, Roshani Patel, Joan S Lewis-Wambi, and Ramona F Swaby, Breast Cancer Research, Volume 10, Supplement 4, 2008, p 1
3	Haddow, Alexander	1907	1976	http://www.aim25.ac.uk/cgi-bin/vcdf/detail?coll_id=10923&inst_id=20
4	Haddow, Alexander	1907	1976	Obituary, Professor Sir Alexander Haddow, by E. Boyland and R. J. C. Harris, Cancer Research, Volume 37, p 1586
1	Pirie, Norman Wingate	1907	1997	The Independent, 22 April 1997

2	Pirie, Norman Wingate	1907	1997	Norman Wingate Pirie, 1 July 1907-29 March 1997, by W.S. Pierpoint, Biographical Memoirs of Fellows of the Royal Society, London, Volume 45, 1999, p 401
1	Todd, Alexander Robertus	1907	1997	http://worldchanging.gla.ac.uk/article/?id=71
2	Todd, Alexander Robertus	1907	1997	Oxford Dictionary of National Biography
3	Todd, Alexander Robertus	1907	1997	http://www.emsb.qc.ca/laurenhill/science/nobelcm.html
4	Todd, Alexander Robertus	1907	1997	Oxford Dictionary of National Biography
1	Brown, George Harold	1908	1987	http://www.ieeeghn.org/wiki/index.php/George_Brown
2	Brown, George Harold	1908	1987	Memorial Tributes, Volume 4, National Academy of Engineering, Washington D.C. 1991, p 35
1	Mellanby, Kenneth	1908	1993	Obituary, The Independent, 11 January 1994
2	Mellanby, Kenneth	1908	1993	http://www.scottish-places.info/scotgaz/people/famousfirst2985.html
3	Mellanby, Kenneth	1908	1993	Obituary, The Independent, 11 January 1994
1	Waland, Robert Louis	1908	1999	http://www.futuremuseum.co.uk/collections/people/key-people/science-invention/robert-waland.aspx
2	Waland, Robert Louis	1908	1999	Dictionary of Minor Planet Names, 6th edition, by Lutz D. Schmadel, Springer, 2012, p 296
3	Waland, Robert Louis	1908	1999	The Herald, 22 March 1999
1	Wilson, John Tuzo	1908	1993	http://hrsbstaff.ednet.ns.ca/bowiet/Geology%2012/Lesson%20_3%20-%20J%20Tuzo%20Wilson%20Plate%20Tectonics%20Theory[1].doc
2	Wilson, John Tuzo	1908	1993	https://www.e-education.psu.edu/earth520/content/l2_p7.html
3	Wilson, John Tuzo	1908	1993	This Dynamic Earth: The Story of Plate Tectonics, by W. Jacquelyne Kious, Robert I. Tilling, published by Geological Survey (USGS), 1 May 1996, p 49
4	Wilson, John Tuzo	1908	1993	http://particle.physics.ucdavis.edu/bios/wilson.html
1	King, Alexander	1909	2007	Oxford Dictionary of National Biography
2	King, Alexander	1909	2007	Alexander King 1909-2007, Obituary, by Keith Suter, The Guardian, 2 May 2007

3	King, Alexander	1909	2007	How "Silent Spring" Ignited the Environmental Movement, by Eliza Griswold, New York Times, 21 September 2012
4	King, Alexander	1909	2007	http://www.clubofrome.org/?p=375
5	King, Alexander	1909	2007	http://www.epa.gov/pesticides/factsheets/chemicals/ddt-brief-history-status.htm
6	King, Alexander	1909	2007	http://www.uow.edu.au/~sharonb/STS300/limits/writings/corinfo2.html
1	Donald, Ian	1910	1987	http://www.ob-ultrasound.net/brown.html
2	Donald, Ian	1910	1987	https://www.birthinternational.com/articles/birth-intervention/82-ultrasound-more-harm-than-good
3	Donald, Ian	1910	1987	http://www.ob-ultrasound.net/brown.html
1	Loutit, John Freeman	1910	1992	Oxford Dictionary of National Biography
2	Loutit, John Freeman	1910	1992	http://www.ggs.wa.edu.au/About-Us/Rhodes-Scholars.aspx
3	Loutit, John Freeman	1910	1992	John Freeman Loutit, 19 February 1910-11 June 1992, by Mary Lyon and P. L. Mollison, Biographical Memoirs of Fellows of the Royal Society, Volume 40, November 1994, pp 238-252
1	Sinclair, Hugh Macdonald	1910	1990	http://www.epi.umn.edu/cvdepi/essay.asp?id=120
2	Sinclair, Hugh Macdonald	1910	1990	http://www.reading.ac.uk/merl/collections/Archives_A_to_Z/merl-D_HS.aspx
3	Sinclair, Hugh Macdonald	1910	1990	http://www.nutritionsociety.org/sites/www.nutritionsociety.org/files/Hugh%20Sinclair%20-%20full%20story.pdf
1	Aitken, Yvonne	1911	2004	http://www.science.org.au/scientists/interviews/a/ya.html
1	Cameron, Alexander Bryce	1911	X	http://www.demko.com/cs000316.htm
1	Ogston, Alexander George	1911	1996	http://www.bookadda.com/books/fellows-trinity-college-oxford-books-llc-1156467411-9781156467411
2	Ogston, Alexander George	1911	1996	The Independent, 9 July 1996
3	Ogston, Alexander George	1911	1996	http://oa.anu.edu.au/obituary/ogston-alexander-george-sandy-779
4	Ogston, Alexander George	1911	1996	The Independent, 9 July 1996
5	Ogston, Alexander George	1911	1996	Ibid.
1	Bruce, Frederick Malloch	1912	1997	http://www.royalsoced.org.uk/cms/files/fellows/obits_alpha/bruce_frederick.pdf

1	Curran, Samuel Crowe	1912	1998	Oxford Dictionary of National Biography
1	Lickley, Robert Lang	1912	1998	http://www.royalsoced.org.uk/cms/files/fellows/obits_alpha/Lickley_r.pdf
2	Lickley, Robert Lang	1912	1998	http://heritage.imeche.org/Biographies/RLLickley
3	Lickley, Robert Lang	1912	1998	http://www.royalsoced.org.uk/cms/files/fellows/obits_alpha/Lickley_r.pdf
4	Lickley, Robert Lang	1912	1998	http://www.nycaviation.com/2012/03/on-this-day-in-aviation-history-march-10th/
5	Lickley, Robert Lang	1912	1998	http://www.royalsoced.org.uk/cms/files/fellows/obits_alpha/Lickley_r.pdf
1	MacKenzie, Kenneth Ross	1912	2002	http://www.redorbit.com/education/reference_library/science_1/elements/2582888/astatine/
2	MacKenzie, Kenneth Ross	1912	2002	Los Angeles Times, 11 July 2002
1	Watt, William	1912	1985	http://www.acs.org/content/acs/en/education/whatischemistry/landmarks/carbonfibers.html
2	Watt, William	1912	1985	http://www.topbritishinnovations.org/PastInnovations/StrongCarbonFibres.aspx
3	Watt, William	1912	1985	http://royalsociety.org/exhibitions/sovereign-science/carbon/
4	Watt, William	1912	1985	http://www.ccm.udel.edu/Intro/MoE/1987-tri.pdf
1	Bigelow, Wilfred Gordon	1913	2005	Wilfred G Bigelow, by Barbara Kermode-Scott, British Medical Journal, Volume 330, No 7497, 23 April 2005, p 967
2	Bigelow, Wilfred Gordon	1913	2005	Dr. Wilfred G. Bigelow; a pioneer in heart surgery, Jeremy Pearce, New York Times News Service, The San Diego Union-Tribune, 1 April 2005
3	Bigelow, Wilfred Gordon	1913	2005	http://www.cdnmedhall.org/laureates/?laur_id=27
1	Falconer, Douglas	1913	2004	The Scotsman, 9 April 2004
2	Falconer, Douglas	1913	2004	D. S. Falconer and Introduction to Quantitative Genetics, by William G. Hill and Trudy F. C. Mackay, Genetics, Volume 167, No 4, 1 August 2004, pp 1529-1536
3	Falconer, Douglas	1913	2004	The Scotsman, 9 April 2004
1	Geddes, William George Nicholson	1913	1993	Encyclopedia Britannica 2009 Deluxe Edition
2	Geddes, William George Nicholson	1913	1993	http://rse.mtcserver6.com/cms/files/fellows/obits_alpha/geddes_william.pdf
1	Leakey, Mary Douglas	1913	1996	New York Times, 10 December 1996

2	Leakey, Mary Douglas	1913	1996	http://www.talkorigins.org/faqs/homs/mleakey.html
3	Leakey, Mary Douglas	1913	1996	New York Times, 10 December 1996
4	Leakey, Mary Douglas	1913	1996	Oxford Dictionary of National Biography
5	Leakey, Mary Douglas	1913	1996	New York Times, 10 December 1996
1	Martin-Scott, Ian	1913	2002	Obituaries, Ian Martin-Scott, by Stephen H Martin-Scott, BMJ (British Medical Journal), Volume 325, 30 November 2002, p 1306
2	Martin-Scott, Ian	1913	2002	Annual Clinical Meeting: Middlesbrough, October 6-9, British Medical Journal Supplement, London, 10 September1960, p 2903
3	Martin-Scott, Ian	1913	2002	Soap and Skin, by Ian Martin-Scott and A. G. Ramsay, British Medical Journal, 30 June 1956, p 1528
1	Silver, Robert Simpson	1913	1997	http://www.swcc.gov.sa/files/assets/Research/Technical%20Papers/Thermal/PROSPECTS%20OF%20IMPROVING%20ENERGY%20CONSUMPTION%20OF%20THE%20MULT-STAGE%20.pdf
2	Silver, Robert Simpson	1913	1997	Memorial Tributes: National Academy of Engineering, Volume 10, 2002, pp 217-220
1	Fergusson, Mary Isolen	1914	1997	http://www.newscientist.com/article/mg19325874.600-this-week-50-years-ago.html
2	Fergusson, Mary Isolen	1914	1997	The New Scientist, 24 January 1957, p 20
1	Reid, Donald Darnley	1914	1977	Biography: Professor D. D. Reid, by Geoffrey Rose, Journal of Epidemiology and Community Health, Volume 32, 1978, pp 229-230
2	Reid, Donald Darnley	1914	1977	http://www.jameslindlibrary.org/illustrating/articles/donald-darnley-reid-1914-1977
1	Ritchie, George Stephen	1914	2012	The Telegraph, 13 August 2012
1	Munro, Hamish Nisbet	1915	1994	The Seattle Times, 6 November 1994
2	Munro, Hamish Nisbet	1915	1994	Star News, 6 November 1994
3	Munro, Hamish Nisbet	1915	1994	The New York Times, 5 November 1994
4	Munro, Hamish Nisbet	1915	1994	http://www.royalsoced.org.uk/cms/files/fellows/obits_alpha/munro_hamish.pdf
1	Rankin, Robert Alexander	1915	2001	http://www.mathcs.emory.edu/~ono/publications-cv/pdfs/076.pdf

2	Rankin, Robert Alexander	1915	2001	http://www-history.mcs.st-andrews.ac.uk/Printonly/Rankin.html
3	Rankin, Robert Alexander	1915	2001	Ibid.
4	Rankin, Robert Alexander	1915	2001	http://en.wikipedia.org/wiki/Rankin%E2%80%93 Selberg_method
1	Grant, James Kerr	1916	2004	www.royalsoced.org.uk/cms/files/fellows/obits_a lpha/grant_j.pdf
2	Grant, James Kerr	1916	2004	http://www.elliottsimpson.com/history/glasgowen docrine.html
1	Macfarlane, George Gray	1916	2007	Oxford Dictionary of National Biography
2	Macfarlane, George Gray	1916	2007	Obituary, The Guardian, 30 July 2007
3	Macfarlane, George Gray	1916	2007	Oxford Dictionary of National Biography
1	Simpson, John Alexander	1916	2000	http://www.lib.uchicago.edu/e/scrc/findingaids/vi ew.php?eadid=ICU.SPCL.JASIMPSON
2	Simpson, John Alexander	1916	2000	Biographic Memoirs, Volume 81, The National Academies Press, 2002, p 320
3	Simpson, John Alexander	1916	2000	http://www.lib.uchicago.edu/e/scrc/findingaids/vi ew.php?eadid=ICU.SPCL.JASIMPSON
4	Simpson, John Alexander	1916	2000	Biographic Memoirs, Volume 81, The National Academies Press, 2002, p 320
1	Strath, John Alexander Wiseman	1916	2009	http://www.eoas.info/biogs/P003976b.htm
2	Strath, John Alexander Wiseman	1916	2009	Air Force, Volume 52, No 16, 2 September 2010, p 18
1	Waterhouse, Douglas Frew	1916	2000	http://science.org.au/fellows/memoirs/waterhouse 2.html
2	Waterhouse, Douglas Frew	1916	2000	Ibid.
3	Waterhouse, Douglas Frew	1916	2000	http://www.csiropedia.csiro.au/display/CSIROpe dia/Aerogard
4	Waterhouse, Douglas Frew	1916	2000	http://science.org.au/fellows/memoirs/waterhouse 2.html
1	Bowie, Stanley Hay Umphray	1917	2008	http://www.royalsoced.org.uk/cms/files/fellows/o bits_alpha/Bowie_s.pdf
2	Bowie, Stanley Hay Umphray	1917	2008	Pollutants, Human Health and the Environment: A Risk Based Approach, edited by Jane A. Plant, Nick Voulvoulis, K. Vala Ragnarsdottir, Nikolaos Voulvoulis, Wiley-Blackwell, 2012, p viii

1	Coughtrie, Thomas Robb	1917	2008	http://www.militarian.com/threads/thomas-coughtrie-rip.3583/
1	Dickson, James Tennant	1917	1991	Biographical Dictionary of the History of Technology, by Lance Day, Ian McNeil, Published by Taylor & Francis, 1996, p 208
2	Dickson, James Tennant	1917	1991	http://www.akzonobel.com/system/images/Akzo Nobel_Historybook_LoRes_tcm9-8568.pdf
1	Paton, William Drummond MacDonald	1917	1993	http://www.readcube.com/articles/10.1111/j.2042 -7158.1949.tb12470.x?locale=en
2	Paton, William Drummond MacDonald	1917	1993	Obituary, Professor William Paton, The Independent, 6 November 1993
3	Paton, William Drummond MacDonald	1917	1993	http://munksroll.rcplondon.ac.uk/biography/Detai ls/3477
4	Paton, William Drummond MacDonald	1917	1993	Oxford Dictionary of National Biography
5	Paton, William Drummond MacDonald	1917	1993	Sir William Drummond Macdonald Paton, C. B. E. 5 May 1917-17 October 1993, by H. P. Rang and Lord Perry of Walton, Biographical Memoirs of Fellows of the Royal Society, Volume 42, November 1996, pp 290-314
6	Paton, William Drummond MacDonald	1917	1993	Ibid. pp 290-314
1	Dewar, Michael James Steuart	1918	1997	Biographical Memoirs, by Office of the Home Secretary, National Academy of Sciences, Washington DC, 1999, p 65
2	Dewar, Michael James Steuart	1918	1997	Ibid. pp 64-77
1	Gibson, Quentin Howieson	1918	2011	http://biochem.rice.edu/Content.aspx?id=633
2	Gibson, Quentin Howieson	1918	2011	www.apiindia.org/medicine_update_2013/chap77 .pdf
3	Gibson, Quentin Howieson	1918	2011	http://www.asbmb.org/asbmbtoday/asbmbtoday_ article_print.aspx?id=13060
1	Cram, Donald James	1919	2001	http://senate.universityofcalifornia.edu/inmemoria m/donaldjamescram.html
2	Cram, Donald James	1919	2001	http://books.google.com.au/books/about/Fundame ntals_of_Carbon_Chemistry.html?id=6HKpMQE ACAAJ&redir_esc=y
1	Hammersley, John Michael	1920	2004	http://www.statslab.cam.ac.uk/~grg/papers/jmh_b iom.pdf

2	Hammersley, John Michael	1920	2004	The Independent, 14 May 2004
3	Hammersley, John Michael	1920	2004	http://www.statslab.cam.ac.uk/~grg/papers/jmh_biom.pdf
1	Pilkington, Lionel Alexander Bethune	1920	1995	Oxford Dictionary of National Biography
2	Pilkington, Lionel Alexander Bethune	1920	1995	Obituaries, The Independent, 6 May 1995
1	Russell, William Morris	1920	2006	http://www.findagrave.com/cgi-bin/fg.cgi?page=gr&GRid=26125570
2	Russell, William Morris	1920	2006	Oxford Dictionary of National Biography
1	Simpson, David Cumming	1920	2006	Obituary, David Simpson, British Medical Journal, Volume 333, No 150, 13 July 2006
2	Simpson, David Cumming	1920	2006	Obituaries, Professor David Simpson, Pioneer of powered prosthetic limbs, by Tam Dalyell, The Independent on Sunday, 23 June 2006
3	Simpson, David Cumming	1920	2006	Prevention of pressure sores: engineering and clinical aspects, by John G. Webster, Taylor & Francis Group, New York, 1991, p 96
4	Simpson, David Cumming	1920	2006	Scope, Volume 22, Issue 2, June 2013, p 12
1	Brass, William	1921	1999	http://www.tandfonline.com/doi/abs/10.1080/713779083
2	Brass, William	1921	1999	2000 Lectures and Memoirs edited by British Academy, The British Academy, 2001, p 413
3	Brass, William	1921	1999	Oxford Dictionary of National Biography
1	Brown, William Piper	1921	2004	Australian Dictionary of Biography
1	Dalziel, Keith	1921	1994	The Independent, 13 January 1994
2	Dalziel, Keith	1921	1994	Keith Dalziel 24 August 1921-7 January 1994, by H. Gutfreund, Biographical Memoirs of Fellows of the Royal Society, Volume 42, November 1996, p 119
1	Geddes, Leslie Alexander	1921	2009	http://www.uspto.gov/about/nmti/recipients/2006.jsp
2	Geddes, Leslie Alexander	1921	2009	http://web.mit.edu/invent/iow/geddes.html
1	Isaacs, Alick	1921	1967	http://science.jrank.org/pages/3637/Interferons.html
2	Isaacs, Alick	1921	1967	http://www.newworldencyclopedia.org/entry/Interferon

3	Isaacs, Alick	1921	1967	Trends in Science: Medicine and Health Science, edited by Jon Turney, Helicon Publishing, Chicago, 2001, p 76
4	Isaacs, Alick	1921	1967	http://www.discoveriesinmedicine.com/Hu-Mor/Interferon.html
5	Isaacs, Alick	1921	1967	Tumor Immunology and Interferon, by Feinerman, Burton, Southern Medical Journal, Volume 71, Issue 11, November 1978
6	Isaacs, Alick	1921	1967	http://www.medicinenet.com/interferon/article.htm
1	Lawther, Patrick	1921	2008	Patrick Lawther, by Alison Snyder, The Lancet, Volume 372, Issue 9639, 23 August 2009, p 624
1	Boyd, Robert Lewis Fullarton	1922	2004	http://www.theguardian.com/science/2004/feb/11/obituaries.spaceexploration
1	Cairns, Hugh John Foster	1922	X	http://www.cartage.org.lb/en/themes/Biographies/MainBiographies/C/Cairns/1.html
1	Cochran, William	1922	2003	http://www.scottish-places.info/scotgaz/people/famousfirst2328.html
2	Cochran, William	1922	2003	Obituaries, The Times, 10 October 2003
3	Cochran, William	1922	2003	William Cochran, by Michael Woolfson, Biographical Memoirs of Fellows of The Royal Society, 1 December 2005, p 73
4	Cochran, William	1922	2003	William Cochran, by Michael Woolfson, Biographical Memoirs of Fellows of The Royal Society, 1 December 2005, p 75
1	McCallum, Donald Murdo	1922	2011	http://www.heraldscotland.com/comment/obituaries/sir-donald-mccallum-1.1131131?53487
1	McGregor, Ian Alexander	1922	2007	Oxford Dictionary of National Biography
2	McGregor, Ian Alexander	1922	2007	Ian McGregor, Obituary, by Andrew Prentice, The Guardian, 9 March 2007
3	McGregor, Ian Alexander	1922	2007	Sir Ian Alexander McGregor, by Hannah Brown, The Lances, Volume 369, Issue 9570, 21 April 2007, p 1,340
4	McGregor, Ian Alexander	1922	2007	Oxford Dictionary of National Biography
1	Paul, John	1922	1994	Obituary, John Paul, British Medical Journal, Volume 309, 10 December 1994, pp 1577-1578
2	Paul, John	1922	1994	http://www.independent.co.uk/news/people/obituary-dr-john-paul-1411175.html
1	Smith, Alexander Mair	1922	2003	How to Build a Jet Engine (Television production). BBC, 2010
1	Hamilton, James Arnot	1923	2012	The Houghton Mifflin dictionary of biography, Houghton Mifflin Company, 2003, p 674

2	Hamilton, James Arnot	1923	2012	http://heritage.imeche.org/honoraryfellows/home
3	Hamilton, James Arnot	1923	2012	http://www.kosmoid.net/technology/hamilton
1	Michie, Donald	1923	2007	Obituaries: Professor Donald Michie, The Times, 12 July 2007
2	Michie, Donald	1923	2007	Professor Donald Michie, The Telegraph, 9 July 2007
3	Michie, Donald	1923	2007	Donald Michie, 83, Theorist of Artificial Intelligence, Dies: by Jeremy Pearce, The New York Times, 23 July 2007
4	Michie, Donald	1923	2007	Professor Donald Michie, The Telegraph, 9 July 2007
5	Michie, Donald	1923	2007	Obituaries: Professor Donald Michie, The Times, 12 July 2007
1	Moodie, Alexander Forbes	1923	X	http://www.mx.iucr.org/iucr-top/people/moodie.html
2	Moodie, Alexander Forbes	1923	X	http://www.eoas.info/biogs/P003867b.htm
1	Black, James Whyte	1924	2010	Sir James Black and propranolol, by M. P. Stapleton, University of Calgary, Texas Heart Institute Journal, Volume 24, No 4, p 336
2	Black, James Whyte	1924	2010	Beta-Blockers after Myocardial Infarction – For Few Patients, or Many? The New England Journal of Medicine, Volume 339, No 8, 20 August 1998, pp 551-553
3	Black, James Whyte	1924	2010	http://www.britannica.com/EBchecked/topic/674 55/Sir-James-Black
1	Cormack, Allan MacLeod	1924	1998	Imagining the elephant: a biography of Allan MacLeod Cormack, by Christopher L. Vaughan, Imperial College Press, London, 2008, p 148
2	Cormack, Allan MacLeod	1924	1998	http://www.britannica.com/EBchecked/topic/137 722/Allan-MacLeod-Cormack
1	Fraser, Robert Donald Bruce	1924	X	http://science.org.au/scientists/interviews/f/bf.html
2	Fraser, Robert Donald Bruce	1924	X	http://www.csiropedia.csiro.au/display/CSIROpe dia/Fraser,+Robert+Donald+Bruce
3	Fraser, Robert Donald Bruce	1924	X	Ibid.
1	Iggo, Ainsley	1924	2012	The Telegraph, 13 May 2012
2	Iggo, Ainsley	1924	2012	The Scotsman, 4 April 2012
1	MacIntyre, Iain	1924	2008	http://neiladamandrews.com/wp-content/uploads/2013/01/Calcitonin.pdf
2	MacIntyre, Iain	1924	2008	http://rsbm.royalsocietypublishing.org/content/ear ly/2012/02/15/rsbm.2011.0025.full.pdf

3	MacIntyre, Iain	1924	2008	http://munksroll.rcplondon.ac.uk/Biography/Details/6092
4	MacIntyre, Iain	1924	2008	http://rsbm.royalsocietypublishing.org/content/early/2012/02/15/rsbm.2011.0025.full.pdf
1	Cameron, Alastair Graham Walter	1925	2005	Memorial: Alastair Graham Walter Cameron (1925–2005), Meteoritics & Planetary Science, Volume 41, No. 1, 2006, p 151
2	Cameron, Alastair Graham Walter	1925	2005	http://news.harvard.edu/gazette/story/2009/12/alastair-graham-walter-cameron/
1	Glennie, Alick Edwards	1925	2003	http://www.britannica.com/EBchecked/topic/725676/Autocode
2	Glennie, Alick Edwards	1925	2003	http://www.rickmaybury.com/bootpages/other/backuo001.htm
3	Glennie, Alick Edwards	1925	2003	http://www.turing.org.uk/publications/physics.html
4	Glennie, Alick Edwards	1925	2003	http://www.chessgames.com/perl/chessplayer?pid=96118
1	McFadzean, James Anderson	1925	2002	http://www.ncbi.nlm.nih.gov/pmc/articles/PMC1124880/bin/bmj_325_7377_1424_e_index.html
2	McFadzean, James Anderson	1925	2002	The Use of Metronidazole for the Treatment of Non-Specific Anaerobic Infections in Dogs and Cats, by P. Carwardine, Veterinary Research Communications, Volume 7, 1983, p 261
1	Meek, Marshall	1925	2013	http://www.rjerrard.co.uk/royalnavy/memoir/memoir.html
2	Meek, Marshall	1925	2013	Biographical Dictionary of the History of Technology, edited by Lance Day, Ian McNeil, Routledge, London, 1996, p 477
3	Meek, Marshall	1925	2013	The Telegraph, 29 September 2013
1	Morrison, Andrew William	1925	2006	In Memoriam: Andrew William Morrison, by Richard T. Ramsden, Otology & Neurology, Volume 27, Issue 5, August 2006, pp 586-587
2	Morrison, Andrew William	1925	2006	Andrew William Morrison, British Medical Journal, Volume 332, No 7549, 6 May 2006, p 1097
3	Morrison, Andrew William	1925	2006	Andrew William Morrison, British Medical Journal, Volume 332, No 7549, 6 May 2006, p 1097
1	Shepherd-Barron, John Adrian	1925	2010	The Telegraph, 20 May 2010
2	Shepherd-Barron, John Adrian	1925	2010	Ibid.
1	Gray, George William	1926	2013	The Guardian, 22 May 2013

2	Gray, George William	1926	2013	The Telegraph, 6 June 2013
3	Gray, George William	1926	2013	http://www.exchangerates.org.uk/GBP-USD-exchange-rate-history-full.html
1	Kerr, Allen	1926	X	http://www.appsnet.org/public/about/kerr.aspx
2	Kerr, Allen	1926	X	http://biotechnology-innovation.com.au/innovations/agriculture/and_gene_splicing.html
3	Kerr, Allen	1926	X	http://www.apsnet.org/members/awards/Fellows/Pages/AllenKerr.aspx
1	Mathieson, Ian James	1927	2010	The Telegraph, 8 July 2010
2	Mathieson, Ian James	1927	2010	http://www.saqqara.nl/excavations/other-excavations/saqqara-geophysical-survey-project-(sgsp)
1	West, Thomas Summers	1927	2010	http://www.royalsoced.org.uk/cms/files/fellows/obits_alpha/west_ts.pdf
1	Scott, Alastair Ian	1928	2007	http://www.science.tamu.edu/articles/546/
2	Scott, Alastair Ian	1928	2007	http://www.royalsoced.org.uk/208_RoyalGoldMedalsforoutstandingachievement.html
3	Scott, Alastair Ian	1928	2007	http://www.chemistry.illinois.edu/events/lectures/Nelson_J_Leonard_Distinguished_Lecturers/Alastair_Scott.html
4	Scott, Alastair Ian	1928	2007	http://www.royalsoced.org.uk/232_HRHTheDukeofEdinburghtoawardRoyalGoldMedalstooutstandingScots.html
1	Watson, James Dewey	1928	X	http://www.theinfidels.org/zunb-jamesdwatson.htm
2	Watson, James Dewey	1928	X	http://www.nobelprize.org/nobel_prizes/medicine/laureates/1962/watson-bio.html
3	Watson, James Dewey	1928	X	http://www.abebooks.com/book-search/title/double-helix/author/watson/first-edition/pub-min/1968/pub-max/1968/pics/sortby/1/page-1/
1	Brown, Alexander	1929	1975	Oxford Dictionary of National Biography
1	Frame, Alexander Gilchrist	1929	1993	Oxford Dictionary of National Biography
1	Graham, Robert M	1929	X	http://people.cs.umass.edu/~bob/bio.html
2	Graham, Robert M	1929	X	http://web.mit.edu/multics-history/
1	Higgs, Peter Ware	1929	X	http://www.bppimt.ac.in/BPPIMT_Newsletter_July_2012.pdf
2	Higgs, Peter Ware	1929	X	http://www.kcl.ac.uk/aboutkings/history/famouspeople/peterhiggs.aspx

3	Higgs, Peter Ware	1929	X	http://www.unifiedfieldtheory.org/peter-ware-higgs.html
4	Higgs, Peter Ware	1929	X	"Higgsogenesis" proposed to explain dark matter, by Eugenie Samuel Reich, Nature, 4 October 2013
5	Higgs, Peter Ware	1929	X	http://home.web.cern.ch/about/physics/search-higgs-boson
6	Higgs, Peter Ware	1929	X	https://www.gov.uk/government/news/pm-statement-on-discovery-of-new-sub-atomic-particle
7	Higgs, Peter Ware	1929	X	http://www.abc.net.au/news/2013-10-08/nobel-prize-in-physics-higgs-boson-particle/5009942
1	MacLeod, Norman Alexander	1929	X	100 Military Inventions That Changed The World by Rod Green, Constable & Robinson Ltd, London, 2013, p26
2	MacLeod, Norman Alexander	1929	X	http://www.arrse.co.uk/wiki/Norman_A_MacLeod
3	MacLeod, Norman Alexander	1929	X	http://www.militaryfactory.com/smallarms/detail.asp?smallarms_id=35
4	MacLeod, Norman Alexander	1929	X	100 Military Inventions That Changed The World by Rod Green, Constable & Robinson Ltd, London, 2013, p27
1	Metcalf, Donald	1929	X	http://www.wehi.edu.au/about_us/achievements/professor_don_metcalf/
2	Metcalf, Donald	1929	X	http://www.filmaust.com.au/australianbio11/Aus%20bio%2011%20Press%20kit.pdf
3	Metcalf, Donald	1929	X	http://www.amazon.com/Summon-Blood-dogged-pursuit-regulators/dp/1880854287
1	Monteith, John Lennox	1929	2012	Newsletter of the Association of Applied Biologists: Issue 77, Autumn/Winter, 2012/13, p 15
2	Monteith, John Lennox	1929	2012	http://www.fao.org/docrep/x0490e/x0490e06.htm
3	Monteith, John Lennox	1929	2012	http://www.agrometeorology.org/topics/history-of-agrometeorology/john-monteith-2013-obituary-for-insam-international-society-for-agricultural-meteorology
1	Almeida, June Dalziel	1930	2007	British Medical Journal, Volume 336: No 7659, 26 June 2008, p 1511
2	Almeida, June Dalziel	1930	2007	Obituary: The Times, 18 February 2008

1	Ferguson-Smith, Malcolm Andrew	1931	X	Malcolm Ferguson-Smith, by Peter Pearson, Cytogenetic and Genome Research, No 111, 2005, pp 2-4
1	Cruickshank, Arthur Richard Ivor	1932	2011	The Guardian, 26 December 2011
2	Cruickshank, Arthur Richard Ivor	1932	2011	The Southern Reporter, 22 December 2011, p 12
3	Cruickshank, Arthur Richard Ivor	1932	2011	http://www.geolsoc.org.uk/en/About/History/Obituaries%202001%20onwards/Obituaries%202011/Arthur%20Richard%20Ivor%20Cruickshank%201932-2011
1	Kibble, Thomas Walter Bannerman	1932	2016	http://plato.tp.ph.ic.ac.uk/conferences/Kibble80/about.html
2	Kibble, Thomas Walter Bannerman	1932	2016	http://plato.tp.ph.ic.ac.uk/conferences/Kibble80/about.html
1	Smith, Charles	1932	1997	http://www.royalsoced.org.uk/cms/files/fellows/obits_alpha/smith_charles.pdf
1	Brown, Thomas Graham	1933	X	Classic papers in modern diagnostic radiology, by Adrian Thomas, Arpan K. Banerjee, Uwe Busch, Springer, Berlin, 2005, p 215
2	Brown, Thomas Graham	1933	X	http://www.ob-ultrasound.net/brown3d.html
1	Arnott, Struther	1934	2013	Popular Mechanics, November 1983, p 44
2	Arnott, Struther	1934	2013	The Telegraph, 17 June 2013
1	Miller, Stuart Crichton	1934	1999	http://rsbm.royalsocietypublishing.org/content/48/323.short
2	Miller, Stuart Crichton	1934	1999	http://www.royalsoced.org.uk/cms/files/fellows/obits_alpha/miller_stewart.pdf
1	Thouless, David James	1934	X	http://www.mit.edu/~levitov/8.334/notes/topol.pdf
2	Thouless, David James	1934	X	http://en.inforapid.org/index.php?search=Hexatic%20phase
1	Leslie, Frank Matthews	1935	2000	Frank Matthews Leslie, 8 March 1935–15 June 2000, by R.J. Atkin and T.J. Sluckin, Biographical Memoirs of the Royal Society, Volume 49, 2003, pp 315-33
2	Leslie, Frank Matthews	1935	2000	Ibid.
1	Whitelaw, James Hunter	1936	2000	Oxford Dictionary of National Biography

1	Goodfellow, James	1937	X	http://www.scribd.com/doc/37538742/3/INVENTION-OF-ATM
1	Duncan, Alan James	1938	1999	www.royalsoced.org.uk/cms/files/fellows/obits_alpha/duncan_alan.pdf
2	Duncan, Alan James	1938	1999	The Herald, 24 July 1999
1	Molloy, Bryan Barnet	1939	2004	http://www.invent.org/hall_of_fame/105.html
2	Molloy, Bryan Barnet	1939	2004	http://www.chemheritage.org/discover/online-resources/chemistry-in-history/themes/pharmaceuticals/restoring-and-regulating-the-bodys-biochemistry/fuller--wong--molloy.aspx
3	Molloy, Bryan Barnet	1939	2004	The 100 most important chemical compounds: a reference guide, by Richard L. Myers, Greenwood Publishing Group, 2007, p 128
4	Molloy, Bryan Barnet	1939	2004	http://www.emedexpert.com/facts/fluoxetine-facts.shtml
1	Napier, William	1940	X	Napier W. M., Paleolithic extinctions and the Taurid Complex, Monthly Notices of the Royal Astronomical Society, 1 April 2010
1	Donaldson, Gordon Bryce	1941	2012	Obituary: Prof Gordon Bryce Donaldson, The Herald [Scotland], 26 January 2013
2	Donaldson, Gordon Bryce	1941	2012	Christ's College Magazine, No. 238, 2013, p 110
3	Donaldson, Gordon Bryce	1941	2012	http://ewh.ieee.org/tc/csc/europe/newsforum/Obituaries.html#PO17
1	Hamilton, Ronald Shade	1941	X	http://www.ronhamilton.co.uk/birth-of-daily-disposables
2	Hamilton, Ronald Shade	1941	X	http://www.lens101.com/october-2004/36-new-contact-lens-triumph-man-vision.html
3	Hamilton, Ronald Shade	1941	X	http://www.ronhamilton.co.uk/about-daysoft/
1	Lipinski, Christopher Andrew	1941	X	http://www.google.com/patents/WO2007148130A1?cl=en
2	Lipinski, Christopher Andrew	1941	X	http://www.biosolveit.com/people/vips/lipinski.html?ct=1
3	Lipinski, Christopher Andrew	1941	X	http://new.tballiance.org/newscenter/view-brief.php?id=98
1	Irvine-Halliday, David	1942	X	http://solar.calfinder.com/blog/news/how-one-man-solar-illuminated-25000-lives/

2	Irvine-Halliday, David	1942	X	http://gchandler.ehclients.com/index.php/graham/imperialoil2/david_irvine-halliday/
3	Irvine-Halliday, David	1942	X	http://lutw.org/
1	Hawking, Stephen William	1942	X	http://www.bookrags.com/Stephen_Hawking/
2	Hawking, Stephen William	1942	X	Stephen Hawking, His Life and Work by Kitty Ferguson, Bantam Press, London, 2011, p 26
3	Hawking, Stephen William	1942	X	http://www.physicsoftheuniverse.com/scientists_hawking.html
4	Hawking, Stephen William	1942	X	Stephen Hawking, His Life and Work by Kitty Ferguson, Bantam Press, London, 2011, p 130
5	Hawking, Stephen William	1942	X	Principia Logica by Alec Misra, Lulu.com, ISBN-10: 141164025X, 2005 p 30
6	Hawking, Stephen William	1942	X	http://www.physicsoftheuniverse.com/scientists_hawking.html
7	Hawking, Stephen William	1942	X	The Telegraph 27 April 2007
8	Hawking, Stephen William	1942	X	http://iphone.metricscat.com/brief-history-time-audio-book/
1	Milne, Alastair David	1942	X	http://www.wolfsonmicro.com/investor/milestones/
2	Milne, Alastair David	1942	X	http://www.bristol.ac.uk/pace/graduation/honorary-degrees/hondeg07/milne.html
1	Skinner, Gordon Robert Bruce	1942	2013	http://www.vri.org.uk/people.html
2	Skinner, Gordon Robert Bruce	1942	2013	http://www.ncbi.nlm.nih.gov/pubmed/9255764
3	Skinner, Gordon Robert Bruce	1942	2013	http://www.thyroiduk.org.uk/tuk/news_and_media/Dr_Skinner.html
1	Stoddart, James Fraser	1942	X	https://www.amacad.org/content/news/pressReleases.aspx?pr=167
2	Stoddart, James Fraser	1942	X	http://stoddart.northwestern.edu/Index.php?View=Fraser_Stoddart/General.php
3	Stoddart, James Fraser	1942	X	http://www.kff.com/en01/kfip/1428H2007G/KFIPWinners6WWW1428H2007G.html
4	Stoddart, James Fraser	1942	X	http://stoddart.northwestern.edu/Index.php?View=Fraser_Stoddart/General.php
5	Stoddart, James Fraser	1942	X	http://umanitoba.ca/faculties/science/alumni/805.html
1	Forrest, Archibald Robin	1943	X	http://www.youtube.com/watch?v=2S3RqGVIdng
2	Forrest, Archibald Robin	1943	X	http://www.cadazz.com/cad-software-history.htm

3	Forrest, Archibald Robin	1943	X	Handbook of computer aided geometric design, edited by Gerald E. Farin, Josef Hoschek, Myung-Soo Kim, published by Elsevier, Amsterdam, 2002, p 11
4	Forrest, Archibald Robin	1943	X	An Introduction to NURBS: With Historical Perspective, by David F Rogers, Academic Press, London, 2001, p 14
5	Forrest, Archibald Robin	1943	X	Ibid. p 15
1	Copus, Johnathan	1944	X	http://care.diabetesjournals.org/content/29/5/1176.1.full
2	Copus, Johnathan	1944	X	http://news.bbc.co.uk/2/hi/uk_news/wales/3386071.stm
3	Copus, Johnathan	1944	X	http://www.medica-tradefair.com/cipp/md_medica/custom/pub/content,oid,14427/lang,2/ticket,g_u_e_s_t/~/World_s_first_electronic_antibiotic_at_MEDICA.html
1	Grant, Peter Mitchell	1944	X	http://archive.is/YJw58
2	Grant, Peter Mitchell	1944	X	http://www.china-scotland-sipra.org/KeyPersonnel/Pages/PeterGrant.aspx
1	Henderson, Richard	1945	X	http://www2.mrc-lmb.cam.ac.uk/groups/rh15/Biographical.html
2	Henderson, Richard	1945	X	http://archive.is/C3CRp
3	Henderson, Richard	1945	X	http://www.iavireport.org/Back-Issues/Pages/IAVI-Report-13(6)-TheBeautyBehindtheBeasts.aspx
1	Plotkin, Gordon David	1946	X	http://www.sigplan.org/Awards/Achievement/2010
2	Plotkin, Gordon David	1946	X	Ibid.
1	Hill, William	1949	2012	The Herald, 23 October 2012
2	Hill, William	1949	2012	Defeating the computer's arch enemy: unreadability, by Kim Honey (Microsoft), The Globe and Mail, 5 March 2001
3	Hill, William	1949	2012	Ibid.
4	Hill, William	1949	2012	http://www.microsoft.com/typography/cleartype/billhill.htm
5	Hill, William	1949	2012	http://scien.stanford.edu/pages/labsite/2007/psych221/projects/07/ClearType/
1	Browne, Leslie Johnston	1950	X	http://www.princetoninfo.com/index.php?option=com_us1more&Itemid=6&key=06-02-2010%20fastlane

2	Browne, Leslie Johnston	1950	X	http://www.bloomberg.com/apps/news?pid=news archive&sid=ar21ksyM89eg
3	Browne, Leslie Johnston	1950	X	http://www.prnewswire.com/news-releases/novartis-researcher-honored-for-breast-cancer-drug-femarar-letrozole-tablets-75575817.html
1	Anderson, Douglas Crombie	1951	X	http://spie.org/x84626.xml
1	Prosser, Patrick	1952	X	http://www.webopedia.com/TERM/D/disk_thrashing.html
2	Prosser, Patrick	1952	X	http://4c.ucc.ie/web/displaybio.jsp?id=73
1	Frazer, Ian Hector	1953	X	http://royalsociety.org/people/ian-frazer/
2	Frazer, Ian Hector	1953	X	Cervical cancer vaccine brings hope to patients, by Amanda Spratt, The New Zealand Herald, 16 October 2005
3	Frazer, Ian Hector	1953	X	http://www.abc.net.au/einsteinfactor/txt/s2664925.htm
4	Frazer, Ian Hector	1953	X	http://www.fiercevaccines.com/story/merck-readies-fda-submission-son-gardasil/2013-11-06
5	Frazer, Ian Hector	1953	X	http://www.gardasil.com/
6	Frazer, Ian Hector	1953	X	Important Information About Gardasil http://www.gardasil.com/ Viewed 24 November 2009
7	Frazer, Ian Hector	1953	X	http://www.uq.edu.au/news/article/2012/07/gardasil-vaccine-be-available-boys-2013
8	Frazer, Ian Hector	1953	X	http://www.fiercevaccines.com/story/merck-sanofi-granted-european-commission-thumbs-gardasil-9/2015-06-17
1	Campbell, Keith Henry Stockman	1954	2012	The Telegraph, 11 October 2012
2	Campbell, Keith Henry Stockman	1954	2012	The Guardian, 17 October 2012
3	Campbell, Keith Henry Stockman	1954	2012	The Scotsman, 12 October 2012
4	Campbell, Keith Henry Stockman	1954	2012	The Telegraph, 11 October 2012
1	Fraser, Bruce	1954	2006	http://www.ppmag.com/web-exclusives/2006/12/obituary-bruce-fraser-19542006.html
2	Fraser, Bruce	1954	2006	http://www.photoshoplab.com/bruce-fraser-receives-lifetime-achievement-award-from-the-national-association-of-photoshop-professionals.html
3	Fraser, Bruce	1954	2006	http://www.peachpit.com/authors/bio.aspx?a=35C6A590-6AFD-4BFF-8E11-7B11840DCCC5

1	Scott, David	1955	X	http://www.ctbuh.org/Information/Committees/ScientificPeerReview/DavidScott/tabid/3215/language/en-US/Default.aspx
2	Scott, David	1955	X	http://www.skyscraper.org/PROGRAMS/VERTICAL_DENSITY/vertical_density_participants.php
3	Scott, David	1955	X	http://web.mta.info/capital/sas_alt.html
1	McNaught, Robert Houston	1956	X	http://www.skyandtelescope.com/news/The-Saga-of-the-Astronomers-Hat-187467971.html
2	McNaught, Robert Houston	1956	X	http://www.distantsuns.com/distant-suns-astronomy-app-makes-tracking-comet-pan-starrs-easy/
3	McNaught, Robert Houston	1956	X	http://www.sciencephoto.com/media/227234/view
4	McNaught, Robert Houston	1956	X	http://mbtimetraveler.com/tag/robert-mcnaught/
1	Gow, David James	1957	X	http://www.europeanvoice.com/page/european-inventor-award-2013-smes/3768.aspx
2	Gow, David James	1957	X	http://www.epo.org/learning-events/european-inventor/finalists/2013/gow/feature.html
3	Gow, David James	1957	X	http://edition.cnn.com/2013/02/01/tech/bionic-hand-ilimb-prosthetic/index.html
4	Gow, David James	1957	X	http://www.dailymail.co.uk/health/article-469272/Revolutionary-bionic-hand-sale-8-500.html
1	Reid, Iain Neill	1957	X	http://www.phschool.com/science/science_news/articles/milky_way_merger.html
2	Reid, Iain Neill	1957	X	Measuring the Universe: The Cosmological Distance Ladder, by Stephen Webb, springer-Praxis, 2001, p 158
3	Reid, Iain Neill	1957	X	http://hubblesite.org/newscenter/archive/releases/2008/26/image/a/
1	Underwood, Ian	1959	X	http://www.royalsoced.org.uk/126_ScotlandsTopInnovator.html
2	Underwood, Ian	1959	X	http://www.oled-info.com/MED_Interview_November2006
3	Underwood, Ian	1959	X	Ibid.
1	Waldron, John Duncan	1959	X	http://www.eaae-astronomy.org/cas//Cruithne.pdf
1	Black, Alan Wilson	1962	X	http://www.cs.cmu.edu/~awb/bioawb2013.pdf
1	Tait, Richard John	1964	X	http://www.fundinguniverse.com/company-histories/cranium-inc-history/
1	Devine, Graeme John	1966	X	http://www.gameinformer.com/b/features/archive/2012/11/26/horror-story-an-oral-history-of-the-7th-guest.aspx

2	Devine, Graeme John	1966	X	http://au.games.ign.com/top-100-game-creators/90.html
3	Devine, Graeme John	1966	X	http://appleinsider.com/articles/10/12/08/ios_game_designer_graeme_devine_leaves_apple_to_make_mac_ios_games
1	Jones, David	1966	X	http://kotaku.com/5830192/what-do-grand-theft-auto-and-lemmings-have-in-common
2	Jones, David	1966	X	http://vgsales.wikia.com/wiki/Grand_Theft_Auto
3	Jones, David	1966	X	http://www.mobygames.com/developer/sheet/view/developerId,13393/
1	McEwan, Ian Kenneth	1966	X	http://www.raeng.org.uk/about/fellowship/pdf/newfels2008.pdf
1	MacKay, David John Cameron	1967	X	https://connect.innovateuk.org/web/nick-kirkwood/~/405026/blogs
2	MacKay, David John Cameron	1967	X	http://www.inference.phy.cam.ac.uk/dasher/DasherSummary2.html
1	Watson, Brian	1967	X	http://www.mobygames.com/developer/sheet/view/developerId,16743/
1	McInnes, Colin Robert	1968	X	http://lifeboat.com/ex/bios.colin.r.mcinnes
1	MacMillan, David William	1968	X	http://www.princeton.edu/admission/whatsdistinctive/facultyprofiles/macmillan/
2	MacMillan, David William	1968	X	http://royalsociety.org/people/david-macmillan/
3	MacMillan, David William	1968	X	http://www.iupac.org/news/news-detail/article/david-wc-macmillan-is-to-be-awarded-the-2006-thieme-iupac-prize.html
1	Tweedie, Stephen Cochran	1969	X	Linux Clustering: Building and Maintaining Linux Clusters, by Charles Bookman, New Riders Publishing, 2003, p 75
1	Benzies, Leslie	1971	X	http://www.imdb.com/name/nm1267734/
2	Benzies, Leslie	1971	X	http://www.fool.com/investing/general/2013/09/28/gta-5-sales-hit-1-billion.aspx
3	Benzies, Leslie	1971	X	http://metro.co.uk/2015/08/11/gta-v-sales-hit-54-million-as-2k-insist-mafia-iii-will-not-use-rockstar-tech-5337625/
1	Mone, Michelle Georgina	1971	X	http://books.google.com.au/books/about/Clothing_Companies_of_Scotland.html?id=QRtHSwAACAAJ&redir_esc=y
2	Mone, Michelle Georgina	1971	X	http://www.dailymail.co.uk/femail/article-1320567/New-Ultimo-Extreme-Cleavage-bra-best-thing-breast-surgery.html
1	Love, Gordon	1974	X	http://newsroom.ucr.edu/2016
1	Grieve, Alison May	1977	X	http://www.fsrmagazine.com/content/safetray-serving-tray-reduces-accidents

1	McGrath, Matthew	1977	X	http://www.aircraftmedical.com/index.php?option=com_content&view=article&id=612:aircraft-medical-launch-the-mcgrathr-x-blade-at-euroanaesthesia-europes-largest-annual-meeting-of-anesthesiologists&catid=52:latest-news&Itemid=168
2	McGrath, Matthew	1977	X	http://www.aircraftmedical.com/index.php?option=com_content&view=article&id=268&Itemid=182
3	McGrath, Matthew	1977	X	http://www.scribd.com/doc/140581295/Review-of-Session-2010-11
4	McGrath, Matthew	1977	X	http://www.prnewswire.com/news-releases/aircraft-medical-launches-mcgrath-x-blade-for-extreme-airways-209633271.html
1	Conclusion			http://www.scran.ac.uk/scotland/pdf/SP2_1Education.pdf
2	Conclusion			The History of Modern Japanese Education: Constructing the National School System, 1872-1890, by Benjamin C. Duke, Rutgers University Press, 2009, p 174

Other Principal Names Included Within Main Articles

Adie, Alexander James	1808	1879	See Alexander Adie 1775-1858
Aird, John	1833	1911	See John Aird 1801-1876
Aitken, John	X	1790	See James Jeffray 1759-1848
Banks, James Arthur	1897	1967	See William George Nicholson Geddes 1913-1993
Bell, Chichester Alexander	1848	1924	See Alexander Graham Bell 1847-1922
Bell, Henry	1848	1931	See John Bell 1850-1929
Callender, Thomas Octavius	1855	1938	See William Marshall Callender born 1859
Clark, Patrick	1742	X	See James Clark 1747-1829
Crawford, John William Croom	1901	1989	See William Malcolm Chalmers 1905-1995
Dalzell, Gavin	1812	1863	See Kirkpatrick McMillan 1812-1878
Dick, James	1823	1902	See Robert Dick 1820-1902
Fraser, Thomas	1872	1951	See John James Rickard Macleod 1876-1935
Gilchrist, Percy Carlyle	1851	1935	See Sidney Gilchrist Thomas
Grieve, John	1905	X	See David Kay born 1900
Johnson, Thomas	1808	X	See John Paterson Reid 1796-1854

Kermack, William Ogilvy	1898	1970	See Anderson Gray McKendrick 1876-1943
McCall, Thomas	1834	1904	See Kirkpatrick McMillan 1812-1878
McConnel, James	1762	1831	See John Kennedy 1769-1855
McCririck, William	1788	X	See Robert Wilson 1803-1882
McCulloch, John Ramsay	1789	1864	See James Chalmers 1782-1853
Macdonald, George	1903	1967	See Ronald Ross 1857-1932
MacGregor, John	1802	1858	See David Tod 1795-1859
McKinlay, Peter Laird	1901	1972	See Anderson Gray McKendrick 1876-1943
Mather, William	1838	1920	See William Colin 1812-1864
Meik, Patrick Walter	1851	1910	See Charles Scott Meik 1853-1923
Meikle, George	1712	1811	See Andrew Meikle 1719-1811
Menzies, Alan Wilfrid Cranbrook	1877	1966	See Alexander Smith 1865-1922
Mitchell, Alexander Philp	1885	1959	See John Fraser 1885-1947
Rennie, John	1865	1928	See John James Rickard Macleod 1876-1935
Ritchie, William Alexander	1951	X	See Keith Henry Stockman Campbell 1954-2012
Steedman, James	1790	1865	See Robert Wilson 1803-1882
Thom, James	X	X	See William Allen unknown date-1840
Wallace, Robert	1782	1855	See James Chalmers 1782-1853
Wallace, William	1881	1963	See Maurice Edward Denny 1886-1955
Webster, Alexander	1708	1784	See Robert Wallace 1697-1771
Wilson, George Fergusson	1822	1902	See William Wilson 1772-1860
Young, George	1692	1757	See Alexander Wood 1817-1884